CLIMATE CHANGE AND
THE LAW

CLIMATE CHANGE AND THE LAW

Chris Wold
Associate Professor of Law & Director International
Environmental Law Project
Lewis & Clark Law School

David Hunter
Associate Professor of Law
American University Washington College of Law

Melissa Powers
Assistant Professor of Law
Lewis & Clark Law School

Library of Congress Cataloging-in-Publication Data

Wold, Chris.
Climate change and the law / Chris Wold, Melissa Powers, David Hunter.
p. cm.
Includes index.
ISBN 978-1-4224-1912-0 (hard cover)
1. Global warming--Law and legislature. 2. Liability for environmental damages. I. Powers, Melissa. II. Hunter, David.
III. Title.
K3593.W65 2009
344.04'6342—dc22

2009003816

NOTE TO USERS

To ensure that you are using the latest materials available in this area, please be sure to periodically check the LexisNexis Law School web site for downloadable updates and supplements at www.lexisnexis.com/lawschool.

Editorial Offices
744 Broad Street, Newark, NJ 07102 (973) 820-2000
201 Mission St., San Francisco, CA 94105-1831 (415) 908-3200
www.lexisnexis.com

MATTHEW BENDER

Dedication

To Sue, Zach, and Mats—C.W.

To Mark, with love—M.P.

To Margaret, Danielle, and Edward—D.H.

Preface

Climate change has become the defining environmental legal and policy challenge of the 21st century, as well as one of the most dynamic. If there is any doubt, consider just some of the events of the past eighteen months since we began writing this book. The Intergovernmental Panel on Climate Change (IPCC) issued its Fourth Assessment, concluding, with 90 percent certainty, that the observable increases in temperature are the result of human activities. The IPCC, along with Al Gore, shared the Nobel Peace Prize in 2007 "for their efforts to build up and disseminate greater knowledge about man-made climate change, and to lay the foundations for the measures that are needed to counteract such change." The United States Supreme Court ruled in *Massachusetts v. EPA* that the U.S. Environmental Protection Agency has authority under the Clean Air Act to regulate carbon dioxide. The United States Fish & Wildlife Service listed the polar bear as a threatened species under the Endangered Species Act principally because its habitat, the Arctic sea ice upon which it is almost entirely dependent, is melting due to increased temperatures and other factors. The Inupiat Village of Kivalina has sued ExxonMobil and other leading energy companies for the costs of relocating their village, which is subsiding into the ocean due to climate change. Due to the high demand for development of solar power in six western states, the Bureau of Land Management and Department of Energy put a moratorium on such projects until it could prepare a programmatic Environmental Impact Statement to assess the environmental, social, and economic impacts associated with solar energy development — and then lifted moratorium. At the international level, governments agreed to an action plan laying out the negotiating framework for concluding a climate change treaty by 2009 to follow the Kyoto Protocol in 2012.

Climate change will continue to occupy center stage as individuals and governments wrestle with mitigating their emissions and adapting to the impacts of climate change at a time when the gravity of climate change becomes increasingly apparent. Seemingly every day, scientists announce new studies showing that the impacts of climate change are more severe or occurring more rapidly than previously predicted. For example, Arctic sea ice is melting faster than predicted and sea levels have risen more than originally thought. Moreover, citizens and governments continue to press for change, using every legal tool at their disposal. Municipalities are developing climate-friendly building codes. States continue to enact renewable portfolio standards that require electricity producers to obtain a certain percentage of energy from renewable sources. Citizens have brought legal actions against major emitters of greenhouse gases for causing a public nuisance. In addition to such common law claims, citizens have also sued the federal government under the Clean Air Act, the Endangered Species, and the National Environmental Policy Act, as well as made petitions under the Clean Water Act, to compel the United States government to mitigate greenhouse gas emissions. At the international level, citizens have used international processes, such as the Inter-American Human Rights Commission and the World Heritage Convention, to compel governments to act more aggressively to mitigate greenhouse gas emissions or adapt to climate change impacts. And many businesses are voluntarily reducing their carbon footprints and trading for increasing amounts of carbon credits in both international and domestic carbon markets.

Given the all-encompassing reach of climate change, it presents both unique challenges and opportunities for teaching. The subject allows students to study how many different areas of law — public international law, public administrative law, federal environmental law, state and municipal regulations, and the common law — can be implicated in

Preface

addressing such a major social issue. The subject thus allows for an integrated experience to study the law generally, as well as to understand in detail the many climate-related challenges facing the next generation of lawyers. To reflect the breadth of legal responses to climate change, this book takes a comprehensive approach to climate change and the law, covering everything from municipal building codes that incorporate climate-friendly requirements, to state efforts to reduce carbon dioxide emissions from automobiles and other sources of greenhouse gases, to federal litigation involving both the common law and statutory law, as well as to the international climate treaty regime. As such, this book could be used as a first-year introduction to the law, a capstone course, or simply as an issue-specific course.

The book is roughly organized in three parts. The first part of the book reviews the background scientific and policy issues surrounding climate change. Chapter 1 summarizes the scientific basis of climate change, relying principally on the IPCC's Fourth Assessment, but supplementing the IPCC's reports with the fast-growing scientific literature that is making the IPCC's 2007 Fourth Assessment seemingly already out of date. Chapter 2 describes the policies and measures that are or could be used to mitigate greenhouse gas emissions, as well as the economic costs of some of those strategies. Recognizing that climate change impacts will occur regardless of how quickly we act to mitigate greenhouse gas emissions, Chapter 3 explores adaptation strategies.

Part two delves deeply into the international framework of the climate change regime. Chapters 4 and 5 introduce the 1992 United Nations Framework Convention on Climate Change (UNFCCC) and the subsequent 1997 Kyoto Protocol, which requires developed countries to reduce or limit their emissions of six greenhouse gases: carbon dioxide, methane, nitrous oxide, hydrofluorocarbons, sulphur hexafluoride, and perfluorocarbons. Subsequent chapters provide a detailed investigation of specific aspects of the international climate change regime. Chapter 6 explores the different types of emissions trading, collectively known as the flexibility mechanisms, under the Kyoto Protocol. Chapter 7 reviews the complicated and controversial regime for reducing greenhouse gas emissions through land use and forest management practices. Chapter 8 describes the Kyoto Protocol's compliance regime. Chapter 9 then explores development of the post-Kyoto Protocol regime, an issue of particular importance as countries struggle to meet their existing obligations under the Kyoto Protocol while scientists make clear that the Kyoto Protocol's commitments fall far short of the greenhouse gas emissions reductions necessary to avoid catastrophic climate change. Finally, Chapter 10 introduces other international laws affecting climate change. The Kyoto Protocol's climate change regime is not the only international law relevant for mitigating emissions and adapting to climate change. Thus, Chapter 10 describes policies affecting climate change within other international conventions, including the Montreal Protocol on Substances that Deplete the Ozone Lawyer, the World Heritage Convention, and the World Trade Organization, among others.

Part three then explores U.S. domestic law. Chapter 11 begins this part by reviewing general U.S. policy concerning climate change. Much of the action, however, has taken place in the courts, so Chapter 12 starts with a discussion of threshold issues, such as Constitutional standing, that determine whether a climate change litigant can even use the judicial system. Chapter 13 then discusses the role existing federal environmental statutes — the Clean Air Act, in particular — may play in mitigating climate change. Chapters 14 and 15 then look at how U.S. energy and transportation policies affect and intersect with climate change policies. Chapter 16 turns back to the courts to discuss the role of the common law in addressing climate change. As Chapters 11 through 16 reveal, the United States does not have a uniform or cohesive climate change policy. Indeed, in many

Preface

situations, the U.S. government has refused to act and thus prompted state and local governments to adopt their own climate change laws and regulations. Chapter 17 reviews the most common and/or aggressive sub-federal actions and explores the roles that all levels of government should and legally can play in mitigating climate change. Chapter 18 looks at the role that private actors have take on their own to reduce greenhouse gas emissions. Finally, Chapter 19 attempts to peer into the future to discuss whether and how governments may move toward a low-carbon future.

Editor's Note

Most footnotes and internal citations have been omitted without indication. Those footnotes that have been retained are numbered as they are in the original text. Deletions of text within an excerpt are indicated in two ways. Small deletions of a sentence or two are indicated with ellipses. The deletion of larger blocks of text is denoted with asterisks. Deletions of dissenting or concurring opinions are generally not noted.

Acknowledgements

This book would not have been possible without the assistance of many people. We thank Wil Burns, David M. Driesen, Sanford Gaines, Royal Gardner, Lesley McAllister, Marcos Orellana, Dan Rohlf, Kassie Siegel, Erica Thorson, Glenn Wiser, and Durwood Zaelke for their thoughtful comments which have improved this book tremendously. We also thank Moses Alajijian, Duncan Delano, Lisa Frenz, Tami Gierloff, Bonnie Green, Amy Lubrano, Nicolas Mansour, Andy Marion, James Mitchell, Courtney McAnn, Stacie Pacheco, Rowan Smith, and Lynn Williams for their excellent research and administrative support.

Table of Contents

Table of Contents

Table of Contents

Table of Contents

Table of Contents

Table of Contents

Table of Contents

Table of Contents

Table of Contents

Table of Contents

Table of Contents

Table of Contents

Table of Contents

Table of Contents

Table of Contents

Table of Contents

Table of Contents

Table of Contents

Table of Contents

Table of Contents

Table of Contents

Table of Contents

Abbreviations & Conversion Units

AA	Assigned Amount
AAU	Assigned Amount Unit
CAA	Clean Air Act
CAFE	Corporate Average Fuel Economy
CCX	Chicago Climate Exchange
CDM	Clean Development Mechanism
CER	Certified Emissions Reduction
CH_4	Methane
CO_2	Carbon Dioxide
CO_2eq	Carbon Dioxide Equivalent
CWA	Clean Water Act
EISA	Energy Independence and Security Act
ERU	Emission Reduction Unit
EPA	United States Environmental Protection Agency
EPAct	Energy Policy Act
ESA	Endangered Species Act
EU	European Union
GEF	Global Environment Facility
GHG	Greenhouse Gas
GWP	Global Warming Potential
HCFCs	Hydrochlorofluorocarbons
HFCs	Hydrofluorocarbons
IPCC	Intergovernmental Panel on Climate Change
JI	Joint Implementation
lCERs	Long-term Certified Emission Reductions
$MtCO_2eq$	Million Tons Equivalent of Carbon Dioxide
MW	Megawatt
NEPA	National Environmental Policy Act
NHTSA	National Highway Traffic Safety Administration
N_2O	Nitrous Oxide
PHEV	Plug-in Hybrid Electric Vehicles
RMU	Removal Unit
RFS	Renewable Fuel Standard
RPS	Renewable Portfolio Standard
SF_6	Sulfur Hexafluoride
tCERs	Temporary Certified Emission Reductions
UNFCCC	United Nations Framework Convention on Climate Change
VMT	Vehicle Miles Traveled

Conversion Units

1 tonne (t)	1,000 kilogram (kg)	10^6 gram (g)	1 Megagram (Mg)
1 Megatonne (Mt)*	1,000,000 t	10^{12} g	1 Teragram (Tg)
1 Gigatonne (Gt)	1,000,000,000 t	10^{15} g	1 Petagram (Pg)
1 hectare (ha)	10,000 square metre (m^2)		
1 square kilometer (km^2)	100 hectare (ha)		
1 tonne per hectare	100 gram per square metre (g m^2)		
1 tonne carbon	3.67 tonne carbon dioxide (tCO_2)		
1 tonne carbon dioxide	0.273 tonne carbon (t C)		
1 tonne	0.984 imperial ton = 1.10 US ton = 2,204 pounds		
1 hectare (ha)	2.471 acre		
1 square kilometer (km2)	0.386 square mile		

Putting Emissions in Context

1 Metric Ton CO_2. Producing one ton of cement releases 1 metric ton CO_2 into the atmosphere (each new average home built uses 19 tons of cement). In Honolulu, the city with the lowest carbon footprint per capita in the U.S., each resident accounts for 1.5 metric tons CO_2 emissions per year.

100 Tons CO_2. Driving an automobile with an average fuel economy of 15 miles per gallon 12,000 miles a year over the course of 10 years would emit close to 100 metric tons CO_2 (or, more precisely, 94.2 metric tons CO_2).

1,000 Metric Tons CO_2. The U.S. produces roughly 1,000 metric tons CO_2 every 5.4 seconds.

---

* Some authors quoted in this book use the abbreviation $MMtCO_2$ to refer to million metric tons of carbon dioxide. $1MMtCO_2$ and $1MtCO_2$ are equivalent.

Chapter 1

THE SCIENCE OF CLIMATE CHANGE

I. INTRODUCTION

Human activity is changing the global climate with unpredictable and potentially profound consequences for global weather patterns, ecosystems, food security, and human health. Water vapor and gases such as carbon dioxide and methane allow energy from the sun to pass through the atmosphere to the earth's surface, and then trap a portion of that energy before it is radiated back into space. This so-called "greenhouse effect" is a natural process; without it the energy from the sun would be lost in space, leaving the earth cold and lifeless. It is also a homeostatic process, or a process tending toward equilibrium. The concentration of greenhouse gases in the atmosphere is kept relatively constant over time by complex natural cycles. Carbon dioxide, for example, is absorbed by plants, released when the plants burn or decompose, and re-absorbed when new plants grow, only to be released again in an endless cycle.

Climate change refers to the response of the planet's climate system to altered concentrations of carbon dioxide and other "greenhouse gases" in the atmosphere.

1

If all else is held constant (e.g., cloud cover, capacity of the oceans to absorb carbon dioxide, albedo, aerosols, etc.), increased concentrations of greenhouse gases lead to "global warming" — an increase in global average temperatures — and associated changes in the earth's climate patterns. Indeed, the basic mechanism of how carbon dioxide (CO_2) and other greenhouse gases warm the planet (i.e., the "greenhouse effect") has been well known since 1896, when the Swedish chemist Svante Arrhenius suggested that carbon dioxide emissions from combustion of coal would lead to global warming.

This chapter provides the scientific and factual basis for climate change. Although areas of uncertainty still exist with respect to the ultimate impacts of climate change, dozens of scientific studies and real-time observations around the world clearly indicate that: (a) the earth's climate is changing; (b) the changes are the result of human activity; (c) the changes are happening at both a faster rate and with greater impacts than previously projected; and (d) immediate action is needed to reduce greenhouse gas emissions to avoid reaching more harmful levels. Indeed, a consensus has existed for more than a decade within the international scientific community that we are witnessing discernible and serious impacts on our climate and natural systems due to human activities. Virtually every day, new observations solidify that consensus and confirm the increasing accuracy of global climate models for predicting both global and regional impacts.

Despite the fact that a vast majority of the world's atmospheric scientists have long agreed that climate change was a serious threat, debates over whether climate change was a "myth" or a "conspiracy of environmentalists" continued well into this century. With the exception of a handful of "climate skeptics," no such debate now exists in the scientific community. The debate has moved from *whether* humans are causing climate change to *what* will be the magnitude and impacts of that change and, more importantly, *how* we should respond to it. In these latter issues, there remain significant areas of uncertainty, but over time the observed and predicted future impacts have almost all led to the conclusion that climate change is accelerating and impacts will be profound. Much of this chapter explores what is known and predicted about these impacts.

The world's ability to move beyond the question of *whether* climate change is occurring to *how* to respond to it owes much to the international community's deliberate attempt to organize and present climate science in a policy-relevant way. Anticipating the critical role that scientific consensus would play in building the political will to respond to climate change, the United Nations Environment Programme (UNEP) and the World Meteorological Organization (WMO) created the Intergovernmental Panel on Climate Change (IPCC) in 1988. The IPCC was initially charged with assessing the scientific, technical, and economic basis of climate change policy in preparation for the 1992 Earth Summit and the negotiations of the UN Framework Convention on Climate Change (discussed in Chapter 5). After the Convention entered into force, the IPCC continued to provide technical reports to the parties and to the public. The IPCC's Second Assessment, for example, concluded in 1995 that the observed warming trend was "unlikely to be entirely natural in origin" and that the balance of evidence suggested a "discernible human influence" on the Earth's climate. IPCC, WORKING GROUP I, THE SCIENCE OF CLIMATE CHANGE, 3–5 (Second Assessment Report 1995). This conclusion informed negotiations of the 1997 Kyoto Protocol.

The IPCC issued its Fourth (and latest) Assessment in 2007 and found that "warming of the planet is unequivocal" and that "most of the observed increase in globally averaged temperatures since the mid-20th century is very likely [i.e., more than 90% likely] due to the observed increase in anthropogenic greenhouse gas concentrations." IPCC WORKING GROUP I, THE PHYSICAL SCIENCE BASIS: SUMMARY FOR POLICYMAKERS (Fourth Assessment Report 2007). For this report and the public awareness its release raised, the IPCC shared the 2007 Nobel Peace Prize with former Vice President Al Gore. Much of the ensuing discussion of facts comes from these IPCC reports.

QUESTIONS AND DISCUSSION

1. The IPCC is organized into three working groups: Working Group I concentrates on the science of the climate system, Working Group II on impacts of climate change and policy options for response, and Working Group III on the economic and social dimensions of climate change. The Working Groups' reports have been designed to inform the policy debate with thorough assessments every five years. The 1990 Assessments built momentum for the 1992 Framework Convention, and the 1995 Assessment's conclusion that climate change was already occurring helped to build the political commitment to establish clear targets and timetables in the Kyoto Protocol. The Fourth Assessment, which was released in November 2007, is being used as the scientific basis for negotiations of the post-Kyoto commitments.

2. The IPCC Assessments are intended to summarize the accepted state of the climate science at a given point in time, but the process of reviewing and summarizing the science and reaching consensus on the text necessarily takes several years. With the recent rapid changes in climate science, the IPCC reports are arguably out of date by the time they are published. Given this conservative nature of the IPCC, how safe are we in relying on its assessments? What other governance mechanisms could you design to ensure that the most accurate and timely science is available for policymakers, industry, and NGOs?

3. *The Carbon Cycle.* To understand climate change, we must understand the global carbon cycle:

> The atmosphere is a critical part of two carbon cycles, which distribute a chemical raw material required by all living organisms. In the shorter cycle carbon is fixed in green plants and in certain microorganisms, such as algae, through the process of photosynthesis. This process takes place when sunlight is absorbed by chlorophyll, which powers a process that breaks down CO_2 from the atmosphere to form organic molecules, such as glucose and amino acids, that accumulate in the biomass of the plants. Animals, which are not capable of photosynthesis, obtain the carbon they need to produce energy for maintaining their bodily processes by eating plants or other animals that are primary or secondary consumers of plants. Carbon is returned to the atmosphere in the form of CO_2 through the cellular respiration of living plants and animals and their decomposition upon death. The carbon in vegetation is also released to the atmosphere when it's burned, as in forest and range fires or slash-and-burn farming. The oceans absorb and release vast quantities of CO_2 and thus serve as a buffer that keeps the level of CO_2 in the atmosphere relatively stable.

> There is also a geological carbon cycle that takes place naturally on a much longer scale of time. The cycle begins when organic material from plants and animals slowly becomes locked into sedimentary deposits, where

it may remain for hundreds of millions of years in the form of either
carbonates containing the shells of marine organisms or organic fossils,
such as coal, oil, and natural gas. Some of the carbon is eventually released
when the geological formations in which it is locked are exposed to
weathering and erosion. Human beings have greatly accelerated the
release of this carbon by mining and drilling large quantities of fossil fuels
and burning them to produce energy while in the process emitting CO_2.

M. SOROOS, THE ENDANGERED ATMOSPHERE 31 (1997).

Figure 1-1: The Carbon Cycle (in billions of tons)

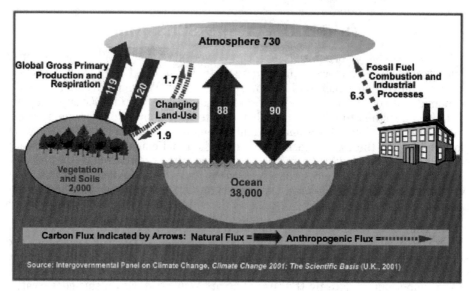

4.   Although the phrase "greenhouse effect" derives its name from an analogy
to greenhouses, the process by which gases warm the atmosphere is actually quite
different from the way a greenhouse warms air. A greenhouse heats the air inside
it primarily by allowing the sun's solar radiation to warm the ground inside it. The
ground turns this solar radiation into heat which is reflected back into the
atmosphere as waves of infrared radiation. Inside the greenhouse, this infrared
radiation is absorbed by gases, thus warming the air. However, the glass of the
greenhouse prevents the warmed air from escaping; that is, it prevents *convection*
— the transfer of heat by motion. The temperature of a greenhouse will quickly
drop, if a window is opened. In contrast, the "greenhouse effect" reduces *radiation
loss*, not convection. In other words, greenhouse gases are transparent to solar
energy and thus allow solar radiation to warm the ground. As in a greenhouse, the
ground releases heat as infrared radiation; instead of preventing convection,
however, greenhouse gases absorb this infrared radiation. Unlike a greenhouse, the
atmosphere has no window to open. Although the "greenhouse effect" may be an
imperfect metaphor, it provides a useful way to describe a complex natural process.

II. THE CAUSES OF CLIMATE CHANGE

Since the beginning of the Industrial Revolution in the early 19th century, human activity has interfered with the homeostatic processes that make up the carbon cycle, releasing carbon dioxide and other greenhouse gases into the atmosphere more quickly than they are absorbed by natural "sinks," primarily oceans and forests. The result is that concentrations of these gases are increasing in the atmosphere. Due to the burning of fossil fuels, such as coal and oil, and the destruction of forests, the atmospheric concentration of carbon dioxide has increased by 35 percent, from 280 parts per million (ppm) to 381 ppm between 1750 and 2005, and, if current trends in fossil fuel use continue, concentrations would reach 600–700 ppm by the end of the 21st century. (One part per million of CO_2 means there is one molecule of CO_2 to every million molecules of air.) Concentrations of methane, nitrous oxide, and other greenhouse gases are rising as well, with methane increasing more than 150 percent from its 1750 level. As a result, an ever-greater proportion of the sun's energy is trapped within the atmosphere, and the planet is heating up.

A.   Increasing Greenhouse Gas Emissions

The six man-made (or "anthropogenic") greenhouse gases currently regulated at the international level are carbon dioxide (CO_2), methane (CH_4), nitrous oxide (N_2O), hydrofluorocarbons (HFCs), perfluorocarbons (PFCs), and sulfur hexafluoride (SF_6). A seventh category, chlorofluorocarbons (CFCs), are also greenhouse gases (GHGs), but regulated under the Montreal Protocol on Substances that Deplete the Ozone Layer because of their ozone-depleting effects. These greenhouse gases collectively account for only three percent of the earth's atmosphere, but relatively small increases in their concentrations are altering the climate system. In addition, many land-use and agricultural practices directly contribute to GHG emissions or reduce the Earth's capacity to assimilate greenhouse gases. For example, forest loss both releases carbon stored in the felled trees and reduces the remaining forest's capacity to absorb carbon from the atmosphere. Also many substances not yet addressed internationally, such as black carbon (or soot), are also significant contributors to global warming. The primary sources of greenhouse gas emissions are discussed below.

Sources of Greenhouse Gases. Each of the six major greenhouse gases currently regulated under the Kyoto Protocol (and CFCs, regulated under the Montreal Protocol) has different sources.

Carbon dioxide, composing nearly 50 percent of all anthropogenic greenhouse gases, is by far the most important. Eighty percent of all carbon dioxide is emitted by fossil fuel burning, in everything from large power plants to automobiles. Much of the remaining 20 percent of CO_2 emissions comes from cement manufacturing and deforestation. Despite growing calls for reducing CO_2 emissions, the U.S. Department of Energy predicts that global CO_2 emissions will increase 70 percent from 2003 to 2030. Contrast this prediction with the view by many climatologists that to avoid substantial climate impacts we need to cap global CO_2 emissions by 2015 and see significant reductions by 2050.

Methane is produced by waste decomposition, the decay of plants, from certain agricultural practices (such as large-scale cattle and pork production, and the flooding of rice fields), and from coal mines. Livestock production produces 37 percent of methane worldwide, and contributes more to GHG emissions than the transportation sector. Solid waste landfills are also a significant source of methane. As temperatures rise, significant methane may also be seeping from the ocean floor and frozen lake beds.

Nitrous oxide (N_2O) is produced from automobile exhaust and other industrial processes, but the largest sources may be from livestock production and the poor management of manure.

Chlorofluorocarbons (CFCs) and hydrochlorofluorocarbons (HCFCs) were used in refrigerants, air conditioners, and other products, until their phase-out under the Montreal Protocol regime. Unfortunately, among the most potent greenhouse gases are the common alternatives to CFCs, including hydrofluorocarbons (HFCs) and other industrial gases such as perfluorocarbons (PFCs) and sulphur hexafluoride (SF_6).

Other gases, such as sulfur dioxide (SO_2), nitrogen oxides (NOx) (not to be confused with nitrous oxide (N_2O)), carbon monoxide (CO), hydrogen sulfide (H_2S), ozone (O_3), and volatile organic compounds (VOCs) also contribute to global warming, but are not yet covered by the Kyoto Protocol. The potential warming impacts of these non-Kyoto GHGs are not as well known. *See The Greenhouse Gas Protocol: A Corporate Accounting and Reporting Standard*, WORLD BUSINESS COUNCIL FOR SUSTAINABLE DEVELOPMENT AND WORLD RESOURCES INSTITUTE 46 (2001).

Black Carbon. Another significant cause of climate change is black carbon, now suspected to be second only to CO_2 in its contribution to climate change. In fact, recent studies suggest that black carbon (i.e., soot) may account for as much as one-third of the warming that is occurring in the Arctic. Black carbon is produced by the incomplete combustion of coal, diesel, wood, and biomass fuels. It is technically a solid, not a gas, and is thus often ignored in policy discussions over greenhouse gases. Black carbon warms the atmosphere by absorbing incoming sunlight, whereas GHGs absorb infrared radiation reflected from the earth's surface. Thus, black carbon emissions and some of its impacts are localized, as opposed to GHG emissions, which uniformly contribute to climate change irrespective of where they are emitted. For example, the accumulation of black carbon on ice sheets, which absorbs heat from sunlight that would otherwise be reflected back into space, is roughly twice as effective as CO_2 in thinning Arctic sea ice and melting land ice and permafrost. William L. Chameides & Michael Bergin, *Soot Takes Center Stage*, 297 SCIENCE, Sept. 27, 2002 at 2214; *see also* S. Menon, et. al., *Climate Effects of Black Carbon Aerosols in China and India*, 297 SCIENCE, Sept. 27, 2002 at 2250; James Hansen & Larissa Nazarenko, *Soot Climate Forcing via Snow and Ice Albedos*, 101 PROCEEDINGS OF THE NATIONAL ACADEMY OF SCIENCES (January 13, 2004); Mark G. Flanner, Charles S. Zender, James T. Randerson, & Philip J. Rasch, *Present-Day Climate Forcing and Response from Black Carbon in Snow*, 112 J. GEOPHYS. RES., D11202 (2007).

QUESTIONS AND DISCUSSION

1. *Atmospheric Lifetimes and Global Warming Potential.* Not all greenhouse gases are created equally; different gases have different warming impacts and different atmospheric lifetimes. The concept of "global warming potentials"

(GWPs) was developed to reflect these differences and allow comparisons of the different impacts each gas has on the climate over a specific period of time. All GWPs are measured relative to CO_2, and the GWP for CO_2 over any timeframe is always 1. Over a 100-year timeframe, the GWP of methane is 23, which means that one unit of methane released into the atmosphere will have a warming impact 23 times greater than the same amount of CO_2 over 100 years. Each gas also has a different atmospheric lifetime. For example, methane's atmospheric lifetime is 12 years, while CO_2's atmospheric lifetime is up to 200 years. As a result, a chemical's GWP changes when a different timeframe is used. Thus, because methane has a shorter atmospheric lifetime than CO_2, over a 20-year timeframe its GWP increases from 23 to 62. Policymakers and scientists rely on the different timeframes for different types of issues. For instance, the 20-year timeframe is useful when considering how much the earth's temperature might change as a result of near-term emissions of a gas, and the 100-year timeframe is useful when considering long-term effects of emissions, such as sea-level rise. Table 1-1 below shows the GWPs and atmospheric lifetimes for several of the major GHGs. Note that GWP is not a perfect measurement, as the warming impacts of substances with atmospheric lifetimes in the thousands of years, such as PFCs and sulfur hexafluoride, may not be accurately reflected over a 100-year timeframe.

Table 1-1: Global Warming Potential of Major Greenhouse Gases

Substance	Atmospheric Lifetime	GWP over 20 years	GWP over 100 years	Substance	Atmospheric Lifetime	GWP over 20 years	GWP over 100 years
CO_2	5 to 200 yrs	1	1	HFC-23	260–270 yrs	9400	12,000
Methane	12 yrs	62	23	PFCs	2600+ yrs	3900+	5700+
N_2O	114 yrs	275	296	SF$_6$	3,200 yrs	15,100	22,200
CFC-11	45 yrs	4500	3400				

Review the GWPs in the above table. Why is establishing GWPs critical for policy setting?

2. *Carbon Dioxide Equivalent (CO_{2eq}) Emissions.* A gas's GWP provides a useful measure for comparing different greenhouse gases — a gas's radiative forcing equivalence compared to carbon dioxide. In the climate change context, radiative forcing measures the factors that affect the balance between incoming solar radiation and outgoing infrared radiation within the Earth's atmosphere. Positive forcing leads to global warming. Simplistically stated, radiative forcing for a greenhouse gas essentially boils down to a measure of how much infrared radiation is captured by a gas. A gas's carbon dioxide equivalence — abbreviated as either CO_{2eq} or CO_{2e} — is defined by the IPCC as:

> The amount of *carbon dioxide* emission that would cause the same integrated *radiative forcing*, over a given time horizon, as an emitted amount of a well mixed *greenhouse gas* or a mixture of well mixed greenhouse gases. The equivalent carbon dioxide emission is obtained by multiplying the emission of a well mixed greenhouse gas by its [GWP] for a given time horizon. For a mix of greenhouse gases, it is obtained by summing the equivalent carbon dioxide emissions of each gas.

IPCC, Glossary of Terms Used in the IPCC Fourth Assessment Report, at 945, *available at* http://www.ipcc.ch/glossary/index.htm (emphasis in original).

3. *Banked Carbon.* Because most GHGs, including CO_2, NOx, PFCs, and HFCs, remain in the atmosphere and contribute to the greenhouse effect for many decades or centuries, we have already "banked" substantial amounts of greenhouse gases, and any emissions reductions taken today will not significantly reduce the overall impact until this bank is exhausted. As a result, anthropogenic warming and sea level rise are likely to continue for centuries due to the time scales associated with climate processes and feedbacks, even if greenhouse gas concentrations were to be stabilized. For example, the IPCC concluded that even if CO_2 emissions were maintained at 1994 levels, they would lead to a nearly constant rate of increase in atmospheric CO_2 concentrations for at least two centuries. This means that even larger reductions in GHG emissions would be needed to avoid dangerous interference with the climate. It may even be necessary to pursue a "carbon negative" strategy, where the net amount of carbon added to the atmosphere is less than what is taken out of the atmosphere through sequestration techniques.

4. GHG emissions (and thus atmospheric concentrations) are expected to rise considerably in the next few decades. The U.S. Department of Energy's Energy Information Administration projects global CO_2 emissions will rise 75 percent from 2003 levels by 2030 (from 25.0 to 43.7 billion metric tons). North American emissions are estimated to reach 9.7 billion tons per year, while emissions from Asian developing countries, particularly China and India, are estimated to reach 16 billion tons per year. By 2050, the International Energy Agency (IEA) projects CO_2 emissions will double from current levels if no new policies are adopted to curb global warming. *See* U.S. Department of Energy, Energy Information Administration, International Energy Outlook 2006, Report #:DOE/EIA-0484 (2006); Muriel Boselli, IEA *Warns G8 of Sharp Rise in CO2 Emissions*, REUTERS, June 22, 2006.

B.   Declining Natural Carbon Sinks

As suggested by Figure 1-1, only about 40 percent of annual GHG emissions remain in the atmosphere, with the remainder being sequestered or absorbed by the earth's "carbon sinks." The oceans, forests, and soils are all critical carbon sinks and reservoirs. "Carbon reservoirs" currently store carbon *previously* removed from the atmosphere. Carbon sinks withdraw carbon from the atmosphere. If carbon reservoirs or sinks are disturbed they can release carbon and add to the atmospheric concentrations of greenhouse gases. Our understanding of carbon sinks and reservoirs is still incomplete. As the IPCC puts it:

> A sustainably managed forest comprising all stages of a stand life cycle operates as a functional system that maintains an overall carbon balance, retaining a part in the growing trees, transferring another part into the soils, and exporting carbon as forest products. Recently disturbed and regenerating areas lose carbon; young stands gain carbon rapidly, mature stands less so; and overmature stands may lose carbon . . . During the early years of the life cycle, when trees are small, the area is likely to be a source of carbon; it becomes a sink when carbon assimilation exceeds soil respiration. * * *

> Human activities modify carbon flows between the atmosphere, the land, and the oceans. Land use and land-use change are the main factors that affect terrestrial sources and sinks of carbon. Clearing of forests has resulted in a reduction of the global area of forests by almost 20 percent during the past 140 years. However, [improved] management practices can restore, maintain, and enlarge vegetation and soil carbon stocks. * * *

Reducing the rate of forest clearing can reduce carbon losses from terrestrial ecosystems. Establishing forests on previously cleared land provides an opportunity to sequester carbon in tree biomass and forest soils, but it will take decades to centuries to restore carbon stocks that have been lost as a result of land-use change in the past. * * *

IPCC, LAND USE, LAND-USE CHANGE, AND FORESTRY, at 26–27 [hereinafter IPCC SPECIAL REPORT ON LAND USE AND FORESTRY]. Thus, forests and soils can act as reservoirs (storing carbon), sinks (actively removing, or sequestering, carbon), or sources (emitting carbon) depending on the relative maturity of the forest as well as the human-caused interferences and uses of the land.

Other critical sinks are the oceans. Oceans have absorbed about one-quarter of all man-made CO_2 released since the industrial revolution, but recent studies suggest that their ability to absorb CO_2 may be declining significantly. A recent 10-year study by researchers from the University of East Anglia, for example, showed that the uptake of CO_2 by the North Atlantic Ocean halved between the mid-1990s and 2002–2005. Similarly, studies found in 2007 that the Southern Ocean's ability to absorb carbon has weakened considerably. *See, e.g.*, Paul Rincon, *Polar Ocean "Soaking up Less CO_2"*, BBC NEWS, May 17, 2007.

QUESTIONS AND DISCUSSION

1. As suggested by the above, deforestation and land-use changes play a complex and critical role in climate change. Over time, changes in forest cover, for example through deforestation and conversion to agriculture, have contributed significantly to the level of carbon in the atmosphere. From 1850 to 1998, approximately one-third of man-made GHG emissions into the atmosphere came from releases due to land-use changes, mostly through deforestation. Wildfires in the United States, for example, have been estimated to contribute emissions equal to 4–6 percent of all fossil fuel use. Fully three-quarters of Brazil's GHG emissions come from deforestation.

Not surprisingly, forest management has become a major issue in climate policy. Many carbon offset programs at both the national and international level involve reforestation initiatives. Conservationists and developing countries hope that they can be paid to conserve forests and avoid deforestation. This raises difficult questions for policy makers. The science is very complex for measuring the rates of forest sequestration and thus for measuring how many carbon "credits" should be awarded when a forest is conserved. It appears, for example, that droughts, which are likely to increase in severity with climate change, may reduce a forests' ability to sequester carbon by about 20 percent. Recent studies also suggest that while reforestation in tropical areas undoubtedly has a net positive impact in removing carbon, reforestation in some temperate areas may actually *add* to warming. Where dark leafy temperate forests replace lighter grasslands, the amount of light (and warmth) absorbed by the darker service may actually offset the impact of the carbon sequestered from the atmosphere. These and other forest issues relevant for climate policy are discussed in Chapter 7.

2. In addition to the natural processes for removing and storing carbon, new technologies are being developed for creating and enhancing carbon sinks. These include carbon capture and sequestration (CCS) technologies that will capture and store carbon produced from the combustion of fossil fuels in geological formations. Other proposals include fertilizing the oceans to enhance algal blooms so they increase their CO_2 uptake, or "vacuuming" CO_2 directly from the atmosphere. Not all methods of sequestration rely on such modern approaches. Ancient land use practices among South America indigenous groups, for example, involve actually cooking wood underground instead of open to the air in a way that results in a high-carbon biochar; replacing "slash and burn" techniques of land-clearing with "slash and char" could sequester large amounts of carbon that would otherwise be released into the atmosphere. These proposals are explored further in Chapter 2's discussion of possible mitigation measures.

C.   The Relationship between GHG Concentrations and Temperature

On one level, climate change is simple. Our use of fossil fuels and land-use practices are unlocking and releasing carbon dioxide taken out of the atmosphere over millennia and stored in fossil fuels, wood, or soil. According to the IPCC, global GHG emissions due to human activities have grown since pre-industrial times, with an increase of 70 percent since 1970. A bit more than half of the additional carbon emitted appears to be removed from the atmosphere and assimilated, either through plants and the soil or through increased absorption by the oceans. The remainder of the emissions remains in the atmosphere, significantly increasing atmospheric concentrations of greenhouse gases. Ice core samples taken from the Antarctic and Greenland ice caps show that atmospheric concentrations of anthropogenic greenhouse gases — carbon dioxide, methane, and nitrous oxide — have increased by about 30 percent, 145 percent, and 15 percent, respectively, in the industrial era.

Increasing concentrations. No one seriously questions that atmospheric concentrations of greenhouse gases have increased. The IPCC's Fourth Assessment issued in 2007 made the following conclusions regarding atmospheric concentrations of greenhouse gases:

> Global atmospheric concentrations of CO_2, methane (CH_4) and nitrous oxide (N_2O) have increased markedly as a result of human activities since 1750 and now far exceed pre-industrial values determined from ice cores spanning many thousands of years. Atmospheric concentrations of CO_2 (379 ppm) and CH_4 (1774 ppb) in 2005 exceed by far the natural range over the last 650,000 years. Global increases in CO_2 concentrations are due primarily to fossil fuel use, with land-use change providing another significant but smaller contribution. It is very likely that the observed increase in CH_4 concentration is predominantly due to agriculture and fossil fuel use. Methane growth rates have declined since the early 1990s, consistent with total emissions (sum of anthropogenic and natural sources) being nearly constant during this period. The increase in N_2O concentration is primarily due to agriculture.

IPCC, CLIMATE CHANGE 2007: SYNTHESIS REPORT, at 4 (Fourth Assessment Report 2007).

Increasing Temperatures. There is also no longer any significant question that average global temperatures have increased over the past century. The IPCC's Fourth Assessment concluded in language meant to put the debate over temperature to rest:

arming of the climate system is unequivocal, as is now evident from observations of increases in global average air and ocean temperatures, widespread melting of snow and ice, and rising global average sea level. . . . Eleven of the last twelve years (1995–2006) rank among the twelve warmest years in the instrumental record of global surface temperature (since 1850). The 100-year linear trend (1906–2005) of 0.74 [0.56 to 0.92]°C is larger than the corresponding trend of 0.6 [0.4 to 0.8]°C (1901–2000) given in the Third Assessment Report (TAR). . . . The temperature increase is widespread over the globe, and is greater at higher northern latitudes. Land regions have warmed faster than the oceans.

Id. at 1. Thus, according to the IPCC, the global average surface temperature has increased from 1906 to 2005 approximately 1.3° Fahrenheit (0.74° Celsius). Additionally, the last two decades have likely been the warmest decades in at least the past 1,000 years, and 2005 was the warmest year in the instrumental record for the northern hemisphere. Moreover, the National Oceanic and Atmospheric Administration (NOAA) has determined that seven of the eight warmest years on record have taken place since 2001. The only exception is 1998, which was influenced by a strong El Niño effect. Moreover, 2007 marked the 29th consecutive year that average global temperatures exceeded historical averages.

Human influences will continue to change atmospheric composition throughout the 21st century. As a result, the IPCC estimates that global average surface temperature is projected to increase by 2.5 to 5.6°F (1.8 to 4.0°C) by 2100 relative to 1990, depending on broad assumptions about future climate policy and economic growth. Some computer models predict substantially higher temperature increases, and many scientists believe the IPCC estimates are too low, given revised predictions based on data developed in the past two years. *See* J. Hansen, R. Ruedy, M. Sato & K. Lo, *Global Temperature Trends: 2005 Summation*, NASA GODDARD INSTITUTE FOR SPACE STUDIES AND COLUMBIA UNIVERSITY EARTH INSTITUTE, Dec. 15, 2005; National Research Council, *Surface Temperature Reconstructions for the Last 2000 Years* (June 2006); D. Stainforth, et al., *Uncertainty in Predictions of the Climate Responses to Rising Levels of Greenhouse Gases*, NATURE, Jan. 27, 2005, at 403–406.

Global average temperatures only tell part of the story, because regional variations will make many regions even hotter, and some even colder. Temperatures over land and particularly over the northern hemisphere, for example, are anticipated to be even higher than these global averages. In Alaska, Western Canada, and Eastern Russia, for example, average winter temperatures have already risen by as much as 4–7°F (3–4°C) over the past 50 years and are projected to rise 7–13°F (4–7°C) over the next 100 years. *See* James Hansen, et al., *Global Temperature Trends: 2005 Summation* (NASA Goddard Institute for Space Studies & Columbia University Earth Institute: Dec. 15, 2005); *see also Arctic Climate Impact Assessment* (2004); James Hansen, et al., *Earth's Energy Imbalance: Confirmation and Implications*, 308 SCIENCE, June 5, 2005, at 1431. By the end of the century, Northeastern U.S. winters are expected to warm by an average of 8–12°F, and summers by 6–14°F. Such a rate of warming is without precedent for at least the last 10,000 years.

The Causal Link Between Concentrations and Temperature. To the extent that any climate skeptics continue to deny the basic facts of climate change, it is not because of changes either in GHG concentrations or in temperature; both of those are observable and well established. Harder to establish is the causal link between the two data sets. Is the observed increase in temperature due to the observed increase in GHG concentrations?

This question has been of primary concern to the IPCC, and over each successive report, evidence has mounted demonstrating that the observed warming was causally linked to increased GHG concentrations. By the 2007 Fourth Assessment, the IPCC could conclude:

> Most of the observed increase in globally averaged temperatures since the mid-20th century is *very likely* [i.e., between 90–95% likely] due to the observed increase in anthropogenic greenhouse gas concentrations. This is an advance since the [Third Assessment Report's (TAR's)] conclusion that "most of the observed warming over the last 50 years is *likely* [i.e., greater than 66% likely] to have been due to the increase in greenhouse gas concentrations." Discernible human influences now extend to other aspects of climate, including ocean warming, continental-average temperatures, temperature extremes and wind patterns . . .
>
> - It is *likely* that increases in greenhouse gas concentrations alone would have caused more warming than observed because volcanic and anthropogenic aerosols have offset some warming that would otherwise have taken place.
>
> - The observed widespread warming of the atmosphere and ocean, together with ice mass loss, support the conclusion that it is *extremely unlikely* [less than 5%] that global climate change of the past fifty years can be explained without external forcing, and *very likely* that it is not due to known natural causes alone.
>
> - Warming of the climate system has been detected in changes of surface and atmospheric temperatures, temperatures in the upper several hundred metres of the ocean and in contributions to sea level rise. Attribution studies have established anthropogenic contributions to all of these changes. The observed pattern of tropospheric warming and stratospheric cooling is *very likely* due to the combined influences of greenhouse gas increases and stratospheric ozone depletion.
>
> - It is *likely* that there has been significant anthropogenic warming over the past 50 years averaged over each continent except Antarctica. . . . The observed patterns of warming, including greater warming over land than over the ocean, and their changes over time, are only simulated by models that include anthropogenic forcing. The ability of coupled climate models to simulate the observed temperature evolution on each of six continents provides stronger evidence of human influence on climate than was available in the TAR.

IPCC, Working Group I, at 10. Thus, the IPCC could conclude with "*very high confidence* [more than 90%] that the net effect of human activities since 1750 has been one of warming." The 2007 IPCC report has substantially quelled most serious questions about the causal link between observed warming trends and increased anthropogenic emissions of greenhouse gases.

QUESTIONS AND DISCUSSION

1. *Feedback Loops.* Among the important factors for predicting the ultimate ramifications of climate change are a series of "feedback loops" in the planet's climate system. Some of these feedback loops may intensify the global warming impact of climate change (positive feedback loops), while others may tend to minimize the impacts of global warming (negative feedback loops). For example, as the atmosphere warms, it should hold more water vapor, which in turn will cause an increase in temperature. More clouds are also expected to form, but their effect on temperature will depend on whether they are low cumulus clouds, which tend to reflect sunlight, or high cirrus clouds, which tend to trap heat. The reduction in ice and snow cover because of an increase in temperature will provide a positive feedback, as the so-called albedo effect (the earth's reflectivity) will decrease, reflecting less sunlight away from the earth's surface. Melting permafrost is another example of a positive feedback loop, where the thawing soil releases massive quantities of methane into the atmosphere. So is forest die-off. On the other hand, CO_2 can spur the growth of plants (all other factors being equal), which in turn increases the amount of carbon removed from the atmosphere by photosynthesis. This latter negative feedback loop is often emphasized by those who argue that climate change will not be significant. And the possible shut-down of the thermohaline circulation (the Atlantic ocean current that brings warm water from the gulf to northern Europe) is expected to lead to a much cooler northern Europe (although the shut-down also will slow the ocean current that carries CO_2 to the deep ocean, which will be another positive feedback).

2. *Sulfates and Global Cooling.* In the past, the role of sulfate particulate emissions in the global climate system has caused confusion among policymakers and the public. Sulfate particulates (also called sulfate aerosols) are also emitted from the combustion of fossil fuels and biomass. Unlike CO_2, however, sulfate particulates have a cooling effect on the planet, essentially because they reflect sunlight away from the earth's surface. The relative magnitude of this cooling effect was not well understood until recently. Indeed, in the 1970s the relative effect of aerosol cooling was thought by some scientists to be greater than the global warming effect of fossil fuel combustion. As a result, some scientists were for a short time worried about a global cooling, and global cooling was one of the major concerns in the early 1970s.

Since then, our understanding of the effect of aerosols has increased. The net effect of sulfate aerosols is now recognized to be less than the warming effect of other greenhouse gases, although locally the cooling from aerosol emissions can completely mask or offset the warming effect due to greenhouse gases. While the cooling is typically focused in particular regions, it can have impacts on a continent's or hemisphere's overall climate patterns. This means some areas of the globe may be experiencing cooling as a result of fossil fuel combustion. Moreover, anthropogenic sulfate aerosols are short-lived in the atmosphere (a matter of weeks as compared to decades for CO_2 and N_2O). As a result, the cooling effect of sulfate aerosols on climate adjusts rapidly to increases or decreases in emissions. Thus, as we reduce fossil fuel emissions, the masking effect of the aerosols will end sooner than the warming effects of most greenhouse gases. The cooling effect of aerosols has led some scientists to consider how aerosols could be used to counter-act the impact of global warming. They are now researching whether we should deliberately seed the upper atmosphere with massive amounts of aerosol particles in an effort to cool the planet. These and other "geoengineering" proposals are discussed in Chapter 3.

3. Although uncertainty surely exists on the extent and scale of impacts and, particularly, on what levels of greenhouse gas concentrations will lead to what impacts, no significant doubt exists among scientists that climate change is happening, is serious, is caused by human activity, and demands real attention at all levels. The few remaining "climate skeptics" typically try to obscure the basic understanding and consensus that exists. Some of these efforts have received substantial press, including Michael Crichton's 2004 fictional novel *State of Fear* and the continued publications from conservative think tanks such as the Cato Institute and the American Enterprise Institute. But the uncertainty portrayed in the press or in popular culture is not reflected in the scientific community — at least about the basic consensus that greenhouse gas concentrations are increasing due to human activities and having a discernible impact on global average temperature. In the United States alone, the National Academy of Sciences, the American Meteorological Society, the American Geophysical Union, and the American Association for the Advancement of Science have all issued statements in recent years stating that the evidence of human-induced climate change is compelling. To determine whether a significant minority opinion was being ignored, Naomi Oreskes surveyed the abstracts of every published article in refereed scientific journals from 1993 to 2003. Of the over 600 journal articles that addressed contemporary issues of climate change, *not one* of them challenged the basic consensus that the climate is changing due to man-made increases in greenhouse gases. *See* Naomi Oreskes, *Beyond the Ivory Tower: The Scientific Consensus on Climate Change*, 306 SCIENCE, Dec. 3, 2004, at 1686.

4.   Until recently, climate skeptics raised three basic arguments against the link between greenhouse gas concentrations and temperature increases: (1) that long-term temperature trends of the earth's surface do not show a meaningful increase, (2) that discrepancies between satellite and ground-level data disproved climate models, and (3) that variations in the changes in solar activity can account for the observed warming. As pointed out in the following excerpt, all three of these arguments have effectively been rebutted in peer-reviewed scientific literature in the past few years:

THOMAS HOMER-DIXON, POSITIVE FEEDBACKS, DYNAMIC ICE SHEETS, AND THE RECARBONIZATION OF THE GLOBAL FUEL SUPPLY: THE NEW SENSE OF URGENCY ABOUT GLOBAL WARMING

in STEVEN BERNSTEIN, ET AL., A GLOBALLY INTEGRATED CLIMATE POLICY FOR CANADA 39–40 (2007)[*]

The first argument concerns the long-term trend of Earth's average surface temperature. In 1999, Mann, Bradley, and Hughes released a paper that estimated average global temperature for the last millennium. This work was subsequently updated by Mann and Jones in 2003 to provide a temperature record from the years 200 to 2000 AD. M. Mann, R. Bradley, & M. Hughes, *Northern Hemisphere Temperatures during the Past Millennium: Inferences, Uncertainties, and Limitations*, 26(6) GEOPHYSICAL RESEARCH LETTERS 759 (1999); M. Mann & P. Jones, *Global Surface Temperatures over the Past Two Millennia*, 30(15) GEOPHYSICAL RESEARCH LETTERS (2003). These researchers combined a number of different paleoclimatological records — like tree rings and coral growth rates — that are "proxy" measures of atmospheric temperature during various historical epochs. They cobbled these proxy measures together to get a long-term record of the planet's temperature. Their graph famously showed a sharp uptick over the last half century, which is why it was widely labeled the "hockey stick" graph. It has been one of the most contentious pieces of evidence used to support the claim that

---

[*] Copyright ©2008 by University of Toronto Press, Inc. Reprinted with permission from publisher.

we are experiencing an abnormally warm period.

. . . In response to criticism of the statistical methodology used to cobble these records together, the National Academy of Sciences in the United States created a panel to examine the Mann et al. methodology. The panel released its results last year, saying that, overall, while some questions remained about the methodology, the original study's conclusions were largely correct: the warming of the last 40 years very likely made Earth hotter than anytime in the last 1000 years, and it certainly made Earth hotter than anytime in the last 400 years. I think the National Academy of Sciences report dealt with the hockey stick issue; it's off the table now . . . . *See* National Research Council of the National Academies, Committee on Surface Temperature Reconstructions for the Last 2,000 Years, Board on Atmospheric Sciences and Climate, Division on Earth and Life Sciences, *Surface Temperature Reconstructions for the Last 2,000 Years* (National Academies Press: 2006).

The second argument concerns satellite data. There has been an enormous debate about an apparent discrepancy between data from satellites that show no warming in the troposphere and data from ground level instruments that show warming. The argument was originally made by John Christy of the University of Alabama in Huntsville. R.W. Spencer & J.R. Christy, *Precise Monitoring of Global Temperature Trends from Satellites*, 247 (4950) SCIENCE 1558 (1990). But recent studies have looked very carefully at this apparent discrepancy between satellite and ground-level data and have shown that Christy and his colleagues made a number of methodological and statistical errors. Once these errors are corrected, the discrepancy disappears. [*See* B.D. Santer et al., *Influence of Satellite Data Uncertainties on the Detection of Externally Forced Climate Change*, 300(5623) SCIENCE 1280 (23 May 2003); C. Mears & F. Wentz, *The Effect of Diurnal Correction on Satellite-Derived Lower Tropospheric Temperature*, 309(5740) SCIENCE 1548 (2 Sept. 2005). On errors in interpreting weather balloon data, see S. Sherwood, J. Lazante, and C. Meyer, *Radiosonde Daytime Biases and Late-20th-Century Warming*, 309(5740) Science 1556 (2 Sept. 2005).] The satellite record actually shows tropospheric warming — in fact, it shows both tropospheric warming and, as we would expect from global warming theory, stratospheric cooling.

The third argument concerns radiation from the sun. The most common argument now put forward by climate skeptics is that the recent warming is a result of changes in the intensity of the sun's radiation. But a major review article last year in the journal *Nature* showed that it's virtually impossible to explain the warming we've seen in the last 40 years through changes in solar radiation. [See P. Foukal et al., *Variations in Solar Luminosity and Their Effect on the Earth's Climate*, 443 NATURE 161 (Sept. 14, 2006).] This research is pretty well definitive, too.

Most of the remaining climate skeptics use vague references to the "uncertainty" of modeling, but no current alternative theory for the observed global warming has any significant following. The more important debate over science is no longer *whether* increased concentrations of greenhouse gases is causing global warming, but what is the *rate* of that warming and what will be the short-term and long-term *impacts* of the warming. These are obviously important issues and will be discussed in the following sections.

III. THE ENVIRONMENTAL IMPACTS OF CLIMATE CHANGE

So what if the planet's temperature increases? Understanding the ultimate impact of climate change on human health and the environment is of course critical for policymaking. As early as 2001, the third IPCC Assessment found that climate change was *already* having a discernible impact on many different environmental systems. The evidence of impacts caused by global warming has increased substantially since 2001. In fact, according to the IPCC Fourth Assessment, based on a "review of more than 29,000 observational data series, from 75 studies that show significant change in many physical and biological systems, more than 89 percent are consistent with the direction of change expected as a response to warming." The Fourth Assessment further concluded:

Observational evidence from all continents and most oceans shows that many natural systems are being affected by regional climate changes, particularly temperature increases.

With regard to changes in snow, ice and frozen ground (including permafrost), there is high confidence [about 8 out of 10 chance of being correct] that natural systems are affected. Examples are:

- enlargement and increased numbers of glacial lakes;

- increasing ground instability in permafrost regions, and rock avalanches in mountain regions;

- changes in some Arctic and Antarctic ecosystems, including those in sea-ice biomes, and also predators high in the food chain [such as polar bears].

Based on growing evidence, there is high confidence that the following types of hydrological systems are being affected around the world:

- increased run-off and earlier spring peak discharge in many glacier- and snow-fed rivers;

- warming of lakes and rivers in many regions, with effects on thermal structure and water quality.

There is very high confidence [about 9 out of 10 chance of being correct], based on more evidence from a wider range of species, that recent warming is strongly affecting terrestrial biological systems, including such changes as:

- earlier timing of spring events, such as leaf-unfolding, bird migration and egg-laying;

- poleward and upward shifts in ranges in plant and animal species.

Based on satellite observations since the early 1980s, there is high confidence that there has been a trend in many regions towards earlier "greening' " of vegetation in the spring linked to longer thermal growing seasons due to recent warming.

There is high confidence, based on substantial new evidence, that observed changes in marine and freshwater biological systems are associated with rising water temperatures, as well as related changes in ice cover, salinity, oxygen levels and circulation. These include:

- shifts in ranges and changes in algal, plankton and fish abundance in high-latitude oceans;

- increases in algal and zooplankton abundance in high-latitude and high-altitude lakes;

- range changes and earlier migrations of fish in rivers.

The uptake of anthropogenic carbon since 1750 has led to the ocean becoming more acidic with an average decrease in pH of 0.1 units [IPCC Working Group I Fourth Assessment]. However, the effects of observed ocean acidification on the marine biosphere are as yet undocumented.

IPCC, Working Group II, Summary for Policymakers, Climate Change 2007: Impacts, Adaptation, and Vulnerability 1-2 (Fourth Assessment Review 2007). Think carefully about what is being said in the IPCC report. Behind the stilted language, IPCC is confirming that summer river flows are declining, polar bears are threatened, and natural ecosystems and migration patterns are already disrupted by climate change. The impacts already observed from climate change are widespread and significant; the future, anticipated impacts even more so. The IPCC presented the expected impacts as a function of potential temperature increases, reproduced in Table 1-2. Note that we have already increased greenhouse gas concentrations sufficiently to virtually guarantee we will see a 1°C (1.8°F) increase, and a 2°C (3.6°F) increase will be very difficult to avoid without substantial reductions in greenhouse gas emissions.

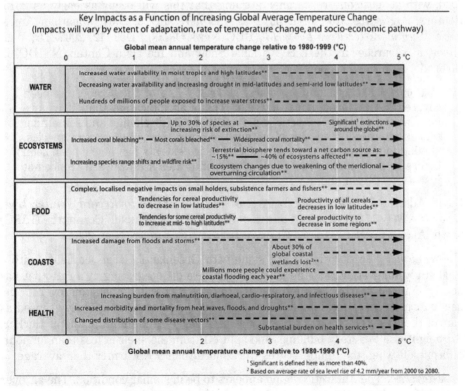

Selected potential environmental impacts from climate change are discussed further below, followed by sections on regional impacts and socio-economic impacts.

A.   Melting Ice

In the past few years, scientists have had to re-assess their predictions about melting polar ice as evidence is emerging that current melting in both the Antarctic and Arctic is more extensive and more rapid than previously predicted.

Melting Arctic Ice. In 2004, the Arctic Climate Impact Assessment (ACIA) found that the Arctic was warming much more rapidly than anticipated — at nearly twice the rate of the rest of the planet. The ACIA reported that temperatures in the region will increase by 4–7°C (7–13°F) by 2100, melting half of the Arctic's summer sea ice and a significant portion of the Greenland Ice Sheet. The report also suggested that it was possible for the Arctic to lose all its summer sea ice by 2100.

But even these estimates may have been too benign. In September, 2006, NASA released three reports showing that Arctic perennial sea ice (ice that survives the summer melt season) had shrunk by 14 percent between 2004 and 2005. The summer sea ice is now approximately half as extensive as 50 years ago. Just as alarming, the Arctic sea ice is not recovering during the winter, reaching all-time lows in 2006 and 2007 with declines of over 20 percent in ice cover from previous years. Researchers now believe that Arctic sea ice is melting faster than climate models predict and is about 30 years ahead of predictions made by the IPCC. If these current rates continue, the Arctic Ocean could be ice-free in the summers by 2020, with at least one researcher arguing that this will occur as early as 2013. Reuters, *Arctic Ice May Melt 30 Years Sooner*, May 3, 2007; Jonathan Amos, *Arctic Summers Ice-Free by '2013'*, BBC NEWS ONLINE, Dec. 12, 2007. Dr. Walt Meier, a researcher at the U.S. National Snow and Ice Data Center (NSIDC) in Colorado, puts this into perspective:

> For 800,000 to a million years, at least some of the Arctic has been covered by ice throughout the year. That's an indication that, if we are heading for an ice-free Arctic, it's a really dramatic change and something that is unprecedented almost within the entire record of human species. Having four years in a row with such low ice extents has never been seen before in the satellite record. It clearly indicates a downward trend, not just a short-term anomaly.

David Adam, *Meltdown Fear as Arctic Ice Cover Falls to Record Winter Low*, GUARDIAN, May 15, 2006; *see also* INTERNATIONAL ARCTIC SCIENCE COMMITTEE (IASC) & THE ARCTIC COUNCIL, ARCTIC CLIMATE IMPACT ASSESSMENT (Nov. 2004).

Greenland. The situation is the same with Greenland's large ice fields, with a 2006 study suggesting that the large glaciers are disintegrating at a rate that has nearly doubled in the last ten years. In May 2007, scientists discovered the newly-formed Ayles Ice Island, which for 3,000 years had been firmly secured as part of the Ayles Ice Shelf. The iceberg was as large as Manhattan and as thick as the height of a ten-story building, and split off from the shelf in less than an hour. It broke off when the temperatures were more than 5°F warmer than average.

Antarctica. The Antarctic region appears to be in similar condition. The air over the western Antarctic peninsula has warmed by nearly 6°F since 1950. Until recently, however, warming in Antarctica was thought to be restricted to the peninsula, but a team of NASA researchers found more widespread warming at least during 2005. *See Snow Accumulation and Snowmelt Monitoring in Greenland and Antarctica*, NASA Press Release, May 15, 2007.

Although for many years scientists thought global warming would cause Antarctica to gain mass, as warmer temperatures would increase precipitation in Antarctica's center, recent studies suggest that it, like the Arctic, is already melting significantly. According to a recent study, the Antarctic ice sheets are melting at a rate of approximately 150 cubic kilometers per year (+/- 80), which is roughly the total U.S. water consumption over three months and is projected to result in a 0.4 millimeter (mm) rise in sea level each year. In a report released in January, 2008, Eric Rignot, a senior scientist at NASA's Jet Propulsion Laboratory, stated that "without doubt, Antarctica as a whole is now losing ice yearly, and each year it's losing more." Most scientists believe this is the result of warmer oceans and ocean breezes that have changed ocean currents around the continent, bringing warmer water into contact with the ice. *See* Andrew C. Revkin, *Antarctica Surveys Show Melting Ice Is Causing Rising Sea Levels*, N.Y. TIMES, Mar. 3, 2006; Eric Rignot, et al., *Recent Antarctic Ice Mass Loss from Radar Interferometry and Regional Climate Modeling*, NATURE GEOSCIENCE, Jan. 13, 2008.

Also, scientists now understand how climate change likely contributed to the spectacular collapse of Antarctica's Larsen B Ice Shelf in 2002. The ice shelf was more than twice the size of Manhattan and its unprecedented collapse sent thousands of icebergs adrift in the Weddell Sea. The collapse was aided by stronger and warmer westerly winds as well as a process of surface lubrication, whereby surface meltwater percolates through the ice sheet down to the bedrock and lubricates the bedrock surface. Ice sheets can then slide more easily into the sea, without fully melting. Through the use of sonar and satellites, scientists have now identified many such meltwater channels in Antarctica, and are increasingly concerned that there could be broader deterioration of Antarctica's ice sheets.

Declining Glaciers and Permafrost. Polar ice caps are not the only areas that are melting due to global warming. A recent study estimated that virtually all of the world's glaciers are receding and that this is in direct response to global warming. Around the world, there are significant observed and predicted declines in glaciers, with significant implications for long-term availability of freshwater as well as for biodiversity. Recent estimates include, for example, that Europe's Alps could lose 80 percent of their glaciers by the end of the century, Glacier National Park is likely to have no glaciers by 2030, and Nepali glaciers are shrinking at a rate of 30 to 60 meters per decade. The impact of receding glaciers can be significant on downstream users. Consider for example that 500 million people use water from the Ganges River, and yet 70 percent of the Ganges' low summer flows come from just one massive glacier which is receding at 40 meters a year. James Owen, *Alps Could Be Ice Free by 2100, Study Warns*, NAT'L GEOG. NEWS, July 11, 2006; *Glaciers Melting In Montana Park: U.N. Is Asked To Declare Park An Endangered World Heritage Site*, CBS NEWS, Mar. 13, 2006; David Cyranoski, *Climate Change: The Long-Range Forecast*, NATURE 438, 275–276 (Nov. 17, 2005); Emily Wax, *A Sacred River Endangered by Global Warming: Glacial Source of Ganges Is Receding*, THE WASHINGTON POST, June 17, 2007, at A14.

Of equal concern is the loss of permafrost across vast reaches of Alaska, Canada, and Russia. Warming temperatures could thaw the top ten or more feet of permafrost across the Northern Hemisphere by 2050, and as much as 90 percent by 2100. Such a thawing would alter ecosystems and substantially damage buildings and roads. It would also release massive amounts of CO_2 (doubling current atmospheric levels) and methane into the atmosphere, as permafrost is estimated to hold 30 percent or more of all carbon stored in soils worldwide.

B.   Rising Sea Levels

According to the IPPC 2007 Report, global average sea level rose at an average rate of 1.8 mm per year from 1961 to 2003. The rate was faster from 1993 to 2003, about 3.1 mm per year. Total sea level rise in the last century is estimated at a modest 0.17 meters. Moreover, under a range of future scenarios, the IPCC estimates a maximum 21st century sea level rise of no more than an additional 0.59 meters. This means that the IPCC estimated total sea level rise by the end of the century to be less than 1 meter.

Since its release in November 2007, however, some experts have criticized the IPCC's treatment of sea level rise for two reasons. First, data released since the IPCC report suggest that the rate of sea level rise is more than previously believed and predicts levels of up to 1.4 meters by the end of the century. *See* Susan Solomon, et al., *A Closer Look at the IPCC Report*, 319 SCIENCE, Jan. 25, 2008, at 409–10. Further, researchers studying the last period (about 120,000 years ago) when temperatures were as warm as they are predicted to be by the end of this century found that sea levels could rise as much as 64 inches, or more than five feet (about twice that predicted by the IPCC). *See Rising Seas "to Beat Predictions,"* BBC NEWS ONLINE, Dec. 17, 2007. The new understanding of sea level rise suggests that even based on current temperature trends, the IPCC's Fourth Assessment significantly underestimates the sea level rise and its impacts on coastal states and landowners.

The second criticism of the IPCC report argues that it only takes into account impacts on sea level rise from temperature increases and linear predictions of ice melting. The growing understanding of the pace and mechanism of polar ice melting (suggested in the section above) has made some scientists re-assess the likelihood of even more significant sea-level rise due to the rapid disintegration of either the Greenland or West Antarctic ice sheets, or both. Indeed, the primary variable in accurately modeling future sea level rise, at least over the long term, is the stability of the ice sheets. Most models have assumed that the Antarctic ice sheet would likely gain mass because of greater precipitation over the next century, but as the reports noted above suggest, this may not be true. Moreover, significant melting of the polar ice sheets appears to be possible at lower temperatures than previously thought.

As noted *infra* in the discussion of rapid climate change events, the U.S. Geological Survey projects that a complete melting of the current Greenland ice sheet would raise sea levels by about 6.5 meters, and a melting of the West Antarctic ice sheet, or a release of the ice sheet from its mooring on the ocean floor, would raise sea levels by about 8 meters. Adding the East Antarctic Ice Sheet could raise sea levels by 80 meters! To put this in perspective, a 10-meter rise in sea levels would flood about 25 percent of the U.S. population, including most of southern Florida, lower Manhattan and portions of southern California. U.S. GEOLOGICAL SURVEY, SEA LEVEL AND CLIMATE (2000). Increasing concern over rapid melting led Rajendra Pachauri, head of the IPCC, to announce that "future reports from the IPCC should look at the 'frightening' possibility that ice sheets in Greenland and Antarctica could both begin melting rapidly. . . . If, through a process of melting, they collapse and are submerged in the sea, then we really are talking about sea-level rises of several meters." Associated Press, *U.N. Climate Chief: World Should Watch Poles: Previous Reports Didn't Factor in "Frightening" Possibility of Significant Melt*, Jan. 8, 2008.

C.   Changing Ocean Ecology

Sea level rise gets a lot of attention because of its impacts on coastal settlements, but other significant impacts on the oceans arise from increased concentrations of atmospheric greenhouse gases. These include changes in ocean temperature, salinity, acidity, and currents.

Ocean Acidification. Increased atmospheric concentrations of CO_2 and other greenhouse gases in the atmosphere are altering ocean chemistry in ways that threaten corals and other marine organisms. The oceans have absorbed so much additional CO_2 in recent years (approximately 118 billion tons since 1800) that they are becoming measurably more acidic, which in turn makes it more difficult for corals, plankton, and tiny marine snails to form their body parts. Worldwide we may be approaching irreversible damage to coral reefs from mass coral bleaching, disease, and mortality. Some scientists now predict that all ocean corals may disappear in fifty years. Moreover, the productivity of plankton, krill, and marine snails, which compose the base of the ocean food-chain, declines as the ocean acidifies. Reductions in their productivity will affect populations of everything from whales to salmon. Joan A. Kleypas, *Impacts of Ocean Acidification on Coral Reefs and Other Marine Calcifiers*, NATIONAL CENTER FOR ATMOSPHERIC RESEARCH (June 2006).

Ocean Warming. Measuring average ocean temperature over time is complex, particularly given that the limited historical data that does exist was not gathered for the purpose of monitoring climate change. Nonetheless, most recent studies conclude that surface temperature of the oceans has increased over the past decades, which is consistent with climate modeling. *See, e.g.*, Catia M. Dominguez, et al., *Improved Estimate of Upper-Ocean Warming and Multi-Decade Sea Level Rise*, 450 NATURE 1090–1093 (June 19, 2008). Warming of the ocean contributes to sea level rise (through thermal expansion) and could significantly alter ocean ecology.

Ocean Currents. Even slight changes in ocean temperature and salinity (due, for example, to ice melt) may alter ocean circulation and vertical mixing in the ocean, which threaten nutrient availability, biological productivity, and the functions of marine ecosystems. According to one recent study, the Walker Circulation, which drives the trade winds and guides ocean behavior across the tropical Pacific, has weakened 3.5 percent since the mid-1800s and may weaken another 10 percent by 2100. These Pacific currents supply important nutrients to ocean ecosystems across the equatorial Pacific, a vital fishing region. Perhaps most important for climate change are the currents of the Southern Ocean around Antarctica. Although significant uncertainty still exists about how the Southern Ocean is responding to global warming, the ocean is responsible for absorbing a significant amount of carbon (perhaps as much as 15 percent of the earth's total carbon sink). Changes in winds and currents in the Southern Ocean could thus have a significant impact in the overall rate of warming. For another important potential impact on ocean currents, see the discussion, *infra*, regarding the Atlantic Ocean's thermohaline circulation.

D.   Intensifying Weather Events

Climate is of course different from weather, and among the most hotly debated questions in the current climate debate is the extent to which extreme weather events are caused or exacerbated by global warming. The IPCC's 2007 report noted that the intensity and frequency of hurricanes, floods, droughts, storms, and other extreme climate events are likely to increase as temperatures increase. An increasing number of studies have begun to show the impact generally of climate change on intensifying extreme weather, including droughts, floods, and hurricanes. *See, e.g.*, U.S. Climate Change Science Program, *Weather and Climate Extremes in a Changing Climate. Regions of Focus: North America, Hawaii, Caribbean, and U.S. Pacific Islands* (June 2008). It is still difficult, however, to attribute all or part of a particular weather event to anthropogenic climate change, although the methodologies for doing so are improving all the time.

Hurricanes, Cyclones, and Tornadoes. In 2005, the Atlantic hurricane season saw a record 28 named storms (including the devastating hurricanes Katrina and Rita), causing approximately $100 billion in damages. According to the National Center for Atmospheric Research, "[g]lobal warming accounted for around half of the extra hurricane-fueling warmth in the waters of the tropical North Atlantic in 2005, while natural cycles were only a minor factor." Press Release, *Global Warming Surpassed Natural Cycles in Fueling 2005 Hurricane Season, NCAR Scientists Conclude*, NATIONAL CENTER FOR ATMOSPHERIC RESEARCH, June 22, 2006. A 2005 study found that hurricanes have become more destructive over the past 30 years and that rising temperatures could increase their intensity in the coming decades. Press Release, *Hurricanes Growing More Fierce Over Past 30 Years*, NATIONAL SCIENCE FOUNDATION (July 31, 2005). Another study suggested the number of Category 4 and 5 hurricanes worldwide has nearly doubled over the past 35 years, even though the total number of hurricanes has dropped since the 1990s. P. J. Webster, G. J. Holland, J. A. Curry, H.-R. Chang, *Changes in Tropical Cyclone Number, Duration, and Intensity in a Warming Environment*, 309 SCIENCE 1844–46 (Sept. 16, 2005). In general, increasing evidence does suggest that the intensity and frequency of hurricanes and other storms will likely increase with global warming. *See, e.g.*, U.S. Climate Change Science Program, *Weather and Climate Extremes in a Changing Climate. Regions of Focus: North America, Hawaii, Caribbean, and U.S. Pacific Islands* (June 2008) (concluding that more intense hurricanes in the Atlantic are "likely" because of climate change).

Freshwater, Floods, and Droughts. Climate change will likely intensify the global hydrological cycle, which could affect the magnitude and timing of floods and droughts. A warmer climate could decrease the proportion of precipitation falling as snow, reducing spring runoffs available for the growing season. Annual streamflows are expected to decline in already arid areas such as central Asia, the Mediterranean region, southern Africa, and Australia. In China's Yellow River, continued rising temperatures are projected to decrease water availability 20 to 40 percent by 2040 and reduce total agricultural output 10 percent by 2030 to 2050. Africa's available surface water is expected to be reduced 25 percent by 2100.

Several regions of the United States are currently suffering from significant droughts, which may be exacerbated by climate change. One study found that the declining snowpack in the western United States is primarily attributable to human-made climate change. According to the report, since 1950, the water content of the snowpack in the western United States has decreased in eight of nine mountain regions, ranging from 10 percent in the Colorado Rockies to 40 percent in the Oregon Cascades, and this decline cannot be explained by natural variability. *See* Marc Kaufman, *Decline in Snowpack Is Blamed On Warming: Water Supplies In West Affected*, WASH. POST, Feb. 1, 2008, at A01. A 2007 study found that the Great Lakes will suffer significant declines primarily due to increased evaporation, because the lakes do not freeze over as much as before. The study estimates that water levels in Lake Erie could drop more than 6 feet by 2066. *See* Detroit River-Western Lake Erie Basin Indicator Project, State of the Strait, Status and Trends of Key Indicators (2007). A recent U.S. government scientific assessment concluded that North America was "very likely" to experience more frequent heat waves and more frequent and intense rainstorms, and that the Southwest was "likely" to see increased drought conditions. U.S. Climate Change Science Program, *Weather and Climate Extremes in a Changing Climate. Regions of Focus: North America, Hawaii, Caribbean, and U.S. Pacific Islands* (June 2008).

E.   Declining Forests and Increasing Desertification

Changing Forests. Sustained climate change is expected to lead to substantial regional changes in the extent and type of forest cover, with some regions gaining and some losing forest productivity. For example, forests from central Europe to Siberia and to a lesser extent in North America have been growing more vigorously during the past two decades, presumably because warmer temperatures have lengthened the growing season by nearly three weeks. Long-term forest trends are hard to predict. Essentially, warmer temperatures will shift climate zones northward, with more southern species being able to tolerate more northern regions. Of course, this assumes that soil, precipitation, and other factors allow for the orderly spread of forest species.

But an orderly transition is doubtful; other forces are likely to limit forest productivity. In 2003, for example, forest fires in Europe, the United States, Australia, and Canada accounted for more global emissions than any other source, and at least one study by the Scripps Institute has suggested that warmer springs and summers may be increasing the number and severity of fires in the western United States. NASA scientists have observed significant browning in Arctic boreal forests, thought to be due to drier and warmer conditions. Even if GHG emissions stopped today, Eurasia, eastern China, Canada, Central America, and Amazonia are estimated to be at a 30 to 60 percent risk of forest loss. One recent study suggests that if left unchecked, increasing temperatures and declining rainfall could transform Brazil's entire Amazon Rainforest into a grassy savanna by the end of the century. Michael Astor, *Researchers: Warming May Change Amazon*, WASH. POST., Dec. 29, 2006.

Diseases may also spread to new areas. As a result of warmer average temperatures in British Columbia, for example, the mountain pine beetle extended its range north and has destroyed an area of soft-wood forest three times the size of Maryland, killing 411 million cubic feet of trees — double the annual take by all the loggers in Canada. Alaska has also lost up to three million acres of old growth forest to the pine beetle. Forests and their implications for climate policy are discussed further in Chapter 7.

Increasing Desertification. Deserts, covering nearly a fourth of the world's land mass and home to more than 500 million people, are expected to be among the hardest hit areas from climate change. Temperatures in desert regions have increased 0.5° to 2°C over the period 1976–2000, which was higher than the average global rise of 0.45°C. In general, deserts are likely to become more extreme and larger; with few exceptions, they are projected to become hotter but not significantly wetter. Shifts in temperature and precipitation in temperate rangelands may result in altered growing seasons and boundary shifts between deserts, grasslands, and shrublands. UNEP's 2006 GLOBAL DESERTS OUTLOOK described the impact of climate change on deserts this way:

> Because deserts are driven more by climatic pulses than by average conditions, even moderate changes in precipitation and temperature may create severe impacts by shifting the intensity and frequency of extreme periods, and subsequently creating catastrophic effects on plants, animals, and human livelihoods.

> Climate change is expected to affect less the total amount of available water, and more the overall water regime and the timing of water availability in deserts. Deserts and desert margins are particularly vulnerable to soil moisture deficits resulting from droughts, which have increased in severity in recent decades and are projected to become even more intense and frequent in the future. Conversely, flood events are expected to be fewer but more intense, in which case less moisture would infiltrate into soils, and run-off and eroded sediment would concentrate in depressions, reinforcing the patchiness of desert ecosystems.

> Deserts fed by melting snow or ice, such as the deserts of Central Asia and the Andean foothills, will be particularly vulnerable to a changing climate. As the volume of snowpack diminishes, river regimes will change from glacial to pluvial and, as a result, total run-off is expected to increase temporarily and then to decline. Peak discharges will shift from the summer months, when the demand is highest, to the spring and winter, with potentially severe implications for local agriculture.

UNEP, GLOBAL DESERT OUTLOOK, Ex. Summ., at x (2006).

F.   Impacts on Ecosystems and Wildlife

As suggested by the impacts described above on different ecosystems, including forests, freshwater, deserts, and oceans, it should be no surprise that climate change is likely to have profound and sweeping impacts on the world's biological diversity. In 2001, the IPCC concluded that:

> Distributions, population sizes, population density, and behavior of wildlife have been, and will continue to be, affected directly by changes in global or regional climate and indirectly through changes in vegetation. Climate change will lead to poleward movement of the boundaries of freshwater fish distributions along with loss of habitat for cold- and cool-water fishes and gain in habitat for warm-water fishes. . . . Many

species and populations are already at high risk, and are expected to be placed at greater risk by the synergy between climate change rendering portions of current habitat unsuitable for many species, and land-use change fragmenting habitats and raising obstacles to species migration. Without appropriate management, these pressures will cause some species currently classified as "critically endangered" to become extinct and the majority of those labeled "endangered or vulnerable" to become rarer, and thereby closer to extinction, in the 21st century.

IPCC, WORKING GROUP II, SUMMARY FOR POLICYMAKERS 11 (Third Assessment Report 2001).

In the past six years, theory has become reality; climate change impacts have already had significant impacts on a wide variety of animal behavior, with scientists reporting changes in populations, migration patterns, hibernation, and reproduction as animals adapt to earlier spring temperatures. Dr. William E. Bradshaw and Dr. Christina M. Holzapfel of the Center for Ecology and Evolutionary Biology have noted that climate change effects penetrate to the genetic level in a wide variety of organisms, with heritable genetic changes in populations such as birds, squirrels, and mosquitoes. Long term, they project that:

> small animals with short lifecycles and large population sizes will probably adapt to longer growing seasons and be able to persist; however, populations of many large animals with longer life cycles and smaller population sizes will experience a decline in population size or be replaced by more southern species. . . . [W]hile questions remain about the relative rates of environmental and evolutionary change . . . it is clear that unless the long-term magnitude of rapid climate change is widely acknowledged and effective steps are taken to mitigate its effects, natural communities with which we are familiar will cease to exist.

William E. Bradshaw & Christina M. Holzapfel, *Evolutionary Response to Rapid Climate Change*, 312 SCIENCE, June 9, 2006, at 1477–1478.

Although by no means the only impact on wildlife, extinctions from climate change are expected to be significant and widespread. The IPCC's Fourth Assessment found that "[a]pproximately 20–30 percent of plant and animal species assessed so far are likely to be at increased risk of extinction if increases in global average temperature exceed 1.5–2.5 degrees Celsius." IPCC, WORKING GROUP II, SUMMARY FOR POLICYMAKERS 8 (Fourth Assessment Report 2007). This suggests that roughly a quarter of all biological diversity may go extinct at temperatures that may be hard to avoid. Several currently rare (and not so rare) species may go extinct if they are unable to evolve or adapt to rapidly changing conditions.

Many examples of climate change impacts on biodiversity exist, reflecting the varied threats facing the planet's biodiversity. Between the 1980s and 1990s, almost two-thirds of the 110 known species of frogs in Central America became extinct. The direct cause of many of the extinctions appears to be a fungus now able to multiply due to warmer, cloudier nighttime weather. A 70-mile wide area off of Oregon's coast has become a dead zone due to low levels of oxygen linked to global warming. Bears in northern Spain have stopped hibernating. The U.S. Geological Survey predicts that as Arctic sea ice loss increases in the coming years, polar bear populations could decline by two-thirds by 2050. Other recent studies have linked global warming to declines in such disparate species as pikas, blue crabs, penguins, gray whales, salmon, walruses, and ringed seals. Bird extinction rates are predicted to be as high as 38 percent in Europe and 72 percent in northeastern Australia, if global warming exceeds 2°C above pre-industrial levels.

In sum, it is hard to comprehend the breadth and gravity of impacts on wildlife and natural ecosystems due to climate change, particularly when other ecological stresses are considered. As the IPCC's Fourth Assessment puts it: "the resilience of many ecosystems is likely to be exceeded this century by an unprecedented combination of climate change, associated disturbances (e.g., flooding, drought, wildfire, insects, ocean acidification) and other global change drivers (e.g., land-use change, pollution, over-exploitation of resources)." IPCC, WORKING GROUP II, SUMMARY FOR POLICYMAKERS 8 (Fourth Assessment Report 2007).

G.   Regional Impacts

The impacts from climate change are expected to be significantly different across regions. Indeed, regional variability is already being seen in the relatively higher temperature increases experienced in the Arctic, for example. Moreover, an increasing amount of time is now being spent in refining climate models to predict regional or local impacts. To help understand some of the differences across regions, the IPCC collected and published the following table that provides some examples.

Table 1-3: Climate Change Impacts by Region, reprinted from IPCC, SYNTHESIS REPORT, SUMMARY FOR POLICYMAKERS, at 10–11 (Fourth Assessment Report 2007)

Africa	• By 2020, between 75 and 250 million of people are projected to be exposed to increased water stress due to climate change.
	• By 2020, in some countries, yields from rain-fed agriculture could be reduced by up to 50%. Agricultural production, including access to food, in many African countries is projected to be severely compromised. This would further adversely affect food security and exacerbate malnutrition.
	• Towards the end of the 21st century, projected sea-level rise will affect low-lying coastal areas with large populations. The cost of adaptation could amount to at least 5–10% of Gross Domestic Product (GDP).
	• By 2080, an increase of 5–8% of arid and semi-arid land in Africa is projected under a range of climate scenarios.
Asia	• By the 2050s, freshwater availability in Central, South, East and South-East Asia, particularly in large river basins, is projected to decrease.
	• Coastal areas, especially heavily-populated megadelta regions in South, East and South-East Asia, will be at greatest risk due to increased flooding from the sea and, in some megadeltas, flooding from the rivers.
	• Climate change is projected to compound the pressures on natural resources and the environment, associated with rapid urbanization, industrialization and economic development.

	• Endemic morbidity and mortality due to diarrheal disease primarily associated with floods and droughts are expected to rise in East, South and South-East Asia due to projected changes in the hydrological cycle.
Australia and New Zealand	• By 2020, significant loss of biodiversity is projected to occur in some ecologically rich sites including the Great Barrier Reef and Queensland Wet Tropics.
	• By 2030, water security problems are projected to intensify in southern and eastern Australia and, in New Zealand . . . .
	• By 2030, production from agriculture and forestry is projected to decline over much of southern and eastern Australia, and over parts of eastern New Zealand, due to increased drought and fire. However, in New Zealand, initial benefits are projected in some other regions.
	• By 2050, ongoing coastal development and population growth in some areas of Australia and New Zealand are projected to exacerbate risks from sea level rise and increases in the severity and frequency of storms and coastal flooding.
Europe	• Climate change is expected to magnify regional differences in Europe's natural resources and assets. Negative impacts will include increased risk of inland flash floods, and more frequent coastal flooding and increased erosion (due to storminess and sea-level rise).
	• Mountainous areas will face glacier retreat, reduced snow cover and winter tourism, and extensive species losses (in some areas up to 60% under high emissions scenarios by 2080).
	• In Southern Europe, climate change is projected to worsen conditions (high temperatures and drought) in a region already vulnerable to climate variability, and to reduce water availability, hydropower potential, summer tourism and, in general, crop productivity.
	• Climate change is also projected to increase the health risks due to heat-waves, and the frequency of wildfires
Latin America	• By mid century, increases in temperature and associated decreases in soil water are projected to lead to gradual replacement of tropical forest by savanna in eastern Amazonia. Semi-arid vegetation will tend to be replaced by arid-land vegetation.
	• There is a risk of significant biodiversity loss through species extinction in many areas of tropical Latin America.
	• Productivity of some important crops is projected to decrease and livestock productivity to decline, with adverse consequences for food security. In temperate zones soybean yields are projected to increase. Overall, the number of people at risk of hunger is projected to increase.
	• Changes in precipitation patterns and the disappearance of glaciers are projected to significantly affect water availability for human consumption, agriculture and energy generation.

North America	• Warming in western mountains is projected to cause decreased snowpack, more winter flooding, and reduced summer flows, exacerbating competition for over-allocated water resources.
	• In the early decades of the century, moderate climate change is projected to increase aggregate yields of rain-fed agriculture by 5–20%, but with important variability among regions. Major challenges are projected for crops that are near the warm end of their suitable range or which depend on highly utilized water resources.
	• During the course of this century, cities that currently experience heatwaves are expected to be further challenged by an increased number, intensity and duration of heatwaves during the course of the century, with potential for adverse health impacts. Coastal communities and habitats will be increasingly stressed by climate change impacts interacting with development and pollution.
Polar Regions	• The main projected biophysical effects are reductions in thickness and extent of glaciers and ice sheets and sea ice, and changes in natural ecosystems with detrimental effects on many organisms including migratory birds, mammals and higher predators.
	• For human communities in the Arctic, impacts, particularly those resulting from changing snow and ice conditions, are projected to be mixed.
	• Detrimental impacts would include those on infrastructure and traditional indigenous ways of life.
	• In both polar regions, specific ecosystems and habitats are projected to be vulnerable, as climatic barriers to species invasions are lowered.
Small Islands	• Sea-level rise is expected to exacerbate inundation, storm surge, erosion and other coastal hazards, thus threatening vital infrastructure, settlements and facilities that support the livelihood of island communities.
	• Deterioration in coastal conditions, for example through erosion of beaches and coral bleaching is expected to affect local resources.
	• By mid-century, climate change is expected to reduce water resources in many small islands, e.g. in the Caribbean and Pacific, to the point where they become insufficient to meet demand during low-rainfall periods.
	• With higher temperatures, increased invasion by non-native species is expected to occur, particularly on mid- and high-latitude islands.

QUESTIONS AND DISCUSSION

1. Regional variations are particularly important, because some regions, particularly in developing countries, do not have the capacity to adapt well to the changes and impacts that are coming.

The ability of human systems to adapt to and cope with climate change depends on such factors as wealth, technology, education, information, skills, infrastructure, access to resources, and management capabilities. There is potential for developed and developing countries to enhance and/or acquire adaptive capabilities. Populations and communities are highly variable in their endowments with these attributes, and the developing countries, particularly the least developed countries, are generally poorest in this regard. As a result, they have lesser capacity to adapt and are more vulnerable to climate change damages, just as they are more vulnerable to other stresses. This condition is most extreme among the poorest people. * * *

The effects of climate change are expected to be greatest in developing countries in terms of loss of life and relative effects on investment and the economy. For example, the relative percentage damages to GDP from climate extremes have been substantially greater in developing countries than in developed countries.

IPCC WORKING GROUP II, SUMMARY FOR POLICYMAKERS, at 8. For more on adaptation responses to climate change, see Chapter 3.

2.   For a good recitation of some potential local and regional impacts from climate change, see the complaint filed in *State of Connecticut v. American Electric Power, Inc.*, Civ. No. 04-5669 (S.D.N.Y.); *see also* the Arctic Climate Impact Assessment, *supra*. As another example, a 2004 California study projected the potential impacts of climate change under two scenarios: one where emissions reduction policies are implemented and temperatures only increase by 2.3 to 3.3°C (4–5.9°F) by the end of the century, and the "business-as-usual" scenario, which projects a temperature increase of 3.8 to 5.8°C (6.8 to 10.4°F). Under the first scenario, the report predicts that heat waves become four times more frequent, increasing heat-related deaths by two or three times current rates. It also predicts the Sierra Nevada snow pack, which is a large source of water for municipal and agricultural areas in the state, decreases by 30 to 70 percent. Under the second scenario, heat waves and extreme heat in Los Angeles are projected to be six to eight times more frequent, with heat-related mortality increasing by five to seven times the current rate. Snow pack reduction ranges from 73 to 90 percent, causing "devastating impacts" throughout California as already tight water resources are strained beyond capacity. The higher temperatures in both scenarios would also shorten the ripening period for grapes, significantly degrading the state's ability to produce world class wine. Higher temperatures are also expected to cause a reduction in milk production by as much as 7 to 10 percent. *See* Katharine Hayhoe, et. al., *Emissions pathways, climate change, and impacts on California*, PROCEEDINGS OF THE NATIONAL ACADEMY OF SCIENCES (August 2004). What steps can the State of California take to respond to climate change — either to reduce the effects of climate change or to prepare for a different future? How do scenarios help to shape climate policy?

3.   Often the media and others confuse weather with climate. Weather refers to meteorological conditions at a specific place and time, including temperature, humidity, wind, precipitation, and barometric pressure. Climate refers to weather patterns that prevail over extended periods of time, including both average and extreme weather. While a temperature change of 6° F in a single day may be trivial, a permanent 6° F change in the average global temperature is not. In addition, weather's inherent variability masks the long-term trends of climate, making it even more difficult to actually measure changes in climate. Climate change often receives front-page media coverage only during hurricanes, droughts, or floods, even though it is difficult to say that any single weather event was caused by climate

change. Moreover, as soon as the weather breaks or appears to go back to normal, media coverage wanes and many people are left believing that the climate change stories were a false alarm.

IV. SOCIO-ECONOMIC IMPACTS

The breadth and magnitude of the environmental and physical impacts from climate change described above come into clearer focus when one analyzes the socio-economic impacts that will inevitably follow. Consider the effect that changing climates will have on food production or increasing temperatures could have on public health. Some socio-economic impacts, organized by sector, are summarized below in Table 1-4, reprinted from the Fourth Assessment of the IPCC, and then discussed further in this Section.

Table 1-4: Socio-Economic Impacts of Climate Change

Phenomenon[a] and direction of trend	Likelihood of future trends based on projections for 21st century	Examples of major projected impacts by sector			
		Agriculture, forestry and ecosystems	Water resources	Human health	Industry, settlement and society
Over most land areas, warmer and fewer cold days and nights, warmer and more frequent hot days and nights	*Virtually certain*	Increased yields in colder environments; decreased yields in warmer environments; increased insect outbreaks	Effects on water resources relying on snowmelt; effects on some water supplies	Reduced human mortality from decreased cold exposure	Reduced energy demand for heating; increased demand for cooling; declining air quality in cities; reduced disruption to transport due to snow, ice; effects on winter tourism
Warm spells/heat waves. Frequency increases over most land areas	*Very likely*	Reduced yields in warmer regions due to heat stress; increased danger of wildfire	Increased water demand; water quality problems, e.g. algal blooms	Increased risk of heat-related mortality, especially for the elderly, chronically sick, very young and socially isolated	Reduction in quality of life for people in warm areas without appropriate housing; impacts on the elderly, very young and poor

Heavy precipitation events. Frequency increases over most areas	Very likely	Damage to crops; soil erosion, inability to cultivate land due to waterlogging of soils	Adverse effects on quality of surface and groundwater; contamination of water supply; water scarcity may be relieved	Increased risk of deaths, injuries and infectious, respiratory and skin diseases	Disruption of settlements, commerce, transport and societies due to flooding; pressures on urban and rural infrastructures; loss of property
Area affected by drought increases	Likely	Land degradation; lower yields/crop damage and failure; increased livestock deaths; increased risk of wildfire	More widespread water stress	Increased risk of food water shortage; increased risk of malnutrition; increased risk of water- and food-borne diseases	Water shortage for settlements, industry and societies; reduced hydropower generation potentials; potential for population migration
Intense tropical cyclone activity increases	Likely	Damage to crops; windthrow (uprooting) of trees; damage to coral reefs	Power outages causing disruption of public water supply	Increased risk of deaths, injuries, water- and food-borne diseases; post-traumatic stress disorders	Disruption by flood and high winds; withdrawal of risk coverage in vulnerable areas by private insurers, potential for population migrations, loss of property
Increased Incidence of extreme high sea level (excludes tsunamis)	Likely	Salinisation of irrigation water, estuaries and freshwater systems	Decreased freshwater availability due to saltwater intrusion	Increased risk of deaths and injuries by drowning in floods; migration-related health effects	Costs of coastal protection versus costs of land-use relocation; potential for movement of populations and infrastructure; also see tropical cyclones above

---

A.   Agriculture, Drought, and Famine

Existing models suggest that global agricultural production could remain relatively stable in the face of anticipated climate change, but crop yields and changes in productivity could vary considerably across regions and among localities. Severe hardships could occur in specific regions, unless agricultural methodologies and distribution chains adapt successfully to relatively rapid and unpredicted changes in climate patterns.

According to three reports published in the December 2007 Proceedings of the National Academies of Science, such smooth transitions should not be assumed; the studies estimate that 1 to 5°C warming could result in "catastrophic" impacts on agriculture due to seasonal extremes of heat, drought or rain, the multiplier effects of spreading diseases or weeds, and other ecological upsets. *Toll of Climate Change on World Food Supply Could Be Worse than Thought*, SCIENCEDAILY (Dec. 4, 2007). The challenge is even more acute when one considers that we will need to double grain production by 2100 just to keep up with expected population and demographic changes.

Recent observations tend to support the position that productivity in many regions may decline. A 2007 report found that rising temperatures between 1981 and 2002 caused an estimated loss in production of wheat, corn, and barley of approximately 40 million tons a year worth about $5 billion (over what would otherwise have been produced). Although relatively modest compared to global production, it does suggest that global warming is already having a negative impact on agriculture. Steve Connor, *World's Most Important Crops Hit by Global Warming Effects*, THE INDEPENDENT, March 19, 2007. Recent studies have also linked global warming to shortened growing seasons and exacerbated drought conditions with significant negative impacts on rice farmers in Bangladesh, cotton farmers in Africa, ranchers in Australia, and dairy producers in California.

In 2008, the world suffered a severe food crisis, due to a combination of low harvests due to severe weather, rising fuel costs, growing demand for beef, and increased demand for biofuels. The World Bank reported that food prices had risen 75% since 2000, with wheat prices increasing by 200%. The cost of rice hit record highs and corn was the highest in more than a decade. Food-related riots or civil unrest erupted in several countries, including Indonesia and Haiti. Some countries were accused of hoarding rice from the international markets. The situation prompted the World Food and Agricultural Organization to hold a "high level conference" on food security, which was attended by more than 180 countries and focused on the challenges posed by climate change and the demand for biofuels. *See Declaration of the High Level Conference on Food Security: Challenges from Climate Change and Bioenergy*, June 5, 2008.

Future impacts are anticipated to be even worse, especially in the tropics and subtropics. For example, by 2080 the FAO predicts a 5 to 8 percent increase in the amount of arid lands in sub-Saharan Africa, resulting in a loss of about 280 million tons of cereal production (16 percent of their agricultural output). According to some estimates, extreme drought (where virtually no farming will be possible), which currently encompasses 1 percent of land area at any given time, could increase to 30 percent of land area by 2100.

B.   Public Health Impacts

A variety of public health impacts have also been linked to current and future climate change, including generally: increased illnesses and deaths from heat waves and air pollution; increased outbreaks of some insect-borne infectious diseases, most notably malaria; increased cases of diarrhea and other water-borne diseases from increased flooding; and increased malnutrition due to reduced agricultural yields in drought-ridden areas. The ultimate impacts of climate change on health will vary widely from region to region. Indeed, we might expect fewer people to freeze to death (even while more die from heat exposure), but we can also expect that the areas hardest hit by climate change (tropical and subtropical developing countries) are also areas with generally poor health care or sanitation and thus the least likely to be able to treat the increased health impacts.

Nor are public health impacts only a concern for the future. In 2002, the World Health Organization (WHO) reported that anthropogenic climate change *already* results in at least 5.5 million cases of illness and more than 150,000 deaths each year. The report projects that these rates could double by 2030. THE WORLD HEALTH ORGANIZATION, THE WORLD HEALTH REPORT 2002 — REDUCING RISKS, PROMOTING HEALTHY LIFE 72 (2002). Anecdotal evidence also now links public health threats specifically to global warming. In the winter of 2007, more than 3,000 cases of infections caused by the rat-transmitted hanta virus were reported in Russian cities and towns, attributed to an unusually warm winter and the presence of rats that should have been hibernating. Italy is now experiencing outbreaks of dengue, a tropical disease from the tropical tiger mosquito, now thriving in southern Europe, and spreading to France and Switzerland. In the United States, the National Environmental Trust reported that heat-related deaths may double due to climate change by 2050.

C.   Climate Refugees

As early as 1993, Oxford Visiting Fellow Dr. Norman Myers estimated that by 2050 approximately 150 million "climate" refugees would be forced from their homes due to agricultural changes and sea level rise brought about by global warming. *See* N. Myers, *Environmental Refugees in a Globally Warmed World*, 43 BIOSCIENCE 752 (Dec. 1993). Estimates have changed little in the last fifteen years as most researchers estimate that anywhere from 20 to 200 million refugees will be displaced by climate change-related impacts. Nor, as suggested by the following excerpt, are the impacts all in the future.

TERESITA PEREZ, CLIMATE REFUGEES: THE HUMAN TOLL OF GLOBAL WARMING
(Center for American Progress, Dec. 7, 2006)*

The number of people affected [by climate change] is uncertain since these "climate refugees" are not granted official refugee status under the Geneva Convention, and the United Nations therefore keeps no central tally. According to the International Federation of Red Cross [and Red Crescent Societies], however, climate change disasters are currently a bigger cause of population displacement than war and persecution. Estimates of climate refugees currently range from 25 to 50 million, compared to the official refugee population of 20.8 million. Rising sea levels, increasing desertification, weather-induced flooding, and other environmental changes, will likely displace many more hundreds of millions of people.

Accidents of geography have caused the countries least able to prevent climate change to become the most vulnerable to its earliest effects. Developing countries bear minimal responsibility for climate change because they have little industry and produce relatively small amounts of pollution. But their populations — often the poorest of the world's poor — are more likely to occupy dangerous locations, such as coast lines, flood plains, steep slopes, and settlements of flimsy shanty homes. The governments of these poor countries therefore carry the largest burden associated with climate refugees though they are already failing to meet the basic needs of their citizens and are ill-equipped to recover from disasters.

We can already see the effects that global warming has on some island nations. The inhabitants of the Carteret Islands were the first climate refugees forced to relocate due to sea level rise attributed to global warming. The Papua New Guinean government authorized a total evacuation of the islands in 2005 — the evacuation is expected to be complete by 2007. Estimates show that by 2015 Carteret will be largely submerged and entirely uninhabitable.

Floods and other weather-related disasters have also caused nearly 10 million people to migrate from Bangladesh to India over the past two decades, creating immense population pressures. A one-meter rise in sea level will, in turn, inundate three million hectares in Bangladesh, and displace another 15–20 million people.

The climate refugee problem will intensify as global warming increases, potentially yielding between 150 million and 200 million refugees as early as 2010. Despite the scale of the problem, no one is really addressing the needs of these refugees, and much of the discussion about them has been limited to defining their official legal status — whether they should be officially classified as refugees or not.

———

Of course, not all climate refugees are due to anthropogenic climate changes; some refugees would need to leave their homes for "natural" weather events as well. But the long-term impacts of climate change are clearly going to increase the number of such refugees and stretch the international community's ability to deal with them.

———

QUESTIONS AND DISCUSSION

1. One particularly dramatic localized impact from climate change is the potential of glacial lake outburst floods or "GLOFs." Freshwater lakes often form at the base of many glaciers, held back by naturally occurring earthen dams or moraines. As glaciers recede more rapidly from climate change, the amount of water in these lakes can expand significantly, as does the pressure resulting on the earthen dam. GLOFs occur when the soil moraine holding back the lake bursts. As with any sudden dam burst, significant damage can occur in a short period of time. GLOFs are not a new phenomenon, but UNEP and other international agencies are concerned that many glacial lakes may now be filling too rapidly due to climate change. A UNEP study identified 20 glacial lakes in Nepal and 24 in Bhutan that they believe are at "high risk" of bursting within the next decade. The impact of a GLOF can be significant; in August 1985, a sudden outburst flood from the Dig Tsho glacial lake in Nepal killed four people, destroyed fourteen bridges and caused $1.5 million in damage to a nearly completed hydropower plant. What policy measures could Nepal and Bhutan implement to protect against such floods? Who should pay for such measures? U.N. Chronicle, *Global Warming Triggers Glacial Lakes Flood Threat*, UNITED NATIONS ENVIRONMENT PROGRAMME, Nov. 3, 2002, at 48.

2. Food security issues will not only be limited to changes in agricultural production. Fish production may also decline due to climate change. A December 2006 report in Nature showed that as climate warms, phytoplankton production declines. Not only does this mean that less phytoplankton is available to remove carbon from the atmosphere (producing a warming feedback loop), but phytoplankton is also the base of the ocean food chain. Less phytoplankton production inevitably means less fish production. Scott C. Doney, *Oceanography: Plankton in a Warmer World*, 444 SCIENCE 695 (Dec. 7, 2006); NASA, *Climate Warming Reduces Ocean Food Supply*, Dec. 6, 2006.

3. For many types of impacts, the portion attributable to global warming cannot easily be separated from the interactions with other causes. For example, global warming will be exacerbated in many cities by the urban heat island effect, where the cumulative impact of few trees and dark pavements can cause temperatures during heat waves to be 6–7° C higher in cities than in surrounding areas. Similarly, higher carbon dioxide levels in already polluted areas are expected to lead to as much as 20,000 more air pollution deaths annually due to CO_2's chemical and meteorological effects. In part, this is due to synergistic impacts between increased temperatures and asthma and other air pollutant-related health effects.

4. As you consider the plight of climate refugees, consider whether a moral responsibility exists for wealthier countries, particularly those that have contributed disproportionately to climate change, to provide support or even citizenship to displaced communities. Is there any argument for a legal responsibility? In this regard, think of the differing responses to Tuvalu's plight from New Zealand and Australia, as depicted in the following excerpt from Friends of the Earth-Australia:

> Tuvalu is the first country in which residents have been forced to evacuate because of rising sea levels. Nearly 3000 Tuvaluans have already left their homelands. In support of their crisis, the New Zealand government has established an immigration programme called the Pacific Access Category, which currently sees seventy-five residents migrate to NZ each year. . . .

> The Pacific Access Category (PAC) is an immigration deal that was formed in 2001 between the governments of Tuvalu, Fiji, Kiribati, Tonga and New Zealand, to enable environmental refugees who are displaced from their homes by the effects of climate change to move to a less vulnerable environment. Each country has been allocated a set quota of citizens who can be granted residency in New Zealand each year. The PAC allows 75 residents each from Tuvalu and Kiribati, whereas Tonga and Fiji have a quota of 250.

> Following the Australian government's refusal to accept any Tuvaluan environmental refugees, New Zealand agreed to accept the entire Tuvaluan population of 11,000. Although New Zealand's immigration policies are far more supportive towards environmental refugees than Australia's policies, Pacific Islanders still face a number of impediments to reaching safer ground. Principal applicants must meet set requirements before being eligible to enter the PAC ballot.

> These requirements exclude part of the Tuvaluan population by stipulating that: applicants possess citizenship status for Kiribati, Tuvalu, Tonga or Fiji; are aged between 18 and 45; have an acceptable offer of employment in New Zealand; have a minimum level of skills in English language; have a minimum income requirement if the applicant has a dependant; exhibit certain health and character requirements; and have no history of unlawful entry into New Zealand since July 1, 2002.

In short, this means that the elderly and the poor — those most vulnerable — may have trouble being accepted as principal applicants. Furthermore, an "acceptable" offer of employment is defined as "permanent, full-time, genuine, and paid by a salary or wages". Considering their location and level of access to required resources, Tuvaluans may have difficulty gaining employment in New Zealand before they arrive in the country, thereby excluding them from access to the program. . . .

In 2000, the Tuvaluan government appealed to both Australia and New Zealand to take in Tuvaluan residents if rising sea levels reached the point where evacuation would be essential. The Australian government refused to implement a program to grant Tuvaluan environmental refugees residency in Australia. In response to Tuvalu's crisis, Immigration Minister Phillip Ruddock stated that accepting environmental refugees from Tuvalu would be "discriminatory".

With regard to Australia's response, Senior Tuvalu official, Mr Paani Laupepa expressed that while New Zealand has helped out their neighbours, "Australia on the other hand has slammed the door in our face".

FRIENDS OF THE EARTH AUSTRALIA, A CITIZEN'S GUIDE TO CLIMATE REFUGEES, 6–7. In light of its concern that the number of climate refugees may be increasing, New Zealand recently created a climate ambassador.

5.   When we think of environmental refugees generally or climate refugees more specifically, we almost always think of the poor from developing countries such as Bangladesh or island states such as Tuvalu. But an argument can be made that the United States is already struggling to support 250,000 climate refugees — the number of people that seem to have been permanently displaced from Hurricane Katrina. Nearly three years after the hurricane, the United States has still not adequately provided for many of the poor affected by the hurricane. *See, e.g.*, Lester R. Brown, *Global Warming Forcing U.S. Coastal Population to Move Inland: An Estimated 250,000 Katrina Evacuees Are Now Climate Refugees*, ECO-ECONOMY UPDATE (Aug. 16, 2006). What does this suggest about the ability of other countries to respond to people internally displaced by an increasing number of natural disasters?

6.   ***Problem Exercise on Impacts.*** Any resuscitation of general impacts from climate change can seem sterile and largely divorced from the reality of law students. But in recent years, an increasing number of studies are being done to identify potential climate change impacts for virtually all regions or states of the United States. Research the potential impacts of climate change on the location where you are attending law school.

V.   RAPID CLIMATE CHANGE EVENTS AND LIVING WITH UNCERTAINTY

Most of the impacts described above, significant as they may be, are relatively straightforward and linear results from increasing temperatures due to climate change. Even more disturbing is the increasing evidence that climate change may be leading us toward a non-linear "environmental cliff," where climate change triggers rapid, irreversible, and unpredictable results. Such abrupt or rapid climate change events could occur suddenly, and drastically, when certain thresholds are crossed, tipping the climate into a new state of equilibrium — one that could change the planet's global ecology and create millions of climate refugees. As a 2007 study on the implications of climate change for national security explained:

> Abrupt climate changes present the most worrisome scenario for human societies because of the inherent difficulties in adapting to sudden changes. Abrupt sea level rise is particularly worrisome. The great ice sheets along the edges of Greenland and the West Antarctic are vulnerable to sudden breakup: as the edges of the sheet thaw and meltwater seeps to the ice-ground boundary, the meltwater will act as a lubricant and facilitate a slippage into the sea. This physical phenomenon is an example of a positive feedback mechanism that, once started, is difficult to reverse. Melting of these ice sheets would be catastrophic. The Greenland Ice Sheet could raise sea levels by twenty-three feet over a millennium; the West Antarctic Ice Sheet would have a more immediate impact, raising sea levels more than three feet per century for five centuries. The probability of a collapse of the West Antarctic Ice Sheet before 2100 is estimated to be between 5 and 10 percent.
>
> None of these abrupt climate changes are projected by the climate models driven by the IPCC's 2007 future scenarios. However, if temperature increases were at the high end of the ranges projected by the models, abrupt climate changes such as those discussed above are more likely to occur. Such abrupt climate changes could make future adaptation extremely difficult, even for the most developed countries.

The CNA Corporation, *National Security and the Threat of Climate Change* 60 (2007). Although substantial sea level rise is the best known possible form of abrupt climate change, it is not the only one that concerns scientists. Of potentially equal concern is the way in which changes in ocean temperatures and salinity may alter major ocean currents, most notably the ocean's Thermohaline Circulation. The following excerpt from the Union of Concerned Scientists describes how global warming might weaken or shut down the thermohaline circulation.

> Thermohaline circulation is a global ocean circulation pattern that distributes water and heat both vertically, through the water column, and horizontally across the globe. As cold, salty water sinks at high latitudes, it pulls warmer water from lower latitudes to replace it. Water that sinks in the North Atlantic flows down to the southern hemisphere, skirts the Antarctic continent, where it is joined by more sinking water, and then crosses south of the Indian Ocean to enter the Pacific Ocean basin. There, the cold deep water rises to the surface, where heat from the tropical sun warms the water at the ocean's surface and drives evaporation, leaving behind saltier water. This warm, salty water flows northward to join the Gulf Stream, traveling up the Eastern coast of the United States and across the Atlantic Ocean into the North Atlantic region. There, heat is released to the atmosphere, warming parts of Western Europe. Once this warm, salty water reaches the North Atlantic and releases its heat, it again becomes very cold and dense, and sinks to the deep ocean. * * *
>
> Thermohaline circulation is [thus] driven by the sinking of cold, salty water at high latitudes. Fresh water flowing into the North Atlantic Ocean from rainfall or the melting of ice and permafrost can make the ocean water less salty, and therefore less dense. If it becomes "light" enough, it will not sink any more, possibly slowing or shutting down global thermohaline circulation. Indeed, during some of the abrupt events in Earth's past climate, scientists find evidence of large catastrophic flows of fresh water into the North Atlantic from the melting of glaciers and ice caps, and due to flooding from glacier-dammed lakes. Without the large-scale sinking of

salty water in the North Atlantic the influx of warm water to replace it from the tropics would not occur, effectively switching off the thermohaline circulation.

Past changes in thermohaline circulation have occurred during periods of relatively rapid climate change, such as transitions in and out of glaciations. Similarly, the rapid warming we are currently experiencing could trigger an abrupt thermohaline shutdown and subsequent regional cooling. While a shutdown of thermohaline circulation is unlikely to occur in the next century, scientists have recently found that freshwater inputs have already caused measurable "freshening" of North Atlantic surface waters over the past 40 years. Human activities may be driving the climate system toward a threshold and thus increasing the chance of abrupt climate changes occurring.

Union of Concerned Scientists, *Abrupt Climate Change FAQ, available at* www.uc-susa.org. The following excerpt is from a National Academies of Science report on the potential reduction of the thermohaline circulation (THC). As you read it, consider how much is still unknown about the THC and what the appropriate policy response should be in the face of such uncertainty.

NATIONAL RESEARCH COUNCIL, ABRUPT CLIMATE CHANGE: INEVITABLE SURPRISES (2002)*

[In the past,] abrupt climate changes were especially common when the climate system was being forced to change most rapidly. Thus, greenhouse warming and other human alterations of the earth system may increase the possibility of large, abrupt, and unwelcome regional or global climatic events. The abrupt changes of the past are not fully explained yet, and climate models typically underestimate the size, speed, and extent of those changes. Hence, future abrupt changes cannot be predicted with confidence, and climate surprises are to be expected. * * *

If the increase in atmospheric greenhouse gas concentration leads to a collapse of the Atlantic THC, the result will not be global cooling. However, there might be regional cooling over and around the North Atlantic, relative to a hypothetical global-warming scenario with unchanged THC. By itself, this reduced warming might not be detrimental. However, we cannot rule out the possibility of net cooling over the North Atlantic if the THC decrease is very fast. Such rapid cooling would exert a large strain on natural and societal systems. The probability of this occurring is unknown but presumably much smaller than that of any of the more gradual scenarios included in the Intergovernmental Panel on Climate Change report. The probability is not, however, zero. Obtaining rational estimates of the probability of such a low-probability/high-impact event is crucial. It is worth remembering that models such as those used in the Intergovernmental Panel on Climate Change report consistently underestimate the size and extent of anomalies associated with past changes of the THC. * * *

Even if no net cooling results from a substantial, abrupt change in the Atlantic THC, the changes in water properties and regional circulation are expected to be large, with possibly large effects on ecosystems, fisheries, and sea level. There are no credible scenarios of these consequences, largely because the models showing abrupt change in the THC have too crude spatial resolution to be used in regional analyses. To develop these scenarios would require the combination of physical and biological models to investigate the effects on ecosystems. . . .

If we are to develop the ability to predict changes in the THC, we must observe its strength and structure as a fundamental requirement, akin to the necessity to observe the equatorial Pacific if one wants to forecast El Niño. So far, however, no observational network exists to observe the THC on a continuous basis. * * *

Arctic sea-ice volume appears to have shrunk dramatically in recent decades. . . . The influence of that decline on the freshwater budget of the Atlantic THC is unknown but could be critical. It is crucial to know the net freshwater flux from the Arctic Ocean to the Nordic Seas, in the form of both sea ice and low-salinity surface water. . . . Given the importance of freshwater forcing for the stability of the THC, such events might presage change in the circulation.

QUESTIONS AND DISCUSSION

1.   Given the large gaps identified above in our understanding of the THC, what should the appropriate policy response be? In general, how should policy makers address low probability/high impact risks? Moreover, not only is the probability low, but we also know so little about the underlying mechanism of the THC that we have little confidence in our analysis of the probability. In this respect, consider how the precautionary principle, discussed further in Chapter 4, could guide policymakers. Under the precautionary principle, policymakers are encouraged to take cost-effective measures to prevent potential irreversible impacts even if there is less than full scientific certainty about the probability and scale of the impacts. Can you see how this approach differs from the normal regulatory approach taken in the United States, where we must demonstrate that an impact will, or is at least likely to, occur before we regulate to prevent the impact? How does the precautionary principle help us, if at all, in addressing rapid climate change events like those described above?

2.   As noted above in the discussions of sea level rise, the latest IPCC reports and supportive modeling do not include estimates based on rapid polar ice melting or the shutdown of the thermohaline circulation. Does such an approach properly inform policymakers of the known potential risks from climate change? How should they report on low probability/high impact possibilities?

VI. NATIONAL SECURITY AND CLIMATE CHANGE

In recent years as the potential impacts from climate change have become clearer, many people are viewing climate change in terms of national security. Partly this is because efforts to address climate change by, for example, shifting to renewable energy or energy conservation will reduce our oil dependency and strengthen our national security at the same time. But the national security discussion also recognizes that climate change may lead to significant instability in the economies and societies of strategically important regions of the world. The discussion of climate refugees, above, is just one dimension of the instability that can trigger security concerns. Consider in this regard the findings from a 2007 report issued by an independent research organization advised by former U.S. military officials:

THE CNA CORPORATION, NATIONAL SECURITY AND THE THREAT OF CLIMATE CHANGE
Ex. Summ., at 6–7 (2007)

Projected climate change poses a serious threat to America's national security. The predicted effects of climate change over the coming decades include extreme weather events, drought, flooding, sea level rise, retreating glaciers, habitat shifts, and the increased spread of life-threatening diseases. These conditions have the potential to disrupt our way of life and to force changes in the way we keep ourselves safe and secure.

In the national and international security environment, climate change threatens to add new hostile and stressing factors. On the simplest level, it has the potential to create sustained natural and humanitarian disasters on a scale far beyond those we see today. The consequences will likely foster political instability where societal demands exceed the capacity of governments to cope.

Climate change acts as a threat multiplier for instability in some of the most volatile regions of the world. Projected climate change will seriously exacerbate already marginal living standards in many Asian, African, and Middle Eastern nations, causing widespread political instability and the likelihood of failed states.

Unlike most conventional security threats that involve a single entity acting in specific ways and points in time, climate change has the potential to result in multiple chronic conditions, occurring globally within the same time frame. Economic and environmental conditions in already fragile areas will further erode as food production declines, diseases increase, clean water becomes increasingly scarce, and large populations move in search of resources. Weakened and failing governments, with an already thin margin for survival, foster the conditions for internal conflicts, extremism, and movement toward increased authoritarianism and radical ideologies.

The U.S. may be drawn more frequently into these situations, either alone or with allies, to help provide stability before conditions worsen and are exploited by extremists. The U.S. may also be called upon to undertake stability and reconstruction efforts once a conflict has begun, to avert further disaster and reconstitute a stable environment.

Projected climate change will add to tensions even in stable regions of the world. The U.S. and Europe may experience mounting pressure to accept large numbers of immigrant and refugee populations as drought increases and food production declines in Latin America and Africa. Extreme weather events and natural disasters, as the U.S. experienced with Hurricane Katrina, may lead to increased missions for a number of U.S. agencies, including state and local governments, the Department of Homeland Security, and our already stretched military, including our Guard and Reserve forces.

The connection between climate change and national security has not been lost on the U.S. military. At the same time that the Bush Administration was denying the scientific evidence for climate change, the military was basing its strategic planning for the coming century in part on scenarios premised on substantial climate impacts. A Pentagon scenario prepared in 2003 describes the national security threats posed by a rapid climate change event, such as the shutdown of the North Atlantic thermohaline conveyor (described above in Section V).

The Pentagon scenario is based on today's global warming trends and studies of previous sudden changes in climate, most notably the so called "Little Ice Age" during the Middle Ages. It depicts a world in which much of the Northern Hemisphere sees a drop in annual average temperature of 5° to 6°F, while the Southern Hemisphere's temperatures increase by as much as 4°F. Along with widespread drought and intensified winter storms, the abrupt climate change causes shortages in food, water, and energy supplies. The collapse in the thermohaline system, which is what will trigger the change, is assumed to begin between 2010 and 2020. Europe becomes an arctic tundra, and southern areas are swarmed with refugees fleeing from Scandinavia and other northern areas. Ocean levels rise, causing emigration from inundated coastal areas. An increase in intensity of monsoons and hurricanes plagues several areas of the globe. All of these predicted changes in climate ultimately impact global security as humankind resorts to warfare to obtain scarce resources:

> Violence and disruption stemming from the stresses created by abrupt changes in the climate pose a different type of threat to national security than we are accustomed to today. Military confrontation may be triggered by a desperate need for natural resources such as energy, food, and water rather than by conflicts over ideology, religion, or national honor. The shifting motivation for confrontation would alter which countries are most vulnerable and the existing warning signs for security threats.

Peter Schwartz and Doug Randall, *An Abrupt Climate Change Scenario and Its Implications for United States National Security*, at 14 (Oct. 2003). As journalist David Stipp, who first reported on the Pentagon scenario, observed: "as abrupt climate change hits home, warfare may again come to define human life." Despite the ominous predictions, the report indicates the United States, while being greatly affected, will be able to protect itself as the nation turns inward and becomes self sufficient. According to the report, the United States will have the wealth, technology, and resources to support its population in the face of food and energy shortages. However, as a defensive measure the United States will have to tighten its borders to prevent mass immigration from Canada, Mexico, and the Caribbean, areas severely predicated to be impacted by harsher winters, drought, or rising sea levels. *Id.; see also* David Stipp, *The Pentagon's Weather Nightmare*, FORTUNE, Feb. 9, 2004.

QUESTIONS AND DISCUSSION

1. The 2003 Pentagon report received significant attention in the press, in part because the military appeared to be taking the threat of climate change more seriously than the Bush Administration's environmental officials. What do you think led to the different approaches of these agencies? Is it consistent to prepare for a rapid climate change event militarily (perhaps as a precautionary step), while at the same time denying that the risk of such an event warrants taking any steps to curb climate change?

2. The United States is not the only country that is evaluating the national security implications of climate change. A 2006 report by the UK's Oxford Research Group called terrorism "a relatively minor threat" compared to the threats posed by climate change, highlighting displacement of large populations, worldwide food shortages, and social unrest. Chris Abbott, Paul Rogers, and John Sloboda, *Global Responses to Global Threats: Sustainable Security for the 21st Century*, OXFORD RESEARCH GROUP (June 2006); *see also* CHRIS ABBOTT, AN UNCERTAIN FUTURE: LAW ENFORCEMENT, NATIONAL SECURITY AND CLIMATE CHANGE (Oxford Research Group, Jan. 2008).

3. On April 17, 2007, the United Kingdom, sitting as President of the UN Security Council, held the first-ever discussion of climate change at the Security Council. Although the decision to use that forum to discuss climate change was controversial, over fifty delegations spoke at the hearing with many supporting the Security Council's attention on climate change as a long-term risk to international security. The following excerpt from the UN's official summary of the meeting provides a flavor of the controversy:

> The session was chaired by British Foreign Secretary, Margaret Beckett . . . . She said that recent scientific evidence reinforced, or even exceeded, the worst fears about climate change, as she warned of migration on an unprecedented scale because of flooding, disease and famine. She also said that drought and crop failure could cause intensified competition for food, water and energy.
>
> She said that climate change was a security issue, but it was not a matter of narrow national security — it was about "our collective security in a fragile and increasingly interdependent world". By holding today's debate, the Council was not seeking to pre-empt the authority of other bodies, including the General Assembly and the Economic and Social Council. The decisions that they came to, and action taken, in all those bodies required the fullest possible understanding of the issues involved. "[So] climate change can bring us together, if we have the wisdom to prevent it from driving us apart," she declared.

*   *   *

> China's representative was among those who argued that the Council was not the proper forum for a debate on climate change. "The developing countries believe that the Security Council has neither the professional competence in handling climate change — nor is it the right decision-making place for extensive participation leading up to widely acceptable proposals," he said. . . . The issue could have certain security implications, but, generally speaking, it was, in essence, an issue of sustainable development. * * *
>
> But Papua New Guinea's representative, who spoke on behalf of the Pacific Islands Forum, said that the impact of climate change on small islands was no less threatening than the dangers guns and bombs posed to large nations. Pacific island countries were likely to face massive dislocations of people, similar to population flows sparked by conflict. The impact on identity and social cohesion were likely to cause as much resentment, hatred and alienation as any refugee crisis.
>
> * * * The Forum did not expect the Council to get involved in Climate Change Convention negotiations, but it did expect the 15-member body to keep the issue of climate change under continuous review, to ensure that all countries contributed to solving the problem and that those efforts were commensurate with their resources and capacities. It also expected the Council to review sensitive issues, such as implications for sovereignty and international legal rights from the loss of land, resources and people.
>
> Singapore's speaker said that . . . [w]hile it might be difficult to quantify the relationship between climate change and international peace and security, there should be no doubt that climate change was an immediate global challenge, whose effects were transboundary and multi-faceted. He was not advocating that the Security Council play a key role on climate change, but neither could he deny that body "some sort of a role,

because it seems obvious to all but the wilfully blind that climate change must, if not now, then eventually have some impact on international peace and security."

See UN Division of Public Information, *Security Council Holds First-Ever Debate on Impact of Climate Change on Peace, Security, Hearing over 50 Speakers* (April 17, 2007). What difference would it make if the Security Council were to keep climate change "under review" as suggested by the Pacific Island Forum? Why are China and the other developing countries insistent that this should remain an issue of sustainable development? The excerpt also provides some initial insights into the conflicts that occur in global negotiations over climate change. The global politics of climate are discussed further in both Chapter 4 and Chapter 9.

4. In July 2006, New Zealand named its former Ambassador to France to be its first Climate Change Ambassador. The Ambassador is responsible for handling New Zealand's international negotiations on climate change, both as part of the Kyoto process and in various bilateral negotiations. For example, the Ambassador has led the delegation to the bilateral negotiations with the United States over the U.S.-New Zealand Climate Change Partnership and the discussions with South Pacific Islanders over New Zealand's policies towards climate refugees. What are the advantages of creating a "Climate Change Ambassador"? Does it more adequately reflect the far-reaching foreign policy implications of climate change? Would it allow countries to respond to climate change more directly as a national security issue?

5. The unprecedented melting of the Arctic Ocean's summer ice has sparked an international land grab between Russia, Denmark, the United States, and Canada. At stake are claims to potentially vast natural resources that may now (due to receding polar ice) be economically feasible to exploit. In 2007, Russia took the remarkable step of sending a submarine to plant a Russian flag under the North Pole to stake its claim to vast parts of the territory. This has prompted renewed focus on the rules for claiming territorial areas of the continental shelf, which are set by the UN Convention on the Law of the Sea. In addition to raising diplomatic concerns, Russia's move also led for further calls in the United States to ratify the Law of the Sea Convention. *See generally* Duncan Currie, *Sovereignty and Conflict in the Arctic Due to Climate Change: Climate Change and the Legal Status of the Arctic Ocean* (Aug. 5, 2007); *see alo* discussion of the law of the sea in Chapter 10.

6. For a readable and interesting account of how past variations in climate played a role in history, see BRIAN FAGAN, THE LITTLE ICE AGE: HOW CLIMATE MADE HISTORY: 1350–1800 (2000). Although the book's description of this era in Europe is interesting for showing how climate affects human development, it is addressing a period of regional climate variability in Europe and has little direct relationship to today's global climate change.

7. In June 2008, the National Intelligence Council provided a report to Congress identifying the national security threats to the United States and the world posed by climate change. The report, which is the first formal report of its kind in the United States, warned that climate change could threaten U.S. security by leading to political instability, mass movements of refugees, terrorism, and conflicts over water and other resources. The report was based in part on assessments conducted by Columbia University's Center for International Earth Science Information Network (CIESIN), which ranked countries by looking at their relative vulnerability to sea-level rise, increased water scarcity, and higher temperatures, compared with their ability to adapt. *See, e.g., Climate Change May Challenge National Security, Classified Report Warns*, SCIENCE DAILY, June 26, 2008.

VII. KEEPING OUR EYE ON THE BALL: LONG-TERM STABILIZATION TARGETS TO AVOID THE WORST CLIMATE IMPACTS

It is easy to get lost (and depressed) in the details of GHG concentrations, carbon dioxide emission levels, parts per million, surface air temperatures, sea level rise, and all the other climate impacts. This section is meant to simplify the way of thinking about climate change impacts and policy — by working backwards from the world in which we want to live to the current policies necessary to get there. We can break this down into a series of five questions:

First, what impacts must we avoid to ensure a livable planet for future generations?

Second, what is the maximum average temperature increase that is allowable to ensure that we avoid the worst climate impacts?

Third, what is the maximum atmospheric concentration of greenhouse gases that is allowable to ensure that we do not exceed the average temperature increase identified in Question 2?

Fourth, what is the amount of net greenhouse gas emissions into the atmosphere that are allowable to stabilize atmospheric concentrations below the level identified in Question 3?

Fifth, what policies will be required to achieve the necessary reductions in greenhouse gas emissions identified in Question 4?

What impacts must we avoid to ensure a livable planet? Although policymakers can differ over what modest impacts are tolerable from climate change, almost every one would agree that we must avoid the worst potential impacts. As discussed in the previous sections of this chapter, many impacts are already occurring and cannot be reasonably avoided in the future (for example, extensive glacier melting and many changes in natural ecosystems). Compared to the anticipated future impacts from a "business-as-usual" scenario, however, today's impacts are relatively modest. Although we will necessarily incur some costs from climate change, we can still avoid the most significant impacts — for example, the wholesale crash of food production or of natural ecosystems, the melting of the Greenland or West Antarctic ice sheets or the shutdown of the thermohaline circulation.

What is the maximum level of temperature increase that can occur without the risk of massive climate impacts? Some scientists recommend a limit of 1°C beyond 1990 temperatures to protect coral reefs, 2°C to protect the Greenland and West Antarctic ice sheets; and 3°C to protect the thermohaline circulation. B.C. O'Neill & M. Oppenheimer, *Climate Change — Dangerous Climate Impacts and the Kyoto Protocol*, 296 SCIENCE 1971–72 (2002). Similarly, NASA's Dr. James Hansen set his long-term temperature target at a 1°C increase above 2005 temperatures (roughly equivalent to a 2°C total increase), based on an estimate of how much more warming the planet could tolerate before triggering a 1.5 m sea level rise. *See* James A. Hansen, *Defusing the Global Warming Time Bomb*, 290 SCI. AM. 68–77 (2004); James Hansen, *A Slippery Slope: How Much Global Warming Constitutes 'Dangerous Anthropogenic Interference', An Editorial Es-*

say, 68 CLIMATE CHANGE (2005). Although there is obviously some uncertainty over this question, most scientists agree with this assessment that we must limit our total temperature increase to 2°C (approximately 1°C more than current warming), to have confidence that we can avoid significant negative change. *See also, e.g.,* Christan Azar & Henning Rodhe, *Targets for Stabilization of Atmospheric CO₂,* 276 SCIENCE 1818–19 (1997) (calling for global warming not to exceed 2°C); H. Grassl, J. Kokott, et al., *Climate Protection Strategies for the 21st Century: Kyoto and Beyond,* (German Advisory Council on Global Change 2003) (calling for a maximum 2°C warming as "acceptable").

This position comports as well with what we know of historical temperatures. A recent study shows that current warming has made global average temperatures higher than any since the end of the last ice age 12,000 years ago, and we are now within 1.0°C (1.8°F) of the highest temperatures in the past million years. In reporting on the study, NASA's Dr. James Hansen, said:

> That means that further global warming of 1°C defines a critical level. If warming is kept less than that, effects of global warming may be relatively manageable. During the warmest interglacial periods the Earth was reasonably similar to today. But if further global warming reaches 2–3°C, we will likely see changes that make Earth a different planet than the one we know. The last time it was that warm was in the middle Pliocene, about three million years ago, when sea level was estimated to have been about 25 meters (80 feet) higher than today. . . . This evidence implies that we are getting close to dangerous levels of human-made (anthropogenic) pollution.

NASA, Press Release, *NASA Study Finds World Warmth Edging Ancient Levels,* Sept. 25, 2006. The study reached its conclusion by focusing on two specific impacts: sea level rise and widespread species extinctions and concluding that avoiding these would require limiting global warming to a 2°C increase. *See* James A. Hansen, et al., *Global Temperature Change,* PROC. NAT'L ACAD. SCI., Sept. 25, 2006.

Thus, if our goal is to lower our risks of significant sea level rise or other ecological change, we need to limit global warming to a total 2°C increase. This would also allow us to avoid many of the other linear impacts described in this chapter.

At what level must we stabilize atmospheric GHG concentrations to limit warming to a total of 2°C? Here, too, there is some bounded uncertainty in the relationship between atmospheric greenhouse gas concentrations and temperature rise. Studies of ice cores in Antarctica show that levels of CO_2, as well as other GHGs, including methane and nitrous oxide, are higher than at any time in the past 800,000 years, with CO_2 increasing at a rate 200 times faster than at any time over that span. The amount of CO_2 in the atmosphere has increased from its preindustrial level of approximately 280 ppm in 1750 to 381 ppm in 2005. The pre-industrial level serves as an important baseline for the current policy debate. Until recently, most climate policymakers have been aiming at atmospheric concentration levels at slightly less than twice the preindustrial level — i.e., 550 ppm. In 2001, the IPCC indicated that such a doubling of atmospheric CO_2 concentrations would result in temperature increases between 1.5° and 4.5°C, although recent studies suggest that this may underestimate the temperature increases. *See, e.g.,* David A. King, *Climate Change Science: Adapt, Mitigate, or Ignore?* 303 SCIENCE 176 (Jan. 9, 2004).

Most observers now recognize that the risks from doubling greenhouse gas concentrations are unacceptably high and thus argue for lower stabilization targets. A study in 2004 found that stabilization at the equivalent of 550 ppm CO_2 provides only a 10–20 per cent chance of limiting global average temperature rise to 2°C, while stabilizing atmospheric concentrations to 400 ppm CO_2 would yield an 80 percent chance of limiting global average temperature rise to 2°C above preindustrial levels. Paul Baer, *Probabilistic Analysis of Climate Stabilization Targets and the Implications for Precautionary Policy*, presented at the Am. Geo. Union Ann. Mtg., Dec. 17, 2004; Paul Baer & Tom Athanasiou, *Honesty about Dangerous Climate Change*, 8 CLIMATE EQUITY OBSERVER, 2004. The German Advisory Council on Climate Change recommended that we "hedge" our bets with a goal of 450 ppm, while NASA's lead climate scientist, Dr. James Hansen, argues for a stabilization target of 350 ppm.

What level of greenhouse gas emissions reductions is necessary to reach the desired stabilization levels? Here again there is general consensus emerging around the goal of 50 percent reductions worldwide by 2050 (involving 80 percent reductions for industrialized countries), and significant interim reduction targets by 2020 or 2030. In 2003, the German Advisory Council on Global Change found that worldwide carbon dioxide emissions must be cut globally by 45–60 percent by the year 2050 relative to 1990. This means that industrialized countries have to reduce their greenhouse gas emissions by at least 20 percent by 2020 and make substantially higher cuts (around 80 percent) by 2050.

What policies and measures will allow us to attain the reductions identified above? This is the subject of the next chapter.

QUESTIONS AND DISCUSSION

1. The objective adopted by the UN Framework Convention on Climate Change (UNFCCC) is to stabilize atmospheric greenhouse gas concentrations "at a level that would prevent dangerous anthropogenic interference with the climate system." *See* UNFCCC, Article 2; *see also* Chapter 4 discussing this objective. The International Climate Task Force calls for an international objective that would limit temperatures from "rising more than 2°C (3.6°F) above the pre-industrial level". Are these two objectives consistent? Given the unprecedented scope of the linear and non-linear impacts from climate change, what should the ultimate objective of climate policy be? Put another way, what risks should be considered as the baseline for setting international policy? A rapid climate change event such as the shutdown of the thermohaline circulation? Or the more linear risks associated with polar ice melt, drought, or coral loss?

2. Meeting this long-term stabilization target means unprecedented reductions in greenhouse gas emissions over the next 50 years, with consensus estimates focusing on a 60 to 80 percent reduction from 1990 levels by 2050, followed by a near-complete transition to a carbon-free economy by 2100. By comparison, the Kyoto Protocol, discussed in Chapter 5, aims at a 5.2 percent reduction from 1990 levels in most developed countries (excluding the United States) by 2012. It is acknowledged to be only the first step, and many world leaders are calling for the more ambitious reductions suggested by the above analysis. The European Union has proposed cuts of up to 80 percent by 2050. The U.S. Senate has been debating cuts at levels ranging from achieving 1990 levels by 2020 to 80 percent reductions by 2050. *See also* State of California Executive Order S-3-05 (June 1, 2005) (setting emissions target at 80 percent below 1990 levels by 2050); State of New Mexico Executive Order 05-033 (June, 2005) (setting emissions target at 75 percent below 2000 level by 2050); Tony Blair, *Global Warming: "We Must Do More to Beat Climate Change,"* THE INDEPENDENT, Nov. 19, 2005. Such deep reductions will not be easy and presume a massive investment in a "new energy economy." The policies to get us there are discussed in Chapter 2.

3.   Talking about the potential impacts from climate change poses significant challenges for environmentalists and policymakers, particularly with respect to complex and potentially catastrophic impacts like the shutdown of the thermohaline current. The first challenge is not to make policymakers or the public feel as if any action is hopeless. In fact, the worst climate impacts happen only at higher temperatures and higher concentrations. The "business-as-usual" scenario is a bleak one — but humans are adaptive and innovative, and we should be able to move significantly away from the business-as-usual future if we have the will to do so. We are essentially in a fight over degrees — at what level of warming will we finally stabilize before bringing greenhouse gas concentrations down. In such a fight over degrees, every small step that policymakers (or individuals) take contributes to the solution.

The second challenge is how to sound the alarm about climate change without sounding like an alarmist. Because the worse predicted impacts from climate change are still decades away, the public can be inured over time to warnings and begin to believe that "chicken little is simply announcing that the sky is falling again." If you were advising an environmental organization (or former Vice President Al Gore) on their communications policy, what advice would you give them?

4.   Many organizations, publications, and websites regularly report on developments in climate science. *See, e.g.,* www.climatescience.gov (information provided by the U.S. government's Climate Science Program, an integrated effort of several government agencies); www.pewclimate.org (the Pew Center on Global Climate Change); www.ucsusa.org/global_warming/ (the Union of Concerned Scientists); *see also* the online publications of *Science* or *Nature*, which frequently publish articles on climate change. For an informative explanation of, and commentary on, current climate science, see www.realclimate.org. An engaging and readable (although ultimately disturbing) depiction of the impacts from climate change can be found in MARK LYNAS, SIX DEGREES: OUR FUTURE ON A HOTTER PLANET (2006).

Chapter 2

RESPONDING TO CLIMATE CHANGE: MITIGATION

SYNOPSIS

I. Introduction
II. General Mitigation Approaches
    A. Climate Change as a Market Failure
    B. Internalizing External Costs: Cures for Market Failure
        1. Traditional Regulation
        2. Emissions Trading
        3. Carbon Taxes
        4. Information-Based Approaches
        5. Investment and Technology Approaches
III. Mitigation Policies At the Sector Level
    A. Mitigation Measures
    B. Stabilization Wedges: Mitigation One Step at a Time
IV. The Benefits And Costs of Climate Mitigation
    A. The Stern Review of Climate Economics
    B. The Critique of Cost-Benefit Analysis

I. INTRODUCTION

The potential economic, environmental, and social impacts of climate change can no longer be ignored, and policymakers at all levels and in all sectors are beginning to respond to climate change. At the same time, foregoing development now to avoid even relatively certain climate impacts in the future is not easy, either in industrialized countries concerned about unemployment and energy prices or, more acutely, in developing countries concerned with alleviating poverty, hunger, and illiteracy. The goal is to choose a proportionate, equitable, and effective policy response that will prevent or reduce the anticipated impacts of climate change, while not unduly burdening economic well-being.

The first step in developing a set of policy responses to climate change is to identify the long-term goal we are trying to achieve. As suggested in Chapter 1, the long term goal is typically discussed in terms of a stabilization goal — the concentration of greenhouse gases in the atmosphere that will allow us to avoid the most serious climate change impacts. Although policymakers have long aimed at a concentration goal of 550 ppm, in recent years knowledge about climate change impacts has moved the goal. Most analysts now argue that we must stabilize greenhouse gas concentrations at 350 ppm or even lower. This debate is important because it sets the broad parameters for the speed, extent and scale of the needed policy and technological responses. But to some extent, consensus over a precise concentration level is not necessary; we know that we must adopt widespread policy changes and we must do so quickly. This chapter describes the range of policy options available for reducing atmospheric greenhouse gas concentrations.

These policy options are generally divided into two broad categories: mitigation and adaptation. This lexicon is derived from the UNFCCC, which defines "mitigation" or preventative responses, as those meant to "reduce the sources of greenhouse gases or enhance the sinks"; and "adaptation" responses as those "adjustment[s] in natural or human systems in response to actual or expected climatic stimuli or their effects, which moderate harm or exploit beneficial opportunities." In other words, mitigation includes all efforts to prevent or avoid climate change, and adaptation includes all efforts to reduce or adjust to the anticipated impacts of climate change.

To some extent, the entire rest of this book relates either to mitigation or adaptation. Discussions of the Kyoto Regime's cap-and-trade system in Chapter 6, for example, are a discussion of mitigation policy responses, as is Chapter 13's discussion of how we address climate change under the Clean Air Act. Efforts to list the polar bear under the Endangered Species Act (also in Chapter 13), if successful, would lead to a recovery plan — a form of adaptation response. We leave such specifics to the ensuing chapters; this chapter introduces more generally the broad types of policy responses that are relevant to mitigation of climate change. Chapter 3 discusses adaptation.

When most lawyers discuss responses to climate change, they are usually discussing mitigation strategies. All pollution control efforts — i.e., efforts to curb emissions of carbon dioxide or other greenhouse gases — fall into the category of mitigation. At every level from the international Kyoto Protocol to local building codes, the majority of our climate policies are aimed at reducing GHG emissions. Emissions reductions are not the only form of mitigation policies, however. Concentrations of GHGs can also be reduced by steps to enhance the removal of GHGs from the atmosphere. These "sequestration" efforts, which may include everything from planting a tree to capturing and injecting carbon dioxide deep underground, are also forms of mitigation.

From the policy-makers' perspective, it is worthwhile to look at mitigation strategies in two ways. First, what general policy approach should we take? Will we choose command-and-control technologies, emissions trading, carbon taxes, or some mixture of these and other approaches? Second, what types of mitigation responses are possible at the industry sector or factory level? As we adopt general efforts to reduce GHG concentrations, what practically does this mean for the energy or transportation sectors, for example? General overall mitigation approaches discussed below and sector-specific questions are introduced in Section III.

II. GENERAL MITIGATION APPROACHES

The debate over what policies are best to reduce atmospheric GHG concentrations is a rich and complicated one. As with many discussions over environmental policy, some of the debate is over whether to use traditional regulatory approaches, such as standards, prohibitions, or other "command-and-control" approaches, or more market-based approaches, such as emissions trading or carbon taxes. Others argue that we should focus on getting information to consumers or on providing incentives to accelerate innovation and investments in newer cleaner technologies.

Climate change is such a massive and wide-ranging issue, of course, that we should not be surprised to see policies being debated that fit all of these descriptions. Indeed, particularly at the national and subnational level, examples exist of traditional regulation, carbon taxes, eco-labeling, government-funded research of new technologies, and virtually every other type of regulatory approach imaginable. What is rather unique about climate change policy, however, is that this debate has been taken to a *global* level. The Kyoto Protocol's cap-and-trade approach is by far the most complicated and ambitious market-based regulatory approach ever taken in the environmental field. Yet, many are critical of the emissions trading approach and argue for more traditional regulations (also known as "policies and measures" under the Kyoto Protocol), including a heavier reliance on carbon-based taxes. Even the Kyoto Protocol is not exclusively an emissions trading system, and we can expect in the future to see widely divergent and innovative examples of policies both internationally and nationally. Moreover, current debate over U.S. national climate legislation also reflects a debate over the most appropriate policy mix for responding to climate change. Because this debate will animate climate policy into the future, some exposure to the conceptual bases for different forms of regulation is important and provided in this section.

A.   Climate Change as a Market Failure

Climate change is arguably the most far-reaching market failure ever. To understand this, we need to understand the economic concept known as "externalities." To show this in the climate context, assume you own a factory. You have to pay basic costs to operate (such as labor, materials, utilities, and so on), but absent government regulation you do not have to pay for the costs of emitting greenhouse gases into the air. In this context, the atmosphere's ability to absorb carbon dioxide and other greenhouse gases are known as "public goods." Public goods are owned by no one and not traded in any market; thus, absent government regulation, public goods are free and open to all users. As a result, public goods become "overused." In seeking to maximize short term profits, for example, the factory will "overuse" the atmosphere and continue polluting. To be sure, the factory owner is causing real costs in the form of climate change, but all these costs are *external* to the costs the factory owner currently pays to operate. These external costs are borne by the public in the form of the impacts from climate change identified in Chapter 1. Thus, injury to coastal landowners from sea level rise or to farmers from drought caused by climate change are costs of the factory's operations — but costs the factory doesn't have to pay. Economists call such costs negative externalities.

If, on the other hand, the factory owner has to pay for the external harm caused by its emissions, then the factory will look for ways to reduce its emission of greenhouse gases. The process for forcing the factory to recognize environmental and social costs is known as *internalizing externalities*. By internalizing externalities, we provide more accurate price signals to buyers. Thus, if climate-related externalities were internalized, the more environmentally harmful products and processes would be relatively more costly. As the economist, David Pearce, explains:

The most desirable feature of the price mechanism is that it signals to consumers what the cost of producing a particular product is, and to producers what consumers' relative valuations are. In a nutshell, this is the elegance and virtue of free markets which economists have (generally) found so attractive since the time of Adam Smith. . . . [M]any environmental products, services and resources do not get represented in the price mechanism. This effectively amounts to them being treated as "free goods", i.e., they have zero prices. It follows that an *unfettered* price mechanism will use too much of the zero-priced good. Resources and environments will become degraded on this basis alone, i.e., because the price mechanism has wrongly recorded environmental goods as having zero prices when, in fact, they serve economic functions which should attract positive prices.

But economic goods and services themselves "use up" some of the environment. Trace gases "use" the atmosphere and troposphere as a waste sink; municipalities use rivers and coastal waters as cleansing agents for sewage, and so on. The cost of producing any good or service therefore tends to be a mixture of priced "inputs" (labour, capital, technology) and unpriced inputs (environmental services). The market price for goods and services does not therefore reflect the true value of the totality of the resources being used to produce them. Unfettered markets fail to allocate resources efficiently. Or, in the economists' language, there is a divergence between private and social cost.

DAVID PEARCE ET AL., BLUEPRINT FOR A GREEN ECONOMY 154–157 (1989).

In this way, climate change can be seen as the market's failure to reflect the external or "social" costs of greenhouse gas emissions. The global atmosphere is a classic case of a global commons where no concepts of private property prevail. The failure of the market to price the commons leads to its "overuse" and to its long-term deterioration. This is known as the "tragedy of the commons." *See* Garrett Hardin, *The Tragedy of the Commons*, 168 SCIENCE 1243 (1968).

DAVID HUNTER, JAMES SALZMAN & DURWOOD ZAELKE, INTERNATIONAL ENVIRONMENTAL LAW AND POLICY
125–26 (3d ed. 2007)*

To understand the causes of the tragedy, Harden asks you to imagine a common pasture shared by an entire village for grazing sheep. Everyone in the village has the right to unlimited use of the pasture. You have a flock of twenty sheep and bring them every day to graze beside all your neighbors' sheep. With each hour your flock spends in the pasture, the amount of future forage available for other flocks — and your own — is reduced. But, of course, the same rule holds with respect to your neighbors' flocks. The more the pasture is over-grazed now, the fewer sheep it will be able to support in the long term. If maximizing short-term economic gain is your primary goal, however, are you going to let your sheep graze until they have eaten as much as they can, or will you stop their feeding earlier?

The more they feed, the more they will weigh and be worth when it comes time to sell them. And if you stop your sheep from feeding as much as they want, of course, there is no guarantee your fellow shepherds will cut back on their flocks' grazing. As a result, you may well encourage your sheep to feed as much as possible, and your fellow shepherds will do the same. Soon, however, the grass on the village pasture will be nibbled down to the roots and not provide enough grazing for *anyone's* flock, including your own. While each shepherd's decision was individually rational in the short run, it proved collectively foolish in the long run. It would have been far wiser for every shepherd to restrain his or her flock's grazing, but seeking to maximize short term economic gain ensured long term economic — and environmental — disaster. As Hardin wrote: * * *

> In a reverse way, the tragedy of the commons reappears in problems of pollution. Here it is not a question of taking something out of the commons, but of putting something in; sewage, or chemical, radioactive, and heat wastes into water; noxious and dangerous fumes into the air; and distracting and unpleasant advertising signs into the line of sight. The calculations of utility are much the same as before. The rational man finds that his share of the cost of the wastes he discharges into the commons is less than the cost of purifying his wastes before releasing them. Since this is true for everyone, we are locked into a system of "fouling our own nest," so long as we behave only as independent, rational, free-enterprisers. * * *

Hardin, *The Tragedy of the Commons*, at 1244–1245. The implication is that the free market will treat open-access resources or public goods as being free. If the primary objective of the market participants is individual wealth maximization, the market's failure to place limits on use of the resource will invariably result in the degradation of that resource.

In the case of climate change, the global atmosphere is no different than the village commons, and emitters of greenhouse gases are no different than the shepherds.

QUESTIONS AND DISCUSSION

What insights for policymakers can be taken from recognizing the economic root causes of climate change as revealed through the concepts of externalities, public goods, and the tragedy of the commons? What options are available to internalize the "external" costs of climate change?

B.   Internalizing External Costs: Cures for Market Failure

If one understands climate change as a failure of the market to reflect the external environmental and social costs of climate change, then the theoretical answer to climate change is to *internalize* those costs. In international environmental law, the polluter pays principle has emerged as the general principle promoting the internalization of environmental and social costs. Under the polluter pays principle, States should take those actions necessary to ensure that polluters and users of natural resources bear the full environmental and social costs of their activities. For example, under Principle 16 of the Rio Declaration on Environment and Development: "National authorities should endeavour to promote the internalization of environmental costs and the use of economic instruments, taking into account the approach that the polluter should, in principle, bear the cost of pollution, with due regard to the public interest and without distorting international trade and investment." UN DOC A/CONF.151/5/Rev. 1, Principle 2, June 13, 1992, *reprinted in* 31 I.L.M. 874 (1992). The principle seeks the reflection of the full environmental and social costs (including costs associated with climate change) in the ultimate market price for a good or service. In theory, at least, environmentally harmful or unsustainable goods will tend to cost more, and consumers will switch to less polluting substitutes. This will result in a more efficient and sustainable allocation of resources.

The principle emerged in the Organization for Economic Cooperation and Development (OECD) in the 1970s as developed countries sought to maintain a level economic business environment by ensuring that every country regulated pollution. The early OECD Council recommendations provide still relevant summaries of the purpose of the principle:

> 1. Environmental resources are in general limited and their use may lead to their deterioration. When the cost of this deterioration is not adequately taken into account in the price system, the market fails to reflect the scarcity of such resources both at the national and international levels. Public measures are thus necessary to reduce pollution and to reach a better allocation of resources by ensuring that prices of goods, depending on the quality and/or quantity of environmental resources, reflect more closely their relative scarcity and that economic agents concerned react accordingly.

> 2. In many circumstances, in order to ensure that the environment is in an acceptable state, the reduction of pollution beyond a certain level will not be practical or even necessary in view of the costs involved.

> 3. The principle to be used for allocating costs of pollution prevention and control measures to encourage rational use of scarce environmental resources and to avoid distortions in international trade and investment is the so-called "Polluter-Pays Principle." The Principle means that the polluter should bear the expenses of carrying out the above-mentioned measures decided by public authorities to ensure that the environment is in an acceptable state. In other words, the cost of these measures should be reflected in the cost of goods and services which cause pollution in production and/or consumption. Such measures should not be accompanied by subsidies that would create significant distortions in international trade and investment.

OECD Council, Recommendation of the Council on Guiding Principles Concerning International Economic Aspects of Environmental Policies, Annex I, adopted at the Council's 239th meeting (May 26, 1972).

The question remains how can one implement the polluter pays principle and internalize costs. The polluter pays principle can be implemented through a variety of methods aimed generally at internalizing environmental costs, including, for example, traditional regulation or the use of a variety of market-based mechanisms. In the climate context, many different types of policy approaches are debated, although the most prominent is the use of emissions trading. The Kyoto Protocol, the European Union, as well as several regional initiatives in the United States all rely heavily on a "cap-and-trade" system, whereby greenhouse gas emissions from one or more sectors are capped, and the regulated community can trade their "rights" to emit among one another. The conceptual basis for this and other regulatory approaches is described in the following sections.

1. *Traditional Regulation*

By far the most common way to control pollution, like the emissions of greenhouse gases, is to adopt prescriptive regulations mandating what parties can and cannot do. These regulations range from outright bans on the use or production of certain substances to "command-and-control" regulations that restrict end-of-pipe emissions, or require specific technologies, design specifications, or processes. With some notable exceptions, most U.S. pollution control laws, including the Clean Air Act, are primarily based on the command-and-control model. *See, e.g.*, Chapter 13 (discussing the potential for regulating CO_2 under the Clean Air Act). In short, the water and air are cleaner today in the United States than 40 years ago largely because of the application of strict command-and-control pollution laws. Moreover, the international response to ozone depletion was also based primarily on a clear phase-out period for the consumption and production of chlorofluorocarbons (CFCs) and other ozone depleting substances. *See* Chapter 10 (discussing the Montreal Protocol on Substances that Deplete the Ozone Layer).

In the climate change arena, many traditional regulatory approaches have already been implemented or are being discussed. U.S. corporate average fuel efficiency (CAFE) standards, for example, set fuel efficiency standards for cars and trucks. Many U.S. states have adopted renewable portfolio standards, which require utilities to produce a minimum percentage of their energy from renewable sources. California and several other states have also tried to impose vehicle emissions standards for carbon dioxide as a direct control measure to ensure lower emissions from automobiles. These and other state policies are discussed further in Chapter 17.

Prescriptive command-and-control regulations have a history of working to protect the environment, but they are often criticized by economists and industry as inefficient in many circumstances. Economists argue that command-and-control approaches disfavor innovation because once the regulated party has installed the required technology or met the appropriate standard, the law creates no further incentive to reduce pollution. Moreover, every polluter has to adopt the same approaches at least in technology-based regulations, regardless of whether they could reduce their emissions at a lower cost some other way. For these and related reasons, many policymakers argue for the use of market-based mechanisms such as emissions trading.

---

2. *Emissions Trading*

As suggested by the above, traditional regulatory approaches are often criticized for being inefficient and inflexible. Better, economists argue, is to allow individual firms the flexibility to work with one another so that those firms that can reduce pollution at a lower cost get paid from other firms to reduce pollution beyond what they otherwise would. The Driesen article below explains this basic argument in favor of using emissions trading approaches to air pollution issues generally. These general arguments are a major reason why the Kyoto Protocol is built around the creation of an emissions trading regime.

Proponents of emissions trading assert that trading provides a number of advantages over traditional regulation. In particular, they claim that emissions trading provides a more cost-effective approach to achieving environmental goals than traditional regulation. Second, they argue that emissions trading stimulates innovation, because regulated facilities are not directed to use specific types of pollution control technologies. Consequently, this innovation may spur pollution reductions beyond those required. The merits of these claims, as well as the critiques of them, provide important lessons for the desirability and design of any greenhouse gas trading regime.

The underlying economic philosophy for emissions trading is relatively straightforward: cost-effectiveness. Emissions trading programs allow polluters the flexibility to reduce their own emissions or, depending on how the program is structured, either reduce emissions from a combination of sources within a single facility or purchase emissions reductions from another facility. T. H. TIETENBERG, EMISSIONS TRADING: PRINCIPLES AND PRACTICE 1 (2D ED. 2006). The virtue of such programs, according to proponents of emissions trading, is that the reductions are made in the most cost-effective way, because polluters decide whether it is cheaper to reduce their own emissions or purchase emissions reductions.

Professor David M. Driesen illustrates the efficiencies that can be created through emissions trading.

> Suppose, for example, that a 100 ton reduction in aggregate sulfur dioxide (SO_2) emissions could protect a lake from acid rain. Assume that two power plants, called Cheap and Expensive, cause this problem and each emits 150 tons of SO_2. If no other sources of this pollutant existed, the government could address this problem by requiring each pollution source to reduce emissions by 50 tons. This involves setting a uniform standard for an industrial category, an approach found in many environmental statutes. Equalized emission reduction does not necessarily imply equalized cost, since one plant's equipment may make pollution control more expensive than that of another. Suppose that Cheap has control costs of $1,000 per ton, but that Expensive has control costs of $2,000 per ton. A uniform standard demanding fifty ton reductions would then produce $150,000 in pollution control expenditures, $50,000 at Cheap ($1,000 X 50) and $100,000 at Expensive ($2,000 X 50).

> Suppose, however, that the government writes the same emission limitations, but allows the pollution sources to trade reductions. Presumably, Expensive will pay Cheap to make fifty tons of reductions in its stead. Cheap will cut its emission by 100 tons below its baseline level at a cost of $100,000 ($1,000 per ton X 100 tons). Expensive will not cut its emissions at all. The public will secure the 100 tons of reduction needed to protect the lake from acidification, but the pollution sources will pay $100,000 instead of $150,000. In theory, emissions trading offers a more cost effective means of meeting an environmental goal than a uniform standard, whenever marginal costs vary between plants.

David M. Driesen, *Free Lunch or Cheap Fix?: The Emissions Trading Idea and the Climate Change Convention*, 26 B.C. ENVTL. AFFAIRS L. REV. 1, 35–36 (1998).

The appeal of this model has led to the growth of emissions trading programs in the United States, China, the European Union, and elsewhere to manage a range of pollutants, including mercury, greenhouse gases, and other air pollutants.

Cap-and-trade programs are perhaps the best known form of emissions trading. Under cap-and-trade programs, regulators first establish a maximum pollution limit — a cap on total mass emissions — for the resource and divide the allocation into allowances (e.g., one allowance equals one ton of carbon). Next, the regulated facilities buy, or far more typically, receive free of charge, the allowances from the regulatory body. Allowances are generally allocated below a facility's baseline emissions. Programs may also gradually reduce the total emissions target and individual allowances. In either case, a facility must either reduce its own emissions to match the number of allowances it holds or purchase credits to cover any emissions above its allowances. A facility that reduces its emissions below its allowance holdings may sell the excess. To ensure that emissions are within applicable limits, a facility must report its emissions to the regulatory body. If a facility's emissions are greater than its allowance holdings at the end of the compliance period, and it has not purchased credits to cover its excess emissions, the regulatory body can impose fines or take other enforcement actions.

Project-based programs allow polluters not subject to mass-based emission caps to generate credits to sell to a buyer, typically another polluter who needs credits to cover its shortfall. In some project-based programs, polluters may purchase allowances from a project that generates emissions reductions of the regulated pollutant compared to emissions in the absence of that project. For example, a coal-fired power plant that must reduce emissions of carbon dioxide could finance the reforestation of forests (which absorb carbon dioxide) or invest in clean technology at another electricity-producing facility. A regulatory body or other entity must certify that the purchase of emission credits resulted in emission reductions that would not have otherwise occurred. As described in Chapter 6, this is the approach of Joint Implementation and the Clean Development Mechanism under the Kyoto Protocol. Another project-based approach allows a facility to average its emissions from any combination of sources within the plant. Facilities create "bubbles" in which the entire facility, regardless of the number of pollution sources, is considered a single pollution source.

In some respects, the nature of climate change is ideal for establishing global trading markets in pollution; reducing one ton of carbon dioxide emissions anywhere in the world mitigates climate change as much as reducing any other ton of carbon dioxide. In addition, disparities in regulatory systems also make carbon dioxide emissions trading potentially extremely cost effective. For example, countries like the United States and Germany have well developed pollution control regimes, and, consequently, cuts in emissions from these countries will be relatively more expensive than in many developed countries where few if any pollution control requirements currently exist. Under a global trading system, the United States or Germany could lower their costs of reducing greenhouse gas emissions by investing in reforestation projects in Costa Rica or technology that reduces carbon dioxide emissions in India or China.

For these reasons, the Kyoto Protocol, which is discussed in Chapters 5 through 8, established a cap-and-trade system for reducing greenhouse gas emissions from industrialized countries. Industrialized countries accepted an overall cap on their emissions and then are permitted to trade among each other to lower their overall compliance costs. The Protocol also created the Clean Development Mechanism, described in Chapter 6, which allows industrialized countries to invest in developing countries that have no cap. These investments can result in emission reduction credits that can help industrialized countries meet their obligations.

Today, active and vibrant carbon trading is happening around the world. Carbon trading increased from about \$10.8 billion and 710 $MtCO_2e$ in 2005 to \$30 billion and

1,639 MtCO$_2$e in 2006. Karan Capoor & Philippe Ambrosi, *State and Trends of the Carbon Market 2007* 3 (2007). In 2006, companies traded more than one billion allowances, three times the amount in 2005, under the European Union's Emissions Trading Scheme. The New South Wales Market and the Chicago Carbon Exchange also recorded record volumes and values of trade in 2006. Programs within the United States, including the Regional Greenhouse Gas Initiative established by nine Northeast states, have initiated carbon trading even in the absence of federal regulation or U.S. participation in the Kyoto Protocol. With the commitment by governments to a post-Kyoto Protocol regime that includes further quantifiable emissions limitations, it seems clear that the carbon market will continue to be one tool for reducing greenhouse gas emissions. The development of the carbon market under the Kyoto Protocol and in Europe is discussed in Chapter 6.

QUESTIONS AND DISCUSSION

1. The Kyoto Protocol's cap-and-trade system was largely inspired by the U.S. Acid Rain Program, which is widely viewed as having achieved its environmental goals with less private sector cost than traditional regulatory approaches. Enacted in 1990, the Acid Rain Program, 42 U.S.C. §§ 7651–7651o, mandates electric power generators to reduce annual emissions of sulfur dioxide (SO$_2$). Sulfur dioxide causes respiratory and other human health problems, and is an important precursor to acid rain, which acidifies lakes, making them incapable of supporting aquatic life.

To achieve the required reductions, the Acid Rain Program adopted a nationwide cap-and-trade regime. The annual nationwide emissions cap for sulfur dioxide, to be achieved by 2010, was set at 8.95 million tons, about half the emissions from power plants in 1980. Individual plants were given sulfur dioxide emission allowances based on past emissions and fuel consumption. These allowances could then be bought and sold as needed to meet annual reductions. In 2005, 3,456 electric generating units were participating in the program.

The Program has been widely viewed as successful. The Acid Rain Program has reduced SO$_2$ emissions from power plants by more than 7 million tons, or about 41 percent, from 1980 levels, cut sulfate deposition by about 36 percent in some regions, and reduced acidification of lakes. Moreover, it achieved these environmental goals with nearly 100 percent compliance through "rigorous emissions monitoring, allowance tracking, and an automatic, easily understood penalty system for noncompliance." Environmental Protection Agency, *Acid Rain Program 2005 Progress Report* 2–3 (2006). One study estimates that in 2010, the Acid Rain Program's annual benefits will be approximately $122 billion (in 2000 dollars), at an annual cost of about $3 billion (less than half of what was estimated in 1990): a 40-to-1 benefit-to-cost ratio. Lauraine G. Chestnut & David M. Mills, *A Fresh Look at the Benefits and Costs of the U.S. Acid Rain Program*, 77 J. ENVTL. MANAGEMENT 252 (2005). Other studies have concluded that the use of a cap-and-trade regime reduced compliance costs by 50 percent relative to the costs of a command-and-control regulatory structure. Denny A. Ellerman, et al., MARKETS FOR CLEAN AIR: THE U.S. ACID RAIN PROGRAM (2000); Curtis P. Carlson, et al., *SO$_2$ Control by Electric Utilities: What Are the Gains from Trade?* 108 J. POL. ECON. 1292 (2000).

2. Publicity surrounding the Acid Rain Program has perhaps masked the mixed environmental performance of other emissions trading programs and the need to focus on critical design and implementation issues to ensure that such programs succeed. The Regional Clean Air Incentives Market (RECLAIM) Program, for example, was designed to reduce emissions of nitrogen oxides (NO$_x$)

and sulfur dioxide (SO_2) from power plants, cement plants, and other large stationary sources in the Los Angeles area. RECLAIM has had substantial noncompliance and high administrative costs. In RECLAIM's initial years, from 1994 to 1999, noncompliance with facility allocations ranged from 4% to 15%, despite the ready availability of inexpensive allowances. When an "energy crisis" sent the average price of NO_x allowances skyrocketing from an average of about $4,000 per ton in 1999 to $45,609 per ton in 2000, RECLAIM's NO_x cap was "significantly exceeded":

> In 2000, power-producing facilities initially were allocated 2,302 tons of allocations, but they emitted 6,788 tons of NO_x. They were able to purchase 2,550 tons of allowances on the market from non-power producing facilities so that their total exceedences amounted to 1,936 tons. Non-power producing facilities sold so many allowances that their holdings did not cover their emissions, and they ended up with exceedences of 1,358 tons. In total, all facilities together exceeded the NO_x cap in 2000 by 3,294 tons, or 19%.

Lesley K. McAllister, *Beyond Playing Banker: The Role of the Regulatory Agency in Emissions Trading*, 59 ADMIN L. REV. 269, 289–290 (2007). *See also* A. DENNY ELLERMAN, ET AL., EMISSIONS TRADING IN THE U.S.: EXPERIENCE, LESSONS, AND CONSIDERATIONS FOR GREENHOUSE GASES (2003).

Despite the exceedences in 2000, covered facilities reduced their NO_x emissions by 19 percent from 1994 to 2000. Nonetheless, that level was significantly less than the 38 percent reductions made by the same facilities from 1989 to 1993, prior to adoption of the cap-and-trade program. Similarly, after power-producing facilities were barred from trading in 2001 and required to install pollution control equipment, emissions plummeted. By 2004, emissions from power producing facilities dropped by more than 90 percent from their 2000 levels while emissions from non-power producing facilities fell by 31 percent. McAllister, at 291.

Research on "bubble" programs has raised similar concerns about their environmental performance:

> The few studies of bubble implementation reveal that polluters often could not document claims that they had made the emission reductions that regulatory requirements underlying bubbles had required. Polluters almost never undertook fresh pollution control projects to satisfy these regulations. Instead, they claimed credits for incidental reductions that would have occurred without the regulation. For example, polluters often claimed credits for routine business decisions to slow down production or shut down facilities. Without the ability to trade, the underlying regulation would trigger a fresh reduction that would supplement any incidental reductions. The trading allowed polluters to claim credit for these incidental reductions in order to avoid any real fresh emission decreases. The bubble regulations, however, did not require polluters to assume debits for incidental emission increases (e.g. from a production increase). Hence, gaming has been a problem.
>
> EPA introduced bubbles primarily as deregulatory mechanisms, and bubbles generally have stimulated neither innovation nor adequate environmental performance at a cheaper price. Rather, they have generated cost savings for industry, often by allowing unverifiable claims of compliance and paper credits to substitute for actual emission reductions and by reducing pollution reduction demands.

David M. Driesen, *Is Emissions Trading an Economic Incentive Program?: Replacing the Command and Control/Economic Incentive Dichotomy*, 55 WASH. &

LEE L. REV. 289, 315–316 (1998).

3. These criticisms do not invalidate the emissions trading model. Practical experience supports the view that a marketable permits system can reduce costs, but most studies also show that adequate enforcement and monitoring are necessary for positive environmental outcomes. Tom Tietenberg, *Tradable Permits in Principle and Practice*, 14 PENN ST. ENVTL. L. REV. 251, 259–61 (2006) (the success of a trading program in meeting its environmental objectives was tied to a number of factors, including adequate enforcement); Jeffrey C. Fort & Cynthia A. Faur, *Can Emissions Trading Work Beyond a National Program?: Some Practical Observations on the Available Tools*, 18 U. PA. J. INT'L ECON. L. 463, 467 (1997); David M. Driesen, *Trading and Its Limits*, 14 PENN ST. ENVTL. L. REV. 169 (2006). Emissions trading must be accompanied by accurate and rigorous monitoring of emissions and trades. Indeed, effective monitoring is one critical reason why the Acid Rain Program succeeded. The program required facilities to install a continuous emission monitoring system (CEMS) — electronic devices that measure actual emissions on a continuous basis and automatically transmit data to the Environmental Protection Agency (EPA) — or an equivalent emissions monitoring system. In addition, EPA established an Allowance Tracking System to monitor trades. McAllister, at 285.

4. ***Administrative Costs.*** The academic literature suggests that the administrative costs of implementing emissions trading programs may not necessarily be less expensive than traditional regulation, although over the long-term, after staff become familiar with the program, fewer administrative hours should be necessary to implement emissions trading programs. Administrative costs may increase, because of the need to verify actual emissions against authorized emissions, rather than simply ensure that mandated equipment functions properly: "Focusing on emissions requires increases in both administrative resources (in the areas of compliance, inspections, and audits), and emitter resources over and above investments in abatement (planning a compliance strategy, implementing the appropriate combination of abatement and acquiring permits, monitoring emissions, and reporting compliance)." Tietenberg, at 264.

5. ***Allocation of Allowances.*** A main source of controversy in any cap-and-trade program, and the climate trading system is no exception, is the initial allocation of the resource (i.e., pollution permits/amounts). For many, the free allocation of allowances provides beneficiaries with "windfall profits," as they benefit from a one-time transfer of wealth. Should countries allocate carbon permits at no charge, based on a lottery, or auction them to the highest bidder? Consider the following concerning implementation of the EU's Emissions Trading Scheme (ETS):

> Despite concerns about windfall profits and economic distortions resulting from the free allocation of allowances, there will be little change in basic allocation philosophy for Phase 2. No country has proposed auctioning the maximum percentage of allowances allowed (10%). Most do not include auctions at all. The unwillingness of governments to employ auctions as an allocating mechanism revolve around equity considerations, including: (1) inability of some covered entities to pass through cost because of regulation or exposure to international competition; (2) potential drag on a sector's economic performance from the up-front cost of auctioned allowances; and, (3) the potential that government will not recycle revenues to alleviate compliance costs, international competitiveness impacts, or other equity concerns, resulting in the auction costs being the same as a tax.

> Against these concerns, economic analysis provides several arguments in favor of auctions in general, and in the case of the EU ETS in particular.

General arguments in favor of auctions include:

- Purest embodiment of the "polluter pays" principle;

- Reduces distributional distortions that free allocation (and accompanying "windfall profits") can create;

- Creates a "level playing field" for existing and new covered entities;

- Potential for reducing the impact of compliance on the economy as a whole if auction revenues are used to reduce more distorting taxes on investment . . . ; and

- Can improve emission market liquidity and transparency.

Larry Parker, *Climate Change: The EU Emissions Trading Scheme (ETS) Gets Ready for Kyoto* (CRS Report, Aug 27, 2007). What type of allocation scheme would you recommend for emissions trading in the climate change context?

6. ***Technological Innovation.*** Proponents of emissions trading also argue that allowing emissions trading will spur technological innovation. But is this always true? Professor David Driesen summarizes the argument before countering that emissions trading may actually provide less innovation than traditional regulation of identical stringency:

DAVID M. DRIESEN, FREE LUNCH OR CHEAP FIX?: THE EMISSIONS TRADING IDEA AND THE CLIMATE CHANGE CONVENTION
26 B.C. ENVTL. AFFAIRS L. REV. 1, 41–46 (1998)*

Many economists assume that emissions trading generates innovation, because trading encourages the pollution source with the cheapest control options to make more reductions than the government requires of it in order to sell credits to other sources for which emissions control is more expensive. These economists assume, correctly, that making more reductions will generally require more innovation than making fewer reductions. Accordingly, cheap sources wishing to sell credits to polluters with more expensive control options innovate more than they would absent emissions trading. This argument focuses very narrowly on pollution sources with relatively cheap control options and does not consider how emissions trading might effect innovation at the pollution sources with relatively expensive control options.

Broadening the analysis to include all of the pollution sources eligible to trade casts grave doubts on the theory that emissions trading encourages more innovation than a comparable traditional regulation. . . . An emissions trading program creates two incentives: an incentive for the cheaper facility to emit less pollution than the government will authorize; and an incentive for the more expensive facility to emit more pollution than the government will authorize under a comparable traditional regulation. In emissions trading, foregoing normally required emission reductions at plants with relatively expensive control options finances "additional" reductions (reductions going beyond requirements) at cheaper facilities. The money saved by foregoing emission reductions at one facility finances the "extra" emission reductions at another.

At a minimum, this means that an emissions trading program decreases the incentives for innovations at relatively expensive facilities, since operators of these

---

facilities will emit more than they would under a comparable uniform standard. These operators, who might have tried to innovate to escape expensive pollution control requirements under a traditional performance standard, will tend to purchase credits instead.

Emissions trading may induce less net innovation than traditional regulation. The trading program effectively lessens or eliminates the pollution control obligations of the sources having the greatest need for innovation, those facing high control costs. It provides an incentive for low cost sources to make more reductions than a regulation would otherwise require. But the low cost sources may meet their needs with conventional technology, since achieving reductions for them is relatively cheap. Emissions trading, by shifting reductions from high cost to low cost facilities, may weaken incentives for innovation, even while it generates short-term cost savings.

Traditional regulation requires emission reductions from specifically targeted pollution sources. It does not allow polluters to forego control of a targeted source in exchange for a reduction elsewhere. This locational constraint may increase the need for innovation by requiring very focused pollution control efforts that might be expensive absent innovation. Easing the spatial constraints of traditional regulation may make it easier to choose some standard technology at a pollution source where control costs are inexpensive, rather than encourage innovation. If countries trade a large volume of environmental benefits under the Climate Change Convention, this may impede innovation for similar reasons. * * *

Trading offers a country the opportunity to make less domestic change to the degree it purchases credits abroad. Since innovation often involves significant initial costs, trading may create an economic incentive to deploy existing technology abroad in lieu of innovation at home.

Suppose, for example, that an American electric utility faces emission limitations stringent enough to force it to increase reliance on renewable energy sources and fuel cells. Given an international trading option, the utility may earn equivalent credits building a coal-burning power plant using standard technologies in a country that burns coal directly to heat buildings, cook, and power small industries. Or it may retrofit an existing dirty coal-fired power plant abroad. Even if use of standard technology abroad produces equivalent emission reductions at less cost than domestic reductions, the use of standard technology does nothing to support the process of developing renewable energy resources or advanced technologies. It consequently does nothing to change the cost differential that prevents the widespread deployment of technologies with much lower emissions. More initially expensive investments in developing and applying renewable energy might lower this cost differential over time; past investments have already substantially lowered the cost of producing renewable energy. A decision to retrofit a Russian power plant (for example) resembles homeowner's decision to patch a leaky spot on the roof, rather than to begin building a new roof capable of withstanding future storms.

* * *

The broader the universe of trading opportunities, the greater the potential to find cheap fixes that avoid long-term investments. In crafting agreements about trading, the international community faces important issues about the appropriate geographic breadth of trading and about which countries may trade. The degree of the threat to innovation depends on the particulars of the law governing trading. Geographically broad trading opportunities to realize credits for using standard technologies or planting trees may facilitate avoidance of investments in energy efficiency and renewable energy.

If Driesen is right that emissions trading may produce less innovation than expected, what should the climate change regime do to encourage greater technological innovation and investments?

7.   The emissions trading provisions of the Kyoto Protocol were controversial in part because developing countries viewed emissions trading as a means for the developed countries to avoid the difficult task of reducing greenhouse gas emissions at home. Does Driesen's analysis support their concerns? Or does the ability to achieve compliance at lower costs translate into greater political will to accept more stringent long-term caps on emissions?

3.   *Carbon Taxes*

Many economists favor environmental taxes over emissions trading systems as a more direct way to establish market incentives for reducing pollution or other forms of waste. In the climate context, this typically translates into proposals for a carbon-based tax that would encourage energy conservation and fuel-switching to less polluting fuels. A carbon tax on the order of $100 per ton of carbon (approximately 30 cents per gallon of gasoline) is a common estimate of what it would take to change consumption significantly. By increasing the costs of greenhouse gas emitting activities, such a tax would discourage unnecessary pollution and energy use. One could levy the penalty directly on carbon emissions, on the energy input (e.g., oil or coal), or on the final product (e.g., a gas-guzzling car). The following excerpt compares the carbon tax proposals with cap-and-trade proposals:

GILBERT E. METCALF, et al., ANALYSIS OF U.S. GREENHOUSE GAS TAX PROPOSALS
(National Bureau of Economic Research, April 2008)

In a cap-and-trade system a government agency sets the number of emissions allowances, and trading among them determines their price. Firms make abatement decisions based on the relative cost of purchasing (or not selling) allowances compared to the cost of abatement. Even if allowances are given for free, firms face an opportunity cost — the price they could sell them for in the market — if they choose to emit greenhouse gases. Under a tax approach the government sets the emissions price directly, and firms respond through decisions to pay the tax or abate. Under either policy emitters will tend to abate to the point where the marginal cost of emissions reduction is equal to the emissions price. * * *

. . . [T]here is not a stark either-or choice between tradable allowances and taxes. Hybrid instruments can be constructed, for example the addition of a safety valve to a cap-and-trade system where the government stands ready to sell permits at a fixed price thereby preventing permit prices from exceeding this level. With a safety valve, a cap-and-trade system works as a constraint on emissions only so long as the permit price is below the safety level; above that level the system works like a tax. Also, to the degree that allocations are auctioned rather than freely distributed, a cap-and-trade system has many characteristics of a tax. Still, even though either instrument, or various hybrids, can be effective at pricing GHGs, the pure versions differ in important respects.

*   *   *

2.2 Political Feasibility

It is argued that a major advantage of cap-and-trade over an emissions tax is its political feasibility. It is noted, for example, that the EU Emissions Trading System (ETS) is a demonstration that a cap-and-trade system can be implemented whereas an effort in the 1990s to implement an EU-wide GHG tax was a failure. A key factor in this EU experience was the fact that a decision to implement a tax required unanimity among EU members whereas the ETS required only majority approval. Political feasibility may thus depend in part on the specific features of different political systems. It is important to keep this factor in mind when considering instrument viability in the United States.

At first glance, U.S. experience also appears to support the argument that a cap-and-trade system is the more likely to be politically feasible. First, the U.S. has successfully implemented several cap-and-trade systems, $e.g.$, for NO_x emissions in some regions and for sulfur dioxide emissions from electric utilities on a national basis. Second, the most recent effort to employ a tax instrument in this context was the BTU tax proposed by President Clinton in 1994. While the BTU tax passed the House, it failed in the Senate and was ultimately replaced by a 4.3¢ per gallon increase in the federal motor vehicle fuels tax, justified as part of a deficit reduction package.

Analysis of why the Clinton tax proposal failed is beyond the scope of this paper, but one factor is that a BTU tax is not an efficient penalty on CO_2 or GHGs because of the differences in emissions among fuels per heat unit. The tax did not have a sharply articulated focus but rather was a compromise between a carbon tax to address global warming and a broad-based energy tax. A tax based on carbon content would have provided incentives to substitute natural gas for coal, and the tax base was designed to win support from coal state legislators. The lack of a focus and the fundamental compromise embedded in the tax design made it difficult to fend off requests for exemptions and other loopholes. Moreover, the scientific case that climate change is a serious threat has become much more compelling in the past decade. Also, while the Clinton Administration was not successful with the BTU tax, it also made no progress in Congress with the idea of a cap-and-trade system. It may well be that, in a changed political climate motivated by growing concern about climate change, the opposition to a tax instrument will be lower.

2.3 Revenue Generation

A GHG tax would raise revenue that could be used to lower other taxes, reduce the federal deficit or finance new government spending. A cap-and-trade system can raise revenue if the government auctions the permits rather than giving them away. While there is precedent in the U.S. for auctioning valuable rights ($e.g.$, broadcast spectrum, offshore oil leases), experience to date with cap-and-trade programs has been that the permits are given to regulated entities for free. . . . . Similarly, in its 2005–07 trial period the EU ETS allocated all allowances for free, but small percentages of auctioning are planned in some EU parties in the 2008–2012 Kyoto commitment period. Whether a GHG tax or cap-and-trade system with auctioning is chosen, a sizable economic literature demonstrates a "double dividend" that can be gained from a revenue-raising instrument if the funds collected are used to lower other distorting taxes, such as those on labor and capital.

2.4 Incentives for Rent-Seeking Activity

One reason for the perceived political advantage of cap-and-trade systems is the historic granting of free permits to the regulated entities, usually industrial and commercial firms. Permits are valuable assets and their allocation becomes a tool to help build support for the program. This creates incentives for industries to lobby to receive a large share of these assets. Commonly referred to as *rent seeking*, expenditure of resources to obtain valuable assets from governments is a socially wasteful activity and can lead to particularly inefficient outcomes. In addition, free distribution of allowances to entities that are the point of accounting and regulation can create an inequitable outcome because some firms will receive a valuable asset for free while passing most of the cost of abatement on to downstream fuel or electricity users. * * *

Experience in the EU ETS suggests that rent seeking can lead to restrictions on permits that may undermine some of their efficiency characteristics. For example, the ETS retains some allowances for new entrants, an incentive to create a new entity that would be eligible for some of these assets. It also requires that firms return allowances if an entire facility shuts down. The cheapest abatement option may be to simply shut down some of the highest emitting facilities, but this rule in the ETS creates an incentive to keep them operating at a low level, or to install more expensive abatement technology so that they do not have turn back in valuable allowances. These rules lead firms in these particular situations to equate the marginal cost of abatement to the price of emissions plus the value of the expected additional allocation of allowances or the value of all of the allowances they would have to turn in if they shut down. This result violates the efficiency criteria that all firms face the same marginal cost of abatement. * * *

Though competing interests may seek earmarks of expected revenue, a GHG tax does not create the same type of valuable financial asset to be allocated, as does a cap-and-trade system. While this may raise the political barrier to enacting a tax, it also may avoid an industry giveaway that is weakly connected to the points where the costs will be felt. A concern with carbon taxes that has been frequently raised is that industry concessions will be required to obtain political support for carbon pricing and that providing free permits is more efficient than excluding industries from a tax. This is unquestionably true, but exclusion is not the only way concessions can be provided to the energy sector through a carbon tax. One alternative approach would be to provide an *emissions floor* similar to the health spending deduction in the personal income tax. An emissions floor would only levy a carbon tax on emissions above a given floor (*e.g.*, 3 percent of a three year moving average of emissions).

2.5 Administrative Cost

The U.S. already has a well-developed administrative structure to collect taxes. Levying the tax at an upstream level on a relatively small number of firms, all of which already pay taxes, would reduce the administrative and compliance costs of the tax considerably. The farther downstream the implementation, the greater the implementation cost. In contrast, a new structure would be needed if a cap-and-trade system were put in place.

Moreover, benchmarking would be required for a cap-and-trade system if permits were allocated on the basis of historic emissions — as was done with the U.S. Acid Rain Program and the EU ETS.

Finally, if the European experience is followed and a downstream cap-and-trade program put in place, administrative complexity would rise considerably. In fact, the ETS exempts emitters of less than 10,000 tons of CO_2 per year and thereby only covers about 50% of the EU's emissions. . . . [By contrast,] since fuel sales are well recorded and already taxed, there does not appear to be much reason that nearly 100% of emissions of carbon dioxide from fossil fuel combustion could not be covered with little administrative burden. The Acid Rain program, a very successful cap-and-trade system, was limited to a small number of large electric utilities in the United States, and other sources of SO_2, from transportation fuels for example, were regulated through other measures.

QUESTIONS AND DISCUSSION

1. As the excerpt suggests, the carbon tax has proven to be politically controversial in the United States, but European countries and Canadian provinces, among others, have been experimenting with such taxes on gasoline and other products in the past few years. Why do you think it is so difficult to get carbon taxes approved in the United States? What steps would you recommend to make a carbon tax more politically acceptable? Do you think Metcalf, et al., are correct that the current political climate may be increasingly amenable to a carbon tax?

2. Experience with carbon taxes to control greenhouse gases is growing. The Nordic countries (Finland, Sweden, Norway and Denmark) instituted greenhouse gas taxes in the early 1990s. The first climate-motivated greenhouse gas taxes in North America have recently passed in Quebec and British Columbia. *See* Jonathan Fowlie & Fiona Anderson, *B.C. Introduces Carbon Tax*, VANCOUVER SUN (Feb. 19, 2008).

3. ***Carbon Trading vs. Taxes.*** What are the relative advantages and disadvantages of carbon trading versus a carbon tax? There are strong adherents on both sides. Robert Shapiro, for example, argues that taxes are preferable because they directly control price, whereas cap-and-trade regimes control the quantity of emissions. By controlling price, a tax system does not have the price volatility that has been prevalent in cap-and-trade regimes. Price stability provides businesses with the price signal they need to make investment decisions, even if the tax cannot predetermine levels of emission reductions. Under the European Trading System, prices have fluctuated wildly. They have been as high as $30 per ton in late 2006 before crashing to about $1 a ton. Prices have subsequently risen to $20 per ton. Second, he argues that a carbon tax would have comparable effects from country to country, while a global cap-and-trade program would not. Third, Shapiro argues that cap-and-trade programs "are more difficult to administer and more vulnerable to evasion, corruption and manipulation than carbon taxes" because they create scarcity (for emitting carbon) where none previously existed. ROBERT J. SHAPIRO, ADDRESSING THE RISKS OF CLIMATE CHANGE: THE ENVIRONMENTAL EFFECTIVENESS AND ECONOMIC EFFICIENCY OF EMISSIONS CAPS AND TRADABLE PERMITS, COMPARED TO CARBON TAXES (2007). He ultimately concludes that "[g]lobal, harmonized net carbon taxes could contain those risks in an economically-efficient and politically-feasible way." Others have taken the opposing view, arguing that a cap-and-trade program would raise prices as a carbon tax would (although not fix prices), while also accomplishing its environmental goals by a specific date. William Chameides & Michael Oppenheimer, *Carbon Trading Over Taxes*, SCIENCE 1670 (March 23, 2007). Which do you prefer? Why?

4. ***Imposing Liability.*** In theory, at least, the imposition of a tax is an administrative mechanism for internalizing the environmental and social costs of pollution. Another way of applying the polluter pays principle, and one particularly interesting to lawyers, is to impose liability for actual damage caused. The

European Union has recognized this in a paper on environmental liability presented by the European Commission:

> One way to ensure that greater caution will be applied to avoid the occurrence of damage to the environment is indeed to impose liability on the party responsible for an activity that bears risks of causing such damage. This means that, when such an activity really results in damage, the party in control of the activity (the operator), who is the actual polluter, has to pay the costs of repair. * * *
>
> Liability for damage to nature is a prerequisite for making economic actors feel responsible for the possible negative effects of their operations on the environment as such. So far, operators seem to feel such responsibility for other people's health or property — for which environmental liability already exists, in different forms, at the national level — rather than for the environment. They tend to consider the environment "a public good" for which society as a whole should be responsible, rather than an individual actor who happened to cause damage to it. Liability is a certain way of making people realize that they are also responsible for possible consequences of their acts with regard to nature. This expected change of attitude should result in an increased level of prevention and precaution.

See European Commission, *White Paper on Environmental Liability* 66 (Feb. 9, 2000). Can you see how the imposition of liability through a torts system or any other system of compensation is another form of internalizing costs, not conceptually that different from imposing a carbon tax? We will consider the role of liability in internalizing climate change costs and providing incentives to reduce greenhouse gas emissions when we discuss climate change litigation in Chapter 16.

———

4.   *Information-Based Approaches*

If prescriptive regulation and market-based instruments represent "hard" regulatory approaches, then a softer approach may be found in laws requiring information production and dissemination. Sometimes described as *the third wave of environmental lawmaking*, the theory behind these reflective approaches is that the government can change people's behavior by forcing them to think about the harm they are causing and by publicizing that harm. There is a wide spectrum of such approaches, ranging from compulsory or voluntary labeling requirements, to public disclosure of pollution levels, to government-sponsored reports, studies or brochures.

Perhaps most important are the requirements to measure and report net greenhouse gas emissions. The international climate treaty regime requires developed countries to provide reports on their net emissions. Some countries also require project-level emissions reporting. Indeed, this is a prerequisite for effective emissions control regulation.

In the climate context, the U.S. government has tried several information-based approaches, including, for example, the Energy Star labelling system for informing consumers of the most energy efficient appliances. Energy Star is discussed further in Chapter 14. EPA also has a series of climate-related awards meant to highlight innovation and leadership relating to climate change. Governments at all levels also issue large numbers of brochures, web-sites, studies and reports relating to climate change.

5.   *Investment and Technology Approaches*

In addition to cap-and-trade, carbon taxes or other regulatory approaches, some observers argue for complementary pro-active efforts to spark private sector investment. According to this approach:

> the key to achieving deep reductions is to drive down the real price and improve the performance of clean energy technology as rapidly as possible. . . . [T]argeted public investment is the most likely path to this outcome. . . . These investments should include dramatic increases in funding for basic research in the energy sciences, a ten-year commitment to buy down the price of solar technology and battery and other energy storage technologies, and a commitment to build a smarter and more efficient electricity grid that can support energy generation that is both more widely distributed and, in many cases, more remote. * * *

> We are proposing a ten-year, $300 billion public investment into accelerating the transition to a clean energy economy. The goal of the program is to bring the price of clean energy down to the price of coal and natural gas as quickly as possible. Other values also should be built into the structure of the investment, such as labor, health, and other environmental standards.

Michael Shellenberger, et al., *Fast, Clean & Cheap: Cutting Global Warming's Gordian Knot*, 2 HARV. L. & POL'Y REV. 93, 115–16 (2008). The converse of subsidizing renewable energy is to remove subsides that make fossil fuel use artificially low or promote land-use practices that increase net climate emissions.

QUESTIONS AND DISCUSSION

1.   In certain respects, some subsidies cost us twice, first as we pay the initial tax to raise the funds needed for the subsidy, and second when we suffer the environmental damage encouraged by the subsidy.

> Energy subsidies — government interventions that affect energy prices or costs — are large, widespread and diverse. They vary greatly in size and type among fuels, end-use sectors and countries. They also fluctuate markedly over time. Today, energy subsidies are of the order of $250 to $300 billion per year net of taxes worldwide, equal to 0.6% to 0.7% of world GDP, according to the latest estimates by the International Energy Agency. . . . Non-OECD countries account for the bulk of these subsidies, with most of them going to consumption by lowering prices paid by consumers. In OECD countries, most subsidies go to production, usually in the form of direct payments to producers or support for research and development.

> Worldwide, fossil fuels are the most heavily subsidised energy sources, totalling an estimated $180 to 200 billion per year. Support to the deployment of low-carbon energy sources currently amounts to an estimated $33 billion each year: $10 billion to renewables, $16 billion to existing nuclear power plants and $6 billion on biofuels. Overall energy subsidies fell sharply in the early to mid-1990s, with the transition to market economies in the former communist bloc countries. But they may have risen in recent years as many non-OECD countries have sought to prevent higher international energy prices from feeding into final prices for social reasons.

Energy subsidies deliberately distort price signals and, therefore, investment in infrastructure to supply different fuels and in the capital stock that transform or consume energy. Because the bulk of energy subsidies worldwide result in a lower price for fossil fuels to end users, they cause more of those fuels to be consumed, increasing carbon-dioxide and other greenhouse-gas emissions and contributing to climate change. Empirical studies suggest that the potential emissions reductions from removing all subsidies that encourage fossil energy consumption could be substantial. Moreover, such a move could bring major economic benefits too. In many cases, the social costs of eliminating those subsidies would be small.

Trevor Morgan, *Energy Subsidies: Their Magnitude, How they Affect Energy Investment and Greenhouse Gas Emissions, and Prospects for Reform*, Report prepared for the UNFCCC Secretariat, June 10, 2007. What do you think the major impediments are for dismantling subsidies to fossil fuels?

2. Simply measuring the total subsidies to the fossil fuel industry can be difficult. A recent review of studies on U.S. fossil fuel subsidies found the estimates ranged from $2.6 to $121 billion. The disparity partly results from different definitions of what is a subsidy, but it also reflects a deliberate lack of transparency in reporting on the level and type of subsidy. *See* Doug Koplow & John C. Dernbach, *Federal Fossil Fuel Subsidies and Greenhouse Gas Emissions: A Case Study of Increasing Transparency for Fiscal Policy*, 26 ANN. REV. OF ENERGY AND THE ENV'T 361 (2001), *available at* http://ssrn.com/abstract=1090718 (recommending that basic information about proposed subsidies be subject to the same kind of public justification requirements to which proposed regulations are subject).

3. Not all subsidies, of course, are environmentally harmful. Indeed, just as with green taxes, green subsidies can promote environmental protection. Many climate-friendly subsidies have been proposed. For example, many states provide tax credits for purchasing fuel-efficient hybrid cars, installing solar or other renewable sources of energy, or purchasing energy efficient appliances. Some general subsidies also support the development of solar or wind power technologies, but in general these subsidies have been less than those provided for the exploration and production of fossil fuels.

4. In the end, climate change is so complex and affects so many sectors that no one category of policy approaches will do. Most policymakers that have addressed climate change have done so through a mix of policies that utilize traditional regulation, market-based mechanisms and other approaches. Even the international climate regime promotes the use of other "policies and measures" beyond cap-and-trade. As you learn the different sectoral challenges to mitigating climate change, outlined in Section III below, consider which policy mix you would recommend for each sector.

III.   MITIGATION POLICIES AT THE SECTOR LEVEL

A.   Mitigation Measures

To some extent, no matter which general approach is taken, mitigation priorities and approaches will have to depend on different factors in each industrial sector. Priorities to reduce greenhouse gas concentrations will partly depend, for example, on an understanding of the relative contribution to climate change from various economic sectors. As shown in Figure 2-1, nearly 60 percent of global carbon-equivalent greenhouse gas emissions come from energy use while another 30 percent comes from land-use conversion and agriculture.

Percentage of GHG Emissions by Sector

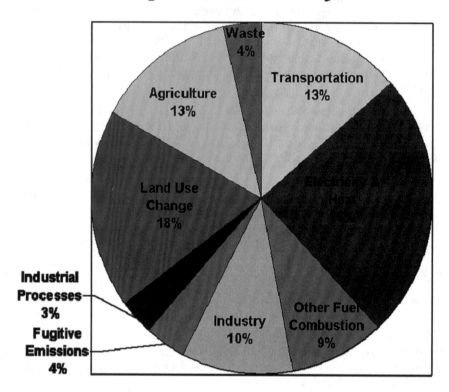

Source: Kevin A. Baumert, et al., *Navigating the Numbers: Greenhouse Gas Data and International Climate Policy* (World Resources Institute, 2005). Table 2-1 illustrates GHG emissions according to end-uses or economic activities, instead of sectors, which gives a more detailed view of the relative contributions of various activities. These statistics can indicate what sectors and activities are the major contributors to climate change, and thus potentially the most important targets for climate policy.

TABLE 2-1: Global GHG Emissions by End Use (adapted from Baumert, et al., *Navigating the Numbers*)	
End Use/Activity	**Percentage of GHG Emissions**
Road (Automobile, trucks, etc)	9.9%
Air	1.6%
Rail, Ship, and Other Transport	2.3%
Residential Buildings	9.9%
Commercial Buildings	5.4%
Unallocated Fuel Combustion	3.5%
Iron and Steel	3.2%
Aluminum/Non-Ferrous Metals	1.4%

TABLE 2-1: Global GHG Emissions by End Use (adapted from Baumert, et al., *Navigating the Numbers*)	
End Use/Activity	**Percentage of GHG Emissions**
Machinery	1.0%
Pulp, Paper and Printing	1.0%
Food and Tobacco	1.0%
Chemicals	4.8%
Cement	3.8%
Other Industry	5.0%
Transmission & Distribution Losses	1.9%
Coal Mining	1.4%
Oil/Gas Extraction, Refining, and Processing	6.3%
Forestation	18.2%
Agricultural Energy Use	1.4%
Agricultural Soils	6.0%
Livestock and Manure	5.1%
Rice Cultivation	1.5%
Other Agriculture	0.9%
Landfills	2.0%
Wastewater, Other Waste	1.6%

The wide range of end-use activities that contribute to climate change shows just how deeply the regulation of greenhouse gases will affect the economy. It also suggests that a wide variety of possible policy approaches can help to reduce climate change. Indeed, most national and subnational climate policies invoke a diverse range of policies aimed at different sectors or activities. Some of the general approaches for each sector are set forth below.

The Energy Sector. The energy sector is obviously inextricably linked to any climate change strategy. The reduction of carbon dioxide cannot be done without a major re-orientation of the energy sector away from fossil fuels. This will not be easy as current energy production is heavily dependent on coal and oil; 50 percent of U.S. electricity, for example, comes from coal. And projections of energy demand, particularly in high-growth countries such as China and India, are hard to square with the goal of reducing CO_2 emissions. In 2006 alone, China received 80 percent of its electricity from coal and reportedly added over 90 Gigawatts of new coal-fired power plant capacity — the equivalent of almost 2 large coal power plants a week. Moreover, the energy sector is capital-intensive, heavily subsidised, politically powerful, and often slow to respond to environmental criticism. Many older U.S. power plants, for example are essentially exempted from the Clean Air Act's strictest provisions and do not currently use modern emission control technologies. Oil producers in Nigeria and other developing countries routinely flare natural gas directly into the air, contributing tons of GHGs unnecessarily and in direct violation of recent judicial holdings there.

The two major strategies for reducing reliance on fossil fuels are increasing energy efficiency and switching to less carbon-intensive forms of fuel. By increasing energy efficiency, we can get the same amount of "work" or benefits from burning less fossil fuels. Energy efficiency technologies are frequently a win-win opportunity — they protect the environment and save energy costs. Innovations like high-efficiency light-bulbs, refrigerators, and other household appliances can greatly reduce the amounts of energy use and reduce overall operating costs. They also offer every individual an opportunity to participate in responding to climate change. Efficiency standards for appliances and other electronic equipment can also reduce emissions now and catalyze future innovation.

Fuel switching to move the economy away from fossil fuels and towards cleaner, renewable technologies will be even more important. Leading green energy alternatives are solar, wind power, and hydrogen fuel cells — but hydroelectric, biofuels, geothermal and nuclear sources of energy also result in lower GHG emissions than traditional fossil-fuel sources. Even switching from coal and oil to natural gas, which is more efficient, can result in significantly lower emissions. As an example, an estimated one gigaton of carbon emissions per year would be reduced if an equivalent amount of fossil-fuel electricity was replaced with approximately 300,000 5MV wind turbines (which would cover an area the size of Portugal). Renewable portfolio standards, which require utilities to supply a percentage of energy from renewable sources, are increasingly common at the state level in the United States.

Important in assessing energy alternatives is to consider all lifetime impacts on climate change. For example, nuclear power may emit few GHGs, but the mining and processing of uranium ore into nuclear fuel is energy-intensive and can contribute significantly to GHG emissions. Some biofuels, particularly corn, have high life-cycle climate impacts. Many alternatives also have significant negative environmental and social externalities not related to climate change. Greater demand for biofuels, for example, may already be partly to blame for the higher food prices and food shortages experienced in 2008; nuclear power raises serious issues of waste disposal; and large hydroelectric dams frequently destroy freshwater ecosystems.

Many climate change policies discussed in later chapters target the energy sector specifically. Many states have adopted renewable portfolio standards, for example, which typically require utilities to ensure that their energy portfolios include a minimum percentage of solar, wind or other renewables. The New England states' Regional Greenhouse Gas Initiative is an example of a cap-and-trade system primarily targeting the emissions from large utilities. Subsidies for renewables or non-fossil fuel energy sources are common policy approaches, as are efficiency standards for appliances and other efforts to reduce energy demand.

The Transportation Sector. Transportation accounts for 27 percent of greenhouse gas emissions in the United States and about 13 percent worldwide. Most transportation-related emissions come from automobiles and trucks (9.6 percent), but air (1.6 percent) and shipping (2.3 percent) are also significant contributors to global emissions. Transportation-related emissions are increasing considerably as growing middle classes in China, India, and Brazil aspire to automobiles. Also significant is the growing distance that people and goods travel in an age of globalized travel and free trade. In Europe, for example, emissions from air travel grew 73 percent from 1990 to 2005, just under 5% a year.

The technical solutions for reducing transportation-related emissions include increasing efficiency in transportation, shifting to cleaner modes of transportation, and reducing the amount of transportation (particularly of goods) altogether. The growth of hybrid technology cars in the United States (now representing 2.5 percent of the market) has been astounding. Unfortunately, newer and greener technologies such as fuel cell, hydrogen-based or electric cars have been discussed for years, but are still not widely available. Motivated mostly by higher fuel costs, the airline industry, through both technological and operational changes, became 23% more efficient from 2000 to 2006. Of course, shifting fuels or building more efficient engines will only partly address the issue; we also need major shifts towards public transportation or bicycles.

Policies in the transportation sector include tougher fuel-efficiency standards on automobiles, trucks, airplanes, and ships. Additionally, enhanced public transportation either through subsidies or other policies and improved land-use patterns could significantly reduce the use of automobiles and thus the resulting GHG emissions. Local transportation decisions can make a big difference. Portland, Oregon, for example, has adopted a wide range of policies to make its city more bike and pedestrian friendly. And in 2008 Washington, D.C. began offering free bicycles for daily use, with the hope of reducing congestion and emissions. The "shop local" movement is also important for reducing the emissions associated with food and other goods that we purchase. Local climate initiatives are discussed further in Chapter 17.

The Industrial Sector. As can be seen in Table 2-1, GHG emissions from chemical plants, aluminum smelters, cement manufacturers, and other industrial plants are significant contributors to global climate change. Cement manufacturing, alone, contributes 3.8 percent of global emissions. Certain industrial gases, including HCFCs, perfluorocarbons, and sulfur hexafluoride, that are used for specific purposes often have global warming potentials thousands of times higher than carbon dioxide.

Key to reducing emissions from the industrial sector is finding alternative substances and technologies and disseminating these innovations to developing countries. Under the guidance of the World Business Council on Sustainable Development, the cement industry, for example, has launched a Cement Sustainability Initiative to cooperate in modernizing the industry with new technologies and new fuels that reduce climate change. *See* www.wbcsd.org. Chemicals with specialized uses and high global warming potentials may also be targeted for phase-outs to force the development of substitute technologies. The Montreal Protocol, for example, agreed in 2007 to accelerate the phase-out of HCFCs, primarily for climate change reasons. *See* discussion of the Montreal Protocol in Chapter 10. Methane emissions from solid waste landfills can be recovered and used to produce energy. *See* Chapter 11 (discussing the U.S. Methane program).

Forestry and Agriculture. Forestry, agriculture, and other land uses have complicated and substantial impacts on climate change. The widespread burning of forests to convert them to agricultural or range lands, for example, is the primary source of net emissions in many developing countries. Significant changes in forests and land-use patterns also reduce or eliminate important carbon sinks and reservoirs, critical for removing carbon from the atmosphere. Thus, improvements in forestry, agriculture, and land use can provide double benefits — both reducing emissions and maintaining carbon sinks.

Changing forestry, agriculture, and land-use practices presents unique challenges because one must often influence rural, widely disbursed, and traditional communities slow to change. Reducing deforestation and encouraging sustainable forestry practices are among the highest priorities in the international climate negotiations. Tree planting and reforestation efforts generally can also increase carbon sequestration. Controlling fires, including eliminating the practice of burning lands for agriculture, is an important priority. Forestry issues are discussed in detail in Chapter 7.

The agricultural sector also offers opportunities for reducing climate impacts, through better land-use practices. Rice production methods are being developed to reduce the amount of methane emitted from rice paddies. Beef production is also inefficient and growing considerably, particularly in China. In response, agronomists have actually been experimenting with different cattle feeds to reduce the amount of methane "emitted" from the digestive tracts of cattle.

QUESTIONS AND DISCUSSION

1. **The Solar Revolution.** Solar power remains one of the most promising alternatives to fossil fuels. Current global installed capacity of photovoltaic solar power since 1996 is more than 9,740 megawatts, enough to meet the electricity demand of more than 3 million European homes each year. Janet L. Sawin, *Another Sunny Year for Solar Power* (Worldwatch Institute, May 8, 2008). And the price of solar is dropping considerably and becoming competitive with fossil fuels in some areas. Solar will undoubtedly continue to expand, but some scientists believe we need a much more pro-active public-private partnership to build a solar infrastructure that can really drop the price and make it widely available. A recent article in *Scientific American* proposed a detailed framework costing $10 billion per year for forty years to create a "solar revolution" that would provide nearly 70 percent of U.S. electricity demand from solar by 2050. *See* Ken Zweibel, et al., *A Solar Grand Plan*, Sci. Am., Dec. 2007, at 64.

2. **Carbon Capture and Storage.** Carbon capture and storage, or CCS, involves the pumping of CO_2 emissions from power plants and other large emission sources into reservoirs located deep underground or beneath the sea, which effectively reduces emissions from that source to near-zero levels. The pipe-line building and well-drilling infrastructure used to extract fossil fuels from the earth uses the same technology that CCS would use to pump CO_2 back into the ground — but virtually none of this technology is now deployed for CCS purposes. CCS is now being conducted at industrial levels in pilot projects in Norway, Canada, and Algeria, but with only minimal amounts of CO_2. One of the main barriers to deploying CCS technology is cost. In December 2005, the U.S. Department of Energy estimated that it costs about $150 per tonne to sequester carbon with current technologies, noting that at that time the price of a carbon allowance under the European Union's Emissions Trading System was around $25 per tonne. In 2008 the U.S. government cancelled its planned joint efforts with U.S. utilities to develop CCS pilot projects, because the projected costs of CCS technology was too high. As a result, the near-term future of CCS technology is decidedly mixed. But companies interested in CCS predict that at some point, as emissions regulations grow more stringent, it will eventually be cheaper to store carbon underground than to emit it into the atmosphere. CCS thus figures to play a prominent role in future climate mitigation, particularly given that the global capacity of coal-fired power plants is projected to double by 2030. *See* IPCC, *Special Report: Carbon Dioxide Capture and Storage*

(2005); "Communique and Plan of Action on Global Energy Security," (July 16, 2006) (announcing that G8 parties will take measures to facilitate investments in the "sustainable global energy value chain," including CCS technologies, and encourage the introduction of CCS technologies wherever appropriate).

3. *Going Carbon Negative.* Some analysts are now promoting "carbon negative" strategies to increase the pace at which the world can return to pre-industrial levels of atmospheric carbon. Peter Read and Jonathan Lermit, for example, suggest combining bio-fuels and CCS technologies; by growing biofuel crops on surplus agricultural land and then capturing emissions from the biofuels and storing them underground, they contend the world could return to pre-industrial CO_2 levels by as early as 2070. *See* Peter Read & Jonathan Lermit, *Bio-Energy with Carbon Storage (BECS): A Sequential Decision Approach to the Threat of Abrupt Climate Change*, 30 ENERGY 2654 (2005). Their approach is predicated on policymakers instituting a "Manhattan Project" type strategy for changing global land uses. Such a strategy would involve three stages of implementation: establishing plantations of biofuel crops eventually large enough to restore preindustrial levels of forest-cover; harvesting the biomass for both energy and timber needs; and capturing emissions and storing them in underground reservoirs with CCS technology. *Id.* New technologies may also make going "carbon negative" less expensive over time. For example, some engineers are beginning to develop air scrubbers that can capture carbon dioxide from the air. These machines still face technical and financial hurdles, but initial prototypes do hold some promise for the future. *See Scrubbing the Skies*, ECONOMIST TECH. Q. 22 (Mar. 7, 2009).

4. *Biochar.* Another "carbon negative" strategy involves a process of burning or smoldering organic material under ground to create "biochar." Developed by the original inhabitants of the Amazon Basin several thousand years ago to produce a highly fertile soil, the process could also be used to sequester significant amounts of carbon. Excess biomass — essentially left-over agricultural material that isn't useful as food — has already drawn carbon from the atmosphere as part of its lifecycle. If burnt or left to decay, most of that carbon is re-released into the atmosphere. But if converted into char, the carbon is held in the ground. A hectare of meter-deep char can store 250 tons of carbon, as opposed to 100 tons from more typical soils. The carbon negative potential of char can be enhanced when used in conjunction with biofuels programs. Researchers have estimated that by the end of the 21st century, the combination of biofuels and char could store up to 9.5 gigatons of carbon per year — which is more than the world's current fossil fuel emissions. Dan Day, *Carbon Negative Energy to Reverse Global Warming*, ENERGY BULLETIN (Aug. 1, 2004); Emma Marris, *Putting the Carbon Back: Black is the New Green*, 442 NATURE (Aug. 10, 2006).

B.   Stabilization Wedges: Mitigation One Step at a Time

One encouraging aspect of the climate change issue is that a diverse menu of policy options is available for reducing GHG emissions. Some options require significant restructuring of our economies and others require new technological innovations, but some require only the dissemination and "scaling up" of technologies and practices already well known. Princeton researchers Stephen Pacala and Robert Socolow, for example, have devised a portfolio of what they call "stabilization wedges" — technological or policy innovations that would make significant progress towards reducing greenhouse gas emissions. In this 2004 article, Pacala and Socolow use as an overall goal stabilizing GHG concentrations at levels "less than double pre-industrial concentrations." This would put atmospheric concentrations at roughly 550 ppm (they are currently at 380). Although this stabilization goal has since been shown to be too high, the article is still helpful in understanding the possible policy mix for responding to climate change. To achieve this level, Pacala and Socolow estimated that in 50 years the global economy would have to be emitting 7 Gigatons of carbon per year less than what current trends suggest is "business as usual." They divided the needed reductions in greenhouse gas emissions into seven equal "stabilization wedges," each representing 1 Gigaton of reductions per year in carbon emissions by 2054. They then list fifteen policy options that could yield the equivalent of a "stabilization wedge" of reductions (i.e., a 1 Gigaton reduction per year). The following excerpt describes these options.

STEPHEN PACALA & ROBERT SOCOLOW, STABILIZATION WEDGES: SOLVING THE CLIMATE PROBLEM FOR THE NEXT 50 YEARS WITH CURRENT TECHNOLOGIES
305 SCIENCE 968 (Aug. 13, 2004)[*]

Humanity already possesses the fundamental scientific, technical, and industrial know-how to solve the carbon and climate problem for the next half-century. A portfolio of technologies now exists to meet the world's energy needs over the next 50 years and limit atmospheric CO_2 to a trajectory that avoids a doubling of the preindustrial concentration. Every element in this portfolio has passed beyond the laboratory bench and demonstration project; many are already implemented somewhere at full industrial scale. Although no element is a credible candidate for doing the entire job (or even half the job) by itself, the portfolio as a whole is large enough that not every element has to be used. * * *

To keep the focus on technologies that have the potential to produce a material difference by 2054, we divide the . . . [total amount of greenhouse gas emissions over time] into seven equal "wedges." A wedge represents an activity that reduces emissions to the atmosphere that starts at zero today and increases linearly until it accounts for 1 GtC/year of reduced carbon emissions in 50 years. It thus represents a cumulative total of 25 GtC of reduced emissions over 50 years. In this paper, to "solve the carbon and climate problem over the next half-century" means to deploy the technologies and/or lifestyle changes necessary to fill all seven wedges [necessary to meet the stabilization goal]. * * *

It is important to understand that each of the seven wedges represents an effort beyond what would occur under BAU [Business As Usual]. Our BAU simply continues the 1.5% annual carbon emissions growth of the past 30 years. This historic trend in emissions has been accompanied by 2% growth in primary energy consumption and 3% growth in gross world product (GWP). If carbon emissions were to grow 2% per year, then [approximately] 10 wedges would be needed instead of 7, and if carbon emissions were to grow at 3% per year, then [approximately] 18 wedges would be required. Thus, a continuation of the historical rate of decarbonization of the fuel mix prevents the need for three additional wedges, and ongoing improvements in energy efficiency prevent the need for eight additional wedges. Most readers will reject at least one of the wedges listed here, believing that the corresponding deployment is certain to occur in BAU, but readers will disagree about which to reject on such grounds. On the other hand, our list of mitigation options is not exhaustive.

What Current Options Could Be Scaled Up to Produce at Least One Wedge?

Wedges can be achieved from energy efficiency, from the decarbonization of the supply of electricity and fuels (by means of fuel shifting, carbon capture and storage, nuclear energy, and renewable energy), and from biological storage in forests and agricultural soils. Below, we discuss 15 different examples of options that are already deployed at an industrial scale and that could be scaled up further to produce at least one wedge . . . . Although several options could be scaled up to two or more wedges, we doubt that any could [meet] the stabilization [goal], or even half of it, alone. * * *

Category I: Efficiency and Conservation

Improvements in efficiency and conservation probably offer the greatest potential to provide wedges. For example, in 2002, the United States announced the goal of decreasing its carbon intensity (carbon emissions per unit GDP) by 18% over the next decade, a decrease of 1.96% per year. An entire wedge would be created if the United States were to reset its carbon intensity goal to a decrease of 2.11% per year and extend it to 50 years, and if every country were to follow suit by adding the same 0.15% per year increment to its own carbon intensity goal. However, efficiency and conservation options are less tangible than those from the other categories. Improvements in energy efficiency will come from literally hundreds of innovations that range from new catalysts and chemical processes, to more efficient lighting and insulation for buildings, to the growth of the service economy and telecommuting. Here, we provide four of many possible comparisons of greater and less efficiency in 2054. . . .

Option 1: Improved fuel economy. Suppose that in 2054, 2 billion cars (roughly four times as many as today) average 10,000 miles per year (as they do today). One wedge would be achieved if, instead of averaging 30 miles per gallon (mpg) on conventional fuel, cars in 2054 averaged 60 mpg, with fuel type and distance traveled unchanged.

Option 2: Reduced reliance on cars. A wedge would also be achieved if the average fuel economy of the 2 billion 2054 cars were 30 mpg, but the annual distance traveled were 5000 miles instead of 10,000 miles.

Option 3: More efficient buildings. According to a 1996 study by the IPCC, a wedge is the difference between pursuing and not pursuing "known and established approaches" to energy efficient space heating and cooling, water heating, lighting, and refrigeration in residential and commercial buildings. These approaches reduce mid-century emissions from buildings by about one-fourth. About half of potential savings are in the buildings in developing countries.

Option 4: Improved power plant efficiency. In 2000, coal power plants, operating on average at 32% efficiency, produced about one-fourth of all carbon emissions: 1.7 GtC/year out of 6.2 GtC/year. A wedge would be created if twice today's quantity of coal-based electricity in 2054 were produced at 60% instead of 40% efficiency.

Category II: Decarbonization of Electricity and Fuels

Option 5: Substituting natural gas for coal. Carbon emissions per unit of electricity are about half as large from natural gas power plants as from coal plants. Assume that the capacity factor of the average baseload coal plant in 2054 has increased to 90% and that its efficiency has improved to 50%. Because 700 GW of such plants emit carbon at a rate of 1 GtC/year, a wedge would be achieved by displacing 1400GWof baseload coal with baseload gas by 2054. The power shifted to gas for this wedge is four times as large as the total current gas-based power.

Option 6: Storage of carbon captured in power plants. Carbon capture and storage (CCS) technology prevents about 90% of the fossil carbon from reaching the atmosphere, so a wedge would be provided by the installation of CCS at 800 GW of baseload coal plants by 2054 or 1600 GW of baseload natural gas plants. The most likely approach has two steps: (i) precombustion capture of CO_2, in which hydrogen and CO_2 are produced and the hydrogen is then burned to produce electricity, followed by (ii) geologic storage, in which the waste CO_2 is injected into subsurface geologic reservoirs. Hydrogen production from fossil fuels is already a very large business. Globally, hydrogen plants consume about 2% of primary energy and emit 0.1 GtC/year of CO_2. The capture part of a wedge of CCS electricity would thus require only a tenfold expansion of plants resembling today's large hydrogen plants over the next 50 years.

The scale of the storage part of this wedge can be expressed as a multiple of the scale of current enhanced oil recovery, or current seasonal storage of natural gas, or the first geological storage demonstration project. Today, about 0.01 GtC/year of carbon as CO_2 is injected into geologic reservoirs to spur enhanced oil recovery, so a wedge of geologic storage requires that CO_2 injection be scaled up by a factor of 100 over the next 50 years. To smooth out seasonal demand in the United States, the natural gas industry annually draws roughly 4000 billion standard cubic feet (Bscf) into and out of geologic storage, and a carbon flow of 1 GtC/year (whether as methane or CO_2) is a flow of 69,000 Bscf/year (190 Bscf per day), so a wedge would be a flow to storage 15 and 20 times as large as the current flow. Norway's Sleipner project in the North Sea strips CO_2 from natural gas offshore and reinjects 0.3 million tons of carbon a year (MtC/year) into a non-fossil-fuel-bearing formation, so a wedge would be 3500 Sleipner-sized projects (or fewer, larger projects) over the next 50 years. * * *

Option 7: Storage of carbon captured in hydrogen plants. The hydrogen resulting from precombustion capture of CO_2 can be sent offsite to displace the consumption of conventional fuels rather than being consumed onsite to produce electricity. The capture part of a wedge would require the installation of CCS, by 2054, at coal plants producing 250 MtH2/year, or at natural gas plants producing 500 MtH2/year. The former is six times the current rate of hydrogen production. The storage part of this option is the same as in Option 6.

Option 8: Storage of carbon captured in synfuels plants. Looming over carbon management in 2054 is the possibility of large-scale production of synthetic fuel (synfuel) from coal. Carbon emissions, however, need not exceed those associated with fuel refined from crude oil if synfuels production is accompanied by CCS. Assuming that half of the carbon entering a 2054 synfuels plant leaves as fuel but the other half can be captured as CO_2, the capture part of a wedge in 2054 would be the difference between capturing and venting the CO_2 from coal synfuels plants producing 30 million barrels of synfuels per day. (The flow of carbon in 24 million barrels per day of crude oil is 1 GtC/year; we assume the same value for the flow in synfuels and allow for imperfect capture.) Currently, the Sasol plants in South Africa, the world's largest synfuels facility, produce 165,000 barrels per day from coal. Thus, a wedge requires 200 Sasol-scale coal-to-synfuels facilities with CCS in 2054. The storage part of this option is again the same as in Option 6.

Option 9: Nuclear fission. On the basis of the Option 5 estimates, a wedge of nuclear electricity would displace 700 GW of efficient baseload coal capacity in 2054. This would require 700 GW of nuclear power with the same 90% capacity factor assumed for the coal plants, or about twice the nuclear capacity currently deployed. The global pace of nuclear power plant construction from 1975 to 1990 would yield a wedge, if it continued for 50 years. Substantial expansion in nuclear power requires restoration of public confidence in safety and waste disposal, and international security agreements governing uranium enrichment and plutonium recycling.

Option 10: Wind electricity. We account for the intermittent output of windmills by equating 3 GW of nominal peak capacity (3 GWp) with 1 GW of baseload capacity. Thus, a wedge of wind electricity would require the deployment of 2000 GWp that displaces coal electricity in 2054 (or 2 million 1-MWp wind turbines). Installed wind capacity has been growing at about 30% per year for more than 10 years and is currently about 40 GWp. A wedge of wind electricity would thus require 50 times today's deployment. The wind turbines would "occupy" about 30 million hectares (about 3% of the area of the United States), some on land and some offshore. Because windmills are widely spaced, land with windmills can have multiple uses.

Option 11: Photovoltaic electricity. Similar to a wedge of wind electricity, a wedge from photovoltaic (PV) electricity would require 2000 GWp of installed capacity that displaces coal electricity in 2054. Although only 3 GWp of PV are currently installed, PV electricity has been growing at a rate of 30% per year. A wedge of PV electricity would require 700 times today's deployment, and about 2 million hectares of land in 2054, or 2 to 3 m^2 per person.

Option 12: Renewable hydrogen. Renewable electricity can produce carbonfree hydrogen for vehicle fuel by the electrolysis of water. The hydrogen produced by 4 million 1-MWp windmills in 2054, if used in high-efficiency fuel-cell cars, would achieve a wedge of displaced gasoline or diesel fuel. Compared with Option 10, this is twice as many 1-MWp windmills as would be required to produce the electricity that achieves a wedge by displacing high-efficiency baseload coal. This interesting factor-of-two carbon-saving advantage of wind-electricity over wind-hydrogen is still larger if the coal plant is less efficient or the fuel-cell vehicle is less spectacular.

Option 13: Biofuels. Fossil-carbon fuels can also be replaced by biofuels such as ethanol. A wedge of biofuel would be achieved by the production of about 34 million barrels per day of ethanol in 2054 that could displace gasoline, provided the ethanol itself were fossil-carbon free. This ethanol production rate would be about 50 times larger than today's global production rate, almost all of which can be attributed to Brazilian sugarcane and United States corn. An ethanol wedge would require 250 million hectares committed to high-yield (15 dry tons/hectare) plantations by 2054, an area equal to about one-sixth of the world's cropland. An even larger area would be required to the extent that the biofuels require fossil-carbon inputs. Because land suitable for annually harvested biofuels crops is also often suitable for conventional agriculture, biofuels production could compromise agricultural productivity.

Category III: Natural Sinks

Although the literature on biological sequestration includes a diverse array of options and some very large estimates of the global potential, here we restrict our attention to the pair of options that are already implemented at large scale and that could be scaled up to a wedge or more without a lot of new research. . . .

Option 14: Forest management. Conservative assumptions lead to the conclusion that at least one wedge would be available from reduced tropical deforestation and the management of temperate and tropical forests. At least one half-wedge would be created if the current rate of clear-cutting of primary tropical forest were reduced to zero over 50 years instead of being halved. A second half-wedge would be created by reforesting or afforesting approximately 250 million hectares in the tropics or 400 million hectares in the temperate zone (current areas of tropical and temperate forests are 1500 and 700 million hectares, respectively). A third half-wedge would be created by establishing approximately 300 million hectares of plantations on nonforested land.

Option 15: Agricultural soils management. When forest or natural grassland is converted to cropland, up to one-half of the soil carbon is lost, primarily because annual tilling increases the rate of decomposition by aerating undecomposed organic matter. About 55 GtC, or two wedges' worth, has been lost historically in this way. Practices such as conservation tillage (e.g., seeds are drilled into the soil without plowing), the use of cover crops, and erosion control can reverse the losses. By 1995, conservation tillage practices had been adopted on 110 million hectares of the world's 1600 million hectares of cropland. If conservation tillage could be extended to all cropland, accompanied by a verification program that enforces the adoption of soil conservation practices that actually work as advertised, a good case could be made for the IPCC's estimate that an additional half to one wedge could be stored in this way.

Conclusions

In confronting the problem of greenhouse warming, the choice today is between action and delay. Here, we presented a part of the case for action by identifying a set of options that have the capacity to provide the seven stabilization wedges and solve the climate problem for the next half-century. None of the options is a pipe dream or an unproven idea. Today, one can buy electricity from a wind turbine, PV array, gas turbine, or nuclear power plant. One can buy hydrogen produced with the chemistry of carbon capture, biofuel to power one's car, and hundreds of devices that improve energy efficiency. One can visit tropical forests where clear-cutting has ceased, farms practicing conservation tillage, and facilities that inject carbon into geologic reservoirs. Every one of these options is already implemented at an industrial scale and could be scaled up further over 50 years to provide at least one wedge.

QUESTIONS AND DISCUSSION

1. Does the article on "stabilization wedges" give you confidence that we can address climate change effectively in the near term? What policies or laws at the national or international level would be necessary or helpful in achieving the necessary seven Gigaton reduction? Which of the fifteen strategies would you choose? As you think about the scale and impacts of the various options, consider the external costs that may be incurred in addressing climate change. For example, what might be the other environmental impacts of expanding the geological storage of carbon or of building 100 new nuclear power plants? What are the implications for food security of any plan that contemplates converting one-sixth of the world's croplands to growing fuel instead of food? On the other hand, some positive externalities would also occur. For example, biodiversity and soil conservation benefits would result from better forestry and land management practices.

2. Pacala and Sokolow's approach of breaking the climate change problem down into manageable wedges has proven quite popular, particularly given changing perceptions of how fast and significantly the climate is changing. As discussed in Chapter 1, most observers now believe we must stabilize GHG emissions at levels far below 550 parts per million. Thus, Pacala and Socolow's conclusion that we need 7 gigatons of GHG reductions is too optimistic. This means we must adopt a larger number of wedges.

3. From the survey of the various sectors above, it becomes obvious that avoidance of the most severe impacts of climate change will be dependent on the widespread dissemination of new technological innovations. The law's role may be simply to ensure that the right incentives are being put in place for the development and distribution of climate-sensitive technologies.

4. Given Pacala & Socolow's discussion of stabilization wedges, if you were proposing a $300 billion program for sparking investments in climate-related technology as suggested by Shellenberger, et al., in Section II.B.5, where would you put your investment dollars? Where could the government get the revenues for such a major investment?

5. After reading Chapter 1 on the impacts, you may wonder what you as an individual can do to address a global problem that may appear overwhelming. In recent years, much more effort has gone into reducing individual contributions to climate change. Many websites now offer both corporations and individuals opportunities to measure their carbon footprints and purchase verified carbon credits to achieve "carbon neutrality." *See, e.g.*, www.earthfuture.com/climate/calculators (listing various carbon calculators for individuals); www.terrapass.com (facilitates carbon offsets for automobile use); http://www.self.org/cnc.asp (invests in solar power as carbon credits). Law students can also work with the National Association for Environmental Law Societies (NAELS) to promote their Campus Climate Neutral campaign. *See also* Michael P. Vandenbergh & Anne C. Steinemann, *The Carbon-Neutral Individual*, 82 N.Y.U. L. Rev. 1673 (2007).

IV.   THE BENEFITS AND COSTS OF CLIMATE MITIGATION

In recent years, some economists have tried to calculate the global costs and benefits of climate change, and responses to it. Cost-benefit analyses (CBA) are a common way to try to evaluate an issue economically. In CBA the benefit is calculated and weighed against the cost of a certain course of action.

Using CBA to evaluate the pros and cons of climate change generally (and thus, the pros and cons of addressing it) is fraught with uncertainty and, not surprisingly, such efforts have resulted in vastly different estimates. In terms of the global cost of climate change, estimates range from 1.7 percent global Gross Domestic Product (GDP) to as high as 20 percent. Some studies, however, have concluded that the benefits of climate change may actually outweigh the cost in certain areas of the world, provided that temperatures increase by no more than 2°C. Of course, any economic estimates must be closely scrutinized and kept in perspective, as one is overlaying economics on to future predictions, which themselves are fraught with uncertainty. In this regard, one should also evaluate whether CBA is an appropriate tool to try to predict future costs of something as massive and pervasive as climate change. *See, e.g.*, WILLIAM D. NORDHAUS & JOSEPH BOYER, WARMING THE WORLD: ECONOMIC MODELS OF GLOBAL WARMING (2000); NICHOLAS STERN, THE STERN REVIEW: THE ECONOMICS OF CLIMATE CHANGE (2006); Richard S.J. Tol, *Estimates of the Damage Costs of Climate Change*, 21 ENVTL. & RES. ECON. 47 (2002).

A.   The Stern Review of Climate Economics

One of the most comprehensive and widely acclaimed studies about the costs of climate change is the report prepared for the UK government by Nicholas Stern, the former World Bank Chief Economist. The Stern Review's major findings are excerpted below:

NICHOLAS STERN, THE STERN REVIEW: THE ECONOMICS OF CLIMATE CHANGE (2006)*

Climate change presents a unique challenge for economics: it is the greatest and widest-ranging market failure ever seen. The economic analysis must therefore be global, deal with long time horizons, have the economics of risk and uncertainty at centre stage, and examine the possibility of major, non-marginal change. To meet these requirements, the Review draws on ideas and techniques from most of the important areas of economics . . . .

The Review considers the economic costs of the impacts of climate change, and the costs and benefits of action to reduce the emissions of greenhouse gases (GHGs) that cause it. . . . [T]he evidence gathered by the Review leads to a simple conclusion: the benefits of strong, early action considerably outweigh the costs.

The evidence shows that ignoring climate change will eventually damage economic growth. Our actions over the coming few decades could create risks of major disruption to economic and social activity, later in this century and in the next, on a scale similar to those associated with the great wars and the economic depression of the first half of the 20th century. And it will be difficult or impossible to reverse these changes. Tackling climate change is the pro-growth strategy for the longer term, and it can be done in a way that does not cap the aspirations for growth of rich or poor countries. The earlier effective action is taken, the less costly it will be. * * *

Formal modelling of the overall impact of climate change in monetary terms is a formidable challenge, and the limitations to modelling the world over two centuries or more demand great caution in interpreting results. However, as we have explained, the lags from action to effect are very long and the quantitative analysis needed to inform action will depend on such long-range modelling exercises. The monetary impacts of climate change are now expected to be more serious than many earlier studies suggested, not least because those studies tended to exclude some of the most uncertain but potentially most damaging impacts. Thanks to recent advances in the science, it is now possible to examine these risks more directly, using probabilities.

Most formal modelling in the past has used as a starting point a scenario of 2–3°C warming. In this temperature range, the cost of climate change could be equivalent to a permanent loss of around 0–3% in global world output compared with what could have been achieved in a world without climate change. Developing countries will suffer even higher costs. * * *

With 5–6°C warming — which is a real possibility for the next century — existing models that include the risk of abrupt and large-scale climate change estimate an average 5–10% loss in global GDP, with poor countries suffering costs in excess of 10% of GDP. Further, there is some evidence of small but significant risks of temperature rises even above this range. Such temperature increases would take us into territory unknown to human experience and involve radical changes in the world around us. * * *

Using this model, and including those elements of the analysis that can be incorporated at the moment, we estimate the total cost over the next two centuries of climate change associated under BAU [business-as-usual] emissions involves impacts and risks that are equivalent to an average reduction in global per-capita consumption of at least 5%, now and forever. While this cost estimate is already strikingly high, it also leaves out much that is important. The cost of BAU would increase still further, were the model systematically to take account of three important factors:

- First, including direct impacts on the environment and human health (sometimes called 'non-market' impacts) increases our estimate of the total cost of climate change on this path from 5% to 11% of global per-capita consumption. There are difficult analytical and ethical issues of measurement here. The methods used in this model are fairly conservative in the value they assign to these impacts.

- Second, some recent scientific evidence indicates that the climate system may be more responsive to greenhouse-gas emissions than previously thought, for example because of the existence of amplifying feedbacks such as the release of methane and weakening of carbon sinks. Our estimates, based on modelling a limited increase in this responsiveness, indicate that the potential scale of the climate response could increase the cost of climate change on the BAU path from 5% to 7% of global consumption, or from 11% to 14% if the non-market impacts described above are included.

- Third, a disproportionate share of the climate-change burden falls on poor regions of the world. If we weight this unequal burden appropriately, the estimated global cost of climate change at 5–6°C warming could be more than one-quarter higher than without such weights.

Putting these additional factors together would increase the total cost of BAU climate change to the equivalent of around a 20% reduction in consumption per head, now and into the future.

In summary, analyses that take into account the full ranges of both impacts and possible outcomes — that is, that employ the basic economics of risk — suggest that BAU climate change will reduce welfare by an amount equivalent to a reduction in consumption per head of between 5 and 20%. Taking account of the increasing scientific evidence of greater risks, of aversion to the possibilities of catastrophe, and of a broader approach to the consequences than implied by narrow output measures, the appropriate estimate is likely to be in the upper part of this range.

* * *

This Review has focused on the feasibility and costs of stabilisation of greenhouse gas concentrations in the atmosphere in the range of 450–550ppm CO_2e. Stabilising at or below 550ppm CO_2e would require global emissions to peak in the next 10–20 years, and then fall at a rate of at least 1–3% per year. . . . By 2050, global emissions would need to be around 25% below current levels. These cuts will have to be made in the context of a world economy in 2050 that may be 3–4 times larger than today — so emissions per unit of GDP would need to be just one quarter of current levels by 2050. * * *

Achieving these deep cuts in emissions will have a cost. The Review estimates the annual costs of stabilisation at 500–550ppm CO_2e to be around 1%

of GDP by 2050 — a level that is significant but manageable.

Reversing the historical trend in emissions growth, and achieving cuts of 25% or more against today's levels is a major challenge. Costs will be incurred as the world shifts from a high-carbon to a low-carbon trajectory. But there will also be business opportunities as the markets for low-carbon, high-efficiency goods and services expand.

Greenhouse-gas emissions can be cut in four ways. Costs will differ considerably depending on which combination of these methods is used, and in which sector:

- Reducing demand for emissions-intensive goods and services

- Increased efficiency, which can save both money and emissions

- Action on non-energy emissions, such as avoiding deforestation

- Switching to lower-carbon technologies for power, heat and transport

Estimating the costs of these changes can be done in two ways. One is to look at the resource costs of measures, including the introduction of low-carbon technologies and changes in land use, compared with the costs of the BAU alternative. This provides an upper bound on costs, as it does not take account of opportunities to respond involving reductions in demand for high-carbon goods and services.

The second is to use macroeconomic models to explore the system-wide effects of the transition to a low-carbon energy economy. These can be useful in tracking the dynamic interactions of different factors over time, including the response of economies to changes in prices. But they can be complex, with their results affected by a whole range of assumptions.

On the basis of these two methods, our central estimate is that stabilisation of greenhouse gases at levels of 500–550ppm CO_2e will cost, on average, around 1% of annual global GDP by 2050. This is significant, but is fully consistent with continued growth and development, in contrast with unabated climate change, which will eventually pose significant threats to growth.

———————

Thus, assuming only a 2°C increase, the Stern Report concluded that costs of climate change would range from 0 to 3 percent of GDP, but the costs go up to as much as 20 percent of GDP at higher levels of (5°–6°C) warming. The question then becomes what would it cost to reduce the risks of that higher warming through mitigation, and the report concludes that stabilizing levels of CO_2e at 500–550 ppm would cost approximately 1 percent of GDP. The Report concludes that immediate efforts to reduce greenhouse gas emissions are cost-effective and warranted to avoid the worse long-term climate impacts.

These findings are generally consistent with other cost-benefit studies. For example:

> One estimate, from the German Institute for Economic Research (DIW), is that if nothing is done to restrain greenhouse gas emissions, annual economic damages could reach U.S.$20 trillion by 2100 (expressed in U.S. dollars at 2002 prices), or 6 to 8 percent of global economic output at that time. The same study found that immediate adoption of active climate protection policies could limit the temperature increase to 2° and eliminate more than half of the damages; by 2100 this would avoid $12 trillion in annual damages by spending $3 trillion per year on climate protection. If, however, climate protection efforts do not begin until 2025, the same model

estimates that it will be impossible to limit warming to 2° by 2100 — and climate protection in general will be more expensive, the later it starts.

Another . . . model . . . estimates that in the absence of new policies, the discounted present value of all cumulative climate damages from now through 2200 will amount to U.S.$74 trillion (at 2000 prices). The average annual damages, from 2000 through 2200, will be $26 trillion, reasonably close to the DIW model estimate for 2100. Again, the . . . model finds that more than half of those damages can be avoided by immediate adoption of active climate protection policies.

Frank Ackerman & Elizabeth Stanton, *Climate Change: the Costs of Inaction, Report to Friends of the Earth England, Wales and Northern Ireland* (Oct. 11, 2006).

Not all cost-benefit analyses have concluded that climate change is worth significant mitigation efforts. Several studies have suggested that, particularly for rich countries in temperate climates like the United States, climate change by 2100 may impose limited costs or even provide net benefits. Bjorn Lomborg, for example, concluded that the social cost of carbon from climate impacts was only $7.50 per ton, which suggests that only a limited amount of abatement would be economically justified. He argues for a policy aiming at 4 percent cuts from 1995 levels. BJORN LOMBORG, THE SKEPTICAL ENVIRONMENTALIST: MEASURING THE REAL STATE OF THE WORLD 306 (2001). These studies assume a net increase in temperature of 2° Celsius or less and typically do not account for potential impacts from greater warming. They are also based on assumptions of no significant sea level rise or other catastrophic event, and, as suggested by the Kysar excerpt below, exclude categories of costs that are too uncertain or difficult to quantify.

QUESTIONS AND DISCUSSION

1. Although the studies may disagree on the aggregate financial impact of climate change, they all recognize that the costs will be spread unevenly around the globe. Developed countries will face lower costs and developing countries will be affected the most. Geographic regions will also be affected differently and face different costs of climate change. The countries that get hit the hardest may be least likely to have the resources to adapt to their new environment. The Kyoto Protocol has tried to address these concerns by creating several international funds, but the amount of money and the effectiveness of these funds has yet to be determined (see discussion of adaptation in Chapter 3).

2. Because estimating climate change costs generally is a huge and complex task given the many different impacts across different sectors, some studies have looked at the costs of different types of impacts:

- A study by Nordhaus in 2006 addressing hurricane damage and costs showed that an increase of 2°–3°C would increase hurricane intensity up to 10 percent, doubling their damage in the United States to 0.13 percent of U.S. Gross Domestic Product. William D. Nordhaus, *The Economics of Hurricanes in the United States* (Dec. 21, 2006).

- A recent article conservatively estimated that the lost use values from extinctions caused by climate change at between $0.5 and $1.3 trillion annually worldwide and between $58 and $144 billion in the United States. Inclusion of lost non-use values for these extinct species would more than double these totals. Although such an analysis has many inherent uncertainties, it does show us how important and widespread climate change impacts may be. *See* Wayne Husing & Cass Sunstein, *Climate Change and Animals*, 155 U. PA. L. REV. 1695, 1740 (2007).

3.   Another form of expressing a cost-benefit analysis is to compare the costs of mitigating a ton of carbon with the "social cost of carbon" (SCC). The implication is that, if carbon emissions can be reduced at a cost per ton less than or equal to the social cost of carbon, society as a whole is better off because the reduction in damages is worth more than the cost of reducing emissions. As noted above, Lomborg concluded that the social cost of carbon was a modest $7.50 per ton, where as the Stern Report concluded the following about the social cost of carbon:

> The third approach to analysing the costs and benefits of action on climate change adopted by this Review compares the marginal costs of abatement with the social cost of carbon. This approach compares estimates of the changes in the expected benefits and costs over time from a little extra reduction in emissions, and avoids large-scale formal economic models.

> Preliminary calculations adopting the approach to valuation taken in this Review suggest that the social cost of carbon today, if we remain on a BAU trajectory, is of the order of $85 per tonne of CO_2 — higher than typical numbers in the literature, largely because we treat risk explicitly and incorporate recent evidence on the risks, but nevertheless well within the range of published estimates. This number is well above marginal abatement costs in many sectors. Comparing the social costs of carbon on a BAU trajectory and on a path towards stabilisation at 550ppm CO_2e, we estimate the excess of benefits over costs, in net present value terms, from implementing strong mitigation policies this year, shifting the world onto the better path: the net benefits would be of the order of $2.5 trillion. This figure will increase over time. This is not an estimate of net benefits occurring in this year, but a measure of the benefits that could flow from actions taken this year; many of the costs and benefits would be in the medium to long term.

> Even if we have sensible policies in place, the social cost of carbon will also rise steadily over time, making more and more technological options for mitigation cost effective. This does not mean that consumers will always face rising prices for the goods and services that they currently enjoy, as innovation driven by strong policy will ultimately reduce the carbon intensity of our economies, and consumers will then see reductions in the prices that they pay as low-carbon technologies mature. * * *

> Preliminary work for this Review suggests that, if the target were between 450–550ppm CO_2e, then the social cost of carbon would start in the region of $25–30 per tonne of CO_2 — around one third of the level if the world stays with BAU. The social cost of carbon is likely to increase steadily over time because marginal damages increase with the stock of GHGs in the atmosphere, and that stock rises over time. Policy should therefore ensure that abatement efforts at the margin also intensify over time. But it should also foster the development of technology that can drive down the average costs of abatement; although pricing carbon, by itself, will not be sufficient to bring forth all the necessary innovation, particularly in the early years.

The great disparities in the social costs of carbon reflect the wide range of economic estimates that are possible, depending on the assumptions that go into the estimates. Given such a wide range, how do you think these general economic analyses of climate change should be used, if at all, by policymakers?

4.   Based on his economic analysis, Lomborg and some industry-backed groups argue against taking any significant steps to mitigate fossil fuel emissions. Rather, they argue, we should rely on further fossil fuel use to grow the economy so that we are better able to afford adaptation measures in the future. Do you agree with their analysis? Consider this again after reading the Kysar excerpt below and after considering the difficulties and costs associated with adaptation discussed in Chapter 3.

B.   The Critique of Cost-Benefit Analysis

Heavy reliance on cost-benefit analysis for guiding decisions has always been viewed with skepticism by environmentalists who fear that most environmental damage gets lost in attempts to reduce environmental damage down to monetary terms. This seems particularly relevant for discussions around climate change, where many impacts are uncertain or present a low-risk of catastrophic damage. Douglas Kysar has recognized four serious limitations on the use of cost-benefit analysis in the climate change context: (1) the difficulty in reflecting the tremendous uncertainty surrounding climate change; (2) the inability of valuation methodologies to reflect appropriately the anticipated losses of human life and environmental resources; (3) the intergenerational inequity of using exponential discounting to resolve decisions regarding the intertemporal distribution of costs and benefits; and (4) the inherent orientation of cost-benefit analysis toward the status quo. In Kysar's view, these limitations suggest that "CBA is an unacceptably crude device for guiding policy choices in the context of a massively complex and morally imbued problem such as global climate change." As you read his critique, do you agree?

DOUGLAS A. KYSAR, CLIMATE CHANGE, CULTURAL TRANSFORMATION, AND COMPREHENSIVE RATIONALITY
31 B.C. ENVTL. AFF. L. REV. 555 (2004)[*]

The normative premise of CBA is that its use will lead society to maximize the efficiency with which it devotes resources to policy goals. . . . In theory, therefore, the results of CBA should afford no basis for serious objection or dissent, as all important considerations will have been identified, tabulated, and weighed in a manner that leads to the identification of a first-best social outcome. There will be particular winners and losers, of course, as costs and benefits are not necessarily distributed equitably by policy interventions that are designed to maximize efficiency. But, according to proponents of CBA, any "disinterested observer" will conclude that CBA has led to the "right answer" in terms of aggregate social welfare. [This Part] explains why this is not the case.

A. Uncertainty

The CBA methodology presumes by its very nature the availability of good data and understanding regarding the magnitude of physical and economic effects of various climate change scenarios, as well as the probability that those scenarios will occur. Yet uncertainty pervades, we might even say defines, the climate change problem. We are unsure how much of observed warming is attributable to greenhouse gas emissions. We do not know with certainty what the size of the human population will become over the next century. We do not know what the reference case of economic growth will be. We do not understand and therefore cannot model how sulfate particles, water vapor, and clouds interact in the atmosphere to mitigate or to enhance warming effects. We do not know with any degree of precision how temperature increases will impact agriculture, forests, vector-related diseases, heat-related deaths, flood zones, coastlines, storm intensity levels, freshwater supplies, or species extinctions. Perhaps most troubling, we cannot begin to pinpoint the likelihood of catastrophic climate-related events such as the disintegration of the West Antarctic Ice Sheet, the shutdown of thermohaline circulation in the Atlantic, or the release of frozen methane deposits. In short, we do not know with anything other than an anemic level of confidence what will be the consequences of our atmospheric experiment.

By providing a semblance of order and exactitude where none exists, therefore, the results of CBA implicitly obscure the severity of climate change uncertainties. Consider as a simple example Lomborg's treatment of the human health toll threatened by climate change. To calculate potential climate-induced losses of human life, Lomborg relies upon Nordhaus's calculation of human health impacts from climate change which in turn relies upon a study that is restricted to climate-related diseases. The IPCC meanwhile reports with high confidence that climate change also will result in an increase in heat-related deaths and illnesses due to more frequent heat waves, an increase in drowning, intestinal, and respiratory diseases due to more frequent flooding, and an increase in malnutrition due to reduced crop yields in certain regions of the world. Nevertheless, because these health effects have not been estimated with sufficient precision to calculate a damages function, Lomborg's CBA simply pretends that they do not exist.

The uncertainties of climate change, moreover, go to our very ability to identify and understand categories of costs and benefits, not just our ability to measure them and to predict their likelihood. In this regard, CBA seems especially ill-equipped to address the threat of potentially catastrophic consequences of climate change. Although several scenarios have been discussed in the scientific literature in which climate change spins dramatically and irreversibly out of control, at present our understanding of such scenarios is limited simply to assessing their scientific plausibility, rather than estimating their empirical likelihood. . . . In sum, climate change poses real, but as yet non-quantifiable, catastrophic threats that must be considered as part of any complete policymaking process. * * *

B. Valuation

As noted already, CBA seeks to do more than simply generate a systematic list of the pros and cons of climate change or of efforts to mitigate or adapt to climate change. In addition, CBA seeks to provide a common metric for them, such that policymakers need only run a spreadsheet in order to determine the optimal policy intervention into the carbon economy. Obviously, then, the policymaker and her constituent public must have a great deal of faith in the valuation methodologies used in order for CBA to generate democratically acceptable results. For good reason, however, CBA practitioners have been unable to come up with widely agreeable methods for determining the monetary value of non-marketed goods such as the Great Barrier Reef, a child's life, or an endangered species.

*   *   *

Such problems are in many respects magnified in the global policymaking context, where potential distortions due to divergent resource endowments are likely to be even more pronounced. Nevertheless, many analyses of the costs and benefits of climate change do in fact distinguish between the value of lives on a country by country or a region by region basis. One prominent analyst, for instance, first divided countries into high income, middle income, and low income categories, and then assumed a value of human life of $1,500,000, $300,000, and $100,000, respectively, for the three categories. Although purportedly a value-neutral approach based only on varying willingness-to-pay calculations for the three regions, this method of valuation nevertheless entails a willingness to invest resources to protect Americans at a level fifteen times higher than sub-Saharan Africans. One might think that such an approach has it exactly backwards. After all, the majority of human-induced greenhouse gas concentrations currently in the atmosphere are traceable to the industrial activities of the developed world, while the majority of premature deaths and other adverse health effects expected from climate change threaten to strike the developing world. Speaking in terms of moral responsibility, then, rather than merely in terms of credits and debits in a greenhouse ledger stripped of human context, one naturally might think that the interests of the developing world should count at a rate greater than those of the developed world. One would, however, have reached a conclusion opposite to the approach often implicitly taken by CBA.

*   *   *

C. Discounting

Given the atmospheric persistence of greenhouse gases, relevant time frames for climate change CBA stretch into the hundreds of years. As a result, many of the benefits of climate change mitigation policies consist of deaths and illnesses that otherwise would afflict generations far into the future. Faced with these time horizons, researchers must articulate some method of comparing the impacts of atmospheric warming across time, even if it is the simple method of assuming that a life today is "worth" the same amount as a life tomorrow. Practitioners of CBA typically attempt to normalize the intertemporal distribution of costs and benefits through the use of an exponential discount rate, which is the logical converse of compounding interest. Accordingly, lives that will be lost in the future due to increased carbon loading of the atmosphere typically are not valued by CBA at the going rate for lives today. Instead, they are discounted to a present value, which often results in numbers that are vanishingly small: one million lives discounted over 145 years at ten percent are "worth" less than a single life today.

The moral basis for discounting in this manner is rarely articulated. Sometimes it is argued that discounting future harms is appropriate because future generations will be richer and therefore better able to handle the harmful consequences of climate change. But this is not an argument that we should discount something because it will occur in the future; it is an argument that we should discount something because it will happen to better off individuals. As a matter of distributive justice, we may agree with such an argument, but it requires a much different implementation device than numerical discounting. Moreover, if we use the standard income-dependent or income-influenced economic methods of valuing life, then an anticipated rise in future incomes suggests that future lives are more worth saving than present lives, not less. Therefore, rather than discount future benefits of climate change mitigation, on this view, we should magnify them. The fact that this result is counterintuitive suggests that the normative justification for discounting has been insufficiently established.

A stronger defense of discounting invokes the economic concept of opportunity costs. By discounting future lives to a present value, the argument goes, governments ensure that climate change mitigation policies produce a "return on investment" at least as high as the discount rate that is being utilized. In that manner, regulatory expenditures can be avoided that might have been invested more profitably in other social projects or in capital markets. Strangely enough, therefore, it seems that future generations will be better off if we discount the value of their lives, because we will leave them with a resource base that has taken advantage of the best available investment opportunities. Along these lines, Lomborg concludes that "a sensible investment with a good yield will leave our descendants and future generations of poor people with far greater resources, and this is probably a far better way of looking after their interests than investing in low-yielding greenhouse gas reductions."

This line of reasoning appears compelling until one recalls that the benefits of climate change mitigation consist at least partially of human lives that might otherwise have been lost in the future. The normative case for discounting — that it will leave future generations with a more valuable stock of resources — is in considerable tension with the fact that some members of those future generations are sacrificed in order to make the very alternative investments that are supposed to inure to their benefit. Obviously, if one takes seriously the moral injunction that human lives should not be used instrumentally without the consent of the sacrificed, then discounting demands still further justification. All the CBA apologist demonstrates by appealing to opportunity costs is the fact that a life lost in the future may be compensated for at lower cost than a life lost today. The decision actually to sacrifice the life — and thereby to bring about a situation in which compensation becomes relevant — remains an entirely separate, and philosophically more problematic, matter. * * *

The situation is even worse than this, for not only are we currently choosing to sacrifice future lives in order to preserve two to four percentage points of GDP, but we also are failing to ensure that resources actually are transferred to those future generations whose members we are sacrificing. To give the opportunity cost argument any practical significance, we would need some reliable intergenerational transfer mechanism to ensure that the resource base actually is expanded for the benefit of surviving members of future generations. As it is, however, we have inadequate means of knowing whether the resources intended to make future generations better off are being conserved as durable capital or whether instead they are being consumed for the fleeting pleasure of the currently living. National income measures such as GDP are notoriously bereft of information about non-marketed goods such as environmental and social capital. GDP simply measures the absolute flow of commodities through the economy over a given time period; it makes no effort to measure the stock of resources from which that flow ultimately originates or to otherwise determine whether the flow is sustainable. The CBA discounter may take comfort in the knowledge that, in some purely hypothetical sense, future generations may be better off for having been discounted. Future generations themselves may not feel as sanguine. * * *

[U]pon reflection, the choice of discount rate often seems downright trivial in comparison to the underlying distributive judgment that the discounting methodology is attempting, however awkwardly, to subsume. Consider, for example, the following question: "At what rate should the benefits of future timber harvesting be discounted when using CBA to determine the appropriate current level of harvesting from a particular forest?" If one's response is some variation of, "at whatever rate results in a sustainably managed forest," then one is in agreement with the view that distributive judgments precede the choice of discount rate. To be sure, the example uses a context in which the distributive judgment is relatively tractable and even appears to admit of an "optimal" outcome: Renewable resources should be harvested at a level that ensures maximum sustainable yield. Nevertheless, the same conceptual framework underlies all issues of intergenerational resource distribution, including the intertemporal distribution of our atmosphere's capacity to absorb persistent greenhouse gases. Discounting cannot resolve these issues; it can only obscure them.

*   *   *

D. Vision

As we have seen, CBA attempts to subsume a variety of important ethical and practical judgments within the rubric of a purportedly straightforward efficiency-maximization exercise. Decisions about how to behave in the face of true uncertainty concerning potentially devastating consequences of human action are masked by statistical uncertainty procedures that, despite their technical sophistication, may depend on flatly unwarranted assumptions about the operations of the physical world. Society's level of commitment to the preservation of species, ecosystems, and human lives is divined from real or contrived individual market decisions in a process that, at best, is beset by a variety of methodological problems and, at worst, fundamentally misconstrues the nature of the very public goods problem that demands collective judgment. Finally, difficult and unavoidable choices about how to distribute potentially massive costs and benefits among generations are elided through an elaborate mathematical fiction, the discount rate. At bottom, each of these features of CBA exhibits a common flaw, observed long ago by Laurence Tribe: "[Q]uantitative decision-making techniques . . . reduce[] entire problems to terms that misstate their underlying structure, typically collapsing into the task of maximizing some simple quantity an enterprise whose ordering principle is not one of maximization at all."

Indeed, this tendency to obscure difficult judgments through mischaracterization or misspecification seems to follow from the very structure of the CBA project. As intimated above, CBA practitioners typically treat individual preference formation as a process that is entirely exogenous to their analysis. Thus, the many internal compromises, hesitancies, and regrets that characterize individual behavior and choice never register a blip on the practitioner's radar. Instead, whatever preferences individuals seem to reveal through their market behavior are taken to be the best measure of true "wants" or "desires" and, therefore, also are taken exclusively to provide the valuation inputs that in critical part determine the policy outputs of CBA. * * *

The deeper problem is that the neoclassical economic project, as exemplified by CBA, excludes from consideration the very feature that many philosophers identify as uniquely constitutive of humanity. That is, what distinguishes us from other animals and makes us distinctly human is not the ability to satisfy our goals, but the ability to reason and deliberate about the content of those goals. Indeed, the very project of life might be said to consist of shaping, revising, and reflecting on one's goals or, put differently, on what one wants to want. A final concern with CBA, then, is that the methodology seems ill-suited to grapple with this central project of life.

In very simplistic terms, CBA asks whether diverting resources from current patterns of production and consumption toward climate change mitigation would produce a net enhancement of social welfare. The benefits of mitigation — avoided human deaths, preservation of ecosystems, survival of other species, and so on — are compared to the opportunity cost of whatever utility would have been provided by the foregone combustion of fossil fuels. The reference case for defining and measuring utility in this process remains unequivocally focused on the status quo pattern of production and consumption. No allowance therefore is made for the possibility of individuals to adapt their preferences in light of changed circumstances, to acknowledge the moral responsibility created by climate change, to accept as being well and just any newly imposed constraints on their harmful activities, or simply to get on with the project of life by deriving utility in new but not necessarily inferior ways. In short, no allowance is made for the possibility of individuals to grow. * * *

CBA, by its very design, is ill-equipped to grapple with deep scientific uncertainty, to reliably value human life and respect the existence of other beings, to assess and honor the needs and rights of future generations, or to contemplate, discuss, and pursue as-yet-unrealized ways and modes of living. Without these capabilities, CBA offers only meager assistance to climate change policymaking.

QUESTIONS AND DISCUSSION

1. *Discount Rates.* As suggested by Kysar, a key issue for cost-benefit analysis is the choice of discount rates. What if an action taken today will have little effect in the present but will prove harmful and entail costs 50 or 100 years hence (such as emission of greenhouse gases in the last several decades)? Put another way, if you were offered $100 today or $110 a year from now, which would you accept? The answer would depend on what you would do with the money during the year. If you could place it in a bank account with 12% interest, presumably you would take the money now and invest it. In this manner, $100 today is the equivalent of $112 in a year. While this may seem an eminently reasonable way to take future costs and benefits into account, it poses serious problems over extended time periods. For instance, assume you want to grow a forest that will generate $1,000,000 in pleasure to recreationists in its 100th year. How much is that future $1,000,000 benefit worth today? If one uses the discount rate of 10% (which is the standard rate for these calculations used by the Office of Management and Budget), the answer is $73. Over long periods of time the choice of discount rates can significantly affect the interests of future generations. *See* FRANCES CAIRNCROSS, COSTING THE EARTH at 32 (1991). Can you see from this example how important discounting is to the ultimate outcome of a cost-benefit analysis for climate change? The Stern report has been criticized for using a zero percent discount rate. Given the arguments in Kysar, do you think such a rate is justified in the climate change context?

2. Much of the criticism of cost-benefit analysis is rooted in the concern that as we monetize all environmental impacts, we lose much of what we value in nature and the environment. Just as not all aspects of a high quality of life come from goods purchased in the market, cost-benefit analysis is imperfect in capturing all the lost values. Do you agree? Is this a critique of cost-benefit analysis or simply a critique of how policy-makers use it?

3. A related source of underestimating the benefits from reducing greenhouse gas emissions is that these studies rarely take into account non-climate benefits from mitigation. Yet, steps to reduce greenhouse gas concentrations may alleviate other important social concerns, including most notably air pollution and energy security. Indeed some estimates suggest that when these other considerations are

taken into account, the costs attributable solely to responding to climate change are reduced from 30 to 100%.

4.   In his article critiquing cost-benefit analysis in the context of climate change, Professor Kysar suggests the use of multiple, complex, and descriptive scenarios of possible climate futures as a preferred way of informing policy discussions over climate change. This is the approach taken by the IPCC reports and others that rely on modelling multiple scenarios. Can such an approach fill the same role for informing decision-makers as CBA? Given the difficulties identified by Professor Kysar with CBA, do you think reliance on scenarios could result in better policy choices or at least richer policy discussions? Put another way, CBA reduces the complexity of decisionmaking to one single parameter (money) — albeit one that can easily be compared across possible climate futures. In what ways, does this help (or hinder) decision-makers?

Chapter 3

RESPONDING TO CLIMATE CHANGE: ADAPTATION

I. INTRODUCTION

Adaptation strategies — i.e., those strategies meant to alleviate the impacts of climate change (as opposed to mitigation strategies meant to avoid climate change) — are becoming increasingly important in discussions of how to respond to climate change. Examples of adaptation run the range from building higher levees, to making evacuation and disaster relief plans, to the relocation of coastal and island communities. Adaptation strategies can involve local, national, or international responses and can include changes in behavior, infrastructure, governance, technology, management, or a wide range of policies. While adaptation is not designed to solve the problem of climate change, it will be crucial for reducing the socio-economic damage caused by climate change.

The increasing focus on adaptation is largely a response to the recognition that many climate impacts are virtually certain at this point and that human suffering and economic losses can be reduced through some adaptive strategies. Mitigation measures are unlikely to prevent climate change before it results in significant environmental and social impacts, and adaptation policies are necessary to alleviate future suffering. As the Intergovernmental Panel on Climate Change (IPCC) points out in its 2007 Report, "even the most stringent mitigation efforts cannot avoid further impacts of climate change in the next few decades, making adaptation unavoidable." IPCC, WORKING GROUP II, CLIMATE CHANGE IMPACTS, ADAPTATION AND VULNERABILITY 747 (Fourth Assessment Report, 2007) [hereinafter IPCC 2007: ADAPTATION AND VULNERABILITY]. Indeed, where the need for adaptation was formerly viewed as decades away, recognition of current climate impacts such as melting glaciers and sea ice and deeper droughts in the interior West and Southeast has brought the timeframe for discussing adaptation forward, even in the United States.

As Warwick McKibbin and Peter Wilcoxen put it:

> [B]oth (mitigation and adaptation) activities are likely to be important as responses to potential climate change. The difference between choosing between these responses to climate change is analogous to the decision to wear seat belts versus installing anti-lock brakes on a car. The anti-lock brakes help to reduce the likelihood of an accident (mitigation) whereas the seat belts help to prevent catastrophe if there is an accident (adaptation). With both options available few sensible people would choose only one or the other since they both act to minimize the risk of serious injury.

See Warwick J. McKibbin & Peter J. Wilcoxen, *Climate Policy and Uncertainty: The Roles of Adaptation Versus Mitigation* 3 (Austl. Nat'l Univ. Econ. & Env't Network, Working Paper EENO306, 2003).

Focusing on adaptation is not without controversy, however, because many observers fear that money and attention spent on adaptation will detract from efforts to mitigate (or prevent) climate change in the first place. If priorities have to be set, critics argue, they should be set on preventing the injury — not on band-aids to reduce the impact. Moreover, a focus on adaptation could implicitly signal that we cannot avoid climate change, thus weakening the resolve of countries to reduce net greenhouse gas emissions. Internationally, the United States and other industrialized countries are reluctant to embrace adaptation measures, because they will be expected to pick up the costs. Thus, to some extent the international dialogue over adaptation is really a dialogue over how much financial responsibility industrialized countries are willing to accept for the impacts expected from climate change. Complicating the discussion further is that developing countries do not want funding for adaptation to substitute for other forms of assistance.

II. ADAPTATION STRATEGIES

In many respects, adaptation to climate change is nothing new. Humans have been adapting to weather events and climate variability since the beginning of time. For example, people have historically adapted to weather variations by crop diversification, climate forecasting, famine early warning systems, and increasing water storage capacity. We also frequently take adaptation measures in response to specific catastrophic events, like hurricanes, floods, or heat waves. Evacuations in anticipation of such events or humanitarian relief in their aftermath are familiar forms of adaptive responses.

What is unique about adaptation in the context of climate change is the need to plan for long-term adaptive measures not to address weather variability but in response to a world in which climate generally is more unpredictable — a world in which future rainfall, temperature, sea levels, river flows, growing seasons, and snowfall (to name just a few) are all different and maybe radically so. In such a context, anticipating possible risks and managing them becomes both more complicated and more urgent.

Virtually every economic sector will need longer term planning to manage potential climate risk. Project developers, for example, will need to assess the impacts of various climate scenarios on the costs and benefits of their proposed projects. Construction companies may need to consider stronger building materials to resist more intense storms. Hazardous waste companies may have to relocate further inland to avoid flood-related contamination like that seen in Hurricane Katrina. Health care professionals may need to prepare for new diseases brought by warmer temperatures. Adaptation strategies thus cover a wide range of possible policies and actions — from individual farming decisions about where or what to plant to collective decisions about whether to build a retaining sea wall. The diversity of potential adaptation measures can be seen in Table 3-1, adapted from the IPCC 2007: ADAPTATION AND VULNERABILITY, at 722.

Table 3-1: Possible Adaptation Practices for Responding to Climate Change Impacts

Country	Climate-related stress	Adaptation Practices
Egypt	Sea-level rise	Adoption of law regulating setback distances for coastal infrastructure; installation of hard structures in areas vulnerable to coastal erosion.
Sudan	Drought	Expanded use of rainwater harvesting and water conserving techniques; building of wind-breaks to improve resilience of rangelands; monitoring the number of grazing animals and cut trees; establishment of revolving credit funds.
Botswana	Drought	National government programmes to re-create employment options after drought; capacity building of local authorities; assistance to small subsistence farmers to increase crop production.
Bangladesh	Sea-level rise; salt-water intrusion	Consideration of climate change in the National Water Management Plan; building of flow regulators in coastal embankments; use of alternative crops and low-technology water filters.
Philippines	Drought; floods	Shift to drought-resistant crops; rotation method of irrigation during water shortage; construction of water impounding basins; construction of fire lines and controlled burning; adoption of soil and water conservation measures for upland farming.
	Sea-level rise; storm surges	Capacity building for shoreline defence system design; provision of grants to strengthen coastal resilience and rehabilitation of infrastructures; construction of cyclone-resistant housing; review of building codes; reforestation of mangroves.
Canada	Permafrost melt; change in ice cover	Changes in livelihood practices by the Inuit, including: change of hunt locations; diversification of hunted species; use of Global Positioning Systems (GPS) technology; encouragement of food sharing.
	Extreme temperatures	Implementation of heat health alert plans in Toronto; operation of an information line to answer heat-related questions; availability of an emergency medical service vehicle with specially trained staff and medical equipment.

Country	Climate-related stress	Adaptation Practices
United States	Sea-level rise	Land acquisition programmes taking account of climate change; establishment of a "rolling easement" in Texas, an entitlement to public ownership of property that 'rolls' inland with the coastline as sea-level rises; other coastal policies that encourage coastal landowners to act in ways that anticipate sea-level rise.
Mexico and Argentina	Drought	Adjustment of planting dates and crop variety (e.g., inclusion of drought-resistant plants such as agave and aloe); accumulation of commodity stocks as economic reserve; spatially separated plots for cropping and grazing to diversify exposures; diversification of income by adding livestock operations; set-up/provision of crop insurance; creation of local financial pools (as alternative to commercial crop insurance).
The Netherlands	Sea-level rise	Adoption of Flooding Defence Act and Coastal Defence Policy as precautionary approaches to climate change; building of a storm surge barrier taking a 50 cm sea-level rise into account; use of sand supplements added to coastal areas; improved management of water levels through dredging, widening of river banks, allowing rivers to expand into side channels and wetland areas; conduct regular 5-year reviews of safety of all protecting infrastructure (dykes, etc.); identifying areas for reinforcement of dunes.
Austria, France, Switzerland	Snow line shift; glacier melt	Artificial snow-making; grooming of ski slopes; moving ski areas to higher altitudes and glaciers; use of white plastic sheets as protection against glacier melt.
	Perma-frost melt; debit flows	Erection of protection dams in Pontresina (Switzerland) against avalanches and increased magnitude of potential debris flows stemming from permafrost thawing.
United Kingdom	Floods; sea-level rise	Coastal realignment under the Essex Wildlife Trust, converting arable farmland into salt marsh and grassland to provide sustainable sea defences; maintenance and operation of the Thames Barrier to address flooding linked to climate change.

Several categories of adaptation measures are discussed further below.

A.   Adaptive Infrastructure

Significant climate change impacts may seem to occur only in the long-term (e.g., in 25–100 years), but this is well within the expected life of most infrastructure projects being built today. Bridges, dams, dikes, even houses, have a life-expectancy of greater than 100 years. Integrating climate uncertainty into the planning and building of infrastructure is critical for long-term adaptation efforts. Think, for example, about decisions to locate major chemical facilities near a vulnerable coastline or to rebuild a coastal community after a storm. To what extent should we take climate change into account in making these decisions today? Consider these questions in light of the examples of adaptive infrastructure designs provided by the IPCC below:

IPCC 2007: ADAPTATION AND VULNERABILITY, AT 724

Early examples where climate change scenarios have already been incorporated in infrastructure design include the Confederation Bridge in Canada and the Deer Island sewage treatment plant in Boston harbour in the United States. The Confederation Bridge is a 13 km bridge between Prince Edward Island and the mainland. The bridge provides a navigation channel for ocean-going vessels with vertical clearance of about 50 m. Sea-level rise was recognized as a principal concern during the design process and the bridge was built one metre higher than currently required to accommodate sea-level rise over its hundred-year lifespan. In the case of the Deer Island sewage facility, the design called for raw sewage collected from communities onshore to be pumped under Boston harbour and then up to the treatment plant on Deer Island. After waste treatment, the effluent would be discharged into the harbour through a downhill pipe. Design engineers were concerned that sea-level rise would necessitate the construction of a protective wall around the plant, which would then require installation of expensive pumping equipment to transport the effluent over the wall. To avoid such a future cost the designers decided to keep the treatment plant at a higher elevation, and the facility was completed in 1998. Other examples where ongoing planning is considering scenarios of climate change in project design are the Konkan Railway in western India; a coastal highway in Micronesia; the Copenhagen Metro in Denmark; and the Thames Barrier in the United Kingdom. * * *

In addition to specific infrastructure projects, there are now also examples where climate change scenarios are being considered in more comprehensive risk management policies and plans. . . . In the Netherlands, for example, the Technical Advisory Committee on Water Defense recommended the design of new engineering works with a long lifetime, such as storm surge barriers and dams, to take a 50 cm sea-level rise into account. Climate change is explicitly taken into consideration in the National Water Management Plan (NWMP) of Bangladesh, which was set up to guide the implementation of the National Water Policy. It recognizes climate change as a determining factor for future water supply and demand, as well as coastal erosion due to sea level rise and increased tidal range.

There are now also examples of consideration of climate change as part of comprehensive risk management strategies at the city, regional, and national level. France, Finland and the United Kingdom have developed national strategies and frameworks to adapt to climate change. At the city level, meanwhile, climate change scenarios are being considered by New York City as part of the review of its water supply system. Changes in temperature and precipitation, sea-level rise, and extreme events have been identified as important parameters for water supply impacts and adaptation in the New York region.

Adaptations can be divided into managerial, infrastructure, and policy categories and assessed in terms of time frame (immediate, interim, long-term) and in terms of the capital cycle for different types of infrastructure. As an example of adaptation measures that have been examined, a managerial adaptation that can be implemented quickly is a tightening of water regulations in the event of more frequent droughts. Also under examination are longer-term infrastructure adaptations such as the construction of flood-walls around low-lying wastewater treatment plants to protect against sea-level rise and higher storm surges.

B.   Response to Sea-level Rise: Defend or Retreat

One of the most vexing and important adaptation questions is how coastal communities should respond to the potential for sea-level rise. In a nutshell, coastal communities have two choices against rising sea levels and higher storm surges: (1) armor the coasts with dikes, concrete, and steel bulworks or (2) retreat strategically over time by moving costly and sensitive infrastructure inland. Choosing between these two strategies is made more difficult because of the wide range of sea-level scenarios that are part of the climate debate. The IPCC's 2007 Fourth Assessment projects a relatively modest sea level rise of less than a meter by the end of the century, which makes a "defense" strategy more defensible, but loss of one or more of the planet's great ice sheets results in sea-level rises of 6 to 10 to even 20 meters, which makes "retreat" the only plausible scenario. Of course, one strategy will not fit all of the world's coastal areas, but throughout the world, communities are starting to make their decisions.

> Hard engineering — involving the construction of groynes, seawalls, breakwaters, and bulkheads — has long been the traditional response to coastal erosion and flooding in many small island states. Unfortunately, this approach has not always been efficiently implemented and has even helped to increase coastal vulnerability in some cases. In these specific circumstances, the term "maladaptation" (which refers to a response that does not succeed in reducing vulnerability but increases it instead . . . may be applied. Realistically, however, for some islands the application of hard solutions may be the only practical option along well-developed coasts, where vital infrastructure is at immediate risk.

> There are other potential options available to small island states, including enhancement and preservation of natural protection (e.g., replanting of mangroves and protection of coral reefs), use of softer options such as artificial nourishment, and raising the height of the ground of coastal villages. Raising the height of the ground requires additional aggregate such as sand and stone and a lot of pumping, in which many small islands are seriously deficient. Removal of materials from "unimportant" islands to build up important islands via sand transfer by pipes and barges has been suggested by the IPCC. Some island states may be faced with few practical options. Thus, it might be necessary for them to lose some islands so that the entire nation is not completely inundated.

> Similarly, beach nourishment may not be a practical or economical option for many island nations because sand often is a scarce resource. Moreover, beach nourishment requires maintenance in the form of periodic sand replenishment, sometimes every 5–10 years or less. Such a requirement could prove to be unsustainable in small economies. In contrast, on some islands such as Singapore, where the technology and resources are more readily available, beach fill projects (used in combination with offshore breakwaters to form artificial headlands) is a feasible option. As a general strategy to respond to sea-level rise, it is likely that Singapore will focus on three main types of responses: coastal protection for developed or heavily populated areas and reclaimed land, anti-salt-intrusion measures for coastal reservoirs, and flood prevention measures (such as tidal gates) for major canals.

In some islands, such as those in the Caribbean, more emphasis is being placed on the application of "precautionary" approaches, such as enforcement of building set-backs, land-use regulations, building codes, and insurance coverage. In addition, application of traditional, appropriate responses (e.g., building on stilts and use of expendable, readily available indigenous building materials), which have proven to be effective responses in many islands in the past, ought to be more widely considered. * * *

Enhancing the resilience of coastal systems has been suggested as an appropriate proactive adaptive response to reduce vulnerability. [T]his could be a more cost-effective way to prepare for uncertain changes such as sea-level rise, rather than relying entirely on building traditional, more costly coastal defenses. . . . One of the ways in which a dynamic and resilient coast can be created is by managed retreat, based on an enforced building set-back that allows the coastline to recede to a new line of defense, thus restoring natural coastal processes and systems. An orderly plan to retreat could be a feasible option on larger islands that cannot commit the resources necessary to prevent coastal land loss in the face of rising sea levels.

IPCC, Working Group II, Impacts, Adaptation and Vulnerability, § 17.2.3.1 (Third Assessment Report, 2001). Small island states are not the only ones facing difficult decisions of how to plan for coastal development in the future. All coastal communities around the world are being forced to adapt to eroding beaches and higher sea levels. Consider the challenges facing relatively wealthy resort communities in the United States:

JAMES G. TITUS, PLANNING FOR SEA LEVEL RISE BEFORE AND AFTER A COASTAL DISASTER
in Michael G. Barth & James G. Titus, Greenhouse Effect and Sea Level Rise: A Challenge for This Generation (1984)

The most important issue for resort communities to resolve will be whether to hold back the sea or retreat landward. The previous section assumed that the major impact of sea level rise on a homeowner's post-disaster decisions will be property losses from increased storm damage and erosion. However, public officials must also consider the impact of rebuilding oceanfront houses on the recreational use of the beach. The fact that a property owner might choose to rebuild his house in spite of projected erosion does not necessarily imply that the community's interest would be served by allowing the owner to do so.

Whether or not a community decides that a retreat is inevitable, the post-disaster period will be a critical time for implementing its response to sea level rise. If the community intends to defend its shoreline, it must do so soon after the storm, or redevelopment activities will be vulnerable to even a moderately severe storm. If it does not intend to fight erosion, deciding not to redevelop oceanfront lots can save the expense of later removing or protecting these properties. Finally, a major storm would increase the public's awareness of the consequences of sea level rise and thereby create a political climate more favorable to the difficult decisions that must be made.

Most measures by which resort communities can respond to sea level rise have been implemented or proposed in existing coastal hazard mitigation programs. These measures include building seawalls and other structures, pumping sand, restricting development or redevelopment, purchasing land, and modifying building codes and zoning.

Defending the Shoreline

The most commonly used measures to curtail erosion have been groins and beach nourishment. By groins, we mean long, thin structures perpendicular to the shore that collect sand moving downshore, including jetties on the updrift side of inlets. By beach nourishment, we mean dredging sand from a channel or offshore and pumping it onto the beach.

Groins cannot prevent erosion caused by sea level rise, but they can move the problem downshore. A jetty at the south end of Ocean City, Maryland (acting as a long groin) has collected enough sediment to allow the shore to advance hundreds of feet, while to the south, Assateague Island National Seashore is eroding rapidly. As sea level rises, communities may use increasingly sophisticated methods to trap sand as it moves along the shore, in spite of the problems these measures may cause their neighbors. In contrast, beach nourishment does not adversely affect neighboring areas, although it may be more expensive than groins.

[B]eaches follow characteristic profiles. A 1 ft rise in sea level would eventually require raising the entire beach profile 1 ft. A profile that extended out to sea 0.5 mi would ultimately require 500,000 yd^3 of sand for every mile of beach. Estimates . . . suggest that this would cost \$2–5 million. In many resorts, the value of the property that would be protected could justify this level of expenditure. However, sand pumping costs could vary considerably. Profiles extend to sea by very different amounts. For example, the profile of San Francisco may extend out several times farther than most profiles . . . implying that protection costs would be several times greater. The availability of sand also varies considerably. Finally, the costs of beach nourishment may escalate as inexpensive supplies are exhausted. In spite of these uncertainties, such extremely valuable real estate as Miami Beach and Atlantic City could probably justify the costs in any event.

Communities that could not afford to raise their entire beach profiles might still use beach nourishment as a temporary measure until depreciation of oceanfront development or a storm makes retreat economical. * * *

Planning a Retreat

Communities that decide to migrate landward could combine engineering and planning measures. One possible engineering response for barrier islands would be to preserve their total acreage by pumping sand to their bayside, imitating the natural overwash process. This option might require bayfront property owners to be compensated for their loss of access to the water. Furthermore, care would have to be taken to ensure that marine life was not irreparably damaged. But because less sand would be necessary, such a program would be less expensive than pumping sand to the Oceanside. In the long run, it would probably be less environmentally disruptive than any of the alternatives, particularly if mainland marshes are also allowed to migrate landward.

Planning measures will be important. North Carolina already requires most new home construction to be set back from the shore a distance equal to 30 years of erosion. For existing construction, communities could implement strong post-disaster plans. Humphries et al. (1983) recommend that Ocean City, Maryland impose a temporary building moratorium after a major storm to give authorities time to decide which redevelopment is appropriate. However, the need to repair damages quickly may inhibit the careful debate necessary to adequately consider sea-level rise.

Although many post-disaster development decisions cannot be made until local officials assess the damages, the general principles of redevelopment should probably be decided in advance of a storm. An assemblyman once introduced a bill to the New Jersey legislature that would have forbidden people to rebuild oceanfront houses that were more than 50 percent destroyed by a storm. That bill was extremely unpopular, in part because it made no provision to compensate property owners. Our analysis of individual decisions suggests that if sea level rise is anticipated, many property owners who are offered some compensation will be willing to sell their land and write off their partly damaged houses; some might even do so without compensation.

In some instances, public officials might have to resort to eminent domain to purchase oceanfront property. Partly because of flood mitigation programs that require houses to be built on pilings sunk far into the ground, erosion from sea level rise will not always destroy the oceanfront houses now being built. Instead, some houses will continue to stand on the beach and perhaps even in the water. Although the owners of these houses might not want to move, the obstruction of the beach might be intolerable to the community and hence necessitate purchases under eminent domain.

Reaching a Decision

Public officials can use the same type of analysis as individual property owners to select the best policy, but they must also convince the public that they have reached the correct decision. Until the general public is convinced of the validity of the sea level rise projections, officials on coastal barriers may have trouble adopting the necessary responses.

Nevertheless, these officials should not defer all action until a scientific consensus emerges. [P]roperty owners in a community could save millions of dollars if they could be certain about the government's intentions. For example, property owners might conclude that sea level rise will make their property too hazardous to rebuild. If the government would stabilize the shoreline in the face of sea level rise, then announcing this policy in advance would enable these people to enjoy their properties rather than mistakenly assume that sea level rise threatens them.

Deciding on the best response to sea level rise could take communities many years. By the time this process is complete, better forecasts of sea level rise may be available. Because we cannot know when a major storm will occur, the time saved by initiating the planning process sooner rather than later may be the critical difference between being ready to act and being unprepared.

QUESTIONS AND DISCUSSION

1. If you were representing a poor, small island state, what options would you recommend to your government? How would the options differ if you represented a wealthy resort community in the United States?

2. Can you see how expectations about government behavior, particularly in the United States, will impact property values? What expectations are reasonable? Should the government be expected to protect property from rising sea levels? Who should pay for this? Could property owners in the United States who lose their property to a storm surge argue that the government's failure to protect them was a "takings" under the Fifth Amendment to the Constitution?

3. The coast is a naturally dynamic place where "the sledgehammer seas and . . . the inscrutable tides of God" (HERMAN MELVILLE, MOBY DICK) constantly erode the coastline in some places and add sand and rock to other places. Rising sea levels will make the coasts an even more dynamic place. How do the processes of erosion and accretion affect a property owner's title to land? Although the rules may vary from state to state, generally speaking a property owner is divested of title to eroded land. She cannot bring a claim to recover land eroded by the ebb and flow of the tides. On the other hand, a property owner is entitled to all accretions. Thus, a waterfront owner may find that her property has been enlarged by dynamic ocean processes. What are the justifications for these traditional property law concepts? What are their implications in light of climate change?

4. The excerpts above describe the three general approaches to protecting beaches from erosion: (1) restoration through beach replenishment, (2) armoring through the construction of groins, seawalls, rip-rap, and other fixed structures intended to stabilize the shoreline, and (3) retreat, through the establishment of setbacks. All three approaches raise legal questions that climate change and rising sea levels will bring into sharp focus. For example, if the groin built by Joe Beachcomber to protect his seafront property from erosion leads to the erosion of his neighbor's property, what legal remedies does the neighbor have? If Sandy Shore spends considerable resources to replenish her beach, but the sand erodes and drifts to the beach of Lucky George, who owns the sand? If a property owner buys a piece of coastal property, and the state later prevents construction seaward of a setback line, does the state's new setback law constitute a Fifth Amendment takings? Can a state prevent a property owner from armoring her property? *See* JOSEPH J. KALO, ET AL., COASTAL AND OCEAN LAW: CASES AND MATERIALS 275–287 (2d ed. 2002).

———————

C.   Expanding Disaster Relief

Climate change is predicted to make many natural disasters, such as floods, droughts, and hurricanes, more frequent and intense. The result will be more people in need of humanitarian assistance to address shortages in food, water, and housing. Because of the uncertainty, speed, and severity of extreme weather events, relief networks often cannot be set up beforehand and, although resources may be available, the problem will be one of distribution.

Because climate change is expected to make large-scale disasters worse, disaster relief organizations expect that existing resources and distribution networks will be increasingly stressed and less effective. To some extent, the problem will be simply one of funding. More disasters will mean more demands on limited supplies of humanitarian relief. Although some types of disasters may become relatively more common with climate change, no meaningful differentiation can currently be made about which disasters are caused by anthropogenic climate change and which would have occurred anyways with "natural" climate variability. Moreover, this question is only relevant if special funds are set aside for responding to climate change-related disasters. In short, climate change suggests a planned expansion of our humanitarian assistance programs, particularly for those types of events related to extreme weather. At least to some extent, better planning today can ensure more effective relief delivery tomorrow.

———————

D.   Adaptive Agriculture

All sectors that are dependent on the land or natural resources will be particularly affected by climate change. Not surprisingly, this means that agriculture will be faced with significant challenges in adapting to a more uncertain weather future. Consider that most agricultural expertise in most countries is the product of centuries, if not longer, of cumulative trial and error passed down from generation to generation. This traditional and localized knowledge has been based on certain set assumptions about the climate of particular regions — yet those very assumptions now may be changing.

As suggested by the following excerpt, many adaptive techniques exist for agriculture, including planting earlier in the year, adopting a different crop rotation, and selecting different varieties of crops. For example, different rice varieties have different abilities to tolerate high temperature, salinity, drought, and floods.

INTERDEPARTMENTAL WORKING GROUP ON CLIMATE CHANGE, FOOD & AGRIC. ORG. OF THE U.N., ADAPTATION TO CLIMATE CHANGE IN AGRICULTURE, FORESTRY AND FISHERIES: PERSPECTIVE, FRAMEWORK AND PRIORITIES 6–7 (2007) [Hereinafter FAO Adaptation Report]

Two main types of adaptation are autonomous and planned adaptation. Autonomous adaptation is the reaction of, for example, a farmer to changing precipitation patterns, in that s/he changes crops or uses different harvest and planting/sowing dates.

Planned adaptation measures are conscious policy options or response strategies, often multisectoral in nature, aimed at altering the adaptive capacity of the agricultural system or facilitating specific adaptations. For example, deliberate crops selection and distribution strategies across different agriclimatic zones, substitution of new crops for old ones and resource substitution induced by scarcity.

Farm level analyses have shown that large reductions in adverse impacts from climate change are possible when adaptation is fully implemented. Short-term adjustments are seen as autonomous in the sense that no other sectors (e.g., policy, research etc.) are needed in their development and implementation.

Long-term adaptations are major structural changes to overcome adversity such as changes in land-use to maximize yield under new conditions; application of new technologies; new land management techniques; and water-use efficiency related techniques. . . . [T]he following "major classes of adaptation" [have been defined]:

- seasonal changes and sowing dates;

- different variety or species;

- water supply and irrigation system;

- other inputs (fertilizer, tillage methods, grain drying, other field operations);

- new crop varieties;

- forest fire management, promotion of agroforestry, adaptive management with suitable species and silvicultural practices.

Accordingly, types of responses include:

- reduction of food security risk;

- identifying present vulnerabilities;

- adjusting agricultural research priorities;

- protecting genetic resources and intellectual property rights;

- strengthening agricultural extension and communication systems;

- adjustment in commodity and trade policy;

- increased training and education;

- identification and promotion of (micro-) climatic benefits and environmental services of trees and forests.

With changes in precipitation and hydrology, temperature, length of growing season and frequency of extreme weather events, considerable efforts would be required to prepare developing countries to deal with climate-related impacts in agriculture. Among the key challenges will be to assist countries that are constrained by limited economic resources and infrastructure, low levels of technology, poor access to information and knowledge, inefficient institutions, and limited empowerment and access to resources. * * *

Climate change and variability are among the most important challenges facing Least Developed Countries because of their strong economic reliance on natural resources and rain-fed agriculture. People living in marginal areas such as drylands or mountains face additional challenges with limited management options to reduce impacts. Climate adaptation strategies should reflect such circumstances in terms of the speed of the response and the choice of options.

———————

As the above excerpt suggests, the problem is not that adaptive technologies do not exist. The challenge is recognizing the need for adaptive steps before we have suffered through significant years of declining harvests. Long-term changes in agricultural practices may also be beyond the reach of those countries most in need of them, requiring resources and governance structures that are simply not in place in many developing countries.

———————

E. Adaptive Water Management

Closely related to agricultural management will be challenges to managing water resources. As the FAO points out:

A broad range of agricultural water management practices and technologies are available to spread and buffer production risks. Enhancing residual soil moisture through land conservation techniques assists significantly at the margin of dry periods while buffer strips, mulching and zero tillage help to mitigate soil erosion risk in areas where rainfall intensities increase.

The inter-annual storage of excess rainfall and the use of resource efficient irrigation remain the only guaranteed means of maintaining cropping intensities. Beyond the direct agricultural interventions, water resource management responses for river basins and aquifers, which are often transboundary, will be forced to become more agile and adaptive (including near real-time management), as variability in river flows and aquifer recharge becomes apparent. Competing sectoral demands for water will place more pressure on allocations to agriculture to account for its dominant use of raw water. Additionally there may be increased water demand for irrigated systems.

FAO ADAPTATION REPORT, at 12. Table 3-2, adapted from IPCC 2007: ADAPTATION AND VULNERABILITY, at 197, details some additional adaptation options for water management:

Table 3–2: Examples of Adaptive Water Management

Supply-side	Demand-side
Prospecting and extraction of ground-water	Improvement of water-use efficiency by recycling water
Increasing storage capacity by building reservoirs and dams	Reduction in water demand for irrigation by changing the cropping calendar, crop mix, irrigation method, and area planted
Desalination of sea water	Reduction in water demand for irrigation by importing agricultural products
Expansion of rain-water storage	Promotion of indigenous practices for sustainable water use
Removal of invasive non-native vegetation from riparian areas	Expanded use of water markets to reallocate water to highly valued uses
Water transfer	Expanded use of economic incentives including metering and pricing to encourage water conservation

As is obvious from reviewing these adaptation options, conflicts over water uses are likely to increase over time. Increased dams, reservoirs, irrigation works, or desalinization plants will all come with an environmental price, and over-allocated rivers in current dry areas will face greater stress. In-stream uses for ecological purposes are likely to suffer. Climate-related stress on water systems will also make reaching the Millennium Development Goal of halving the number of people without sanitation or fresh drinking water by 2015 more difficult.

F.   Relocation of Climate Refugees

As noted in Chapter 1, sea-level rise and other impacts may force a growing number of people permanently from their homes. Some put the estimates as high as 150 million "environmental" refugees by 2050, most of which would be displaced by conditions exacerbated or caused by climate change. In 2005, the 100 people in the village of Lateu on Vanuatu became one of the first communities forced to evacuate because of climate change. Although storm surges had occasionally swept over the village in the past, in recent years such storm surges became more frequent and intense, presumably because of global warming. The villagers of Lateu moved inland to higher ground on Vanuatu, with financial and technical support from the United Nations Environmental Programme (UNEP) and the

Canadian Government. Such international cooperation is likely to become increasingly necessary in the future. Nor are climate refugees just an issue for distant small island states; the Alaskan Native Village of Kivalina must be relocated due to climate change, at an estimated cost of $95 to $400 million.

Relocating a community is a difficult and complex task. Besides the enormous costs of moving the population, critical "social capital" is also lost through the breakdown of traditional care-giving networks, access to employment, or other social and economic relationships. In fact, it is not certain whether communities can be successfully relocated, even when more resources are made available. The situation of climate refugees is discussed further in Chapter 10 on Human Rights. See also the complaint filed on behalf of the Village of Kivalina seeking damages for relocating their village, excerpted in Chapter 16.

G.   Enhancing Natural Resilience and Ecosystem Services

Climate change will have significant impacts on natural systems and, at the same time, natural systems can be important for the adaptive capacity of different regions. The resilience of natural systems and their ability to absorb the stresses brought about by climate change have been weakened in the past century by other man-made impacts, such as pollution or habitat fragmentation. The resilience of these systems can be proactively restored, and in many instances these natural systems can provide effective defenses against climate change. In particular, the protection of natural coastal buffer zones can reduce the impacts from storm surges or general sea-level rise. The disastrous flooding of Hurricane Katrina was in part due to the widespread loss of coastal dunes and wetlands in the Gulf Coast over the past decades. In response, many coastal regions are setting aside or restoring areas to provide adaptive buffer zones. New Jersey's Coastal Blue Acres program, for example, is acquiring coastal lands vulnerable to storms and returning them to recreational and conservation uses. The State of Georgia is expanding protection of its coastal salt marshes to better withstand the expanded storm surges expected as sea levels rise. *See also* the discussion of recovery plans for endangered species threatened by climate change in Chapter 13. For a comprehensive treatment of the world's ecosystem services, see MILLENNIUM ECOSYSTEM ASSESSMENT, ECOSYSTEMS AND HUMAN WELL-BEING (2005).

H.   Insurance as Adaptation

In wealthier countries, insurance has been used for years to spread the risks of extreme weather events such as floods, hurricanes, or droughts. The purchaser of insurance pays a premium to be protected against catastrophic or substantial loss. Because climate change will (if it hasn't already) increase the frequency and intensity of storm events, private insurance is getting more difficult to find in some coastal areas in the United States. A recent survey of industry officials by Ernst & Young found that climate change is currently the top insurance risk. Insurance companies are beginning to not only raise rates for homeowners in threatened coastal areas, but are also cutting them off from renewing their policies. The following *New York Times* article discusses the current state of insurance as nonrenewal is spreading to the northeast regions as well:

In the last three years, more than three million homeowners have received letters from their insurers as insurance companies, determined to avoid another $40 billion Katrina bill, have essentially begun to redraw the outline of the eastern United States somewhere west of the Appalachian Trail.* * *

Companies including Allstate, State Farm and Liberty Mutual have "nonrenewed" policies not only in hurricane-battered places like Florida and Louisiana, but in New York and other Northern states that have not seen hurricanes in years. Since last year, Allstate has turned down all new homeowners' insurance business in New Jersey, Connecticut, Rhode Island, Maryland, Massachusetts and the eight downstate counties of New York.* * *

The companies say they are obliged to avoid undue risks where they see them, and to remain solvent. "Considering what happened between 2003 and 2005," said Robert P. Hartwig, president of the Insurance Information Institute, an industry lobbying group, "and considering that the best meteorological minds are telling us that for the next 15 to 20 years hurricane activity will be heavier than normal, if we didn't do something to reduce our exposure, we'd be out of business."

Paul Vitello, *Home Insurers Canceling in the East*, N.Y. TIMES, Oct. 16, 2007.

In response, states have had to pick up where insurance companies leave off, finding creative ways to offer publicly-supported insurance. The state of Florida, for example, created the Citizen's Property Insurance Corporation, which, with nearly 1.5 million policies, is Florida's largest homeowner insurer. At the national level, the National Flood Insurance Program, which provides federally-backed flood insurance to homeowners, renters, and business owners in communities that adopt and enforce floodplain management ordinances to reduce flood damage, is coming up for renewal in the Senate and is on the verge of bankruptcy after huge losses from Katrina and other Gulf Coast storms. The Florida delegation is pushing for a measure that would make the U.S. Treasury the insurer of last resort for future catastrophic storms, and other measures are being proposed to expand federal insurance programs to cover wind-related damage. As of April 2008, the House had passed both measures. These measures are controversial. Some insurance companies argue that they keep insurance rates artificially low. Environmentalists and taxpayer groups argue that they subsidize risky developments and encourage unsustainable land-use patterns. *See* John J. Fialka, *Will Climate Change Shrink the Insurance Industry*, EARTHNEWS, Apr. 1, 2008, *available at* www.earthportal.org/news/?p=992. Indeed, some homes in flood-prone areas have been rebuilt multiple times with the assistance of federally supported insurance. Does this seem like a good use of taxpayer money?

Insurance may also have a role in international adaptation policy. Both the Kyoto Protocol and UNFCCC recognize the role of insurance as a possible adaptation response. The following excerpt from the Pew Center explains international insurance strategies:

The insurance sector is growing rapidly in emerging economies, which, at current growth rates, will represent half the world market by 2050. But this growth is unlikely to reach many among the populations most vulnerable to climate change. Donor governments, possibly in partnership with the private sector, could support insurance-type approaches in vulnerable countries by subsidizing premiums or by pledging backup capital to reduce risks to public or private providers. A variety of risk-transfer instruments could be supported for different sectors and types of risk. * * *

The insurance industry and developing country governments are exploring or testing a number of [other] insurance-type approaches to cover climate-related risks. Examples include:

Pooling Cash Reserves. As a form of collective self-insurance, the Eastern Caribbean Central Bank is accumulating cash reserves through mandatory contributions by member governments, which can then draw loans if struck by natural disasters.

Indemnifying Debts. The Commonwealth and Smaller States Disaster Management Scheme provides insurance to risk-prone governments so they can continue to service outstanding debt following natural disasters. Countries pay a flat-rate premium of 1 percent of the sum insured.

Catastrophe Bonds. The World Bank is exploring whether catastrophe bonds, now in use in developed countries, might be extended to developing country markets. "Cat" bonds insure against a predefined event. Investors who purchase them realize a return if the event does not occur but may lose their entire investment if it does.

Indexed Insurance for Agriculture. These contracts, also known as weather derivatives, provide payments to farmers under predetermined conditions (such as number of days with temperatures above a set threshold) without requiring proof of loss. The World Bank is studying their feasibility in Ethiopia, Morocco, Nicaragua, and Tunisia.

The World Bank is developing a proposal for a Global Index Insurance Facility, with $100 million in public and private capital, to reinsure governments and primary insurers providing index-based coverage against weather and other risks. Reinsurance — or "backstopping" — also could be provided for acute losses from extreme events such as hurricanes or typhoons. One potential model is the Turkish Catastrophe Insurance Pool, a national earthquake insurance program backed by a standby line of credit from the World Bank, the first instance of an international financial institution absorbing developing country risk. Backstopping also could take the form of catastrophe bonds, in which investors funding a reinsurance pool receive above-market returns if no losses occur but risk their full investment should there be a major disaster. Mexico plans to issue catastrophe bonds on the private market to reinsure its national catastrophe relief fund. Donor governments, alone or with private investors, could use the same mechanism to back climate relief in vulnerable countries.

See Ian Burton, Elliot Diringer & Joel Smith, *Adaptation to Climate Change: International Policy Options* 19–21 (Pew Center on Global Climate Change, 2006) [hereinafter *Pew Center, Adaptation Policy Options* (2006)].

QUESTIONS AND DISCUSSION

1. ***Adaptive Capacity.*** Adaptive capacity is the ability or potential of a system to adjust behavior and resources to respond to change. Unfortunately, the capacity to adapt to climate change is unequal across and within societies. Generally speaking, developing countries have fewer resources to respond to immediate threats and adapt for potential future impacts, but adaptive capacity can also vary within developed countries. Consider, for example, the relative capacity of Louisi-

ana to respond to Hurricane Katrina. As the following excerpt from the IPCC explains, adaptive capacity is influenced by social factors like human capital, community networks, and governance structure, perhaps as much as by the level of economic development or access to technology:

> [A]daptive capacity is influenced not only by economic development and technology, but also by social factors such as human capital and governance structures. Furthermore, recent analysis argues that adaptive capacity is not a concern unique to regions with low levels of economic activity. Although economic development may provide greater access to technology and resources to invest in adaptation, high income per capita is considered neither a necessary nor a sufficient indicator of the capacity to adapt to climate change. Some elements of adaptive capacity are not substitutable: an economy will be as vulnerable as the 'weakest link' in its resources and adaptive capacity. . . . Within both developed and developing countries, some regions, localities, or social groups have a lower adaptive capacity. There are many examples where social capital, social networks, values, perceptions, customs, traditions and levels of cognition affect the capability of communities to adapt to risks related to climate change. Communities in Samoa in the south Pacific, for example, rely on informal non-monetary arrangements and social networks to cope with storm damage, along with livelihood diversification and financial remittances through extended family networks. Similarly, strong local and international support networks enable communities in the Cayman Islands to recover from and prepare for tropical storms. Community organization is an important factor in adaptive strategies to build resilience among hillside communities in Bolivia. Recovery from hazards in Cuba is helped by a sense of communal responsibility. Food-sharing expectations and networks in Nunavut, Canada, allow community members access to so-called country food at times when conditions make it unavailable to some. The role of food sharing as a part of a community's capacity to adapt to risks in resource provisioning is also evident among native Alaskans.

IPCC 2007: ADAPTATION AND VULNERABILITY, at 728. What challenges do the variations in adaptive capacity present for the international community? How should the international community respond to these differences?

2. Another complexity in considering future adaptation measures is how such measures may create positive feedback loops to further exacerbate climate change. If adaptation plans include increased use of air conditioners in the summers, for example, the expanded use of energy could in turn lead to greater greenhouse gas emissions. Similarly, as agriculture adapts to warming climates by requiring more irrigation, energy demand for pumping water will increase. What other potential feedback loops can you identify where adaptation measures could make achieving our mitigation goals that much harder? What procedural or other steps should be taken in developing adaptation plans to ensure they are not contributing further to climate change? See generally IPCC 2007: ADAPTATION AND VULNERABILITY, at 759–62.

3. Given that adaptive capacity is at least partly dependent on social and economic factors, effective adaptation will require sensitivity to gender disparities in both climate vulnerability and capacity. Consider the following discussion in the IPCC 2007: ADAPTATION AND VULNERABILITY, Box 17.5:

> Empirical research has shown that entitlements to elements of adaptive capacity are socially differentiated along the lines of age, ethnicity, class, religion and gender. Climate change therefore has gender-specific implications in terms of both vulnerability and adaptive capacity. There are

structural differences between men and women through, for example, gender-specific roles in society, work and domestic life. These differences affect the vulnerability and capacity of women and men to adapt to climate change. In the developing world in particular, women are disproportionately involved in natural resource-dependent activities, such as agriculture, compared to salaried occupations. As resource-dependent activities are directly dependent on climatic conditions, changes in climate variability projected for future climates are likely to affect women through a variety of mechanisms: directly through water availability, vegetation and fuel-wood availability and through health issues relating to vulnerable populations (especially dependent children and elderly). Most fundamentally, the vulnerability of women in agricultural economies is affected by their relative insecurity of access and rights over resources and sources of wealth such as agricultural land. It is well established that women are disadvantaged in terms of property rights and security of tenure, though the mechanisms and exact form of the insecurity are contested. This insecurity can have implications both for their vulnerability in a changing climate, and also their capacity to adapt productive livelihoods to a changing climate.

A body of research argues that women are more vulnerable than men to weather-related disasters. The impacts of past weather-related hazards have been disaggregated to determine the differential effects on women and men. Such studies have been done, for example, for Hurricane Mitch in 1998 and for natural disasters more generally. These differential impacts include numbers of deaths, and well-being in the post-event recovery period. The disproportionate amount of the burden endured by women during rehabilitation has been related to their roles in the reproductive sphere. Children and elderly persons tend to be based in and around the home and so are often more likely to be affected by flooding events with speedy onset. Women are usually responsible for the additional care burden during the period of rehabilitation, whilst men generally return to their pre-disaster productive roles outside the home. Fordham (2003) has argued that the key factors that contribute to the differential vulnerability of women in the context of natural hazards in South Asia include: high levels of illiteracy, minimum mobility and work opportunities outside the home, and issues around ownership of resources such as land.

The role of gender in influencing adaptive capacity and adaptation is thus an important consideration for the development of interventions to enhance adaptive capacity and to facilitate adaptation. Gender differences in vulnerability and adaptive capacity reflect wider patterns of structural gender inequality. One lesson that can be drawn from the gender and development literature is that climate interventions that ignore gender concerns reinforce the differential gender dimensions of vulnerability. It has also become clear that a shift in policy focus away from reactive disaster management to more proactive capacity building can reduce gender inequality.

IPCC 2007: ADAPTATION AND VULNERABILITY, at 730. What types of policies could address these gender imbalances in the context of climate change?

4. Concerns that adaptation would be considered an *alternative* to mitigation are not completely unfounded. Most observers understand adaptation as a second-best response to climate change, necessary to reduce human suffering as much as possible while we find ways to reduce long-term climate change. Some conservative commentators, however, promote adaptation as an alternative to mitigation,

arguing that the costs of adaptation are lower than mitigation and that the costs of mitigation would unduly slow the growth in our economy. Better, they say, to allow the economy to grow so a wealthier world — better able to afford adaptation — would result. How would you respond to these arguments, particularly in light of the discussion of cost-benefit analysis in Chapter 1?

5.   Relocating communities of climate refugees raises interesting international law questions. International humanitarian institutions differ in their definitions of refugees, and many definitions don't easily cover environmental refugees. The Global Governance Project, a European research program aimed at improving global governance, has proposed creation of a Climate Refugee Protection and Resettlement Fund. Money could be raised through a levy on air travel or similar mechanism. Funds could be provided as grants, completely separate from other adaptation and sustainable development funds. The legal framework would be established in a separate protocol to the UNFCCC on the Recognition, Protection, and Resettlement of Climate Refugees. *See generally* Frank Biermann & Ingrid Boas, *Preparing for a Warmer World; Towards a Global Governance System to Protect Climate Refugees* 17–18, 29–30 (Global Governance Working Paper No. 33, 2007), *available at* www.glogov.org (last visited Mar. 20, 2008). What value is there to a separate protocol focused specifically on climate refugees? Are there any arguments for treating climate refugees differently than refugees displaced by other environmental causes? By non-environmental causes? These questions are discussed further in Chapter 10 in the section on human rights and climate change.

6.   Adaptation has only recently received attention from environmental lawyers. At first glance, adaptation does not seem to raise significant legal questions, but, as climate change impacts are better understood, the law, too, may have to adapt. Many of our laws dealing with property (tidal land ownership) or sovereignty (the extent of the territorial sea), for example, assume that sea levels are essentially constant. *See* Charles Di Leva & Sachiko Morita, *Maritime Rights of Coastal States and Climate Change: Should States Adapt to Submerged Boundaries?*, World Bank Law & Dev. Ser. No. 5 (2008); David D. Caron, *Climate Change, Sea Level Rise and the Coming Uncertainty in Oceanic Boundaries: A Proposal to Avoid Conflict, in* SEOUNG-YONG HONG AND JON M. VAN DYKE EDS., MARITIME BOUNDARY DISPUTES, SETTLEMENT PROCESSES AND THE LAW OF THE SEA (forthcoming 2009). Can you think of other examples where the legal system may be predicated on assumptions that will change as climate changes? How can we develop laws that are adaptive over time to a changing climate?

7.   A wide range of international and national organizations currently exists to support disaster relief. The UN Office for the Coordination of Humanitarian Affairs (OCHA) assembles and updates information on current disasters in order to help the international humanitarian community coordinate emergency assistance. *See* ReliefWeb (www.reliefweb.int). The recently launched Central Emergency Response Fund (CERF) provides urgent aid to regions in crisis within 72 hours of the emergency. Generally least-developed countries have been the recipients of these UN-governed funds. The CERF is funded by voluntary contributions from UN member States, private businesses, individuals, and foundations. The private sector organized the Disaster Resource Network (DRN) as part of the World Economic Forum to catalyze and coordinate private sector support for disaster management in developing countries. The DRN believes that the private sector must not only supply funds for relief organizations but must also proactively participate to prevent and mitigate effects of disasters by providing access to resources, knowledge, and assets. In the United States, organizations like the American Red Cross, provide shelter, food, and health services to individuals and families affected by the disaster, as well as resources to help them get back to a more normal life after the emergency is over.

III. INTERNATIONAL CHALLENGES OF ADAPTATION

Until recently, adaptation has mostly taken a backseat to mitigation in the international negotiations. The UNFCCC acknowledged adaptation in general terms, but its primary focus, as well as that of the Kyoto Protocol, is clearly on mitigation.

The relative lack of emphasis on adaptation has begun to change, however, particularly as developing countries have placed increasing demands on the industrialized countries to provide funding for adaptation. From the developing country perspective, substantial financial support for adaptation from industrialized countries is warranted, both because industrialized countries are the primary contributors to climate change and because they have greater resources generally. Funding for adaptation is at least implicitly understood as part of the political price that industrialized countries must pay for developing country participation in the international climate regime.

Under the UNFCCC, the parties agree to prepare for adaptation, assist developing countries in creating appropriate adaptation plans, and promote sustainable economic growth to facilitate coping with climate change. Under the Kyoto Protocol, parties are to implement adaptation programs and provide funding for vulnerable developing countries and high-risk areas. In the first UNFCCC meeting in 1995, the parties established a three-stage framework for addressing adaptation. Stage I was to identify vulnerable countries, Stage II was to start building capacity to prepare for adaptation, the Stage III was to implement measures to facilitate adaptation. So far, the focus has been on Stages I and II, assessing countries' vulnerabilities and setting up National Adaptation Programmes of Action (NAPAs) for these countries. *See Pew Center, Adaptation Policy Options* (2006), *supra*, at 13.

Adaptation also presents significant institutional challenges. Although adaptation is seen as an integral part of the international political bargain reached under the climate regime — i.e., that developing countries' participation in mitigating climate change may be conditioned on financial support for adaptation, the UNFCCC is not necessarily an appropriate institution for directing or managing many adaptation efforts. For example, adaptation in the international context often relates to disaster relief, typically carried out by well-established humanitarian organizations. Proactive adaptation strategies may require civil engineering, long-term agricultural or ecological planning, or other areas of expertise that are not necessarily found in the climate regime. Nor is there an obvious reason why those activities should be brought under the UNFCCC. Consider the following analysis by the Pew Global Center for Climate Change:

IAN BURTON, ELLIOT DIRINGER, & JOEL SMITH, ADAPTATION TO CLIMATE CHANGE
15–17 (Pew Center on Global Climate Change 2006)*

From a political standpoint, it may be most plausible to pursue future adaptation efforts within the Framework Convention. To the degree that additional adaptation support is bound with the question of future commitments on climate mitigation, the UNFCCC negotiating process is the most obvious venue for structuring agreements that speak to both. Further, it makes sense to build on, or where appropriate redirect, the adaptation apparatus already established under the Convention. There may be constraints, however, on what can be achieved within a regime created specifically to address climate change. First, the climate regime has not traditionally engaged many of the agencies and actors whose participation in adaptation is essential. Even if the regime assigned a higher priority to adaptation, it still might not be the best channel for engaging relevant policymakers and stakeholders. Second, the regime's inherent focus on climate change may not easily lend itself to a comprehensive effort addressing both climate change and natural climate variability.

Still, a proactive approach under the regime could help to address urgent climate change-specific impacts while also facilitating comprehensive long-term climate risk management at the national level. Specific elements of a Convention-based approach could include:

- Support to vulnerable countries for the development of comprehensive national adaptation strategies;

- Reliable funding to assist countries with approved national strategies to implement high-priority measures, with priority given to those addressing impacts reasonably attributable to climate change; and

- Establishment or designation of an international body to provide technical support, judge the adequacy of national strategies, and select high-priority projects for funding.

Convention support for developing national adaptation strategies would help establish frameworks for action and strengthen capacity in vulnerable countries. The strategies could build on the NAPAs, which target urgent priorities, to map out comprehensive long-term plans identifying: climate risks (from both climate change and climate variability); existing and needed adaptation capacities; risk reduction objectives; high priority adaptation measures; and national policies and measures to integrate climate risk management fully into development decision-making. In addition to organizing national-level adaptation efforts, the strategies could serve as a basis for targeting implementation assistance through the regime or other channels. Such assistance could be made conditional on a country's completion of an adequate national strategy.

If assistance is provided for specific adaptation measures, parties would need to establish parameters for qualifying projects. Given that assistance through the Convention would likely be limited, and that the Convention concerns itself specifically with climate change, such funds presumably would be targeted to urgent needs arising directly from climate change impacts. This determination may be possible only in a narrow range of circumstances — such as sea-level rise or glacial melting — which could be agreed as classes of impact eligible for funding. Beyond such readily identifiable priorities, Convention funds could be packaged with other assistance through development channels to support broader climate risk management efforts in vulnerable countries.

Institutionally, such an approach would require means to support development of national plans and capacity, assess the adequacy of national plans, and allocate any implementation assistance made available under the Convention. These functions could be performed by a new or existing body, which, in coordination with other expert and implementing agencies, could serve as a clearinghouse for information, expertise, and funding. This institution would need political legitimacy with both donor and recipient countries, and sufficient independence to credibly pass judgment on national plans and to choose among competing projects. Some form of political oversight, perhaps by the Conference of the Parties, also would be needed.

A Convention-based approach, whether initiated through an "adaptation protocol" or another instrument, would most likely be agreed as part of a broader package that also addresses mitigation. In the long term, a Convention-based strategy would be effective only insofar as it succeeded in institutionalizing adaptation in vulnerable countries. To the degree possible, assistance provided for planning or implementation should serve simultaneously to build or strengthen national capacities so that, over time, countries are better able to adapt on their own. Also critical to long-term success would be adequate, predictable, and sustained funding. This would require supplementing or replacing the present system of pledging-plus-CDM levy with a stronger, dedicated source such as a wider levy on the emissions market or funding commitments under an agreed formula.

Given the ubiquitous nature of climate change, adaptation planning should likely be integrated into all sustainable development planning. The IPCC and other observers thus argue that adaptation must be "mainstreamed" into the planning of all development institutions. Existing infrastructure lending from the World Bank, for example, should now take into account changing priorities due to climate change. Disaster relief efforts, too, should mainstream planning based on future climate scenarios. Such efforts that already have community-based delivery mechanisms in place may provide the core capacity for responding to climate change-related disasters.

QUESTIONS AND DISCUSSION

1.   One of the biggest constraints on adaptation is financing. A UNFCCC estimate puts the cost to developing countries between $28–67 billion per year by 2030, which is generally consistent with a 2007 estimate from Oxfam ($50 billion dollars/year) and the World Bank (up to $41 billion for developing countries). Charlotte Sterrett, *Financing Adaptation: Why the UN's Bali Climate Conference Must Mandate the Search for New Funds*, OXFAM BRIEFING NOTE, Dec. 4, 2007; UNFCCC, *Investment and Financial Flows Relevant to the Development of an Effective and Appropriate International Response to Climate Change* (2007). Although great uncertainty exists around these numbers, what is certain is that finding the money is not going to be easy and serious questions arise about how to allocate costs.

2.   Assessing the costs and benefits of adaptation measures is difficult because of uncertainty in climate change projections. Some studies have been done on

various sectors to try to estimate costs and benefits of adaptation, but any benefits from adaptation measures will only be successful if the local community can adapt and implement these measures. *See generally* NICHOLAS STERN, THE STERN REVIEW ON THE ECONOMICS OF CLIMATE CHANGE 410–412 (2006). The agriculture sector has been studied extensively for costs and benefits of adaptation. At first, the focus was on benefits such as increased crop yields, but gradually studies have recognized that changing planting dates and crop diversification have costs as well. Additionally, many of these studies assume that farmers can adapt immediately to changing climate conditions. Even if farmers and agricultural regions could adapt perfectly, costs of adapting to a different climate would still be significant. *See generally* IPCC 2007: ADAPTATION AND VULNERABILITY, at 725–726 (2007).

3. Given that adaptive capacity is so dependent on the level of development, many adaptation strategies are indistinguishable from development generally. Building capacity for a country to address climate risk necessarily means that it will be better off in addressing other risks as well. Viewed in this light, is it easier to see why we may understate the benefits of adaptation? Is there good reason to separate those adaptation measures that are simply development efforts relabelled from those adaptation measures specifically tailored to respond to climate risk?

4. Moreover, the issue is not only about the amount of money. Under the UNFCCC's general financing approach, donor countries agree to provide financial support to pay only the incremental costs incurred by developing countries in responding to global environmental issues. Thus, for example, assistance is available to cover the additional costs of installing new pollution control equipment to reduce greenhouse gas emissions for purposes of addressing climate change. This criterion to address the incremental costs has a different twist when applied to adaptation. In adaptation, the question of what costs are incremental would require scientists to be able to differentiate between disaster impacts caused by anthropogenic climate change and disasters caused by natural causes. Why should donor countries be more concerned about providing disaster relief from climate-induced changes than from, for example, victims of earthquakes or the tsunami that struck Thailand and Indonesia in 2006? Does this argue that adaptation be addressed generally through expanded disaster assistance? Why establish a special Adaptation Fund at all? Is this related to the question of responsibility and liability?

5. Adaptation raises difficult issues of fairness in the international context. Developing countries are generally more vulnerable to climate change impacts because they have fewer resources for adaptation. Countries that have more resources or better adaptive capacity can anticipate climate change and begin to address projected impacts faster. Developing countries have also not contributed as much to climate change historically as the industrialized countries. Is there a way to link responsibility and adaptive capacity? In an article exploring the social justice implications of adaptation, Paul Baer briefly considers various theories on how to assess and distribute the costs of climate change:

> Given the disproportionate share of emissions from the industrialized countries of the North and that the developing countries of the South are more vulnerable to climate impacts, plausible interpretations of "common but differentiated responsibilities" imply that the North should shoulder the major part of the costs of adaptation. . . . [A]ll the donors to the [existing Adaptation Funds] are wealthy countries with significant responsibility. However, the funds' voluntary nature allows other countries with equal or greater wealth or responsibility to avoid paying for adaptation. . . . It seems likely that Northern governments are resistant to explicit claims for "polluter pays" liability for adaptation investments because there is a clear link between current responsibility for adaptation

and eventual liability for compensation for actual climate damages. Northern governments might reasonably fear that acknowledging such claims would obligate northern countries to the largest share of a potentially enormous financial liability. Direct "polluter pays" liability has been avoided so far by emphasizing ability to pay rather than responsibility for climate change, while continuing to give rhetorical support to the importance of the responsibility. The strong correlation between responsibility and capacity has allowed this compromise to justify an initial round of adaptation-related funding. However, reliance on capacity as the basis for sharing burdens implies that the magnitude of funding is determined by capacity limits or, in the end, on the limit on willingness to pay.

Paul Baer, *Adaptation: Who Pays Whom? in* W. NEIL ADGER, ET AL., FAIRNESS IN ADAPTATION TO CLIMATE CHANGE 131, 132–33 (2006). As suggested by the Baer excerpt, any significant discussion of adaptation immediately leads to discussions of who should pay for adaptation, particularly for responding to events after they have happened. In those situations, the discussion over adaptation is closely linked to one of liability or responsibility. In your view, who should bear the costs of adapting to climate change? On what basis should these costs be allocated across countries? Does it matter how wealthy a country is? Should the countries with the highest emissions pay? The highest past emissions? Why do you think industrialized countries have thus far only supported voluntary contributions to adaptation funds?

6. Oxfam has created an index to assess responsibility and how much a country should contribute to the assistance funds to address climate change:

Oxfam's Adaptation Financing Index (AFI) calculates shares based on the principles of responsibility and capability set out in the UNFCCC. Taking account of population size, the AFI measures responsibility based on a country's excessive CO_2 emissions per person since 1992, and measures capability based on each country's current score in the UNDP's Human Development Index. According to the AFI, of the 28 countries both responsible for, and capable of, financing adaptation in developing countries:

- The USA and the EU should contribute over 75 per cent of the finance needed, with over 40 per cent coming from the USA, and over 30 per cent from EU members;

- Within the EU, the top five contributors should be (in order): Germany, the UK, Italy, France, and Spain: together they account for over three-quarters of Europe's share;

- Japan, Canada, Australia, and the Republic of Korea should together contribute a further 20 per cent of the finance, with Japan providing over half of that;

See Oxfam Briefing Note. Do you agree with Oxfam's approach? If not, what other criteria would you use?

7. Some observers believe an insurance approach could avoid or at least reduce tensions over whether adaptation costs should be paid based on liability. Consider the insurance-type instruments described above. How could they reduce tension over legal claims of liability? Does it help if insurance-type instruments address all impacts whether due to climate variability or long-term climate change?

8. ***Problem Exercise.*** Climate change impacts affect every economic sector of society, and every sector will need to adapt to climate change. The class may be divided into groups corresponding to different sectors of the economy, including, for example: fisheries, forestry, agriculture, urban planning, homeowners, health care

providers, and insurance. Each group should evaluate the impact climate change will have on their sector and make specific recommendations of how the laws, policies and practice in their area can be adapted to reflect a future with significant climate impacts.

IV. GEOENGINEERING

In the climate change context, geoengineering is the intentional, large-scale manipulation of the planet's climate. As the evidence of climate change impacts mount, ideas of re-engineering the planet's basic ecosystems — ideas once dismissed as ridiculous — are now gaining more interest and credibility. And as climate change impacts worsen with only tepid efforts to avoid it, geoengineering proponents can make increasingly plausible arguments that we may have little choice than to use geoengineering at least to some extent. Some geoengineering proposals, like sending a million tiny mirrors into orbit or pulling the earth further away from the sun, sound like science fiction and are currently only theoretical possibilities. Others, for example, launching sulfates or other aerosols into the upper atmosphere to deflect solar radiation or fertilizing the oceans with iron to enhance carbon sequestration, are already technically feasible, relatively easy to understand, and in some cases already the subject of design studies or pilot tests.

A.   What is Geoengineering?

Geoengineering is an expansive term encompassing a wide array of proposals for mitigating the effects of global warming through the deliberate, large-scale manipulation of various environmental systems. Most geoengineering proposals fall within two distinct categorical approaches to the problem of global warming. "Sequestration," or those steps that directly remove CO_2 or other GHGs from the atmosphere, include ocean fertilization, large scale forest management, and other sequestration efforts discussed previously in Chapter 2. "Screening" techniques involve enhancing the planet's albedo — or reflectivity — to effectively shade the Earth from solar radiation. Methods within this category reduce the sun's energy input without reducing atmospheric GHG levels. What sets geoengineering apart, as suggested by the following excerpt, is the focus on intent and scale:

> While the scope of human impact is now global, we have yet to make a deliberate attempt to transform nature on a planetary scale. I call such transformation geoengineering. More precisely, I define geoengineering as intentional, large-scale manipulation of the environment. Both scale and intent are important. For an action to be geoengineering, environmental change must be the goal rather than a side effect, and the intent and effect of the manipulation must be large in scale. Two examples demonstrate the roles of scale and intent. First, consider intent without scale: Ornamental gardening is the intentional manipulation of the environment to suit human desires, yet it is not geoengineering because neither the intended nor realized effect is large-scale. Second, consider scale without intent: Climate change due to increasing carbon dioxide (CO_2) has a global effect, yet it is not geoengineering because it is a side effect of the combustion of fossil fuels to provide energy. Pollution, even pollution that alters the planet, is not engineering. It's just making a mess.

Manipulations need not be aimed at changing the environment, but rather may aim to maintain a desired environment against perturbations — either natural or anthropogenic. Indeed, the term has most commonly been applied to proposals to engineer climate, so as to counteract climate change caused by rising CO_2 concentrations. In this context, the primary focus of this essay, geoengineering implies a countervailing measure or a "technical fix"; an expedient solution that uses additional technology to counteract unwanted effects without eliminating their root cause.

David W. Keith, *Geoengineering*, forthcoming in STEVEN SCHNEIDER & MIKE MASTRANDREA, CLIMATE CHANGE SCIENCE AND POLICY (Island Press).

Geoengineering proposals come in many different variations. Some are based on relatively proven technologies, while others assume dramatic advances in technology and would be very expensive. The following is a summary of a cross-section of some geoengineering proposals.

Sulfate Aerosols. Several proposals have been made to launch sulfate or aluminum particles into the atmosphere to scatter or reflect incoming light from the sun, which shades and cools the Earth's surface by preventing solar energy from hitting the planet's surface. Such proposals are based on the documented impacts of volcanic eruptions like that of the Philippines' Mt. Pinatubo, which lowered the earth's average temperature significantly. Sulfate aerosols could be added to the emissions of power plants or to the fuel emissions from commercial airliners.

Orbiting Reflectors. Similar to the proposals to use aerosols to scatter solar light away from the planet is to use orbiting mirrors or other reflective materials. One proposal is to release millions of tiny hydrogen-filled mylar balloons into an orbit 25 kilometers above the surface. Another proposal would launch 55,000 orbiting mirrors, each approximately 100 square kilometers to reflect solar energy away from the earth. Proposals to ring the planet with satellites or a particle ring like that found around Saturn are aimed at the same effect.

Solar Orbiting Reflectors. Further afield (or more precisely further in space) are proposals to orbit a reflector around the sun. Such solar shields have been proposed of glass, opaque thin film, or metal. These systems are more theoretical and expensive.

Moving the Earth. In a particularly ambitious proposal, several scientists have suggested moving the Earth farther away from the sun. *See* D. Korycansky, G. Laughlin & F. Adams, *Astronomical Engineering: A Strategy for Modifying Planetary Orbits*, ASTROPHYSICS & SPACE SCIENCE 275, 349–66 (2001).

Ocean Fertilization. In recent years, two private companies have been actively pursuing the widespread distribution of iron particles in certain parts of the ocean. This iron would fertilize the ocean, causing rapid growth in certain algae that would consume significant amounts of CO_2. As the algae die, they would sequester this CO_2 on the ocean floor. Depending on the scale, ocean fertilization may or may not always be considered geoengineering, but widespread ocean fertilization shares similarly high levels of uncertainty and risk with other forms of geoengineering.

Each of these geoengineering proposals, even the more prosaic among them, raise significant legal, ethical and governance issues. Many policymakers are fearful that time and resources spent in developing and debating geoengineering proposals will detract from the higher priority of avoiding emissions in the first place.

B.   The Geoengineering Debate

The most important argument for geoengineering is simply that we may have no choice if we hope to avoid catastrophic impacts from anthropogenic climate change. To be sure, the potential impacts from climate change outlined in Chapter 1 argue persuasively for looking at all feasible options. In light of the growing climate threat it becomes less likely with each passing year that relying solely on the reduction of greenhouse gas emissions, even with better management of existing carbon sinks, will enable us to avoid substantial economic and ecologic dislocation. While not suggesting that we reduce efforts to mitigate climate change, some geoengineering proponents argue that we need to evaluate all possible responses and need to be testing the more promising geoengineering approaches at least as a sort of short-term insurance policy against cataclysmic climate change.

Geoengineering proponents also argue that, at least as compared to some cost estimates for reducing GHG emissions, some geoengineering proposals are cheap. The introduction of atmospheric aerosols appears to be very cost-effective. For $500 million in annual costs, some geoengineering proponents argue that you could place enough aerosol particles above the poles to reverse the current levels of ice melt. Moreover, given the well-documented global temperature drops from massive volcanic eruptions, few doubt the cooling effect of such aerosols. *See generally* Alan Carlin, *Global Climate Change Control: Is There a Better Strategy than Reducing Greenhouse Gas Emissions?*, 155 U. PA. L. REV. 1401 (2007).

The anticipated timelines for climate change also argue for a closer look at geo-engineering. Even if we are able to muster the political will to make deep cuts in CO_2 emissions and move significantly towards a carbon-neutral era, this may not be done in time to avoid significant climate impacts. We may need to bridge the gap between the time when emissions are reduced substantially and the decline of atmospheric concentrations of GHGs. These timing considerations may change the risk analysis around geoengineering options. Even if some unintended (and unknown) consequences are likely from geoengineering, those risks must be measured against the unintended (and unknown) consequences of living for that same period of time with an atmosphere exceedingly high in carbon. The choice becomes with which of the two devils we most want to dance. Particularly, if geoengineering is viewed as a temporary step, the risk analysis could swing in its direction.

Opponents of geoengineering rebut many of the proponents' arguments, but add significant arguments about the ethics and uncertainty of tinkering so fundamentally with the earth's life support systems. Deliberately manipulating the planetary climate regime reflects, to some, an act of hubris beyond almost anything humanity has tried before. Although we have undoubtedly changed the earth's climate through human activities, that has been (at least until recently) without intent. To *intentionally* try to manage God's design takes climate change into a different set of ethical debates. The "end of nature" is no longer an accident, but a decision. BILL MCKIBBEN, THE END OF NATURE (1989).

Beyond ethical issues are arguments about the unintended consequences that will occur from any deliberate manipulation of the climate system. Many scientists do not believe that we have sufficient knowledge about the planet to predict what potentially serious impacts could occur from most geoengineering proposals. Purporting to evaluate the potential benefits and costs of geoengineering processes paints geoengineering discussions with a patina of legitimacy that may, in some views, not be warranted by the state of scientific knowledge. The potential unknowns are substantial and in fact we may make matters worse — we may be "swallowing the spider to catch the fly." For many ecologists, the record of human intervention in trying to improve nature is rich with examples where the best of human intentions have resulted in significant calamities. Often these calamities have been felt in local ecosystems (for example, with the deliberate introduction of invasive species to control other invasive species). Geoengineering has the potential for massive mistakes.

Even the known potential negative impacts are significant. A recent study showed that, along with cooling, volcanic eruptions also brought global drought. Moreover, it is not clear what public health impacts, including impacts on the ozone layer, might come from annually sending the equivalent of a volcano's worth of particulate matter into the atmosphere.

Many climate change followers fear that focusing on geoengineering will distract policymakers from making the hard decisions to reduce GHGs. It could, for example, divert funding — both public and private — away from clean technologies that would reduce GHG emissions. And it could lull the general public into thinking that we do not need to make the difficult cultural and economic decisions necessary to address climate change.

In this context, opponents fear that we will become addicted to geoengineering. If, in fact, we do not take the steps necessary to substantially reduce GHG emissions, then any reliance on geoengineering will be forever and the commitment to use geoengineering only as a temporary fix will be forgotten.

Those geoengineering screening techniques that are meant to shade the planet or "manage" solar radiation are not designed to reduce GHG concentrations but rather simply to mask the impacts of GHGs. Once the geoengineering is put in place (for example, aerosol particles or sun shading), any removal (or failure to maintain the geoengineering practice) might result in rapid climate change once the geoengineering is stopped. With no time for natural adaptation to occur, such rapid heating up might have particularly severe impacts. Moreover, such screening techniques will not reduce ocean acidification or other impacts from increased CO_2 concentrations. Ocean acidification (discussed in Chapter 1) is a direct result of increasing concentrations of CO_2 in the atmosphere, independent of climate change or temperature. To the extent that a geoengineering strategy, for example sun-shading or aerosol scattering, does not reduce atmospheric GHG concentrations, it will not reduce ocean acidification.

QUESTIONS AND DISCUSSION

1.   What is your view of the concept of geoengineering? What other arguments for or against the intentional manipulation of the earth's climate do you find compelling?

2.   The prospect of geoengineering raises unique and difficult institutional challenges for the international system. No organization is tasked with taking an

integrated look and managing the unintended consequences of something as substantial as the geoengineering proposals being discussed. What do you think may be the legal implications of these geoengineering proposals? What type of regulatory or governance regime would you recommend, before allowing such geoengineering proposals to proceed? Should there be liability for any unintended consequences?

3. The geoengineering proposals gaining the most support currently are proposals to scatter sulfur or other aerosols in the upper atmosphere. The idea is grounded in strong evidence that aerosols emitted from major volcanic eruptions lead to a reduction in global temperatures. In fact, the volcanic eruption of Mt. Pinatubo is why for some years we thought the planet might face global cooling. We now know this was a temporary impact from the Pinatubo eruption.

Not only is aerosol scattering already tested in a sense, but it is also not very expensive to carry out. Some proposals would have aerosols added to jet fuel to be released as airplanes travel around the globe. Other proposals place the aerosols into electric utilities to be emitted along with their carbon emissions. Aerosols can also be sent into the atmosphere by rockets. The costs for this have been estimated from $500 million to $1 billion per year. Thus, the advantages of aerosol scattering are that it is relatively inexpensive and we are fairly certain it will lower global temperatures almost immediately. Alan Carlin, *Global Climate Change Control: Is There a Better Strategy than Reducing Greenhouse Gas Emissions?*, 155 U. Pa. L. Rev. 1401, 1459–63 (2007).

Aerosol scattering sounds too good to be true, and it likely is. Major concerns have emerged. First, aerosol scattering cools the planet by reflecting sunlight away from the earth's surface, but it does not reduce GHG concentrations. It would do nothing to reduce ocean acidification, which is caused by GHG concentrations. Also, aerosols fall out of the atmosphere relatively quickly and must be replenished annually. Like all geoengineering proposals, the unintended consequences are likely substantial. In the case of aerosol scattering, evidence suggests that the aerosol emissions from volcanoes also lead to significant changes in micro-climates, including drier conditions and increased droughts. *See* Kevin E. Trenberth & Aiguo Dai, *Effects of Mount Pinatubo Volcanic Eruption on the Hydrological Cycle as an Analog of Geoengineering*, Geophys. Res. Lett., Vol. 34, L15702 (Aug. 1, 2007).

The relative feasibility and low cost of aerosol scattering also raises specific types of issues. Either large private sector actors or individual governments could afford to finance aerosol scattering on their own. What would happen if the climate impact on Russia's far north became too acute? What would stop Russia from unilaterally deciding to launch aerosols into the atmosphere? What kind of governance structure would you want in place? Do you think we have the international laws and institutions to prevent or restrict Russia? What types of restrictions would you like to see?

4. Private companies might also promote geoengineering and indeed this has happened with ocean fertilization. In 1999 to test ocean fertilization, an international research team dumped over 8,600 kilograms of iron into the ocean off the coast of Tasmania. One month later, the algae bloom could be seen from satellites and an estimated 3,000 tons of carbon were removed from the atmosphere to the sea. Margaret Munro, *Ironing Out Global Warming*, The National Post, A18 (Oct. 17, 2000); Phillip Boyd, et al, *A Mesoscale Phytoplankton Bloom in the Polar Southern Ocean Stimulated by Iron Fertilization*, Nature 695–702 (Oct. 12, 2000). Subsequently, three companies — Planktos and Climos in the United States and Ocean Nourishment in Australia — were created with the goal of sequestering massive amounts of carbon through ocean fertilization, which would be financed by the sale of emission reduction credits in the carbon market under the Kyoto

Protocol. Planktos' plans in 2007 for a major pilot project off the coast of the Galapagos sparked significant opposition from environmental groups and the U.S. government. But it also showed the potential loopholes that existed in regulating such an activity in the high seas. The United States had no jurisdiction over the activity, and the International Maritime Organization's Conventions to prevent high seas dumping of wastes arguably didn't apply because the iron filings weren't "waste" — the activity was just a form of aquaculture, argued the companies. The iron filings were fertilizers and the crop was plankton and sequestration. Both the International Maritime Organization and the Convention on Biological Diversity have expressed their opposition to the concept of commercial-scale ocean fertilization, but this has not deterred the companies. *See* Chapter 10, Section III (discussing the Convention on Biological Diversity) and Section IV (discussing the International Maritime Organization). Although Planktos ultimately ran out of money, Climos has reportedly received $3.5 million in venture capital investments to continue pilot testing iron fertilization. *See* Martin LaMonica, *Ocean Fertilization firm Climos gains financial backing*, http://news.cnet.com, Mar. 5, 2008; Rachel Petkewitch, *Fertilizing The Ocean With Iron*, CHEM & ENG.NEWS, Vol. 86, No. 12, at 30 (Mar. 31, 2008). For more on Climos, visit their website at http://www.climos.com/.

5.   As suggested above, a comprehensive international legal framework for geoengineering does not yet exist. The climate regime does not speak of geoengineering directly, but it does clearly set down some relevant parameters. The objective of the climate regime is written in terms of the stabilization of GHG concentrations in the atmosphere, and not more generally in preventing climate change. *See* UNFCCC, art. 2. As a result, we would not expect the climate regime to treat all geoengineering proposals the same. Those geoengineering techniques that screen solar radiation and do not address atmospheric concentrations of GHGs would not fall within the ambit of the climate regime. Ocean fertilization and other sequestration efforts, on the other hand, which are designed to reduce CO_2 concentrations, would fall within the regime.

The regime clearly contemplates providing credit for at least some sequestration efforts. Net changes of a country's emissions under the regime include any changes due to the enhancement of sinks, although this is currently limited to changes in land-use and forest projects. Similarly, credits for sinks under the Clean Development Mechanism (CDM) are limited to land-use and forest-related projects. Thus, proponents of ocean fertilization will likely require some changes in the current regime to receive carbon credits under the climate regime. Before such changes are made, significant technical issues regarding verification and validation will have to be resolved. Given the climate regime's current broad approach to sinks and given the effort that continues to go into measuring and verifying carbon sequestration, the technical issues for ocean fertilization may not be insurmountable. Certainly, the private sector firms believe ocean fertilization has a commercial future. Consider their business plan again after reading how the climate regime treats sequestration from forest activities. *See* Chapter 7.

6.   Geoengineering proposals aimed at screening the sun (or shading the earth) would arguably be a form of environmental modification covered by the Convention on the Prohibition of Military or Any Other Hostile Use of Environmental Modification Techniques, signed May 18, 1977, *reprinted in* 16 I.L.M. 88 (Jan. 1977) [hereinafter ENMOD Convention]. The primary purpose of the ENMOD Convention is to prohibit military or hostile use of such techniques, but in so doing it clearly contemplates their peaceful use. Indeed, the ENMOD Convention states that Parties "shall not hinder the use of environmental modification techniques for peaceful purposes. . . . " The Convention clearly makes environmental modification techniques a focus of international law and may implicitly at least be viewed as

prohibiting the unilateral use of environmental modification techniques. In this regard, Parties to the Convention "undertake to facilitate, and have the right to participate in, the fullest possible exchange of scientific and technological information on the use of environmental modification techniques for peaceful purposes." What are the implications of a finding that geoengineering should be a focus of international law?

7.   Geoengineering proposals that assume specific use of outer space may also fall under the Outer Space Conventions. *See* Treaty on Principles Governing the Activities of States in the Exploration and Use of Outer Space, Including the Moon and Other Celestial Bodies, done January 27, 1967, 610 U.N.T.S. 205(1967), *reprinted in* 6 I.L.M. 386 (1967); Agreement Governing the Activities of States on the Moon and Other Celestial Bodies, done Dec. 5, 1979. Under these treaties, outer space is the common heritage of humankind and must be managed for peaceful purposes for the benefit of all humanity. Scientific studies of space must avoid adverse environmental impacts on Earth, and any State is internationally liable for any damage caused by articles launched from their territory. How could geoengineering proposals lead to claims of damage on Earth? Would States participating in geoengineering to change the climate be more susceptible to liability claims than States that have changed the climate indirectly through burning fossil fuels?

8.   Lawyers, even international lawyers, find it difficult to talk about "managing the planet" because we know how inadequate our legal institutions are for effective, democratic, and fair planetary management. Planetary management presumes "world government" — impossible, even if desirable. But the technical manipulation of the planet is becoming more realistic. Climate change, itself, is essentially accidental geoengineering, and now the question is whether we need to *intentionally* re-engineer the climate to manage our way out of the mess. If scientists tell us it is technologically and economically feasible to geoengineer the planet, then should we not also evaluate our institutional and legal structures to determine whether they are able to manage such geoengineering? Or should ethical considerations prevent us from going down the geoengineering path? Is such manipulation of the planet more like building a dam to control river flows, which we consider open to reasonable debate, or more like human cloning, which we have essentially prohibited as spiritually and ethically suspect?

Chapter 4

THE UNITED NATIONS FRAMEWORK CONVENTION ON CLIMATE CHANGE

I. AN INTRODUCTION TO INTERNATIONAL TREATIES

Climate change is inherently a global issue. Not only are the impacts of climate change felt by all countries, but greenhouse gas emissions mix in the atmosphere evenly and contribute to global climate change the same no matter where on the planet they are emitted. Even if one (or several) countries stopped emitting all of their greenhouse gases, those countries would neither solve the problem of climate change nor prevent impacts to their countries from the rest of the world's emissions. For these reasons, solving climate change requires international cooperation.

International cooperation can be both formal and informal. The most important and dominant form of cooperation in the climate context is clearly the negotiation of binding treaties — the UN Framework Convention on Climate Change (UNFCCC or Framework Convention), which established an institutional framework for addressing climate change, and the Kyoto Protocol, which imposed binding emission limitations on developed countries. These are discussed in this Chapter and Chapter 5, respectively. Other treaties may also relate to climate change and those are discussed in Chapter 10. Beyond treaties, other less formal forms of cooperation exist and may be just as important to solving climate change. Thus, pronouncements of sustainable energy goals by the G-8, regional agreements to adopt sustainable energy policies, or action-oriented partnerships to implement climate-friendly research or transfer renewable energy technology are all examples of the many international initiatives aimed at addressing climate change.

International law has its own unique processes for lawmaking. As compared to national law-making with its strong legislatures to pass laws, robust executive agencies to implement the laws, and independent courts to enforce the law, the international law-making system is far less developed. Under the principles of international law, each State is independent and sovereign. No supra-national legislature exists with the power to create laws applicable to the entire world, nor is there a supra-national administrative structure to implement international laws, nor a supra-national court with mandatory jurisdiction to interpret and enforce international law. (Although there is a "World Court," the International Court of Justice (ICJ) lacks both mandatory jurisdiction and the power to enforce its judgments). Moreover, the subjects of international law (States) are also the lawmakers, who can easily defeat the application of the law by refusing or withdrawing consent.

Given how jealously each country protects its own sovereignty and self interest, it is perhaps not surprising that international law is tightly circumscribed. In traditional public international law, all sources of law emanate either explicitly or implicitly from a State's consent to the rule. An international lawyer's general task is thus to look for evidence of consent to prove that international law on a particular subject exists with respect to a particular State. The most widely recognized definition of the sources of international law comes from the agreement creating the ICJ, which is the primary judicial organ of the United Nations and plays a leading role in identifying and developing international law. Article 38(1) of the ICJ Statute identifies the four traditional sources of international law that the Court applies. According to Article 38(1):

> The Court, whose function is to decide in accordance with international law such disputes as are submitted to it, shall apply:
>
> (a) international conventions, whether general or particular, establishing rules expressly recognized by the contesting states;
>
> (b) international custom, as evidence of a general practice accepted as law;
>
> (c) the general principles of law recognized by civilized nations; and
>
> (d) . . . judicial decisions and the teachings of the most highly qualified publicists of the various nations, as subsidiary means for the determi-

nation of rules of law.

The most important source of international law in the climate change field is clearly treaties. Both the UNFCCC and the Kyoto Protocol are treaties, and there are many bilateral and regional treaties aimed for example at enhancing research on climate change or promoting transfers of climate-friendly technology. The following excerpt provides a general introduction to treaties as a source of international law.

DAVID HUNTER, JAMES SALZMAN & DURWOOD ZAELKE, INTERNATIONAL ENVIRONMENTAL LAW AND POLICY
301–09 (3d ed. 2007)*

A. Treaties

1. Definition of a Treaty

Article 2.1(a) of the Vienna Convention [on the Law of Treaties] defines a "treaty" as "an international agreement concluded between States in written form and governed by international law, whether embodied in a single instrument or in two or more related instruments and whatever its particular designation." This definition, of course, is somewhat circular: a treaty is an instrument governed by international law. A more useful definition might be that a treaty is any instrument between two or more States that fulfills the requirements for valid treaties set out in the Vienna Convention itself. Note that the instrument need not be called a treaty; it can be called an agreement, convention, pact, covenant or virtually any other name. A treaty is a contract between States and, just as with commercial contracts, what is important is the manifest intent of the parties — in this case States — to be bound by their agreement. It is the obligatory character of the terms of a treaty, not its nominal designation, that determines whether a binding rule of international law has been created.

The only formal requirement is that there be a writing. While States may undertake binding international agreements without concluding a written instrument, the Vienna Convention does not govern such agreements, although they may be governed by general principles of international law. Nor does it govern agreements between State and non-State actors, or agreements entirely among non-State actors. This limitation is made explicit in Article 1 of the Convention, which states that "The present Convention applies to treaties between States." This provision reflects the traditional view that non-State actors can be neither subjects nor authors of international law. Because the ICJ has now recognized the international personality of certain international organizations, a second Vienna Convention was negotiated to govern agreements among these organizations or between an international organization and a State. Vienna Convention on the Law of Treaties Between States and International Organizations or Between International Organizations, 25 I.L.M. 543 (March 21, 1986). Agreements between States and private individuals, organizations or corporations are not governed by international law, but by the law of contracts — either as applied in the territory of the contracting State or as otherwise specified in the contract itself. Aside from these requirements, however, the only limitation on the scope, form or subject matter of a treaty is that the terms of the treaty must

---

not violate a peremptory norm of international law. This restriction is roughly analogous to domestic laws that prohibit contracts made for illegal purposes.

The Vienna Convention does not distinguish between the various forms that a treaty may take, such as multilateral or bilateral, nor the diverse legal functions that they perform. . . . Most treaties, particularly bilateral treaties, are much like contracts, creating legal obligations that are relatively narrow in scope and strictly limited to the parties involved in the negotiations. Some multilateral treaties, however, are considered to be "law-making" treaties in that they create general norms for future conduct. Almost like international legislation, these "law-making" treaties are more broadly applicable and are open even to States that did not participate in the negotiations. Although in principle binding only on the parties, in some cases these treaties may codify and develop customary law or general principles. The . . . UN Convention on the Law of the Sea, for example, both codified existing customary international law and catalyzed the further development and "crystallization" of customary international law. * * *

2. The Treaty-Making Process

Just as there is no prescribed form for treaties, neither is there a prescribed process for initiating the treaty-making process or for negotiating a treaty. . . . [Nonetheless,] four basic steps are inherent in the conclusion of any international agreement: 1) identification of needs and goals; 2) negotiation; 3) adoption and signature; and 4) ratification. Even after these steps are completed, treaties must be implemented, monitored for compliance, enforced, and, if necessary, modified or amended. For now, however, we will focus on treaty creation. . . .

a. Identification of Needs and Goals

Before an international agreement can be concluded, certain preliminary steps must be taken. The first step, of course, is that the need for action must be discovered — someone must conduct the research and synthesize the data that demonstrate, for example, that a particular substance harms the environment or a particular species is in danger of extinction. This seems an obvious point, yet it bears mention for two reasons. First, many important environmental problems have gone unaddressed for years or even decades before someone accumulated sufficient data to convince the international community to address them. Second, because there is neither a prescribed process for identifying treaty needs, nor any group of actors vested with primary responsibility for doing so, need identification has proven an important strategy for non-State actors to influence the international environmental law-making process. * * *

b. Negotiation

[I]n recent decades, a somewhat standardized negotiating process has emerged. Negotiations may be initiated by individual States; more often, however, a State will recommend that an international organization, particularly the United Nations General Assembly (UNGA) or the UN Economic and Social Council (ECOSOC), establish a committee or convene an international conference to consider a particular issue. The host organization will then organize preparatory committees, working groups of technical and legal experts, scientific symposia and preliminary conferences. Increasingly, the organizing body will invite, or at least accept, comments from NGOs, scientific unions and other private groups. During these informal discussions, information is disseminated, the preliminary positions of interested States are established, the parameters of a possible agreement are narrowed, and the slow process of building international consensus begins.

This process of informal exchange may continue for years before a conference of plenipotentiaries (representatives with the authority to approve an international agreement on behalf of their respective governments) is convened. In the interim, the host government or organization, or some other qualified international body, will develop a draft convention to serve as the basis for discussions at the plenipotentiary conference. Generally, draft conventions are prepared with significant participation by the interested parties, and many disagreements among States are likely to be ironed out before the final conference convenes. At the plenipotentiary conference, delegates will seek to resolve their remaining disputes, and produce a final, authoritative version of the treaty, an "authentic text". [For a description of the negotiating process for the UNFCCC, see Section II.] * * *

c. Adoption and Authentication

Before the negotiation phase of the treaty-making process can be concluded, and the treaty "opened" for signature and ratification, the text must be adopted. Unless a State has specified otherwise, adoption of a treaty text does not make the treaty binding on that State. Adoption simply signifies the participants' agreement that the text of the treaty is acceptable in principle. * * * Because it does not create binding obligations for any State, a treaty can be adopted at an international conference with less than full consensus. [Article 9 of the Vienna Convention, for example, requires only a two-thirds majority vote for adoption of treaty text negotiated at an international conference. This lack of the need for full consensus partly explains why oil-rich countries could not block final negotiation of the UNFCCC.] Nonetheless, many international conferences will still seek widespread agreement among participating States to ensure that States will sign and ratify the treaty once it is adopted.

When the final draft of the treaty has been adopted, it must be "authenticated" by a representative of each State, generally by signing the treaty. Authentication identifies the treaty text as the actual text the negotiating States agreed to and establishes that each signing State agrees in principle to its terms. Although there are exceptions, a State's signature on a treaty generally does not signify its consent to be bound by the treaty. By signing a treaty, however, a State does agree to refrain from acts "which would defeat the object and purpose of the treaty," until it has made clear its intention not to become a treaty party. [See Vienna Convention, Article 18.]

d. Ratification and Accession

As should already be clear, a State will be bound by the terms of a treaty only if it takes affirmative steps to demonstrate its consent to be bound. . . . . The means of expressing consent to a treaty include: "signature, exchange of instruments constituting a treaty, ratification, acceptance, approval or accession, or by any other means if so agreed." Vienna Convention, Article 11. With respect to multilateral agreements, the most common method of demonstrating consent is by ratification. Ratification is any authoritative act whereby a State declares to the international community that it considers itself bound by a treaty. Multilateral environmental treaties are typically ratified by depositing an "instrument of ratification" with the United Nations or another designated depositary organization. Only States that participated in the negotiation of, and subsequently signed, the treaty may bind themselves through ratification. Other States often may join by accession. Accession simply means that a State declares its intent to be bound by the treaty. The procedures for acceding often are specified in the treaty. Vienna Convention, Article 15.

In many States, a treaty must be approved through domestic political processes before the treaty can be ratified. In the United States, for example, [all treaties must be approved by] the Senate. . . . The Senate may make its consent contingent on certain changes or exceptions. If these cannot be accommodated through reservations to the treaty, the United States must renegotiate the treaty to incorporate the changes or the treaty cannot be ratified.

Because of the Senate ratification process in the United States, and similar processes in other States — which are a matter of domestic law, and not international law — months or even years may pass between the time a State signs a treaty and the time it ratifies. . . . And until the treaty is ratified and has entered into force, the State's obligations with respect to the treaty are limited.
* * *

f. Entry Into Force

The parties to a treaty are not bound by its terms until the treaty enters into force. No treaty enters into force for a specific State until that State ratifies the treaty according to its national law, deposits its instrument of ratification with the appropriate depository, and any conditions for the treaty's entry into force have been satisfied. If the treaty makes no special provision for entry into force, it enters into force as soon as all the negotiating States have ratified. More often, however, the treaty will provide for its entry into force after a certain minimum number of States have ratified, even if other States have not. Vienna Convention, Article 24. The treaty then becomes effective as between the ratifying States.

QUESTIONS AND DISCUSSION

1. The Vienna Convention on the Law of Treaties, cited throughout the above discussion of treaties, governs the major aspects of treaties, including negotiation, conclusion, interpretation, amendment, and termination. Even for non-Parties to the Vienna Convention, the Convention is widely accepted as a codification of customary international law. For example, although the United States has never ratified the Vienna Convention, the U.S. Department of State has declared that the principles expressed in the Convention are binding upon the United States. Thus, questions of how to interpret the climate treaties or other treaties that may affect climate change — for example, trade treaties or other environmental treaties — will be illuminated by reference to the Vienna Convention.

2. *Custom.* In addition to treaty-making, international law is also created through the customary practice of States, where such practice is done under the belief that it is required by law. Custom requires that you both articulate a rule of law, and then prove that State's behave in such a way that demonstrates they accept the rule as law. Thus, a customary rule of law is binding on all nations, "not because it was prescribed by any superior power, but because it has been generally accepted as a rule of conduct." *The Scotia*, 14 Wall. 170, 187 (1876) *quoted in The Paquete Habana*, 175 U.S. 677, 20 S. Ct. 290 (1900). To prove that a customary norm exists, a court must establish two things (1) state practice — that states generally follow the rule in practice; and (2) *opinio juris* — that states act in accordance with the rule from a sense of legal obligation to do so. Once a custom is established it becomes binding on all States, regardless of whether those States follow the practice or express a belief that the practice was law. However, a State may exclude itself from the obligations of a particular customary rule by persistent conduct exhibiting an unwillingness to be bound by the rule or a refusal to recognize it as law. RESTATEMENT OF FOREIGN RELATIONS LAW OF THE UNITED STATES, section 102, comment b. Customary law in the context of climate change is discussed further in Chapter 8.

   3. ***General Principles, Judicial Opinions and the Writing of Publicists.*** In addition to treaties and customary norms, general principles of civilized nations, judicial decisions and the writings of publicists are also listed under Article 38 of the ICJ Statute as sources of international law. These sources of law are more controversial and are generally viewed as supplementary sources to the primary sources of treaties or custom. Thus, courts may look to divine "general principles" of law accepted by the majority of the world's great legal systems in order to fill in gaps in custom or treaty law, but are necessary to decide a case. Courts may also look to earlier decisions of the ICJ or other international tribunals for guidance, but in general the concept of *stare decisis* does not prevail in international law. Nonetheless, ICJ cases are regularly cited in subsequent cases and are clearly considered to be authoritative statements of international law — if not strictly binding on the future behavior of states. Finally, courts may also look to the writings of publicists, such as the International Law Association or the International Law Commission, to discern what the law is or what it should be — but they have no independent binding force.

   4.   Under the principle of State responsibility, States are generally responsible for breaches of their obligations under international law. Thus, states can be held responsible for violations of international legal obligations — either treaties like the climate treaties or customary obligations such as the obligation to cooperate or the obligation not to "harm" the environment of other States. State responsibility is the set of rules that define the consequences of a State's breach of international law. According to the International Law Commission, States responsible for an internationally wrongful act must:

   (1)   make restitution (i.e., to re-establish the situation which existed before the wrongful act was committed),

   (2)   compensate for any damage caused, and

   (3)   give satisfaction (for example acknowledge the breach, express regret, or formally apologize).

See ILC Draft Articles, *supra*, at paras 34–37. *See* International Law Commission, Draft Articles on the Responsibility of States for Internationally Wrongful Acts, Arts. 1–2, in Report of the International Law Commission on the Work of its Fifty-third Session, UN GAOR, 56th Sess., Supp. No. 10, at 43, UN Doc. A/56/10 (2001). State responsibility in the climate context is discussed again in Chapter 8.

   5.   In recent years, many commentators have noted the rise of so-called "soft law" as an important innovation in international law-making, particularly in new fields like international environmental law. Soft law reflects a more flexible process for developing and testing new non-binding norms before states accept them as binding upon the international community. The soft law process is more dynamic and democratic than traditional lawmaking, embracing a broader range of societal actors (including scientific organizations, academic specialists, NGOs, and industry). It has become a critical part of the consensus-building that is ultimately needed to negotiate environmental treaties. The distinction between "soft" and "hard" law is not precise; it is possible to have "soft" obligations in "hard" law form, for example in a framework treaty, such as the "Principles" found in Article 3 of the UNFCCC. *See generally* Pierre-Marie Dupuy, *Soft Law and the International Law* *of the Environment*, 12 MICH. J. INT'L L. 420, 420–35 (1991).

The most important soft law document in international environmental law is the 1992 *Rio Declaration on Environment and Development*, UN DOC A/CONF.151/ 5/Rev. 1, Principle 2, June 13, 1992, *reprinted in* 31 I.L.M. 874 (1992). Although not binding law, the *Rio Declaration* is recognized as an important reflection of the political consensus around international environmental principles as of 1992. The *Rio Declaration* is probably most noteworthy for its integration of development concerns with environmental protection and its resulting affirmation of the concept of sustainable development. Because of the careful North-South compromises found within so many of the *Rio Declaration's* principles, it is often viewed as the starting point for discussions concerning specific global environmental issues, including climate change.

II.   THE GLOBAL POLITICS OF CLIMATE CHANGE

Now that we have discussed the general way in which international treaties are negotiated, we will turn to the negotiations of the UN Framework Convention on Climate Change (UNFCCC). This section provides the geopolitical context for those negotiations. Section III describes the negotiations, themselves, and Section IV summarizes the Framework Convention.

A.   National and Regional Contributions to Climate Change

From the perspective of international cooperation, it is important to understand which countries are the primary contributors to climate change and how current trends will change this overtime. Not surprisingly, the United States and other industrialized countries are the primary contributors to the increase in atmospheric concentrations of greenhouse gases. As shown in Table 4-1, with only 4% of the world's population, the United States now emits an estimated 20% of the world's greenhouse gases each year. China is next at approximately 15%, with the twenty-five countries of the European Union collectively third at 14%. Developed countries and developing countries as a group are nearly equal with 52% and 48% respectively of current emissions. Emission growth rates are highest in developing countries, however, and they will soon represent a majority of all emissions. By most estimates, China passed the United States in total annual emissions in 2007. *See* Table 4-1, adapted from Kevin A. Baumert, et. al, *Navigating the Numbers*, Fig. 3.1 (World Resources Institute, 2005).

Table 4-1: Top GHG Emitting Countries Carbon Equivalent Emissions for Six GHGs: CO_2, CH_4, N_2O, HFCs, PFCs, SF_6				
Country (ranked by total emissions)	$MtCO_2$ Equivalent	% of World GHGs	Tons eCO_2/ capita	Rank for Emissions per Capita
1. United States	6928	20.6	24.5	6
2. China	4938	14.7	3.9	99
3. EU-25	4725	14.0	10.5	37
4. Russia	1915	5.7	13.2	22
5. India	1884	5.6	1.9	140
6. Japan	1317	3.9	10.4	39

Table 4-1: Top GHG Emitting Countries Carbon Equivalent Emissions for Six GHGs: CO_2, CH_4, N_2O, HFCs, PFCs, SF_6				
Country (ranked by total emissions)	MtCO$_2$ Equivalent	% of World GHGs	Tons eCO$_2$/ capita	Rank for Emissions per Capita
7. Germany	1009	3.0	12.3	27
8. Brazil	851	2.5	5.0	83
9. Canada	680	2.0	22.1	7
10. UK	654	1.9	11.1	32
11. Italy	531	1.6	9.2	48
12. South Korea	521	1.5	11.1	33
13. France	513	1.5	8.7	50
14. Mexico	512	1.5	5.2	76
15. Indonesia	503	1.5	2.4	122
16. Australia	491	1.5	25.6	4
17. Ukraine	482	1.4	9.7	44
18. Iran	480	1.4	7.5	60
19. South Africa	417	1.2	9.5	46
20. Spain	381	1.1	9.4	47

Aggregate totals, however, represent only part of the picture, because they depend on both population size and the level of industrial activity. Per capita emissions may provide a more equitable comparison of a region's contribution to climate change. The United States has the 6th highest per capita emissions — 24.5 metric tons of CO_2 equivalent emissions per person per year (trailing only four oil-rich middle eastern countries and Australia). By contrast, per capita emissions in India and China were 1.9 and 3.9 tons per year, ranking them 140th and 99th, respectively. A representative review of other countries also demonstrates the significantly disproportionate amount of per capita emissions contributed by the United States — Germany 12.3 metric tons, Japan 10.4, Canada 22.1, Indonesia 2.4, and Brazil 5.0. *See* Kevin A. Baumert, Timothy Herzog & Jonathan Pershing, *Navigating the Numbers: Greenhouse Gas Data and International Climate Policy*, Fig. 3.1, (World Resources Institute, 2005).

B.   Global Divides in Climate Politics

At times, divisions between blocs of countries over the negotiations of the climate change regime have been as intense as virtually any issues outside the realm of war and national security. The most consistent divisions have included a split between the North and South; between various countries within the G-77, for example differences between low-lying states (the victims of climate change) and the oil-producing states (primary beneficiaries of fossil fuel dependence); and between the European Union and the United States. Although these divisions have ebbed and flowed, most of these tensions have persisted throughout the negotiation of the climate regime beginning before the 1992 Earth Summit (the United Nations Conference on Environment and Development, held in Rio de Janeiro) and continuing through to today's negotiations over a post-Kyoto agreement.

1. *The North-South Split*

As in many global environmental issues, differences exist between the industrialized and developing countries, particularly because consumption of fossil fuels (and thus the release of greenhouse gases) is viewed as inextricably linked to economic development. Developing countries have not yet accepted any requirement through the climate change negotiations that will slow their economic growth. The international concern with climate change arguably distracts attention from the more pressing national environmental concerns of urban air pollution and lack of safe drinking water. Moreover, by most measures, industrialized countries are primarily responsible for the current composition of the atmosphere. Although China now ranks as the highest annual emitter of greenhouse gases, its *per capita* emissions are less than 1/5th that of the United States. India's per capita emissions are less than 1/10th of the United States. Furthermore, given that most greenhouse gases remain in the atmosphere for decades or more, the industrialized countries have "banked" an even greater percentage of the total responsibility for global warming. The United States, for example, has contributed an estimated 30% of all CO_2 emissions from fossil fuel use over the past century (although its percentage contribution decreases as other GHGs are included). China's aggregate contribution to current concentrations of greenhouse gases, and thus to current climate change problems are a fraction of the historical contribution of the United States. To developing countries, this historical, aggregate contribution is compelling justification for requiring industrialized countries to make significant reductions in greenhouse gas emissions first. On the other hand, emissions are growing fastest in the global South, and no effort to curb climate change solely by reducing emissions in industrialized countries will be successful.

The North-South debate will likely come to a head in the near future. Most developing countries are already parties to the UNFCCC and the Kyoto Protocol, but the next step of that process is to assign developing country parties some targets and timetables as part of the post-Kyoto negotiations. The terms for setting developing country targets and timetables are not clear and will be fiercely debated — even assuming developed countries offer a recipe similar to that of the Montreal Protocol process, involving a package of financial support, technology transfer, and flexibility in setting and achieving targets and timetables. Particularly if the United States remains outside of any binding targets, however, the largest and fastest growing countries — countries like China, Brazil, and India — are unlikely to agree to any binding targets in the near future.

2. *Divisions within the G-77*

Developing countries cannot be viewed uniformly, however, as they are far from unified in their positions on climate change. Not surprisingly, the group of countries taking the strongest position on climate change are those countries that have the most to lose — small island States and those States like Bangladesh that are barely above sea level. About thirty small island states have joined the Alliance of Small Island States (AOSIS), which promotes the interests of island nations in the climate change negotiations. According to the current best estimates of sea level rise, some island States like the Maldives will be totally inundated by the middle part of the next century. AOSIS originally supported a 20% cut in GHG emissions from 1990 levels for all industrialized countries by the year 2005. AOSIS has also sought a funding mechanism for countries most vulnerable to climate change. Countries would have access to these funds as compensation for damages incurred due to sea-level rise and increased storm activity, as well as to finance climate change adaptation strategies, such as the construction of sea-walls.

At the opposite extreme are the oil-producing nations, which have not supported any specific measures to curb global warming. Some delegates believe the OPEC nations joined the UNFCCC simply to block any international agreement that would reduce global oil demand. The OPEC countries also promote a compensation fund, but their version of the fund would be used to reimburse oil-producing states for any financial losses incurred due to reduced oil demand (and prices) resulting from the climate change regime.

Brazil and the countries of the Amazon Basin as well as other heavily forested countries bring an additional perspective to climate negotiations. They see the focus of the industrialized countries on forest conservation and climate sinks as an effort to shift the responsibility and costs for responding to climate change to developing countries. Brazil objects to the "internationalization" of the Amazon as a sink under the UNFCCC. They particularly object to the U.S. and other industrialized countries using their countries as a merely something to absorb the wastes they put out. At the same time, many forest-rich countries recognize that the climate regime could provide significant financial support for forest conservation and management. They have recently proposed an ambitious program for the North to compensate forest-rich countries that slow their rate of deforestation.

---

3.   *The Persistent EU-U.S. Division*

Serious differences also exist within the industrialized world. The publicly articulated position of the United States has always been significantly weaker than that of the European Union. In addition, differences between the industrial sectors of Europe and the United States led to conflicts over which gases should be included and to what extent production of these gases should be restricted. The United States has always sought unlimited carbon trading and unrestricted credits for its substantial and growing forests. Europe has always sought the flexibility and cost-savings that would come with regional trading between countries within the European Union, but has sought limits to trading outside such regional blocs.

These differences came to a head in 2001, when the United States under newly elected President George W. Bush announced its unilateral renunciation of the Kyoto Protocol. Since then the policies of the two regions have diverged considerably, with the European Union supporting a multilateral response with clear targets and timetables under the Kyoto regime and the United States pursuing a foreign policy that engaged a relatively few countries on joint research, technology transfer, and investment.

The United States has not always been alone in its opposition to European climate policies. In most of the Kyoto Protocol parties, the non-EU heavy emitting countries — namely Japan, the United States, Canada, Australia and New Zealand (JUSCANZ) often negotiated as a bloc. What kept them together was the need for more flexible targets and strong trading mechanisms. Since the Kyoto negotiations these countries have not been a bloc. Only Australia joined the United States in refusing to ratify Kyoto, although Australia flipped its position and joined Kyoto in 2007. Canada, on the other hand, has ratified the Protocol, but announced again recently that it did not intend to comply fully with the binding commitments.

---

4.   *Special Situation of Countries in Economic Transition*

The industrialized countries of the former Soviet bloc brought slightly different concerns to the table than most other industrialized countries. Their economies, which had been among the most inefficient in the world, have undergone significant restructuring and transition since the collapse of the Soviet system. Production at many of the largest polluting factories came to a standstill due to severe economic conditions during the early 1990s. Their rates of GHG emissions were expected to remain well below their 1990 baseline year through the first reporting period (2008–2012). These countries were also facing a severe economic crisis and were hoping to receive funding from the climate regime, making them in this respect more like developing countries. During the Kyoto negotiations, these countries insisted on receiving sellable allowances for the difference between their actual emissions and the amount they are allowed to emit under the Protocol. Their position was ultimately accepted because countries like the United States saw this as a convenient mechanism for helping meet their own commitments through trading carbon allowances (discussed below).

QUESTIONS AND DISCUSSION

1.   At first glance, the demand by OPEC nations to be compensated for declines in demand of their oil products seems to turn the concept of compensation for damages on its head. We do not typically think about the need to compensate States for stopping production of something that international society has decided causes widespread harm. But is their position any different than the forest-rich countries asking for financial support to avoid deforestation? *See* Chapter 7. Is that not compensation for lost opportunities from developing the forests?

2.   The climate change negotiations place developing countries in an unusually powerful position. Unlike most other fields of international law, the cooperation of key developing countries is required for a successful climate change regime. For example, the World Trade Organization managed to operate successfully for many years without China's participation; the climate regime will clearly not be a success without China. Although the industrialized countries currently emit a majority of greenhouse gases, this is expected to change within the next decade. Without the cooperation of the developing countries, greenhouse gas reductions made in the North will not make a significant difference in the overall warming trend if the South does not eventually agree to some limitations as well. How should the South use this leverage? Should they use it with respect to issues of development?

III.   THE NEGOTIATIONS OF THE UN FRAMEWORK CONVENTION

Although climate change now grabs the headlines almost daily, it is not a new issue. Environmentalists and climatologists have known for some time that the build-up of atmospheric greenhouse gas concentrations was likely to lead to significant changes in global climate. International negotiations over climate change now date back more than twenty years, and during that time the science regarding climate change has only become clearer and the problem more urgent.

Given the high stakes involved in global climate negotiations and the widely divergent interests of various countries, it is no wonder that the climate regime is taking years to develop. Although at times the pace is maddeningly slow with significant backward steps (for example, the U.S. withdrawal of support for the Kyoto Protocol), international cooperation with respect to climate change has continued to march forward and promises to be even more significant in years to come. The chronology provided in Table 4-2, should help you to understand the development of the climate regime.

Table 4-2: Development of the Climate Change Regime

1979	World Meteorological Organization (WMO) convenes First World Climate Conference
1985	Scientific meeting in Villach, Austria, concludes it is "highly probable" that increasing concentrations of greenhouse gases will produce significant climate change."
1988	WMO and UNEP establish the IPCC
1988	Toronto Conference on the Changing Atmosphere issues a call for 20% reduction of carbon dioxide by 2005
1990	Second World Climate Conference recommends a framework climate change convention
1990	IPCC issues First Assessment Report predicting that business as usual would result in "unprecedented" warming.
1990	UN General Assembly establishes the Intergovernmental Negotiating Committee for a Framework Convention on Climate Change (FCCC)
1992	UN FCCC Signed at the Rio Earth Summit
1994	UN FCCC enters into force
1995	Berlin Mandate Agreed by the First Conference of Parties to the UN FCCC
1995	IPCC's Second Assessment concludes that human activities are changing the climate
1997	Kyoto Protocol is concluded
2000	IPCC's Third Assessment identifies discernible man-made effect on the environment
2001	President George W. Bush takes office and unilaterally withdraws from the Kyoto Protocol
2001	Europe, Japan, and the rest of the world agree to the Marrakesh Accords implementing the Kyoto Protocol
2005	Kyoto Protocol enters into force
2005	EU launches European Trading System, a continent-wide carbon trading system
2007	Fourth IPCC Assessment concludes that observed climate change is "very likely" caused by GHG emissions

2007	All countries agree to the Bali Plan of Action to agree to post 2012 commitments by 2009
2008	First four-year reporting period begins under the Kyoto Protocol
2009	President Obama takes office and announces that the U.S. will aim toward reducing GHG emissions 80% by 2050
2009	A new Post-Kyoto agreement?

A.   The Early Years: Building Support for an International Convention on Climate Change

The following excerpt describes some of the early years of negotiations leading up the Earth Summit's adoption of the UN Framework Convention on Climate Change:

DANIEL BODANSKY, THE UNITED NATIONS FRAMEWORK CONVENTION ON CLIMATE CHANGE: A COMMENTARY
8 Yale J. Int'l L. 451, 458–63 (1993)[*]

Although scientists have understood the general theory of greenhouse warming for more than a century, widespread concern emerged only in the last two decades. This resulted from several scientific developments. First, in the 1960s and 1970s atmospheric chemists conclusively established that concentrations of carbon dioxide were in fact increasing. Since 1958, when direct measurements first began, atmospheric carbon dioxide concentrations have risen from 315 ppm to more than 350 ppm today. Second, in the 1980s scientists began to focus on trace gases other than carbon dioxide that trap heat and contribute to the greenhouse effect, chief among them methane, nitrous oxide, and chlorofluorocarbons (CFCs). In 1985, the global warming effect of these gases was estimated to be roughly equal to the effect of carbon dioxide, indicating that the problem was twice as serious as previously believed.

Third, as computing power grew, climatic models became much more sophisticated and complex, increasing the credibility of global warming predictions. Models of the atmosphere must take into account many factors, including the heat-trapping characteristics of greenhouse gases, ocean and wind currents, soil moisture, the reflectivity of the Earth's atmosphere and surface to sunlight, and an array of feedback mechanisms. Early simulations of the atmosphere were very crude, and did not come close to approximating the complexity of atmospheric dynamics. The advent of supercomputers permitted the development of more realistic general circulation models, which represent the atmosphere in three dimensions and in greater spatial detail, and take better account of feedback mechanisms and ocean-atmosphere interactions. Although a high degree of uncertainty still exists, most climate scientists believe that general circulation models are now sufficiently reliable to provide a basis for policy decisions.

Finally, new studies in the 1980s indicated that the temperature record is broadly consistent with global warming forecasts. In the mid-twentieth century, such forecasts had had limited impact, given what appeared to be a cooling trend.

As recently as the mid-1970s, when a series of climatological disasters drew attention to the climate change issue, scientists were still split between "coolers" and "warmers," and some feared the onset of another ice age. Today, in contrast, a careful re-examination of the historical data has produced a general consensus that the Earth is warming. * * *

By 1985, these scientific developments had combined to make the theory of greenhouse warming more convincing and urgent. In October of that year, a scientific conference held in Villach, Austria concluded that "[a]lthough quantitative uncertainty in model results persists, it is highly probable that increasing concentration of the greenhouse gases will produce significant climatic change." The conference statement recommended that since "the understanding of the greenhouse question is sufficiently developed, scientists and policy-makers should begin an active collaboration to explore the effectiveness of alternative policies and adjustments."

However, whether scientific evidence alone would have been sufficient to spur the international community to action is questionable. Three additional factors catalyzed governmental and public interest in global warming and helped transform it from a scientific to a political issue. First, a number of scientists acted as promoters, publicizing the threat of greenhouse warming through conferences, reports, and personal contacts. The 1985 and 1987 Villach Conferences and the 1987 Bellagio Conference helped to consolidate the scientific consensus regarding global warming and to communicate that consensus to policymakers. Second, the discovery of the ozone hole in 1987, which dramatically demonstrated that human activities can indeed affect the global atmosphere, raised the prominence of atmospheric issues generally. Finally, the heat wave and drought of the summer of 1988 gave an enormous popular boost to greenhouse warming proponents. In June, the testimony of James Hansen, a NASA climate modeler, to the Senate Energy Committee on the greenhouse effect made front-page news. Although most scientists believed it was unproven whether the hot weather was due more to the greenhouse effect or to normal climate variability, the climate change issue had emerged politically, even prompting [the first] President Bush to address it during his election campaign. * * *

Just as concern about global warming was mounting, Canada sponsored an international conference in Toronto. The Conference on the Changing Atmosphere sought to bridge the gap between scientists and policymakers. More than 340 individuals from forty-six countries, including two heads of government, more than one hundred other government officials, and numerous scientists, industry representatives, and environmentalists, attended the conference. * * *

In many respects, the Toronto Conference Statement was the high water mark of policy declarations on global warming. On the one hand, although the conference was not officially governmental in nature (the government participants attended in their personal capacities), it had far more status and influence than other non-governmental meetings held before or since. In part, this was due to Canada's sponsorship and the substantial participation by high government officials, including the Prime Ministers of Canada and Norway. In part, the Toronto Conference came at the right time: it was an "event waiting to happen." On the other hand, because of its non-governmental character, the Toronto Conference Statement was not a negotiated document. It was drafted by a committee composed mostly of environmentalists and discussed in less than a day. Flush with the success of the Montreal Protocol, many participants did not fully appreciate the political difficulties of addressing the climate change issue. Moreover, as with many new environmental issues, environmental activists — who discovered and pushed the issue — had a head start, while opponents in industry and government took longer to mobilize. Following the Toronto Conference, the climate change issue continued to attract substantial attention. Increasingly, however, the discussions moved onto an inter-governmental track, where agreement proved more difficult to reach and conference statements became more carefully qualified. Indeed, as states became increasingly aware of the stakes and uncertainties involved in the climate question, even states that had initially supported a strong policy response became more cautious.

As you read the following excerpt from the Toronto Conference Statement consider how far (or not) international negotiations have advanced in the twenty years since this meeting. Consider, too, how much better off we would be in addressing climate change today, if governments had implemented the recommendations outlined in Toronto.

CONFERENCE STATEMENT, THE CHANGING ATMOSPHERE: IMPLICATIONS FOR GLOBAL SECURITY
(June 27–30, 1988), reprinted in 5 Am. U. Int'l L. & Pol'y 515 (1990)

1. Humanity is conducting an unintended, uncontrolled, globally pervasive experiment whose ultimate consequences could be second only to a global nuclear war. The Earth's atmosphere is being changed at an unprecedented rate by pollutants resulting from human activities, inefficient and wasteful fossil fuel use and the effects of rapid population growth in many regions. These changes represent a major threat to international security and are already having harmful consequences over many parts of the globe.

2. Far-reaching impacts will be caused by global warming and sea level rise, which are becoming increasingly evident as a result of continued growth in atmospheric concentrations of carbon dioxide and other greenhouse gases. Other major impacts are occurring from ozone-layer depletion resulting in increased damage from ultra-violet radiation. The best predictions available indicate potentially severe economic and social dislocation for present and future generations, which will worsen international tensions and increase risk of conflicts among and within nations. It is imperative to act now. * * *

5. The Conference called upon governments to work with urgency towards an Action Plan for the Protection of the Atmosphere. This should include an international framework convention while encouraging other standard-setting agreements along the way, as well as national legislation to provide for protection of the global atmosphere. The Conference also called upon governments to establish a World Atmosphere Fund financed in part by a levy on the fossil fuel consumption of industrialized countries to mobilize a substantial part of the resources needed for these measures. * * *

9. The Conference calls for urgent work on *an Action Plan for Protection of the Atmosphere*. This Action Plan, complemented by national action, should address the problems of climate warming, ozone layer depletion, long-range transport of toxic chemicals and acidification. * * *

21. In order to reduce the risks of future global warming, energy policies must be designed to reduce emissions of CO_2 and other trace gases. Stabilizing atmospheric concentrations of CO_2 is an imperative goal. It is currently estimated to require reductions of more than 50% from present emission levels. Energy research and development budgets must be massively directed to low and non-CO_2

emitting energy options and to studies undertaken to further refine the target reductions.

22. An initial global goal should be to reduce CO_2 emissions by approximately 20 percent of 1988 levels by the year 2005. Clearly the industrialized nations have a responsibility to lead the way, both through their national energy policies and their bilateral and multilateral assistance arrangements. About one-half of this reduction would be sought from energy efficiency and other conservations measures. The other half should be effected by modifications in supplies.

23. Targets for energy efficiency improvements should be directly related to reductions in CO_2 and other greenhouse gases. A challenging target would be to achieve the 10 percent energy efficiency improvements by 2005. Improving energy efficiency is not precisely the same as reducing total carbon emissions and the detailed policies will not all be familiar ones. A detailed study of the systems implications of this target should be made. Equally, targets for energy supply should also be directly related to reductions in CO_2 and other greenhouse gases. As with efficiency, a challenging target would again be to achieve the 10 percent energy supply improvements by 2005. * * *

25. Apart from efficiency measures, the desired reduction will require (i) switching to lower CO_2 emitting fuels, (ii) reviewing strategies for the implementation of renewable energy especially advanced biomass conversion technologies; (iii) revisiting the nuclear power option, which lost credibility due to problems related to nuclear safety, radioactive wastes, and nuclear weapons proliferation. If these problems can be solved, through improved engineering designs and institutional arrangements, nuclear power could have a role to play in lowering CO_2 emissions.

26. Negotiations on ways to achieve the above mentioned reactions should be initiated now.

27. Systems must be initiated to encourage, review and approve major new projects for energy efficiency.

28. There must be vigorous application of existing technologies to reduce (i) emissions of acidifying substances to reach the critical load that the environment can bear; (ii) substances which are precursors of tropospheric ozone; and (iii) other non-CO_2 greenhouse gases, in addition to gains made through reduction of fossil fuel combustion.

29. Products should be labeled to allow consumers to judge the extent and nature of contamination of the atmosphere which arises from the manufacture and use of the product. * * *

30. Initiate the development of a comprehensive global convention as a framework for protocols on the protection of the atmosphere. The convention should emphasize such key elements as the free international exchange of information and support of research and monitoring, and should provide a framework for specific protocols for addressing particular issues, taking into account existing international law. This should be vigorously pursued . . . with a view to having the principles and components of such a convention ready for consideration at the inter-governmental Conference on Sustainable Development in 1992. These activities should in no way impede simultaneous national, bilateral and regional actions and agreements to deal with specific problems such as acidification and greenhouse gases.

QUESTIONS AND DISCUSSION

1. The drafters of the Toronto Statement envisioned a global framework on the atmosphere analogous to the Law of the Sea Convention. Separate protocols would then be adopted to address different atmospheric issues, including climate change, acid rain and the dispersal of persistent organic pollutants. The ozone depletion regime would also have been brought into this institutional arrangement. Instead, today we have the Montreal Protocol regime, the climate regime and the Stockholm Convention on Persistent Organic Pollutants (POPs), all with separate institutional and policy structures. What advantages, if any, do you think the Toronto Statement's approach would have had? What disadvantages?

2. What specific goals for addressing climate change were identified in the 1988 Toronto Statement? How many of these climate-related goals have been achieved? Note, for example, that where the Conference participants called for a 20 percent reduction of CO_2 emissions by 2005, we have actually seen an increase of global CO_2 emissions of more than 20 percent. How much harder does this make today's challenge for addressing climate change?

3. As you read the UNFCCC and the subsequent Kyoto Protocol, consider what elements of the Toronto Conference Statement are reflected in the ultimate approach taken by the governments? Does this suggest a more general role for more informal conferences in the development of international treaties? Can you think of other examples where unofficial conferences have helped to build political will for policy change?

4. As it became increasingly clear that there would be an international negotiation to address climate change, both UNEP and the WMO were vying to be the lead agency to host the negotiations. In December 1990, however, the U.N. General Assembly opted for an International Negotiating Committee (INC) under its own auspices with both UNEP and WMO playing supportive roles. As suggested by the excerpt below, the U.N. General Assembly Resolution also set a firm schedule for the negotiations with the goal of having a proposed convention ready to sign at the 1992 UN Conference on Environment and Development (the Earth Summit).

The General Assembly, . . .

1. Decides to establish a single intergovernmental negotiating process under the auspices of the General Assembly, supported by the United Nations Environment Programme and the World Meteorological Organization, for the preparation by an Intergovernmental Negotiating Committee of an effective framework convention on climate change, containing appropriate commitments, and any related instruments as might be agreed upon, taking into account proposals that may be submitted by States participating in the negotiating process, the work of the Intergovernmental Panel on Climate Change and the results achieved at international meetings on the subject, including the Second World Climate Conference; . . .

2. Decides that the International Negotiating Committee should be open to all States Member to the United Nations or members of the specialized agencies with the participation of observers in accordance with the established practice of the General Assembly; . . .

4. Decides that the first negotiating session should be held in Washington, D.C, in February 1991 and that . . . further meetings should be held at Geneva and at Nairobi, in May/June, September and November/December 1991 and, as appropriate, between January and June 1992; . . .

6. *Decides* that maximum duration of each of the negotiating sessions should be two weeks;

7. *Considers* that the negotiations for the preparation of an effective framework convention on climate change, containing appropriate commitments, and any related legal instruments as might be agreed upon should be completed prior to the United Nations Conference on Environment and Development in June 1992 and opened for signature during the Conference.

Protection of Global Climate for Present and Future Generations of Mankind, U.N.G.A. Res. 45/212 (Dec. 21, 1990). What substantive parameters did the General Assembly place on the negotiations of the climate change convention? For example, how did the General Assembly settle the debate at the time of whether the convention should be a framework convention only, or one with specific emission reduction targets? Whatever substantive guidance the Resolution did or did not provide, it did unmistakably commit the governments to a short timetable for negotiations (less than 18 months). As you read the following section consider how this timetable affects the outcome of the negotiations.

B.   Negotiations of the UNFCCC

After the end of the Cold War, the United Nations and many world leaders were looking to the Earth Summit to launch a major global partnership for sustainable development. The UN organizers of the Summit hoped that one of the centerpieces of that partnership for the conference would be a convention to address climate change. The 1990 UN General Assembly Resolution committed negotiators to this time frame, even if the ultimate substance of the convention remained uncertain. The following is a summary of the negotiations immediately leading up to the 1992 Framework Convention on Climate Change, written by Donald Goldberg, the first NGO observer on the U.S. delegation to the climate negotiations.

DONALD GOLDBERG, AS THE WORLD BURNS: NEGOTIATING THE FRAMEWORK CONVENTION ON CLIMATE CHANGE
5 Geo. Int'l Envtl. L. Rev. 239, 244-51 (1993)[*]

By the time of the opening session of the Climate Convention negotiations [in February 1991], a number of countries had already committed to reducing GHG emissions. The European Community (EC) had committed to returning its joint CO_2 emissions to 1990 levels by the year 2000. The EC . . . also promised to provide financial assistance to help developing countries respond to climate change. Its position was based on individual country commitments by Germany, Denmark, Switzerland, Sweden, Australia, Austria, Norway, and Canada. Many of these commitments went beyond stabilization at 1990 levels or promised deeper CO_2 cuts in later years.

Japan had previously stated that its "emissions of CO_2 should be stabilized on a per capita basis in the year 2000 and beyond at about the same level as in 1990," and "the emission of methane should not exceed the present [1990] level." In the opening round, Japan called for negotiation first of a basic framework, but suggested the convention might also contain concrete measures to be taken by the parties.

The Group of 77 developing countries (actually composed of 127 developing countries) made a point of the fact that 75% of energy-related CO_2 emissions are attributable to industrialized countries, but acknowledged, nevertheless, that developing countries have a responsibility not to follow the same path. They called for industrialized countries to transfer environmentally sound technologies to developing countries on preferential and non-commercial terms to help developing countries avoid the environmentally destructive aspects of development. They also called for the creation of a differentiated regime under the climate convention for developing countries, along the lines of the Montreal Protocol.

The United States, as expected, rejected targets and timetables, instead advocating a "no regrets" policy of actions that would be taken only insofar as they produced benefits having nothing to do with global warming. For example, the U.S. might promote the use of a new energy technology that would have global warming benefits if it could be shown to be more cost-effective, or to reduce urban pollution, but not merely for the purpose of reducing GHG emissions. The U.S. also supported further research to resolve uncertainties and a "comprehensive approach" to reducing emissions, which would take into account not just CO_2, but all greenhouse gases.

The United States attempted to deflect some of the criticism aimed at it during the first negotiating round by releasing a White House "Action Agenda," intended to demonstrate that the U.S. was acting responsibly with regard to its GHG emissions. The Action Agenda purported to show that U.S. policies would result in GHG emissions in the year 2000 at or below 1987 levels. Unlike the European plan, however, the U.S. approach contemplated significant increases in domestic CO_2 emissions. To achieve its year 2000 target, the U.S. plan relied heavily on the phase-out of CFCs, thought to account for approximately 11% of radiative forcing. Both the Europeans and environmentalists objected that the U.S. plan was disingenuous, since CFCs were already scheduled to be phased out under the Montreal Protocol on Substances That Deplete the Ozone Layer, and were not included in other countries' emissions reduction plans. * * *

The first round ended with the U.S. and the EC deadlocked on the question of whether the agreement should include firm commitments to reduce greenhouse gases. To break the deadlock, the U.K. Environment Secretary, Michael Heseltine, traveled to the United States shortly before the start of the second round with an offer of compromise. The EC would accept the U.S.'s comprehensive approach — excluding gases already controlled by the Montreal Protocol — if the U.S. would accept targets and timetables. The U.S. declined, and little additional progress was made in the second round. In hopes of moving the process incrementally forward, Japan, with the support of the U.K. and France, floated an informal paper proposing a "pledge and review" approach, under which parties would pledge to undertake actions to reduce emissions, and an international body would review the implementation of those pledges. Environmentalists were quick to lampoon this approach as "hedge and retreat."

Supporters of pledge and review — stung by environmentalists' criticism — backed away from the proposal at the next negotiating round, in Nairobi in September 1991, and reaffirmed their support for stabilization of CO_2 emissions at 1990 levels by 2000. The EC also called for a treaty objective to stabilize greenhouse gases at levels that would "prevent dangerous anthropogenic interference with climate" within a timeframe that would "allow ecosystems to adapt naturally." The U.S. continued to resist any binding commitments on targets and timetables.

But cracks in the U.S. position were beginning to appear. In December 1991, when White House Chief-of-Staff John Sununu — the Administration's strongest opponent of greenhouse gas controls — resigned, the White House began to review its position. EPA Director William Reilly argued that stabilization tied to population growth was achievable, based on EPA's innovative "Green" Programs. By the start of the last negotiating round, in February 1992, Administration officials were reporting that a change in U.S. policy was in the making. The first complete draft text was introduced at the fourth negotiation, held in Geneva in December 1991. The draft was over 110 pages long, and most of the text was bracketed, indicating that the text was controversial and had not yet been approved by the full Committee. Nevertheless, its introduction signaled that the Committee might yet complete its work in time for the Rio Earth Summit in June.
* * *

Meanwhile, it was becoming clear that negotiators would never resolve all the issues under discussion in time for Rio, and a wholesale jettisoning of bracketed provisions began. As time grew short, negotiators agreed to return to the UN at the end of April, to try to finish their work. During the interim the INC Chairman, in consultation with a number of countries, substantially revised the text, paring it down to a third of its previous size.

The Chairman's text was in many respects a fait accompli — there was simply not enough time to make large-scale revisions. Ground-breaking approaches to dispute settlement, a financial mechanism, technology transfer, amendments, annexes, protocols, and entry into force provisions contained in earlier drafts were dropped in favor of formulations that in some respects actually marked a retreat from previous international environmental agreements.

The commitment section of the Chairman's text acknowledged the fact that a legally binding commitment to reduce greenhouse gases was beyond reach, if the U.S. was to be a signatory. It reflected a consensus of the other industrial countries that an agreement would not be meaningful without the participation of the U.S. The EC and Japan mildly protested the weak commitment section, but made clear they would not hold out for stronger language. The Chairman blamed the weak and ambiguous GHG commitment language squarely on the U.S.

Had the U.S. not taken such a hard line on commitments, the Convention would no doubt have been stronger. But the difference a more constructive U.S. approach might have made should not be overstated. Not every industrialized country other than the U.S. was prepared to make commitments to deep cuts in CO_2 or other GHG emissions. Indeed, the best the EC could offer was to stabilize its emissions at 1990 levels by the year 2000. Japan's commitment was even weaker, though it probably would have accepted the EC target. Nevertheless, a firm commitment to any targets and timetables would have been a significant improvement . . .

QUESTIONS AND DISCUSSION

1. It is easy to forget that actual people negotiate international environmental agreements and that the final outcomes may in fact reflect specific choices or ideas of individuals. In the case of the UNFCCC, many observers attribute the ability of the countries to reach consensus to Chairman Ripert's deft handling of the final negotiations. Consider the following account by one of India's lead negotiators:

It was remarkable that it proved possible to bridge this chasm in ten days of negotiations during the resumed fifth session in New York. How did it prove possible to achieve this in a few days when efforts over the past fifteen months had yielded such limited and disappointing results?

Two new factors enabled the finalization of the Convention apart from the high political priority which delegations placed on completing a Convention before the UNCED meeting in Rio that was scheduled for June. First, at long last, the North arrived at a common formulation of its commitment concerning emissions. Second, connected with this breakthrough and at the initiative of the chairman, a new negotiating procedure was adopted to hasten an agreement.

On the very first day of the final round, Chairman Ripert announced his intention to seek a speedy conclusion of the negotiations on the basis of a Working Paper that he would present to the plenary. The first installment of the draft was distributed immediately following his announcement and the second installment — covering the crucial areas of "commitments" and "mechanisms for transfer of finance and technology" — was made available on the following day, after finalization of a common U.S.-EC formulation on their commitments regarding emissions. The chairman explained that the Working Papers were based on the Revised Text prepared at the conclusion of the previous round and that he had used his best judgment to produce a clean text without brackets. In another major procedural change, it was accepted, at the chairman's suggestion, that negotiations on the basis of this text should initially be confined to an "Enlarged" Bureau. This included about two dozen countries . . . .

The chairman explained in the Enlarged Bureau that plenary meetings were unnecessary at this stage since the formulations in his text were not new and had been debated in earlier sessions of the plenary. * * *

Negotiations within the Enlarged Bureau commenced on the basis of the chairman's Working Paper. The chairman argued that the formulation on emission commitments of developed countries, which had emerged after very difficult and delicate negotiations, should not be reopened. The Indian delegate expressed the view that the paper as a whole was under negotiation, including the new formulation on the emissions commitments of developed countries. In the end, India did not press for action on this proposal, in light of bearing in mind also the importance of securing a consensus Convention. The EU-U.S. formulation itself was later revised slightly by its authors. It was finally incorporated into the Convention in this revised form, with only a few very minor changes.

Vigorous negotiations took place in the Enlarged Bureau over the next several days, often lasting until the early hours of the morning. There were also frequent consultations among delegations outside the Bureau. Efforts were made by group representatives to inform and consult countries not represented in the Enlarged Bureau, but these efforts could not keep pace with the rapid development of text within the Bureau. After agreement had been reached within the Enlarged Bureau, texts were circulated to the plenary for wider discussion and approval. But, since some of the crucial elements relating to "Commitments" were finalized only on the final day, a majority of delegations saw the full text of the convention just hours before its adoption by consensus. The discussion did not significantly alter the text emerging from the Enlarged Bureau.

Chandrashekhar Dasgupta, *The Climate Change Negotiations*, *in* IRVING M. MINTZER, ET AL., NEGOTIATING CLIMATE CHANGE: THE INSIDE STORY OF THE RIO CONVENTION 129, 142–44(1994). Chairman Ripert took two "tried and true" steps to facilitate the last negotiating session: (1) he introduced a "chairman's" draft and (2) he reduced the number of parties involved in the principle negotiations by creating an "Enlarged Bureau" of just 24 countries. Can you see why these steps may be necessary to reach consensus? Can you see why they may breed resentment among many of the parties?

2.   As you read the description of the negotiations leading up to the UNFCCC, consider the extent to which they match the general model outlined in Section I. Can you identify the different stages in the negotiating process? What entity, for example, hosted or organized the negotiations? Also, review the Convention itself and determine how it addresses issues such as ratification, accession, and entry into force.

IV. THE UNITED NATIONS FRAMEWORK CONVENTION ON CLIMATE CHANGE

Lacking in any binding commitments to reduce greenhouse gases, the resulting UNFCCC was somewhat disappointing to environmentalists. It nonetheless marked significant progress in the international commitment to address climate change. Most importantly, the Convention established the policy and institutional framework for the continued implementation and progressive development of the regime into the future. Indeed, more than fifteen years later, the UNFCCC still embodies the basic framework for the international response to climate change. The Kyoto Protocol nests within the UNFCCC, supplementing it with binding commitments but not replacing most of its provisions. Moreover, although the United States has never ratified the Kyoto Protocol, the United States remains a party to the UNFCCC and is bound by whatever obligations it contains. As the world moves beyond Kyoto and looks for ways to gain commitments from developing countries and the United States, the open-ended flexibility of the UNFCCC may prove to be critical in shaping the post-Kyoto consensus.

PROBLEM EXERCISE: READING THE UNFCCC

The following sections describe different aspects of the UNFCCC, including the basic principles, objective, commitments, and institutional arrangements. Before reading these sections, we recommend that you review the Convention, reproduced as Appendix I, to gain some understanding of the Convention in its entirety. In addition, work with the treaty by finding answers to the following questions in its text:

(1)   Why are some countries included in Annex I not included in Annex II? What is the difference in their commitments under the Convention?

(2)   How many parties does it take to amend the Convention? Do amendments apply to parties who do not vote for the amendment?

(3)   What is the difference between a "reservoir" and a "sink" in the Convention? What, if anything, are Parties supposed to do with respect to their reservoirs and sinks?

(4)   Find at least four decisions or actions the Conference of the Parties is supposed to make at their first meeting. When does the first meeting of the Conference of the Parties take place?

(5)   What requirements to actually reduce greenhouse gas emissions, if any, are developed countries required to take under the Convention?

(6)   What steps can one Party take to force a resolution of any dispute it has under the Convention with another Party?

A.   Selected Principles Underlying the UNFCCC

Many international environmental agreements include general principles, typically in the preamble of the convention. The UNFCCC is no exception, but it also repeats some of the principles, such as state sovereignty, common but differentiated responsibilities, and the precautionary principle, among others, in the main text of the Convention in Article 3. The debate over the "general principles" provision is explained in the following excerpt:

DANIEL BODANSKY, THE UNITED NATIONS FRAMEWORK CONVENTION ON CLIMATE CHANGE: A COMMENTARY
8 Yale J. Int'l L. 451, 501-02 (1993)*

Most developing countries supported the inclusion of an article on general principles, arguing that such an article would serve as the lodestar or compass to guide the parties in implementing and developing the Convention. Some even argued that the Convention should include only principles and leave commitments to future protocols. In contrast, developed countries generally questioned the inclusion of a principles article. The United States in particular insistently opposed its inclusion, arguing that its legal status was unclear. The United States maintained that if the principles merely stated the intentions of the parties or provided a context for interpreting the Convention's commitments, they served the traditional functions of the preamble, and placing them in the operative part of the Convention would be unnecessary and even misleading. On the other hand, the United States argued, if the principles were themselves commitments, they should be designated in the Convention as such.

The U.S. reasoning, however, fails to take into account that principles may serve a third function, different from those of either preambles or commitments: unlike preambular paragraphs, principles embody legal standards, but the standards they contain are more general than commitments and do not specify particular actions. As Ronald Dworkin explains, both legal principles and legal rules:

> point to particular decisions about legal obligation in particular circum-stances, but they differ in the character of the direction they give. Rules are applicable in an all-or-nothing fashion. . . . [A principle] states a reason that argues in one direction, but does not necessitate a particular decision. . . . All that is meant, when we say that a particular principle is a principle of our law, is that the principle is one which officials must take into account, if it is relevant, as a consideration inclining in one way or another.

Because of the open-ended character of principles, a government cannot be certain of where they will eventually lead. This may explain why the United States, which is deeply skeptical of the international lawmaking process, opposed a principles article and preferred more clearly enunciated commitments.

Although developing countries ultimately prevailed in obtaining the inclusion of a principles article, the United States successfully pressed for several changes to Article 3 to reduce its potential legal implications. First, a chapeau was added, specifying that the principles are to "guide" the parties in their actions to achieve the objectives of the Convention and to implement its provisions. Second, the term "states" was replaced by "Parties." Finally, the term "inter alia" was added to the chapeau to indicate that the parties may take into account principles other than those listed in Article 3 in implementing the Convention. These three modifications were intended to forestall arguments that the principles in Article 3 are part of customary international law and bind states generally. Instead, the principles clearly apply only to the parties and only in relation to the Convention, not as general law.

Developing countries also had to compromise on the substance of the principles. In some cases, Western opposition led to the transfer of proposed principles to the preamble; in other cases, principles proposed by developing countries were not included in the final text at all. In general, Western countries were able to define the principles more narrowly than in the parallel negotiations on the Rio Declaration, possibly because the INC was a less politicized, less public forum than the UNCED Preparatory Committee.

As suggested by the above, the legal status and effect of these principles may not be clear, but they are still important to the climate regime. Some of the principles shaped the Kyoto negotiations and continue to influence the long-term global dialogue around climate change. Indeed, it is difficult to fully understand current negotiations of the Post-Kyoto regime without some understanding of these general principles. Some of these key principles are described in the sections below.

QUESTIONS AND DISCUSSION

1.   What general concepts or principles of international environmental law are found in the UNFCCC? What purpose does including such broad principles serve?

2.   In general, preambles to conventions are not considered binding, but provide guidance regarding the negotiating history, purpose, and general approach of the treaty. Review the preamble to the UNFCCC reproduced in Appendix I. Can you see how the preamble to the UNFCCC reflects many of the compromises and tensions between industrialized and developing countries that are further reflected throughout the body of the Convention? What other functions do you think the preamble serves?

---

1.   *State Sovereignty*

Lurking behind the scenes in any treaty negotiation is the pre-eminence of state sovereignty in international law. In fact, any discussion of international law must begin with the concept of state sovereignty. States have the sovereign right to govern the affairs that occur within their territorial areas. State sovereignty in the legal sense thus signifies independence — that is, the right to exercise, within a portion of the globe and to the exclusion of other States, the functions of a State such as the exercise of jurisdiction and enforcement of laws over persons and resources therein. Among a State's sovereign authority is the authority to consent (or not) to the creation of international law that binds them.

The entire international legal system is thus premised on each State having control over the activities that occur within their jurisdiction. This necessarily includes the authority to choose whether to control the emission of greenhouse gases, to slow the rate of deforestation or to take any other action implicated by climate change. On the other hand, just the act of negotiating a treaty necessarily means that countries are willing to cede some of their sovereignty to the international community — presumably in the furtherance of some greater mutual benefit. For this reason, the UNFCCC's preamble reaffirms "the principle of sovereignty of States in international cooperation to address climate change" and recalls the basic relationship of State sovereignty to environmental harm that:

> States have, in accordance with the Charter of the United Nations and the principles of international law, the sovereign right to exploit their own resources pursuant to their own environmental and developmental policies, and the responsibility to ensure that activities within their jurisdiction or control do not cause damage to the environment of other States or of areas beyond the limits of national jurisdiction,

UNFCCC, Preamble; *see also* Stockholm Declaration on the Human Environment, Principle 21 (1972); Rio Declaration on Environment and Development, Principle 2 (1992). In some ways, the entire UNFCCC and the subsequent Kyoto Protocol can be seen as the articulation of how states balance their sovereign rights to follow their own development path (i.e., to burn fossil fuels) with their responsibility under international law not to harm areas beyond the limits of their jurisdiction (i.e., the global atmosphere's role in regulating climate). The question facing the negotiators of the UNFCCC was how to characterize conceptually the international nature of climate change in a way that could explain why states should relinquish some of their sovereignty.

But neither State sovereignty generally, nor the State's right to development, is absolute. State sovereignty is limited first and foremost by the territorial extent of the State. Thus, while States may enjoy the right to follow their own development and environment policies inside their territorial jurisdictions, their sovereign powers do not typically reach beyond those State territories — either to the territory of one State or to areas beyond the jurisdiction of any State. Thus, as described by international scholar Ian Brownlie:

> In spatial terms the law knows four types of regime: territorial sovereignty, territory not subject to the sovereignty of any state or states and which possesses a status of its own (trust territories, for example), the *res nullius*, and the *res communis*. Territorial sovereignty extends principally over land territory, the territorial sea appurtenant to the land, and the seabed and subsoil of the territorial sea. The concept of territory includes islands, islets, rocks, and reefs. A *res nullius* consists of the same subject-matter legally susceptible to acquisition by states but not as yet placed under territorial sovereignty. The *res communis*, consisting of the high seas which for present purposes include exclusive economic zones and also outer space, is not capable of being placed under state sovereignty. In accordance with customary international law and the dictates of conve-

nience, the airspace above and subsoil beneath state territory, the *res nullius*, and the *res communis* are included in each category.

Ian Brownlie, Principles of Public International Law 105 (6th ed. 2003). Thus territorial sovereignty extends to the geographic borders of the country and to the airspace overhead (generally defined as the height that can be reached by ordinary manned flight), while outer space is considered *res communis* and is beyond the reach of any State's sovereignty. Changes to the Earth's atmosphere, including increases in greenhouse gas emissions, fall somewhere in between.

As Professors Patricia Birnie and Alan Boyle put it:

> The atmosphere is not a distinct category in international law. Because it consists of a fluctuating and dynamic airmass, it cannot be equated with airspace, which, above land, is simply a spatial dimension subject to the sovereignty of the subjacent states. But this overlap with territorial sovereignty also means that the atmosphere cannot be treated as an area of common property beyond the jurisdiction of any state, comparable in this sense to the high seas. The alternative possibility of regarding it as a shared resource is relevant in situations of bilateral or regional trans-boundary air pollution, affecting other states. . . . UNEP has referred to 'air-sheds' as examples of shared natural resources, and this status is consistent with regional approaches to the control and regulation of transboundary air pollution. . . .

> The shared resources concept is of less use, however, in relation to global atmospheric issues such as ozone depletion or climate change. What is needed here is a legal concept which recognizes the unity of the global atmosphere and the common interest of all states in its protection. The traditional category of common property, is, as we have seen, an inadequate one for this purpose. The same objection applies to the use of 'common heritage' in this context, with the additional difficulty that this concept has so far been applied only to mineral resources of the deep seabed and outer space and that its legal status remains controversial. The atmosphere is clearly not outer space, despite the difficulty of defining the boundaries of that area. * * *

> Significantly, common heritage was not employed in the 1985 Vienna Convention for the Protection of the Ozone Layer, or in the 1992 Convention on Climate Change (UNFCCC). The 1985 Convention defines the 'ozone layer' as 'the layer of atmospheric ozone above the planetary boundary layer'. This does not mean that the ozone layer is either legally or physically part of outer space. It remains part of the atmosphere, and falls partly into areas of common property, and partly into areas of national sovereignty. One purpose of the Convention's definition is to indicate that it is concerned with stratospheric ozone, and not with low-level ozone, which . . . is an air pollutant. More importantly, however, the definition treats the whole stratospheric ozone layer as a global unity, without reference to legal concepts of sovereignty, shared resources, or common property. It points to the emergence of a new status for the global atmosphere, which makes it appropriate to view the ozone layer as part of a common resource or common interest, regardless of who enjoys sovereignty over the airspace which it occupies.

> The same conclusion can also be drawn from UN General Assembly resolution 43/53 which declares that global climate change is 'the common concern of mankind'. This phraseology was the outcome of a political compromise over Malta's initial proposal to treat the global climate as the

common heritage of mankind. . . . What it suggests is that the global climate should have a status comparable to the ozone layer, and that the totality of the global atmosphere can now properly be regarded as the 'common concern of mankind'. By approaching the issues from this global perspective, the UN has recognized both the artificiality of territorial boundaries in this context, and the inadequacy of treating global climate change in the same way as transboundary air pollution, for which regional or bilateral solutions remain more appropriate.

[T]he status of 'common concern' is primarily significant in indicating the common legal interest of all states in protecting the global atmosphere, whether directly injured or not, and in enforcing rules concerning its protection. While it is not clear that a General Assembly resolution alone is sufficient to confer this status, the 1985 Ozone Convention and the 1992 UNFCCC unquestionably do so.

PATRICIA BIRNIE & ALAN BOYLE, INTERNATIONAL LAW & ENVIRONMENTAL PROTECTION, 502–503 (2d ed. 2004). Thus, the answer to why climate change required international cooperation came in the form of the principle of "common concern," described further in the next section.

QUESTIONS AND DISCUSSION

1. Although States enjoy sovereign rights to follow their own environment and development policies *within* their jurisdiction, such sovereign rights are limited by reciprocal obligations vis-à-vis other equally sovereign states. Foremost among these "good neighborly" international obligations is the obligation for States to cooperate generally with their neighbors in addressing international issues:

States have the duty to co-operate with one another, irrespective of the differences in their political, economic and social systems, in the various spheres of international relations, in order to maintain international peace and security and to promote international economic stability and progress, the general welfare of nations and international co-operation free from discrimination based on such differences.

Declaration of Principles on International Law Concerning Friendly Relations and Cooperation Among States in Accordance with the Charter of the United Nations, U.N.G.A. Res. 2625 (Oct. 24, 1970), *reprinted in* 9 I.L.M. 1292 (1972). The UNFCCC's preamble recognized that the duty to cooperate extends to the climate context, with Parties "*Acknowledging* that the global nature of climate change calls for the widest possible cooperation by all countries and their participation in an effective and appropriate international response."

The duty to cooperate is widely viewed as a binding principle of customary international law. The precise contours of the principle are not completely certain, however. Although the duty to cooperate probably includes a duty to provide notice and to consult in good faith with neighboring countries or other countries affected by a state's activities, the principle does not require the countries to reach an agreement.

2. As suggested by the UNFCCC's preamble, state sovereignty is also limited by the principle that each State has an obligation not to harm the sovereign interests of other States, including their environment. The obligation not to cause environmental harm has its roots in the common law principle of *sic utere tuo ut alienum non laedus* (i.e., do not use your property to harm another). In the international law context, States are under a general obligation not to use their territory, or to allow others to use their territory, in a way that can harm the interests of another State. The obligation not to cause harm to other States was extended to environmental damage as early as 1941 in the well-known *Trail Smelter* arbitration (involving a U.S. action brought against Canada for damages caused by air pollution from a Canadian smelter). The principle was subsequently restated in both Principle 21 of the 1972 *Stockholm Declaration on the Human Environment* and Article 2 of the 1992 *Rio Declaration.*

The obligation not to harm another state is clearly meant to limit the extent of each State's sovereign right to develop in any way it wants. The principle is now generally considered a binding principle of international law. The contours of this principle, probably more than any other, will determine the legal rights and responsibilities in any international dispute brought by states harmed from climate change. To apply the principle, however, requires detailed answers to several significant issues. How should the balance between sovereignty and transboundary harm be struck in the climate context? Should all damage be prohibited? What level of harm should trigger the obligation? To what standard of care should the State be held? What activities should be considered under the "jurisdiction and control" of a State? What remedies should be available to States who suffer such damage? These questions are discussed in Chapter 8.

----

2.   *Common Concern of Humankind*

The very first paragraphs of the UNFCCC preamble introduce the concept of common concern and explain exactly what it is that the Parties are concerned about:

> *The Parties,*
>
> *Acknowledging* that change in the Earth's climate and its adverse effects are a common concern of humankind,
>
> *Concerned* that human activities have been substantially increasing the atmospheric concentrations of greenhouse gases, that these increases enhance the natural greenhouse effect, and that this will result on average in an additional warming of the Earth's surface and atmosphere and may adversely affect natural ecosystems and humankind,

The prominence of the principle reveals its importance to the conceptual foundation of the Convention; the concept of common concern is the explanation that justifies why States are required to cooperate in an international agreement to address climate change. The principle of common concern is thus in tension with the principle of State sovereignty. Prior to the negotiations of the Climate Change Convention, for example, States were assumed to have complete control and discretion with respect to air pollution emissions that did not directly cause transboundary environmental impacts on a neighboring country. After the emergence of the concept of common concern, States are expected to cede some of their sovereignty to the pursuit of collective action to address recognized "common concerns," including climate change. The UNFCCC invokes the concept of common concern as the theoretical basis for why States must constrain their sovereign right to continue changing the composition of the atmosphere.

Although the role that the principle plays — legitimizing international cooperation in the climate context is clear — the substantive meaning of the principle is not.

In general, the principle of common concern does not yet independently imply any specific legal obligation beyond cooperation. But this too was important for the negotiations of the climate regime. The parties did not want to accept any status for the atmosphere that connoted any legal meaning, or put another way that prejudged or preordained the outcome of the negotiations. An area (the atmosphere) or an activity (emitting greenhouse gases) that could be considered "of common concern" necessitated international cooperation without necessitating any specific international legal rights or responsibilities. The negotiators could write on a clean slate.

QUESTIONS AND DISCUSSION

1. The concept of common concern should not be confused with common heritage of humankind. The common heritage principle applies to the high seas, outer space, the moon, and possibly Antarctica. Areas that are considered part of humanity's common heritage are governed by four principles: (1) non-appropriation — no State could colonize or appropriate the resources in the global commons; (2) joint management — common heritage resources should be managed jointly by the international community; (3) shared benefits — benefits from these commons areas should be shared among all humanity; and (4) non-militarization — the global commons should be reserved for peaceful purposes. *See, e.g., Treaty on Principles Governing the Activities of States in the Exploration and Use of Outer Space, Including the Moon and Other Celestial Bodies, done* January 27, 1967, 610 U.N.T.S. 205 (1967), *reprinted in* 6 I.L.M. 386 (1967) [referred to as the *1967 Outer Space Treaty*]; *Agreement Governing the Activities of States on the Moon and Other Celestial Bodies, done* Dec. 5, 1979 [referred to as the *1979 Moon Treaty*].

In the first proposal addressing climate change at the U.N. General Assembly, Malta (who had championed the concept of common heritage in the law of the sea) also proposed a "Declaration proclaiming climate as part of the common heritage of mankind." The General Assembly subsequently adopted a resolution recognizing the urgency of the climate change issues, but refused to characterize the principle of the common heritage of mankind — opting instead for a more ambiguous reference to climate as a "common concern of mankind."

Common heritage was thus specifically considered and rejected by the negotiators of the UNFCCC (as well as the Convention on Biological Diversity negotiated at the same time). Developing countries rejected application of the common heritage principle in these conventions because they thought it would subject their natural resources to too much international control. Developed countries rejected common heritage because of the implication that benefits would have to be shared from these resources. Common concern was an acceptable compromise, in part because it did not carry with it any preconceived notions of benefit sharing or of joint management. As noted above, the constructive ambiguity of the concept of common concern provided the framework for international climate negotiations (and thus for the abdication of some aspects of State sovereignty), while still allowing full flexibility in negotiating the specific contours of the climate regime.

2. What is meant in the Birnie and Boyle excerpt above by reference to the "global unity" of the atmosphere? How is this related to the international legal status of an issue like climate change? Can you see why neither State sovereignty nor *res communis* neatly fits the issue of climate change?

3.   How are the duty to cooperate and the principle of common concern related? Is the principle of common concern just a label placed on an issue where global cooperation is necessary? Does it suggest more than a procedural obligation to negotiate?

4.   The concept of common concern extends to climate change and the conservation of biological diversity. It may extend more generally to the concept of sustainable development. A growing consensus is emerging that because the planet is ecologically interdependent, humanity may have a collective interest in many activities that take place, or resources that are located, wholly within State boundaries. All international environmental treaties and instruments arguably reflect a growing acceptance that protecting the environment and achieving sustainable development generally are "common concerns of humanity." Article 3 of the *IUCN Draft Covenant on Environment and Development*, states that the "global environment is a common concern of humanity." The commentary to the *Draft Covenant* offers the following explanation:

> Article 3 states the basis upon which the international community at all levels can and must take joint and separate action to protect the environment. It is based on the scientific reality that harm to the environment resulting from human activities (e.g., depletion of the stratospheric ozone layer, climate modification, and the erosion of biological diversity) adversely affect all humanity. World-wide cooperation to take concerted action is necessary to avoid environmental disaster. This implies acceptance of both the right and the duty of the international community as a whole to have concern for the global environment. * * *

> The conclusion that the global environment is a matter of "common concern" implies that it can no longer be considered as solely within the domestic jurisdiction of states due to its global importance and consequences for all. It also expresses a shift from classical treaty-making notions of reciprocity and material advantage, to action in the long-term interests of humanity.

> The concept of "common concern" is not new and has been applied in other fields. It forms the basis for international laws relating to human rights, humanitarian relief and international labour relations. Those obligations are now recognized as obligations *erga omnes*, owed by all States to the entire international community.

> The inter-dependence of the world's ecosystems and the severity of current environmental problems call for global solutions to most, if not all, environmental problems, thereby justifying designation of the global environment as a matter of "common concern".

IUCN, *Draft Covenant on Environment and Development*, 32 (1995). The IUCN Draft Covenant has never been adopted by the governments, but reflects a progressive perspective on the future development of environmental principles such as common concern. *See also* the New Delhi Declaration of Principles of International Law Relating to Sustainable Development (2002) (declaration at the 70th Conference of the International Law Association). Do you think the global environment or sustainable development generally has become a matter of common concern? Would such a finding require that all States achieve sustainable development? Consider this question again after the following discussion of sustainable development as a principle in the UNFCCC.

3.   *The Right to Sustainable Development*

Although State sovereignty has many aspects, perhaps the most important for understanding the international law of climate change is a State's sovereign right to follow its own development path. A State's sovereign right to control its own development has been a high priority of developing countries ever since the post-colonial period, and they see it as a fundamental principle for achieving their aspirations of greater economic independence and a more equitable international economic order. To ensure the right to development, developing countries jealously protect the right of all countries to choose their own development path — even if that means emitting greenhouse gases and contributing to global climate change. In this way, the continued ability of developing countries to emit greenhouse gases is tied not only to economic growth but to the right to development and its associated goals of economic justice and poverty alleviation. *See generally* Declaration on the Right to Development, UNGA Res. No. 41/128, Annex (Dec. 4, 1986).

Given the scope and tremendous potential impact of the climate regime on the economy, it should come as no surprise that the climate negotiations were permeated with concerns and dialogue about development impact. One cannot separate an effort to regulate emissions from fossil fuels (the primary energy source for industrialization) or to improve the management of forests or land-use practices from questions of development. Moreover, the UNFCCC was also to be signed at the Earth Summit where the discussion about development was taking a marked shift from one of a "right to development" to a right to "sustainable development." The UNFCCC reflects this shift:

> The Parties have a right to, and should, promote sustainable develop-ment. Policies and measures to protect the climate system against human-induced change should be appropriate for the specific conditions of each Party and should be integrated with national development programmes, taking into account that economic development is essential for adopting measures to address climate change.

UNFCCC, Article 3.4. Although relatively non-objectionable in its ultimate word-ing, the negotiation of the provision reflected the conflict at the time between developing and developed countries over the right to development:

> Initially, developing countries pressed for inclusion of a principle recognizing that "the right to development is an inalienable human right" and that "[a]ll peoples have an equal right in matters relating to reasonable living standards." Meanwhile, some developed countries wished to include a principle that states have a duty to aim at sustainable development. Both proposals raised serious problems for some delegations. On the one hand, the United States has long refused to accept the "right to development" as advanced in the human rights field, on the grounds that it is vague and could be used by developing countries to demand financial assistance from developed countries. In contrast, developing countries, fearing that "sus-tainability" might become a new conditionality on financial assistance and ultimately inhibit their development plans, have traditionally expressed doubts about the concept of "sustainable development."
>
> The Convention finesses both issues by stating that "the Parties have a right to, and should, promote sustainable development," thereby address-ing the concerns of both developing and developed countries. The Conven-tion speaks of a "right," thereby satisfying developing countries, but the

right relates to the "promotion of sustainable development," which is arguably different from the traditional "right to development" . . . . With respect to sustainable development, paragraph 4 states that parties "should promote sustainable development," an important recognition by developing states but less than the "duty" sought by developed countries.

Bodansky, *A Commentary*, at 504–05.

QUESTIONS AND DISCUSSION

1. In an economic sense, the principle of sustainable development recognizes each generation's responsibility to be fair to the next generation, by leaving an inheritance of wealth no less than they themselves had inherited. It may thus influence the choice of economic discount rates that we use in evaluating the costs and benefits of climate change. In this regard, recall Chapter 2's discussion of discount rates.

2. A State's rights and responsibilities with respect to development are outlined in the 1986 UN Declaration on the Right to Development, UNGA Res. 41/128, Annex (Dec. 4, 1986):

Article 1

1. The right to development is an inalienable human right by virtue of which every human person and all peoples are entitled to participate in, contribute to, and enjoy economic, social, cultural and political development, in which all human rights and fundamental freedoms can be fully realized.

2. The human right to development also implies the full realization of the right of peoples to self-determination, which includes, subject to the relevant provisions of both International Covenants on Human Rights, the exercise of their inalienable right to full sovereignty over all their natural wealth and resources.

Article 2

* * * 3. States have the right and the duty to formulate appropriate national development policies that aim at the constant improvement of the well-being of the entire population and of all individuals, on the basis of their active, free and meaningful participation in development and in the fair distribution of the benefits resulting therefrom. * * *

Article 4

1. States have the duty to take steps, individually and collectively, to formulate international development policies with a view to facilitating the full realization of the right to development.

2. Sustained action is required to promote more rapid development of developing countries. As a complement to the efforts of developing countries, effective international co-operation is essential in providing these countries with appropriate means and facilities to foster their comprehensive development.

Virtually every year, the United Nations reaffirms the right to development and a State's responsibility to fulfill that right. *See, e.g.*, The Right to Development, UNGA Res. No. 62/161, Mar. 13, 2008; The Right to Development, UNGA Res No. 56/150, 8 Feb. 2002; Report of the World Summit on Sustainable Development, A/Conf. 199/20, paras. 62a, 138, 169 (2002); Principle 3 of the 1992 *Rio Declaration* ("The right to development must be fulfilled so as to equitably meet developmental and environmental needs of present and future generations.").

3.   The United States has consistently objected to the right to development. For example, in signing the *Rio Declaration*, the United States attached the following interpretative statement concerning Principle 3:

> The United States cannot agree to, and would disassociate itself from, any interpretation of principle 3 that accepts a "right to development," or otherwise goes beyond that understanding. The United States does not, by joining in consensus on the Rio Declaration, change its long-standing opposition to the so-called "right to development." Development is not a right. On the contrary, development is a goal we all hold, which depends for its realization in large part on the promotion and protection of human rights set out in the Universal Declaration of Human Rights.

A/Conf.151/26/Rev.1 (vol. II). Do you agree with the U.S. position? Why is the United States so intent on distinguishing development as a goal versus development as a right? Since the adoption of the *Rio Declaration*, the U.S. position has been refined somewhat and the United States now appears to support an individual's right to develop to his or her full potential. The United States still resists the right of development as a right of States to demand a certain level of development or, for example, to demand foreign assistance or technology transfers. In recent years, developing countries have softened their rhetoric as well, dropping demands that the right to development could lead to a legal obligation on developed countries to provide greater development assistance or otherwise transfer greater amounts of wealth. This lowered rhetoric on both sides has allowed for considerable progress in the negotiations of development-related instruments, including most notably the 2000 Millennium Development Goals, which establishes a set of universal development objectives and global action plan for reducing poverty. *See* United Nations Millennium Declaration, *A/55/L.2* (Sept. 8, 2000).

4.   The final principle in UNFCCC, Article 3, was aimed at ensuring that climate change policies reinforced the push for free trade:

> The Parties should cooperate to promote a supportive and open international economic system that would lead to sustainable economic growth and development in all Parties, particularly developing country Parties, thus enabling them better to address the problems of climate change. Measures taken to combat climate change, including unilateral ones, should not constitute a means of arbitrary or unjustifiable discrimination or a disguised restriction on international trade.

The potential conflict between trade and environment had just emerged prior to the 1992 Earth Summit, and the Parties desired that trade and climate policies would be mutually supportive. Do you think this language limits in any way the possible future use of trade measures in the climate regime? The relationship between international trade and climate change is explored further in Chapter 10.

5.   Recognition that the climate change would be part of an international system that had sustainable development as an overall goal continues to be important for the development of the climate regime. The Kyoto Protocol, for example, acknowledges the importance of sustainable development in several provisions, and makes it an explicit goal of the Protocol's Clean Development Mechanism: "The purpose of

the clean development mechanism shall be to assist Parties not included in Annex I in achieving sustainable development and in contributing to the ultimate objective of the Convention . . . ." Kyoto Protocol, Article 12; *see also* Kyoto Protocol, Articles 2, 10 (referencing sustainable development). The Clean Development Mechanism is discussed further in Chapter 6.

---

4.   *Common but Differentiated Responsibilities*

One of the most important and controversial principles shaping the climate regime is the principle of common but differentiated responsibility. According to this principle, all States have common responsibilities to protect the environment, including the climate, but because of different social, economic, and ecological situations, countries must shoulder different responsibilities. The principle reflects core elements of equity, placing more responsibility on wealthier countries and those that are more responsible for causing specific global environmental problems. Differentiated responsibility also allows for ecological differences in countries — for example, the particular vulnerability of small island states to the flooding that may result from global warming.

The principle emerged from the general North-South dialogue at the Rio Earth Summit, and its articulation in the controversial Principle 7 of the Rio Declaration reveals its general parameters:

> States shall cooperate in a spirit of global partnership to conserve, protect and restore the health and integrity of the Earth's ecosystem. In view of the different contributions to global environmental degradation, States have common but differentiated responsibilities. The developed countries acknowledge the responsibility that they bear in the international pursuit of sustainable development in view of the pressures their societies place on the global environment and of the technologies and financial resources they command.

Thus, the principle was tied closely to the grand global partnership that was the centerpiece of the Earth Summit. The partnership in general terms was that the Global South agreed to participate in making the resolution of global environmental problems a priority, but it would do so only with the recognition that the primary responsibility — and thus the primary actions — must be taken by the North, who after all were mostly at fault.

This general compromise was also an integral part of the UNFCCC, forming the basis on which developing countries would agree to join in the regime. The principle permeates the preamble and is central to the first two principles in Article 3.

UNFCCC, PREAMBLE

*The Parties to this Convention, * * ***

Noting that the largest share of historical and current global emissions of greenhouse gases has originated in developed countries, that per capita emissions in developing countries are still relatively low and that the share of global emissions originating in developing countries will grow to meet their social and development needs, * * *

Acknowledging that the global nature of climate change calls for the widest possible cooperation by all countries and their participation in an effective and appropriate international response, in accordance with their common but differentiated responsibilities and respective capabilities and their social and economic conditions, * * *

Recognizing also the need for developed countries to take immediate action in a flexible manner on the basis of clear priorities, as a first step towards comprehensive response strategies at the global, national and, where agreed, regional levels that take into account all greenhouse gases, with due consideration of their relative contributions to the enhancement of the greenhouse effect,

Have agreed as follows: * * *

UNFCCC, ARTICLE 3

In their actions to achieve the objective of the Convention and to implement its provisions, the Parties shall be guided, inter alia, by the following:

1. The Parties should protect the climate system for the benefit of present and future generations of humankind, on the basis of equity and in accordance with their common but differentiated responsibilities and respective capabilities. Accordingly, the developed country Parties should take the lead in combating climate change and the adverse effects thereof.

2. The specific needs and special circumstances of developing country Parties, especially those that are particularly vulnerable to the adverse effects of climate change, and of those Parties, especially developing country Parties, that would have to bear a disproportionate or abnormal burden under the Convention, should be given full consideration.

On one level, "common but differentiated responsibilities" simply presents a conceptual framework for compromise and cooperation in meeting future environmental challenges, because it allows countries that are in different positions with respect to specific environmental issues to be treated differently. In the climate context, the principle has a more specific implication — that developed countries must go first and make demonstrable progress in curtailing greenhouse gas emissions before developing countries will agree to take on any firm reduction commitments.

The concept of common but differentiated responsibilities remains controversial in the climate context. The concept is used to justify why only industrialized countries were required to accept binding emission reduction levels in the Kyoto Protocol. This issue — whether developing countries should be allowed less rigorous compliance requirements — was one of the most difficult issues in negotiations over binding targets and timetables under the Kyoto Protocol and remains a major impediment to consensus in the post-Kyoto negotiations. It was also one of the primary reasons the United States offered in pulling back from the Protocol in 2001. Well-funded industry advertisements during the Kyoto negotiations as well as after argued that the Protocol "is not global and won't work."

QUESTIONS AND DISCUSSION

1.   The principle is also referenced again in the chapeau to Article 4.1 as a condition on commitments that all Parties accept under the Convention: "All Parties, taking into account their common but differentiated responsibilities and their specific national and regional development priorities, objectives and circumstances, shall. . . . " Article 4 can also be seen as providing some clarification as to what precisely was meant by common but differentiated responsibilities. All Parties agreed to the commitments in Article 4.1, but only developed countries (Annex I countries) agreed to the commitments in Article 4.2. Review these articles in the Convention. Does it give you more of a sense of how the Parties intended to allocate responsibilities? Do developing countries have any binding responsibilities under the convention?

2.   The climate negotiators were influenced by the success of the Montreal Protocol in gaining broad-based developing country support for restrictions on the production and use of ozone depleting substances. Although the principle of common but differentiated responsibilities is not explicitly identified as such in the Montreal Protocol, the Protocol did provide significant financial and technical assistance to developing countries and, most importantly, explicitly delayed the imposition of any restrictions on developing countries' production and consumption of ODSs for at least ten years as compared to developed countries. This approach was widely viewed as effective and working in the ozone regime, and was part of the "formula" that the climate negotiators hoped to follow. See Montreal Protocol, Article 5.

3.   Consider the following discussion of "differentiated responsibilities," offered by Professor Ileana Porras:

> There are two distinct ways in which Principle 7 of the *Rio Declaration* begins to define "differentiated responsibility." First, it imputes differentiated responsibility to States in accordance with their different levels of responsibility for causing the harm. Second, it ties differentiated responsibility to the different capacities of States, by referring to the differentiated responsibility for sustainable development, acknowledged by developed countries in view of the "technologies and financial resources they command." Together, these two elements of differentiated responsibility provide the beginnings of a philosophical basis for international cooperation in the fields of environment and development. It is a basis that allows the characterization of the transfer of resources from developed to developing countries as "obligation" rather than as "aid" or assistance and provides a theoretical basis to justify different environmental standards, in view of the different capacities of States and their different contributions to environmental degradation.

Ileana Porras, *The Rio Declaration: A New Basis for International Cooperation, in* PHILIPPE SANDS, GREENING INTERNATIONAL LAW 25, 29 (1994). What difference does it make to developing countries whether foreign assistance is based on a sense of obligation as opposed to aid? To developed countries?

4.   In signing the Rio Declaration, the United States attached an interpretive statement to Article 7 clarifying that it entailed no legal responsibility for global environmental problems.

> The United States understands and accepts that principle 7 highlights the special leadership role of the developed countries, based on our industrial development, our experience with environmental protection policies and actions, and our wealth, technical expertise and capabilities.

> The United States does not accept any interpretation of principle 7 that would imply a recognition or acceptance by the United States of any international obligations or liabilities, or any diminution in the responsibilities of developing countries.

What exactly do you think concerned the United States?

5. Some economists argue that developing countries should be allowed to continue polluting as they develop their economies, and that this is a legitimate "comparative advantage" they should be able to exploit to compete in the global economy. Should this be considered as part of common but differentiated responsibilities?

6. Consider the principle in light of the following from Chris Stone:

> On first acquaintance, the wide appeal of CDR seems unsurprising. Is it not right that the law should subject the rich to higher demands than the poor? But a moment's reflection will show that the principle is neither universal nor self-evident. True, the rich pay a higher marginal tax rate than the poor. But differentiations in municipal legal systems are the exception. Poverty does not excuse theft. Domestic environmental regulations do not hold marginally profitable polluters to lower standards than their wealthy competitors.

> Why should our posture be different — that is, why should we differentiate more liberally — in the international arena?

> To begin with the principles of "customary international law," I can think of none that does differentiate on the basis of wealth. Surely, the customary rules against piracy and abusing diplomats carve out no exceptions for the needy. * * *

> Nonetheless, despite the inducements to differentiate, uniform terms remain the rule. Under the conventions governing the conduct of war, a belligerent's use of poison gas is not excused because it cannot afford cannonry. The Stockholm Declaration's principle 21 speaks in universal terms that "States have . . . the responsibility to ensure that activities within their jurisdiction or control do not cause damage to the environment of other States or of areas beyond the limits of national jurisdiction." There is no qualification that a lack of resources to mitigate damage constitutes a defense. No one proposes adjusting the international standards for radioactive emissions to account for a nation's difficulties in meeting them.

Christopher D. Stone, *Common But Differentiated Responsibilities in International Law*, 98 AM. J. INT'L L. 276, 281–82 (2004). Do you agree with Professor Stone's assessment? For further discussion of common but differentiated responsibilities, see ANITA HALVORSSEN, EQUALITY AMONG UNEQUALS IN INTERNATIONAL ENVIRONMENTAL LAW: DIFFERENTIAL TREATMENT FOR DEVELOPING COUNTRIES (1999).

---

5. *Equity*

Closely related to the principle of common but differentiated responsibilities is the concept of "equity." Article 3.1 of the UNFCCC states that parties should protect the climate system "on the *basis of equity* and in accordance with their common but differentiated responsibilities" (emphasis added). Although the principle of equity may refer generally to concepts of fairness and environmental justice, it also has a relatively specific connotation in the context of the UNFCCC.

To many developing countries the only fair way of allocating the right to emit greenhouse gases is on a per capita basis. Thus, when the Convention speaks of addressing the climate system on the basis of equity, this has come to suggest, at least implicitly, that each country's commitments should in some ways be tied to its per capita emissions.

In this respect, the Kyoto Protocol would be a disappointment to developing countries. Even though the Protocol seemed to reflect the concept of common but differentiated responsibilities by imposing emissions limitations only on industrialized countries, those emissions limitations were allocated among the industrialized countries through a process of negotiation that reflected political expediency and the economic conditions of each country. The allocation of emissions limitations was not based on per capita emissions or any other equitable factor. Indeed, the term "equity" is found nowhere in the Kyoto Protocol, but the concept continues to influence post-Kyoto discussions relating to developing country commitments. Because of this debate around the proper way to allocate emissions limitations, the term "equity" remains a hot-button issue in the climate negotiations.

---

6.   *Intergenerational Equity*

Because of the long lag-time between when greenhouse gas emissions occur and when they are naturally removed from the atmosphere (measured in decades to centuries, depending on the gas), decisions we make today to reduce our emissions will have profound impacts on the quality of life 100 years hence. Similarly, investments made today in researching and developing environmentally sustainable energy sources (as opposed to, for example, investing further in coal-fired power plants) also shape and constrain the energy choices available to future generations. For this reason, international climate negotiations often invoked the concept of intergenerational equity. Article 3.1 of the Framework Convention asks parties to protect the climate system for "the benefit of present and future generations of humankind."

In essence, the principle is one of fairness, that present generations not leave future generations worse off by the choices we make today regarding development. By explicitly recognizing that future generations are among the beneficiaries of our actions in the climate regime, the parties are reminded to take a long-term view.

Intergenerational equity thus requires that we take into consideration the impact of our activities on future generations, giving them a "seat at the table" in making current decisions. At a minimum, implementing this principle requires using natural resources sustainably and avoiding irreversible environmental damage. It may also require modifications to our procedures for conducting environmental impact assessments and expansion of our concepts of judicial standing to future generations.

QUESTIONS AND DISCUSSION

1. Beginning with the 1972 *Stockholm Declaration*, international environmental instruments have emphasized the interests of future generations. The *Stockholm Declaration's* preamble notes that "To defend and improve the human environment for present *and* future generations has become an imperative goal of humankind. . . . " Principle 1 states that "Man . . . bears a solemn responsibility to protect and improve the environment for present and future generations," and Principle 2 requires the safeguarding of natural resources and ecosystems "for the benefit of present and future generations," Similarly, Principle 3 of the *Rio Declaration* states: "The right to development must be fulfilled so as to equitably meet developmental and environmental needs of present and future generations." *See also, e.g., United Nations General Assembly Resolution on the Historical Responsibility of States for the Protection of Nature for the Benefit of Present and Future Generations*, G.A. Res. 35/8 (Oct. 30, 1980); *Declaration of the Hague*, Mar. 11, 1989, 28 I.L.M. 1308 (1989). For a thorough treatment of the principle, see EDITH BROWN WEISS, IN FAIRNESS TO FUTURE GENERATIONS: INTERNATIONAL LAW, COMMON PATRIMONY, AND INTERGENERATIONAL EQUITY 37–39 (1996).

2. What concrete steps would be required in our national laws if we took seriously the rights of future generations? How do the principles of inter- and intra-generational equity relate to the environmental justice movement in the United States? Given that many of the impacts of climate change will be visited primarily on future generations, some of which are as yet unborn, should future generations have standing to bring suit? *Cf. Minors Oposa v. Secretary of the Department of Environment and Natural Resources*, 33 I.L.M. 168, 185 n. 18 (1994) (decision by the Philippines Supreme Court citing the principle of intergenerational equity in granting standing to future generations to bring an action to protect the Philippines' forests).

---

7.   *The Precautionary Principle*

Experience in the past decades with environmental problems such as ozone depletion and the accumulation of persistent chemicals in even the most remote parts of the earth, as well as climate change, have jolted some observers to re-evaluate how we address potential environmental harm. At the center of that re-evaluation is the precautionary principle, which reflects the recognition that scientific certainty about environmental harm often comes too late to design effective legal and policy responses for preventing potential environmental threats. Particularly with respect to environmental issues like climate change that involve complex analyses of scientific, technical, and economic factors, policymakers rarely have anything approaching perfect knowledge when asked to make decisions whether to respond or not.

The precautionary principle addresses how environmental decisions are made in the face of scientific uncertainty. The principle is concerned with taking anticipatory actions to avoid environmental harm *before* it occurs. Principle 15 of the 1992 *Rio Declaration* is the most widely accepted elaboration of the precautionary principle:

> In order to protect the environment, the precautionary approach shall be widely applied by States according to their capabilities. Where there are threats of serious or irreversible damage, lack of scientific certainty shall

not be used as a reason for postponing cost-effective measures to prevent environmental degradation.

Principle 15 thus forbids using scientific uncertainty as a reason for postponing cost-effective measures to prevent environmental harm. This focus on avoiding delay and on acting before environmental harm occurs illustrates the principle's emphasis on anticipating and avoiding harm. In this respect, the principle speaks more to *when* policy measures can be taken and on what basis, than to *what* type of measures should be taken. Although not clearly supported by the *Rio Declaration*, many commentators also argue that the precautionary principle acts to switch the burden of proof necessary for triggering policy responses from those who support prohibiting or reducing a potentially offending activity to those who want to continue the activity. Such a shift in the burden of proof can shorten the time period between when a potential threat to the environment is identified and when a legal response can be developed.

The precautionary principle as set forth in the *Rio Declaration* does not prescribe what type of policies and measures should be used — except that such policies and measures should be "cost-effective." This proved to be the most difficult issue with respect to the principle in the climate negotiations. The United States wanted the cost-effectiveness language included to condition the principle's application but this was opposed by some European countries. In the end, a compromise was reached by adding a separate statement about cost-effectiveness to the same paragraph as the precautionary principle:

UNFCCC, ARTICLE 3.3

The Parties should take precautionary measures to anticipate, prevent or minimize the causes of climate change and mitigate its adverse effects. Where there are threats of serious or irreversible damage, lack of full scientific certainty should not be used as a reason for postponing such measures, taking into account that policies and measures to deal with climate change should be cost-effective so as to ensure global benefits at the lowest possible cost. To achieve this, such policies and measures should take into account different socio-economic contexts, be comprehensive, cover all relevant sources, sinks and reservoirs of greenhouse gases and adaptation, and comprise all economic sectors.

QUESTIONS AND DISCUSSION

1.   The precautionary principle is not meant to supplant science; it provides a framework for governments to set preventative policies where existing science is incomplete or where no consensus exists regarding a particular threat. The principle is not intended to downgrade the role of science, and the fact that there is scientific uncertainty does not alleviate the need to take into account whatever science does exist. Existing science may, for example, identify the potential scale and seriousness of potential harm as well as the adequacy or effectiveness of policy measures, even where uncertainty remains regarding cause and effect. Indeed, this was arguably the situation in 1992 when the UNFCCC was being negotiated. In that context, can you see the role the precautionary principle could play in the climate regime?

The state of climate science has progressed considerably since 1992, and for the most part much of the cause-and-effect of climate change no longer presents significant uncertainties. What is uncertain is the rate and ultimate impact from climate change. Consider the various forecasts of possible climate impacts identified in Chapter 1. Is the precautionary principle still relevant? In what ways, could a precautionary approach shape current climate negotiations?

2. In recent years, the precautionary principle has emerged as perhaps the most controversial of all international environmental principles. The strongest controversies have erupted as a result of different approaches that Europe and the United States take to the precautionary principle in the context of international trade and environment issues. In fact, precaution has probably always been an element of both European and U.S. environmental and health policy, but a strong World Trade Organization (WTO) now provides an opportunity to challenge precaution-based policies as being trade-restrictive. The WTO's apparent preference for scientifically based environmental policies has provided opponents an opportunity to depict precaution as unscientific and protectionist.

The controversy over the precautionary principle is not just about law, however; it is about the pace, methodology, and extent of environmental regulation. Experience with environmental problems such as ozone depletion and now climate change have taught us that current activities may have serious and irreversible environmental impacts in the distant future or in distant places. We also recognize that the increasing pace of the global economy provides shorter lead time for making key regulatory decisions over products that may have substantial, but not proven, environmental impacts. This has led to the growing interest inside and outside governments for anticipating environmental damage and taking precautionary actions. On the other hand, industry supporters argue that the costs of such an approach in foregone economic opportunities would ultimately be too high for society, particularly if no science exists to justify the expense.

3. The precautionary principle in slightly different formulations has been included in many international environmental instruments. Indeed, despite the controversy over the precautionary principle in the trade field it continues to play a key role in most recent international instruments, albeit often over U.S. opposition. *See, e.g., World Charter for Nature*, Principle 11, G.A. Res. 37/7 (Oct. 28, 1982); *London Adjustments and Amendments to the Montreal Protocol on Substances that Deplete the Ozone Layer, and Non-Compliance Procedure*, at Annex II, Article I.A.1 (amendment to 6th preambular paragraph), Decision IV/18, Nov. 25, 1992, UNEP/Oz.L.Pro.4/15; *Treaty Establishing the European Economic Community*, Mar. 25, 1957, 294 U.N.T.S. 17, U.K.T.S. 15 (1979) *as amended by Treaty on European Union*, Title XVI, Article 130r, Feb. 7, 1992; *Biodiversity Convention*, Preamble; *Agenda 21*, para. 18.40(b)(iv) (1992); *Cartagena Protocol on Biosafety*, Article 10 (Jan. 28, 2000); *Stockholm Convention on Persistent Organic Pollutants*, Articles 1, 8 (2001); Report of the World Summit on Sustainable Development, A/Conf. 199/20, paras. 23, 109(f) (2002); Conference of the Parties to the Convention on Biological Diversity, Decision VI/23: Guiding Principles for the Prevention, Introduction and Mitigation of Impacts of Alien Species that Threaten Ecosystems, Habitats or Species, Annex I (2004); *see also* DAVID FREESTONE, THE PRECAUTIONARY PRINCIPLE IN INTERNATIONAL ENVIRONMENTAL LAW (1996); C. RAFFENSPERGER & J. TICKNER, PROTECTING PUBLIC HEALTH & THE ENVIRONMENT: IMPLEMENTING THE PRECAUTIONARY PRINCIPLE (1999).

B.   The UNFCCC Objective

Article 2 of the UNFCCC sets out the climate regime's overall objective:

UNFCCC, ARTICLE 2
Objective

The ultimate objective of this Convention and any related legal instruments that the Conference of the Parties may adopt is to achieve, in accordance with the relevant provisions of the Convention, stabilization of greenhouse gas concentrations in the atmosphere at a level that would prevent dangerous anthropogenic interference with the climate system. Such a level should be achieved within a time frame sufficient to allow ecosystems to adapt naturally to climate change, to ensure that food production is not threatened and to enable economic development to proceed in a sustainable manner.

The phrasing of the objective is important for several reasons. First, the objective clarifies that the Convention is not only about curbing greenhouse gas emissions. The objective is not written in terms of "reducing emissions," but rather in terms of the "stabilization of greenhouse gas *concentrations* in the atmosphere." In this way, the objective signals the tremendous ambition of the climate regime to cover not only fossil-fuel emissions, but land-use and forestry policies that relate to the ultimate concentrations of greenhouse gases. The breadth of the climate regime is further signaled by reference to the goal of avoiding impacts on the "climate system," which is defined in Article 1 of the Convention to mean the "totality of the atmosphere, hydrosphere, biosphere and geosphere and their interactions."

The objective is necessarily written in general terms — i.e., to stabilize greenhouse gas concentrations at a level necessary to prevent anthropogenic interference with the climate system — but it also provides some additional potential benchmarks for determining whether we have stabilized greenhouse gas concentrations at an appropriate level. The acceptable level is defined as that level that allows us to avoid impacts on (1) the ability of natural ecosystems to adapt to climate change; (2) impacts on food production; and (3) the achievement of sustainable development. These benchmarks are important because it means that the debate over whether we have met our objective — on whether we can be satisfied with progress under the climate regime — will be partially determined by reference to things that can be measured objectively and that are not inherently political. Particularly for impacts on natural ecosystems or food production, scientists and other presumably apolitical experts will be important for informing the discussion of whether more action is needed under the climate regime. Although that decision will ultimately be made by diplomats and politicians, it is more difficult to announce "mission accomplished" if experts in the field can point to objective evidence that the stated objective of the Convention has not been met.

And as long as the international community's climate objective — as defined in the Convention is not met — then the parties must continue to strengthen their policies and commitments. Under Articles 4(2)(d) and 7(2)(a), for example, the Conference of the Parties is charged with periodically evaluating implementation of the Convention to ensure that commitments are adequate to meet this overall objective. It was just such an evaluation that ultimately led to the recognition that binding targets were necessary in the Kyoto Protocol. Fifteen years later, the failure to reach Article 2's objective still sets the general frame for ongoing post-Kyoto negotiation.

QUESTIONS AND DISCUSSION

1. The UNFCCC's objective continues to drive further development of the climate regime. Given the discussion of climate impacts, including rapid climate change events, in Chapter 1, how would you operationalize the objective? Should the objective be set at stabilizing greenhouse gas concentrations at pre-industrial levels? Should it be set with reference to a certain allowed temperature increase?

2. The breadth of the UNFCCC is generally seen as an asset. One can not solve climate change with out also addressing unsustainable land-use practices and deforestation. Conceptually, therefore, an agreement that brought all impacts on the climate system together makes logical sense for fashioning a comprehensive global response to the problem. Given where we are today in discussions over the post-Kyoto strategy, do you agree that the comprehensive approach was the best one? Is the system too complicated? Would we, for example, be better off addressing climate change with sector-by-sector responses? Is such an approach precluded by the Convention?

3. The breadth of the UNFCCC was a subject of significant debate in the negotiations. Some European countries desired a convention that focused primarily on reducing carbon dioxide emissions — in part because those countries had significant methane emissions. The United States supported a broader approach that would deal with all greenhouse gases, primarily because it wanted greater flexibility in designing policy responses. The Convention's objective reveals that it is concerned with all greenhouse gases, which is defined broadly to mean "those gaseous constituents of the atmosphere, both natural and anthropogenic, that absorb and re-emit infrared radiation." The United States did not get everything it wanted, however, because all of the commitments under the Convention relate only to those greenhouse gases "not regulated under the Montreal Protocol." The United States had hoped to get credit for the considerable amount of global warming it had avoided by phasing out chlorofluorocarbons and other ozone depleting substances (that are also greenhouse gases). The Europeans and developing countries believed that countries should not receive credit under the climate regime for reductions that they were already legally obligated to make.

4. Can you see how the UNFCCC's objective could be used to depoliticize the decision of whether stronger commitments are needed? Who should make the assessment about whether greenhouse gas concentrations are going to stabilize at an acceptable level? Do you see a role for other international institutions such as the IPCC, the Food and Agriculture Organization, or the United Nations Development Program in assisting the Parties to evaluate progress in meeting the goal?

5. Recall the framework for thinking about climate change impacts and responses offered at the end of Chapter 1. The UNFCCC's objective helps to answer the first question — what impacts are we trying to avoid (impacts on food production, natural ecosystems and sustainable development). Left to other provisions in the Convention and to be debated over time as the climate change regime evolves are the rest of the questions: what concentrations, temperatures, and emissions reductions will ensure that we avoid these impacts, and what policies and commitments can we agree to take to meet those targets?

6. The UNFCCC framework is arguably biased against adaptation, because it only contemplates the costs of adaptation. No benefits are assumed from adaptation because by definition they are implemented only to respond to expected impacts from climate change, Roger Pielke explores this topic below:

> Under the FCCC definition, "adaptation" refers only to actions in response to climate changes attributed to greenhouse gas emissions.

Absent the increasing greenhouse gases, climate — by definition — would not change and the adaptive measures would be unnecessary. This means that under the FCCC adaptation can have only costs because the measures represent costs that would be incurred only because of the changes in climate that result from greenhouse gas emissions. That is, the narrow definition excludes other benefits of adaptive measures. This exclusion of benefits may seem like a peculiarity of accounting but it has practical consequences. One IPCC report used the FCCC definition to discuss climate policy alternatives in exactly this way, affecting how policy makers perceive alternative courses of action. The IPCC report discusses mitigation policies in terms of both costs and benefits, but discusses adaptation policies only in terms of their costs. The bias against adaptation comes from disallowing consideration of its ancillary benefits while by contrast mitigation's ancillary benefits are considered. This "stacks the deck" against adaptation policies and ensures that mitigation will look better from a benefit-cost standpoint.

The bias against adaptation is particularly unfortunate not only because the world is already committed to some degree of climate change (as the IPCC makes inescapable), but also because many communities around the world are maladapted to current climate. Many, if not most, adaptive measures would make sense even if there were no greenhouse gas-related climate change. The FCCC definition of climate change provides little justification for efforts to reduce societal or ecological vulnerability to climate variability and change beyond those impacts caused by greenhouse gases. From the perspective of the broader IPCC definition of climate change, adaptation policies also have benefits to the extent that they lead to greater resilience of communities and ecosystems to climate change, variability and particular weather phenomena.

The restricted perspective of the FCCC definition makes adaptation and mitigation seem to be opposing strategies rather than complements, and creates an incentive to recommend adaptive responses only to the extent that proposed mitigation strategies cannot prevent changes in climate. From the perspective of adaptation, the FCCC approach serves as a set of blinders, directing attention away from adaptation measures that make sense under any scenario of future climate change. As nations around the world necessarily move toward a greater emphasis on adaptation in the face of the unavoidably obvious limitations of mitigation-only policies, reconciling the different definitions of climate change becomes more important.

R.A. Pielke Jr., *Misdefining "Climate Change": Consequences for Science and Action*, 8 ENVTL SCI. & POL'Y, 548, 555 (2005). Do you agree that most adaptation strategies would make sense with or without a need to respond to man-made climate change? Why do you think the UNFCCC defined adaptation in this way?

C.   Commitments

As suggested by the negotiating history described above, perhaps the most controversial provisions were those that addressed the specific commitments of the Parties. The Parties are essentially divided into three categories: all Parties; Parties listed in "Annex I," which includes all industrialized country Parties; and Parties included in "Annex II," which includes all industrialized country Parties except those from the former Soviet bloc in a process of economic transition. All

Parties must meet some general commitments, for example to cooperate, exchange information, create national inventories and report certain information. *See* Article 4.1. Annex I countries agreed to more specific commitments on reducing sources and enhancing sinks. *See* Article 4.2. Annex II countries agreed further to the provisions requiring financial assistance and technology transfers. *See* Articles 4(3)–4(5). Each of these categories of commitments are discussed below.

1.   *General Commitments of All Parties*

General commitments applicable to all Parties, including all developing country parties, were set forth in Article 4.1.

UNFCCC, ARTICLE 4

1.   All Parties, taking into account their common but differentiated responsibilities and their specific national and regional development priorities, objectives and circumstances, shall:

   (a)   Develop, periodically update, publish and make available to the Conference of the Parties, in accordance with Article 12, national inventories of anthropogenic emissions by sources and removals by sinks of all greenhouse gases not controlled by the Montreal Protocol, using comparable methodologies to be agreed upon by the Conference of the Parties;

   (b)   Formulate, implement, publish and regularly update national and, where appropriate, regional programmes containing measures to mitigate climate change by addressing anthropogenic emissions by sources and removals by sinks of all greenhouse gases not controlled by the Montreal Protocol, and measures to facilitate adequate adaptation to climate change;

   (c)   Promote and cooperate in the development, application and diffusion, including transfer, of technologies, practices and processes that control, reduce or prevent anthropogenic emissions of greenhouse gases not controlled by the Montreal Protocol in all relevant sectors, including the energy, transport, industry, agriculture, forestry and waste management sectors;

   (d)   Promote sustainable management, and promote and cooperate in the conservation and enhancement, as appropriate, of sinks and reservoirs of all greenhouse gases not controlled by the Montreal Protocol, including biomass, forests and oceans as well as other terrestrial, coastal and marine ecosystems;

   (e)   Cooperate in preparing for adaptation to the impacts of climate change; develop and elaborate appropriate and integrated plans for coastal zone management, water resources and agriculture, and for the protection and rehabilitation of areas, particularly in Africa, affected by drought and desertification, as well as floods;

   (f)   Take climate change considerations into account, to the extent feasible, in their relevant social, economic and environmental policies and actions, and employ appropriate methods, for example impact assessments, formulated and determined nationally, with a view to minimizing adverse effects on the economy, on public health and on the quality of the environment, of projects or measures undertaken by them to mitigate or adapt to climate change;

(g)   Promote and cooperate in scientific, technological, technical, socio-economic and other research, systematic observation and development of data archives related to the climate system and intended to further the understanding and to reduce or eliminate the remaining uncertainties regarding the causes, effects, magnitude and timing of climate change and the economic and social consequences of various response strategies;

(h)   Promote and cooperate in the full, open and prompt exchange of relevant scientific, technological, technical, socio-economic and legal information related to the climate system and climate change, and to the economic and social consequences of various response strategies;

(i)   Promote and cooperate in education, training and public awareness related to climate change and encourage the widest participation in this process, including that of non-governmental organizations; and

(j)   Communicate to the Conference of the Parties information related to implementation, in accordance with Article 12.

*   *   *

UNFCCC, ARTICLE 12

1.   In accordance with Article 4, paragraph 1, each Party shall communicate to the Conference of the Parties, through the secretariat, the following elements of information:

(a)   A national inventory of anthropogenic emissions by sources and removals by sinks of all greenhouse gases not controlled by the Montreal Protocol . . . using comparable methodologies to be promoted and agreed upon by the Conference of the Parties;

(b)   A general description of steps taken or envisaged by the Party to implement the Convention; and

(c)   Any other information that the Party considers relevant to the achievement of the objective of the Convention and suitable for inclusion in its communication, including, if feasible, material relevant for calculations of global emission trends.

The following excerpt from Professor Dan Bodansky highlights some of the conflicts and compromises that shaped the commitments made under the UN-FCCC:

DANIEL BODANSKY, THE UNITED NATIONS FRAMEWORK CONVENTION ON CLIMATE CHANGE: A COMMENTARY
8 YALE J. INT'L L. 451, 508–09 (1993)*

2. General Commitments (Articles 4(1), 5, 6, and 12(1))

From the beginning, the negotiators viewed general commitments as qualitative rather than quantitative in nature. An extensive list of general commitments was proposed, including use of best available technology to limit greenhouse gas emissions; promotion of energy efficiency and conservation; development of renewable energy sources; promotion of sustainable forest management; removal of subsidies that contribute to global warming; harmonization of national policies, taxes, and efficiency standards; internalization of costs; and development and coordination of market instruments. During the negotiations, these proposals were slowly pared away (in some cases, becoming specific commitments) or watered down, and the general commitments became general not only in their application to all parties, but also in their content.

Perhaps the most important general commitments to survive the negotiating process are those designed to promote long-term national planning and international review of national actions — in essence, those embodying the concept of "pledge and review." Article 4(1) requires each party to develop, periodically update, and publish national inventories of greenhouse gas emissions and removals by sinks, using "comparable methodologies" to be agreed on by the COP. These inventories are to lay the basis for national planning and to provide more accurate information for use in future scientific assessments of the greenhouse problem. Each party must also formulate, implement, and regularly update programs to mitigate and adapt to climate change, and communicate information to the COP on its national inventories and the steps it has taken to implement the Convention. The COP is then to review the national reports and assess the parties' implementation, the overall effects of the measures taken pursuant to the Convention, and the progress towards meeting the Convention's objective. * * *

In contrast to these provisions, which survived the negotiations relatively intact, the general commitments relating to sources and sinks were progressively weakened. Oil-producing states such as Saudi Arabia and Kuwait objected to the regulation of sources, while countries with large forests such as Malaysia and Brazil fought substantial commitments on enhancing sinks. As a result, Article 4(1)(c) (dealing with greenhouse gas emissions) makes no mention of energy efficiency measures or renewable energy sources, and seems to place all relevant economic sectors (energy, transport, industry, agriculture, forestry, and waste management) on an equal footing. Similarly, Article 4(1)(d) fails to single out forests for special consideration in requiring states to promote the sustainable management and enhancement of sinks and reservoirs. * * *

---

2. *Developed Country Commitments: Policies and Measures*

In addition to the general commitments agreed to by all Parties, developed countries listed in Annex I to the Convention also agreed to some more specific commitments aimed at reducing sources, and enhancing sinks, of greenhouse gases. It is these provisions that embody the ultimate compromise between Europe and the United States over whether to commit to targets or timetables to reduce greenhouse gas concentrations. The compromised and therefore somewhat ambiguous text is found in Articles 4(2) and 12(2):

UNFCCC, ARTICLE 4

2. The developed country Parties and other Parties included in annex I commit themselves specifically as provided for in the following:

    (a) Each of these Parties shall adopt national policies and take corresponding measures on the mitigation of climate change, by limiting its anthropogenic emissions of greenhouse gases and protecting and enhancing its greenhouse gas sinks and reservoirs. These policies and measures will demonstrate that developed countries are taking the lead in modifying longer-term trends in anthropogenic emissions consistent with the objective of the Convention, recognizing that the return by the end of the present decade to earlier levels of anthropogenic emissions of carbon dioxide and other greenhouse gases not controlled by the Montreal Protocol would contribute to such modification, and taking into account the differences in these Parties' starting points and approaches, economic structures and resource bases, the need to maintain strong and sustainable economic growth, available technologies and other individual circumstances, as well as the need for equitable and appropriate contributions by each of these Parties to the global effort regarding that objective. These Parties may implement such policies and measures jointly with other Parties and may assist other Parties in contributing to the achievement of the objective of the Convention and, in particular, that of this subparagraph;

(b)   In order to promote progress to this end, each of these Parties shall communicate, within six months of the entry into force of the Convention for it and periodically thereafter, and in accordance with Article 12, detailed information on its policies and measures referred to in subparagraph (a) above, as well as on its resulting projected anthropogenic emissions by sources and removals by sinks of greenhouse gases not controlled by the Montreal Protocol for the period referred to in subparagraph (a), with the aim of returning individually or jointly to their 1990 levels these anthropogenic emissions of carbon dioxide and other greenhouse gases not controlled by the Montreal Protocol. This information will be reviewed by the Conference of the Parties, at its first session and periodically thereafter, in accordance with Article 7;

(c)   Calculations of emissions by sources and removals by sinks of greenhouse gases for the purposes of subparagraph (b) above should take into account the best available scientific knowledge, including of the effective capacity of sinks and the respective contributions of such gases to climate change. The Conference of the Parties shall consider and agree on methodologies for these calculations at its first session and review them regularly thereafter;

(d)   The Conference of the Parties shall, at its first session, review the adequacy of subparagraphs (a) and (b) above. Such review shall be carried out in the light of the best available scientific information and assessment on climate change and its impacts, as well as relevant technical, social and economic information. Based on this review, the Conference of the Parties shall take appropriate action, which may include the adoption of amendments to the commitments in subparagraphs (a) and (b) above. The Conference of the Parties, at its first session, shall also take decisions regarding criteria for joint implementation as indicated in subparagraph (a) above. A second review of subparagraphs (a) and (b) shall take place not later than 31 December 1998, and thereafter at regular intervals determined by the Conference of the Parties, until the objective of the Convention is met;

(e) Each of these Parties shall: (i) Coordinate as appropriate with other such Parties, relevant economic and administrative instruments developed to achieve the objective of the Convention; and (ii) Identify and periodically review its own policies and practices which encourage activities that lead to greater levels of anthropogenic emissions of greenhouse gases not controlled by the Montreal Protocol than would otherwise occur; * * *

(g) Any Party not included in Annex I may, in its instrument of ratification, acceptance, approval or accession, or at any time thereafter, notify the Depositary that it intends to be bound by subparagraphs (a) and (b) above. The Depositary shall inform the other signatories and Parties of any such notification. * * *

UNFCCC, ARTICLE 12

*　　*　　*

2. Each . . . Party included in Annex I shall incorporate in its communication the following elements of information:

(a) A detailed description of the policies and measures that it has adopted to implement its commitment under Article 4, paragraphs 2(a) and 2(b); and

(b) A specific estimate of the effects that the policies and measures referred to in subparagraph (a) immediately above will have on anthropogenic emissions by its sources and removals by its sinks of greenhouse gases during the period referred to in Article 4, paragraph 2(a).

The compromise language on targets and timetables is not a shining light of clarity, precisely because it is the product of compromise between those who wanted commitments to reduce emissions (i.e., Europe) and those who did not (i.e., the United States). As Professor Bodansky explained:

DANIEL BODANSKY, THE UNITED NATIONS FRAMEWORK CONVENTION ON CLIMATE CHANGE: A COMMENTARY
8 YALE J. INT'L L. 451, 512–17 (1993)*

a. Targets and Timetables

In connection with the specific commitments to adopt and report on national policies and measures [Article 4.2], the Convention establishes a quasi-target and quasi-timetable for greenhouse gas emissions. The targets and timetables issue was perhaps the most controversial in the entire negotiation. Although, in common parlance, the term "target" means an object or goal, in the context of international environmental negotiations the phrase "targets and timetables" means quantitative limitations, including those that are legally-binding commitments. In recent years, targets and timetables have become the preferred form of international regulation of atmospheric pollution. They tend to be easier to negotiate than uniform international regulatory rules, because they allow countries to choose how to meet overall national emissions levels, for example, by direct regulation, market mechanisms, or taxes. * * *

Both before and during the negotiations, most Western states pressed vigorously for the adoption of an internationally-defined stabilization target and timetable to stabilize greenhouse gas emissions, particularly carbon dioxide emissions. For example, the European Community supported an immediate commitment by developed countries to stabilize carbon dioxide emissions at 1990 levels by the year 2000. In fact, many OECD countries unilaterally adopted national targets and timetables. The main holdout against the adoption of targets and timetables was the United States, which derided the targets and timetables adopted by most other countries as political in nature, not backed by concrete measures designed to achieve them. * * *

A compromise was finally reached in two highly ambiguous subparagraphs of Article 4(2). By way of setting a quasi-target, Article 4(2) states that developed countries are to adopt and report on national policies to limit emissions and enhance sinks with the "aim of returning to" 1990 emissions levels. Although this phrase has been equated with stabilization, the term "return" unlike "stabilize" does not necessarily have an ongoing temporal dimension. Thus, a state could potentially argue that, once it had achieved a "return" to 1990 levels, emissions increases would be allowed. The "time-table" is even more ambiguous: the Convention simply states that developed countries recognize that a return by the year 2000 to earlier (unspecified) emissions levels would contribute to a modification of longer-term emissions trends.

Article 4(2)'s quasi-target and quasi-timetable are not only highly ambiguous, but also heavily qualified. Because some eastern European countries were concerned about meeting the quasi-target . . . , the COP is to allow countries with economies in transition "a certain degree of flexibility." The Convention does not limit the type of "flexibility" that may be accorded, but identifies the baseline emissions level as a potential subject of flexibility. Additionally, the quasi-timetable is to take into account differences in the parties' starting points and approaches, economic structures, and resource bases; the need to maintain strong and sustainable economic growth; available technologies and other individual circumstances; and the need for equitable and appropriate contributions by each party to the global effort.

Indeed, it is questionable whether the Convention creates a legally binding target and timetable at all. Article 4(2) states that parties "shall" adopt national policies and take corresponding measures to mitigate climate change, and "shall" communicate information on these policies and measures and on the resulting projected emissions. For the quasi-target and quasi-timetable, however, the Convention uses less obligatory language. The target is phrased as an "aim," and the verbs used to characterize the timetable are all descriptive rather than imperative. These ambiguous formulations allow states to put their own spin on the requirements imposed by Article 4(2). Indeed, within days after the Convention was adopted, various countries advanced divergent interpretations. For example, [the first] President Bush's domestic policy advisor stated, "there is nothing in any of the language which constitutes a commitment to any specific level of emissions at any time." In contrast, the chief British negotiator characterized the provisions as "indistinguishable" from an absolute guarantee. These widely divergent interpretations illustrate the limitations of the quasi-target and quasi-timetable contained in Article 4(2). * * *

QUESTIONS AND DISCUSSION

1. If you were advising the Clinton Administration, which took office shortly after the United States signed the UNFCCC, what would you advise the United States was legally required to do to comply with the treaty? Do you think there would be any need for new regulations or policies?

2. In fact, the Clinton Administration prepared a national plan to address climate change based entirely on voluntary incentives and measures. The plan was widely criticized as having no chance of achieving 1990 levels of emissions. Read again Article 4(2) and the commentary by Bodansky. Can you make an argument that the United States was out of compliance with the UNFCCC?

3. The question of U.S. compliance arose again after the United States repudiated the Kyoto Protocol in 2001. The United States remains a party to the UNFCCC. Can you make any arguments that the United States was out of compliance, particularly given that U.S. emissions were nowhere near 1990 levels by 2000? What commitments, if any, are imposed by the Convention after the year 2000?

4. Re-read the obligations found in Article 4 regarding Annex I countries (i.e., industrialized countries). How does this provision reflect a compromise between those wanting a clear target and timetable and those countries wanting no target?

5. One of the most controversial aspects of the commitments and one that continues to shape the Kyoto Protocol was the concept of "joint implementation," found in the last sentence of Article 4.2(a): "These Parties may implement such policies and measures jointly with other Parties and may assist other Parties in contributing to the achievement of the objective of the Convention and, in particular, that of this subparagraph." This seemingly benign reference to acting "jointly" was short-hand for the intentions of the United States and other countries to meet their obligations in part by investing in projects in developing countries. This general idea — that developed countries can meet their treaty obligations by choosing to reduce emissions off-shore in developing countries that have no binding cap on emissions — continued to be a major issue in the Kyoto Protocol negotiations. Ultimately joint implementation would be the conceptual predecessor to the Protocol's Clean Development Mechanism, which has led to billions of dollars in investments in developing countries while continuing to raise significant questions regarding the climate and development benefits. The Clean Development Mechanism is described further in Chapter 6.

---

3.   *Developed Country Commitments: Financial Assistance and Technology Transfer*

As is the case in almost all environmental agreements, financial issues were among the most controversial in the UNFCCC negotiations, and were critical to gaining full participation by developing countries. Moreover, countries of the former Soviet bloc who were facing significant financial uncertainties in their economic transitions would not commit to providing financial assistance. Thus, the financial and related technology transfer provisions would apply only to developed countries not undergoing economic transition. They are listed in Annex II of the Convention. The primary financial and technology provisions were provided in Articles 4(3) and 12.

UNFCCC, ARTICLE 4

3. The . . . Parties included in Annex II shall provide new and additional financial resources to meet the agreed full costs incurred by developing country Parties in complying with their obligations under Article 12, paragraph l. They shall also provide such financial resources, including for the transfer of technology, needed by the developing country Parties to meet the agreed full incremental costs of implementing measures that are covered by paragraph l of this Article and that are agreed between a developing country Party and the international entity or entities referred to in Article 11, in accordance with that Article. The implementation of these commitments shall take into account the need for adequacy and predictability in the flow of funds and the importance of appropriate burden sharing among the developed country Parties.

4. The . . . Parties included in Annex II shall also assist the developing country Parties that are particularly vulnerable to the adverse effects of climate change in meeting costs of adaptation to those adverse effects.

5. The . . . Parties included in Annex II shall take all practicable steps to promote, facilitate and finance, as appropriate, the transfer of, or access to, environmentally sound technologies and know-how to other Parties, particularly developing country Parties, to enable them to implement the provisions of the Convention. In this process, the developed country Parties shall support the development and enhancement of endogenous capacities and technologies of developing country Parties. Other Parties and organizations in a position to do so may also assist in facilitating the transfer of such technologies. * * *

7. The extent to which developing country Parties will effectively implement their commitments under the Convention will depend on the effective implementation by developed country Parties of their commitments under the Convention related to financial resources and transfer of technology and will take fully into account that economic and social development and poverty eradication are the first and overriding priorities of the developing country Parties. * * *

ARTICLE 12

*   *   *

3. In addition, each . . . Party included in Annex II shall incorporate details of measures taken in accordance with Article 4, paragraphs 3, 4 and 5.

4. Developing country Parties may, on a voluntary basis, propose projects for financing, including specific technologies, materials, equipment, techniques or practices that would be needed to implement such projects, along with, if possible, an estimate of all incremental costs, of the reductions of emissions and increments of removals of greenhouse gases, as well as an estimate of the consequent benefits.

5. Each . . . Party included in Annex I shall make its initial communication within six months of the entry into force of the Convention for that Party. Each Party not so listed shall make its initial communication within three years of the entry into force of the Convention for that Party, or of the availability of financial resources in accordance with Article 4, paragraph 3. Parties that are least developed countries may make their initial communication at their discretion. The frequency of subsequent communications by

all Parties shall be determined by the Conference of the Parties, taking into account the differentiated timetable set by this paragraph. * * *

7.   From its first session, the Conference of the Parties shall arrange for the provision to developing country Parties of technical and financial support, on request, in compiling and communicating information under this Article, as well as in identifying the technical and financial needs associated with proposed projects and response measures under Article 4. ***

The following excerpt, again from Professor Bodansky, describes the compromises shaping the Convention's treatment of financial resources and technology transfer.

DANIEL BODANSKY, THE UNITED NATIONS FRAMEWORK CONVENTION ON CLIMATE CHANGE: A COMMENTARY
8 Yale J. Int'l L. 451, 523–30 (1993)*

Transfers of financial resources to developing countries were proposed for two general purposes: (1) to offset the various costs of implementing the Convention's general commitments, and (2) to aid developing countries in adapting to the adverse effects of climate change if steps taken under the Convention fail to abate global warming adequately.

(1) Implementation Costs (Articles 4(3) and 12(3))

. . . [D]eveloping countries argued that they would assume general commitments to combat climate change only if they received financial resources from developed countries to cover their increased (or "incremental") costs. Developed countries generally accepted this position, but insisted in return that the channeling of money occur through an appropriate financial mechanism; that developing countries accept at least some binding commitments, in particular, commitments to report on their greenhouse gas emissions and national programs; and that developing countries agree to establish institutions with adequate authority to implement the Convention effectively. Although this quid pro quo was rarely stated explicitly, it shaped the package that ultimately emerged from the negotiations. * * *

[Although the requirement on developed countries to provide financial resources is mandatory,] the Convention does not mandate a specific level of funding, . . . [and] specific figures for financial transfers were never proposed. . . . [S]ome developing countries suggested that developed countries be required to make "assessed" contributions — that is, to provide specified amounts, possibly determined by the COP. This proposal was unsuccessful. Instead, Article 4(3) simply stresses the "need for adequacy and predictability in the flow of funds and the importance of appropriate burden sharing among the developed country Parties." While this provision lays down important guidelines, the Convention allows each developed country to determine for itself the size of its financial contribution. * * *

Instead of seeking specific minimum sums, some developing countries sought a more general commitment by developed countries to provide "adequate, new and additional" financial resources. Although the exact meaning of this phrase was never fully explained, the general thrust of the developing countries' demands was clear: money to implement the Convention should not be diverted from existing development aid, but should consist of "new and additional" resources . . . [M]ost Western countries were willing to accept language requiring the provision of "new and additional" financial resources, although the United States opposed this formulation until near the end of the negotiations.

Also problematic was the demand by developing countries that financial transfers should cover their "full incremental costs" in implementing the Convention. Although the general concept of "incremental costs" is clear, identifying these costs can be very difficult, if not impossible, since for many types of actions there is no baseline from which to measure a country's incremental costs. For this reason, states in general can more easily agree on specific categories of costs to be funded rather than on a general definition of "incremental costs." * * *

Ultimately, the parties resolved the financial resources issue by distinguishing between two types of financial transfers: (1) transfers to help developing countries comply with their reporting obligations under Article 12(1); and (2) transfers to help developing countries implement other aspects of the Convention, such as mitigation measures, research, information exchange, education, training, and public awareness. Developing countries were most immediately concerned with the former category of costs, because those costs were their only definite costs of joining the Convention. Developed countries were amenable to underwriting these costs fully, both because they want developing countries to develop and publish inventories and reports and because the costs of doing so will be limited. In contrast, developed countries resisted underwriting the other costs that may be incurred by developing countries in addressing climate change, because such costs are open-ended and potentially great. They could include the costs of building hydroelectric or nuclear facilities to replace coal-fired power plants, or the opportunity costs of not clearing forests for timber sales. Developed countries, particularly the United States and the United Kingdom, wanted to ensure that in accepting the Convention they would not be writing a blank check. * * *

Technology cooperation and transfer is closely related to the issue of financial resources. Delegations generally agreed on the importance of technology transfer and on the need to view technology broadly (to include "know how" as well as hardware). Discussions on this issue centered on the terms of technology transfer. Developing countries initially sought a commitment by developed countries to transfer technology on "concessional and preferential terms." They argued that, to implement the Convention, they needed access to environmentally sound technologies at an affordable cost. Some even suggested that the Convention provide for "assured access to technology" or "compulsory licensing."

In contrast, developed countries emphasized technology "cooperation" rather than "transfer" and the need to protect intellectual property rights in order to preserve incentives for innovation. Most were willing to agree to the transfer of technology only on "fair and most favorable terms." Since the rights to most technologies are privately held, developed countries argued that governments could not commit to their transfer. For reasons not fully apparent, developing countries . . . accepted a quite moderate provision in the Convention which does not define the terms on which transfers will occur. Instead, Article 4(5) requires developed countries simply "to take all practicable steps to promote, facilitate and finance, as appropriate, the transfer of, or access to, environmentally sound technologies and know-how to other Parties," and to support the "development and enhancement of endogenous capacities and technologies of developing country Parties."

QUESTIONS AND DISCUSSION

1. Review Articles 4 and 12. What specific financial assistance did the developed countries agree to provide? Article 4.7 ties the fulfillment of developing country obligations under the Convention to the developed countries meeting their financial assistance and technology transfer obligations. Does the language relieve developing countries of any legal obligation to comply with their Article 4.1 obligations if the developed countries fail to provide sufficient financial and technical support?

2. Recall that the Toronto Conference Statement leading up to the formal climate negotiations had "called upon governments to establish a World Atmosphere Fund financed in part by a levy on the fossil fuel consumption of industrialized countries." What other mechanisms or fees could the climate regime impose to generate a regular flow of revenue for supporting activities in developing countries? What are the advantages and disadvantages of such an approach? See also discussion of the surcharge imposed by the Clean Development Mechanism, discussed in Chapter 6.

3. Not only did the North and South split over the amount and nature of the financing, but also over what the delivery mechanism should be. The United States and other donor countries did not want to create a new mechanism, particularly if it was going to be controlled by developing countries. They argued that funding under the regime should be done through the Global Environment Facility (GEF), a mechanism operated jointly by UNEP, UNDP, and the World Bank but essentially controlled by the World Bank. Donor countries retain a majority of the votes at the World Bank. The Convention ultimately agreed to allow the GEF to be the interim financial mechanism, until a mechanism could be found that met certain criteria set forth in Article 11 of the Convention. Several years later the continued controversy would be resolved by a restructuring of the GEF; the World Bank's dominant role was reduced and the GEF adopted a complicated, but arguably more democratic, governance structure.

As of 2007, GEF's committed grants in the climate change focal area totalled $1.75 billion. One example is a $3.3 million GEF grant to Costa Rica to install wind turbines to generate power that would otherwise have been provided by thermal plants was classified as a climate-change grant. . . . For updated information, see the Global Environment Facility's website at http/www.gefweb.org. For information about other climate-related funding mechanisms, see discussion of the Clean Development Mechanism and the new Adaptation Fund in Chapter 6.

4. Some countries wanted Parties to the Convention to cover social and economic costs that could result from implementation of the Convention. Oil producing states for example sought compensation for the expected reductions in fossil fuel consumption by other states. Does the Convention cover these costs? Consider in this regard the wording of articles 4(3) and 4(4).

E.   Institutional Architecture

One of the most important, though often overlooked, aspects of international environmental agreements is the institutional architecture that they establish. Lawyers often focus only on the legal norms and binding commitments included in a treaty. Yet, in many cases (and the climate regime is no exception) the ability of the regime to respond over time to changing scientific, economic and political conditions is as important as the initial binding norms. The flexibility of any regime and its long-term effectiveness depends on having an institutional framework that allows for dynamic evolution of the regime over time.

In the case of the UNFCCC (as with most environmental treaties), the top policymaking authority is vested in a Conference of the Parties (CoP), which meets annually. Each Party sends a diplomatic delegation to represent it at the CoP. Some delegations may be only one person, but the United States often comes with dozens of members. The CoP issues broad policy decisions that interpret the treaty as well as detailed decisions that guide implementation of the treaty, such as detailed guidelines for the submission of greenhouse gas inventories. It also issues mandates to the Secretariat and the Convention's subsidiary bodies. *See* Article 7 in Appendix I, for the CoP's specific responsibilities. Day-to-day implementation of the Convention is the responsibility of a permanent Secretariat, now located in Bonn, Germany. The Secretariat's duties include compiling and transmitting to the parties the various reports submitted to it, as well as providing technical and other assistance to the Parties. The Secretariat also organizes the meetings of the CoP. *See* Article 8 in Appendix I for the precise functions of the Secretariat.

QUESTIONS AND DISCUSSION

1. The best way to understand the function and role of the Conference of the Parties and the Secretariat of the UNFCCC is to visit its website, see www.unfc-cc.org, and spend some time reviewing the various decisions, reports, workshops, and other activities that these bodies carry out. Given the complexity of the climate change issue, and particularly of the Kyoto Protocol described in the next chapter, it should not be surprising to find that the Secretariat is a burgeoning bureaucracy that plays a critical role in the development of the climate regime generally and the carbon market more specifically.

2. Perhaps the most important function of the Convention's CoP is to periodically review the state of the science regarding climate change and to evaluate the ultimate effectiveness of the regime in meeting its objective. For example, after determining that the Convention would not meet its objective of stabilizing atmospheric greenhouse gas concentrations at safe levels, the CoP became the primary forum for the negotiation of binding targets and timetables under the 1997 Kyoto Protocol.

3. In addition to the Conference of the Parties and Secretariat, the Convention also establishes two subsidiary bodies (essentially specialized working groups of the Parties) — the Subsidiary Body for Scientific and Technical Advice (SBSTA) and the Subsidiary Body on Implementation (SBI). See Articles 9 and 10 of the Convention, respectively.

4. The UNFCCC also sets forth some general provisions regarding implementation and dispute resolution. Under Article 13, Parties at the first CoP established a "multilateral consultative process," which was meant to provide the procedural approach to monitoring implementation and compliance with the Convention. This process was largely eclipsed by the compliance mechanism created under the Kyoto Protocol and discussed further in Chapter 8. Under Article 14, the Convention addressed dispute resolution and set forth a procession of increasingly formal steps that could be taken to resolve disputes that arise under the Convention. These include: settlement of the dispute through "negotiation or any other peaceful means of their own choice"; establishment of a "conciliation commission"; submission of the dispute to the International Court of Justice; or arbitration in accordance with procedures adopted subsequently by the Conference of the Parties.

V. EVALUATING THE UNFCCC: THE FRAMEWORK-PROTOCOL MODEL

If one is looking for binding commitments to address climate change, then the UNFCCC must be considered a disappointment. But that is probably not the appropriate standard to use. The negotiators of the UNFCCC had learned from prior negotiations relating to ozone depletion and to a lesser extent transboundary air pollution that gaining broad participation was just as important initially as imposing binding commitments. Binding commitments could then be added incrementally over time through subsequent protocols. This model of environmental treatymaking would become known as the "framework-protocol" approach. While the climate negotiators failed to achieve binding reduction commitments, they were more successful in gaining nearly universal participation in a framework that could, if parties proved amenable, lead to incrementally stronger steps to address climate change.

Thus, the climate regime's framework-protocol approach was self-consciously designed to start with a general convention with the full expectation that further agreements (i.e., Protocols) would follow to add specific commitments as science or technology expanded our understanding. Supporters of this approach argued that it would allow for broad initial participation by many countries, even those not yet willing to take any significant steps to curb climate change. Reaching consensus was also possible because, lacking any specific obligations, neither States nor special interests like the fossil fuel industry would incur sufficient costs to lead them to try to block the consensus. In this way, it was hoped that a framework convention would help to build political will around the general need for an international response, while allowing time to establish the institutional structures that would be needed later to negotiate and implement stronger commitments. In this way, the UNFCCC envisioned a dynamic regime that could evolve to reflect shifts in scientific understanding, technological innovation or value changes. As was the case with the Montreal Protocol regime, the climate negotiators fully expected that trends in science and technology would lead to greater political will for stronger commitments over time. And in fact that is exactly what would happen with the completion of the Kyoto Protocol in 1997.

Of course, the framework-protocol approach can also be criticized for providing recalcitrant governments with a politically acceptable way of participating. Parties that may never have any intention of ever complying with international targets and timetables, for example, may be able to continue to participate in the UNFCCC without facing significant political isolation or pressure. Certainly as compared to an agreement with substantive commitments, the framework-protocol approach delays meaningful commitments and simply puts off the difficult political decisions until later. The calculation inherent in this approach was that sufficient time existed to allow for this incremental approach before the planet would face irreversible and catastrophic climate change. We likely still do not know the answer to whether the Parties to the UNFCCC were correct in that calculation.

QUESTIONS AND DISCUSSION

1. Given the general framework-protocol approach to treaty-making that has emerged in international environmental treatymaking, we can expect that framework conventions would include the following elements:

(1)   Legitimize the "internationalization" of the issue by explaining the justification for why the subject matter should not be left to each state under the principle of state sovereignty;

(2)   Set out the basic goals or objectives of the regime;

(3)   Set out basic principles that will help guide interpretation and development of the regime;

(4)   Establish and organize the collection of baseline information and promote relevant scientific research, including, for example, by requiring national reporting on emissions and other activities, creating coordinated research agendas, and establishing or identifying an international scientific community to organize and present the scientific data;

(5)   Establish the institutional structure of the regime, including the role of the conferences of the parties and the secretariat as well as various other bodies or mechanisms to address topics such as science and technology, implementation, compliance, dispute resolution or financing;

(6)   Create the process for the dynamic evolution of the regime, including the process for amending the treaty or creating or revising protocols to the convention.

What elements of the UNFCCC fulfill these functions? Does it fulfill these functions well? Does this change your opinion about the relative merits of the UNFCCC?

2.   *Epistemic Communities.* As you consider the relative merits of the Framework Convention, consider the role of the Conference of the Parties and of the Secretariat in building and strengthening an international cohort of climate experts to work on the issue. The annual meetings of the climate regime are now massive affairs, providing a forum for thousands of climate experts to gather and share information and ideas. Known as "epistemic communities," such international communities of experts provide "a network of professionals with recognized expertise and competence in a particular domain and an authoritative claim to policy-relevant knowledge within that domain or issue-area." Peter Haas, *Introduction: Epistemic Communities and International Policy Coordination*, 46 INT'L ORG. 1, 3 (1992). Such communities play a critical role in the development and implementation of international environmental regimes. Consider the observations in two influential international relations articles.

> In articulating the cause-and-effect relationships of complex problems, helping states identify their interests, framing the issues for collective debate, proposing scientific policies, and identifying salient points for negotiation . . . [m]embers of transnational epistemic communities can influence state interests either by directly identifying them for decision makers or by illuminating the salient dimensions of an issue from which the decision makers may then deduce their interests. The decision makers in one state may, in turn, influence the interests and behaviors of other states, thereby increasing the likelihood of convergent state behavior and international policy coordination, informed by the causal beliefs and policy preferences of the epistemic community.

Id. at 2, 4.

> When the same officials meet recurrently, they sometimes develop a sense of collegiality which may be reinforced by their membership in a common profession, such as economics, physics, or meteorology. Individual officials may even define their roles partly in relation to their transnational reference group rather than in purely national terms. . . . Regularized patterns of policy coordination can therefore create attitudes and relationships that will at least marginally change policy or affect its implementation. . . .

> As such practices [i.e., patterns of regularized policy coordination] become widespread, transgovernmental elite networks are created, linking officials in various governments to one another by ties of common interest, professional orientation, and personal friendship. Even where attitudes are not fundamentally affected and no major deviations from central policy positions occur, the existence of a sense of collegiality may permit the development of flexible bargaining behavior in which concessions need not be required issue by issue or during each period.

Robert Keohane & Joseph Nye, *Transgovernmental Relations and International Organizations*, 27 WORLD POLITICS 39, 44–45 (1974). The development of an epistemic climate community is quite clear to anyone who has participated in the annual meeting of the Conference of the Parties. More than 10,000 people participated in the 2007 Bali meeting and hundreds of side events were held, in addition to the formal negotiations. Although perhaps hard to measure, over time the level of trust that is built, information that is shared, and partnerships that are formed may be as important to addressing climate change as the formal negotiated text.

3.   In evaluating the UNFCCC shortly after its negotiation, Professor Bodansky offered another set of criteria against which to measure the Convention:

> First, it should be politically acceptable to a wide variety of states, given the global nature of the climate change problem. Second, it should be equitable, that is, it should encourage burden-sharing and treat developing countries fairly. Third, it should promote economic efficiency, by encouraging states to consider the cost-effectiveness of measures to address climate change. Fourth, and perhaps most critical, the convention should be flexible. Flexibility is essential, given the long-term nature of the climate change problem and current uncertainties about both scientific predictions of global warming, and the costs and benefits of response measures. Fifth, it should lay a foundation for future work by reducing uncertainties, promoting consensus, and building a base of information. Finally, it should establish targets and timetables for greenhouse gas limitations.

Bodansky, *A Commentary*, at 555–56. How do you think the UNFCCC measures up against these criteria? Would your assessment have been different in 1992 as compared to now? As we turn to a discussion of the Kyoto Protocol in Chapter 5, consider what additional criteria you would suggest for evaluating the Protocol and any future climate agreement?

4.   One proposal put forward at the time of the negotiations was to develop a General Agreement on Climate Change modeled on the GATT, involving a semi-continuous process of negotiation "rounds," see David G. Victor, *How to Slow Global Warming*, 349 NATURE 451 (1991). How would this differ from the approach we have now? What topical priorities might various rounds have addressed?

5.   On the use of the Montreal Protocol ozone regime as a model for the climate negotiations, see Winfried Lang, *Is the Ozone Depletion Regime a Model for an Emerging Regime on Global Warming?*, 9 U.C.L.A. J. ENVTL. L. & POL'Y 161 (1991); Peter M. Morrisette, *The Montreal Protocol: Lessons for Formulating Policies for Global Warming*, 19 POL'Y STUD. J. 152 (1991). For critical evaluations of the framework convention/protocol approach to climate change, *see* David G. Victor, *How to Slow Global Warming*, 349 NATURE 451, 454 (1991), (questioning whether framework convention/protocol model allows sufficient issue linkages to gain widespread acceptance); James K. Sebenius, *Designing Negotiations Towards a New Regime: The Case of Global Warming*, INT'L SECURITY 114–18 (1991).

Chapter 5

INTRODUCTION TO THE KYOTO PROTOCOL

I. INTRODUCTION

Even as governments took the first steps to address climate change in the United Nations Framework Convention on Climate Change (UNFCCC or Framework Convention), most observers knew that it was just a starting point for the real negotiations that would certainly have to come in the future. The Framework Convention would only be as good as its ability to respond to emerging science and to establish a process for negotiating further commitments. The first test would come soon after the UNFCCC came into force, because the convention required the Conference of the Parties (CoP) at its first meeting to "review the adequacy" of the developed countries' commitments "in light of the best available scientific information and assessment on climate change and its impacts. . . . "

Although the UNFCCC did not include a legally binding obligation to meet 1990 levels of greenhouse gas (GHG) emissions by the year 2000, Article 4 required at least that developed country Parties try to meet that target. To outside observers, two things were clear by 1995 when the CoP met for the first time: first, the original target of freezing emissions at 1990 levels for Annex I countries was not going to be sufficient to meet the Convention's Article 2 objective — i.e., to achieve stabilization of greenhouse gas concentrations at a safe level; and second, even if it was sufficient, few developed countries were even going to come close to meeting the 1990-level target.

As described below, the negotiations for the Kyoto Protocol were complex, intense, and, until the final hours, filled with uncertainty. Ultimately, the Parties would agree to an ambitious — if somewhat ambiguous — agreement that would set clear targets for reducing the net greenhouse gas emissions of most developed countries while allowing them to meet these targets by trading emission credits among themselves or investing in climate-friendly projects in developing countries. While the United States withdrew from the Protocol, Europe and other developed countries went forward. Once only theoretical, the Kyoto Protocol's "cap-and-trade" system has now entered into force and a dynamic market for buying and selling greenhouse gas emissions has been created. *See* Kyoto Protocol to the United Nations Framework Convention on Climate Change, FCCC/CP/1997/L.7/Add.1 (Dec. 11, 1997), entered into force (Feb. 16, 2005) [hereinafter Kyoto Protocol].

This chapter introduces the negotiating process that led to the Kyoto Protocol, followed immediately by a summary of the basic provisions of the Protocol. The details of several particularly complicated issues, including the rules for the trading system and other "flexibility mechanisms," the treatment of forests and other sinks, and the compliance system, were largely deferred to negotiations immediately following Kyoto. These issues are addressed in Chapters 6, 7, and 8, respectively.

II. NEGOTIATING THE KYOTO PROTOCOL

A.   The First CoP and the Berlin Mandate

Environmentalists and most developing countries came to Berlin for the first meeting of the Conference of the Parties (CoP1) hoping to persuade the Annex I countries to step up their level of commitment, both financially and politically. A group of developing countries offered a first draft of what became known as the "Berlin Mandate," which would establish a timetable for developed countries to negotiate a protocol with clear "quantifiable emissions limitation and reduction objectives" (QELROs) — a new term for "targets and timetables."

CONCLUSION OF OUTSTANDING ISSUES AND ADOPTION OF DECISIONS
FCCC/CP/1995/L.14 (April 7, 1995) (The Berlin Mandate)

The Conference of the Parties, at its first session, having reviewed Article 4, paragraph 2 (a) and (b) and concluded that these are not adequate, agrees to begin a process to enable it to take appropriate action for the period beyond 2000, including the strengthening of the commitments of Annex I Parties in Article 4, paragraph 2 (a) and (b) through the adoption of a protocol or another legal instrument. * * *

2. The process will, *inter alia*:

(a)   Aim, as the priority in the process of strengthening the commitments in Article 4.2 (a) and (b) of the Convention, for developed country/other Parties included in Annex I, both to elaborate policies and measures, as well as to set quantified limitation and reduction objectives within specified time-frames, such as 2005, 2010 and 2020, for their anthropogenic emissions by sources and removals by sinks of greenhouse gases not controlled by the Montreal Protocol taking into account the differences in starting points and approaches, economic structures and resource bases, the need to maintain strong and sustainable economic growth, available technologies and other individual circumstances, as well as the need for equitable and appropriate contributions by each of these Parties to the global effort, and also the process of assessment and analysis referred to in section III, paragraph 4, below;

(b)   Not introduce any new commitments for [developing country] Parties . . . , but reaffirm existing commitments in Article 4.1 and continue to advance the implementation of these commitments in order to achieve sustainable development, taking into account Article 4.3, 4.5 and 4.7;* * *

3. The process will be carried out in the light of the best available scientific information and assessment on climate change and its impacts, as well as relevant technical, social and economic information, including, inter alia, IPCC reports. It will also make use of other available expertise. * * *

The Berlin Mandate thus set the Parties on a path to negotiate targets and timetables for developed countries by the third meeting of the CoP, which was scheduled for December 1997 in Kyoto, Japan. The Ad Hoc Working Group on the Berlin Mandate (AGBM) was tasked with the negotiations.

QUESTIONS AND DISCUSSION

1. In the Berlin Mandate, the Parties have essentially "agreed to agree" to a treaty with certain general characteristics. What are the primary parameters established in the Berlin Mandate for the ensuing negotiations? What role does such a document play? As you read the description of the Kyoto negotiations below, consider how the Mandate influences the outcome. These preliminary agreements on workplans or negotiating parameters are often overlooked by the media but they are important for setting the agenda and aligning the parties in anticipation of the actual negotiations.

2. Can you see how the Framework Convention's mechanism for reviewing progress was critical for pushing the parties toward the Berlin Mandate?

B.   Prelude to Kyoto: Building Political Will

The Berlin Mandate establishes the parameters for what would eventually become the Kyoto Protocol: targets and timetables (though named "quantified limitation and reduction objectives") were in; developing country commitments to reduce emissions were out. Nevertheless, reaching agreement on the Kyoto Protocol would prove very difficult and involve massive efforts to build political will domestically for binding commitments, while trying to negotiate an acceptable formula for compromise internationally. Ultimately, negotiations over the Kyoto Protocol would continue past the scheduled end of the meeting.

In 1995, the IPCC released a report that would become a significant milestone in the development of the climate regime. For the first time, the IPCC formally reported a consensus among scientists that "the balance of evidence suggests that there is a discernible human influence on global climate." The climate was changing and humans were causing it. This conclusion sparked considerable debate, pitting the great majority of atmospheric scientists and environmentalists who endorsed the IPCC report, against a small but vocal group of "climate skeptics" funded substantially by the fossil fuel industry. *See* Ozone Action, Ties that Blind (1996).

Despite the initial controversy, the IPCC Report catalyzed the negotiation of the Kyoto Protocol. The scientific consensus that climate change was not only a serious long-term problem but was actually occurring now provided the political leaders with critical support for adopting targets and timetables. On the other hand, global emissions of greenhouse gases had increased in the years since the 1992 UNFCCC was adopted, making efforts based on a 1990 baseline even more difficult for some countries, including the United States, to achieve.

At Berlin, several key Parties re-tabled their negotiating positions for the UNFCCC three years earlier. The Europeans for the most part maintained their position of calling for 15 percent reductions in CO_2 from 1990 levels by the year 2010. The Association of Small Island States (AOSIS) continued their call for 20 percent reductions in CO_2 by the year 2005, by far the most progressive stance of any official delegation or negotiating bloc, and one that gained little support from other governments.

The United States, meanwhile, continued its lack of clear commitment to any target or timetable, although this position was an increasingly isolated one. Finally, in part because of the findings in the 1995 IPCC Report and because of growing public pressure, the United States surprised climate negotiators by announcing for the first time that it would support binding targets and timetables for greenhouse gas emissions. The United States was silent, however, on what specific levels it would support. Nonetheless, the public announcement gave a shot in the arm to the negotiations and offered the first promise that a meaningful regime might be negotiated at Kyoto.

Through the next year the United States remained silent about specific targets and timetables. Increasing pressure built from Europe as well as the developing countries for the United States to show leadership on this issue by announcing support for a strong target. Instead, President Clinton announced at the "Rio+5" Session of the United Nations in June 1997 (marking the five-year anniversary of the Earth Summit and the signing of the UNFCCC) that he would use the six months remaining before Kyoto to educate the American public about the need for greenhouse gas reductions.

The Europeans and others were not pleased with the U.S. position. Perhaps the loudest cheers during the entire Rio+5 Session greeted British Prime Minister Tony Blair when he indirectly criticized the United States by saying "some of the greatest industrialized nations" have not lived up to their promises. He stated further that: "The biggest responsibility falls on those countries with the biggest emissions. . . . We in Europe have put our cards on the table. It is time for the special pleading to stop and for others to follow suit." The G-77 Chairman, Daudi Mwakawago was even clearer: "[President Clinton] articulated the problems very clearly, but when it came to global action, joining the rest of humanity to address them, there wasn't very much there."

Clinton's announcement that he would build political will over the next six months catalyzed both sides of the U.S. climate debate to rally their troops and build political support for either a stronger or weaker protocol. Just a few months after Clinton's June speech, industry announced a $13 million dollar campaign under the ambiguous name of the "Global Climate Information Project." Amid a refrain of "It's not global, and it won't work," industry first attacked the

Framework Convention as being unfair to U.S. industry because it let developing countries off the hook for binding commitments. Other ads in the campaign claimed that energy prices would rise more than 20 percent. Over 1500 utilities, trade associations, labor unions, and other corporations signed on to an advertisement asking the President not to "rush into an unwise and unfair United Nations Agreement that's bad for America." WASHINGTON POST, Oct. 6, 1997, at A9. The U.S. Senate added its support to this position by passing a resolution urging the President not to agree to any convention that did not include binding targets on developing countries. The Byrd-Hagel Resolution, as it has since been referred to, strongly influenced both the Kyoto negotiations and the ensuing national dialogue over whether to support the Kyoto Protocol.

S. RES. 98, REPORT NO. 105–54, 105TH CONG.
(July 25, 1997)

Expressing the sense of the Senate regarding the conditions for the United States becoming a signatory to any international agreement on greenhouse gas emissions under the United Nations Framework Convention on Climate Change. * * *

Whereas the 'Berlin Mandate' calls for the adoption, as soon as December 1997, in Kyoto, Japan, of a protocol or another legal instrument that strengthens commitments to limit greenhouse gas emissions by Annex I Parties for the post-2000 period and establishes a negotiation process called the 'Ad Hoc Group on the Berlin Mandate';

Whereas the 'Berlin Mandate' specifically exempts all Developing Country Parties from any new commitments in such negotiation process for the post-2000 period; * * *

Whereas greenhouse gas emissions of Developing Country Parties are rapidly increasing and are expected to surpass emissions of the United States and other OECD countries as early as 2015; * * *

Whereas the exemption for Developing Country Parties is inconsistent with the need for global action on climate change and is environmentally flawed; [and]

Whereas the Senate strongly believes that the proposals under negotiation, because of the disparity of treatment between Annex I Parties and Developing Countries and the level of required emission reductions, could result in serious harm to the United States economy, including significant job loss, trade disadvantages, increased energy and consumer costs, or any combination thereof; * * *

Now, therefore, be it

Resolved, That it is the sense of the Senate that—

(1)   the United States should not be a signatory to any protocol to, or other agreement regarding, the United Nations Framework Convention on Climate Change of 1992, at negotiations in Kyoto in December 1997, or thereafter, which would—

  (A)   mandate new commitments to limit or reduce greenhouse gas emissions for the Annex I Parties, unless the protocol or other agreement also mandates new specific scheduled commitments to limit or reduce greenhouse gas emissions for Developing Country Parties within the same compliance period, or

(B)   result in serious harm to the economy of the United States; and

(2)   any such protocol or other agreement which would require the advice and consent of the Senate to ratification should be accompanied by a detailed explanation of any legislation or regulatory actions that may be required to implement the protocol or other agreement and should also be accompanied by an analysis of the detailed financial costs and other impacts on the economy of the United States which would be incurred by the implementation of the protocol or other agreement.

Environmental groups countered by launching media and public information campaigns and grassroots actions to raise awareness and garner support for U.S. commitments to cut greenhouse gases. Some environmental groups attacked Vice President Gore, quoting passages from his book *Earth in the Balance* and running advertisements with the words "Withdrawn by the author" superimposed over a copy of the book's cover. A scientist's statement signed by over 2600 leading scientists was handed to the President on June 18, 1997, endorsing strong and clear commitments at Kyoto. A similar statement from over 1000 leading economists argued that the United States could meet the objectives of the Framework Convention without harming the national economy.

The Administration also engaged in a flurry of public relations actions; Vice President Gore, for example, hiked five miles to the base of the shrinking Grinnell Glacier in Glacier National Park, to dramatize the current impacts of climate change. Inside the White House, however, infighting continued between those pushing the Administration to come as close as possible to the European position and others cautioning that dramatic steps could harm the robust U.S. economy. Even a Department of Energy study, which concluded that energy efficiency technologies could allow the United States to reach 1990 levels by the year 2010 with little or no overall cost to the economy, did not unify the Administration's position.

With time running out on the eve of the final formal negotiating meeting before Kyoto, the Clinton Administration announced its long-awaited policy on October 22, 1997. The U.S. position proposed a binding target of stabilizing emissions at 1990 levels by the year 2008 to 2012, and further unspecified reductions by the year 2017. To meet these targets, the President outlined a program of $5 billion in tax and other incentives to spur energy efficiency technologies; endorsed the concept of an international pollution trading system that would allow for reduced costs of compliance; and emphasized the restructuring of the electric industry concurrent to deregulation (a process that was already beginning). The Administration's position drew immediate criticism from both U.S. environmentalists and industry groups, and by governments around the world, especially European, which had hoped for stronger leadership from the world's only remaining superpower.

With the U.S. position finally known, the major proposals for targets and timetables leading up to Kyoto could be identified. See Box 5-1.

Box 5-1: Kyoto Negotiating Positions on GHG Reductions

Country/Bloc	Negotiating Position
Alliance of Small Island States	20% below 1990 levels by 2005
G-77	35% below 1990 levels by 2020
European Union	7.5% below 1990 levels by 2005; 15% below by 2010
Russia	1990 levels by 2010
Czech Republic	5% below 1990 levels by 2005; 15 % below by 2010
Eastern Europe	1990 levels by 2005
Peru	15% below 1990 levels by 2005
Brazil	30% below 1990 levels by 2020
Switzerland	10% below 1990 levels by 2010 based on per capita consumption
Japan	0–5% below 1990 levels by 2008–2012, depending on economic factors
United States	1990 levels by 2008–2012; further unspecified cuts by 2017

Differences over the targets and timetables were not the only differences separating the Parties as they entered the last year of negotiations for the Kyoto Protocol. Differences also existed on whether and to what extent emissions trading would be allowed, whether the experiment of joint implementation found in the UNFCCC would be expanded, whether developing countries would commit to making binding future commitments, and to what extent countries such as the OPEC countries would be compensated for taking steps to address climate change.

QUESTIONS AND DISCUSSION

1. The Berlin Mandate set out certain parameters for the negotiation of the Kyoto Protocol. For example, the mandate states that the Kyoto negotiations should "not introduce any new commitments" on developing countries. During the Kyoto negotiations, this aspect of the Berlin Mandate would come under intense criticism in the United States, particularly from industry. What justification is there for treating developing countries differently?

2. President Clinton quite explicitly made the run-up to Kyoto an exercise in building political support. He challenged environmentalists to show that the U.S. population would support strong action on climate change. On one hand, this seems a fair role for environmental groups to play — but what does it say about the President's own willingness to take a bold leadership position? How would you advise the President to build political will for strong and controversial international action? What if you were head of an environmental organization? How, then, would you seek to build political will?

3. The Byrd-Hagel Resolution substantially shaped the national debate over climate change for more than a decade. For example, when the Bush Administration repudiated the Protocol in 1992, it cited the same two reasons highlighted in the Byrd-Hagel Resolution — i.e., that the Protocol did not include developing countries and that domestic economic costs would be too high. What legal significance does the Byrd-Hagel Resolution have? How does this Resolution

comport with the principle of common but differentiated responsibilities discussed in Chapter 4?

C.   Negotiations at Kyoto

Not since the 1992 Earth Summit had so much press and attention been paid to an international environmental negotiation as was paid to the Kyoto negotiations. Kyoto teemed with thousands of official delegates, reporters, scientists, activists, industry officials — and not one of them went to Kyoto knowing how the Protocol would turn out, or indeed even if there would be a Protocol. The various positions of the key parties — the European Community, the United States, and the G-77 — seemed too distant for any meaningful agreement to be reached. In addition to being far apart on the size of commitments, the major negotiating blocs could not agree on such basic issues as whether all countries had to accept the same commitment; the extent to which emissions trading would be allowed; and what the consequences for noncompliance would be. Entering the final negotiations at Kyoto, virtually the entire text of the draft Protocol was still heavily bracketed, often with more than two alternative provisions elaborated. Yet, the public scrutiny was such that failure to reach an agreement would have been an embarrassing failure for many of the governments. And no one wanted to be blamed for "killing Kyoto."

One highly publicized turning point was the visit of U.S. Vice President Al Gore midway in the negotiations. Although he did not make any specific commitments, he publicly instructed the U.S. delegation to be "flexible" in order to reach an agreement. More important than what he said was that he was there at all — his presence in Kyoto raised the political stakes of failure. Within a few days, the United States announced that it would consider flexible targets and timetables, meaning that all the industrialized Parties did not have to agree to the same emission reductions and the same baseline year. Japan immediately tabled a new proposal that had the EU reducing emissions more than either the United States or Japan. Not surprisingly, the European Union criticized the Japanese position, claiming that they were failing to play the traditional role of a host to facilitate consensus. The European Union insisted on being able to use a regional bubble concept, by which it could meet the emissions reductions through a system of trading between member countries. The United States, complaining that the Europeans had an unfair economic advantage in complying with any emissions standards, announced that it was considering creating its own emissions trading bloc with Japan, Russia, Canada, Australia, and New Zealand (collectively referred to as the Umbrella Group).

With two days left to go, the United States had finally agreed to a three percent reduction in emissions from 1990 levels and deals were starting to be made. The final negotiating session went essentially non-stop for forty-eight hours and the end of the session had to be extended for several hours. Even so, only the heavy-handed work of the negotiation's Argentinian Chairperson, Raul Estrada, averted last minute disputes between the G-77 and the industrialized countries that could have derailed the entire agreement. A hastily crafted compromise put off for one year any further discussions about developing country commitments, thus paving the way for final adoption of the Protocol. In the end, the Parties agreed to a set of clear targets and timetables, coupled with a decidedly unclear and complex trading structure that was meant to provide flexibility and lower costs of compliance for the Parties. Some of the last-minute political trade-offs and the tension in the negotiations can be seen in the following excerpt, written shortly after the negotiations ended:

MICHAEL GRUBB, et al., THE KYOTO PROTOCOL: A GUIDE AND ASSESSMENT
89–114 (1999)

*3.5.3. International emissions trading * * ***

The first reaction to the U.S. proposal [for emissions trading] was one of uncertainty, backed with a lot of suspicion. For most negotiators, the concept was entirely new. Indeed the United States itself was at the time unclear as to how it would develop the proposal in the context of an international agreement, and it mixed references to governmental commitments with examples of its sulphur trading programme, citing the need to let industry invest in emissions reductions wherever it was cheapest to do so. The import of the U.S. proposals only really became clear after a group of U.S. officials retreated over Christmas 1996 to hammer out specific textual proposals. Their subsequent Protocol proposal stated that countries — Parties to the Protocol — should agree to a specific commitment of 'carbon equivalent emissions allowed for a budget period', and that then: 'A Party . . . may . . . transfer to, or receive from, any other [participating] Party, any of its tonnes of carbon equivalent emissions allowed for a budget period, for the purpose of meeting its obligations.' The proposed basis on which governments could exchange their emission commitments was not specified and did not need to be: all that matters is that combined emission allowances after the 'trade' do not exceed the initial combined total allocation. The responsibility rests with the governments, but the way in which countries limit emissions internally would remain entirely a sovereign issue, as would the terms of trading.

The U.S. draft language then stated that: 'A Party may authorize any domestic entity . . . to participate in actions leading to transfer and receipt . . . of tonnes of carbon equivalent emissions allowed.'

This could allow a government to create an internal system of tradable emission permits along the lines of the system used for controlling sulphur in the United States, and then to engage in international trading. Each participating industry would be required to obtain permits equivalent to its emissions. Direct participation in such a system could be limited to major industries (such as power generators). The new feature would be that industries could trade internationally with companies in other countries that adopted a similar system.

Although many details remained to be resolved . . . , the essence of the U.S. proposal on emissions trading was now clear; and the United States embarked upon strenuous diplomatic efforts to explain and promote the concept to other countries.

* * *

Initial reactions included concern that emissions trading would somehow confer a morally objectionable right to pollute. In the OECD, this concern did not go far beyond bar-room rhetoric and denunciations in the press. Every country was emitting and would continue to emit greenhouse gases at some level; indeed the very concept of emission targets could be similarly construed as condoning this. It was hard to argue that making targets tradable necessarily makes them immoral.

A more practical objection raised in Europe was that such a novel and complex idea in the international scene could not possibly be negotiated in time for Kyoto. More Machiavellian commentators suspected the United States of introducing emissions trading as a way of deliberately confounding the negotiations. For Kyoto to establish industry-level trading — in which industries hold the permits and can trade them internationally — would indeed have been an impossibly complex task in the time available. But the U.S. submission of its negotiating text made it plain that the goal for Kyoto was altogether more practical, focusing upon a structure of intergovernmental trading that could allow the subsequent evolution of industry-level trading by those countries desiring to participate. It sounds complex but is in fact astonishingly simple: the text would just establish that governments can exchange their 'tonnes of CO_2,' allowed under the Protocol, and that they are entitled to pass this authority on to subnational entities (e.g., industries) providing that the governments ensure the integrity of any resulting trades.

Thus concerns that such a system was not practical, that there was not enough time to set it up, or that administrative requirements would be too onerous, proved hard to sustain. As these objections foundered, two core concerns emerged.

The first was the general concern that international flexibility might provide a way for the leading emitters to avoid serious domestic action. As the Kyoto debate proceeded, this began to take a very specific and startling form, arising from the peculiarities of the situation in the EITs [Economies in Transition]. In most of the OECD, as noted, emissions had continued rising. But in the EITs, and most notably Russia, emissions fell dramatically with the economic transition. If emissions there stayed quite low, a flat-rate emissions target with unconstrained trading could imply a huge transfer of allowances from most of the transition economies, which would have a surplus, to the OECD countries, above all the United States and Japan. The United States understood this, and over successive months teams of U.S. officials went to the East to explain the windfall that could be waiting. No specific deal was concluded but the Russians got the point, and in March they submitted their own negotiating proposals in favour of emissions trading with flat-rate initial allocations from 1990 levels.

There are two ways of looking at this. The primary incentive for the United States is that trading provides perhaps the only means by which it can agree to substantial flat-rate emission reductions. It was obvious that the U.S. Congress would never agree to bind the country to significant cuts in its domestic emissions, and it was equally obvious that the EU would place intense pressure for such cuts on the United States and the rest of the OECD. The only way of squaring the circle was to have emissions trading, preferably with a big seller in the market. Russia, with its probable surplus allowances, was the only player big enough.

A more charitable interpretation was possible. To help sustain its old foe in its conversion from communism, the United States was proposing to use the Climate Change Convention as a way of endowing Russia with desperately needed resources. Additionally, Russia would be given an incentive to restructure its staggeringly inefficient and polluting economy in more efficient and sustainable ways, so as to enhance the allowances it could sell. * * *

The problem was that it still looked like cheating on the basic commitment. The EU concern that emissions trading would undermine any success in imposing more stringent U.S. emission targets was reinforced by the east European situation. The United States might not even have to take significant action at home; it might simply buy a surplus of what the EU termed 'hot air' from Russia. . . .

Against this background the European Council of Ministers met in June, just before the Denver Summit, and under the guidance of the Dutch presidency crafted a compromise between the majority of governments that remained hostile to emissions trading and the small band of supporters. "The Council considers", they concluded, "that mechanisms such as emissions trading are supplementary to domestic action and common coordinated policies and measures, and that the inclusion of any trading system in the Protocol and the level of the targets to be achieved are interdependent. It therefore calls upon all industrialized countries to indicate the targets they envisage for 2005 and 2010." In other words, the EU was prepared to accept the logic of emissions trading, but only if it resulted in practice in the benefits which its proponents claimed, with greater efficiency enabling a stronger overall outcome. The EU had worked out how to catch the ball tossed by the United States, and thrown it down as a gauntlet.

The Japanese focused on a different concern. They were worried that the United States would use its enormous political leverage over Russia to monopolize that country's surplus, and so — along with several other countries — Japan demanded conditions that any trading should be transparent, competitive and open. To this were added other factors. As the EU recognized that the overall level of commitments would indeed be much weaker than its proposed 15% reduction, it pressed for constraints to ensure that any international action would be supplementary to domestic action — a 'supplementary cap" on international trading. . . . The French, in particular, also pressed for some common rules about how any domestic allocations of emission permits might be made. Against this complex background, in Kyoto the OECD countries edged towards an agreed text on emissions trading; for whatever doubts the EU had about emissions trading, it knew full well by now that an agreement was impossible without it.

But the OECD was overlooking a deeper challenge. Developing countries had been almost ignored in the internecine OECD debate on emissions trading. This fed a resentment that grew as they began to understand the game: not only might such trading allow the United States to avoid serious domestic action, but Russia, an industrialized country, could be the major beneficiary. Behind this was a more principled objection. Although the United States was at pains to emphasize that the allowances agreed at Kyoto would not constitute any more basic or long-term 'right' to emit, there was a deep fear that the whole question of long-term emission entitlements was being pre-empted. African countries had already started supporting a principle that emission entitlements should be allocated on a per capita basis, or at least that they should converge towards this. China and, most stridently, India backed similar proposals, arguing that fundamental issues of principle were at stake on which they had not been adequately consulted and on which they could not retreat.

The OECD, having spent much of its energies on internal debate, hit a brick wall when it then tried to place its delicately crafted (and still not finalized) proposed text into the final negotiating texts at the climax to the Kyoto conference. The G77 adamantly refused to accept an article on emissions trading. Chairman Estrada rejected the OECD's complex text on the grounds that it was submitted too late; in reality, he knew that every sentence would be opposed as a matter of principle and that such complexity at the final hour would destroy the negotiations. The proposed article was omitted and replaced by a simple paragraph allowing countries to exchange parts of their assigned amounts.

But developing-country opposition to emissions trading was rooted in principles, fed by anger that it might enable the United States to avoid significant domestic action, and magnified by resentment about the prospective Russian windfall. They were not going to budge. * * *

At about 2.00 a.m. on 11 December, with the conference already long past its official deadline, the negotiations reached the offending paragraphs. On behalf of the EU, the UK proposed an amendment that trading could not start until rules were agreed at the subsequent Conference of Parties, a condition that the United States resisted, fearing it would be used to block emissions trading altogether. Then China said it could not accept the paragraph, amended or not, as there had not been sufficient time to consider the implications. India followed with its fundamental objections to the ad-hoc creation of tradable entitlements without debate about the global principles involved. A dozen developing countries raised their objections.

At 4.00 a.m. Ambassador Estrada called a halt to the negotiations, for short consultations. A pleasant (alas, unconfirmed) rumour holds that instead of yet more frantic consultations, he went back to his hotel room for a short rest, a shower and a change of clothes. In reality he remained locked in consultations, testing out compromises on emissions trading repeatedly, also in relation to other parts of the package. Nevertheless, he returned with renewed vigour. He reconvened the conference and announced that he proposed to delete the offending paragraphs, and instead insert a new article within the section on implementation procedures. The new article would consist of three short sentences stating basically that the Parties would subsequently negotiate principles, rules, etc. for emissions trading; that they may trade emissions; and that any trading would be supplemental to domestic action. He read the sentences twice, very slowly, and paused. He asked if there were any objections and brought down his gavel as India — some say joined by both China and the EU — raised flags to object. He ignored the flags and stormed ahead to the next paragraph on commitments. Any country that openly challenged his authority would almost certainly have been held responsible for destroying the Kyoto negotiations. None did. Thus in the defining moment of the Kyoto conference, the objections in principle of major developing countries to emissions trading — and countries altogether probably representing almost half the world's population — were overridden. In another area of the agreement, however, they were to get their *quid pro quo*. First, however, the Kyoto negotiations had another surprise in store in the area of international flexibility. * * *

3.6.1 Objections to North-South 'joint implementation'

The concept of joint implementation — generating emission credits by investing in projects outside the industrialized world — faced far more severe opposition in relation to developing countries than when applied between industrialized countries. This sprang from a number of long- standing concerns.

Locus of responsibilities and 'cream-skimming'. Perhaps the most fundamental and principled criticism of JI was that it could allow developed countries — those with the highest emissions and an acknowledged responsibility to lead — to achieve their emission targets without taking adequate action at home. JI was seen as enabling developed countries to escape their prime responsibility to put their own house in order.

Related to this was the fear that JI projects would focus on and 'use up' the cheapest reduction options in developing countries, so that if and when developing countries came to adopt emission commitments, they would only have more expensive options left. While, strictly speaking, this is an issue that could be simply resolved in terms of allocations, the underlying fear was a potent one. Many developing countries consequently suggested that current JI proposals should be re-evaluated in order to reflect the total economic cost of carbon abatement in the short and long term, rather than on the basis of short-term single projects undertaken by individual companies, but this was anathema to the idea of a market-based process promoting private investment.

Baselines for measuring 'additional' emission reductions. There are serious methodological difficulties in estimating the emissions saving resulting from a JI project, since this hinges upon an estimate of how much higher emissions would have been without it. It is a 'counterfactual' problem of measuring emissions avoided rather than simply the emissions themselves. Would certain alternative projects really have gone ahead? Whose assessment of the alternative favoured and feasible options should be believed? Developing countries have feared that investing countries would get unfairly high credits for JI projects. One solution is to incorporate wide margins of error into the predicted savings achieved by JI projects. However, this would reduce the scope and profitability of projects. * * *

Jl for carbon sequestration or technology transfer? The difficulties were aggravated by the dispute about the role of sinks. To many in the North, forest management and reforestation offered an obvious and cheap way to offset emissions, a view supported by some organizations seeking to protect wildlife and biodiversity in the developing world, and also by some forestry organizations in developing countries that welcomed the opportunity to attract more resources. Costa Rica led the field with extensive offers of forest protection under the aegis of JI.

However, many other developing countries opposed using their land to generate credits that would allow industrialized countries to continue emitting GHGs. Furthermore, many reforestation or land-management schemes in developing countries risk being ineffective or politically unsettling if they take land away from agriculture or otherwise cut across already disputed aspects of land rights. Concentrating on carbon sequestration projects in the developing world provoked the accusation of imposing developed-world environmental values onto the poor and weak — at worst, cast as 'carbon colonialism' — as well as being difficult to measure and enforce.

[The depth of feelings — and the complexities — became visible from an early stage. The most striking example the author witnessed was at a meeting in the early 1990s. An economist from a U.S. environmental NGO (one long associated with promoting market instruments) had expounded the virtues of JI and explained how much cheaper it could be to absorb CO_2 in Africa than to limit emissions in the United States. Shaking with anger, an African present rose and asked 'why should African governments let their land be used as a toilet for absorbing emissions from Americans' second cars?' Needless to say, the ensuing debate was not a very productive one.]

3.6.3 The 'Kyoto surprise'

It was against this background that the single most remarkable development of the entire Kyoto negotiations occurred. It arose from a most unexpected quarter. One element of the sweeping proposals that Brazil had put forward in June 1997 was that Annex I Parties should be subject to a financial penalty if they did not comply with their quantified commitments under the Protocol, with the fine being levied in proportion to the degree of non-compliance. The money would be paid into a Clean Development Fund that would be used to support appropriate projects in developing countries, for limiting emissions and potentially for adaptation. The proposal included ways of apportioning the proceeds between developing countries, and suggested a level of $10 per tonne of excess carbon-equivalent emitted.

The idea that industrialized countries would agree to being subject to assessed financial penalties as a compliance measure seemed far-fetched to any seasoned politician — the debate about enforcement mechanisms had barely begun — and Ambassador Estrada omitted it (along with the rest of the complex Brazilian proposal) from the chairman's negotiating text for the final pre-Kyoto session in October. But the G77, while uneasy about several aspects of the Brazilian proposal, could unite around the suggestion for financial penalties channelled into a Clean Development Fund, and they insisted that it be reinserted into the text.

The Annex I countries pronounced their opposition and it seemed a fruitless debate. But by the end of the final pre-Kyoto negotiating session, a remarkable twist on the proposal had occurred to one or two key people. If the penalty were levied at a sufficient rate to fund carbon-saving projects in the developing countries that would save emissions equivalent to the excess emissions from Annex I, the practical consequence would be almost identical to JI, though the legal and institutional framework would be completely different. From this perspective, one of the most apparently aggressive proposals from the G77 could be considered as consonant with the U.S. proposals for JI that they had been fiercely rejecting for five years.

The idea was first floated in the negotiations at the small ministerial discussions that Japan hosted early in November 1997. Fired with the possibilities, a U.S. team dashed down to Rio to explore the options. The United States managed to shift the line on compliance to encompass such investments as *contributing to* compliance, rather than being a *penalty for not* complying. The idea of a penalty on governments was transformed into a mechanism for investment by companies. The multilateral character of the framework was retained, but it became a 'mechanism' rather than a 'fund'; and in the final days of Kyoto, the clean development mechanism . . . was born. * * *

3.8 Extending commitments to new countries: evolution and voluntary accession

The most divisive North-South issue of all in the Kyoto negotiations concerned the desire of most OECD countries — but especially the United States — to draw developing countries into specific quantified emission limitation commitments, or at least into a process that might visibly lead to this conclusion.

The reasons why this was (and remains) such a divisive issue are easy to see. From one standpoint, it is quite unreasonable to expect the developing countries to commit themselves to adopting binding emission constraints at present. Most of them have contributed hardly anything to the climate change problem and their per capita emissions are still but a small fraction of those in the industrialized world. . . . Why should they devote resources towards a diffuse and long-term problem, largely caused by others, when they have more basic and pressing priorities ranging from simple health and sanitation to basic infrastructure developments?

From the other perspective, it is equally apparent that the climate change problem cannot ultimately be solved without action by the developing countries. Their emissions are growing rapidly, especially in percentage terms (though less rapidly since the Asian financial crisis ended), since they comprise more than three-quarters of the world's population, their long-term potential emissions growth could ultimately swamp any restraint by the current industrialized world. Furthermore, many of the cheapest options for limiting emissions may lie in developing countries, whose economies are inevitably less efficient (in carbon per unit of GDP) than most OECD economies. Altering the trajectory of emissions growth in developing countries is probably the biggest low-cost long-term opportunity for limiting global emissions that exists. From this perspective, excluding them makes economic nonsense.

If the divide itself derives from a classic clash of perspectives, and potentially a clash of equity vs. efficiency (though it need not take this form), it became poisoned during the negotiations as a result of the long history of North-South politics, the internal politics of the G77 group (which encompasses hugely diverse interests) and the specific legacy of the debate on developing-country involvement in the climate change regime.

The Convention had little choice but to enshrine the basic structural division between the Annex I countries and the developing countries. Already by the time of the Berlin conference, the pressures in the United States to include developing countries in negotiations on any new commitments were very strong. However, since the industrialized countries had done so little towards establishing leadership through their domestic actions, and most of the OECD was far from ready to achieve the indicative aim of returning emissions to 1990 levels by 2000, there was never any chance of the Mandate including anything that might lead to new commitments by developing countries.

In fact it was the EU which first formally proposed extending the net of commitments, recommending that they be applied in all countries listed in an Annex X, which was clearly intended to go beyond the existing Annex I. The EU belatedly indicated that this should include at least South Korea and Mexico, and also Turkey which was trying to withdraw from Annex I. It was also implied that this same list should undertake quantified emission limitations. Since the core EU proposal on quantified commitments focused on flat-rate reductions from 1990 levels, this seemed a clear provocation to countries whose emissions in 1990 were relatively low but had already grown by as much as 25–40%. Quite apart from being outside the terms of the Berlin Mandate, the resultant perception that any talk of extending commitments to some new countries might require them to reduce below 1990 levels — clearly impossible and inequitable for most developing countries — was a fear that was very slow to dissipate.

The pressures in the United States were for far broader participation, and they took on concrete form with the specific U.S. protocol proposal of January 1997. This included a section on the 'evolution of commitments' which stated that all countries should have binding quantified commitments by a certain date — 2005 was suggested as a negotiating basis in the U.S. proposal. This was clearly outside the terms of the Berlin Mandate and aroused predictable anger across most of the developing world. 'Evolution of commitments' were dirty words in the negotiations thereafter.

Attempts to extend the negotiations to include new commitments for developing countries continued right up to Kyoto itself, where New Zealand, supported by the other [non-EU developed countries] and by Poland and Slovenia, proposed that conditional upon industrialized countries having fulfilled their commitments in the first period, developing countries should agree to binding commitments applicable in a subsequent period. This at least attempted to acknowledge the agreed principle of industrialized-country leadership, and universal participation was not proposed (they called for 'progressive engagement' according to levels of development, and explicitly excluded the least developed), but it was still clearly outside the terms of the Berlin Mandate. The proposal provoked several hours of angry rejection from the developing countries, which saw such linkage as a betrayal of trust about the whole purpose of the Kyoto negotiations.

The only creative approach towards developing-country commitments that could plausibly be argued to fall within the terms of the Berlin Mandate was the proposal crafted by Chairman Raul Estrada-Oyuela to include an article explicitly providing a path for voluntary adoption of quantified commitments — Article 10 (later 9) in the draft Protocol. This appeared innocuous, but many developing countries saw it as a Trojan horse which would leave them vulnerable to being subjected, perhaps one by one, to pressure to adopt commitments. The G77 always felt that its only protection against the might of the OECD was collective strength. Though at least 35 developing countries registered their support for the proposed article in the final night at Kyoto, core countries, which felt they had been slighted in some of the earlier debates, remained adamantly opposed to it. With China, India and Brazil lining up with the OPEC countries and others, forcing the article through could have alienated half the world from the Kyoto regime for years to come. In what must have been the most difficult decision of that long night, Ambassador Estrada declared that the article on voluntary commitments — his own creation and the only credible attempt to resolve the impossible division — had failed to gain sufficient support and had to be removed.

The deletion of the proposed article on voluntary accession was the other major plenary decision in the long night at Kyoto, a *quid pro quo* for riding roughshod over the objections of China and India to emissions trading; given the weight that the United States had placed upon developing-country commitments, some waited to see if its delegation would walk out. But the clean development mechanism and slightly strengthened references to enhancing the existing commitments of developing countries (shortly to be confirmed) were enough for the U.S. delegation to stay. No one else walked out; half of the delegates anyway were asleep from sheer exhaustion.

The meeting proceeded to more detailed wrangles over aspects of the CDM and confirmation of the procedural articles . . . and the struggle over improving the implementation of existing commitments, noted above. With the full terms of the instruments and the political package in place, the final points of the specific numerical commitments were agreed and brought to the plenary hall. Given the delicate balance between the varied concerns finally reached after two and a half years of negotiations, not a single Party wanted to risk the opprobrium of objecting. Ambassador Estrada brought down his gavel, and declared that the Kyoto Protocol had been agreed unanimously and could now be forwarded for formal adoption.

3.9 Conclusions

What general conclusions can be drawn from the negotiations of the Kyoto Protocol? It was an extraordinary process, grappling with an unprecedented problem. Trying to get more than 150 countries with hugely divergent interests and perceptions to agree was bound to be extremely difficult. That it succeeded at all was a considerable achievement, due in no small measure to the generosity of Japan in funding a host of additional facilitating activities, and the skill and authority ultimately wielded by the chairman of the negotiations, Ambassador Estrada-Oyuela.

QUESTIONS AND DISCUSSION

1. Does it surprise you how much of the Protocol negotiations depended on the actions or decisions of individuals? Consider particularly the sensitive and important role of the chairperson to encourage and cajole, sometimes even force, a consensus among the Parties.

2. In reviewing the excerpt above, recall the discussion of global climate politics in Chapter 4. Can you see how the different voting blocs affected the Kyoto Protocol negotiations? What techniques are used to get countries to move away from their more self-interested positions?

3.   There were obviously many different viewpoints that had to be considered and reflected throughout the negotiations, but some countries still emerge as the most important. One of the great ironies is that the United States achieved virtually every one of the major policy goals it had in negotiating the Protocol, but yet would still be one of the only developed countries to reject it. As Grubb et al. conclude in their treatment of the negotiations:

> U.S. dominance is striking. The United States got virtually everything it wanted in respect of flexibility for Annex I commitments with the sole exception of 'borrowing'. The EU, with greater population and GDP, did score important successes: through its efforts, the United States (and other OECD countries) made a stronger commitment than they otherwise would have done; the EU headed off many of the most potentially dangerous proposals on sinks, and at least kept the door open on aspects of its policies and measures proposals. But to discover the source of most of the ideas in the Protocol, one only needs to read the U.S. proposal of January 1997. The coherence of the U.S. administration contrasted with . . . the unwieldy (and introspective) morass of EU decision making during the negotiating process. This reflects the EU's broader foreign policy difficulties, and should provoke a lot of thought among member states. Only in respect of developing countries did the United States not get what it wanted; indeed U.S. pressure on developing countries frequently served only to inflame their resistance.

Grubb, at 114. Can you see why this would make Parties to the Protocol even more upset when the United States subsequently withdrew from the agreement? In what specific ways did the United State achieve its policy goals? In what ways, were its goals rejected?

4.   As you read the Kyoto Protocol and begin to learn about the global carbon market it created, you may at times be frustrated with the dizzying and technical issues that emerge. At those times, pause to consider what an amazing and ambitious achievement in international cooperation the Protocol represents. The countries are struggling, usually in good faith, to find a compromise that will address the complexities of global climate change while leaving room for economic development. They are also creating an entire carbon market out of nothing other than mutual promises; it is a market completely born out of international law. It may ultimately not work, but there is still great hope in the Kyoto Protocol for successfully responding to climate change and more generally for other international negotiations in the future.

III.   THE KYOTO PROTOCOL

The core of the Kyoto Protocol is targets and timetables, or "quantified emissions limitation and reduction objectives" (QELROs), for industrialized (Annex I) Parties to reduce their net emissions of greenhouse gases over a five-year reporting period, 2008–2012. Together, QELROs and the deadline for compliance are commonly called "targets and timetables." In aggregate, developed countries aimed at a 5 percent reduction from 1990 levels by the first reporting period, 2008–2012. Most European countries agreed to lower their emission 8 percent below 1990 levels, while the United States agreed to a 7 percent reduction. *See* Annex B to the

Protocol for the full listing of commitments (reprinted in Annex 2 of this casebook). Countries in economic transition were allowed to select an alternative baseline year other than 1990, and several countries did so. In addition, all countries had the option of choosing 1995 as the baseline year for three relatively minor but potent greenhouse gases (hydrofluorocarbons, perfluorocarbons, and sulphur hexafluoride). The Protocol envisions that the first reporting period would be followed by subsequent commitment periods and presumably stricter emission targets. For a further summary of the Kyoto Protocol, see Don Goldberg, *A Legal Analysis of the Kyoto Protocol* (CIEL, 1998).

In addition to the targets and timetables, the Kyoto Protocol also set forth general parameters for four different flexibility mechanisms, including emissions trading, joint implementation, an emissions bubble, and a new initiative called the "Clean Development Mechanism." In this way, Kyoto created a "cap-and-trade" system whereby developed country emissions were capped, but they would be allowed to lower their costs of compliance through trading in one or more of the flexibility mechanisms. Parameters were also set for a compliance and monitoring system and for the consideration of at least certain land-use and forestry activities that could alter carbon reservoirs or sinks. Many of these provisions raised as many questions as they answered, and set the stage for further negotiations after Kyoto.

As can be seen from the above discussion, the Kyoto Protocol is a complicated agreement, but one that also left considerable details to be worked out subsequently by the parties. Indeed, all of the Parties knew that the Protocol could not be ratified without further negotiations. At this point, you should review the Kyoto Protocol, reproduced in Annex 2. The rest of this chapter summarizes briefly the basic structure of the Kyoto Protocol. The following four chapters will address in detail key implementation challenges in the Kyoto regime, including emissions trading and other flexibility mechanisms, forests and land-use changes, compliance mechanisms and the negotiation of post-Kyoto commitments.

QUESTIONS AND DISCUSSION

1. *Reading the Treaty.* Before proceeding further, review the Kyoto Protocol in Annex 2 of this book. To become better familiar with its provisions, answer the following questions from the Kyoto Protocol.

- a) By what year must Annex I countries show demonstrable progress toward their target emissions level? How must they show "demonstrable progress"?

- b) What are the conditions placed on trading emissions reduction units?

- c) What is the purpose of the Clean Development Mechanism?

- d) What number of Parties is necessary for the Protocol to enter into force?

- e) What functions, authorities and responsibilities does the Conference of the Parties meeting as the Parties to the Protocol have? Are these sufficient to ensure the success of the Protocol?

- f) How does the Protocol penalize non-Parties?

2. After reviewing the Kyoto Protocol, evaluate its terms against the negotiating framework of the Berlin Mandate. In what ways does the Protocol meet the

parameters of the Berlin Mandate?

3. As you review the Protocol, consider how it relates to the UNFCCC's framework. The Protocol implements the Convention and incorporates many of its provisions, such as the overall objective and institutional architecture, explicitly into the Protocol. The Parties meet for both agreements at the same time. But when the Parties want to discuss the Framework Convention they meet as the Conference of the Parties (CoP), and when they meet to discuss the Protocol, they meet as the "Conference of the Partings meeting as the Parties to the Protocol," which has become known as the "CoP/MoP" — one of the more memorable acronyms. As a Party to the Framework Convention, the United States can join fully in discussions of interpreting or revising the Convention, but when the Protocol is being discussed at the CoP/MoP, the United States is merely an observer (albeit still an influential one).

A.   Emission Reduction Targets and Timetables

The following excerpt from an article published shortly after the Protocol negotiations describes the basic quantified emissions level reduction objectives — i.e., the targets and timetables — to which the developed countries agreed under the Kyoto Protocol. That is followed immediately by excerpts from the Protocol's text.

CLAIRE BREIDENRICH, et al., THE KYOTO PROTOCOL TO THE UNITED NATIONS FRAMEWORK CONVENTION ON CLIMATE CHANGE
92 Am. J. Int'l L. 315 (1998)[*]

Emission Reduction Targets

Article 3 of the Protocol establishes QELROs or emission targets for FCCC Annex I countries, with the exception of Turkey. The Protocol sets targets against base year emission levels. For most parties, 1990 is the official base year. However, certain countries with economies in transition are authorized by a decision of the Conference of the Parties to use a different base year, and other countries with economies in transition may apply to use a different base year. Also, as described in greater detail below, any Annex I country may select 1995 as the base year for the three synthetic GHGs (HFCs, PFCs and SF_6).

The negotiated emission targets for each Annex I country are contained in Annex B to the Protocol, and are listed as percentages of base year emission levels. For example, the target for the United States, which is listed as 93, corresponds to a 7 percent reduction from 1990 levels (or from 1995 levels for the three synthetic GHGs, as explained below). The targets range from an 8 percent reduction (i.e., 92) in the base year emissions level for the European Community (Community or EC) to a 10 percent increase (i.e., 110) in the base year emissions level for Iceland. Overall, the emission reduction among countries listed in Annex B is equivalent to about 5.2 percent of their emissions, if one does not take into account the possible use of 1995 as a base year for synthetic GHGs and the possible use of the Clean

---

Development Mechanism by industrialized countries. . . .

The difference in parties' individual targets is the outcome of contentious negotiations. Several parties, notably EC member states and the United States (until the last stages of the negotiations), called for a uniform target for all industrialized-country parties (although the Community envisioned differentiation among its own member states). Other parties, led strongly by Australia, and including Japan, Norway and Iceland, argued that differentiated targets, rather than a uniform target, were appropriate, owing to the vast differences in countries' national circumstances, particularly natural resources and energy production and consumption profiles. In the final negotiations, parties were not able to reach agreement on a uniform target and opted for individual, differentiated targets.

The uniform 8 percent reduction target for the EC member states is also noteworthy. With respect to the FCCC's aim of returning emissions of Annex I countries to 1990 levels by the year 2000, parties are allowed to achieve that aim individually or jointly. Consequently, the Community developed an arrangement, often referred to as the "EC bubble," to share emission reductions among its member states. This arrangement was fundamental to the Community's ability to gain member state support for a reduction target in the Protocol. Under the EC internal burden-sharing agreement, certain member states such as Portugal and Ireland will be allowed to increase their emissions from 1990 levels. Thus, for the Community as a whole to reach the 8 percent reduction target, other member states will be required to reduce emissions by more than 8 percent. Originally, the Community based its burden-sharing arrangement on an overall 10 percent reduction. Although the FCCC allows for internal burden sharing among Annex I countries with respect to its aim of reducing GHG emissions from those countries to 1990 levels, such burden sharing was not automatically a part of the Kyoto Protocol and had to be negotiated. Under Article 4 of the Protocol, Annex B countries may jointly fulfill their commitments. * * *

Rather than a single-year, fixed target, the Protocol establishes a cumulative target that applies to a multiyear "commitment period." Each Annex I country must ensure that its aggregate emissions during the commitment period do not exceed its "assigned amount." The first commitment period is established by the Protocol as 2008–2012. This multiyear formulation was devised to give parties greater flexibility in meeting their emission reduction commitments and to take into account annual fluctuations, for example, from business cycles. Article 3 implies that there will be subsequent commitment periods of unspecified duration.

Each party's initial "assigned amount" is calculated by multiplying its base year emissions by its individual target in Annex B and then multiplying the result by five — the number of years in the first commitment period. However, the assigned amount may increase or decrease, depending on the party's participation in market-based mechanisms authorized by the Protocol.

GHG Coverage

All of the significant GHGs not controlled by the Montreal Protocol are included in parties' targets under the Protocol, as are all sources and sectors of GHG emissions, other than CO_2 from the land use and forestry sector. . . . These GHGs and source categories are listed in Annex A to the Protocol.

The inclusion of the three synthetic GHG categories, HFCs, PFCs and SF_6, was the subject of lengthy debate in the negotiations. Because these gases are primarily used as substitutes for the stratospheric ozone-depleting substances controlled by the Montreal Protocol, their emissions have grown rapidly since 1990 and are projected to continue to grow. Unfortunately from a climate change perspective, these gases are also potent GHGs with long atmospheric residence times and high radiative forcing effects. For these reasons, several of the parties insisted that the synthetic gases be included in the Protocol's emission targets. Some parties, however, adamantly opposed their inclusion, arguing that to do so would greatly increase the difficulty of attaining overall emission targets. As a compromise, the Kyoto Protocol requires Annex I countries to include the synthetic gases in their emission targets but allows them to use 1995 as the base year for emission reductions of those gases. Since the later base year accounts for an additional five years of growth in emissions, the target is effectively increased for these gases.

KYOTO PROTOCOL, ARTICLE 3

1. The Parties included in Annex I shall, individually or jointly, ensure that their aggregate anthropogenic carbon dioxide equivalent emissions of the greenhouse gases listed in Annex A do not exceed their assigned amounts, calculated pursuant to their quantified emission limitation and reduction commitments inscribed in Annex B and in accordance with the provisions of this Article, with a view to reducing their overall emissions of such gases by at least 5 per cent below 1990 levels in the commitment period 2008 to 2012.

2. Each Party included in Annex I shall, by 2005, have made demonstrable progress in achieving its commitments under this Protocol.

                              *   *   *

7. In the first quantified emission limitation and reduction commitment period, from 2008 to 2012, the assigned amount for each Party included in Annex I shall be equal to the percentage inscribed for it in Annex B of its aggregate anthropogenic carbon dioxide equivalent emissions of the greenhouse gases listed in Annex A in 1990, or the base year or period determined in accordance with paragraph 5 above, multiplied by five. Those Parties included in Annex I for whom land-use change and forestry constituted a net source of greenhouse gas emissions in 1990 shall include in their 1990 emissions base year or period the aggregate anthropogenic carbon dioxide equivalent emissions by sources minus removals by sinks in 1990 from land-use change for the purposes of calculating their assigned amount.

8. Any Party included in Annex I may use 1995 as its base year for hydrofluorocarbons, perfluorocarbons and sulphur hexafluoride, for the purposes of the calculation referred to in paragraph 7 above.

                              *   *   *

10. Any emission reduction units, or any part of an assigned amount, which a Party acquires from another Party in accordance with the provisions of Article 6 [Joint Implementation] or of Article 17 [Emissions Trading] shall be added to the assigned amount for the acquiring Party.

11. Any emission reduction units, or any part of an assigned amount, which a Party transfers to another Party in accordance with the provisions of Article 6 or of Article 17 shall be subtracted from the assigned amount for the transferring Party.

12. Any certified emission reductions which a Party acquires from another Party in accordance with the provisions of Article 12 [Clean Development

Mechanism] shall be added to the assigned amount for that Party.

13.   If the emissions of a Party included in Annex I in a commitment period are less than its assigned amount under this Article, this difference shall, on request of that Party, be added to the assigned amount for that Party for subsequent commitment periods.

QUESTIONS AND DISCUSSION

1.   The Kyoto Protocol, like the Framework Convention before it, anticipated continual amendments and changes to the commitments, particularly for periods beyond the initial reporting period of 2008–2012. Under Article 3.9, the CoP/MoP was tasked with beginning negotiations of a second round of commitments at least "seven years before the end of the first commitment period," which meant that consideration of a post-Kyoto agreement had to begin in 2005. In this way, the Parties back in 1997 tried to tie their own hands a little by placing post-Kyoto commitments on an agenda some eight years in the future. The post-Kyoto negotiations are discussed further in Chapter 9.

2.   The Protocol's commitments are based on total net emissions for the six greenhouse gases not covered by the Montreal Protocol that were specified in Annex A: carbon dioxide (CO_2), methane (CH_4), nitrous oxide (N_2O), hydrofluorcarbons (HFCs), perfluorocarbons (PFCs), and sulphur hexafluoride (SF_6). The Parties had decided not to address each gas separately but to treat them as one "basket of gases." But not all of the gases are equal when it comes to their global warming effect. Thus, to create a unified market of greenhouse gases, the Parties had to accept a unified "currency" for each of the gases and an exchange rate for determining, for example, how much reduction in CO_2 was worth in terms of reduced methane. The "currency" in the market would be tons of carbon dioxide equivalent (CO_{2eq}), and the exchange rate would be determined by the "global warming potential" of each greenhouse gas, relative to the global warming potential of CO_2. In this way, a ton of reductions in any gas could be compared (and traded) with a ton of reductions in any other gas. The global warming potentials for the six gases are established by the IPCC. Kyoto Protocol, Article 5.3. For further discussion of global warming potentials and carbon dioxide equivalency, see Chapter 1, Section I (Questions and Discussions). Can you see why this "basket of gases" approach provides additional flexibility for the Parties to be able to meet their Kyoto commitments?

3.   Ultimately, the decision of what targets each country would have to meet under the Kyoto Protocol was left to the give-and-take of the negotiations. No systematic approach was taken. Interestingly, it was the developing countries who were most disappointed that no formula was discussed. When it comes time for developing countries to take a binding commitment they will push for a rights-based formula that reflects basic concepts of equity. This is discussed further in Chapter 9, Section IV.A.

B.   Policies and Measures

From the start of negotiations, the United States and Europe disagreed on whether to adopt, in addition to targets and timetables, a list of mandatory "policies and measures" that countries would have to adopt to lower greenhouse gas emissions. The European Union supported harmonized policies and measures, because they would be required to harmonize their measures inside the European

Union anyway. Enshrining these policies and measures in the Protocol itself would eliminate any competitive disadvantage Europe's industries might face compared to the United States and Japan. The United States adamantly opposed this approach, however, insisting that each country should retain flexibility to choose its own policies and measures that would minimize domestic costs. The Protocol's ultimate language on policies and measures is not mandatory, and the measures listed in Article 2 — for example, enhancement of energy efficiency, protection of sinks and reservoirs, promotion of sustainable agriculture, and promotion of renewable energy — are fairly general and, by-and-large, uncontroversial.

KYOTO PROTOCOL, ARTICLE 2

1. Each Party included in Annex I, in achieving its quantified emission limitation and reduction commitments under Article 3, in order to promote sustainable development, shall:

    (a) Implement and/or further elaborate policies and measures in accordance with its national circumstances, such as:

        (i) Enhancement of energy efficiency in relevant sectors of the national economy;

        (ii) Protection and enhancement of sinks and reservoirs of greenhouse gases not controlled by the Montreal Protocol, taking into account its commitments under relevant international environmental agreements; promotion of sustainable forest management practices, afforestation and reforestation;

        (iii) Promotion of sustainable forms of agriculture in light of climate change considerations;

        (iv) Research on, and promotion, development and increased use of, new and renewable forms of energy, of carbon dioxide sequestration technologies and of advanced and innovative environmentally sound technologies;

        (v) Progressive reduction or phasing out of market imperfections, fiscal incentives, tax and duty exemptions and subsidies in all greenhouse gas emitting sectors that run counter to the objective of the Convention and application of market instruments;

        (vi) Encouragement of appropriate reforms in relevant sectors aimed at promoting policies and measures which limit or reduce emissions of greenhouse gases not controlled by the Montreal Protocol;

        (vii) Measures to limit and/or reduce emissions of greenhouse gases not controlled by the Montreal Protocol in the transport sector;

        (viii) Limitation and/or reduction of methane emissions through recovery and use in waste management, as well as in the production, transport and distribution of energy; * * *

2. The Parties included in Annex I shall pursue limitation or reduction of emissions of greenhouse gases not controlled by the Montreal Protocol from aviation and marine bunker fuels, working through the International

Civil Aviation Organization and the International Maritime Organization, respectively.

3. The Parties included in Annex I shall strive to implement policies and measures under this Article in such a way as to minimize adverse effects, including the adverse effects of climate change, effects on international trade, and social, environmental and economic impacts on other Parties, especially developing country Parties . . . .

4. The [CoP/MoP] . . . , if it decides that it would be beneficial to coordinate any of the policies and measures in paragraph 1(a) above, taking into account different national circumstances and potential effects, shall consider ways and means to elaborate the coordination of such policies and measures.

* * *

KYOTO PROTOCOL, ARTICLE 10

All Parties, taking into account their common but differentiated responsibilities and their specific national and regional development priorities, objectives and circumstances, without introducing any new commitments for Parties not included in Annex I [of the Convention] . . . shall:

(a) Formulate, where relevant and to the extent possible, cost-effective national and, where appropriate, regional programmes to improve the quality of local emission factors, activity data and/or models which reflect the socio-economic conditions of each Party for the preparation and periodic updating of national inventories of anthropogenic emissions by sources and removals by sinks of all greenhouse gases not controlled by the Montreal Protocol. . . .

(b) Formulate, implement, publish and regularly update national and, where appropriate, regional programmes containing measures to mitigate climate change and measures to facilitate adequate adaptation to climate change:

(i) Such programmes would, *inter alia*, concern the energy, transport and industry sectors as well as agriculture, forestry and waste management. Furthermore, adaptation technologies and methods for improving spatial planning would improve adaptation to climate change. . . .

QUESTIONS AND DISCUSSION

1. The voluntary approach in Article 2 meant that countries would not be required to take any specific policies or measures to address climate change, as long as they reached their overall cap. As a result, relatively little attention has been given to the provision on "policies and measures." Nonetheless, the policies-and-measures approach may prove to be the most important in post-Kyoto negotiations. Countries that do not want to agree to a binding overall cap — for example developing countries and possibly the United States — may nonetheless be willing to accept an internationally mandated restriction on specific activities or emissions sources. It is conceivable that countries could accept binding standards for vehicle emissions or for the proportion of new electricity that must be generated by renewable energy sources — even if they were unable to accept an overall emissions cap.

2. Article 10 applies to all Parties, including developing countries and is thus necessarily general. The Protocol negotiators did not have authority under the Berlin Mandate to negotiate any new obligations for developing countries, so the requirements in Article 10 to develop improved emissions data or national or regional mitigation and adaptation plans were carefully crafted not to introduce any new obligations on developing countries — but just to reaffirm and clarify existing obligations already enumerated in Article 4 of the Convention.

C.   Forests and Other Sinks

Both the Framework Convention and the Kyoto Protocol clearly contemplate that sinks such as forests would be within the ambit of the climate regime. As noted in the discussion of the Framework Convention, by choosing an objective framed in terms of "concentrations" and focussing on the enhancement of sinks as well as the reduction of emissions, the Parties clearly enlarged the climate talks to encompass forestry and land-use management. But the actual practice of Parties under the Framework Convention varied with respect to land-use change and forestry practices. Many countries had prepared no baseline for the impact of these sectors on their net emissions. Those that did measure them calculated emissions from the sector as a net annual flow rate of carbon sequestered or emitted. Because the ability of trees to sequester carbon declines over time, a country with a large proportion of forested area will have a high rate of carbon sequestration in the base year and thus relatively lower net emissions, but will have difficulty maintaining the rate of sequestration as the country's forests mature. Conversely, countries with heavy deforestation may have had net emissions from the forestry sector contributing to their base year, and they can contribute to their target simply by decreasing the rate of deforestation or by reforesting. Thus, a system that includes sequestered carbon in sinks as part of a country's baseline emissions would paradoxically reward countries that historically had been deforesters and penalize countries that had been better forest managers during their baseline years.

Facing a system with built-in perverse incentives, the Kyoto Protocol took some initial general steps toward better integrating land-use change and forestry into the countries' overall targets and timetables. Article 3.3 allows for Parties to meet their target level by counting the net changes in greenhouse gas emissions resulting from human-induced "afforestation, reforestation, and deforestation" since 1990. Thus, sinks were generally not included in calculating base year emissions, but Annex I countries were to report on the man-made net changes in emissions from the land-use and forestry sector that occurred from the baseline year to the end of the reporting period. This was intended to benefit countries that were enhancing their forest sinks and penalize those where sinks were declining. Those countries that had net emissions from the land-use and forestry sector in the baseline year could also include them in the baseline, so that their target in the reporting period would be higher. In this way, the incentives were overall better aligned with sustainable land-use and forestry practices.

The Kyoto Protocol's treatment of forests was nonetheless both narrow and deliberately ambiguous. Article 3.3 is limited only to afforestation, reforestation, and deforestation. Article 3.4 provides that additional activities, presumably including for example conservation, forest management, and sustainable harvesting, could be considered in meeting targets and timetables only in subsequent commitment periods. Article 3.4 prepared for broader treatment of the land-use and forestry sectors in the future by requiring each country in Annex I to provide the data necessary to establish a 1990 baseline for its carbon stock (i.e., the amount of carbon held in forests and other terrestrial sinks and reservoirs). The Kyoto Protocol's coverage of land-use change and forests raised many difficult and controversial issues. Afforestation, reforestation, and deforestation were not defined in the Protocol, leaving them open for a wide range of definitions that could fundamentally change the effect of the Protocol in reducing greenhouse gas emissions. The widely varying interpretations of Articles 3.3 and 3.4 made forest issues central to the post-Kyoto negotiations. The ultimate rules for land-use, land-use changes, and forests are discussed in detail in Chapter 7.

QUESTIONS AND DISCUSSION

1. With large areas of growing forests, the United States in particular argued for an expansive application of Article 3.3. For example, although harvesting was specifically rejected as an activity that must be counted in the first commitment period, the United States at one point suggested that restocking of harvested areas could be counted as reforestation. The impact of such an interpretation could be huge. In 1995, some 1.6 billion seedlings were planted to replace recently harvested trees in the United States, according to the American Forest and Paper Association. A tree removes roughly a ton of CO_2 and takes 40 or so years to mature. Assuming a steady rate of planting and growth from 1990 on, in 2010 the carbon sequestered in trees planted in the United States since 1990 would be roughly 800 million tons, or about 16 percent of total U.S. 1990 emissions. In other words, simply by defining reforestation to include restocking after harvesting, the United States could meet its commitments under Kyoto and be having a greater impact on the climate system in the year 2008! Similarly, despite the rejection of forest management as a credited activity under Article 3.3, the United States also considered taking credit for reforestation and afforestation initiated before 1990 but that required some form of post-1990 management. As you think about these proposals, can you see how important interpretation of the Protocol's ambiguous terms would be for determining whether Parties should ratify the Protocol or not.

2. Article 3.3 could also have been read to require Annex I Parties only to report emissions and removals that occur during commitment periods. Such an interpretation, however, would have created a perverse incentive to deforest areas before the year 2008 (i.e., the beginning of the first commitment period), thus creating more land for afforestation activities that could be counted if conducted during the reporting period. Consider, too, that under IPCC Guidelines, emissions from deforestation are all counted in the year the activity takes place, while removals from reforestation are counted over decades, as the carbon accrues. Parties that follow such a strategy would have reported no emissions from the deforestation, but most or all of the removals from subsequent reforestation.

3. What should be clear from this analysis is that the science, politics, and economics associated with land-use changes and forest management are complex and dynamic. The deliberately ambiguous terms of the Protocol allowed all Parties to sign on in 1997, but all the Parties knew at the time that they would have to revisit land-use change and forest management issues soon. These issues were

among the most contentious and important issues addressed in the Marrakesh Accords. The current treatment of land-use change and forests under the international climate regime is addressed in Chapter 7.

D.   Emissions Trading and Other Flexibility Mechanisms

The Kyoto Protocol takes a "cap-and-trade" approach, and the most difficult and interesting questions arising from Kyoto relate to the "trade" part of that approach. For example, on what terms would industrialized (Annex I) countries be allowed to meet their own obligations by trading emission credits or financing or undertaking activities in other countries? Would Europe be allowed to meet its obligations under the Protocol by investing in energy efficiency in China? In some respects, the global nature of climate change is ideal for establishing global trading markets in pollution; the reduction of one ton of carbon dioxide emissions anywhere in the world reduces climate change as much as any other ton of reduction carbon dioxide equivalent emissions. Trading carbon credits would allow greater flexibility and thus lower costs in meeting climate change targets.

The Protocol contains four mechanisms (collectively know as "flexibility mechanisms") that allow Parties to meet their commitments jointly through cooperating with other countries.

Emissions Trading. Emissions trading under Article 17 of the Kyoto Protocol allows one Annex I Party to purchase or otherwise transfer part of its assigned amount to another Annex I Party. As noted above, the expectation was that Russia and other economies in transition would have substantial carbon emissions to trade.

KYOTO PROTOCOL, ARTICLE 17

The Conference of the Parties shall define the relevant principles, modalities, rules and guidelines, in particular for verification, reporting and accountability for emissions trading. The Parties included in Annex B may participate in emissions trading for the purposes of fulfilling their commitments under Article 3. Any such trading shall be supplemental to domestic actions for the purpose of meeting quantified emission limitation and reduction commitments under that Article.

Joint Implementation. Like emissions trading, joint implementation (JI) under Article 6 may take place only between Annex I countries. JI involves the sale of "emission reduction units" (ERUs) from one Annex I Party, or private enterprise, to another Annex I party or enterprise. Reduction credits are generated by specific projects that reduce emissions or increase removals in the selling country. JI may be distinguished from emissions trading in that emissions trading is program-based, while JI is project-based. Emissions trading may also occur before associated emissions reductions are achieved, while JI reduction credits can be transferred only after they have accrued. Emissions trading may be government-to-government, while JI may be initiated and undertaken by private sector entities. But in the final analysis, emissions trading and JI are closely linked; a country may not credit any ERUs generated by a JI project without a concurrent emissions trade (or its equivalent) at the country's program-wide level.

KYOTO PROTOCOL, ARTICLE 6

1. For the purpose of meeting its commitments under Article 3, any Party included in Annex I may transfer to, or acquire from, any other such Party emission reduction units resulting from projects aimed at reducing anthropogenic emissions by sources or enhancing anthropogenic removals by sinks of greenhouse gases in any sector of the economy, provided that:

(a)   Any such project has the approval of the Parties involved;

(b)   Any such project provides a reduction in emissions by sources, or an enhancement of removals by sinks, that is additional to any that would otherwise occur;

(c)   It does not acquire any emission reduction units if it is not in compliance with its obligations under Articles 5 and 7; and

(d)   The acquisition of emission reduction units shall be supplemental to domestic actions for the purposes of meeting commitments under Article 3.

*   *   *

3. A Party included in Annex I may authorize legal entities to participate, under its responsibility, in actions leading to the generation, transfer or acquisition under this Article of emission reduction units.

Article 4 "Bubbles." The third approach, joint fulfillment of commitments under Article 4 allows an agreement between two or more Parties to meet their combined commitments by reducing their aggregated emissions. Article 4 essentially allows Parties to create a bubble around one or more of them to create their own targets and timetables, as long as the aggregate emissions from the Parties do not exceed the aggregate allowances under the Protocol. Article 4 allows the European Union, for example, to operate essentially as one entity within the Protocol.

KYOTO PROTOCOL, ARTICLE 4

1. Any Parties included in Annex I that have reached an agreement to jointly fulfil their commitments under Article 3 jointly, shall be deemed to have met those commitments provided that their total combined aggregate anthropogenic carbon dioxide equivalent emissions of the greenhouse gases listed in Annex A do not exceed their assigned amounts calculated pursuant to their quantified emission limitation and reduction commitments inscribed in Annex B and in accordance with the provisions of Article 3. The respective emission level allocated to each of the Parties to the agreement shall be set out in that agreement.

*   *   *

4. If Parties acting jointly do so in the framework of, and together with, a regional economic integration organization, any alteration in the composition of the organization after adoption of this Protocol shall not affect existing commitments under this Protocol. Any alteration in the composition of the organization shall only apply for the purposes of those commitments under Article 3 that are adopted subsequent to that alteration.

5. In the event of failure by the Parties to such an agreement to achieve their total combined level of emission reductions, each Party to that agreement shall be responsible for its own level of emissions set out in the agreement.

6. If Parties acting jointly do so in the framework of, and together with, a regional economic integration organization which is itself a Party to this Protocol, each member State of that regional economic integration organization individually, and together with the regional economic integration organization acting in accordance with Article 24, shall, in the event of failure to achieve the total combined level of emission reductions, be responsible for its level of emissions as notified in accordance with this Article.

Clean Development Mechanism under Article 12. The Clean Development Mechanism (CDM), which is defined in Article 12, replaces joint implementation (available under Article 4 of the Framework Convention) with respect to investments in developing countries. Article 12 provides that Annex I (developed) Parties, or private entities from those Parties, may fund activities in non-Annex I (developing) countries that result in certified emissions reductions (CERs) and apply those reductions toward meeting their emissions target.

KYOTO PROTOCOL, ARTICLE 12

1. A clean development mechanism is hereby defined.

2. The purpose of the clean development mechanism shall be to assist Parties not included in Annex I in achieving sustainable development and in contributing to the ultimate objective of the Convention, and to assist Parties included in Annex I in achieving compliance with their quantified emission limitation and reduction commitments under Article 3.

3. Under the clean development mechanism:

(a)   Parties not included in Annex I will benefit from project activities resulting in certified emission reductions; and

(b)   Parties included in Annex I may use the certified emission reductions accruing from such project activities to contribute to compliance with part of their quantified emission limitation and reduction commitments under Article 3, as determined by the [CoP/MoP]. . . .

4. The clean development mechanism shall be subject to the authority and guidance of the [CoP/MoP] . . . and be supervised by an executive board of the clean development mechanism.

5. Emission reductions resulting from each project activity shall be certified by operational entities to be designated by the [CoP/MoP] . . . , on the basis of:

(a)   Voluntary participation approved by each Party involved;

(b)   Real, measurable, and long-term benefits related to the mitigation of climate change; and

(c)   Reductions in emissions that are additional to any that would occur in the absence of the certified project activity.

6. The clean development mechanism shall assist in arranging funding of certified project activities as necessary.

7. The [CoP/MoP] . . . shall, at its first session, elaborate modalities and procedures with the objective of ensuring transparency, efficiency and accountability through independent auditing and verification of project activities.

8. The [CoP/MoP] . . . shall ensure that a share of the proceeds from certified project activities is used to cover administrative expenses as well as to assist

developing country Parties that are particularly vulnerable to the adverse effects of climate change to meet the costs of adaptation.

9. Participation under the clean development mechanism, including in activities mentioned in paragraph 3(a) above and in the acquisition of certified emission reductions, may involve private and/or public entities, and is to be subject to whatever guidance may be provided by the executive board of the clean development mechanism.

10. Certified emission reductions obtained during the period from the year 2000 up to the beginning of the first commitment period can be used to assist in achieving compliance in the first commitment period.

Many controversies continued beyond Kyoto regarding how the flexibility mechanisms would operate. Among the most complicated was the debate over the technical rules to ensure the flexibility mechanisms are in fact leading to additional reductions (i.e., reductions over and above what would have occurred without the trade or investment). These issues are even more complex when it comes to the CDM or other mechanisms that allow Annex I countries to invest in or trade with developing countries, which have no quantified targets on emissions under the Protocol.

These provisions in the Protocol are somewhat vague, and the Parties expected to develop them in negotiations after the Protocol. The implementation of the flexibility mechanisms is now well under way and is discussed in Chapter 6.

QUESTIONS AND DISCUSSION

1. The CDM was outlined only in its broadest terms in the Protocol. But Article 12 also tasked the CoP with developing the rules and modalities for emissions trading, including, for example, rules concerning accounting, verification and reporting. These and other rules implementing the CDM have been passed by the CoP in various decisions, including as part of the Marakesh Accords. As a result, the CDM is now up-and-running and substantial investments have been flowing into developing countries. Significant questions still persist, however, about whether the CDM will be able to verify real and permanent positive climate benefits specifically and sustainable development benefits more generally. How should Parties determine whether any reductions in greenhouse gas emissions are "additional to" any that would otherwise occur, when a developing country has no commitment to limit its overall emissions? The CDM is discussed further, along with the other flexibility mechanisms, in Chapter 6.

2. Consider the flexibility mechanisms under the Kyoto Protocol in light of the information presented in Chapter 6, regarding emissions trading. How should Parties verify that Clean Development Mechanism and Joint Implementation projects achieve emissions reductions beyond those that would otherwise occur? What kind of system should be devised for tracking trades, which will occur on a global basis? What other design and implementation features should be included?

3. Each of the various flexibility mechanisms has different nomenclature for their contribution to a country's efforts to comply with the Kyoto Protocol, making the Protocol even more confusing than it otherwise would be. In the end, a country's total emissions for purposes of compliance with the Protocol will be compared to the following:

5 x (AAUs) + (ERUs) + (CERs) + (RMUs), where:

AAUs = Assigned Amount Units (determined by the target taken under the Kyoto Protocol +/- any AAUs traded directly under Article 17);

ERUs = Emission Reduction Units (received from investing in any Joint Implementation (JI) project);

CERs = Certified Emissions Reductions (received from investing in any the Clean Development Mechanism);

RMUs = Removal Units (received from the management of forests or land-use practices).

If we assume that Country X emitted 100 tons CO2eq in 1990 and it has committed to a 5 percent emissions reduction under the Kyoto Protocol, then its Assigned Amount for the total 5-year commitment period is 95 x 5 = 475 tons CO2eq. Let's assume further that Country X has received 10 ERUs through investing in JI projects, 15 CERs through investing in CDM projects and 5 RMUs through domestic improvements in forest management. All of these are denominated in tons CO2eq. At the end of the commitment period, Country X reports that its net emissions for their commitment period were 497 tons CO2eq. Is Country X in compliance with the Kyoto Protocol? The answer is "yes." Country X has a final allocation of 475 AAUs + 10 ERUs +15 CERs + 5 RMUs, giving Country X total allowances to emit up to 505 tons CO2eq for the full Kyoto commitment period.

E.   Implementation and Compliance

The Protocol envisioned an international regime unlike any attempted in international environmental law — the creation of a global pollution market. That market would require exponentially greater amounts of information for the Parties to police one another than other forms of regulation. A centralized accounting system — like a central bank for carbon trading — would need to be established, and national governments would have to provide more information about their annual net emissions and any trades or investments they had made to adjust their allowances.

The Framework Convention had created some reporting requirements, but they were insufficient to support the Protocol. Under the Framework Convention, Annex I parties had to provide annual inventories of their anthropogenic sources and sinks and accounts of GHG emission budgets, and periodic reports on all aspects of their implementation of the Convention. Article 5 of the Protocol requires Annex I Parties to put in place a system at the national level for measuring net emissions and for tracking trades made under the flexibility mechanisms. The Protocol then adds a general requirement that the Parties submit "necessary supplementary information for the purposes of ensuring compliance." To ensure that greenhouse gases were measured and counted in the same way — critical for ensuring that one ton of emissions traded or purchased in the market was roughly equivalent to any other — the Parties agreed to develop over time a common set of methodologies for counting and tracking net greenhouse gas emissions. The Secretariat was tasked with publishing national emissions data and eventually would establish a centralized accounting system for tracking each country's net emissions and their participation in the carbon market.

A primary strategy for ensuring implementation piloted in the Framework Convention and expanded in the Kyoto Protocol is the use of "expert review teams" to ensure the veracity and integrity of the information reported by each of the Parties. Under Decision 3/CP.1 made by the Parties under the Framework Convention, the Secretariat was tasked with leading in-country technical reviews of each Annex I Party's reports. Although visits by the expert review teams were voluntary under the Decision, all Annex I Parties had had their initial reports verified by in-country reviews by the time of the Kyoto negotiations. The negotiators built on this experience and strengthened the composition and use of these expert review teams. Under Article 8 of the Protocol, expert review teams coordinated by the Secretariat will conduct comprehensive technical assessments of the full range of a Party's implementation of the Protocol and will report any potential compliance problems to the CoP/MoP:

KYOTO PROTOCOL, ARTICLE 8

1. The information submitted under Article 7 by each Party included in Annex I shall be reviewed by expert review teams . . .

2. Expert review teams shall be coordinated by the secretariat and shall be composed of experts selected from those nominated by Parties to the Convention and, as appropriate, by intergovernmental organizations, in accordance with guidance provided for this purpose by the Conference of the Parties.

3. The review process shall provide a thorough and comprehensive technical assessment of all aspects of the implementation by a Party of this Protocol. The expert review teams shall prepare a report to the [CoP/MoP] . . . , assessing the implementation of the commitments of the Party and identifying any potential problems in, and factors influencing, the fulfilment of commitments. Such reports shall be circulated by the secretariat to all Parties to the Convention. The secretariat shall list those questions of implementation indicated in such reports for further consideration by the [CoP/MoP]. . . .

5. The [CoP/MoP] . . . shall . . . consider:

(a)   The information submitted by the Parties under Article 7 and the reports of the expert reviews thereon conducted under this Article; and

(b)   Those questions of implementation listed by the secretariat under paragraph 3 above, as well as any questions raised by Parties.

6. Pursuant to its consideration of the information referred to in paragraph 5 above, the [CoP/MoP] . . . shall take decisions on any matter required for the implementation of this Protocol.

The expanded national reporting verified by expert review teams strengthened the ability of the Parties to monitor implementation; more problematic, however, was what measures should be taken against Parties that were found to be in non-compliance. Given that the Protocol would include binding commitments to reduce greenhouse gases, these issues of compliance — and non-compliance — took on additional significance. What should the sanctions be if a country, having committed to reduce its net emissions by 7 percent by 2008–2012, misses its target? What can the Parties do to penalize the non-compliant country? Does it matter if the country made a good faith effort and missed by just a little, or if it did little and announced on the eve of the first reporting period that it expects to miss its Kyoto targets? These are difficult issues and some would argue are the most important for ensuring that the Protocol results in real climate benefits. Ultimately, like many of the most difficult issues, the Kyoto Protocol would only provide a general framework for how to respond to non-compliance:

> The [CoP/MoP] . . . shall, at its first session, approve appropriate and effective procedures and mechanisms to determine and to address cases of non-compliance with the provisions of this Protocol, including through the development of an indicative list of consequences, taking into account the cause, type, degree and frequency of non-compliance. Any procedures and mechanisms under this Article entailing binding consequences shall be adopted by means of an amendment to this Protocol. * * *

Kyoto Protocol, Article 18. This provision committed the Parties to develop an "indicative list of consequences" for noncompliance, which could presumably be implemented if they were nonbinding consequences. Any "binding consequences" had to be adopted by amending the Protocol (requiring a three-fourths vote). The details of the noncompliance procedures, including the indicative list of consequences, has been developed further as part of the Marrakesh Accords, and are described in Chapter 8.

QUESTIONS AND DISCUSSION

Technology Transfer and Financial Resources. Although technology transfer and financial assistance issues are always a major point of discussion in international climate negotiations, under the Berlin Mandate the developing countries were not supposed to take on any additional commitments. Under the guise of "advancing implementation of the Convention," some new language regarding essentially voluntary measures to reduce emissions was included in Article 10. But because new developing country commitments were minimal, relatively little attention was paid to the technical assistance or financial resource provisions, other than to reaffirm commitments to cooperate in technology transfer and to provide "new and additional financial resources to meet the agreed full costs incurred by developing country Parties in advancing the implementation of existing commitments" under the Framework Convention. *See* Kyoto Protocol, Article 10(c); Article 11.

IV. TOWARDS RATIFICATION: NEGOTIATING THE MARRAKESH ACCORDS

No sooner had the ink dried on the Kyoto Protocol than it became clear that significant ambiguities existed in the text of the Protocol that could lead to vastly different reduction requirements for the United States and other Annex I countries. Several provisions of the Protocol were deliberately left ambiguous in order to reach consensus at Kyoto, thus allowing countries to make their own interpretations and thus their own calculations of the costs they faced in meeting their emission reduction targets. With the clock already ticking toward the first reporting period of 2008, however, all of the Parties recognized some urgency in clarifying a unified interpretation of the Protocol. At the very least the institutional, procedural and reporting requirements for the first reporting period needed to be established.

In order to build the political momentum for an agreement and given the lesson of the Berlin Mandate, the Parties meeting in Buenos Aires in 1999 agreed to a "Buenos Aires Workplan," which among other things set forth a negotiating schedule that would clarify all major ambiguities in the Kyoto Protocol by the Sixth Meeting of the Conference of the Parties (CoP-6), scheduled in late 2000 for the Hague. All negotiations then began to aim at CoP-6 as the determinative meeting for the Kyoto Protocol. Whether signatories to the Protocol would be willing to ratify the agreement would depend on whether and how agreement was reached in clarifying the Protocol's approach.

The run-up to CoP6 was also intertwined with U.S. politics, because the meeting was scheduled for just a few weeks after the U.S. Presidential elections. Because the 2000 election was shrouded with confusion, the U.S. delegation actually went to CoP6 at The Hague not knowing for sure whether Al Gore, a promoter of climate policies, or George W. Bush, a self-avowed oil and gas man, would replace President Clinton.

Given the political uncertainties and the inherent complexities, the United States and European Union could not bridge their remaining differences. Rather than closing the meeting, the Chairman suspended discussions until further negotiations (what would become known as CoP6-bis) was scheduled for Bonn in July of 2001. The failure to reach consensus at The Hague was particularly important, because with the new year (2001) came a new U.S. Presidency, and in February 2001 President Bush reversed his campaign pledge and announced that the United States would no longer support the Kyoto Protocol.

The Bush Administration offered neither an apology nor an alternative, leaving Europeans and others furious at the unilateral and unexplained shift. Protests occurred at U.S. Embassies around the world, and Bush was widely decried as a "climate criminal." Europe quickly called for other countries to join it in negotiating the outstanding issues under the Protocol so it could be ratified without the United States.

That would prove to be easier said than done. Under Article 25 of the Protocol, it would enter into force once it was ratified by at least 55 Parties to the Convention, and sufficient Annex I Parties to account for at least 55 percent of the total carbon dioxide emissions from all Annex I countries based on their 1990 baseline years. This meant it was theoretically possible that the Protocol could enter into force without the United States, but only if the European Union convinced virtually all of the rest of the Annex I countries, including Japan, Canada, Australia, New Zealand, and Russia.

Given that the United States was actively lobbying others to reject the Protocol, most observers thought little progress would be made at the Bonn CoP6-bis meeting. But Europe was undeterred. The Chairperson of the negotiations, Dutch Environment Minister Jan Pronk, issued a paper (known as the Second Pronk Paper) that essentially outlined a proposed set of policies he believed could be accepted by all the countries, now that the United States was not at the table.

In part because of Pronk's effort, European resolve more generally, and the United States' failure to offer even a cosmetic alternative, the remaining Kyoto Parties surprised most observers by reaching an agreement on the key elements of the Protocol. The United States had undermined its own position by promising to offer an alternative policy approach to the Protocol and then delivering nothing but a commitment to research the causes and impacts of climate change.

The July agreement clarifying the details of the Protocol set the stage for a ratification fight. First Japan and then Russia would milk this position for concessions from both sides. Japan gained support from the United States in propping up Japan's ailing banking industry and then subsequently gained concessions from Europe in the climate negotiations before announcing that it would indeed ratify the Kyoto Protocol. Aiding the effort to woo Japan was the fact that the Protocol bore the name of one of Japan's most important cities. Buttons at subsequent climate negotiations were passed out with the flag of Japan, saying "Honour Kyoto" — reminding the Japanese that as the hosts of the Protocol negotiations they had a special interest in ensuring its success. For its part, Russia negotiated favorable support from the European Union for its membership bid into the World Trade Organization. After flip-flopping several times, Russia finally ratified the Kyoto Protocol, and it entered into force in 2005.

With ratification of Kyoto, the world formally adopted a three-tiered approach to international climate policy. Most OECD countries led by the European Union would embark on an aggressive effort to implement the Kyoto Protocol, including creation of a major regional carbon market. Implementation of the Protocol regime is both complicated and exciting, and is discussed in the next four Chapters. The United States, initially with Australia, would follow another strategy, effectively turning their back on global cooperation in favor of limited engagement with selected partners on research, investment, energy efficiency and clean development. The U.S. approach is described in Chapter 11. Developing countries represent a third category — deliberately left out of the Kyoto Protocol targets and timetables. Pressure continues, at least on the rapidly growing middle income countries like China and India, to accept some commitments in the next reporting period under Kyoto.

QUESTIONS AND DISCUSSION

1. Ever since the Rio Earth Summit in 1992 when the UNFCCC was adopted, climate negotiations have become huge affairs, with literally thousands of official delegates, industry leaders, environmental advocates, professional climatologists, and other members of the climate community. Along with the official negotiations, literally hundreds of side events are held at each CoP/MoP to highlight different policy initiatives, scientific developments or technological innovations. These meetings are enormous venues for addressing the full range of climate-related issues.

Environmental NGOs are well represented in these negotiations. Many coordinate through an international network called the Climate Action Network to develop and promote joint policy statements that can significantly influence the direction of the negotiations. The NGOs are also present to monitor the situation and to build political pressure among the negotiators — with the hope that this will move the parties to swifter and stronger action. In the negotiations at CoP6, for example, environmental activists symbolically sandbagged the entire building where the negotiations were being held to underscore the perils of sea level rise. Even the chair of the negotiations, Jan Pronk, came outside to lay a sandbag. Meanwhile, the United States was widely seen as slowing progress at the negotiations so some of the nearly 200 students brought over to the negotiations by Greenpeace USA, feigned sleep at a table under the banner "U.S. delegation Hard at Work on Negotiations." These types of stunts can backfire, of course, but they can also break the ice of tense negotiations while reminding negotiators of their responsibility to address climate change.

2. It is easy to criticize the Kyoto Protocol, particularly in hindsight a decade later. For sure, the Protocol has its flaws and at best was never more than a first step toward a global resolution of climate change. Yet one should not underestimate the potentially profound impact at the time of the industrialized countries agreeing to *limit* their emissions of greenhouse gases. Why did they do it? What factors influenced their decision to complete an agreement at all in Kyoto? What pressures drove governments to negotiate for forty-eight hours and to continue the negotiations a full day longer than was scheduled? Does the Kyoto process provide general lessons about how international law is made?

3. In evaluating the Kyoto Protocol, it is also important to recall the overall strategy embodied by the climate regime at this point in time. The Kyoto Protocol was viewed by climate advocates as a next step — just as the Montreal Protocol was a next step in phasing out ozone depleting substances. The Montreal Protocol has been significantly revised or amended every two or three years since its initial negotiation and many of the most important provisions (including the full inclusion of developing countries) did not occur until the 1990 London Revisions. Does this understanding, coupled with the discussion of the Framework-Protocol method of treatymaking in Chapter 4, influence your view of the Kyoto Protocol?

4. To be sure, all the parties at the time of the UNFCCC and of the Kyoto Protocol (including the United States) expected to follow in the steps of the Montreal Protocol. By taking significant steps to reduce greenhouse gas emissions first, the argument was that the Annex I countries would be in a better position to negotiate with the developing countries in the second reporting period. Consider the current state of affairs now, given that the United States never joined Kyoto. How much stronger would the industrialized countries be in trying to gain deeper commitments from China and India if the United States had joined Europe and other countries in making at least some efforts to curb greenhouse gas emissions? Is there any reason to believe that the United States rhetorically demanding a "global" commitment adds more pressure on China and India than if the United States sought their cooperation after making its own commitments?

5. The Kyoto Protocol was clearly never meant to be the end-point of the climate regime. The Parties clearly contemplated that additional commitments would be required beyond the 2008–2012 reporting period. Moreover, all Parties understood that eventually developing countries would be asked to take additional responsibilities under the regime. The posture of the United States in rejecting the Protocol complicated matters but did not derail the structure of the climate regime altogether. In the end, all Parties including the United States have agreed to continue negotiations for a post-Kyoto time period. The outlines of this negotiation (not unlike the Berlin Mandate) is known as the Bali Action Plan, UNFCCC Decision 1/CP.13 and is discussed further in Chapter 9 on the post-Kyoto negotiations.

Chapter 6

IMPLEMENTING THE KYOTO PROTOCOL

I. INTRODUCTION

Perhaps the most controversial aspect of the climate change negotiations and the Kyoto Protocol itself has been the extent to which the developed (Annex I) countries may meet their own obligations by financing or undertaking activities in other countries. For example, would France or the United States be allowed to meet its emissions limitations by investing in reforestation projects in Costa Rica or technology that reduces carbon dioxide emissions in India and HFC emissions in China? In some respects, the nature of climate change is ideal for establishing global trading markets in pollution; reducing one ton of carbon dioxide anywhere in the world mitigates climate change as much as reducing any other ton of carbon dioxide. In addition, disparities in regulatory systems also make emissions trading potentially cost effective. For example, countries like the United States and Germany have well developed pollution control regimes. Consequently, cuts in

225

emissions from these countries will be relatively more expensive than in many developing countries where few if any pollution control requirements currently exist. Nonetheless, many countries, particularly developing countries, view emissions trading as a means for the developed countries to avoid the difficult task of reducing greenhouse gas emissions at home.

Emissions trading is simply one means for implementing environmental goals; Article 2 of the Kyoto Protocol recognizes this by calling on Annex I Parties to implement a wide range of policies to reduce greenhouse gas emissions. Nonetheless, as introduced in Chapter 5, the Kyoto Protocol has embraced carbon markets, and so too have polluters and investors. Today, active and vibrant carbon trading is happening around the world. Carbon trading increased from about $10.8 billion and 710 MtCO$_2$eq in 2005 to $30 billion and 1,639 MtCO$_2$eq in 2006. Karan Capoor & Philippe Ambrosi, *State and Trends of the Carbon Market 2007*, 3 (2007). In 2006, companies traded more than one billion allowances, three times the amount in 2005, under the European Union's Emissions Trading Scheme. The New South Wales Market and the Chicago Carbon Exchange also recorded record volumes and values of trade in 2006. Programs within the United States, including the Regional Greenhouse Gas Initiative established by nine Northeast states, have initiated carbon trading even in the absence of federal regulation or U.S. participation in the Kyoto Protocol.

With the commitment by governments to a post-Kyoto Protocol regime that includes further quantifiable emissions limitations, it seems clear that the carbon market will continue to be one tool for reducing greenhouse gas emissions. How has emissions trading developed and how can it be improved? Has it resulted in significant emissions reductions, at least compared to other strategies for mitigating climate change? Section II of this chapter begins by reviewing the implementation of emissions trading, joint implementation, and the Clean Development Mechanism under the Kyoto Protocol. Section III explores some key implementation issues, such as ensuring that emissions trading is supplemental to reductions made at home. Section IV describes implementation of the mandatory emissions trading regime in the European Union. The voluntary, private sector regime established in North America, the Chicago Climate Exchange, is discussed in Chapter 18.

II. THE KYOTO PROTOCOL'S FLEXIBILITY MECHANISMS

As described in the previous chapter, Annex B of the Kyoto Protocol establishes targets — quantifiable emissions limitations and reduction commitments — for six greenhouse gases that must be met by developed countries during the 2008 to 2012 commitment period. Each Party with a target established in Annex B is given an "assigned amount" (AA) — the emissions that a Party may emit over the commitment period. Thus, if Country Z must reduce its emissions by eight percent based on 1990 emissions, and its 1990 emissions for the six greenhouse gases was 500 million metric tons of carbon dioxide equivalent (MtCO$_2$eq), then it must reduce its emissions to 460 MtCO$_2$eq. Because actual emissions will vary from year to year, depending on economic activity and other factors, achieving a specific reduction target may be difficult in any given year. As a consequence, the Kyoto Protocol establishes a five-year commitment period — 2008 to 2012 — that allows the Party to aggregate its emissions over this period and eliminate year-to-year emission variances. Thus, a country's total allowable emissions must be multiplied by five. In our example, County Z's total allowable emissions — its AA — will be 2300 $MtCO_2eq$ (460 x five) for the full five-year period. In the Kyoto Protocol's jargon, the AA is then broken down into "assigned amount units" (AAUs), where each AAU is equal to one $MtCO_2eq$ and calculated using the global warming potentials for the various greenhouse gases. Country Z has 2300 AAUs.

To help the Parties achieve their targets, the Kyoto Protocol includes a number of market instruments that allow the Parties to buy and sell their AAUs. These "flexibility mechanisms" were introduced in Chapter 5. The remainder of this Section explains these flexibility mechanisms in greater detail: bubbles, joint implementation, the Clean Development Mechanism, and emissions trading. Section III then looks more closely at a number of implementation issues, such as supplementarity and additionality.

A.   Bubbles

Article 4 of the Kyoto Protocol permits Annex I Parties "to jointly fulfil their commitments under Article 3." This allows two or more Annex I Parties to aggregate their emissions and reduce them together. This instrument is called a "bubble" because it acts like an imaginary bubble over a group of Parties (or facilities at the domestic level) so that they may be treated as one entity. Assume Countries A and B establish a bubble and that Country A must reduce its emissions by 500 $MtCO_2eq$ and Country B must reduce its emissions by 5 $MtCO_2eq$. In a bubble, the two countries must reduce their emissions collectively by 505 $MtCO_2eq$. Even if Country A reduces its emissions by 250 $MtCO_2eq$ and Country B reduces its emissions by 260 $MtCO_2eq$, both countries will be deemed to be in compliance, because their aggregate emissions reductions of 510 $MtCO_2eq$ exceed 505 $MtCO_2eq$.

Although any group of countries may establish a bubble, it was designed for the EU and only the EU has established a bubble to redistribute emissions reductions. While each of the original EU member states pledged to reduce emissions by eight percent under the Kyoto Protocol, the EU members negotiated a burden-sharing agreement to re-allocate allowances within the bubble. Under this burden-sharing agreement, Germany and Denmark each agreed to reduce their greenhouse gas emissions by 21 percent and the United Kingdom by 12.5 percent because of their relatively high per capita emissions. Meanwhile, Ireland, Greece, and Portugal are allowed to grow their emissions by 13 percent, 25 percent, and 27 percent, respectively. The countries that joined the EU after the Kyoto Protocol was negotiated are not part of the bubble and are not participating in the burden sharing agreement. *See* European Environment Agency, *Greenhouse Gas Emission Trends and Projections 2006* 8, Table 0.1 (2006).

Table 6-1: Greenhouse Gas (CO_2, CH_4, and N_2O) Emissions in the EU

	Share of EU Emissions in 1990	Emissions in 1990 in Mt Eq CO_2	Emissions in 1990 in t eq CO_2 per capita	Reductions Due to Burden Sharing	Burden Sharing in Mt eq CO_2
Austria	1.7	74	9.2	-13%	64
Belgium	3.2	139	13.7	-7.5%	129
Denmark	1.7	72	13.7	-21%	57
Finland	1.7	73	14.2	0%	73
France	14.7	637	11.0	0%	637
Germany	27.7	1201	14.7	-21%	949
Greece	2.4	104	9.9	25%	130
Ireland	1.3	57	16.0	13%	64
Italy	12.5	542	9.5	-6,5%	506
Luxembourg	0.3	14	34.7	-28%	10
Netherlands	4.8	208	13.5	-6%	196
Portugal	1.6	69	7.0	27%	87
Spain	7.0	301	7.6	15%	347
Sweden	1.6	69	7.9	4%	72
UK	17.9	775	13.3	-12.5%	678
Total EU	**100**	**4334**	**13.1**		3998

Source: *Annual European Community Greenhouse Gas Inventory 1990–1996, submission to UNFCCC*, prepared by the European Environment Agency for the European Commission (DGXI), April 1999.

QUESTIONS AND DISCUSSION

Why do you think other countries have not followed the EU's lead and formed a bubble? For example, why wouldn't other regional blocs, such as the United States, Canada, and Mexico, or the JUSCANZ alliance, create an Article 4 bubble? Read Article 4.6 of the Kyoto Protocol. What obligations does it impose on members of a bubble? Do you think those obligations explain why other Parties have not created a bubble?

B.   Joint Implementation

The idea for joint implementation — that countries could obtain credits for climate mitigation projects in other countries — originates in Article 4.2(a) of the UNFCCC, which provides that Parties may implement climate change mitigation policies and measures *jointly* with other Parties. Prior to the Kyoto Protocol, the parties adopted a joint implementation pilot phase for "activities implemented jointly" (AIJ), that allowed projects between Annex I and non-Annex I Parties. FCCC, Decision 5/CP.1 (1995). Even though no credits could issue from such projects, because they pre-dated any caps under the Kyoto Protocol, more than 150 AIJ projects were developed.

The negotiation of the Kyoto Protocol finally led to a more concrete framework for joint implementation. During these negotiations, many Annex I Parties continued to press for a definition of joint implementation that would allow Annex I Parties to meet their commitments through projects in non-Annex I countries that reduce emissions or increase sinks. The G77-China objected to such a scheme, because they wanted to see Annex I Parties make emissions reductions at home. They countered with a much different plan for financing projects in developing countries: a Clean Development Fund that would impose financial penalties on Annex I Parties that failed to meet their targets. Those penalties would be diverted to fund climate change mitigation projects in non-Annex I countries. FCCC/AGBM/1997/MISC.1/Add.3. Not surprisingly, many Annex I Parties opposed penalties for noncompliance. Moreover, a number of developing countries, having received financial and technological benefits from AIJ projects under the pilot phase, softened their opposition to projects in developing countries that would assist Annex I Parties meet their commitments. These factors opened some negotiating space and led to a compromise. "Joint implementation" was restricted to projects between Annex I Parties. In addition, the Clean Development Fund was transformed into the "Clean Development Mechanism" (CDM). The CDM would not be funded by penalties for noncompliance and would establish separate rules for projects between Annex I Parties and non-Annex I Parties.

Under Article 6 of the Kyoto Protocol, joint implementation (JI) allows an Annex I Party to "transfer to, or acquire from, any other such Party, emission reduction units from projects aimed at reducing anthropogenic emissions" of greenhouse gases. Article 6.1 sets out four conditions for JI projects:

(a)   The project has the approval of the Parties involved;

(b)   The project provides "a reduction in emissions by sources, or an enhancement of removals by sinks, that is additional to any that would otherwise occur";

(c)   A Party may not acquire any emission reduction units if it is not in compliance with its obligations under Articles 5 and 7 to estimate and report its emissions from sources and removals by sinks of greenhouse gases; and

(d)   The acquisition of emission reduction units "shall be supplemental to domestic actions for the purposes of meeting commitments under Article 3."

JI requires an actual project that reduces emissions (e.g., an energy efficiency scheme or the acquisition of pollution control equipment for an industrial facility) or increases removals by sinks (e.g., a reforestation project) in the territory of another Annex I Party. As an example, Germany (or a company based in Germany) could reforest 1,000 acres of forest in the Russian Far East. Germany (or the company making the investment) would receive all or some credit (depending on how the project is structured) for reducing GHGs in an amount equivalent to the amount of GHGs absorbed by the trees planted. Provided that the project reduces emissions or enhances removals by sinks that are "additional to any that would otherwise occur," then Germany would receive *emission reduction units* (ERUs) to help meets its target.

The Parties have established two tracks for verifying whether ERUs may be issued for a JI project. To use "Track 1," both the host country and the ERU-receiving country must meet all of the eligibility requirements to engage in JI projects. The eligibility requirements are discussed in Section III.C, below. If these conditions are met, then the host Party may verify that the project creates "additional" reductions in emissions by sources or enhancements of removals by sinks. After verifying that the project indeed creates reductions or removals additional to those that would otherwise occur, the host Party may issue the appropriate quantity of ERUs. Decision 9/CMP.1, para. 23.

Failure to meet all of the eligibility requirements, however, does not foreclose the possibility to obtain ERUs; it merely takes away the authority of the host Party to verify reductions or enhancements and issue ERUs. Under "Track 2," a host Party that fails to meet all of the eligibility requirements must have an independent entity verify any reductions or enhancements from a JI project. The independent entity must be accredited by the Protocol's Joint Implementation Supervisory Committee (JISC), which has established verification procedures that must be used by the independent entity. A host Party that meets all the eligibility requirements may choose to use either Track 1 or Track 2. Decision 9/CMP.1, paras. 23–24.

JI procedures have been slow to develop. For example, because Parties have not been verified as meeting the eligibility requirements to host JI projects, only five countries have approved JI projects under Track 1. In addition, the JISC adopted approval rules and procedures for Track 2 only in October 2006. As a consequence, the JISC had approved only six JI projects as of January 2009.

Nonetheless, interest in JI has been intensifying, largely because of the potential for projects in Russia, Ukraine, and countries of Central and Eastern Europe.

> The market's interest in JI is growing because of its potential size as a supplier. Some estimate that Russia and Ukraine together could produce 70 million–80 million ERUs or more per year. For example, total credit supply from JI in 2008–12 is estimated at 475 million tonnes (Mt) by New Carbon Finance. Others expect JI volumes to be significantly higher: ICF International estimates volumes from Russia alone could be 500Mt over the next five years. * * *

> With the highest energy intensities amongst the 25 largest global emitters, Russia and Ukraine have a huge potential to generate emission reductions. In Ukraine, energy use per unit of production is 3.3 times that of the EU 25, and 3.2 times in Russia. It is therefore not surprising that most of the emission reductions of the validated projects are expected to be generated from energy efficiency projects and reduction of fugitive gas emissions from gas transport and distribution (see Figure 2).

John Paul Miller & Egbert Liese, *What Is to Become of JI?*, ENVIRONMENT FINANCE (updated Dec. 10, 2007). Figure 6-1 underscores the enormous bias for potential JI projects in these countries, while Figure 6-2 identifies the expected types of JI projects.

Figure 6-1: JI Supply Expected From Validated Projects by County/Region

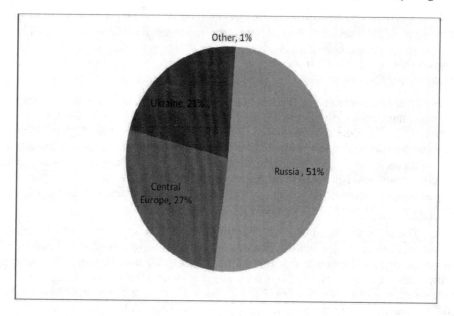

Source: UNEP Risø Centre.

Figure 6-2: JI Supply Expected From Validated Projects by Technology

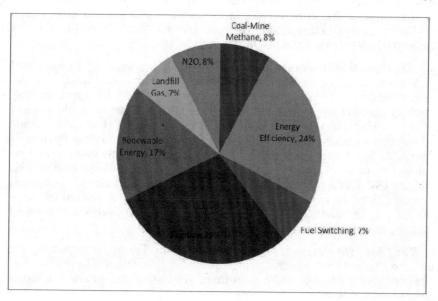

Source: UNEP Risø Centre.

QUESTIONS AND DISCUSSION

1. Of the 150 AIJ projects developed as part of the pilot phase, only projects starting as of 2000 are eligible as JI projects under the Kyoto Protocol. In addition, ERUs will be issued only for a crediting period starting after the beginning of 2008. Decision 9/CMP.1, *Guidelines for the Implementation of Article 6 of the Kyoto Protocol*, para. 5.

2. In 2006, commercial transactions for projects between Annex I Parties, although not necessarily in the JI pipeline yet, were valued at $141 million with a volume of 16.7 million metric tons of CO_2 ($MtCO_2eq$). More than 60 percent of the total volume derived from projects in Bulgaria, Russia, and Ukraine. The average price was $8.70 per ERU. Energy efficiency and fuel switching projects accounted for 28 percent of JI projects, with biomass, wind, and hydro projects constituting respectively 13 percent, 12 percent, and 10 percent of the market. *State and Trends of the Carbon Market 2007*, at 4, 21, 29.

3. The over-allocation of ERUs poses substantial risks to an emissions trading program, because "[t]he availability of a large number of low-cost allowances will lower the price of carbon and potentially increase price volatility of CO_2 emissions allowances." Craig A. Hart, *The Clean Development Mechanism: Considerations for Investors and Policymakers*, 7 SUSTAINABLE DEV. L. & POL'Y, 41, 43–44 (Spring 2007). This will likely make more costly projects financially unattractive because investors will have a variety of low-cost options from which to choose. In fact, excess emissions from Russia and Ukraine may exceed 791.5 Mt CO_2eq annually by 2010 from fossil fuel emissions alone. *Id.* Indeed, the combination of excess allowances and "hot air" from Ukraine could theoretically meet *all* the reductions of *all* developed countries. Energy Information Administration, *International Energy Outlook 2005* 83 (2005). Moreover, the large volume of excess allowances and hot air from Russia and Ukraine could depress the market for certified emissions reductions (CERs) pursuant to CDM projects:

> To place this in perspective, if 791.5 million tonnes of Russian and Ukrainian annual excess allowances produced from fossil fuel CO_2 emissions enter the market, this additional supply would be approximately twenty times larger in volume than the 41 million tonne over-allocation of CO_2 in May 2006 that caused the price of EUAs [European Union Allowances, under the EU Emissions Trading Scheme] to drop by over 67 percent. The same 791.5 million metric tonnes CO_2 per year would be almost three times greater than the validated annual emissions reductions of the 1835 CDM projects filed as of May 1, 2007, and almost four times greater than the expected annual volume of CERs to be issued by these CDM projects assuming that validations continue to overestimate actual issuances of CERs by a 27 percent error margin.

Hart, *The Clean Development Mechanism*, at 44–45. Trading in excess allowances would also eliminate any climate change mitigation benefits of JI projects, because no real emissions would actually be retired. How should the Parties address the issue of over-allocation?

C.   The Clean Development Mechanism

Article 12 of the Kyoto Protocol establishes the Clean Development Mechanism (CDM), essentially JI between Annex I Parties and non-Annex I Parties (the developing country Parties). The twin purposes of the CDM are to assist developing countries in achieving sustainable development while contributing to the ultimate objective of the Convention and to assist Annex I Parties in meeting their quantified emission limitation and reduction commitments. Assuming that Annex I Parties invest in technologies to reduce greenhouse gas emissions in developing countries, the CDM promises to support developing country efforts to develop their economies in a sustainable, climate-friendly manner while also allowing Annex I Parties a cost-effective means for achieving their GHG emissions targets.

With the CDM, an Annex I Party may undertake qualifying projects that reduce GHG emissions in non-Annex I countries and use the resulting *certified emission reductions* (CERs) to help meet their own targets. Non-Annex I Parties may also initiate their own projects and generate CERs (a "unilateral" CDM project). In both situations, CERs are tradable. Starting in 2000, reductions resulting from CDM projects could be counted towards satisfying an Annex I Party's quantifiable emission limitations. Article 12(5) of the Kyoto Protocol states that participation in the CDM must be voluntary and any project must provide "real, measurable, and long-term benefits related to the mitigation of climate change" as well as reductions that are "additional to any that would occur in the absence of the certified project activity."

Beyond these requirements, the Kyoto Protocol provided almost no guidance for operating the CDM. To develop the necessary institutional framework to operate the CDM, the Parties have adopted a substantial body of Decisions at meetings of the Parties. In particular, ensuring that projects actually lead to "real, measurable, and long-term" climate change benefits and reductions that are "additional to any that would occur in the absence of the certified project activity" requires an institutional framework designed to review and approve project proposals and monitor project implementation. To that end, Article 12 of the Kyoto Protocol called for the establishment of an Executive Board to supervise implementation of the CDM. The Executive Board operates under the authority of the Kyoto Protocol Parties, but is provided substantial administrative support by the UNFCCC Secretariat. The ten members of the Executive Board consist of one representative from each of the five official UN regions (Africa, Asia, Latin America and the Caribbean, Central and Eastern Europe and OECD), one representative from the small island developing countries, and two representatives each from developed and developing countries. The Executive Board, among many other things, maintains the CDM registry for issuance of CERs, approves methodologies for measuring baselines and additionality, and accredits entities that verify CERs for CDM projects. Decision 3/CMP.1, *Modalities for a Clean Development Mechanism as Defined in Article 12 of the Kyoto Protocol*, Annex, Parts C, D.

Article 12 of the Kyoto Protocol also requires that a CDM project have the approval of the Parties involved in the project. To ensure that such approval is granted, Parties must identify a Designated National Authority (DNA or National Authority) to serve as the focal point for consideration and approval of CDM project proposals. Decision 3/CMP.1, Annex, para. 29. Project proponents submit a Project Design Document (PDD) to the host country National Authority. The PDD should provide the technical and financial details of the proposed project, including the proposed baseline methodology for ascertaining emissions reductions, estimated operational life time of the project, description of how the additionality requirements are met through the project, documentation of environmental impacts, sources of funding, stakeholders' comments, and a monitoring plan. Decision 3/CMP.1, at Annex B. The National Authority evaluates the PDD and issues a letter of approval with the confirmation as to how the project will help the host country achieve sustainable development.

While the National Authority is responsible for ensuring that a project has been approved at the country level, a Designated Operational Entity (DOE) certifies the project proponent's proposed methodology for measuring emissions reductions, validates project proposals, and verifies the emission reductions resulting from the project that could be considered for issuance of CERs. Institutions or agencies with the requisite professional expertise to assess projects and which have no conflict of interest with the project participants may be accredited as DOEs by the Executive Board. To validate a project, the DOE reviews and assesses the PDD. The DOE is also responsible for publishing the PDD and for soliciting comments of stakeholders. Decision 3/CMP.1, at Annex, Part G. Based on the validation report of the operational entity, the CDM Executive Board registers the project.

As part of the PDD, participants in the CDM project must include a monitoring plan that allows for collecting data to estimate emissions reductions within the project boundary. Moreover, the DOE must verify and certify, based on the periodic review of the project, actual emissions reductions at the project. The DOE then submits a verification report to the project participants and the Executive Board and certifies the emissions reductions generated by the project. Based on the DOE's report, the Executive Board issues CERs for the project. Decision 3/CMP.1, at Annex, Part H-J.

BOX 1 — ANATOMY OF A DEAL — THE LIAONING HUANREN NIUMAODASHAN WIND POWER PROJECT

The Liaoning Huanren Niumaodashan Wind Power Project is a grid-connected renewable energy CDM project located in Liaoning Province, in Northeast China. The proposed project will reduce CO_2 emissions by replacing electricity produced from a fossil fuel fired power plant with electricity generated from 29 state-of-the-art wind turbines with a total generating capacity of 24.65 megawatts to the Northeast China Power Grid. The proposed project is expected to reduce emissions annually by 61,737 $MtCO_2eq$ per year. The project will be developed by EDF Trading Company of the United Kingdom and CASC Longyuan (Benxi) Wind Power Co., Ltd of China. Although neither China nor the United Kingdom is directly involved, both have given their approval to the project. The project proponents used methodologies for calculating additionality and monitoring approved by the CDM's Executive Board. Consistent with CDM requirements, the project proponents solicited stakeholder comments. A total of six stakeholders, representatives from the local Government, local Environmental Protection Bureau, local Development and Reform Bureau, local Agricultural Power Bureau, and Wafangdian Village in Huanren County, participated in a meeting to discuss the project. These stakeholders provided no negative comments. The project proponents also concluded that the project would lead to no significant environmental impacts. Although the installation of the wind turbines would generate some solid waste and vegetation would be destroyed, the waste would be transported to landfills and the vegetation replanted. Noise from the project would be minimal as the turbines would be placed on top of a mountain. These findings were confirmed by the DOE, Det Norske Veritas Certification AS. Details of the project can be found at:

http://cdm.unfccc.int/Projects/DB/DNV-CUK1199956532.2/view.

QUESTIONS AND DISCUSSION

1. The cost-effectiveness of reducing emissions through investments in developing countries and the development procedures and methodologies for CDM projects by the CDM Executive Board and its subsidiary panels and working groups have helped create a vibrant market for CDM projects. As of February 2009, the CDM Executive Board had registered 1390 projects, which are expected to deliver more than 2.9 billion CERs by 2012. CDM projects reduced emissions by 450 $MtCO_2eq$ in 2006. With more than 3,000 projects in the pipeline, CDM projects could generate another 2.7 billion or more CERs by 2012. The average price of a CER in 2006 was $8.70. *State and Trends of the Carbon Market 2007*, at 4, 20.

2. *Suing the Executive Board.* The Argentinean utility company Capex is threatening to sue the CDM's Executive Board because the Board rejected its CDM project — the conversion of a gas-fired power plant from open to combined cycle. Capex claims that the project would have generated 2.65 million CERs over the project's six-year crediting period. The Executive Board rejected the project due to concerns about whether the project would reduce emissions beyond "business as usual" and because the project was started prior to January 1, 2000, the date such projects became eligible under the CDM. Capex, of course, disputes the Executive Board's conclusions. Carbon Finance, *Executive Board Faces Legal Threat over Rejected Project* (May 21, 2008).

Does Capex have a case? Within the United States, an aggrieved party would look to the statute authorizing agency action as well as the Administrative Procedure Act, which allows lawsuits against agencies for agency action that is arbitrary, capricious or otherwise not in accordance with law. 5 U.S.C. § 706. However, international law has no equivalent to the Administrative Procedure Act. Moreover, the rules of the CDM do not provide any recourse to private parties to challenge the Board's decisions, although they do allow private parties to provide the Board with additional information. Instead, the Executive Board, as with other international institutions, has immunity to enable it to exercise its functions or fulfill its purposes without the threat of litigation. What type of recourse, if any, should private parties have? Should private parties be able to sue individual board members in their personal capacity in national courts? Are these the types of claims that should be raised in national courts or should these disputes be subject to some process within the UNFCCC? For a thorough treatment of these issues, see Ernestine E. Meijer, *The International Institutions of the Clean Development Mechanism Brought Before National Courts: Limiting Jurisdictional Immunity to Achieve Access to Justice*, 39 N.Y.U. J. INT'L L. & POL'Y 873 (2007).

3. The role of the DOE in verifying emissions reductions is obviously critical. In practice, the project participants choose and often pay DOEs, who are private consultants and not governmental officials. Even though the CDM Executive Board accredits DOEs, is an accreditation process adequate to prevent conflicts of interest? To help answer this question, you may wish to compare PDDs prepared by project proponents with the validations prepared by the DOEs. *See* CDM, Projects Registered, *at*: http://cdm.unfccc.int/Projects/registered.html.

4. As with over-allocation of ERUs for JI projects, the problem of over-allocation plagues CDM projects. For the first 175 CDM projects that issued CERs, the validation procedure overestimated the number of CERs produced by an average of approximately 27 percent. Hart, *The Clean Development Mechanism*, at 45, citing UNEP Risø Centre, *Overview of CDM Pipeline as of May 1, 2007*. If the risks of over-allocation are so great, then why does over-allocation occur? CDM participants have identified the following as contributing factors:

CRAIG A. HART, THE CLEAN DEVELOPMENT MECHANISM
7 SUSTAINABLE DEV. L. & POL'Y 41, 43 (Spring 2007)*

The leading explanation of validation/verification error was inadequate technology or methodology to measure emissions reductions. For example, with respect to methane landfill projects, several respondents identified the primary cause of error to be the lack of adequate technology to measure low concentrations of gases over large areas. Survey respondents noted that measurements are typically not conducted under ideal conditions (as assumed in the standard methodologies), and very little is known about the quality of waste in landfill sites, which affects decomposition rates and the selection of appropriate methods for analyzing data. Further, models and assumptions used for estimation are often not reliable or appropriate for local conditions.

With respect to environmental conditions, the performance of projects that depend upon wind, precipitation, river flow, or heat (as in the case of decomposition of waste) will be affected by fluctuations in weather conditions. These factors will significantly influence the outcome of verification results.

Supply and demand conditions also influence the verification results of projects whose performance is linked to market conditions. For example, electricity generation projects are verified based on the actual amount of electricity supplied to the grid. Furthermore, delay of project completion or operation can significantly affect the economic feasibility of a project and its verification results. In particular, hydroelectric plants are highly sensitive to construction delays.

Several firms identified the use of inappropriate assumptions in the validation stage and conservative assumptions in the verification stage as potential factors influencing validation/verification error. Several respondents noted that CDM methodologies often use generalized Intergovernmental Panel on Climate Change ("IPCC") estimates that do not take local conditions into account. For example, the use of IPCC estimates for methane projects fails to take into account local agricultural conditions. Several individuals noted that because the validation stage involves estimation, it is inherently subject to error, and one respondent noted that project sponsors are often optimistic in the validation stage. Others suggested that firms conducting the verification may use conservative assumptions in accordance with best practices recommended by the International Organization for Standardization and other organizations, thereby further increasing the difference between validation estimates and verification results.

With respect to the adequacy of guidance or change in procedures, several respondents noted that the CDM Executive Board has not provided adequate guidance for validation and verification procedures. CDM methodologies have been frequently revised, which has greatly contributed to uncertainty. One respondent noted that some of these methodologies have been revised several times already since their inception and that CDM guidelines do not specify exactly what steps need to be taken to validate or verify emissions. Another person indicated that CDM rules which prohibit direct contact between project sponsors and reviewing personnel have slowed approvals and prevented project sponsors from receiving timely or detailed guidance.

Do you think that the complexity of verifying emissions reductions outweighs the potential climate change mitigation gains from these projects? How should the Parties redress this issue?

5. *The CDM and Removals by Sinks.* Whereas Article 6 concerning JI refers to both "reduction in emissions by sources, or an enhancement of removals by sinks," Article 12 concerning the CDM refers only to emissions reductions. Is this difference in language intended to exclude forestry and other land use projects that remove carbon dioxide from the atmosphere from the CDM? The Parties had many concerns about such projects, including whether it was possible to ensure removals from sinks over time, because disease, natural disturbances, and other factors could eliminate any gains made from tree planting or other activities. As a consequence, they limited the use of the CDM to "afforestation" and "reforestation" projects,

terms defined to exclude forest management practices. Decision 5/CMP.1, *Modalities and Procedures for Afforestation and Reforestation Project Activities under the Clean Development Mechanism in the First Commitment Period of the Kyoto Protocol* (2005). These issues are covered in much greater detail in Chapter 8.

6. *Financing.* Developing countries worried that government funded CDM projects might reduce other sources of development assistance. As a result, the parties adopted a Decision providing that public funding for CDM projects from Annex I Parties should not result in the diversion of official development assistance and should be separate from financial obligations of Annex I Parties under the convention. *See, e.g.*, Decision 3/CMP.1, at Appendix B, para. 2(f).

D.   Emissions Trading

In addition to project-based emissions trading through JI and CDM projects, the Kyoto Protocol also allows emissions trading in the absence of a specific project. Through procedures developed pursuant to Article 17 of the Kyoto Protocol, Annex I Parties with quantified emissions limitations may buy and sell "carbon" credits that result from non-project-based activities, such as policy changes that improve fuel efficiency of automobiles or energy efficiency of appliances. They may also buy and sell credits generated from JI and CDM projects. Even in the absence of policies and projects that reduce emissions, the Kyoto Protocol regime is primed for emissions trading. For example, many developed countries agreed to reduce their emissions by seven or eight percent below 1990 levels. Yet, Russia and Ukraine, which negotiated the right to stabilize their emissions at 1990 levels, have seen their emissions drop dramatically due to the substantial contraction of the industrial sector after the fall of communism. As noted above, by one 2006 estimate, Russia will have 3.1 billion tonnes of carbon dioxide equivalent (tCO_2eq) and Ukraine another 1 billion tCO_2eq of surplus AAUs to sell during the 2008–2012 commitment period, provided they are willing to forgo their right to increase their own emissions. Natalia Gorina, *Cooling Down Hot Air*, *in* GLOBAL CARBON 2006 (May 2006).

The Kyoto Protocol itself does not establish rules for emissions trading, but Article 17 calls on the Parties to establish principles and criteria for verification, reporting, and accountability for emissions trading by Annex I Parties. The Parties have developed those rules at various meetings of the Parties. For example, "carbon" credits from each of the flexibility mechanisms may be bought and sold: assigned amount units (AAUs) issued by an Annex I Party on the basis of its assigned amount; ERUs generated through joint implementation projects, and CERs generated through CDM projects. In addition, removal units (RMUs) issued by an Annex I Party on the basis of removals from sinks from land use activities may be traded.

As a technical matter, all forms of emissions trading — JI, CDM, and Article 17 emissions trading — are only available to Parties. Nonetheless, decisions of the Parties authorize a Party to open up each of these mechanisms to businesses, non-governmental organizations and other private entities. Thus, private entities may develop JI and CDM projects and engage in emissions trading. Decision 11/CMP/.1, *Modalities, Rules, and Guidelines for Emissions Trading under Article 17 of the Kyoto Protocol*, Annex, para. 5 (2005).

Despite private involvement, any transaction pursuant to the flexibility mechanisms becomes a "government" matter by virtue of accounting registries required by Decisions of the Parties. The Parties track the various transfers and acquisitions through a series of registries. Perhaps the most important is the national registry. Each Annex I party must establish and maintain a national registry "to ensure the accurate accounting of the issuance, holding, transfer, acquisition, cancellation, and retirement of ERUs, CERs, AAUs and RMUs." Decision 13/CMP/.1, *Modalities for the Accounting of Assigned Amounts under Article 7, paragraph 4, of the Kyoto Protocol*, Annex, para. 17 (2005). If a Party has authorized private entities to participate in any of the flexibility mechanisms, the Party must establish an account in the national registry for that entity. *Id.* at para. 21(b). As a result, any transaction between account holders or between Parties takes place within and between the national registries.

In addition, the CDM registry, which the UNFCCC Secretariat administers, issues and distributes CERs to national registries. Thus, CERs are not issued directly to a private entity. The UNFCCC Secretariat also administers the International Transaction Log, which verifies registry transactions, in real time, for consistency with rules of the Kyoto Protocol and subsequent Decisions of the Parties. The Log requires registries to terminate transactions that are inconsistent with those rules.

III. IMPLEMENTATION ISSUES

Many have heralded emissions trading and the Kyoto Protocol's flexibility mechanisms as a win-win-win situation: developed countries can reach their targets in a cost-effective way, global climate change is mitigated, and much needed infusions of cash and technology flow to developing countries.

Whether the flexibility mechanisms actually do reflect a win-win-win situation depends on how they are implemented. Many of the most challenging and controversial implementation issues were left unresolved by the Kyoto Protocol negotiations, leaving the Parties to clarify the use of the flexibility mechanisms at subsequent meetings. For example, given the presence of the flexibility mechanisms, to what extent should countries be required to make domestic reductions to meet their targets? For both JI and CDM, projects must provide climate change benefits that are "additional to any that would otherwise occur." How should that be determined? Which Parties are eligible to use the flexibility mechanisms? Moreover, CDM projects are being developed in disproportionate amounts in just a few developing countries like India and China. Is that a problem? The remainder of this section explores these and other issues.

A.   Supplementarity

While agreement was reached on the use of emissions trading by Annex I Parties to meet their commitments, no consensus could be reached on the extent to which those Parties could use emissions trading to meet their commitments. Could the United States meet its targets exclusively from emissions trading and JI and CDM projects? In the alternative, should Annex I Parties be required, as a moral imperative or legal obligation, to make some emissions reductions at home?

Articles 6 and 17 of the Kyoto Protocol provide only that any emissions trading "shall be supplemental to domestic actions" for the purpose of meeting a Party's commitments. Article 12 allows an Annex I party to use the CDM to meet "part" of its commitments. The Kyoto Protocol thus left for future negotiations the difficult decision of defining what constitutes "supplemental." Hoping to take advantage of Russia's "hot air" and championing the economic efficiency of making reductions elsewhere, the United States advocated for unlimited trading. The European Union sought a cap on emissions trading of 50 percent of the total reductions required. Europe's position only underscored its regulatory advantage over other countries and regions. Because of the European Union's well-developed regulatory and institutional structures, it could implement a "bubble" pursuant to Article 4 and average emissions across the EU. Importantly, the requirements for supplementarity do not apply to bubbles.

In choosing an approach to supplementarity, the Parties have faced a number of dilemmas. First, despite the express incorporation of the flexibility mechanisms into the Kyoto Protocol, the moral and legal argument for supplementarity is strong. Shouldn't the developed countries, which have contributed far more to climate change than the developing countries, "take the lead" by reducing emissions at home? Doesn't the principle of "common but differentiated responsibilities" require developed countries to do more? At the same time, the flexibility mechanisms are designed to encourage cost-effective GHG reductions, and without them, many Annex I Parties may not have adopted the Kyoto Protocol or, in the alternative, would have insisted on much lower targets.

Second, while recognizing the cost-effectiveness of reducing GHG emissions through the flexibility mechanisms, strict requirements for Annex I Parties to reduce greenhouse gas emissions domestically could provide a powerful incentive to develop climate-friendly technologies. By keeping the pressure on for reductions in the more technologically advanced countries, additional reductions are more likely to come from new technological innovations. These new climate-friendly technologies could become the first choice for use in both developed and developing countries. How should the Parties balance cost-effectiveness with incentives for the development of climate-friendly technology?

On the other hand, rigid requirements for supplementarity may minimize economic benefits of the flexibility mechanisms, particularly for developing countries. By requiring substantial reductions in Annex I Parties, investors would have little incentive to develop CDM projects. Just how significant would be the lost economic opportunities for developing countries? Researchers evaluated the effects on developing countries of imposing limits on the number of CERs that Annex I Parties with commitments under the Kyoto Protocol ("Annex B Parties") could use to meet their commitments. They concluded that:

> [T]he effects of the three levels of supplementarity restrictions are straightforward. By forcing Annex B Parties to reduce more internally, by definition importing less CERs, the demand for developing nations' CDM projects falls. As the limit on the use of CERs is tightened from 75% to 50% to 25%, the price of CERs falls, fewer CDM projects are financed, and the potential economic benefits to developing nations fall accordingly. The restriction severely reduces the potential for developing nations to contribute to the mitigation of climate change, constrains their ability to assist Annex B [Parties] in achieving their targets, and minimizes the economic benefits of CDM for sustainable development.

Thomas Black-Arbelaez et al., *Contributions from the National Strategy Studies Program to COP6 Negotiations Regarding CDM and JI* (Sept. 2000); *see also* A. Denny Ellerman, et al, *The Effects on Developing Countries of the Kyoto Protocol and Carbon Dioxide Emissions Trading* 9–11 (MIT Policy Research Paper, 1998).

These studies have shown that the impacts on developing countries could be significant. For example, one study concluded that emissions trading would generate $6.1 billion a year for five developing countries (Thailand, Pakistan, the Philippines, Korea, and Vietnam), but only $1.4 billion if developed countries were required to make 75% of their reductions domestically. Thomas Black-Arbelaez, *Supplementarity at COP6: Fewer Benefits and Less Development for Asian Countries*, in AUSTRALIAN BUREAU OF AGRICULTURAL AND RESOURCE ECONOMICS, OUTLOOK 2001, at 35 (2001). *See also* Thomas Black-Arbelaez et al., *Contributions from the National Strategy Studies Program to COP6 Negotiations Regarding CDM and JI* (Sept. 2000) (finding similar results for Zimbabwe, Argentina, and Colombia); A. Denny Ellerman & Ian Sue Wing, *Supplementarity: An Invitation to Monopsony* (2000).

The European Union eventually relented and withdrew its proposal for establishing specific supplementarity limits on a Party's use of the flexibility mechanisms. Instead, the Parties established some general guidance on supplementarity.

DECISION 2/CMP.1
PRINCIPLES, NATURE AND SCOPE OF THE MECHANISMS PURSUANT TO ARTICLES 6, 12 AND 17 OF THE KYOTO PROTOCOL
(2005)

The Conference of the Parties serving as the meeting of the Parties to the Kyoto Protocol, * * *

Emphasizing that the Parties included in Annex I shall implement domestic action in accordance with national circumstances and with a view to reducing emissions in a manner conducive to narrowing per capita differences between developed and developing country Parties while working towards achievement of the ultimate objective of the Convention, * * *

1. *Decides* that the use of the mechanisms shall be supplemental to domestic action and that domestic action shall thus constitute a significant element of the effort made by each Party included in Annex I to meet its quantified emission limitation and reduction commitments under Article 3, paragraph 1;

2. *Requests* the Parties included in Annex I to provide relevant information in relation to paragraph 1 above, in accordance with Article 7 of the Kyoto Protocol, for review under its Article 8;

3. *Decides* that the provision of such information shall take into account reporting on demonstrable progress as contained in decision 15/CMP.1;

4. *Requests* the facilitative branch of the Compliance Committee to address questions of implementation with respect to paragraphs 2 and 3 above;

QUESTIONS AND DISCUSSION

1. In what way is the supplementarity requirement enforceable? For example, can a Party be challenged for failing to take "significant" domestic action to achieve its commitment? As described in more detail in Chapter 9, the Compliance Committee does not have the authority to penalize a Party for noncompliance with this supplementarity guidance. Instead, through its facilitative branch, the Compliance Committee provides advice and facilitates compliance with the Kyoto Protocol. If that is so, what is the value of referring the question of supplementarity to the facilitative branch?

2. A stated purpose of the CDM is to promote sustainable development in developing countries and to allow developing countries to contribute to climate change mitigation. If supplementarity requirements would diminish economic opportunities that could spur sustainable development, should any restrictions be placed on emissions trading? *See* Sangmin Shim, *Korea's Leading Role in Joining the Kyoto Protocol with the Flexibility Mechanisms as "Side-Payments"*, 15 GEO. INT'L ENVTL. L. REV. 203 (2003) (calling for the abolishment of supplementarity).

B.   Additionality

Articles 6(1)(b) and 12(5)(c) of the Kyoto Protocol require that JI and CDM projects provide emissions reductions that are "additional" to any that would otherwise occur. The establishment of technical rules for determining when a JI or CDM project actually achieves "additional" reductions has been one of the most challenging tasks for Parties. Indeed, whether a project provides "additional" reductions involves a number of related, complex issues.

The initial question is just how to conceptualize when a project might generate emissions reductions that would not otherwise occur, because emission reductions often occur as a result of natural economic progression. For example, U.S. carbon intensity — a measure of carbon emissions per unit of economic activity, such as gross domestic product — fell by 21 percent in the 1980s and 16 percent in the 1990s. Pew Center on Global Climate Change, "Analysis of President Bush(s Climate Change Plan" (Feb. 2002). Although overall emissions grew in the United States during these periods as a result of an expanding economy, emissions fell at the project or facility level due to technological and other improvements. Similarly, energy efficiency gains in China avoided 432 metric tons of carbon emissions from 1980 to 1997, again, in the absence of any CDM projects. Kevin A. Baumert, et al., *What Might a Developing Country Commitment Look Like?*, CLIMATE NOTES 4 (May 1999). Producers either became more energy efficient by purchasing more modern and efficient technologies or shifted to less carbon intensive fuels as China made policy choices, such as sharp reductions in coal and petroleum subsidies, that eliminated economic incentives to use large amounts of high carbon fuels. *See id.* at 9. In any event, emissions reductions in China and the United States occurred without JI or CDM projects.

The challenge for the Kyoto Protocol is to sort out these "business-as-usual" factors from emissions reductions that simply would not have occurred absent the JI or CDM project. If the Parties do not establish credible rules for doing so, they will allow the issuance of CERs and ERUs for emissions reductions that would have occurred regardless of the existence of the JI or CDM project or the entire climate change regime. In other words, there would be no additional emissions reductions from JI or the CDM.

Assessing a project's additionality is without question extremely complex. The Parties have established a two-step process to assess what is "business as usual." First, the project participants must establish the project baseline, an assessment of what is actually happening and will happen without the JI or CDM project. Second, the project participants must assess the proposed project against this baseline. A third issue, leakage, further complicates the additionality finding. Leakage occurs when the reduction or sequestration of emissions in one place shifts emissions to another site. For example, energy efficiency investments may produce cost savings that encourage increased production — and emissions. An afforestation project may enhance removals of carbon dioxide but force subsistence farmers to cut forests elsewhere to meet their basic needs. Under these scenarios, should emissions reductions from a JI or CDM project be considered additional? These challenges are explored below.

---

1.   *Establishing Baseline Emissions*

The process for assessing additionality starts with establishing a project baseline. For both JI and CDM projects, baseline emissions should "reasonably represent[] the anthropogenic emissions by sources or anthropogenic removals by sinks of greenhouse gases that would occur in the absence of the proposed project." In establishing the baseline, the project proponents must include all anthropogenic GHG emissions by sources and anthropogenic removals by sinks within the project boundary. Decision 9/CMP.1, *Guidelines for the Implementation of Article 6 of the Kyoto Protocol*, Appendix B (2005); Decision 3/CMP.1, *Modalities and Procedures for a Clean Development Mechanism as Defined by Article 12 of the Kyoto Protocol*, Annex, paras. 44–52.

This baseline must also be established conservatively, in a transparent manner, and on a project-by-project basis. The Parties have established three basic approaches for establishing baselines, summarized by UNEP as follows:

RAM M. SHRESTHA et al., BASELINE METHODOLOGIES FOR CLEAN DEVELOPMENT MECHANISM PROJECTS: A GUIDEBOOK
21–22 (UNEP Risø Centre, Nov. 2005)

a) The first approach involves existing actual or historical emissions (hereafter "Approach A"). This is applicable to cases where the analysis of the baseline scenario indicates that the most likely activities implemented in absence of the proposed CDM project is the continuation of existing activities. To continue with the Landfill CDM project example, recall that the current practice in the host country is zero collection of methane generated from MSW [municipal solid waste] disposed at the landfills. The analysis of the situation indicates that though there are other options available for curtailing emissions from a landfill (e.g., treatment of organic waste before disposal in a landfill or systems for methane collection at the landfill), the most likely scenario is continuation of present practice. The baseline approach to be used in such a case is Approach A.

b) The second approach (hereafter, "Approach B") is based on emissions from a technology that represents an economically attractive course of action, taking into account barriers to investment. This approach is applicable to situations, where economic analysis is undertaken to identify [the] most attractive option among various options, which includes the CDM project activity. The emissions from the economically most attractive alternative are the baseline. For the Landfill CDM project example, say the alternatives available are: continuation of the current practice, i.e., zero collection of methane generated from landfill; treatment of organic waste before disposal to landfill (methane emissions from landfill are from decay of organic matter); and, a collection system for landfill methane. Suppose the analysis of the situation indicates that treatment of organic waste before disposal at the landfill site is the economically most attractive alternative. Then, the baseline scenario is treatment of organic waste before its disposal to landfill and the baseline approach is Approach B. In this example, the baseline is in terms of emissions from the landfill under the condition that organic waste disposed at the site is pre-treated.

c) The third approach is based on the average emissions of similar project activities undertaken in the previous five years, in similar social, economic, environmental and technological circumstances, and whose performance is among the top 20 percent of their category (hereafter "Approach C"). To continue with the Landfill CDM project, say there are four alternatives, other than the proposed CDM project alternative, available to curtail the methane emission from the landfill. None of the four alternatives can be clearly demonstrated as economically most attractive. The baseline scenario then is based on analysis of alternatives implemented during the last five years. The baseline approach in this case will be Approach C. The baseline is the average emission of the options most commonly used in the previous five years and whose performance is among the top 20 percent.

The three are akin to options available for implementing a project. Project proponents choose either to continue with an existing commonly used process/technology or to adopt a newer option available in the market that has come to be preferred over a more commonly used option in recent years. If more than one new option is available, the proponents choose the most economical option that meets all the regulatory requirements. But in absence of adequate information or differences among various new options, any of the options from the basket of new options could be chosen.

---

2.   *Additionality Assessment*

Identifying whether a specific project actually yields reductions "additional to" any that would otherwise occur is perhaps the most complex issue for both JI and CDM projects. Without an honest appraisal of additionality, the environmental integrity of the Kyoto Protocol is jeopardized and efforts to mitigate climate change seriously undermined. As a consequence, the Parties have provided guidance on making additionality assessments to ensure climate change mitigation benefits are actually achieved.

As designed under the Kyoto Protocol, calculating additionality is not simply a measurement of the greenhouse gas emissions of a JI or CDM project. Instead, additionality is intended to assess whether the project avoids business-as-usual activities and emissions. To assist with this analysis, the CDM's Executive Board has developed a voluntary "additionality tool" to clarify elements of additionality and guide assessment of additionality on a project-specific level. In this way, the questions help gauge whether the project's emissions — to the extent that they are less than other options — provide reductions that would not otherwise occur. CDM Executive Board, *Methodological Tool for the Demonstration and Assessment of Additionality (Version 04)*. If project participants propose another methodology for assessing additionality, they must justify it.

The Executive Board's tool establishes a four-step process for assessing additionality. First, the project participants must identify realistic or credible alternatives comparable to the proposed project. The second and third steps are combined: the project participants must prepare either an investment analysis or a barriers analysis, or both, to compare the proposed project with the alternatives. The project participants have the discretion to choose which analysis they want to use. The investment analysis is designed to determine whether the proposed project activity, without revenue from the sale of CERs, is economically or financially less attractive than at least one of the identified alternatives.

If the project is financially attractive, then step three requires the project participants to show that other realistic and credible barriers would prevent the development of the proposed project but not prevent at least one of the alternatives. These barriers could include technological barriers, the lack of funding for innovative projects, and the inability to manage state-of-the-art technology.

If the investment analysis shows that the proposed CDM project is not financially attractive or not likely to be the most financially attractive, depending on which analytical tool is used to assess investment barriers, or the barriers analysis indicates that the project faces barriers that do not affect other alternatives, then the project participants need to complete step four, the common practice analysis.

The common practice analysis assesses the extent to which the proposed project type has already been deployed in the relevant sector and region. This analysis is designed as a credibility check on the investment and barriers analysis: if similar projects already exist in the area, it is difficult to claim that investment or other barriers prevent the development of the proposed project in the absence of the CDM. If similar activities cannot be observed or similar activities are observed, but essential distinctions between the project activity and similar activities can reasonably be explained, then the proposed project activity is additional. However, if similar projects exist and essential differences cannot be explained, then the project is not additional. For additional information on the additionality tool, see Ram M. Shrestha, et al., *Baseline Methodologies for Clean Development Mechanism Projects: A Guidebook* 35–45 (UNEP Risø Centre, Nov. 2005).

BOX 2 — ASSESSING ADDITIONALITY — THE LIAONING HUANREN NIUMAODASHAN WIND POWER PROJECT

To demonstrate that their project would be additional to those that would otherwise occur, the project proponents of the **Liaoning Huanren Niumaodashan Wind Power Project** began Step 1 of their additionality analysis by suggesting alternatives to the proposed project:

a)   A thermal power plant with the same capacity or the same annual electricity output as the proposed project.

b)   The proposed project not undertaken as a CDM project activity but as a commercial project.

c)   Another renewable energy power plant with the same capacity or the same annual electricity output as the proposed project.

d)   The Northeast China Power Grid as the provider for the same capacity and electricity output as the proposed project.

Under Step 1, the project proponents concluded that building a thermal power plant with comparable output would not be reasonable because it would not be permitted under Chinese law. Similarly, building a different type of renewable energy project was also not reasonable. While wind energy, solar, geothermal, biomass, and other renewable energy sources could be used to supply the power to the Northeast China Power Grid, the Chinese partner in this venture, CASC Longyuan (Benxi) Wind Power Company, Ltd., did not have a license to produce power in Liaoning Province from sources other than wind.

Using the investment analysis of Step 2, the project proponents eliminated as an option undertaking the same project as a commercial project without CERs. According to the project proponents, such a project would produce a financial rate of return below that expected for electricity generating projects. The rate of return could exceed the benchmark rate of return only if operational and maintenance costs dropped significantly or if other factors, such as an 8 percent change in the tariff, applied to electricity. However, these changes were considered improbable. Applying the common practice analysis of Step 3, the proponents found that wind power was uncommon in Northeast China, with only 3 percent of energy deriving from wind power. While other wind power projects existed in the area, they were built with lower international interest rates than would apply to the proposed project or more generous Chinese policies supporting wind power projects. In addition, the owner of some of the other projects had applied for CERs to help ensure the profitability of its wind power projects. Thus, it could not be expected that the proposed project would be developed as a non-CDM project. As a consequence, the Designated Operational Entity concluded that "it is sufficiently demonstrated that the project is not a likely baseline scenario and that emission reductions occurring from this will hence be additional." Det Norske Veritas, Validation Report: Liaoning Huanren Niumaodashan Wind Power Project, Report No. 2007–1256, 10 (Revision No. 01, Jan. 1, 2008).

3.   *Leakage*

As described in the introduction to this section, leakage occurs when reducing or sequestering emissions in one place shifts the pollution-causing activity to another place. The accurate accounting of leakage is obviously central for calculating the "additional" reductions from a project. If leakage is not accounted for or underreported, then too many CERs or ERUs will be issued and the overall goal of mitigating climate change undermined. Studies underscore the importance of accurate accounting of leakage to the credibility of the Kyoto Protocol regime: most estimates suggest leakage rates of GHG abatement policies in Annex I countries to non-Annex I countries are between 5 percent and 20 percent. *See* Frank Vöhringer, et al., *A Proposal for the Attribution of Market Leakage to CDM Projects* 13 (HWWA Discussion Paper, 2004) (summarizing research on leakage). As the following article describes, leakage can happen in a variety of ways, which explains why leakage is so prevalent and difficult to measure.

THE CDM GUIDEBOOK: A RESOURCE FOR CLEAN DEVELOPMENT MECHANISM DEVELOPERS IN SOUTHERN AFRICA
¶ 3.1.3 (Randall Spalding-Fecher, ed. 2002)*

Leakage is a measurable emissions increase that is caused by the project, but is outside of a CDM project boundary or timeframe. Leakage occurs when system boundaries are drawn in such a way as to ignore some emission changes caused by the project. In some cases there can be a positive leakage (known as spillover) if the CDM project leads to reduced emissions elsewhere, or after the project ends. Sources of leakage vary according to project type and according to which emission sources or effects are components of the project baseline. Leakage may be influenced by the type of baseline used. An example would be a physical displacement of the baseline technology to a location where a more modern and efficient technology was intended to be used, but where technology was chosen because it was readily available and possibly cheaper. A more common example would be a large CDM project lowering the price of its products or services, and so increasing the demand. For instance, a large energy-efficiency programme may decrease the price of electricity and increase the total demand for power. The fuel emissions offset by the project would then be reduced by the increase in emissions from the additional demand. Similarly, a large afforestation project may depress the market price for timber, thereby increasing demand for timber products and reducing net carbon reductions. Another example would be a project to reduce deforestation displacing the pressure on forest resources to somewhere else outside the project boundary.

Positive leakage or spillover could happen when CDM project technology is emulated by other projects in the same country or elsewhere, through a demonstration effect. If this replication of technology is planned, the spillover may be termed an intended consequence of the project, or market transformation. CDM project developers who adopt innovative technology may also patent it and market it to other producers. An example of a spillover in the [land management] sector would be if products from sustainably managed afforestation projects replaced products from unsustainably managed forests. If the reduction of deforestation outside the CDM project boundary reduces total emissions from the country, this should be considered as spillover. On the other hand, if the CDM project displaced subsistence farmers from the project area, and these farmers engaged in deforestation in other areas, the additional emissions would have to be counted against the project as leakage.

To measure the emissions impacts, it may be necessary to monitor changes in emissions outside the official project boundary, bearing in mind that widening the monitoring domain will entail greater costs. The secondary impacts of a project are likely to be modest in the beginning, and the monitoring of such impacts may not be a priority — for small-scale projects they may even be insignificant. In such circumstances, the project developer may be justified in disregarding these impacts and simply focussing on energy savings and direct emissions reduction. As the project becomes larger and more linked to market transformation, however, these impacts may become significant and may have to be evaluated.

As can be imagined, measuring leakage is challenging. First, activities causing leakage by definition occur outside a project's boundary. Because it is not typical to monitor for such changes, they may not be noticed. With respect to an afforestation project, for example, how should project participants ascertain whether displaced subsistence farmers have engaged in deforestation? Second, even if such changes are detected, proving that they resulted from the CDM or JI project and not other economic or other factors will be challenging.

Despite these difficulties, project participants must account for and subtract any leakage from a project's on-site greenhouse gas reductions. For both JI and CDM projects, leakage is defined as "the net change of anthropogenic emissions by sources and/or removals by sinks of greenhouse gases which occurs outside the project boundary, and which is measurable and attributable to the CDM project activity." The project boundary encompasses all anthropogenic emissions by sources of greenhouse gases "under the control of the project participants that are significant and reasonably attributable to the CDM project activity." Decision 3/CMP.1, *Modalities and Procedures for a Clean Development Mechanism as Defined in Article 12 of the Kyoto Protocol*, paras. 50–52 (2005); Decision 9/CMP.1, *Guidelines for the Implementation of Article 6 of the Kyoto Protocol*, Appendix B, para. 4(f) (2005); Joint Implementation Supervisory Committee, *Guidance on Criteria for Baseline Setting and Monitoring*, Annex 2 (Version 01).

The discussion of leakage begins at the project design stage — the project design document must include a description of formulae used to calculate and to project leakage that is measurable and attributable to the project. To assist with the calculation of leakage, the CDM Executive Board has approved a number of methodological tools for particular types of projects. *See, e.g.*, CDM Executive Board, *Tool to Calculate Project or Leakage CO_2 Emissions from Fossil Fuel Combustion* (Version 01), *available at* http://cdm.unfccc.int/Reference/Guidclarif/index.html. In some cases, a highly pragmatic approach has been taken. For example, market leakage — leakage effects that are transmitted through changes in price, supply, or demand of goods — are considered to be unmeasurable or insignificant for some projects. Vöhringer, et al., *Market Leakage*, at 1. One can easily imagine the challenges of determining whether a particular CDM afforestation project has had an impact on the price or the manufacture and sale of wood-based products produced from wood harvested outside the project's boundary. The CDM Executive Board thus decided to exclude "market leakage" from consideration of afforestation/reforestation projects. CDM Executive Board, *Guidance Related to Market Leakage* (March 3, 2006).

QUESTIONS AND DISCUSSION

1. *Baselines.* The three approaches for establishing baselines provide general guidance to project participants. The Parties have adopted highly technical guidance, including formulae and algorithms, for calculating actual baselines for specific types of projects. UNFCCC, *Approved Baseline and Monitoring Method-*

ologies. Despite this technical detail, the general approaches remain the starting point for establishing baselines. Consider the range of options under the three approaches. Why are three approaches necessary for ascertaining baseline emissions? In other words, why is it insufficient in some cases to establish baseline emissions using actual or historical emissions?

2.   After reviewing the additionality analysis for the Liaoning Huanren Niu-maodashan Wind Power Project, how confident are you that that CDM investment in the project will result in additional climate benefits?

3.   Despite the central importance of additionality, a review by the CDM's Panel on Methodologies has revealed some deficiencies in assessing additionality:

CDM EXECUTIVE BOARD, TWENTY-SEVENTH MEETING, PROPOSED AGENDA-ANNOTATIONS
(Oct. 29–Nov. 1, 2006)

(a) From review of available documentation it appears that current methodological guidance from the Board is either not applied or, if applied, is not always documented. For example, several project activities, which use the additionality tool have not assessed whether the proposed project carried out without the CDM is a realistic and credible alternative scenario. Most projects requesting a crediting period that started prior to registration have not provided evidence in the CDM-PDD to support the claim that CDM was considered in the decision to proceed with the project activity, while some have provided evidence that appeared inconsistent with the claim. For a majority of PDDs examined, the method for conducting the common practice analysis is not documented, as is requested by the additionality tool. In many of the PDDs considered, key underlying assumptions and rationales related to additionality are not substantiated. Documented evidence tends to be more complete and sufficient in cases where the project activity does not generate significant revenues other than those related to CERs.

(b) Paragraph 27(h) of the annex to decision 3/CMP.1 ("Information used to determine additionality . . . shall not be considered as proprietary or confidential") is interpreted differently by various project participants. In approximately half the PDDs examined, key information used to demonstrate additionality was not included in the PDD. It is possible that such information was shared privately with the DOEs or the Board, or may be available elsewhere.

(c) Current assessment of additionality by DOEs is varied. While validation reports for some registered CDM projects indicate that efforts to corroborate additionality claims were undertaken, other cases with no such indications were found. Some validation reports acknowledge or restate claims made in PDDs, but do not explain whether or how such claims (and their underlying assumptions) have been validated. In cases where one or more alternatives are not under the control of project participants, a different procedure would be required to demonstrate additionality and identify the baseline scenario than provided in the draft. Such cases might include grid-connected power projects (where an alternative might be electricity produced by other facilities not under the control of project participants) or other projects that increase the delivery of a given product to a competitive local, regional or global market. In such cases, baseline scenarios might be rather complex (such as the combined margin scenario in ACM0002), and the methods for comparing alternatives may differ from those provided in the draft (e.g., benchmark analysis or other methods that utilize information about the markets in which such projects might compete). * * *

Among the project activities examined, there was no indication of a DOE requiring corrective action related to additionality. In summary, the available documentation reviewed by the consultants provides little evidence of external validation by DOEs of key assumptions and data used for additionality assessment, though such evidence may exist elsewhere. As noted above, such documentation (PDDs and validation reports) may not tell the full story; at the same time, such a gap in documentation should be rectified in the future.

Why might compliance with the information requirements be so problematic? What does this assessment suggest about the effectiveness of the CDM for providing climate change benefits?

4. Commentators widely agree that additionality determinations are very subjective. *See, e.g.*, Axel Michaelowa, et al., *COP 10: Getting the CDM Started and Pondering the Future of the Climate Policy Regime* (Jan. 2005). As a consequence, interest has grown for simpler approaches for measuring project additionality and establishing project baselines. The simplified procedures for small-scale projects are one response (*see infra* Section III.D.1., note 4). Other approaches have also been proposed for simplifying the measurement of additionality. The "benchmark" approach involves establishing quantitative benchmarks expressed in terms of tons of carbon per unit of output and judged against "best practices" or some other agreed upon criteria that represents baseline emissions. A project would be deemed "additional" if its emissions were below the relevant benchmark. A second approach would establish lists of specific technologies that represent baseline technologies (and emissions) for different economic sectors. The baseline technologies could be universal or limited to specified countries or regions. Projects that use technologies with lower GHG emissions than the baseline technology would be deemed additional. While these approaches may be easier to measure, what additional challenges do they introduce? Does the language of Articles 6.1(b) and 12.5(c) of the Protocol pose any problems for these approaches?

5. The World Wildlife Fund has established the Gold Standard, a set of expanded procedures and standards based on the CDM framework and rules of the CDM Executive Board. The goal of the Gold Standard is to ensure that CDM and JI projects achieve additional reductions from business-as-usual activities and provide sustainable development benefits in the host country. The Gold Standard applies exclusively to projects employing renewable energy and energy efficiency technologies "to encourage the shift from a fossil fuel based economy to a renewable energy economy." It also requires technology transfer and that project proponents use the Executive Board's additionality tool. Project proponents must also invite local stakeholders to two consultation meetings (one in the initial stages of the project and one prior to validation) and ensure that the project responds to local concerns regarding the environmental, social, and economic impacts of the project. To ensure sustainable development benefits flow from the project, they must also calculate the environmental, social, and economic impacts of the project by scoring the project's impacts (from -2 to +2) with respect to several specific questions (e.g., what is the impact on water quality and livelihoods of the poor?). Only projects with overall positive environmental, social, and economic impacts are given the Gold Standard. *The Gold Standard: Manual for Project Developers (Version 3)* (May 2006). To date, about 240 projects have completed the registration process or are in some stage of the Gold Standard pipeline. WWF admits that the Gold Standard adds evaluation costs for project developers. What are the benefits of seeking the Gold Standard? Do such private efforts provide an important supplementary means for ensuring that projects provide real benefits to climate mitigation and sustainable development?

6. Some business leaders and environmentalists worry that the development of additionality methodologies and actually ascertaining additionality has been too time-consuming and has resulted in high transactions costs. They argue that additionality may not even be "the most important factor at this stage in the development of offset-based emissions trading mechanisms." Instead, they argue that it is more important to get "emissions trading frameworks into place for the future, noting that near-term emissions reduction targets and trading are only a first step toward long-term climate policy." These observers are willing to trade "near-term environmental integrity in favor of getting a trading system into place." Mark C. Trexler et al., *A Statistically-Driven Approach to Offset-Based GHG Additionality Determinations: What Can We Learn?*, 6 SUSTAINABLE DEV. L. & POL'Y 30, 34–35 (Winter 2006). Do you agree?

7. Because leakage is defined as occurring outside the project's boundaries, leakage will very likely be beyond the control of the project participants, unless the project participant is a government or governmental body. While a government may be able to control some leakage through extensive national planning, it will not be able to control "international leakage," where companies or individuals move operations to another country. Consider potential leakage from a Bolivian afforestation CDM project. What kind of plan should project participants develop to measure leakage? Are there any steps they can take to avert leakage?

C.   Eligibility of Parties

The establishment of eligibility requirements for use of the flexibility mechanisms proved to be yet another contentious issue. The Kyoto Protocol itself is silent on whether a Party must meet certain requirements before it is eligible to use the flexibility mechanisms and when eligibility can be withdrawn. Yet, the majority of Parties wanted eligibility criteria; they wanted the flexibility mechanisms to act as an inducement for compliance with other Kyoto Protocol objectives and requirements.

The issue came to a head during the negotiations at the seventh meeting of the UNFCCC Parties in Marrakech in 2001. These negotiations were contentious because some Parties wanted to tie use of the flexibility mechanisms to acceptance of a compliance agreement. In their view, such a requirement would have two major benefits. First, it would help ensure the integrity of the flexibility mechanisms by making them subject to the compliance regime. Second, because Annex I Parties wanted to use the flexibility mechanisms, an express link to the compliance regime would help ensure the adoption of the compliance regime. Although the final criteria do not condition eligibility on the adoption of a compliance regime, they do authorize the enforcement branch of the Compliance Committee to assess whether a Party has met its eligibility requirements. Decision 2/CMP.1, *Principles, Nature and Scope of the Mechanisms Pursuant to Articles 6, 12 and 17 of the Kyoto Protocol* (2005). In addition, separate decisions on JI, the CDM, and emissions trading require that, to participate in these mechanisms, an Annex I Party must:

(a)   be a Party to the Protocol;

(b)   have calculated its assigned amount pursuant to relevant decisions;

(c)   have established a national system for estimating emissions and removals;

(d)   have established its national registry;

(e)   have submitted its most recent required inventory; and

(f)   have submitted the "supplementary information" required to show that it is in compliance with its emissions commitments.

Decision 9/CMP.1, *Guidelines for the Implementation of Article 6 of the Kyoto Protocol*, Annex, para. 21 (2005); Decision 3/CMP.7, *Modalities and Procedures for a Clean Development Mechanism as Defined by Article 12 of the Kyoto Protocol*, Annex, para. 31 (2005); Decision 11/CMP.1, at Annex, para. 2 (2005).

An Annex I Party may not participate in emissions trading or use CERs to meets its commitments under the CDM if it fails to meet any of the six criteria. Decision 27/CMP.1, *Procedures and Mechanisms Relating to Compliance under the Kyoto Protocol*, Annex XV, para. 5(c) (2005); Decision 3/CMP.1, Annex, paras. 31–33. Similarly, an Annex I Party may not participate in JI if it fails to meet criteria (a), (b) or (d). However, if an Annex I Party fails to meet criteria (c), (e), or (f), it may still participate in JI, but it must use "track two" for verifying emissions reductions from JI projects. *See* Section II.B, *infra. See also* Decision 9/CMP.1, Annex, para. 24.

QUESTIONS AND DISCUSSION

1.   ***Banking.*** Article 3.13 of the Kyoto Protocol allows Parties to bank emissions units from one commitment period and use or sell them in subsequent periods. The Parties later adopted additional rules that allow banking of AAUs without restriction. ERUs and CERs may be banked up to a maximum of 2.5 percent of a country's assigned amount. In contrast, because some Parties had concerns about accounting for sinks, RMUs may not be banked. Decision 13/CMP.1, *Modalities for the Accounting of Assigned Amounts under Article 7, Paragraph 4, of the Kyoto Protocol*, Annex, paras. 15–16. Are there any reasons to treat AAUs differently from ERUs and CERs?

2.   ***Commitment Period Reserve.*** The Parties also established the Commitment Period Reserve to prevent Parties from selling more assigned amount units than they have accumulated. The Commitment Period Reserve requires each Annex I party to hold a minimum number of emission credits (i.e., ERUs, CERs, AAUs, and RMUs) in its national registry. A party cannot transfer such credits if its credits fall below the level of the reserve. This reserve is calculated as the lower of the following:

(a)   90% of the Party's assigned amount; or

(b)   100% of a Party's most recently reviewed emissions inventory multiplied by five (for the five years of the commitment period).

Decision 11/CMP.1, at Annex, para. 6. Why would the Parties want to place these limits on trading?

D.   Problems of Project Breadth and Equity in the CDM

At first glance, the statistics for CDM projects suggest a broad range of projects in a broad range of countries: as of February 2009, the CDM has registered 1,390 projects in 53 countries. With many more projects in the pipeline, the CDM is helping to reduce greenhouse gas emissions that would not otherwise have occurred. However, a closer look at the statistics reveals both a skewing of projects toward big projects with big CER payoffs as well as an inequitable distribution of projects among a small subset of developing countries. These issues have led some to question whether the CDM could be more effective in meeting its twin goals of helping developing countries contribute to climate change mitigation and promoting sustainable development.

1.   *Breadth of CDM Projects*

Not surprisingly, investors have gravitated towards those projects that give them the biggest CER bang for their buck. As a consequence, CDM projects have skewed towards particular sectors that, according to some, do not address climate change in the most cost-effective way. The elimination of HFC-23 is particularly illustrative. HFC-23 is a powerful greenhouse gas created as a by-product of the production of HCFC-22, an industrial coolant until recently promoted as an alternative to CFCs because it is a less potent ozone depleting substance. Although HCFC-22 is scheduled for phaseout under the Montreal Protocol on Substances that Deplete the Ozone Layer, its current production continues to produce HFC-23 with a global warming potential of 11,700. Regulation of HCFCs under the Montreal Protocol is addressed in Chapter 10. The following excerpt nicely summarizes the economic and other issues at play as investors seek cheap CERs.

KEITH BRADSHER, OUTSIZE PROFITS, AND QUESTIONS, IN EFFORT TO CUT WARMING GASES
N.Y. TIMES, Dec. 21, 2006[*]

Under the [CDM], businesses in wealthier nations of Europe and in Japan help pay to reduce pollution in poorer ones as a way of staying within government limits for emitting climate-changing gases like carbon dioxide, as part of the Kyoto Protocol.

Among their targets is a large rusting chemical factory here in southeastern China. Its emissions of just one waste gas contribute as much to global warming each year as the emissions from a million American cars, each driven 12,000 miles.

Cleaning up this factory will require an incinerator that costs $5 million — far less than the cost of cleaning up so many cars, or other sources of pollution in Europe and Japan.

Yet the foreign companies will pay roughly $500 million for the incinerator — 100 times what it cost. * * *

The huge profits from that will be divided by the chemical factory's owners, a Chinese government energy fund, and the consultants and bankers who put together the deal from a mansion in the wealthy Mayfair district of London.

Arrangements like this still make sense to the foreign companies financing them because they are a lot less expensive, despite the large profit for others, than cleaning up their own operations. * * *

With so much money flowing to a few particularly lucrative cleanup deals, the danger is that they will distract attention from the broader effort to curb global warming gases, and that the lure of quick profit will encourage short-term fixes at the expense of fundamental, long-run solutions, including developing renewable energy sources like solar power. * * *

Another concern is that the program can have unintended results. The waste gas [HFC-23] to be incinerated here is emitted during the production of a refrigerant [HCFC-22] that will soon be banned in the United States and other industrial nations because it depletes the ozone layer that protects the earth from ultraviolet rays.

Handsome payments to clean up the waste gas have helped chemical companies to expand existing factories that make the old refrigerant and even build new factories, said Michael Wara, a carbon-trading lawyer at Holland & Knight in San Francisco.

Moreover, air-conditioners using this Freon-like refrigerant are much less efficient users of electricity than newer models. The expansion of large middle classes in India and China has led to soaring sales of cheap, inefficient air-conditioners, along with the building of coal-fired plants to power them, further contributing to global warming and the depletion of the ozone layer. * * *

[A recent] study . . . found that the profits are enormous in destroying trifluoromethane, or HFC-23, a very potent greenhouse gas that is produced at the factory here and several dozen other plants in developing countries. The study calculated that industrial nations could pay $800 million a year to buy credits, even though the cost of building and operating incinerators will be only $31 million a year. * * *

Richard Rosenzweig, chief operating officer of Natsource, a company in Washington arranging emissions deals between poor and rich countries, said it was not fair to look only at incineration costs and compare them with the size of payments from industrial nations. The administrative costs of the program are high, he said, and at least disposal of the waste gas is taking place. * * *

Environmental groups say that governments in developing countries should either require factories to incinerate the waste gas as a cost of doing business, or receive aid from wealthier countries to cover the relatively modest cost of incinerators.

"Couldn't we pay for the cost, or even twice the cost, of abatement and spend the rest of the money in better ways?" Mr. Wara asked. * * *

James Cameron, the vice chairman of Climate Change Capital, which organized the chemical factory deal here, said there were considerable costs and risks in setting up plans that required elaborate certification by consultants, acceptance by developing-country governments and approval by a United Nations secretariat.

For small projects involving less than $250,000 worth of credits, fees for deal makers, consultants and lawyers can far exceed the cost of installing equipment to clean up emissions.

Even the Chinese government, the main seller of carbon credits and a defender of the program, is expressing some misgivings.

"We do not encourage more HFC projects," a statement by Lu Xuedu, deputy director of the Office of Global Environment Affairs at the Ministry of Science and Technology, said. "We would prefer to have more energy efficiency and renewable-energy projects that could help alleviate poverty in the countryside."

———————

As suggested by the article, many CDM projects have involved the destruction of HFC-23, which is relatively inexpensive to destroy and yields significant CERs per dollar invested. In fact, 99 percent of HFC-23 emissions can be destroyed by thermal oxidation at a cost of $2 to $8 million plus annual operating costs of $189,000–$350,000, depending on the facility's capacity (less than $0.20 per tonne of CO_2eq). Technology and Economic Assessment Panel, *Response to Decision XVIII/12: Report of the Task Force on HCFC Issues (With Particular Focus on the Impact of the Clean Development Mechanism) and Emissions Reduction Benefits Arising from Earlier HCFC Phase-Out and Other Practical Matters* 51 (Aug. 2007). Consequently, HFC-23 destruction projects accounted for 67 percent of CDM CERs contracted in 2005 and 34 percent in 2006 (compared to just 16 percent for renewable energy projects in 2006). Karan Capoor & Philippe Ambrosi, *State and Trends of the Carbon Market 2007* 27–28 (2007). Some estimate that the sale of HFC-23 credits will fetch €4.7 *billion* ($6.4 billion) by 2012, even though the cost of capturing and destroying the gas is only €100 *million* ($150 million). Economist-.com, *Perverse Incentives*, Apr. 23, 2007.

Given these financial incentives, the rush to HFC-23 projects is easy to understand. In contrast, the following excerpt looks at the challenges facing CDM-project developers as they seek CERs through renewable energy projects.

RENEWABLE ENERGY AND INTERNATIONAL LAW PROJECT, THE CLEAN DEVELOPMENT MECHANISM: SPECIAL CONSIDERATIONS FOR RENEWABLE ENERGY PROJECTS
2–3 (Nov. 2006)[*]

The first year after the Kyoto Protocol's entry into force has revealed some hurdles in the operation of the CDM which renewable projects must overcome if the CDM is to be a meaningful driver for significant market growth of the renewable energy industry to meet the growing energy demand of developing countries in a sustainable manner. . . .

- Due to the differentiated global warming potentials of greenhouse gases (carbon dioxide, which is displaced by renewable energy, being the least "potent" in terms of its global warming effect), the volume of emission reductions from renewable energy projects is much smaller per unit of output than the volumes created by projects which abate other greenhouse gases such as nitrous oxide, HFC or methane.

- Conversely, the equipment cost of most renewable energy projects is significantly higher per emission reduction than the cost of other types of potential CDM projects, such as agricultural methane flaring projects. The overall contribution of the revenue stream from Certified Emission Reductions (CERs) is therefore comparatively smaller for renewable

———————

energy projects than for other types of potential CDM projects. As the CDM is essentially a market, CDM project equity investors will tend to go to where "manufacturing costs" are cheapest and purchasers will tend to seek out a plentiful supply of CERs for minimum transaction costs. Renewable energy projects are therefore at a comparative disadvantage in the CDM compared to projects which reduce other types of greenhouse gases.

- In addition, renewable energy projects such as wind farms have a long operation life which (for projects being constructed today), will extend far beyond the Kyoto Protocol's first commitment period. Until very recently, there was a significant amount of uncertainty as to whether the Kyoto Protocol would be continued beyond its first commitment period (i.e., 2012). CER purchasers have therefore been reluctant to make binding commitments to purchase CERs post-2012, such that the financial incentive created by CERs has in many cases been insufficient to support renewable energy projects for their entire operational life.

- As a result, many renewable energy projects which may be eligible under the CDM have had difficulty attracting project finance to support the projects. CER purchasers have tended to restrict their involvement in CDM projects to a commitment to pay for CERs upon delivery, rather than provide financial support for the underlying project. Registration as a CDM project does not necessarily mean that a renewable energy project will achieve project finance and become operational. Issues such as perceived regulatory and political risk in developing countries and the higher level of technology risk involved in renewable energy projects (as opposed, for example, to traditional fossil fuel projects) have meant that those renewable energy projects which have achieved external finance have tended to be smaller scale projects, rather than projects to create the optimum number of CERs. In addition, local host country regulations (such as grid connection, distribution or electricity tariff arrangements) may not provide renewable energy projects with the priority or support needed to make them feasible in the existing electricity market.

- Therefore, the transaction costs of developing these smaller scale projects as CDM projects (including the costs of external auditors, registration fees, consultants' fees and legal fees for the negotiation of CER purchase agreements and power purchase agreements) may be prohibitively high compared to the volume of CERs expected to be generated by the projects.

QUESTIONS AND DISCUSSION

1. Both of the excerpts above suggest that the current market for CERs is biased against energy efficiency projects. Should we be concerned with that? Isn't the market "bias" simply a reflection that the lowest cost approach to mitigating climate change is the destruction of HFCs? Isn't the point of Kyoto's flexibility mechanisms to allow capital to flow to the lowest cost opportunities for abatement?

As you think about those questions, consider the discussion of HCFCs in Chapter 10. As noted there, concern over the climate impacts of HFCs led Parties to the Montreal Protocol to accelerate the phase out of HCFCs. This will mean that most HCFC production facilities even in developing countries will be phased out over the next few decades. How does this change the "additionality" of HFC destruction under the CDM? How will this regulatory change alter the market value of CERs from HFC destruction in the future?

2. During the Kyoto Protocol negotiations, some NGOs sought to limit CDM eligibility to an exclusive list of projects relating to renewable energy and demand-side energy efficiency technologies. *See* Climate Action Networks Climate Negotiations Newsletter Eco 4, June 12, 2000. By rejecting the "list" approach to CDM eligibility, the Parties not only allowed a much broader range of projects to be eligible for CDM approval, but also required renewable energy and other projects to compete for CDM investment. Consequently, investments have skewed towards projects with much larger emissions reductions (and therefore CERs) and profit margins. By way of comparison:

> a 50MW wind farm in India (a large scale wind farm, compared to the size of most wind farms which have been successful in attracting project finance, due to perceived technology risk) is estimated to cost around US$58 million to develop and create around 112,500 CERs per year. On the other hand, two HCFC22 plants in China, from which the World Bank's Umbrella Carbon Fund purchased HFC23-based CERs in December 2005, [are] expected to generate 19 million CERs per year. HFC23 destruction technology is generally much less cost-intensive than wind farm turbines.

Renewable Energy and International Law Project, *The Clean Development Mechanism: Special Considerations for Renewable Energy Projects* 8 (Nov. 2006). Would a "list" approach help ensure that CDM investment is appropriately targeted towards sustainable development projects? What other approaches might encourage investment in renewable energy projects?

3. ***Transaction Costs.*** Both excerpts above emphasize the high transaction costs for CDM projects. According to one report:

> EcoSecurities has estimated that the consultancy costs for project assessment and completion of the project documentation necessary to register a large scale (i.e., >15 MW) renewable energy project range between £23,000 and £122,000 [eds. note: $46,000 to $244,000 in January 2008], plus additional fees for the Designated Operational Entity's validation and verification. The Executive Board will also require payment of US$21,000 upon registration of such a project to cover administrative expenses, plus US$0.20 per CER issued (with a discount of US$0.10 for the first 15,000 CERs issued each year). For a 50MW renewable energy plant expected to produce around 112,500 CERs per year, the transaction costs can eat away much of the first year's expected CER revenues from the project.

Renewable Energy and International Law Project, *The Clean Development Mechanism: Special Considerations for Renewable Energy Projects* 12 (Nov. 2006). As the New York Times excerpt reports, transaction costs frequently far exceed the actual costs of GHG abatement. How should the Parties address this issue, if at all? Should governments find alternative ways to pay for such projects, as environmentalists have suggested?

4. ***Simplified Procedures for Small Projects.*** The Parties recognized that many smaller projects could have cumulatively large climate benefits. However, each small project may not be profitable due to high transaction costs and modest CER value. Also, whereas the consulting fees must generally be paid upfront, the CERs gain value over a number of years. Ecosecurities, *Clean Development Mechanism (CDM): Simplified Modalities and Procedures for Small-Scale Projects*, para. 3.2.1 (May 2002); *see also* Mindy G. Nigoff, *The Clean Development Mechanism: Does the Current Structure Facilitate Kyoto Protocol Compliance?*, 18 GEO. INT'L ENVTL. L. REV. 249 (2006) (finding the registration process "too cumbersome"). To reduce transaction costs and encourage smaller projects with climate benefits, the Parties developed simplified procedures for validation and verification of "small projects": renewable energy projects with a maximum output of 15 megawatts; energy efficiency projects that reduce consumption by at least 60 Gigawatts/hours per year, and "other projects," such as waste management, fuel switching, and agricultural projects, that reduce emissions by sources and directly emit fewer than 60 kilotons of CO_2equivalent annually. Decision 17/CP.7, *Modalities and Procedures for a Clean Development Mechanism as Defined in Article 12 of the Kyoto Protocol*, para. 6(c), (2001), as amended by Decision 1/CMP.2, para. 28 (2006). These thresholds also apply to JI projects. Decision 3/CMP.2, *Guidance on Implementation of Article 6 of the Kyoto Protocol*, para. 14 (2006)). By simplifying the procedures, small-scale projects are intended to benefit developing countries that perhaps do not have the capacity to undertake larger CDM projects and thus enhance the sustainable development aspect of the CDM. At the same time, the rules developed by the Executive Board are intended to ensure that such projects do not undermine the climate benefits of the CDM. Under the simplified procedures, projects fitting these categories must follow less rigorous requirements for the different aspects of CDM projects: project design, selection of baseline methodologies, proof of additionality, and monitoring.

In addition, "small-scale afforestation and reforestation project activities under the CDM" are eligible for the simplified procedures. The original decision establishing a category of small-scale afforestation and reforestation projects limited such projects to removals by sinks of less than 8 kilotonnes of CO_2 per year. Decision 5/CMP.1, *Modalities and Procedures for Afforestation and Reforestation Project Activities under the Clean Development Mechanism in the First Commitment Period of the Kyoto Protocol*, para. 20(d) (2005). Projects of this size were widely considered unprofitable; Bolivia estimated that removals of 24 kilotonnes of CO_2 were needed to break even on a project and proposed increasing the limit to 48 kilotonnes of CO_2. In the end, the Parties increased the limit to 16 kilotonnes, provided that the project is "developed or implemented by low-income communities and individuals as determined by the host Party." Decision 9/CMP.3, *Implications of Possible Changes to the Limit for Small-Scale Afforestation and Reforestation Clean Development Mechanism Project Activities* (2007); *see also* Decision 4/CMP.1, *Guidance Relating to the Clean Development Mechanism* (2005).

---

2.   *Inequitable Distribution of CDM Benefits*

The distribution of CDM projects has been a source of complaint among NGOs as well as governments. As of February 2009, 396 projects had been registered in Latin America and the Caribbean and 957 projects in Asia and the Pacific Islands. Meanwhile, only 29 had been registered in Africa and 8 in other parts of the world. Inside each region, one or two countries have attracted an overwhelming number of CDM projects. For example, India (392 projects) and China (410 projects) account for 84 percent of all CDM projects in Asia. In fact, India and China alone account for 59 percent of *all* CDM projects. Similarly, Brazil (150 projects) and Mexico (111 projects) account for 66 percent of CDM projects in Latin America. South Africa's 13 projects account for just under 50 percent of all CDM projects in Africa. UNFCCC, *CDM Registration, available at* http://cdm.unfccc.int/Statistics/ Registration/NumOfRegisteredProjByHostPartiesPieChart.html.

The inequitable distribution of projects means that the CDM is failing to assist the vast majority of developing countries to achieve sustainable development, one of the CDM's two principal goals. An important aspect of achieving sustainable development is the transfer of technology. Indeed, the CDM is designed to promote the transfer of environmentally-friendly technologies for sustainable development. In a study of all 644 CDM projects registered as of May 2007, however, researchers found that only certain types of projects lead to transfers of technology and that certain countries received technology more frequently than other countries. Some of the paper's key findings are:

- Only 43 percent of CDM projects involved technology transfer.

- CDM projects in Malaysia (87 percent), Mexico (68 percent) and China (59 percent) involved much greater rates of technology transfer than Brazil (40 percent), Chile (35 percent), and India (12 percent).

- Some types of projects, such as biomass energy (19 percent) and supply side energy efficiency (14 percent) had relatively low levels of technology transfer compared to landfill gas recovery (80 percent) and N_2O destruction projects (100 percent).

- 70 percent of agriculture, including reforestation, projects involved technology transfer, whereas energy (39 percent) and industrial (27 percent) projects had much lower rates of technology transfer.

Matthieu Glachant et al., *The Clean Development Mechanism and the International Diffusion of Technologies: An Empirical Study* (Fondazione Eni Enrico Mattei, Nota de Lavoro 105, 2007). Why? The researchers sought to answer whether technology transfer was more likely in countries with greater technological capabilities, due to the type of project involved, or other factors. Some answers were explained easily. For example, China has had a high rate of technology transfer because all HFC-23 destruction projects, many of which have occurred in China, involve technology transfer. Other explanations for the data were not as easily explained.

MATTHIEU GLACHANT et al., THE CLEAN DEVELOPMENT MECHANISM AND THE INTERNATIONAL DIFFUSION OF TECHNOLOGIES: AN EMPIRICAL STUDY
(Fondazione Eni Enrico Mattei, Nota de Lavoro 105, 2007)

From a descriptive point of view, the data shows that technology transfers take place in more than 40% of the CDM projects. Very few projects involve the transfer of equipment only. Instead, projects often include the transfer of knowledge and operating skills, allowing project implementers to appropriate the technology.

Technology transfer mainly concern two areas. The first one is the end-of-pipe destruction of non-CO_2 greenhouse gas with high global warming potentials, such as HFCs, CH_4 and N_2O. This concerns the chemicals industry, the agricultural sector and the waste management sector. The second one is wind power. Other projects, such as electricity production from biomass or energy efficiency measures in the industry sector, mainly rely on local technologies. Moreover, Mexican and Chinese projects more frequently attract technology transfers while European countries are the main technology suppliers. We have also developed econometric models in order to characterize the factors underlying these patterns. They show that there are economies of scale in technology transfer: all other things being equal, transfers in large projects — in terms of emissions reductions — are more likely. Furthermore, the probability of transfer is 50% higher when the project is developed in a subsidiary of Annex 1 companies. Having an official credit buyer in the project also exerts a positive influence on transfer likeliness, albeit much smaller (+16%).

As regards the host countries' features, the most interesting econometric results deal with technological capabilities. In theory, this factor has ambiguous effects. On the one hand, high capabilities may be necessary to adopt a new technology. On the other hand, high capabilities imply that many technologies are already available locally, thereby reducing transfer likeliness. Our estimations show that the first effect strongly dominates in the energy sector and in the chemicals industry. By contrast, the second effect is stronger for agricultural projects. This suggests that the agricultural technologies transferred in these projects tend to be simple.

What are the policy implications? First, these results suggest policy lessons on CDM design. Encouraging large projects — or project bundling — allows . . . increasing returns in technology transfer. Promoting projects in subsidiaries of Annex 1 companies could also be of great use to foster technology transfer. In practice, one could imagine different ways of providing incentives for companies to do so (e.g., additional credits, simplified administrative procedures). To a lesser extent, credit buyers, which are generally not pure financial actors, can also play a positive role. Our analysis may also give lessons on general measures. In particular, the study suggests that programs of technological capacity building would be particularly profitable in the energy sector and in the chemicals industry.

QUESTIONS AND DISCUSSION

1.   The inequitable distribution of projects towards a small subset of developing countries has raised questions about the ability of the CDM to deliver on its promise to help developing countries achieve sustainable development objectives. To fulfill its goal of providing sustainable development opportunities and to overcome the inequitable distribution of CDM projects, some have proposed different approaches to CDM approval. One such proposal would establish quotas for CDM investment (e.g., one-third of CDM projects must be in Africa), in the hope of equalizing investment opportunities among the developing countries. Youba Sokona et al., *The Clean Development Mechanism: What Prospects for Africa?* 109, 115–116, *in* THE CLEAN DEVELOPMENT MECHANISM: ISSUES AND OPTIONS (José Goldemberg, ed. 1998). Do you think that such a quota system would improve opportunities for sustainable development through the CDM?

2.   In some countries, opportunities for CDM projects may be limited. For example, in Uganda and Zambia only about 10 percent of the population has access to the grid for electricity. To be an eligible CDM project, an electricity-generating project must displace "carbon-intensive" electricity. *See* CDM Executive Board, *Consolidated Baseline Methodology for Grid-connected Electricity Generation from Renewable Sources*, ACM0002 (version 7). Where hydroelectric facilities generate existing energy, it is difficult to conceive of a CDM project that would displace carbon-intensive electricity. At the same time, many African countries plan to develop major new sources of electricity. Whether this energy will come from renewable resources or CO_2-producing fossil fuels is not known. Should the rules of the CDM be changed to encourage investment in renewable energy resources where countries do not have current, but may have future, greenhouse gas emissions? Or should the Parties develop a separate program distinct from the CDM to encourage new clean power development and other projects that do not produce climate change benefits that are "additional" to those that would otherwise occur?

3. ***Sustainable Development Criteria.*** The Parties have not established rules to ensure that CDM projects as a whole promote sustainable development. Instead, each Party hosting a CDM project determines on a case-by-case basis whether a project meets that country's sustainable development objectives. While the Parties have adopted various criteria, they have, on the whole, developed criteria that align with the three pillars of sustainable development: environmental, economic, and social development. A comprehensive review of national sustainable development criteria reports that environmental criteria include, for example, levels of CO_2 equivalent reduction in local areas or some other measurement of climate change mitigation, improvements to air quality, increased efficiency in resource use, or conservation of local resources. Economic criteria include job creation and improved working conditions, poverty reduction, technology transfer, and development in particular regions. Social criteria include training and technological development, improved quality of life, better income distribution, poverty relief, or increased energy supply. Bruce P. Chadwick, *Sustainable Development Criteria and the Clean Development Mechanism* (2005). Regardless of the criteria, Designated National Authorities do not appear to be influencing decisions to approve or reject CDM projects: projects are approved because of the desire for investment. Is it true that any investment assists in some way with achieving sustainable development? Should the CDM Executive Board review projects against some minimum sustainable development criteria as part of the registration process? As an international institution, should the CDM at least ensure that all approved projects are consistent with norms found in other international environmental, human rights or labor agreements? Would it be acceptable to focus only on climate benefits, for example, if a project were shown to involve child labor? To have resulted in the dispossession of indigenous lands?

4. ***The Buyers.*** Given the presence of the European Union's mandatory emissions reduction scheme and an active emission trading program, it is not surprising that Europeans have bought the overwhelming majority of CERs and ERUs — 86 percent. Whereas private sector entities bought 90 percent of CERs, public entities bought 92 percent of ERUs. *State and Trends of the Carbon Market 2007*, at 22–23.

5. ***Adaptation Fund.*** Article 12 of the Kyoto Protocol requires 2 percent of the proceeds from each CDM project to be used to cover the administrative expenses and to assist developing countries that are particularly vulnerable to the adverse effects of climate change to meet the costs of adaptation. In December 2008, the Parties to the Kyoto Protocol agreed to operationalize the Adaptation Fund. The Fund's 16-member Adaptation Fund Board will decide on projects, including the allocation of funds, to finance concrete adaptation projects and programs. Decision 1/CMP.3, *Adaptation Fund* (2007). Review the discussion of adaptation in Chapter 3. If you were a member of the Adaptation Fund Board, what criteria would you set for funding adaptation projects? To what extent will the Fund's available resources, which could reach as much as $5 billion per year, for less than tens of billions some think necessary, influence your criteria?

IV. IMPLEMENTATION OF KYOTO'S FLEXIBILITY MECHANISMS: THE EUROPEAN UNION'S EMISSIONS TRADING SCHEME

All over the world, regional and national governments are using the Kyoto Protocol's flexibility mechanisms to meet their commitments or are hosting CDM and JI projects. Most countries are doing so either by engaging in trading themselves or by authorizing private entities under their jurisdiction to do so. Other jurisdictions are building on the Kyoto Protocol's flexibility mechanisms by developing carbon markets that allow intra- and inter-jurisdictional carbon trading. These efforts range from the private and voluntary Chicago Climate Exchange (discussed in Chapter 18) to the robust and active European Union's Emissions Trading System (ETS). In addition, exchanges in Tokyo, Buenos Aires, Australia, and elsewhere are trading carbon credits. In all, some 58 different carbon markets exist.

The most ambitious of these efforts is the European Union's ETS, which the European Union (EU) launched in January 2005. The EU ETS is the first emissions trading program to struggle with the many issues associated with linking different international and national emissions trading programs. In addition, the EU has had little experience with emissions trading, and it is integrating the less developed regulatory systems of the new EU members of Central and Eastern Europe. Thus, the EU is building essentially from scratch a complex trading program and institutional structures that cover thousands of GHG-emitting installations. For that reason, the ETS built in an early commitment period, which ended in December 2007, to allow EU regulators and businesses time to familiarize themselves with carbon trading and improve the program for the more important second commitment period, which coincides with the 2008–2012 commitment period of the Kyoto Protocol. A third commitment period runs from 2013 to 2020.

A.   Key Features of the ETS

1.   *Scope of the ETS*

The EU ETS is the first large-scale attempt to regulate greenhouse gases. It covers all 27 member States of the EU. The trading program covers only carbon dioxide, which accounts for about 80 percent of the EU's total greenhouse gas emissions. It applies to more than 11,500 energy intensive installations in four sectors: production and processing of iron and steel, minerals (such as cement, glass, and ceramic production), energy (including electric power and emissions from oil refineries), and pulp and paper installations. These covered entities emit 40 to 45 percent of the EU's carbon dioxide emissions. The EU may add additional greenhouse gases or installations in subsequent commitment periods, and it has already agreed to add the aviation sector to the list of covered sectors by 2012. At this time, the EU does not intend to add the transportation sector, which accounts for about 25 percent of the EU's total greenhouse gas emissions. Directive 2003/87/EC of the European Parliament and of the Council of 13 October 2003 establishing a scheme for greenhouse gas emission allowance trading within the Community and amending Council Directive 96/61/EC, OJ 2003 L 275, art. 2, Annexes I, II.

2.   *Emission Allowances*

As in other carbon trading systems, emission allowances are the heart of the ETS, where one allowance equals the right to emit one metric ton of carbon dioxide. Each member State must develop National Allocation Plans (NAPs), which allocate allowances to covered installations. EU legislation provides that at least 95 percent of allowances during the first commitment period and 90 percent during the second commitment period must be allocated free of charge. *Id.* at arts. 9, 10. While only covered installations are granted allowances, any person, including nongovernmental organizations and individuals, may purchase and resell the allowances. *Id.* at art. 12(1).

Each year, installations must reduce their emissions by a specified amount. Those installations that exceed their emissions reduction target may sell their extra allowances; those that fail to meet their target may purchase allowances. *Id.* at art. 12. Those that fail to meet their reduction target must pay a fine, now set at 100 Euros per metric ton, and purchase allowances to cover the shortfall in the following year. *Id* at art. 16.

---

3.   *National Allocation Plans*

If emission allowances are the heart of the ETS, then the NAPs are its backbone. The NAPs include critical decisions, including how many allowances to issue to covered installations and how many to distribute to each of the four sectors. These decisions are politically and economically challenging. Because each EU member has an obligation to limit its nationwide emissions by a specified amount under the burden sharing agreement, if a member grants a large number of allowances to the four sectors covered by the ETS, then all other economic sectors must reduce their emissions by a larger amount to meet the nationwide emissions limits. In addition, a decision to grant a large percentage of allowances to, for example, the cement industry, will necessarily curtail activity in the other three economic sectors covered by the ETS.

The member States have some flexibility in making their choices, but they must be based on objective and transparent criteria and comply with criteria established by Annex III of the ETS Directive. *Id.* at art. 9. These criteria include the following:

- Quantities of allocated allowances must be consistent with a member State's Kyoto Protocol and EU targets, and the potential, including the technological potential, of activities covered by this scheme to reduce emissions.

- The NAP as a whole must "not discriminate between companies or sectors in such a way as to unduly favour certain undertakings or activities" and include information on the manner in which new entrants will be able to begin participating in the ETS.

- The NAP must establish a limit on the number of allowances from joint implementation and CDM projects that may be used to achieve an installation's target.

- The NAP must contain information about how many allowances will be reserved for new installations ("new entrants") in the four sectors covered by the ETS.

To ensure compliance with EU legislation, each member State must submit its NAP to the European Commission for review and approval at least 18 months prior to the beginning of the next commitment period. *Id* at art. 9(3). The Commission assesses NAPs on the basis of these rules and other relevant EU legislation (such as EU rules on State aid and competition). If it concludes that the

NAP is not consistent with these criteria, it may reject or require changes to the plan. Once the Commission approves a NAP, a member State may not change the total quantity of allowances to be issued. In addition, a member State may not change the number of allowances issued to each installation after it makes its final allocation.

---

4.   *Monitoring and Reporting*

EUROPEAN COMMISSION, EU ACTION AGAINST CLIMATE CHANGE: EU EMISSIONS TRADING — AN OPEN SCHEME PROMOTING GLOBAL INNOVATION
12–14 (2005)

Each installation in the ETS must have a permit from its competent authority for its emissions of all six greenhouse gases controlled by the Kyoto Protocol. A condition for granting the permit is that the operator is capable of monitoring and reporting the plant's emissions. A permit is different from the allowances: the permit sets out the emissions monitoring and reporting requirements for an installation, whereas allowances are the scheme's tradable unit.

Installations must report their CO_2 emissions after each calendar year. The European Commission has issued a set of monitoring and reporting guidelines [Commission Decision 2004/156/EC of 29 January 2004]) to be followed. Installations' reports have to be checked by an independent verifier on the basis of criteria set out in the ETS legislation, and are made public. Operators whose emission reports for the previous year are not verified as satisfactory will not be allowed to sell allowances until a revised report is approved by a verifier.

Allowances are not printed but held in accounts in electronic registries set up by Member States. The European Commission has set out specific legislation for a standardised and secured system of registries based on UN data exchange standards to track the issue, holding, transfer and cancellation of allowances. Provisions on the tracking and use of credits from JI and CDM projects in the EU scheme are also included. The registries system is similar to a banking system which keeps track of the ownership of money in accounts but does not look into the deals that lead to money changing hands.

The system of registries is overseen by a central administrator at EU level who, through an independent transaction log, checks each transaction for any irregularities. Any irregularities detected prevent a transaction from being completed until they have been remedied. The EU registries system is being integrated with the international registries system used under the Kyoto Protocol.

---

5.   *Linkages to Other Emissions Trading Regimes*

Like the Kyoto Protocol, the ETS is not a closed system. Just as the Kyoto Protocol allows Annex I Parties to buy CERs from non-Annex I parties (i.e., countries without emissions limitations), EU member States may buy allowances from public and private entities outside the ETS. The "Linking Directive" of the ETS allows companies in the second commitment period to use credits from JI and the CDM projects, up to a certain proportion of their allocation of emission allowances, to cover their emissions. However, CERs and ERUs generated from nuclear facilities and land use, land-use change and forestry activities cannot be used. *See* Directive 2004/101/EC of the European Parliament and of the Council of 27 October 2004 amending Directive 2003/87/EC establishing a scheme for greenhouse gas emission allowance trading within the Community, in respect of the Kyoto Protocol's project mechanisms.

The Linking Directive requires that the use of such allowances be supplemental to domestic action. At the national level, each member State determines the percentage of CERs and ERUs that installations may use to meet their obligations. Member States are given the choice of applying the same limit on use of CERs and ERUs to all installations or on an installation-by-installation basis. Whatever approach is taken, the limit on use of CERs and ERUs does not restrict a company from generating and selling them in excess of the limit; excess CERs and ERUs may be sold to other installations, governments, or others outside the ETS regime. They may also be banked.

The EU Directive also allows linkages to the national greenhouse gas trading schemes of Kyoto Protocol Parties with commitments under Annex B, provided that an agreement is concluded to ensure mutual recognition of allowances. ETS Directive, art. 25. A subsequent "Linking Directive" directs the European Commission to examine whether similar linkages are possible with the trading schemes of Parties that have yet to ratify the Kyoto Protocol but that have mandatory caps on GHG emissions. Directive 2004/101/EC of the European Parliament and of the Council of 27 October 2004 amending Directive 2003/87/EC establishing a scheme for greenhouse gas emission allowance trading within the Community, in respect of the Kyoto Protocol's project mechanisms, L 338/18 (Nov. 13, 2004). The EU has considered linkages with subnational trading schemes, such as the Regional Greenhouse Gas Initiative among states in Northeastern United States. It concluded, however, that U.S. Constitutional issues — i.e., states cannot enter into treaties — may prevent such linkages. Ralf Schüle & Wolfgang Sterk *Options and Implications of Linking the EU ETS with other Emissions Trading Schemes* (prepared for the European Parliament, Mar. 2008). *See* Chapter 17 for a discussion of this initiative.

QUESTIONS AND DISCUSSION

1.   The ETS allows a member State to issue as many allowances as it wants so long as the NAP otherwise meets the Directive's 12 criteria for NAPs, including ensuring that the NAP is "consistent with achieving the overall Kyoto target." While this could result in over-allocating allowances, a member State would probably fail to comply with some of the allocation criteria if it issued too many allowances. In the broader picture, the member State would fail to produce the "carbon" scarcity necessary to develop a vibrant market. Is that enough to keep member states from over-allocating allowances? What incentives exist for over-allocating allowances?

2.   The EU ETS has now linked to the Kyoto Protocol and, more recently, to the emissions trading systems of Norway, Iceland, and Liechtenstein. As in the Kyoto Protocol, critics such as Greenpeace complain that the Linking Directive does not promote emissions reductions at home and does not establish any concrete limits on the use of allowances from JI and CDM projects. According to Greenpeace, even an eight percent limit (about 120 $MtCO_2$) would be "unacceptably high." Greenpeace,

Seven Reasons to Reject the Linking Directive (24 October 2003). The European Commission has used 10 percent of a country's allocation as the maximum acceptable level of allowances that may be obtained from other emissions trading systems. According to the Commission, the 10 percent limit "reflects a reasonable balance between domestic reductions and giving operators of installations an incentive to invest in projects in developing countries." European Commission, COM(2006) 725 final 10 (Nov. 29, 2006). Nonetheless, it has approved JI/CDM limits of as much as 20 percent for Lithuania and Spain. European Commission, *Emissions Trading: Commission Adopts Decision on Cyprus' National Allocation Plan for 2008–2012* (July 18, 2007). Based on Commission limits and JI/CDM activities, the World Bank estimates that EU installations will purchase about 1,000 to 1,200 $MtCO_2$ of allowances in the second commitment period — roughly the combined greenhouse gas emissions of Denmark and Ireland in 1990. *State and Trends of the Carbon Market 2007*, at 16. Recall that the Parties to the Kyoto Protocol were unable to quantify a limit on use of the flexibility mechanisms. Why has the EU been able to do so? Does a 10 percent limit reflect the "reasonable balance" that the Commission suggests?

3. ***Banking.*** Under Article 13 of the ETS Directive, the ETS, member States had the discretion to permit banking of allowances from the first to the second trading period, but only "if it did not lead to an allocation beyond the total allocation approved by the Commission for the second trading period. Therefore, for each allowance allowed to be banked, an allowance must be deducted from the total quantity issued for the second trading period." Press Release, *Emissions Trading: Commission Decides on First Set of National Allocation Plans for the 2008–2012 Trading Period*" IP/06/1650 (Nov. 29, 2006). Thus, a company may be allowed to bank allowances for the second trading period, but the country's overall tradable allowances would have to be reduced by the same amount. Some member States had hoped to use banked allowances in the first trading period to offset emissions from sectors not allowed to be traded (e.g., the transport sector) in the second period, but this was effectively blocked by the Commission's decision.

The Commission viewed discretionary banking from the first to the second trading period as an impermissible trade-distorting measure — essentially a subsidy known as "State aid" — under Article 87 of the EC Treaty, "because the Member State would issue allowances for free where it could otherwise have sold them."

Banking would not be considered state aid, however, if it was supported by "proven real emission reductions during the first period." *See* European Commission, COM(2006) 725 final, 11–12 (Nov. 29, 2006). These decisions of the Commission greatly limited the use of banking. As a consequence, only Poland and France — just 2 of 25 member States at that time — allowed banking from the first to the second trading period. This led to a substantial devaluation of allowances in the last months of the first commitment period, because excess allowances from the first commitment period became virtually worthless. Do you understand why? Banking is expressly allowed in the second commitment period, and thus, it will not constitute impermissible State aid.

B.   Implementation of the ETS

The EU ETS capped carbon dioxide emissions from covered facilities at 6,600 $MtCO_2$ during the first phase. The EU granted Germany about 15 percent of the allocations, while Italy, Poland, and the United Kingdom received about 10 percent each. At the country level, members allocated almost 55 percent of allowances to the power and heat sector, 12 percent each to the minerals and metals sectors, and 10 percent each to the oil and gas sector. *State and Trends of the Carbon Market 2007*, at 15. For 2005, member States as a whole exceeded the caps established by the ETS, although six countries (Austria, Greece, Ireland, Italy, Spain, and the United Kingdom) did not. In addition, 8,980 installations representing more than 99 percent of allocated allowances in the 21 member States with functioning electronic registries had fulfilled their obligations. European Commission, COM(2006)676 final, 3 (Nov. 13, 2006). Overall, total GHG emissions in 2006 for the 23 EU member States that have Kyoto Protocol emissions targets were 5 percent below 1990 levels. (Cyprus and Malta, as non-Annex I Parties, do not have targets, although they do under EU law.)

Despite meeting the ETS's goals for emissions reductions, questions have arisen concerning the achievements of the ETS. For example, Germany has reduced its emissions by 18 percent from 1990 levels, but those reductions have been fueled by energy efficiency improvements, legislation that encourages energy efficiency, subsidies for renewable energy, and other policies (as well as emissions reductions from the loss of industry in the former East Germany).

Moreover, Phase 1 of the ETS was plagued by problems, leading many to question whether the ETS resulted in any real emissions reductions. Allowances, for example, were over-allocated. In fact, some suggest that annual average 2005-2007 allocations were actually 44.2 million metric tons higher than the reported 2005 emissions. Larry Parker, *Climate Change: The European Union's Emissions Trading System (EU-ETS)*, 5 (CRS Report for Congress, July 31, 2006). Gaps and variances in data caused some of this allocation, *See* Joseph A. Kruger & William A. Pizer, *Greenhouse Gas Trading in Europe: The Grand New Policy*, 46 ENV'T 8 (Oct. 2004). However, excessive over-allocation was caused primarily by "states that left a gap in how they would achieve their target, to be filled with measures to be defined later; insufficiently delineated plans to purchase allowances; and unrealistic economic or emissions growth assumptions." Parker, *The European Union's Emissions Trading System*, at 4.

This over-allocation led to significant price volatility. While the volume of trade in allowances tripled to more than one billion allowances by 2006, the price of allowances hit a high of €30 in April 2006 from an earlier low of less than €1. *State and Trends of the Carbon Market 2007*, at 11–12. In May 2006, the price plummeted based on news from several EU member States that their 2005 emissions would be less than predicted. The price had dropped below €10 in February 2009.

As part of six new pieces of climate change legislation, including requirements to reduce emissions by 20 percent and mandatory requirements to use renewable energy, the EU recently adopted significant changes for Phase 3 of the ETS, beginning in 2013. Phase 3 is expected to reduce emissions by 21 percent below 2005 levels by 2020. This equates to an emissions cap of 1.72 billion $MtCO_2$ for facilities covered by the ETS. Phase 3 also expands its scope to include new sectors and gases, including GHG emissions from petrochemicals, ammonia and aluminum industries, N_2O emissions from the production of nitric, adipic and glyoxalic acids, and perfluorocarbon emissions from the aluminum sector. With this expansion, the ETS will cover about 50 percent of all EU GHG emissions. European Commission, "Questions and Answers on the Revised EU Emissions Trading System," MEMO/08/796, 5–6, 9 (Dec. 17, 2008).

Some of the major changes respond directly to the problems of over-allocation in previous phases. For example, member States will no longer develop NAPs. Because country-specific NAPs established significant differences in allocation rules and tended to favor a member State's own industries, navigating the different rules became complex and inefficient. As a consequence, the European Commission will establish and allocate EU-wide emissions allowances based on harmonized rules. In addition, to ensure consistency in measuring emissions and reductions, the EU will also establish common rules for monitoring, reporting, and verification of emissions. *Id.* at 4–5.

Moreover, Phase 3 reserves five percent of total allowances for installations or airlines entering the ETS after 2013. A harmonized system was thought desirable, because some over-allocation resulted from member States saving allowances for "new entrants", i.e., new GHG-emitting facilities covered by the ETS. In addition, different member States had established different rules for allocating allowances to new entrants and how many allowances to grant new entrants, such as the use of best practices or best technology. Larry Parker, *Climate Change: The EU Emissions Trading Scheme (ETS) Gets Ready for Kyoto* 16 (CRS Report, Aug. 27, 2007).

Moreover, Phase 3 will place greater emphasis on auctioning allowances. Allowances for certain industries, such as the electricity generators, will be completely auctioned beginning in 2013, although this requirement is subject to exceptions. On the other hand, "exposed industries"—a category to be defined later—will receive free allowances to the extent that they use the most efficient technology. Other sectors will begin with the majority of allowances allocated free of charge but with auctioning increasing to 100% by 2027. European Commission, "Questions and Answers," at 3–4, 7–8.

Phase 3 further envisages linking with the Kyoto Protocol and national cap-and-trade regimes. The overall use of such credits is not to exceed 50 percent of total credits for the period 2008–2020. However, credits from LULUCF projects, whether from the CDM or otherwise, are not permissible. *Id.* at 9–11.

QUESTIONS AND DISCUSSION

1. The European Commission has used its authority to approve NAPs to improve them and reject them. For example, the Commission objected to the 2005–2007 NAP of the United Kingdom because it failed to (1) provide information on the manner in which new entrants will be able to begin participating in the Community scheme; and (2) include installations situated within the territory of Gibraltar and the quantities of allowances allocated to each such installation. *See* United Kingdom v. European Commission, Case T-178/05, Nov. 23, 2005. When the UK amended its NAP to include installations in Gibraltar, it also increased its allowances. The Commission thus rejected the UK's NAP. However, the European Court of Justice annulled the Commission's rejection of the UK's NAP because it ruled that Member States have the authority to amend their NAPs to account for comments of the public as well as the Commission. *Id.*

2. Because of the over-allocation problems identified in the preceding section, the European Commission has increased the rigor with which it is reviewing NAPs for the 2008–2012 commitment period. For example, the Commission has reduced proposed allocations of allowances by an average of 9.5 percent for 23 member States with approved NAPs as of August 2007. Larry Parker, *Climate Change: The*

EU Emissions Trading Scheme (ETS) Gets Ready for Kyoto, 4 (CRS Report, Aug. 27, 2007).

The Commission's decision with respect to Germany's NAP further shows the tensions that allocating allowances creates between sectors included in the ETS and non-ETS sectors as well as between EU member States. For the second commitment period, Germany proposed to allocate 482 million metric tons of allowances, even though the actual emissions for the covered ETS sectors in 2005 were 474 million metric tons. Its Kyoto Protocol target is 971.7 million metric tons for the 2008–2012 commitment period and its actual emissions for 2004 were 1015.3 million metric tons. The Commission concluded, among other things, that Germany's NAP failed to demonstrate that it would meet its Kyoto and EU targets. Based on an assessment of Germany's anticipated GDP growth, carbon-intensity improvements, and the effect of the increase in scope of the ETS, the Commission concluded that Germany's proposed allocations exceeded emissions by 28.93 million tons.

Germany also proposed to allocate 11 million metric tons to new combustion facilities, i.e., coal-fired power plants. It further proposed that new power stations built between 2008 and 2012 could opt out from CO_2 caps and the ETS for 14 years. Without commenting on the 14-year opt out provision, the Commission concluded that Germany's allocation guarantees for new combustion facilities unduly discriminates against comparable existing facilities in other member States in contravention of the Treaty Establishing the European Community, because the allocation guarantee constituted State aid that distorted or threatened to distort competition by favoring certain undertakings. European Commission. *Decision concerning the National Allocation Plan for the Allocation of Greenhouse Gas Emission Allowances Notified by Germany in accordance with Directive 2003/87/EC of the European Parliament and of the Council* (Nov. 29, 2006). Each country's NAP, as well as the Commission's decision concerning each NAP, can be found at: European Commission, National Allocation Plans: Second Phase (2008–2012), http://ec.europa.eu/environment/climat/2nd_phase_ep.htm.

3.   The Climate Action Network (CAN), a network of 365 nongovernmental organizations, described the emissions limits set by EU member States for the first phase as a major disappointment. In contrast, the European Union sees the over-allocation issue as part of the learning process that will only strengthen the ability of the EU to meet its Kyoto Protocol targets. Do the changes made for Phase 3 suggest that the EU has learned from Phases 1 and 2?

Chapter 7

LAND USE AND FORESTRY

I. INTRODUCTION

While climate change mitigation has focused largely on reducing emissions of carbon dioxide and other greenhouse gases, our use of land and forests for agriculture, cities, timber production, and other activities also plays a critical role in climate change. Because trees and other plants absorb carbon dioxide, sequester carbon, and release that carbon when they die, the way we use and manage land greatly affects the climate outcome. Decisions that land managers make all the time — whether to clear land to expand towns and cities, the selection of trees to plant, the length of the harvest rotation, or the use of particular harvest techniques (till versus no-till for agricultural practices or selective logging versus clearcutting in forest management) — will determine whether land use activities help mitigate or exacerbate climate change. If those decisions and practices retain or restore habitat, then land use activities can help mitigate climate change.

As the following materials make clear, land use activities, which account for 31 percent of total greenhouse gas emissions, are an important aspect of climate change policy. T. Barker et al., *Technical Summary, in* CLIMATE CHANGE 2007: MITIGATION: CONTRIBUTION OF WORKING GROUP III TO THE FOURTH ASSESSMENT REPORT OF THE INTERGOVERNMENTAL PANEL ON CLIMATE CHANGE 27 (B. Metz et al. eds., 2007) [hereinafter IPCC WORKING GROUP III, *Technical Summary*]. What is less clear is how the climate change regime should address land use. For example, should the climate change regime provide certified emissions reductions (CERs) for activities that restore or maintain forests? Because forests can be easily cleared by humans or destroyed by natural events, such as disease or hurricanes, any reductions may only be temporary and thus the issuance of the CERs would not help mitigate climate change. Should conservation-based land use activities, which retain forests and other habitat but do not reduce emissions below business-as-usual levels, be eligible for CERs under the Clean Development Mechanism (CDM)? To what extent, if at all, should the Parties create incentives for developing countries to reduce deforestation? Before exploring these issues, Section II of this chapter summarizes how land use activities affect carbon stocks. Section III explores some special attributes of land use activities that make their incorporation into the climate change regime problematic. It further describes how the Kyoto Protocol addresses land use activities. Section IV explores recent proposals to address deforestation within the climate change regime.

II. THE ROLE OF LAND USE ACTIVITIES IN CLIMATE CHANGE

The role of carbon and carbon dioxide in land use activities is complex and depends on a number of factors. Critically, carbon sequestration is not simply about forests and forest protection. A large range of land use activities, including agricultural practices, plays an important role in carbon sequestration. In addition, in some habitats, far more carbon is stored in soil than in vegetative matter.

A.   Nature's Carbon Warehouse

Photosynthesis and respiration are the starting points for discussing the role of land use activities in climate change, because they are the essential mechanisms by which forests store and release carbon. As plants grow, they absorb carbon dioxide from the air and, through photosynthesis, use solar energy to convert carbon dioxide into carbon, which is stored throughout the plant. Through respiration, plants release some carbon into the atmosphere as carbon dioxide.

Overall, trees and forests are carbon "sinks" — they remove more carbon than they release. In the absence of major disturbances, trees continue to accumulate carbon for 20 to 50 years or more, depending on the species and site conditions. At maturity, about half of the average tree's dry weight is carbon.

> Depending on the stage of stand development, individual stands are either carbon sources or carbon sinks (1 m^3 of wood stores ~ 0.92 tCO$_2$). For most immature and mature stages of stand development, stands are carbon sinks. At very old ages, ecosystem carbon will either decrease or continue to increase slowly with accumulations mostly in dead organic matter and soil carbon pools. In the years following major disturbances, the losses from decay of residual dead organic matter exceed the carbon uptake by regrowth. While individual stands in a forest may be either sources or sinks, the forest carbon balance is determined by the sum of the net balance of all stands. The theoretical maximum carbon storage (saturation) in a forested landscape is attained when all stands are in

old-growth state, but this rarely occurs as natural or human disturbances maintain stands of various ages within the forest.

G.J. Nabuurs et al., *Forestry, in* Climate Change 2007: Mitigation. Contribution of Working Group III to the Fourth Assessment Report of the Intergovernmental Panel on Climate Change 549 (2007) [hereinafter IPCC Working Group III, *Forestry*].

When trees decay and die, plant material is decomposed largely by microorganisms, and the trees become a net source of carbon dioxide emissions as they begin to release more carbon than they absorb. In addition, when forests are harvested, burned, or cleared, or are affected by natural disturbances (e.g., fire or disease), carbon dioxide is released into the atmosphere. Wood that is converted to forest products, such as furniture, lumber, and other products, stores carbon for the life of the product.

Soils also store carbon. When plants decay, they leave behind organic residues, often called humus, which may "persist in soils for hundreds or even thousands of years. At the same time, many factors can slow the decay of organic materials and, as a result, affect a soil's capacity for storing carbon. Inherent factors include climate variables (temperature and rainfall), clay content and mineralogy." Charles, W. Rice, *Storing Carbon in Soil: Why and How?*, Geotimes (Jan. 2002). Overall, however, soils store far more carbon than either vegetation or the atmosphere: global carbon stocks in soils are estimated to be about 1,100 to 1,600 petagrams (one petagram is one billion metric tons), at least twice the carbon in living vegetation (560 petagrams) or in the atmosphere (750 petagrams). *Id.* An IPCC comparison of carbon stocks in various ecosystems is presented in Table 7-1.

Table 7-1: Global Carbon Stocks in Vegetation and Soil Carbon Pools Down to a Depth of 1 Meter

Biome	Area (10^9 ha)	Global Carbon Stocks (Gt C)		
		Vegetation	Soil	Total
Topical Forests	1.76	212	216	428
Temperate Forests	1.04	59	100	159
Boreal Forests	1.37	88	471	559
Tropical Savannas	2.25	66	264	330
Temperate Grasslands	1.25	9	295	304
Deserts and semideserts	4.55	8	191	199
Tundra	0.95	6	121	127
Wetlands	0.35	15	225	240
Croplands	1.60	3	128	131
Total	15.12	466	2,011	2,477

IPCC Special Report: Land Use, Land-Use Change, and Forestry: Summary for Policy Makers, 4 (2000). While these numbers suggest some level of uniformity in the carbon stocks of habitat types, substantial variations also exist among similar habitats within the same region and in different regions.

B.   Land Use Factors Affecting Carbon Stocks

How we manage land use activities plays a substantial role in determining whether those activities are a net source of greenhouse gas emissions or a net sink (sequestering more carbon than they emit). Below, the IPCC summarizes the influence of land use activities on sources and sinks of carbon dioxide (CO_2), methane (CH_4), and nitrous oxide (N_2O), opportunities to reduce the impact of land use activities on climate change, and uncertainties that challenge our ability to address such activities effectively.

IPCC, IPCC SPECIAL REPORT: LAND USE, LAND-USE CHANGE, AND FORESTRY
(2000)

1.4.1. Land-Use Change

Different factors and mechanisms drive land use and land cover transformation. In many cases, climate, technology, and economics appear to be determinants of land-use change at different spatial and temporal scales. At the same time, land conversion seem[s] to be an adaptive feedback mechanism that farmers use to smooth the impact of climate variability, especially in extremely dry and humid periods. Land-use change is often associated with a change in land cover and an associated change in carbon stocks. For example, . . . if a forest is cleared, the carbon stocks in aboveground biomass are either removed as products, released by combustion, or decay back to the atmosphere through microbial decomposition. Stocks of carbon in soil will also be affected, although this effect will depend on the subsequent treatment of the land. Following clearing, carbon stocks in aboveground biomass may again increase, depending on the type of land cover associated with the new land use. During the time required for the growth of the new land cover — which can be decades for trees — the aboveground carbon stocks will be smaller than their original value. * * *

When forests are cleared for conversion to agriculture or pasture, a very large proportion of the aboveground biomass may be burned, releasing most of its carbon rapidly into the atmosphere. Some of the wood may be used as wood products; these carbon stocks could thereby be preserved for a longer time. Forest clearing also accelerates the decay of dead wood and litter, as well as below-ground organic carbon. Local climate and soil conditions will determine the rates of decay; in tropical moist regions, most of the remaining biomass decomposes in less than 10 years. Some carbon or charcoal accretes to the soil carbon pool. When wetlands are drained for conversion to agriculture or pasture, soils become exposed to oxygen. Carbon stocks, which are resistant to decay under the anaerobic conditions prevalent in wetland soils, can then be lost by aerobic respiration.

Forest clearing for shifting cultivation releases less carbon than permanent forest clearing because the fallow period allows some forest regrowth. On average, the carbon stocks depend on forest type and the length of fallow, which vary across regions. Some soil organic matter is also oxidized to release carbon during shifting cultivation — but less than during continuous cultivation. Under some conditions, shifting cultivation can increase carbon stocks in forests and soils, from one cut-regrowth cycle to another. Because shifting cultivation usually has lower average agricultural productivity than permanent cultivation, however, more land would be required to provide the same products. In addition, shorter rotation periods deplete soil carbon more rapidly.

Abandonment of cultivated land and pastures may result in recovery of forest at a rate determined by local conditions. Selective logging often releases carbon to the atmosphere through the indirect effect of damaging or destroying up to a third of the original forest biomass, which then decays as litter and waste in the forest (although there are techniques that may reduce these consequences). The harvested wood decays at rates dependent on their end use; for example, fuel wood decays in 1 year, paper in less than a few years, and construction material in decades. The logged forest may then act as a sink for carbon as it grows at a rate determined by the local soil and climate, and it will gradually compensate for the decay of the waste created during harvest. Clear-cutting of forest can also lead to the release of soil carbon, depending on what happens after harvesting. For example, harvesting followed by cultivation or intensive site preparation for planting trees may result in large decreases in soil carbon — up to 30 to 50 percent in the tropics over a period of up to several decades. Harvesting followed by reforestation, however, in most cases has a limited effect ($\pm$ 10 percent). This effect is particularly prevalent in the tropics, where recovery to original soil carbon contents after reforestation is quite rapid. There are also some cases in which soil carbon increases significantly, probably because of the additions of slash and its decomposition and incorporation into the mineral soil. [The IPCC also explained that tree plantations exhibit variations in carbon accumulation depending on site conditions, species grown, and pattern of rotational harvests.]

1.4.2. Land-Use Management

Management of forests, croplands, and rangelands affects sources and sinks of CO_2, CH_4, and N_2O. On land managed for forestry, harvesting of crops and timber changes land cover and carbon stocks in the short term while maintaining continued land use. Moreover, most agricultural management practices affect soil condition. A forest that is managed in a wholly sustainable manner will encompass stands, patches, or compartments comprising all stages from regeneration through harvest, including areas disturbed by natural events and management operations. Overall, a forest comprising all stages in the stand life cycle operates as a functional system that removes carbon from the atmosphere, utilizing carbon in the stand cycle and exporting carbon as forest products. Forests of such characteristics, if well managed, assure rural development through working opportunities at the beginning and establishment of forest industries in later stages of the development process. In addition, such forests provide other benefits, such as biodiversity, nature conservation, recreation, and amenities for local communities. For historical and economic reasons, however, many forests today depart from this ideal and are fragmented or have strongly skewed stand age distribution that influences their carbon sequestration capability.

Forest soils present opportunities to conserve or sequester carbon. Several long-term experiments demonstrate that carbon can accrete in the soil at rates of 0.5 to 2.0 t ha^{-1} yr^{-1}. Management practices to maintain, restore, and enlarge forest soil carbon pools include fertilizer use; concentration of agriculture and reduction of slash-and-burn practices; preservation of wetlands, peatlands, and old-growth forest; forestation of degraded and nondegraded sites, marginal agricultural lands, and lands subject to severe erosion; minimization of site disturbance during harvest operations to retain organic matter; retention of forest litter and debris after silvicultural activities; and any practice that reduces soil aeration, heating, and drying.

Cropland soils can lose carbon as a consequence of soil disturbance (e.g., tillage). Tillage increases aeration and soil temperatures, making soil aggregates more susceptible to breakdown and physically protected organic material more available for decomposition. In addition, erosion can significantly affect soil carbon stocks through the removal or deposition of soil particles and associated organic matter. . . . Soil carbon content can be protected and even increased through alteration of tillage practices, crop rotations, residue management, reduction of soil erosion, improvement of irrigation and nutrient management, and other changes in forestland and cropland management. * * *

Croplands and pastures are the dominant anthropogenic source of CH_4 and N_2O, although estimates of the CH_4 and N_2O budgets remain uncertain. Rice cultivation and livestock (enteric fermentation) have been estimated to be the two primary sources of CH_4. The primary sources of N_2O are denitrification and nitrification processes in soils. Emissions of N_2O are estimated to have increased significantly as a result of changes in fertilizer use and animal waste. Alteration of rice cultivation practices, livestock feed, and fertilizer use are potential management practices that could reduce CH_4 and N_2O sources.

Ecosystem conservation may also influence carbon sinks. Many forests, savannas, and wetlands, if managed as nature reserves or/and recreation areas, can preserve significant stocks of carbon, although these stocks might be affected negatively by climate change. Some wetlands and old-growth forests exhibit particularly high carbon densities; other semi-natural ecosystems (e.g., savannas) may conserve carbon simply because of their large areal extent.

C. Greenhouse Gas Emissions from Land Use

At present, land use activities are causing large-scale loss of forests and other habitat and massive emissions of CO_2, CH_4, and N_2O. Land-use change and forestry operations, exclusive of agriculture, accounted for 17 percent of all greenhouse gas emissions in 2004. When agriculture is added, global emissions from land use increase to 31 percent of total greenhouse gas emissions. IPCC WORKING GROUP III, *Technical Summary*, at 27. From 1850 to 1998, net cumulative global carbon dioxide emissions from land-use change are estimated to have been 136 +/- 55 billion tons of carbon. Of these emissions, about 87 percent were from forest areas and about 13 percent from cultivation of mid-latitude grasslands. By comparison, 270 +/- 30 billion tons of carbon were emitted from fossil fuel burning and cement production during the same period. IPCC, IPCC SPECIAL REPORT: LAND USE, LAND-USE CHANGE, AND FORESTRY, § 1.2.1.1 (2000).

Deforestation accounts for a large percentage of emissions from land use activities, particularly in developing countries. Deforestation has remained at high levels since 1990 when annual deforestation rates were about 13.1 million hectares per year (131,000 km^2, or roughly an area the size of England or Arkansas). From 2000 to 2005, deforestation rates slowed somewhat to about 12.9 million hectares annually. This deforestation is due largely to the conversion of forests to agricultural land, but unsustainable logging practices and the expansion of settlements and infrastructure are also leading causes of deforestation. When afforestation, restoration, and the natural expansion of forests are included in the ledger, net loss of forest is about 7.3 million hectares per year, down from 8.9 million hectares annually in the 1990s. The IPCC estimates emissions from deforestation, exclusive of other land use activities, at 5,800 million tons of CO_2 per year during the 1990s. IPCC WORKING GROUP III, *Forestry*, at 543.

Losses at the country level underscore the significance of deforestation to climate change mitigation. Brazil lost 23,750 km² (roughly the size of Vermont or Kuwait) of Brazilian Amazon in 2004, while Indonesia lost nearly the same amount (21,000 km²) in 2003. At these rates of deforestation, Brazil's and Indonesia's emissions from deforestation alone would equal about four-fifths of the emissions reductions gained by implementing the Kyoto Protocol in its first commitment period. Márcio Santilli et al., *Tropical Deforestation and the Kyoto Protocol: An Editorial Essay*, 71 Climatic Change 267 (2005).

For some countries, emissions from deforestation and other land use activities grossly exceed all other sources (*See* Table 7-2). In Bolivia, for example, emissions from land use activities, including deforestation, constitute about 82 percent of its greenhouse gas emissions. G. A. Silva-Chávez, *Reducing Greenhouse Gas Emissions from Tropical Deforestation by Applying Compensated Reduction to Bolivia, in* Tropical Deforestation and Climate Change 73, 73 (Paulo Moutinho & Stephan Schwartzman eds., 2005). Indeed, when cumulative emissions from 1950 to 2000 account for emissions from deforestation, Indonesia moves from the 27th largest emitter to the fourth, and Brazil moves from the 18th to the fifth largest emitter. Larry Parker & John Blodgett, *Greenhouse Gas Emissions: Perspectives on the Top 20 Emitters and Developed Versus Developing Nations* 6 (CRS Report, updated April 27, 2007).

Table 7-2: Emissions from Land Use as Percentage of Total GHG Emissions

Country	Land Use Emissions
Argentina	19%
Bolivia	82%
Brazil	69%
Indonesia	86%
Malaysia	82%
Mexico	16%

QUESTIONS AND DISCUSSION

1. Given the large variations and uncertainties concerning carbon stocks in different habitats and different regions, are you convinced that land-use activities should be a central feature of the climate change regime? Significant technical and methodological questions exist for measuring changes in carbon stocks. Consider, for example, the difficulties a government will have in assessing emissions from agricultural activities when emissions are dependent on the individual actions of thousands of farmers.

2. The IPCC outlines the many impacts of land use activities on carbon stocks. It also summarizes some cost-effective strategies for reducing greenhouse gas emissions from land use activities. What are they? What are the principal barriers to implementing these strategies? Consider, for example, that when the entire commodity chain is accounted for, livestock are responsible for 18 percent of greenhouse gas emissions — more than the transport sector. Henning Steinfeld, Livestock's Long Shadow: Environmental Issues and Options (Food and Agriculture Organization, 2006). In fact, the methane produced by the manure of a typical 1,330-pound cow translates into about five tons of CO_2 per year. That is about the same amount generated annually by a typical U.S. car getting 20 miles per gallon and driven 12,000 miles per year. Jeffrey Ball, *Cows, Climate Change and Carbon Credits*, WALL STREET JOURNAL June 14, 2007. What are some of the obstacles to reducing emissions from livestock? Can they be overcome?

3.   The IPCC, in its comparison of carbon stocks in soils, concluded that current carbon stocks are "much larger in soils than in vegetation, particularly in non-forested ecosystems in middle and high latitudes." *IPCC Special Report: Land Use, Land-Use Change, and Forestry*, at para. 6. In broad terms, what might be some of the political implications of this finding? Does this require a shift in focus from reducing deforestation in Brazil's Amazon to ensuring that Canada's tundra is not disturbed?

4.   In the United States, forests, grasslands, and agricultural lands form a sizable carbon sink, absorbing 1.1 to 2.6 million metric tons of CO_2 annually. This is equivalent to 20 to 46 percent of total U.S. greenhouse gas emissions. However, this "sink appears to be shrinking. Carbon sequestration by forests and other lands decreased by approximately 20 percent from 1990 to 2001, a decline stemming primarily from unsustainable timber management (especially on privately owned forests) and the clearing of forests for development." Michelle Manion, *Forest Carbon Sequestration* 3 CATALYST (Union of Concerned Scientists, Fall 2004).

III.   INCORPORATING LAND USE INTO THE CLIMATE REGIME

The importance of reducing deforestation and other habitat loss and increasing reforestation and habitat restoration is unquestioned. Since the negotiations of the United Nations Framework Convention on Climate Change (UNFCCC), governments have contemplated the role of sequestration in the climate change regime. Article 3 of the UNFCCC declares a basic policy to mitigate climate change from "all relevant sources, sinks and reservoirs of greenhouse gases." Article 4 calls on all Parties to develop national inventories of anthropogenic emissions by sources and removals by sinks of all greenhouse gases. It also calls on Parties to formulate and implement national programs containing measures to mitigate climate change by addressing anthropogenic emissions by sources and removals by sinks of all greenhouse gases. The Berlin Mandate, which laid the groundwork for the Kyoto Protocol, called for "coverage of all greenhouse gases, their emissions by sources and removals by sinks."

The question then was not whether the climate change regime would account for land use activities, but how to incorporate them into the regime. Section A introduces the accounting challenges created by land use activities. Section B describes how these challenges influenced the negotiations of the Kyoto Protocol. Section C then explores the accounting and emissions trading issues concerning land use activities under the Kyoto Protocol generally, and Section D addresses the specific issues raised by the Clean Development Mechanism (CDM).

A.   Accounting Challenges of Land Use Activities

Land use activities pose special accounting and other challenges that do not necessarily apply to emissions from industrial sources. For example, unlike industrial sources, land use activities are subject to natural events and disturbances, such as hurricanes and diseases, as well as human activities that call into question whether any reductions in emissions from land use activities will survive the next year or the next decade. When considering how the climate change regime can accommodate land use activities, three fundamental issues must be addressed:

- *Permanence.* Can we guarantee that trees planted to offset carbon dioxide emissions will not be destroyed in a natural disaster or cut down for firewood?

- *Saturation:* Are there limits to the amount of carbon benefits that can be achieved?

- *Verifiability:* Can removals of carbon dioxide from land use activities be accurately measured and verified?

The following excerpt takes a closer look at these issues.

BERNHARD SCHLAMADINGER & GREGG MARLAND, LAND USE & GLOBAL CLIMATE CHANGE: FORESTS, LAND MANAGEMENT, AND THE KYOTO PROTOCOL
8–12 (Pew Center on Global Climate Change, June 2000)[*]

Permanence

Emission reductions in the energy sector can be regarded as permanent. For [land use] activities, on the other hand, there is a possibility that any carbon accumulated or protected in the biosphere might be released at a later time.

To suggest that reductions in the energy sector are permanent is not to say that an activity will continue forever or that reductions achieved in one year will be achieved again the following year. It is not to say that the same molecule of carbon that has been kept out of the atmosphere in one year will be kept out of the atmosphere in the next year. However, achieving lower emissions in one year will seldom lead to higher emissions in later years. If less automotive fuel is used in one year, emissions will not increase in the next as a result. The total, cumulative emissions up to any given time will be smaller. This is true so long as the potential supply of fossil fuels is very large and the question is not simply how soon the fuel supply is fully converted to CO_2. . . .

For [land use] activities, on the other hand, changes in land ownership, public policy, commitment by the landowner, climate, or natural disturbances such as fire or pests could cause accumulated carbon to be released back to the atmosphere. In fact, increased carbon stocks in the biosphere could increase their vulnerability to subsequent release to the atmosphere by, e.g., accumulating combustible material in fire-prone areas. * * *

Saturation

The potential of the terrestrial biosphere to take up additional carbon is limited by the total land area available and by the amount of additional carbon that can be stored by the plants and soils per unit area. This means that at some point in time any net removals of carbon will, of necessity, diminish. The point at which this saturation will occur will vary for different places and will depend on the history of land management. It will sometimes be true that places with the greatest loss of forest and soil carbon in the past will have the largest opportunities for uptake of carbon in the future. * * *

Opportunities to reduce emissions in the energy sector will not be limited by saturation effects. Assuming that the resource of carbon-based fuels is not constraining CO_2 emissions, there will be continuous benefits from limiting use of fossil fuels through energy efficiency or the use of renewable energy. An activity that conserves use of fossil fuels this year can do the same next year and in succeeding years. An activity that increases the carbon in the biosphere this year may or may not be able to do so again next year. * * *

Verifiability

If carbon emissions to the atmosphere are to be offset by increasing the amount of carbon in the terrestrial biosphere, is it possible to accurately measure what has been accomplished? Can measurements affirm that one ton of carbon emissions has been offset by one ton of carbon sequestered in the biosphere? Estimating changes in carbon stocks in the biosphere is not as simple and straightforward as estimating carbon emissions from fossil-fuel combustion. One reason for the difference in uncertainty of the estimates is that fossil fuels are a traded commodity whereas, except for timber, most biospheric carbon is not traded in commercial markets. In the case of fossil fuels, there is an economic incentive for accurately measuring energy flows, and hence the related carbon flows. For carbon in the biosphere, however, there are trade-offs among the economic incentive[s] for measuring changes, the cost of measuring changes in carbon stocks, and the uncertainty in the measurement.

The CO_2 discharged from fossil-fuel burning can be estimated with an uncertainty of perhaps +/-10% on a global basis, and the uncertainty is much less for countries or projects with good statistical data on energy consumption. If energy consumption is reduced with more energy-efficient devices or there is a shift toward fuels with less carbon content, it is straightforward to estimate the amount by which CO_2 emissions have been reduced. Brown et al. suggest that similar uncertainty (+/-10%) can be achieved for [land use] activities at the project level. However, many groups believe that accounting for changes in carbon stocks in the biosphere is inherently more difficult than accounting for carbon emitted by burning fossil fuels. Two significant problems are resolution (recognizing small changes in large numbers) and maintaining the infrastructure needed for regular measurement of changes in carbon stocks. Temporal and spatial variability contribute to high variability in estimates of soil carbon at all scales. Uncertainty can be reduced at the cost of more intense sampling and analysis.

For carbon stored in tree stems, it is estimated that changes in carbon stocks over a ten-year interval can be approximated within +/-10% for a specific project. Uncertainty will usually be larger for the below-ground carbon in roots and soils, although for some projects a precision level of +/-10% has been achieved. Because changes in soil carbon are likely to involve small changes in large numbers, accurate estimates of the change in soil carbon may require longer time intervals (to achieve a more readily distinguishable change) and extensive and/or expensive sampling. Current methods are effective for evaluating changes in soil organic carbon at relatively low precision (20–50% error) and at widely spaced time intervals (minimum three to five years) with levels of effort that are reasonably affordable. If more sampling is required to improve the quality of estimates, the trade-off between the uncertainty and the cost of the estimate is likely to be encountered.

QUESTIONS AND DISCUSSION

1.   The issues of non-permanence and verifiability in particular have slowed the development of rules concerning land use activities within the climate change regime. For example, if removals are not permanent, then it may not be feasible to include removals in any kind of emissions trading. If removals cannot be verified, then it may not be appropriate to consider such removals as "additional." On the other hand, given the large emissions from land use activities, the inclusion of land use activities in the climate change regime can provide an incentive to improve land management and decrease emissions. In order to take advantage of the tremendous opportunities for climate change mitigation from land use activities, should the climate regime sacrifice some of the certainty that removals of carbon are real and permanent? What mechanisms might you propose to limit the uncertainties posed by land use activities (i.e., better ensure permanence and verifiability of removals)?

2.   The non-permanence and unpredictability of carbon storage from forests and other types of land is highlighted by data on the impacts of recent storms, fires, and insects on North American forests. For example, in 2005 Hurricane Katrina killed an estimated 320 million trees, creating a major carbon source that totally nullified the carbon sink of the rest of the U.S. forests for that year. The mountain pine beetle epidemic raging through western North America has flipped nearly 500,000 square kilometers of forests from being a net carbon sink to being a net carbon source. Fires are even more influential on carbon balances as they emit tremendous amounts of carbon and change the albedo effect of wide regions. Significantly, current climate models do not yet adequately take these episodic events and related forest impacts into account. *See* Steven W. Running, *Ecosystem Disturbance, Carbon, and Climate*, 321 Science 652 (2008).

3.   The conservation and restoration of forests produce a large number of non-climate benefits ("co-benefits") for wildlife, clean water, and other ecosystem functions and social services. How should these positive externalities be considered, if at all, in addressing land use activities under the climate regime? Should measures that have positive co-benefits be taken, regardless of uncertainties in the magnitude of their climate benefits?

B.   The Kyoto Protocol Negotiations

Despite the recognition that removals by sinks should be included in the climate change regime, concerns over permanence, saturation, and verifiability made it unclear how removals should be addressed. During the Kyoto Protocol negotiations, these concerns raised two sets of issues:

- *Accounting.* In calculating whether countries have met their commitments, how should emissions and sequestration from land use activities be counted? Should emissions from land use activities be calculated as part of a country's 1990 baseline emission levels and/or its emissions during the 2008–2012 commitment period?

- *Emissions Trading.* To what extent, if at all, should land use projects that sequester carbon generate credits under joint implementation (JI) or the CDM?

As the following discussion underscores, the Kyoto Protocol negotiations laid bare not only the differences of opinion about how to address land use activities but also the status of forests and other land use activities around the world.

SCHLAMADINGER & MARLAND, LAND USE & GLOBAL CLIMATE CHANGE: FORESTS, LAND MANAGEMENT, AND THE KYOTO PROTOCOL
15–16

In the weeks before convening in Kyoto, it appeared that sinks were likely to be omitted from consideration entirely. Topics of concern included permanence, saturation, and verifiability, and the ability of accounting systems to be equitable and to encourage desired objectives such as sustainable development. . . . Consensus on inclusion of sinks was not resolved until the late stages of the Kyoto negotiations. A sense of the intense, late negotiations leading to the final version of the Kyoto Protocol can be gained by noting that three key sentences relative to [land use] that are found in the final, 10 December, version of the Protocol, were not in the 9 December draft. The text was in flux right to the very end of the negotiations.

Land use and land-use change are, and have historically been, a source of anthropogenic emissions of carbon dioxide to the atmosphere, primarily through deforestation. They also present opportunities to reduce net CO_2 emissions to the atmosphere or to increase the net uptake of carbon from the atmosphere. For one or both of these reasons, many observers felt that it was desirable to include [land use] activities in a binding treaty limiting greenhouse gas emissions. The potential for ancillary benefits in terms of forest protection, biodiversity, water quality, and soil quality further encouraged inclusion.

Another argument for including [land use] options was that they provide a cost-effective means of reducing net emissions to the atmosphere, especially in the short term. This is particularly relevant if the decision is made to limit the atmospheric CO_2 level to a value not too much larger than the current value. Model calculations show, for example, that if the atmospheric CO_2 concentration is to be limited to 450 ppm, and if cumulative fossil-fuel emissions between 1990 and 2100 are limited to 600 billion tons carbon (i.e., slightly below current levels for the next 100 years), carbon stocks in the terrestrial biosphere would have to increase by 120 billion tons carbon. However, when the Ad Hoc Group on the Berlin Mandate (AGBM) invited Parties to submit views on the inclusion of sinks in meeting emission commitments, many Parties expressed fears that carbon sequestration would result in reduced commitments to limiting emissions from energy use, that there were important problems in measuring and verifying carbon sinks, and that accounting methods for sinks could create perverse incentives in forest management. Questions about permanence and leakage were also raised.

. . . [T]here was considerable concern leading into Kyoto that some countries would try to meet much of their obligation by increasing carbon stocks in the terrestrial biosphere and would thus avoid having to confront the primary cause of increasing atmospheric CO_2: the emissions of CO_2 from combustion of fossil fuels. It was argued that the largest contribution to increasing atmospheric CO_2, especially in the future, is the use of fossil fuels, and that any solution must concentrate on fossil-fuel emissions. Inexpensive compliance achieved by using the terrestrial biosphere in the initial phase might not lead toward the long-term goals of the UNFCCC — stabilization of the greenhouse gas concentrations in the atmosphere. The use of cost-effective [land use] measures now might increase the cost of mitigation in the medium to long term if sufficient motivation for developing the innovative technologies needed for deeper reductions is not provided early enough. Others have argued conversely, that lower compliance costs in the first commitment period may lead to countries negotiating deeper cuts for future commitment periods, thus providing greater impetus toward the long-term goals of the UNFCCC.

———————

Recall that Parties under the Kyoto Protocol must establish baseline emissions levels, generally based on emissions in 1990, and that they must reduce their emissions during the commitment period by some percentage of these baseline emissions. As a consequence, negotiators needed to answer two questions with respect to accounting of land use activities. First, when establishing baseline emissions, must Parties account for emissions from industrial sources only or all emissions, including removals from sinks? Second, would Parties be allowed to account for removals by sinks to achieve their commitments? The negotiators presented a number of possible answers.

As an initial matter, the term "gross" emissions of greenhouse gases under the climate change regime refers to total emissions from all industrial sources; it does not include emissions or removals from sinks, such as land-use activities, deforestation, and reforestation. "Net" emissions include emissions from industrial sources in addition to emissions or removals from sinks. Consider the difference between "gross" emissions and "net" emissions. Assume Country Z has emissions of 100 million metric tons carbon dioxide equivalent ($MtCO_2eq$) emissions from industrial sources in 1990. These are its "gross" emissions. If Country Z also has emissions from sinks of 20 $MtCO_2eq$ in 1990, its net emissions would be 120 $MtCO_2eq$.

Given the disparities in emissions and removals from sinks in countries around the world, it is not surprising that Parties came to the Kyoto Protocol negotiations with distinctly different proposals for treating sinks and land use activities. The European Union simply wished to defer inclusion of sinks until better accounting rules were developed. The United States, seeking to take advantage of its net removals from sinks and anticipated increases in removals by sinks, proposed that both commitments and the means to meet them should be based on net emissions, the so-called "net-net" approach. Other countries, such as New Zealand, proposed "gross-net" accounting that would allow them to set their baseline only on industrial emissions; many of these countries had significant removals from land-use sinks around 1990 and were concerned that they could not maintain them throughout the commitment period. Thus, if net emissions from land use were included, their baseline for emissions reductions would be relatively low and they would have greater difficulty reaching their commitments.

Under *net-net accounting*, removals from sinks would be used to establish baseline emissions in 1990 and emissions levels during the 2008–2012 commitment period. Thus, if Country Z has 1990 emissions from industrial sources of 80 $MtCO_2eq$ and emissions from land use activities of 20 $MtCO_2eq$, then its baseline emissions would be 100 $MtCO_2eq$. If Country Z had agreed to reduce emissions by eight percent, then it would need to ensure that emissions from sources and removals by sinks were no more than 460 $MtCO_2eq$ for the 5-year commitment period (an average of 92 $MtCO_2eq$ per year). For a country like Country Z with large emissions from sinks, net-net accounting makes it easier to meet its commitment, because it increases baseline year emissions. On the other hand, countries with large removals from sinks in the base year may have greater difficulties in meeting their commitments, because they will need to maintain the size of the sink to avoid increasing their emissions in the commitment period.

Gross-net accounting has different costs and benefits. Under this approach, baseline emissions would be based only on gross emissions (i.e., emissions from industrial sources). However, countries could count removals from sinks when calculating their emissions levels during the commitment period. Thus, if Country X has gross emissions in 1990 of 100 $MtCO_2eq$ and emissions from sinks of 50 $MtCO_2eq$, its baseline emissions would be 100 $MtCO_2eq$. In this scenario, Country X may have difficulties meeting its commitment, because it will need to reverse emissions from sinks.

However, if countries have large removals from sinks, the gross-net approach provides countries with the opportunity to grow emissions. For example, if Country W has gross emissions in 1990 of 100 $MtCO_2eq$ and removals from sinks of 20 $MtCO_2eq$, its baseline emissions would be 100 $MtCO_2eq$, when in fact its "real" emissions were only 80 $MtCO_2eq$ for each year of the 5-year commitment period. If Country W has agreed to reduce its emissions by eight percent, it must reduce its emissions to an average of 92 $MtCO_2eq$. Because Country W's net emissions are already 80 $MtCO_2eq$ using gross-net accounting, it can actually grow its emissions by 12 $MtCO_2eq$ and still achieve compliance with its commitment.

Negotiators discussed variations on these approaches. For example, both accounting approaches could be limited to certain types of land use activities or to specific time periods. In the jargon of the Parties, an accounting approach that was restricted in some way would be "limited," for example, "limited gross-net" accounting. If no such restrictions were imposed, then the approach would be considered "full," as in "full net-net" accounting.

C.   The Rules of the Kyoto Protocol

1.   *Defining Land Use Activities: LULUCF*

The unease that some countries had concerning permanence, saturation, and verifiability are manifest not only in the accounting rules, which are described in the following section, but also in the distinctions the Kyoto Protocol makes among different types of land-use activities. Rather than treat all land-use activities the same, the Parties distinguished reforestation from afforestation (*See* Table 7-3). Both of these terms have meanings different from replanting as part of forest management. While the Parties could not agree on definitions at the time of the Kyoto Protocol, they created a series of *sui generis* definitions for land-use activities captured collectively in the term "land use, land-use changes, and forestry," or LULUCF. The importance of these definitions is readily apparent: whereas Article 3.3 requires Parties to account for emissions and removals from afforestation, reforestation, and deforestation activities, Article 3.4 grants the Parties discretion to account for other land use activities, such as forest management, cropland and grazing management, and other "land-use change."

Table 7-3: Definitions of Land Use Activities under the Kyoto Protocol, Decision 16/CMP.1, *Land Use, Land-Use Change and Forestry*, para. 1 (2005)

Land Use Activity	Definition
Afforestation	"the direct human-induced conversion of land that has not been forested for a period of at least 50 years to forested land through planting, seeding and/or the human-induced promotion of natural seed sources[.]"
Reforestation	"the direct human-induced conversion of non-forested land to forested land through planting, seeding and/or the human-induced promotion of natural seed sources, on land that was forested but that has been converted to non-forested land. For the first commitment period, reforestation activities will be limited to reforestation occurring on those lands that did not contain forest on 31 December 1989[.]"
Deforestation	"the direct human-induced conversion of forested land to nonforested land[.]"
Forest Management	"a system of practices for stewardship and use of forest land aimed at fulfilling relevant ecological (including biological diversity), economic and social functions of the forest in a sustainable manner."
Cropland Management & Grazing Land Management	These terms are generally defined as systems of practices on land on which agricultural crops are grown or livestock produced.
Revegetation	"a direct human-induced activity to increase carbon stocks on sites through the establishment of vegetation that covers a minimum area of 0.05 hectares and does not meet the definitions of afforestation and reforestation contained here[.]"

QUESTIONS AND DISCUSSION

Review the definitions carefully. How does afforestation differ from reforestation? What is the affect of requiring lands to be the result of "direct human-induced conversion"? Does either include "forest management"? Does logging without the replanting of trees constitute "deforestation" or "forest management"? Keep these definitions in mind as you consider the different provisions of the Kyoto Protocol regime, discussed below.

---

2.   *Accounting for LULUCF Activities*

The Kyoto Protocol's accounting rules for LULUCF ultimately reflect a series of compromises. Article 3 of the Kyoto Protocol adopts neither "full gross-net" nor "full net-net" accounting but rather includes two "limited" approaches that appear to provide accounting benefits regardless of a country's emissions from LULUCF activities. For most countries, it adopts a "limited gross-net" approach, but also includes the possibility of "limited net-net" accounting. These approaches are "limited" because only a limited number of land use activities are covered. The Kyoto Protocol also limits its accounting to emissions "since 1990."

KYOTO PROTOCOL, ARTICLE 3

3. The net changes in greenhouse gas emissions from sources and removals by sinks resulting from direct human-induced land use change and forestry activities, limited to afforestation, reforestation, and deforestation since 1990, measured as verifiable changes in stocks in each commitment period shall be used to meet the commitments in this Article of each Party included in Annex I. The greenhouse gas emissions from sources and removals by sinks associated with those activities shall be reported in a transparent and verifiable manner and reviewed in accordance with Articles 7 and 8.

4. . . . The Conference of the Parties serving as the meeting of the Parties to this Protocol shall, at its first session or as soon as practicable thereafter, decide upon modalities, rules and guidelines as to how and which additional human-induced activities related to changes in greenhouse gas emissions and removals in the agricultural soil and land use change and forestry categories, shall be added to, or subtracted from, the assigned amount for Parties included in Annex I, taking into account uncertainties, transparency in reporting, verifiability, the methodological work of the Intergovernmental Panel on Climate Change, the advice provided by the Subsidiary Body for Scientific and Technological Advice in accordance with Article 5 and the decisions of the Conference of the Parties. Such a decision shall apply in the second and subsequent commitment periods. A Party may choose to apply such a decision on these additional human-induced activities for its first commitment period, provided that these activities have taken place since 1990. * * *

7. * * * Those Parties included in Annex I for whom land use change and forestry constituted a net source of greenhouse gas emissions in 1990 shall include in their 1990 emissions base year or period the aggregate anthropogenic carbon dioxide equivalent emissions minus removals in 1990 from land use change for the purposes of calculating their assigned amount.

From a legal perspective, the number of issues that the Kyoto Protocol leaves unresolved is remarkable. In addition to leaving key land-use activities undefined, the Kyoto Protocol left the following issues needing resolution before a country could begin accounting for its LULUCF emissions:

- What constitutes a forest?
- How should possible non-permanence and leakage be calculated, if at all?
- What counts as a "verifiable change[] in stocks"?
- What are "direct human-induced . . . activities"?
- Are there any limits on how much credit from LULUCF activities a Party may use to meet its commitments?

Because of the large number of critical issues left unanswered, Article 3 of the Kyoto Protocol at best established only a framework for future negotiations. Indeed, the Parties later developed a complex set of rules at the seventh meeting of the Conference of the Parties (CoP7) in Marrakesh in 2001. Decision 11/CP.7 (2001); Decision 16/CMP.1 (2005). These rules define key LULUCF activities, establish a multi-tiered capping system that limits the use of LULUCF activities to meet emission targets, and limit the development of LULUCF activities in the Clean Development Mechanism. Some of the more important aspects of this decision are summarized below, with Table 7-4 outlining the applicable accounting rules.

Table 7-4: Summary of LULUCF Accounting Rules

Activity	Kyoto Protocol Article	Start Date	Accounting	Accounting Method	Cap
Afforestation	3.3	"to have begun on or after 1 January 1990"	Mandatory	Gross-Net	
Reforestation					
Deforestation					
Forest Management	3.4	"to have occurred since 1 January 1990"	Voluntary		Cap Per Country
Revegetation				Net-Net	No cap
Cropland Management					
Grazing-Land Management					

a.   *Afforestation, Reforestation, and Deforestation*

Several features of the provisions relating to afforestation, reforestation, and deforestation raised important issues for the post-Kyoto negotiations. For example, the Parties limited accounting under Article 3.3 to afforestation (A), reforestation (R), and deforestation (D) projects initiated *since 1990*. However, 1990 is not a baseline for measuring whether a Party's ARD projects have resulted in net emissions or removals; it is only the date by which the Parties determine whether ARD projects are subject to accounting. Instead, a Party measures changes in GHG emissions and removals from those projects during the commitment period (2008–2012). Thus, if a Party has removals of 100 $MtCO_2eq$ in 2008 and 175 $MtCO_2eq$ in 2012, then it would report net removals of 75 $MtCO_2eq$ for the commitment period.

While appearing straightforward, the negotiators recognized that Article 3.3 could create "odd results":

> The "since 1990" starting date set forth by the Protocol will account for only those stands harvested or regenerated since 1990. The benchmark chosen will result in either net credits or net debits being falsely created. For example, a state that deforested its land before 1990 at the beginning of the first commitment period, but then reforests in the following decade would obtain windfall credits toward carbon reduction without ever having taken into account the emissions associated with the earlier deforestation. Likewise, if land was reforested prior to 1990, but harvested before 2008, the state's emissions would appear to increase. This failure to account for a state's initial condition when calculating its net carbon emissions creates odd results.

Alexander Gillespie, *Sinks and the Climate Change Regime: The State of Play*, 13 DUKE ENVTL. L. & POL'Y F. 279, 289–90 (2003).

To avoid the appearance of new emissions for countries that had begun reforesting before 1990, the Parties agreed to exclude GHG removals attributable to activities and practices before 1990. To avoid penalizing Parties that began harvesting mature forests during the first commitment period, they also agreed that emissions from harvesting (following afforestation and reforestation) could not be greater than the removals earned on that unit of land. Decision 16/CMP.1, at para. 4. Thus, if emissions are larger than removals on a specific unit of land, then a net balance of zero should be recorded.

The Parties developed another set of protocols to ensure consistent reporting of removals and emissions from afforestation, reforestation, and deforestation. First, the Parties must classify particular lands as afforestation or reforestation (AR) lands or deforestation (D) lands, based on the definitions included in Decision 16/CMP.1. If land meets one of these definitions, a Party must designate it as such unless the Party chooses to report changes in GHG emissions and removals on that land as an elected activity under Article 3.4. Once a Party classifies land as AR or D, it must account for all subsequent changes in GHG emissions or removals, including changes resulting from natural regeneration and natural disasters. The difference between GHG emissions or removals (and other greenhouse gases) in 2008 and 2012 is reported as net sequestration. Since the reporting obligations of Article 3.3 are mandatory, a Party may not reclassify AR or D as Article 3.4 lands, which are subject to voluntary reporting. Thus, even if land designated as AR later comes under forest management, it must remain classified as AR land under Article 3.3 for the entire commitment period. However, a Party may reclassify AR land as deforested land if land that was afforested or reforested after 1989 is later deforested prior to the end of the commitment period. The classification of deforested land is permanent for the commitment period.

b. *Revegetation and Cropland and Grazing Land Management*

In contrast to mandatory reporting of Article 3.3 emissions and removals, accounting for other LULUCF activities — revegetation, cropland management, grazing land management activities, and forest management — is voluntary under Article 3.4. Parties were able to choose, by 2007, which Article 3.4 LULUCF activities they will count.

Accounting for revegetation and cropland and grazing land management activities (not forest management) is on a net-net basis. *See* Decision 16/CMP.1, para. 9. Net-net accounting differs from the gross-net accounting method used for Article 3.3. Thus, a Party must subtract net GHG emissions or removals for the chosen activities during the commitment period from net emissions or removals in 1990 (multiplied by five to account for the five-year commitment period).

c. *Forest Management*

As with other Article 3.4 LULUCF activities, Parties have discretion to account for forest management. If they choose to account for forest management activities, then they must follow a third accounting approach developed specifically for forest management activities in the first commitment period. *See* Decision 16/CMP.1, paras. 10–12.

Under this accounting approach, if a Party's afforestation, reforestation, and deforestation activities result in net emissions, then the Party may offset these emissions through forest management activities, but only up to 9 megatons of carbon per year for the five-year commitment period. A Party may include forest management activities to help meet emission targets beyond 9 megatons of carbon per year, but only up to the individual cap specified for each Annex B Party in the Appendix to Decision 16/CMP.1. These caps vary substantially. Twenty-five countries have a limit of 0.50 MtC per year or less, but Japan, Canada, and Russia have much larger caps of 13 MtC per year, 22 MtC per year, and 33 MtC per year, respectively. *Id.* at Appendix; Decision 12/CP.7 (2001).

Where did these limits come from? Prior to walking out of the negotiations at the sixth meeting of the Conference of the Parties, the United States had estimated that removals from sinks could provide as much as half of its annual reduction commitment by 2010, and it wanted to claim all of these removals in its accounting. The EU, pointing to the scientific uncertainty in calculating removals from sinks, insisted on limits. At one point, the United States reduced its claim from sinks from 312 to 20 million tons, but the talks collapsed nonetheless. With the United States no longer participating in the negotiations, entry into force of the Kyoto Protocol hinged on Canada, Japan, and Russia ratifying the Protocol. With the potential collapse of the Protocol looming, the Parties granted these three countries disproportionate forest management allowances. *See* Gillespie, *Sinks and the Climate Change Regime*, at 289–90 (providing a history of the forest management negotiations).

The actual limits were derived based on an 85 percent discount factor (i.e., a value representing 15 percent of actual forest sequestration) and a cap of 3 percent of a Party's base year emissions for forest management removals. The Parties discounted 85 percent of forest management removals to avoid crediting removals resulting from elevated carbon dioxide concentrations above their pre-industrial level (many plants photosynthesize faster and thus sequester carbon more rapidly when CO_2 concentrations are higher). In addition, because most Annex I countries primarily had rapidly growing young forests in 1990, management *since* 1990 would not produce "the majority of carbon sequestration occurring during the commitment period in these forests, but simply business-as-usual management and the existing age structure. By restricting the amount of credits that most Annex I countries may earn for 'forest management' in forests that existed before 1990 to roughly 15 percent of actual national forest carbon increment, Parties found a practical solution to this vexing problem." Kenneth L. Rosenbaum et al., *Climate Change and the Forest Sector: Possible National and Subnational Legislation* 10 (FAO 2004).

QUESTIONS AND DISCUSSION

1.   Contrast the accounting methods under Article 3.3 and Article 3.7. How do the accounting rules differ? Australia reported LULUCF emissions in 1990 that were 14 percent of its total greenhouse gas emissions. Why would Australia benefit from the "limited net-net" accounting rules of Article 3.7?

2.   Commentators have argued that "[t]his new accounting system will reward countries that are increasing their forestry sinks, and penalize those whose sinks are decreasing." Clare Breidenich et al., *"The Kyoto Protocol to the United Nations Framework Convention on Climate Change,"* 92 A.J.I.L. 315, 322–323 (1998). Do you agree?

3.   Although the inclusion of gross-net and net-net accounting allows countries to select the accounting method that provides the most beneficial accounting strategy for that country, Article 3 does eliminate some potentially advantageous accounting rules. For example, what is the effect of limiting removals by sinks to "net changes . . . since 1990"?

4. *"Forest."* To ensure consistency and comparability among Parties, the Parties created a common definition of the term "forest" based on the UN Food and Agriculture Organization's definition. "Forest" is defined as an area with minimum tree crown cover value between 10 and 30 per cent, a single minimum land area value between 0.05 and 1 hectare and a single minimum tree height value between 2 and 5 metres. Decision 16.CMP.1, at para. 1(a). While Parties have some flexibility to define "forest" within the ranges included in the definition, once a Party makes its choice, that definition remains fixed. *Id.* at para. 16. Although these figures may appear arbitrarily chosen, they were not:

> The amount of canopy cover has a strong impact in the context of the Kyoto Protocol. For example, if a high threshold was set (e.g., 70 percent canopy cover) then many areas of sparse forest and woodland could be cleared or planted and the resultant carbon losses or gains would not be accounted in determining forest emissions/sequestration under the Protocol. If a low threshold was set (e.g., 10 percent canopy cover) then dense forest could be heavily degraded and significant amounts of carbon released, without the actions being registered as "deforestation." Similarly, a forest with low canopy cover (15 percent, for example), could be considerably enhanced without the actions actually qualifying as "reforestation" or "afforestation."

Gillespie, *Sinks and the Climate Change Regime*, at 297. The practical effect of the definition under Decision 16/CMP.1 is to exclude road side tree plantings and other "minor" tree planting efforts as qualifying as AR lands. What are the advantages and disadvantages from limiting afforestation and reforestation to larger projects?

5. *Harvested Wood Products.* The challenges of accounting for greenhouse gas emissions is underscored by the question of how to account for harvested wood. Not only is carbon dioxide released during harvesting, it is also released during the manufacture of wood products and by the use and disposal of wood. On the other hand, carbon is stored in finished products. How should the release of carbon dioxide during the harvesting and manufacturing process be accounted for, if at all? The IPCC has recommended that the storage of carbon in forest products be included in a Party's national inventory only in the case where a country can document that existing stocks of long-term products are in fact increasing. Where carbon storage in forest products is reported, the IPCC recommends that all CO_2 emissions and removals associated with forest harvesting and the oxidation of wood products are accounted for by the country in the year of harvesting. IPCC, *Revised 1996 IPCC Guidelines for National Greenhouse Gas Inventories: Volume 3: Reference Manual*, page 5.17 and box 5. The reporting on harvested wood products is optional, but the Subsidiary Body on Scientific and Technological Assessment has invited Parties to report voluntarily on harvested wood products in their national inventories (only four Parties have done so: Australia, Canada, the United Kingdom, and the United States). Is it realistic for Parties to report on the amount of carbon stored in wood products, such as paper? Do you think that Parties should account for wood products traded internationally? If Germany imports wooden desks from Canada, how should that be reported?

6. *Removal Units.* To distinguish removals by sinks from other types of emissions reductions, the Parties created a new unit — removal units (RMUs). RMUs are generated from removals of greenhouse gases from eligible LULUCF activities under Articles 3.3 and 3.4. Annex I Parties may use RMUs to help meet their emissions targets. RMUs, as with certified emissions reductions and emission reduction units, must be verified by expert review teams under the Kyoto Protocol's reporting and review procedures. In addition, they may not be banked. Where a Party's LULUCF activities result in a net source of greenhouse gas emissions, they count against the country's assigned amount.. Decision 13/CMP.1, *Modalities for the Accounting of Assigned Amounts under Article 7, Paragraph 4, of the Kyoto Protocol*, Annex (2001).

7. The complexity of accounting for carbon from LULUCF raises a more general question about the effectiveness of the Kyoto Protocol approach: Does the complexity introduced by trying to include net emissions from LULUCF in the carbon market nullify the value of taking such a comprehensive approach to reducing greenhouse gas concentrations? What alternative policies and measures for LULUCF could the Parties adopt outside the carbon trading market set up in Kyoto?

D.   LULUCF and the CDM

As with other LULUCF issues, the Parties struggled with concerns over permanence and verifiability to determine whether to make LULUCF projects eligible under the Clean Development Mechanism (CDM). Other issues were also at play. Because Article 12 of the Kyoto Protocol refers to "emissions" but excludes references to "removals by sinks," it was unclear whether LULUCF projects were permissible under the CDM. In addition, most of the developing countries considered LULUCF projects under the CDM as yet another loophole for developed countries to meet their commitments without decreasing their own domestic emissions. Further, because LULUCF projects do not require any technology, their inclusion in the CDM would reduce technology transfers to developing countries while still giving developed countries what they want — certified emissions reductions (CERs). From a technical perspective, some cited the lack of permanence of carbon sequestration from LULUCF activities as a reason to exclude them from the CDM. Others, particularly Brazil, feared an erosion of sovereignty if developed countries and their corporate citizens established long-term interests — CERs — in developing country forests.

On the other hand, LULUCF-CDM advocates, such as the Umbrella Group (a loose coalition of non-EU developed countries that usually includes Australia, Canada, Iceland, Japan, New Zealand, Norway, the Russian Federation, Ukraine, and the United States) and many Latin American countries that would benefit from LULUCF projects, argued that the severity of climate change compelled the use of all abatement strategies. In any event, they argued that because deforestation caused significant carbon dioxide emissions, the CDM should be used to help prevent deforestation. *See* Emily Boyd, et al., *The Politics of Afforestation and Reforestation Activities at COP-9 and SB-20* (Tyndall Briefing Note No. 12, Dec. 2003), at: http://www.tyndall.ac.uk/publications/briefing_notes/note12.shtml.

Eventually, the arguments of LULUCF-CDM proponents prevailed, but not before the Parties developed a comprehensive array of Decisions to address the concerns of LULUCF-CDM opponents. First, the Parties sought to reduce uncertainties due to non-permanence and verifiability by limiting LULUCF-CDM activities to afforestation and reforestation. They also limited use of CDM-related afforestation and reforestation projects to one percent of an Annex I Party's base year emissions, times five (to account for the five years of the 2008–2012 commitment period). Decision 16/CMP.1, *Land Use, Land-Use Change and Forestry*, paras. 13–14 (2005).

The Parties also addressed non-permanence through an innovative crediting system. Decision 5/CMP.1, *Modalities and Procedures for Afforestation and Reforestation Project Activities under the Clean Development Mechanism in the First Commitment Period of the Kyoto Protocol* (2005). The first step in the CDM's temporary crediting system is for the project participants to choose one of two crediting periods. They may choose a non-renewable crediting period of a maximum of 30 years or a 20-year crediting period that may be revised and renewed up to two times for a possible crediting period of 60 years. *Id.*, para. 23. These projects enjoy long crediting periods, because AR activities are unlikely to generate any removals for a number of years, yet they may incur emissions early on as project participants clear land and disturb soil to initiate the project.

Second, project participants must choose to receive one of two new CERs: "temporary CERs (tCERs)" or "long-term CERs (lCERs)." Both types of CERs have limited applicability, but they differ in how they are issued. tCERs are issued each time a project is certified (i.e., every five years) based on the net increase in GHG removals *since the start of the project*. Thus, assume that an afforestation project starts in 2005 and the first accounting period ends in 2010. If removals in 2005 were zero and removals in 2010 were 100 $MtCO_2$, then the project participant will be issued tCERs in 2010 worth 100 $MtCO_2$ (100 − 0 = 100). If the removals at the end of the next 5-year certification period in 2015 total 300 $MtCO_2$, then the project participant will be issued tCERs worth 300 $MtCO_2$ (300 − 0 = 300). To protect against non-permanence, tCERs expire at the end of the commitment period (e.g., 2012, not the 2015 *certification* period) subsequent to the one in which they were issued.

In contrast, lCERs are issued after each five-year certification corresponding to the increase in GHG removals *since the previous certification*. Assume again that an afforestation project starts in 2005 and the first accounting period ends in 2010. If removals in 2005 were zero and removals in 2010 were 100 $MtCO_2$, then the project participant will be issued lCERs in 2010 worth 100 $MtCO_2$ (100 − 0 = 100), just as with tCERs. If the removals at the end of the next 5-year certification period in 2015 total 300 $MtCO_2$, then the project participant will be issued lCERs worth 200 $MtCO_2$ (300 − 100 = 200). The project participant receives a smaller number of lCERs. However, lCERs may have greater economic value because they do not expire until the end of the *crediting* period (e.g., at the end of 20 or 30 years), as opposed to the end of the next *commitment* period.

This system provides another safeguard against non-permanence. With lCERs, a project participant must replace any "lost" emissions. Thus, if removals in 2005 were zero but the project had emissions of 50 $MtCO_2$ because of a fire, then the project participant would need to obtain 50 $MtCO_2$ of AAUs, ERUs, or some other "permanent" emission credit. With tCERs, on the other hand, if CO_2 removals have decreased since the previous certification, project participants will be issued fewer tCERs.

Box 1 — Guangxi Watershed CDM AR Project

This project, the first AR-CDM project, was registered in November 2006. The project will replant 4,000 hectares of heavily degraded land to pine, oak and other species in southern China. The project will sequester about 26,000 $MtCO_2eq$/year, which will be sold via the World Bank BioCarbon Fund to the Governments of Spain and Italy.

The project will have sites in 2 districts, and about 5000 households in 10 communes will be involved. In this part of China land is communally owned. However, many households have abandoned agriculture and their collective lands lie idle. These communes will surrender the title of this land to a local forestry company which, in exchange, will pay for the establishment and management of plantations, and then share with households 60% of the revenue from the sale of forest products and 40% of the revenue from sale of CERs. In addition, the company will employ local labour. About 80% of the land will be managed in this way. The remaining 20% of the land will be planted up by independent farmer groups. They have to lease the land from their communes for 50 years, and cover establishment costs, but they will be the sole beneficiaries of income from sale of forest products and CERs [from this land]. Their scheme will be registered by the forest company, which will sell the CERs on their behalf.

Over the 30 year life of the project, total income of $21 million ($4200/household, or $140/hh/year) will be generated, 75% from employment, 15% from forest products and 10% from sale of CER[s], estimated at $3/[metric tons]$CO_2$e. So the annual net benefit from the CDM will be around $14 per household.

Ben Vickers & Catherine Mackenzie, *Forestry in the Clean Development Mechanism: Potential Benefits for the Rural Poor* (undated), *available at* www.recoftc.org/.

QUESTIONS AND DISCUSSION

1. Although tCERs have an estimated cost of just 14 to 30 percent of the cost of CERs from emission reduction projects, only 0.08 percent of CDM projects have been AR projects. Do you think it is worth the time and expense of developing rules to help ensure permanence and verifiability for such a small percentage of projects?

2. The Parties chose to address non-permanence through the issuance of expiring tCERs and lCERs. During negotiations, however, Canada and several Latin American countries supported an insurance approach under which project participants would insure the CERs generated by the project against non-permanence. If any removals were lost during the life time of the project plus 10 years, the insurer would be required to replace the CERs with other permanent carbon credits, such as ERUs, AAUs, or RMUs. Insured CERs could command a higher price because they would be considered permanent. However, concerns were raised that the volatility in CER prices would prevent insurers from establishing a fixed premium to insure CERs. If prices for CERs eventually stabilize, would you favor an approach that spreads the risk of non-performance through insurance?

    3.   *Environmental and Socio-Economic Impacts.* To ensure that afforestation and reforestation projects do not cause adverse environmental and socio-economic impacts, project participants must analyze these impacts. Decision 5/CMP.1, Annex, para. 12(c). Project participants must assess the impact of the project on biodiversity and natural ecosystems, as well as impacts outside the proposed project boundary. Specific environmental impacts that should be described include impacts on hydrology, soils, risk of fires, pests, and diseases. Decision 5/CMP.1 does not require project participants to analyze specific socio-economic impacts of the proposed project, but provides that they should assess impacts on local communities, indigenous peoples, land tenure, local employment, and food production, among other things. *Id.*, Appendix B, paras. (j)–(k). If the project participants or the host Party believe that any of the impacts are significant, the project participants must prepare a socio-economic or environmental impact assessment consistent with national regulation of the host country. They must also describe any mitigation measures that will be taken to avoid those impacts. *Id.*, Annex, para. 12(c). When verifying additionality and other aspects of the project, the designated operational entity must determine whether the project participants monitored socio-economic and environmental impacts consistently with their monitoring plan. These provisions, however, are tied to the host country's procedures for impact assessment. What should happen if the host country does not have such procedures or they are inadequate to address the impacts addressed by Decision 5/CMP.1?

    These rules differ from the requirements for other CDM projects. For example, the rules for non-AR small-scale CDM projects do not require an assessment of socio-economic impacts and require an environmental assessment only if the host country requires it. Decision 4/CMP.1, *Guidance Relating to the Clean Development Mechanism*, Annex II, para. 22(c) (2005). For "regular" CDM projects with potential significant impacts, however, project participants must prepare an environmental impact assessment in accordance with the laws of the host country. Decision 3/CMP.1, Annex, para. 37(e).

    4.   *Additionality.* With respect to additionality, the Parties adopted rules essentially the same as those for other projects. The Parties agreed that projects must increase actual net greenhouse gas removals by sinks "above the changes in carbon stocks in the carbon pools within the project boundary that would have occurred in the absence of the CDM afforestation or reforestation project." This is defined as the "actual net greenhouse gas removals by sinks" minus the "baseline net greenhouse gas removals by sinks" minus "leakage." "Actual greenhouse gas removals by sinks" are the actual removals due to the project minus any emissions caused by the implementation of the project. Rules and definitions for "leakage" and the establishment of baselines are the same as for other CDM projects. Decision 5/CMP.1, *Modalities and Procedures for Afforestation and Reforestation Project Activities under the Clean Development Mechanism in the First Commitment Period of the Kyoto Protocol*, Annex, paras. 1, 18–22.

    5.   *Small-scale Afforestation and Reforestation Projects.* The Parties have also established simplified procedures for small-scale afforestation and reforestation projects under the CDM. These are discussed in Chapter 6, Section III.D.1., at note 4.

IV.   DEFORESTATION AND CLIMATE CHANGE

Deforestation remains an untapped element of climate change mitigation under the Kyoto Protocol. Because of concerns about how to address additionality, non-permanence, leakage, and a range of other issues, the Parties omitted deforestation projects from the CDM. Yet, the climate change benefits of reducing deforestation are clear. Tropical forests, in particular, hold great value for climate change mitigation:

> Tropical forests account for slightly less than half of the world's forest area, yet they hold about as much carbon in their vegetation and soils as temperate-zone and boreal forests combined. Trees in tropical forests hold, on average, about 50% more carbon per hectare than trees outside the tropics. Thus, equivalent rates of deforestation will generally cause more carbon to be released from the tropical forests than from forests outside the tropics. Although the soils in temperate zone and boreal forests generally hold more carbon per unit area than tropical forest soils, only a fraction of this carbon is lost with deforestation and cultivation.

R. A. Houghton, *Tropical Deforestation As a Source of Greenhouse Gas Emissions*, *in* TROPICAL DEFORESTATION AND CLIMATE CHANGE 13, 15 (Paulo Moutinho & Stephan Schwartzman eds., 2005).

If deforestation can be arrested and reversed, the world's forests may play a significant role in mitigating rather than exacerbating climate change. According to the IPCC, the carbon mitigation benefits of reducing deforestation, at least in the short term, are greater than the benefits of afforestation, simply because of the scale of deforestation. In the long term, however, forest management that maintains or increases forest carbon stocks, while also producing sustainable harvests of forest products, should provide the largest sustained climate mitigation benefits. IPCC WORKING GROUP III, *Forestry*, at 543.

Many obstacles, however, stand in the way of reversing deforestation rates and building sustainable forest management practices.

IPCC WORKING GROUP III, FORESTRY
566, 569

Realization of the mitigation potential requires institutional capacity, investment capital, technology RD [research and development] and transfer, as well as appropriate policies and incentives, and international cooperation. In many regions, their absence has been a barrier to implementation of forestry mitigation activities. Notable exceptions exist, however, such as regional successes in reducing deforestation rates and implementing large-scale afforestation programmes. Considerable progress has been made in technology development for implementation, monitoring and reporting of carbon benefits but barriers to technology transfer remain. . . . " * * *

The causes of tropical deforestation are complex, varying across countries and over time in response to different social, cultural, and macroeconomic conditions. Broadly, three major barriers to enacting effective policies to reduce forest loss are: (i) profitability incentives often run counter to forest conservation and sustainable forest management; (ii) many direct and indirect drivers of deforestation lie outside of the forest sector, especially in agricultural policies and markets; and (iii) limited regulatory and institutional capacity and insufficient resources constrain the ability of many governments to implement forest and related sectoral policies on the ground. * * *

The lack of robust institutional and regulatory frameworks, trained personnel, and secure land tenure has constrained the effectiveness of forest management in many developing countries. Africa, for example, had about 649 million forested hectares as of 2000. Of this, only 5.5 million ha (0.8%) had long-term management plans, and only 0.9 million ha (0.1%) were certified to sound forestry standards. Thus far, efforts to improve logging practices in developing countries have met with limited success. For example, reduced-impact logging techniques would increase carbon storage over traditional logging, but have not been widely adopted by logging companies, even when they lead to cost savings.

———————

Funding is another major hurdle. The *Stern Review on the Economics of Climate Change* has estimated that investments of $5 to $15 billion per year are needed to reduce emissions from deforestation by 50% globally. The IPCC's estimate may be higher; it has reported that reducing emissions from deforestation by 50% could save 1.6 billion tons of carbon dioxide annually at cost under $20/t CO_2eq. IPCC WORKING GROUP III, *Forestry*, at 543.

To overcome these challenges, a number of governments and nongovernmental organizations have turned to the climate change regime. Papua New Guinea and Costa Rica are credited with initiating formal discussions within the climate change regime in 2005 for providing compensation to developing countries for reducing emissions from deforestation. Their proposal led to a series of workshops to discuss how such a scheme might address leakage, non-permanence, and other issues. These discussions have generated a number of proposals to provide compensation to countries that reduce deforestation rates. Some proposals envisage the creation of tradable emissions credits to developing countries that reduce their emissions from deforestation below some country-specific baseline. Other proposals would place funds from developed countries — bilateral and multilateral development assistance and other sources — into a compensation fund. In either case, the funds generated would be earmarked for enforcing environmental laws and regulations, supporting economic alternatives to land use activities that result in deforestation, and building the institutional capacity to manage forests sustainably. As you read excerpts for a couple of these proposals, consider which might best provide incentives to reduce deforestation.

A.   Compensated Reductions in Deforestation

MÁRCIO SANTILLI et al., TROPICAL DEFORESTATION AND THE KYOTO PROTOCOL: AN EDITORIAL ESSAY
71 CLIMATIC CHANGE 267, 269–273 (2005)*

Compensated reductions

We suggest the concept of *compensated reduction* as a means of both reducing the substantial emissions of carbon from deforestation and facilitating significant developing country participation in the Kyoto Protocol framework. Developing countries that elect to reduce their national emissions from deforestation during

———————

the 5 years of the first commitment period (taking average annual deforestation over some agreed period in the past, measured with robust satellite imagery techniques, as a baseline), would be authorized to issue carbon certificates, similar to the Certified Emissions Reductions (CERs) of the CDM, which could be sold to governments or private investors. Once having received compensation, countries would agree not to increase, or to further reduce, deforestation in future commitment periods (provided that Annex I countries fulfill their obligations). A country that committed to reducing deforestation and was compensated, but instead increased deforestation, would take the increment increased as a mandatory cap in the next commitment period.

Baselines

Baselines should be designed in accordance with different regional dynamics of deforestation in the tropics. In the Amazon with ~80% of original forest cover, and high current deforestation rates, a baseline of the average annual deforestation in the 1980s (since 1990 is the year of reference for the Kyoto targets) would be adequate. Any historical average since the 1970s over a sufficient time period to compensate for anomalous yearly highs and lows would be adequate, provided that the baseline refers to a period prior to adopting compensated reductions, so that no incentive to increase deforestation in order to get credit for reductions is created. The specific period (1980s, 1990s, 1995–2005) will determine how much deforestation must be reduced in order to obtain credit, and so will necessarily be a political negotiation. Countries with substantial tropical forests, but relatively little deforestation to date (e.g., Peru, Bolivia) might be allowed baselines higher than their recent deforestation rates (along the lines of Australia's "growth cap") as an inducement to participate and avoid future increases. For heavily logged regions such as Kalimantan, Sumatra and Sulawesi, for example, where 70–80% of lowland dipterocarp forest cover has been removed in logged areas and conversion to oil palm plantations is underway a baseline could be expressed in terms of existing carbon stocks at some point in the past, with crediting for any increase in total carbon stocks between 2008–2012, making reforestation or re-growth an alternative to oil palm plantations. . . .

The principle in all cases is to set baselines in terms of historic deforestation or destruction of carbon stocks and create incentives for progressive reductions, or avoiding future increases. As a motivation for countries to continue reducing their deforestation rates, the historic baseline might be revised downwards in 20 years, a plausible time period for a nation such as Brazil to reorder its land use practices.

Leakage, additionality and permanence

Calculating reductions against a national baseline and monitoring system for deforestation addresses the problem of leakage that ha[s] vexed the CDM. Deforestation does not "leak" into the energy or transport sectors, and if reductions in one region are equaled or exceeded by increases in another, this will be apparent in comparing national rates over time. Deforestation can be measured at the beginning and end of a commitment period just as can national emissions for Annex I countries. International "market leakage" for timber exports, where a participating country ceases to export timber to get carbon investments, and a non-participating country increases its exports correspondingly, is an issue. But international market leakage is potentially a much bigger issue under current Kyoto Protocol rules — forest sinks, and activities that increase carbon stocks in Annex I countries are credited, but developing country forest destruction is not debited. An Annex I country could in principle cease timber harvests altogether at home and replace them with tropical imports and still receive credit under Article 3.3 of the Kyoto Protocol. Enlisting any tropical forest countries to compensated reduction programs would, by creating a framework for engaging tropical countries in emissions controls, begin to address this problem. Leakage of deforestation from one country to another (e.g., Brazilians who cease clearing in Brazil and move to Bolivia) could in principle occur if only one or a few countries elect to participate in compensated reductions. The same risk, however, obtains for all sectors as long as only some countries have emissions caps — multinational corporations might for example reduce emissions in Kyoto countries and invest in high-emissions operations in non-Kyoto countries. While remote sensing monitoring of deforestation rates could be used to mitigate international leakage, ultimately only drawing more major emitters into an international reductions regime will solve the problem.

The most recent and thorough deforestation studies offer no suggestion that deforestation is decreasing, either of its own accord or in consequence of policy interventions; to the contrary, increasing global integration of markets and demand for agricultural commodities appears to be driving substantial increases in deforestation rates. Hence, there is no need to show that sustained reductions in deforestation rates would not have occurred without compensated reductions, even though deforestation rates will eventually decline as forests disappear. Deforestation in all major tropical forest regions can certainly be expected to continue for the 20 years following 2008, after which time compensated reductions baselines should be adjusted, and global time horizons for forest carbon crediting based on total forest carbon stocks should be calculated.

The security of emissions offsets, or "permanence," would be assured by the provision that participating countries that increased deforestation above their baseline take the increment as a mandatory target in the following commitment period. The security of emissions offsets could be enhanced by a system of "banking" forest carbon credits: a portion of the reductions achieved in a 5-year commitment period could be made available for emissions offsets in the following period, while others could be banked for use in future commitment periods (unlike CERs, which are only valid for the first commitment period under the Marrakech Accords). Banked carbon credits could be used to insure offsets. Permanence of reductions is also an issue for all sectors — a country that meets commitments in the first period might opt out of the second and increase emissions. Carbon insurance mechanisms for all emissions offsets should be developed, and their costs incorporated into emissions trading.

B.   Brazil's Reduced Rate of Emissions Proposal

BRAZIL, BRAZILIAN PERSPECTIVE ON REDUCING EMISSIONS FROM DEFORESTATION
FCCC/SBSTA/2007/MISC.2, 22–24 (March 2, 2007)

The main objective of this proposal is the development of an arrangement under the Framework Convention on Climate Change aimed at providing positive incentives for the net reduction of emissions from deforestation in developing countries that voluntarily reduce their greenhouse gas emissions from deforestation in relation to a rate of emissions from deforestation. . . .

The proposal is based on the distribution of financial incentives to countries that demonstrate, in a transparent and credible manner, a reduction in their emissions from deforestation. These financial incentives should be provided by Annex I countries that voluntarily engage in the arrangement, and shall be new and additional to financial resources provided for other activities (according to Art. 4.3 of the UNFCCC). * * *

Participating countries are entitled to financial incentives from the arrangement after they demonstrate, in a transparent and credible manner, that they have reduced their emissions from deforestation. This approach is based on demonstrable reduction of emissions from deforestation, or *ex-post* results.

The positive incentives system should be based on a comparison between the rate of emissions from deforestation (RED) for a certain past time period with the reference emissions rate (RER). This should be achieved through a transparent, consistent and scientifically-based method.

The incentive will be quantified taking into account the reference emissions rate:

- if emissions from deforestation have decreased, the difference is converted into a financial incentive to be received (credit); and

- if emissions from deforestation have increased, the difference is converted into an amount to be subtracted (debit) from future financial incentives to be received.

The amount of the incentive per carbon tonne is to be calculated by a set amount to be agreed and to be reviewed periodically.

All the reduced emissions of a country are to be added together for an agreed period, and the total reduced carbon tonnes is to be converted into a monetary sum, divided among the participating developing countries in the same ratio as the emissions reductions they have achieved.

Financial incentives should be received only when this net accounting results in a number below the RER. In this case, this number should be converted into a monetary sum. The positive incentives will be provided by developed country Parties, taking into account their obligations under the UNFCCC.

The proposal is based on actual demonstration of reduced emissions from deforestation, relative to a reference emission rate, built on the basis of past emissions from deforestation. Hence, it does not recognize "virtual" emission reductions resulting from a projected deforestation rate, such as those from the avoided deforestation concept.

Countries that voluntarily participate in the arrangement should be able to develop public policies and measures to reduce emissions from deforestation. It must be stressed that consistent emission reductions from deforestation requires continuous investments.

At the start of the implementation of the arrangement, two categories of countries are likely to emerge: (1) countries that are ready for a prompt start; and (2) countries that require capacity-building and enhancement of endogenous capacities and technology transfer to adequately implement their policies and measures to reduce emissions from deforestation. Adequate efforts to ensure financing for capacity-building and technology-transfer for category 2 countries should be pursued, including through relevant multilateral financing institutions as well as voluntary contributions from Annex I countries. * * *

The monitoring of the reduction in emissions from deforestation shall be based on a transparent and credible system that reliably provides estimates of the annual emissions from deforestation, by biome. All data and information shall be disclosed publicly, and should allow for the analysis of data of the estimated reduction from deforestation by all interested stakeholders.

[Brazil's proposal alsp establishes a methodology for estimating carbon stocks within different types of forested land. Countries then set a deforestation reference emission rate (RER) for the different forest types based on emissions from deforestation. The RER is established based on the average of emission rates from a minimum of 4 representative years in the last 10 years. RERs will be recalculated every three years, based on average emission rates from the last three years, and applied for purposes of receiving financial incentives provided that it falls below the previous RER.]

C.   Bolivia's Proposed REDD Mechanism

Bolivia and 16 other developing countries from Africa, Asia, Central and South America, and Oceania also submitted a proposal for reducing emissions from deforestation in developing countries (REDD). Their proposed REDD Mechanism would establish baseline emissions based on deforestation rates over a period of not less than five years. The REDD Mechanism would provide positive incentives, to be determined later for countries that reduce their emissions from deforestation. The proposal does not describe exactly what these incentives are, but they would not include penalties against countries that fail to reduce emissions from deforestation. In addition, it would establish two distinct funds for reducing emissions from deforestation in developing countries. The REDD Stabilization Fund would provide financial support to developing countries that have very low rates of deforestation and that seek to maintain existing forest areas. The funds would be supported through a tax on emission reduction units created through joint implementation projects or based on countries' original assigned amounts, a tax on carbon intensive commodities and services that are currently excluded from emissions reductions policies, and/or new and additional overseas development assistance or voluntary contributions. Lastly, a REDD Enabling Fund would provide financial assistance to developing countries to establish and improve data collection and carry out policies and measures, among other things, to facilitate participation in the REDD Mechanism and Stabilization Fund. Bolivia, *Reducing Emissions from Deforestation in Developing Countries: Approaches to Stimulate Action, in* FCCC/SBSTA/2007/MISC.2, 14–16 (March 2, 2007).

QUESTIONS AND DISCUSSION

1.   These proposals for compensation have generated substantial interest as a means to reduce deforestation and provide climate mitigation benefits. While similar, they differ in important ways. Consider the following issues:

a.   *Market vs. Non-market Approaches.* Do you think any of the proposals provide the right mix of market and non-market incentives to overcome the institutional and other problems identified by the IPCC?

b.   *Additionality, Leakage, Permanence.* Additionality, leakage, and permanence are major concerns with respect to all forest-related issues under the climate change regime. Do the proposals adequately address these issues?

c. **Compliance.** All three proposals carefully point out that the proposed mechanisms are voluntary. If the mechanism is voluntary, should a country be penalized for allowing deforestation to increase above the target rate?

d. **Low Deforestation Rates.** Not all countries have deforestation rates similar to Brazil and Indonesia. It would be perverse to reward countries with high rates of deforestation, like Brazil and Indonesia, without providing some reward for those countries already managing their forests effectively. How do the proposals address this issue? Do you agree that countries with relatively modest deforestation rates should be encouraged to participate by giving them a deforestation growth cap similar to the one Australia was given for its emissions cap? Under such a plan, a country that had a baseline deforestation rate of, for example, 5,000 km^2 per year might be given a cap of 10,000 km^2 per year. If they are not rewarded with growth caps, how should they be rewarded to prevent an incentive to deforest in order to take advantage of the compensation scheme?

2.   Supporters of a market-based approach point to the much larger financial benefits of a market-based approach. For example, if Brazil reduced deforestation by 10 percent against a baseline of average annual deforestation of about 20,000 km^2 for the 1980s, Brazil could earn $495 million per year, or $2.47 billion over five years based on a weighted average carbon price in 2004–2005 of $5.63/tCO$_2$. Paulo Moutinho et al., *Introduction, in* TROPICAL DEFORESTATION AND CLIMATE CHANGE (Paulo Moutinho & Stephan Schwartzman eds., 2005). According to these supporters, "It is hard to envision that ODA funds could increase to the hundreds of millions or even billions of dollars necessary to achieve large-scale reductions in emissions. It is even harder to envision why developed countries would invest in reducing deforestation emissions when those reductions would not be creditable and freely tradable in a global carbon market." Environmental Defense & Amazon Institute for Environmental Research, *Reducing Emissions from Deforestation in Developing Countries: Policy Approaches to Stimulate Action* 4–5 (Feb. 23, 2007). Do you agree? What are some of the advantages of a purely non-market-based compensation fund?

3.   **Value of Credits.** The market-based approaches will only work if the price of sequestering carbon is greater than the income derived from alternative economic uses of the land, such as logging or farming. Further, because the price of different crops varies, the scheme may be economically attractive in some places and not in others. To stimulate the market and ensure that a significant level of funding is available to developing countries, Greenpeace has proposed that Annex I Parties must purchase a minimum number of "deforestation credits." To ensure the price remains high enough to encourage developing countries to take action to avoid deforestation, it has also proposed a cap on the supply of "deforestation credits." Bill Hare & Kirsten Macey, *Tropical Deforestation Emission Reduction Mechanism: A Discussion Paper* 4 (Greenpeace, Dec. 2007). Does this strategy provide an effective strategy for overcoming the potential shortcomings of market-based approaches?

4.   One concern with providing tradeable credits for avoiding deforestation is that the credit will be relatively inexpensive compared to other credits. That could reduce the value of credits under the CDM. In addition, there is deep concern that project-based efforts to avoid deforestation under the CDM will not be able to control for leakage and non-permanence or adequately establish baselines for additionality. As a result, many view the country-wide, non-project-based approach of a REDD as more feasible, although it would be difficult to link such a scheme to the existing project-based Kyoto Protocol mechanisms. To what extent should a system of compensation for avoiding deforestation be tied to existing Kyoto Protocol mechanisms, such as the CDM?

5. *National Implementation.* To implement the compensated reductions plan, governments would have to adopt national level policies that encourage private landowners not to deforest their lands. What types of policies would you recommend?

6. The various compensation schemes are trumpeted as mechanisms that achieve an equitable distribution of the costs and allocation of benefits for reducing deforestation and implement the principle of common but differentiated responsibilities. Do you agree?

7. The climate change regime is rapidly becoming the most important international forest management regime, in part because governments have never been able to agree to a binding set of principles for sustainable forest management. Numerous global "dialogues" regarding forests have resulted in many non-binding statements or action plans. *See, e.g.*, Non-Legally Binding Authoritative Statement of Principles for a Global Consensus on the Management, Conservation and Sustainable Development of All Types of Forests, U.N.Doc.A/conf.151/26 (Vol III), reprinted at 31 I.L.M. 881 (1992). But despite nearly two decades of negotiations, no binding forest conservation regime yet exists. Those regimes that do exist, such as the International Tropical Timber Agreement, are criticized for being primarily commodity agreements focused on expanding timber production and trade. The UN Food and Agricultural Organization has primary authority to address forests in the UN system, but it too views forests primarily as units of production. To what extent do you think the climate change regime will be an appropriate or effective forum for forest conservation? Can it adequately address the many, sometimes conflicting, non-carbon values of forests, such as wood production, biodiversity conservation or protection of indigenous lands? Do any of the proposals outlined in this chapter address these non-climate values of forests?

8. Indigenous peoples and other traditional users of forests are in fact quite concerned that the climate change regime will catalyze further incursions into their territories with limited consultation or participation from forest dwellers. Forests and climate change were a major topic at the last meeting of the Permanent Forum on Indigenous Issues, which made the following recommendations:

> 44. The Permanent Forum recommends that the renewed political focus on forests stimulated by current policy debates on reducing emissions from deforestation and degradation (REDD) under the United Nations Framework Convention on Climate Change be used towards securing the rights of indigenous peoples living in forests and rewarding their historical stewardship role and continuing conservation and sustainable use of forests. According to the principle of free, prior and informed consent, indigenous peoples must not be excluded from, and should be centrally involved in and benefit from, deciding forest policies and programmes at all levels that deliver justice and equity and contribute to sustainable development, biodiversity protection and climate change mitigation and adaptation.

> 45. The Permanent Forum notes that the current framework for REDD is not supported by most indigenous peoples. It is argued that existing REDD proposals reinforce centralized top-down management of forests, and undermine indigenous peoples rights. In order to directly benefit indigenous peoples, new proposals for avoided deforestation or reduced emissions from deforestation must address the need for global and national policy reforms and be guided by the United Nations Declaration on the Rights of Indigenous Peoples, respecting rights to land, territories and resources; and the rights of self-determination and the free, prior and informed consent of the indigenous peoples concerned.

Report of the Seventh Session of the Permanent Forum on Indigenous Issues, E/2008/4, E/C.19/2008/13, paras 44–45 (21 April–2 May 2008). Should the climate regime accept these recommendations? For further discussion of the relationship between climate change and human rights, see Chapter 10, Section V.

9.   *Current Status.* At the Thirteenth Meeting of the Conference of the Parties (CoP13) in Bali in 2007, the Parties agreed on a negotiating framework for an agreement to follow the Kyoto Protocol. Among other things, the Parties agreed to consider "[p]olicy approaches and positive incentives on issues relating to reducing emissions from deforestation and forest degradation in developing countries; and the role of conservation, sustainable management of forests and enhancement of forest carbon stocks in developing countries." Decision 1/CP.13, *Bali Action Plan*, para. 1(b)(iii) (2007). A separate decision taken at CoP13 established a mandate for actions by the Parties to reduce emissions from deforestation in developing countries. The decision encourages Parties to "support capacity-building, provide technical assistance, facilitate the transfer of technology to improve, *inter alia*, data collection, estimation of emissions from deforestation and forest degradation, monitoring and reporting, and address the institutional needs of developing countries to estimate and reduce emissions from deforestation and forest degradation." It further encourages Parties "to explore a range of actions, identify options and undertake efforts, including demonstration activities, to address the drivers of deforestation." The Subsidiary Body on Scientific and Technological Assessment (SBSTA) will investigate methodological issues related to a range of policy approaches and positive incentives that reduce emissions from deforestation and forest degradation in developing countries. The SBSTA is expected to report on the outcomes, including any recommendations on possible methodological approaches, to the CoP in December 2008. Decision 2/CP.13, *Reducing Emissions from Deforestation in Developing Countries: Approaches to Stimulate Action* (2007).

As suggested by the proposals described above, the Parties have significantly divergent views on a number of major issues. In addition to the methodological issues surrounding additionality, leakage, and non-permanence, the "submissions of Parties" concerning this issue indicates that serious negotiations over the next two years are needed to address the following issues:

a)   whether market-based mechanisms should be used, alone or in combination with nonmarket mechanisms;

b)   whether (or to what extent) Annex I Parties may use credits from reduced emissions to meet their reduction commitments;

c)   whether and how to compensate countries without significant deforestation or that have net removals due to afforestation and other forest management practices;

d)   whether and how to compensate reduced emissions from forest degradation;

e)   whether gross or net emissions should be used; and

f)   whether non-CO_2 emissions will be included;

See generally FCCC/SBSTA/2007/MISC.2, 14–16 (March 2, 2007). How do you think these issues should be resolved?

Chapter 8

COMPLIANCE AND DISPUTE SETTLEMENT

Almost all nations observe almost all principles of international law and almost all of their obligations almost all of the time.
—LOUIS HENKIN, HOW NATIONS BEHAVE: LAW AND FOREIGN POLICY 47 (1979)

SYNOPSIS

I. **Introduction**
II. **Compliance under Multilateral Environmental Agreements**
III. **Compliance Within the Climate Change Regime**
    A. **The Climate Change Convention**
    B. **The Kyoto Protocol**
        1. **The Kyoto Protocol's Compliance Mechanism**
        2. **The Consequences of Noncompliance**
IV. **Dispute Settlement**
    A. **Settlement of Disputes under the Climate Change Regime**
    B. **Climate Disputes under Customary International Law**
        1. **The Duty Not to Cause Environmental Harm**
        2. **State Responsibility**

I. INTRODUCTION

The success of any international treaty depends on whether the Parties to the treaty implement the treaty through national legislation and comply with the treaty's obligations. Often nations comply with their international obligations out of national interest: they comply because the advantages of compliance outweigh the benefits of noncompliance. At other times, these countries may be *unwilling* to comply or, as is the case for many developing countries, they may be *unable* to comply due to a lack of resources or technical capacity. For these reasons, multilateral environmental agreements frequently include provisions for enforcement, including deterrence- and sanctions-based penalties and other measures levied against violators, as well as provisions to facilitate compliance through capacity building, technology transfer, education, and other "carrots." Thus, compliance strategies may differ depending on the severity of the problem or the underlying cause of the noncompliance. The goal is to develop both an equitable and effective approach to compliance — one flexible enough to treat different countries differently, yet strong enough to ensure that commitments are met over time.

The use of multiple compliance strategies is particularly important at the international level, because simply litigating a Party's noncompliance is almost never a realistic option — litigation before the International Court of Justice (ICJ) rarely occurs in any context and has never occurred to enforce compliance with an international environmental treaty. As a result, enforcement of treaty rules tends to occur within the treaty regime itself. While treaties typically include provisions for binding dispute settlement through the ICJ or arbitration, they tend to use a mix of capacity building, self reporting on implementation, review of the reports by Parties or technical bodies, and, sometimes, an assessment of a Party's compliance.

With respect to climate change, the success of the Kyoto Protocol quite obviously depends on whether the Parties meet their targets and timetables. In turn, whether Parties meet their targets and timetables depends on the quality and timeliness of the data on greenhouse gas emissions provided by the Parties and the reliability of the Parties to determine whether Joint Implementation and Clean Development Mechanism projects result in reductions in emissions that are additional to any that would have occurred in the absence of the project. For many countries, however, the benefits of noncompliance — the avoidance of costs to domestic industries to reduce greenhouse gas emissions — may outweigh the more diffuse, largely global, benefits of compliance. Thus, it is essential that the Kyoto Protocol have an equitable and effective means for ensuring compliance.

Section II of this chapter explores the emerging trends in compliance mechanisms now found within international environmental treaties. As you read these materials, consider what types of compliance measures the UNFCCC and the Kyoto Protocol *should* include. Section III then provides an overview of the actual compliance mechanisms of the UNFCCC and the Kyoto Protocol and assesses their strengths and weaknesses. Section IV briefly describes the process for international dispute resolution for both climate-related disputes brought under the UNFCCC or Kyoto Protocol and disputes brought more generally under emerging principles of customary international environmental law — for example, claims brought by a low-lying island nation against a major emitter of greenhouse gases.

II. COMPLIANCE UNDER MULTILATERAL ENVIRONMENTAL AGREEMENTS

Multilateral environmental agreements (MEAs) have adopted a large number of compliance strategies. Xeuman Wang and Glenn Wiser explore these strategies in the following excerpt.

XEUMAN WANG & GLENN WISER, THE IMPLEMENTATION AND COMPLIANCE REGIMES UNDER THE CLIMATE CHANGE CONVENTION AND ITS KYOTO PROTOCOL
11 RECIEL 181, 181–184 (2002)[*]

Since the 1972 Stockholm Conference on the Human Environment, more than 200 MEAs have been developed. An important challenge confronting governments and the international community has been how best to implement and comply with the commitments under environmental treaties, including how to deal with countries that fail to meet their treaty obligations.

The traditional, adversarial approach to addressing non-compliance — in which States seek damages for harm caused by injurious behaviour, or in which they suspend their performance under a treaty in response to another's failure to perform — has inherent disadvantages for MEAs. Many MEAs deal with the

---

'global commons,' such as the atmosphere, oceans, or biological diversity. Thus, it can be difficult or impossible for a State to establish the causal link between an injury it suffers and a specific act of non-compliance by another State. Moreover, States have been reluctant to use the International Court of Justice (ICJ) to resolve cases of non-compliance under MEAs, because ICJ proceedings tend to be very time-consuming and inherently confrontational, thereby posing political risks to bilateral relationships. For similar reasons, the dispute-settlement mechanisms provided in most MEAs have rarely been used. Instead, a discrete compliance theory has gradually evolved in which compliance under MEAs is addressed in three ways: preventing non-compliance, facilitating compliance and managing compliance.

Preventing Non-Compliance

Most MEAs are intended to protect the global commons. One country's non-compliance thus harms everyone, and reciprocating that country's non-compliance by suspending one's own compliance with the treaty will only make the situation worse. Consequently, the task of devising effective mechanisms for compliance and enforcement in MEAs is difficult. Because reciprocity will mean only greater environmental damage, MEAs must, in the first instance, strive to prevent non-compliance. States have tried to accomplish this by concentrating on facilitating and managing compliance, rather than punishing non-compliance.

Facilitating Compliance

The capacity of a State to comply with its commitments under an MEA is often the key factor that determines its status of compliance. Building up a domestic compliance system to implement an MEA requires sufficient technical, bureaucratic and financial resources. A party may adopt a commitment in good faith, but nevertheless fail to comply due to lack of resources or capacity. * * *

Lack of sufficient capacity for compliance is common in developing countries. Environmental issues do not receive priority in the agendas of many developing country governments because limited resources must be allocated to more pressing concerns. In many cases, developing countries are unable to comply with their MEA obligations unless they receive outside assistance.

As non-compliance is thus often due not to willful disobedience, but instead to a lack of capability, approaches for addressing non-compliance must be directed at the root of the problem. Two policy instruments, among others, are now used in MEAs to induce compliance: capacity building and reduction of compliance costs.

Capacity building strives to enhance the ability of States to implement and comply with their commitments. In MEAs, capacity building may include technical and financial assistance, transfer of technology, training and education. For example, the Global Environmental Facility (GEF) administered by the World Bank Group funds developing countries to assist them in implementing their obligations in focal areas such as climate change and biodiversity. Outside of the World Bank system, the Montreal Protocol Fund has successfully supported projects in developing countries that have resulted in a considerable phase-out of the consumption of ozone-depleting substances.

Some MEAs affirmatively link [developing-country] compliance with the availability of financial resources. For instance, Article 20(4) of the Convention on Biological Diversity states that:

the extent to which developing country Parties will effectively implement their commitments under this Convention will depend on the effective implementation by developed country Parties of their commitments under this Convention related to financial resources and transfer of technology and will take fully into account the fact that economic and social development and eradication of poverty are the first and overriding priorities of the developing country Parties.

The second policy instrument is intended to make compliance easier by lowering its costs. Some commentators predict that compliance costs in MEAs like the Kyoto Protocol could be substantial. To encourage compliance, the Kyoto Protocol creates market-based mechanisms to increase flexibility and cost effectiveness. As discussed in the third part of this article, these mechanisms will facilitate the attainment of the Protocol's environmental obligations, while assisting States to secure economic and social policy objectives as well.

Managing Compliance

Policy instruments alone are insufficient to address compliance in MEAs. To address this gap, managerial approaches have been developed to handle compliance in a systematic manner. The most common of these is the establishment of a regulatory framework, or compliance system. The purpose of these systems is to make compliance processes transparent, to identify any potential compliance problems at an early stage, to help parties fix problems and, finally, to respond to non-compliance.

A comprehensive compliance system may contain three steps: (1) reporting, (2) verification, and (3) assessing compliance and responding to non-compliance. Each is reviewed in turn below.

Reporting. The first step in the compliance systems of most MEAs is self-reporting by parties. Parties report information on their performance in implementing their treaty commitments. They may also include information submitted by international organizations or non-government organizations (NGOs), as is the practice under the Convention on International Trade in Endangered Species (CITES). To improve the quality of data and ensure timely reporting, technical and financial assistance may be needed to help parties — in particular developing countries — collect and prepare their national reports. As the data generated in the reports constitute the basis for assessing compliance in the future, it is important to establish a uniform format of reporting, with clear and precise requirements as to how and what to report.

Verification. The second compliance step is verification of the reported information. Key considerations are who will conduct the verification and how they will do it. The Convention Secretariats or a group of experts may undertake the task of checking the reliability and accuracy of data. On-site monitoring with the consent of parties may also be an option to verify compliance. The UNFCCC and the Ramsar Convention on Wetlands authorize country visits to review implementation of their obligations. However, unlike the practice in arms-control agreements, such as the Chemical Weapons Convention, verification processes under MEAs are generally non-confrontational, and have the aim of discovering problems and helping parties to fix them so that they can avoid non-compliance.

Assessing Compliance and Responding to Non-Compliance. One of the most common features of compliance assessments under MEAs is their non-judicial nature. Most assessments are conducted in a facilitative, cooperative manner aimed at helping to bring parties back to compliance. The Montreal Protocol was the first major environmental treaty to create an institutionalized non-compliance procedure. The Protocol's Implementation Committee identifies facts and possible causes of individual cases of non-compliance. It makes recommendations to the party concerned on ways to remedy the non-compliance, and can provide and arrange for assistance, including technical assistance for data collection, financial assistance and transfer of technology. More MEAs now follow the Montreal Protocol model, calling for the establishment of specialized compliance procedures carried out by a standing compliance committee empowered to assess the compliance of parties.

Backing up the compliance assessment are the responses to non-compliance mandated under the regime. So far, only a few MEAs explicitly provide for response measures to non-compliance. These measures may include the provision of technical and financial assistance, publication of cases of non-compliance, issuance of cautions, or suspension of treaty rights and privileges. . . . Stronger enforcement measures ('sticks'), in which trade sanctions or threats of trade sanctions have been used to enforce compliance, have been explored in MEAs such as CITES.

It should be noted that the strictness and comprehensiveness of a compliance regime under an MEA depends to a significant extent on the nature of the commitment embodied in the agreement. Not all MEAs need to adopt the full three-step system outlined above. If the nature of the commitments in the agreement is both general and soft (thus, leaving much of its interpretation and implementation up to the discretion of individual parties), a strong compliance system may not be appropriate. On the other hand, if an MEA contains hard, precise and measurable commitments, a comprehensive compliance regime with 'teeth' may provide an effective way to prevent free riders and ensure the full implementation of the obligations.

QUESTIONS AND DISCUSSION

1.   The mix of carrots and sticks has been essential to the effectiveness of the compliance mechanisms of the Montreal Protocol and CITES. Ultimately, however, the threat of trade sanctions or other penalty appears essential. For example, when the Montreal Protocol's Implementation Committee publicly invited nine Parties to explain their persistent failure to supply their baseline data, only five of those countries submitted their data before the meeting. Another 17 Parties submitted missing data only after the Implementation Committee recommended that they lose their Article 5 status — a status that makes them eligible for funding under the Montreal Protocol's Multilateral Fund and the Global Environment Facility. David G. Victor, *The Operation and Effectiveness of the Montreal Protocol's Non-Compliance Procedure, in* THE IMPLEMENTATION AND EFFECTIVENESS OF INTERNATIONAL ENVIRONMENTAL COMMITMENTS 137 (David G. Victor et al. eds., 1998).

Under CITES, which regulates international trade in species of conservation concern, all Parties are required to have adequate implementing legislation. If a Party does not have adequate legislation, it is offered technical assistance from the Secretariat. Nonetheless, this assistance is sometimes refused. If after a period of years the Party fails to implement adequate legislation, then the Parties recommend the suspension of trade in CITES-listed wildlife with that Party.

A situation involving seven parties highlights how the positive and negative incentives of the CITES compliance process operate. These seven parties were known to have significant implementation problems and the parties had worked for several years to help them. Finally, the parties directed the CITES Standing Committee to determine if trade should be suspended in CITES specimens with these seven countries. Doc. SC.42.12.2, "Implementation of the Convention in individual countries: Implementation of Decisions 10.18 and 10.64."

The Standing Committee noted that only Indonesia, Malaysia-Sabah, and Nicaragua had demonstrated that they had adopted new legislation that generally met the requirements for the implementation of CITES. The four remaining parties, the Democratic Republic of the Congo, Egypt, Guyana, and Senegal, had failed to adopt appropriate legislation. As a result, the Standing Committee recommended to the parties that the trade in specimens of CITES-listed species with Egypt, Guyana, and Senegal be suspended unless the Secretariat verified in the meantime that the countries had enacted legislation that generally meets the requirements of CITES. It agreed, however, that in the case of Senegal, there would be no such suspension if the Standing Committee agreed, at its next meeting, on a recommendation from the Secretariat, that Senegal enacted legislation that generally meets the requirement for the implementation of CITES. Regarding the Democratic Republic of the Congo, the Standing Committee agreed to defer a decision for two meetings. The Secretariat then sent three letters of reminder to these Parties, pointing out the need to adopt legislation meeting the criteria specified in Resolution Conf. 8.4 and, in particular, advising Senegal that its case would be considered again at the next meeting of the Standing Committee. By the time the Standing Committee met one month later, Egypt had adopted adequate legislation and averted trade sanctions. Without progress from Guyana and Senegal, the Secretariat notified the parties that they should refuse any trade with Senegal and Guyana in CITES specimens until further notice. Five days after the recommendation to impose trade sanctions, Guyana submitted regulations to the Secretariat that adequately implemented CITES; Senegal took about 75 days to adopt adequate legislation and, as with Guyana, the recommendation of trade sanctions was withdrawn.

CHRIS WOLD, SANFORD GAINES, & GREG BLOCK, TRADE AND THE ENVIRONMENT: LAW AND POLICY 661–62 (2005). For a comprehensive analysis of CITES and compliance, see ROSALIND REEVE, POLICING INTERNATIONAL TRADE IN ENDANGERED SPECIES: THE CITES TREATY AND COMPLIANCE (2002); *see also* Marceil Yeater & Juan Carlos Vasquez, *Demystifying the Relationship between CITES and the WTO*, 10 RE-CEIL 271, 274–275 (2000).

2.   Unlike the Montreal Protocol and CITES, which cover trade in specific substances or species, the UNFCCC and Kyoto Protocol seek to reduce emissions of certain gases which derive from a large variety of sources. Are trade sanctions a realistic option for penalizing noncompliance with a Party's commitment to reduce or limit greenhouse gas emissions? If not, what types of penalties might be effective for ensuring that Parties submit their inventories of greenhouse gases and meet their targets and timetables? For further information on trade sanctions and the rules of the World Trade Organization, see Chapter 10, Section VI.

III.   COMPLIANCE WITHIN THE CLIMATE CHANGE REGIME

A.   The Climate Change Convention

Although the UNFCCC does not set any targets and timetables or otherwise commit Parties to reduce emissions of greenhouse gases, it does establish a three-step process for reporting, reviewing, and assessing a Party's performance of certain provisions. Article 12 requires Parties to report their greenhouse gas inventories each year. Annex I Parties must also periodically submit national reports on their overall implementation of the UNFCCC — known as "national communications" — according to dates set by the Conference of the Parties (CoP). The fourth national communications were due on January 1, 2006. Non-Annex I Parties must also submit national communications, but they do not have fixed dates for submitting them. Nonetheless, 132 of 148 non-Annex I Parties have submitted their initial national communications. They have been asked to submit their second national communications (or in some cases their third), although the Parties have made clear that the least developed countries have flexibility in completing their communications. Decision 8/CP.11, *Submission of Second and, Where Appropriate, Third National Communications from Parties Not Included in Annex I to the Convention* (2005).

The Secretariat is charged with compiling the information, which is then reviewed by technical experts. Unlike the communication from non-Annex I Parties, the national communications of Annex I Parties then undergo an "in-depth" review by a team of international experts, coordinated by the UNFCCC Secretariat, which results in an "in depth review report." With the consent of the reporting Party, the technical experts may make an in-country visit to ensure the accuracy and consistency of the information. These reports have, at times, identified implementation problems or suggested areas where implementation could be improved. However, because the UNFCCC does not commit Parties to concrete actions, other than the reports themselves, it is almost impossible to determine whether a Party is in noncompliance. To address specific implementation concerns in a less political forum, the Parties contemplated the establishment of a ten-member multilateral consultative committee. However, they failed to agree on the committee's composition and size.

In addition, the Parties directed two subsidiary bodies, the Subsidiary Body for Implementation (SBI) and the Subsidiary Body for Technological Advice (SBSTA) to provide the CoP with scientific and technical information and guidance on the steps that Parties have taken to implement their obligations. While the two bodies have "actively promoted the implementation process of the UNFCCC and have provided a forum for Parties to conduct a constructive dialogue on the general problems of implementation," the politicized nature of their processes has stifled actions to improve implementation. Wang & Wiser, at 185.

QUESTIONS AND DISCUSSION

In negotiating the UNFCCC, the Parties well understood that developing countries would need assistance in implementing the treaty. To that end, Article 4.3 directs developed countries to provide "new and additional financial resources to meet the agreed full costs incurred by developing country Parties in complying with their [reporting] obligations." That article also directs developed countries to "provide such financial resources, including for the transfer of technology," that developing countries need to meet "the agreed full incremental costs" of implementing measures under Article 4.1, such as the development of programs for greenhouse gas mitigation. This emphasis on capacity-building has been an important part of the successful implementation of the Montreal Protocol and is widely seen as critical to the future of the climate change regime.

B.   The Kyoto Protocol

The inclusion of specific targets and timetables in the Kyoto Protocol, as well as the perceived economic benefits that noncompliance could bring, helped push compliance mechanisms to the forefront of the Kyoto Protocol negotiations. Given the difficulties of negotiating agreement on any commitments, the negotiators were unable to develop a fully fledged compliance regime. However, the Kyoto Protocol inherited the UNFCCC's procedures and institutions, including the SBSTA and SBI. With respect to reporting, the Parties have continued to improve the quality and ensure the comparability of the data submitted by Parties.

Moreover, Article 8 of the Kyoto Protocol requires expert review teams to review Annex I Parties' annual inventory of anthropogenic emissions by sources and removals by sinks of greenhouse gases. The expert review teams also review each Annex I Party's submissions concerning its compliance with its commitments under the Protocol. The expert review teams, composed of experts nominated by the Parties and, as appropriate, by intergovernmental organizations, are expected to provide a comprehensive technical assessment of all aspects of a Party's implementation of the Protocol.

1.   *The Kyoto Protocol's Compliance Mechanism*

In negotiating the Kyoto Protocol, the Parties could not reach consensus on the details of a compliance regime. Instead, Article 18 committed the Parties, at their first meeting, to adopt "appropriate and effective procedures and mechanisms to determine and to address cases of non-compliance." Article 18 placed an importation limitation on any future compliance regime, however, by requiring any mechanism with legally binding compliance measures to be adopted by means of an amendment to the Protocol. Despite this limitation, the Parties developed a compliance mechanism with consequences, if not legally binding measures, through Decision 27/CMP.1, Annex, *Procedures and Mechanisms Relating to Compliance under the Kyoto Protocol* (2005). That compliance mechanism, described below, includes two separate branches: a "facilitative" branch and an "enforcement" branch.

UNFCCC SECRETARIAT, AN INTRODUCTION TO THE KYOTO PROTOCOL COMPLIANCE MECHANISM
available at,
http://unfccc.int/kyoto_protocol/compliance/introduction/items/3024.php

The Kyoto Protocol compliance mechanism is designed to strengthen the Protocol's environmental integrity, support the carbon market's credibility and ensure transparency of accounting by Parties. Its objective is to facilitate, promote and enforce compliance with the commitments under the Protocol. . . .

The Compliance Committee is made up of two branches: a facilitative branch and an enforcement branch. As their names suggest, the facilitative branch aims to provide advice and assistance to Parties in order to promote compliance, whereas the enforcement branch has the responsibility to determine consequences for Parties not meeting their commitments. Both branches are composed of 10 members, including one representative from each of the five official UN regions (Africa, Asia, Latin America and the Caribbean, Central and Eastern Europe, and Western Europe and Others), one from the small island developing States, and two each from Annex I and non-Annex I Parties. The Committee also meets in a plenary composed of members of both branches, and a bureau, made up of the chairperson and vice-chairperson of each branch, supports its work. Decisions of the plenary and the facilitative branch may be taken by a three-quarters majority, while decisions of the enforcement branch require, in addition, a double majority of both Annex I and non-Annex I Parties.

Through its branches, the [Compliance] Committee considers questions of implementation which can be raised by expert review teams under Article 8 of the Protocol, any Party with respect to itself, or a Party with respect to another Party (supported by corroborating information). Each Party designates an agent who signs submissions containing such questions, as well as comments. The bureau of the Committee allocates a question of implementation to the appropriate branch, based on their mandates. In addition, at any time during its consideration of a question of implementation, the enforcement branch may refer a question of implementation to the facilitative branch.

The enforcement branch is responsible for determining whether a Party included in Annex I (Annex I Party) is not in compliance with its emissions targets, the methodological and reporting requirements for greenhouse gas inventories, and the eligibility requirements under the mechanisms. In case of disagreements between a Party and an expert review team, the enforcement branch shall determine whether to apply adjustments to greenhouse gas inventories or to correct the compilation and accounting database for the accounting of assigned amounts.

The mandate of the facilitative branch is to provide advice and facilitation to Parties in implementing the Protocol, and to promote compliance by Parties with their Kyoto commitments. It is responsible for addressing questions of implementation by Annex I Parties of response measures aimed at mitigating climate change in a way that minimizes their adverse impacts on developing countries and the use by Annex I Parties of the mechanisms as "supplemental" to domestic action. Furthermore, the facilitative branch may provide "early warning" of potential non-compliance with emissions targets, methodological and reporting commitments relating to greenhouse gas inventories, and commitments on reporting supplementary information in a Party's annual inventory.

* * *

In the case of the enforcement branch, each type of non-compliance requires a specific course of action. For instance, where the enforcement branch has determined that the emissions of a Party have exceeded its assigned amount, it must declare that that Party is in non-compliance and require the Party to make up the difference between its emissions and its assigned amount during the second commitment period, plus an additional deduction of 30%. In addition, it shall require the Party to submit a compliance action plan and suspend the eligibility of the Party to make transfers under emissions trading until the Party is reinstated.

No such correspondence exists in the case of the facilitative branch, which can decide to provide advice and facilitation of assistance to individual Parties regarding the implementation of the Protocol, facilitate financial and technical assistance to any Party concerned, including technology transfer and capacity building and/or formulate recommendations to the Party concerned.

In the enforcement branch, questions of implementation will be resolved within approximately 35 weeks from receipt by the branch of the question of implementation. In time-sensitive requests, including those relating to eligibility to participate in the mechanisms, the expedited procedures involving shorter periods will apply. Apart from the three-week deadline given to complete its preliminary examination, no fixed deadlines are provided for the facilitative branch.

The branches of the Compliance Committee will base their deliberations on reports from expert review teams, the subsidiary bodies, Parties and other official sources. Competent intergovernmental and non-governmental organizations may submit relevant factual and technical information to the relevant branch after the preliminary examination.

There are detailed procedures with specific timeframes for the enforcement branch, including the opportunity for a Party facing the Compliance Committee to make formal written submissions and request a hearing where it can present its views and call on expert testimony.

Any Party not complying with reporting requirements must develop a compliance action plan as well, and Parties that are found not to meet the criteria for participating in the mechanisms will have their eligibility withdrawn. In all cases, the enforcement branch will make a public declaration that the Party is in non-compliance and will also make public the consequences to be applied.

If a Party's eligibility is withdrawn or suspended, it may request, either through an expert review team or directly to the enforcement branch, to have its eligibility restored if it believes it has rectified the problem and is again meeting the relevant criteria.

In the case of compliance with emission targets, Annex I Parties have 100 days after the expert review of their final annual emissions inventory has finished to make up any shortfall in compliance (e.g., by acquiring AAUs, CERs, ERUs or RMUs through emissions trading). If, at the end of this period, a Party's emissions are still greater than its assigned amount, the enforcement branch will declare the Party to be in non-compliance and apply the consequences outlined above.

As a general rule, decisions taken by the two branches of the Committee cannot be appealed. The exception is a decision of the enforcement branch relating to emissions targets. Even then, a Party can only appeal [to the Conference of the Parties serving as the meeting of the Parties to the Protocol] if it believes it has been denied due process.

2. *The Consequences of Noncompliance*

The Kyoto Protocol's compliance mechanism treats different noncompliance issues differently. For example, the duty to establish a national system for estimating anthropogenic emissions of greenhouse gases is subject to the facilitative branch's carrot approach to compliance. In contrast, the penalty provisions of the enforcement branch apply to noncompliance with binding targets and timetables. As a consequence, only Annex I Parties are currently subject to the enforcement branch.

DECISION 27/CMP.1, ANNEX, PROCEDURES AND MECHANISMS RELATING TO COMPLIANCE UNDER THE KYOTO PROTOCOL (2005)

XIV. Consequences applied by the Facilitative Branch

The facilitative branch, taking into account the principle of common but differentiated responsibilities and respective capabilities, shall decide on the application of one or more of the following consequences:

(a)   Provision of advice and facilitation of assistance to individual Parties regarding the implementation of the Protocol;

(b)   Facilitation of financial and technical assistance to any Party concerned, including technology transfer and capacity building from sources other than those established under the Convention and the Protocol for the developing countries;

(c)   Facilitation of financial and technical assistance, including technology transfer and capacity building, taking into account Article 4, paragraphs 3, 4 and 5, of the Convention; and

(d)   Formulation of recommendations to the Party concerned, taking into account Article 4, paragraph 7, of the Convention.

XV. Consequences applied by the Enforcement Branch

1.   Where the enforcement branch has determined that a Party is not in compliance with Article 5, paragraph 1 or paragraph 2, or Article 7, paragraph 1 or paragraph 4, of the Protocol, it shall apply the following consequences, taking into account the cause, type, degree and frequency of the non-compliance of that Party:

　　(a)   Declaration of non-compliance; and

　　(b)   Development of a plan in accordance with paragraphs 2 and 3 below.

2.   The Party not in compliance under paragraph 1 above, shall, within three months after the determination of non-compliance, or such longer period that the enforcement branch considers appropriate, submit to the enforcement branch for review and assessment a plan that includes:

　　(a)   An analysis of the causes of non-compliance of the Party;

　　(b)   Measures that the Party intends to implement in order to remedy the non-compliance; and

(c)   A timetable for implementing such measures within a time frame not exceeding twelve months which enables the assessment of progress in the implementation.

3.   The Party not in compliance under paragraph 1 above shall submit to the enforcement branch progress reports on the implementation of the plan on a regular basis.

4.   Where the enforcement branch has determined that a Party included in Annex I does not meet one or more of the eligibility requirements under Articles 6, 12 and 17 of the Protocol, it shall suspend the eligibility of that Party in accordance with relevant provisions under those articles. At the request of the Party concerned, eligibility may be reinstated in accordance with the procedure in section X, paragraph 2 [requiring a finding by an expert review team indicating that the eligibility requirements are met].

5.   Where the enforcement branch has determined that the emissions of a Party have exceeded its assigned amount . . . it shall declare that that Party is not in compliance with its commitments under Article 3, paragraph 1, of the Protocol, and shall apply the following consequences:

(a)   Deduction from the Party's assigned amount for the second commitment period of a number of tonnes equal to 1.3 times the amount in tonnes of excess emissions;

(b)   Development of a compliance action plan in accordance with paragraphs 6 and 7 below; and

(c)   Suspension of the eligibility to make transfers under Article 17 of the Protocol until the Party is reinstated in accordance with section X, paragraph 3 or paragraph 4.

6.   The Party not in compliance under paragraph 5 above shall, within three months after the determination of non-compliance or, where the circumstances of an individual case so warrant, such longer period that the enforcement branch considers appropriate, submit to the enforcement branch for review and assessment a compliance action plan that includes:

(a)   An analysis of the causes of the non-compliance of the Party;

(b)   Action that the Party intends to implement in order to meet its quantified emission limitation or reduction commitment in the subsequent commitment period, giving priority to domestic policies and measures; and

(c)   A timetable for implementing such action, which enables the assessment of annual progress in the implementation, within a time frame that does not exceed three years or up to the end of the subsequent commitment period, whichever occurs sooner. At the request of the Party, the enforcement branch may, where the circumstances of an individual case so warrant, extend the time for implementing such action for a period which shall not exceed the maximum period of three years mentioned above.

7.   The Party not in compliance under paragraph 5 above shall submit to the enforcement branch a progress report on the implementation of the compliance action plan on an annual basis.

8.   For subsequent commitment periods, the rate referred to in paragraph 5 (a) above shall be determined by an amendment.

Designing appropriate and effective noncompliance measures in an international regime is always a difficult tight-rope walk: if the consequences are too severe, governments simply refuse to consent to the mechanism; if they are too soft, then they are unlikely to deter noncompliance. Did the Parties get the balance right?

XEUMAN WANG & GLENN WISER, THE IMPLEMENTATION AND COMPLIANCE REGIMES UNDER THE CLIMATE CHANGE CONVENTION AND ITS KYOTO PROTOCOL
11 RECIEL 181, 196–197 (2002)

Two types of consequences were adopted for the Protocol . . . This first type of consequences includes those associated with the facilitative branch. They are purely facilitative in nature, such as advice, financial and technical assistance, and recommendations. These measures aim to assist parties in their efforts to avoid non-compliance or return to compliance. Due to their generally non-confrontational nature, the facilitative consequences received relatively little attention from the JWG [Joint Working Group].

The second type includes the consequences imposed by the enforcement branch. Regarding these consequences, the most contentious issues were what would happen if a party failed to honour its Protocol, Article 3(1) emissions reduction target, and what would be the nature of those consequences. The remainder of this section discusses those consequences related to Article 3(1).

Deduction of Excess Emissions from a Party's Future Emissions Allowance (Assigned Amount). The deduction proposal was also known as "restoration of tonnes" and — derisively by many environmentalists — as "borrowing." The rationale behind deduction was partly based on the assumption that it would provide incentives for parties to comply with their targets during the first commitment period, because deducting excess tonnes from the subsequent commitment period would significantly increase the difficulty and cost of compliance for that period. Yet several problems were identified for this consequence. First, deduction from the second commitment period will not truly make up for the excess emissions in the first unless there is some extra means of ensuring that the non-complying party does, in fact, reduce its emissions during the second period. Many commentators predicted that the party would in fact simply "borrow" from commitment period to commitment period, in the same way that someone might pass on debt indefinitely into the future until the system was forced to accept that the debt would never be repaid.

Second, commentators were concerned that the party facing deduction would simply negotiate its second (or third) commitment period targets to a higher amount of emissions, to accommodate for the deduction. As stated by the Australian Department of Foreign Affairs and Trade, "[p]arties would simply take into account any anticipated subtraction of emission in negotiating their targets for the subsequent commitment period, thus removing the incentive." Moreover, there was little agreement on what the correct deduction rate should be or how it should be calculated, with some parties arguing that a one-to-one deduction rate would provide the proper compliance incentives, while others replying that discount rates, opportunity costs of money, compliance theory and various other analyses should be taken into account in arriving at the number.

Despite the well-recognized shortcomings of deduction, parties eventually consented to it because no other politically feasible or realistic non-compliance response seemed possible. While most Annex I parties agreed that the Protocol would require a strong compliance system, they were generally loath to expose themselves to the possibility of non-compliance consequences with "teeth", such as financial penalties or trade measures. The deduction rate that was finally adopted, 1.3-to-1, "split the difference" between those who wanted a higher penalty rate and those who preferred a one-to-one deduction.

Compliance Action Plan. The compliance action plan was proposed by the EU as a way to make deductions more palatable to parties that supported stronger consequences. This consequence requires an Annex I party that has exceeded its emissions target to submit a plan explaining specifically how it will comply with its emissions reduction targets for the subsequent commitment period. The plan is subject to "review and assessment" by the enforcement branch. The rationale of the compliance action plan is that it will provide a means for the enforcement branch to remain involved in the efforts of a non-complying party to meet its subsequent, reduced target, thereby reducing the likelihood that the party will simply 'roll-over' its emissions excess into commitment period after commitment period.

The major concern of some negotiators was that the enforcement branch might use the compliance action plan requirement to dictate to a party the specific means by which it must return to compliance; in particular, the extent to which it could use the Kyoto flexible mechanisms instead of purely domestic actions. These negotiators believed that such a situation would amount to the enforcement branch being able to order a party to adopt specific policies and measures to reach its targets, which was an approach that was specifically rejected during the Kyoto negotiations (and consequently not included in the Protocol). In the end, the compliance action plan language that was adopted did not give the enforcement branch the power to "approve" a compliance action plan. Instead, the enforcement branch is empowered to 'review and assess' the plan after the party submits it.

Suspension of Eligibility to Participate in International Emissions Trading. Many multilateral treaty regimes provide for suspension of a State's rights and privileges when a State fails to honour its treaty obligations. Because participation in the Protocol's emissions trading mechanism will be an important part of many parties' efforts to comply with their targets in a cost-effective manner, the prospects of losing that privilege could provide parties with a powerful incentive to restore themselves to compliance or avoid non-compliance in the first place. Moreover, because the integrity of the trading regime is predicated on the notion that a party will only transfer surplus, valid emissions credits, and not credits that it needs for its own compliance, most negotiators agreed that a non-compliant party should not be allowed to make any emissions trading transfers until it has demonstrated that it will be able to comply with its current emissions target.

The only major point of contention regarding this consequence was how a suspended party would have its eligibility to trade reinstated. In the final Marrakesh rules, parties agreed upon specific reinstatement procedures that create a presumption that the enforcement branch will reinstate a party's eligibility after the party requests it to do so. However, the rules allow the enforcement branch to deny reinstatement if it believes the party has not complied, or will not be able to comply, with its emissions targets for the subsequent commitment period.

Compliance Fund. One alternative to deductions that was considered by negotiators was a compliance fund, which was included in the various compliance negotiating drafts prior to the adoption of the Bonn Agreement. The compliance fund was intended as a mechanism that would allow parties to remedy or avoid a finding of non-compliance by making payments to a fund that would invest the proceeds in GHG mitigation projects. Either a domestic or an international entity could have administered the fund. While one version or another of the compliance fund attracted the support of many parties, it was eventually dropped because some countries perceived it as a potential form of financial penalty, while others suspected that it would be used to set a "price cap" on the compliance cost of parties.

Financial Penalty. Financial penalties are rarely used in multilateral agreements, partly because there are few effective ways to ensure that they will be paid. During the JWG's discussions, many parties felt that the prospect of financial penalties for non-compliance with their emissions targets would make it politically difficult for them to win domestic support for the Protocol. Although financial penalties appeared in some of the compliance text drafts during the negotiations, they never received broad enough support from parties to make them a realistic prospect for adoption.

QUESTIONS AND DISCUSSION

1.   Carefully review the compliance procedures above and answer the following questions:

- Which compliance issues are allocated to the facilitative branch and which are allocated to the enforcement branch? Considering the consequences of noncompliance, do you think this allocation is appropriate?

- Which body makes the final decision concerning compliance measures, the Compliance Committee or the CoP/MoP? Which body do you think should make such decisions?

- Which compliance measures may be appealed? On what grounds may a Party appeal? To whom is the appeal directed?

2.   Wang and Wiser note that the Parties adopted the emissions deduction scheme for noncompliance with emission targets because "no other politically feasible or realistic non-compliance response seemed possible." Do you agree? As mentioned earlier in this chapter, the use of trade measures has been very effective within the Convention on International Trade in Endangered Species of Wild Fauna and Flora (CITES). What kind of trade measures, if any, would be appropriate in the climate change context? Can you think of alternative penalties to trade measures or emissions deductions?

3.   *Proportionality.* A major issue concerning any international compliance scheme is proportionality — that is, penalties or other measures to redress noncompliance should be proportionate to the nature of the obligation and seriousness of the breach, taking into account the cause, type, degree, and frequency of noncompliance. If a Party fails to report its emissions, it is impossible to ascertain what its baseline emissions are and whether it is meeting its targets and timetables. What measure is proportional to this offense? If a party fails to meet its target by one percent, what constitutes a proportionate response? What if a Party misses its target by 30 percent? In establishing two different branches of the Compliance Committee and imposing different penalties for different noncompliance issues, have the Parties created an equitable compliance regime?

4.   Because the targets and timetables do not apply until 2008–2012, only the facilitative branch of the Compliance Committee has been active. At the second meeting of the facilitative branch, South Africa, on behalf of developing countries, submitted questions of implementation concerning 15 Annex I Parties, including

Bulgaria, Germany, France, Russia, and others. In each case, South Africa reported that the 15 Parties had not submitted their national communication submissions detailing whether they were making "demonstrable progress" towards meeting their commitments, as required by Article 3.2 of the Kyoto Protocol. South Africa's submissions can be found at http://unfccc.int/kyoto_protocol/compliance/facilitative_branch/items/3786.php.

The facilitative branch voted not to proceed against Latvia and Slovenia. Votes to proceed and not proceed against the other Parties did not receive the required three-fourths majority and those decisions were not adopted. Compliance Committee, Facilitative Branch, *Report of the Third Meeting*, CC/FB/3/2006/2 (Sept. 6 2006); *see also* Report to the Compliance Committee on the Deliberations in the Facilitative Branch Relating to the Submission Entitled "Compliance with Article 3.1 of the Kyoto Protocol" (CC-2006-1/FB to CC-2006-15/FB). Are you surprised by the inertia of the facilitative branch, which was designed to assist with implementation and not to impose punitive measures? If the facilitative branch had pursued these compliance matters, what would have been an appropriate response for a Party's failure to make "demonstrable progress" in achieving its commitments?

5.   Under the dispute settlement provisions of the World Trade Organization (WTO), the WTO members are not only subject to compulsory dispute settlement, but also to binding arbitral awards. If a member fails to comply with the rulings of a WTO panel or the WTO's Appellate Body, the prevailing member in the dispute may impose trade sanctions against the losing member. These sanctions take the form of increased tariffs — taxes imposed on products as the price of admission to the importing country's market. These economic sanctions can be significant. In one case, an arbitrator authorized the European Community to impose $4 billion in additional tariffs on imports of certain goods from the United States to offset an impermissible subsidy granted by the United States to certain U.S. exporters. United States-Tax Treatment for Foreign Sales Corporations: Recourse to Arbitration under Article 22.6 of the DSU and Article 4.11 of the SCM Agreement by the United States, Decision of the Arbitrator, WT/DS108/ARB (Aug. 30, 2002). Why do you think governments are willing to submit disputes regarding environmental and other laws affecting trade to binding dispute settlement and possible economic sanctions within the WTO but unwilling to adopt similar processes and remedies within an environmental forum? Is a World Environmental Organization needed that could adjudicate allegations of breaches of international environmental treaties?

6.   ***Composition of the Compliance Committee.*** Within international agreements, the establishment of any committee raises questions about its composition. Should composition be based on geographic representation? Should members serve in their individual capacities? Should the Committee include members of nongovernmental organizations? (At least one compliance committee, the Independent Review Panel of the Agreement on International Dolphin Conservation Program, includes a representative of a nongovernmental organization.) In the end, the Parties agreed that both the facilitative and enforcement branches would have ten members serving in their individual capacity, selected on the basis of equitable geographic representation. If only Annex I Parties are subject to enforcement proceedings, do you think that the majority of the Compliance Committee or at least the enforcement branch should be represented by Annex I Parties?

7.   ***Triggering the Compliance Procedure.*** The compliance mechanism can be triggered in three distinct ways. First, the reports of the expert review teams may point to implementation problems. Second, a party may request assistance if it is struggling to meets its obligations. This approach is consistent with the facilitative approach to redressing injuries to collective or commons resources. Self reporting

of noncompliance has become a common and effective feature of the Implementation Committee of the Montreal Protocol. Third, a party may initiate a claim against another party. Although this approach is used in both the Montreal Protocol and CITES, it is viewed as confrontational and is thus more controversial. Do you agree? Do you think the success of self reporting is due to the threat of a more adversarial process? What else might motivate self-reporting of noncompliance?

In both CITES and the Montreal Protocol, the Secretariat may trigger the compliance mechanism. As the recipient of the various reports from the Parties and as an important conduit for technical and other expertise, the Secretariat is strategically placed to identify potential compliance problems. Nevertheless, the Parties to the Kyoto Protocol refused to grant authority to the climate change secretariat to trigger the compliance mechanism. Are there valid grounds for restricting the role of the secretariat to administrative functions within the compliance regime?

8. *Expert Review Teams under Article 8.* Perhaps the most innovative aspect of the Kyoto Protocol is Article 8, which calls for the establishment of expert review teams to analyze a Party's annual inventory of anthropogenic emissions by sources and removals by sinks of greenhouse gases. Most environmental treaties do not authorize the independent verification of information submitted by Parties, because governments view such verification as an infringement of State sovereignty. Thus, incidents of noncompliance are often uncovered by nongovernmental organizations that use informal channels to bring such cases to the attention of Parties. As a consequence, the authorization of formal expert review teams to verify information submitted by governments is quite an innovation. The compliance mechanism broadens that innovation. Where an expert review team uncovers evidence of noncompliance, that information will automatically be forwarded to the Compliance Committee. Consequently, a State's compliance with the Kyoto Protocol will be subject to technical review by independent experts, and then to a legal assessment by a group of experts, acting in their personal capacities, on the Compliance Committee. This level of non-State involvement in compliance matters is quite extraordinary. Why do you think it is necessary to bypass governments when assessing information concerning a Party's emissions of greenhouse gases?

9. *Expedited Review.* To ensure the integrity of the Kyoto Protocol's flexibility mechanisms, the Parties designed an expedited review of cases of noncompliance with the flexibility mechanisms. While the process is more or less the same as the standard procedure, the timelines for review of information and submission of documents are all shorter than those of the standard procedure.

10. Some observers have been critical of Kyoto's compliance mechanism, questioning whether it provides any real binding teeth to the Parties' reduction commitments:

> [A]ccording to Article 18, "any procedures and mechanism . . . entailing binding consequences shall be adopted by means of an amendment to this Protocol." Under the rules of international law, an amendment is binding only on the countries that ratify it, and on the countries that accede to the original agreement after the amendment enters into law. Since any party to Kyoto could decline to ratify a subsequent compliance amendment, it can avoid being punished for failing to comply. In other words, there is nothing in the agreement that actually makes countries do what they said they would do. As matters now stand, the Kyoto emission limits are more "political" than "legal."

*   *   *

This is a defective mechanism, and not only because it cannot be binding for the first control period, except by means of an amendment. First, the mechanism relies on every party punishing itself for failing to comply. But what happens if a country doesn't implement the compliance punishment in the second control period? How is the enforcement mechanism to be enforced? This problem has not yet been addressed. Second, the emission limits for the second control period have yet to be negotiated. A country that worries that it may not be able to comply in the first control period may thus hold out for easy targets in the second control period — so that the punishment, if triggered, doesn't actually bite. Finally, and perhaps most importantly, a country can always avoid the punishment — by not ratifying the Protocol, or by not participating in a future protocol or amendment, or even by withdrawing from the Protocol. Since this is the easiest option available, participation is a key challenge for enforcement.

Scott Barrett, *U.S. Leadership for a Global Climate Change Regime*, 14–15 (Climate Policy Center 2003), *available at* http://www.cleanair-coolplanet.org/cpc/library_cpc.php. Do you agree with this assessment? Realistically, we won't know how effective the compliance mechanism is until the close of the reporting period in 2012. What criteria would you use at that point to evaluate the fairness and effectiveness of the Kyoto compliance regime?

IV. DISPUTE SETTLEMENT AND RESOLUTION

International disputes in the climate context may arise in two different ways. First, Parties to the Convention or Protocol may have disputes that arise under the climate treaty regime and involve an interpretation or application of the Convention or Protocol. Such disputes would be addressed by the dispute settlement provisions of the Convention and are discussed in Section A. The second type of dispute might be brought by either Parties or non-Parties to the Convention that raise claims rooted in customary international law — not based on the Convention or Protocol. The most widely discussed example of such a claim is one brought by a low-lying island State threatened by sea level rise from climate change that seeks compensation or other remedies for harms caused by the major emitters of greenhouse gases. This type of dispute is discussed further in Section B.

A.   Settlement of Disputes under the Climate Change Regime

Most international environmental agreements include provisions for resolving disputes that arise in the application or interpretation of the agreement. These are frequently distinct from compliance mechanisms as discussed above. Article 14 of the UNFCCC provides the provisions for dispute settlement, which Article 19 of the Kyoto Protocol adopts by reference for disputes arising under the Protocol:

UNFCCC, ARTICLE 14

1. In the event of a dispute between any two or more Parties concerning the interpretation or application of the Convention, the Parties concerned shall seek a settlement of the dispute through negotiation or any other peaceful means of their own choice.

2. When ratifying, accepting, approving or acceding to the Convention, or at any time thereafter, a Party which is not a regional economic integration organization may declare in a written instrument submitted to the Depositary that, in respect of any dispute concerning the interpretation or application of the Convention, it recognizes as compulsory ipso facto and without special agreement, in relation to any Party accepting the same obligation:

(a)   Submission of the dispute to the International Court of Justice, and/or

(b)   Arbitration in accordance with procedures to be adopted by the Conference of the Parties as soon as practicable, in an annex on arbitration.

These provisions of the UNFCCC mirror those of many other international environmental agreements. The resort to negotiation as a first step for settling disputes is an almost universal element of dispute settlement in international treaties. Such negotiations do not have to be disclosed, and thus it is not known to what extent climate-related disputes have been resolved through negotiation. On the other hand, no dispute concerning a multilateral environmental agreement has ever been resolved by arbitration or the ICJ. Perhaps as a consequence, the Parties to the UNFCCC have yet to develop procedures for arbitration.

As a result, any dispute outside of the compliance mechanism would take place before the ICJ, provided that each Party in the dispute has consented to the jurisdiction of the ICJ. Because the ICJ does not have compulsory jurisdiction to hear disputes, nations must provide their consent to the ICJ's jurisdiction for climate change disputes through their ratification documents to the UNFCCC. They may also submit to the ICJ's jurisdiction through official declarations to the ICJ, although they may limit their consent to certain types of disputes.

QUESTIONS AND DISCUSSION

1.   What is the relationship, if any, between the compliance mechanism on the one hand and the dispute settlement provisions of Article 14 of the UNFCCC and Article 19 of the Kyoto Protocol on the other hand? Do you agree with the following position of Saudi Arabia?

> Difficult issues arise concerning the relationship between Articles 18 and 19 of the Protocol. This is because Article 19 applies Article 14 of the Convention (Settlement of Disputes) to the Protocol; and Article 14 of the Convention concerns a dispute between as few as two Parties regarding "interpretation or application of the Convention" (and, therefore, the Protocol); yet "non-compliance [by a Party] with the provisions of this Protocol," which is the subject of Article 18, is a matter of concern to all Parties to the Protocol. If Party X believes it is aggrieved by Party Y's non-compliance with a provision of the Protocol, the settlement of their dispute pursuant to Article 14 of the Convention/Article 19 of the Protocol, even though satisfactory to them, may or may not be satisfactory to the other Parties to the Protocol. The decisions of the COP/MOP concerning procedures for compliance/noncompliance should make clear that resolution of disputes between Parties, pursuant to Article 14 of the Convention/ Article 19 of the Protocol, is without prejudice to full use of the compliance/ non-compliance procedures under the Protocol.

UNFCCC, *Procedures and Mechanisms relating to Compliance under the Kyoto Protocol*, Submissions from Parties, 53–54 (Sept. 29, 1999).

2. Although their historic and current contributions to climate change are insignificant, small island developing States (SIDS) and some other developing countries are bearing disproportionate effects of climate change. Do they have a claim that they can bring against major emitters? If all of the concerned countries are Parties to the Kyoto Protocol, then a small island State could bring their claim under Article 14 of the Convention as discussed above — but those dispute settlement provisions are limited to disputes "concerning the interpretation or application of the Convention." What if they want to bring an action against the United States, which is not a Party to the Protocol? Moreover, even if all countries comply with the Protocol, small island states are still expected to suffer considerable damage from climate change. What recourse do they have? We turn our attention to this situation in the next section.

B.   Climate Disputes under Customary International Law

For many years, representatives of island States and their allies have considered litigation as a possible means for redressing climate change. As early as 1990, two environmental attorneys in analyzing the possibility of an international climate action wrote:

> Of all the geographic areas, low-lying reef and atoll islands, such as those found in the South Pacific and Indian Oceans, may be the most threatened by sea-level rise. These islands are rarely more than three meters above sea level and some are considerably less. Within only a few decades the islands of Kiribati could disappear beneath the Pacific, making refugees of the islands' 60,000 inhabitants. The Republic of the Maldives, in the Indian Ocean, is also vulnerable; a two-meter rise in sea level would flood the capital and over one-half the populated atoll islands of the republic. The Pacific atoll island nations of Tokelau, Tuvalu, and the Marshall Islands are similarly threatened.

> Even a moderate rise in sea level could have serious consequences for small coastal and island states. Despite their small size, many have relatively large populations. Existing problems caused by rapid population growth and development would be exacerbated as floods, and possibly storms, become more frequent and severe. Erosion, already a problem, due in part to the diversion of currents by man-made structures, would be accelerated. Saltwater would displace freshwater, diminishing already strained supplies of drinking water and damaging crops which cannot tolerate salt. Tourism and fishing, economic staples for small coastal and island states, will also suffer as beaches erode and dying coral reefs cease to yield their plentiful supply of bait.

Durwood Zaelke & James Cameron, *Global Warming and Climate Change — An Overview of the International Legal Process*, 5 Am. U. J. Int'l L. & Pol'y 249, 259–260 (1990).

As noted in Chapter 1, these scenarios are not far fetched. To the contrary, citizens of Tuvalu, as well as the Carteret Islands in Papua New Guinea, already have become climate change refugees. Moreover, the most recent reports of the IPCC confirm the dire environmental prospects for developing countries as a whole and SIDS in particular. Both the IPCC and the UNFCCC report that SIDS are already feeling the impacts from climate change and that they have few resources to help them adapt.

UNFCCC, CLIMATE CHANGE: IMPACTS, VULNERABILITIES AND ADAPTATION IN DEVELOPING COUNTRIES
24, 26 (2007)

In SIDS, arable land, water resources and biodiversity are already under pressure from sea level rise. Increases in population and the unsustainable use of available natural resources add further problems. Tropical storms and cyclones cause storm surges, coral bleaching, inundation of land, and coastal and soil erosion with resulting high-cost damages to socio-economic and cultural infrastructure. For example, in the Pacific islands region, cyclones accounted for 76 per cent of the reported disasters between 1950 and 2004, with the average costs relating to damage caused per cyclone standing at USD 75.7 million in 2004 value. In the Caribbean region, the 2004 hurricane season alone caused damages estimated at USD 2.2 billion in four countries: the Bahamas, Grenada, Jamaica and the Dominican Republic. * * *

Water supply in SIDS is likely to be exacerbated by future climate change. Freshwater lenses are predicted to reduce in size due to increased demand and reduced rainfall. It has been estimated that a 10 per cent reduction in average rainfall by 2050 could produce a 20 per cent reduction in the size of the freshwater lens on the Tarawa Atoll, Kiribati, and reduce the thickness of the freshwater lens on atolls by as much as 29 percent. Freshwater supplies are also threatened by saltwater intrusion due to storm surge and sea level rise.

The projected impacts of climate change on agriculture include extended periods of drought, loss of soil fertility and shortening of the growing season which will lead to major economic losses and seriously affect food security.

On many islands, prime agricultural land is located on the coastal plains which are already threatened by sea-level rise. The relative magnitude of economic losses due to climate change is likely to differ among islands. For example, in the absence of adaptive measures on a high island such as Viti Levu in Fiji, the cost of damages could be in the range of USD 23–52 million per year (2–3 per cent of GDP) by 2050 whereas in a low island such as Tarawa, Kiribati, the annual average cost of damages would be in the order of USD 8–16 million (17–18 per cent of GDP) by 2050.

In SIDS, increasing extreme events such as tropical cyclones are predicted to have huge impacts on forest cover and biodiversity, particularly as adaptation responses on small islands are expected to be slow, and impacts of storms may be cumulative. Changes in temperature are likely to particularly affect high elevation SIDS, and biological invasions are predicted to drive several species, including many endemic birds, to extinction. Increasing temperatures and decreasing water availability due to climate change may also increase the burden of diarrhoeal and other infectious diseases in some small island States. Increases in tropical cyclones, storm surges, flooding, and drought are likely to have both short and long-term effects on human health, including drowning, injuries, increased disease transmission, decreases in agricultural productivity and subsequent malnutrition.

Coastlines will almost certainly suffer from accelerated coastal erosion as well as inundation of settlements and arable land with associated social and economic consequences. For example, in Grenada, a 50 cm rise in sea level could lead to serious inundation with 60 per cent of beaches in some areas being lost. A one-metre rise in sea level is expected to cost Jamaica USD 462 million, 19 per cent of its GDP; while for the Maldives a one-meter rise in sea level would mean the complete disappearance of the nation.

Sea level rise, increasing sea surface temperatures and acidification of the oceans will entail a loss of mangrove forests and coral reefs and reduced fish stocks throughout this region. For example, studies have projected that 3 per cent of Cuba's mangrove forests may be lost with a one meter rise in sea level. For the same rise in sea level a complete collapse of the Port mangrove wetland in Jamaica is predicted, since this system has shown little capacity to migrate over the last 300 years.

Climate change is also likely to have a negative effect on tourism in SIDS, seriously affecting the economy of many small islands. The increasing frequency and severity of extreme weather, sea-level rise and accelerated beach erosion, degradation of coral reefs (including bleaching), and the loss of cultural heritage on the coasts through inundation and flooding are likely to reduce the attractiveness of small island States to tourists. For example, in Barbados 70 per cent of the hotels are located within 250 m of the high water mark. This suggests that many hotels are almost exclusively within the 1 in 500 and 1 in 100 inundation zones, placing them at risk of major structural damage.

Assuming that the ICJ has jurisdiction over a dispute, the question is: what law would apply to such a dispute? As described in Chapter 4 Section I, the ICJ may resort to treaties, custom, and general principles of law to determine the obligations of nation States. Recall that treaty provisions may emerge as customary norms through State practice and *opinio juris*. Do you think any provisions of the UNFCCC or Kyoto Protocol have attained the status of custom?

A large number of international law principles have guided the creation of international treaties, international declarations, and domestic law, and these principles may also provide the basis for claims to mitigate climate change. The precautionary principle (*see* Chapter 4, Section IV.A.7), polluter pays principle (*see* pages Chapter 2, Section II.B), and duty to cooperate (*see* Chapter 4, Section IV.A.1) are bedrocks of international environmental law. However, the obligation not to cause environmental harm, together with the principle for assessing liability, State responsibility, provide the most compelling basis for redressing harms caused by climate change.

1.   *The Duty Not to Cause Environmental Harm*

The roots of the obligation not to cause environmental harm are found in the *Trail Smelter Arbitration*, a dispute involving transboundary pollution from Canada into the United States in the 1920s and 1930s. Perhaps the most famous international environmental dispute, the *Trail Smelter Arbitration* centered on a smelter in Trail, British Columbia, which emitted thousands of pounds of sulfur dioxide (SO_2) annually. Those emissions crossed the U.S.-Canada border just a few miles away, causing hundreds of thousands of dollars in damage to crops, buildings, and livestock. The tribunal ultimately concluded that "under the principles of international law, as well as of the law of the United States, no State has the right to use or permit the use of its territory in such a manner as to cause injury by fumes in or to the territory of another or the properties or persons therein, when the case is of serious consequence and the injury is established by clear and convincing evidence." Trail Smelter Case (United States v. Canada), Arbitral Tribunal, 1941, 3 UN Rep. Int'l Arb. Awards (1941). The tribunal imposed monetary penalties on Canada and required the smelter to undertake investments costing some $20 million to reduce its emissions.

The tribunal does not provide much formal legal precedent, because Canada and the United States negotiated a special treaty to establish the tribunal and resolve this dispute. The treaty specified the sources of law to be reviewed and directed the tribunal to "give consideration to the desire of the high contracting parties to reach a solution just to all parties." Nevertheless, the obligation not to cause environmental harm can be viewed as an extension of the general international norm that prohibits a State from using its territory, or to allow others to use its territory, in a way that can harm the interests of another State. The ICJ has affirmed the obligation not to cause harm in several rulings, perhaps most notably in the *Corfu Channel* case, which concerned damage to British warships caused by mines placed in Albanian waters. In holding Albania responsible, the ICJ stated:

> From all the facts and observations mentioned above, the Court draws the conclusion that the laying of the minefield which caused the explosions on October 22nd, 1946, could not have been "accomplished without the knowledge of the Albanian Government." The obligations resulting for Albania from this knowledge are not disputed between the Parties. Counsel for the Albanian Government expressly recognized that [translation] "if Albania had been informed of the operation before the incidents of October 22nd, and in time to warn the British vessels and shipping in general of the existence of mines in the Corfu Channel, her responsibility would be involved. . . . "

> The obligations incumbent upon the Albanian authorities consisted in notifying, for the benefit of shipping in general, the existence of a mine field in Albanian territorial waters and in warning the approaching British warships of the imminent danger to which the minefield exposed them. Such obligations are based, not on the Hague Convention of 1907, No. VIII, which is applicable in time of war, but on certain general and well-recognized principles, namely: elementary considerations of humanity, even more exacting in peace than in war; the principle of the freedom of maritime communication; *and every State's obligation not to allow knowingly its territory to be used for acts contrary to the rights of other States* [emphasis added.]

Corfu Channel (U.K. v. Alb.), Merits, 1949 I.C.J. Rep. 4, 22 (Judgment of April 9).

Trail Smelter and *Corfu Channel* provide clear precedents for the development of international environmental law. At the first major multilateral meeting to develop international environmental policy, governments adopted the Stockholm Declaration on the Human Environment, including Principle 21 which provides:

> States have . . . the sovereign right to exploit their own resources pursuant to their own environmental policies, and the responsibility to ensure that activities within their jurisdiction or control do not cause damage to the environment of other States or of areas beyond the limits of national jurisdiction."

Stockholm Declaration on the Human Environment, UN Doc. A/CONF.48/14 and Corr.1, June 16, 1972 (1972), *reprinted in* 11 I.L.M. 1416 (1972). *See also* Rio Declaration on Environment and Development, UN DOC A/CONF.151/5/Rev. 1, Principle 2, June 13, 1992, *reprinted in* 31 I.L.M. 874 (1992); *Lac Lanoux*

Arbitration, (Spain v. Fr.) XII R.I.A.A. 281 (1957); *UNEP Principles for Shared Natural Resources*, Principle 3; *United Nations Convention on the Law of the Sea*, Part XII; *IUCN Draft Covenant*, at Principle 4; *IUCN Draft Covenant on Environment and Development*, at Article 11.

Principle 21 of the Stockholm Declaration appears to be broader than the holdings in *Trail Smelter* and *Corfu Channel*. Whereas *Trail Smelter* limited its conclusions to transboundary pollution between States, the Stockholm Declaration applies to "areas beyond the limits of national jurisdiction," including, for example, the oceans and Antarctica. In addition, the ICJ in *Corfu Channel* suggested that a violation of another legal norm, such as the duty to notify, is required as a prerequisite to finding a breach of the duty not to cause harm to another State. In contrast, the Stockholm Declaration, as well as subsequent iterations in other declarations and treaties, makes clear that the harm itself is sufficient to trigger a breach of the duty not to cause environmental harm. Nonetheless, Principle 21 prohibits only the impacts from activities under a State's "jurisdiction or control."

Principle 21 is widely accepted as customary international law. Indeed, the ICJ, in its advisory opinion on the Legality of the Threat or Use of Nuclear Weapons, declared:

> The Court recognizes that the environment is under daily threat and that use of nuclear weapons could constitute a catastrophe for the environment. The Court also recognizes that the environment is not an abstraction but represents the living space, the quality of life and the very health of human beings, including generations unborn. *The existence of the general obligation of States to ensure that activities within their jurisdiction and control respect the environment of other States or of areas beyond national control is now a part of the corpus of international law relating to the environment.*

Para. 29–30 (emphasis added). While the Court's formulation differs from that of Principle 21, it nonetheless seems to endorse the general obligation not to cause environmental harm.

---

2. *State Responsibility*

The concept of State responsibility establishes a set of rules that describe the consequences of a State's breach of its international obligations. As Ian Brownlie puts it:

> Today one can regard responsibility as a general principle of international law, a concomitant of substantive rules and of the supposition that acts and omissions may be categorized as illegal by reference to the rules establishing rights and duties. Shortly, the law of responsibility is concerned with the incidence and consequences of illegal acts, and particularly the payment of compensation for loss caused. However, this, and many other generalizations offered on the subject, must not be treated as dogma, or allowed to prejudice the discussion which follows. Thus the law may prescribe the payment of compensation for the consequences of legal or "excusable" acts, and it is proper to consider this aspect in connection with responsibility in general.

IAN BROWNLIE, PRINCIPLES OF PUBLIC INTERNATIONAL LAW 433 (6th ed. 2003).

International tribunals have several times affirmed State responsibility as an international legal norm. In the *Chorzow Factory* case, for example, the Permanent Court of International Justice, the predecessor to the ICJ, held:

> It is a principle of international law, and even a general conception of law, that any breach of an engagement involves an obligation to make reparation. In judgement No. 8 . . . the Court has already said that reparation is the indispensable complement of a failure to apply a convention, and there is no necessity for this to be stated in the convention itself.

PCIJ (1928), Ser. A, no. 17, p. 29. Subsequently, the ICJ held in the *Corfu Channel* case that Albania was "responsible under international law" for allowing the use of its territory to harm British vessels and that Albania must pay compensation for the loss of property and human life.

Principle 21 of the Stockholm Declaration explicitly extends State responsibility to breaches of the obligation not to cause environmental harm. As noted above, Principle 21 of the Stockholm Declaration and Principle 2 of the Rio Declaration refer to States' "responsibility to ensure that activities within their jurisdiction or control do not cause damage to the environment."

QUESTIONS AND DISCUSSION

1. ***Due Diligence.*** The duty to prevent environmental harm is not absolute. In practice it appears to require States to use due diligence in taking all practicable steps to prevent harm. For example, Article 194 of the UN Convention on the Law of the Sea requires that:

> States shall take, individually or jointly as appropriate, all measures consistent with this Convention that are necessary to prevent, reduce and control pollution of the marine environment from any source, using for this purpose the best practicable means at their disposal and in accordance with their capabilities, and they shall endeavor to harmonize their policies in this connection.

See also Convention on Environmental Impact Assessment in a Transboundary Context, Article 2(1), *done* Feb. 25, 1991, 30 I.L.M. 800, 803 (providing that "[t]he Parties shall, either individually or jointly, take all appropriate and effective measures to prevent, reduce and control significant adverse transboundary environmental impact from proposed activities"). Other Conventions link the general principle to avoid harm to one that requires due diligence in environmental management. The Basel Convention, for example, requires the "environmentally sound management of hazardous wastes and other wastes," which is defined as: "taking all practicable steps to ensure that hazardous wastes or other wastes are managed in a manner which will protect human health and the environment against the adverse effects which may result from such wastes." Basel Convention, Article 2(8); *see also, e.g.*, London Convention, 1972. How should the principle of common but differentiated responsibilities be reflected in a due diligence standard? Does the due diligence standard suggest that a negligence standard applies when seeking to hold a State responsible for environmental harm? Or should the focus of the inquiry simply be on the extent and nature — the "significance" — of the resulting harm, regardless of whether the acting State was at fault?

2. ***Jurisdiction and Control.*** Principle 21 of the Stockholm Declaration limits a State's responsibility (i.e., when it must pay compensation) for harm to those

activities under that State's "jurisdiction and control." How far does a State's responsibility extend? Is a State responsible for transboundary pollution caused by individuals and corporations within its "jurisdiction"? Because individuals and corporations emit most greenhouse gases, as well as other transboundary pollution, the answer to this question is of obvious importance. Decisions of international tribunals do not provide much guidance. The U.S. *Restatement* (Third) *of the Law of Foreign Relations*, a scholarly review of what leading U.S. academics believe to be the state of international law from a U.S. perspective (but which is *not* a statement of the law *per se*), provides the following description of these terms in *Comments c* and *d* to Section 601 on State Obligations with Respect to the Environment of Other States and the Common Environment:

> c. *"Activities within its jurisdiction" and "significant injury."* An activity is considered to be within a state's jurisdiction under this section if the state may exercise jurisdiction to prescribe law with respect to that activity under sections 402–403. The phrase "activities within its jurisdiction or control" includes jurisdiction, Part V, as well as activities on ships flying its flag or on installations on the high seas operating under its authority. . . . International law does not address internal pollution, but a state is responsible under this section if pollution within its jurisdiction causes significant injuries beyond its borders. "Significant injury" is not defined but references to "significant" impact on the environment are common in both international law and United States law. The word "significant" excludes minor incidents causing minimal damage. . . . In special circumstances, the significance of injury to another state is balanced against the importance of the activity to the state causing the injury.

> d. *Conditions of responsibility.* A state is responsible . . . for both its own activities and those of individuals or private or public corporations under its jurisdiction. The state may be responsible, for instance, for not enacting necessary legislation, for not enforcing its laws against persons acting in its territory or against its vessels, or for not preventing or terminating an illegal activity, or for not punishing the person responsible for it. In the case of ships flying its flags, a state is responsible for injury due to the state's own defaults . . . but is not responsible for injury due to fault of the operators of the ship. In both cases, a state is responsible only if it has not taken "such measures as may be necessary" to comply with applicable international standards and to avoid causing injury outside its territory. . . . In general, the applicable international rules and standards do not hold a state responsible when it has taken the necessary and practicable measures; some international agreements provide also for responsibility regardless of fault in case of a discharge of highly dangerous (radioactive, toxic, etc.) substances, or an abnormally dangerous activity (e.g., launching of space satellites) . . . . In all cases, however, some defenses may be available to the state: e.g., that it had acted pursuant to a binding decision of the Security Council of the United Nations, or that injury was due to the failure of the injured state to exercise reasonable care to avoid the threatened harm. . . . A state is not responsible for injury due to a natural disaster such as an eruption of a volcano, unless such disaster was triggered or aggravated by a human act, such as a nuclear explosion in a volcano's vicinity. But a state is responsible if after a natural disaster has occurred it does not take necessary and practicable steps to prevent or reduce injury to other states.

3.   Given the above discussions, outline the primary elements that must be demonstrated to bring a climate change claim against a State with large greenhouse

gas emissions for violating Principle 21's obligation not to cause environmental harm.

4.   Consider the various obligations of the UNFCCC and the Kyoto Protocol as well as relevant principles of international environmental law. What legal advice would you give to the government of Tuvalu if it asks you to help it build a case seeking damages and injunctive relief to mitigate climate change? What problems will you have in bringing your claim? Consider the following questions:

- Will you have a better chance of success against the United States or another State?

- Although the United States is not a Party to the Kyoto Protocol, can you claim that the commitments to reduce emissions in the Kyoto Protocol have become customary international law?

- What level of harm should trigger any obligation to avoid harm from greenhouse gas emissions?

- To what standard of care should the State be held?

- What activities should be considered under the "jurisdiction and control" of a State?

- What remedies should be available to States who suffer such damage?

See generally RODA VERHEYEN, CLIMATE CHANGE DAMAGE AND INTERNATIONAL LAW: PREVENTION DUTIES AND STATE RESPONSIBILITY (2005); Durwood Zaelke & James Cameron, *Global Warming and Climate Change — An Overview of the International Legal Process*, 5 AM. U. J. INT'L L. & POL'Y 249 (1990).

5.   Do the UNFCCC and the Kyoto Protocol help define the contours of the obligation not to cause environmental harm or establish other obligations upon which Tuvalu could base its claim? Consider the following.

DAVID M. DRIESEN, FREE LUNCH OR CHEAP FIX?: THE EMISSIONS TRADING IDEA AND THE CLIMATE CHANGE CONVENTION
26 B.C. ENVTL. AFF. L. REV. 1, 58–61 (1998)*

The Framework Convention articulates a broad normative idea that nations should avoid dangerous climate change. It translates this broad norm into a developed country "aim" of returning greenhouse gas emissions to 1990 levels by the year 2000. This locution makes it difficult to give national leaders either credit or blame for committing to stabilize emissions (or deciding not to do anything). The phrasing makes it difficult to state whether the leaders have agreed to a binding limit stabilizing emissions or not. The mention of a concrete target certainly suggests a serious commitment. But the use of the term "aim" might suggest something more akin to a goal than a binding commitment.

Furthermore, this ambiguity made it difficult to hold nations accountable for emission increases after the adoption of the Framework Convention. It is difficult to argue that developed countries that increased their emissions (such as the United States) violated an international agreement. Hence, the Framework Convention had little normative force as a generator of concrete actions.

Annex B to the Kyoto Protocol, however, seems to help clarify national obligations under the Climate Change Convention. It establishes national quantified emission limitations, stated as a percentage reduction in greenhouse gas emissions below 1990 levels. Article 3, section 1 clearly establishes these limits as binding, stating that the developed country parties "shall . . . ensure that their . . . emissions of . . . greenhouse gases . . . do not exceed their assigned amounts." This means that while holding the international community accountable for any particular accomplishment is difficult, the Protocol, absent trading, establishes a clear basis for holding each developed nation accountable for meeting a quantifiable national commitment. The national caps in Annex B seem to translate an amorphous international goal, preventing dangerous climate change, into fairly specific national obligations aimed at moving toward this goal.

However, these seemingly concrete physical national obligations vanish before the eyes of a careful reader, because of provisions designed to facilitate trading. In fact, the treaty may instead create a much less specific "virtual" obligation, a developed country's obligation to either make the required reduction or earn credits abroad deemed equivalent to the specified reduction under rules yet to be defined. Indeed, the Kyoto Protocol may be read as not requiring any emission reductions at all, to the extent it allows tree planting to substitute for emission reductions. The Kyoto Protocol now contains more amorphous commitments than the Protocol would have if the countries of the world had agreed to the reductions specified in Annex B without trading.

This vagueness creates real difficulties in determining what precisely the parties have agreed to do. A post-Kyoto dispute concerning trading of so-called "hot air" illustrates this vagueness. Because of the economic collapse of Eastern Europe and the former Soviet Union, emissions have fallen in this area since 1990, in spite of antiquated energy systems. A dispute has arisen about whether other developed countries may purchase credits reflecting this downturn in emissions in lieu of physical national compliance.

If the CoP allows trading of "hot air" credits, the developed countries will likely realize less aggregate emission reductions than national compliance without trading would generate. But to the extent the five percent aggregate developed country reduction target in the Kyoto Protocol already takes the economic downturn of countries in transition to market economies into account, the developed countries may realize this five percent target, even if they trade "hot air." Accepting this use of hot air involves interpreting the treaty as using the five percent target, rather than the results of each nation complying with its binding national cap, as the measuring rod of effective implementation. But the Protocol creates no binding obligation to meet the five percent target. Rather, it states that the developed countries "shall, individually or jointly ensure that their aggregate . . . emissions . . . do not exceed their assigned amounts . . . with a view to reducing their overall emissions of such gases by at least 5 percent." This language resembles the amorphous language expressing the Framework Convention's aim to stabilize emissions at 1990 levels by the year 2000. If compliance with this language provides the measuring rod for assessing implementation of the Kyoto Protocol, the world has made little progress in clarifying the Framework Convention.

One might hypothesize that the Kyoto Protocol clearly requires that developed countries at least collectively ensure that their aggregate emissions equal the aggregate of their national targets. But to the extent the COP allows developed countries to claim credits for reductions in developing countries under Article 12, developed country emissions will likely exceed the aggregate limits as well. The provisions introduced to facilitate trading make definite simple statements about what precisely the parties have agreed to accomplish very difficult. This hinders public understanding of the agreement and accountability.

———————

Do you agree with these conclusions? Are there alternative ways to interpret the obligations of the Parties to the Kyoto Protocol, even in light of emissions trading?

6.   Given the dire consequences of sea level rise for many of the small island States, it may at first be surprising that none of them have yet turned to the International Court of Justice to press their claims. Indeed, some countries have seriously considered bringing such a case. *See, e.g.,* Kalinga Seneviratne, *Tiny Tuvalu Steps up Threat to Sue Australia, U.S.,* INTERPRESS SERV., Sept. 5, 2002, found at http://www.commondreams.org/headlines02/0905-02.htm. Why do you think no such cases have been brought? Even if the island States thought they could prevail (and this is not at all clear), many island States are heavily dependent on larger countries. It is thus important to see possible litigation before the ICJ as part of a broader set of diplomatic relationships.

Chapter 9

BEYOND 2012: THE POST-KYOTO CLIMATE REGIME

There is no Plan B. There is no escaping to another planet.
—Kevin Rudd, Australia's new prime minister, declaring Australia's support for the Bali negotiations

I. INTRODUCTION

The future of international cooperation to mitigate climate change is at a critical and uncertain juncture. The Fourth Assessment Report of the Intergovernmental Panel on Climate Change (IPCC) issued in early 2007 has strengthened the existing consensus that anthropogenic greenhouse gas GHG emissions are causing global temperatures to rise. Moreover, the Kyoto Protocol's first reporting period ends in 2012. Governments have entered negotiations for a post-2012 climate regime with enormous differences about how to address climate change and even who should address it. As a result, no one can predict for certain whether governments will be able to construct a meaningful climate change regime for beyond 2012 or what that regime might look like.

The primary framework for negotiating the post-Kyoto climate regime is the "Bali Action Plan," which the UNFCCC Parties adopted in December 2007. The Action Plan put the world on a schedule to agree to a post-Kyoto regime by the end of 2009. The Action Plan also reflected important concessions by many of the Parties in framing the negotiations, but it still left unresolved the three most important issues threatening the success of future negotiations. First, although the Action Plan calls for developed countries to make measurable reductions in

335

greenhouse gases, the countries must still reach agreement on what specifically those new commitments will be.

Second, although the Bali Action Plan commits developing countries to adopt "nationally appropriate mitigation actions," it does not clarify what the nature of those mitigation actions might be. With aggregate annual GHG emissions of developing countries set to exceed developed country emissions before any new agreement comes into force, the success of any future climate regime seems dependent on meaningful commitments from developing countries. Yet, historical emissions by industrialized countries, and thus their contribution to current climate change, still far exceed that of developing countries. The nature and extent of developing country obligations remains a central part of the current negotiations.

A third issue also lingers: what will be necessary for the United States to join a post-Kyoto regime? Although the United States joined the consensus Bali Action Plan, it was the last country to do so and then only reluctantly after being jeered by virtually the entire international community. Complicating predictions about the U.S. negotiating position is the timing set forth in the Action Plan, which calls for agreement only ten months after President Obama has taken office.

This chapter explores the politics shaping the Bali Action Plan and the post-Kyoto climate negotiations. It then discusses a wide range of options for thinking about the post-Kyoto future. As you read the materials that follow, consider what that future should be. Is it a future only of Kyoto-like "targets and timetables" or is it one that focuses on transforming specific economic sectors, such as requirements to use renewable energy sources for generating electricity? Is it one where developing countries may have completely different obligations from developed countries? Where island States have different obligations than China? If targets are set, what should the targets be and when should they be met? The sky is the limit, both figuratively and literally.

II. THE ROAD TO BALI

Negotiators under the climate change regime agreed in May 2006 that there should be "no gap" between the end of the first commitment period in 2012 and the beginning of a new commitment period and that the Annex I countries will adopt further mandatory reductions after 2012. The Parties also committed to establishing a framework at their meeting in Bali, Indonesia in December 2007. As the meeting approached, it was not at all clear that an agreement would be reached. Prior to the meeting, Europe proposed that all developed countries commit to substantial cuts in Bali. The United States initially refused to commit to any negotiations under the Kyoto Protocol (to which it was not a Party) and any binding commitments at least until major developing countries did. At the same time, the United States hoped to open up an alternative negotiation with the large developing countries that focused on voluntary commitments and technology cooperation. Meanwhile, major developing countries such as China and India remained deeply reluctant to commit to GHG reductions or other commitments, especially if developed countries refused to do so. These divisions posed substantial challenges to establishing even a framework for negotiating a post-Kyoto Protocol agreement, much less the actual agreement itself.

A.   Europe and Other Annex I Parties

Having committed through the Kyoto Protocol and European Trading System to the establishment and maintenance of a carbon market, the European Union (EU) not surprisingly has been committed to seeing the post-Kyoto regime continue the basic institutional structure of targets and timetables and flexibility mechanisms found in the Kyoto Protocol. In March 2005, the EU's Council of Ministers created a stir by suggesting ambitious GHG reduction targets for the post-Kyoto process (15–30 percent by 2020 and 60–80 percent by 2050). The subsequent summit of EU leaders backpedaled from the Council proposal, stating that a 15–30 percent cut in GHG emissions "should be considered" for 2020, but only "in the light of future work on how the objective can be achieved, including the cost-benefit aspect." At the insistence of Germany and Austria, precise targets for periods after 2020 were withdrawn, calling into question the 60–80 percent cuts proposed by the environment ministers. Finally, in February 2007, the EU announced an agreement calling for 20 percent reductions by 2020 if there is no post-Kyoto Protocol accord and 30 percent if there is. The 2020 target is binding on all 27 EU countries and was designed to both set a benchmark and provide an incentive for other Parties to join in the post-Kyoto process.

Other non-EU industrialized Parties to the Kyoto Protocol have offered a less unified approach to the post-Kyoto regime. Perhaps most importantly, Australia which had for many years been the United States' strongest ally in opposing the Kyoto Protocol, flipped its position (in light of a change of governments), ratified the Kyoto Protocol just days before the Bali meeting, and dramatically promised a 60 percent reduction in greenhouse gases by 2050 from 1990 levels. Japan has made no dramatic announcements but is taking steps to ensure its compliance with its Kyoto obligations. Less constructively Canada's has announced that it has no intention of complying with Kyoto, and by implication, that it does not plan to take a leadership role in more expansive targets post-Kyoto. Canada thus replaced Australia as the strongest ally for the United States in opposing a post-Kyoto agreement.

QUESTIONS AND DISCUSSION

1. What impact do you think the Australian and EU proposals will have on the post-Kyoto negotiations? What are the advantages in announcing the negotiating position as early as did the Europeans? Are there disadvantages? How can the EU justify its proposal to increase the required reductions from 20 percent to 30 percent if there is a broader international agreement?

2. In addition to creating an overall emissions cap, the EU proposal established a binding target for renewable energy, requiring that 20 percent of all of Europe's energy needs be met by renewable sources by 2020. Some observers believe this could potentially open another possible negotiating avenue with the United States and developing countries, namely to agree to binding sector-specific policies and measures rather than overall emission caps. Do you agree? What advantages might there be for the United States or developing countries to emphasize policies and measures? The policies-and-measures approach is discussed further, below.

3. In addition to the collective action being taken by the EU, individual EU members are also taking bold and substantial steps to position themselves as climate change leaders. For example, in November 2007, the United Kingdom committed to reduce carbon dioxide emissions by 60 percent before 2050. In December 2007, the United Kingdom also announced that agencies must include the economic cost of climate change in their assessments of proposed projects, such as airport expansions or coal-fired power plants. The government set the "shadow price for carbon" at £25.50 (about $50 in January 2008) for each metric ton of carbon in 2007 with the price rising annually to £59.60 a metric ton in 2050. Thus, if a new power plant will cost £1 billion but it will add £200 million worth of carbon emissions, the project will be evaluated as if it costs £1.2 billion to construct. Patrick Wintour, *Ministers Ordered to Assess Climate Cost of All Decisions*, THE GUARDIAN, Dec. 22, 2007, at A1. Could such legislation form the basis for part of the international negotiations? What advantages, if any, do you think the United Kingdom will gain from being the first to enact such legislation? Should international financial institutions such as the World Bank be required to include a shadow price of carbon as part of their project assessment?

B.   The United States and the Major Emitters' Process

Given its repudiation of the Kyoto Protocol, the United States obviously remains outside the mainstream of international climate negotiations as long as those negotiations remain focused on expanding the Kyoto Protocol's targets and timetables into a second reporting period. The Bush Administration was heavily criticized not only for repudiating the Protocol, but also for offering no alternative other than some relatively minor support for technology cooperation. As the Kyoto Protocol Parties began to explore arrangements for the period after 2012, the United States hoped that it could isolate Europe and the Kyoto Protocol supporters by convincing developing countries to join it in seeking only voluntary measures outside of the existing climate regime. This initial effort did not succeed, however, and the United States ultimately agreed in Montreal in 2006 to continue to participate in negotiations under the Framework Convention.

The second effort by the United States to end-run the Kyoto Protocol has met with greater success. In particular, the Bush Administration's call for broader participation by developing countries has gained traction, in large part because GHG emissions from middle income developing countries, particularly China, have grown at much faster rates than expected when the Kyoto Protocol was negotiated. China's annual emissions now exceed those of the United States and aggregate developing country emissions will soon exceed emissions from industrialized countries. Although both historic and per capita emissions from developing countries remain small, and often miniscule, compared to U.S. emissions, the failure to include commitments of some kind for developing countries has become harder to defend. In response, the Bush Administration has called for a new process of "major emitters" (including both developed and developing countries) to come to agreement on a strategy for addressing climate change in the future.

PRESIDENT BUSH DISCUSSES UNITED STATES INTERNATIONAL DEVELOPMENT AGENDA
(May 31, 2007)

[M]y proposal is this: By the end of next year [2008], America and other nations will set a long-term global goal for reducing greenhouse gases. To help develop this goal, the United States will convene a series of meetings of nations that produce most greenhouse gas emissions, including nations with rapidly growing economies like India and China.

In addition to this long-term global goal, each country would establish midterm national targets, and programs that reflect their own mix of energy sources and future energy needs. Over the course of the next 18 months, our nations would bring together industry leaders from different sectors of our economies, such as power generation and alternative fuels and transportation. These leaders will form working groups that will cooperate on ways to share clean energy technology and best practices.

It's important to ensure that we get results, and so we will create a strong and transparent system for measuring each country's performance. This new framework would help our nations fulfill our responsibilities under the U.N. Framework Convention on Climate Change. The United States will work with all nations that are part of this convention to adapt to the impacts of climate change, gain access to clean and more energy-efficient technologies, and promote sustainable forestry and agriculture.

The way to meet this challenge of energy and global climate change is through technology[.] * * *

We're also going to work to conclude talks with other nations on eliminating tariffs and other barriers to clean energy technologies and services by the end of year. If you are truly committed to helping the environment, nations need to get rid of their tariffs, need to get rid of those barriers that prevent new technologies from coming into their countries. We'll help the world's poorest nations reduce emissions by giving them government-developed technologies at low cost, or in some case, no cost at all.

After outlining this broad framework, President Bush initiated an alternative to the main climate change negotiations — known as the "major emitters' process" — which includes the 16 largest emitters of greenhouse gases (the United States, Australia, Brazil, Britain, Canada, China, France, Germany, India, Indonesia, Italy, Japan, South Korea, Mexico, Russia, and South Africa). These 16 countries account for approximately 80 percent of the world's GHG emissions. While President Bush said that the largest emitters of greenhouse gases should all set goals for reducing GHG emissions, he did not specify what those goals should be nor did he intend them to be binding. Under the President's proposal, countries could choose their own strategies for meeting their goals and they would not be required to meet mandatory targets for limiting GHG emissions.

Regardless of whether the major emitters' process was intended in part to shift the discussion away from a Kyoto-like agreement, the process has at this point largely been incorporated into the broader negotiations. Other countries in the major emitters' process have proposed cuts of 50 percent by 2050, similar to proposals made in the broader climate talks. President Bush also proposed an international fund to help developing nations benefit from clean energy technology, which has drawn some interest. To date, none of these ideas has generated anything close to consensus but the countries involved have agreed to continue meeting in parallel to discussions taking place under the Bali Action Plan.

Predicting the future posture of the United States towards international climate cooperation is difficult, because President Obama took office January 2009 amid a vast financial crisis. However, he continues to support cap-and-trade approaches to climate change. Thus, the United States is likely to be more in line with the mainstream of developed country positions in the future. Moreover, the U.S. Congress is slowly moving comprehensive climate legislation forward. At this point, Congress is unlikely to have passed legislation before the end of 2009, but signals from Congress will be critical in shaping the U.S. negotiating position for a post-Kyoto climate future.

QUESTIONS AND DISCUSSION

1.   President Bush's plan emphasized the need for vast improvements in technology. In his speech excerpted above, he noted that the United States has taken the lead in spending on clean technologies, including "safe nuclear power," clean coal technologies, biofuels, and alternative power for automobiles, such as hydrogen cells. How did the President propose to promote the development of technologies? How can international cooperation enhance the development and dissemination of climate-friendly technologies?

2.   The Bush Administration's call for greater developing country participation in post-Kyoto negotiations has gained traction. Scott Barrett writes that:

> In principle, the difference between the Bush Administration and developing countries is easily bridged. It is only essential to distinguish between the question of which countries should mitigate climate change and which should pay for mitigation. If developing countries were assigned emission limits with "headroom," say, then they could not lose by participating and may gain by trading their emission surpluses. That is, mitigation might be in the interests of developing countries under a trading regime.

Scott Barrett, *U.S. Leadership for a Global Climate Change Regime* 10 (Climate Policy Center, 2003), *available at* http://www.cpc-inc.org/library/index.php. While it may be too much to say that the differences are "easily bridged," the idea has taken hold that a broader range of countries should be responsible for mitigating climate change and a smaller group of developed countries should be responsible for paying for mitigation. Barrett also suggests that U.S. objections to the Kyoto Protocol could be resolved "by getting the developing countries to accept emission limits; lowering the limits overall; and redistributing the total volume of allowances, with the United States being given more, and countries such as Russia less." *Id.* at 12. Do you think such changes would be sufficient to bring the United States back to the international climate negotiations? What other steps do you believe are necessary?

3.   The United States cannot take all of the credit for raising questions of developing country participation in the climate regime. Indeed, the whole approach established under the UNFCCC and the principle of common but differentiated responsibilities presumes that at some point developing countries will also make binding commitments. Indeed, the Bush Administration's criticism of the Kyoto Protocol for not including developing countries was viewed by many as a convenient smokescreen for U.S. repudiation of its commitments. All Parties to the Kyoto Protocol, including developing country Parties, knew that at some point — either in the second or subsequent reporting periods — developing countries would be expected to take on binding commitments. The theory was that developing countries would be more likely to do so if industrialized countries had already shown the way. In this regard, how different do you think current negotiations with China, India, and other large developing countries would be if the United States had

joined Europe in striving to cut emissions during the past decade? Would this have increased or decreased pressure on developing countries?

4.   The major emitters' process has become a significant negotiating forum, even if it has yet to produce any results. Is this process a distraction from the main international negotiations or does it complement those efforts? What do you think the United States hopes to achieve in the major emitters' process that it cannot achieve in negotiations involving all Parties to the climate change regime? Why would Europe agree to participate? To some extent, Europe views the major emitters' negotiations as just another "contact group" for advancing negotiations that will ultimately have to be incorporated into the UNFCCC/Kyoto process.

5.   China would not agree to participate unless the formal name was changed to a "major economies" meeting. Although semantic, it also suggests that the price for China to make climate commitments may be in part greater respect for its role in the global economy. Is there any advantage to negotiating with a relatively few developing countries as opposed to the broader negotiations in the climate change regime? Are there disadvantages?

6.   As discussed further in Chapter 11 regarding U.S. national policy, the climate is changing in the U.S. Congress, and federal legislation is now more a question of *when*, rather than *whether*. Much of the proposed climate legislation, like that in California, will impose national caps on emissions. Assuming that the U.S. Congress does enact a national emissions cap and approve national and international carbon trading, how will this affect the post-Kyoto negotiations? On the one hand, it would seem to support the United States re-engaging in post-Kyoto negotiations, but might it also constrain the ability of the executive branch to negotiate a treaty? How likely is it, for example, that after agreeing to set specific national caps, Congress would ratify an international agreement that sets more stringent caps?

C.   The G8

The major industrial democracies have met annually since 1975 to address major economic and political issues facing their domestic societies as well as the international community. Starting with a group of six countries (France, the United States, Britain, Germany, Japan and Italy), these meetings now also include Canada and Russia, with the European Community also represented. Acknowledging that climate change could seriously damage our natural environment and the global economy, this group of countries, known as the G8, has addressed climate change in many of its recent meetings. Like the major emitters' process identified above, the G8 presents an alternative forum for building consensus among industrialized countries to address climate change. In 2007, the G8 made the following proposal for climate change action. These commitments are not legally binding, but important politically as they can signal the direction of future negotiations. In particular, as you read this excerpt consider both the compromise language meant to bridge the EU-U.S. gap and the specific signals being sent to China, India, and other large developing countries.

G8, GROWTH AND RESPONSIBILITY IN THE WORLD ECONOMY
Summit Declaration (June 7, 2007)

Fighting Climate Change

49. We are . . . committed to taking strong and early action to tackle climate change in order to stabilize greenhouse gas concentrations at a level that would prevent dangerous anthropogenic interference with the climate system. Taking into account the scientific knowledge as represented in the recent IPCC reports, global greenhouse gas emissions must stop rising, followed by substantial global emission reductions. . . .

50. As climate change is a global problem, the response to it needs to be international. We welcome the wide range of existing activities both in industrialised and developing countries. We share a long-term vision and agree on the need for frameworks that will accelerate action over the next decade. Complementary national, regional and global policy frameworks that co-ordinate rather than compete with each other will strengthen the effectiveness of the measures. Such frameworks must address not only climate change but also energy security, economic growth, and sustainable development objectives in an integrated approach. They will provide important orientation for the necessary future investment decisions.

51. We stress that further action should be based on the UNFCCC principle of common but differentiated responsibilities and respective capabilities. We reaffirm, as G8 leaders, our responsibility to act. We acknowledge the continuing leadership role that developed economies have to play in any future climate change efforts to reduce global emissions, so that all countries undertake effective climate commitments tailored to their particular situations. We recognise however, that the efforts of developed economies will not be sufficient and that new approaches for contributions by other countries are needed. Against this background, we invite notably the emerging economies to address the increase in their emissions by reducing the carbon intensity of their economic development. Action of emerging economies could take several forms, such as sustainable development policies and measures, an improved and strengthened clean development mechanism, the setting up of plans for the sectors that generate most pollution so as to reduce their greenhouse gas emissions compared with a business as usual scenario. * * *

53. To address the urgent challenge of climate change, it is vital that major economies that use the most energy and generate the majority of greenhouse gas emissions agree on a detailed contribution for a new global framework by the end of 2008 which would contribute to a global agreement under the UNFCCC by 2009. We therefore reiterate the need to engage major emitting economies on how best to address the challenge of climate change. . . . This major emitters' process should include, inter alia, national, regional and international policies, targets and plans, in line with national circumstances, an ambitious work program within the UNFCCC, and the development and deployment of climate-friendly technology. This dialogue will support the UN climate process and report back to the UNFCCC.

Technology

54. Technology is a key to mastering climate change as well as enhancing energy security. We have urgently to develop, deploy and foster the use of sustainable, less carbon intensive, clean energy and climate-friendly technologies in all areas of

energy production and use. We have to develop and create supportive market conditions for accelerating commercialisation of new less carbon intensive, clean-energy and climate-friendly technologies. Furthermore, to ensure sustainable investment decisions worldwide, we need an expanded approach to collaboratively accelerate the widespread adoption of clean-energy and climate-friendly technologies in emerging and developing economies. Therefore, we will

- stimulate global development, commercialisation, deployment and access to technologies,

- promote major emerging and developing economies' participation in international technology partnerships and collaborations,

- scale up national, regional and international research and innovation activities, and

- undertake strategic planning and develop technology roadmaps to strengthen the role of advanced technology in addressing climate change.

Market Mechanisms

55. Private sector investment is and will remain the primary means of technology deployment and diffusion. Strong economies and a wide range of policy instruments are required to develop, deploy and foster climate-friendly technologies. Market mechanisms, such as emissions-trading within and between countries, tax incentives, performance-based regulation, fees or taxes, and consumer labelling can provide pricing signals and have the potential to deliver economic incentives to the private sector. Fostering the use of clean technologies, setting up emissions-trading systems and, as many of us are doing, linking them are complementary and mutually reinforcing approaches. Therefore, we will share experience on the effectiveness of the different policy instruments in order to

- better provide the international business community with a predictable and long-term perspective, and

- strengthen and extend market mechanisms by, inter alia, developing and extending existing programmes, taking into account the appropriate metrics for such systems.

Reducing Emissions by Curbing Deforestation

56. We are determined to assist in reducing emissions from deforestation, especially in developing countries. Reducing, and in the long term halting deforestation provides a significant and cost-effective contribution toward mitigating greenhouse gas emissions and toward conserving biological diversity, promoting sustainable forest management and enhancing security of livelihoods. To this end, we will

- encourage the establishment of a pilot project dedicated to building capacity, creating and testing performance-based instruments to reduce emissions from deforestation in developing countries, in support of and without prejudice to ongoing UN climate change discussions. We therefore encourage the World Bank, in close cooperation with the G8, developing countries, the private sector, NGOs and other partners, to develop and implement such a forest carbon partnership as soon as possible.

- continue to support existing processes to combat illegal logging. Illegal logging is one of the most difficult obstacles to further progress in realising sustainable forest management and . . . in protecting forests worldwide.

- remain engaged in supporting developing countries to achieve their self-commitments for halting forest loss and to implement sustainable forest management, as stated in various regional initiatives, i.e., the Congo Basin and the Asia Forest Partnerships. Good results and good practice in international cooperation have also been achieved through ITTO projects and the Brazilian Pilot Program to conserve the tropical rain forests.

* * *

Adapting to Climate Change

58. We acknowledge that even implementing the ambitious mitigation steps described above will not avoid further climate impacts, especially in those developing countries and regions which are most vulnerable to climate change. We are committed to enhancing resiliency to climate variability and climate change in a way that fully supports our common goal of sustainable development. We welcome the adoption of the Nairobi work programme on impacts, vulnerability, and adaptation to climate change. We also note the importance of the UN adaptation funds in helping developing countries mainstream adaptation into policies and programming. We emphasise our willingness to continue and enhance cooperation with and support for developing countries in adapting to climate change and enhancing their resilience to climate variability, in particular those most vulnerable to the negative impacts of climate change. We also emphasise our willingness to work with developing countries on the costs and benefits of climate change adaptation measures to help integrating them in national development planning. We reaffirm our commitment to assist with climate research and risk assessments including through helping developing countries benefit from satellite observation systems.

[The G8 also noted that, according to the International Energy Agency (IEA), successfully implemented energy efficiency policies could contribute up to 80% of avoided greenhouse gases while substantially increasing security of supply. The G8 members thus agreed to improve energy efficiency in the building, transport, and power sectors, promote policy frameworks to support the use of clean fuels, including clean coal, renewable energy sources (wind, solar, geothermal, bioenergy, hydro power), and pledged to use nuclear energy peacefully.]

65. Against this background we commit ourselves to a model of efficient energy systems and call on other countries with high energy demand, including the major emerging economies, to join us in this endeavour. Our goal of building less energy intensive economies will also advance economic growth and competitiveness. To this end, we will promote the appropriate policy approaches and instruments, including inter alia economic incentives and sound fiscal policies, minimum standards for energy efficiency, sound and ambitious energy performance labelling, information campaigns aimed at consumers and industry that enhance national awareness, sector-based voluntary commitments agreed with industry, investment in research and development and guidelines for public procurement. We will develop and implement national energy efficiency programmes and advance international cooperation on energy efficiency, notably on efficiency standards. We ask the IEA to continue to support our national efforts by appropriate advice and make proposals for effective international co-operation.

QUESTIONS AND DISCUSSION

1.   Although the majority of G8 members are European, the G8 position on climate change is substantially different from the European Union's approach. Clearly, the United States and Japan have influenced the G8's position. For example, the G8 declaration does not include a call to reduce greenhouse gas emissions by a fixed amount. Do you think the European members of the G8 have moved the United States toward a more progressive position on climate change?

2.   The G8 declaration links climate change to energy security as well as economic growth and sustainable development. Do you think that including these issues opens opportunities for negotiating a future agreement on climate change or do they complicate the negotiations?

3.   If you were a representative of a large developing country, how would you interpret the G8 statement? Have they made concessions? What are the major points of potential consensus? What is the G8 asking from the large developing countries?

4.   The G8 issues a new declaration every year, although it does not always address climate change. Find the most recent declaration and compare it to the 2007 declaration. What explains any significant differences?

D.   Developing Countries

Both the UNFCCC and the Kyoto Protocol are premised on the notion of "common but differentiated responsibilities." For that reason, the UNFCCC imposes obligations on developed countries that are not imposed on developing countries. Developed countries agreed to "take the lead" due to their much greater contribution to climate change, higher per capita greenhouse gas (GHG) emissions, and more abundant financial and technological resources to mitigate climate change. For example, developed countries are responsible for about 72 percent of carbon dioxide emissions that accumulated in the atmosphere from 1750 to 1990. The average American emits about 10 times more carbon than the average Chinese and 20 times the average Indian.

At the same time, GHG emissions from the developing world are rapidly increasing. While developed countries have a projected annual growth rate for energy of 1.1 percent over the next 20 years, developing countries have a 3.2 percent projected annual growth rate over the same period. Because GHG emissions are closely correlated with economic growth, developing countries with robust economic growth will see their GHG emissions increase. Indeed, some predict that by as early as 2020, GHG emissions of developing countries will exceed those of developed countries. According to the Netherlands Environmental Assessment Agency, China's emissions of greenhouse gases exceeded those of the United States in 2007.

While it seems clear that mitigating climate change must eventually involve developing countries in some way, the willingness of developing countries to negotiate any mandatory obligations will probably depend on several issues. These issues include the extent to which industrialized Parties comply with the Protocol's first reporting period's commitments, the growth and profitability of developing country participation in the CDM and the global carbon market, progress in negotiating strong caps for the Annex I countries in the second reporting period, and the willingness of the United States to impose mandatory limits on its GHG emissions (either unilaterally or multilaterally). *See* Thomas C. Heller & P.R. Shukla, *Development and Climate: Engaging Developing Countries, in* BEYOND KYOTO: ADVANCING THE INTERNATIONAL EFFORT AGAINST CLIMATE CHANGE 111, 116–117 (Pew Center on Global Climate Change, 2003).

Perhaps because these issues have not been resolved or cannot be known until the first commitment period is well underway, the current position of the developing countries with respect to the post-Kyoto negotiations has remained unclear. Nonetheless, the G77 and China have outlined the two general elements of their position: climate change must be addressed "on the basis of equity, common but differentiated responsibilities and respective capabilities" and include "major and significant reductions" in greenhouse gas emissions by all Annex I countries. At the Bali negotiations, Pakistan's Ambassador to the UN, Mr. Munir Akram, speaking on behalf of the G77 and China, stated this point succinctly:

> The major responsibility rests on the developed countries. No significant progress can be made without major and significant reductions in emissions of Greenhouse Gases by all Annex-1 countries. Therefore, the G77 and China attaches particular significance to the new commitments, which Annex 1 countries are to make in the second commitment period after 2012. This will be the single most vital determinant of success or failure in meeting the Climate Change challenge.

Third World Network, *G77-China Warns Against Erosion of UNFCCC, Kyoto Protocol*, BALI NEWS UPDATE, Dec. 14, 2007.

As the following excerpt makes clear, however, the position of the developing countries is more nuanced than simply calling for deep cuts by developed countries.

STATEMENT BY H. E. MUKHDOOM SYED FAISAL SALEY HAYAT ON BEHALF OF THE GROUP OF 77 AND CHINA
(New York, 24 September 2007), *available at,*
http://www.g77.org/statement/getstatement.php?id=070924

5. The Group of 77 and China has consistently called for efforts to address climate change in a manner that enhances and ensures the sustainable development and sustained economic growth of the developing countries and the universal elimination of poverty, hunger and disease. To this end, all three pillars of sustainable development i.e., economic development, social development and environmental protection, should be addressed in an integrated, coordinated and balanced manner.

* * *

8. In elaborating a global strategy to address climate change, we must continue to adhere to the Rio principles and in particular the Principle of Common but Differentiated Responsibility. This central principle must be given tangible content. We would like to highlight that effective mitigation efforts are essential to address the challenges posed by climate change. Developed countries must continue to take the lead, as they have committed to, in combating climate change and the adverse effects thereof including through significantly reducing GHG emissions.

9. The developed countries also have an obligation to support the developing countries to adapt an environment-friendly path to development and growth by providing additional and substantial financial and technological assistance. Clearly,

the challenge of sustaining economic development and achieving social development and ensuring environmental protection is too overwhelming and beyond the capacity of the developing countries to address on their own. It can only be effectively addressed through international cooperation as well as a partnership with the developed countries, premised on the principle of common but differentiated responsibilities. It is the view of the G-77 and China that the decisions on Climate Change should, therefore, fulfill the commitments, undertaken at the Rio and Johannesburg Conferences, including Agenda 21 and the Rio Principles.

10. Developed countries should support and assist the efforts of developing countries to adapt to climate change and the response measures designed to address climate change.

11. We strongly believe that no adaptation plan or strategy would be effective without enhanced financing and greater technological support and access for developing countries.

12. Enabling the developing countries to respond to climate change will require substantial additional official assistance, over and above the long standing 0.7 ODA target as well as the 0.15-0.20 ODA target for LDCs. In this context, the recent negative trend in ODA levels is highly regrettable. [eds. note: In 1970, donor governments committed to providing 0.7 percent of their Gross National Income to Official Development Assistance (ODA) to developing countries and more than twice that to the least developed countries (LDCs)].

13. Similarly, technology is essential to address the climate change challenge. The present restraint on access to advanced technologies, imposed particularly by the IPR regime, need to be lifted, at least for technologies that can assist in meeting the climate change challenge. The developing countries must also be helped, on affordable preferential and concessional terms, through technology transfer, directed R&D and other assistance, to acquire and build capacity for the application of technologies to meet sustainable development targets and goals.

14. The Group of 77 and China would also like to emphasize the urgent need for building the resilience of communities and nations to natural disasters, including those related to Climate Change, and establishing early warning systems in order to prevent and reduce the adverse impacts of such events.

*   *   *

17. Equally important is to work towards strengthening North-South, South-South and triangular cooperation in research, development and demonstration (RD&D) and to undertake initiatives towards mitigation and adaptation to climate change and its adverse impacts.

QUESTIONS AND DISCUSSION

1.   Like the G8, the G77 and China have broadened the debate about future commitments beyond reductions in GHG emissions. In what ways do the positions of the G8 and G77 and China overlap? In what ways do the positions differ? Do you think the commonalities are sufficient to form the basis of a deal?

2.   The position of G77 and China calls for much greater technological and financial assistance as well as participation in research development, and demonstration of new initiatives towards mitigation and adaptation. In so doing, the G77 and China appear to be conditioning their acceptance of commitments on extensive

infusions of funding. Consider the following critique of the Kyoto Protocol with regard to financing:

THOMAS C. HELLER & P.R. SHUKLA, DEVELOPMENT AND CLIMATE: ENGAGING DEVELOPING COUNTRIES

in BEYOND KYOTO: ADVANCING THE INTERNATIONAL EFFORT AGAINST CLIMATE CHANGE 111, 116–117 (Pew Center on Global Climate Change 2003)*

Under the UNFCCC, developed countries pledged to provide "new and additional" resources and to promote technology transfer to support climate action in developing countries. They also pledged adaptation assistance to developing countries particularly vulnerable to climate impacts. These are general commitments with no specific formula or schedule for flows. The adequacy of the assistance provided has been a chronic source of friction between developed and developing countries in the climate negotiations.

In their national communications to the UNFCCC Secretariat, developed countries report a wide assortment of bilateral and multilateral projects and contributions. The level of support varies from donor to donor and from year to year. Some funding covers the cost to developing countries of fulfilling Convention commitments such as preparing emission inventories and national communications. Some reported flows are for projects such as forest protection, in which climate is one among many benefits. From 1997 to 2000, the combined flows reported by developed countries were in excess of $12 billion.

Some of the funding reported by developed countries flows through the Global Environment Facility (GEF), which was established in 1992 to fund projects in areas of global environmental concern (these also include biodiversity, international waters, ozone depletion, land degradation, and persistent organic pollutants). From 1991 to 2001, GEF funding for climate projects amounted to $3 billion, or 37 percent of the GEF disbursal. In 2001, GEF disbursed $472 million in climate funds, with nearly 80 percent directed to renewable energy and energy efficiency projects.

GEF funding follows the "incremental cost" principle established in the UNFCCC: developed countries are to pay the "agreed full incremental costs" of developing country efforts under the Convention. Incremental funding has helped push advanced technologies, such as solar photovoltaics, fuel cells, biomass gasifier engines, and electrical vehicles, which may face high initial costs or other barriers. However, while GEF programs are often input-based, there is no stipulated or evident tie between the environmental goals of the GEF and leading political priorities in developing nations. In addition, concerns have been raised about GEF program implementation, including its weak incentives for discovering least-cost mitigation options and inadequate replication of successful projects.

UNFCCC Parties agreed in 2001 to establish three new funds to support technology transfer, capacity building, adaptation planning, and other needs in developing countries. They are the Special Climate Change Fund, which also aims to assist countries whose economies are highly dependent on income generated from fossil fuels; the Least Developed Countries Fund; and the Adaptation Fund, to be financed in part by a charge of 2 percent of the certified emission reductions issued for CDM projects. Developed countries, however, have not committed to particular levels of funding. Apart from the CDM surcharge for the Adaptation

Fund, the funds are supported entirely by discretionary contributions. To date, developed countries have announced commitments of 450 million Euro per year by 2005. However, the funds are not yet operational and no disbursals have taken place.

Heller and Shukla conclude that, because of the Kyoto Protocol's focus on channeling investments to emissions reductions rather than to fundamental climate-friendly development needs, "it is understandable if there is only limited interest among developing countries in exploring the road beyond Kyoto." What type of activities do you think Heller and Shukla would want to see funded? How would the negotiation dynamics change if instead of funding projects the Parties agreed to fund large-scale, climate-friendly development needs?

3. Both the G8 and G77-China link climate change to growth and development. Although the Clean Development Mechanism provides some linkage between climate change and development, Heller and Shukla believe a much closer linkage is necessary:

> Climate is not an arcane or peripheral question for development. Both concern fundamental issues of energy, transport, land use, and food security that are priorities for developing countries. Development and climate intersect across two broad dimensions. First, the localized impacts of climate change — including water shortages, agricultural disruption, and coastal flooding — pose serious long-term threats to development. These impacts will be felt disproportionately in developing countries. At the same time, development is itself the driving force behind climate change. In the long run, achieving the deep reductions in global emissions necessary to stabilize the climate will require fundamental shifts in development pathways.

Id. at 111. To what extent, if at all, should the international climate treaty relate to development goals instead of focusing on emissions reductions? To what extent should developed countries be responsible for financing development that is consistent with climate change mitigation?

4. As might be expected, the developing countries do not always speak with one voice. Small Island Developing States (SIDS) clearly have different interests than China and have, for example, called for stronger climate commitments from all major emitters. A representative of India, although speaking in an unofficial capacity, suggested that agreement at Bali might be contingent upon which countries are asked to reduce greenhouse gas emissions, such as "one big country" — meaning, of course, China. Malaysia at one point called for a "flexible" and "non-binding" agreement. Heavily forested countries, such as Brazil and Indonesia, also have their own priorities and approaches to the negotiations.

III. THE BALI ACTION PLAN

In December 2007, more than 10,000 governmental representatives and observers from intergovernmental and nongovernmental organizations from 187 countries met in Bali, Indonesia, to negotiate a roadmap for a future international agreement on climate change. The rollercoaster negotiations had a movie thriller atmosphere to them. The negotiations nearly collapsed on several occasions and needed to be extended. Then, just as agreement was within reach, at least among current Kyoto

Parties, developing countries asked for additional technological help from developed nations. U.N. Secretary-General Ban Ki-moon flew back to the negotiations to make an unscheduled last-minute appeal for a deal. In his impassioned speech, he pleaded with governments to "seize the moment, this moment, for the good of all humanity" and to overcome their differences. India and others then suggested minor adjustments to the text, supported by the European Union, that encouraged monitoring of technological transfer to ensure that developed countries meet the needs of developing countries.

With the international community ready to adopt the proposal, known as the "Bali Action Plan," the United States voiced its rejection and called for additional talks. The U.S. statement drew loud boos and sharp floor rebukes, a rarity in the formal world of international diplomacy. Finally, the delegate from Papua New Guinea took the floor and said, "If you are not willing to lead, then get out of the way!" Less than an hour later, the United States dramatically reversed its position and accepted the Bali Action Plan, with the changes requested by developing countries. That reversal then brought cheers from governments and observers.

In the final agreement, governments agreed to reach a new agreement on climate change by the end of 2009. The resulting Bali Action Plan, however, is just that, an agreement to agree and a broad plan for the negotiations. Nonetheless, the Bali Action Plan is a crucial document that sets the parameters and goals for the negotiations. As one might expect from a document as contentious as this, reviews of the Bali Action Plan were mixed. Yvo de Boer, the Executive Secretary of the UNFCCC Secretariat, called the plan "a real breakthrough, a real opportunity for the international community to successfully fight climate change." Environmentalists were more subdued in their comments. According to Marcelo Furtado of Greenpeace Brazil: "The people of the world wanted more. They wanted binding targets." Others, such as the World Wildlife Fund, thought the world caved to U.S. pressure. They may all be right.

UNFCCC, DECISION 1/CP.13
Bali Action Plan

The Conference of the Parties,

Resolving to urgently enhance implementation of the Convention in order to achieve its ultimate objective in full accordance with its principles and commitments,

Reaffirming that economic and social development and poverty eradication are global priorities,

Responding to the findings of the Fourth Assessment Report of the Intergovernmental Panel on Climate Change that warming of the climate system is unequivocal, and that delay in reducing emissions significantly constrains opportunities to achieve lower stabilization levels and increases the risk of more severe climate change impacts,

Recognizing that deep cuts in global emissions will be required to achieve the ultimate objective of the Convention and emphasizing the urgency to address climate change as indicated in the Fourth Assessment Report of the Intergovernmental Panel on Climate Change,

1. *Decides* to launch a comprehensive process to enable the full, effective and sustained implementation of the Convention through long-term cooperative action,

now, up to and beyond 2012, in order to reach an agreed outcome and adopt a decision at its fifteenth session, by addressing, inter alia:

(a) A shared vision for long-term cooperative action, including a long-term global goal for emission reductions, to achieve the ultimate objective of the Convention, in accordance with the provisions and principles of the Convention, in particular the principle of common but differentiated responsibilities and respective capabilities, and taking into account social and economic conditions and other relevant factors;

(b) Enhanced national/international action on mitigation of climate change, including, inter alia, consideration of:

(i) Measurable, reportable and verifiable nationally appropriate mitigation commitments or actions, including quantified emission limitation and reduction objectives, by all developed country Parties, while ensuring the comparability of efforts among them, taking into account differences in their national circumstances;

(ii) Nationally appropriate mitigation actions by developing country Parties in the context of sustainable development, supported and enabled by technology, financing and capacity-building, in a measurable, reportable and verifiable manner;

(iii) Policy approaches and positive incentives on issues relating to reducing emissions from deforestation and forest degradation in developing countries; and the role of conservation, sustainable management of forests and enhancement of forest carbon stocks in developing countries;

(iv) Cooperative sectoral approaches and sector-specific actions, in order to enhance implementation of Article 4, paragraph 1(c), of the Convention;

(v) Various approaches, including opportunities for using markets, to enhance the cost-effectiveness of, and to promote, mitigation actions, bearing in mind different circumstances of developed and developing countries;

(vi) Economic and social consequences of response measures;

(vii) Ways to strengthen the catalytic role of the Convention in encouraging multilateral bodies, the public and private sectors and civil society, building on synergies among activities and processes, as a means to support mitigation in a coherent and integrated manner;

(c) Enhanced action on adaptation, including, inter alia, consideration of:

(i) International cooperation to support urgent implementation of adaptation actions, including through vulnerability assessments, prioritization of actions, financial needs assessments, capacity-building and response strategies, integration of adaptation actions into sectoral and national planning, specific projects and programmes, means to incentivize the implementation of adaptation actions, and other ways to enable climate-resilient development and reduce vulnerability of all Parties, taking into account the urgent and immediate needs of developing countries that are particularly vulnerable to the adverse effects of climate change, especially the least developed countries and small island developing States, and further taking into account the needs of countries in Africa affected by drought, desertification and floods;

(ii) Risk management and risk reduction strategies, including risk sharing and transfer mechanisms such as insurance;

(iii) Disaster reduction strategies and means to address loss and damage associated with climate change impacts in developing countries that are particularly vulnerable to the adverse effects of climate change;

(iv) Economic diversification to build resilience;

(v) Ways to strengthen the catalytic role of the Convention in encouraging multilateral bodies, the public and private sectors and civil society, building on synergies among activities and processes, as a means to support adaptation in a coherent and integrated manner;

(d) Enhanced action on technology development and transfer to support action on mitigation and adaptation, including, inter alia, consideration of:

(i) Effective mechanisms and enhanced means for the removal of obstacles to, and provision of financial and other incentives for, scaling up of the development and transfer of technology to developing country Parties in order to promote access to affordable environmentally sound technologies;

(ii) Ways to accelerate deployment, diffusion and transfer of affordable environmentally sound technologies;

(iii) Cooperation on research and development of current, new and innovative technology, including win-win solutions;

(iv) The effectiveness of mechanisms and tools for technology cooperation in specific sectors;

(e) Enhanced action on the provision of financial resources and investment to support action on mitigation and adaptation and technology cooperation, including, inter alia, consideration of:

(i) Improved access to adequate, predictable and sustainable financial resources and financial and technical support, and the provision of new and additional resources, including official and concessional funding for developing country Parties;

(ii) Positive incentives for developing country Parties for the enhanced implementation of national mitigation strategies and adaptation action;

(iii) Innovative means of funding to assist developing country Parties that are particularly vulnerable to the adverse impacts of climate change in meeting the cost of adaptation;

(iv) Means to incentivize the implementation of adaptation actions on the basis of sustainable development policies;

(v) Mobilization of public- and private-sector funding and investment, including facilitation of carbon-friendly investment choices;

(vi) Financial and technical support for capacity-building in the assessment of the costs of adaptation in developing countries, in particular the most vulnerable ones, to aid in determining their financial needs;

QUESTIONS AND DISCUSSION

1. At the Bali meeting, the Parties agreed to structure future negotiations around four main themes, or building blocks: mitigation, adaptation, financing, and technology. How does the Bali Action Plan address these issues?

2. How are the various positions of the main negotiating blocs reflected in the Bali Action Plan? For example, did the United States, or China for that matter, agree to negotiate any future binding commitments? Does the Action Plan suggest the broader focus on development that developing countries wanted?

3. An earlier version of the Bali Action Plan included a proposal from the European Union and G77-China that developed (Annex I) countries reduce their emissions by 25–40% below 1990 levels by 2020. This proposal relied upon the most recent scientific findings of the IPCC, which reported that greenhouse gas emissions would peak within 10 to 15 years with emissions reductions of this size. At the insistence of the United States, but joined by Japan, Canada, and Russia, the adopted agreement excludes specific greenhouse gas emissions reduction targets. Instead it calls for agreement on a "shared vision for long-term cooperative action, including a long-term global goal for emission reductions." What are the advantages and disadvantages of excluding a specific target in the Bali Action Plan?

4. Developing countries committed to taking "nationally appropriate mitigation actions" to address climate change, provided that they receive sufficient financial, technical, and capacity building support to do so; both the mitigation actions and the provision of support would be "measurable, reportable and verifiable." As the Center for International Environmental Law writes, "This marks an important evolution of thinking among the G-77 and China, reflecting the urgency of climate change and the understanding that the UNFCCC principle of 'common but differentiated responsibility' should define not only the relationship between Annex I and non-Annex countries, but also the relationships among non-Annex I countries with different social, economic, and other relevant characteristics." Center for International Environmental Law, *Bali Action Plan: Key Issues* (Dec. 21, 2007). Do you agree?

IV. OPTIONS FOR A POST-KYOTO PROTOCOL AGREEMENT

The international community now faces the daunting task of reaching agreement on a post-Kyoto Protocol agreement by the end of 2009. To be sure, the negotiations will not be orderly or logical. Three major trends outside the global negotiations will substantially influence international climate policy in ways difficult to predict. First, the evidence is mounting of serious and relatively imminent climate change. The IPCC's Fourth Assessment may have already catalyzed agreement in Bali and is likely to provide a scientific catalyst for mobilizing public opinion and strengthening global climate policy. Since publication of the Fourth Assessment, however, studies have shown that Arctic ice and glaciers are melting even faster than predicted. The scientific case for strong and urgent action has thus grown and will act as a counterforce to the Parties' inherent self-interests in the negotiations. Second, the global carbon market appears to be vibrant and growing. Substantial economic forces are now profiting from the carbon market. These forces will welcome a global regulatory system that sets clear and predictable guidance for carbon trading, but they may also obscure the need to investigate other policies and measures for reducing greenhouse gas emissions. The negotiations over the respective caps (targets and timetables) will be important, but pressure may build for all countries to agree to a cap — any cap — in order to be a full participant in the emerging carbon market. Third, the economic collapse will undoubtedly influence governments' willingness to commit to new obligations and perhaps further emissions reductions unless they perceive some economic advantage in doing so.

The Bali Action Plan also creates expectations for what might be included in a post-Kyoto Protocol agreement. First, the Action Plan strongly suggests that developing countries — or at least some of them — will have commitments of some kind. Section A reviews some of the issues surrounding developing country commitments. Second, the Plan's call for "commitments or actions" for developed countries and "appropriate mitigation actions . . . in the context of sustainable development" for developing countries strongly hints that the post-Kyoto Protocol agreement may include strategies unrelated to specific reduction commitments. Section B describes the major strategies being discussed.

A.   Who Will be Subject to Commitments?

The Bali Action Plan clearly anticipates that both developed and developing countries will agree to some form of commitments. Given the history of the UNFCCC and the Kyoto Protocol, it is relatively clear that all developed countries (i.e., Annex I countries), including the United States, are expected to have commitments in the post-Kyoto period. It is not at all clear, however, which developing countries will or should have commitments.

As the United States has argued, at least some indicators suggest that developing countries need to accept obligations of some kind. China has already exceeded the United States as the largest emitter of greenhouse gases. Aggregate emissions from developing countries, excluding land use activities, are expected to exceed developed country emissions by 2020. However, when land use activities are included, developing countries (non-Annex I countries) already account for 54 percent of emissions. IPCC, Working Group III, *Summary for Policymakers* 3 (2007). Moreover, their greenhouse gas intensity — essentially an energy efficiency measure — was 1.06 kilograms CO_2 equivalent per dollar of GDP compared to just 0.68 kilograms CO_2 equivalent per dollar of GDP for Annex I Parties.

The Bali Action Plan provides that developing country commitments should reflect national circumstances and it seems obvious that not all developing countries will be treated alike. First, emissions vary widely among reporting Parties, with Tuvalu reporting a low of 4,660 tonnes CO_2 equivalent (for CO_2, CH_4, and N_2O) and China reporting a high of more than 4 billion tonnes CO_2 equivalent (or 863,257 times more than Tuvalu). A total of 19 non-Annex I Parties reported emissions smaller than 1 mt CO_2 equivalent and 22 Parties reported emissions greater than 100 mt CO_2 equivalent.

Second, the sources of greenhouse gases vary widely across developing countries. Unlike emissions for Annex I Parties, where the energy sector constitutes the largest source of greenhouse gas emissions, the energy sector was the largest source of emissions for just 70 non-Annex I Parties, with agriculture the largest source for the other 45 non-Annex I Parties reporting. FCCC/SBI/2005/18/Add.2, paras. 21–24, 27 (Oct. 25, 2005). Only 55 percent of non-Annex I Parties reported CO_2 emissions as their primary greenhouse gas. One-third of non-Annex I Parties reported methane as their most significant greenhouse gas, and 14 Parties (12 percent) emitted more nitrous oxide than any other greenhouse gas. Presumably the needs of countries with large agricultural emissions will require solutions that differ from those countries with a majority of emissions from the energy sector.

In apparent recognition that a one-size-fits-all approach may not be appropriate, after adoption of the Bali Action Plan the United States issued a statement that it considers a framework for addressing differentiated commitments:

> First, the negotiations must proceed on the view that the problem of climate change cannot be adequately addressed through commitments for emissions cuts by developed countries alone. Major developing economies must likewise act. Just as the work of the IPCC has deepened our scientific understanding of the scope of the problem and action required, so too empirical studies on emission trends in the major developing economies now conclusively establish that emissions reductions principally by the developed world will be insufficient to confront the global problem effectively.

> Second, negotiations must clearly differentiate among developing countries in terms of the size of their economies, their level of emissions and level of energy utilization, and sufficiently link the character or extent of responsibility to such factors. We must give sufficient emphasis to the important and appropriate role that the larger emitting developing countries should play in a global effort to address climate change.

> Third, the negotiations must adequately distinguish among developing countries by recognizing that the responsibilities of the smaller or least developed countries are different from the larger, more advanced developing countries. In our view, such smaller and less developed countries are entitled to receive more differentiated treatment so as to more truly reflect their special needs and circumstances.

White House, *Statement by the Press Secretary* (Dec. 15, 2007), *available at* http://www.whitehouse.gov/news/releases/2007/12/20071215-1.html.

While the U.S. statement did not identify which developing nations constituted "major developing economies," the United States is clearly referring to the developing countries among the 16 largest emitters involved in the major emitter's process that are responsible for about 80 percent of the world's CO_2 emissions from fossil fuel combustion. At a minimum, then, the United States appears to seek commitments from the seven developing countries (i.e., non-Annex I countries) included in the major emitter's process — China, India, South Korea, Mexico, South Africa, Indonesia, and Brazil.

QUESTIONS AND DISCUSSION

1. Based on the information above, which developing countries do you think should have obligations under a post-Kyoto Protocol agreement? Would all developing countries be subject to similar obligations? For example, while emissions from some developing countries, such as China and South Korea, are predominately from industrial sources, the emissions from other countries are primarily agricultural. Should any commitments be specific to particular gases or sectors? What would be the advantage of such an approach?

2. Many believe the U.S. position has been somewhat disingenuous, hiding its own desire to avoid binding targets behind the claim that all major emitters should have obligations. A focus on current annual emissions shifts the focus from the historical, cumulative, and disproportionate contribution of the United States and away from any discussion of per capita emissions, where the United States far exceeds China.

3. Deciding which developing countries will now or in the future be asked to make binding commitments under the Kyoto regime is only the first, and maybe the easiest, step. Next, the Parties will have to determine on what basis the obligations will be distributed. Put another way, if the climate regime eventually places a global cap on GHG emissions into the atmosphere, how will we allocate the right to pollute across all countries? Many human rights observers view the right to an equal percentage of the climate's atmosphere as part of an individual's human rights. Indeed, it is hard to accept any other position for allocating future climate emissions limits, once one accepts a rights-based approach. Consider in this regard the views of Professor Wolfgang Sachs:

WOLFGANG SACHS, HUMAN RIGHTS AND CLIMATE CHANGE
in INTERACTIONS BETWEEN GLOBAL CHANGE AND HUMAN HEALTH 349
(Pont. Acad. of Sci, 2006)*

During climate negotiations, both developed and developing countries — apart from the Island States — have shown little interest in defining low danger emission caps. All parties disregard the fact that, when it comes to capping emissions, the choice is between livelihood rights and the desire for affluence. The task of keeping the temperature rise below 2°C appears too large and too threatening to the economic interests of consumers and corporations. In particular, it still seems to have escaped the attention of developing countries that climate protection is of the utmost importance for the dignity and survival of their own people. It is time they became protagonists of climate protection, because climate protection is not simply about crops and coral reefs, but fundamentally about human rights. * * *

[T]he way in which reduction commitments have been distributed among the industrial countries in Kyoto was a matter of accident and political shrewdness rather than systematic consideration. There is no explanation why, for instance, Australia, was granted a further rise in emissions of 8% while Japan was forced to reduce emissions by 6%. In any case, rules for the distribution of reduction commitments will be at the centre of attention the moment developing countries are expected to come onboard a governance system for climate protection. The atmosphere, however, belongs to nobody in particular and to everybody equally; in other words, the atmosphere is a global common good. In the future, who should be

---

allowed to use it, and by how much? What principles should determine the fair distribution of the 'cake' that is available?

Among observers of the negotiations, this issue has been hotly debated for some time. For instance, some put forth the grandfathering principle, according to which each nation has to accept equal reduction commitments, disregarding the present unequal distribution of emissions. However, as such a principle would maintain the global welfare gap; it can hardly be considered fair. Brighter prospects are offered by the capabilities principle that demands commitments according to the capability of countries to reduce emissions. Economically strong countries are expected to carry the bulk of the reduction load, regardless of how efficiently they use energy. This proposal may be fair, but it is ecologically counterproductive, as wasteful countries would enjoy an advantage. A third principle calls for a distribution of commitments according to the historical responsibility of countries for loading the atmosphere with greenhouse gases. Each country's obligation would be measured by its relative contribution to global warming. Indeed, in 1997 Brazil introduced a proposal along these lines to the climate negotiations; the issue of equity has been squarely on the agenda of environmental diplomacy ever since. Countries are expected to assume obligations according to their share of cumulative emissions, given that the ominous concentration of greenhouse gases in the atmosphere has been built up over 150 years. Such a scheme would place the biggest burden by far on industrial countries. However, it is doubtful to what extent responsibility can be assumed for actions that have been adopted in ignorance of their consequences. After all, the possibility of a greenhouse effect was known to just a handful of specialists before the 1980s.

The situation is different when it comes to the equal entitlement approach. This calls for a framework that respects the principle of an equal per capita right to the Earth's atmosphere. Most other allocation schemes would repeat a colonial style approach, granting disproportionate shares to the North. If the use of a global common good has to be restrained through collective rules, it would violate the principle of equity to design these rules to the advantage of some and the disadvantage of many. The equal right of all world citizens to the shared atmosphere is therefore the cornerstone of any viable climate regime. Therefore, for the second commitment period of the Kyoto Protocol, a process should be initiated whereby each country is allocated emission allowances based on equal rights per capita. This is hard on the North, but not unfair, as in exchange for accepting the rule of egalitarianism in the present, industrial countries would not be held liable for emissions accumulated in the past.

Assuming an equal right to the Earth's atmosphere, broadly speaking it is possible to envisage different development paths for North and South. All countries are expected in the long run, to converge upon a similar level of fossil energy-use per capita. The North will contract, while the South will expand towards a convergence with the North. Over-users will have to come down from their present level, while under-users are permitted to raise their present level, albeit at a gradient that is much less steep than the one industrial countries went through historically, levelling off at the point of convergence. However, the convergence of North and South on equal emission levels cannot be achieved at the expense of contraction, i.e., the transition to globally sustainable levels of emissions. Once again, sustainability gives rise to equity. Indeed, the vision of 'contraction and convergence' combines ecology and equity most elegantly; it starts with the insight that the global environmental space is finite, and attempts to fairly share its permissible use among all world citizens, taking into account the future generations as well.

In light of this human-rights perspective, how would you allocate emissions? Should emissions be allocated on a per capita basis? Should each country get the same allocation so that the United States and Mozambique each would be allowed, say, 100 million tons of GHG emissions? On what basis were the emission caps allocated under the Kyoto Protocol?

B.   The Nature of the Commitments

Given the complexity and uncertainty regarding climate negotiations, the nature of post-Kyoto commitments is not predictable. The agreement could resemble the existing Kyoto Protocol, with additional overall caps and expansive use of flexibility mechanisms. The caps could also take on a variety of different shapes, or there could be an emphasis on other policy prescriptions besides caps. However, it seems clear that developing countries, at least the vast majority of developing countries, will not agree to caps, although they may agree to other types of obligations.

What, then, are viable approaches for a future climate agreement that meet the concerns of the United States and developing countries, while also preventing catastrophic impacts of climate change? Even before the ink was dry on the Kyoto Protocol, some governments and commentators questioned whether a focus on outputs (emissions) only was the best strategy for mitigating the impacts of climate change. Instead, they sought to broaden the scope of possible strategies to address inputs, such as energy use and other emissions-generating activities.

Section 1 below addresses the question of how to frame the overall goal for the post-Kyoto agreement. Section 2 then describes specific types of obligations that may integrate the concerns of developing and developed countries alike while also mitigating climate change.

1.   *The Commitment Goal*

The Bali Action Plan ties future negotiated commitments back to meeting the "ultimate objective" of the UNFCCC. Found in Article 2, that objective is to achieve "stabilization of greenhouse gas concentrations in the atmosphere at a level that would prevent dangerous anthropogenic interference with the climate system." In adopting an overall five percent reduction in greenhouse gas emissions, Parties to the Kyoto Protocol recognized that they were taking only the first step in reaching that objective. The Protocol's commitments reflect political expediency, not a scientific judgment that those reductions would by themselves prevent particular impacts. Implicit in that judgment, however, was that the world had several decades to achieve stabilization of greenhouse gases at a safe concentration, which at the time was generally viewed as approximately double pre-industrial levels (i.e., about 550 ppm).

Current scientific understanding, including the findings in the IPCC's Fourth Assessment, suggest that the situation is more urgent and the overall goal must now be more ambitious. Most scientists propose a long-term goal of preventing average temperatures from rising more than 2 degrees Celsius (3.6 degrees Fahrenheit) above pre-industrial average temperatures, because beyond 2 degrees Celsius, "the risks to human societies and ecosystems grow significantly [and] the risks of abrupt, accelerated, or runaway climate change also increase," such as loss of the West Antarctic and Greenland ice sheets. INTERNATIONAL CLIMATE CHANGE

TASK FORCE, MEETING THE CLIMATE CHALLENGE: RECOMMENDATIONS OF THE INTERNATIONAL CLIMATE CHANGE TASK FORCE 3 (2005). Yet, as explored in Chapter 2, significant uncertainty still exists in every step of the equation: what temperature increase will allow us to avoid the worst impacts? What concentrations of greenhouse gases will ensure that global average temperatures do not exceed the target? What emission caps will result in the desired atmospheric concentrations? Finally, what curbs on human activities will result in the emission reductions?

In light of these inherent uncertainties, whether a temperature-based goal is the most appropriate is not completely clear. The next excerpt by Jonathan Pershing and Fernando Tudela explores the stages of the climate cycle, from human activities to impacts, to assess the advantages and disadvantages of different targets.

JONATHAN PERSHING & FERNANDO TUDELA, A LONG-TERM TARGET: FRAMING THE CLIMATE EFFORT

in BEYOND KYOTO: ADVANCING THE INTERNATIONAL EFFORT AGAINST CLIMATE CHANGE 17–28 (Pew Center on Global Climate Change 2003)*

Stage V — Impacts

One approach to setting a long-term climate target would be to cast it in terms of the level of climate change impacts, or damages, to be avoided. Such a target could take many forms: avoiding substantial damage to coastal zones; minimizing climate-related migration of disease vectors or of natural or managed ecosystems; avoiding shifts in ocean circulation. There are compelling reasons for setting a target at this stage:

- As stated before, avoiding damages is the ultimate rationale for any action to mitigate climate change. An impacts target makes explicit the intent of the near-term effort.

- Many types of damage can be assessed in terms of cost, which can be weighed against the cost of mitigation. This allows an assessment of the value of any given level of effort.

- Many impacts are local. An impacts target with local resonance can provide a more compelling political rationale for action.

An impact-based approach is implicit in the UNFCCC's ultimate objective: avoiding *"dangerous"* anthropogenic interference." However, translating "dangerous" into concrete terms is anything but clear-cut. It requires consensus on the level of acceptable risk, an inherently political determination resting on value judgments.

More broadly, any impact-based target requires an adequate understanding of the likely magnitude, timing, and distribution of future climate impacts, as well as the potential steps that might be taken to offset the damages (e.g., through adaptation). However, even assuming sufficient knowledge and consensus on acceptable risk, an impacts target can effectively drive action only if it can be reflected back through the earlier stages — temperature, concentrations, and emissions — to human activities.

* * *

[E]ven if we were able to accurately forecast future temperature rises, our understanding of the climate responses, and therefore our ability to model them, remains limited, particularly at local and regional scales. . . .

Some impacts, particularly those on ecosystems, are quite sensitive not only to the magnitude of local climatic shifts but also to the rate of change. A slow change may allow for adaptation or shifts in the spatial distribution of species, while a quick one may accelerate the rate of extinction or disrupt ecological functions in an irreversible way. Some ecosystems, such as coral reefs, are particularly sensitive to climate changes and may be irreversibly affected in a matter of a few years.

Any attempt to project climate impacts also is made difficult by the long time lags involved. Even once global temperatures re-stabilize, already a distant outcome, sea level may still keep rising for centuries, driven by the slow process of ice cap melting. In setting a target, would the appropriate time frame be a century? Ten centuries? A millennium? The local nature of many impacts — and their sheer diversity — would further complicate a negotiation that arguably must be global in scope. Impacts will not be evenly spread throughout spatial scales, social groups, or ecosystems. Indeed, some are likely to be felt most acutely by those contributing least to their generation. Further, what is "dangerous" for one region or group might be less so or even beneficial for others.

One approach might be to define "dangerous" in larger structural terms — for example, irreversible or non-linear changes in ecosystems or societal systems. A long-term target may be more acceptable if it could define a threshold below which events perceived as catastrophic would be much less likely. Some have suggested that preventing the loss of "charismatic" ecosystems like coral reefs, or averting low-probability catastrophic events like the collapse of the West Antarctic Ice Sheet, could serve as powerful markers framing the long-term climate effort. Yet it is in understanding the triggers for, and therefore likelihood of, such events that science and modeling are in some cases at their weakest.

Even if consensus on what constitutes "dangerous" could be reached, to be of real utility, an impacts target would have to be translated back through the other stages of the climate cycle to in some fashion redirect human activities. It is important, then, to understand the additional uncertainties that enter at each stage.

Stage IV — Temperature

The most direct consequence of rising GHG concentrations is their thermody-namic effect on the atmosphere and the planet — i.e., rising temperatures. There are strong reasons to cast a long-term climate target in terms of global mean temperature [eds. note: e.g., a maximum temperature increase of 1.5 degrees Celsius]:

- Temperature and concomitant sea level rise are the primary climate change effects we are concerned with; establishing an explicit long-term target at this stage places the emphasis on those variables.

- Thermodynamic effects are global and thus are shared by all countries and individuals.

- The link between concentrations and temperatures has been well established; it thus can serve as a useful proxy.

- Temperature is an indicator that is readily understandable by the average citizen and therefore helps make an arcane debate more accessible.

- Global temperatures are now routinely monitored in a reasonably accurate fashion.

* * *

Focusing on temperature, rather than impacts, may bypass one broad set of uncertainties: the specific impacts linked to a change in temperature. However, this stage presents its own set of uncertainties. For instance, how are we to assess the global variability in the temperature change? Temperature is projected to increase faster in the polar regions, so must we set our global target correspondingly lower, below the desired average, to ensure an acceptable level of risk at the polar extremes? Or do we set different targets for different regions? Also, while the timescales are not as open-ended as at the previous stage, we continue to face very large time lags. Do we assess the acceptability of change as a function of the long-term equilibrium effect or of the effect over the next 100 years only? And how do we know when the effects of temperature stop being linear and cross some threshold to become sudden or catastrophic?

Finally, there are uncertainties in the link between temperature and GHG concentrations, one stage back in the cycle. For any given level of stable concentrations, we can at best project a range of temperature increase, with dramatic variations in the likely impacts at the upper and lower bounds of the estimate. . . .

Stage III — Concentrations

In both technical and political analyses of a potential long-term climate target, the metric most often employed is GHG concentrations. This is not surprising as it is the metric enshrined in the ultimate objective of the Framework Convention: " . . . stabilization of greenhouse gas concentrations in the atmosphere. . . . " This alone may suggest to some that this is the appropriate form for a long-term climate target and could impede any effort to negotiate a target of a different type. There are a number of persuasive rationales for setting a target at this stage of the cycle:

- Increased GHG concentrations in the global atmosphere are the most direct cause of climate change.

- Even more accurately than global temperatures, global GHG concentrations are now routinely monitored.

- The dynamics of GHG concentrations are commensurate with the long-term time frame of mitigation action, reflecting, as it does, not marginal change, but the cumulative total of all global activities.

- Finally, the UNFCCC reflects a political consensus that was difficult to achieve and, as it casts its ultimate objective in terms of stabilizing concentrations, politically this may be the easiest path to a specific long-term target.

* * *

A concentration target effectively sets an upper bound on allowable cumulative emissions over a given period. But it leaves open the question of the most feasible or cost-effective emission trajectories consistent with that target. The higher the near-term emissions, the sharper and greater the magnitude of the future decrease that will be required if any given concentration level is to be met. Analysts have run the models "backwards" to define possible emission pathways that would lead to stabilized CO_2 concentrations at levels ranging from 450 ppm to 1,000 ppm. They conclude that any given level of stabilization would require emissions to peak and then fall well below current levels. These analyses lead to a further inescapable conclusion: in the long run, regardless of what concentration level is set, it can be achieved only when net emissions (emissions minus removals by sequestration) effectively are reduced to zero. . . .

Stage II — Emissions

There are several compelling rationales for casting a long-term target in terms of emissions:

- Excess GHG emissions are readily understood as the cause of climate change; an emissions target is readily understood as an effort against an undesirable effluent.

- GHG emissions are frequently associated with other pollutants whose elimination is sought anyway for public health reasons.

- Every government has the authority to fully control domestic GHG emissions. As a consequence, it may adopt commitments related to these emissions and be held accountable in case of non-compliance.

- Based upon the work of the IPCC, clear methodologies, procedures, and formats exist to monitor, review, and report emissions in national inventories.

*   *   *

At the emissions stage of the cycle, however, we are yet further removed from climate impacts. Setting a target at this stage thus injects another layer of uncertainty in the correlation between the chosen metric and the ultimate goal of impacts avoided. The flip side, however, is that the metric is now more closely related to the underlying causes of climate change — human activities amenable to human control. This allows a more direct assessment of the kinds of actions that would be required and the costs they might entail.

As we have already seen, such assessments rest in part on assumptions about future emission trends. These, in turn, rest on assumptions about a host of variables, including economic growth, population growth, and the rate of technological change. As no one set of assumptions can be deemed reliable, the IPCC has developed a set of scenarios illustrating potential alternative futures and their associated emission trajectories, all in the absence of specific climate initiatives. . . . [T]he potential emission paths vary enormously. In some cases, CO_2 emissions peak around 2040–2050 and then decline; in others, these emissions keep growing throughout the 21st century and beyond. As of 2100, the projected levels of CO_2 emissions range from below 5 GtC to above 20 GtC [eds. note: a gigaton (Gt) equals one billion tons]. This enormous variability in emission forecasts provides considerable room for conflicting assessments of the effort required to meet a given emissions target.

*   *   *

Stage I — Human Activities

Arriving finally at the first stage of the climate cycle places the focus squarely on the human activities at the root of climate change. There are strong rationales for establishing a long-term target at this stage:

- Ultimately, human activities are the proximate cause of climate change; changing these activities will change the climate system.

- We — individually and through government policies — have the capacity to change behavior and technology to curb emissions and climate impacts. Few other points in the cycle can be so directly affected.

- Long-term goals set at this stage in the cycle may have ancillary benefits (e.g., local pollution reduction and improvements in trade competitiveness) and thus bring additional political support.

- Characterizing the challenge as technological, rather than exclusively environmental, may also help broaden political support.

What might an activities-based target look like? One option is to focus on outcomes — for instance, fully decarbonizing the energy sector by 2100. Another option is to set a particular technology goal — for instance, replacing internal combustion engines with fuel cell vehicles by 2030. Both approaches define the goal in concrete terms that, in theory at least, can be readily translated into a detailed program of action. The effects these targets have for subsequent stages in the climate cycle, while not easily quantified, are nonetheless obvious.

At the first stage evaluated above — stage V, impacts — the focus is primarily on damages to be avoided and, only secondarily, on the implications for other stages, from temperature to concentrations, emissions and, ultimately, human activity. The middle stage — concentrations — allows a more balanced view extending in both directions around the climate cycle. The present stage is the furthest removed from impacts; any attempt to calculate the benefits of an activities-based target in terms of impacts avoided is thus subject to all the uncertainties introduced at each intervening stage. Such a target can be correlated to the ultimate goal of avoiding impacts only in the most general sense.

Conversely, an activities-based target minimizes uncertainties about what effort will be required. The metric employed is the variable over which we have the greatest control. . . . Our influence is most direct at the stage of human activity: we can discourage activities that generate emissions, encourage activities that emit less or that capture emissions from the atmosphere, or live with the consequences and try to adapt. A long-term target set at any stage of the climate change cycle would, in any event, have to be translated into policies reshaping human behavior.

There are, of course, drawbacks. Unless the goal is sufficiently broad or stringent (e.g., full energy decarbonization), there is no assurance that it will in fact deliver the desired outcome of reduced climate change impacts. As with an emission target, the benefits are thus far more opaque than the costs of whatever action is required. At the same time, the costs are less diffuse here than they would be at other stages in the cycle. A focus on major emissions-generating activities places the burden much more immediately on specific sectors with significant political influence. Finally, a target cast in terms of a particular technology runs the risk of locking in a less-than-ideal technology and discouraging investment and innovation that could produce a better one. From a narrow economic standpoint, it may also be less cost-effective than a target that sets a desired environmental outcome and allows the market to choose the means of achieving it.

QUESTIONS AND DISCUSSION

1.   After reviewing the advantages and disadvantages of the various approaches described by Pershing and Tudela, which approach do you think governments should take? Do you think it is possible to devise an agreement with a meaningful scientific target or should the negotiating goal be to find a goal that is politically acceptable to all Parties?

2.   In choosing a goal, the negotiators will also need to address a number of other key issues. For example, to the extent that the goal allows some level of climate change to occur, then the negotiators must decide to what extent, if at all, adaptation should be included in the post-Kyoto Protocol agreement. Some proposals include liability or insurance mechanisms to compensate countries adversely affected by climate change. In addition, negotiators will need to decide whether new institutions are needed or existing ones replaced. To the extent that quantifiable commitments are not part of the new agreement, new compliance strategies must be considered. *See* Daniel Bodansky, *International Climate Efforts Beyond 2012: A Survey of Approaches*, 3–4 (Pew Center on Global Climate Change, 2004) (summarizing key issues).

3.   *Class Exercise.* The class may be divided into five groups representing stages I to V of the climate cycle: impacts, temperature, concentrations, emissions, and human activities. Each group should research, choose, and be ready to defend a commitment goal (for example, a maximum two degree Celsius temperature increase for the temperature group). Each group should explain why they have chosen that limit by describing the environmental, economic, and political implications of that choice.

---

2.   *Options for Mitigation Commitments*

Even if a goal can be chosen for designing international commitments, governments must achieve that goal through specific national commitments. As described above, an international goal that focuses on avoiding impacts still leaves unanswered whether those impacts will be avoided by demanding changes in policies or reductions in emissions. Similarly, quantitative targets could take the form of Kyoto-like targets and timetables where countries agree to reduce emissions of a certain amount by a specific date. They could also establish targets based on a percentage of actual emissions during a specific period. Regardless of the goal, governments will need to develop specific commitments for implementing the chosen goal. Governments, NGOs, academics, and others have proposed a wide variety of proposals. For some, the Kyoto Protocol's structure provides all the flexibility needed to ensure cost-effective emissions reductions as well as the participation of developing countries. For them, the only questions to be negotiated are the stringency of the commitments and timetable for meeting those commitments. *See* Cedric Philibert, *Approaches for Future International Co-operation*, COM/ENV/EPOC/IEA/SLT(2005)6, (OECD Environment Directorate & International Energy Agency, 2005) (summarizing the approaches for a post-Kyoto agreement). A number of proposals also rely on a quantitative approach, but would focus not on actual emissions, but on other thresholds, such as per capita emissions or emissions intensity. Still others take a non-quantitative approach that would focus on technology transfer, research and development, or changes in policies. *Id.*

By one count, more than 40 different proposals have been produced. Bodansky, *A Survey of Approaches*, at 1. Rather than summarize all 40 proposals, we focus on three alternative approaches that have garnered significant attention and represent broadly different approaches: indexed intensity targets, action targets, and sustainable development policies and measures (also known as SD-PAMs or PAMs). As you read the excerpts below, consider which of the approaches best meets the concerns of the various negotiating blocs and which may best avoid climate change impacts. In addition, because of the substantial and vibrant carbon market, it is highly likely that any future regime will include carbon trading. Which approach would work best with current carbon trading mechanisms?

a.   *Intensity Targets*

KEVIN A. BAUMERT, et al., WHAT MIGHT A DEVELOPING COUNTRY COMMITMENT LOOK LIKE?
CLIMATE NOTES 4–16 (World Resources Institute, May 1999)[*]

Measuring Climate Performance

Because carbon emission levels in most countries are closely correlated with economic growth, a country's *absolute* emission level may not always be a good indicator of "climate performance." . . .

In some cases, rapidly growing GHG emission levels are not necessarily indicative of poor climate performance. For example, even though China's annual GHG emissions grew by nearly 500 million tons of carbon (MtC) between 1980 and 1997, energy efficiency gains achieved during this period resulted in avoided emissions of 432 MtC. Although not done to protect the climate, without the price reforms and other measures that improved energy efficiency, China's carbon emissions in 1997 would have been more than 50 percent higher than its actual emissions. This decoupling of economic development and emissions growth is evident in terms of China's carbon intensity, which has declined by about 45 percent since 1980. Unfortunately, China's rapidly declining carbon intensity is the exception rather than the rule for most countries.

In the Ukraine, carbon emissions from 1990 to 1995 dropped by more than 40 percent. However, this decrease is due primarily to economic decline, rather than energy efficiency, fuel saving, or any other climate- or energy-related policy. In fact, the Ukraine's carbon intensity actually worsened during this period, increasing 20 percent from 994 to 1,194 tons of carbon per million dollars of gross domestic product (GDP) (measured in purchasing power parity). Similarly, absolute carbon emissions in the Russian Federation fell by more than 169 MtC between 1990 and 1995 (26 percent) while the economy became *more* carbon intensive, increasing in carbon intensity from 807 to 950. Thus, although overall levels of carbon emissions have decreased, neither Russia nor the Ukraine has become more sustainable this decade.

Climate performance can be better expressed through emissions *per unit of GDP*. This measure illustrates how well countries are decoupling the typically high correlation between carbon emissions and GDP . . . Indeed one could argue that the path toward achieving the Climate Convention's objective will necessarily require decoupling economic output and GHG emissions, much in the way conventional air pollution has been delinked from GDP in many industrialized countries. . . . A carbon intensity indicator measures tons of carbon emissions per million dollars of GDP.

*   *   *

EXPLORING THE CARBON INTENSITY INDICATOR

[The relationship between GDP and emissions, the two components of the carbon intensity indicator is intuitive — most economic activity typically results in GHG emissions.]

The key determinants of a national-level indicator are a country's economic structure, geography, fuel mix, and the energy efficiency of its production processes. Argentina and Brazil, for example, have low intensities partly due to the widespread use of carbon-free hydroelectric power. China and India have high intensities (although their trend lines differ) due partially to exploitation of domestic coal resources.

More important, however, the main *drivers of change* in developing country carbon intensities are policies and measures (or external shocks) that affect a country's economic structure, energy efficiency, and fuel choices. For example, China's successful decoupling of economic growth and carbon emissions (demonstrated by the steep decline in the carbon intensity indicator) is due largely to energy price reforms. Coal subsidies in China fell from 61 percent in 1984 to 29 percent in 1995, and petroleum subsidies dropped from 55 percent in 1990 to 2 percent in 1995. Shifts in economic activity to lower or higher carbon sectors as well as technological progress also contribute to variations in intensity trends. Disaggregating the carbon intensity indicators by sector and subsector would help reveal where fossil fuel use is most efficient and inefficient, shedding light on which sectors and industries drive the country-level indicators.

Finally, carbon intensity indicators differ from other measures, such as total carbon emissions or emissions per capita, in that they are not driven primarily by economic growth. Typically, during economic decline, both GDP and energy-related carbon emissions fall (while the opposite is true for economic growth). Which figure falls faster, and how a country's carbon intensity changes, is less clear. In some cases, such as economic decline in the Russian Federation and the Ukraine, GDP fell faster than carbon, signaling an increase in carbon intensity. In other cases, such as Bulgaria, Poland, Hungary, and other Eastern European countries, carbon intensity levels fell when economies declined (i.e., carbon emissions fell faster than GDP). This is often the result of deliberate energy policy reforms, including price liberalization and energy restructuring.

[The authors then note that the most important consideration is not a comparison of carbon intensity between countries but rather an assessment of "a country's performance *relative to itself*, taking into account both absolute intensity levels and changes over time." They also report that, among developing countries, "there is no discernible relationship between carbon intensity and level of development. For example, China and India have similar per capita income levels, yet China's intensity is falling rapidly while India's is rising." On the other hand, "for mature, industrialized economies . . . carbon intensity decreases consistently over time because GDP growth typically outpaces energy consumption."]

What Might a Developing Country Commitment Look Like?

A carbon intensity indicator, or another more comprehensive intensity-based measure, could also be used as a measure for a country commitment under the Climate Convention or Kyoto Protocol. Such a commitment might represent an agreement to *improve* intensity levels relative to past performance. In other words, the commitment might take the form of lowering the country's carbon or GHG intensity indicator. Determining compliance would be simple and straightforward in this case — a country would be in compliance if its actual intensity indicator was less than or equal to a target intensity indicator (i.e., the commitment) during the compliance period.

However, a country making a binding commitment might want to engage in international emissions trading. In this case, the intensity indicator could be translated into an absolute level of emissions during the compliance period. (*See the equation below.*)

Allowable GHG emissions = (GDP) (GHG emissions/GDP) where *GHG emissions / GDP* is the target intensity indicator and *GDP* is the total economic output during the compliance period. For the purposes of an individual country commitment, GDP would likely be measured in *local currency* rather than PPP or market exchange rates. This could eliminate possible controversy over exchange rate variations or PPP [purchasing power parity] conversion factors. * * *

Bringing an Intensity Indicator into Practice * * *

Data Coverage of the Intensity Indicator

Ideally, a voluntary commitment would factor in all gases and sinks included in the Kyoto Protocol. However, this may not be possible for some countries that may wish to make a commitment in the foreseeable future. Because of a lack of data availability in developing countries, the analysis here includes only carbon emissions from fossil fuel burning, cement manufacture, and gas flaring. Other GHGs and carbon emissions from land-use change (including biomass burning) . . . may, in many cases, be significant.

While comprehensive coverage of sources and sinks is desirable, data accuracy and consistency are crucial both for determining the magnitude of an initial commitment and ensuring its compliance — a fact true regardless of how commitments are measured. The current data limitations seriously constrain any focused discussion of voluntary commitments. In fact, the lack of technical capacity to measure and report emissions may be an important signal that a developing country is not ready to assume binding commitments. Remedying this data deficiency should be an objective of developing country governments, relevant multilateral bodies, *and* Annex I countries, which are required to provide "financial resources to meet the agreed full costs incurred by developing country Parties" in complying with their reporting obligations under the Climate Convention. * * *

In addition to the importance of GHG emissions data, using intensity indicators raises the added issue of scrutiny over reported GDP levels. In at least one recent case, officials have raised doubts about the validity of reported economic growth rates. Currently, the World Bank relies on countries to supply GDP data in their own local currencies. A common understanding of methodologies and full transparency would be required to ensure that GDP figures are not purposefully inflated in order to lower the reported intensity level.

Agreeing on a Commitment Level

Another issue inherent in any discussion of developing country commitments is agreeing on an acceptable target level. As noted above, a carbon intensity indicator removes the need to engage in an emissions "guessing game." However, negotiators will still need to consider what constitutes good performance and the intensity level from which to judge progress.

For many countries, progress could be benchmarked against a base year intensity indicator. Because the carbon intensity indicator internalizes fluctuations in economic growth, it is significantly less variable over time. The carbon intensity levels of Argentina, Brazil, Ghana, Indonesia, Korea, and Mexico have changed less than 10 percent over a 17-year period from 1980 to 1996. (*See* Table 9-1.) The Republic of Korea, for example, increased its absolute level of emissions by more than 225 percent during the 1980–1996 period. Over the same period, however, the carbon intensity indicator changed a mere 1.1 percent. For countries that experience more noticeable increases or declines in carbon intensity, projections may be needed. [P]rojections [based on] a continuation of the past performance of an economy's changing "carbon structure" — not a prediction of either GDP or annual carbon emission levels . . . may be a starting point for identifying a country's business-as-usual path, although factors unique to individual countries should color the detailed discussions on refining projection figures.

For example, carbon-reduction measures already taken and any future planned initiatives may help refine predictions and help shape a more plausible business-as-usual path from which to gauge progress. Carbon intensity indicators *disaggregated by sector* could also help forecast intensities by revealing where opportunities for reducing emissions exist and how existing policies and measures may alter future intensity levels.

*   *   *

Table 9-1: Percent Changes in Carbon Intensity and Carbon Emissions from 1980 to 1996

Country	Percent Change in Carbon Intensity	Percent Change in Total Carbon Emissions
Argentina	-5.8	20.8
Brazil	6.4	49.0
Chile	-18.5	74.6
China	-47.2	127.8
Ghana	5.5	66.8
India	29.1	187.2
Indonesia	-4.9	159.0
Rep. of Korea	-1.1	226.1
Malaysia	57.6	325.6
Mexico	1.8	38.4
Australia	-5.4	51.2
European Union	-29.2	-2.5
Japan	-20.4	26.9
United States	-20.3	15.9

Compliance and Emissions Trading

Although there are environmental advantages to intensity indicators, countries will be uncertain of their exact allowable emission levels until the *end* of the compliance period (unlike an Annex I-style commitment, where a country's allowable amount is calculated on the basis of the 1990 emission level). The time lag is necessary because GDP levels are needed to calculate allowable emissions. Thus, until emissions and GDP data are compiled at the end of the compliance period, a country will be unsure of both actual and allowable emissions. This added uncertainty has implications for compliance and emissions trading.

Annual assessments during the multiyear compliance period are one means of gauging country progress. However, an interim period at the conclusion of the compliance period would be needed during which countries could purchase allowances to come into compliance if necessary. Such a grace period is already envisioned by some as a desirable, or necessary, feature of an Annex I compliance system.

Emissions trading might also be inhibited by the absence of specific targets expressed in tons per year. However, options and futures markets could increase market efficiency and enable market transactions before or during the compliance period, with the final trades for compliance purposes occurring during the grace period. More significantly, again, multiyear compliance periods allow for *annual* assessments that would help countries gauge the amount of allowances needed to purchase or available to sell. After the first year of the compliance period, for example, a country could compare its actual emissions with the year's "allowable amount."

Thus, emissions trading could be far more dynamic than the simplistic example in Box 3 suggests. The possible shortcomings of emissions trading under an intensity indicator should be weighed against the dangers of operating a trading system that would combine existing Annex I targets with large emission growth commitments from non-Annex I countries.

Box 3 — Applying a GHG Intensity Indicator: A Thought Exercise

STEP 1. Formulating the Target

IF: *Country A, a rapidly growing developing country, agrees to lower its greenhouse gas (GHG) intensity by 40 percent below 1996 levels between the 2013–2017 period, and 1996 data are:*

Greenhouse gas emissions = 1,000 tons of carbon equivalent

Gross domestic product = $2 million

GHG intensity = 500 tons of greenhouse gas per million dollars of GDP

THEN: *The target GHG intensity for 2013–2017 = 300 (40 percent below the 1996 level of 500).*

STEP 2. Determining Allowable Emissions

IF: *During 2013–2017, Country A actually has:*

Gross domestic product = $30 million (average of $6 million per year for 5 years — three times higher than 1996 levels)

THEN: *Country A's allowable greenhouse gas emissions = 9,000 metric tons of carbon equivalent over the 5-year period (30 x 300) (i.e.,GDP times the target GHG intensity indicator).*

Despite this reduction in intensity, absolute levels of GHG emissions are still allowed to increase by 80 percent (from 1,000 tons of carbon equivalent in 1996 to 1,800 tons of carbon equivalent yearly during the 2013–2017 period).

STEP 3. How Much to Trade?

Outcome 1: If GHG emissions equal 8,000 tons of carbon equivalent during the 2013–2017 period, Country A may *sell* 1,000 tons of allowances through international emissions trading (i.e., the allowable amount exceeds actual emissions by 1,000 tons).

Outcome 2: If GHG emissions equal 10,000 tons of carbon equivalent, Country A must *buy* 1,000 allowances through emissions trading (actual emissions exceed the allowable amount by 1,000 tons).

QUESTIONS AND DISCUSSION

1.   Baumert et al. agree that a "carbon intensity indicator is a possible next step, but not the last step," and that future absolute limits or reductions may be needed. Nevertheless, they defend intensity indicators because they help address the climate challenge by decoupling economic development and GHG emissions growth.

Given our current understanding of climate change science, are intensity indicators a viable next step for developing countries?

2.   The United States has been a proponent of intensity targets, because it has not wanted to accept any absolute limits on its own emissions. As discussed in Chapter 11, President Bush set a goal for the United States to reduce its greenhouse gas intensity by 18 percent in ten years through voluntary measures. According to President Bush, this plan "will achieve 100 million metric tons of reduced emissions in 2012 alone, with more than 500 million metric tons in cumulative savings over the entire decade" and that this "is comparable to the average progress that nations participating in the Kyoto Protocol are required to achieve." White House, "Global Climate Change Policy Book" (Feb. 14, 2002). This policy would lead to an increase in U.S. GHG emissions and, because U.S. carbon intensity is declining anyway, President Bush's goal represents only a slight change from "business as usual." Many proponents of intensity targets, including Baumert, et al., do not believe they are appropriate for developed countries, because of their larger historical contribution to climate change. Do you agree?

---

b.   *Action Targets*

KEVIN A. BAUMERT & DONALD M. GOLDBERG, ACTION TARGETS: A NEW APPROACH TO INTERNATIONAL GREENHOUSE GAS CONTROLS
5 CLIMATE POLICY 567, 568–579 (2006)[*]

Mechanics of an action target

An action target is an obligation to achieve or acquire an agreed amount of GHG emission reductions. The amount of reductions required by the action target is expressed as a percentage of the country's actual emissions during the compliance period. For example, if a country adopted an action target of 2% for the period 2013–2017, it would need to demonstrate emission reductions equal to 2% of its actual emissions during this period. In this way, an action target defines the amount of abatement to be achieved during a commitment period. This differs from Kyoto-style or dynamic [i.e., intensity] targets, which define a level of *emissions* (or *emissions per unit of GDP*) to be achieved during a particular period.

Mathematically, an action target can be illustrated as:

$$RR = AT \times E \text{ (1)}$$

where required reductions (RR) is the number of reductions a country must achieve, the action target (AT) is the percentage by which the country has agreed to reduce its emissions, and E is the country's emissions during a given compliance period. Required reductions (RR) is equal to the action target (AT) multiplied by the country's emissions (E). To illustrate, suppose Country A agrees to an action target (AT) of 5% for the year 2015. If Country A's emissions (E) in that year are 100 million tons of carbon (MtC), then the required amount of reductions is 5 MtC. According to Equation 1:

$$RR = AT \times E \text{ (1)}$$

$$RR = 5\% \text{ x } 100 \text{ MtC}$$

$$RR = 5 \text{ MtC}$$

This illustration demonstrates that action targets would have the effect of bending the emissions trajectory of a country downward. It follows that, if emissions are *actually* 100 MtC during the compliance year *and* the country has demonstrated 5 MtC of domestic reductions, then emissions *would have been* 105 MtC in the absence of any actions taken to reach the target.

Because the required emission reduction is a function of the actual emissions during the commitment period (100 MtC, see above), large fluctuations in economic and emission levels have only moderate effects on the level of abatement required. In the example above, suppose that Country *A*'s economy grew faster than expected, causing emissions to rise to 120 MtC during the commitment period. In this case, Country *A* would need to demonstrate 6 MtC of reductions (5% of 120), either domestically or through international purchases. Conversely, economic stagnation would have the opposite effect. If emissions turn out to be only 80 MtC during the commitment period, Country *A*'s required reductions drop to 4 MtC (5% of 80). Thus, extremely large emission fluctuations, on the order of 40 MtC, have the effect of altering this particular target by only 2 MtC.

This contrasts with Kyoto-style fixed targets, which are formulated as a percentage change in emissions relative to a fixed base year. If Country *A*, in the example above, had agreed to a fixed target of 100 MtC, then this target could turn out to be extremely onerous (e.g., if Country *A* ended up on an emissions path of 120 MtC) or require no effort at all (e.g., if economic stagnation put Country *A* on a path toward 80 MtC) resulting in a windfall of excess emission allowances.

As the name implies, some amount of 'action' — in the form of domestic reductions or international purchases — is required to meet any target. This is true for very small targets (e.g., 0.5%) or more ambitious action targets (e.g., 10%). The amount of action can be tailored to a relatively high level of certainty. As the above example illustrates, a country could adopt an action target and be relatively certain, even a decade in advance, of the level of effort (i.e., emission reductions) that will be required to meet that target. * * *

Emissions trading and environmental performance

Action targets could operate in a manner that is complementary and consistent with the prevailing Kyoto system of fixed targets, emissions trading and the CDM. Like countries with emissions targets, a country adopting an action target could comply with its obligation by purchasing Kyoto-compliant emission allowances or credits in lieu of (or in concert with) taking domestic action. Likewise, countries could be permitted to sell allowances if they over-comply with their action targets. * * *

Assessing compliance

Compliance assessments under action targets would entail two basic steps. First, a determination of required reductions would need to be made at the end of the commitment period (or, during a 'trueup' period following the commitment period). To do this, according to Equation 1 . . . , a country's action target would simply be multiplied by its actual emissions during the commitment period. This is not to suggest that countries should wait until the end of the commitment period to determine what actions are needed to meet their action targets. Just as fixed targets require countries to look ahead to determine the actions they will need to take during, or even preceding, the commitment period, action targets require countries to assess the number of reductions they are likely to need to meet their target . . . and to have a plan in place to achieve the amount of required reductions.

To undertake this first step, a national GHG emissions inventory would be needed. However, the degree of accuracy and international oversight such inventories would require is less under action targets than under fixed or dynamic targets. This is because measurement inaccuracies have a relatively small effect on the required reductions (RR) under an action target. Repeating the Country A example used above: if the action target (AT) is 5%, and the emissions (E) inventory during the commitment period is understated by 10% (90, instead of 100 MtC), then the required reduction will be 4.5 MtC (5% of 90). Similarly, a 10% overstatement in emissions during the commitment period would increase the reduction requirement to 5.5 MtC (5% of 110). Thus, the same dynamics that reduce uncertainty in target setting also help to offset the potentially deleterious effects of inaccurate national inventories.

By contrast, under a system of fixed or dynamic targets, a bias of a few percentage points might substantially alter the level of effort needed to achieve compliance. Accordingly, inventories must be prepared to a higher degree of quality and are subject to rigorous international standards and oversight procedures. Were developing countries to adopt such targets, achieving high quality inventories would entail major financial and institutional capacities, which might otherwise be directed toward substantive action. Indeed, almost all developing countries have reported difficulty in compiling their emissions inventories under the Climate Convention.

The second step in a compliance assessment is determining the amount of reductions a country has generated domestically and transacted internationally (purchases and sales). Thus, for action targets, the compliance assessment would need to be directed primarily at assessing the efficacy of pledged *actions*, rather than a Kyoto-style assessment of actual *emissions*. . . . This kind of process — examining actions, or the lack thereof — might help accelerate learning in climate protection efforts and help build capacity to take further actions. Emissions inventories may tell policy makers whether emissions have gone up or down, but they do not explain the reasons for those changes. In contrast, the information required to assess compliance with action targets should enhance the ability of regulators and stakeholders to distinguish between actions that were effective from those that failed to produce desired reductions.

QUESTIONS AND DISCUSSION

1. One reason for preferring intensity or action targets to absolute (fixed) emissions limitations is that they reduce the uncertainty caused by emissions projections based on uncertain assumptions of economic growth. For example, emissions projections for China made in the late 1990s varied by as much as 519 MtC in 2010 — an amount that exceeded the combined 1990 carbon emissions of Brazil, India, Indonesia, Korea, and Mexico. If a developing country's caps on emissions growth are based on high projections of economic growth, or an economic downturn causes growth to slow, countries would have substantial "hot air" to trade. Both intensity targets and action targets seek to eliminate uncertainties in projecting economic growth and the possibility for hot air by establishing targets that adjust according to changes in GDP or another variable.

2.   Action targets require countries to reduce emissions by some amount based on actual emissions during a specific time period. If that is so, how can a country reduce emissions by the end of the commitment period when actual emissions for the commitment period cannot be counted until the end of that year? Each time a country emits a ton, it incurs an obligation to reduce its emissions by one ton multiplied by the action target. So, if Country A has an action target of 5%, each ton it emits gives rise to an obligation to reduce emissions by 1/20th of a ton (5%). Thus, Country A must keep track of emissions in real time. In practice, countries would be more likely to estimate their ongoing emissions and reduce accordingly. Another possibility would be to require the reductions to be made in the following compliance period.

3.   A fundamental aspect of action targets is to devise a method for developing countries to take on commitments with little or no economic risk. To ascertain the level of economic and climate change risk, Baumert and Goldberg compared a 2 percent target in 2015 using fixed (Kyoto-style), intensity, and action targets in five large developing countries where emissions are expected to grow significantly (Brazil, China, India, South Korea, and Mexico). Their results showed that a fixed target set at 2 percent below business-as-usual could result in high economic and climate change risk. Depending on whether economic growth was higher or lower than expected, fixed targets would result in large reductions (-9 percent to -13 percent) or significant surplus emissions (+3 percent to +22 percent), creating uncertain mitigation results. Higher than expected growth would also create economic uncertainty by requiring countries to finance greater reductions than expected.

Intensity targets substantially reduce uncertainty in the level of abatement effort required. However, while almost all growth scenarios require some emissions reductions, amounts were, overall, much less than for fixed targets under the high growth scenario: zero for Brazil and South Korea under a high GDP scenario and as much as a 7 percent reduction for Brazil under a low GDP scenario. The authors, however, noted a potentially troubling aspect to intensity targets: "that *higher* levels of effort tend to be needed when GDP is *lower* than expected (i.e., targets are most stringent in the Low GDP scenarios). This could be problematic, as economic stagnation will reduce the capacity of countries to take actions on climate, as other social and economic issues rise in priority." Baumert & Goldberg, at 570.

For action targets, reductions varied little between scenarios, because the reduction requirement is based on actual rather than projected emissions. Although the actual reductions in metric tons were small compared to intensity targets, Baumert and Goldberg conclude that by eliminating much of the uncertainty in target setting, developing countries might be more likely to commit to binding obligations. Do you agree? If you were representing a developing country, what would you see as the major advantages and disadvantages of each of the three types of targets: emission caps, intensity targets and action targets? What if you were representing environmentalists?

---

c.   *Policies and Measures*

A policies-and-measures approach (PAMs), also called sustainable development policies and measures (SD-PAMs), that focuses not on emissions but rather on a country's laws and policies, such as requiring the use of renewable energy, has generated much enthusiasm for a number of reasons. First, the PAMs approach could transform entire economic sectors, such as the transportation sector, if governments mandate specific technological or fuel efficiency requirements for automobiles. Second, many believe it is the only way to obtain commitments from developing countries. Developing countries have adamantly opposed quantifiable emissions limits, because such limits are viewed as constraining economic development. Developing countries may be more willing to accept PAMs that place the same or similar requirements on everyone and may also bring development opportunities to them. Third, assuming that the PAMs lead to greater country participation, leakage will be reduced or eliminated: companies will not have an incentive to move their production, because all countries will have obligations to adopt certain policies. A PAMs approach can be implemented in many ways as suggested in the following excerpt:

DANIEL BODANSKY, CLIMATE COMMITMENTS: ASSESSING THE OPTIONS

in BEYOND KYOTO: ADVANCING THE INTERNATIONAL EFFORT AGAINST CLIMATE CHANGE 37, 41–43 (Pew Center on Global Climate Change 2003)*

In contrast to a target-based approach, a commitment regarding policies and measures (PAMs) is an obligation of conduct rather than an obligation of result: it requires countries to act in certain ways, but does not require them to achieve any particular level of emissions or financial contribution. During the negotiation of the Kyoto Protocol, the European Union pushed for the inclusion of commitments related to policies and measures, but due to strong resistance from the United States, the Protocol includes only an illustrative list of possible PAMs, without requiring states to adopt them. Examples of PAMs include:

Technology and performance standards — An international commitment can address the use of emission-reduction technologies. For example, it could specify mandatory standards relating to appliance efficiency, residential insulation, or the use of renewable or other non-emitting energy sources. The international commitment can either require the use of particular technologies (which would tend to lock in those technologies) or set forth a performance standard (for example, relating to energy efficiency) that allows private entities flexibility as to the choice of particular technologies. Among the relatively few examples of international technology standards are the construction, design, and equipment standards for oil tankers set forth in the Marine Convention (MARPOL) including, for example, segregated ballast tanks.

Taxes — An international commitment can provide for a common or harmonized tax on GHG emissions. So long as a country had the required tax in place, it would satisfy its international commitment, regardless of the actual level of emissions reduction achieved.

Subsidy removal — An international commitment can require countries to remove specified subsidies, for example, on energy production or consumption. The Kyoto Protocol includes in its illustrative list of PAMs for developed countries "the progressive reduction and phasing out of subsidies." Subsidies are a problem not only in industrialized countries: the International Energy Agency estimates that removing energy subsidies in just eight developing and transition countries would reduce their CO_2 emissions by 17 percent and global emissions by 4.6 percent.

Emissions trading — An emissions commitment can be coupled with a PAM requiring countries to implement a domestic emissions trading program with specified features (including possible linkages with other national programs and with an international emissions trading system, or a safety-valve device). The European Union directive on emissions trading represents an effort of this kind: it sets forth the parameters of a required emissions trading system for EU member states.

Technology R & D and incentives — To address the low rates of investment in research and development concerning emission-reducing technologies, a commitment might require states to devote additional resources for R & D, as well as for deployment of existing and new technologies. For example, countries could commit to various forms of participation in an international hydrogen initiative. The agreement on the international space station is one illustration of an international agreement focusing on cooperative research, development, and deployment.

Since a targets-based approach and a PAM-based approach are often seen as competitors, it is worth emphasizing that they could complement one another: a target could be used to specify the overall result to be achieved, while PAMs could specify the means for reaching that result. Indeed, in some cases the relationship could be even stronger. As some commentators have noted, an international target-and trading approach would be most cost-effective if combined with national PAMs ensuring that domestic trading systems are complementary.

Policies and measures may be most effective when developed and applied at an industry sector level. Examples might include:

- Achieving specific high levels of efficiency (measured as an output per unit of energy) in home or industrial appliances, transportation systems, utilities or production processes;

- Eliminating the use of sulfur hexafluoride (SF_6) or perfluorocarbons (PFCs) in the industrial sector;

- Developing the technology for cost-effective capture and storage of CO_2 by 2025;

- Replacing gasoline in the transport sector with hydrogen produced by non-carbon emitting sources by 2050;

- Eliminating carbon emissions from the energy sector by 2060.

Pershing & Tudela, *A Long-Term Target: Framing the Climate Effort*, at 30.

In the next excerpt, Scott Barrett argues that, to make a difference to the climate, "a treaty has to create incentives for long-term technical innovation." To that end, he would couple a policies and measures approach with cooperative research and development, a "big science" collaboration comparable to the International Space Station, that would focus on electric power and transportation. Concerning the policies and measures aspect of his proposal, he makes the following observations:

SCOTT BARRETT, U.S. LEADERSHIP FOR A GLOBAL CLIMATE CHANGE REGIME
17–18 (Climate Policy Center: March 2003), *available at,*
http://www.cleanair-coolplanet.org/cpc/library_cpc.php*

[W]e must rely on business to develop and produce new energy technologies. Supplemental protocols should establish a system for agreeing on common standards for technologies that can be developed using the R&D. Economists normally reject the setting of technology standards. But they have a strategic advantage. The standard of requiring catalytic converters on automobiles, coupled with the use of unleaded gasoline, has effectively spread this technology around the world. Why? One reason is that a combination of economies of scale and learning has lowered the costs of producing both technologies. A second reason is that countries manufacturing either autos or gasoline want to be able to sell their products in the leading markets — so they will produce to these standards for commercial reasons. A third reason is that network externalities mean that every country wants to do what its neighbors are doing. If your neighbor requires catalytic converters, your own gas stations will supply unleaded gasoline to meet the demand of cars and trucks crossing your border. Having done so, it then becomes cheaper to require catalytic converters domestically. Fourth, there will be a domestic demand for the new technologies. It is hard for a country to argue for an environmental standard that is weaker than available abroad; why should our country's public health be valued less than that of other countries? Finally, standards create automatic trade restrictions — restrictions that are easy to monitor and enforce, and that are permitted by the rules of the World Trade Organization.

Again, notice the strategic effect of this approach. As more countries adopt a standard, it becomes more attractive for others to adopt the same standard. This kind of incentive is lacking in the Kyoto approach. In contrast to Kyoto, compliance with the protocol would also be easy to monitor and verify. Standards agreements already exist in related areas. One multilateral agreement establishes auto standards. Another establishes standards for oil tankers.

There are, to be sure, problems with the standards approach. One problem is that standards will work better for some sectors than for others. For automobiles, network externalities are relatively important, leading to a positive feedback in the adoption of new technologies such as the fuel cell. For other sectors, such as electric power generation, economies of scale may be important, but network externalities will be less so.

Another disadvantage is that standards are not always the most cost-effective way of reducing emissions. Certain parts of the economy will not be affected by the standards protocols. Standards may "lock in" a technology, rather than promote continuous innovation and improvement. The standards approach is very much a second best proposal. . . .

I have emphasized the strategic advantage of standards, but others have noted a different advantage to any policy and measure as compared to an emission limit. When countries sign up to an emission limit, they do so without knowing how much implementation will cost. With policies and measures, including standards, it is harder to know the final effect of implementation on emissions, but it is easier to estimate the cost. The allocation problems associated with Kyoto — in which the United States is given a very stringent target and Russia an overly generous one — are thus eased by a policies-and-measures approach. This advantage would be especially important if the system were subject to unanticipated shocks. Timing of the economic cycle and fluctuations in energy prices can have a huge effect on emissions, but they would have little effect on the adoption of technologies.

I should emphasize, however, that standards, like targets, must be carefully chosen. They must, in particular, offer every party a benefit in excess of the cost. The standards approach is basically intended to affect a technological transformation of the global economic system, but the extent of the transformation could be large or small, depending partly on the success of the joint R&D and partly on the level of mitigation countries think is justified. At the one extreme, standards could mandate hybrid engines for new automobiles. At the other extreme, they could mandate fuel cells or electric vehicles coupled with carbon capture and storage in electricity supply. The essential point is that, for strategic reasons, it may be better to negotiate agreements promoting the development and diffusion of new technologies directly. The Kyoto approach promotes technological development and diffusion indirectly, by raising the cost of emitting greenhouse gases. Both approaches have to make choices about the policy goals or *ends*, which are substantial versus modest mitigation. Where they differ is in the choice of the policy instrument or *means*.

QUESTIONS AND DISCUSSION

1.   The economist Joseph Stiglitz has proposed a common environmental tax on emissions of greenhouse gases as part of the post-Kyoto regime.

> There is a social cost to emissions, and the common environmental tax would simply make everyone pay the social cost. This is in accord with the most basic of economic principles, that individuals and firms should pay their full (marginal) costs. The world would, of course, have to agree on assessing the magnitude of the social cost of emissions; the tax could, for instance, be set so that the level of (global) reductions is the same as that set by the Kyoto targets. As technologies evolve, and the nature of the threat of global warming becomes clearer, the tax rate could adjust, perhaps up, perhaps down.

Joseph E. Stiglitz, *A New Agenda for Global Warming*, ECONOMISTS' VOICE 3 (July 2006). Review the discussion of carbon taxes in Chapter 2, Section II.3. What advantages and disadvantages does such a proposal have? What challenges must be overcome to impose a *global* tax?

2.   Daniel Bodansky summarizes a number of other proposals:

> **No lose targets** — "No lose" targets are another type of target that some have suggested for less developed countries (or possibly for all developing country's). No lose targets are non-binding and, if exceeded, do not have any compliance consequence. But if a [developing country's] emissions are below the no lose target, it would be allowed to sell surplus emissions to other countries and thereby receive a benefit.

> **Dual intensity targets** — Dual intensity targets combine dynamic and no lose targets in a further effort to address the problem of economic uncertainty. Under this approach, developing countries would receive two targets: a relatively weak "compliance" target and a more stringent "selling" target. Both targets would be carbon intensity targets, indexed to the country's GDP. The compliance target would be legally binding; if a country exceeded the target, it would suffer compliance consequences. In

contrast, the selling target would be no lose: if a country exceeded its target, it would not suffer any compliance consequence but, if it bettered the target, then it could sell its excess allowances internationally. Because different targets would be established for compliance and emissions trading purposes, developing countries could be given a comparatively easy compliance target that does not unduly constrain economic growth or create the danger of hot air, since a more stringent target would be defined for emissions trading purposes.

Conditional targets — The Human Development Goals proposal suggests that, to the extent that a developing country target goes beyond projected business-as-usual improvements in carbon intensity, it should be made conditional on the receipt of financial assistance or technology from developed countries.

Sectoral targets — Although most target-based proposals set a target for a country's national emissions, a target could apply to a limited number of sectors — for example, energy production. The Growth Baselines and the Converging Markets proposals, for example, envision the possibility of sector-based targets. The Technology Backstop Protocol would, in effect, define long-term zero emission targets for particular sectors: fossil fuel electric power generation, synthetic fuels, and fossil fuel refining.

Safety valve — Several target-based proposals, including the Hybrid International Emissions Trading and the Dual Track approaches, include a safety valve mechanism. A safety valve allows states (and possibly individual companies or other entities) to buy additional allowances at a predetermined "safety valve" price. This makes an emissions target conditional: if the marginal cost of abatement rises above the safety valve level, then the target is relaxed through the sale of additional allowances. If the price is set above the projected marginal cost of compliance, the safety valve serves as insurance against unexpectedly high costs. Setting a low price can effectively turn the emissions target into a tax. A safety valve could be implemented by individual countries or internationally. One design issue in either case is how the proceeds, if any, would be spent.

Daniel Bodansky, *International Climate Efforts Beyond 2012: A Survey of Approaches*, 67–68 (Pew Center on Global Climate Change 2004).

Under another approach, the climate change regime would act as a facilitator of national level actions to mitigate climate change. Rather than negotiate global or country-specific commitments, governments would inform the Parties to the climate change regime of the commitments they are taking and will take in the future. This approach recognizes that the very different and entrenched views of countries concerning climate change may weaken any eventual international agreement, if an agreement can be reached at all. It also recognizes each country's economic circumstances, capacities to address climate change, and emissions levels. What are the advantages and disadvantages of this approach?

3.   Others have taken a more interventionist view of what needs to be done. In addition to reducing emissions and developing adaptation strategies at the local, national, and regional levels, some have argued that countries need to begin now to negotiate the terms and conditions for employing geo-engineering to respond to climate change. Scott Barrett, for example, argues:

[W]e need to begin to consider the possibility of removing carbon dioxide (CO_2) directly from the atmosphere . . . by fertilizing the oceans with iron to stimulate the growth of CO_2-eating phytoplankton. . . . [W]e must also contemplate the possibility of reducing the amount of solar radiation that strikes the Earth, to counteract the effects of increasing atmospheric concentrations of greenhouse gases. . . . "Geoengineering" would essentially fabricate a similar effect; the most developed proposals would throw sulfate or engineered particles into the stratosphere, where they would linger for a few years before being "rained out" over the poles. Such an intervention would introduce new risks, but it may help to reduce the risk of abrupt and catastrophic climate change.

Scott Barrett, *Proposal for a New Climate Change Treaty System*, ECONOMISTS' VOICE 2 (Oct. 2007). Review the discussion of these geoengineering proposals in Chapter 3, Section IV. Should a post-Kyoto agreement include plans for these technological interventions? If so, who should be responsible for undertaking such activities and who should be liable for any unintended consequences?

4. ***Climate Change and Development.*** As noted earlier in this chapter, climate change and development are clearly linked. It should also be readily apparent that development is the key issue for developing countries in the climate change context and other contexts. Food security, access to clean water, clean air, energy, and transportation are all issues that all developing countries must address. The PAMs approach is thought to provide the best opportunities for linking climate change and development because policies and measures could be tied to sustainable development *and* climate goals. How should an PAMs approach be constructed to ensure climate change policy leads to development gains for developing countries?

5. ***Problem Exercise.*** Your instructor will divide you into groups representing different sectors, such as the transportation, energy, forestry, and chemicals sectors. Identify what these sectors are doing at the national level to reduce GHG emissions. Do any of these strategies provide the basis for an international agreement to reduce emissions within that sector? What policies and measures being taken nationally or subnationally would be appropriate for international cooperation?

6. ***Class Exercise.*** Your instructor will divide the class into four groups: (1) Annex 1 Parties to the Kyoto Protocol; (2) Large, middle-income developing countries represented by India and China; (3) Small Island Developing States and other developing countries likely to be seriously affected by climate change; and (4) industrialized countries, such as the United States, Japan, and Canada, that have strong reservations about the Kyoto Protocol. Taking into account the latest science and policy developments (including the release of the IPCC's latest report), negotiate a post-Kyoto international response to climate change. To be successful in reversing climate change, assume that the policy response must strive: (1) to reduce GHG emissions worldwide by 60-80 percent and (2) to deploy technologies or land-use practices capable of drawing down atmospheric carbon dioxide concentrations close to pre-industrial levels. You must accomplish these goals in about 50 years. In addition to the issues and approaches described in this chapter, consider both the Bali Action Plan and the following general issues for your negotiations.

DANIEL BODANSKY, A SURVEY OF APPROACHES
67–68*

Form and Forum of Negotiations

Should international efforts continue to focus on the development of a single, comprehensive global regime and, if so, does the UNFCCC provide the most appropriate forum? Or should negotiations proceed in a more flexible, decentralized manner, involving multiple agreements and/or smaller groups of countries or private-sector parties (for example, like-minded states or companies)? If this more variable geometry is pursued, should it be in addition, or as an alternative, to the UNFCCC process?

Time Frame

What is the appropriate time frame — the Kyoto Protocol's second commitment period, a somewhat longer medium-term time frame, or the long-term evolution and development of the regime?

Mitigation Commitments

Approaches to defining commitments — Should the climate regime continue to operate in a top-town manner, involving the multilateral negotiation of commitments? Or should it proceed in a bottom-up fashion, seeking to encourage countries to make (and implement) pledges of domestic measures to mitigate climate change? Can the two be combined?

Type of commitments — What types of mitigation commitments should be included? Should the climate regime continue to emphasize quantitative emission targets and, if so, should they be fixed, national, Kyoto-like targets, or some alternative form of target (dynamic, dual, sectoral, no lose, etc.)? Or are non-target-based approaches preferable — for example, harmonized domestic policies and measures, development-focused approaches, financial transfers, or technology standards?

Stringency of commitments — How should the stringency of commitments be determined? Is it better to begin with relatively weak commitments, to encourage broad participation, or more stringent commitments?

Differentiation and burden sharing — How should the burden of commitments be shared among countries? For example, if a target-based approach is adopted, how should targets be allocated (for example, on the basis of population, historical responsibility, basic human needs)? What is the pathway, if any, towards global coverage? Should the differentiation in the UNFCCC and the Kyoto Protocol between developed and developing countries continue, or should additional categories of countries be defined and, if so, on what basis (e.g., per capita GDP, per capita emissions, total emissions)? Should criteria be developed for graduation of countries from one category to another?

Adaptation

What approach should be taken to the issue of adaptation? Can existing approaches under the UNFCCC be improved or expanded? Should a liability or insurance scheme be established to provide compensation to countries adversely affected by climate change?

Implementation and Compliance

Are new institutions or approaches needed to assure that international climate commitments are implemented and enforced?

Good luck in your negotiations. The future response to climate change, if effective, will mark a historic high point in international cooperation. If it fails, then climate change may reshape the future of international cooperation in ways we can only imagine.

Chapter 10

CLIMATE CHANGE AND OTHER INTERNATIONAL LAW REGIMES

SYNOPSIS

4. **Fuel Efficiency Standards and Ecolabels**
5. **Subsidies**

I. INTRODUCTION

This chapter explores implications of climate change for other areas of international law, and vice-versa. Not surprisingly given its pervasive impacts, the phenomenon of climate change will raise significant new issues for other international law fields. Climate change, for example, may lead to the large-scale displacement of people, thus raising issues of how human rights and humanitarian law will address climate refugees. The significant deterioration of natural ecosystems expected from climate change will undermine the effectiveness of international legal regimes aimed at protecting our natural heritage. The international climate regime, particularly with its unique cap-and-trade approach, also raises significant questions of overlaps and gaps with other existing international legal regimes. The relationship between the climate regime and efforts to control ozone depletion is one such example, as is the relationship between climate change and international trade law.

In general, international law is ill-equipped to deal with overlapping jurisdictions, gaps in the law, or unintended consequences that require policy trade-offs between regimes. International environmental law comprises a relatively ad hoc set of treaties, each aimed at a different environmental issue. To make matters worse, no one institution is in charge of international environmental law. To be sure, questions regarding the climate regime will be addressed by the climate Secretariat in Bonn or the Conference of the Parties — but it is not authorized to interpret other environmental regimes or to make decisions binding on the Parties of other regimes. The Vienna Convention on the Law of Treaties provides general guidance on interpreting treaties that may be in potential conflict, but this provides little specific guidance to ensure a balanced and well-reasoned outcome. Moreover, no overarching international environmental agreement sets forth either procedures or principles for resolving conflicts between environmental regimes. Nor does the United Nations Environment Programme or any other institution have the authority to ensure policy coherence among the environmental regimes. The situation is even starker when environmental rules come into conflict with or otherwise raise issues of international trade or human rights. Who decides? Under what rules? These questions are explored further in this chapter.

II. THE OZONE REGIME AND CLIMATE CHANGE

A.   Introduction to Ozone Depletion

Ozone depletion and climate change are frequently confused. For most purposes they should be considered two completely separate environmental issues. They involve different chemical processes, have mostly different causes, and result in different threats to human health and the environment. Ozone depletion is itself a major environmental threat, but one that is being addressed effectively through the Montreal Protocol regime. The following excerpt provides a brief overview of ozone depletion and the Montreal Protocol regime.

DAVID HUNTER, JAMES SALZMAN & DURWOOD ZAELKE, INTERNATIONAL ENVIRONMENTAL LAW & POLICY
5–7 (3d ed., 2007)*

The stratospheric ozone layer is a blanket of diffuse gases encircling the earth at a distance of 12 to 50 kilometers above the surface. Named for the molecule of three weakly bound oxygen atoms (O_3 or ozone) that concentrate there, the stratospheric ozone layer shields the earth from high-energy ultraviolet (UV-B) radiation from the sun. UV-B radiation is extremely harmful to human health and the environment.

Like greenhouse gases, stratospheric concentrations of ozone have maintained relatively constant levels through natural, homeostatic processes. By interfering with these processes, chlorofluorocarbons (CFCs) and certain other widely used synthetic chemicals, can destroy stratospheric ozone more quickly than natural processes can replenish it. CFCs and similar chemicals, used as refrigerants, aerosols and other common applications, migrate into the upper atmosphere, where they are broken down by high-energy radiation. As these compounds break down, they release chlorine and bromine ions. These ions, in turn, catalyze a reaction that breaks down ozone molecules. The chlorine and bromine ions are not destroyed in this reaction, and each ion can destroy thousands of ozone molecules. Beginning in the 1940s, global use of CFCs and other ozone depleting substances expanded dramatically, with a corresponding increase in atmospheric chlorine and bromine.

In Antarctica, where the greatest losses have occurred, up to 60% of stratospheric ozone is depleted each September, resulting in an "ozone hole" larger than the entire United States. A similar hole also exists above the Arctic. The thinning of the ozone layer is not confined to the poles. Unprecedented levels of ozone depletion have been measured over Europe, North America, Australia, and New Zealand, with as much as a 10% decline over northern middle latitudes, and 35% over parts of Siberia.

The increased amounts of UV-B radiation striking the Earth's surface endanger human health, agriculture and the environment. Rates of skin cancer, for example, may increase by 2% for every 1% loss in ozone coverage. A 10% reduction of atmospheric ozone could result in an additional 300,000 cases of skin cancer and up to 1.75 million additional cases of cataracts *each year*. UV-B exposure also suppresses the body's immune response system, making it more vulnerable to certain diseases. Under laboratory conditions, increased radiation at the levels expected from ozone depletion inhibits the growth of many plants, including important commercial species such as soybeans, cotton, and certain trees. Not only could this impair crop production, but it may also alter the biodiversity of terrestrial ecosystems. UV-B radiation causes developmental abnormalities in fish, shellfish and amphibians, threatening hundred of species. The global decline of frogs, for example, has been attributed in part to increased UV-B exposure. Such exposure also reduces the productivity of phytoplankton, the base of the ocean's food web. Reductions in this fundamental food source could dramatically affect the biodiversity of the oceans, potentially threatening the entire marine food chain.

Beginning with the Vienna Convention on Ozone Depletion in 1985 and the Montreal Protocol in 1987, the international community has taken a series of increasingly restrictive steps to phase out global production and consumption of ozone depleting substances. Known as the Montreal Protocol regime, these treaties have led to the nearly complete ban of CFCs and other ozone depleting substances.

Because of the steps taken under this regime, global consumption of chlorofluorocarbons (CFCs), the most used ozone-depleting substance, has dropped from 1.1 million tons in 1986 to less than 70,000 tons in 2006. Atmospheric concentrations of ozone-depleting substances appear to have peaked in the late 1990s, and stratospheric ozone levels are expected to begin to increase over time. In 1999, the United Nations Environment Program (UNEP) predicted that the ozone layer would recover to its pre-1980 levels by 2050, UNEP, GLOBAL ENVIRONMENT OUTLOOK 2000, AT 26 (1999), but more recent data suggests the ozone hole's recovery may be delayed. A 2006 study by NASA pushed the anticipated recovery schedule back to 2068, nearly a 20-year delay. NASA Press Release, *NASA Finds Clock Ticking Slower on Ozone Hole Recovery*, June 29, 2006. Nonetheless, without the Protocol, UNEP predicted that levels of ozone-depleting substances would have been five times higher than they are today and surface UV-B radiation levels would have doubled at mid-latitudes in the northern hemisphere. *See* UNEP, GLOBAL ENVIRONMENT OUTLOOK 2000, at 26 (1999); *see also* UNEP & WMO, Scientific Assessment of Ozone Depletion (2002).

———————

The Montreal Protocol regime is widely viewed as the most effective environmental treaty regime and was the explicit model for the international negotiations over climate change. Consider in this regard the following comments from U.S. ozone negotiator Richard Benedick, written on the eve of the United Nations Conference on Environment and Development in 1992.

> The current debate about greenhouse warming conveys a distinct sense of déjà vu. The world again confronts a classic situation: weighing the risks of action and inaction in the face of uncertainties. Short-term costs loom large; long-term dangers seem remote . . . The Antarctic ozone hole is an example of what scientists call a nonlinear response; that is, the ozone layer kept absorbing ever more chlorine from man-made sources without revealing any problem, until the concentrations reached a breaking point, and collapse ensued. With respect to greenhouse warming, scientists warn that the billions of tons of carbon dioxide and other gases being emitted by modern industrial economies constitute an unpredictable experiment on the atmosphere. Are we approaching other unknown thresholds? ***

> Had CFCs been permitted to continue growing, they would have wrought irreparable damage on the ozone layer. And yet at the time, powerful voices in government and industry strongly opposed regulations, on the grounds of incomplete scientific evidence. Under these circumstances, the lesson for the policymaker seems clear: if we are to err, let us err on the side of caution. The very existence of scientific uncertainty about global warming should lead us to action rather than delay, especially when most of the international scientific community persistently warns of the risks. . . . Significantly, the Montreal Protocol on Substances that Deplete the Ozone Layer departed from the customary accommodation of environmental regulation to commercial convenience. It did not merely prescribe "best available technology" to replace CFCs. Rather the designers of the treaty mandated a timetable for deep cuts in consumption of these useful chemicals with full knowledge that the technology "did not yet exist to achieve those cuts." The treaty furnished an unmistakable market signal that made it worthwhile for companies to invest in research into new chemicals and processes they had previously eschewed . . . I suspect we would find the same forces at work if we would focus on reducing dependence on fossil fuels in the current international negotiations on a climate treaty.

Richard Benedick, *Essay: A Case of Déjà Vu*, Sci. Am., April 1992, at 160.

The Montreal Protocol's precautionary, technology-forcing approach significantly influenced the climate negotiations. In particular, climate negotiators recognized that the Montreal Protocol's success was largely due to its ability to respond over time to advances in scientific understanding. By first establishing an institutional and policy framework, the Vienna Convention allowed the Parties to take periodic, incremental steps to strengthen the regime. It is in this respect that the Montreal Protocol became the model for climate negotiators. Indeed as early as 1989, the intergovernmental working group charged with developing the elements of a climate convention, turned to the Montreal Protocol regime's Framework/Protocol approach as the model for the UNFCCC.

Despite the value of understanding climate change and ozone depletion as separate problems, they do overlap in important ways. Both CFCs, the main cause of ozone depletion, and ozone itself are greenhouse gases. Thus, the addition of CFCs to the atmosphere adds directly to global warming, but in destroying ozone it leads to global cooling. The two effects partly cancel each other out, but overall the warming impact of CFCs is now thought to be considerably greater than the cooling impact of ozone depletion. Complicating the situation further is that the substitutes allowed for CFCs under the Montreal Protocol regime are more potent greenhouse gases than CFCs or result in by-products that are more potent. Thus, as countries have expanded their production of HCFCs, a CFC substitute, their impact on climate change has increased as well.

The complex relationship between ozone depleting substances and greenhouse gases has, not surprisingly, resulted in a complicated relationship within international law. Although the climate and ozone regimes generally recognize the importance of having a mutually reinforcing set of policies, the two regimes still act largely independent of one another and, at least until recently, do not take explicit steps to address one another's goals. We will look first at how the climate regime addressed ozone depleting substances and then how the Montreal Protocol regime has begun to address global warming.

B.   The UNFCCC's Treatment of Ozone Depleting Substances

During the negotiations of the UNFCCC, the Parties disagreed as to how to treat CFCs and other substances controlled under the Montreal Protocol. The United States sought to include CFCs, but other countries opposed their inclusion because CFCs were already scheduled to be phased out under the Protocol. Opponents thought that including CFCs would give industrialized countries credit for something they already agreed to do and would allow certain countries (particularly the United States) to increase substantially their emissions of other greenhouse gases. To some extent, this argument became less important at least with respect to CFC reductions, because the IPCC reported that ozone itself was a greenhouse gas and thus the elimination of CFCs (and the resulting increase in stratospheric ozone) would essentially cancel one another's global warming impact.

Given this new evidence, the United States and others allowed the UNFCCC to exempt substances regulated under the Montreal Protocol. Thus, in Article 4 of the

UNFCCC the various commitments of developed countries repeatedly exempt greenhouse gases "not controlled by the Montreal Protocol." Similar language is found throughout the Kyoto Protocol, and the six greenhouse gases specifically listed in Annex A to the Kyoto Protocol do not include CFCs, HCFCs, or any other substance specifically controlled by the Montreal Protocol.

Thus, the general approach of the Kyoto Protocol was to keep its market-based approach to the regulation of greenhouse gases separate from the control of ozone-depleting substances under the Montreal Protocol. Countries that had made or will make significant reductions in their ozone depleting substances would not be able to gain credit for this under the Kyoto Protocol's cap-and-trade system.

Although Kyoto's approach clarified the overall relationship between the two regimes to some extent, important difficulties in coordination would emerge over time. The Montreal Protocol's preference for HCFCs as a substitute for CFCs would eventually have significant climate implications because HCFCs are a more potent greenhouse gas. Moreover, the manufacture of HCFCs results in by-products (HFCs) that are regulated *only* under the Kyoto Protocol. Under Kyoto's Clean Development Mechanism, industrialized countries could partly meet their Kyoto commitments by investing in the destruction of HFCs produced as by-products at HCFC manufacturing facilities in developing countries. In this way, the Kyoto regime essentially provided subsidies for the growth of the HCFC industry in developing countries. As suggested by the following excerpt, this arguably leads to greater production of HCFCs than would otherwise occur:

> In addition to delaying the recovery of the ozone layer at mid-latitudes, the production of HCFC-22 results in emissions of trifluoromethane ("HFC-23"), an unwanted by-product that is a "super greenhouse gas" 11,700 times more powerful at warming the planet than CO_2. The combined climate emissions of HCFC-22, with a GWP of 1,780, and its HFC-23 byproduct, with GWP of 11,700, are projected to reach 1 $GtCO_2eq.$ by 2015 — roughly equal to the emissions reductions presently required under the Kyoto Protocol. * * *

> The projected increase in HCFC production is being driven by the transfer of the old technology from developed to developing countries, as well as by rapid economic growth in the developing countries. The Kyoto Protocol's Clean Development Mechanism ("CDM"), as applied to HFC-23, also is partly to blame.

> Under Kyoto's CDM, the capture and destruction of HFC-23 emissions at facilities producing HCFC-22 can generate Certified Emissions Reductions ("CERs"). Given the relatively low cost of HFC-23 destruction compared to the value of CERs on the global carbon market, the CDM is inadvertently creating a "perverse incentive" that has created windfall profits for HCFC-22 producers — effectively acting as a subsidy that is driving the expanded production of HCFC-22. HFC-23 destruction projects have dominated the CDM market, accounting for 52 percent of all project-based carbon volumes transacted in 2006 and 64 percent in 2005. The abundance of CERs from HFC-23 destruction projects appears to be depressing the price of carbon, which in turn harms the competitiveness of other CDM projects.

Donald Kaniaru, Rajende Shende, Scott Stone & Durwood Zaelke, *Strengthening the Montreal Protocol: Insurance against Abrupt Climate Change*, Sust. Dev. L & Pol'y 3, 4–5 (Winter 2007). Moreover, if no action was taken this situation could continue at least until 2040 when the Montreal Protocol's phase-out of HCFCs would kick in for developing countries. This problem created by the interplay of the climate and ozone regimes could have been solved by actions taken in either regime, but as we will see below it would be the Montreal Protocol that would take the necessary steps.

C.   The Montreal Protocol Regime's Treatment of Greenhouse Gases

Although the focus of the Montreal Protocol regime has always been on avoiding ozone depletion, it has incidentally had an enormous positive impact on reducing global warming. Indeed, the Montreal Protocol has already led to the reduction of substances having a total global warming impact equivalent to 135 gigatons (Gt) of CO_2. This means that the Montreal Protocol, alone, has slowed global warming by twelve years. If voluntary and domestic measures preceding the Montreal Protocol are taken into account, the effort to avoid ozone depletion has slowed global warming by an astonishing 41 years. *See* Guus J. M. Velders, et al., *The Importance of the Montreal Protocol in Protecting Climate Change*, 104 Proc. Nat'l Acad. Sci., Mar. 20, 2007. The significant impact of the Montreal Protocol is partly due to the fact that it has been curtailing global warming substances for decades, but it also reflects the effective nature of the Protocol's regulatory and technology-forcing approach in changing State behavior.

Even as early as the 1987 Montreal Protocol, the Parties emphasized that they were "conscious of the climatic effect of the emissions of [ODS]s." *See* Montreal Protocol, preamble, para. 4. Throughout the next two decades the Montreal Protocol Parties would periodically affirm the need to consider the full environmental (presumably including climatic) effects of the substances they were regulating. In establishing the control measures for HCFCs, for example, Article 2F(7) of the Montreal Protocol noted that in addition to reducing ozone depletion, the decision to use HCFCs should meet other "environmental, safety and economic considerations." Subsequently, the Parties would direct their technical bodies to consider such factors as "energy efficiency, total global warming impact, potential flammability, and toxicity" in evaluating substances under the regime. *See* Decision VI/13 (Sixth Meeting of the Parties, Nairobi 1994). Finally, sparked by increasing concern over climate change, the Parties to the Montreal Protocol in 2007 clarified further their intention to build greater policy coherence between their efforts to reverse ozone depletion and climate change. They decided:

> 9. To encourage Parties to promote the selection of alternatives to HCFCs that minimize environmental impacts, in particular impacts on climate, as well as meeting other health, safety and economic considerations; * * *

> 11. To agree that the Executive Committee, when developing and applying funding criteria for projects and programmes, and taking into account paragraph 6, give priority to cost-effective projects and programmes which focus on, *inter alia*: . . .

> (b) Substitutes and alternatives that minimize other impacts on the environment, including on the climate, taking into account global-warming potential, energy use and other relevant factors.

Decision XIX/6: Adjustments to the Montreal Protocol with regard to Annex C, Group I, Substances (hydrochlorofluorocarbons), Report of the 19th Meeting of the Parties to the Montreal Protocol (2007). Although this formal agreement to consider climate impacts was important, more important was the specific action the Parties took to accelerate the phase-out of HCFCs.

Under the 2007 Adjustments, production of HCFCs is to be frozen in 2013 at the average production level in 2009–2010. The phase-out of HCFCs would then be accelerated in both developed and developing countries. Developed countries agreed to a slightly more accelerated phase-out of HCFCs than previously agreed, culminating with the complete phase-out in 2020. Interim goals for developed countries are 75 percent by 2010 and 90 percent by 2015. Developing countries also agreed to a step-by-step phase-out on their way to a total phase-out in 2030. After freezing production and consumption in 2013, developing countries would reduce their HCFC production and consumption by 10 percent by 2015, 35 percent by 2020, and 67.5 percent by 2025. Developing countries will be eligible for up to a 2.5 percent "servicing" exemption, which will allow some grandfathered, capital-intensive equipment to continue to operate on HCFCs through 2040. The Parties also agreed that additional funding would be made available under the Multilateral Fund to assist developing countries in meeting the incremental costs of accelerating the phase-out of HCFCs. Decision XIX/6: Adjustments to the Montreal Protocol with regard to Annex C, Group I, substances (hydrochlorofluorocarbons) (2007). The differences between the "before" and "after" status of HCFCs is shown in the following table:

Table 10-1: The Acceleration of HCFCs

Developed Countries	Original Schedule	2007 Acceleration
	65% reduction by 2010	75% reduction by 2010
	90% reduction by 2015	90% reduction by 2015
	Phase-out by 2020	Total phase-out by 2020
	0.5% service tail	Service tail ends 2030
Developing Countries		
	Freeze production in 2016	Freeze production in 2013
		10% reduction by 2015
		35% reduction by 2020
		67.5% reduction by 2025
		97.5% reduction by 2030
	Total Phase-out by 2040	2.5% service tail ends 2040

As the table suggests, the key difference is that the developing country Parties agreed to a gradual reduction with interim phase-out targets as opposed to waiting until 2040 for the ban to kick in. This eliminates significant quantities of HCFCs along the way and reduces the risk that the 2040 ban would present an "all-or-nothing" compliance challenge, where countries might pretend to be reducing HCFC use along the way and simply wait to 2040 to disclose their noncompliance.

The Montreal Protocol's acceleration of the phase-out of HCFCs is one of the most meaningful international steps yet taken to combat climate change. It will have a significant role in reducing greenhouse gas emissions and, just as importantly, provide hope that the international community will step up to meet the climate challenge. Consider the following excerpt describing the importance of the

HCFC accelerated phase-out.

> Last September's historic agreement under the Montreal Protocol to accelerate the phase-out of hydrochlorofluorocarbons ("HCFCs") marked the first time both developed and developing countries explicitly agreed to accept binding and enforceable commitments to address climate change. This is particularly significant because the decision was taken by consensus by all 191 Parties to the Protocol — all but five countries recognized by the United Nations. Accelerating the HCFC phase-out could reduce emissions by 16 billion tons of carbon dioxide-equivalent ("$GtCO_2e$") through 2040. In terms of radiative forcing, this will delay climate change by up to 1.5 years. . . . Thus, from September 2007 both Montreal and Kyoto can be considered climate protection treaties.

Donald Kaniaru, Rajendra Shende, & Durwood Zaelke, *Landmark Agreement To Strengthen Montreal Protocol Provides Powerful Climate Mitigation*, SUST DEV. L. & POL'Y 46, 46 (Winter 2008).

QUESTIONS AND DISCUSSION

1. Do you agree with the view that clear standards like those in the Montreal Protocol create a strong market signal for technological innovation? If clear legal standards, including prohibitions, provide market incentives and economic opportunities, why does the climate regime rely so heavily on the market-based cap-and-trade approach? What are the major advantages and disadvantages between the approaches taken by the ozone and climate regimes? Which do you think has the greatest potential to drive technological innovation?

2. How could coordination be improved further between the ozone and climate regimes? In the future, how should the Montreal Protocol address substances that both destroy the ozone layer and contribute to climate change? Industry argues that industrial gases, such as HFCs, should not be regulated solely under the Montreal Protocol, because inclusion of those gases in the Kyoto Protocol expands the supply of credits in the trading system, broadens its flexibility and reduces overall compliance costs. Is the Montreal Protocol's regulatory approach incompatible with the market trading system of Kyoto? If so, which would you prefer? What steps can be taken in the climate regime to better reflect the approach taken in the Montreal Protocol?

3. *Reducing ODS Banks.* Another existing gap in the Montreal Protocol that has significant climate change implications is the treatment of existing "banks" of ozone depleting substances:

> The Montreal Protocol does not place any controls on emissions from "banks" and provides minimal incentives for their recovery and destruction. Banks are defined as the chemicals contained in equipment and products or stored in tanks. Large amounts of CFCs and other ODS substitutes such as HCFCs and HFCs (not an ODS but a GHG) currently exist in refrigerators, air conditioners, insulating foams, and chemical stockpiles, where they can leak. When equipment reaches the end of its useful life, the chemicals inside are usually released into the atmosphere.

> With limited incentives for recovery and destruction of ODS banks, most of the CFCs in banks will be emitted into the atmosphere over the next decade, with detrimental impacts for both the ozone layer and the climate. In addition to contributing to the expected delay in ozone recovery,

emissions from CFC banks by 2015 could equal approximately 7.4 $GtCO_2$-eq. yr-1 — more than seven times the size of the emissions reductions initially targeted by the Kyoto Protocol.

Kaniaru, et al., *Strengthening the Montreal Protocol, supra*, at 5–6. How would you recommend governments address these banks? Which regime would be more effective — the regulatory approach of the Montreal Protocol or the market incentives of the Kyoto Protocol? In November 2008, the Montreal Protocol Parties began to address this gap by launching initial pilot projects, cost-benefit analyses and other consultations to promote the destruction of ODSs in stockpiles and discarded products such as refrigerators.

    4. *Improving Energy Efficiency of ODS Alternative Technologies.* The Montreal Protocol Parties' general decision to consider energy efficiency and other non-ozone environmental impacts paves the way for the Parties to address the climate change implications of future decisions they make. This is an important step in improving the coherence of global environmental governance generally and of the climate-ozone connection more specifically. It should allow the Montreal Protocol regime to address each substance in terms of its combined impacts on ozone and climate, using an integrated life-cycle analysis. Such an analysis would consider a chemical's ozone depleting potential, its global warming potential, the energy efficiency of the equipment in which it is used, and the potential for leaks and containment thereof. From this broader perspective, it may make sense for overall environmental purposes to exempt certain HCFCs from accelerated phase-out, perhaps in exchange for corresponding offsets (i.e., destruction of an equal or even greater amount of ODS), at least until an overall environmentally superior alternative emerges. *See* Stephen O. Andersen & Durwood Zaelke, Industry Genius: People and Inventions Protecting Climate and the Fragile Ozone Layer 168–69 (2003) (discussing the climate benefits from exempting HCFC-123 for use in low-pressure chillers where its leakage is near zero and its energy efficiency is superior to other refrigerants). *See also* Environmental Investigation Agency, *Turning Up the Heat: Linkages between Ozone Layer Depletion and Climate Change: The Urgent Case of HCFCs and HFCs* (2006).

    5. To describe the Montreal Protocol as only a "regulatory" approach admittedly misses a significant part of its effectiveness. The Protocol mixes its clear targets and timetables with strong financial and technical assistance to developing countries, thus minimizing their costs of compliance. In accelerating HCFCs as it did in 2007, the Montreal Protocol Parties also agreed to make sufficient financial resources available to meet the developing country costs of switching to alternative substances. The next year, the Parties replenished the Montreal Protocol Fund with $490 million, in part to assist developing countries in accelerating their phase-out of HCFCs. Developing countries are of course demanding similar support in the climate regime, but the costs of reducing GHGs will be substantially higher than was the case in the ozone regime, and industrialized countries will be reluctant to agree to provide all the financial and technical assistance necessary.

III.   BIODIVERSITY-RELATED TREATIES

    Frustrated by the slow pace of progress with the climate change regime, environmentalists have sought other forums to compel Parties to reduce their greenhouse gas emissions or take action to adapt to the adverse impacts of climate change. Many of these efforts have focused on biodiversity-related conventions, because of the important two-way links between climate change and biodiversity.

For example, while biodiversity is threatened by climate change, it can also reduce the impacts of climate change. Forests and other habitats have great capacity to store carbon, while deforestation and other land use practices currently release about 20 percent of the world's anthropogenic emissions of carbon dioxide. The conservation of mangroves and other coastal ecosystems can help retard storm surges that can flood coastal areas. More generally, ecosystems that are more biodiverse are more resilient to disturbances, which are expected to increase in frequency and intensity due to climate change.

As reported by the Intergovernmental Panel on Climate Change (IPCC), climate change is already forcing species to adapt either through shifting habitat, changing life cycles, or developing new physical traits. The Secretariat to the Convention on Biological Diversity (CBD) provides the following examples of climate impacts on biodiversity:

- Rising temperatures have caused coral bleaching — massive die offs — of coral reef communities from Australia to the Caribbean.

- The Common Murre has advanced breeding by 24 days per decade over the past 50 years due to rising temperatures.

- Polar bear populations face dwindling access to food sources as Arctic ice melts.

The question for species is whether they can adapt quickly enough to these types of changes. For some species, changes in temperatures are likely to have irrevocable impacts. Some estimates suggest that as many as one million species may become extinct due to climate change. The recently extinct Golden Toad and Gastric Brooding Frog have already been labeled as the first victims of climate change. *See* CBD Secretariat, *The International Day for Biological Diversity: Biodiversity and Climate Change: 22 May 2007, available at* http://www.cbd.int/programmes/outreach/awareness/biodiv-day-2007.shtml.

Some biodiversity-related conventions have begun to recognize the need to link biodiversity conservation and climate change. For example, Decision VIII/30 of the CBD encourages Parties and other governments to integrate biodiversity considerations into all relevant national policies, programs, and plans in response to climate change, and encourages governments and relevant organizations to develop rapid assessment tools for the design and implementation of biodiversity conservation and sustainable use activities that contribute to adaptation to climate change. The International Tropical Timber Organization (ITTO) recently decided to study the implications of climate change for tropical forests and the contribution of tropical forests to the mitigation of the effects of climate change. To that end, it will "assist members in formulating and implementing an integrated forest sector response to climate change." Decision 2(XLII), ITTO Biennial Work Programme for the Years 2008–2009, ITTC(XLIII)/15, at 5 (Nov. 10, 2007).

While these agreements have not yet taken any specific action to address climate change, others have or are actively contemplating it. As described below, the World Heritage Convention is studying how it can play a role in climate change mitigation and adaptation within World Heritage Sites. The Convention on Wetlands of International Importance, Especially as Waterfowl Habitat (Ramsar Convention) has begun assessing the impacts of climate change on wetlands. As you read about the activities of these treaties, ask yourself what their role should be. Should they engage in climate change mitigation or should they restrict their activities to adaptation? Or should they step aside completely and leave the business of climate change to the UNFCCC and Kyoto Protocol? How should multilateral environmental regimes structure their cooperation on overlapping issues, given that each regime is limited in authority to issues that fall within the substantive scope of their respective treaties?

A.   The World Heritage Convention

1.   *Background*

The Convention Concerning the Protection of the World Cultural and Natural Heritage, more commonly called the World Heritage Convention, directs the convention's Parties to protect areas representing "universal outstanding heritage" that are part of "the world [natural and cultural] heritage of mankind as a whole." Convention Concerning the Protection of the World Cultural and Natural Heritage, Nov. 16, 1972, 27 U.S.T. 37, 1037 U.N.T.S. 151 (entered into force Dec. 17, 1975). To date, the World Heritage Convention's 186 Parties have placed 851 properties on the World Heritage List. These sites include 669 cultural, 174 natural, and 25 mixed properties in 145 countries. UNESCO, *World Heritage List, available at* http://whc.unesco.org/en/list.

The criteria for inclusion in the World Heritage List are rigorous. For example, Parties seeking to list a site due to its biodiversity values must demonstrate that the site includes "superlative natural . . . formations," such as "the most important ecosystems"; or "the most important and significant natural habitats where threatened species of animals or plants of outstanding universal value from the point of view of science or conservation still survive." *Operational Guidelines for the Implementation of the World Heritage Convention*, para. 77 WHC. 05/2 (Feb. 2, 2005), *available at* http://whc.unesco.org/en/guidelines [hereinafter WHC Operational Guidelines].

As a consequence of these rigorous criteria, the inclusion on the World Heritage List gives a site special international legal status that can enhance its protection. The Convention itself does not impose many specific obligations, but, once a site is included on the List, the host government must do its "utmost" to protect and conserve the site. The host government must also "endeavor, in so far as possible, and as appropriate for each country," to establish services and training for the protection, conservation and presentation of cultural and natural heritage; and to take the appropriate legal, scientific, technical, administrative and financial measures necessary for the identification, protection, conservation, presentation, and rehabilitation of this heritage. Each Party is also precluded from taking "any deliberate measures" that might directly or indirectly damage listed sites. *World Heritage Convention*, at arts. 4–6.

2.   *World Heritage Sites in Danger Due to Climate Change*

The World Heritage Convention also includes a List of World Heritage in Danger.   UNESCO,   *World   Heritage   in   Danger,   at* http://whc.unesco.org/pg.cfm?cid=86. The danger list is designed to inform the international community of "serious and specific dangers" that threaten the very characteristics for which a site was originally included on the World Heritage List. Article 11(4).

The World Heritage Convention's List of World Heritage in Danger has been of particular interest to environmentalists looking to raise awareness of the impacts of climate change. Beginning in 2005, environmental lawyers from around the world coordinated efforts to petition the World Heritage Committee to list five World Heritage Sites as in danger due to climate change. *See Climate Justice, available at* http://www.climatelaw.org. The petitioners sought out sites where the effects of climate change were best understood, in particular, sites with bleaching coral reefs and shrinking glaciers. Thus, they petitioned to list as "in danger" the following World Heritage Sites: Belize Barrier Reef, Huarascán National Park in Peru, Sagarmatha National Park in Nepal, the Great Barrier Reef in Australia, and Waterton-Glacier International Peace Park. For example, Glacier National Park, the U.S. portion of Waterton-Glacier International Peace Park, once boasted approximately 150 glaciers, but only 27 remain, and those are rapidly melting. Scientists estimate that the glaciers in Glacier National Park will vanish entirely by 2030.

The World Heritage Committee has identified two broad categories of the types of danger facing World Heritage sites that may warrant listing a site on the List of World Heritage in Danger: ascertained danger and potential danger. According to the *Operational Guidelines for the Implementation of the World Heritage Convention,* an "ascertained danger" exists when a site faces "specific and proven imminent danger," such as a serious decline in the population of the endangered species or other species of outstanding universal value for which the property was legally established to protect. Other ascertained dangers include severe deterioration of the natural beauty or scientific value of the property due to human settlement and industrial and agricultural development.

A "potential danger" exists when a site faces "major threats which could have deleterious effects on [a site's] inherent characteristics." These threats include a modification of the legal protective status of the area, planned development projects that may affect the site, or an inadequate management plan.

Prior to listing a site as "in danger," the World Heritage Committee must determine whether the threats facing the site are amenable to corrective actions. This raises particularly difficult questions with respect to World Heritage Sites threatened due to climate change. Does the World Heritage Convention require all Parties — or at least the Party hosting a World Heritage Site in danger due to climate change — to reduce greenhouse gas emissions to protect the site? If Parties are not required to reduce their greenhouse gas emissions as a necessary corrective action, must they take site-level adaptation measures to address the effects of climate change? In this regard, consider first Articles 4 through 6 of World Heritage Convention, followed by an article from the lead attorney of the petition to list Waterton-Glacier International Peace Park as in danger due to climate change:

CONVENTION FOR THE PROTECTION OF THE WORLD CULTURAL AND NATURAL HERITAGE

Article 4

Each State Party to this Convention recognizes that the duty of ensuring the identification, protection, conservation, presentation and transmission to future generations of the cultural and natural heritage . . . situated on its territory, belongs primarily to that State. It will do all it can to this end, to the utmost of its own resources. . . .

Article 5

To ensure that effective and active measures are taken for the protection, conservation and presentation of the cultural and natural heritage situated on its territory, each State Party to this Convention shall endeavor, in so far as possible, and as appropriate for each country:

1. To adopt a general policy which aims to give the cultural and natural heritage a function in the life of the community and to integrate the protection of that heritage into comprehensive planning programmes;

2. To set up within its territories, where such services do not exist, one or more services for the protection, conservation and presentation of the cultural and natural heritage with an appropriate staff and possessing the means to discharge their functions. * * *

4. To take the appropriate legal, scientific, technical, administrative and financial measures necessary for the identification, protection, conservation, presentation and rehabilitation of this heritage. * * *

Article 6

1. Whilst fully respecting the sovereignty of the States on whose territory the cultural and natural heritage mentioned in Articles 1 and 2 is situated, and without prejudice to property rights provided by national legislation, the States Parties to this Convention recognize that such heritage constitutes a world heritage for whose protection it is the duty of the international community as a whole to co-operate. * * *

3. Each State Party to this Convention undertakes not to take any deliberate measures which might damage directly or indirectly the cultural and natural heritage referred to in Articles 1 and 2 situated on the territory of other States Parties to this Convention. * * *

ERICA J. THORSON, ON THIN ICE: THE FAILURE OF THE UNITED STATES AND THE WORLD HERITAGE COMMITTEE TO TAKE CLIMATE CHANGE MITIGATION PURSUANT TO THE WORLD HERITAGE CONVENTION SERIOUSLY
38 ENVTL. L. 139, 149, 160–65 (2008)*

Together, [Articles 4–6] . . . represent the responsibility to cooperate in global efforts to protect world heritage and to ensure that actions taken within a national territory do not cause damage or deterioration of the world heritage situated in any other national territory.

*   *   *

Although the Petitioners employed the "in danger" listing process to highlight the devastating consequences of climate change and to urge immediate attention for particular areas, the language of the Convention text, which is implicated when a site is listed simply as "world heritage," demands that State Parties engage in effective climate change mitigation even before a site is listed as "in danger." Climate change mitigation is defined as "an anthropogenic intervention to reduce the sources of greenhouse gases or enhance their sinks." Certainly, if climate change is causing deterioration of World Heritage sites, then climate change mitigation is at least one of the "appropriate" legal, scientific, and technical undertakings that the WHC references because mitigation is necessary to prevent total deterioration of many vulnerable World Heritage sites. Moreover, Article 6 requires that State Parties avoid undertakings that will damage World Heritage sites; in the context of climate change, this means that State Parties must limit their emissions of greenhouse gases.

A. The Nature and Extent of State Parties' Obligations under Articles 4, 5, and 6

The nature and extent of how the obligations set forth in Articles 4, 5, and 6 bind State Parties — namely, whether the operative provisions impose mere recommendations entirely left to State Party discretion to implement or whether, in a given context, like climate change, they impose substantive obligations — is a key interpretive question. Articles 4 and 5 are broad, potentially leaving much room for State Party discretion as to the exact nature of the respective responsibilities. They contain qualifying language such as "as far as possible," employ precatory verbs such as "endeavor," and merely require that State Parties "recognize" certain responsibilities. In fact, some would argue that the language of Articles 4 and 5 is so broad and imparts so much discretion that it eviscerates any binding obligation. However, the High Court of Australia and established principles of international law have defined the limits of this discretion.

1. The Limits of Discretion under Articles 4 and 5

The only case to examine the nature of the obligations imposed by Articles 4 and 5 is *Commonwealth v. Tasmania*, a case of the High Court of Australia [(Tasmanian Dam Case), 158 CLR1 (1983)]. Despite the qualifying language of Articles 4 and 5, a majority of the High Court of Australia determined that both Articles impose legally binding obligations, essentially because the qualifying language would be

---

superfluous if, in fact, no obligation existed. Although having found that Articles 4 and 5 of the WHC impose binding legal obligations, the Court nonetheless recognized that the duties are so broadly articulated that State Parties have much latitude as to how they implement the Convention. As one judge stated in his opinion: "[T]here may be an element of discretion and value judgment on the part of the State to decide what measures are necessary and appropriate." This discretion, however, is not without bounds. This judge further noted, "There is a distinction between a discretion as to the manner of performance and a discretion as to performance or non-performance."

The Australian case clarifies that Articles 4 and 5 impose discretionary obligations, but international law defines the nature of State Parties' discretion. With respect to treaty implementation, the principle of *pacta sunt servanda* guides State Party discretion. This principle provides that States are bound by their international agreements and that they must implement such agreements in good faith. Thus, Articles 4 and 5 of the WHC impose discretionary obligations, but "good faith" is the touchstone for implementation, and the aims of the Convention — namely, the protection and conservation of world heritage — guide operationalization of State Parties' good faith.

2. Article 6: No Deliberate Damage

Unlike Articles 4 and 5, Article 6 is not qualified with language of limitation. The provisions of Article 6 are less discretionary, stating that State Parties are not to undertake deliberate measures that might damage world heritage. A simple textual analysis of the plain meaning of the provision supports this interpretation. Under fundamental rules of treaty interpretation, as provided by the Vienna Convention [on the Law of Treaties], a treaty must "be interpreted in good faith in accordance with the ordinary meaning of the terms of the treaty in their context and in light of its object and purpose." The plain language of Article 6(3) sets forth a non-discretionary duty to forgo deliberate undertakings that may damage world heritage.

The *travaux preparatoires* (the negotiating history of the treaty) supports this plain language interpretation. Early drafts of the Convention did contain qualifying language, but the drafters pointedly excluded it from the final version of Article 6. In early drafts, Article 6(3) read:

> The States Parties to this Convention undertake to respect the cultural and natural heritage enjoying international protection under this Convention by refraining so far as possible from acts which might damage them.

The adopted language is far less discretionary and imposes a binding, articulable legal obligation on State Parties. In fact, the drafters specifically eliminated "in so far as possible," indicating that this provision was meant to be implemented in a less discretionary manner than Articles 4 and 5. Article 6, as adopted, codifies the object and purpose of the Convention — international cooperation for the protection of world heritage.

As the Preamble evinces, the WHC's object and purpose is two-fold. First, protection of "[world] heritage at the national level often remains incomplete because of the scale of the resources which it requires and of the insufficient economic, scientific, and technological resources of the country where the property" is located. In other words, the State Parties recognized that in many circumstances national-level efforts are insufficient to provide adequate protection. Second, to work toward resolving the inadequacies inherent in national-level protection, . . . "it is incumbent on the international community as a whole to participate in the protection of the cultural and natural heritage of outstanding universal value, by the granting of collective assistance which, although not taking the place of action by the State concerned, will serve as an efficient complement thereto." Essentially, the Preamble, while recognizing the primary nature of national effort, makes clear that . . . to ensure protection they must engage in an internationally cooperative effort.

. . . The WHC Preamble supports the interpretation that Articles 4, 5, and 6 impose binding legal obligations. It makes clear that the WHC's object and purpose is to foster international cooperation, coupled with national efforts, to protect world heritage.

B. The Mitigation Strategy Required by the World Heritage Convention

The obligations imposed by Articles 4, 5, and 6 of the WHC require that State Parties engage in an aggressive climate-change mitigation strategy because they mandate the protection of World Heritage sites and the "outstanding universal values" therein. Articles 4 and 5 call for State Parties to act aggressively to protect world heritage within their territories, and Article 6 obliges all State Parties to forgo actions that might damage World Heritage sites. Together, these provisions require that all State Parties engage in an aggressive climate change mitigation strategy entailing sharp reductions in greenhouse gas emissions.

As a consequence of this interpretation of the World Heritage Convention, the Waterton-Glacier petitioners did not ask for corrective actions relating to the park itself, such as removal of automobiles from the park in favor of buses to reduce carbon dioxide emissions or the creation of wildlife corridors so that species could migrate as their habitat changed. Instead, they recommended the following nationwide corrective actions:

> Because electricity generation accounts for thirty-nine percent of all carbon dioxide emissions, a program of corrective measures should include a plan to reduce reliance on coal to produce electricity through the promotion of alternative energy sources, like wind power. In addition, a significant corrective measure could be regulation of emissions from coal-fired power plants; this could be achieved efficiently and economically with a cap-and-trade program for carbon dioxide emissions. Moreover, a program of corrective measures could achieve significant progress toward reducing greenhouse gas emissions if it included transportation sector reductions, including increases in fuel efficiency standards, regulation of tail-pipe emissions, and increased reliance on non-petroleum-based fuels, like ethanol and biodiesel. Finally, the World Heritage Committee could also include programs aimed at achieving greater energy efficiency through appliance efficiency standards.

Petition to the World Heritage Committee Requesting Inclusion of Waterton-Glacier International Peace Park on the List of World Heritage in Danger as a Result of Climate Change and for Protective Measures and Actions, viii (Feb. 16, 2006).

To date, the World Heritage Committee has not acted on any of the climate-related petitions. The petitions have, however, initiated a process to consider how the World Heritage Committee and the convention's Parties should address climate change. The World Heritage Committee first initiated an assessment of the impacts of climate change on World Heritage Sites and concluded that climate change was already affecting many World Heritage Sites. Decision 29 COM 78.a.Rev (2005), *available at* http://whc.unesco.org/archive/2005/whc05-29com-22e.pdf. The Committee then organized a meeting specifically to discuss the impacts of climate change on World Heritage Sites. That meeting led to the development of a report on predicting and managing the effects of climate change on World Heritage and a strategy to assist the Parties to implement appropriate management responses, which the World Heritage Committee endorsed at its 2006 annual meeting. World Heritage Committee, *The Impacts of Climate Change on World Heritage Properties*, WHC-06/30.COM/7/1 (including May Cassar et al., *Predicting and Managing the Effects of Climate Change on World Heritage*, at Annex 4).

The World Heritage Committee made very clear, however, that the "UNFCCC is the instrument through which mitigation strategies at the global and State Parties level is being addressed," not the World Heritage Convention. World Heritage Committee, *The Impacts of Climate Change on World Heritage Properties*, WHC-06/30.COM/7.1, para. 13 (2006). Instead, the Committee has reported that World Heritage Convention Parties must consider "*site-level* monitoring, mitigation and adaptation measures, where appropriate." World Heritage Committee, *Draft of the Policy Document on the Impacts of Climate Change on World Heritage Properties*, WHC-07/31.COM/7.1, at 4 (June 2007) (emphasis added). Possible adaptation strategies available to Parties could include enlarging existing protected areas, creating buffer zones of natural habitat around protected areas, and restoration of natural habitat, among others. *Predicting and Managing the Effects of Climate Change on World Heritage*, at 56, Box 11. Site-level mitigation activities could include conservation for carbon sequestration.

QUESTIONS AND DISCUSSION

1.   Environmentalists have decried the World Heritage Committee's response to these petitions. As Erica Thorson writes:

> Many World Heritage sites will never be preserved for transmission to future generations unless the State Parties, led by the World Heritage Committee, act more proactively than merely supporting site-specific mitigation. For example, any climate-change mitigation occurring within Glacier National Park's boundaries, while commendable, is inevitably inadequate to address the devastating consequences of climate change within the park. Even a total ban on greenhouse gas emissions within the park would not slow, and could never reverse, the climate change effects on glacial melt within the Park. Yet this type of mitigation is all that the Joint Report and the Strategy suggest should occur — a wholly inadequate response to the threat of climate change because it will not protect the outstanding universal values of the Park. The World Heritage Committee's weak approach may be politically palatable, especially to State Parties like the United States, but it falls far short of the type of mitigation required to protect World Heritage sites.

Thorson, *On Thin Ice*, at 170–71. Her comment raises the important distinction between legal obligations and political realities. Are the Parties to the World Heritage Convention required to take action beyond site-level adaptation and mitigation? If so, should they?

2. In a series of case studies, the World Heritage Convention summarized some possible adaptation strategies for World Heritage Sites affected by climate change. For example, Australia has increased the percentage of no-take areas from 5 percent to 33 percent, which should improve the resilience of biodiversity within the Great Barrier Reef Marine Park. State and federal officials are also collaborating to improve water quality. For Sagarmatha National Park in the Himalayas of Nepal, the case study noted that 50 percent of the park includes high altitude ice, glaciers, snow, and rocks. With rising temperatures, glaciers are melting and causing the rapid expansion of glacial lakes whose banks are unstable. The retention of glaciers and glacial lakes is essential, because mountain glaciers account for half of the freshwater used by humankind, and the glaciers of Sagarmatha are no exception. Moreover, the banks of these glacial lakes in Sagarmatha (and elsewhere) have burst, leading to "Glacial Lake Outburst Floods" (GLOFs). GLOFs in Sagarmatha have already destroyed power stations and houses and killed at least 20 people. The Imja Lake in Sagarmatha is considered "one of the largest and most threatening lakes" needing preventive action. To respond to these and other threats caused by climate change, the case study suggests an early warning system to notify people downstream in case of a GLOF. It also suggests that artificially draining a lake could avoid a GLOF. Augustin Collette et al., *Case Studies on Climate Change and World Heritage* (2007). Do any of these facts and possible adaptation strategies lead you to reconsider your responses to the questions posed in note 1, above?

3. The response of the United States to these petitions has been unsurprising. In addition to challenging whether climate change is caused by human activities, the United States also argued that citizens do not have the right to submit petitions to list sites as "in danger" and that the designation of a site as "in danger" requires the consent of the Party concerned. United States, *Position of the United State [sic] of America on Climate Change with Respect to the World Heritage Convention and World Heritage Sites*, available at http://www.elaw.org/assets/word/u.s.climate.US%20position%20paper.doc. The United States is wrong on both accounts. Nothing in the Convention or Operational Guidelines bars such petitions from citizens and other provisions of the Convention and documents expressly call for contributions and collaboration with nongovernmental organizations. Moreover, while Article 11.3 of the Convention expressly provides that State consent is needed for inclusion of a site on the World Heritage List, Article 11.4 directs the World Heritage Committee to maintain the List of World Heritage in Danger. Even if consent of the Party concerned is not required, from a practical standpoint, coordination is necessary in order to implement the corrective actions. Perhaps aware of the shortcomings of its legal analysis, the United States proposed the following amendment to the Operational Guidelines, which the World Heritage Committee adopted:

> [T]he decisions to include properties on the List of World Heritage in Danger because of threats resulting from climate change are to be made by the World Heritage Committee, on a case-by-case basis, in consultation and cooperation with States Parties, taking into account the input from Advisory Bodies and NGOs, and consistent with the *Operational Guidelines for the Implementation of the World Heritage Convention.*

World Heritage Committee, *Issues Relating to the State of Conservation of World Heritage Properties: The Impacts of Climate Change on World Heritage Properties*, Decision 30 COM 7.1, para. 14 (July 2006).

4. The International Environmental Law Project of Lewis & Clark Law School, the author of the petition to list Waterton-Glacier International Peace Park as "in Danger due to Climate Change," has provided links to a variety of sources concerning shrinking glaciers, including time-lapse photography of Glacier National Park's vanishing glaciers. *See* http://law.lclark.edu/org/ielp/glacierpetition.html. Information concerning the other petitions can be found on the website of the Climate Justice Programme, http://www.climatelaw.org.

B.   Convention on Biological Diversity

The Convention on Biological Diversity (CBD) is the most comprehensive treaty aimed at conserving biological diversity. United Nations Convention on Biological Diversity, June 5, 1992, S. TREATY DOC. 20 (1993), *reprinted in* 311.L.M. 818 (entered into force Dec. 29, 1993). It establishes three laudable and reinforcing goals: (1) the conservation of biological diversity, (2) the sustainable use of components of biological diversity, and (3) the equitable sharing of benefits from the use of genetic resources. To achieve these goals, the CBD establishes general obligations to, *inter alia*, develop national biodiversity conservation strategies, protect threatened species, establish protected areas, and integrate conservation and sustainable use into relevant sectoral policies. Like the World Heritage Convention, the CBD leaves implementation of these obligations to national governments. There are, for example, no requirements to establish a certain number of protected areas or adopt any particular policy for the conservation and sustainable use of biodiversity. The CBD specifically recognizes that differing economic circumstances and biodiversity endowments will lead the Parties to different biodiversity conservation strategies.

The strength of the CBD has been in developing frameworks and principles for conservation and sustainable use to guide the management of particular resources. For example, the Parties developed groundbreaking guidelines on the conservation and use of marine and coastal biodiversity, although, consistent with CBD experience, it has allowed Parties the discretion to implement those guidelines as they see fit. CBD, Decision II/10, *Conservation and Sustainable Use of Marine and Coastal Biological Diversity* (1995). Similarly, the Parties developed guidelines and principles for protected areas (Decision VII/28 (2004)) and ecosystem management (Decision V/6 (2000)).

The CBD has undertaken a similar approach to climate change. In 2000, at their fifth meeting, the Parties to the CBD called for collaboration with the appropriate bodies of the UNFCCC and the IPCC to understand better the impact of climate change on forest biological diversity, marine and coastal biodiversity, and other habitats. The Parties also directed its scientific body, the Subsidiary Body on Scientific, Technical and Technological Advice (SBSTTA), to consider the impact of climate change on these habitats. Those recommendations led to the establishment of an Ad Hoc Technical Expert Group on Biological Diversity and Climate Change to analyze possible adverse impacts on biological diversity of measures taken under the climate change regime, identify factors influencing biodiversity's capacity to mitigate climate change and contribute to adaptation and the likely effects of climate change on that capacity, and identify options for future work on climate change that also contribute to the conservation and sustainable use of biological diversity. SBBSTA, Recommendation VI/7, para. 1. Relying on the IPCC's Third Assessment Report and other documents, the Ad Hoc Technical Expert Group documented the effects of climate change on biodiversity and described tools, such as criteria and indicators and environmental impact assessment, for integrating climate change into biodiversity conservation planning. UNEP/CBD/SBSTTA/9/INF/12.

This report, while not necessarily breaking new ground, placed climate change impacts squarely in the context of biodiversity conservation planning. The expert group noted that the "protection, restoration or establishment of biologically diverse ecosystems that provide important goods and services may constitute important adaptation measures to supplement existing goods and services, in anticipation of increased pressures or demand, or to compensate for likely losses." *Id.*, Executive Summary, para. 36. The protection or restoration of mangroves, for example, may protect coastal areas from sea level rise and extreme weather events.

Subsequent to the report, the Parties have adopted two decisions that encourage the Parties to integrate biodiversity conservation into climate change adaptation. The decisions further encourage Parties to develop assessment tools for the design and implementation of biodiversity conservation and sustainable use activities that contribute to adaptation to climate change. The CBD Parties also committed to work closely with the Ramsar Convention on Wetlands, the Convention on Migratory Species, the World Heritage Convention, and the UN Convention to Combat Desertification to support the preparation of adaptation activities and plans; these activities may include assistance in the areas of financial resources, technology transfer, education and outreach, capacity-building, research and systemic observation, and harmonized reporting. In addition, the CBD, through a new Ad Hoc Technical Expert Group on Biodiversity and Climate Change, has placed itself in the position to provide biodiversity-related information to the climate change regime. Decision VIII/30, *Biodiversity and Climate Change: Guidance to Promote Synergy among Activities for Biodiversity Conservation, Mitigating or Adapting to Climate Change and Combating Land Degradation* (2006); Decision IX/16, *Biodiversity and Climate Change* (2008).

QUESTIONS AND DISCUSSION

1. ***Invasive Species.*** The CBD provides the general framework for international efforts to control invasive species. Invasive species are those plants, animals, and microbes not native to a region that, when introduced either accidentally or intentionally, out-compete native species for available resources, reproduce prolifically, and dominate regions and ecosystems. Because they often arrive in new areas unaccompanied by their native predators, invasive species can be difficult to control. The resulting damage can have broad economic impacts and threaten human health and well-being. The introduction of invasive species has escalated in recent years, largely due to increased international trade and travel. But climate change, too, can create conditions favoring introduced species over native species. Left unchecked, many climate-aided invasive species have the potential to transform entire ecosystems, as native species and those that depend on them for food, shelter, and habitat disappear. The CBD calls on governments to "control or eradicate those alien species which threaten ecosystems, habitats or species." In 2004, the CBD Parties adopted *Guiding Principles for the Prevention, Introduction and Mitigation of Impacts of Alien Species that Threaten Ecosystems, Habitats or Species*, Decision VI/23, Annex I (2004). How should such principles address climate change, if at all? *See generally* HAROLD A. MOONEY & RICHARD J. HOBBS, INVASIVE SPECIES IN A CHANGING WORLD (2000).

2. *Genetically Modified Organisms.* In 2000, the CBD Parties signed the Cartagena Protocol on Biosafety, creating an international regime for importing and exporting genetically modified organisms (GMOs). The Protocol establishes an elaborate notification and prior informed consent procedure for living modified organisms intended to be released into the environment (for example, seeds or live fish), but requires only labeling of bulk commodities of GMOs. *See* Cartagena Protocol on Biosafety to the Convention on Biological Diversity, *adopted* Jan. 29, 2000, *reprinted in* 31 I.L.M. 1257 (2000). The Cartagena Protocol does not explicitly address climate change, but climate change is expected to increase the use and distribution of GMOs. Many agricultural companies are developing drought- or heat-resistant crops to increase yields in a warmer planet. Although many people hope this will soften the potential food security issues raised by climate change, others are concerned that the risks of GMO crops are not well understood. Managing those risks in the future will fall in part to the Parties to the Biosafety Protocol.

3. *Ocean Fertilization.* The CBD Parties have also expressed their concern about the potential impacts of iron fertilization as a step to mitigate climate change. In 2008, the 9th Conference of the Parties made the following decision:

> *Bearing in mind* the ongoing scientific and legal analysis occurring under the auspices of the London Convention (1972) and the 1996 London Protocol, *requests* Parties and *urges* other Governments, in accordance with the precautionary approach, to ensure that ocean fertilization activities do not take place until there is an adequate scientific basis on which to justify such activities, including assessing associated risks, and a global, transparent and effective control and regulatory mechanism is in place for these activities; with the exception of small scale scientific research studies within coastal waters. Such studies should only be authorized if justified by the need to gather specific scientific data, and should also be subject to a thorough prior assessment of the potential impacts of the research studies on the marine environment, and be strictly controlled, and not be used for generating and selling carbon offsets or any other commercial purposes;

Conference of the Parties to the Convention on Biological Diversity, *Decision IX/16, Biodiversity and Climate Change*, para. C.4. (2008). What legal effect, if any, does this have on the status of ocean fertilization? See further discussion in Section IV (describing steps to address ocean fertilization under the London Dumping Convention).

4. One of the key challenges for international environmental governance is how to increase policy coordination among the many different environmental Secretariats and institutions with overlapping or interconnected missions. This is particularly important for developing countries that do not have the capacity and resources to address a growing number of obligations under an increasingly large number of conventions. What steps would you recommend that the Secretariats take to improve coordination? Are there steps that can be taken to consolidate reporting and other requirements to reduce the burden on developing countries? *See, e.g.,* Conference of the Parties to the Convention on Biological Diversity, *Decision IX/16, Biodiversity and Climate Change*, Annex II: Indicative List of Activities by Parties to Promote Synergies Among the Rio Conventions (2008).

C. Convention on International Trade in Endangered Species of Wild Fauna and Flora

The Convention on International Trade in Endangered Species of Wild Fauna and Flora (CITES) establishes permitting requirements for species of conservation concern that may be adversely affected by international trade for pets, trinkets, clothing, and other purposes. Convention on International Trade in Endangered Species of Flora and Fauna (CITES), Mar. 3, 1973, 27 U.N.T.S. 243. Species covered by CITES are listed on one of three appendices. Appendix I species are those that "are threatened with extinction [and] which are or may be affected by trade." This list of approximately 900 species includes the black rhinoceros, orangutan, and monkey-puzzle tree. Appendix II species are those that "although not necessarily now threatened with extinction may become so unless trade in specimens of such species is subject to strict regulation in order to avoid utilization incompatible with their survival." Appendix II contains more than 33,000 species, including the pygmy hippopotamus, American alligator, and several hundred genera of orchids. The Parties vote to include species in Appendix I and II species after a review of biological and trade data. Species are listed in Appendix III solely on the basis of a decision by the country of origin.

CITES does not require Parties to protect the habitat of listed species but rather requires the Parties engaged in trade to issue permits and make certain scientific and management findings as a condition of trade in "specimens" — readily recognizable parts and derivatives — of the listed species. CITES, arts. III, IV. The permit system is central to CITES' ability to monitor trade so as to prevent further endangerment or the loss of species due to trade. For Appendix I species, the importing country must make a variety of findings, including a determination that the specimen is not to be used for primarily commercial purposes.

For both Appendix I and Appendix II species, the exporting country must also make a number of findings. The most important finding generally and for climate change purposes specifically is the requirement that the export will not be detrimental to the survival of the species. This biological finding, known as the "non-detriment finding," is crucial for ensuring that trade does not undermine the conservation status of species in the wild.

As argued by the Species Survival Network, a coalition of wildlife conservation organizations, the CITES Parties have several opportunities to take the impacts of climate change into account, particularly when listing a species in the Appendices and when making non-detriment findings.

SPECIES SURVIVAL NETWORK, CITES AND CLIMATE CHANGE: INTERACTIONS, IMPACTS AND POTENTIAL RESPONSES

3–4 (June 6, 2007), *available at,*
http://www.ssn.org/Meetings/cop/cop14/cites_cop14_EN.htm#fs*

Although consideration of climate change has taken place in other conservation agreements, Parties to CITES have yet to directly address the relationship between species conservation and climate change. After considerable discussion during the revision of the CITES Listing Criteria, Resolution Conf. 9.24 (Rev. CoP13) was amended to specifically recognize "climate regime shifts" as an extrinsic factor affecting a species' vulnerability to over-exploitation for purpose of listing decisions. To date, however, Parties have made little direct reference to climate change in listing proposals. Climate change is referenced in Proposal 18 to list the European Eel (*Anguilla anguilla*) on Appendix II at CoP14, which notes that declines in European and American eels, which both spawn in the Sargasso Sea, provide evidence that changes in ocean currents resulting from climate change may have interfered with larval transport, leading to reduced recruitment in eel stocks. Surprisingly, it goes unmentioned in the U.S. proposal to list red and pink corals in Appendix II, despite substantial scientific evidence that warmer seas pose a major threat to coral species.

More significantly, there is little evidence that the impacts of climate change are being considered at all in the context of transfers between appendices, or in the making of non-detriment findings. Nor has CITES considered how to factor the threat posed to species by climate change into its deliberations. Considering the clear and immediate relevance of climate impacts to managing wildlife sustainably, this is a serious omission.

The text of the Convention provides both the authority and the mandate for Parties to take climate change into account. Article III, paragraph 2(a) and Article IV, paragraph 2(a) of the Convention provide that export permits shall only be granted, *inter alia*, upon a determination by a Scientific Authority of the State of export that such export will not be detrimental to the survival of that species (non-detriment findings or NDFs). Resolution Conf. 10.3 recommends that the findings and advice of the Scientific Authority of the country of export be based on the scientific review of available information on the population status, distribution, population trend, harvest and other biological and ecological factors, as appropriate. Climate change is clearly an appropriate ecological factor to be considered in this context. CITES also requires that exports be regulated to maintain a traded species "at a level consistent with its role in the ecosystem in which it occurs" (Art. IV(3)). Fulfilling that mandate adequately will require far greater attention to what each species' role may be in an ecosystem that is changing rapidly.

———

QUESTIONS AND DISCUSSION

1. As the Species Survival Network states, the impacts of climate change clearly fit within the range of factors affecting a species: species' population status, distribution, population trend, and other biological and ecological factors affecting the species. How should Parties evaluate climate change impacts when making a

———

non-detriment finding? For example, if a specific export of a polar bear skin will not be detrimental to the survival of the species, but climate change is considered to be a key factor threatening the very survival of polar bears, should the trade in a polar bear skin be allowed?

2.   The Secretary General of the CITES Secretariat has called the issuance of adequate non-detriment findings "obviously essential for achieving the aims of the Convention" and has said, "[i]t is also obvious that this advice requires sufficient knowledge of the conservation status of the species and that a positive advice should not be given in the absence thereof." WILLEM WIJNSTEKERS, THE EVOLUTION OF CITES 67 (7th ed. 2003). Nonetheless, many Parties lack the technical expertise, financial resources, or political will to make appropriate non-detriment findings — problems that have been widely acknowledged. For example, one CITES report has acknowledged that "Clearly, action is needed to improve the situation and to assist Scientific Authorities in making non-detriment findings." CITES Inf. Doc. 11.3, *CITES Scientific Authorities Checklist to Assist in Making Non-Detriment Findings for Appendix II Exports*, 1. The International Union for the Conservation of Nature (IUCN) has reported that "many species continue to be traded in the absence of information about the impact of such exploitation on the wild population." A.R. ROSSER & M.J. HAYWOOD, OCCASIONAL PAPER OF THE IUCN SPECIES SURVIVAL COMMISSION NO. 27, GUIDANCE FOR CITES SCIENTIFIC AUTHORITIES: CHECKLIST TO ASSIST IN MAKING NON-DETRIMENT FINDINGS FOR APPENDIX II EXPORTS 3 (2002). If the Parties are already struggling to make adequate non-detriment findings because they lack basic biological information concerning a species, how will they be able to factor in climate change? If they cannot, should trade be permitted? For more information on non-detriment findings, see Erica Thorson & Kim McCoy, *IELP White Paper on Non-Detriment Finding Criteria* (March 2, 2006), *available at* http://www.lclark.edu/org/ielp/cites.html.

D.   The Ramsar Convention on Wetlands of International Importance

The 1971 Convention on Wetlands of International Importance especially as Waterfowl Habitat (known as the Ramsar Convention, because it was signed in Ramsar, Iran) provides the framework for the conservation and wise use of wetlands. Convention on Wetlands of International Importance, Especially As Waterfowl Habitat, Feb. 2, 1971, 11 I.L.M. 969 (1972). To that end, the Ramsar Convention's 158 Parties must designate at least one of their own wetlands for inclusion in the Ramsar List of Wetlands of International Importance. To date, they have included more than 1800 wetland sites encompassing a surface area of over 170 million hectares. *See* Ramsar homepage, www.ramsar.org. In addition, the Parties must promote the conservation of the wetlands included in the List and the wise use of all wetlands in their territory. They must also establish wetland nature reserves for waterfowl. Ramsar Convention, arts. 2–4.

The Ramsar Convention originally focused on wetland protection for waterbird habitat, but its scope has subsequently broadened to cover all aspects of wetland conservation and wise use. Ramsar's broader scope recognizes the substantial ecological, economic, and social benefits that derive from wetlands. More recently, it has begun to examine its mission and goals in the context of climate change, with efforts to assess the value of wetlands for carbon sequestration. Along with forests, wetlands, particularly boreal peatlands and tropical peat swamps, are the world's principal mechanisms to sequester carbon. Draining and drying these wetlands releases both carbon dioxide and methane. CBD Secretariat, *Biodiversity and Climate Change* 29 (2007) (citing D. Dudgeon, et al. *Freshwater Biodiversity: Importance, Threats, Status and Conservation Challenges*, 81 BIOL. RES. 163–82 (2006)). Conservation and restoration of these wetlands will thus avoid the release of carbon dioxide and methane in addition to providing other important ecological services.

In 2002, the Ramsar Parties adopted Resolution VIII.3, which calls on Parties to manage wetlands so as to increase their resilience to climate change and extreme climatic events. It also called on Parties to minimize the degradation, promote restoration, and improve management practices of wetland types that are significant carbon reservoirs, or have the ability to sequester carbon. They were further asked to study the role of wetlands in carbon storage and sequestration and in mitigating the impacts of sea-level rise. Ramsar, Resolution VIII.3, *Climate Change and Wetlands: Impacts, Adaptation, and Mitigation* (2002).

The Parties subsequently embraced climate change under the Ramsar Strategic Plan 2003–2008 as a major global challenge to conservation and wise use of wetlands. Indeed, a number of climate change-related effects will present challenges to wetlands conservation, including: more extreme droughts, storms and floods; rises in sea temperature and level; permafrost and glacier thawing; and changes in the distribution and quality of ecosystems that will negatively impact species survival. The Ramsar Strategic Plan 2003–2008, § 12(b). As a consequence, managing wetlands adaptively in response to the impacts of global climate change and sea-level rise has become a stated objective of the Parties. *Id.* at § 27(b). Other climate change-related activities identified in the Strategic Plan, include:

- developing methodologies to assess the vulnerability of wetlands to the impacts of climate change and sea-level rise. *Id.* at paras. 1.2.4–1.2.5.

- ensuring that their wetlands policies "are fully integrated into and harmonized with" other strategic or planning processes and documents relating to, *inter alia*, climate change. *Id.* at para. 2.1.2.

- analyzing the values and functions of Ramsar sites with respect to coastal protection, flood control, and climate change mitigation, among other things. *Id.* at para. 3.3.2.

- promoting the management of wetlands in relation to adaptive management and mitigation of the impacts of climate change. *Id.* at para. 3.4.8.

A 2008 resolution of the Parties updates Resolution VIII.3, encourages cooperation with other biodiversity-related conventions and institutions, and implements elements of the Strategic Plan. Resolution IX.24, *Climate Change and Wetlands* (2008).

In addition to the general strategies to address the relationship between climate change and wetlands, the Ramsar Convention also provides at least two potential processes for protecting a Ramsar wetlands site that is adversely affected by climate change. First, the Parties established a process for deleting or restricting a site if the site "unavoidably loses the values, functions and attributes for which it was included." Ramsar, Decision IX.6, *Guidance for Addressing Ramsar Sites or Parts of Sites which No Longer Meet the Criteria for Designation* (2005). To delete a site, a Party must assess the present ecological character of the site and establish whether the site still qualifies as a Ramsar site. As part of this assessment, the

Party must establish whether the change in ecological character is truly irreversible. If the change may be reversible, then the Party must "define the conditions under which the change may reverse or be reversed, and the management actions (including restoration) needed to secure this, as well as the likely timescales needed to permit the recovery of the character of the site." *Id.* at Annex, para. 25. If there is potential for reversibility, the Party must monitor the key ecological features of the site, reevaluate whether the site meets the criteria for inclusion in the Ramsar List, and report to the Parties on the recovery of the site. If the loss of part or all of the listed site is irreversible, and the attempts at recovery or restoration have failed, then the Party must report to the Parties on the new boundaries of the site or the site's removal from the List.

The second potential process for responding to sites threatened by climate change is to use the "Montreux Record." The Parties may use the Montreux Record to highlight Ramsar sites "where an adverse change in ecological character has occurred, is occurring, or is likely to occur, and which are therefore in need of priority conservation attention." Ramsar, Resolution VI.1, *Working Definitions of Ecological Character, Guidelines for Describing and Maintaining the Ecological Character of Listed Sites, and Guidelines for Operation of the Montreux Record,* Annex, Section 3 (1996). Although a Party normally requests that one of its own sites be included in the Montreux Record, the Ramsar Secretariat may also suggest that a site be included in the Montreux Record. However, a site may only be included in the Record with the consent of the Party concerned. The convention's Scientific and Technical Review Panel (STRP) will then provide comments and advice to the Party on what steps might be taken, including whether the site should be included in the Montreux Record. If a site is included in the Montreux Record, then the Ramsar Secretariat will prioritize the use of the Ramsar Advisory Mission mechanism. Ramsar, Recommendation 4.8, *Change in Ecological Character of Ramsar Sites* (1990). The Ramsar Advisory Mission is a technical mission that provides "advice on the measures to be taken, and assess the desirability of removing a site from the Montreux Record when measures have been implemented successfully." RAMSAR CONVENTION SECRETARIAT, THE RAMSAR CONVENTION MANUAL: A GUIDE TO THE CONVENTION ON WETLANDS, § 4.3.6 (4th ed. 2005).

QUESTIONS AND DISCUSSION

1.　The Montreux Record is analogous to the "in danger" listings under the World Heritage Convention, and Ramsar Parties have reported that inclusion of a site in the Montreux Record has improved the conservation of the affected wetland. For example, a Ramsar Advisory Mission in 1992 made recommendations to reverse the negative changes to the ecological character of the Srebarna Nature Reserve in Bulgaria. Ramsar's Small Grants Fund provided the means for the development of a management plan for the site, and a second Advisory Mission in 2001 reported "a stable and sustained trend towards improvement of the ecological character" of Srebarna Nature Reserve. *Id.* at § 1.5.

2.　Compare the process and impact of an "in danger" listing under the World Heritage Convention with the two processes for protecting wetlands under the Ramsar Convention. If you were representing an environmental organization hoping to highlight the impacts of climate change, how would you advise them about the relative potential impact of using these two conventions? Would petitioners obtain similar results in the Ramsar Convention as they did by petitioning to list sites as "in danger" under the World Heritage Convention? What are the relative advantages and disadvantages of using the two mechanisms under the Ramsar Convention to raise climate-related issues?

E.   The Convention on the Conservation of Migratory Species of Wild Animals

The Convention on the Conservation of Migratory Species of Wild Animals (CMS), June 3, 1979, 19 I.L.M. 15, focuses solely on the conservation of migratory species. It requires Parties to "endeavour" to conserve and, where feasible, restore essential habitat of endangered migratory species — those species "in danger of extinction throughout all or a significant portion of [their] range" — included in Appendix I. Party Range States (i.e., those Parties where the species occurs) must also endeavour to prevent or mitigate obstacles to the migration of the species, and "to the extent feasible," reduce factors leading to endangerment. Range States also "shall prohibit" the "taking," including the "capturing" and "harassing," of Appendix I species, subject to some exceptions. It also establishes a process for creating specific agreements for the conservation of species or groups of species listed in Appendix II. A species in Appendix II either has an "unfavourable conservation status" which requires international conservation and management or "a conservation status which could significantly benefit" from international cooperation. Thus, unlike species in Appendix I, Appendix II species do not need to be endangered with extinction before the Parties implement conservation obligations (although a species can be included in both Appendices). On the other hand, Parties have no conservation obligations regarding species included only in Appendix II until they conclude a separate agreement specifically addressing that species.

The CMS Secretariat has published a significant report on the effects of climate change on migratory species. UNEP/CMS Secretariat, *Migratory Species and Climate Change: Impacts of a Changing Environment on Wild Animals* (2006). In addition, the CMS Parties have adopted two resolutions to reduce the impacts of climate change on CMS-listed species. First, a 2006 resolution directed the CMS Scientific Council to identify those migratory species that are particularly threatened by climate change and review the distribution of CMS-listed species for climate change consequences. Resolution 8.13, *Climate Change and Migratory Species* (2005). A 2008 resolution goes further, recommending that the Parties reduce the impacts of climate change and climate change mitigation or adaption activities on CMS-listed species. CMS Parties are also to design and implement adaptation strategies for migratory species threatened by climate change. The Parties and the CMS Secretariat are also requested "to coordinate the incorporation of climate change impacts and relevant adaptation measures into species-specific Action Plans." Resolution 9.7, *Climate Change Impacts on Migratory Species* (2008).

QUESTIONS AND DISCUSSION

The ability to craft species-specific or taxon-specific agreements for migratory species included in Appendix II provides a unique opportunity to develop conservation approaches to address the effects of climate change on those species. The task of establishing appropriate conservation strategies for species affected by climate change is indeed daunting. The United Kingdom's Department for Environment Food and Rural Affairs commissioned an extraordinary document that analyzes the impacts of climate change on a wide variety of migratory species and underscores the challenges of conserving migratory species. The report found, for example, that 84 percent of bird species protected by CMS are threatened to some degree by climate change. Even if those species are affected by the same vector, such as changes in water supplies or alterations in habitat, each may require a separate set of conservation measures to help adapt to climate change. Where one species needs year-round glacial melt for the breeding of prey species, another needs an ice pack from which to hunt. In considering these issues, the report made the following recommendations for addressing the effects of climate change on migratory species. In making its recommendations, the authors distinguished between what they called "broad-front" migrants — those species that "migrate in short hops, stopping frequently on route, and often have geographically diffuse migration routes (most bats, insects, passerine birds and marine animals)"; and "leap migrants" — those species that "migrate in long-haul journeys stopping at only a few, usually discrete, sites, such as wetlands, often in large numbers; the primary example of these would be migrating shorebirds and waterfowl."

ROBERT A. ROBINSON, et al., CLIMATE CHANGE AND MIGRATORY SPECIES
25–28 (2005)[*]

6.1. In terrestrial ecosystems, two issues potentially affect a large range of migratory species: (i) **changes in water resources** — particularly wetland quality, site maintenance and increased desertification; (ii) **loss of vulnerable habitats** — particularly tundra, cloud forest, sea ice and low-lying coastal areas, especially in small island states. Many of these areas also face severe anthropogenic threats.

6.2. Different conservation approaches are required for 'broad-front' and 'leap' migrants. Broad-front migrants will benefit from modifications to extensive land-use along the migratory route, whereas, leap migrants require a coherent site network, with the quality of individual sites being of critical importance. **In most cases, the impacts of climate change need to be integrated with other economic, social and conservation objectives.**

6.3. **For leap migrants, maintenance of a coherent network of stopover sites will be required.** Currently there is a lack of even some of the most basic syntheses of information that are required for conservation action. **There is an urgent need to collate information on migratory stopover sites to identify coherent migratory networks.** This would provide a strategic, international overview and enable clear identification of site protection priorities for leap migrants. Much of this information is available for birds, so this could be achieved relatively straightforwardly for the key flyways. The same consideration may also apply to other taxonomic groups.

6.4. For broad-front terrestrial migrants, the creation of suitable migratory habitat, such as wildlife-friendly field margins, hedgerows, small copses and ponds have potential to allow migrants to adapt to climate change. Where these are absent, populations may not be able to adapt sufficiently and hence will suffer negative impacts. . . .

6.5. In areas with remaining pristine habitat, the creation of protected trans-boundary habitat corridors is likely to be a great benefit. This will help broad-front migrants as well as migrants at the end of their migrations. Currently it is an approach applied particularly in the Americas, e.g., the Meso-American Corridor, through Central America.

6.6. The priority for adapting to change in the marine environment will be to manage human impacts on the resources required by migratory species through ecosystem-based management. One way to achieve this would be to designate marine protected areas (a.k.a. 'no-take zones') for the prey of marine mammals at key sites. However, the locations of such areas are likely to change over time, and protection will require very different legislation than anything that has been developed to date. There will need to be a degree of flexibility in the establishment of protected areas for marine mammals, such as Special Areas of Conservation (SAC) to take account of the potential for shifts in the range of species with climate change.

6.7. Maintain large population sizes. Successful adaptation to changed climatic factors (and consequently habitat) will require sufficient genetic variation present in the population, which will be related to population size.

Given the species-specific nature of climate change threats to migratory species, what kind of measures would you recommend to conserve such species? Does the flexibility to negotiate separate agreements under CMS provide the best opportunity for developing adaptation strategies for migratory species?

IV. CLIMATE CHANGE AND THE LAW OF THE SEA

A.   Introduction

The UN Convention on the Law of the Sea, which along with associated treaties, provides the basic legal and institutional framework for governing our oceans. Not surprisingly, given the many interactions between climate change and the oceans, ocean governance has important implications for how we respond to climate change. As already suggested in other chapters, climate change is having substantial impacts on ocean ecology. The top layers of the oceans appear to be warming, sea levels are rising, and ocean salinity in some areas may be changing. In addition, increased concentrations of greenhouse gases are turning the oceans measurably more acidic. The net results are that climate change threatens the future of coral reefs as well as the productivity of the ocean's basic food pyramid (zooplanktons, planktons and algae). *See* Chapter 1.

At the same time oceans are one of the most important elements in the self-regulation of the earth's climate. The oceans collectively are the largest carbon sink and reservoir on the planet, although evidence is mounting that the ability of the oceans to sequester carbon from the atmosphere is slowing. This has prompted serious proposals to fertilize the oceans with iron to spark greater algal blooms, which in turn would remove more carbon from the atmosphere. Ocean fertilization is discussed in Section D.

This section introduces the Law of the Sea and highlights some of its implications for climate change, as well as the challenges that climate change may present for application of the Law of the Sea.

B.   The Law of the Sea Regime

The modern law of the sea is built upon a small number of basic principles. The most important of these is the "freedom of the seas" — the oceans' status as a global commons upon which nations' freedom to travel and extract resources is unimpeded. By the early 1800s this legal principle was universally accepted by major powers, largely as a result of State practice and the powerful Dutch and British fleets' establishment of naval dominance around the globe to protect their commerce and colonies.

Grotius' principle is straightforward. One nation's use of a sea-lane for passage does not impede any other nation's right to travel on the sea-lane, nor does one nation's fishing in an area impede other nations from fishing there. In terms of fisheries, this principle allocates property rights on the basis of the law of capture. Yet such an arrangement provides a perfect setting for the tragedy of the commons, where individual actors' interests to exploit an open-access resource for short-term benefits are stronger than the common interest to restrict short-term exploitation and conserve the resource. *See* Chapter 3. With rights come duties, yet the right of unimpeded resource extraction granted by the traditional freedom of the seas doctrine did not impose a parallel responsibility to work collectively to conserve ocean resources. If every nation can fish unimpeded on the high seas, no nation can effectively manage the resource for the benefit of all. Since the oceans' resources were thought inexhaustible, though, this lack of parallel obligations was not a concern.

After nearly a decade of negotiations, the UN Third Conference on the Law of the Sea concluded in 1982, when governments signed the UN Convention on the Law of the Sea (UNCLOS). U.N.Doc. A/CONF.62/122, *reprinted in* 21 I.L.M. 1261 (1982). UNCLOS, which came into force in 1994, is a massive document, consisting of 320 articles and nine annexes. It outlines the global framework for governing virtually all aspects of the oceans — think of it as a constitution for the seas, providing broad rules to guide general behavior but requiring issue-specific agreements to give its provisions concrete meaning. Over 150 countries have ratified UNCLOS, but the United States is not one of them. *See generally* http://www.un.org/depts/los/>.

The basic tension in the UNCLOS negotiations was one between the interests of maritime nations who rely on the seas for commerce and navigation and the interests of coastal States who rely on the natural resources of the adjacent sea. For obvious reasons, maritime nations favor expansive freedom of the seas and limited national jurisdiction over coastal waters while coastal States seek enlarged national jurisdiction over adjacent waters.

UNCLOS resolved this basic tension by establishing a series of jurisdictional zones, moving outward from a baseline that in general reflects a nation's coast line. The ports of a coastal State are regarded as *internal waters* and, with few exceptions relating to inspections and enforcement, ports are subject to the full range of the coastal State's national authority. UNCLOS, art. 11. The freedom of the seas has always been limited by a customary law of *territorial seas*, permitting exclusive national jurisdiction over a narrow marine zone off the coast (originally three miles). This was known popularly as the "cannon shot rule," reflecting the fact that shore-based cannons could not fire farther than three miles out to sea. Over time, the law evolved as reflected in UNCLOS to extend the territorial seas to twelve nautical miles offshore. *Id.* art. 3. Subject to the right of innocent passage (i.e., the right to freedom of navigation), the coastal State exercises almost complete authority in the territorial sea. From 12 to 24 miles is the *contiguous zone*. *Id.* art. 33. Here the coastal State's sovereignty is more limited, though it may enforce its customs, fiscal, immigration or sanitary laws and regulations. From the boundary of the territorial sea (generally 12 miles) up to 200 nautical miles is the *exclusive economic zone* (EEZ). Within the EEZ, coastal States have the sovereign right to explore, exploit, conserve and manage the natural resources, both mineral and living. *Id.* arts. 56–57. Beyond the EEZ, more than 200 nautical miles off the coast, lie the *high seas*, an area beyond national jurisdictions that are part of the global commons.

UNCLOS embodied a fundamental shift in the way the seas were regulated. The historical "freedom of the seas" approach meant that few rules restricted activities such as fishing or pollution. UNCLOS shifts much of this focus from one of "freedom" to one of "rights and responsibilities." Restrictions, for example to fish sustainably or to limit ocean dumping, were now a central part of the law of the sea. UNCLOS includes the following relatively general provisions concerning environmental protection:

U.N. CONVENTION ON THE LAW OF THE SEAS

Article 192

General obligation

States have the obligation to protect and preserve the marine environment.

Article 193

Sovereign right of States to exploit their natural resources

States have the sovereign right to exploit their natural resources pursuant to their environmental policies and in accordance with their duty to protect and preserve the marine environment.

Article 194

Measures to prevent, reduce and control pollution of the marine environment

1. States shall take, individually or jointly as appropriate, all measures consistent with this Convention that are necessary to prevent, reduce and control pollution of the marine environment from any source, using for this purpose the best practicable means at their disposal and in accordance with their capabilities, and they shall endeavour to harmonize their policies in this connection.

2. States shall take all measures necessary to ensure that activities under their jurisdiction or control are so conducted as not to cause damage by pollution to other States and their environment, and that pollution arising from incidents or activities under their jurisdiction or control does not spread beyond the areas where they exercise sovereign rights in accordance with this Convention.

3. The measures taken pursuant to this Part shall deal with all sources of pollution of the marine environment. These measures shall include, *inter alia*, those designed to minimize to the fullest possible extent:

    (a) the release of toxic, harmful or noxious substances, especially those which are persistent, from land-based sources, from or through the atmosphere or by dumping;

    (b) pollution from vessels, in particular measures for preventing accidents and dealing with emergencies, ensuring the safety of operations at sea, preventing intentional and unintentional discharges, and regulating the design, construction, equipment, operation and manning of vessels;

    (c) pollution from installations and devices used in exploration or exploitation of the natural resources of the sea-bed and subsoil, in particular measures for preventing accidents and dealing with emergencies, ensuring the safety of operations at sea, and regulating the design, construction, equipment, operation and manning of such installations or devices;* * *

4. In taking measures to prevent, reduce or control pollution of the marine environment, States shall refrain from unjustifiable interference with activities carried out by other States in the exercise of their rights and in pursuance of their duties in conformity with this Convention.

5. The measures taken in accordance with this Part shall include those necessary to protect and preserve rare or fragile ecosystems as well as the habitat of depleted, threatened or endangered species and other forms of marine life.

Article 195

Duty not to transfer damage or hazards or transform one type of pollution into another

In taking measures to prevent, reduce and control pollution of the marine environment, States shall act so as not to transfer, directly or indirectly, damage or hazards from one area to another or transform one type of pollution into another.

Article 196

Use of technologies or introduction of alien or new species

1. States shall take all measures necessary to prevent, reduce and control pollution of the marine environment resulting from the use of technologies under their jurisdiction or control, or the intentional or accidental introduction of species, alien or new, to a particular part of the marine environment, which may cause significant and harmful changes thereto.

2. This article does not affect the application of this Convention regarding the prevention, reduction and control of pollution of the marine environment.* * *

Article 204

Monitoring of the risks or effects of pollution

1. States shall, consistent with the rights of other States, endeavour, as far as practicable, directly or through the competent international organizations, to observe, measure, evaluate and analyse, by recognized scientific methods, the risks or effects of pollution of the marine environment.

2. In particular, States shall keep under surveillance the effects of any activities which they permit or in which they engage in order to determine whether these activities are likely to pollute the marine environment. * * *

Article 206

Assessment of potential effects of activities

When States have reasonable grounds for believing that planned activities under their jurisdiction or control may cause substantial pollution of or significant and harmful changes to the marine environment, they shall, as far as practicable, assess the potential effects of such activities on the marine environment and shall communicate reports of the results of such assessments . . . .

Article 207

Pollution from land-based sources

1. States shall adopt laws and regulations to prevent, reduce and control pollution of the marine environment from land-based sources, including rivers, estuaries, pipelines and outfall structures, taking into account internationally agreed rules, standards and recommended practices and procedures.

2. States shall take other measures as may be necessary to prevent, reduce and control such pollution. * * *

4. States, acting especially through competent international organizations or diplomatic conference, shall endeavour to establish global and regional rules, standards and recommended practices and procedures to prevent, reduce and control pollution of the marine environment from land-based sources, taking into account characteristic regional features, the economic capacity of developing States and their need for economic development. Such rules, standards and recommended practices and procedures shall be re-examined from time to time as necessary.

In addition to these general obligations, more specific treaty regimes have been adopted for managing ocean fisheries and for controlling pollution. In addition, many regional seas agreements exist to provide clearer governance for enclosed or semi-enclosed ocean areas. Separate regional seas agreements cover the Mediterranean, Black, Caspian, and Baltic Seas as well as areas around the Caribbean and South Pacific. UNEP supports these treaties through its regional seas programme. There are more than fifteen conventions under the UNEP framework with provisions addressing land-based sources of marine pollution, in every region except East Asia, South Asia, and the Northwest Pacific.

QUESTIONS AND DISCUSSION

1. Review the description in Chapter 1 of ocean acidification caused by increasing concentrations of carbon dioxide in the atmosphere. Do the general provisions of the Law of the Sea Convention provide any legal basis for addressing the emission of greenhouse gases?

2. Assuming that climate change is causing substantial impacts on ocean ecology, do the general environmental principles excerpted above in UNCLOS provide any arguments for bringing climate change claims? *See, e.g.*, William C.G. Burns, *Potential Causes of Action for Climate Change Damages in International Fora: The Law of the Sea Convention*, 2 INT'L J. OF SUST. DEVT. L. & POL'Y 27 (2006).

C.   Shifting Baselines Due to Climate Change

In addition to the potential ecological impacts on the oceans, climate change may also have significant impacts for other aspects of ocean governance. Most notably, if climate change results in even modest amounts of sea level rise, then maritime boundaries between countries may be affected because these boundaries are often based on geographic features that will be inundated by rising seas. UNCLOS includes an elaborate set of rules for establishing maritime boundaries based on the determination of baselines for each coastal country. The rules allow countries to extend their territorial seas or exclusive economic zones (EEZs) on the basis of any territory (or rock) that can support habitation. The value of these areas for fisheries and oil and gas development, for example, can be quite substantial, and a number of international disputes persist over claimed maritime boundaries. As sea levels rise, many observers argue that under UNCLOS the baselines for demarking the maritime boundaries also change, adding uncertainty and increasing the potential for conflict.

CHARLES DI LEVA & SACHIKO MORITA, MARITIME RIGHTS OF COASTAL STATES AND CLIMATE CHANGE: SHOULD STATES ADAPT TO SUBMERGED BOUNDARIES
WORLD BANK LAW & DEV. WORKING PAPER SER. NO. 5 (2007)

The baseline points that would be most threatened by rising sea levels include the following:

* low-tide elevations (drying rocks). These can serve as a baseline point if they are located within the territorial sea. According to some commentators, if a drying rock is located within 12 nautical miles from shore, . . . permanent submergence of this rock by a rising sea level could mean a loss of territorial sea generated by the rock.

* fringing reefs. In the case of islands having fringing reefs, the baseline for measuring the breadth of the territorial sea is the seaward low-water line of the reef. With rising sea levels, therefore, the extent of the territorial sea may change for these islands.

* riverbanks. Article 9 of UNCLOS provides that "if a river flows directly into the sea, the baseline shall be a straight line across the mouth of the river between points on the low-water line of its banks." Riverbanks, however, are subject to constant erosion and accretion. Therefore, a maritime zone generated using the riverbank as a base point may shift.

* islands. UNCLOS Article 121 provides that islands are entitled to a 200-mile wide EEZ as well as a territorial sea, contiguous zone, and the continental shelf. According to most commentators, an island in the legal sense has to meet two conditions: (i) it must be natural and not an artificial installation and (ii) it must always be above sea level. Formations visible only at low tide, and permanently submerged banks and reefs, do not in general produce a territorial sea. . . . [T]he issue of climate change as discussed here is that the rising sea level could submerge part of or an entire island, thereby potentially giving rise to the claim that the impacted island state has been deprived of its right to use that part of its island group to extend its EEZ.

UNCLOS does not expressly provide that boundaries should move with baselines. * * * [N]o provisions . . . "fix" the outer boundary of the EEZ, the contiguous zone, or the territorial sea. Many scholars have therefore considered the legal and physical boundary of these maritime zones to be ambulatory. For example, one expert who has been involved in maritime boundary issues for almost four decades concludes that "as [the normal low-water line] moves landward and seaward with accretion and erosion, so does the baseline. As the baseline ambulates,

so does each of the maritime zones measured from it." This view, perhaps more than any other, makes clear how rising sea levels may soon affect boundary lines. . . .
* * *

Although it is difficult to predict with certainty all the possible legal implications of . . . [ambulatory baselines in an era of sea level rise], we can list some potential consequences here. For example, if the outer limit of the territorial sea shifts landward, it could mean that some area that now falls in territorial sea becomes part of the EEZ, and what is now within the EEZ would become part of the high seas. This, in turn, would imply that a coastal state can start exercising its "sovereign rights" granted to it in the EEZ for the "economic exploitation and exploration" in what is now the territorial sea, but that it could lose part of its current EEZ In addition, if such a shift occurs, other states would have "freedom of navigation" instead of "innocent passage" in certain parts of the coastal state's waters. This change could in turn mean that a warship would possibly gain increased flexibility in its navigation in those parts of the water.

One could postulate that rising sea levels may lead some states to try to preserve the current baselines by arguing that it would promote stability in boundaries (less uncertainty), be fair (in that it maintains the present allocation of authority over the oceans and their resources, preserving the "historic use" of the waters), and be efficient (in that it avoids the costs of adjustment). In addition, constant changes to boundaries have the potential to cause confusion and possibly reduce confidence in the location of maritime limits. Some scholars have also argued that tying maritime boundaries to ambulatory baselines would encourage wasteful spending by states to protect the baselines. Alternatively, other states may try to take advantage of these shifting coastlines and argue that they should be entitled to augment their baselines and their maritime boundaries accordingly. * * *

[Moreover,] many maritime zones are subject to bilateral or multilateral maritime boundary delimitation treaties, and these treaties may further complicate the situation, especially where not all countries involved are party to UNCLOS. Maritime boundary delimitation treaties generally define the maritime boundaries, as well as the access rights that each state has over their various maritime zones. Given that more than 90 percent of the global fish catch is taken within zones that are under national jurisdiction, states are increasingly turning to these treaties to define their own rights and obligations, as well as those of others. Negotiations of these treaties entail extensive preparatory work, expertise, and substantial amounts of data. Thus, once they are negotiated, they are unlikely to change for a long time. It is therefore important that these maritime boundary delimitation treaties adequately take account of possible future shifts in baselines and that developing countries receive appropriate and sufficient technical support when negotiating these treaties so that their interests are effectively represented.

QUESTIONS AND DISCUSSION

1.   What solutions could you consider for solving the ambiguity caused by the current rules for setting national boundaries under UNCLOS? Professor David Caron suggests that coastal states should move toward a system of permanent, fixed boundaries rather than the ambulatory approach currently assumed to be part of UNCLOS. David D. Caron, *Climate Change, Sea Level Rise and the Coming Uncertainty in Oceanic Boundaries: A Proposal to Avoid Conflict,* in MARITIME BOUNDARY DISPUTES, SETTLEMENT PROCESSES, AND THE LAW OF THE SEA (Seoung-Yong Hong & Jon M. Van Dyke, eds., forthcoming 2008). What do you think of this proposal? What political obstacles do you think would hinder such an approach?

What steps would you recommend a coastal State take to secure its baselines?

2. The U.S. Supreme Court has affirmed the ambulatory nature of setting maritime boundaries under U.S. law. In *United States v. Alaska*, the Court in a conflict over whether certain submerged lands were federal or state lands ruled that "the shifts in a low-water line along the shore . . . could lead to a shift in the baseline for measuring a maritime zone." As a result, a state's entitlement to submerged lands beneath the territorial sea could change as the baseline changes. *See United States v. Alaska*, 521 U.S. 1 (1997); *United States v. Louisiana*, 394 U.S. 11 (1969).

3. As Professor Caron points out, islands are potentially the most vulnerable to shifting baselines due to sea level rise:

> This is because islands, as opposed to uninhabitable rocks, are entitled to a 200-mile-wide EEZ. An island could be an offshore barrier island which in a practical sense, only extends the maritime zones of a coastal state somewhat in the same way as a drying rock. An offshore island could also be an anchor point of a straight baseline. Most significantly, a small island could be an island state or, more likely, one of a group of islands that form a state. This is significant because such island states do not merely extend the zones of the related adjacent coastal state, but can potentially generate an EEZ of their own, enclosing some 125,664 square nautical miles of ocean. Numerous island states exist. A rising sea level could taint the freshwater reservoir of an island, potentially rendering it an uninhabitable rock, submerge enough of it to leave only an uninhabitable rock, or submerge it entirely. In any of these circumstances, the island state would potentially lose its right to use that part of the island group to extend its EEZ. Consequently, for the island state, there is little doubt that the combination of a rise in sea level and the contingent nature of boundaries is, or will be, of grave concern.

David D. Caron, *Climate Change, Sea Level Rise and the Coming Uncertainty in Oceanic Boundaries: A Proposal to Avoid Conflict*, *in* MARITIME BOUNDARY DISPUTES, SETTLEMENT PROCESSES, AND THE LAW OF THE SEA (Seoung-Yong Hong & Jon M. Van Dyke, eds., forthcoming 2008).

4. Just as rising sea levels may submerge islands or alter baselines for establishing territorial seas and EEZs, melting ice may give rise to territorial claims. In August 2007, for example, a Russian submarine dramatically planted the Russian flag on the seabed at the North Pole. Russia's action was by no means a publicity stunt. With billions of barrels of oil and gas thought to be untapped in the Arctic, Russia was attempting to assert territorial claims to the continental shelf. Just days after Russia's stunt, the United States sent a team of 20 scientists to the Arctic to continue its efforts to map the undersea regions of the Arctic. All five Arctic nations — Canada, Denmark (Greenland), Norway, Russia, and the United States — are known to be mapping the Arctic.

These activities are clearly intended to assert claims in the UNCLOS continental shelf sweepstakes, which grants a coastal state "sovereign rights" to the resources of the continental shelf. The value of the resources at stake are potentially enormous — UNCLOS defines the continental shelf as the area comprising the sea-bed and subsoil extending at least 200 nautical miles from the baseline from which the territorial sea is measured (assuming a coastal state's claim does not run into the claim of another coastal State) and may extend up to 350 nautical miles from a State's baseline. UNCLOS, art. 76. A coastal State claiming a continental shelf beyond 200 nautical miles must submit its claim to the Commission on the Limits of the Continental Shelf. *Id.*, at Annex II, art. 3. The Commission will consider data and other material submitted by coastal States concerning the outer limits of the continental shelf in areas where those limits extend beyond 200 nautical miles. States must submit their claims within 10 years of the entry into force of this Convention for that State. *Id.*, at Annex II, art. 4. The Commission will make recommendations to coastal States on their respective claims, which the coastal state must take into account when establishing the outer limits of its continental shelf.

Territorial claims to the continental shelf in the Arctic have always been a possibility, but with the vast amount of sea ice that has historically persisted there, little motivation existed for countries to pursue their claims. With the ice melting and large areas of ocean now open year-round, offshore drilling for oil and gas could become technically and economically feasible; new fishing grounds will also open. *See generally* Duncan Currie, *Sovereignty and Conflict in the Arctic Due to Climate Change: Climate Change and the Legal Status of the Arctic Ocean* (Aug. 5, 2007), available at www.globelaw.com.

5. Beyond the continental shelf claims, the melting Arctic is giving rise to other territorial disputes, including a Canadian-United States dispute over the Northwest passage.

> The impacts of climate change heighten the existing dispute over the status of the Northwest Passage. Canada claims that the Arctic waters of the Northwest Passage constitute "historic internal waters," and thus fall under Canadian jurisdiction and control. However, this claim has been disputed, especially by the United States and the European Union. The United States has consistently argued that the Northwest Passage represents an international strait (international waters), which allows the right of transit passage (beyond "innocent passage").

> The requirements of an international strait are both "geographic" and "functional." An international strait must connect two bodies of the high seas, in this case the Atlantic and Pacific oceans. However, an international strait must also satisfy the criterion of being a useful (not just potentially useful) route for navigation, and must have experienced a sufficient number of transits. Considering the International Court of Justice's ruling in the Corfu Channel Case, "it becomes readily available that [this criterion] fails to be met" in the case of the Northwest Passage, as there has not yet been a sufficient number of transits to qualify it as a "useful route for international maritime traffic." However, if a sufficient number of vessels transit the passage without seeking Canadian permission, Canada's claims to the legal status of the passage could be challenged, as there would be an increasing claim and perception that the passage constitutes an international strait. This international status would limit Canada's ability to control these waters, especially in terms of rules governing environmental issues and shipping practices, which would potentially be governed by the International Maritime Organization. Most agree that ensuring control requires a Government of Canada presence in the region, to monitor the passage and ensure compliance with Canadian sovereign claims.

Matthew Carnaghan & Allison Goody, *Canadian Arctic Sovereignty* 3–4 (Library of Parliament, Jan. 26, 2006). Is the United States' position even in its best interest?

D.   Ocean Fertilization and Climate Change

How we respond to climate change may also raise questions relating to the international law of the seas. As noted in Chapter 3, Section IV, in recent years at least three private companies have been actively exploring the possibility of sequestering carbon by fertilizing the ocean with iron. Their business model is to put tons of iron into parts of the ocean that are iron-poor, thus catalyzing an algal bloom. The algae will ingest carbon dioxide from the atmosphere, which will then be sequestered in the ocean floor as the algae die. The companies then plan to measure the amount of carbon removed from the atmosphere and attempt to sell the carbon removal credits in the global carbon offset market. Thus far, twelve open ocean experiments have been held, ranging from 1–4 weeks, with 1–2 tons of elemental iron, covering approximately 100 km^2 in the ocean. These experiments have been inconclusive on the effectiveness of ocean iron fertilization, which has led some in the scientific community as well as the private companies to expand the experiments to 10,000 km^2, using 10–20 tons of iron so they can analyze the full growth cycle of plankton and find out where the carbon actually ends up (at the bottom or surface of the ocean). *See* Carlie Ghelfi, *Despite Opposition, Ocean Iron Fertilization Forging Ahead,* available at http://media.cleantech.com, June 10, 2008; Phillip Boyd, et al., *A Mesoscale Phytoplankton Bloom in the Polar Southern Ocean Stimulated by Iron Fertilization,* NATURE, Oct. 12, 2000, at 695–702; Martin LaMonica, *Ocean Fertilization Firm Climos Gains Financial Backing,* available at http://news.cnet.com, Mar. 5, 2008; Rachel Petkewitch, *Fertilizing The Ocean With Iron,* 86 CHEM & ENG.NEWS, Mar. 31, 2008, at 30.

For obvious reasons, the companies' plans to discharge such large amounts of iron deliberately into the oceans raise questions under international law. The operational discharges, spills, and intentional dumping from ships are an important source of pollution to the marine environment. At least eight international agreements address threats posed by vessel pollution and dumping. The most relevant for iron fertilization is the Convention on the Prevention of Marine Pollution by Dumping of Wastes and Other Matter, 11 I.L.M. 129 (known as the 1972 London Convention). The London Convention and subsequent protocols establish international controls regulating the dumping and incineration of wastes at sea. The term "dumping" is defined broadly in Article III as the deliberate disposal of wastes and other matter at sea by ships, aircraft, and man-made structures at sea. The Convention covers all wastes, including sewage sludge, dredged materials, construction and demolition debris, explosives, chemical munitions, radioactive wastes, and other materials loaded on a vessel for the purpose of dumping. Periodic resolutions and amendments since 1978 have both strengthened its controls and extended its breadth of coverage.

When it became clear that Planktos, one of the private companies interested in iron fertilization was planning a major pilot project of the coast of the Galapagos, environmentalists and several countries sought the intervention of the International Maritime Organization (IMO). The IMO's view, however, was that iron fertilization did not necessarily involve the "deliberate disposal of wastes," and thus that the London Convention could not address the issue without amendments or a separate decision of the Parties. Although Planktos ran out of money before it could go through with its plans, the other private companies are better funded and still planning the commercialization of iron fertilization. This led to calls for the IMO to place a moratorium on iron fertilization.

Greenpeace International initially petitioned the scientific groups under the IMO to address and evaluate iron fertilization as a way to try to catalyze further action by the IMO. In Greenpeace's petition they invited the IMO Scientific Groups to:

1. give the matter of iron fertilization its urgent consideration, taking account of, in particular, the scale of uncertainties and potential for unpredictable and irreversible adverse impacts on marine ecosystems which may result from such activities; and

2. identify iron fertilization as an issue requiring urgent consideration by Contracting Parties during the 29th Consultative Meeting of the London Convention/2nd Meeting of the Parties to the London Protocol given the current absence of international regulations under which these activities may be properly evaluated and controlled.

Challenging "Geo-engineering Solutions" to Climate Change: The Urgent Need for Detailed Scientific Scrutiny and International Regulations to Protect the Oceans from Large-scale Iron Fertilization Programmes, LC/SG 30/12/1 (May 8, 2007) (submitted by Greenpeace International to the Scientific Groups of the London Convention and Protocol). Greenpeace also worked to get the U.S. Environmental Protection Agency to make a similar submission to the IMO seeking action against iron fertilization.

In response the Scientific Groups to the London Convention and the London Protocol issued the following decision in July 2007:

STATEMENT OF CONCERN REGARDING IRON FERTILIZATION OF THE OCEANS TO SEQUESTER CO_2

Introduction

1. At the 30th meeting of the Scientific Group under the London Convention, convened in conjunction with the 1st meeting of the Scientific Group under the London Protocol, (Santiago de Compostela, Spain: 18 to 22 June 2007), a number of documents were considered concerning large-scale ocean iron fertilization: (LC/SG 30/12 (IUCN); LC/SG 30/12/1 (Greenpeace International); and (LC/SG 30/INF.28 (United States)). In light of these submissions, the Scientific Groups developed the following "statement of concern":

Statement of Concern

"Large-scale fertilization of ocean waters using micro-nutrients such as iron to stimulate phytoplankton growth in order to sequester carbon dioxide is the subject of recent commercial interest. The Scientific Groups of the London Convention and the London Protocol take the view that knowledge about the effectiveness and potential environmental impacts of ocean iron fertilization currently is insufficient to justify large-scale operations.

According to the Intergovernmental Panel on Climate Change (IPCC), iron fertilization of the oceans may offer a potential strategy for removing carbon dioxide from the atmosphere by stimulating the growth of phytoplankton and thereby sequestering the carbon dioxide in the form of particulate organic carbon. However, the IPCC also stated that ocean iron fertilization remains largely speculative, and many of the environmental side effects have yet to be assessed.

The Scientific Groups of the London Convention and London Protocol note with concern the potential for large-scale ocean iron fertilization to have negative impacts on the marine environment and human health. They therefore recommend that any such operations be evaluated carefully to ensure, among other things, that such operations are not contrary to the aims of the London Convention and London Protocol." * * *

2. The Scientific Groups agreed that the evaluation referred to in the above statement should include, among other things, consideration of:

.1 the estimated amounts and potential impacts of iron and other materials that may be released with the iron;

.2 the potential impacts of gases that may be produced by the expected phytoplankton blooms or by bacteria decomposing the dead phytoplankton;

.3 the estimated extent and potential impacts of bacterial decay of the expected phytoplankton blooms, including reduced oxygen concentrations;

.4 the types of phytoplankton that are expected to bloom and the potential impacts of any harmful algal blooms that may develop;

.5 the nature and extent of potential impacts on the marine ecosystem including naturally occurring marine species and communities;

.6 the estimated amounts and timescales of carbon sequestration, taking account of partitioning between sediments and water; and

.7 the estimated carbon mass balance for the operation.

Action requested

3. The Scientific Groups requested the 29th Consultative Meeting of Contracting Parties to the London Convention and the 2nd Meeting of Contracting Parties to the London Protocol (5 to 9 November 2007) to consider the issue of large-scale ocean iron fertilization operations with a view to ensuring adequate regulation of such operations. In particular, the Scientific Groups requested that the following issues be addressed by the Contracting Parties:

.1 the purposes and circumstances of proposed large-scale ocean iron fertilization operations and whether these are compatible with the aims of the Convention and the Protocol;

.2 the need, and potential mechanisms, for regulation of such operations; and

.3 the desirability of bringing to the attention of other international instruments and institutions proposals for such operations.

4. Contracting Parties to the London Convention and the London Protocol are invited to:

.1 take into account the above-mentioned statement of concern when considering experimental or large-scale ocean iron fertilization to sequester CO_2; and

.2 provide further information relating to proposed large-scale ocean iron fertilization operations to the Secretariat and to the Scientific Groups as and when such information becomes available.

International Maritime Organization, *Statement of Concern regarding Iron Fertilization of the Oceans to Sequester CO_2*, LC-LP.1/Circ.14 (13 July 2007). In October 2008, the Parties to the London Convention reviewed the legal and technical issues surrounding ocean iron fertilization and agreed to a non-binding resolution prohibiting ocean fertilization activities other than "legitimate scientific research." The resolution further states that other ocean fertilization activities "should be considered as contrary to the aims of the Convention and Protocol and not currently qualify for any exemption from the definition of dumping." The Parties agreed that scientific research proposals should be assessed on a case-by-case basis using an assessment framework to be developed by the Scientific Groups under the London Convention and Protocol. The Parties agreed to consider further a potential legally binding resolution or amendment to the London Protocol at their next session in 2009. *See* IMO Announcement, *available at* http://www.imo.org/home.asp?topic_id=1488.

QUESTIONS AND DISCUSSION

1.   Greenpeace was important in bringing the IMO's attention to this issue. Can you see how environmental groups can play an important monitoring and agenda-setting role? Do you think Greenpeace received everything it wanted from the Scientific Groups?

2.   Serious questions remain about whether iron fertilization will even result in any significant, long-term removal of carbon from the atmosphere. *See* S. Blain, et al., *Effect of Natural Iron Fertilization on Carbon Sequestration in the Southern Ocean*, 446 NATURE, April 26, 2007, at 1070–74. How much of the decision by the IMO Scientific Groups seems to have been motivated by the unknown effectiveness of iron fertilization?

3.   Concerned countries and environmental groups also raised ocean fertilization under the Convention on Biological Diversity, described in Section III.B above. In May 2008, the Conference of the Parties agreed to a statement that:

> urges other Governments, in accordance with the precautionary approach, to ensure that ocean fertilization activities do not take place until there is an adequate scientific basis on which to justify such activities, including assessing associated risks, and a global transparent and effective control and regulatory mechanism is in place for these activities; with the exception of small scale research studies within coastal waters.

Unlike the IMO, the CBD has no enforcement mechanism so the moratorium has little practical effect on any country that wants to allow iron fertilization.

4.   Not all marine scientists endorse the idea of a moratorium on large-scale iron fertilization experiments. Some scientists believe experiments of at least 200 sq. km in size are necessary to understand the impacts on ocean ecology. They also objected to the CBD's statement limiting experiments to coastal areas. Moreover, they do not want to foreclose the possibility of conducting other experiments that could be important for understanding the oceans. *See* Intergovernmental Oceanographic Commission, Statement of the IOC Ad Hoc Consultative Group on Ocean Fertilization, June 14, 2008.

5.   In 2009, the Parties to the London Convention are expected to consider a legally binding resolution on ocean fertilization. What elements would you hope to

see in such a resolution? What steps, if any, could Parties to the London Convention take to influence non-Parties regarding ocean fertilization?

V.   HUMAN RIGHTS CONVENTIONS

A.   Introduction

In the wake of the atrocities of World War II, the international community recognized that certain fundamental rights inhere in individuals, not simply in the States of which they are subjects. The new United Nations Charter included as one of its purposes "promoting and encouraging respect for human rights and for fundamental freedoms for all without distinction as to race, sex, language, or religion." UN Charter, Art. 1(3). In 1948, the United Nations enshrined certain fundamental human rights in the Universal Declaration of Human Rights. *See* U.N.G.A. Res. 217A (III) U.N.Doc. A/810 (Dec. 10, 1948). The Declaration was later followed by two human rights covenants adopted in 1966 and that entered into force in 1976: the International Covenant on Civil and Political Rights (ICCPR) and the International Covenant on Economic, Social and Cultural Rights (ICESCR). The full body of human rights law now includes approximately twenty universal treaties, more than a dozen regional conventions, and scores of declarations, resolutions and soft law instruments. Just as importantly, regional human rights institutions in Europe, the Americas and more recently Africa provide opportunities for individuals to pursue their basic human rights. At the United Nations level, the UN Commission on Human Rights is empowered to examine, monitor, and publicly report either on human rights situations in specific countries or on major phenomena of human rights violations worldwide. *See generally* Philip Alston, Ryan Goodman, & Henry J. Steiner, International Human Rights in Context: Law, Politics, Morals (2007).

Human rights evolved directly from moral principles set in philosophical views of what it means to be human and of the value and dignity of humanity. This foundation strengthens human rights law and gives it coherence and legitimacy as a counter-weight to a States-centered system of international law. It is this moral authority, along with the relatively robust mechanisms for individuals to vindicate their rights, that attracts some environmental activists to look at the human rights system for promoting environmental protection.

If left unaddressed, climate change will have significant adverse impacts on the quality of human life — impacts that implicate many internationally recognized and protected human rights. In general, climate change threatens the achievement of sustainable levels of development necessary for the fulfillment of economic, social, and cultural rights. Climate change may also lead to or exacerbate specific violations of human rights, including the right to life, health, habitation, culture, equality before the law, and the right to property. Indeed, many of the impacts of climate change discussed in Chapter 1, including, for example, the destruction of property and the creation of climate refugees, clearly affect human rights. Climate change's impacts on human rights are not going to be equally felt; the rights of the poor, of politically marginalized communities and of future generations are particularly at risk. How we respond to climate change may also give rise to human rights violations, and a rights-based approach might lead to different preferences among otherwise equivalent responses.

Although the moral authority of human rights makes it tempting for climate advocates, the structure of human rights — placing responsibilities on the government for the respect and promotion of its citizens' absolute human rights — may not be a perfect match for addressing the complexity of an issue like climate change. This complexity makes some argue that climate change should be "managed" free from the need to guarantee certain rights. A rights-based approach, by contrast, implies that some positions or interests cannot so easily be compromised. Consider the relative merits of framing climate change as a rights-based issue as you read the following excerpt from Professor Wolfgang Sachs:

WOLFGANG SACHS, HUMAN RIGHTS AND CLIMATE CHANGE

in INTERACTIONS BETWEEN GLOBAL CHANGE AND HUMAN HEALTH
349 (PONT. ACAD. OF SCI (2006)[*]

Climate perturbations are likely to be superimposed on economic insecurity. As a consequence, climate impacts are at times likely to aggravate the living conditions of people up to a point where their basic rights are in jeopardy. It is for this reason that climate impacts may turn into a matter of human rights. As people already living at the edge see themselves pushed over into disaster, climate effects may trigger an infringement upon economic and social human rights. This is not to say that climate-related threats (hurricanes or heat waves, for instance) to human physical integrity under conditions of greater affluence may not constitute a human rights violation as well, but they are going to be more occasional and less structural in terms of their occurrence, just as they are going to be more accidental and less predictable in terms of their location. Impacts in poorer regions, in contrast, often add to an already structurally precarious livelihood situation; it is the compounded effect of economic insecurity and climate stress for large numbers of people that centres around the question of how much climate change should be allowed into a human rights issue.

However, climate-related human rights are matched only by imperfect, not by perfect duties. Like with most economic, social and cultural rights, the link between the right and the corresponding duty is blurred. Just as a violation of the right to food, health, or shelter, can often not be traced back to the action of a clearly identifiable duty-bearer, also climate effects cannot be attributed to a culprit with name and address. Who exactly should be held responsible for hunger and widespread illness? While it might be possible to identify the victims, it is often impossible to identify the responsible agent or the causal relationship between a specific action and a specific damage. In fact, an objection often raised against the concept of economic, social and cultural rights holds that rights make no sense unless they are combined with exact duties imposed on specified actors who would make sure that these rights are fulfilled. But the objection is flawed, for it militates against the basic idea that people have some claims on others and on the design of social arrangements regardless of what laws happen to be enforced. The absence of culprits or judges does not nullify rights. A strictly legal conception, which maintains that there are no rights unless they are justiciable, misses out on the universalist nature of human rights entitlements.

Furthermore, climate rights call for extra-territorial responsibility, even more so than do economic, social and cultural rights. Climate perturbations most clearly surpass the jurisdiction of single states, they are in fact a striking example of the transnational character of threats in a highly interdependent world. Under such circumstances, the human rights obligations of states and non-state actors cannot simply stop at territorial borders; rather, they reach geographically to other countries as well. As the Special Rapporteur to the Human Rights Commission on the Right to Food has recently stated: 'Governments must recognize their extra-territorial obligations towards the right to food. They should refrain from implementing any policies or programs that might have negative effects on the right to food of people living outside their territories'. When the right to food is threatened by climate change, the principle of extra-territorial obligations becomes even more relevant, given that rich countries are largely responsible for climate perturbations in poorer countries. Just as climate effects reach to the ends of the earth, the geographical scope of responsibility has become global as well.

However, this responsibility is in the first place a negative one; it implies avoiding harmful action rather than intervening to provide conditions for an unmutilated life. In other words, climate responsibility is first of all a matter of self-limitation on the part of high-emitting nations and social groups, not a matter of benevolent imperialism bent on improving the world. It is, incidentally, the liberal core of human rights law to emphasize negative obligations, i.e., to call on power-holders to refrain from actions that infringe upon people's integrity. Since institutions are nothing but consolidated systems of action, the human rights imperative can be reformulated by saying that social institutions — including, one might add, energy systems — should be shaped in such a way that they do not structurally and permanently undermine fundamental rights. . . .

Under human rights law, governments are supposed to carry out a triple task with regard to the rights to food, health, and housing. They are first and foremost obliged to respect these rights by avoiding violating them through state measures; they are further required to protect them against powerful third parties, such as industries or landlords; and they are, in the end, expected to fulfill them only through positive action by facilitating access to food, health or housing. It would follow to apply the same hierarchy of obligations to climate rights; the right to live in freedom from human-induced climate perturbations has first to be respected by avoiding harmful emissions nationally, it has, secondly, to be protected against third-party emissions of countries or corporations through international cooperation, and it has, thirdly, to be fulfilled by upgrading people's capability to cope with climate change through adaptation measures, such as dam building, resettlement, or land redistribution. * * *

From a human rights point of view, the classical policy responses to dangerous climate change, mitigation and adaptation, acquire an additional urgency. As to mitigation, human rights considerations need to enter into the definition of what constitutes dangerous climate change. They direct attention to the most vulnerable sections of the world population, suggesting a frame of evaluation that is consistent with the basic law that governs world society. However, negotiations at present fail to define a target of tolerable climate change that would sufficiently protect the fundamental rights of the most vulnerable people. . . . [A] survey of possible impacts suggests that a target that avoids systematic threats to human rights would need to keep the global mean temperature increase below 2°C above pre-industrial levels. It is obvious that such a target calls for mitigation commitments far beyond the Kyoto Protocol.

One reason, however, for the neglect of a human rights approach so far is the prevalence of a utility-based framework of evaluation in climate research and politics. In this framework, benefits of climate mitigation are weighed against its cost in order to optimize both the amount and the time of protection measures. Achieving optimal welfare on the national or global level is the overriding goal. Yet the focus on aggregate welfare is largely incompatible with a focus on rights. For a rights-based framework centres on individual, local or ethnic rights that are not to be violated even at the expense of the aggregate good. It concentrates on the distribution of advantages/disadvantages across single groups, not on the maximization of welfare at the collective level. . . . It is therefore immune against considerations like the one, for example, that the flooding of the Maldives might be a cost to be justified by the aggregate benefit of unhindered growth. The utility approach is all too often inclined to trade away rights for higher aggregate welfare, while human rights are clearly absolute rights; they cannot be traded for higher incomes or disregarded because of a majority opinion.

Finally, human rights considerations also call for vigorous measures to facilitate adaptation to unavoidable climate change. . . . [I]n a human rights perspective, [high-emitting nations] are obliged to prevent violations of economic, social and cultural rights by adequate protective measures. These may range from upgrading health care, to investments in construction, to the building of dams. Governments, however, have so far not been very forthcoming; only a levy on projects in the framework of the Clean Development Mechanism is earmarked for this purpose up to this date. In any case, there can be no doubt that the adherence of the more affluent countries to human rights principles will be put to a hard test as long as emissions remain at current levels.

QUESTIONS AND DISCUSSION

1. What are the main arguments raised by Professor Sachs in favor of framing climate change as a human rights issue? What are the disadvantages?

2. In addition to the substantive perspectives that a rights-based approach brings to climate change, the human rights field provides unique institutional advantages for those affected by climate change. Several human rights fora allow individuals to press their claims for human rights violations. Communities, particularly indigenous and other resource-dependent communities, who are facing specific, climate-induced hardships, are increasingly reframing their concerns in human rights terms. If nothing else, these communities gain the moral (if not legal) standing to participate in dialogues about climate change. Climate change, for example, is already demonstrably deteriorating the quality of life for many island communities and communities in the Arctic. In response, both of these two groups of communities have taken significant steps to invoke the legal and moral authority of human rights in their effort to build political support for responding to climate change — although their approaches have differed. The Inuit have filed a petition to the Inter-American Commission on Human Rights, while small island States have called for the UN High Commissioner on Human Rights to address climate change. These two initiatives are discussed below.

3. What are some of the advantages of using a human rights approach to addressing climate change, as opposed to a regulatory approach, or an approach based on tort law? Professor Michael Anderson, notes that "[o]ften, the real value of a human right is that it is available as a moral trump card precisely when legal arrangements fail." *Human Rights Approaches to Environmental Protection: An Overview in* HUMAN RIGHTS APPROACHES TO ENVIRONMENTAL PROTECTION 12–13 (Alan E. Boyle & Michael R. Anderson eds., 1996). How can such a moral trump card be used in practice to address climate change? If you cannot appeal to courts or to

international processes for protection of a right, to whom can you appeal? The government itself? The public? By what means? Is the availability of a "moral trump card" an adequate substitute for binding obligations on the State to protect human rights, or should it instead be considered a supplement to such obligations?

4. Sometimes climate change is framed in human rights terms as a legal argument based on specific provisions of international human rights law, but just as frequently human rights language is invoked for the moral authority it supports. In its 2007 Human Development Report, the United Nations Development Programme (UNDP) described climate change in this way:

> The values that inspired the drafters of the Universal Declaration of Human Rights provide a powerful point of reference. That document was a response to the political failure that gave rise to extreme nationalism, fascism and world war. It established a set of entitlements and rights — civil, political, cultural, social and economic — for "all members of the human family". The values that inspired the Universal Declaration were seen as a code of conduct for human affairs that would prevent the "disregard and contempt for human rights that have resulted in barbarous acts which have outraged the conscience of mankind".

> The drafters of the Universal Declaration of Human Rights were looking back at a human tragedy, the second world war, that had already happened. Climate change is different. It is a human tragedy in the making. Allowing that tragedy to evolve would be a political failure that merits the description of an "outrage to the conscience of mankind". It would represent a systematic violation of the human rights of the world's poor and future generations and a step back from universal values. Conversely, preventing dangerous climate change would hold out the hope for the development of multilateral solutions to the wider problems facing the international community. Climate change confronts us with enormously complex questions that span science, economics and international relations. These questions have to be addressed through practical strategies. Yet it is important not to lose sight of the wider issues that are at stake. The real choice facing political leaders and people today is between universal human values, on the one side, and participating in the widespread and systematic violation of human rights on the other.

United Nations Development Programme, Fighting Climate Change: Human Solidarity in a Divided World, Human Development Report, Summ. 10 (2007/2008). Who do you think the UNDP believes is "participating in the widespread and systematic violation of human rights?" Does this rhetoric help to build political will to address climate change?

B.   The Inuit Petition to the Inter-American Commission

The unique dependence of the Inuit people of the Arctic led them to submit a petition to the Inter-American Commission on Human Rights to highlight the impact of global warming on their culture, livelihoods, and survival. The petition is a serious and innovative effort to use human rights to influence the debate on a global environmental issue. As you read the excerpted summary of the petition, consider whether framing climate change concerns in the language of human rights is an effective way of building support for policy response. What are the specific human rights claims and remedies put forward by the Inuit?

PETITION TO THE INTER-AMERICAN COMMISSION ON HUMAN RIGHTS SEEKING RELIEF FROM VIOLATIONS RESULTING FROM GLOBAL WARMING CAUSED BY ACTS AND OMISSIONS OF THE UNITED STATES

(Dec. 7, 2005)

I. Summary of the Petition

In this petition, Sheila Watt-Cloutier, an Inuk woman and Chair of the Inuit Circumpolar Conference, requests the assistance of the Inter-American Commission on Human Rights in obtaining relief from human rights violations resulting from the impacts of global warming and climate change caused by acts and omissions of the United States. Ms. Watt-Cloutier submits this petition on behalf of herself, 62 other named individuals, and all Inuit of the arctic regions of the United States of America and Canada who have been affected by the impacts of climate change described in this petition. * * *

The Inuit, meaning "the people" in their native Inuktitut, are a linguistic and cultural group descended from the Thule people whose traditional range spans four countries — Chukotka in the Federation of Russia, northern and western Alaska in the United States, northern Canada, and Greenland. While there are local characteristics and differences within the broad ethnic category of "Inuit," all Inuit share a common culture characterized by dependence on subsistence harvesting in both the terrestrial and marine environments, sharing of food, travel on snow and ice, a common base of traditional knowledge, and adaptation to similar Arctic conditions. Particularly since the Second World War, the Inuit have adapted their culture to include many western innovations, and have adopted a mixed subsistence- and cash-based economy. Although many Inuit are engaged in wage employment, the Inuit continue to depend heavily on the subsistence harvest for food. Traditional "country food" is far more nutritious than imported "store-bought" food. Subsistence harvesting also provides spiritual and cultural affirmation, and is crucial for passing skills, knowledge and values from one generation to the next, thus ensuring cultural continuity and vibrancy.

Like many indigenous peoples, the Inuit are the product of the physical environment in which they live. The Inuit have fine-tuned tools, techniques and knowledge over thousands of years to adapt to the arctic environment. They have developed an intimate relationship with their surroundings, using their understanding of the arctic environment to develop a complex culture that has enabled them to thrive on scarce resources. The culture, economy and identity of the Inuit as an indigenous people depend upon the ice and snow.

Nowhere on Earth has global warming had a more severe impact than the Arctic. Building on the 2001 findings of the Intergovernmental Panel on Climate Change, the 2004 Arctic Climate Impact Assessment [ACIA] — a comprehensive international evaluation of arctic climate change and its impacts undertaken by hundreds of scientists over four years — concluded that:

The Arctic is extremely vulnerable to observed and projected climate change and its impacts. The Arctic is now experiencing some of the most rapid and severe climate change on Earth. Over the next 100 years, climate change is expected to accelerate, contributing to major physical, ecological, social, and economic changes, many of which have already begun.

Because annual average arctic temperatures are increasing more than twice as fast as temperatures in the rest of the world, climate change has already caused severe impacts in the Arctic, including deterioration in ice conditions, a decrease in the quantity and quality of snow, changes in the weather and weather patterns, and a transfigured landscape as permafrost melts at an alarming rate, causing slumping, landslides, and severe erosion in some coastal areas. Inuit observations and scientific studies consistently document these changes. For the last 15 to 20 years, Inuit, particularly hunters and elders who have intimate knowledge of their environment, have reported climate-related changes within a context of generations of accumulated traditional knowledge.

[The Petition then summarizes the current impacts of global warming on the Arctic environment. For example, increased temperatures and sun intensity have heightened the risk of previously rare health problems such as sunburn, skin cancer, cataracts, immune system disorders, and heat-related health problems. Warmer weather has increased the mortality and decreased the health of some harvested species, impacting important sources of protein for the Inuit. Due to these and other changes, the ACIA has stated: "For Inuit, warming is likely to disrupt or even destroy their hunting and food sharing culture as reduced sea ice causes the animals on which they depend on to decline, become less accessible, and possibly become extinct."]

Several principles of international law guide the application of the human rights issues in this case. Most directly, the United States is obligated by its membership in the Organization of American States and its acceptance of the American Declaration of the Rights and Duties of Man to protect the rights of the Inuit described above. Other international human rights instruments give meaning to the United States' obligations under the Declaration. For example, as a party to the International Convention on Civil and Political Rights ("ICCPR"), the United States is bound by the principles therein. As a signatory to the International Convention on Economic, Social, and Cultural Rights ("ICESCR"), the United States must act consistently with the principles of that agreement.

The United States also has international environmental law obligations that are relevant to this petition. For instance, the United States . . . has an obligation to ensure that activities within its territory do not cause transboundary harm or violate other treaties to which it is a party. As a party to the UN Framework Convention on Climate Change, the United States has committed to developing and implementing policies aimed at returning its greenhouse gas emissions to 1990 levels. All of these international obligations are relevant to the application of the rights in the American Declaration because, in the words of the Inter-American Commission, the Declaration "should be interpreted and applied in context of developments in the field of international human rights law . . . and with due regard to other relevant rules of international law applicable to [OAS] member states."

The impacts of climate change, caused by acts and omissions by the United States, violate the Inuit's fundamental human rights protected by the American Declaration of the Rights and Duties of Man and other international instruments. These include their rights to the benefits of culture, to property, to the preservation of health, life, physical integrity, security, and a means of subsistence, and to residence, movement, and inviolability of the home.

Because Inuit culture is inseparable from the condition of their physical surroundings, the widespread environmental upheaval resulting from climate change violates the Inuit's right to practice and enjoy the benefits of their culture. The subsistence culture central to Inuit cultural identity has been damaged by climate change, and may cease to exist if action is not taken by the United States in concert with the community of nations

The Inuit's fundamental right to use and enjoy their traditional lands is violated as a result of the impacts of climate change because large tracks of Inuit traditional lands are fundamentally changing, and still other areas are becoming inaccessible. Summer sea ice, a critical extension of traditional Inuit land, is literally ceasing to exist. Winter sea ice is thinner and unsafe in some areas. Slumping, erosion, landslides, drainage, and more violent sea storms have destroyed coastal land, wetlands, and lakes, and have detrimentally changed the characteristics of the landscape upon which the Inuit depend. The inability to travel to lands traditionally used for subsistence and the reduced harvest have diminished the value of the Inuit's right of access to these lands.

The Inuit's fundamental right to enjoy their personal property is violated because climate change has reduced the value of the Inuit's personal effects, decreasing the quality of food and hides, and damaging snowmobiles, dog sleds and other tools. Their right to cultural intellectual property is also violated, because much of the Inuit's traditional knowledge, a formerly priceless asset, has become frequently unreliable or inaccurate as a result of climate change.

The Inuit's fundamental rights to health and life are violated as climate change exacerbates pressure on the Inuit to change their diet, which for millennia has consisted of wild meat and a few wild plants. Climate change is accelerating a transition by Inuit to a more western store-bought diet with all of its inherent health problems. Life-threatening accidents are increasing because of rapid changes to ice, snow, and land. Traditional food preservation methods are becoming difficult to practice safely. Natural sources of drinking water are disappearing and diminishing in quality. Increased risks of previously rare heat and sun related illnesses also implicate the right to health and life.

The Inuit's fundamental rights to residence and movement, and inviolability of the home are likewise violated as a result of the impacts of climate change because the physical integrity of Inuit homes is threatened. Most Inuit settlements are located in coastal areas, where storm surges, permafrost melt, and erosion are destroying certain coastal Inuit homes and communities. In inland areas, slumping and landslides threaten Inuit homes and infrastructure.

The Inuit's fundamental right to their own means of subsistence has also been violated as a result of the impacts of climate change. The travel problems, lack of wildlife, and diminished quality of harvested game resulting from climate change have deprived the Inuit of the ability to rely on the harvest for year-round sustenance. Traditional Inuit knowledge, passed from Inuit elders in their role as keepers of the Inuit culture, is also becoming outdated because of the rapidly changing environment.

The United States of America, currently the largest contributor to greenhouse emissions in the world, has nevertheless repeatedly declined to take steps to regulate and reduce its emissions of the gases responsible for climate change. As a result of well-documented increases in atmospheric concentrations of greenhouse gases, it is beyond dispute that most of the observed change in global temperatures over the last 50 years is attributable to human actions. This conclusion is supported by a remarkable consensus in the scientific community, including every major U.S. scientific body with expertise on the subject. Even the Government of the United States has accepted this conclusion.

However, and notwithstanding its ratification of the UN Framework Convention on Climate Change, United States has explicitly rejected international overtures and compromises, including the Kyoto Protocol to the U.N. Framework Convention on Climate Change, aimed at securing agreement to curtail destructive greenhouse gas emissions. With full knowledge that this course of action is radically transforming the arctic environment upon which the Inuit depend for their cultural survival, the United States has persisted in permitting the unregulated emission of greenhouse gases from within its jurisdiction into the atmosphere. * * *

Because this petition raises violations of the American Declaration of the Rights and Duties of Man by the United States of American, the Inter-American Commission on Human Rights has jurisdiction to receive and consider it. The petition is timely because the acts and omissions of the United States that form the basis for the petition are ongoing, and the human rights violations they are causing is increasing. Because there are no domestic remedies suitable to address the violations, the requirement that domestic remedies be exhausted does not apply in this case.

The violations detailed in the petition can be remedied. As such, the Petitioner respectfully requests that the Commission:

1. Make an onsite visit to investigate and confirm the harms suffered by the named individuals whose rights have been violated and other affected Inuit;

2. Hold a hearing to investigate the claims raised in this Petition;

3. Prepare a report setting forth all the facts and applicable law, declaring that the United States of America is internationally responsible for violations of rights affirmed in the American Declaration of the Rights and Duties of Man and in other instruments of international law, and recommending that the United States:

   a. Adopt mandatory measures to limit its emissions of greenhouse gases and cooperate in efforts of the community of nations — as expressed, for example, in activities relating to the United Nations Framework Convention on Climate Change — to limit such emissions at the global level;

   b. Take into account the impacts of U.S. greenhouse gas emissions on the Arctic and affected Inuit in evaluating and before approving all major government actions;

   c. Establish and implement, in coordination with Petitioner and the affected Inuit, a plan to protect Inuit culture and resources, including, inter alia, the land, water, snow, ice, and plant and animal species used or occupied by the named individuals whose rights have been violated and other affected Inuit; and mitigate any harm to these resources caused by U.S. greenhouse gas emissions;

   d. Establish and implement, in coordination with Petitioner and the affected Inuit communities, a plan to provide assistance necessary for Inuit to adapt to the impacts of climate change that cannot be avoided;

   e. Provide any other relief that the Commission considers appropriate and just.

QUESTIONS AND DISCUSSION

1. On November 16, 2006, the Inter-American Commission on Human Rights wrote the Inuit that it cannot process the petition "at present" because the petition "does not enable [it] to determine whether the alleged facts would tend to

characterize a violation of rights protected by the American Declaration." The Commission subsequently invited the petitioners to testify at an information hearing on March 1, 2007 to investigate the relationship between global warming and human rights. For an audiotape of the hearing, see http://www.cidh.org/ audiencias/select.aspx. Links to the testimony can be found at http://www.ciel.org/ Climate/IACHR_Inuit_5Mar07.html. Although not successful legally, the Inuit petition brought substantial international attention to the Inuit's plight and undoubtedly increased the overall sense of urgency in international climate negotiations. Do you think that raising the political will for action was a significant reason for filing the petition in the first place? If you were the attorney representing the Inuit, how important would it be to identify from the beginning the specific goals for filing the petition? How would different possible goals affect your strategy?

2.   At least one Inuit village, which is being forced to relocate, has chosen to pursue its rights to compensation in U.S. Federal Court. On February 26, 2008, the Native Village of Kivalina filed a tort suit based on theories of public nuisance, private nuisance, and conspiracy to commit a tortious wrong. *See* Complaint, Kivalina v. Exxon Mobil Corp., (N.D. Cal. Feb. 26, 2008). Climate change and torts is discussed further in Chapter 16. Plaintiffs claim that the relocation will cost about $400 million.

C.   The Small Island States

As part of their effort to raise awareness of the long-term implications of climate change for their continued existence, small island states have also begun to frame their concerns in terms of human rights, although they have taken a less adversarial approach than the Inuit. In November 2007, in the preparation for the Bali Conference of the Parties under the UNFCCC, the Small Island Developing States issued the following declaration:

MALÉ DECLARATION ON THE HUMAN DIMENSION OF GLOBAL CLIMATE CHANGE
Nov. 14, 2007

We the representatives of the Small Island Developing States having met in Malé from 13 to 14 November 2007,

Aware that the environment provides the infrastructure for human civilization and that life depends on the uninterrupted functioning of natural systems;

Accepting the conclusions of the WMO/UNEP Intergovernmental Panel on Climate Change (IPCC) including, *inter alia*, that climate change is unequivocal and accelerating, and that mitigation of emissions and adaptation to climate change impacts is physically and economically feasible if urgent action is taken; * * *

Emphasizing that small island, low-lying coastal, and atoll states are particularly vulnerable to even small changes to the global climate and are already adversely affected by alterations in ecosystems, changes in precipitation, rising sea-levels and increased incidence of natural disasters;

Reaffirming the United Nations Charter and the Universal Declaration of Human Rights; * * *

Noting that the fundamental right to an environment capable of supporting human society and the full enjoyment of human rights is recognized, in varying formulations, in the constitutions of over one hundred states and directly or indirectly in several international instruments; * * *

Concerned that climate change has clear and immediate implications for the full enjoyment of human rights including *inter alia* the right to life, the right to take part in cultural life, the right to use and enjoy property, the right to an adequate standard of living, the right to food, and the right to the highest attainable standard of physical and mental health;

Do solemnly request:

1. The international community to commit in Bali to a formal process that will ensure a post-2012 consensus to protect people, planet and prosperity by taking urgent action to stabilize the global climate and ensure that temperature rises fall well below 2°C above pre-industrial averages, and that greenhouse gas concentrations are less than 450ppm, consistent with the principles of common but differentiated responsibilities.

2. The members of AOSIS in New York to consider including the human dimension of global climate change as one of the agenda items for the meeting of AOSIS Ministers in Bali, and to explore possible alternatives for advancing this initiative in Bali in order to stress the moral and ethical imperatives for action.

3. The Conference of the Parties of the United Nations Framework Convention on Climate Change, with the help of the Secretariat, under article 7.2(l), to seek the cooperation of the Office of the United Nations High Commissioner for Human Rights and the United Nations Human Rights Council in assessing the human rights implications of climate change.

4. The Office of the United Nations High Commissioner for Human Rights to conduct a detailed study into the effects of climate change on the full enjoyment of human rights, which includes relevant conclusions and recommendations thereon, to be submitted prior to the tenth session of the Human Rights Council.

5. The United Nations Human Rights Council to convene, in March 2009, a debate on human rights and climate change.

QUESTIONS AND DISCUSSION

1.   What specifically do you think the small island States hope to achieve by appealing to the UN human rights bodies? What advantages or disadvantages does their approach have when compared to that of the Inuit?

2.   Led by the Maldives, the small island States called upon the UN Human Rights Council to address the relationship between human rights and climate change. The Council issued a resolution recognizing the linkage between human rights and climate change, decided in March 2008 to:

> request the Office of the United Nations High Commissioner for Human Rights, in consultation with and taking into account the views of States, other relevant international organizations and intergovernmental bodies, including the Intergovernmental Panel on Climate Change, the secretariat of the United Nations Framework Convention on Climate Change and other stakeholders, to conduct, within existing resources, a detailed analytical study of the relationship between climate change and human rights, to be submitted to the Council prior to its tenth session.

UN Human Rights Council, A/HRC/7/L.21/Rev.1, 26 March 2008. Would it surprise you that the United States did not support the resolution? The UN High

Commissioner's Report called for by the Council was released on January 15, 2009. *See* REPORT OF OHE OFFICE OF THE UN HIGH COMMISSIONER FOR HUMAN RIGHTS ON THE RELATIONSHIP BETWEEN CLIMATE CHANGE AND HUMAN RIGHTS, A/HRC/10/61 (15 Jan. 2009) [hereinafter High Commissioner Report]. The High Commissioner Report found that climate change is closely linked to the satisfaction of many human rights, including the rights to life, food, health, water and self-determination. The Report further found:

> The physical impacts of global warming cannot easily be classified as human rights violations, not least because climate change-related harm often cannot clearly be attributed to acts or omissions of specific States. Yet, addressing that harm remains a critical human rights concern and obligation under international law. Hence, legal protection remains relevant as a safeguard against climate change-related risks and infringements of human rights resulting from policies and measures taken at the national level to address climate change.

High Commissioner Report, at para. 96. What is the legal significance of saying that climate change is related to certain human rights, but denying that it is a human rights violation? Does this seem like an appropriate compromise? The next step is for the Council to accept the Report and make it available to the UNFCCC as part of the negotiations leading to Copenhagen. What impact, if any, do you think the High Commissioner Report will have on the climate negotiations? The Council could also decide to identify a Special Rapporteur on climate change or otherwise agree to keep the relationship between human rights and climate change under review. Would such a decision help to keep pressure on developed countries to address climate change and its impacts? *See also generally* Submission of the Maldives to the UN Office of the High Commissioner for Human Rights under Human Rights Council Resolution 7/23, Sept. 25, 2008 (elaborating the link between climate change and human rights).

3.   As no binding human rights treaty explicitly establishes a human right to a stable climate, activists have to rely on other provisions. What provisions in human rights law form the basis for the Inuit petition? What provisions, if any, are invoked by the small island States?

———

D.   Human Rights Implications of Climate Change Policies

Not all of the linkages between human rights and climate change result from climate impacts. Human rights are also implicated by the various policy interventions designed to mitigate or adapt to climate change. Greater reliance on biofuels, for example, has led to increases in food prices that implicate the right to food. Land conversion for biofuels has also led to concerns by indigenous peoples and other forest dwelling communities that their rights will not be protected in the rush to convert land to agro-fuel crops. And as the impacts of climate change become more serious, many observers fear that governments will respond in ways that ignore or even exacerbate human rights violations. A potential influx of climate refugees could be met with military force or border fences, for example.

Currently, the most active human rights concerns relate to the potential impacts of projects financed by northern countries to address climate change but located in developing countries where indigenous peoples or other vulnerable groups may be at risk. This has led indigenous and other human rights advocates to argue for procedural and substantive safeguards on the Protocol's implementation. They argue that investments promoted under the CDM, for example, may lead to new pressures to encroach on indigenous lands or that the rules for CDM investments, particularly in forests, will not promote procedural rights for community-based participation and decisionmaking. Conversely, they worry that adaptation measures will ignore the special needs of resource-dependent communities.

These concerns have led indigenous leaders to call for a greater voice in climate change deliberations. In particular, indigenous leaders have repeatedly called on the UNFCCC to create, among other things, an Ad Hoc Working Group on Indigenous Peoples and Climate Change within the UNFCCC framework:

MILAN DECLARATION OF THE SIXTH INTERNATIONAL INDIGENOUS PEOPLES FORUM ON CLIMATE CHANGE
COP 9, UNFCCC, Milan, Italy, Nov. 29–30, 2003

We, the representatives of the Indigenous Peoples of the world present at the 6th International Indigenous Peoples Forum on Climate Change held prior to the 9th Conference of the Parties of the United Nations Framework Convention on Climate Change (UNFCCC) in Milan, Italy, restate our principles and * * * **call upon the States Parties of the United Nations Framework Convention on Climate Change that:**

a. COP 9 to the . . . [UNFCCC] recognizes the fundamental role of Indigenous Peoples in addressing climate change and environmental degradation to restore the natural balance.

b. COP 9 considers the creation of the Inter-sessional Ad hoc Working Group on Indigenous Peoples and Climate Change for the timely, effective and adequate solutions in response to the urgent situation caused by climate change.

c. COP 9 provides necessary support to indigenous peoples for their full and effective participation in all levels of discussion, decision making and implementation as well as ensuring that the necessary funding be provided to guarantee such participation and to strengthen their capacities.

d. Include Indigenous Peoples and climate change as items in the agenda of the COP and the Subsidiary Bodies meetings with specific reference to vulnerability, adaptation, poverty, and other climate change related issues.

e. The Clean Development Mechanism (CDM) and Joint Implementation (JI) must incorporate principles which address transparency, free, prior and informed consent and equitable benefit sharing with Indigenous Peoples in order to accomplish the objectives of lowering greenhouse gas emissions and achieving sustainable development in developed and developing countries.

f. All development projects within indigenous ancestral territories must respect our fundamental rights to lands, territories, self-determination and ensure our right to our free, prior and informed consent. Sinks project do not contribute to climate change mitigation and sustainable development. The modalities and procedures for afforestation and reforestation project activities under the CDM do not respect and guarantee our right to lands, territories, and self-determination.

g. We vigorously support the creation and financing of the Adaptation Fund to be accessed by Indigenous Peoples to address the potential and actual impacts of climate change in a manner compatible with our traditional knowledge, customs, culture and lifestyles.

h. We express our desire to be included in UNFCCC capacity building initiatives and propose that special capacity building be undertaken for Indigenous Peoples. Such capacity building would strengthen our ability to exercise our right to fully participate in climate change negotiations.

i. We call upon all governments to implement Climate Impact Assessments which take into account indigenous knowledge systems, culture, social values, spirituality and ecosystems; as well as the full and equal participation of Indigenous Peoples in all aspects and stages of the assessment.

Recognizing all of the above, we call upon the UNFCCC to recognize that through the protection and promotion of Indigenous Peoples' rights and through recognizing and integrating our dynamic and holistic visions, we are securing not only our future, but the future of humanity and social and environmental justice for all.

Despite repeated calls, the UNFCCC has not yet agreed to such a working group, and at this point indigenous peoples' organizations are allowed to participate in the climate negotiations on essentially the same terms as any NGO observer.

QUESTIONS AND DISCUSSION

1. Having failed to gain significant support for their positions within the UNFCCC, indigenous peoples have begun to raise climate change concerns within the UN Permanent Forum on Indigenous Issues. In April 2008, the Permanent Forum issued a set of recommendations aimed at climate mitigation and adaptation efforts:

6. Strategies for mitigation and adaptation must be holistic, taking into account not only the ecological dimensions of climate change, but also social impacts, human rights, equity and environmental justice. Indigenous peoples, who have the smallest ecological footprints, should not be asked to carry the heavier burden of adjusting to climate change. * * *

36. The Permanent Forum recommends that the Framework Convention on Climate Change, in cooperation with States, provide adaptation funds to indigenous peoples affected by climate change-related disasters. Indigenous peoples whose lands have already disappeared or have become uninhabitable or spoilt due to seawater rise, floods, droughts or erosion, and who have thus become environmental refugees or displaced persons, should be provided with appropriate relocation with the support of the international community.

37. The Permanent Forum recommends following the example of indigenous peoples, who have been the stewards of the land and sea for millenniums. When allocating research and development funding and setting the criteria for clean development mechanism projects, policymakers at the State and multilateral levels must look beyond the simple question of whether a particular form of alternative energy or carbon absorption technique can provide a short-term reduction in greenhouse gases. Policymakers should consider the long-term sustainability of any mitigation policy they choose. * * *

41. The Permanent Forum urges the Human Rights Council expert mechanism on indigenous peoples to evaluate whether existing and pro-

posed climate change policies and projects adhere to the standards set by the United Nations Declaration on the Rights of Indigenous Peoples. These bodies, together with the members of the Inter-Agency Support Group for Indigenous Issues, should collaborate with States, multilateral bodies, donors and indigenous peoples to effectively ensure that the implementation of the Declaration is central to the design and implementation of climate change policies and programmes.

42. The Permanent Forum reaffirms the need for all actors to respect the right to self-determination of indigenous peoples to decide on mitigation and adaptation measures in their lands and territories.

Permanent Forum on Indigenous Issues, Declaration, *Climate Change, Biocultural Diversity and Livelihoods: The Stewardship Role of Indigenous Peoples and New Challenges, in* U.N. Economic and Social Council, Report on the Seventh Session (21 April–2 May 2008), E/2008/43, E/C.19/2008/13. Which is the better mechanism for addressing human rights and climate change: the UNFCCC or human rights fora? *See also* Chapter 7, Section IV.C, note 8 (discussing indigenous peoples' concerns over proposals to address deforestation under the climate change regime).

2. Ensuring greater public participation in the CDM has been the focus of significant attention, because of the potentially adverse environmental and social impact that CDM projects can have on specific communities, even if the project provides some climate benefits. Consider the following request from the Center for International Environmental Law for greater transparency and participatory rights:

While opportunities for vigorous public participation in CDM governance and project planning and implementation will likely prove essential for the CDM's long-term success, neither the Convention nor Protocol texts provide much indication of what these public participation rights and mechanisms should entail.

Under the Convention, all developed and developing country parties agreed to "promote and cooperate in education, training and public awareness related to climate change and encourage the widest participation in this process, including that of non-governmental organizations." Implementation of these provisions has been left to the discretion of individual parties, with effectively no oversight from the Convention's Conference of the Parties (COP). Article 12 of the Protocol, which defines the CDM, contains no mention of any role for the public.

Accordingly, neither the Convention nor the Protocol contains provisions that properly can be described as creating "rights" to public participation in CDM processes. Instead, the CDM public participation rights that presently exist were established as part of the "Marrakech Accords," which were adopted by the COP in November 2001. * * *

[But] it is important to bear . . . in mind . . . [that] CDM rules established at the international level under the auspices of the Protocol generally pertain either to CDM governance (e.g., the CDM executive board) or to the setting of minimum performance standards for projects. Since all CDM projects must be approved by both the "home" (investor/developer's) country and the "host" (project site) country, Protocol parties that participate in the CDM will have an opportunity under their domestic laws to establish and enforce more liberal standards for public participation, if they wish.

Nathalie Eddy & Glenn Wiser, *Public Participation in the Clean Development Mechanism of the Kyoto Protocol*, THE NEW PUBLIC: THE GLOBALIZATION OF PUBLIC PARTICIPATION (Carl Bruch ed., 2002). The CDM executive board has clarified that CDM projects should be open to public comment and sponsors should engage in consultations with hosting local communities — but implementation at the project level is largely left up to domestic law. Given that any project approved under the CDM must comply with domestic law, is there any need for additional procedural safeguards at the international level? If so, what specific procedures would you recommend be included in the CDM's operating rules?

3. Climate change has potentially disparate impacts on women, and women may also bring different perspectives to the debate. These considerations partly motivate the following recommendations regarding climate change and gender equality:

WOMEN'S ENVIRONMENT AND DEVELOPMENT ORGANIZATION (WEDO), et al., DECLARATION ON CLIMATE CHANGE AND GENDER EQUALITY
(Sept. 2007)

- Given that women's knowledge and participation has been critical to the survival of entire communities in disaster situations, governments should take advantage of women's specialized skills in various aspects of their livelihood and natural resource management strategies that lend themselves to mitigation and adaptation.

- Since climate change disproportionately affects poor women, governments should analyze and identify gender-specific impacts and protection measures related to floods, droughts, heat waves, diseases, and other environmental changes and disasters. The global community should prioritize reducing the high levels of female mortality rates resulting from climate-induced disasters and livelihood changes.

- Given the vulnerability of the poor, and particularly women, to climate change, adequate funds must be allocated by Annex I countries to help these groups adapt to the impacts.

- Practical tools should be developed that allow governments and institutions to incorporate gender equality in climate change initiatives. * * *

- Women's participation in climate change related debates and planning must be enhanced by tools and procedures that augment their capacity and sensitize decisionmakers to the advantages of equal participation.

- The UNFCCC should develop a gender strategy, invest in gender-specific climate change research, and establish a system for the use of gender-sensitive indicators and criteria for governments to use in national reporting to the UNFCCC Secretariat, adaptation planning, or projects under the Clean Development Mechanism (CDM).

- Market-based approaches to curbing climate change, such as the Clean Development Mechanism, should be made accessible to both women and men and ensure equitable benefits, considering that women and men do not have equal access to natural resources such as water and energy, land titles, credit, or information. In particular, the CDM should fund projects that make renewable energy technologies more available to women and meet their household needs.

- The gendered impacts of biofuels and nuclear energy as a solution to reducing greenhouse gas emissions should be assessed, in cooperation with gender experts and women's organizations. * * *

If you were advising the UNFCCC Secretariat, what specific steps do you think it should take to respond to the above recommendations on gender equity? What value is added to the climate debate by invoking gender analysis or concerns?

4. On the relationship between human rights and the environment generally, see SVITLANA KRAVCHENKO & JOHN BONINE, HUMAN RIGHTS AND THE ENVIRONMENT (2008); ALAN BOYLE & MICHAEL ANDERSON, HUMAN RIGHTS APPROACHES TO ENVIRONMENTAL PROTECTION (1996). For a discussion of climate change and refugees or internally displaced people, see the discussion in Chapter 1. Review the other impacts discussed in Chapter 1; many of them may give rise to human rights concerns, particularly relating to economic and social rights. Consider, for example, the public health implications of climate change to the right to life or to health, or the impacts of climate change on food security and the right to food.

VI. CLIMATE CHANGE AND THE INTERNATIONAL TRADE REGIME

A.   Introduction

Since the early 1950s, the volume of trade in manufactured goods has grown at an annual rate of 7.5 percent. During the same period, international trade in agricultural goods grew annually at 3.5 percent and fuels and mining products grew at 4 percent. In 2006, total trade in goods grew by 8 percent and world gross domestic product increased by 3.5 percent. WORLD TRADE ORGANIZATION, INTERNATIONAL TRADE STATISTICS 2007 1–2 (2007). At the regional level, trade is also booming. From 1993 to 2007, trade among Canada, Mexico, and the United States — the three members of the North American Free Trade Agreement (NAFTA) — more than tripled, from $297 billion to $930 billion. U.S. Trade Representative, *NAFTA Facts* (Mar. 2008).

International trade exerts a tremendous influence over climate change. With increased trade, carbon dioxide emissions also grow, principally from transportation, as goods move around the world by trains, planes, trucks, and ships. For example, greenhouse gas emissions from the European transport sector increased by 20 percent between 1990 and 2001. R. Andreas Kraemer, et al., *What Contribution Can Trade Policy Make Towards Combating Climate Change*, 1 (European Parliament, 2007).

At the same time, the international trading system, as administered by the members of the World Trade Organization (WTO), provides opportunities as well as challenges for implementing national strategies to mitigate climate change. For example, carbon taxes, depending on how they are structured, may or may not be consistent with the rules of the General Agreement on Tariffs and Trade (GATT). Requirements to use renewable energy and laws that impose higher taxes on automobiles with low fuel economy than on automobiles with higher fuel economy may run afoul of the GATT's nondiscrimination rules. Efforts to label or subsidize climate-friendly products may violate other agreements of the WTO.

On the other hand, trade liberalization may encourage the dissemination of climate-friendly technologies. An agreement to reduce agricultural subsidies, including the $9 billion in U.S. subsidies for corn in 2005, would encourage the production of ethanol from sugarcane, a superior energy product than corn-based ethanol. Reductions in tariffs — the taxes imposed on imported products — on climate-friendly technologies would reduce the price for these goods and encourage their use. Many developing countries, for example, impose tariffs on compact fluorescent light bulbs exceeding 20 percent *ad valorem*, adding substantially to the cost of a known technology that can significantly reduce greenhouse gas emissions.

This section covers three distinct but related issues concerning international trade and climate change. First, Section B reviews the climate impacts of trade in specific goods to identify the challenges of identifying "climate-friendly" products. Second, Section C examines whether the regulation of greenhouse gas emissions places firms at a competitive disadvantage vis-à-vis firms that are not required to reduce their emissions. Third, Section D summarizes the principal trade rules affecting climate change mitigation policies and assesses specific climate change policies, such as carbon taxes, subsidies, and renewable energy requirements, in light of trade law.

B.   Climate Impacts of International Trade

The sustained growth in international trade is clearly causing carbon dioxide emissions to grow around the world. As products move around the world, fossil fuels are consumed. As discussed below, it is not always clear which products have the worst trade-related impacts on climate change.

First, the way in which products are transported is critical to determining the carbon impact of international trade, because different modes of transport produce considerably different carbon dioxide emissions for each kilometer a metric ton of freight is transported:

Table 10-2: Carbon Dioxide Emissions for Different Modes of Transport

Mode of Transport	CO_2 emissions (in grams/ton km)
Truck (12 ton)	110
Truck (24 ton)	92
Truck (36 ton)	84
Maritime Shipping	14
Train	23
Plane	607

R. Andreas Kraemer et al., at 5. Although maritime shipping is considerably less carbon intensive than other modes of transport, about 90% of world trade moves by ship. As a result, shipping produces between 600 and 800 $MtCO_2$ annually, up to 5% of total global emissions. John Vidal, *CO_2 Output from Shipping Twice as Much as Airlines*, THE GUARDIAN, Mar. 3, 2007.

Moreover, as globalization has moved production of many energy intensive industries from developed to developing countries, so too have carbon dioxide emissions shifted to developing countries. For example, a recent study revealed that U.S. carbon dioxide emissions would have been 3% to 8% higher if goods imported from China had been produced in the United States. At the same time, exports to the United States accounted for 7% to 14% of China's total CO_2 emissions. Not only did this shift emissions from a developed country to a developing country, but the shift resulted in a net increase in carbon dioxide emissions of approximately 720 million metric tons because Chinese production technologies are less energy efficient and more emission intensive than U.S. production methods. B. Shui & R. Harriss, *The Role of Embodied CO_2 in the U.S.-China Trade*, 34 ENERGY POLICY 4063–68 (2006).

The mode of transport and the production method ultimately determine the carbon footprint of a particular product. For example, shipping steel from China to Hamburg results in carbon dioxide emissions 3.5 times higher than producing the same steel in Germany and transporting it by rail to a facility in Hamburg, Germany. Even though shipping produces fewer emissions than rail, Chinese production methods are much less energy efficient than German production methods. Moreover, because steel production is energy intensive, the production process in China accounts for 90 percent of the total emissions and almost 100 percent in Germany. In other words, steel production is so emissions intensive, the mode of transport is not a large factor in the overall carbon footprint of the steel. Greenhouse gas emissions do not necessarily increase simply because they are produced abroad, however; buying local may sometimes be more carbon intensive than buying foreign. Producing fertilizer in New York and sending it thousands of miles by ship and rail to Florence, Italy, for example, would produce 13 percent *less* carbon dioxide emissions than producing it in Ravenna, Italy, a mere 199 kilometers from Florence, because U.S. production processes are so much less emissions intensive. Perhaps most astounding, production of lamb in New Zealand is so efficient that shipping lamb from New Zealand to the United Kingdom would produce one-fourth the carbon dioxide emissions of producing the lamb in the United Kingdom, where more fertilizers are used. R. Andreas Kraemer, et al., *supra*, at 18–21.

QUESTIONS AND DISCUSSION

1. As a result of the shift in production to developing countries, developed countries can show reductions in emissions even though they still use and consume the same products. Should the Kyoto Protocol attempt to account for the consumption patterns of developed countries by attributing to them carbon dioxide emissions from imported products?

2. In the United Kingdom, Tesco, the nation's largest retailer of food, has started placing airplane symbols on the packaging of food products transported by air. It also plans to create labels that indicate a product's carbon emissions and place them on all of its seventy thousand products. Are such ecolabels an effective way to educate consumers about the carbon footprint of the products they buy? How would you design such a label? What factors would you include in determining a product's greenhouse gas emissions?

3. The relative climate change impact of shipping and trucking compared to rail or automobiles is likely understated when only carbon dioxide emissions are compared, because both shipping and trucks release significant quantities of black carbon. Reducing black carbon emissions from shipping is being discussed at the IMO.

C.   Competitiveness Concerns

Because the Kyoto Protocol submits only developed countries to limits on greenhouse gas emissions, many have raised concerns that those limits will place firms in those countries at a competitive disadvantage in global markets. Former President Bush, for example, consistently claimed that the failure to control developing country emissions will hurt U.S. competitiveness. The Confederation of British Industries perhaps best summarized the argument as follows:

> Competitive distortions will arise if companies from one country face different climate burdens to their competitors in other countries. This could lead to relocation of industries or production from countries facing environmental constraints to those with lower or no constraints, resulting in significant 'carbon leakage'. Constraints and restrictions applied on a specific region of the world can affect its competitiveness in the global market, resulting in a loss of jobs and GDP, while failing to achieve significant climate change benefit.

Confederation of British Industries, "Stern Review on Economics of Climate Change: CBI Response," para. 21 (undated).

The competitiveness argument has arisen frequently in the trade context. Businesses argue that regulation will drive companies to countries with less stringent regulations. Environmentalists argue that the inability to erect trade barriers against products produced with environmentally damaging production methods will encourage "pollution havens" and a "race to the bottom" as companies move production to countries with less stringent environmental controls.

Despite this talk of the competitiveness effect, its existence or its magnitude in economic terms has not become apparent, largely because pollution abatement costs are generally small compared to total operating costs. For example, pollution abatement costs for the tobacco products industry were just 0.12 percent of total costs; for fabricated metal products, 0.42 percent; for petroleum and coal products, 1.93 percent; and for all industries evaluated, an average of 0.62 percent. Håkan Nordström & Scott Vaughan, *Trade and Environment* 37 (1999), *available at* http://www.wto.org/english/news_e/pres99_e/environment.pdf.

Several studies do indicate that the costs of mitigating greenhouse gases may be somewhat higher. In an energy-intensive industry, such as the steel industry, the marginal cost increase for steel would be 7.7 percent if the steel industry were required to purchase carbon emissions at a price of $10€/tCO_2$, with the marginal cost rising to 17 percent if emissions must be purchased at a price of $30€/tCO_2$. Similarly, the marginal product cost of cement would increase between 18.6 percent and 144 percent. *See* R. Andreas Kraemer, et al., at 10–12. A recent World Bank study found "some evidence" that carbon taxes imposed on domestic industries do have negative competitiveness effects. WORLD BANK, INTERNATIONAL TRADE AND CLIMATE CHANGE: ECONOMIC, LEGAL, AND INSTITUTIONAL PERSPECTIVES 29 (2007). For more on the relative climate impacts of various sectors, see Chapter 2.

QUESTIONS AND DISCUSSION

The coming years may provide better empirical data concerning competitiveness effects of climate change policy. If the United States remains outside the climate regime, the impacts of climate change policy on business in Annex I countries can be compared with U.S. businesses. Until that data is forthcoming, how would you, as an advocate for climate change mitigation, respond to President Bush and the Confederation of British Industries?

D.   International Trade Rules and Climate Change Policy

Since the emergence of the "trade and environment" debate in the early 1990s, the international community has wrestled with how to incorporate the trade liberalization rules of trade agreements with the use of trade restrictions in multilateral environmental agreements (MEAs). Should the rules of CITES, for example, which ban trade for primarily commercial purposes in highly endangered species such as blue whales, gorillas, and many other species, be exempt from trade rules? Should the Montreal Protocol's bar on trade in ozone depleting substances with non-Parties be exempt? The trade community, through the WTO, has debated these questions extensively. In fact, the WTO ministers have directed the WTO's Committee on Trade and Environment to negotiate, as part of the current round of trade negotiations known as the "Doha Round," an outcome to "the relationship between existing WTO rules and specific trade obligations" of MEAs. Ministerial Declaration, WTO Ministerial Conference, Fourth Session, Doha, Nov. 9–14 2001, WT/MIN(01)/DEC/W/1, para. 31 (Nov. 14, 2001). The resolution of these questions, however, has been tied up with many other issues, such as agricultural subsidies, that are part of the Doha Round. For more on this subject, see CHRIS WOLD, SANFORD GAINES, & GREG BLOCK, TRADE AND THE ENVIRONMENT: LAW AND POLICY 637–95 (2005).

The UNFCCC and the Kyoto Protocol recognize that climate change policy may provide opportunities as well as challenges for the international trading system. Article 3.5 of the UNFCCC states that "Parties should cooperate to promote a supportive and open international economic system" and that climate change mitigation policies "should not constitute a means of arbitrary or unjustifiable discrimination or a disguised restriction on international trade." Article 2.1 of the Kyoto Protocol calls on Parties to reduce or phase out market imperfections, fiscal incentives, tax and duty exemptions, and subsidies in all greenhouse gas emitting sectors that run counter to the objective of the Convention. Article 2.3 further directs Parties to implement policies to minimize adverse effects on international trade. As the following discussion of specific climate change mitigation policies makes clear, the ambiguity in the rules of the international trading system makes it difficult for Parties to know just when they are adopting measures that run counter to WTO rules.

1.   *An Introduction to International Trade Rules*

The WTO administers a number of agreements covering trade in goods and services (e.g., telecommunications and provision of electricity), and disciplining the use of product standards (e.g., fuel efficiency and toxicity limits, as well as some ecolabels), intellectual property rights, and subsidies, among other things. Unlike the climate change regime and other MEAs, the WTO provides for compulsory dispute settlement through which prevailing parties may impose sanctions against losing parties that do not comply with the decisions of the WTO dispute settlement panels or the Appellate Body.

The GATT is the principal WTO agreement governing trade in goods. Originally adopted in 1947, the GATT is designed to ensure the efficient allocation of the world's economic resources by reducing barriers to trade and leveling the conditions for trade in goods. To achieve this goal, the GATT requires each country to bind itself to maximum tariffs that it applies equally to all members. In this regard, the GATT has succeeded; the Parties have reduced tariffs on nonprimary products (manufactured goods) of industrial countries from an estimated 40 percent in 1947 to 3.9 percent today.

The GATT also imposes three core rules to prevent governments from using nontariff barriers — taxes, administrative procedures, and other laws and regulations — to discriminate against imported products. First, the most favored nation (MFN) obligation of Article I requires each WTO member to tax and regulate "like products" from all other WTO members the same. For example, Mexico cannot tax solar panels from Germany less than solar panels from Japan. Second, the national treatment principle of Article III requires a country to tax and regulate imported products "no less favourably" than "like" domestic products. Thus, the United States may impose a tax on imports of HFC-23, a powerful greenhouse gas, provided that the tax rate is no more than the tax imposed on domestic HFC-23. Third, Article XI prohibits members from applying any restrictions, such as quotas and licensing schemes, other than tariffs to imported products. Thus, the U.S. embargo on Mexican tuna in the *Tuna/Dolphin I* dispute violated Article XI.

A central question for both the MFN and national treatment nondiscrimination obligations is whether the trade measure relates to "like products." Quite obviously, governments may tax and regulate wind turbines differently from automobiles and coal differently from solar panels. At some point, however, products become so similar that the trade rules demand equal tax and regulatory treatment to ensure fair competition in the global marketplace. The issue of "like products" raises difficult questions. Is electricity from coal the same as electricity from wind power? Are hybrid, electric, and traditional gas-powered automobiles like products that require equivalent tax and regulatory treatment?

WTO dispute settlement panels make determinations of whether products are "like products" by assessing, on a case-by-case basis, the following four factors: (1) the product's end-uses in a given market; (2) consumers' tastes and habits, which change from country to country; (3) the product's properties, nature and quality; and (4) tariff classification of the products in question. Japan-Taxes on Alcoholic Beverages, Report of the Appellate Body, WT/DS8/AB/R, WT/DS10/AB/R, WT/DS11/AB/R, PAGE (Nov. 1, 1996). The simplicity of this four-part test masks the complexities of the national treatment obligation, which alters the meaning of "likeness" depending on the circumstances. For example, panels have defined "like products" narrowly with respect to taxes, provided they are not imposed to protect domestic production. If that condition is met, then natural gas and coal, because of their different physical characteristics, are probably not like products despite their similar end uses. They could be taxed differently. However, taxes designed to afford protection to domestic production expand the concept of like products to include "directly competitive and substitutable products." Under this expanded concept of likeness, the WTO's Appellate Body has found shochu, whisky, brandy, rum, gin, genever, and liqueurs to be "directly competitive and substitutable." For regulatory measures, the definition of "like product" fits somewhere between these two points but significantly closer to the broader reading of "directly competitive and substitutable products."

Whatever ambiguity exists in the interpretation of "like products," trade panels have been absolutely clear that factors unrelated to the product as a product cannot be used as the basis for taxing or regulating products differently. Thus, in the *Tuna/Dolphin* disputes, the panels found U.S. import restrictions on tuna to be impermissible because the basis for barring imports into the United States related to the way the fish were caught, not some physical characteristic of the tuna itself. Processes and production methods (PPMs) such as fish harvesting techniques that do not affect the product as a product (non-product related PPMs) cannot be used to distinguish otherwise like products for tax and regulatory purposes. United States-Restrictions on Imports of Tuna, GATT Panel Report, DS21/R (Sept. 3, 1991) (unadopted), *reprinted in* 30 I.L.M. 1594 (1991) (*Tuna/Dolphin I*). Similarly, a panel found U.S. rules that imposed different requirements on foreign gasoline than domestic gasoline impermissible because those rules related to data held by a foreign company, not the gasoline itself. United States-Standards for Reformulated and Conventional Gasoline Report of the Panel, WT/DS2/R (May 20, 1996), *reprinted in* 35 I.L.M. 276 (1996) (decided on Jan. 29, 1996). On the other hand, product-related PPMs, such as irradiation and pasteurization, may be used to distinguish products for tax and regulatory purposes (that is, pasteurized milk may be taxed and regulated differently from nonpasteurized milk). As described below, these rulings complicate efforts to tax or regulate climate-friendly technologies more favorably than other products.

The GATT also includes exceptions to these core rules, two of which are relevant to the environment and climate change. Under Article XX, measures otherwise inconsistent with the GATT are allowed if they are measures "necessary" for the protection of "human, animal or plant life or health" (Article XX(b)), or measures "relating to" the "conservation of exhaustible natural resources" (Article XX(g)). Moreover, the introduction to Article XX requires that any measures must be applied in a way that avoids "arbitrary or unjustifiable discrimination" in trade and they must not constitute a "disguised restriction" on trade.

QUESTIONS AND DISCUSSION

1. In addition to the GATT, the WTO also administers agreements relating to services and product standards. These agreements adopt the central nondiscrimination obligations of the GATT. For example, the General Agreement on Trade in Services and the Agreement on Technical Barriers to Trade (TBT Agreement) both require application of the MFN and national treatment obligations. They also adopt other rules that are relevant for climate change. For example, the TBT Agreement provides that technical regulations — those laws or regulations specifying mandatory product characteristics, such as fuel economy standards or emissions limits — "shall not be more trade-restrictive than necessary to fulfill a legitimate objective." In addition, the Agreement on Subsidies and Countervailing Measures (SCM

Agreement) prohibits certain subsidies that distort international trade by, among other things, suppressing world prices of goods.

2.   *Tariff Reductions.* As part of the current Doha Round of negotiations, WTO members have agreed to reduce or eliminate tariffs on environmental goods and services. WTO Ministerial Conference, Fourth Session, Doha, Nov. 9–14, 2001, WT/MIN(01)/DEC/W/1, para. 31(iii) (Nov. 14, 2001). A wide range of climate change-related technologies, including wind turbines, solar panels, geothermal energy sensors, and fuel cells, could be considered environmental goods. Reducing or eliminating tariffs to facilitate trade in, and use of, these technologies would reduce the cost and encourage the use and dissemination of many emission-reduction technologies. A World Bank report concluded that removing tariffs alone for four basic clean energy technologies (wind, solar, clean coal, and efficient lighting) in 18 of the high-GHG-emitting developing countries could result in trade gains of up to 7 percent (and up to 14 percent if nontariff barriers are also removed). WORLD BANK, INTERNATIONAL TRADE AND CLIMATE CHANGE, *supra*, at 45–72. If translated into emissions reductions, these gains suggest that — even within a small subset of clean energy technologies and for a select group of countries — the impact of trade liberalization could be significant.

Nonetheless, WTO members have not been able to agree on the list of qualified goods and services; defining what are "environmental" goods and services has proven more challenging than it appears. Consider two approaches in the climate change context. Under the first approach, climate change mitigation technologies (and services) would be defined in relation to a specific good or end-use. Thus, goods such as solar photovoltaic panels and wind turbines would be slated for tariff reduction or elimination. The second approach would cast a wider net and include "environmentally preferable products" from a climate change perspective. Under this approach, a product that causes less harm to climate than alternative products would be subject to tariff reduction or elimination. Mahesh Sugathan, *Climate Change Benefits from Liberalisation of Environmental Goods and Services*, in LINKING TRADE, CLIMATE CHANGE AND ENERGY 8 (ICTSD 2006). The trouble with this second approach is determining exactly when a product is more climate change friendly than an alternative product. While marginally better than existing fossil fuels, corn-based ethanol is far worse than sugarcane-based ethanol. Moreover, technology developments may make both substantially inferior products to cellulosic ethanol. If current technologies receive preferential treatment, then it will be difficult, if not impossible, to provide trade advantages to future, superior technologies. The same problems hold true for attempts to reduce tariffs for appliances and other products that are energy efficient. In addition, the establishment of separate tariffs for energy efficient dishwashers would require governments to establish a new tariff classification. *Id.* at 84. Another concern with both approaches for many countries is that a reduction in the tariffs to benefit a specific technology may lead to a tariff reduction for other technologies unrelated to climate change. For example, India classifies solar photovoltaic panels as "Other" under the subclassification of light emitting diodes (LEDs). An effort to reduce tariffs for solar photovoltaic panels may thus lead to a tariff reduction in all "other" LEDs. While India could always reclassify photovoltaic panels, the example highlights why the negotiations are not straightforward.

Despite these challenges, do you think that governments should establish lists of climate-friendly goods and pursue tariff elimination for them? If yes, which approach do you prefer? Which products do you think deserve reduced tariffs?

3.   The negotiations to reduce tariffs on environmental goods and services is taking place within the WTO. Should the WTO be involved at all in such negotiations? Should the Parties to the climate change regime negotiate their own

tariff reductions for climate-friendly goods and services? What are the advantages of having these negotiations within the WTO? Within the climate change regime?

4. In light of the slow progress within the WTO on environmental matters, as well as the general difficulty of negotiating with more than 150 WTO members, some have begun to argue that reductions in tariffs and nontariff barriers for climate change technology occur through bilateral and regional trade agreements, such as the North American Free Trade Agreement. What are the advantages and disadvantages of such an approach?

---

2.   *Carbon and Other Taxes*

Governments have proposed or adopted a variety of taxes — gas taxes, automobile taxes, and carbon taxes — to help mitigate climate change and meet their commitments under the Kyoto Protocol. In general, a WTO member is free to impose these taxes on its domestic industry without implicating WTO rules, because no international trade concerns are raised. However, in the absence of a similar tax in the markets of competitors, a government and its industries may feel that the untaxed imported products have an unfair, competitive advantage in the marketplace. A couple of current proposals before the U.S. Congress, for example, would impose a tax on both domestic and imported fossil fuels based on their carbon content. *See, e.g.*, H.R. 2069. Where both domestic and foreign products are taxed, some of these taxes, such as a tax on fuel consumption, are unlikely to raise trade concerns, provided that imported and foreign gas are taxed the same. Other taxes, such as those based on fuel efficiency, pose greater challenges under trade law, because they may discriminate between "like products."

a.   *Automobile Taxes*

A number of countries impose some form of "gas guzzler" tax, a tax on automobiles based on the vehicle's fuel economy. For example, under the U.S. Energy Tax Act of 1978, the United States imposes taxes that increase as the fuel economy of a vehicle decreases. 26 U.S.C. §§ 4064 et seq. Cars with an average fuel economy greater than 22.5 miles per gallon have no tax imposed on them. Cars getting between 21.5 and 22.5 miles per gallon have a tax imposed on them of $1,000. The tax increases as fuel economy decreases with cars getting fewer than 12.5 miles per gallon assessed a tax of $7,700. Currently, sport utility vehicles and trucks, including light-duty trucks, are exempt.

Whether such laws are consistent with the GATT depends on whether cars, irrespective of their fuel economy, are "like products." When the European Communities challenged the U.S. gas guzzler tax in the 1990s, a GATT panel upheld the tax. United States-Taxes on Automobiles, GATT Panel Report, DS31/R (Oct. 11, 1994) (unadopted). The GATT Parties never adopted that decision, however. The panel failed to use the four-part "like product" test described above, to assess whether cars with high and low fuel economy were "like products." *See* Japan-Alcoholic Beverages; United States-Standards for Reformulated and Conventional Gasoline, Report of the Appellate Body, WT/DS2/AB/R (decided Apr. 29, 1996) (adopted May 20, 1996). As a result, whether tax distinctions based on a car's fuel economy are permissible is unclear. Do you think that low mileage vehicles are "like" high mileage vehicles based on the vehicles' end use, physical characteristics, and tariff classification, as well as consumer preferences?

---

b.   *Carbon Taxes*

Many governments believe that a carbon tax — based on the carbon content of fossil fuels or the carbon dioxide emitted in manufacturing a product — provides an attractive means for reducing emissions, creating appropriate market incentives for switching to cleaner fuels and encouraging energy efficiency. Representative Fortnoy's Save Our Climate Act of 2007 (H.R. 2069) proposes a tax of $10 per ton of carbon in natural gas, coal, and other fossil fuels. The tax increases by $10 per year until U.S. CO_2 emissions reach, but do not exceed, 20 percent of 1990 emissions. Similarly, Representative John Larson's America's Energy Security Trust Fund Act of 2007 (H.R. 3416) proposes a tax of $15 per ton on the carbon dioxide content of fossil fuels extracted, manufactured, or produced in the United States or imported into the United States for consumption, use, or warehousing.

If a carbon tax is based on the carbon content of the product, like Representative Fortnoy's bill, or the average BTUs per unit of the fossil fuel, then the carbon taxes should be consistent with the GATT. Under these circumstances, the tax would be based on a physical characteristic of the product, thus avoiding the problem the United States encountered in the *Tuna/Dolphin* disputes. It should also allow a higher tax to be imposed on coal with a higher carbon content than coal with a lower carbon content. Although this appears to be a violation of the rule that prohibits taxing like products differently, here the taxed item is the carbon, not the coal. This arguably avoids any discrimination or "like product" concerns by taxing the carbon in the product, not the product itself. Similar taxes, such as those based on the alcohol content in perfumes and the amount of certain chemicals in other substances, have been upheld by trade panels. In the *Superfund* dispute, for example, a GATT panel allowed the United States to tax the amount of "certain chemicals" that were constituents of other substances, so long as the tax was based on the amount of chemicals in the final product and not the value of the final product. United States-Taxes on Petroleum and Certain Imported Substances, GATT Panel Report, L/6175, BISD, 34th Supp. 136, para. 5.2.8 (1988) (adopted June 17, 1987) (*Superfund*). The panel upheld the tax, because it was imposed "in respect of an article from which the imported product has been manufactured or produced in whole or in part," as allowed by Article II:2(a) of the GATT. Although the energy or carbon naturally found in a product is not used to "manufacture or produce" the final energy product, a tax on the energy or carbon content of the product would seem to be sufficiently analogous, because the tax is on some embedded element of the product.

Some taxes on carbon emissions from the production of imported goods may also violate the GATT under current jurisprudence. Such taxes, like all taxes on pollution discharges or process and production methods, constitute taxes on the manufacturing process, not the product itself. This is the lesson from the *Tuna/Dolphin* dispute. In that case, the GATT panel concluded that U.S. restrictions on the importation of tuna caught by encircling dolphins violated the GATT's prohibition against import restrictions, because the United States was impermissibly distinguishing products based on the way the tuna was produced, not on some characteristic of the product itself. In essence, all tuna, were "like products," and import restrictions based on the method of harvest or production were not allowed. Taxes based on carbon emissions would likely be treated the same way.

c.   Border Tax Adjustments

To ensure that domestic products enter international commerce on a level playing field, not only do countries impose taxes on imported "like" products, but they also exempt or rebate the tax on the domestic product when it is exported. Such "border tax adjustments" are a feature of both the Fortnoy and Larson bills. They are also perhaps the most controversial taxes from a trade perspective. In 1993, President Clinton proposed an energy tax that would have taxed imported products similarly to domestic products and rebated the tax for domestic products that were exported. The proposal was rejected when European and Japanese producers objected that the proposal violated the GATT. *See* DANIEL ESTY, GREENING THE GATT 168 (1994).

Although trade objections stopped the Clinton proposal, border tax adjustments of carbon taxes may in fact be consistent with GATT rules. Consider the Fortnoy and Larson bills, which exempt sales of "taxable fuels" for export from the carbon tax. As described in the previous section, the United States or another WTO member should be able to tax imported products, provided that imported products are taxed the same as domestic products. The only remaining question is whether a WTO member can exempt or rebate the tax for domestic products destined for export. The question hinges on whether the tax is a product tax (also called an "indirect tax"), such as sales, excise, value-added, and other taxes on a product, or a "direct tax," taxes not directly levied on products, such as income, social security, and payroll taxes. Under GATT rules, only indirect taxes are eligible for border tax adjustment. Because a tax on carbon content relates to some physical characteristic of the product, it should be considered an indirect tax and thus eligible for a border tax adjustment.

d.   Taxes on Products Made with Fossil Fuels

Instead of taxing coal or natural gas, a tax could be imposed on the production of chairs, computers, and any other manufactured product based on the amount of energy consumed during the production process, from the operation of the machinery to heating and lighting the factory where the product is made. While such a tax on energy inputs would strongly encourage energy efficiency throughout the entire production cycle, such taxes when imposed on imported products may not be consistent with the GATT.

Taxes on energy, transportation, and equipment used in production, are neither "indirect" nor "direct" taxes; they are *taxes occultes*. As such, they are not impermissible taxes on processes or production methods, such as taxes based on emissions during production of the good, or U.S. restrictions on tuna or shrimp based on the harvest method. At the same time, they are not considered taxes relating to the product itself, which would be a permissible tax and eligible for a border tax adjustment.

Although the GATT has discussed these taxes within the context of border tax adjustments, it has concluded only that there is a "divergence of views" on whether *taxes occultes* are eligible for border tax adjustment. *Border Tax Adjustments*, Dec. 2, 1970, GATT Doc. L/3464, BISD 18th Supp. 97, paras. 14–15. (1972). A number of authors have parsed the distinctions among various taxes to determine whether taxes on products made with energy products are eligible for border tax adjustments. These analyses, which are very complex and require a sophisticated understanding of the Agreement on Subsidies and Countervailing Duties, come to different conclusions about the eligibility of such taxes for border tax adjustments. *See* Thomas J. Schoenbaum, *International Trade and Protection of the Environment: The Continuing Search for Reconciliation*, 91 AM. J. INT'L. L. 268,

310 (1997) (concluding that taxes on imports are not permissible but rebates on exports are); Paul Demaret & Raoul Stewardson, *Border Tax Adjustments under GATT and EC Law and General Implications for Environmental Taxes*, 28 J. WORLD TRADE 5 (1994); Frank Muller and Andrew Hoerner, *Using A Border Adjustment To Take The Lead On Climate Change Without Encouraging Runaway Shops* 5 (Sept. 1997), *available at* www.ies.unsw.edu.au/about/staff/franksFiles/Policy%20Notes/Border%20Adjustment.pdf.

QUESTIONS AND DISCUSSION

1. Consider again the discussion of carbon taxes in Chapter 2, as well as some of the environmental and economic benefits of various taxes discussed below.

Gas Taxes. An assessment of a large number of studies on gas taxes concluded that a tax that increases the price of gas by 10% will cause demand for gas to fall by 5.8% in the long run (defined as longer than one year). Molly Espey, *Explaining the Variation in Elasticity Estimates of Gasoline Demand in the United States: A Meta-Analysis*, 17 ENERGY J. 49–60 (1996).

Automobile Taxes. Taxes such as gas guzzler taxes may create market incentives for improving fuel economy. For consumers, adding $7,700 to the cost of a car no doubt provides a powerful disincentive for its purchase. For producers, improving fuel economy may be cheaper than incorporating the tax into the price of the vehicle. The Union of Concerned Scientists has reported that investments to increase fuel economy pay off if gas guzzler taxes are applied. For example, the Ford Explorer gets 19.3 miles per gallon. While currently exempt from gas guzzler taxes, the Explorer would be assessed a tax of $2,100 if gas guzzler applied. However, a $700 investment in existing technologies could improve its fuel efficiency to 28.4 mpg and it would not have to pay for a gas guzzler tax. Jason Mark, *Greener SUVs: A Blueprint for Cleaner, More Efficient Light Trucks* 3–5 (1999), *available at* http://www.ucsusa.org/publications.

Emissions Taxes. Taxes on carbon emissions may encourage technological innovation more than taxes on carbon content of energy inputs. A tax on carbon content should discourage use of energy products with high carbon levels. On the other hand, if more effective technologies can reduce carbon emissions, manufacturers may continue to use high carbon energy inputs knowing that their emissions can be reduced or eliminated (and thus not taxed). Moreover, economists claim that taxes on externalities from processes and production methods, such as emissions, are more efficient than taxes on products, because the price of the good will better reflect total social costs. Charles S. Pearson & Robert Repetto, *Reconciling Trade and Environment: The Next Steps, in* TRADE AND ENVIRONMENT COMMITTEE OF THE NATIONAL ADVISORY COUNCIL FOR ENVIRONMENTAL POLICY AND TECHNOLOGY, THE GREENING OF WORLD TRADE 83, 96 (1993).

Border Tax Adjustments. Carbon taxes accompanied by border tax adjustments appear to reduce greenhouse gas emissions more effectively than carbon taxes without border tax adjustments. In one study, significant leakage — the portion of cuts in greenhouse gas emissions by countries with targets and timetables that may reappear in other countries not bound by such limits — occurred when modelers imposed a tax of 15 euros per metric ton of carbon dioxide emissions for all Kyoto Protocol Parties with targets and timetables (except the United States and Australia). Under this simulation, emissions were reduced by about 20 percent in the countries with the tax, but emissions increased in the rest of the world by about 20 percent of the emissions reduction. When the tax was transformed into a border tax adjustment, global emissions decreased. Damien Demailly & Philippe Quirion, *Leakage from Climate Policies and Border Tax Adjustment: Lessons from a Geographic Model of the Cement Industry*, available at http://ideas.repec.org/p/hal/papers/halshs-00009337_v1.html.

Assume you are a legislator in Spain, looking for strategies to meet your country's Kyoto Protocol commitment. Based on this information and the information concerning the GATT-consistency of the various taxes, which taxes, if any, would you propose?

2. *Taxes on Products Made with Fossil Fuels.* One considerable challenge for implementing a tax on carbon used to make final products is ascertaining the amount of carbon actually consumed to produce that product. Because carbon is not a component of the final product, it cannot be measured. How, then, can regulators ascertain the carbon used to produce a product? Several options are available. First, producers could be required to submit reports that demonstrate production levels and the amount and type of fuel purchased. From this data, officials in the importing country could determine how much fuel was used per unit of product. As the IPCC has stated, however, "Determining the emissions associated with the manufacture of a particular product, hence the border tax adjustment, is likely to be very complex because of differences in the fuel mix and production techniques used in different regions." IPCC, TECHNOLOGIES, POLICIES AND MEASURES FOR MITIGATING CLIMATE CHANGE, § 9.3 (R. Watson et al. eds., 1996). Joost Pauwelyn describes some other options based on the possibility of the United States imposing a carbon tax:

> An alternative basis for calculation of the carbon tax (or amount of emission credits to be provided) could then be the amount of carbon that would have been emitted had the imported product been produced in the United States using the U.S. *predominant method of production.* * * *

> An alternative method of calculation that has been suggested, largely to avoid any semblance of discrimination, is to calculate a carbon tax or emission allowance requirement on imports based on the carbon emitted using the *best available technology.* This would mean that, for example, Chinese steel made with coal would only have to pay the price of carbon emitted for the same steel produced in the United States with the least polluting technology, say, natural gas. This would, of course, seriously reduce the amount of adjustment that can be imposed on imports and may not be sufficient to address competitiveness concerns. Yet, it would avoid claims of discrimination as all "like" products — for example, all steel — would then be taxed the same.

Joost Pauwelyn, *U.S. Federal Climate Policy and Competitiveness Concerns: The Limits and Options of International Trade Law* 31–32 (2007). Under any of these scenarios, "the process of calculating [border tax adjustments] will be expensive and time-consuming." Richard G. Tarasofsky, *Heating Up International Trade Law: Challenges and Opportunities Posed by Efforts to Combat Climate Change,* 1 CLIMATE CHANGE L. REV. 7, 12 (2008). Despite the cost, is such a border tax adjustment worthwhile? Are there other options that may be easier and less costly to implement?

3.   *Renewable Energy Requirements*

The European Union and numerous states in the United States require a certain percentage of energy sold or consumed in the state to come from renewable sources. For example, Maine requires certain electricity providers to derive at least 30% of their supply sources for retail electricity from "renewable" or "efficient resources." ME. REV. STAT. ANN. tit. 35-A, § 3210(3) (West 2003). Maine defines renewable energy sources to include small hydropower facilities (which are abundant in the state) but not hydroelectric facilities with a production capacity over 100 megawatts (which are prevalent in the Canadian provinces that border Maine). Similarly, under Maryland's renewable energy portfolio standards, eligible hydroelectric facilities must generate 30 megawatts of power or less. Code of Maryland, § 7-701 *et seq.*

Because electricity is commonly bought and sold in international markets, renewable energy requirements pose a number of trade issues. First, while these and other state laws are facially nondiscriminatory — they do not, for example, impose higher taxes on Canadian electricity — they may disadvantage producers from other countries and be considered discriminatory within the meaning of the GATT. In the past, trade panels have found *de facto* discrimination where a facially neutral measure changes the conditions of competition between imported and domestic products. *See, e.g.*, Korea-Measures Affecting Import of Fresh, Chilled & Frozen Beef, Report of the Appellate Body, WT/DS161/AB/R, WT/DS169/AB/R, para. 137 (Jan. 11, 2001) (stating that "a formal difference in treatment" between imported and like domestic products is not necessary to show a violation of Article III:4). The requirements of Maine and Maryland, for example, could disadvantage Canadian producers of energy, because Canada's comparative advantage in electricity generation derives from "big" hydro. In 1998 and 1999, Canada generated about 96 percent of its hydroelectric power from facilities that produce more than 30 megawatts. Because hydroelectric facilities account for about 60–65 percent of Canadian electricity exports to the United States, renewable energy requirements could adversely affect demand for Canadian electricity. Canadian Electricity Association, *Electric Power in Canada 1998–1999* (2000).

Second, renewable energy requirements may violate the GATT's bar against taxing or regulating products differently based on the way they are produced. As described above, GATT and WTO panels have consistently rejected claims that governments could distinguish products based on processes and production methods (PPMs). Instead, distinctions in tax or regulatory treatment must be based on some characteristic of the product. Thus, laws that tax or regulate electricity differently based on the way they are produced (e.g., coal, large-scale hydroelectric facilities, or small-scale hydroelectric facilities) would violate Article XI of the GATT. Renewable energy requirements that merely require electricity providers to use energy from renewable sources may not violate Article XI. On the other hand, they may still violate Article III by creating *de facto* discrimination between foreign and domestic sources. For example, the laws of U.S. states that define renewable hydropower as deriving from facilities of less than 30 megawatts clearly discourage imports from Canada. Previous decisions of trade panels have held that such de facto discrimination affects the internal sale of products in violation of Article III's national treatment obligation. Canada-Administration of the Foreign Investment Review Act, GATT Panel Report, L/5504, BISD, 30th Supp. 140, para. 6.1 (1984) (adopted Feb. 7, 1984).

QUESTIONS AND DISCUSSION

1. *Article XX Exceptions.* In the event that any of the taxes and renewable energy portfolios discussed in this section violate Article III or Article XI of the GATT, they may be justified pursuant to the GATT's exceptions for measures (1) necessary to protect human, animal, or plant life or health or (2) relating to the conservation of an exhaustible natural resource. GATT and WTO panels have interpreted these exceptions very narrowly, finding only a French ban on asbestos and U.S. restrictions on shrimp as meeting the applicable requirements.

Whether a measure is "necessary" under Article XX(b) is determined by weighing and balancing a number of factors, including:

> the relative importance of the interests or values furthered by the challenged measure, the contribution of the measure to the realization of the ends pursued by it and the restrictive impact of the measure on international commerce. Once all those factors have been analyzed, the Appellate Body said a comparison should be undertaken between the challenged measure and possible alternatives. In performing this comparison, the Appellate Body also stated that the weighing and balancing process of the factors informs the determination of whether a WTO-consistent alternative measure, or a less WTO-inconsistent measure, which the Member concerned could reasonably be expected to employ, is available.

Brazil-Measures Affecting Imports of Retreaded Tyres, Report of the Panel, para. 7.104, WT/DS332/R (published June 12, 2007) (adopted Dec. 17, 2007); *see also* Brazil-Measures Affecting Imports of Retreaded Tyres, Report of the Appellate Body, WT/DS332/AB/R, paras. 142–143; 156 (Dec. 3, 2007). A measure "relat[es] to conservation of an exhaustible natural resource," such as clean air, sea turtles, or dolphins, where there is a "substantial relationship" between the conservation objective and the trade measure or "a close and genuine relationship of ends and means." The measure must also be applied in an even-handed manner to both imported and domestic products. United States-Standards for Reformulated and Conventional Gasoline, Report of the Appellate Body, WT/DS2/AB/R, 19–21, (decided Apr. 29, 1996) (adopted May 20, 1996); United States-Import Prohibition of Certain Shrimp and Shrimp Products, Report of the Appellate Body, WT/DS58/AB/R, paras. 136, 143–45 (decided Oct. 12, 1998) (adopted Nov. 6, 1998).

With respect to either exception, a panel will ask whether the measure constitutes arbitrary or unjustifiable discrimination between countries where the same conditions prevail. As an initial matter, the Appellate Body has stated that there is arbitrary or unjustifiable discrimination "when a Member seeks to justify the discrimination resulting from the application of its measure by a rationale that bears no relationship to the accomplishment of the objective that falls within the purview of one of the paragraphs of Article XX, or goes against this objective." Brazil-Retreaded Tyres, Appellate Body Report, para. 246. Thus, although Brazil sought to bar all imports of retreaded tires, a trade panel under MERCOSUR (a customs union of several South American countries) ruled that Brazil must accept such tires from MERCOSUR members. When Brazil sought to use the MERCOSUR decision to justify the difference in treatment between retreaded tires from MERCOSUR members and all other countries, the Appellate Body found that discrimination arbitrary and unjustifiable. According to the Appellate Body, that justification bore no relationship to the goal of preventing malaria and other mosquito-borne diseases, the principal reason offered by Brazil for barring the importation of retreaded tires.

In *Shrimp/Turtle*, the panel found that U.S restrictions on shrimp constituted unjustifiable discrimination in countries where the same conditions prevail, because the United States failed to take into account the individualized circumstances of each country exporting shrimp to the United States. Instead, the United States required each country to adopt a sea turtle conservation program that was essentially the same as that adopted in the United States, which required the use of Turtle Excluder Devices (TEDs). Once the United States allowed for an individualized approach that required a sea turtle conservation program *"comparable in effectiveness"* to that employed in the United States, the panel found the new U.S. approach flexible enough to account for the unique circumstances in each country. WTO panels have also found arbitrary and unjustifiable discrimination where the WTO Member imposing a trade restriction did not seek to negotiate a solution to the problem with relevant governments.

While much more could be said about the Article XX exceptions to the GATT, consider whether various climate friendly policies are GATT consistent. Assuming that the U.S. gas guzzler tax and Maine's renewable energy requirements violate basic GATT principles, could these measures nonetheless be justified pursuant to either Article XX(b) or XX(g)?

2.   *"Like Products."* Many benefits could derive from taxing or regulating products with a high climate change impact more rigorously than products with a lower climate change impact. Vehicles with poor fuel economy could be taxed higher than vehicles with better fuel economy. Vehicles with flex fuel engines — those that can use any blend of gasoline and ethanol — could be taxed differently from cars with conventional engines. Electricity from renewable sources could be preferred to electricity from other sources. The GATT may also allow a differential tax based on the type of engine (flex-fuel, hybrid, electric, conventional), because such taxes would seem to be clearly related to the physical characteristics of the car. Still other distinctions, such as those between coal-based electricity and hydropower, are clearly inconsistent with GATT rules (provided electricity is a good). Implementing such taxes, however, entails risks, because they could be challenged in a WTO dispute. WTO members could adopt a formal interpretation that identifies certain products as "not like products." Do you think it should? If so, what other categories of "not like products" would be valuable from a climate change perspective?

---

4.   *Fuel Efficiency Standards and Ecolabels*

WTO members cannot avoid GATT scrutiny by turning taxes into laws and regulations, because laws and regulations are also subject to the most favored nation and national treatment obligations of the GATT. In addition, technical regulations — mandatory governmental product specifications such as fuel efficiency requirements, technology standards, and emissions standards — fall within the scope of the Agreement on Technical Barriers to Trade (TBT Agreement).

Like the GATT, the TBT Agreement requires WTO members to adopt and implement technical regulations consistent with their MFN and national treatment obligations. In addition, technical regulations must not be "more trade restrictive than necessary to fulfill a legitimate objective." Although the protection of the environment is listed as a legitimate objective, members must nevertheless base their technical regulations on international standards, if they exist, unless such standards are "ineffective or inappropriate." A technical regulation based on an international standard is presumed consistent with the TBT Agreement. The development of technical regulations is also subject to transparency, notification, and consultation requirements.

In *EC-Sardines*, the Appellate Body set out three criteria for defining a "technical regulation": 1) the regulation applies to an identifiable product or group of products, even if not expressly identified; 2) the regulation lays down one or more characteristics of the product; and 3) compliance with the product characteristics is mandatory. Based on these criteria, the Appellate Body found that a regulation that restricted the use of the term "sardine" to a particular fish species constituted a "technical regulation." European Communities-Trade Description of Sardines Report of the Appellate Body, WT/DS231/AB/R, paras. 176–195 (adopted Oct. 23, 2002).

This Appellate Body interpretation of the term "technical regulation" is likely to capture a broad range of measures relating to climate change. For example, regulations requiring appliances to meet certain energy efficiency requirements would certainly constitute a technical regulation — a group of products is identified (appliances) and certain characteristics of the product are mandated (energy efficiency specifications). Even an outright ban on the sale of certain products, for example cars not meeting certain fuel economy standards, would be considered a technical regulation. At the same time, the scant jurisprudence concerning the substantive obligations of the TBT Agreement makes it difficult to analyze technical regulations concerning climate change. The following examples highlight some of the issues:

Fuel Economy and Appliance Efficiency Standards. Countries around the world have adopted fuel economy standards. Of course, they differ from country to country. In the United States, Congress has set fuel economy standards for passenger cars at 27.5 miles per gallon (mpg). China's standards are about 35 mpg while Japan tops the rankings at more than 40 mpg. From an international trade perspective, why do these differences in fuel economy matter? Which substantive rules of the TBT Agreement might allow a WTO member to challenge the fuel economy standards of say, Japan, as being too strict? Consider the following discussion concerning Japan's most recent improvements to its fuel economy standards:

> In 1998, Japan announced that it would be promulgating binding regulations for energy efficiency of nine classes of automobiles grouped by weight of the vehicle. The target in the year 2010 for each class was pegged at the "top runner," which happened to be a Japanese vehicle. Manufacturers selling vehicles in a weight class that cumulatively perform less well on average than the top runner are to be assessed a penalty. Several governments complained about this regulation, and called it a violation of the TBT Agreement. The dispute was never brought to the WTO, however, and Japan has expressed confidence that its regulation conforms to TBT.

> One lesson from this episode is that any national regulation having a disparate trade effect on foreign producers will raise concerns under TBT. The underlying problem is that the regulator may center attention on one attribute that may be relatively less important in other countries. In this episode, Japan was most concerned about fuel economy, but imported vehicles that are heavier may reflect competing concerns in the country of manufacture about pollution or safety.

Steve Charnovitz, *Trade and Climate: Potential Conflicts and Synergies, in* Pew Center on Global Climate Change, Beyond Kyoto: Advancing the International Effort Against Climate Change 141, 149 (2003).

Ecolabeling. Ecolabeling has become an important means for consumers to distinguish products based on their environmental characteristics without actually barring the importation of environmentally "unfriendly" products. Worldwide, thousands of products carry ecolabels, from shade-grown coffee to sustainably harvested timber products to energy efficient appliances. For a list of ecolabels, see http://ecolabelling.org/ecolabel. Some labels simply provide information about a certain characteristic of the product, such as a car's fuel efficiency and carbon dioxide emissions. Review the Appellate Body's definition of a technical regulation. Do you see why, based on the Appellate Body's interpretation of "technical regulation," that a labeling requirement to display information, such as fuel consumption, falls within the scope of the TBT Agreement? Do you think that a label displaying an automobile's fuel economy meets the TBT Agreement's substantive requirements?

Other labels provide information about the way the product was made, such as salmon-safe wine or dolphin-safe tuna. Labels could indicate whether a product was "climate-friendly" based on the amount of carbon dioxide emitted during the production process or on the energy inputs used (e.g., renewable resources versus coal). Whether the TBT Agreement applies to such labels is not clear; due to ambiguity in the definition of "technical regulation," the WTO members cannot agree on whether the TBT Agreement covers ecolabels based on processes and production methods unrelated to a product, such as harvesting techniques or greenhouse gas emissions. *See* Chris Wold, Sanford Gaines & Greg Block, Trade and the Environment: Law and Policy 420–22 (2005) (explaining the different interpretations).

Aside from the legal debate, critics of labels claim that they are discriminatory. For example, developing countries hotly contested an Austrian requirement to label all tropical timber as "Made from Tropical Timber" or "Containing Tropical Timber." They claimed the label was discriminatory because only tropical timber was subject to the label. Do you agree? Does the Austrian label, merely by identifying products as containing tropical timber, violate the MFN or national treatment obligation of the TBT Agreement? For more information on ecolabels and the TBT Agreement, see Wold, Gaines, & Block, *supra*, at 399–434.

QUESTIONS AND DISCUSSION

1.   Under the "Energy Star" program of the United States, dishwashers may be labeled with the Energy Star if they are at least 25 percent more efficient than minimum federal government standards. DVD players receive the Energy Star if they consume three watts or less when switched off. What information, if any, might you need to answer whether either of these labels are consistent with the TBT Agreement?

2.   Design a climate change ecolabel. What criteria will you use to issue your label? For example, will you consider only a product's energy efficiency, like the Energy Star program? Will you provide the label for products that have fewer

climate change impacts than other products (e.g., wind mills receive a label; lignite does not).

3.   Daniel Esty says that ecolabels should be the "default" trade restriction. He argues that ecolabels provide information to consumers while also allowing products to be sold, which "strikes a useful balance between trade and environmental goals in many situations where the appropriateness of more severe restrictions is uncertain." DANIEL C. ESTY: GREENING THE GATT: TRADE, ENVIRONMENT, AND THE FUTURE 134 (1994). Do you agree that ecolabels provide a preferable alternative to trade restrictions? For example, would the "dolphin-safe" label indicating zero dolphin mortality in a tuna fishery adequately protect dolphins if not supplemented with an import ban on tuna caught using dolphin unsafe fishing methods? Would ecolabels be sufficiently effective in the climate change context? Under what conditions would restrictions other than ecolabels be appropriate?

---

5.   *Subsidies*

Subsidies have generated growing interest among governments and environmental organizations that see subsidies as a means either to protect or harm the environment, depending on how they are used. For example, corn subsidies in the United States promote the production of corn-based ethanol, which produces less energy than sugarcane-based ethanol. At the same time, subsidies can encourage the use and production of climate-friendly technologies and the use of farming techniques that store carbon in the soil.

The WTO's Agreement on Subsidies and Countervailing Measures (SCM Agreement) does not judge subsidies based on their policy objective. Rather, it prohibits subsidies that distort trade by causing material injury or serious prejudice to industries in other countries (for example, by suppressing prices or displacing imports of nonsubsidized products). Subsidies that promote climate change mitigation, such as subsidies for solar panels, may result in trade distortions just like any other subsidy by providing an unfair advantage for the country's solar panels in the marketplace. Where a subsidy distorts trade by material injury or serious prejudice to another country's industry, the harmed country may retaliate with countervailing duties, increased duties to offset the harm caused by the subsidy.

To fall within the scope of the SCM Agreement, the government must provide a financial contribution, such as the transfer of funds or the provision of goods or services, that confers a benefit to the recipient. The subsidy must also be "specific" to a limited group of enterprises. For example, a subsidy limited to producers of renewable energy or certain types of climate change mitigation technologies might be deemed a specific subsidy, because it is available in fact or in law to only certain enterprises or industries. The WTO panel's decision in *United States-Cotton* suggests that even a relatively large number of recipients may lead to a "specificity" finding. In that case, the Panel concluded that crop insurance subsidies available for about 100 different crops were available to "a sufficiently discrete segment of the United States economy to qualify as 'specific.'" United States-Subsidies on Upland Cotton, Report of the Panel, WT/DS267/R, para. 7.1150 (Sept. 8, 2004), affirmed by the Report of the Appellate Body, WT/DS267/AB/R, para. 543 (Mar. 3, 2005) (adopted Mar. 21, 2005). Where subsidies distort trade and are considered specific, they are subject to retaliatory trade sanctions.

While the SCM Agreement casts doubt on some efforts to mitigate climate change, it also prohibits actions of WTO members that may hinder climate change mitigation. For example, the U.S. corn economy is supported by vast subsidies: corn farmers received 46 percent of roughly $20 billion in annual subsidies under the 2002 farm bill. *See Uncle Sam's Teat: Can America's Farmers Be Weaned from Their Government Money?*, THE ECONOMIST, Sept. 9, 2006, at 35. WTO panels have concluded that U.S. cotton subsidies and EU sugar subsidies are inconsistent with the SCM Agreement, and it is highly likely that they would draw the same conclusions with respect to U.S. corn subsidies (Canada and Brazil have lodged a WTO dispute). That U.S. corn subsidies distort the world market for corn is plain. For example, Mexican farmers are actually reducing their corn prices below costs of production to compete with U.S. corn. Timothy A. Wise, *The Paradox of Agricultural Subsidies: Measurement Issues, Agricultural Dumping and Policy Reform* (Feb. 2004), *available at* http://ase.tufts.edu/gdae/Pubs/wp/04-02AgSubsidies.pdf. Because sugarcane-based ethanol has an energy balance — the ratio of energy contained in the final biofuel product to the energy used to produce it — about 5.33 times higher than corn-based ethanol, the SCM Agreement could be an effective means for eliminating subsidies for "underperforming" corn-based ethanol.

QUESTIONS AND DISCUSSION

1.   To avoid a specificity finding, WTO members must provide a subsidy based on objective criteria or conditions governing the eligibility that are generally available (i.e., not available only to certain industries or enterprises). Moreover, the subsidy must be granted automatically upon fulfillment of the criteria or conditions; any agency discretion to refuse the subsidy could lead to a "specificity" finding by a trade panel. Consider the following three subsidies: Country X provides a subsidy to any facility that 1) achieves a certain level of carbon dioxide emissions during the production process, 2) reduces carbon dioxide emissions by a certain percentage, or 3) produces products that meet certain energy-efficiency criteria. Would any of these be sufficiently "specific" to be covered by the SCM Agreement? *See* Yulia Selivanova, *Transition to a Sustainable Energy Future: Global Trade Rules and Energy Policies, in* LINKING TRADE, CLIMATE CHANGE AND ENERGY 3, 4 (International Centre for Trade and Sustainable Development 2006).

2.   WTO members could advance the climate change mitigation agenda by ensuring that a range of climate-friendly subsidies are not actionable under the SCM Agreement. They have adopted just this approach for fisheries subsidies. Although the negotiations are not yet finished, the members have found common ground on a range of permissible and prohibited fisheries subsidies. For example, subsidies for artisanal fishing and for the construction of water and sanitary waste systems serving processing facilities for fisheries products, among many others, have been proposed as permissible under the SCM Agreement. *See, e.g.,* New Zealand, *Fisheries Subsidies: Exhaustive List of Non-Prohibited Fisheries Subsidies*, TN/RL/GEN/141 (June 6, 2006). If this approach were adopted for climate change, what would you include in your lists of permissible and prohibited subsidies?

3. ***Trade Sanctions for Nonparticipation.*** A number of climate change proposals have attempted to prevent free-riders — principally the United States — from receiving benefits of other country's climate change mitigation efforts without accepting any of the costs. For example, French Prime Minister de Villepin has proposed a tax, or anti-dumping duty, against those who "dump" their products — that is, sell their products below the cost of production — on the international market because they refuse to include the social cost of carbon dioxide emissions in the price of their goods. Under the WTO's Anti-Dumping Agreement, however, goods are dumped only when the price of the good falls below the price of the good in the market of the country allegedly engaged in dumping. Thus, as long as the exporting country does not tax or regulate carbon dioxide emissions, the failure to internalize the social cost of carbon dioxide emissions in exported goods cannot be considered dumping. *See* Joost Pauwelyn, *U.S. Federal Climate Policy and Competitiveness Concerns: The Limits and Options of International Trade Law* 13–14 (2007). Others, such as Joseph Stiglitz, have called for a countervailing duty on products not subject to a carbon tax based on the idea that such products are "subsidized." Joseph E. Stiglitz, *A New Agenda for Global Warming*, Economists' Voice 3 (July 2006). The SCM Agreement clearly answers that such products are not subsidized, because the government has not provided any financial contribution, i.e., there is no transfer of funds or provision of goods or services. Even if the failure to tax or regulate carbon dioxide emissions was somehow construed as a subsidy, it would not be "specific," because the subsidy would be generally available to everyone. For more on whether the failure to regulate constitutes a subsidy, see Wold, Gaines, & Block, at 573–80 (2005).

4.   The United States also discourages imports of ethanol by imposing a tariff of 54 cents per gallon on imported ethanol. Harmonized Tariff Schedule of the United States, § 9901.00.50. Because ethanol produced from sugarcane in Brazil costs 40 percent to 50 percent less to produce than U.S.-produced ethanol and because U.S. wholesale ethanol prices ranged from $1.80 to $2.06 per gallon at the beginning of 2006, the tariff creates a "significant barrier to imports." Brent D. Yacobucci, *Ethanol Imports and the Caribbean Basin Initiative* 3 (CRS Report for Congress, Updated March 10, 2006). Because tariffs are negotiated, however, the U.S. tariff on ethanol is not inconsistent with WTO rules.

5. ***Carbon Trading and the GATS.*** Even the carbon trading provisions of the Kyoto Protocol raise trade questions. Joint implementation and CDM-related activities are services covered by the General Agreement on Trade in Services (GATS). Some entity, whether private or governmental, must issue ERUs and CERs. The design of a CDM project will require engineering, architectural and planning services, as well as construction, installation, assembly, finishing and, in some cases, landscaping and real estate services. To monitor and maintain the project, additional services may be required, such as accounting, testing and analysis, and consulting services. Securing project funding and executing contracts will necessitate financial, lending, and legal services. If a secondary market exists for ERUs and CERs, brokerage, advisory and ratings services may be needed to buy, sell, or trade them. The extent to which these services are covered, or perhaps of more concern, not covered by the GATS, may determine how effectively and efficiently these services can be provided.

While the GATS includes MFN and national treatment obligations, it also includes an array of exceptions. While a few members, including the United States, have undertaken commitments to apply national treatment and most favored nation obligations to certain energy-related services, the vast majority of members have not. As a consequence, the energy sector in many countries is characterized by discriminatory barriers to trade in services. *See generally*, Office of the United States Trade Representative, *Report of the Office of the United States Trade*

Representative on Trade-Related Barriers to the Export of Greenhouse Gas Intensity Reducing Technologies 2 (Oct. 2, 2006). Because many developing countries often view national control over natural resources generally and energy resources in particular as critical to their identity, sovereignty, and development, they are unlikely to liberalize trade in energy services without substantial concessions from developed countries.

Chapter 11

THE U.S. NATIONAL CLIMATE CHANGE POLICIES

The United States is one of the world's largest per capita emitter of greenhouse gases. Even though China's overall emissions of greenhouse gases exceeded the annual U.S. emissions in 2007, China's per capita emissions remained about one quarter of the U.S. per capita emissions. On average, each person in the United States emits around 20 tons of carbon per year; in contrast, the worldwide average is 4 tons per person. U.S. vehicle emissions are particularly high: the state of California emits more greenhouse gases from motor vehicles than any other country in the world, except the United States. Moreover, the U.S. historical contribution to greenhouse gas concentrations remains by far the largest in the world.

The enormous U.S. carbon footprint has led to worldwide calls for the United States to commit to binding greenhouse gas emissions targets. In addition, the majority of Americans have expressed support for national laws restricting domestic emissions of greenhouse gases. Despite this, the U.S. government has not yet developed a comprehensive national climate change policy. Instead, most of the national climate change activity in the United States has occurred in the courts, as states, municipalities, and environmental organizations have used litigation to try to force regulation of greenhouse gas emissions.

That does not mean, however, that the United States lacks any national climate policies whatsoever. Since 1978, the United States has had a law aimed at studying and understanding the causes and consequences of climate change. National Climate Program Act, 15 U.S.C. §§ 2901–2908 (1978). More recently, in 2002, the Bush Administration developed a policy to address climate change that is discussed further in Section II. In addition, for several years, Congress has toyed with developing new laws specifically focused on reducing U.S. greenhouse gas emissions. Many commentators believe that it is only a matter of time before Congress passes federal climate change legislation. Indeed, President Obama submitted a budget proposal to Congress that would use revenues from a cap-and-trade law to fund renewable energy development and tax cuts for the middle class. At President Obama's urging, congressional leaders have stated they will propose new comprehensive climate change legislation during 2009. While the fate of any federal climate change law remains uncertain, 2009 could be a pivotal year for greenhouse gas regulation.

This chapter first provides the context for the U.S. domestic approach to climate change mitigation. Section I describes the major sources of U.S. greenhouse gas emissions. Section II then summarizes existing U.S. policies addressing climate change. Section II describes the Bush Administration's climate change policy. Section III then discusses the various bills that members of Congress have proposed to address domestic greenhouse gas emissions. While the exact nature and scope of any future climate change legislation remains uncertain, Congress seems most likely to use emissions trading as the primary regulatory tool, although some members of Congress favor carbon taxes. Section III reviews the current proposals and explores whether they would, if adopted, effectively reduce U.S. greenhouse gas emissions.

I. AN OVERVIEW OF GREENHOUSE GAS EMISSIONS IN THE UNITED STATES

Pursuant to the United Nations Framework Convention on Climate Change (UNFCCC), each Party to the convention must develop an inventory of national greenhouse gas emissions. The Environmental Protection Agency (EPA) fulfills this commitment through the U.S. Greenhouse Gas Inventory, a comprehensive overview of the country's greenhouse gas emissions. As the following excerpts of the inventory show, nearly every sector of the U.S. economy contributes significantly to the country's massive carbon footprint.

ADAPTED FROM THE U.S. ENVIRONMENTAL PROTECTION AGENCY, INVENTORY OF U.S. GREENHOUSE GAS EMISSIONS AND SINKS
1990–2006, ES-1 to ES-20, 2-1 to 2-35 (Apr. 15, 2008)

2.1. Recent Trends in U.S. Greenhouse Gas Emissions

In 2006, total U.S. greenhouse gas emissions were 7,054.2 teragrams of carbon dioxide equivalents (Tg CO_2 Eq.). Overall, total U.S. emissions have risen by 14.7 percent from 1990 to 2006, while the U.S. gross domestic product has increased by 59 percent over the same period. Emissions decreased from 2005 to 2006 by 1.1 percent (75.7 Tg CO_2 Eq.). The following factors were primary contributors to this decrease: (1) compared to 2005, 2006 had warmer winter conditions, which decreased consumption of heating fuels, as well as cooler summer conditions, which reduced demand for electricity, (2) restraint on fuel consumption caused by rising fuel prices, primarily in the transportation sector and (3) increased use of natural gas and renewables in the electric power sector. * * *

As the largest source of U.S. greenhouse gas emissions, carbon dioxide (CO_2) from fossil fuel combustion has accounted for approximately 79 percent of global warming potential (GWP) weighted emissions since 1990, growing slowly from 77 percent of total GWP-weighted emissions in 1990 to 80 percent in 2006. Emissions from this source category grew by 19.3 percent from 1990 to 2006 and were responsible for most of the increase in national emissions during this period. From 2005 to 2006, these emissions decreased by 1.6 percent. Historically, changes in emissions from fossil fuel combustion have been the dominant factor affecting U.S. emission trends.

* * *

Figure [11-1] illustrates the relative contribution of the direct greenhouse gases to total U.S. emissions in 2006. The primary greenhouse gas emitted by human activities in the United States was CO_2, representing approximately 84.8 percent of total greenhouse gas emissions. The largest source of CO_2, and of overall greenhouse gas emissions, was fossil fuel combustion. CH_4 emissions, which have declined from 1990 levels, resulted primarily from enteric fermentation associated with domestic livestock, decomposition of wastes in landfills, and natural gas systems. Agricultural soil management and mobile source fossil fuel combustion were the major sources of N_2O emissions. The emissions of substitutes for ozone depleting substances and emissions of HFC-23 during the production of HCFC-22 were the primary contributors to aggregate HFC emissions. Electrical transmission and distribution systems accounted for most SF_6 emissions, while PFC emissions resulted from semiconductor manufacturing and as a by-product of primary aluminum production.

Figure 11-1: 2006 Greenhouse Gas Emissions by Gas
(percents based on Tg CO_2 Eq.)

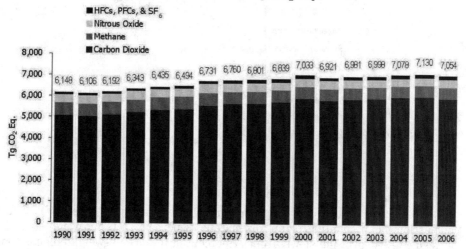

Overall, from 1990 to 2006, total emissions of CO_2 increased by 18.0 percent, while CH_4 and N_2O emissions decreased by 8.4 percent and 4.0 percent, respectively. During the same period, aggregate weighted emissions of HFCs, PFCs, and SF_6 rose by 63.7 percent. HFCs increased by 237.3 percent, while PFCs decreased by 70.9 percent, and SF_6 decreased by 47.0 percent. Despite being emitted in smaller quantities relative to the other principal greenhouse gases, emissions of HFCs, PFCs, and SF_6 are significant because many of them have extremely high global warming potentials and, in the cases of PFCs and SF_6, long atmospheric lifetimes. Conversely, U.S. greenhouse gas emissions were partly offset by carbon sequestration in forests, trees in urban areas, agricultural soils, and landfilled yard trimmings and food scraps, which, in [the] aggregate, offset 12.5 percent of total emissions in 2006. The following sections describe each gas' contribution to total U.S. greenhouse gas emissions in more detail.

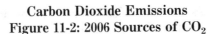

Carbon Dioxide Emissions
Figure 11-2: 2006 Sources of CO$_2$

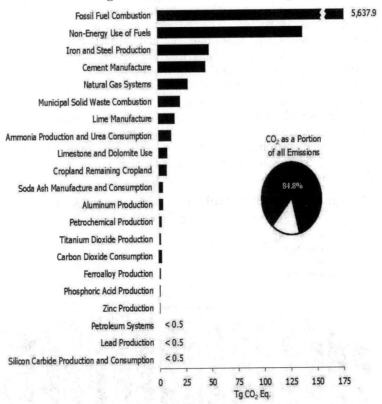

As the largest source of U.S. greenhouse gas emissions, CO$_2$ from fossil fuel combustion has accounted for approximately 79 percent of GWP-weighted emissions since 1990, growing slowly from 77 percent of total GWP-weighted emissions in 1990 to 80 percent in 2006. Emissions of CO$_2$ from fossil fuel combustion increased at an average annual rate of 1.1 percent from 1990 to 2006. The fundamental factors influencing this trend include (1) a generally growing domestic economy over the last 16 years, and (2) significant overall growth in emissions from electricity generation and transportation activities. Between 1990 and 2006, CO$_2$ emissions from fossil fuel combustion increased . . . 19.3 percent. * * *

The four major fuel consuming end-use sectors contributing to CO$_2$ emissions from fossil fuel combustion are industrial, transportation, residential, and commercial. Electricity generation also emits CO$_2$, although these emissions are produced as they consume fossil fuel to provide electricity to one of the four end-use sectors. For the discussion below, electricity generation emissions have been distributed to each end-use sector on the basis of each sector's share of aggregate electricity consumption. * * *

Figure [11-3] and Figure [11-4] summarize CO$_2$ emissions from fossil fuel combustion by end-use sector.

Figure 11-3: 2006 CO$_2$ Emissions from Fossil Fuel Combustion by Sector and Fuel Type

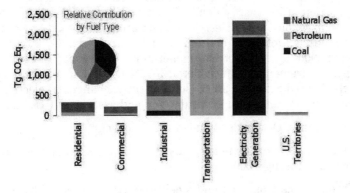

Figure 11-4: 2006 End-Use Sector Emissions of CO$_2$ from Fossil Fuel Combustion

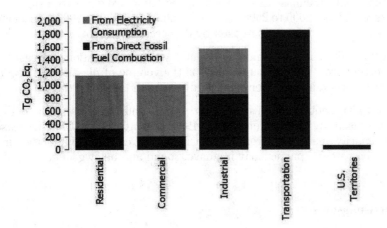

Transportation End-Use Sector. Transportation activities (excluding international bunker fuels) accounted for 33 percent of CO$_2$ emissions from fossil fuel combustion in 2006. Virtually all of the energy consumed in this end-use sector came from petroleum products. Over 60 percent of the emissions resulted from gasoline consumption for personal vehicle use. * * *

Industrial End-Use Sector. Industrial CO$_2$ emissions, resulting both directly from the combustion of fossil fuels and indirectly from the generation of electricity that is consumed by industry, accounted for 28 percent of CO$_2$ from fossil fuel combustion in 2006. Just over half of these emissions resulted from direct fossil fuel combustion to produce steam and/or heat for industrial processes. The remaining emissions resulted from consuming electricity[.] * * *

Residential and Commercial End-Use Sectors. The residential and commercial end-use sectors accounted for 20 and 18 percent, respectively, of CO$_2$ emissions from fossil fuel combustion in 2006. Both sectors relied heavily on electricity for meeting energy demands, with 72 and 79 percent, respectively, of their emissions attributable to electricity consumption for lighting, heating, cooling, and operating appliances. The remaining emissions were due to the consumption of natural gas and petroleum for heating and cooking.

Electricity Generation. The United States relies on electricity to meet a significant portion of its energy demands, especially for lighting, electric motors, heating, and air conditioning. Electricity generators consumed 36 percent of U.S. energy from fossil fuels and emitted 41 percent of the CO_2 from fossil fuel combustion in 2006. . . . [E]lectricity generators rely on coal for over half of their total energy requirements and accounted for 94 percent of all coal consumed for energy in the United States in 2006. Consequently, changes in electricity demand have a significant impact on coal consumption and associated CO_2 emissions.

Other significant CO_2 trends included the following:

- CO_2 emissions from non-energy use of fossil fuels have increased 18 percent from 1990 through 2006 . . . .

- CO_2 emissions from iron and steel production increased by 5.3 percent in 2006, but have declined overall by 43 percent from 1990 through 2006, due to restructuring of the industry, technological improvements, and increased scrap utilization.

- In 2006, CO_2 emissions from cement manufacture decreased slightly by 0.4 percent from 2005 to 2006. . . . Overall, from 1990 to 2006, emissions from cement manufacture increased by 37 percent . . .

- CO_2 emissions from municipal solid waste combustion increased by 91 percent from 1990 through 2006, as the volume of plastics and other fossil carbon-containing materials in municipal solid waste grew. * * *

- Net CO_2 sequestration from Land Use, Land-Use Change, and Forestry increased by 20 percent from 1990 through 2006. This increase was primarily due to an increase in the rate of net carbon accumulation in forest carbon stocks, particularly in aboveground and belowground tree biomass. . . .

Methane Emissions

. . . Anthropogenic sources of CH_4 include landfills, natural gas and petroleum systems, agricultural activities, coal mining, wastewater treatment, stationary and mobile combustion, and certain industrial processes (see Figure [11-5]).

Figure 11-5: 2006 Sources of CH$_4$

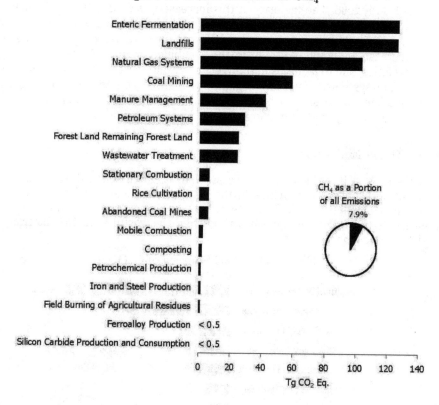

Some significant trends in U.S. emissions of CH$_4$ include the following:

- Enteric [f]ermentation [from livestock] is the largest anthropogenic source of CH$_4$ emissions in the United States. In 2006, enteric fermentation CH$_4$ emissions were approximately 22.7 percent of total CH$_4$ emissions, which represents a decline of 0.6 percent, since 1990. Despite this overall decline in emissions, the last two years have shown a slight increase in emissions.

- Landfills are the second largest anthropogenic source of CH$_4$ emissions in the United States, accounting for approximately 22.6 percent of total CH$_4$ emissions in 2006. From 1990 to 2006, net CH$_4$ emissions from landfills decreased by 16 percent, with small increases occurring in some interim years, including 2006. This downward trend in overall emissions is the result of increases in the amount of landfill gas collected and combusted, which has more than offset the additional CH$_4$ emissions resulting from an increase in the amount of municipal solid waste landfilled.

- CH$_4$ emissions from natural gas systems were 102.4 Tg CO$_2$ Eq. in 2006; down 18 percent since 1990. This decline has been due to improvements in technology and management practices, as well as some replacement of old equipment.

- In 2006, CH$_4$ emissions from coal mining were 58.5 Tg CO$_2$ Eq., a 2.5 percent increase over 2005 emission levels. The overall decline of 30 percent from 1990 results from the mining of less gassy coal from underground mines and the increased use of CH$_4$ collected from degasification systems.

- CH_4 emissions from manure management increased by 34 percent [from 1990 to] 2006. The majority of this increase was from swine and dairy cow manure, since the general trend in manure management is one of increasing use of liquid systems, which tends to produce greater CH_4 emissions. The increase in liquid systems is the combined result of a shift to larger facilities, and to facilities in the West and Southwest, all of which tend to use liquid systems. Also, new regulations limiting the application of manure nutrients have shifted manure management practices at smaller dairies from daily spread to manure managed and stored on site.

Nitrous Oxide Emissions

N_2O is produced by biological processes that occur in soil and water and by a variety of anthropogenic activities in the agricultural, energy-related, industrial, and waste management fields. While total N_2O emissions are much lower than CO_2 emissions, N_2O is approximately 300 times more powerful than CO_2 at trapping heat in the atmosphere. * * *

Figure 11-6: 2006 Sources of N₂O

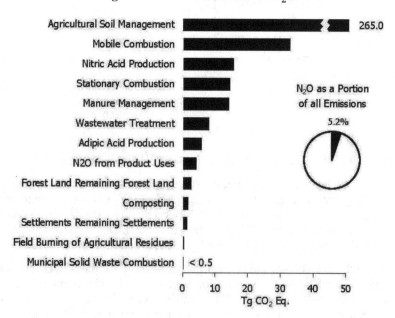

Some significant trends in U.S. emissions of N_2O include the following:

- Agricultural soils produced approximately 72 percent of N_2O emissions in the United States in 2006. . . . N_2O emissions from this source have not shown any significant long-term trend, as they are highly sensitive to the amount of N applied to soils, which has not changed significantly over the time-period, and to weather patterns and crop type.

- In 2006, N_2O emissions from mobile combustion were 33.1 Tg CO_2 Eq. (approximately 9 percent of U.S. N_2O emissions). From 1990 to 2006, N_2O emissions from mobile combustion decreased by 24 percent. * * *

- N_2O emissions from adipic acid production were 5.9 Tg CO_2 Eq. in 2006, and have decreased significantly in recent years from the widespread installation of pollution control measures. Emissions from adipic acid production have decreased 61 percent since 1990. . . .

HFC, PFC, and SF_6 Emissions

HFCs and PFCs are families of synthetic chemicals that are used as alternatives to the ODSs, which are being phased out under the *Montreal Protocol* and Clean Air Act Amendments of 1990. * * *

Other [emission] sources of these gases include HCFC-22 production, electrical transmission and distribution systems, semiconductor manufacturing, aluminum production, and magnesium production and processing (see Figure [11-7]).

Figure 11-7: 2006 Sources of HFCs, PFCs, and SF_6

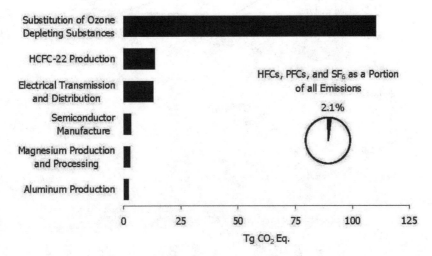

Some significant trends in U.S. HFC, PFC, and SF_6 emissions include the following:

- Emissions resulting from the substitution of ozone depleting substances (e.g., CFCs) have been increasing from small amounts in 1990 to 110.4 Tg CO_2 Eq. in 2006. Emissions from substitutes for ozone depleting substances are both the largest and the fastest growing source of HFC, PFC, and SF_6 emissions. * * *

- HFC emissions from the production of HCFC-22 decreased by 62 percent from 1990 through 2006, due to a steady decline in the emission rate of HFC-23 (i.e., the amount of HFC-23 emitted per kilogram of HCFC-22 manufactured) . . .

- SF_6 emissions from electric power transmission and distribution systems decreased by 51 percent from 1990 to 2006, primarily because of higher purchase prices for SF_6 and efforts by industry to reduce emissions.

- PFC emissions from aluminum production decreased by 87 percent from 1990 to 2006, due to both industry emission reduction efforts and lower domestic aluminum production.

Overview of Sector Emissions and Trends

Over the sixteen-year period of 1990 to 2006, total emissions in the Energy, Industrial Processes, and Agriculture sectors climbed by 17 percent, 7 percent, and 1 percent, respectively. Emissions decreased in the Waste sector by 10 percent, while emissions from the Solvent and Other Product Use sectors [have] been essentially constant. Over the same period, estimates of net carbon sequestration in the Land Use, Land-Use Change, and Forestry sector increased by [17 percent].

Figure 11-8: U.S. Greenhouse Gas Emissions and Sinks by Chapter/IPCC Sector

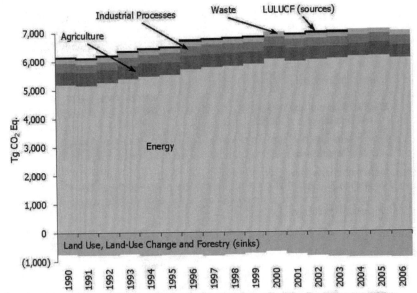

Note: Relatively smaller amounts of GWP-weighted emissions are also emitted from the Solvent and Other Product Use sectors

Energy

The Energy chapter contains emissions of all greenhouse gases resulting from stationary and mobile energy activities including fuel combustion and fugitive fuel emissions. Energy-related activities, primarily fossil fuel combustion, accounted for the vast majority of U.S. CO_2 emissions for the period of 1990 through 2006. In 2006, approximately 83 percent of the energy consumed in the United States (on a Btu basis) was produced through the combustion of fossil fuels. The remaining 17 percent came from other energy sources such as hydropower, biomass, nuclear, wind, and solar energy (see Figure 11-9). Energy-related activities are also responsible for CH_4 and N_2O emissions (37 percent and 13 percent of total U.S. emissions of each gas, respectively). Overall, emission sources in the Energy chapter accounted for a combined 86.1 percent of total U.S. greenhouse gas emissions in 2006.

Figure 11-9: 2006 U.S. Energy Consumption by Energy Source

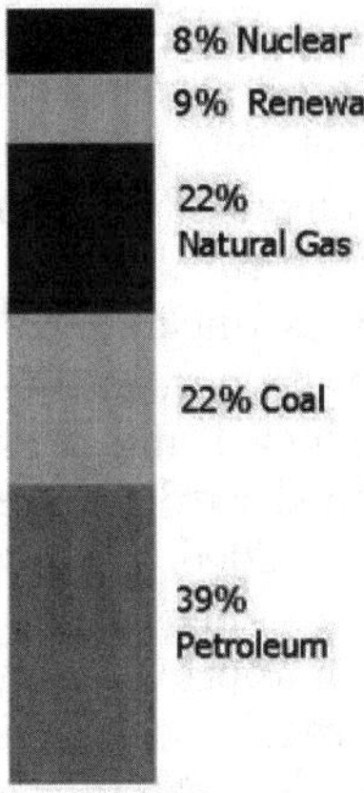

8% Nuclear

9% Renewable

22% Natural Gas

22% Coal

39% Petroleum

Industrial Processes

The Industrial Processes chapter contains by-product or fugitive emissions of greenhouse gases from industrial processes not directly related to energy activities such as fossil fuel combustion. . . . Overall, emission sources in the Industrial Process chapter accounted for 4.5 percent of U.S. greenhouse gas emissions in 2006.

Solvent and Other Product Use

The Solvent and Other Product Use chapter contains greenhouse gas emissions that are produced as a by-product of various solvent and other product uses. In the United States, emissions from N_2O from Product Uses, the only source of greenhouse gas emissions from this sector, accounted for less than 0.1 percent of total U.S. anthropogenic greenhouse gas emissions on a carbon equivalent basis in 2006.

Agriculture

The Agricultural chapter contains anthropogenic emissions from agricultural activities (except fuel combustion, which is addressed in the Energy chapter, and agricultural CO_2 fluxes, which are addressed in the Land Use, Land-Use Change, and Forestry Chapter). Agricultural activities contribute directly to emissions of greenhouse gases through a variety of processes, including the following source categories: enteric fermentation in domestic livestock, livestock manure management, rice cultivation, agricultural soil management, and field burning of agricultural residues. CH_4 and N_2O were the primary greenhouse gases emitted by agricultural activities. CH_4 emissions from enteric fermentation and manure management represented about 23 percent and 7 percent of total CH_4 emissions from anthropogenic activities, respectively, in 2006. Agricultural soil management activities such as fertilizer application and other cropping practices were the largest source of U.S. N_2O emissions in 2006, accounting for 72 percent. In 2006, emission sources accounted for in the Agricultural chapters were responsible for 6.4 percent of total U.S. greenhouse gas emissions.

Land Use, Land-Use Change, and Forestry

The Land Use, Land-Use Change, and Forestry chapter contains emissions of CH_4 and N_2O, and emissions and removals of CO_2 from forest management, other land-use activities, and land-use change. Forest management practices, tree planting in urban areas, the management of agricultural soils, and the landfilling of yard trimmings and food scraps have resulted in a net uptake (sequestration) of carbon in the United States. Forests (including vegetation, soils, and harvested wood) accounted for approximately 84 percent of total 2006 net CO_2 flux, urban trees accounted for 11 percent, mineral and organic soil carbon stock changes accounted for 5 percent, and landfilled yard trimmings and food scraps accounted for 1 percent of the total net flux in 2006. . . . Land use, land-use change, and forestry activities in 2006 resulted in a net carbon sequestration of 883.7 Tg CO_2 Eq. . . . This represents an offset of approximately 14.8 percent of total U.S. CO_2 emissions, or 12.5 percent of total greenhouse gas emissions in 2006. Between 1990 and 2006, total land use, land-use change, and forestry net carbon flux resulted in a 20 percent increase in CO_2 sequestration, primarily due to an increase in the rate of net carbon accumulation in forest carbon stocks, particularly in aboveground and belowground tree biomass. * * *

Waste

The Waste chapter contains emissions from waste management activities (except waste incineration, which is addressed in the Energy chapter). Landfills were the largest source of anthropogenic CH_4 emissions in the Waste chapter, accounting for 23 percent of total U.S. CH_4 emissions. Additionally, wastewater treatment accounts for 4 percent of U.S. CH_4 emissions. . . . Emissions of CH_4 and N_2O from composting grew from 1990 to 2006. . . . Overall, in 2006, emission sources accounted for in the Waste chapter generated 2.3 percent of total U.S. greenhouse gas emissions.

Emissions by Economic Sector

* * * This section reports emissions by the following economic sectors: Residential, Commercial, Industry, Transportation, Electricity Generation, Agriculture, and U.S. Territories. . . .

Figure 11-10: Emissions Allocated to Economic Sectors

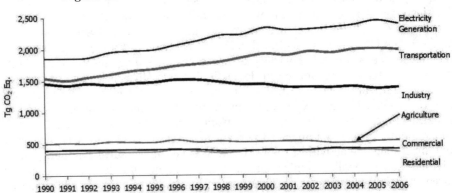

Using this categorization, emissions from electricity generation accounted for the largest portion (34 percent) of U.S. greenhouse gas emissions in 2006.

Transportation activities, in aggregate, accounted for the second largest portion (28 percent). Emissions from industry accounted for 19 percent of U.S. greenhouse gas emissions in 2006. In contrast to electricity generation and transportation, emissions from industry have in general declined over the past decade. The long-term decline in these emissions has been due to structural changes in the U.S. economy (i.e., shifts from a manufacturing-based to a service-based economy), fuel switching, and energy efficiency improvements. The remaining 19 percent of U.S. greenhouse gas emissions were contributed by the residential, agriculture, and commercial sectors, plus emissions from U.S. territories. * * *

Electricity is ultimately consumed in the economic sectors described above. To distribute electricity emissions among end-use sectors, emissions from the source categories assigned to electricity generation were allocated to the residential, commercial, industry, transportation, and agriculture economic sectors according to retail sales of electricity . . . .

When emissions from electricity are distributed among these sectors, industry accounts for the largest share of U.S. greenhouse gas emissions (29 percent) in 2006. Emissions from the residential and commercial sectors also increase substantially when emissions from electricity are included, due to their relatively large share of electricity consumption (e.g., lighting, appliances, etc.). Transportation activities remain the second largest contributor to total U.S. emissions (28 percent). In all sectors except agriculture, CO_2 accounts for more than 80 percent of greenhouse gas emissions, primarily from the combustion of fossil fuels.

Figure [11-11] shows the trend in these emissions by sector from 1990 to 2006.

Figure 11-11: Emissions with Electricity Distributed to Economic Sector

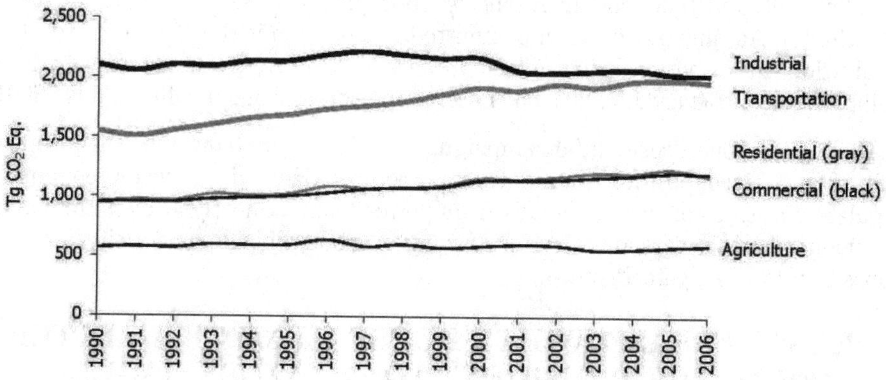

QUESTIONS AND DISCUSSION

1. *Regulating Upstream or Downstream.* Policymakers must decide on whom they should impose greenhouse gas reduction requirements. Consider, for example, the greenhouse gas emissions associated with electricity production and use. Regulating greenhouse gas emissions at the source of electricity production (e.g., the coal-fired power plant) would cover more than 86 percent of all electricity-related U.S. greenhouse gas emissions and yet apply to a relatively small number of facilities. Regulating emissions at the downstream use, in contrast, would probably capture a slightly larger quantity of emissions, but require agencies to develop controls for thousands more facilities in a wide array of industrial

categories. Upstream regulation, therefore, would seem to make more sense administratively. However, some believe that upstream regulation would be unfair, because it would place an undue burden on a handful of facilities to reduce greenhouse gases, when the end users of electricity are responsible for the high energy use in the United States. Regulation of upstream sources may also present risks of leakage, if other new energy sources could develop, but end uses are not regulated. To date, most U.S. policies and regulatory proposals attempt to regulate both upstream and downstream. In so doing, they create very comprehensive, yet extraordinarily complex, regulatory systems. Is this the best approach?

II. THE BUSH ADMINISTRATION'S POLICY ON CLIMATE CHANGE

Until very recently, the United States government has resisted international or domestic actions to mitigate climate change. During the Kyoto Protocol negotiations, the U.S. Senate passed a "Sense of the Senate" resolution, with a 95-0 vote, proclaiming that the United States would not ratify a climate change treaty that did not establish binding emissions limitations for developing countries. When the Clinton Administration nonetheless signed the Kyoto Protocol in September 1998, the Senate responded with an appropriations bill prohibiting EPA from spending any of its funding " propose or issue rules, regulations, decrees or orders for the purpose of implementation, or in preparation for implementation, of the Kyoto Protocol." P. L. 105-276, Departments of Veterans Affairs and Housing and Urban Development, and Independent Agencies Appropriations Act, 1999 (Oct. 21, 1998). The Clinton Administration then committed not to submit the Kyoto Protocol for ratification. *See* George Pring, *The United States Perspective, in* Kyoto: From Principles to Practice 185, 205–06 (Peter Cameron & Donald Zillman eds., 2001).

During the 2000 Presidential campaign, then-Governor George W. Bush repeatedly stated his opposition to the Kyoto Protocol. He did, however, commit to regulate emissions of carbon dioxide from power plants. Shortly after taking office, President Bush reversed course regarding carbon dioxide and reiterated his opposition to the Kyoto Protocol.

PRESS RELEASE, WHITE HOUSE, TEXT OF A LETTER FROM THE PRESIDENT TO SENATORS HAGEL, HELMS, CRAIG, AND ROBERTS
(Mar. 13, 2001)

Thank you for your letter of March 6, 2001, asking for the Administration's views on global climate change, in particular the Kyoto Protocol and efforts to regulate carbon dioxide under the Clean Air Act. My Administration takes the issue of global climate change very seriously.

As you know, I oppose the Kyoto Protocol because it exempts 80 percent of the world, including major population centers such as China and India, from compliance, and would cause serious harm to the U.S. economy. The Senate's vote, 95-0, shows that there is a clear consensus that the Kyoto Protocol is an unfair and ineffective means of addressing global climate change concerns.

As you also know, I support a comprehensive and balanced national energy policy that takes into account the importance of improving air quality. Consistent with this balanced approach, I intend to work with the Congress on a multipollutant strategy to require power plants to reduce emissions of sulfur dioxide, nitrogen oxides, and mercury. Any such strategy would include phasing in reductions over a reasonable period of time, providing regulatory certainty, and offering market-based incentives to help industry meet the targets. I do not believe, however, that the government should impose on power plants mandatory emissions reductions for carbon dioxide, which is not a "pollutant" under the Clean Air Act.

A recently released Department of Energy Report, "Analysis of Strategies for Reducing Multiple Emissions from Power Plants," concluded that including caps on carbon dioxide emissions as part of a multiple emissions strategy would lead to an even more dramatic shift from coal to natural gas for electric power generation and significantly higher electricity prices compared to scenarios in which only sulfur dioxide and nitrogen oxides were reduced.

This is important new information that warrants a reevaluation, especially at a time of rising energy prices and a serious energy shortage. Coal generates more than half of America's electricity supply. At a time when California has already experienced energy shortages, and other Western states are worried about price and availability of energy this summer, we must be very careful not to take actions that could harm consumers. This is especially true given the incomplete state of scientific knowledge of the causes of, and solutions to, global climate change and the lack of commercially available technologies for removing and storing carbon dioxide.

Consistent with these concerns, we will continue to fully examine global climate change issues — including the science, technologies, market-based systems, and innovative options for addressing concentrations of greenhouse gases in the atmosphere. I am very optimistic that, with the proper focus and working with our friends and allies, we will be able to develop technologies, market incentives, and other creative ways to address global climate change.

I look forward to working with you and others to address global climate change issues in the context of a national energy policy that protects our environment, consumers, and economy.

Sincerely,

GEORGE W. BUSH

Approximately a year later, President Bush released a plan which the White House claimed would limit domestic greenhouse gas emissions without jeopardizing economic prosperity.

WHITE HOUSE, THE U.S. GLOBAL CLIMATE CHANGE POLICY: A NEW APPROACH, EXECUTIVE SUMMARY
1–4 (Feb. 14, 2002)

The President announced a new approach to the challenge of global climate change. This approach is designed to harness the power of markets and technological innovation. It holds the promise of a new partnership with the developing world. And it recognizes that climate change is a complex, long-term challenge that will require a sustained effort over many generations. As the President has said, "The policy challenge is to act in a serious and sensible way, given the limits of our knowledge. While scientific uncertainties remain, we can begin now to address the factors that contribute to climate change."

While investments today in science will increase our understanding of this challenge, our investments in advanced energy and sequestration technologies will provide the breakthroughs we need to dramatically reduce our emissions in the longer term. In the near term, we will vigorously pursue emissions reductions even in the absence of complete knowledge. Our approach recognizes that sustained economic growth is an essential part of the solution, not the problem. Economic growth will make possible the needed investment in research, development, and deployment of advanced technologies. This strategy is one that should offer developing countries the incentive and means to join with us in tackling this challenge together. Significantly, the President's plan will:

- Reduce the Greenhouse Gas Intensity of the U.S. Economy by 18 Percent in the Next Ten Years. Greenhouse gas intensity measures the ratio of greenhouse gas (GHG) emissions to economic output. This new approach focuses on reducing the growth of GHG emissions, while sustaining the economic growth needed to finance investment in new, clean energy technologies. It sets America on a path to slow the growth of greenhouse gas emissions, and — as the science justifies — to stop and then reverse that growth:

  - In efficiency terms, the 183 metric tons of emissions per million dollars GDP that we emit today will be lowered to 151 metric tons per million dollars GDP in 2012.

  - Beyond that, the President's commitment will achieve 100 million metric tons of reduced emissions in 2012 alone, with more than 500 million metric tons in cumulative savings over the entire decade.

  - This goal is comparable to the average progress that nations participating in the Kyoto Protocol are required to achieve.

Reduce GHG Emission Intensity 18% Over the Next Decade

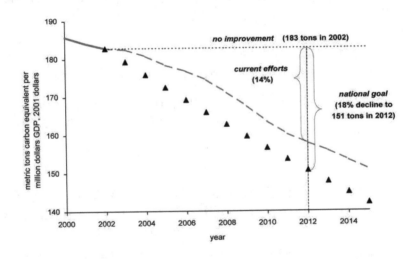

- Substantially Improve the Emission Reduction Registry. The President directed the Secretary of Energy . . . to propose improvements to the current voluntary emission reduction registration program under section 1605(b) of the 1992 Energy Policy Act within 120 days. These improvements will enhance measurement accuracy, reliability and verifiability, working with and taking into account emerging domestic and international approaches.

- Protect and Provide Transferable Credits for Emissions Reduction. The President directed the Secretary of Energy to recommend reforms to ensure that businesses and individuals that register reductions are not penalized under a future climate policy, and to give transferable credits to companies that can show real emissions reductions.

- Review Progress Toward Goal and Take Additional Action if Necessary. If, in 2012, we find that we are not on track toward meeting our goal, and sound science justifies further policy action, the United States will respond with additional measures that may include a broad, market-based program as well as additional incentives and voluntary measures designed to accelerate technology development and deployment.

- Increase Funding for America's Commitment to Climate Change. The President's FY '03 budget seeks $4.5 billion in total climate spending — an increase of $700 million. This commitment is unmatched in the world. . . .

- Take Action on the Science and Technology Review. The Secretary of Commerce and Secretary of Energy have completed their review of the federal government's science and technology research portfolios and recommended a path forward. As a result of their review, the President has established a new management structure to advance and coordinate climate change science and technology research.

  - The President has established a Cabinet-level Committee on Climate Change Science and Technology Integration to oversee this effort.

  - The President's FY '03 budget proposal dedicates $1.7 billion to fund basic scientific research on climate change and $1.3 billion to fund research on advanced energy and sequestration technologies.

- Implement a Comprehensive Range of New and Expanded Domestic Policies, Including:

  - Tax Incentives for Renewable Energy, Cogeneration, and New Technology. The President's FY '03 budget seeks $555 million in clean energy tax incentives, as the first part of a $4.6 billion commitment over the next five years ($7.1 billion over the next 10 years). These tax credits will spur investments in renewable energy (solar, wind, and biomass), hybrid and fuel cell vehicles, cogeneration, and landfill gas conversion. * * *

  - Business Challenges. The President has challenged American businesses to make specific commitments to improving the greenhouse gas intensity of their operations and to reduce emissions.

  - Transportation Programs. The Administration is promoting the development of fuel-efficient motor vehicles and trucks, researching options for producing cleaner fuels, and implementing programs to improve energy efficiency. The President is committed to expanding federal research partnerships with industry, providing market-based incentives and updating current regulatory programs that advance our progress in this important area. This commitment includes expanding fuel cell research, in particular through the "Freedom-CAR" initiative. The President's FY '03 budget seeks more than $3 billion in tax credits over 11 years for consumers to purchase fuel cell and hybrid vehicles. The Secretary of Transportation has asked the Congressional leadership to work with him on legislation that would authorize the Department of Transportation to reform the Corporate Average Fuel Economy (CAFE) program, fully considering the recent National Academy Sciences report, so that we can safely improve fuel economy for cars and trucks.

- Carbon Sequestration. The President's FY '03 budget requests over $3 billion — a $1 billion increase above the baseline — as the first part of a ten year (2002–2011) commitment to implement and improve the conservation title of the Farm Bill, which will significantly enhance the natural storage of carbon. The President also directed the Secretary of Agriculture to provide recommendations for further, targeted incentives aimed at forest and agricultural sequestration of greenhouse gases. The President further directed the Secretary of Agriculture . . . to develop accounting rules and guidelines for crediting sequestration projects, taking into account emerging domestic and international approaches.

- Promote New and Expanded International Policies to Complement Our Domestic Program. The President's approach seeks to expand cooperation internationally to meet the challenge of climate change, including:

  - Investing $25 Million in Climate Observation Systems in Developing Countries.

  - Tripling Funding for "Debt-for-Nature" Forest Conservation Programs. . . . Under [the Tropical Forest Conservation Act (TFCA)] developing countries agree to protect their tropical forests from logging, avoiding emissions and preserving the substantial carbon sequestration services they provide.

QUESTIONS AND DISCUSSION

1. *Elements of the Bush Climate Change Policy.* The overall goal of the Administration's policy was to reduce U.S. greenhouse gas intensity by 18 percent by 2012. To implement this goal, the policy promoted a number of strategies designed to: 1) improve renewable energy and industrial power systems, 2) improve fuel economy, 3) promote domestic carbon sequestration, and 4) encourage businesses to reduce their emissions. Two of the strategies involved mandatory requirements. First, the Administration finalized a rule requiring vehicles to include tire pressure monitoring systems. Second, the Administration promulgated a regulation raising fuel economy standards for light trucks from 20.7 miles per gallon to 22.3 miles per gallon by 2007. All the other strategies either involved funding for research and development, tax deductions or credits to incentivize renewable energy technologies, or other general calls for businesses to voluntarily become more efficient. Based on the Administration's and Congress' stated concerns that climate change policies not disrupt the U.S. economy, does this approach make sense? Beyond those concerns, do you think a climate change policy focused on incentives — rather than mandates — could successfully limit greenhouse gas emissions? To what extent, if at all, does the Bush Administration policy reflect current understanding of climate change impacts or a focus on the long-term goals being championed by climate scientists?

2. *Greenhouse Gas Intensity.* Some policymakers believe that developing countries should seek reductions in "greenhouse gas intensity," rather than

absolute reductions in greenhouse gas emissions. *See* Chapter 9. Should developed countries similarly use targets based on greenhouse gas intensity? Is there a good reason to use greenhouse gas intensity for developing countries, but *not* for developed countries like the United States? Consider the comments of the Pew Center on Global Climate Change.

PEW CENTER ON GLOBAL CLIMATE CHANGE, ANALYSIS OF PRESIDENT BUSH'S CLIMATE CHANGE PLAN
1–3 (Feb. 2002)*

A new climate change strategy for the United States announced by President Bush on February 14, 2002, sets a voluntary "greenhouse gas intensity" target for the nation, expands existing programs encouraging companies to voluntarily report and reduce their greenhouse gas emissions, and proposes increased federal funding for climate change science and technology development. Some elements of the Administration's strategy may provide additional incentive to companies to voluntarily reduce greenhouse gas emissions. However, the Administration's target — an 18 percent reduction in emissions *intensity* between now and 2012 — will allow *actual* emissions to increase 12 percent over the same period. Emissions will continue to grow at nearly the same rate as at present.

Greenhouse Gas Intensity Target

Different types of targets can be used to limit or reduce emissions. One approach is an "absolute" target requiring that emissions be reduced by a specified amount. This is the approach taken by both the United Nations Framework Convention on Climate Change (UNFCCC), which set non-binding emissions targets for developed countries and was ratified by the U.S. Senate; and by the Kyoto Protocol, which sets binding targets but was rejected by the Administration.

The Administration's strategy instead sets a target for greenhouse gas intensity: the ratio of greenhouse gas emissions (GHGs) to economic output expressed in gross domestic product (GDP). This approach minimizes economic impact by allowing emissions to rise or fall with economic output; however, it provides no assurance that a given level of environmental protection will be achieved since the degree of environmental protection is measured in relation to GDP. Theoretically a GHG intensity target can lead to a net reduction in emissions, but only if it is sufficiently stringent. The Administration's target — an 18 percent improvement in GHG intensity over the next decade — allows a substantial increase in net emissions.

In 1990, total U.S. GHG emissions were 1,671 million metric tons in carbon equivalents (MMTCE) or 6,128 million metric tons in carbon dioxide equivalents (MMTCO$_2$E). As of 2000, total U.S. GHG emissions were 14.1 percent above 1990 levels, or 1,907 MMTCE (6,994 MMTCO$_2$E).

Although total emissions continued to rise, greenhouse gas intensity in fact fell over the last two decades. Contributing factors include energy efficiency improvements, the introduction of new information technologies, and the continued transition from heavy industry to less energy-intensive, service-oriented industries. In the 1980s greenhouse gas intensity fell by 21 percent. During the 1990s greenhouse gas intensity fell by 16 percent. The Administration's strategy aims to cut greenhouse gas intensity to a level of 151 metric tons carbon equivalent per million dollars of GDP by 2012, 18 percent below its present level. While this would represent a very modest improvement over the "business as usual" emissions projections for 2012 used by the Administration, it appears to continue the same trend of GHG-intensity reductions and GHG emissions increases experienced over the last two decades.

In terms of actual emissions, total U.S. GHG emissions would grow 12 percent by 2012, resulting in GHG emissions of 2,155 MMTCE (7,900 MMTCO$_2$E). Emissions in 2012 would be 30 percent above 1990 levels . . . The Administration proposes to achieve its GHG intensity target entirely through voluntary measures. Prior experience has shown that despite the existence of a range of voluntary government programs to encourage early reductions, despite significant actions by individual companies, and despite improvements in greenhouse gas intensity, emissions continue to rise as these gains are outpaced by economic expansion, changing consumer preferences, and population growth. Further, because the target (1) is voluntary, (2) represents only a slight change from the "business as usual" path, and (3) does not appear to advance specific policy solutions, it is unclear how this goal will be translated into actual reductions in GHG intensity across various sectors of the economy.

---

3.   In its announcement, the Bush Administration describes its intensity goals as "comparable to the average progress that nations participating in the Kyoto Protocol are required to achieve." Recall that the parties to the Kyoto Protocol agreed to reduce their emissions five percent from 1990 levels by 2012. The Bush Administration's plan allowed an increase in emissions at least through 2012. In what way, then, are the emission reduction goals "comparable"?

4.   In April 2008, President Bush announced that the United States was "on track" toward meeting the Administration's goal of reducing the country's greenhouse gas intensity by 18 percent by 2012. Press Release, President Bush Discusses Climate Change (April 16, 2008). At the same time, the President outlined a new national goal: "to stop the growth of U.S. greenhouse gas emissions by 2025." *Id.* Under this new national goal, what do you think the emissions target in 2025 would be? How does stabilizing greenhouse gas emissions at 2025 levels compare to the commitments recommended by leading scientists (*see* Chapter 1) or proposed by Europe in the post-Kyoto negotiations (*see* Chapter 9)?

5.   The Bush Administration has often stated that the United States cannot afford significant cuts in greenhouse gas emissions. In 2003, the Congressional Budget Office (CBO) released a report analyzing the economics of climate change. The report provided several reasons why the uncertainty associated with potential climate change in the future may not justify the high costs of taking swift action now. These included:

> Much of the energy-using capital stock is in the form of very long lived power plants, buildings, and machinery. Gradual adjustment would give people time to use up the existing stock and replace it with more-efficient equipment.

> When viewed from the present, the cost of reducing emissions in the future is cheaper because of discounting.

> Technological change will probably lower the cost of controlling emissions. (In addition, it might take a long time to develop alternative technologies, and there would be more incentive to engage in research and development over the long term if it was fairly certain that the policies in

place were gradually going to create a large market for nonfossil energy.)

People are likely to be wealthier in the future and therefore may find it easier to pay to reduce emissions. If income and wealth grow and technology improves as expected, future generations may find it relatively easy to cope with the impacts of climate change and to gradually impose increasingly strict restraints on emissions to avert further change.

At least for carbon dioxide, emissions that occur sooner rather than later will have more time to be absorbed from the atmosphere by the oceans. As a result, any given future target for concentrations could be met with somewhat greater total emissions over the next century if the bulk of the emissions occurred early on.

CBO, *The Economics of Climate Change: A Primer* 30 (April 2003). What do you think of these justifications? Are there other, stronger economic reasons that support a delay in taking action to mitigate climate change? What economic reasons argue in favor of taking immediate action to reduce greenhouse gas emissions? Consider these questions in light of the discussion of economics in Chapter 2.

6. Based on early signals sent by the new Obama Administration, it seems likely that President Obama intends to abandon the intensity targets and voluntary aspects of the Bush Climate Change Policy and to pursue legislation requiring mandatory domestic greenhouse gas reductions. Throughout the campaign, then-Senator Obama expressed his support for domestic legislation and U.S. participation in the Kyoto Protocol. Approximately a month after winning the presidential election, President Obama announced that he had selected Carol Browner, the former EPA Administrator during the Clinton Administration, to serve as the White House "climate czar" and run the newly created White House Office on Energy and Climate Change. Ms. Browner had submitted an amicus brief to the Supreme Court in the *Massachusetts v. EPA* litigation, supporting regulation of greenhouse gases under the Clean Air Act. *See* Chapters 12 and 13 for further discussion of *Massachusetts v. EPA*. Ms. Browner has also expressed her support for domestic climate change legislation. Several other new members of the Obama Administration have similarly advocated for mandatory greenhouse gas reductions under either a cap-and-trade program or the Clean Air Act, or both. Finally, President Obama has based portions of his 2010 budget proposal on the assumption that Congress will have enacted a cap-and-trade law by the time the 2010 budget takes effect, in late 2009. The details of this proposal are discussed below in Section II.

7. *Other U.S. Laws Addressing Climate Change.* Although the Congress has not enacted any statute curbing greenhouse gas emissions, it has not been completely silent on climate change. A variety of statutes authorize research or reporting on climate change. *See, e.g.,* National Climate Program Act, § 5, 92 Stat. 601, codified as amended at 15 U.S.C. § 2901 *et seq.* (establishing a National Climate Program to promote climate change research); Global Climate Protection Act of 1987, Pub. L. No. 100–204 § 1103, 101 Stat. 1408–1409 (directing EPA and the Secretary of State to develop a coordinated national policy on global climate change); Global Change Research Act of 1990, Tit. I, 104 Stat. 3097, codified as amended at 15 U.S.C. §§ 2921–2938 (requiring the "development and coordination of a comprehensive and integrated United States research program" to aid in "understand[ing] . . . human-induced and natural processes of climate change"); Global Climate Change Prevention Act of 1990, 104 Stat. 4058, 7 U.S.C. § 6701 *et seq.* (directing the Department of Agriculture to study the effects of climate change on forestry and agriculture); Energy Policy Act of 1992, §§ 1601–1609, 106 Stat. 2999, codified as amended at 42 U.S.C. §§ 13381–13388 (requiring the Secretary of Energy to report on information pertaining to climate change).

8.   The United States has insisted it will not agree to binding international commitments to reduce greenhouse gas emissions until large developing countries like China, India and Brazil also agree to binding commitments. As a result, the United States has initiated a "major emitters" negotiating process in parallel to the post-Kyoto negotiations. The current U.S. negotiating position and that of other countries was discussed further in Chapter 9.

III.   LEGISLATIVE PROPOSALS TO ADDRESS CLIMATE CHANGE

Over the past few years, Congress has become much more active in its efforts to address U.S. contributions to global climate change. In recent years, the Senate has passed various "Sense of the Senate" resolutions, which recognize that human-induced climate change is occurring and that the United States has an obligation to act to curb the country's greenhouse gas emissions. One such resolution, adopted by the Senate on June 22, 2005, as an amendment to the Energy Policy Act of 2005, stated that "Congress should enact a comprehensive and effective national program of mandatory, market-based limits and incentives on emissions of greenhouse gases that slow, stop, and reverse the growth of such emissions. . . . " S. Res. 866, 109th Cong., 151 Cong. Rec. S7033, S7033 (2005). Another recent "Sense of the Senate" resolution, passed by the Senate Foreign Relations Committee, called on the United States to "address global climate change through the negotiation of fair and effective international commitments." S. Res. 312, The Lugar-Biden Climate Change Resolution, 1 (passed by the Senate Foreign Relations Committee on May 23, 2006). Congress has also begun to develop domestic legislation to create a legally binding framework to lower greenhouse gas emissions. The number of proposed bills in Congress that relate to climate change has increased dramatically in the past decade.

> The number of climate change-related legislative proposals increased from seven introduced in the 105th Congress (1997–1998) to 25 in the 106th Congress (1999–2000), to over 80 in the 107th Congress (2001–2002) to 96 in the 108th Congress (2003–2004). Fifty-nine such legislative proposals have been introduced to date in the 109th Congress (2005–2006). Congressional efforts to deal with global warming have increased dramatically over the past few years.

Pew Center on Global Climate Change, *109th Congress Proposals*, Legislation in the 109th Congress Related to Global Climate Change *available at* http://www.pewclimate.org/what_s_being_done/in_the_congress/109th.cfm (last visited Feb. 17, 2009). It seems inevitable that Congress will pass some sort of comprehensive climate change legislation in the near future. The question remains what that legislation will include.

It seems likely, based on the recent legislative proposals, that national legislation will involve an emissions trading (or cap-and-trade) program that will limit the aggregate amount of authorized greenhouse gas emissions and allow covered entities to participate in a market-based system involving the purchase and sale of pollution credits to meet their emissions limitations. Yet legislative proposals differ regarding the initial level of the emissions cap, the amount by which the cap will lower over time, and the level of the final cap. Proposals also vary in terms of the types and numbers of entities that any federal program will cover and how the initial permits will be allocated. Also unclear is whether Congress will accede to industry demands to use national legislation to preempt other federal regulatory laws, such as the Clean Air Act, or state and local laws that address climate change.

In addition to cap-and-trade, legislators and policy analysts have considered a carbon tax to reduce domestic greenhouse gas emissions. According to some analysts, carbon taxes could achieve greenhouse gas reductions sooner with considerably less administrative bureaucracy than other types of climate change legislation. Carbon taxes are discussed in Section B. While several members of Congress have begun to develop carbon tax legislation, such proposals have thus far garnered less support than cap-and-trade.

A.   Emissions Trading: The Lieberman-Warner Climate Security Act

For the past several years, various members of Congress have designed an array of climate change bills that would use emissions trading as the primary regulatory mechanism. In the 110th Congress alone, members of Congress developed at least seven separate emissions trading programs. Only one bill — the Lieberman-Warner Climate Security Act of 2008, S. 3036, 110th Cong., 2nd Sess. (2008) (the Lieberman-Warner Act) — has made it out of committee and onto the Senate floor. It ultimately died on the Senate floor in early June 2008. Despite its failure, the bill is one model for future climate change legislation. A summary of the Lieberman-Warner Act follows.

1. The bill would cap overall greenhouse gas emissions from covered sources and lower the cap over time. Using 2005 emission levels as a baseline, the bill would require a 4 percent reduction by 2012, a 19 percent reduction by 2020, and a 71 percent reduction by 2050.

2. The emissions cap would apply to: any entity that uses more than 5,000 metric tons of coal annually; any entity that produces, processes (except in Alaska), or imports natural gas; any entity that imports or manufactures petroleum-based or coal-based fuel; and any entity that manufactures more than 10,000 metric tons of any greenhouse gas (other than HFCs). The bill sets a separate, and more aggressive, cap and trade regime for any entity that produces more than 10,000 metric tons CO_2eq of HFCs as a byproduct of HCFC production. Based on these categories, the bill's sponsors estimated that the bill would encompass 87 percent of the U.S. GHG emissions and regulate the electricity, transportation, manufacturing, and natural gas production sectors.

3. The bill would initially give 33 percent of the initial emission allowances to covered sources, but later phase out the free distribution of allowances. Of the remaining initial allowances, 11 percent would go to energy customers, 10.5 percent would go to states, 9 percent would be set aside for carbon capture and sequestration projects, 5 percent would go to entities that take early action to reduce their GHG emissions, and 26.5 percent would be auctioned off on the open market.

4. Proceeds from the initial auction would fund technology development, the transition to new energy sources, and climate change adaptation.

5. Covered entities could meet 30 percent of their emissions allocations through offsets. Of this 30 percent, 15 percent could come through domestic carbon

sequestration (both through enhancing natural sinks and developing carbon capture and sequestration projects) and 15 percent could come through international projects.

6. Carbon trading would occur on the open market, and trading would be open to entities without GHG allowances.

7. Covered entities would be allowed unlimited banking of allowances and would also be allowed to borrow up to 15 percent of their compliance obligations. However, any borrowed allowances would need to be repaid within 10 years at an interest rate of 10 percent.

8. The bill would fund research and development into alternative energy technologies, transportation technologies, natural resource protection, and other mitigation strategies.

See Summary, The Lieberman-Warner Climate Security Act (S. 2191) (as reported from the Senate Environment and Public Works Committee on December 5, 2007).

QUESTIONS AND DISCUSSION

1.   Advocates of emissions trading programs often promote the ease of implementation as a benefit of these programs over typical "command-and-control" regulation. Based on the summary of the Lieberman-Warner Act, do you think it will be easy to implement? It seems likely that thousands of entities would be covered under the bill. The bill would require the EPA to establish initial emission allocations for all of these covered facilities and to monitor each facility's compliance with the Act. In addition, the bill would require EPA to administer the research and development program that the emissions auction would fund. The Congressional Budget Office estimated that the bill would require EPA to hire up to 400 new employees to administer the program, at a cost of $1.3 billion from 2009–2013. Congressional Budget Office, Cost Estimate, S. 2191, America's Climate Security Act 16 (April 10, 2008). What do these figures suggest about the complexity of using a cap-and-trade system to regulate greenhouse gases? Who should pay the costs of administering the act?

2.   The initial allocation system in the Lieberman-Warner Act requires EPA to distribute — without an auction — one-third of the allowances to covered sources. What is the rationale behind giving away a portion of the initial allowances? Because all sources have the right to immediately trade any allowances they receive, aren't those sources simply receiving a windfall? As noted below, President Obama has proposed to auction off all credits, rather than distribute any for free.

3.   The Lieberman-Warner Act directs EPA to make its allocation decisions based upon covered entities' recent greenhouse gas emissions. Lieberman-Warner Climate Security Act of 2008, S. 3036, 110th Cong., 2nd Sess. (2008), Section 552, 562, 611(b). What signals does that type of allocation send to regulated facilities? Consider the following comments of Professor Victor Flatt:

> If CO_2 credits are not sold or auctioned, legislators must decide whether to allocate the credits based on energy output or historic CO_2 output. Between the two, allocation based on energy output is preferable since it more accurately prices the externalities of CO_2-producing activities and would tilt energy usage towards renewables and efficiency. An allocation based on energy output would reward those who produce non-CO_2 based

power production but still cost consumers of CO_2 intensive energy more, even without money going to the U.S. treasury. An allocation based on historic CO_2 production, on the other hand, means that CO_2-intensive energy producers will still be able to produce energy for the same cost structure as they have always done, which means that at least theoretically prices would not disproportionately rise in the CO_2 intensive areas. However, since CO_2 would still be rationed, the price of energy would still eventually go up overall. It just wouldn't rise as much in the CO_2 intensive areas and wouldn't affect the bottom line as much as those who sell CO_2 intensive products (such as coal-fired electricity).

As expected, the electric utilities that already consider themselves energy efficient, or those that produce power without fossil fuels, would prefer either a carbon tax or an allocation based on energy production. Doing this imposes the cost of reducing CO_2 on the largest producers of CO_2 and puts the producers (and, by extension, the consumers) of non-CO_2 generating energy or more efficiently produced energy at an advantage. Those that have high CO_2 production, such as coal-fired power plants, would prefer that allocations be distributed based on historic CO_2 production. These producers cite the historic precedent with SO_2 and the costs that would fall on the consumer if allocations are not "given" to coal producers.

*   *   *

It is surprising that whether allocation should be based on energy output or historic CO_2 output has not received more attention. In many of the bills, it is difficult to determine which method is being used (some use terms such as "heat output" rather than CO_2 or energy output), and the legislative press reports do not focus on this distinction. . . . However, since this decision alone is worth billions of dollars to certain segments of the economy and since the initial distribution will have a large impact on how quickly consumers and industry turn to energy with lower CO_2 production, this is a very important point. Part of the tendency to award based on historic CO_2 production may be a hold over from the use of the SO_2 system as a model or a holdover from what was at one time believed to be politically feasible. Closer examination of the costs and benefits of the different allocation systems may push the American public towards a different conclusion.

Victor B. Flatt, *Taking the Legislative Temperature: Which Federal Climate Change Legislative Proposal is "Best"?*, 102 Nw. U. L. Rev. Colloquy 123, 140–141, 142 (2007). Are there any other ways to distribute initial allowances that will not reward large emitters that may have failed to enact conservation measures?

4.   Environmental groups were divided regarding the value of the Lieberman-Warner Act. The Natural Resources Defense Council (NRDC) called the bill "a strong start on cutting global warming pollution." NRDC, Legislative Facts, The Boxer-Lieberman-Warner Climate Security Act Substitute Amendment (May 2008). Other national environmental organizations similarly supported the bill. However, a coalition of environmental groups led by Friends of the Earth and Greenpeace published an advertisement in *Roll Call*, to "fix or ditch" the bill by "[m]aking polluters pay for 100 percent of their pollution credits through auctions" and "[s]etting pollution reduction targets that go to work right away and keep in step with evolving science." *See* Friends of the Earth Action, Press Release, Diverse Coalition Calls on Senate to "Fix or Ditch" Lieberman-Warner Bill in Print Ad (June 2, 2008). Their opposition was based, in part, on the fear that the Lieberman-Warner Act could be the only piece of legislation that would pass for

many years related to climate change. What do you think? Is the Lieberman-Warner Act a "strong start" or a flawed effort? How often can we expect the U.S. Congress to revisit the climate change issue?

5. *Other Cap-and-Trade Proposals in the 110th Congress.* The Pew Center on Global Climate Change has summarized the various cap-and-trade proposals developed in the 110th Congress. Pew Center on Global Climate Change, *Economy-wide Cap-and-Trade Proposals in the 110th Congress*, *available at* http://www.pewclimatecenter.org/federal/analysis/congress/110/cap-trade-bills (Jun. 2008). Although all of the proposals employ emissions trading, they vary regarding: which greenhouse gases are covered; which facilities have emissions caps; which entities may participate in trading; whether facilities may obtain offsets and what limitations should apply to the offsets; and how emissions credits will be allocated.

6. As noted earlier, the Obama Administration has signaled its intention to promote domestic climate change legislation by basing part of its 2010 budget on revenues earned through an auction of greenhouse gas allowances. The budget assumes that greenhouse gas emitters will pay $646 billion from 2012 to 2019 for emissions credits. OFFICE OF MANAGEMENT AND BUDGET, A NEW ERA OF RESPONSIBILITY: RENEWING AMERICA'S PROMISE 119 (Feb. 26, 2009). It then proposes to use, over a ten-year period, $150 billion of the revenue to fund clean energy development. Lori Montgomery, *In $3.6 Trillion Budget, Obama Signals Broad Shift in Priorities*, WASH. POST, Feb. 27, 2009, at A01. The remainder of the auction revenue would fund tax credits for low— and middle-income workers. *Id.*

The idea of a "cap-and-dividend" climate law, in which revenues from a carbon auction are returned to the population at large, has gained traction due to the economic crisis. *See* Peter Barnes, *Cap and Dividend, Not Trade: Making Polluters Pay*, SCIENTIFIC AMERICAN (Dec. 2008). Under some models, all revenues collected through a carbon auction would be distributed equally to all Americans, much like Alaska residents receive equal dividends from proceeds generated from oil and gas leasing. *Id.* Advocates of equitable distribution believe that poor people will gain from a cap-and-dividend system, because they generally consume fewer fossil fuels (and thus will pay less if companies pass on costs associated with purchasing carbon credits to consumers) but will receive an equal percentage of the proceeds earned through a carbon auction. *Id.* Cap-and-dividend advocates also believe that the equitable distribution will ultimately discourage consumption of fossil fuels because it will force consumers to pay more for fossil fuels, but limit each person's dividend to an equitable share determined solely by the U.S. population. *Id.* They believe this system would ultimately create economic incentives to transition away from fossil fuels, while cushioning the economic impact of a straight cap-and-trade program. This, in turn, would ensure political support for a cap on greenhouse gas emissions.

Not everyone favors a strict cap-and-dividend approach, however. *See* Joseph Romm, *Peter Barnes' Cap-and-Dividend Plan is Fatally Incomplete*, GRISTMILL (Jan. 5, 2008). For example, Mr. Romm argues that a cap-and-dividend approach, which attempts to reduce consumers' exposure to costs associated with greenhouse gas reductions, will fail to send appropriate price signals about the need to change behavior. *Id.* He also argues that market-only approaches fail to ensure the necessary transition to renewable energy and energy efficiency. *Id.* Instead, he believes the government must play a much greater role in regulating behavior and establishing mandatory standards to hasten a transition away from fossil fuels. *Id.*

President Obama's plan would not strictly adhere to a cap-and-dividend model. First, it would distribute approximately 23 percent of the proceeds from a greenhouse gas auction to renewable energy development. Second, it would not distribute the remaining proceeds from the auction equitably; families with incomes above $195,000 would not receive the tax credit funded by the auction proceeds. Finally, as noted above, members of the Obama Administration have signaled their intention to use other laws — like the Clean Air Act — to regulate greenhouse gas emissions and force technological changes. Do you think the President's proposal represents a reasonable compromise between top-down regulation and market-based mechanisms?

7.   What role should "offsets" play in cap-and-trade legislation? Advocates of emissions trading programs often argue that trading creates incentives for technological innovation by providing a market for emissions credits created through new technologies. *See* Chapter 2 (discussing whether emissions trading produces the kind of technological innovation advocates claim). Offsets, however, seem to stifle technological innovation — at least initially — by allowing companies to invest in low-tech solutions, such as forest conservation, to generate emissions credits. Do you think the Lieberman-Warner Act strikes the appropriate balance between spurring technological innovation and providing covered entities with flexibility through offsets?

8.   Many industrial groups and politicians have expressed support for a federal cap-and-trade program so long as the legislation preempts both state action on climate change and other federal regulation (such as regulation under the Clean Air Act). Most recently, ten Democratic Senators stated that they would not support the Lieberman-Warner Act, and instead called for a law that would be the "single regulatory regime for controlling greenhouse gas emissions." *See* Letter to Senators Harry Reid and Barbara Boxer 2 (June 6, 2008). Calls for Congress to preempt state and local laws have grown increasingly loud as state and local governments have enacted their own regulations to fill the regulatory void left by federal inaction. In addition, when the Supreme Court concluded that the Clean Air Act could regulate carbon dioxide as an "air pollutant," industrial lobbyists pressed Congress to override the Clean Air Act through a cap-and-trade law. If Congress does ultimately pass a federal emissions trading law, should it preempt other laws, or should entities covered under a federal trading program also have to comply with other federal and state requirements? Do multiple climate change laws create a redundant, unfair, and expensive regulatory system as industry argues, or are they necessary for effective climate change mitigation as many states and environmentalists argue? Most federal environmental statutes allow states to impose more stringent state requirements on federally regulated facilities. Is the nature of climate change so different from other types of environmental pollution that states should not be allowed to impose more stringent requirements on greenhouse gas emitters? For thoughts regarding preemption of state and local laws, *see* Chapter 16. For a discussion of the Clean Air Act, see Chapter 13.

9.   Emissions banking allows a covered entity to save emissions credits earned from early reductions and then apply the credits later, when the cap has declined and emissions allowances have become more expensive. Advocates of emissions banking believe that it encourages prompt action to reduce greenhouse gas emissions. They also contend that emissions banking is necessary for any cap-and-trade legislation to be politically viable. However, unlimited emissions banking has the potential to disrupt emissions trading programs. First, to the extent companies are able to earn emissions credits early through relatively minimal efforts, emissions banking may limit technological innovation. Second, if most covered entities bank emissions credits for future use, overall greenhouse gas emissions may not decline as rapidly as legislative proposals suggest. Third, an influx of banked emissions into a cap-and-trade system may lower the value of the allowances and create uncertainty in the market. If emissions banking is a critical component of any politically viable system, how can it be structured to avoid disruptions to the cap-and-trade scheme?

10. For further discussion of banking in the context of the European Emission Trading System, see Chapter 6. What other lessons can be learned from the European system for designing a U.S. cap-and-trade system?

B.   Carbon Tax Legislation

Various members of Congress have also proposed carbon tax legislation as a tool to reduce domestic greenhouse gas emissions. Under some of these proposals, Congress would tax carbon at an initially modest rate (somewhere between $10 and $15 per ton) and then annually increase the tax until it achieves necessary reductions in greenhouse gas emissions. For example, the Save Our Climate Act of 2007 would initially assess a tax of $10 per ton of carbon on coal, petroleum, and petroleum products, as well as on natural gas extraction, production, and importation. Save Our Climate Act of 2007, H.R. 2069, 110th Cong. (2007). The tax would increase by $10 per ton annually until U.S. carbon dioxide emissions fall to 20 percent of their 1990 levels. *Id.* The America's Energy Security Trust Fund Act of 2007 would initially impose a $15 per ton of carbon tax on coal, petroleum, petroleum products, and natural gas, and then raise the tax by 10 percent annually. America's Energy Security Trust Fund Act of 2007, H.R. 3416, 110th Cong. (2007).

QUESTIONS AND DISCUSSION

1. Some analysts prefer a carbon tax to a cap-and-trade program because of the direct benefits the United States would receive through tax revenues. Consider, for example, the comments of N. Gregory Mankiw, an economics professor at Harvard, who supports Pigovian taxes (i.e., taxes levied to correct negative externalities, such as pollution, of market activity):

> [I]n essence, [cap-and-trade programs] give the revenue from a Pigovian tax lump-sum to a regulated entity. Why should an electric utility, for example, be given a valuable resource simply because it has for years polluted the environment? That does not strike me as equitable. A new firm entering the market should not have to pay for something that an incumbent gets for free. And the fact that the incumbent has for years been taking a valuable resource from the rest of society is no reason to think it deserves a free ride in the future. On equity grounds, one could just as easily argue that the incumbents should compensate society for their past misdeeds.

> Cap-and-trade systems are also relatively inefficient, for two reasons. First, they encourage utilities to pollute more before the cap-and-trade system is put into effect in order to "earn" pollution rights. Second, they waste the opportunity to use the Pigovian tax revenue to reduce distortionary taxes on labor and capital. Of course, cap-and-trade systems are better than heavy-handed regulatory systems. But they are not as desirable, in my view, as Pigovian taxes coupled with reductions in other taxes. One exception: If the pollution rights are auctioned off rather than handed out, then cap-and-trade systems are almost identical to Pigovian taxes, including all the desirable efficiency properties.

N. Gregory Mankiw, *Pigovian Questions* (Dec. 9, 2006), *available at* http:// gregmankiw.blogspot.com/2006/12/pigovian-questions.html. Professor Mankiw's views are shared by both conservative and liberal commentators, who view free allocations of emissions credits as an unfair subsidy to polluting industries. Consider as well the public relations aspect of how we form climate change policies. Normally, we consider taxes to be unpopular, but Mankiw characterizes the tax as a fee for the right to pollute. In this regard, consider the discussion of framing policy options in the excerpt by Joe Brewer and Evan Frisch in Chapter 19.

2.   Representative John Dingell (D. Michigan) has informally proposed one of the most immediately aggressive tax proposals to date. Through his Congressional website, Representative Dingell has suggested a tax on carbon and gasoline, as well as a phase-out of the home mortgage interest deduction for larger homes.

The legislation would impose a $50/ton tax on the carbon content of various fossil fuels, including coal, lignite and peat, petroleum and petroleum products, and natural gas. In addition, a 50 cents/gallon tax would also be imposed on gas, jet fuel, and petroleum-based kerosene, phased in over five years and adjusted for inflation. Both diesel and biofuels are exempt from the tax.

The Dingell bill would also phase out the mortgage interest deduction on large homes to reduce the carbon footprint of new homes, counter urban sprawl, and shorten commutes. Specifically, the proposal phases out the mortgage interest on primary mortgages on houses over 3000 square feet. Homes built prior to 1900 and farm houses are exempt, as are home owners who purchase carbon offsets to make their home carbon neutral or homes that are certified carbon neutral. The deduction would be phased out based on home size:

- An owner would receive 85% of the mortgage interest deduction for homes 3000–3199 square feet;

- 70% for homes 3200–3399 square feet;

- 55% for homes 3400–3599 square feet;

- 40% for homes 3600–3799 square feet;

- 25 % for homes 3800–3999 square feet;

- 10% for homes 4000–4199 square feet;

- 0 for homes 4200 square feet and up.

See Representative John D. Dingell, Summary of Draft Carbon Tax Legislation, available at http://www.house.gov/dingell/carbonTaxSummary.shtml (last visited Feb. 19, 2009). Representative Dingell has long been one of the fiercest defenders of the automobile industry, having once proposed a nuclear waste dump in Nevada in response to a Nevada senator's attempt to raise automobile fuel economy standards. See David Leonhardt, What is John Dingell Really Up To?, N.Y. TIMES, Sept. 5, 2007, at C1. His aggressive carbon tax proposal, therefore, received a skeptical reception when he first sought comments from the public on his website while expressing his doubts that "the American people are willing to pay what this is really going to cost them." Id. Some commentators believed that his proposal to use revenues from the carbon tax to phase out the popular mortgage interest deduction was little more than a cynical attempt to generate opposition to any carbon taxes. See id. In response, Representative Dingell has publicly defended a carbon tax as the "most effective way to curb carbon emissions and make alternatives economically viable." John D. Dingell, The Power in the Carbon Tax, WASH. POST, August 2, 2007, at A21. What do you think of his proposal? Is it a cynical ploy or an innovative effort to use tax policy to effectively reduce greenhouse gas emissions?

3. One concern is that carbon taxes may not yield sufficient greenhouse gas reductions. If a carbon tax is too low, it will not spur investment in alternative energies and conservation that will lead to lower emissions. At the same time, policymakers are wary of setting a carbon tax amount that is, at least initially, too high, because high taxes could send shocks through the economy. The proposed bills attempt to address these concerns by initially setting a modest tax of $10–15 per ton of carbon and then incrementally increasing that tax until greenhouse gas emissions are reduced. Is this a good approach? Professors at the Massachusetts Institute of Technology recently released a report comparing the benefits of proposed cap-and-trade legislation with the benefits of proposed carbon tax legislation. Their analysis concludes:

> [A] low starting tax rate combined with a low rate of growth in the tax rate will not reduce emissions significantly. The Dingell proposal reduces emissions from the reference case by 12 percent over the 2012–2050 control period while the Stark proposal [the Save Our Climate Act of 2007] reduces emissions by 25 percent. The Larson Bill [America's Energy Security Trust Fund Act] with its more rapid growth rate for the tax rate reduces emissions by nearly 50 percent over this period.

> [However], the carbon tax bills that have been proposed or submitted lead to a range of emissions reductions that are comparable to many of the cap-and-trade proposals that have been suggested. Thus the choice between a carbon tax and cap-and-trade system can be made on the basis of considerations other than their effectiveness at reducing emissions over some control period. Either approach (or some hybrid of the two approaches) can be equally effective at reducing GHG emissions in the United States.

Gilbert E. Metcalf et al., *Analysis of U.S. Greenhouse Gas Tax Proposals, National Bureau of Economic Research Working Paper Series No. 13980 38–39* (Apr. 2008). What do these conclusions suggest about the efficacy of the carbon tax proposals and cap-and-trade legislation?

4. Representative Dingell's plan to eliminate the home mortgage interest deduction has also received significant attention. Does his proposal get at the central issue — the amount of energy a home uses? Wouldn't it be better to tax the energy efficiency of a house? Others have linked the home mortgage interest deduction to transportation issues. This is discussed in Chapter 15.

5. In April 2008, Representative Dingell stated that he would not push his carbon tax proposal, due to concerns about the economic downturn and the added burdens a carbon tax could place on Americans. Other members of Congress have similarly eschewed carbon taxes and have introduced legislation to protect various sectors of the U.S. economy from carbon tax regulation. For example, in response to an outcry by the American Farm Bureau Federation, Senators John Thune (R-South Dakota) and Charles Shumer (D-New York) introduced a bill to ban a tax on methane emissions from cattle and other livestock. *See* Press Release, Thune, Schumer Introduce "Cow Tax" Prevention Bill, Puts Nail in Coffin of Inane Proposal that Could Cost SD Farmers an Estimated $367 Million and Put Family Farms at Risk of Going out of Business (Mar. 5, 2009). As noted earlier, enteric fermentation from livestock is the largest U.S. source of methane emissions. What do the senators' preemptive moves suggest about the likelihood of a carbon tax covering other sectors?

6. Some observers thought that a change in leadership of the influential Energy and Commerce Committee, over which Representative Dingell served as the top-ranking Democrat for 28 years, would spur quick Congressional action on climate change. In November 2008, Representative Dingell lost his leadership position over the Energy and Commerce Committee to Representative Henry Waxman, a vocal advocate of climate change regulation. While it is difficult to predict how Representative Waxman's leadership will affect climate change legislation, it appears likely that the so-called "Gang of 16" — a group of mostly moderate Democrats representing industrial Midwestern states — will oppose climate change legislation requiring a complete auction of all emissions allowances. Thus, the change in leadership on the Energy and Commerce Committee does not necessarily augur smooth passage of a climate change bill.

7.   Carbon taxes, if not properly designed, could violate free trade rules under the General Agreement on Tariffs and Trade (GATT). *See* the discussion of international trade law in Chapter 10.

Chapter 12

CLIMATE CHANGE IN THE COURTS

I.   THRESHOLD ISSUES

In response to the U.S. repudiation of the Kyoto Protocol, and the U.S. Environmental Protection Agency's (EPA's) decision not to regulate greenhouse gas (GHGs) emissions at the national level, states, municipalities, private environmental organizations, and private citizens have turned to the courts seeking to compel various federal agencies to regulate GHGs and to challenge industrial polluters and federal, state, and municipal regulatory agencies. In this way, climate change litigants have sought to use existing legislation and common law norms to fill the gap left by executive and legislative branches.

An underlying question raised by this judicial strategy is whether the courts provide an appropriate forum for addressing climate change. In U.S. jurisprudence, the appropriateness of litigation is embraced by the legal concepts of standing, justiciability, and preemption. The courts are just beginning to address these issues in the climate change context. Even the Supreme Court, while addressing plaintiffs' standing to challenge the failure of the EPA to act on a petition to regulate GHG emissions in automobiles, narrowly answered the question by acknowledging the "special solicitude" given to states. It thus left unanswered whether private citizens have standing to challenge climate change-related activities. Given the scale and ubiquity of climate change injuries, can citizens meet standing requirements by showing that they have been injured or are likely to suffer an imminent injury? Can they show that the injury suffered is caused by the action challenged or that a favorable decision would remedy the alleged injury? Section II explores these issues.

Other courts, particularly in the context of public nuisance claims, have wrestled with whether the scale and complexity of climate change make courts suitable fora for granting injunctive or monetary relief or whether the executive or legislative branches are best equipped to address climate change. Again, the scale of climate change makes fashioning a remedy daunting. Consider California's public nuisance claim against six major car manufacturers. In that case, California sought damages for, among other things, "such future monetary expenses and damages as may be incurred by California in connection with the nuisance of global warming." Complaint at 14, California v. Gen. Motors Corp., No. 3:06CV05755 (N.D. Cal. Sept.

20, 2006). In another case, *Comer v. Murphy Oil*, victims of Hurricane Katrina sued major industrial emitters of GHGs for their injuries. The court, in dismissing the case, emphasized that everyone is an emitter of GHGs: we heat and cool our homes, we drive our cars, we eat food. Concerned that everyone might be a potential defendant, the court asked plaintiffs when emissions "reach[] a point of negligence or unreasonable conduct. Where is that . . . point? When do we reach that point? How do we know, for example when a particular coal mining or coal producing defendant has crossed the line between acceptable legal conduct and negligent or unreasonable conduct?" Comer v. Murphy Oil, Transcript of Hearing on Defendants' Motions to Dismiss, Civ. Action No.: 1:05CV436-LG-RHG, at 26 (Aug. 30, 2007). In light of such concerns, Section III explores whether climate-related claims raise nonjusticiable political questions best left to the executive and the legislature.

These claims brought under common law theories of public nuisance and negligence raise another threshold issue: whether any federal environmental statutes, particularly the Clean Air Act, preempt such claims. Although the Clean Air Act does not expressly preempt or save common law claims, except in narrow circumstances, the Act is so comprehensive that it may impliedly preempt common law claims. This question of the preemption of common law claims is discussed in Chapter 16.

II. ARTICLE III STANDING

Article III of the U.S. Constitution limits the authority of federal courts to hear only "Cases or Controversies." Although Article III itself does not define a case or controversy, the Supreme Court has interpreted Article III as requiring plaintiffs to show they have a genuine interest and stake in a case by meeting several standing requirements. To satisfy Article III's standing requirement, a plaintiff must show (1) " 'an injury in fact' that is (a) concrete and particularized and (b) actual or imminent and not conjectural or hypothetical; (2) that the injury is fairly traceable to the challenged action of the defendant; and (3) it is likely, as opposed to merely speculative, that the injury will be redressed by a favorable decision." *See, e.g.*, Friends of the Earth, Inc. v. Laidlaw Environmental Services (TOC), Inc., 528 U.S. 167, 180–81 (2000).

Environmental disputes have led to some of the most important standing jurisprudence. In the 1970s, the Supreme Court ruled that the Sierra Club's special interest in the environment was insufficient to grant it standing to challenge the development of a ski resort. Nonetheless, Sierra Club could file suit on behalf of its members provided that a member could show an aesthetic or recreational injury. Sierra Club v. Morton, 405 U.S. 727 (1972). In *SCRAP*, perhaps the high water mark for permissive standing, the Supreme Court found that members of an environmental group were injured by a railroad freight rate surcharge. The court reasoned that plaintiff's members would be harmed by increased refuse that might appear in parks as a result of the greater use of nonrecyclable goods caused by the higher freight rates. United States v. Students Challenging Regulatory Agency Procedures (SCRAP), 412 U.S. 669 (1973). The Court noted that the widespread nature of the challenged action, which could allegedly impact all railroads in the nation and thus "all the natural resources of the country," did not diminish SCRAP's own claims of injury: "To deny standing to persons who are in fact injured simply because many others are also injured, would mean that the most injurious and widespread Government actions could be questioned by nobody." *Id.* at 687–88. The Court also rejected the contention that plaintiffs must demonstrate a "significant" injury for standing purposes, noting that even an "identifiable trifle" qualifies as a sufficient injury for Article III. *Id.* at 689 n.14.

In the 1990s, however, the Supreme Court tightened standing requirements. In *Lujan v. Defenders of Wildlife*, plaintiffs challenged a revised regulation that limited the geographic scope of the consultation provisions of Section 7 of the Endangered Species Act to federal actions within the United States. *Lujan*, 504 U.S. 555 (1992). The plaintiff claimed it would be injured by the lack of consultation concerning federally funded activities in foreign countries, because the rate of extinction of endangered and threatened species would increase. The plaintiff's members noted that they had traveled to areas, such as Egypt, where the endangered Nile crocodile existed, that they intended to return to these areas, and that U.S. government-funded projects in these areas would further threaten these species. Justice Scalia, writing for the majority, stated that "[s]uch some day intentions — without any description of concrete plans, or indeed even any specification of *when* the some day will be — do not support a finding of the 'actual or imminent' injury that our cases require." *Lujan*, 504 U.S. at 564.

The Supreme Court has also held that an Article III injury cannot take place unless a person uses the actual area affected by an activity. Thus, the Court found that plaintiffs lacked standing when they claimed injury from environmental damage based on using an area "in the vicinity" of the challenged project rather than the area actually affected by the challenged activity. Lujan v. National Wildlife Federation, 497 U.S. 871 (1990).

While these decisions certainly narrowed standing for environmental plaintiffs, the Supreme Court opened the 21st century with a decision that again offered hope to environmental litigants. In *Laidlaw*, the Court held that a person's reasonable concerns about the defendant's pollutant discharges resulted in "injury":

> The relevant showing for purposes of Article III standing, however, is not injury to the environment but injury to the plaintiff. To insist upon the former rather than the latter as part of the standing inquiry . . . is to raise the standing hurdle higher than the necessary showing for success on the merits. . . .

Laidlaw, 528 U.S. at 181. The Court also found that plaintiffs' injuries could be redressed by civil penalties, because civil penalties deter ongoing and future violations of the law. *Id.* at 185–188.

A.   Standing in Early Climate Change Cases

This Supreme Court standing jurisprudence created great uncertainty concerning the ability of environmental litigants to challenge climate change-related activities. Indeed, all three elements of standing pose challenges to plaintiffs. The global nature of climate change, for example, could suggest that no one has a particularized injury because everyone is injured. The scientific uncertainty concerning specific impacts of climate change and the contribution of specific activities, such as GHG emissions from a particular facility, to a specific injury, such as melting ice, make the "fairly traceable" requirement potentially difficult to show. In addition, the contribution to climate change from every single automobile tailpipe and every single coal-fired power plant, in addition to many other activities, could suggest that the injury is not redressable except through the political branches. Several early court cases, in fact, rejected plaintiffs' standing for these reasons.

FOUNDATION ON ECONOMIC TRENDS v. WATKINS
794 F. Supp. 395, 400–01 (D.D.C. 1992)

[Plaintiffs, including the author Jeremy Rifkin, challenged the failure of the Department of Energy under the National Environmental Policy Act (NEPA) to discuss in an Environmental Impact Statement the climate change impacts of forty-two of the department's actions and programs.]

Mr. Rifkin further contends that defendants' failure to take adequate consideration of global warming into account in the challenged NEPA documents "create[s] risks that decisionmakers will overlook the impact of those programs and actions on global warming." As a consequence, the challenged decisions "increase the likelihood that Rifkin's use and enjoyment of the eastern seashore beaches described above will be curtailed or eliminated by the effects of global warming."

There is no question that injury to an individual's recreational use or aesthetic enjoyment of the environment is cognizable for standing under NEPA. Nor does this Court doubt the potentially serious consequences of global warming, or that such consequences may fall within the scope of agency consideration pursuant to NEPA. Rather, the question is whether *Mr. Rifkin* has shown himself to have "a direct stake in the outcome" of the 42 federal actions and programs he seeks to challenge, to invoke the power of this Court to review those actions pursuant to the NEPA statute.

The Court finds that the allegations of injury set forth above fall short of that showing for two reasons. First, Mr. Rifkin's allegations of environmental harm to the beaches he expects to use lack "'a sufficient geographical nexus *to the site of the challenged project* that he may be expected to suffer whatever environmental consequences *the project* may have.'" City of Los Angeles, 912 F.2d at 492 (quoting City of Davis v. Coleman, 521 F.2d at 671) (emphasis added). Moreover, his claim of environmental injury rests merely upon the assertion that he "expects" to rent a cottage in Emerald Beach, North Carolina in June 1992, and that he "expects" to do so in future years. This allegation is a far cry from the situation of the NRDC member whose allegations of injury our court of appeals found sufficient to confer standing in City of Los Angeles. *See id.* at 494 (member-affiant regularly used lands in the vicinity of the challenged action for recreational purposes and gained his livelihood by farming directly from the affected geographic area).

Second, Mr. Rifkin has failed to show that "the alleged injury is 'fairly traceable' to the proposed action." In fact, Mr. Rifkin has failed to relate the environmental harm he claims he may suffer to any of the 42 challenged agency actions. On a motion for summary judgment, it is not for the Court to presume causal connections between the harm alleged and the particular actions challenged. *See* Lujan v. National Wildlife Fed'n, 110 S. Ct. at 3189. Moreover, the Supreme Court has made it abundantly clear that a litigant may no longer obtain across-the-board, nationwide correction of agency actions under the [Administrative Procedure Act] APA simply because his use of one locality may be adversely affected. *See id.* at 3190–91; see also Conservation Law Foundation v. Reilly, 950 F.2d 38, 43 (1st Cir. 1991) (holding that a plaintiff has no standing to challenge, under CERCLA's citizen-suit provision, each and every federal facility in a nationwide program where it has "ties only to a few federal facilities").

In short, under Mr. Rifkin's allegations of environmental injury, "the standing requirement [in NEPA cases] would, as a practical matter, [be] eliminated for anyone with the wit to shout 'global warming' in a crowded courthouse." City of Los Angeles, 912 F.2d at 484 (D.H. Ginsburg, J., dissenting). Notwithstanding the seriousness of the phenomenon, there is no "global warming" exception to the standing requirements of Article III or the APA. Because Mr. Rifkin's claim of direct environmental injury, as set forth in plaintiffs' Second Amended Complaint, would not pass muster to establish his standing to obtain judicial review of the agency actions he seeks to challenge, granting plaintiffs leave to amend their complaint would be futile, and their Motion to Amend will accordingly be denied.

The court's decision in *Foundation on Economic Trends* was not anomalous. In a 1990 suit involving Corporate Average Fuel Economy (CAFE) standards, the overall fuel economy standards that automobile manufacturers must meet, set by the National Highway Traffic Safety Administration (NHTSA), Judge D.H. Ginsburg wrote in a dissent:

> [A]s to redressability: because the increase in greenhouse gases that the NHTSA's decision can be expected to generate is so small a contribution to the quantum necessary to produce the projected catastrophe, I cannot conclude, on the basis of the NRDC's allegations, that the injury asserted is "likely to be redressed by a favorable decision" on its petition. As we said in *Dellums v. U.S. Nuclear Regulatory Comm'n*, 863 F.2d 968, 980 (D.C. Cir. 1988), "When numerous third parties and independent variables lead to an injury, the complainant has the burden of showing that but for the particular governmental action that he is challenging, the injury would abate." The NRDC fails to satisfy these twin causal requirements; absent any allegation that the marginal impact of NHTSA's decision to set the [model year 1989] standard at 26.5 mpg may create a serious environmental harm that, without an EIS, would be overlooked, *see City of Davis v. Coleman*, 521 F.2d at 671, that decision appears to be but an insignificant tributary to the causal stream leading to the overall harm that the petitioners have alleged.

City of Los Angeles v. NHTSA, 912 F.2d 478, 484 (D.C. Cir. 1990). Similarly, in *Massachusetts v. Environmental Protection Agency*, 415 F.3d 50, 60 (D.C. Cir. 2005), Judge Sentelle wrote:

> [E]ven in the light most favorable to the petitioners, in the end they come down to this: Emission of certain gases that the EPA is not regulating may cause an increase in the temperature of the earth — a phenomenon known as "global warming." This is harmful to humanity at large. Petitioners are or represent segments of humanity at large. This would appear to me to be neither more nor less than the sort of general harm eschewed as insufficient to make out an Article III controversy by the Supreme Court and lower courts.

> The courts under Article III stand ready to adjudicate and redress the particularized injuries of plaintiffs, when all other elements of jurisdiction are present. But "when the plaintiff is not himself the object of the government action or inaction he challenges, [although] standing is not precluded, . . . it is ordinarily 'substantially more difficult' to establish." *Lujan*, 504 U.S. at 562 (citations omitted). This time, in my view, it is not only difficult, it is impossible. The generalized public good that petitioners seek is the thing of legislatures and presidents, not of courts. As we stated

in another environmental case, to ascertain standing courts must ask the question, did the "underlying governmental act [or inaction] demonstrably increase[] some specific risk of environmental harm to the interest *of the plaintiff*"? *Florida Audubon Soc'y*, 94 F.3d at 667 (emphasis in original). Here, as in *Florida Audubon*, the alleged harm is not particularized, not specific, and in my view, not justiciable.

Therefore, I would reject and dismiss all the petitions before us. This is not to say that petitioners' complaints are wrong. This is not to say they are without redress. This is to say only that the question is not justiciable in its present form with its present champions in the present forum. A case such as this, in which plaintiffs lack particularized injury is particularly recommended to the Executive Branch and the Congress. Because plaintiffs' claimed injury is common to all members of the public, the decision whether or not to regulate is a policy call requiring a weighing of costs against the likelihood of success, best made by the democratic branches taking into account the interests of the public at large. There are two other branches of government. It is to those other branches that the petitioners should repair.

Not all courts and judges held these views. In *Covington v. Jefferson County*, 358 F.3d 626 (9th Cir. 2004), the court addressed whether injuries caused by another global environmental problem — ozone depletion — could be redressed by courts. In this case, the Covingtons claimed that Jefferson County violated the Clean Air Act (CAA) by not following federal procedures to account for removal or recapture of chlorofluorocarbons (CFCs) and other ozone-depleting substances before disposal or recycling. Despite the global nature of ozone depletion, the court treated the alleged injuries as essentially a local issue:

> The evidence of leakage of white goods provided by the Covingtons is sufficient to show injury in fact because the failure to comply with CAA has increased the risk of harm to the Covingtons' property. The Covingtons have observed liquids leaking from the white goods and they fear that this liquid will contaminate their property. From this, the Covingtons' enjoyment of their property is diminished by the attested leaks. This analysis is parallel to our analysis of injury in fact for the RCRA [Resource Conservation and Recovery Act] violations. A credible threat of risks to their home yields a loss of enjoyment of property. That is enough for injury in fact for the CAA claims.

> There is also causation: Failure of the landfill to follow CAA procedure allowed CFCs and other ozone-depleting substances to be released in the landfill, instead of being recaptured or properly removed. If the CAA regulation had been followed, no liquids would have leaked from the white goods. Or if liquid had leaked, these violations of federal law would have been documented. Redressability is satisfied, as with the RCRA violations, by the fines and penalties applicable for violations of CAA. *Laidlaw*, 528 U.S. at 185–86. Such CAA fines and penalties can cause Jefferson County to bring the landfill into compliance with the CAA. We conclude that the Covingtons have standing to bring the CAA claim.

Id. at 641. However, in a lengthy concurrence, Judge Gould — who also authored the panel's decision — discussed the question of whether "injury to all is injury to none," and concluded that it was not. A short time later, a district court squarely considered a defendant's argument that plaintiffs could not have Article III standing to challenge actions that will cause "global injuries." In *Northwest Environmental Defense Center v. Owens Corning Corporation*, 434 F. Supp. 2d 957 (D. Or. 2006), environmental organizations brought suit against a company for constructing a facility without first obtaining a permit as required under the new source review program of the Clean Air Act. Once operational, the facility would have emitted HCFC-142b, an ozone-depleting substance and greenhouse gas. The defendants argued that the groups' alleged injuries were indistinguishable from any harms that individuals might suffer in Mongolia, Australia, or anywhere else in the world. The court, however, followed Judge Gould's concurrence and rejected the contention that "injury for all is injury for none."

NORTHWEST ENVIRONMENTAL DEFENSE CENTER v. OWENS CORNING CORPORATION
434 F. Supp. 2d 957, 963–64, 967–68 (D. Or. 2006)

1. Injury in Fact

The phrase "injury in fact" notwithstanding, a plaintiff need not wait until after he has been harmed before seeking relief, particularly when the injuries are of a kind not readily redressed by damages. Instead, a plaintiff may petition the court for injunctive relief to prevent the threatened harm. A "concrete risk of harm" to the plaintiff is sufficient to satisfy the injury-in-fact requirement. Covington v. Jefferson County, 358 F.3d 626, 638 (9th Cir. 2004) (risk of harm if landfill not properly operated was sufficient to confer standing, and citing additional authorities); Hall v. Norton, 266 F.3d 969, 979 (9th Cir. 2001) ("evidence of a credible threat to the plaintiff's physical well being from airborne pollutants" sufficient to satisfy injury requirement).

The allegations that Plaintiffs "fear" or are "concerned" they will be harmed if Defendant's facility discharges pollutants — rather than affirmatively alleging that Plaintiffs "will" sustain such harm (or are "informed and believe they will") — do give some pause. However, in environmental litigation, such allegations can be enough to satisfy the injury-in-fact requirement. See Covington, 358 F.3d at 639 (sufficient to allege that defendant's actions "caused 'reasonable concern' of injury to" the plaintiff) and at 641 (evidence that plaintiffs observed leaks from landfill and "fear that this liquid will contaminate their property" was sufficient to show injury-in-fact). See also Laidlaw, 528 U.S. at 182–84 (plaintiffs allegedly altered their behavior because they were "concerned" about harmful effects from Laidlaw's discharges); Central Delta Water Agency v. United States, 306 F.3d 938, 948 (9th Cir. 2002) (" 'to require actual evidence of environmental harm, rather than an increased risk based on a violation of the statute, misunderstands the nature of environmental harm' . . . a credible threat of harm is sufficient to constitute actual injury for standing purposes"). * * *

Of course, the harm must be more than imaginary. See Societe de Conditionnement en Aluminium v. Hunter Engineering Co., Inc., 655 F.2d 938, 944 (9th Cir. 1981) (a "real and reasonable apprehension" is sufficient). Defendant does not suggest, however, that the harm described in the complaint is entirely without any credible scientific basis nor — at this stage of the proceedings — are Plaintiffs required to prove their contentions. The enactment by Congress of laws governing these emissions, and the participation by the United States in related international agreements, also weigh against any suggestion that the threatened harm is entirely chimerical.

*   *   *

Adverse effects from the emissions will not necessarily be limited to Oregon, yet Plaintiffs' injuries are not diminished by the mere fact that other persons may also be injured by the Defendant's conduct. Standing has never required proof that the plaintiff is the only person injured by the defendant's conduct. A class action may be prosecuted on behalf of a class of millions of similarly situated persons, all claiming to have been injured by the same conduct. As Judge Gould's concurrence in Covington ably illustrates, the notion that "injury to all is injury to none" does not correctly reflect the current doctrine of standing. Covington, 358 F.3d at 651–55. If Defendant's theory of standing were correct, no person could have standing to maintain an action aimed at averting harm to the Grand Canyon or Yellowstone National Park, or threats to the giant sequoias and blue whales, as the loss of those treasures would be felt by everyone. For that matter, if the proposed action threatened the very survival of our species, no person would have standing to contest it. The greater the threatened harm, the less power the courts would have to intercede. That is an illogical proposition.

2. Fairly Traceable

The "fairly traceable" element of standing requires the plaintiff to articulate a "causal connection between the injury and the conduct complained of — the injury has to be fairly traceable to the challenged action of the defendant, and not the result of the independent action of some third party not before the court." Defenders of Wildlife, 504 U.S. at 560–61 (internal citations and quotations omitted). Defendant is the entity that commenced construction of the Gresham facility and intends to operate it, and is also the entity answerable for any violations of the Clean Air Act arising from such activities.

While Defendant is not the sole entity allegedly discharging pollutants into the atmosphere that may adversely impact the Plaintiffs, the "fairly traceable" element does not require that a plaintiff show to a scientific certainty that the defendant's emissions, and only the defendant's emissions, are the source of the threatened harm. . . . It is sufficient for Plaintiffs to assert that emissions from Defendant's facility will contribute to the pollution that threatens Plaintiffs' interests. See also Southwest Marine, 236 F.3d at 995 (requirement of traceability does not mean plaintiff must show to a scientific certainty that defendant's effluent caused the precise harm suffered by the plaintiff; rather, the plaintiff must show that a defendant discharges a pollutant that causes or contributes to the kinds of injuries alleged in the specific geographic area of concern).

I also reject Defendant's contention that Plaintiffs lack standing because the challenged conduct is the commencement of construction without the required permit, while the ultimate harm can result only from operation of the plant once construction is completed. That argument improperly compartmentalizes the challenged conduct and the injury.

3. Redressability

The redressability element is satisfied. If Plaintiffs prevail in this action, Defendant's plant cannot open unless and until Defendant complies with all applicable legal requirements. Those requirements are intended to protect the public health and the public's right to participate in the review process. Plaintiffs are not obligated to also show that the permit request would be denied, or that the design of the plant or its emissions will be altered as a consequence of this litigation. . . .

Imposition of civil penalties also would redress, to an extent, the injury caused by Defendant's alleged failure to comply with the law, by deterring future violations. *See* Friends of the Earth, 528 U.S. at 185–86; Covington, 358 F.3d at 641.

Plaintiffs need not show that the entire problem (for instance, global warming) will be cured if the Plaintiffs prevail in this action, or that the challenged action is the exclusive source of that harm. Particularly in environmental and land use cases, the challenged harm often results from the cumulative effects of many separate actions that, taken together, threaten the plaintiff's interests. The relief sought in the Complaint need not promise to solve the entire problem, any more than a legislative body is forbidden to enact a law addressing a discrete part of a problem rather than the entire problem. Cf. Railway Express Agency, Inc. v. New York, 336 U.S. 106, 110, (1949) ("It is no requirement of equal protection that all evils of the same genus be eradicated or none at all").

B. Prudential Limitations

The "prudential limitations" upon standing include (1) a "plaintiff generally must assert his own legal rights and interests, and cannot rest his claim to relief on the legal rights or interest of third parties," (2) the federal courts "refrain[] from adjudicating 'abstract questions of wide public significance' which amount to 'generalized grievances,' pervasively shared and most appropriately addressed in the representative branches," and (3) the complaint must "fall within 'the zone of interests to be protected or regulated by the statute or constitutional guarantee in question.' " Valley Forge, 454 U.S. at 474–75 (citations omitted).

Two of the three prudential limitations are not seriously in dispute. The interests represented by Plaintiffs are their own rights, notwithstanding that other similarly situated persons may benefit collaterally from the outcome. Assuming the "zone of interest" requirement applies here, it is plainly satisfied. The Clean Air Act was intended to protect the interests advanced by Plaintiffs here, and Congress expressly provided for citizen suits to enforce its provisions. Defendant suggests that if Plaintiffs have standing to prosecute this action, then so would "a woman with lupus in Perth, Australia, and a man living in Ulan Bataar, Mongolia . . . ." I express no opinion concerning the rights of such hypothetical litigants. The actual Plaintiffs in this case have a strong geographical nexus to Defendant's Gresham facility.

*   *   *

As for the remaining prudential limitation, issues such as global warming and ozone depletion may be of "wide public significance" but they are neither "abstract questions" nor mere "generalized grievances." An injury is not beyond the reach of the courts simply because it is widespread.

*   *   *

In addition, Defendant's argument presumes that all persons on the planet will suffer the identical injury from global warming. According to some theories, global warming may well alter the lives of every person on the planet, but all will not be affected in the same way. Rising oceans may inundate coastal communities, to the detriment of local residents and property owners, yet the rising waters may benefit some formerly inland property owners who discover they now own oceanfront property. More frequent hurricanes may harm residents of Florida and the Gulf Coast, yet increase business and profits for roofing contractors. Warm temperatures in Alaska may harm indigenous subsistence hunters, yet benefit local air conditioning salesmen. Some farmers will be hurt by warmer temperatures and changing rainfall patterns, yet other farmers may benefit from longer growing seasons or higher commodity prices. Oregonians could be deprived of their traditional summertime skiing on Mount Hood, an injury distinct from the harms likely to be sustained by residents of other states. In short, it is unlikely that all persons will be similarly impacted by global warming. This conclusion further undermines Defendant's shared injury argument.

B.   *Massachusetts v. EPA*

Less than a year after the district court ruled that the plaintiffs had standing in *Northwest Environmental Defense Center*, the Supreme Court addressed standing in the climate context.

MASSACHUSETTS v. ENVIRONMENTAL PROTECTION AGENCY
549 U.S. 497 (2007)

JUSTICE STEVENS delivered the opinion of the Court. * * *

Calling global warming "the most pressing environmental challenge of our time," a group of States, local governments, and private organizations, alleged in a petition for certiorari that the Environmental Protection Agency (EPA) has abdicated its responsibility under the Clean Air Act to regulate the emissions of four greenhouse gases, including carbon dioxide. Specifically, petitioners asked us to answer two questions concerning the meaning of § 202(a)(1) of the Act: whether EPA has the statutory authority to regulate greenhouse gas emissions from new motor vehicles; and if so, whether its stated reasons for refusing to do so are consistent with the statute.

In response, EPA, supported by 10 intervening States and six trade associations, correctly argued that we may not address those two questions unless at least one petitioner has standing to invoke our jurisdiction under Article III of the Constitution. Notwithstanding the serious character of that jurisdictional argument and the absence of any conflicting decisions construing § 202(a)(1), the unusual importance of the underlying issue persuaded us to grant the writ.

*   *   *

III

Petitioners, now joined by intervenor States and local governments, sought review of EPA's order [denying the rulemaking petition] in the United States Court of Appeals for the District of Columbia Circuit. Although each of the three judges on the panel wrote a separate opinion, two judges agreed "that the EPA Administrator properly exercised his discretion under § 202(a)(1) in denying the petition for rule making." 415 F.3d 50, 58 (2005). The court therefore denied the petition for review.

In his opinion announcing the court's judgment, Judge Randolph avoided a definitive ruling as to petitioners' standing, reasoning that it was permissible to proceed to the merits because the standing and the merits inquiries "overlapped-.". . . Judge Sentelle wrote separately because he believed petitioners failed to "demonstrate the element of injury necessary to establish standing under Article III." In his view, they had alleged that global warming is "harmful to humanity at large," but could not allege "particularized injuries" to themselves. While he dissented on standing, however, he accepted the contrary view as the law of the case and joined Judge Randolph's judgment on the merits as the closest to that which he preferred.

Judge Tatel dissented. Emphasizing that EPA nowhere challenged the factual basis of petitioners' affidavits, he concluded that at least Massachusetts had "satisfied each element of Article III standing — injury, causation, and redressability." In Judge Tatel's view, the "'substantial probability,'" that projected rises in sea level would lead to serious loss of coastal property was a "far cry" from the kind of generalized harm insufficient to ground Article III jurisdiction. He found that petitioners' affidavits more than adequately supported the conclusion that EPA's failure to curb greenhouse gas emissions contributed to the sea level changes that threatened Massachusetts' coastal property. As to redressability, he observed that one of petitioners' experts, a former EPA climatologist, stated that "'achievable reductions in emissions of CO_2 and other [greenhouse gases] from U.S. motor vehicles would . . . delay and moderate many of the adverse impacts of global warming.'" He further noted that the one-time director of EPA's motor-vehicle pollution control efforts stated in an affidavit that enforceable emission standards would lead to the development of new technologies that "'would gradually be mandated by other countries around the world.'" On the merits, Judge Tatel explained at length why he believed the text of the statute provided EPA with authority to regulate greenhouse gas emissions, and why its policy concerns did not justify its refusal to exercise that authority.

IV

Article III of the Constitution limits federal-court jurisdiction to "Cases" and "Controversies." Those two words confine "the business of federal courts to questions presented in an adversary context and in a form historically viewed as capable of resolution through the judicial process." It is therefore familiar learning that no justiciable "controversy" exists when parties seek adjudication of a political question, or when the question sought to be adjudicated has been mooted by subsequent developments. This case suffers from none of these defects.

The parties' dispute turns on the proper construction of a congressional statute, a question eminently suitable to resolution in federal court. Congress has moreover authorized this type of challenge to EPA action. See 42 U.S.C. § 7607(b)(1). That authorization is of critical importance to the standing inquiry: "Congress has the power to define injuries and articulate chains of causation that will give rise to a case or controversy where none existed before." *Lujan,* 504 U.S., at 580 (Kennedy, J., concurring in part and concurring in judgment). "In exercising this power, however, Congress must at the very least identify the injury it seeks to vindicate and relate the injury to the class of persons entitled to bring suit." *Ibid.* We will not, therefore, "entertain citizen suits to vindicate the public's nonconcrete interest in the proper administration of the laws." *Id., at 581.*

EPA maintains that because greenhouse gas emissions inflict widespread harm, the doctrine of standing presents an insuperable jurisdictional obstacle. We do not agree. At bottom, "the gist of the question of standing" is whether petitioners have "such a personal stake in the outcome of the controversy as to assure that concrete adverseness which sharpens the presentation of issues upon which the court so largely depends for illumination." *Baker v. Carr,* 369 U.S. 186, 204 (1962). As Justice Kennedy explained in his *Lujan* concurrence:

"While it does not matter how many persons have been injured by the challenged action, the party bringing suit must show that the action injures him in a concrete and personal way. This requirement is not just an empty formality. It preserves the vitality of the adversarial process by assuring both that the parties before the court have an actual, as opposed to professed, stake in the outcome, and that the legal questions presented . . . will be resolved, not in the rarified atmosphere of a debating society, but in a concrete factual context conducive to a realistic appreciation of the consequences of judicial action." *504 U.S., at 581* (internal quotation marks omitted).

To ensure the proper adversarial presentation, *Lujan* holds that a litigant must demonstrate that it has suffered a concrete and particularized injury that is either actual or imminent, that the injury is fairly traceable to the defendant, and that it is likely that a favorable decision will redress that injury. However, a litigant to whom Congress has "accorded a procedural right to protect his concrete interests," — here, the right to challenge agency action unlawfully withheld, § 7607(b)(1) — "can assert that right without meeting all the normal standards for redressability and immediacy," *ibid.* When a litigant is vested with a procedural right, that litigant has standing if there is some possibility that the requested relief will prompt the injury-causing party to reconsider the decision that allegedly harmed the litigant. *Ibid.*; see also *Sugar Cane Growers Cooperative of Fla. v. Veneman*, 289 F.3d 89, 94–95 (D.C. Cir. 2002) ("A [litigant] who alleges a deprivation of a procedural protection to which he is entitled never has to prove that if he had received the procedure the substantive result would have been altered. All that is necessary is to show that the procedural step was connected to the substantive result").

Only one of the petitioners needs to have standing to permit us to consider the petition for review. We stress here, as did Judge Tatel below, the special position and interest of Massachusetts. It is of considerable relevance that the party seeking review here is a sovereign State and not, as it was in *Lujan*, a private individual.

Well before the creation of the modern administrative state, we recognized that States are not normal litigants for the purposes of invoking federal jurisdiction. As Justice Holmes explained in *Georgia v. Tennessee Copper Co.*, 206 U.S. 230, 237 (1907), a case in which Georgia sought to protect its citizens from air pollution originating outside its borders:

> "The case has been argued largely as if it were one between two private parties; but it is not. The very elements that would be relied upon in a suit between fellow-citizens as a ground for equitable relief are wanting here. The State owns very little of the territory alleged to be affected, and the damage to it capable of estimate in money, possibly, at least, is small. This is a suit by a State for an injury to it in its capacity of *quasi*-sovereign. In that capacity the State has an interest independent of and behind the titles of its citizens, in all the earth and air within its domain. It has the last word as to whether its mountains shall be stripped of their forests and its inhabitants shall breathe pure air."

Just as Georgia's "independent interest . . . in all the earth and air within its domain" supported federal jurisdiction a century ago, so too does Massachusetts' well-founded desire to preserve its sovereign territory today. Cf. *Alden v. Maine*, 527 U.S. 706, 715 (1999) (observing that in the federal system, the States "are not relegated to the role of mere provinces or political corporations, but retain the dignity, though not the full authority, of sovereignty"). That Massachusetts does in fact own a great deal of the "territory alleged to be affected" only reinforces the conclusion that its stake in the outcome of this case is sufficiently concrete to warrant the exercise of federal judicial power.

When a State enters the Union, it surrenders certain sovereign prerogatives. Massachusetts cannot invade Rhode Island to force reductions in greenhouse gas emissions, it cannot negotiate an emissions treaty with China or India, and in some circumstances the exercise of its police powers to reduce in-state motor-vehicle emissions might well be pre-empted. See *Alfred L. Snapp & Son, Inc. v. Puerto Rico ex rel. Barez*, 458 U.S. 592, 607 (1982) ("One helpful indication in determining whether an alleged injury to the health and welfare of its citizens suffices to give the State standing to sue *parens patriae* is whether the injury is one that the State, if it could, would likely attempt to address through its sovereign lawmaking powers").

These sovereign prerogatives are now lodged in the Federal Government, and Congress has ordered EPA to protect Massachusetts (among others) by prescribing standards applicable to the "emission of any air pollutant from any class or classes of new motor vehicle engines, which in [the Administrator's] judgment cause, or contribute to, air pollution which may reasonably be anticipated to endanger public health or welfare." 42 U.S.C. § 7521(a)(1). Congress has moreover recognized a concomitant procedural right to challenge the rejection of its rulemaking petition as arbitrary and capricious. § 7607(b)(1). Given that procedural right and Massachusetts' stake in protecting its quasi-sovereign interests, the Commonwealth is entitled to special solicitude in our standing analysis.[17]

With that in mind, it is clear that petitioners' submissions as they pertain to Massachusetts have satisfied the most demanding standards of the adversarial process. EPA's steadfast refusal to regulate greenhouse gas emissions presents a risk of harm to Massachusetts that is both "actual" and "imminent." *Lujan, 504 U.S., at 560* (internal quotation marks omitted). There is, moreover, a "substantial likelihood that the judicial relief requested" will prompt EPA to take steps to reduce that risk. *Duke Power Co. v. Carolina Environmental Study Group, Inc.*, 438 U.S. 59, 79 (1978).

---

[17] The Chief Justice accuses the Court of misreading *Georgia v. Tennessee Copper Co.*, 206 U.S. 230 (1907), see *post*, at 3–4 (dissenting opinion), and "devising a new doctrine of state standing," *id.*, at 15. But no less an authority than Hart & Wechsler's The Federal Courts and the Federal System understands *Tennessee Copper* as a standing decision. R. Fallon, D. Meltzer, & D. Shapiro, Hart & Wechsler's The Federal Courts and the Federal System 290 (5th ed. 2003). Indeed, it devotes an entire section to chronicling the long development of cases permitting States "to litigate as *parens patriae* to protect quasi-sovereign interests — i.e., public or governmental interests that concern the state as a whole." *Id.*, at 289; see, *e.g., Missouri v. Illinois*, 180 U.S. 208, 240–241 (1901) (finding federal jurisdiction appropriate not only "in cases involving boundaries and jurisdiction over lands and their inhabitants, and in cases directly affecting the property rights and interests of a state," but also when the "substantial impairment of the health and prosperity of the towns and cities of the state" are at stake).

Drawing on Massachusetts v. Mellon, 262 U.S. 447 (1923), and Alfred L. Snapp & Son, Inc. v. Puerto Rico ex rel. Barez, 458 U.S. 592 (1982) (citing Missouri v. Illinois, 180 U.S. 208 (1901)), The Chief Justice claims that we "overlook the fact that our cases cast significant doubt on a State's standing to assert a quasi-sovereign interest . . . against the Federal Government." Post, at 5. Not so. Mellon itself disavowed any such broad reading when it noted that the Court had been "called upon to adjudicate, not rights of person or property, not rights of dominion over physical domain, [and] not quasi sovereign rights actually invaded or threatened." 262 U.S., at 484–485 (emphasis added). In any event, we held in Georgia v. Pennsylvania R. Co., 324 U.S. 439, 447 (1945), that there is a critical difference between allowing a State "to protect her citizens from the operation of federal statutes" (which is what Mellon prohibits) and allowing a State to assert its rights under federal law (which it has standing to do). Massachusetts does not here dispute that the Clean Air Act applies to its citizens; it rather seeks to assert its rights under the Act. See also Nebraska v. Wyoming, 515 U.S. 1, 20 (1995) (holding that Wyoming had standing to bring a cross-claim against the United States to vindicate its "'quasi-sovereign' interests which are 'independent of and behind the titles of its citizens, in all the earth and air within its domain'" (quoting Tennessee Copper, 206 U.S., at 237).

The Injury

The harms associated with climate change are serious and well recognized. Indeed, the NRC Report itself — which EPA regards as an "objective and independent assessment of the relevant science," — identifies a number of environmental changes that have already inflicted significant harms, including "the global retreat of mountain glaciers, reduction in snow-cover extent, the earlier spring melting of rivers and lakes, [and] the accelerated rate of rise of sea levels during the 20th century relative to the past few thousand years. . . . "

Petitioners allege that this only hints at the environmental damage yet to come. According to the climate scientist Michael MacCracken, "qualified scientific experts involved in climate change research" have reached a "strong consensus" that global warming threatens (among other things) a precipitate rise in sea levels by the end of the century, "severe and irreversible changes to natural ecosystems," a "significant reduction in water storage in winter snowpack in mountainous regions with direct and important economic consequences," and an increase in the spread of disease. He also observes that rising ocean temperatures may contribute to the ferocity of hurricanes.

That these climate-change risks are "widely shared" does not minimize Massachusetts' interest in the outcome of this litigation. See *Federal Election Comm'n v. Akins*, 524 U.S. 11, 24 (1998) ("Where a harm is concrete, though widely shared, the Court has found 'injury in fact' "). According to petitioners' unchallenged affidavits, global sea levels rose somewhere between 10 and 20 centimeters over the 20th century as a result of global warming. These rising seas have already begun to swallow Massachusetts' coastal land. Because the Commonwealth "owns a substantial portion of the state's coastal property," it has alleged a particularized injury in its capacity as a landowner. The severity of that injury will only increase over the course of the next century: If sea levels continue to rise as predicted, one Massachusetts official believes that a significant fraction of coastal property will be "either permanently lost through inundation or temporarily lost through periodic storm surge and flooding events." Remediation costs alone, petitioners allege, could run well into the hundreds of millions of dollars.[21]

Causation

EPA does not dispute the existence of a causal connection between man-made greenhouse gas emissions and global warming. At a minimum, therefore, EPA's refusal to regulate such emissions "contributes" to Massachusetts' injuries.

EPA nevertheless maintains that its decision not to regulate greenhouse gas emissions from new motor vehicles contributes so insignificantly to petitioners' injuries that the agency cannot be haled into federal court to answer for them. For the same reason, EPA does not believe that any realistic possibility exists that the relief petitioners seek would mitigate global climate change and remedy their injuries. That is especially so because predicted increases in greenhouse gas emissions from developing nations, particularly China and India, are likely to offset any marginal domestic decrease.

---

[21] In dissent, The Chief Justice dismisses petitioners' submissions as "conclusory," presumably because they do not quantify Massachusetts' land loss with the exactitude he would prefer. He therefore asserts that the Commonwealth's injury is "conjectural." Yet the likelihood that Massachusetts' coastline will recede has nothing to do with whether petitioners have determined the precise metes and bounds of their soon-to-be-flooded land. Petitioners maintain that the seas are rising and will continue to rise, and have alleged that such a rise will lead to the loss of Massachusetts' sovereign territory. No one, save perhaps the dissenters, disputes those allegations. Our cases require nothing more.

But EPA overstates its case. Its argument rests on the erroneous assumption that a small incremental step, because it is incremental, can never be attacked in a federal judicial forum. Yet accepting that premise would doom most challenges to regulatory action. Agencies, like legislatures, do not generally resolve massive problems in one fell regulatory swoop. See *Williamson v. Lee Optical of Okla., Inc.*, 348 U.S. 483, 489 (1955) ("[A] reform may take one step at a time, addressing itself to the phase of the problem which seems most acute to the legislative mind"). They instead whittle away at them over time, refining their preferred approach as circumstances change and as they develop a more-nuanced understanding of how best to proceed. Cf. *SEC v. Chenery Corp.*, 332 U.S. 194, 202 (1947) ("Some principles must await their own development, while others must be adjusted to meet particular, unforeseeable situations"). That a first step might be tentative does not by itself support the notion that federal courts lack jurisdiction to determine whether that step conforms to law.

And reducing domestic automobile emissions is hardly a tentative step. Even leaving aside the other greenhouse gases, the United States transportation sector emits an enormous quantity of carbon dioxide into the atmosphere — according to the MacCracken affidavit, more than 1.7 billion metric tons in 1999 alone. That accounts for more than 6% of worldwide carbon dioxide emissions. To put this in perspective: Considering just emissions from the transportation sector, which represent less than one-third of this country's total carbon dioxide emissions, the United States would still rank as the third-largest emitter of carbon dioxide in the world, outpaced only by the European Union and China. Judged by any standard, U.S. motor-vehicle emissions make a meaningful contribution to greenhouse gas concentrations and hence, according to petitioners, to global warming.

The Remedy

While it may be true that regulating motor-vehicle emissions will not by itself reverse global warming, it by no means follows that we lack jurisdiction to decide whether EPA has a duty to take steps to *slow* or *reduce* it. See also *Larson v. Valente*, 456 U.S. 228, 244, n. 15 (1982) ("[A] plaintiff satisfies the redressability requirement when he shows that a favorable decision will relieve a discrete injury to himself. He need not show that a favorable decision will relieve his *every* injury."). Because of the enormity of the potential consequences associated with man-made climate change, the fact that the effectiveness of a remedy might be delayed during the (relatively short) time it takes for a new motor-vehicle fleet to replace an older one is essentially irrelevant. Nor is it dispositive that developing countries such as China and India are poised to increase greenhouse gas emissions substantially over the next century: A reduction in domestic emissions would slow the pace of global emissions increases, no matter what happens elsewhere.

We moreover attach considerable significance to EPA's "agreement with the President that 'we must address the issue of global climate change,' " and to EPA's ardent support for various voluntary emission-reduction programs. As Judge Tatel observed in dissent below, "EPA would presumably not bother with such efforts if it thought emissions reductions would have no discernable impact on future global warming."

In sum — at least according to petitioners' uncontested affidavits — the rise in sea levels associated with global warming has already harmed and will continue to harm Massachusetts. The risk of catastrophic harm, though remote, is nevertheless real. That risk would be reduced to some extent if petitioners received the relief they seek. We therefore hold that petitioners have standing to challenge the EPA's denial of their rulemaking petition.[24]

* * *

CHIEF JUSTICE ROBERTS, with whom JUSTICE SCALIA, JUSTICE THOMAS, and JUSTICE ALITO join, dissenting.

* * *

I would reject these challenges as nonjusticiable. Such a conclusion involves no judgment on whether global warming exists, what causes it, or the extent of the problem. Nor does it render petitioners without recourse. This Court's standing jurisprudence simply recognizes that redress of grievances of the sort at issue here "is the function of Congress and the Chief Executive," not the federal courts. *Lujan v. Defenders of Wildlife*, 504 U.S. 555, 576 (1992). I would vacate the judgment below and remand for dismissal of the petitions for review.

I

Article III, § 2, of the Constitution limits the federal judicial power to the adjudication of "Cases" and "Controversies." "If a dispute is not a proper case or controversy, the courts have no business deciding it, or expounding the law in the course of doing so." *DaimlerChrysler Corp. v. Cuno*, 547 U.S., 126 S. Ct. 1854, (2006) (slip op., at 5). "Standing to sue is part of the common understanding of what it takes to make a justiciable case," *Steel Co. v. Citizens for Better Environment*, 523 U.S. 83, 102 (1998), and has been described as "an essential and unchanging part of the case-or-controversy requirement of Article III," *Defenders of Wildlife, supra*, at 560.

Our modern framework for addressing standing is familiar: "A plaintiff must allege personal injury fairly traceable to the defendant's allegedly unlawful conduct and likely to be redressed by the requested relief." *DaimlerChrysler*, supra, at, 126 S. Ct. 1854(slip op., at 6) (quoting *Allen v. Wright*, 468 U.S. 737, 751 (1984) (internal quotation marks omitted)). Applying that standard here, petitioners bear the burden of alleging an injury that is fairly traceable to the Environmental Protection Agency's failure to promulgate new motor vehicle greenhouse gas emission standards, and that is likely to be redressed by the prospective issuance of such standards.

---

[24] In his dissent, The Chief Justice expresses disagreement with the Court's holding in *United States v. Students Challenging Regulatory Agency Procedures (SCRAP)*, 412 U.S. 669, 687–688 (1973). He does not, however, disavow this portion of Justice Stewart's opinion for the Court:

> "Unlike the specific and geographically limited federal action of which the petitioner complained in *Sierra Club* [*v. Morton*, 405 U.S. 727 (1972)], the challenged agency action in this case is applicable to substantially all of the Nation's railroads, and thus allegedly has an adverse environmental impact on all the natural resources of the country. Rather than a limited group of persons who used a picturesque valley in California, all persons who utilize the scenic resources of the country, and indeed all who breathe its air, could claim harm similar to that alleged by the environmental groups here. But we have already made it clear that standing is not to be denied simply because many people suffer the same injury. Indeed some of the cases on which we relied in *Sierra Club* demonstrated the patent fact that persons across the Nation could be adversely affected by major governmental actions. *To deny standing to persons who are in fact injured simply because many others are also injured, would mean that the most injurious and widespread Government actions could be questioned by nobody.* We cannot accept that conclusion." *Ibid.* (citations omitted and emphasis added).

It is moreover quite wrong to analogize the legal claim advanced by Massachusetts and the other public and private entities who challenge EPA's parsimonious construction of the Clean Air Act to a mere "lawyer's game."

Before determining whether petitioners can meet this familiar test, however, the Court changes the rules. It asserts that "States are not normal litigants for the purposes of invoking federal jurisdiction," and that given "Massachusetts' stake in protecting its quasi-sovereign interests, the Commonwealth is entitled to *special solicitude* in our standing analysis." (emphasis added).

Relaxing Article III standing requirements because asserted injuries are pressed by a State, however, has no basis in our jurisprudence, and support for any such "special solicitude" is conspicuously absent from the Court's opinion. The general judicial review provision cited by the Court, 42 U.S.C. § 7607(b)(1), affords States no special rights or status. The Court states that "Congress has ordered EPA to protect Massachusetts (among others)" through the statutory provision at issue, § 7521(a)(1), and that "Congress has . . . recognized a concomitant procedural right to challenge the rejection of its rulemaking petition as arbitrary and capricious." The reader might think from this unfortunate phrasing that Congress said something about the rights of States in this particular provision of the statute. Congress knows how to do that when it wants to, *see, e.g.*, § 7426(b) (affording States the right to petition EPA to directly regulate certain sources of pollution), but it has done nothing of the sort here. Under the law on which petitioners rely, Congress treated public and private litigants exactly the same.

Nor does the case law cited by the Court provide any support for the notion that Article III somehow implicitly treats public and private litigants differently. The Court has to go back a full century in an attempt to justify its novel standing rule, but even there it comes up short. The Court's analysis hinges on *Georgia v. Tennessee Copper Co.*, 206 U.S. 230 (1907) — a case that did indeed draw a distinction between a State and private litigants, but solely with respect to available remedies. The case had nothing to do with Article III standing.

In *Tennessee Copper*, the State of Georgia sought to enjoin copper companies in neighboring Tennessee from discharging pollutants that were inflicting "a wholesale destruction of forests, orchards and crops" in bordering Georgia counties. Although the State owned very little of the territory allegedly affected, the Court reasoned that Georgia — in its capacity as a "*quasi*-sovereign" — "has an interest independent of and behind the titles of its citizens, in all the earth and air within its domain." The Court explained that while "the very elements that would be relied upon in a suit between fellow-citizens as a ground for equitable relief [were] wanting," a State "is not lightly to be required to give up *quasi*-sovereign rights for pay." Thus while a complaining private litigant would have to make do with a *legal* remedy — one "for pay" — the State was entitled to *equitable* relief.

In contrast to the present case, there was no question in *Tennessee Copper* about Article III injury. There was certainly no suggestion that the State could show standing where the private parties could not; there was no dispute, after all, that the private landowners had "an action at law". *Tennessee Copper* has since stood for nothing more than a State's right, in an original jurisdiction action, to sue in a representative capacity as *parens patriae. See, e.g., Maryland v. Louisiana*, 451 U.S. 725, 737 (1981). Nothing about a State's ability to sue in that capacity dilutes the bedrock requirement of showing injury, causation, and redressability to satisfy Article III.

A claim of *parens patriae* standing is distinct from an allegation of direct injury. Far from being a substitute for Article III injury, *parens patriae* actions raise an additional hurdle for a state litigant: the articulation of a "quasi-sovereign interest" "*apart* from the interests of particular private parties." *Alfred L. Snapp & Son, Inc. v. Puerto Rico ex rel. Barez*, 458 U.S. 592, 607 (1982) (emphasis added). Just as an association suing on behalf of its members must show not only that it represents the members but that at least one satisfies Article III requirements, so too a State asserting quasi-sovereign interests as *parens patriae* must still show that its citizens satisfy Article III. Focusing on Massachusetts's interests as quasi-sovereign makes the required showing here harder, not easier. The Court, in effect, takes what has always been regarded as a *necessary* condition for *parens patriae* standing — a quasi-sovereign interest — and converts it into a *sufficient* showing for purposes of Article III.

What is more, the Court's reasoning falters on its own terms. The Court asserts that Massachusetts is entitled to "special solicitude" due to its "quasi-sovereign interests," but then applies our Article III standing test to the asserted injury of the State's loss of coastal property. See *ante*, at 19 (concluding that Massachusetts "has alleged a particularized injury *in its capacity as a landowner*" (emphasis added)). In the context of *parens patriae* standing, however, we have characterized state ownership of land as a "nonsovereign interest" because a State "is likely to have the same interests as other similarly situated proprietors." *Alfred L. Snapp & Son, supra*, at 601.

On top of everything else, the Court overlooks the fact that our cases cast significant doubt on a State's standing to assert a quasi-sovereign interest — as opposed to a direct injury — against the Federal Government. As a general rule, we have held that while a State might assert a quasi-sovereign right as *parens patriae* "for the protection of its citizens, it is no part of its duty or power to enforce their rights in respect of their relations with the Federal Government. In that field it is the United States, and not the State, which represents them." *Massachusetts v. Mellon*, 262 U.S. 447, 485–486 (1923) (citation omitted). . . .

All of this presumably explains why petitioners never cited *Tennessee Copper* in their briefs before this Court or the D. C. Circuit. It presumably explains why not one of the legion of *amici* supporting petitioners ever cited the case. And it presumably explains why not one of the three judges writing below ever cited the case either. Given that one purpose of the standing requirement is " 'to assure that concrete adverseness which sharpens the presentation of issues upon which the court so largely depends for illumination,' " *ante*, at 13–14 (quoting *Baker v. Carr*, 369 U.S. 186, 204(1962)), it is ironic that the Court today adopts a new theory of Article III standing for States without the benefit of briefing or argument on the point.[1]

II

It is not at all clear how the Court's "special solicitude" for Massachusetts plays out in the standing analysis, except as an implicit concession that petitioners cannot establish standing on traditional terms. But the status of Massachusetts as a State cannot compensate for petitioners' failure to demonstrate injury in fact, causation, and redressability.

---

[1] The Court seems to think we do not recognize that *Tennessee Copper* is a case about *parens patriae* standing, but we have no doubt about that. The point is that nothing in our cases (or Hart & Wechsler) suggests that the prudential requirements for *parens patriae* standing can somehow substitute for, or alter the content of, the "irreducible constitutional minimum" requirements of injury in fact, causation, and redressability under Article III. *Lujan v. Defenders of Wildlife*, 504 U.S. 555, 560 (1992). *Georgia v. Pennsylvania R. Co.*, 324 U.S. 439 (1945), is not to the contrary. As the caption makes clear enough, the fact that a State may assert rights under a federal statute as *parens patriae* in no way refutes our clear ruling that "[a] State does not have standing as *parens patriae* to bring an action against the Federal Government." *Alfred L. Snapp & Son, Inc. v. Puerto Rico ex rel. Barez*, 458 U.S. 592, 610, n. 16 (1982).

When the Court actually applies the three-part test, it focuses, as did the dissent below, on the State's asserted loss of coastal land as the injury in fact. If petitioners rely on loss of land as the Article III injury, however, they must ground the rest of the standing analysis in that specific injury. That alleged injury must be "concrete and particularized," and "distinct and palpable." Central to this concept of "particularized" injury is the requirement that a plaintiff be affected in a "personal and individual way," and seek relief that "directly and tangibly benefits him" in a manner distinct from its impact on "the public at large." Without "particularized" injury, there can be no confidence of 'a real need to exercise the power of judicial review' or that relief can be framed 'no broader than required by the precise facts to which the court's ruling would be applied.' "

The very concept of global warming seems inconsistent with this particularization requirement. Global warming is a phenomenon "harmful to humanity at large," 415 F.3d at 60 (Sentelle, J., dissenting in part and concurring in judgment), and the redress petitioners seek is focused no more on them than on the public generally — it is literally to change the atmosphere around the world.

If petitioners' particularized injury is loss of coastal land, it is also that injury that must be "actual or imminent, not conjectural or hypothetical," "real and immediate," and "certainly impending."

As to "actual" injury, the Court observes that "global sea levels rose somewhere between 10 and 20 centimeters over the 20th century as a result of global warming" and that "these rising seas have already begun to swallow Massachusetts' coastal land." But none of petitioners' declarations supports that connection. One declaration states that "a rise in sea level due to climate change is occurring on the coast of Massachusetts, in the metropolitan Boston area," but there is no elaboration. And the declarant goes on to identify a "significant" *non*-global-warming cause of Boston's rising sea level: land subsidence. Thus, aside from a single conclusory statement, there is nothing in petitioners' 43 standing declarations and accompanying exhibits to support an inference of actual loss of Massachusetts coastal land from 20th century global sea level increases. It is pure conjecture.

The Court's attempts to identify "imminent" or "certainly impending" loss of Massachusetts coastal land fares no better. One of petitioners' declarants predicts global warming will cause sea level to rise by 20 to 70 centimeters *by the year 2100*. Another uses a computer modeling program to map the Commonwealth's coastal land and its current elevation, and calculates that the high-end estimate of sea level rise would result in the loss of significant state-owned coastal land. But the computer modeling program has a conceded average error of about 30 centimeters and a maximum observed error of 70 centimeters. As an initial matter, if it is possible that the model underrepresents the elevation of coastal land to an extent equal to or in excess of the projected sea level rise, it is difficult to put much stock in the predicted loss of land. But even placing that problem to the side, accepting a century-long time horizon and a series of compounded estimates renders requirements of imminence and immediacy utterly toothless. See *Defenders of Wildlife, supra*, at 565, n. 2 (while the concept of " 'imminence' " in standing doctrine is "somewhat elastic," it can be "stretched beyond the breaking point"). "Allegations of possible future injury do not satisfy the requirements of Art. III. A threatened injury must be *certainly impending* to constitute injury in fact." *Whitmore, supra*, at 158.).

III

Petitioners' reliance on Massachusetts's loss of coastal land as their injury in fact for standing purposes creates insurmountable problems for them with respect to causation and redressability. To establish standing, petitioners must show a causal connection between that specific injury and the lack of new motor vehicle greenhouse gas emission standards, and that the promulgation of such standards would likely redress that injury. As is often the case, the questions of causation and redressability overlap. And importantly, when a party is challenging the Government's allegedly unlawful regulation, or lack of regulation, of a third party, satisfying the causation and redressability requirements becomes "substantially more difficult." *Defenders of Wildlife, supra*, at 562.

Petitioners view the relationship between their injuries and EPA's failure to promulgate new motor vehicle greenhouse gas emission standards as simple and direct: Domestic motor vehicles emit carbon dioxide and other greenhouse gases. Worldwide emissions of greenhouse gases contribute to global warming and therefore also to petitioners' alleged injuries. Without the new vehicle standards, greenhouse gas emissions — and therefore global warming and its attendant harms — have been higher than they otherwise would have been; once EPA changes course, the trend will be reversed.

The Court ignores the complexities of global warming, and does so by now disregarding the "particularized" injury it relied on in step one, and using the dire nature of global warming itself as a bootstrap for finding causation and redressability. First, it is important to recognize the extent of the emissions at issue here. Because local greenhouse gas emissions disperse throughout the atmosphere and remain there for anywhere from 50 to 200 years, it is global emissions data that are relevant. According to one of petitioners' declarations, domestic motor vehicles contribute about 6 percent of global carbon dioxide emissions and 4 percent of global greenhouse gas emissions. The amount of global emissions at issue here is smaller still; § 202(a)(1) of the Clean Air Act covers only *new* motor vehicles and *new* motor vehicle engines, so petitioners' desired emission standards might reduce only a fraction of 4 percent of global emissions.

This gets us only to the relevant greenhouse gas emissions; linking them to global warming and ultimately to petitioners' alleged injuries next requires consideration of further complexities. As EPA explained in its denial of petitioners' request for rulemaking,

> predicting future climate change necessarily involves a complex web of economic and physical factors including: our ability to predict future global anthropogenic emissions of [greenhouse gases] and aerosols; the fate of these emissions once they enter the atmosphere (e.g., what percentage are absorbed by vegetation or are taken up by the oceans); the impact of those emissions that remain in the atmosphere on the radiative properties of the atmosphere; changes in critically important climate feedbacks (e.g., changes in cloud cover and ocean circulation); changes in temperature characteristics (e.g., average temperatures, shifts in daytime and evening temperatures); changes in other climatic parameters (e.g., shifts in precipitation, storms); and ultimately the impact of such changes on human health and welfare (e.g., increases or decreases in agricultural productivity, human health impacts).

Petitioners are never able to trace their alleged injuries back through this complex web to the fractional amount of global emissions that might have been limited with EPA standards. In light of the bit-part domestic new motor vehicle greenhouse gas emissions have played in what petitioners describe as a 150-year global phenomenon, and the myriad additional factors bearing on petitioners' alleged injury — the loss of Massachusetts coastal land — the connection is far too speculative to establish causation.

IV

Redressability is even more problematic. To the tenuous link between petitioners' alleged injury and the indeterminate fractional domestic emissions at issue here, add the fact that petitioners cannot meaningfully predict what will come of the 80 percent of global greenhouse gas emissions that originate outside the United States. As the Court acknowledges, "developing countries such as China and India are poised to increase greenhouse gas emissions substantially over the next century," so the domestic emissions at issue here may become an increasingly marginal portion of global emissions, and any decreases produced by petitioners' desired standards are likely to be overwhelmed many times over by emissions increases elsewhere in the world.

Petitioners offer declarations attempting to address this uncertainty, contending that "if the U.S. takes steps to reduce motor vehicle emissions, other countries are very likely to take similar actions regarding their own motor vehicles using technology developed in response to the U.S. program." In other words, do not worry that other countries will contribute far more to global warming than will U.S. automobile emissions; someone is bound to invent something, and places like the People's Republic of China or India will surely require use of the new technology, regardless of cost. The Court previously has explained that when the existence of an element of standing "depends on the unfettered choices made by independent actors not before the courts and whose exercise of broad and legitimate discretion the courts cannot presume either to control or to predict," a party must present facts supporting an assertion that the actor will proceed in such a manner. *Defenders of Wildlife*, 504 U.S. at 562. The declarations' conclusory (not to say fanciful) statements do not even come close.

No matter, the Court reasons, because *any* decrease in domestic emissions will "slow the pace of global emissions increases, no matter what happens elsewhere." Every little bit helps, so Massachusetts can sue over any little bit.

The Court's sleight-of-hand is in failing to link up the different elements of the three-part standing test. What must be *likely* to be redressed is the particular injury in fact. The injury the Court looks to is the asserted loss of land. The Court contends that regulating domestic motor vehicle emissions will reduce carbon dioxide in the atmosphere, *and therefore* redress Massachusetts's injury. But even if regulation *does* reduce emissions — to some indeterminate degree, given events elsewhere in the world — the Court never explains why that makes it *likely* that the injury in fact — the loss of land — will be redressed. Schoolchildren know that a kingdom might be lost "all for the want of a horseshoe nail," but "likely" redressability is a different matter. The realities make it pure conjecture to suppose that EPA regulation of new automobile emissions will *likely* prevent the loss of Massachusetts coastal land.

V

Petitioners' difficulty in demonstrating causation and redressability is not surprising given the evident mismatch between the source of their alleged injury — catastrophic global warming — and the narrow subject matter of the Clean Air Act provision at issue in this suit. The mismatch suggests that petitioners' true goal for this litigation may be more symbolic than anything else. The constitutional role of the courts, however, is to decide concrete cases — not to serve as a convenient forum for policy debates. See *Valley Forge Christian College v. Americans United for Separation of Church and State, Inc.*, 454 U.S. 464, 472 (1982) ("[Standing] tends to assure that the legal questions presented to the court will be resolved, not in the rarified atmosphere of a debating society, but in a concrete factual context conducive to a realistic appreciation of the consequences of judicial action").

When dealing with legal doctrine phrased in terms of what is "fairly" traceable or "likely" to be redressed, it is perhaps not surprising that the matter is subject to some debate. But in considering how loosely or rigorously to define those adverbs, it is vital to keep in mind the purpose of the inquiry. The limitation of the judicial power to cases and controversies "is crucial in maintaining the tripartite allocation of power set forth in the Constitution." *DaimlerChrysler*, 547 U. S., at, 126 S. Ct. 1854 (slip op., at 5) (internal quotation marks omitted). In my view, the Court today — addressing Article III's "core component of standing," *Defenders of Wildlife, supra, at 560* — fails to take this limitation seriously.

To be fair, it is not the first time the Court has done so. Today's decision recalls the previous high-water mark of diluted standing requirements, *United States v. Students Challenging Regulatory Agency Procedures (SCRAP)*, 412 U.S. 669 (1973). *SCRAP* involved "probably the most attenuated injury conferring Art. III standing" and "surely went to the very outer limit of the law" — until today. *Whitmore*, 495 U.S., at 158–159; see also *Lujan v. Nat'l Wildlife Fed'n*, 497 U.S. 871, 889 (1990) (*SCRAP* "has never since been emulated by this Court"). In *SCRAP*, the Court based an environmental group's standing to challenge a railroad freight rate surcharge on the group's allegation that increases in railroad rates would cause an increase in the use of nonrecyclable goods, resulting in the increased need for natural resources to produce such goods. According to the group, some of these resources might be taken from the Washington area, resulting in increased refuse that might find its way into area parks, harming the group's members. 412 U.S., at 688.

Over time, *SCRAP* became emblematic not of the looseness of Article III standing requirements, but of how utterly manipulable they are if not taken seriously as a matter of judicial self-restraint. *SCRAP* made standing seem a lawyer's game, rather than a fundamental limitation ensuring that courts function as courts and not intrude on the politically accountable branches. Today's decision is *SCRAP* for a new generation.[2]

Perhaps the Court recognizes as much. How else to explain its need to devise a new doctrine of state standing to support its result? The good news is that the Court's "special solicitude" for Massachusetts limits the future applicability of the diluted standing requirements applied in this case. The bad news is that the Court's self-professed relaxation of those Article III requirements has caused us to transgress "the proper — and properly limited — role of the courts in a democratic society." *Allen*, 468 U.S., at 750, 104 S. Ct. 3315, 82 L. Ed. 2d 556 (internal quotation marks omitted).

I respectfully dissent.

---

[2] The difficulty with *SCRAP*, and the reason it has not been followed, is not the portion cited by the Court. Rather, it is the *attenuated* nature of the injury there, and here, that is so troubling. Even in *SCRAP*, the Court noted that what was required was "something more than an ingenious academic exercise in the conceivable," 412 U.S., at 688, and we have since understood the allegation there to have been "that the string of occurrences alleged would happen *immediately*," *Whitmore v. Arkansas*, 495 U.S. 149, 159 (1990) (emphasis added). That is hardly the case here.

The Court says it is "quite wrong" to compare petitioners' challenging "EPA's parsimonious construction of the Clean Air Act to a mere 'lawyer's game.' " Of course it is not the legal challenge that is merely "an ingenious academic exercise in the conceivable," *SCRAP, supra,* at 688, but the assertions made in support of standing.

QUESTIONS AND DISCUSSION

1. ***Injury in Fact.*** The federal courts have issued varied decisions regarding whether a widely shared injury may be "concrete and particularized." In *SCRAP*, the Supreme Court observed that "to deny standing to persons who are in fact injured simply because many others are also injured, would mean that the most injurious and widespread Government actions could be questioned by nobody." *SCRAP*, 412 U.S. at 687–88. However, where a plaintiff fails to demonstrate how a widely-shared injury will impact the plaintiff in a particularized way, the Supreme Court has refused to find that the plaintiff has standing. *See, e.g.*, United States v. Richardson, 418 U.S. 166, 176–77 (1974) (stating that generalized grievances do not give rise to a concrete injury); Lujan v. Defenders of Wildlife, 504 U.S. 555, 573–74 (1992) (same). This theory has been characterized as "injury to all is injury to none." As Judge Gould stated in *Covington*, "A theory that 'injury to all is injury to none' seems wrong in theory, for it would deny standing to every citizen such that no matter how badly the whole may be hurt, none of the parts could ever have standing to go to court to cure a harmful violation." 358 F.3d at 651. Has the dissent in *Massachusetts v. EPA* adopted the "injury to all is injury to none" theory? Under the dissenting opinion, could any plaintiff ever be able to bring a case relative to climate change? What would a plaintiff need allege to meet the dissent's theory of standing?

2. ***Injury in Fact: "Actual or Imminent."*** The majority recognized Massachusetts's claim of present and future sea-level rise arising from human contributions of GHGs. While some portion of sea-level rise is due to natural phenomena, the petitioners submitted affidavits detailing estimates and projections of future increases in sea level over the next several decades ("by 2100") that would be due, in part, to human emissions of greenhouse gases. Writing for the dissent, Chief Justice Roberts finds these future projections of injury far too speculative to satisfy the "imminence" requirement. Does he have a point? If an injury will not occur for 100 years, is it really "imminent"? What about five years? 50 years?

3. The courts' approach to addressing future injuries often occurs under a "probabilistic harm" theory. Several courts have held that plaintiffs have Article III standing if they can demonstrate that they will suffer a demonstrable increased risk of death or injury as a result of a challenged action. *See* Baur v. Veneman, 352 F.3d 625, 634 (2d Cir. 2003); Cent. Delta Water Agency v. United States, 306 F.3d 938, 947–48 (9th Cir. 2002); Friends of the Earth, Inc. v. Gaston Copper Recycling Corp., 204 F.3d 149, 160 (4th Cir. 2000) (en banc). Other courts, however, have rejected this approach to standing. Shain v. Veneman, 376 F.3d 815, 818 (8th Cir. 2004); Baur, 352 F.3d at 651 & n.3 (Pooler, J., dissenting). Under this approach, plaintiffs must often submit detailed scientific declarations to demonstrate the likelihood of future injury, and defendants often submit their own declarations refuting plaintiffs' scientific claims. Thus, the standing inquiry often turns into a "battle of the experts," even if the claims on the merits involve purely legal questions. Is this appropriate? How else should courts approach the question of standing for future injuries that will result from present actions?

The D.C. Circuit took this probabilistic approach to standing in a case involving the ozone-depleting chemical, methyl bromide. Natural Resources Defense Council v. Environmental Protection Agency, 440 F.3d 476 (D.C. Cir. 2006), *opinion withdrawn on rhrg.*, 464 F.3d 1 (D.C. Cir. 2006). In that case, NRDC challenged EPA's decision to allow for continued use of methyl bromide, despite the U.S. commitment to phase out the substance pursuant to international agreements. NRDC submitted a scientist's declaration alleging that the continued use would result in "10 deaths, more than 2,000 non-fatal skin cancer cases, and more than 700 cataract cases" over a period of 145 years. 440 F.3d at 481. Relying (or so it appears) on its own calculations, the court concluded that NRDC had not sufficiently proven that its injuries were imminent, because the court's calculations suggested that no NRDC member would die as a result of the challenged action for at least 12,000 years. *Id.* at 481–84. On rehearing, EPA submitted scientific declarations which stated that approximately 1 in every 129,000 people would, over their lifetimes, contract nonfatal cancer as a result of the rule. The court found this threshold of injury sufficient for Article III standing purposes as two to four of NRDC's nearly half a million members could expect to develop cancer as a result of EPA's rule. How would such a quantitative approach to injury apply in the climate change context?

4. *Standing for Private Litigants.* By focusing its standing decision on the unique status of Massachusetts as a state, the Supreme Court left unanswered whether private citizens have standing to challenge actions that contribute to climate change. Consider the district court's decision in *Northwest Environmental Defense Center v. Owens Corning*. Do you think the district court would have reached the same decision if the case had been decided after *Massachusetts?*

Because much of the climate-related litigation to date has involved whether an agency has adequately fulfilled the procedural requirements under the National Environmental Policy Act to prepare an Environmental Impact Statement, one question of importance is whether plaintiffs seeking redress of procedural violations must meet the "normal standards for redressability and immediacy." In dictum, Justice Scalia suggested that the standing requirements may be relaxed:

> There is this much truth to the assertion that "procedural rights" are special: The person who has been accorded a procedural right to protect his concrete interests can assert that right without meeting all the normal standards for redressability and immediacy. Thus, under our case law, one living adjacent to the site for proposed construction of a federally licensed dam has standing to challenge the licensing agency's failure to prepare an environmental impact statement, even though he cannot establish with any certainty that the statement will cause the license to be withheld or altered, and even though the dam will not be completed for many years.

Lujan v. Defenders of Wildlife, 504 U.S. at 572–73, n. 7. Outside of the climate change context, the Ninth and Tenth Circuits have embraced a more relaxed test for standing under NEPA. Citizens for Better Forestry v. United States Dept. of Agriculture, 341 F.3d 961, 972 (9th Cir. 2003) (holding that plaintiffs "need only establish 'the reasonable probability of the challenged action's threat to [their] concrete interest' "); Committee to Save the Rio Hondo v. Lucero, 102 F.3d 445, 447 n.2, 451 (10th Cir. 1996) ("litigants face few standing barriers where an agency's procedural flaw results in concrete injuries" and that under NEPA "a plaintiff need only show its increased risk is fairly traceable to the agency's failure to comply with the [NEPA]"). In contrast, the D.C. Circuit has adopted a more rigorous test. Florida Audubon Society v. Bentsen, 94 F.3d 658, 666 (D.C. Cir. 1996) (en banc) (plaintiffs must demonstrate that the "challenged act is substantially probable to cause the demonstrated particularized injury."). Should standing requirements be more or less rigorous when plaintiffs assert violations of procedural rights? Which view appears to be more consistent with Justice Scalia's passage in *Defenders?*

5. For private litigants, another important question that the Court left unanswered is the extent to which Congress can define injuries. The role of Congress in standing decisions will likely be tested in future climate change litigation as members of Congress prepare legislation to address climate change. Assume that Congress, either in climate change-specific legislation or in the Clean Air Act, defines injury as flood damage from rising sea levels or weather damage or infectious diseases that likely result from climate change, and that it also enacts a citizen suit provision that allows "any person" to challenge emission standards or limitations relating to GHGs. Do you think that the Supreme Court would find that these provisions meet the constitutional elements of standing? For an excellent article on standing and climate change prior to *Massachusetts v. EPA* as well as a view on the question posed, see Bradford C. Mank, *Standing and Global Warming: Is Injury to All Injury to None?*, 35 ENVTL. L. 1, 81–82 (2005).

6. Both the majority and dissenting opinions in *Massachusetts* acknowledge that domestic motor vehicle emissions contribute about 6 percent of world emissions of carbon dioxide — but they reach polar opposite conclusions about the redressability of the harm. In his dissent in *Massachusetts v. EPA*, Chief Justice Roberts concludes that the petitioners' alleged injuries are "too speculative to establish causation." On redressability, he concludes that it is "pure conjecture" to believe that the regulation of new automobile emissions "will *likely* prevent the loss of Massachusetts coastal land." Should the "bit part" that new U.S. auto emissions may play in reducing global GHG emissions be relevant to causation and redressability? How does the majority's approach to redressability differ from the dissent's? What percentage of current and future emissions would have to be involved in a case before the dissent would likely find standing?

7. Ronald Cass has described the majority's decision as "present[ing] as broad a claim as conceivable, involving harm that is remote, debatable, and — if one gets past those problems — ubiquitous." Ronald A. Cass, Massachusetts v. EPA: *The Inconvenient Truth About Precedent*, 93 VA. L. REV. IN BRIEF 73, 76 (2007). Has the Court opened the floodgates to climate change litigation?

8. *The Dissenters in Massachusetts.* The dissent's statements appear to suggest an unwillingness to hold specific parties — or perhaps any party — accountable for pollution to which everyone in the world contributes. Do you agree with that approach? In the Clean Water Act context, courts have routinely allowed plaintiffs to challenge the actions of just one defendant, even though many other parties are contributing pollution to a given waterway. Public Interest Research Group of New Jersey, Inc. v. Powell Duffryn Terminals Inc., 913 F.2d 64, 72 (3d Cir. 1990) ("The requirement that plaintiff's injuries be 'fairly traceable' to the defendant's conduct does not mean that plaintiffs must show to a scientific certainty that defendant's effluent, and defendant's effluent alone, caused the precise harm suffered by the plaintiffs."); Sierra Club, Lone Star Chapter v. Cedar Point Oil Co. Inc., 73 F.3d 546, 558 (5th Cir. 1996) (same); Natural Resources Defense Council v. Southwest Marine, Inc., 236 F.3d 985, 995 (9th Cir. 2000) (same). Should climate change be treated differently?

9. *Zone of Interests.* In addition to the constitutional requirements for standing, the Supreme Court has also added "prudential" requirements to standing. For example, the Supreme Court has held that a plaintiff claiming a right to sue must "establish that the injury he complains of (his aggrievement, or the adverse effect upon him) falls within the 'zone of interests' sought to be protected by the statutory provision whose violation forms the legal basis for his complaint." Lujan v. National Wildlife Fed'n, 497 U.S. 871 (1990). In the context of climate change, one of the possibly more important prudential limitations is that the federal courts "refrain[] from adjudicating 'abstract questions of wide public significance' which amount to 'generalized grievances,' pervasively shared and most appropriately addressed in the representative branches." Valley Forge Christian College v. Americans United for Separation of Church and State, 454 U.S. 464, 475 (1982). How did the district court in *Northwest Environmental Defense Center* address this prudential limitation? Do you agree with that court's approach? Note that, unlike the constitutional requirements to standing, the prudential limits on standing "can be modified or abrogated by Congress." Bennett v. Spear, 520 U.S. 154, 162 (1997).

A NOTE ON *PARENS PATRIAE*

As the Court says, a state may sue as *parens patriae* to assert the claims of its citizens or to protect *quasi*-sovereign interests of the state. The majority bases its view that states should receive "special solicitude" on *Georgia v. Tennessee Copper*. In that case, the Supreme Court stated:

> The state owns very little of the territory alleged to be affected, and the damage to it capable of estimate in money, possibly, at least, is small. This is a suit by a state for an injury to it in its capacity of *quasi*-sovereign. In that capacity the state has an interest independent of and behind the titles of its citizens, in all the earth and air within its domain. It has the last word as to whether its mountains shall be stripped of their forests and its inhabitants shall breathe pure air. . . . The alleged damage to the state as a private owner is merely a makeweight. . . .

Georgia v. Tennessee Copper, 206 U.S. 230, 237 (1907). While the majority declares that states should be given "special solicitude," it never actually says in what way Massachusetts is being given "special solicitude." Is there evidence that the majority relaxed standing requirements for Massachusetts? If so, is there any reason that the constitutional requirements for standing should have been relaxed? As you consider that question, consider the Supreme Court's historical view of *parens patriae* from the following case, in which it ultimately concluded that Puerto Rico could sue a private party as *parens patriae* for alleged violations of employment laws.

ALFRED L. SNAPP & SON, INC. v. PUERTO RICO *EX REL.* BAREZ
458 U.S. 592 (1982)

JUSTICE WHITE delivered the opinion of the Court.

* * *

Parens patriae means literally "parent of the country." The *parens patriae* action has its roots in the common-law concept of the "royal prerogative." The royal prerogative included the right or responsibility to take care of persons who "are legally unable, on account of mental incapacity, whether it proceed from 1st. nonage: 2. idiocy: or 3. lunacy: to take proper care of themselves and their property." At a fairly early date, American courts recognized this common-law concept, but now in the form of a legislative prerogative: "This prerogative of *parens patriae* is inherent in the supreme power of every State, whether that power is lodged in a royal person or in the legislature [and] is a most beneficent function . . . often necessary to be exercised in the interests of humanity, and for the prevention of injury to those who cannot protect themselves." *Mormon Church v. United States*, 136 U.S. 1, 57 (1890).

This common-law approach, however, has relatively little to do with the concept of *parens patriae* standing that has developed in American law. That concept does not involve the State's stepping in to represent the interests of particular citizens who, for whatever reason, cannot represent themselves. In fact, if nothing more than this is involved — *i.e.*, if the State is only a nominal party without a real interest of its own — then it will not have standing under the *parens patriae* doctrine. See *Pennsylvania* v. *New Jersey*, 426 U.S. 660 (1976); *Oklahoma ex rel. Johnson* v. *Cook*, 304 U.S. 387 (1938); *Oklahoma* v. *Atchison, T. & S. F. R. Co.*, 220 U.S. 277 (1911). Rather, to have such standing the State must assert an injury to what has been characterized as a "quasi-sovereign" interest, which is a judicial construct that does not lend itself to a simple or exact definition. Its nature is perhaps best understood by comparing it to other kinds of interests that a State may pursue and then by examining those interests that have historically been found to fall within this category.

Two sovereign interests are easily identified: First, the exercise of sovereign power over individuals and entities within the relevant jurisdiction — this involves the power to create and enforce a legal code, both civil and criminal; second, the demand for recognition from other sovereigns — most frequently this involves the maintenance and recognition of borders. * * *

Not all that a State does, however, is based on its sovereign character. Two kinds of nonsovereign interests are to be distinguished. First, like other associations and private parties, a State is bound to have a variety of proprietary interests. A State may, for example, own land or participate in a business venture. As a proprietor, it is likely to have the same interests as other similarly situated proprietors. And like other such proprietors it may at times need to pursue those interests in court. Second, a State may, for a variety of reasons, attempt to pursue the interests of a private party, and pursue those interests only for the sake of the real party in interest. Interests of private parties are obviously not in themselves sovereign interests, and they do not become such simply by virtue of the State's aiding in their achievement. In such situations, the State is no more than a nominal party.

Quasi-sovereign interests stand apart from all three of the above: They are not sovereign interests, proprietary interests, or private interests pursued by the State as a nominal party. They consist of a set of interests that the State has in the well-being of its populace. Formulated so broadly, the concept risks being too vague to survive the standing requirements of Art. III: A quasi-sovereign interest must be sufficiently concrete to create an actual controversy between the State and the defendant. The vagueness of this concept can only be filled in by turning to individual cases.

That a *parens patriae* action could rest upon the articulation of a "quasi-sovereign" interest was first recognized by this Court in *Louisiana* v. *Texas*, 176 U.S. 1 (1900). In that case, Louisiana unsuccessfully sought to enjoin a quarantine maintained by Texas officials, which had the effect of limiting trade between Texas and the port of New Orleans. The Court labeled Louisiana's interest in the litigation as that of *parens patriae*, and went on to describe that interest by distinguishing it from the sovereign and proprietary interests of the State:

> "In as much as the vindication of the freedom of interstate commerce is not committed to the State of Louisiana, and that State is not engaged in such commerce, the cause of action must be regarded not as involving any infringement of the powers of the State of Louisiana, or any special injury to her property, but as asserting that the State is entitled to seek relief in this way because the matters complained of affect her citizens at large." *Id.* at 19.

Although Louisiana was unsuccessful in that case in pursuing the commercial interests of its residents, a line of cases followed in which States successfully sought to represent the interests of their citizens in enjoining public nuisances. *North Dakota* v. *Minnesota*, 263 U.S. 365 (1923); *Wyoming* v. *Colorado*, 259 U.S. 419 (1922); *New York* v. *New Jersey*, 256 U.S. 296 (1921); *Kansas* v. *Colorado*, 206 U.S.

46 (1907); *Georgia* v. *Tennessee Copper Co.*, 206 U.S. 230 (1907); *Kansas* v. *Colorado*, 185 U.S. 125 (1902); *Missouri* v. *Illinois*, 180 U.S. 208 (1901).

In the earliest of these, *Missouri* v. *Illinois*, Missouri sought to enjoin the defendants from discharging sewage in such a way as to pollute the Mississippi River in Missouri. The Court relied upon an analogy to independent countries in order to delineate those interests that a State could pursue in federal court as *parens patriae*, apart from its sovereign and proprietary interests:

> "It is true that no question of boundary is involved, nor of direct property rights belonging to the complainant State. But it must surely be conceded that, if the health and comfort of the inhabitants of a State are threatened, the State is the proper party to represent and defend them. If Missouri were an independent and sovereign State all must admit that she could seek a remedy by negotiation, and, that failing, by force. Diplomatic powers and the right to make war having been surrendered to the general government, it was to be expected that upon the latter would be devolved the duty of providing a remedy and that remedy, we think, is found in the constitutional provisions we are considering." *Id.*, at 241.

This analogy to an independent country was also articulated in *Georgia* v. *Tennessee Copper Co., supra*, at 237, a case involving air pollution in Georgia caused by the discharge of noxious gasses from the defendant's plant in Tennessee. Justice Holmes, writing for the Court, described the State's interest under these circumstances as follows:

> "[The] State has an interest independent of and behind the titles of its citizens, in all the earth and air within its domain. It has the last word as to whether its mountains shall be stripped of their forests and its inhabitants shall breathe pure air. It might have to pay individuals before it could utter that word, but with it remains the final power. . . .

> " . . . When the States by their union made the forcible abatement of outside nuisances impossible to each, they did not thereby agree to submit to whatever might be done. They did not renounce the possibility of making reasonable demands on the ground of their still remaining quasi-sovereign interests."

Both the Missouri case and the Georgia case involved the State's interest in the abatement of public nuisances, instances in which the injury to the public health and comfort was graphic and direct. Although there are numerous examples of such *parens patriae* suits, *e. g., North Dakota v. Minnesota, supra* (flooding); *New York* v. *New Jersey, supra* (water pollution); *Kansas* v. *Colorado*, 185 U.S. 125 (1902) (diversion of water), *parens patriae* interests extend well beyond the prevention of such traditional public nuisances.

In *Pennsylvania* v. *West Virginia*, 262 U.S. 553 (1923), for example, Pennsylvania was recognized as a proper party to represent the interests of its residents in maintaining access to natural gas produced in West Virginia:

> "The private consumers in each State . . . constitute a substantial portion of the State's population. Their health, comfort and welfare are seriously jeopardized by the threatened withdrawal of the gas from the interstate stream. This is a matter of grave public concern in which the State, as representative of the public, has an interest apart from that of the individuals affected. It is not merely a remote or ethical interest but one which is immediate and recognized by law." *Id.*, at 592.

The public nuisance and economic well-being lines of cases were specifically brought together in *Georgia* v. *Pennsylvania R. Co.*, 324 U.S. 439 (1945), in which Georgia alleged that some 20 railroads had conspired to fix freight rates in a manner that discriminated against Georgia shippers in violation of the federal antitrust laws:

> "If the allegations of the bill are taken as true, the economy of Georgia and the welfare of her citizens have seriously suffered as the result of this alleged conspiracy. . . . [Trade barriers] may cause a blight no less serious than the spread of noxious gas over the land or the deposit of sewage in the streams. They may affect the prosperity and welfare of a State as profoundly as any diversion of waters from the rivers. . . . Georgia as a representative of the public is complaining of a wrong which, if proven, limits the opportunities of her people, shackles her industries, retards her development, and relegates her to an inferior economic position among her sister States. These are matters of grave public concern in which Georgia has an interest apart from that of particular individuals who may be affected." *Id.*, at 450–451.

This summary of the case law involving *parens patriae* actions leads to the following conclusions. In order to maintain such an action, the State must articulate an interest apart from the interests of particular private parties, i.e., the State must be more than a nominal party. The State must express a quasi-sovereign interest. Although the articulation of such interests is a matter for case-by-case development — neither an exhaustive formal definition nor a definitive list of qualifying interests can be presented in the abstract — certain characteristics of such interests are so far evident. These characteristics fall into two general categories. First, a State has a quasi-sovereign interest in the health and well-being — both physical and economic — of its residents in general. Second, a State has a quasi-sovereign interest in not being discriminatorily denied its rightful status within the federal system.

The Court has not attempted to draw any definitive limits on the proportion of the population of the State that must be adversely affected by the challenged behavior. Although more must be alleged than injury to an identifiable group of individual residents, the indirect effects of the injury must be considered as well in determining whether the State has alleged injury to a sufficiently substantial segment of its population. One helpful indication in determining whether an alleged injury to the health and welfare of its citizens suffices to give the State standing to sue as *parens patriae* is whether the injury is one that the State, if it could, would likely attempt to address through its sovereign lawmaking powers.

Distinct from but related to the general well-being of its residents, the State has an interest in securing observance of the terms under which it participates in the federal system. In the context of *parens patriae* actions, this means ensuring that the State and its residents are not excluded from the benefits that are to flow from participation in the federal system. Thus, the State need not wait for the Federal Government to vindicate the State's interest in the removal of barriers to the participation by its residents in the free flow of interstate commerce. See *Pennsylvania* v. *West Virginia*, 262 U.S. 553 (1923). Similarly, federal statutes creating benefits or alleviating hardships create interests that a State will obviously wish to have accrue to its residents. See *Georgia* v. *Pennsylvania R. Co.*, 324 U.S. 439 (1945) (federal antitrust laws); *Maryland* v. *Louisiana*, 451 U.S. 725 (1981) (Natural Gas Act). Once again, we caution that the State must be more than a nominal party. But a State does have an interest, independent of the benefits that might accrue to any particular individual, in assuring that the benefits of the federal system are not denied to its general population.

[The Court then concluded that Puerto Rico could sue as *parens patriae* because a State has "a substantial interest" in protecting its citizens from the "harmful effects of discrimination" and that unemployment was "surely a legitimate object" of Puerto Rico's interests.]

For more on states suing as *parens patriae*, see R. FALLON, D. MELTZER, & D. SHAPIRO, HART & WECHSLER'S THE FEDERAL COURTS AND THE FEDERAL SYSTEM 287–94 (5th ed. 2003); Ann Woolhandler & Michael G. Collins, *State Standing*, 81 VA. L. REV. 387 (1995).

III. IS CLIMATE CHANGE A NONJUSTICIABLE POLITICAL QUESTION?

Like standing, the question of whether a particular dispute raises a nonjusticiable political question rests in Article III of the U.S. Constitution. As the Supreme Court has said, "The requirement that jurisdiction be established as a threshold matter 'spring[s]' from the nature and limits of the judicial power of the United States' and is 'inflexible and without exception.'" Steel Co. v. Citizens for a Better Environment, 523 U.S. 83, 94–95 (1998) (quoting Mansfield, C. & L.M.R. Co. v. Swan, 111 U.S. 379, 382 (1884)). "Either the absence of standing or the presence of a political question suffices to prevent the power of the federal judiciary from being invoked by the complaining party." Schlesinger v. Reservists Committee to Stop the War, 418 U.S. 208, 215 (1974).

The complex and global nature of climate change has invited defendants to argue that climate change is not an issue falling within the limited jurisdiction of federal courts but rather the function of Congress and the Chief Executive. As Judge Preska declared in a public nuisance action against five major emitters of greenhouse gases:

> The Framers based our Constitution on the idea that a separation of powers enables a system of checks and balances, allowing our Nation to thrive under a Legislature and Executive that are accountable to the People, subject to judicial review by an independent Judiciary. *See Federalist Paper* No. 47 (1788); U.S. Const. arts. I, II, III. While, at times, some judges have become involved with the most critical issues affecting America, political questions are not the proper domain of judges. *See, e.g., Baker v. Carr*, 369 U.S. 186 (1962); *Nixon v. United States*, 506 U.S. 224 (1993). Were judges to resolve political questions, there would be no check on their resolutions because the Judiciary is not accountable to any other branch or to the People. Thus, when cases present political questions, "judicial review would be inconsistent with the Framers' insistence that our system be one of checks and balances." *Nixon*, 506 U.S. at 234–35. As set out below, cases presenting political questions are consigned to the political branches that are accountable to the People, not to the Judiciary, and the Judiciary is without power to resolve them.

Connecticut v. American Electric Power Co., Inc., 406 F. Supp. 2d 265, 267 (S.D.N.Y. 2005). Chief Justice Roberts described the issue more succinctly in *Massachusetts v. EPA*: "The constitutional role of the courts . . . is to decide concrete cases — not to serve as a convenient forum for policy debates."

Massachusetts v. EPA, 549 U.S. at 547 (dissenting).

The political question doctrine has presented significant hurdles for plaintiffs making public nuisance and other tort claims against automobile manufacturers and emitters of greenhouse gases. In the following case, *California v. General Motors Corp.*, California sought damages against various automakers for creating, and contributing to, an alleged public nuisance under federal common law or the California Civil Code. Defendants claimed that the entire case should be dismissed because it raises nonjusticiable issues properly reserved for resolution by the political branches of government.

CALIFORNIA v. GENERAL MOTORS CORP.
2007 U.S. Dist. LEXIS 68547 (N.D. Cal. 2007)

Opinion by: MARTIN J. JENKINS, J. * * *

II. Political Question — Justiciability

The threshold issue in this case is whether the complaint raises non-justiciable political questions that are beyond the limits of this Court's jurisdiction. Defendants argue that Plaintiff's nuisance claims present nonjusticiable political questions. According to Defendants, global warming and its causes are issues of public and foreign policy fraught with scientific complexity, as well as political, social, and economic consequences. Defendants contend that the political branches of the federal government, and not the courts, must address and resolve these issues. Plaintiff maintains that its federal common law nuisance claim, although complex, is the type of case that courts routinely resolve. Plaintiff does not directly address the justiciability of its state law nuisance claim in its papers.

Because these claims touch on public policy, foreign policy, and political issues, it is "tempting to jump to the conclusion that such claims are barred by the political question doctrine." *Alperin v. Vatican Bank*, 410 F.3d 532, 537 (9th Cir. 2005). However, "it is error to suppose that every case or controversy which touches foreign relations lies beyond judicial cognizance." *Baker v. Carr*, 369 U.S. 186, 211 (1962). The justiciability inquiry is limited to " 'political questions,' not . . . 'political cases,' " *id.* at 217, and should be made on a "case-by-case" basis, *id.* at 211.

To determine if a case is justiciable in light of the separation of powers ordained by the Constitution, a court must decide "whether the duty asserted can be judicially identified and its breach judicially determined, and whether protection for the right asserted can be judicially molded." *Id.* at 198. Six "formulations" indicate the existence of a non-justiciable political question: (1) a textually demonstrable constitutional commitment of the issue to a coordinate political department; (2) a lack of judicially discoverable and manageable standards for resolving it; (3) the impossibility of deciding without an initial policy determination of a kind clearly for nonjudicial discretion; (4) the impossibility of a court's undertaking independent resolution without expressing lack of the respect due coordinate branches of the government; (5) an unusual need for unquestioning adherence to a political decision already made; or (6) the potentiality of embarrassment from multifarious pronouncements by various departments on one question. *Vieth v. Jubelirer*, 541 U.S. 267, 277–78 (2004) (quoting *Baker*, 369 U.S. at 217). Dismissal on the basis of the political question doctrine is appropriate only if one of these formulations[4] is "inextricable" from the case. *Baker*, 369 U.S. at 217. However, these tests are more discrete in theory than in practice, with the analyses often collapsing into one another. *See Nixon v. United States*, 506 U.S. 224, 228–29 (1993) (describing interplay between the first and second *Baker* tests). This overlap is not surprising given the common underlying inquiry of whether the very nature of the question is one that can properly be decided by the judiciary. *Alperin*, 410 F.3d at 544. Although several of the *Baker* indicators support the Court's conclusion that Plaintiff's current claims raise non-justiciable political questions, the third indicator is most relevant on the current record. *See Connecticut v. American Electric Company, Inc. (AEP)*, 406 F. Supp. 2d 265, 272 (S.D. N.Y. 2005) (stating that third *Baker* factor is most relevant).

A. Indicia of Non-Justiciability

1. Resolution of Plaintiff's Federal Common Law Nuisance Claim Would Require This Court To Make An Initial Policy Decision

The third *Baker* indicator asks whether the Court can decide the case "without [making] an initial policy determination of a kind clearly for nonjudicial discretion." *Baker*, 369 U.S. at 217. This factor largely controls the analysis in the current case due to the complexity of the initial global warming policy determinations that must be made by the elected branches prior to the proper adjudication of Plaintiff's federal common law nuisance claim. *AEP*, 406 F. Supp. 2d at 273. Defendants argue that it is impossible for this Court to decide this case without making an initial policy decision of the kind reserved for the political branches of government. Relying on the chronology of legislative and executive efforts in the field of global warming, Defendants argue that any meaningful reduction in carbon dioxide emissions can be achieved only if a broad array of domestic and international activities are regulated in coordination. According to Defendants, this is a policy determination of the highest order more properly reserved for the political branches of government. In opposition, Plaintiff proffers that resolution of this case does not require the Court to make an initial policy determination, but instead requires the Court to do nothing more than apply facts to well-established law. Plaintiff contends that Defendants are contributing to an interstate nuisance that is causing concrete damage to the State of California, which is properly compensable in damages. Plaintiff asserts that it should not have to await a comprehensive political solution to global warming.

As the Supreme Court has recognized, to resolve typical air pollution cases, courts must strike a balance "between interests seeking strict schemes to reduce pollution rapidly to eliminate its social costs and interests advancing the economic concern that strict schemes [will] retard industrial development with attendant social costs." *AEP*, 406 F. Supp. 2d at 272 (citing *Chevron U.S.A., Inc. v. Natural Res. Def. Council, Inc.*, 467 U.S. 837, 847 (1984)). Balancing those interests, together with the other interests involved, is impossible without an "initial policy determination" first having been made by the elected branches to which our system commits such policy decisions, namely, Congress and the President. *Id.* Courts have recognized the complexity of the "initial policy determinations" that must be made by the elected branches before a non-elected court can properly adjudicate a global warming nuisance claim. *Id.* at 273.

---

[4] Although termed as "formulations" in *Baker*, the plurality in *Vieth v. Jubelirer*, 541 U.S. 267 (2004), recently described these criteria as "six independent tests." *Alperin*, 410 F.3d at 544.

In *AEP*, the court rejected a similar global warming nuisance claim finding that resolution of the issues required "an initial policy determination of a kind clearly for non-judicial discretion." *AEP*, 406 F. Supp. 2d at 274. There, the Attorneys General of California and other States brought a global warming public nuisance claim against certain electric utilities seeking abatement. *Id.* at 267, 270. In particular, the plaintiffs sought an order: (1) holding each of the defendants jointly and severally liable for contributing to an ongoing public nuisance, global warming; and (2) enjoining each of the defendants to abate its contribution to the nuisance [by] capping its emission of carbon dioxide and then reducing those emissions by a specified percentage each year for at least a decade. *Id.* at 270. After outlining the historical legislative and executive efforts to address global warming, the court stated, "[t]he explicit statements of Congress and the Executive on the issue of global climate change in general and their specific refusal to impose the limits on carbon dioxide emissions Plaintiffs now seek to impose by judicial fiat confirm that making the 'initial policy determination[s]' addressing global climate change is an undertaking for the political branches." *Id.* at 274.

Also in *AEP*, the court noted that the EPA's commentary on global warming was compelling support for the notion that the elected branches must make an initial policy determination on global warming before the courts can properly adjudicate such a claim. *See id.* at 273. The EPA, the agency in which "Congress has vested administrative authority" over the "technically complex area of environmental law," has been grappling with the proper approach to the issue of global climate change for a number of years. *Id.* (citation omitted). As the EPA has stated:

> It is hard to imagine any issue in the environmental area having greater "economic and political significance" than regulation of activities that might lead to global climate change. The issue of global climate change . . . has been discussed extensively during the [past] Presidential campaigns; it is the subject of debate and negotiation in several international bodies; and numerous bills have been introduced in Congress over the last 15 years to address the issue." Unilateral [regulation of carbon dioxide emissions in the United States] could also weaken U.S. efforts to persuade key developing countries to reduce the [greenhouse gas] intensity of their economies. Unavoidably, climate change raises important foreign policy issues, and it is the President's prerogative to address them. Virtually every sector of the U.S. economy is either directly or indirectly a source of [greenhouse gas] emissions, and the countries of the world are involved in scientific, technical, and political-level discussions about climate change.

This Court is mindful that the federal common law nuisance claim in *AEP* sought only equitable relief, whereas Plaintiff's current federal common law nuisance claim seeks damages. However, despite this difference, the Court finds that the same justiciability concerns predominate and significantly constrain this Court's ability to properly adjudicate the current claim. Regardless of the type of relief sought, the Court must still make an initial policy decision in deciding whether there has been an "unreasonable interference with a right common to the general public." *In re Oswego Barge Corp.*, 664 F.2d 327, 332 n.5 (2d Cir. 1981) (describing public nuisance). Plaintiff insists that in order to adjudicate its claim, "[t]he Court will not be required to determine whether [D]efendants' actions have been unreasonable, but [instead] whether the interference suffered by California is unreasonable." This distinction is unconvincing because regardless of the relief sought, the Court is left to make an initial decision as to what is unreasonable in the context of carbon dioxide emissions. Such an exercise would require the Court to create a quotient or standard in order to quantify any potential damages that flow from Defendants' alleged act of contributing thirty percent of California's carbon dioxide emissions.

Just as in *AEP*, the adjudication of Plaintiff's claim would require the Court to balance the competing interests of reducing global warming emissions and the interests of advancing and preserving economic and industrial development. *AEP*, 406 F. Supp. 2d at 272. The balancing of those competing interests is the type of initial policy determination to be made by the political branches, and not this Court.

The political branches' actions and deliberate inactions in the area of global warming further highlight this case as one for nonjudicial discretion. An examination of the political branches' consideration of the issues surrounding global climate change counsels against an initial policy determination to be made by the courts. As early as 1978, and as recent as the current administration, the elected branches of government have addressed the issues of climate change and global warming. As the above-referenced chronological policy summary demonstrates, reductions in carbon dioxide emissions is an issue still under active consideration by those branches of government.

[The court then described the comprehensive state and federal scheme to control air pollution found in the Clean Air Act (CAA) and fuel economy requirements of the Energy Policy and Conservation Act (EPCA).]

By themselves, the CAA and EPCA do not directly address the issue of global warming and carbon dioxide emission standards. However, when read in conjunction with the prevalence of international and national debate, and the resulting policy actions and inactions, the Court finds that injecting itself into the global warming thicket at this juncture would require an initial policy determination of the type reserved for the political branches of government. A judicial determination of monetary damages for Plaintiff's global warming nuisance tort would improperly place this Court into precisely the geopolitical debate more properly assigned to the coordinate branches and would potentially undermine the political branches' strategic choices by "weaken[ing] U.S. efforts to persuade key developing countries to reduce the [greenhouse gas] intensity of their economies." Plaintiff has failed to provide the Court with sufficient explanation or legal support as to how this Court could impose damages against the Defendant automakers without unreasonably encroaching into the global warming issues currently under consideration by the political branches. Because a comprehensive global warming solution must be achieved by a broad array of domestic and international measures that are yet undefined, it would be premature and inappropriate for this Court to wade into this type of policy-making determination before the elected branches have done so.

A recent Supreme Court opinion further underscores the conclusion that policy decisions concerning the authority and standards for carbon dioxide emissions lie with the political branches of government, and not with the courts. *See Massachusetts v. Environmental Protection Agency*, 127 S. Ct. 1438 (2007). . . . The Supreme Court's holdings with respect to standing and the reach of the EPA's regulatory authority are particularly relevant to this Court's finding that Plaintiff's claims are non-justiciable.

*   *   *

The underpinnings of the Supreme Court's rationale in *Massachusetts* only reinforce this Court's conclusion that Plaintiff's current tort claim would require this Court to make the precise initial carbon dioxide policy determinations that should be made by the political branches, and to the extent that such determination falls under the CAA, by the EPA. Because the States have "surrendered" to the federal government their right to engage in certain forms of regulations and therefore may have standing in certain circumstances to challenge those regulations, and because new automobile carbon dioxide emissions are such a regulation expressly left to the federal government, a resolution of this case would thrust this

Court beyond the bounds of justiciability. Plaintiff has failed to offer an adequate explanation of how this Court would possibly endeavor to make the initial policy determinations that would be both necessary and antecedent to a resolution of this case.

*   *   *

For these reasons, the Court find[s] that it cannot adjudicate Plaintiff's federal common law global warming nuisance tort claim without making an initial policy determination of a kind clearly for nonjudicial discretion.

2. Plaintiff's Claim Implicates A Textually Demonstrable Constitutional Commitment To The Political Branches

Several other factors outlined by the Supreme Court in *Baker* weigh in favor of the Court's finding that Plaintiff's claim presents a non-justiciable political question. The first *Baker* test requires a court to determine whether the issues before the court implicate a textually demonstrable constitutional commitment to the political branches of government. *Baker*, 369 U.S. at 217. In support of their argument that the Constitution reserves the issues in this case for the political branches of government, Defendants rely on Congress's enumerated power over interstate commerce and the political branches' enumerated power over foreign policy. *See* U.S. Const. art. I, § 8, cl. 3; art. II, § 2, el. 2. Plaintiff disagrees and maintains its environmental nuisance claim is committed to the federal judiciary and has no import on interstate commerce or foreign policy.

"In order to determine whether there has been a textual commitment to a coordinate department of the Government, [a court] must interpret the Constitution." *Powell v. McCormack*, 395 U.S. 486, 519 (1969). The test for a "textual commitment to a coordinate political department" is not completely separate from the test for "a lack of judicially discoverable and manageable standards" for resolving it. *Nixon*, 506 U.S. at 228. The lack of judicially manageable standards may strengthen the conclusion that there is a textually demonstrable commitment to a coordinate branch. *Id.* at 228–29. At issue here are the textual commitment of *interstate commerce and foreign policy* to the political branches of government.

*   *   *

In addressing Congress's power over national and foreign commerce, the Court notes that recognizing such a new and unprecedented federal common law nuisance claim for damages would likely have commerce implications in other States by potentially exposing automakers, utility companies, and other industries to damages flowing from a new judicially-created tort for doing nothing more than lawfully engaging in their respective spheres of commerce within those States. *See Gore*, 517 U.S. at 571–72 (discussing Commerce Clause in tort context and declaring that "a State may not impose economic sanctions on violators of its laws with the intent of changing the tortfeasors' lawful conduct in other States."). The Court finds that the concerns raised by the potential ramifications of a judicial decision on global warming in this case would sufficiently encroach upon interstate commerce, to cause the Court to pause before delving into such areas so constitutionally committed to Congress.

In the area of foreign policy, the Court finds that the political branches have weighed in on the issue, and have made foreign policy determinations regarding the United States' role in the international concern about global warming. The political branches have deliberately elected to refrain from any unilateral commitment to reducing such emissions domestically unless developing nations make a reciprocal commitment. The EPA has recognized that imposing mandatory unilateral restrictions on domestic manufacturers would impede that diplomatic objective. Furthermore, the fact that an award of damages would punish Defendants for lawfully selling their automobiles both within California, and outside of California in the global market, buttresses Defendants' position that a judicial determination of damages for carbon dioxide emissions would run headlong into nonjusticiable foreign policy issues.

For these reasons, the Court finds that Plaintiff's federal common law global warming nuisance tort would have an inextricable effect on interstate commerce and foreign policy — issues constitutionally committed to the political branches of government.

3. There Is A Lack of Judicially Discoverable Or Manageable Standards By Which To Resolve Plaintiff's Claim

The second *Baker* indicator requires a court to determine whether there are judicially discoverable or manageable standards available to resolve the question before it. *Baker*, 369 U.S. at 217. Defendants accord special significance to this indicator of justiciability. Defendants assert that it will be impossible for the Court to determine what constitutes an unreasonable level of carbon dioxide produced by Defendants' vehicles, without making an initial policy determination of national scope. Defendants also point to the difficulty associated in evaluating the essential elements of causation and injury, given the myriad sources of global greenhouse gas emissions and the "[s]ubstantial scientific uncertainties [that] limit [the] ability to separate out those changes resulting from natural variability from those that are directly the result of increases in anthropogenic [greenhouse gases]." 68 Fed. Reg. at 52930. Plaintiff avers that because this action seeks damages only, the legal framework for adjudicating this case is already established.

The crux of this inquiry is not whether the case is unmanageable in the sense of being large, complicated, or otherwise difficult to tackle from a logistical standpoint. *Alperin*, 410 F.3d at 552. Rather, courts must ask whether they have the legal tools to reach a ruling that is "principled, rational, and based upon reasoned distinctions." *Vieth*, 541 U.S. at 278.

In support of its argument that the legal framework is well-established, Plaintiff cites a number of trans-boundary nuisance cases. * * *

Legally, these cases are distinguishable because the remedies sought therein were equitable remedies to enjoin or abate the nuisance, rather than the legal remedy of monetary damages sought in the current case. Additionally, the cases cited by Plaintiff do not provide the Court with legal framework or applicable standards upon which to allocate fault or damages, if any, in this case. The Court is left without guidance in determining what is an unreasonable contribution to the sum of carbon dioxide in the Earth's atmosphere, or in determining who should bear the costs associated with the global climate change that admittedly result from multiple sources around the globe. Plaintiff has failed to provide convincing legal authority to support its proposition that the legal framework for assessing global warming nuisance damages is well-established.

Factually, Plaintiff's cases are distinguishable because none of the pollution-as-public-nuisance cases implicates a comparable number of national and international policy issues. *See AEP*, 406 F. Supp. 2d at 272 (noting that the plaintiffs' reliance on the same decisions was unavailing due to the wide array of policy considerations not suitable for judicial determination). To the contrary, Plaintiff's cited decisions involve primarily issues of local concern involving a state or public entity seeking equitable relief from a source-certain nuisance originating in a neighboring state. Plaintiff's cited decisions are also factually distinguishable because the cases involved transboundary nuisances from identifiable external sources. As more fully discussed below, this is a critical distinction because the limited application of federal common law nuisance claims has been recognized as a means for a State to seek abatement of pollution originating within the borders of another state. In this case, Plaintiff's global warning nuisance tort claim seeks to impose damages on a much larger and unprecedented scale by grounding the claim in pollution originating both within, and well beyond, the borders of the State of California. Unlike the equitable standards available in Plaintiffs' cited cases, here the Court is left without a manageable method of discerning the entities that are creating and contributing to the alleged nuisance. In this case, there are multiple worldwide sources of atmospheric warming across myriad industries and multiple countries.

"Were judges to resolve political questions, there would be no check on their resolutions because the Judiciary is not accountable to any other branch or to the People. Thus, when cases present political questions, 'judicial review would be inconsistent with the Framers' insistence that our system be one of checks and balances.'" *AEP*, 406 F. Supp. 2d at 267. For these reasons, the Court finds that this *Baker* indicator is inextricable from the current case and that there is a lack of judicially discoverable or manageable standards by which to properly adjudicate Plaintiff's federal common law global warning nuisance claim.

Because each of the identified *Baker* indicators is inextricable from Plaintiff's federal common law global warning nuisance claim, the Court finds that the claim presents a non-justiciable political question, and therefore **GRANTS** Defendants' motion to dismiss this claim.

QUESTIONS AND DISCUSSION

1.   The court in *California v. General Motors* references the *AEP* case, in which Connecticut, New York, and other states, as well as a number of environmental organizations, brought a public nuisance claim against five large power generators. According to the plaintiffs, the defendants collectively emit approximately 650 million tons of carbon dioxide annually, "are the five largest emitters of carbon dioxide in the United States," and their emissions "constitute approximately one quarter of the U.S. electric power sector's carbon dioxide emissions." *Connecticut v. American Electric Power Co., Inc.*, 406 F. Supp. 2d 265, 268 (S.D.N.Y. 2005). Nonetheless, the *AEP* court found that the resolution of climate change related issues:

> requires identification and balancing of economic, environmental, foreign policy, and national security interests, [and] "an initial policy determination of a kind clearly for non-judicial discretion" is required. *Vieth*, 541 U.S. at 278 (quoting *Baker*, 369 U.S. at 212). Indeed, the questions presented here "uniquely demand single-voiced statement of the Government's views." *Baker*, 369 U.S. at 211. Thus, these actions present non-justiciable political questions that are consigned to the political branches, not the Judiciary.

Id. at 274. Do you agree?

2.   In *AEP*, plaintiffs sought only injunctive relief, including an order establishing a cap on the allowable carbon dioxide emissions from each facility as well as an annual percentage reduction in these emissions over a decade-long period. In dismissing the plaintiffs' claims, the district court concluded that the plaintiffs' request would have effectively required the court to:

(1) determine the appropriate level at which to cap the carbon dioxide emissions of these Defendants; (2) determine the appropriate percentage reduction to impose upon Defendants; (3) create a schedule to implement those reductions; (4) determine and balance the implications of such relief on the United States' ongoing negotiations with other nations concerning global climate change; (5) assess and measure available alternative energy resources; and (6) determine and balance the implications of such relief on the United States' energy sufficiency and thus its national security — all without an "initial policy determination" having been made by the elected branches.

AEP, 406 F. Supp. 2d at 272. Was the *AEP* court correct that granting plaintiffs' relief would require compliance with all six steps? Wouldn't a court need to undertake the same tasks for other types of pollution (e.g., odors from a pig farm or sulfur dioxide emissions from a smelter)? In *California v. General Motors*, the plaintiff sought monetary damages with hopes of avoiding the issues raised by seeking injunctive relief highlighted in *AEP*. Does a request for monetary damages avoid the need to answer these questions?

3.   The underlying question in these cases is not whether climate change should be addressed but whether the judiciary is the appropriate forum for addressing climate change. Abating climate change requires the reduction of greenhouse gases from a wide variety of sources, each with a different global warming potential and overall contribution to climate change. What then constitutes an unreasonable level of emissions for any of these gases? This issue was addressed prominently in *Comer*, where individuals claimed that the GHG emissions of nine oil companies, thirty-one coal companies, and four chemical companies constituted a public nuisance and contributed to Hurricane Katrina. This court, too, dismissed plaintiffs' claims as nonjusticiable pursuant to the political question doctrine. Comer v. Murphy Oil USA, Inc., Civ. Action No. 1:05-CV-436-LG-RHW (S.D. Miss. Aug. 30, 2007); *see also* Comer v. Nationwide Mut. Ins. Co., No. 1:05 CV-436-LTD-RHW, 2006 WL 1066645, at 3 (S.D. Miss. Feb. 23, 2006) (dismissing without prejudice the claims against insurance companies and mortgage providers, but preserving the claims against the oil and chemical company defendants). The defendants argued that the court was being asked to decide "what is an acceptable level of emissions in a world in which . . . my clients have engaged in nothing but lawful activity." *Comer*, Transcript of Hearing on Defendants' Motions to Dismiss, at 9. Plaintiffs responded that the issue was not to determine an appropriate level of CO_2 emissions but rather to determine "what constitutes unreasonable conduct" based on the "reasonable person" standard common in tort law. *Id.* at 19. The court sided with defendants: "Adjudication of the plaintiffs' claims in this case would necessitate the formulation of standards dictating, for example, the amount of greenhouse gas emissions that would be excessive and the scientific and policy reasons behind those standards." *Id.* at 40. Plaintiffs had argued that no such standard setting was needed because plaintiffs sought monetary damages and not injunctive relief. The court, however, did not see any distinction between injunctive and monetary relief:

> **The Court:** "Wouldn't you agree that any emission or any contribution to greenhouse gases, that cannot be a good thing, and consequently, there must be some standard by which a jury could conclude that at some point . . . so much greenhouse gas has been contributed to the atmosphere that it reaches a point of negligence or unreasonable conduct. Where is that — where is that point? When do we reach that point? How do we know, for example, when a particular coal mining or coal producing defendant has crossed the line between acceptable legal conduct and negligent or unreasonable conduct?"

Mr. Maples [the plaintiffs' attorney]: As an example of crossing the line, I think we have to look at the conduct of the parties, their actions in concert, whether or not they were making a good faith effort to learn the effects of their products, to promote science, or were they in fact doing something else and visiting a giant fraud on the public at large. They cannot say that the public at large are contributors to this cause if it was their conduct that caused a confusion in the eyes of the public at large as far as what the scientific truth was. . . .

The Court: Are you telling me that ultimately the standard that the jury would apply would be what would a reasonable emitter of greenhouse gases do?

*   *   *

Mr. Maples: It doesn't have to be a scientific standard. This court doesn't have to make a determination about what would be a good policy or bad policy decision concerning levels of emissions into the atmosphere. . . . If these defendants knew full well what they were doing, if they knew that this problem was getting worse and worse and worse, if they hid the truth, if they were deceitful about the science, then I think this Court can formulate jury instructions that submit that question to the jury based upon the evidence, but we have to go through the whole discovery process to see what all the evidence is.

Id. at 25–27. The focus on conduct other than emissions foreshadowed the complaint in *Kivalina v. Exxon Mobil*, excerpted *infra* in Chapter 16. In *Kivalina*, plaintiffs alleged defendants collectively conspired to distort the science of global warning to delay public policy responses. Prior to Kivalina, plaintiffs had relied on the use of public nuisance theories to alleviate the need to focus on the reasonableness of defendants' behavior. Rather than identify an unreasonable level of emissions, plaintiffs asked the court simply to find that a defendants' CO_2 emissions caused a public nuisance because they constitute "a substantial interference" with a right held in common by the general public. Public nuisance theories for liability in the climate context are discussed further in Chapter 16. *See also* DAN B. DOBBS, THE LAW OF TORTS, § 467 (2000) (defining a public nuisance).

4. Appeals are pending in all three of these public nuisance cases (*California*, *AEP*, and *Comer*). How would you argue for plaintiffs on appeal? What are the strongest arguments that the courts should treat these climate change claims just like any other public nuisance claim?

5. Many other types of public nuisance and tort actions involve pollutants that move in interstate and international commerce, yet courts have little difficulty applying principles of tort law to resolve the disputes. Shortly after the district court dismissed the plaintiffs' claims in *AEP*, defendants in a case involving the gasoline additive methyl tertiary butyl ether (MBTE) sought dismissal of a products liability and public nuisance action on "political question" grounds. In re Methyl Tertiary Butyl Ether (MBTE) Products Liability Litigation, 438 F. Supp. 2d 291 (S.D. N.Y. 2006). The court rejected each of the defendants' arguments, noting that Congress' deliberations regarding MBTE — which had not resulted in any action — could not provide a basis for dismissing what was otherwise a typical tort action. *Id.* at 301. The court repeatedly referred to the MBTE as an ordinary or typical tort action and refused to allow the political question doctrine to serve as justification for dismissal. Why, in the context of climate change, did the courts reach a different result? Is it really that much easier to determine when odor from a pig farm or sulfur dioxide emissions from a smelter substantially interfere with a person's property (private nuisance) or the general public's interest in health,

safety, and convenience (public nuisance)?

Chapter 13

CLIMATE CHANGE UNDER EXISTING FEDERAL ENVIRONMENTAL STATUTES

This chapter addresses the application of existing U.S. environmental statutes to climate change. In the absence of any comprehensive federal climate change legislation, advocates and policymakers turned to sometimes innovative approaches to tackling climate change through existing statutes. The Clean Air Act, addressed in Section I, is an obvious candidate for addressing climate change and holds significant promise for climate-related regulation. More creative, perhaps, were efforts to use provisions of the National Environmental Policy Act (Section II), the Endangered Species Act (Section III) and the Clean Water Act (Section IV) to force government action on climate change. As you read these sections, consider the creativity of the lawyers who are clearly attempting to extend statutes meant primarily for one purpose to the new purpose of addressing climate change.

I. REGULATING CLIMATE CHANGE UNDER THE CLEAN AIR ACT

On its face, the Clean Air Act (CAA) is the most clearly relevant federal environmental statute for addressing climate change. The emission of carbon dioxide and other greenhouse gases would seem to be exactly the type of activity that would be covered under the Clean Air Act. Indeed, some of the pollutants regulated under the CAA are greenhouse gases, although they were regulated for ground-level environmental impacts and not because of their role in global warming.

It is hard to understand the current relationship of the Clean Air Act with climate change without recognizing the intensely political nature of the issue. Having repudiated the Kyoto Protocol in 2001, the Bush Administration was firmly committed to the position that climate change does not warrant any binding constraints on greenhouse gas emissions. For this reason, until 2009 the Environmental Protection Agency (EPA) opposed the use of any existing authority under the Clean Air Act to regulate greenhouse gases. Indeed, in 2003 the EPA General Counsel reversed the agency's earlier positions and stated that EPA has no authority under the CAA to regulate carbon dioxide emissions. Not surprisingly, this shift in position launched a firestorm of protest and litigation, which resulted in the Supreme Court's decision in *Massachusetts v. EPA*.

Through a series of lawsuits, petitions, and other activities, environmental groups and some states have repeatedly tried to persuade, entice, or even force EPA to regulate greenhouse gases under the Act. Although these efforts have led to important decisions, including *Massachusetts v. EPA*, the strategy has not yet prevailed, and EPA had yet to issue any federal rule or regulation curbing greenhouse gases under the Clean Air Act — at least not for climate change purposes at the time this casebook went to press. However, the Obama Administration seems poised to reverse some of the positions EPA took during the Bush Administration regarding regulation of greenhouse gases under the CAA. Many observers believe it is only a matter of time before EPA exercises its authority under the CAA to regulate greenhouse gas emissions from automobiles, coal-fired power plants, and possibly other major sources of greenhouse gases.

The Clean Air Act is complicated, and understanding its potential implications for climate change even more so. This section first briefly summarizes the Clean Air Act and then discusses major areas of controversy in the climate context: (1) the fight over EPA's authority to regulate carbon dioxide, which led to the Supreme Court decision in *Massachusetts v. EPA*; (2) the dispute over whether the State of California's motor vehicle emission standards are preempted by the Clean Air Act; and (3) ongoing debates regarding regulation of carbon dioxide emissions from coal-fired power plants. The section concludes with a brief overview of future actions the Obama Administration may take to address climate change under the CAA.

A.   Overview of the CAA

The CAA has been described as "without a doubt the most complex environmental regulatory scheme," one "that is bewildering at times to even the most experienced environmental lawyers." SUSAN MANDIBERG & SUSAN SMITH, CRIMES AGAINST THE ENVIRONMENT § 4-2(a) (1997). The CAA simply cannot be learned in a single day. That said, a basic discussion of the main provisions of the CAA will help you navigate your way through the materials.

Generally speaking, the CAA regulates emissions of "air pollutants" from stationary sources and mobile sources. Air pollutant is broadly defined to mean "any air pollution agent or combination of such agents, including any physical, chemical, biological, radioactive . . . substance or matter which is emitted into or otherwise enters the atmosphere." CAA § 302(g); 42 U.S.C. § 7602(g). If EPA determines that an air pollutant "may reasonably be anticipated to endanger public health or welfare," EPA must include that air pollutant on a published list. CAA § 108(a)(1); 42 U.S.C. § 7408(a)(1). Welfare is defined broadly and "includes, but is not limited to, effects on soils, water, crops, vegetation, manmade materials, animals, wildlife, weather, visibility, and climate . . . " CAA § 302(h), 42 U.S.C. § 7602(h). Once an air pollutant is placed on the list, it is considered a "regulated air pollutant" subject to the CAA's various regulatory provisions.

The CAA operates pursuant to a "cooperative federalism" scheme, in which states receive delegated power to administer federal law. States must develop State Implementation Plans (SIPs), which explain how the states plan to administer the CAA within their borders, and submit the SIPs to EPA for review and approval. *See* CAA § 110; 42 U.S.C. § 7410. The SIPs must insure that state-administered programs will be at least as stringent as the federal requirements. Except in specific circumstances described below, states are generally allowed to have more stringent requirements than federal law requires. If a SIP meets the minimum requirements of the CAA, EPA will approve the SIP. *Id.* Once approved, the SIP becomes federal law. *Id.*

The CAA uses several mechanisms to control emissions of regulated air pollutants. These include the establishment of ambient air standards, emissions limitations for stationary sources, emissions limitations for mobile sources, and other regulatory programs designed to address specific environmental problems, including acid rain and ozone depletion.

The Clean Air Act sets forth an elaborate set of standards and requirements that apply differently depending on the type of pollutant, the type and age of the source, and the relative air quality of the region. Thus, the Act differentiates between:

- Criteria pollutants (there are currently six) versus hazardous pollutants (188 regulated hazardous pollutants);

- Stationary sources (e.g., smokestacks) versus mobile sources (e.g., cars, trucks and ships);

- Existing sources (that may be grandfathered under the statute) v. newly proposed sources that must meet federally mandated new source performance standards; and

- Areas that are in compliance with National Ambient Air Quality Standards (NAAQS) versus areas that are not in compliance with those standards.

---

1. *National Ambient Air Quality Standards*

National Ambient Air Quality Standards (NAAQS) are nationwide air quality goals that are meant to protect public health and public welfare. Richard E. Ayres & Mary Rose Kornreich, *Setting National Ambient Air Quality Standards, in* The Clean Air Act Handbook, 13 (2004). NAAQS reflect the maximum concentrations of pollutants in the ambient (i.e., outdoor) air that will still protect health and welfare. *Id.* at 15. The CAA directs EPA to establish a list of air pollutants "the presence of which in the ambient air results from numerous or diverse mobile or stationary sources." CAA § 108(a)(1)(B); 42 U.S.C. § 7408(a)(1)(B). To date, EPA has listed six "criteria" pollutants that are widespread and considered a significant threat to public health and welfare:

1) Sulfur dioxide (SO_2);

2) Particulate matter (PM);

3) Nitrogen oxides (NO_x);

4) Carbon monoxide (CO);

5) Ozone (at the ground level, caused primarily by volatile organic compounds); and

6) Lead.

40 C.F.R. Part 50. Although the Act contemplates that EPA would add new criteria pollutants, only lead has been added by EPA during the life of the Clean Air Act (the other five criteria pollutants were identified by Congress in the original statute).

Once a pollutant is identified as a criteria pollutant, EPA must set both a primary and secondary ambient air quality standard. These are known as National Ambient Air Quality Standards (NAAQS). Once EPA has established NAAQS for a given air pollutant, air emissions may not exceed the applicable NAAQS. The primary NAAQS is intended to protect public health, and the secondary standard is intended to protect public welfare more generally. All areas throughout the country are then labelled either as being in attainment with these standards (i.e., their air quality is at least as good as that required by the NAAQS) or not in attainment with the standards. Achieving and maintaining these ambient standards is left largely up to the states, which must submit a State Implementation Plan to the EPA showing how the State intends to achieve or maintain air pollution levels below the NAAQS. Depending on whether a state is in compliance or non-compliance with the NAAQS for a particular pollutant partly determines how stringent the permitting regulations for air pollution sources have to be.

2.   *Hazardous Air Pollutants*

In addition to the regulation of criteria air pollutants, the Clean Air Act also authorizes EPA to regulate hazardous air pollutants. CAA § 112, 42 U.S.C. § 7412. For the 188 listed hazardous air pollutants (HAPs), none of which has been listed because of its global warming potential, EPA must establish the National Emission Standards for Hazardous Air Pollutants (NESHAPs). Based on the maximum achievable control technology (MACT), NESHAPs should require "the maximum degree of reduction in emissions of the hazardous air pollutants subject to this section (including a prohibition on such emissions, where achievable) that the Administrator, taking into consideration the cost of achieving such emission reduction, and any non-air quality health and environmental impacts and energy requirements, determines is achievable for new or existing sources in the category or subcategory to which such emissions applies." CAA § 112(d)(2), 42 U.S.C. § 7412(d)(2). To implement this standard, EPA sets emission limits that are "no higher than the average emission standards achieved by the best performing 12 percent of sources in each category specified in Section 112 (or the top 5 facilities if the category contains less than 30 sources)." *See* EPA, Module 7: Regulatory Requirements — Title III: Hazardous Air Pollutants.

3.   *Stationary Source Emissions Standards or Limitations*

The Clean Air Act contains two main schemes for regulating emissions of air pollutants from stationary sources. First, the New Source Performance Standards (NSPS) program requires certain categories and classes of stationary sources to comply with specified "standards of performance," which are emissions standards that "reflect[] the degree of emission limitation achievable through the application of the best system of emission reduction which . . . the Administrator [of the EPA] determines has been adequately demonstrated." CAA § 111(a)(1); 42 U.S.C. § 7411(a)(1). NSPS apply to new sources, modified sources, and, at times, existing sources. CAA § 111(a)(2) & (d); 42 U.S.C. § 7411(a)(2) & (d). For NSPS to apply to a particular facility, the facility must fall within a category of sources which, in the EPA Administrator's judgment "causes, or contributes significantly to, air pollution which may reasonably be anticipated to endanger public health or welfare," CAA § 111(b)(1)(A); 42 U.S.C. § 7411(b)(1)(A), and for which EPA has established standards of performance. CAA § 111(b)(4); 42 U.S.C. § 7411(b)(4).

Second, some of the CAA's most important stationary source controls are found in the CAA's new source review (NSR) program. The primary purpose of NSR is to ensure that emissions of air pollutants will not lower ambient air quality. If a stationary source proposes to operate in an area that is in compliance with the NAAQS, that source will be subject to the prevention of significant deterioration (PSD) program. CAA §§ 165–169; 42 U.S.C. §§ 7475–7479. If a stationary source proposes to operate in an area that has not attained any of the NAAQS (i.e., if actual air pollution concentrations exceed the applicable air quality standards), that source will be subject to non-attainment new source review (NNSR).

The PSD and NNSR programs have some similar requirements. First, the programs apply to "major" sources. A source is "major" if it will emit more than a threshold level of pollutants. For most parts of the statute, a facility is considered "major" if it emits or has the potential to emit at least 100 tons per year of any air pollutant. CAA § 302(j); 42 U.S.C. § 7602(j). Under the PSD program, however, the threshold level is 100 tons per year for specifically listed facilities and 250 tons per year for all other facilities. CAA § 169(1); 42 U.S.C. § 7479(1). Second, the programs apply to the construction and operation of any new or modified sources. CAA §§ 165(a), 172(b)(5); 42 U.S.C. §§ 7475(a), 7502(b)(5). Thus, a company must insure that it complies with the new source review requirements before it constructs a new or modified facility.

A facility subject to new source review must install pollution control technology prior to operation. The use of these technology controls is meant to insure compliance with any air quality standards. For the PSD program, the facility must use the "Best Available Control Technology" (BACT). Facilities subject to NNSR must use technology controls that insure that the facility will comply with the "Lowest Achievable Emissions Rate" (LAER). LAER typically requires installation of more effective pollution controls than BACT requires.

While there are other controls on stationary sources, and other important aspects to new source review, the main point to understand is that Congress intended for air emission sources to use pollution control technology to achieve ambient air standards. EPA has been sued recently for failing to include carbon dioxide emissions in its revision of the new source performance standards for power plants. In addition, every coal-fired power plant that is now being proposed is being challenged on grounds that the permit needs to consider regulation of carbon dioxide. This is discussed further in Part D.

----

4. *Mobile Source Emissions Standards*

The CAA also establishes various requirements for mobile sources, including automobiles, trucks, and airplanes. For purposes of climate change, the relevant requirements involve new vehicle emission standards.

The CAA directs the EPA to establish motor vehicle emissions standards for those pollutants which "cause, or contribute to, air pollution which may reasonably be anticipated to endanger public health or welfare." CAA § 202(a)(1); 42 U.S.C. § 7521(a)(1). Unless certain exceptions apply, the emissions standards shall reflect "the greatest degree of emission reduction [technologically and economically] achievable." CAA § 202(a)(3); 42 U.S.C. § 7521(a)(1). The CAA expressly prohibits states from adopting their own motor vehicle emissions standards, with two important exceptions. CAA §§ 209(a)&(b); 42 U.S.C. §§ 7543(a)&(b). First, California is entitled to adopt its own emissions standards for new motor vehicles and engines if EPA grants California a waiver from the prohibition against state-adopted standards. CAA § 209(b)(1); 42 U.S.C. § 7543(b)(1). (The statute does not reference California by name, but allows EPA to waive the prohibition against state-adopted vehicle emission standards for any state which had adopted its own vehicle emissions standards prior to March 30, 1966. CAA § 209(b)(1). California was the only state that had such standards, and thus the only state entitled to the waiver.) EPA "shall" grant the waiver if it determines that, among other requirements, California's standards are at least as protective as the federal standards and California can demonstrate that state standards fulfill a "compelling and extraordinary need." *Id.* Second, once California adopts its own standards, other states may adopt and enforce the California standards, rather than the federal standards. CAA § 177; 42 U.S.C. § 7505. California's efforts to invoke this waiver in order to address climate change are discussed in Part C *infra*.

QUESTIONS AND DISCUSSION

Mandatory Greenhouse Gas Reporting. As a party to the UNFCCC, the United States is obligated to prepare and maintain an inventory of "anthropogenic emissions by sources and removals by sinks of all [greenhouse gases] not controlled by the Montreal Protocol." The Energy Policy Act of 1992 was passed to meet this obligation and directs the Energy Information Agency to "develop [and update annually] . . . an inventory of the national aggregate emissions of each [greenhouse gas] for each calendar year of the baseline period of 1987 through 1990." Under the Act, the United States also established a voluntary greenhouse gas registry where private industry and others could report the results of voluntary efforts to reduce, avoid, or sequester greenhouse gas emissions. For the year 2004, 226 companies reported that they had undertaken 2,154 projects to reduce or sequester approximately 480 million metric tons carbon dioxide equivalent (million $MTCO_2eq$) greenhouse gases in 2004.

In 2007, as part of a massive budget bill, Congress required EPA to establish by June 2009 a mandatory program requiring companies to report their greenhouse gas emissions by mid-2009. Congress left all of the details to EPA's discretion, including which industries will have to report, what threshold levels of emissions will trigger reporting, and how often reporting will be required. *See* H.R. 2764 (Public Law No. 110-161).

B.   *Massachusetts v. EPA*: The Authority to Regulate

Substantial controversy has surrounded the issue of whether and to what extent the Clean Air Act empowers the Administration to regulate greenhouse gases for purposes of addressing climate change. Frustrated with the slow pace of federal climate policy, nineteen environmental organizations petitioned EPA in 1999 to regulate greenhouse gas emissions from new motor vehicles under Section 202 of the Clean Air Act. EPA denied the petition in 2003, arguing that the Act "does not authorize EPA to issue mandatory regulations to address global climate change . . . and (2) that even if the agency had the authority to set greenhouse gas emission standards, it would be unwise to do so." EPA argued that greenhouse gases were not "air pollutants" as defined by the Clean Air Act and, alternatively, that climate change was so important that we would expect Congress to address it explicitly if Congress intended for the Act to cover the issue. The environmental groups, joined by several states and localities, sued EPA claiming that it had misinterpreted the Clean Air Act. The case eventually reached the Supreme Court.

In the resulting *Massachusetts v. EPA* decision, the Supreme Court addressed climate change for the first time. Over a spirited defense, the Court found (5 to 4) that the Clean Air Act had a sufficiently broad definition of "air pollutant" to cover carbon dioxide and the other greenhouse gases at issue. Although Congress in passing the Clean Air Act did not explicitly address climate change, the Court found that it had deliberately provided EPA with sufficient flexibility to address new air pollution threats that might arise over time. Having found that EPA had the regulatory authority to address greenhouse gases, the Court then turned to EPA's argument that now was not the time to regulate greenhouse gases. There the Court found that EPA had not properly evaluated whether greenhouse gases endangered public welfare. As you read the following excerpt, consider what exactly the Court is saying EPA must do:

MASSACHUSETTS v. ENVIRONMENTAL PROTECTION AGENCY
547 U.S. 497 (2007)

JUSTICE STEVENS * * * Petitioners asked us to answer two questions concerning the meaning of § 202(a)(1) of the Act: whether EPA has the statutory authority to regulate greenhouse gas emissions from new motor vehicles; and if so, whether its stated reasons for refusing to do so are consistent with the statute. * * *

Section 202(a)(1) of the Clean Air Act . . . provides:

> "The [EPA] Administrator shall by regulation prescribe (and from time to time revise) in accordance with the provisions of this section, standards applicable to the emission of any air pollutant from any class or classes of new motor vehicles or new motor vehicle engines, which in his judgment cause, or contribute to, air pollution which may reasonably be anticipated to endanger public health or welfare . . . ."

The Act defines "air pollutant" to include "any air pollution agent or combination of such agents, including any physical, chemical, biological, radioactive . . . substance or matter which is emitted into or otherwise enters the ambient air." § 7602(g). "Welfare" is also defined broadly: among other things, it includes "effects on . . . weather . . . and climate." § 7602(h). * * *

II

On October 20, 1999, a group of 19 private organizations filed a rulemaking petition asking EPA to regulate "greenhouse gas emissions from new motor vehicles under § 202 of the Clean Air Act." * * *

On September 8, 2003, EPA entered an order denying the rulemaking petition. The agency gave two reasons for its decision: (1) that contrary to the opinions of its former general counsels, the Clean Air Act does not authorize EPA to issue mandatory regulations to address global climate change,; and (2) that even if the agency had the authority to set greenhouse gas emission standards, it would be unwise to do so at this time.

In concluding that it lacked statutory authority over greenhouse gases, EPA observed that Congress "was well aware of the global climate change issue when it last comprehensively amended the [Clean Air Act] in 1990," yet it declined to adopt a proposed amendment establishing binding emissions limitations. Congress instead chose to authorize further investigation into climate change. EPA further reasoned that Congress' "specially tailored solutions to global atmospheric issues" — in particular, its 1990 enactment of a comprehensive scheme to regulate pollutants that depleted the ozone layer, see Title VI, 104 Stat. 2649, 42 U.S.C. §§ 7671–7671q — counseled against reading the general authorization of § 202(a)(1) to confer regulatory authority over greenhouse gases.

*   *   *

EPA reasoned that climate change had its own "political history": Congress designed the original Clean Air Act to address *local* air pollutants rather than a substance that "is fairly consistent in its concentration throughout the *world's* atmosphere"; declined in 1990 to enact proposed amendments to force EPA to set carbon dioxide emission standards for motor vehicles; and addressed global climate change in other legislation. Because of this political history, and because imposing emission limitations on greenhouse gases would have [great] economic and political repercussions . . . , EPA was persuaded that it lacked the power to do so. In essence, EPA concluded that climate change was so important that unless Congress spoke with exacting specificity, it could not have meant the agency to address it.

Having reached that conclusion, EPA believed it followed that greenhouse gases cannot be "air pollutants" within the meaning of the Act. The agency bolstered this conclusion by explaining that if carbon dioxide were an air pollutant, the only feasible method of reducing tailpipe emissions would be to improve fuel economy. But because Congress has already created detailed mandatory fuel economy standards subject to Department of Transportation (DOT) administration, the agency concluded that EPA regulation would either conflict with those standards or be superfluous.

Even assuming that it had authority over greenhouse gases, EPA explained in detail why it would refuse to exercise that authority. The agency began by recognizing that the concentration of greenhouse gases has dramatically increased as a result of human activities, and acknowledged the attendant increase in global surface air temperatures. EPA nevertheless gave controlling importance to the NRC Report's statement that a causal link between the two " 'cannot be unequivocally established.' " Given that residual uncertainty, EPA concluded that regulating greenhouse gas emissions would be unwise.

The agency furthermore characterized any EPA regulation of motor-vehicle emissions as a "piecemeal approach" to climate change and stated that such regulation would conflict with the President's "comprehensive approach" to the problem. That approach involves additional support for technological innovation, the creation of nonregulatory programs to encourage voluntary private-sector reductions in greenhouse gas emissions, and further research on climate change — not actual regulation. According to EPA, unilateral EPA regulation of motor-vehicle greenhouse gas emissions might also hamper the President's ability to persuade key developing countries to reduce greenhouse gas emissions.

III

*   *   *

The scope of our review of the merits of the statutory issues is narrow. As we have repeated time and again, an agency has broad discretion to choose how best to marshal its limited resources and personnel to carry out its delegated responsibilities. See *Chevron U.S.A. Inc. v. Natural Resources Defense Council, Inc.*, 467 U.S. 837, 842–845 (1984). That discretion is at its height when the agency decides not to bring an enforcement action. Therefore, in *Heckler v. Chaney*, 470 U.S. 821, 105 S.Ct. 1649, 84 L. Ed. 2d 714 (1985), we held that an agency's refusal to initiate enforcement proceedings is not ordinarily subject to judicial review. Some debate remains, however, as to the rigor with which we review an agency's denial of a petition for rulemaking.

There are key differences between a denial of a petition for rulemaking and an agency's decision not to initiate an enforcement action. See *American Horse Protection Assn., Inc. v. Lyng*, 812 F.2d 1, 3–4 (D.C. Cir. 1987). In contrast to nonenforcement decisions, agency refusals to initiate rulemaking "are less frequent, more apt to involve legal as opposed to factual analysis, and subject to special formalities, including a public explanation." *Id.*, at 4; see also 5 U.S.C. § 555(e). They moreover arise out of denials of petitions for rulemaking which (at least in the circumstances here) the affected party had an undoubted procedural right to file in the first instance. Refusals to promulgate rules are thus susceptible to judicial review, though such review is "extremely limited" and "highly deferential." *National Customs Brokers & Forwarders Assn. of America, Inc. v. United States*, 883 F.2d 93, 96 (D.C. Cir. 1989). * * *

VI

On the merits, the first question is whether § 202(a)(1) of the Clean Air Act authorizes EPA to regulate greenhouse gas emissions from new motor vehicles in the event that it forms a "judgment" that such emissions contribute to climate change. We have little trouble concluding that it does. In relevant part, § 202(a)(1) provides that EPA "shall by regulation prescribe . . . standards applicable to the emission of any air pollutant from any class or classes of new motor vehicles or new motor vehicle engines, which in [the Administrator's] judgment cause, or contribute to, air pollution which may reasonably be anticipated to endanger public health or welfare." 42 U.S.C. § 7521(a)(1). Because EPA believes that Congress did not intend it to regulate substances that contribute to climate change, the agency maintains that carbon dioxide is not an "air pollutant" within the meaning of the provision.

The statutory text forecloses EPA's reading. The Clean Air Act's sweeping definition of "air pollutant" includes "*any* air pollution agent or combination of such agents, including *any* physical, chemical . . . substance or matter which is emitted into or otherwise enters the ambient air . . . ." § 7602(g) (emphasis added). On its face, the definition embraces all airborne compounds of whatever stripe, and underscores that intent through the repeated use of the word "any." Carbon dioxide, methane, nitrous oxide, and hydrofluorocarbons are without a doubt "physical [and] chemical . . . substance[s] which [are] emitted into . . . the ambient air." The statute is unambiguous. * * *

EPA finally argues that it cannot regulate carbon dioxide emissions from motor vehicles because doing so would require it to tighten mileage standards, a job (according to EPA) that Congress has assigned to [the Department of Transportation (DOT)]. . . . But that DOT sets mileage standards in no way licenses EPA to shirk its environmental responsibilities. EPA has been charged with protecting the public's "health" and "welfare," 42 U.S.C. § 7521(a)(1), a statutory obligation wholly independent of DOT's mandate to promote energy efficiency. See Energy Policy and Conservation Act, § 2(5), 89 Stat. 874, 42 U.S.C. § 6201(5). The two obligations may overlap, but there is no reason to think the two agencies cannot both administer their obligations and yet avoid inconsistency.

While the Congresses that drafted § 202(a)(1) might not have appreciated the possibility that burning fossil fuels could lead to global warming, they did understand that without regulatory flexibility, changing circumstances and scientific developments would soon render the Clean Air Act obsolete. The broad language of § 202(a)(1) reflects an intentional effort to confer the flexibility necessary to forestall such obsolescence. . . . Because greenhouse gases fit well within the Clean Air Act's capacious definition of "air pollutant," we hold that EPA has the statutory authority to regulate the emission of such gases from new motor vehicles.

VII

The alternative basis for EPA's decision — that even if it does have statutory authority to regulate greenhouse gases, it would be unwise to do so at this time — rests on reasoning divorced from the statutory text. While the statute does condition the exercise of EPA's authority on its formation of a "judgment," 42 U.S.C. § 7521(a)(1), that judgment must relate to whether an air pollutant "cause[s], or contribute[s] to, air pollution which may reasonably be anticipated to endanger public health or welfare," *ibid.* Put another way, the use of the word "judgment" is not a roving license to ignore the statutory text. It is but a direction to exercise discretion within defined statutory limits.

If EPA makes a finding of endangerment, the Clean Air Act requires the agency to regulate emissions of the deleterious pollutant from new motor vehicles. *Ibid.* (stating that "[EPA] shall by regulation prescribe . . . standards applicable to the emission of any air pollutant from any class of new motor vehicles"). EPA no doubt has significant latitude as to the manner, timing, content, and coordination of its regulations with those of other agencies. But once EPA has responded to a petition for rulemaking, its reasons for action or inaction must conform to the authorizing statute. Under the clear terms of the Clean Air Act, EPA can avoid taking further action only if it determines that greenhouse gases do not contribute to climate change or if it provides some reasonable explanation as to why it cannot or will not exercise its discretion to determine whether they do. *Ibid.* To the extent that this constrains agency discretion to pursue other priorities of the Administrator or the President, this is the congressional design.

EPA has refused to comply with this clear statutory command. Instead, it has offered a laundry list of reasons not to regulate. For example, EPA said that a number of voluntary executive branch programs already provide an effective response to the threat of global warming, that regulating greenhouse gases might impair the President's ability to negotiate with "key developing nations" to reduce emissions, and that curtailing motor-vehicle emissions would reflect "an inefficient, piecemeal approach to address the climate change issue."

Although we have neither the expertise nor the authority to evaluate these policy judgments, it is evident they have nothing to do with whether greenhouse gas emissions contribute to climate change. Still less do they amount to a reasoned justification for declining to form a scientific judgment. In particular, while the President has broad authority in foreign affairs, that authority does not extend to the refusal to execute domestic laws. In the Global Climate Protection Act of 1987, Congress authorized the State Department — not EPA — to formulate United States foreign policy with reference to environmental matters relating to climate. See § 1103(c), 101 Stat. 1409. EPA has made no showing that it issued the ruling in question here after consultation with the State Department. Congress did direct EPA to consult with other agencies in the formulation of its policies and rules, but the State Department is absent from that list. § 1103(b).

Nor can EPA avoid its statutory obligation by noting the uncertainty surrounding various features of climate change and concluding that it would therefore be better not to regulate at this time. If the scientific uncertainty is so profound that it precludes EPA from making a reasoned judgment as to whether greenhouse gases contribute to global warming, EPA must say so. That EPA would prefer not to regulate greenhouse gases because of some residual uncertainty . . . is irrelevant. The statutory question is whether sufficient information exists to make an endangerment finding.

In short, EPA has offered no reasoned explanation for its refusal to decide whether greenhouse gases cause or contribute to climate change. Its action was therefore "arbitrary, capricious, . . . or otherwise not in accordance with law." 42 U.S.C. § 7607(d)(9)(A). We need not and do not reach the question whether on remand EPA must make an endangerment finding, or whether policy concerns can inform EPA's actions in the event that it makes such a finding. Cf. *Chevron U.S.A. Inc. v. Natural Resources Defense Council, Inc.*, 467 U.S. 837, 843–844 (1984). We hold only that EPA must ground its reasons for action or inaction in the statute.

VIII

The judgment of the Court of Appeals is reversed, and the case is remanded for further proceedings consistent with this opinion.

It is so ordered.

[Chief Justice Roberts, with whom Justice Scalia, Justice Thomas, and Justice Alito joined, issued an opinion dissenting from the finding that the State of Massachusetts had standing].

Justice Scalia, with whom The Chief Justice, Justice Thomas, and Justice Alito join, dissenting.

I

A

The provision of law at the heart of this case is § 202(a)(1) of the Clean Air Act (CAA), which provides that the Administrator of the Environmental Protection Agency (EPA) "shall by regulation prescribe . . . standards applicable to the emission of any air pollutant from any class or classes of new motor vehicles or new motor vehicle engines, which *in his judgment* cause, or contribute to, air pollution which may reasonably be anticipated to endanger public health or welfare." 42 U.S.C. § 7521(a)(1) (emphasis added). As the Court recognizes, the statute "condition[s] the exercise of EPA's authority on its formation of a 'judgment.' " . . . There is no dispute that the Administrator has made no such judgment in this case. * * *

The question thus arises: Does anything *require* the Administrator to make a "judgment" whenever a petition for rulemaking is filed? Without citation of the statute or any other authority, the Court says yes. Why is that so? . . . Where does the CAA say that the EPA Administrator is required to come to a decision on this question whenever a rulemaking petition is filed? The Court points to no such provision because none exists.

Instead, the Court invents a multiple-choice question that the EPA Administrator must answer when a petition for rulemaking is filed. The Administrator must exercise his judgment in one of three ways: (a) by concluding that the pollutant *does* cause, or contribute to, air pollution that endangers public welfare (in which case

EPA is required to regulate); (b) by concluding that the pollutant *does not* cause, or contribute to, air pollution that endangers public welfare (in which case EPA is *not* required to regulate); or (c) by "provid[ing] some reasonable explanation as to why it cannot or will not exercise its discretion to determine whether" greenhouse gases endanger public welfare (in which case EPA is *not* required to regulate).

I am willing to assume, for the sake of argument, that the Administrator's discretion in this regard is not entirely unbounded — that if he has no reasonable basis for deferring judgment he must grasp the nettle at once. The Court, however, with no basis in text or precedent, rejects all of EPA's stated "policy judgments" as not "amount[ing] to a reasoned justification," effectively narrowing the universe of potential reasonable bases to a single one: Judgment can be delayed *only* if the Administrator concludes that "the scientific uncertainty is [too] profound." The Administrator is precluded from concluding *for other reasons* "that it would . . . be better not to regulate at this time." Such other reasons — perfectly valid reasons — were set forth in the agency's statement. * * *

The Court dismisses EPA's analysis as "rest[ing] on reasoning divorced from the statutory text." "While the statute does condition the exercise of EPA's authority on its formation of a 'judgment,' . . . that judgment must relate to whether an air pollutant 'cause[s], or contribute[s] to, air pollution which may reasonably be anticipated to endanger public health or welfare.' " *Ibid.* True, but irrelevant. When the Administrator *makes* a judgment whether to regulate greenhouse gases, that judgment must relate to whether they are air pollutants that "cause, or contribute to, air pollution which may reasonably be anticipated to endanger public health or welfare." 42 U.S.C. § 7521(a)(1). But the statute says *nothing at all* about the reasons for which the Administrator may *defer* making a judgment — the permissible reasons for deciding not to grapple with the issue at the present time. Thus, the various "policy" rationales that the Court criticizes are not "divorced from the statutory text" except in the sense that the statutory text is silent, as texts are often silent about permissible reasons for the exercise of agency discretion. The reasons the EPA gave are surely considerations executive agencies *regularly* take into account (and *ought* to take into account) when deciding whether to consider entering a new field: the impact such entry would have on other Executive Branch programs and on foreign policy. There is no basis in law for the Court's imposed limitation.

EPA's interpretation of the discretion conferred by the statutory reference to "its judgment" is not only reasonable, it is the most natural reading of the text. The Court nowhere explains why this interpretation is incorrect, let alone why it is not entitled to deference under *Chevron U.S.A. Inc. v. Natural Resources Defense Council, Inc.*, 467 U.S. 837 (1984). As the Administrator acted within the law in declining to make a "judgment" for the policy reasons above set forth, I would uphold the decision to deny the rulemaking petition on that ground alone. * * *

II

A

Even before reaching its discussion of the word "judgment," the Court makes another significant error when it concludes that "§ 202(a)(1) of the Clean Air Act *authorizes* EPA to regulate greenhouse gas emissions from new motor vehicles in the event that it forms a 'judgment' that such emissions contribute to climate change." *Ante*, at 1459 (emphasis added). For such authorization, the Court relies on what it calls "the Clean Air Act's capacious definition of 'air pollutant.' "

"Air pollutant" is defined by the Act as "any air pollution agent or combination of such agents, including any physical, chemical, . . . substance or matter which is emitted into or otherwise enters the ambient air." 42 U.S.C. § 7602(g). The Court is correct that "[c]arbon dioxide, methane, nitrous oxide, and hydrofluorocarbons" fit within the second half of that definition: They are "physical, chemical, . . . substance[s] or matter which [are] emitted into or otherwise ente[r] the ambient air." But the Court mistakenly believes this to be the end of the analysis. In order to be an "air pollutant" under the Act's definition, the "substance or matter [being] emitted into . . . the ambient air" must also meet the *first* half of the definition — namely, it must be an "air pollution agent or combination of such agents." The Court simply pretends this half of the definition does not exist. * * *

In short, the word "including" does not require the Court's (or the petitioners') result. It is perfectly reasonable to view the definition of "air pollutant" in its entirety: An air pollutant *can* be "any physical, chemical, . . . substance or matter which is emitted into or otherwise enters the ambient air," but only if it retains the general characteristic of being an "air pollution agent or combination of such agents." This is precisely the conclusion EPA reached: "[A] substance does not meet the CAA definition of 'air pollutant' simply because it is a 'physical, chemical, . . . substance or matter which is emitted into or otherwise enters the ambient air.' It must also be an 'air pollution agent.' " 68 Fed. Reg. 52929, n. 3. See also *id.*, at 52928 ("The root of the definition indicates that for a substance to be an 'air pollutant,' it must be an 'agent' of 'air pollution' "). Once again, in the face of textual ambiguity, the Court's application of *Chevron* deference to EPA's interpretation of the word "including" is nowhere to be found. Evidently, the Court defers only to those reasonable interpretations that it favors.

B

Using (as we ought to) EPA's interpretation of the definition of "air pollutant," we must next determine whether greenhouse gases are "agent[s]" of "air pollution." If so, the statute would authorize regulation; if not, EPA would lack authority.

Unlike "air pollutants," the term "air pollution" is not itself defined by the CAA; thus, once again we must accept EPA's interpretation of that ambiguous term, provided its interpretation is a "permissible construction of the statute." *Chevron*, 467 U.S., at 843. In this case, the petition for rulemaking asked EPA for "regulation of [greenhouse gas] emissions from motor vehicles to reduce the risk of global climate change." Thus, in deciding whether it had authority to regulate, EPA had to determine whether the concentration of greenhouse gases assertedly responsible for "global climate change" qualifies as "air pollution." EPA began with the common sense observation that the "[p]roblems associated with atmospheric concentrations of CO_2" bear little resemblance to what would naturally be termed "air pollution":

> "EPA's prior use of the CAA's general regulatory provisions provides an important context. Since the inception of the Act, EPA has used these provisions to address air pollution problems that occur primarily at ground level or near the surface of the earth. For example, national ambient air quality standards (NAAQS) established under CAA section 109 address concentrations of substances in the ambient air and the related public health and welfare problems. This has meant setting NAAQS for concentrations of ozone, carbon monoxide, particulate matter and other substances in the air near the surface of the earth, not higher in the atmosphere. . . . CO_2, by contrast, is fairly consistent in concentration throughout the world's atmosphere up to approximately the lower stratosphere."

In other words, regulating the buildup of CO_2 and other greenhouse gases in the upper reaches of the atmosphere, which is alleged to be causing global climate change, is not akin to regulating the concentration of some substance that is *polluting* the *air*.

We need look no further than the dictionary for confirmation that this interpretation of "air pollution" is eminently reasonable. The definition of "pollute," of course, is "[t]o make or render impure or unclean." Webster's New International Dictionary 1910 (2d ed. 1949). And the first three definitions of "air" are as follows: (1) "[t]he invisible, odorless, and tasteless mixture of gases which surrounds the earth"; (2) "[t]he body of the earth's atmosphere; esp., the part of it near the earth, as distinguished from the upper rarefied part"; (3) "[a] portion of air or of the air considered with respect to physical characteristics or as affecting the senses." *Id.*, at 54. EPA's conception of "air pollution" — focusing on impurities in the "ambient air" "at ground level or near the surface of the earth" — is perfectly consistent with the natural meaning of that term.

In the end, EPA concluded that since "CAA authorization to regulate is generally based on a finding that an air pollutant causes or contributes to air pollution" the concentrations of CO_2 and other greenhouse gases allegedly affecting the global climate are beyond the scope of CAA's authorization to regulate. "[T]he term 'air pollution' as used in the regulatory provisions cannot be interpreted to encompass global climate change." *Ibid.* Once again, the Court utterly fails to explain why this interpretation is incorrect, let alone so unreasonable as to be unworthy of *Chevron* deference.

*   *   *

The Court's alarm over global warming may or may not be justified, but it ought not distort the outcome of this litigation. This is a straightforward administrative-law case, in which Congress has passed a malleable statute giving broad discretion, not to us but to an executive agency. No matter how important the underlying policy issues at stake, this Court has no business substituting its own desired outcome for the reasoned judgment of the responsible agency.

After the ruling, the case remanded to EPA for further action. EPA initially announced that it would issue an endangerment finding before the end of 2007, but subsequently changed its mind and announced that it would instead issue an Advanced Notice of Proposed Rulemaking (ANPR) to solicit comments from the public regarding the many issues raised by regulating carbon dioxide under the Clean Air Act. Part E discusses some of the issues raised in the ANPR. Most environmental groups viewed this as a delaying tactic and in early 2008, several of the original plaintiffs filed a writ of mandamus to the D.C. Circuit seeking a court order to compel the EPA to make the endangerment finding. That Court refused to put EPA on any strict timeline, recognizing the inherent complexity of the issue. But in a separate opinion, Judge Tatel recognized the foot-dragging that was apparent: "EPA has postponed — now indefinitely — deciding whether greenhouse gas emissions endanger public health and welfare, calling into question whether the agency's desire to promulgate regulations . . . is simply an excuse to avoid complying with the statute." Order, Massachusetts v. EPA, No. 03–1361 (June 26, 2008). As a result, more than nearly two years after the *Massachusetts v. EPA* ruling, EPA had still not issued an endangerment finding or otherwise responded to the Court's ruling.

QUESTIONS AND DISCUSSION

1. The Court focused on the requirement that EPA must come to a judgment on whether greenhouse gases endanger public health or welfare. Did the Court order EPA to regulate greenhouse gases? If not, what options are left to EPA? In this regard, consider the Court's statement that "EPA can avoid taking further action only if it determines that greenhouse gases do not contribute to climate change or if it provides some reasonable explanation as to why it cannot or will not exercise its discretion to determine whether they do."

2. What do you think of Justice Scalia's effort to distinguish greenhouse gases from the statute's definition of air pollution? Prior to reading this case would you have doubted that greenhouse gas emissions are air pollution? The majority opinion responded to Scalia in a footnote:

> In dissent, Justice Scalia maintains that because greenhouse gases permeate the world's atmosphere rather than a limited area near the earth's surface, EPA's exclusion of greenhouse gases from the category of air pollution "agent[s]" is entitled to deference under *Chevron U.S.A. Inc. v. Natural Resources Defense Council, Inc.* 467 U.S. 837 (1984). EPA's distinction, however, finds no support in the text of the statute, which uses the phrase "the ambient air" without distinguishing between atmospheric layers. Moreover, it is a plainly unreasonable reading of a sweeping statutory provision designed to capture "*any* physical, chemical . . . substance or matter which is emitted into or otherwise enters the ambient air." 42 U.S.C. § 7602(g). Justice SCALIA does not (and cannot) explain why Congress would define "air pollutant" so carefully and so broadly, yet confer on EPA the authority to narrow that definition whenever expedient by asserting that a particular substance is not an "agent." At any rate, no party to this dispute contests that greenhouse gases both "ente[r] the ambient air" and tend to warm the atmosphere. They are therefore unquestionably "agent[s]" of air pollution.

In this regard, consider the discussion of the international law of the atmosphere in Chapter 4. In international law, the global mixing of greenhouse gases makes climate change less like transboundary air pollution. Does this lend support to Justice Scalia's position?

3. As Justice Scalia suggests, *Massachusetts v. EPA* is at root an administrative law case. To what extent does the majority opinion reshape administrative law by eroding the well known *Chevron* doctrine?

4. Justice Scalia's well known rhetorical flare was evident in the following footnote:

> Not only is EPA's interpretation reasonable, it is far more plausible than the Court's alternative. As the Court correctly points out, "all airborne compounds of whatever stripe" would qualify as "physical, chemical-, . . . substance[s] or matter which [are] emitted into or otherwise ente[r] the ambient air," 42 U.S.C. § 7602(g). It follows that *everything* airborne, from Frisbees to flatulence, qualifies as an "air pollutant." This reading of the statute defies common sense.

While cow flatulence is indeed a significant contributor to climate change, are Frisbees covered under the majority's definition?

5. Although *Massachusetts v. EPA* applied only to vehicle emissions, the implications extend to other provisions of the Clean Air Act. Nine states, New York City, the District of Columbia, and three environmental groups sued EPA for failing to include carbon dioxide in revisions to its new source performance standard for electric-generating power plants. Under language very similar to the vehicle emissions language, Section 111(b)(1)(A) of the Clean Air Act requires EPA to include in its categories of stationary sources any category "if in his judgment it causes, or contributes significantly to, air pollution which may reasonably be anticipated to endanger public health or welfare." Once a category of sources is listed, EPA has one year in which to publish new source performance standards for that category of sources. In revising its new source performance standards for power plants, EPA had not included any measures to curb greenhouse gas emissions, arguing as in *Massachusetts v. EPA*, that it did not have the authority. Given the Supreme Court's ruling on the public endangerment language of Section 202, EPA accepted a remand in this case to develop a more comprehensive response under the Clean Air Act. *See New York v. EPA*, No. 06-1322 (D.C. Cir.) (remanded to EPA on Sept. 24, 2007). While still considering its options on remand regarding regulation of coal plant emissions under Section 111 (the New Source Performance Standards, or NSPS, program), EPA issued other NSPS for emissions of pollutants from petroleum refineries in June 2008. EPA, Standards of Performance for Petroleum Refineries: Final Rule, 73 Fed. Reg. 35,838 (June 24, 2008). Over the objections of several states and environmental organizations, EPA refused to regulate greenhouse gas emissions from these sources, even though they may contribute approximately 15 percent of carbon dioxide emissions from industrial sources. *See* Press Release, Cuomo Files Lawsuit to Force Bush EPA to Control Global Warming Pollution from Big Oil Refineries (Aug. 25, 2008). Several states and environmental organizations filed suit against EPA challenging its refusal to regulate greenhouse gas emissions from oil refining.

6.   The Court first had to address whether the parties even had standing to raise a case involving injury from climate change. The Court found (5 votes to 4) that at least the State of Massachusetts in its quasi-sovereign status had alleged a potential threat to its coastline and other interests, and thus had standing to bring a climate change-related action. The standing part of the Supreme Court decision is discussed in Chapter 12, Section II.B.

C.   Regulation of Vehicle Emissions Standards by the States

Whereas the states and environmental organizations sought to compel EPA to regulate carbon dioxide in *Massachusetts v. EPA*, California and several other states have also taken a different approach to the regulation of carbon dioxide and other greenhouse gases that implicates the Clean Air Act: through limits on vehicle emissions. This raises two separate issues. First, under what circumstances does the Clean Air Act allow the states to regulate vehicle emissions, and second, are vehicle emission standards preempted by the Energy Policy and Conservation Act, which directs the Department of Transportation to regulate vehicle *efficiency* standards?

1.   *California's Waiver under the Clean Air Act for Vehicle Emissions Standards*

Under Section 209(a) of the Clean Air Act, states are preempted from adopting any measures that regulate air emissions from new vehicles. This provision was included in the Clean Air Act to protect automobile companies from a hodgepodge of different state regulations, thus ensuring that they would be able to produce uniform automobiles for a national market. If states were allowed to develop their own environmental standards, the argument went, then the automobile companies (and the consumer) could not benefit from the economies of large-scale production.

California, however, was given an exemption. Section 209(b)(1) of the Clean Air Act requires the EPA Administrator to waive the preemption bar for California "if the State determines that the State standards will be, in the aggregate, at least as protective of public health and welfare as applicable Federal standards." However, no such waiver shall be granted if the Administrator finds that: (A) the protectiveness determination of the State is arbitrary and capricious; (B) the State does not need such State standards to meet "compelling and extraordinary conditions"; or (C) such State standards and accompanying enforcement procedures are not consistent with section 202(a) of the Clean Air Act.

Congress granted California this exemption primarily because California had a particularly problematic air pollution problem in the Los Angeles area and had already adopted a robust air quality program prior to the adoption of the vehicle emissions provisions of the Clean Air Act. Moreover, the reason for the preemption provision did not readily apply to California. Its market was so big that automobile companies could still make a sizable profit while producing cars to meet California's idiosyncratic environmental requirements. Moreover, once California passed state-wide standards, the Act allowed other states to pass the same California standards, piggy-backing on any waiver granted to California.

Invoking this provision, the State of California passed legislation in 2002 directing the California Air Resources Board (CARB) to "develop and adopt regulations that achieve the maximum feasible and cost-effective reduction of greenhouse gas emissions from motor vehicles" not later than January 1, 2005. In 2004, CARB adopted limits for four greenhouse gases — carbon dioxide, methane, nitrous oxide and hydrofluorocarbons — that are stricter than federal standards (or for which EPA had not set federal standards at all). Based on the new standards, emissions of these greenhouse gases would drop by 30 percent from 2002 levels by 2016. In response, sixteen states eventually agreed to follow California's vehicle emission standards. All of these regulations were voided (at least temporarily), however, when EPA denied California's petition for a waiver on March 6, 2008. *See* 73 Fed. Reg. 12156 (Mar. 6, 2008). EPA argued that the Clean Air Act waiver provision was intended to protect California's right to address unique regional and local air pollution problems. Because climate change was a global issue, EPA argued, California was not uniquely impacted as compared to the rest of the country. Thus, the state did not have "extraordinary and compelling" reasons to regulate:

NOTICE OF DECISION DENYING A WAIVER OF CLEAN AIR ACT PREEMPTION FOR CALIFORNIA'S 2009 AND SUBSEQUENT MODEL YEAR GREENHOUSE GAS EMISSION STANDARDS FOR NEW MOTOR VEHICLES
73 Fed. Reg. 12,156 (Mar. 6, 2008)

I. Finding

In this decision, I find that the California Air Resources Board's (CARB's) amendments . . . relating to greenhouse gases (GHGs), are not needed to meet compelling and extraordinary conditions. While I recognize that global climate change is a serious challenge, I have concluded that section 209(b) was intended to allow California to promulgate state standards applicable to emissions from new motor vehicles to address pollution problems that are local or regional. I do not believe section 209(b)(1)(B) was intended to allow California to promulgate state standards for emissions from new motor vehicles designed to address global climate change problems; nor, in the alternative, do I believe that the effects of climate change in California are compelling and extraordinary compared to the effects in the rest of the country. Based on this finding, pursuant to section 209(b)(1) of the Clean Air Act (Act), CARB's waiver request for its GHG standards for new motor vehicles must be denied. * * *

III. Analysis of Preemption Under the Clean Air Act * * *

B. Deference

* * * [A]s discussed below, EPA's interpretation of section 209(b)(1)(B) looks at the nature of GHGs as an air pollution problem, and in the alternative looks at the impacts of global climate change in California in comparison to the rest of the nation as a whole. Applying this interpretation to this waiver application calls for EPA to exercise its own judgment to determine whether the air pollution problem at issue — elevated concentrations of GHGs — is within the confines of state air pollution programs covered by section 209(b)(1)(B). EPA's evaluation relates to the limits of California's authority to regulate GHG emissions from new motor vehicles, not to the particular regulatory provisions that California wishes to enforce. California has its own views on this issue, but EPA does not believe it is required or appropriate to give deference to California of the statutory interpretation of the Clean Air Act, including the issue of the confines or limits of state authority established by section 209(b)(1)(B). This does not change EPA's consistent view that within such confines it should give deference to California's policy judgments, as it has in past waiver decisions, on the mechanism used to address local and regional air pollution problems.* * *

IV. Discussion * * *

C. Does California Need Its GHG Standards To Meet Compelling and Extraordinary Conditions? * * *

1. Is It Appropriate To Apply This Criterion to California's GHG Standards Separately, as Compared to California's Motor Vehicle Program as a Whole? * * *

a. EPA's Practice in Previous Waivers

In past waivers that addressed local or regional air pollution, EPA has interpreted section 209(b)(1)(B) as looking at whether California needs a separate motor vehicle program to meet compelling and extraordinary conditions. Under this approach EPA does not look at whether the specific standards at issue are needed to meet compelling and extraordinary conditions related to that air pollutant. For example, EPA reviewed this issue in detail with regard to particulate matter in a 1984 waiver decision. In that waiver proceeding, California argued that EPA is restricted to considering whether California needs its own motor vehicle program to meet compelling and extraordinary conditions, and not whether any given standard is necessary to meet such conditions. Opponents of the waiver in that proceeding argued that EPA was to consider whether California needed these PM standards to meet compelling and extraordinary conditions related to PM air pollution.

The Administrator agreed with California that it was appropriate to look at the program as a whole in determining compliance with section 209(b)(1)(B). One justification of the Administrator was that many of the concerns with regard to having separate state standards were based on the manufacturers' worries about having to meet more than one motor vehicle program in the country, but that once a separate California program was permitted, it should not be a greater administrative hindrance to have to meet further standards in California. The Administrator also justified this decision by noting that the language of the statute referred to "such state standards," which referred back to the use of the same phrase in the criterion looking at the protectiveness of the standards in the aggregate. He also noted that the phrase referred to standards in the plural, not individual standards. He considered this interpretation to be consistent with the ability of California to have some standards that are less stringent than the federal standards, as long as, per section 209(b)(1)(A), in the aggregate its standards were at least as protective as the federal standards.

The Administrator further stated that in the legislative history of section 209, the phrase "compelling and extraordinary circumstances" refers to "certain general circumstances, unique to California, primarily responsible for causing its air pollution problem," like the numerous thermal inversions caused by its local geography and wind patterns. The Administrator also noted that Congress recognized "the presence and growth of California's vehicle population, whose emissions were thought to be responsible for ninety percent of the air pollution in certain parts of California." EPA reasoned that the term compelling and extraordinary conditions "does not refer to the levels of pollution directly." Instead, the term refers primarily to the factors that tend to produce higher levels of pollution — "geographical and climatic conditions (like thermal inversions) that, when combined with large numbers and high concentrations of automobiles, create serious air pollution problems."

The Administrator summarized that the question to be addressed in the second criterion is whether these "fundamental conditions" (i.e., the geographical and climate conditions and large motor vehicle population) that cause air pollution continued to exist, not whether the air pollution levels for PM were compelling and extraordinary, or the extent to which these specific PM standards will address the PM air pollution problem.

From this it can be seen that EPA's interpretation in the context of reviewing standards designed to address local or regional air pollution has looked at the local causes of the air pollution problems — geographic and climatic conditions that turn local emissions into air pollution problems, such as thermal inversions, combined with a large number of motor vehicles in California emitting in the aggregate large quantities of emissions. Under this interpretation, it is the common factors that cause or produce local or regional air pollution problems, and the particular contribution of local vehicles to such problems, that set California apart from other areas when Congress adopted this provision.

EPA's review of this criterion has usually been cursory and not in dispute, as the fundamental factors leading to air pollution problems — geography, local climate conditions (like thermal inversions), significance of the motor vehicle population — have not changed over time and over different local and regional air pollutants. These fundamental factors have applied similarly for all of California's air pollution problems that are local or regional in nature. California's circumstances of geography, climate, and motor vehicle population continue to show that it has compelling and extraordinary conditions leading to such local air pollution problems related to traditional pollutants.

To date, California's motor vehicle program has addressed air pollution problems that are generally local or regional in nature. The emission standards have been designed to reduce emissions coming from local vehicles, in circumstances where these local emissions lead to air pollution in California that will affect directly the local population and environment in California. In that context, EPA's prior interpretation has been and continues to be a reasonable and appropriate interpretation of the second criterion, and EPA is not reconsidering or changing it here for local or regional air pollution problems. The narrow question in this waiver proceeding is whether this interpretation is appropriate when considering motor vehicle standards designed to address a global air pollution problem and its effects, as compared to a local or regional air pollution problem that has close causal ties to conditions in California.

b. The Distinct Nature of Global Pollution as It Relates to Section 209(b)(1)(B)

The air pollution problem at issue here is elevated atmospheric concentrations of greenhouse gases, and the concern is the impact these concentrations have on global climate change and the effect of global climate change on California. In contrast to local or regional air pollution problems, the atmospheric concentrations of these greenhouse gases is basically uniform across the globe, based on their long atmospheric life and the resulting mixing in the atmosphere. The factors looked at in the past — the geography and climate of California, and the large motor vehicle population in California, which were considered the fundamental causes of the air pollution levels found in California — no longer perform the same causal function. The atmospheric concentration of greenhouse gases in California is not affected by the geography and climate of California. The long duration of these gases in the atmosphere means they are well-mixed throughout the global atmosphere, such that their concentrations over California and the U.S. are, for all practical purposes, the same as the global average.

The number of motor vehicles in California, while still a notable percentage of the national total and still a notable source of GHG emissions in the State, bears no more relation to the levels of greenhouse gases in the atmosphere over California than any other comparable source or group of sources of greenhouse gases anywhere in the world. Emissions of greenhouse gases from California cars do not generally remain confined within California's local environment but instead become one part of the global pool of GHG emissions, with this global pool of emissions leading to a relatively homogenous concentration of greenhouse gases over the globe. Thus, the emissions of motor vehicles in California do not affect California's air pollution problem in any way different from emissions from vehicles and other pollution sources all around the world. . . .

Given the different, and global, nature of the pollution at issue, it is reasonable to find that the conceptual basis underlying the practice of considering California's motor vehicle program as a whole does not apply with respect to elevated atmospheric concentrations of GHGs. Therefore EPA has considered whether it is appropriate to apply this criterion in a different manner for this kind of air pollution problem; that is, a global air pollution problem. EPA continues to believe that it is appropriate to apply its historical practice to air pollution problems that are local or regional in nature, and is not suggesting the need to change such interpretation. The only question addressed is whether it is appropriate to employ a different practice to the very different circumstances present for this global air pollution problem. * * *

2. Relationship of California Motor Vehicles, Climate, and Topography to Elevated Concentrations of Greenhouse Gases in California

I recognize that Congress' purpose in establishing the prohibition in section 209(a) and the waiver in 209(b) was to balance the benefit of allowing California significant discretion in deciding how to protect the health and welfare of its population, and that part of that benefit is allowing California to act as a laboratory for potential federal motor vehicle controls, with the burden imposed on the manufacturers of being subject to two separate motor vehicle programs. S. Rep. No. 403, 90th Cong. 1st Sess., at 32–33 (1967). It is clear that Congress intended this balance to be premised on a situation where California needs the state standards to meet compelling and extraordinary conditions. Thus, if I find that California does not need its state GHG standards to meet compelling and extraordinary conditions, it would not be appropriate to grant a waiver of preemption for California's state requirements.

Commenters opposed to EPA granting the waiver commented that California should be denied the waiver because separate state GHG standards are not needed to meet compelling and extraordinary conditions because there is no link between motor vehicle emissions in California and any alleged extraordinary conditions in California. These commenters state that while California spends a great deal of time discussing the effects of climate change in California (discussed below), California does not link these emission standards with such effects. They note that GHGs are not localized pollutants that can affect California's local climate or which are problematic due to California's specific topography. Instead, emissions from vehicles in California become mixed with the global emissions of GHG and affect global climate (including California's climate) in the same way that any GHG from around the world affect global (and California) climate conditions. They claim that Congress authorized EPA to grant a waiver of preemption only in cases where California standards were necessary to address peculiar local air quality problems. They claim that there can be no need for separate California standards if the standards are not aimed at, and do not redress, a California-specific problem. California and others supporting the waiver counter that the reductions in GHG emissions from the standards are needed to reduce future impacts of climate change.

In previous waiver decisions, EPA was asked to waive preemption of standards regulating emissions that were local or regional in effect. Local air pollution problems are affected directly by local conditions in California, largely the emissions from motor vehicles in California in the context of the local climate and topography. As a result state standards regulating such local motor vehicle emissions will have a direct effect on the concentration of pollutants directly affecting California's environment. They are effective mechanisms to reduce the levels of local air pollution in California because local conditions are the primary cause of that kind of air pollution problem. In addition, reductions in emissions from motor vehicles that occur elsewhere in the United States will not have the same impact, and often will have no impact, on reducing the levels of local air pollution in California.

By contrast, GHGs emitted by California motor vehicles become part of the global pool of GHG emissions that affect concentrations of GHGs on a uniform basis throughout the world. The local climate and topography in California have no significant impact on the long-term atmospheric concentrations of greenhouse gases in California. Greenhouse gas emissions from vehicles or other pollution sources in other parts of the country and the world will have as much effect on California's environment as emissions from California vehicles. As a result, reducing emissions of GHGs from motor vehicles in California has the same impact or effect on atmospheric concentrations of GHGs as reducing emissions of GHGs from motor vehicles or other sources elsewhere in the U.S., or reducing emissions of GHGs from other sources anywhere in the world. California's motor vehicle standards for GHG emissions do not affect just California's concentration of GHGs, but affect such concentrations globally, in ways unrelated to the particular topography in California. Similarly, emissions from other parts of the world affect the global concentrations of GHGs, and therefore concentrations in California, in exactly the same manner as emissions from California's motor vehicles.

* * * The legislative history indicates that Congress' intent in the second criterion was to allow California to adopt new motor vehicle standards because of compelling and extraordinary conditions in California that were causally related to local or regional air pollution levels in California. These factors — climate, topography, large population of motor vehicles — cause these kinds of local or regional air pollution levels in California and because of this causal link, California's motor vehicle standards can be effective mechanisms to address these local problems. Reductions outside California would not be expected to be as effective as reductions from California's state motor vehicle standards in addressing California's local or regional air pollution problems, as there is not such a causal link between emissions outside California and local or regional air quality conditions inside California. * * *

Given that Congress enacted section 209(b) to provide California with a unique ability to receive a waiver of preemption, which provides California with authority that it would not otherwise have under section 209, and given the specific language in section 209(b)(2) pointing out the need for extraordinary and compelling conditions as a condition for the waiver, I believe that it is not appropriate to waive preemption for California's standards to regulate GHGs. Atmospheric concentrations of greenhouse gases are an air pollution problem that is global in nature, and this air pollution problem does not bear the same causal link to factors local to California as do local or regional air pollution problems. I believe that atmospheric concentrations of GHGs are not the kind of local or regional air pollution problem Congress intended to identify in the second criterion of section 209(b)(2). As such I find that California does not need its GHG standards to meet compelling and extraordinary conditions.

3. Relationship of Impacts of Global Climate Change in California to the Rest of the Country

As noted above, in section IV.C.1., as an alternative to the approach discussed in section IV.C.2, EPA has also considered the effects of this global air pollutant problem in California in comparison to the rest of the country. While the air pollution concentrations may be relatively uniform around the globe, and GHG emissions distributed globally, EPA has considered whether the potential impact of climate change resulting from these emissions and concentrations will differ across geographic areas and if so whether the likely effects in California amount to compelling and extraordinary conditions.

In determining whether the effect in California is compelling and extraordinary, guidance can be found in the legislative history, which speaks of California demonstrating "compelling and extraordinary circumstances sufficiently different from the nation as a whole to justify standards on automobile emissions which may, from time to time, need to be more stringent than national standards." S. Rep. No. 403, 90th Cong. 1st Sess., at 32 (1967). The history refers to California's "peculiar local conditions" and "unique problems." Id. This indicates a Congressional intent that there be particular circumstances in California sufficiently different from the nation as a whole that justify separate standards in California. Therefore the criterion to apply is whether the effects in California from elevated concentrations of GHGs and any resulting climate change are different enough from the rest of the nation as a whole that California should be considered to have compelling and extraordinary conditions under section 209(b)(1)(B).

In its waiver request CARB restates its need for its own engine and vehicles programs to meet serious air pollution problems. CARB states that climate change threatens California's public health, water resources, agricultural industry, ecology, and economy. Direct health impacts due to climate change that CARB cites include extreme events, such as heat waves, droughts, increased fire frequency, and increased storm intensity. CARB also notes that air quality impacts, such as increases in ground-level ozone due to higher temperatures, will cause secondary health effects. * * *

EPA also received comment from CARB and others supporting the waiver stating that California faces unique and compelling geographical and population issues in their state, which have not changed since Congress and EPA originally recognized California's need to establish separate vehicle standards. According to the comments, along with exacerbating ozone impacts and increasing wildfires, there are a number of other compelling and extraordinary circumstances in California that justify the passage of GHG emission standards, including: declining snowpack and early snowmelt and resultant impacts on water storage and release, sea level rise, salt water intrusion, and adverse impacts to agriculture (e.g., declining yields, increased pests, etc.), forests, and wildlife. During EPA's two public hearings and in written submissions to the docket many commenters provided additional discussion regarding the variety and severity of adverse impacts of GHG emissions and global warming on the environment. In addition, some commenters specifically point to a direct threat to public health (e.g., asthma) since increased temperatures due to increased GHG emissions will lead to increased levels of ozone and other pollutants. Some commenters also assert that there is nothing in section 209(b)(1)(B) of the CAA that limits the "extraordinary and compelling conditions" that should be considered to those associated with smog, and that as a result, California should be able to consider these additional conditions. * * *

While I find that the conditions related to global climate change in California are substantial, they are not sufficiently different from conditions in the nation as a whole to justify separate state standards. As the discussion above indicates, global climate change has affected, and is expected to affect, the nation, indeed the world, in ways very similar to the conditions noted in California. While proponents of the waiver claim that no other state experiences the impacts in combination as does California, the more appropriate comparison in this case is California compared to the nation as a whole, focusing on averages and extremes, and not a comparison of California to the other states individually. These identified impacts are found to affect other parts of the United States and therefore these effects are not sufficiently different compared to the nation as a whole. California's precipitation increases are not qualitatively different from changes in other areas. Rises in sea level in the coastal parts of the United States are projected to be as severe, or more severe, particularly in consequences, in the Atlantic and Gulf regions than in the Pacific regions, which includes California. Temperature increases have occurred in most parts of the United States, and while California's temperatures have increased by more than the national average, there are other places in the United States with higher or similar increases in temperature. * * *

It is true that many of the effects of global climate change (e.g., water supply issues, increases in wildfires, effects on agriculture) will affect California. But these effects are also well established to affect other parts of the United States. Many parts of the United States may have issues related to drinking water (e.g., increased salinity) and wildfires and effects on agriculture are by no means limited to California. These are issues of national, indeed international, concern and Congress has indicated that such conditions do not merit separate standards in California unless the conditions are sufficiently different in California compared to the rest of the nation as a whole. In my judgment, the impacts of global climate change in California, compared to the rest of the nation as whole, are not sufficiently different to be considered "compelling and extraordinary conditions" that merit separate state GHG standards for new motor vehicles.

V. Decision

Having given due consideration to all material submitted for the record and other relevant information and the requisite burden of proof required to deny a waiver, I find that California does not need its GHG standards for new motor vehicles to meet compelling and extraordinary conditions, pursuant to section 209(b)(1)(B). Therefore, I deny California's request to waive application of section 209(a) of the Act with respect to its GHG standards for new motor vehicles. I make no findings with regard to sections 209(b)(1)(A) and 209(b)(1)(C) of the Act.

My decision will affect not only persons in California, but also manufacturers outside the State who would have otherwise had to comply with California's requirements in order to produce new motor vehicles for sale in California. In addition, because other states have adopted or may adopt California's GHG program for new motor vehicles — which is allowed if certain criteria under section 177 of the Act are met, this decision will also affect those states and those persons in such states.

QUESTIONS AND DISCUSSION

1.   In his decision, the Administrator spent considerable effort distinguishing greenhouse gases from other pollutants to conclude that the factors used in previous waiver determinations to interpret "compelling and extraordinary conditions" do not apply to the circumstances of this global air pollution problem. Is his analysis persuasive? Consider the following information and analysis from a report prepared by the Congressional Research Service:

Whether the state's mobile source GHG emission standards are "need[ed]" to meet these conditions poses a more difficult question, however. Climate change is a global issue, and will pose nearly identical challenges to California whether or not the state is permitted to implement the adopted regulations. The reductions in GHG emissions that the regulations would bring about are estimated at 155,200 tons of CO_2 equivalent per day in 2030 (i.e., when the fleet consists of vehicles that meet the 2016 standard) — 56.6 million tons a year compared to a business-as-usual scenario. If all 15 states that have adopted or announced plans to implement the regulations do so, the reductions might be as much as 175 million or 200 million tons annually. Compared to total current U.S. emissions from all sources of about 7 billion tons, California's action alone would reduce emissions less than 1%, and all 15 states would eliminate 2.5% to 3%. Compared to world emissions from all sources (34 billion tons), all 15 states would reduce the total about 0.6%.

* * *

[W]hile the nature of the pollution problem (global vs. local or regional) is clearly different, a case can still be made that the GHG regulations are similar in fundamental respects to the 53 previous sets of regulations for which EPA has granted California waivers. Like the GHG standards, each of the previous sets of regulations were incremental steps that reduced emissions, but in themselves were insufficient to solve the pollution problem they addressed: large portions of the state are still in nonattainment of the ozone air quality standard nearly 40 years after the first of these waivers, despite these incremental steps to reduce emissions.

Furthermore, auto and light truck emissions are major contributors to the total pool of greenhouse gas emissions (about 20% of the total of U.S. emissions), and are growing more quickly than emissions from other sources. In California, according to CARB, the affected vehicles produce about 30% of the state's total GHG emissions. Stabilizing and reducing total GHG emissions would be difficult or impossible without addressing this sector. Thus, a strong case can be made that reducing GHG emissions from mobile sources is necessary if the state is to meet the compelling and extraordinary conditions posed by the increasing concentration of GHGs in the atmosphere.

James E. McCarthy & Robert Meltz, CALIFORNIA'S WAIVER REQUEST TO CONTROL GREENHOUSE GASES UNDER THE CLEAN AIR ACT 10–11 (CRS Report for Congress, updated March 4, 2008).

2. A day before the EPA denied California's waiver, President Bush signed an energy bill that requires a fleet-wide fuel economy average of 35 miles per gallon (mpg) by 2020. Energy Independence and Security Act (EISA), P.L. 110-140 (Dec. 19, 2007). On the other hand, California officials claim that its regulations, which set emissions standards, not fuel economy standards, would achieve an average of 36 mpg by 2016 (although the EPA calculated California's standards as producing a mileage average of 33.8 by 2016). California's law would also regulate emissions from a broader spectrum of greenhouse gases, including refrigerants from vehicle air conditioners, and a range of alternative fuels, not just gasoline. Do any of these facts alter your opinion about the Administrator's decision?

3. In denying California's waiver, the EPA departed from the deference previously given to California in all previous waiver applications. EPA argued that the previous waivers involved local and regional air pollution conditions. In the case of a global pollution problem, EPA argued, California's view that it faced "compelling and extraordinary" circumstances warranted no particular deference under the Clean Air Act. This allowed EPA the freedom to depart from earlier precedent. Do you agree with this view?

4. In order to explain its denial of California's preemption waiver, EPA provided a detailed discussion of climate science and impacts and concluded that climate change was a "critical and substantial challenge to the environment." In essence, EPA confirmed all of the potential climate impacts, but argued that California was not significantly worse off than other parts of the country. Although this might be a strong argument in this case, at the same time EPA had yet to release the 'endangerment' finding required by *Massachusetts v. EPA*. Can you see how the EPA's positions could be hard to reconcile? If real climate impacts were "substantial" all over the country, did they not also pose an endangerment to public welfare under Section 202 of the Act? Anticipating this argument, EPA Adminis-

trator put the following caveat in footnote 1 of his denial of California's waiver.

> This document does not reflect, and nothing in this document should be construed as reflecting, my judgment regarding whether emissions of GHGs from new motor vehicles or engines cause or contribute to air pollution "which may reasonably be anticipated to endanger public health or welfare," which is a separate question involving different statutory provisions and criteria; nor should it be construed as reflecting my judgment regarding any issue relevant to the determination of this question.

73 Fed. Reg. 12,156, at n.1. Do you think this statement provides any cover for EPA? Can you see, as a lawyer, how a response in one case can affect your client's (in this case EPA's) position in other cases?

5. Despite Administrator Johnson's demurral, many observers thought the denial of the waiver portended a finding of endangerment under the Clean Air Act, and indeed there is evidence that such a finding had been made by EPA scientists. The endangerment finding, however, was apparently withdrawn and shelved at the request of political appointees in the White House.

6. California and other petitioners, in separate suits, have challenged the Administrator's decision. *See* State of California v. U.S. EPA, No. 08-70011 (9th Cir. Filed January 3, 2008). If you were representing the State of California, what arguments would you make for overturning the Administrator's decision?

7. On January 26, 2009, President Obama ordered EPA to reconsider its denial of California's waiver request. On February 12, 2009, EPA published a notice that it was reconsidering the denial and seeking further public comments on the waiver request. EPA, California State Motor Vehicle Pollution Control Standards; Greenhouse Gas Regulations; Reconsideration of Previous Denial of a Waiver of Preemption, 74 Fed. Reg 7040-02 (Feb. 12, 2009). If EPA ultimately grants California's waiver request, it will need to explain its change in position from its earlier denial. Otherwise, a court may find EPA's changed position "arbitrary and capricious" under the Administrative Procedure Act. What explanations could EPA offer if it changes its position?

---

2.   *Are California's State Vehicle Emissions Standards Preempted?*

Because the Clean Air Act specifically contemplates a waiver for California's state vehicle emissions standards under specified conditions, California's emission standards would be allowed if EPA's Administrator approves the waiver. But vehicle *emission* standards under the Clean Air Act should not be confused with vehicle *efficiency* standards enacted under the Energy Policy and Conservation Act (EPCA), 49 U.S.C. §§ 32902(a), 32902(c). Under EPCA, the Department of Transportation's National Highway Traffic Safety Administration is authorized to improve the efficiency of motor vehicles by establishing federal fuel economy standards for new vehicles on a fleet-wide basis. These Corporate Automobile Fuel Economy (CAFE) standards were first enacted in the wake of the 1970s energy crisis. They were updated in 2007 and are discussed separately in Chapter 15.

EPCA contains an express preemption provision as follows:

> When an average fuel economy standard prescribed under this chapter is in effect, a State or a political subdivision of a State may not adopt or

enforce a law or regulation related to fuel economy standards or average fuel economy standards for automobiles covered by an average fuel economy standard under this chapter.

Because of the close link between vehicle emission standards for carbon dioxide and fuel efficiency standards, does the EPCA preempt California's attempt to regulate emissions? Unlike the Clean Air Act, EPCA provides no waiver for California or any other state regulation aimed at fuel economy standards. Arguing that California's fuel emissions standards were pre-empted under EPCA because emissions are so closely linked to fuel efficiency, the automobile industry filed suit in California, Vermont, and Rhode Island to invalidate the California-based rules. After the Supreme Court decision in *Massachusetts v. EPA* recognized EPA's authority to regulate carbon dioxide under the Clean Air Act, two courts (in Vermont and California) issued orders denying the auto industry's claims that EPCA pre-empted California's waivers. *See* Central Valley Chrysler Jeep v. Goldstene, 529 F. Supp. 2d 1151 (E.D. Cal. 2007); Green Mountain Chrysler Plymouth Dodge Jeep v. Crombie, 508 F. Supp. 2d 295 (D. Vt., Sept. 12, 2007); *see also* Lincoln-Dodge, Inc. v. Sullivan, 2007 WL 4577377 ((D. R.I., Dec. 21, 2007) (rejecting Rhode Island's motion to dismiss on ripeness grounds).

EPA's denial of California's waiver now makes these challenges of preemption moot, at least until the waiver is revisited. If California's challenge to EPA's denial of the waiver is granted, then these challenges of preemption will likely be renewed. Moreover, the analysis of preemption found in these cases is enlightening for other future potential preemption cases brought against state or local climate-related regulations. In *Green Mountain Chrysler Plymouth Dodge Jeep*, the District Court of Vermont held that the preemption doctrine per se was not applicable because the California state vehicle emissions had essentially been "federalized" through the operation of the waiver clause in the federal CAA. The court then found that the two federal statutes (the Clean Air Act and the EPCA) could be reconciled. The California District Court in *Central Valley Chrysler-Jeep, Inc* chose another approach, without necessarily rejecting the *Green Mountain* court's reasoning:

CENTRAL VALLEY CHRYSLER JEEP v. GOLDSTENE
529 F. Supp. 2d 1151, 1171–89 (E.D. Cal. 2007)

III. Preemption, Preclusion, and EPCA

[The court first concluded that] "where EPA, consistent with its obligation to protect public health and welfare, determines that regulation of pollutants under the Clean Air Act is necessary and where such regulation conflicts with average mileage standards established pursuant to EPCA, EPA is not precluded from promulgating such regulation. The court further concludes the agency designated by EPCA to formulate average mileage standards is obliged to consider such regulations pursuant to 49 U.S.C. § 32902(f) and is further obliged to harmonize average fuel efficiency standards under EPCA with the standards promulgated by EPA. * * *

C. The Status of State Regulations Granted Waiver by EPA

*   *   *

Having now determined that EPA may promulgate regulations that are in conflict with fuel efficiency standards, the court re-posits the question to ask whether a state regulation that is granted waiver of preemption under the Clean Air Act should stand in any different stead with respect to inconsistencies or conflicts it may have with EPCA-established fuel efficiency standards.

Section 209 of the Clean Air Act imposes three conditions on state regulations that are submitted to EPA for waiver of preemption (other than the requirement that they be proposed by California). First, the proposed regulations must "be, in the aggregate, at least as protective of the public health and welfare as applicable Federal standards." 42 U.S.C. § 7543(b)(1). Second, EPA must determine the state regulations are necessary to "to meet compelling and extraordinary conditions," and that the regulations were not promulgated in an arbitrary and capricious fashion. *Id.*; *Motor Equip. & Mfrs. Ass'n v. EPA*, 142 F.3d 449, 462–463 (D.C. Cir. 1998) ("MEMA"). Finally, the proposed regulations must be consistent with section 7521(a), which requires that air pollution standards be formulated in consideration of technological feasibility, the time necessary to apply the requisite technology, the cost of compliance, and energy and safety factors associated the application of the technology. 42 U.S.C. §§ 7543(b)(1)(c) and 7521(a)(2) and (3).

If EPA concludes that California's regulations meet these three requirements, EPA is obliged to grant the waiver application. * * *

Once a proposed California regulation has been granted a waiver of preemption pursuant to section 209 of the Clean Air Act, section 177 of the Clean Air Act, codified at 42 U.S.C. § 7507 (hereinafter "section 177") provides, in pertinent part:

> Notwithstanding section 7543(a) of this title [expressly preempting state regulation of vehicle emissions], any State which has plan provisions approved under this part may adopt and enforce for any model year standards relating to control of emissions from new motor vehicles or motor vehicle engines and take such other actions as are referred to in section 7543(a) of this title respecting such vehicles if-

> (1) such standards are identical to the California standards for which a waiver has been granted for such model year, and

> (2) California and such State adopt such standards at least two years before commencement of such model year (as determined by regulations of the Administrator).

Section 177 further provides that any state adopting a California regulation for which waiver has been granted may not "have the effect of creating [ ] a motor vehicle engine different than a motor vehicle or engine certified in California under California standards (a 'third vehicle') or otherwise create such a "third vehicle." *Id.*

As a consequence of the limited adoption provisions of section 177, "there can be only two types of cars 'created' under emissions regulations in this country: 'California' cars and 'federal' (that is, EPA-regulated) cars." *American Automobile Mfrs. Ass'n v. Com'r, Massachusetts Dep't of Envtl. Prot.*, 31 F.3d 18, 21 (1st Cir. 1994). Once a proposed California vehicle emission regulation is granted waiver of preemption, any other state may, through its own legislative process, adopt vehicle emission regulations in lieu of EPA-promulgated regulations provided: (1) the adopted regulations are " 'identical' to California's (the identicality requirement)," and (2) the adopting state must assure "there is a two-year time lapse between the time the standards are adopted and the first model year affected by those standards (the leadtime requirement)." *Id.*

Defendants contend, and Plaintiffs and AIAM do not directly dispute that a California regulation that has been granted waiver of preemption under section 209 of the Clean Air Act is an "other motor vehicle standard[ ] of the Government" that must be considered by NHTSA in the formulation of average fleet mileage standards under EPCA.

* * *

[W]hen a California regulation is granted waiver of preemption pursuant to section 209 of the Clean Air Act, the California regulation assumes three attributes. First, the California regulation becomes available for adoption by any other state, subject only to the identicality and leadtime requirements. Second, compliance with the California regulation or standard is deemed "compliance with applicable Federal standards for purposes of [Subchapter II-Emissions Standards for Moving Sources]." 42 U.S.C. § 7543(b)(3). Third, as discussed in *Green Mountain*, the California regulation or standard becomes an "other motor vehicle standard[] of the government" that affects fuel economy and that the Secretary of Transportation must consider in formulating maximum feasible average fuel economy standards under EPCA. 49 U.S.C. § 32902(f). *Green Mountain*, 508 F. Supp. 2d at 347; Doc. # 533, at 115.

The court can discern no legal basis for the proposition that an EPA-promulgated regulation or standard functions any differently than a California-promulgated and EPA-approved standard or regulation. Either EPA-promulgated regulations or California-promulgated regulations that are approved by EPA may be implemented to achieve compliance by any state, and both must be considered by NHTSA in formulating average fuel economy standards. In either case, where there is conflict between new EPA-promulgated or California-promulgated regulations that are EPA approved and existing EPCA fuel economy standards, DOT is empowered through EPCA to take the new regulations into consideration when revising its CAFE standards.

The court concludes that, just as the Massachusetts Court held EPA's duty to regulate greenhouse gas emissions under the Clean Air Act overlaps but does not conflict with DOT's duty to set fuel efficiency standards under EPCA, so too California's effort to regulate greenhouse gas emissions through the waiver of preemption provisions of the Clean Air Act overlaps, but does not conflict with DOT's activities under EPCA.

IV. Express Preemption and Conflict Preemption

There remains the question of whether, notwithstanding the non-preclusion of EPA-approved state regulation by EPCA-established fuel economy standards, EPCA either expressly or impliedly preempts states from enforcing EPA-approved California regulations because those regulations impinge on DOT's duty through EPCA to set maximum feasible mileage standards. Preemption of state law may be either express or implied. Express preemption may be found where Congress has explicitly stated "the extent to which its enactments preempt state law." *English v. Gen. Elec. Co.*, 496 U.S. 72, 79 (1990). State law is impliedly preempted where obligations imposed by federal statute "reveal a purpose to preclude state authority." *Rice v. Santa Fe Elevator Corp.*, 331 U.S. 218, 230 (1947).

A. Express Preemption

When a court examines a federal statute to discern the scope of express preemption, that examination is "informed by two presumptions about the nature of the preemption." *Air Conditioning & Refrigeration Inst. v. Energy Res. Conservation & Dev. Comm'n*, 410 F.3d 492, 496 (9th Cir. 2005). . . . First, the court assumes that the " 'historic police powers of the states were not to be superceded by the Federal Act unless that was the clear and manifest purpose of congress.' This presumption against preemption leads [the court] to the principle that express preemption statutory provisions should be given a narrow interpretation." Second the court proceeds on the understanding that " 'the purpose of Congress is the ultimate touchstone in every pre-emption case.' " *Id.* As previously noted, congressional intent is discerned by an examination of the "language, structure, subject matter, context and history-factors that typically help courts determine a statute's objectives and thereby illuminate its text." *Akhtar*, 384 F.3d at 1199.

EPCA provides that " . . . a State or a political subdivision of a State may not adopt or enforce a law or regulation related to fuel economy standards or average fuel economy standards . . . ." 49 U.S.C. § 32919. EPCA's preemptive scope obviously turns on the breadth of regulatory activities embodied in the term "related to." In light of the foregoing discussion, the question to be resolved is not whether California's AB 1493 Regulations will have an effect on fuel economy standards established by EPCA, but whether the definition of "related to" encompasses effects on fuel efficiency that are incidental to the stated purpose of limiting greenhouse gas emissions.

The waiver provision of the Clean Air Act recognizes that California has exercised its police power to regulate pollution emissions from motor vehicles since before March 30, 1966; a date that predates both the Clean Air Act and EPCA. Thus, the court must presume that Congress did not intend that EPCA would supercede California's exercise of its historically established police powers. Second, EPCA's requirement that NHTSA consider "other motor vehicle standards of the government" that affect fuel economy pursuant to 49 U.S.C. § 32902(f) makes it clear that Congress did not intend that EPCA should preempt state laws that serve purposes different from EPCA, but which may have some effect on fuel economy as a byproduct of their enforcement. It makes no logical sense that EPCA would direct NHTSA to give consideration to a law that cannot be enforced because EPCA preempts it. Third, the Supreme Court's decision in *Massachusetts* makes it clear that EPA regulations under the Clean Air Act that control carbon dioxide emissions serve a purpose that is distinct from, and not in conflict with, the purpose of EPCA.

Each of the foregoing considerations support the proposition that EPCA's express preemption of state regulations related to mileage standards be construed as narrowly as the plain language of the law permits. The narrowest interpretation consistent with the plain language of EPCA's preemptive provision is that it encompasses only those state regulations that are explicitly aimed at the establishment of fuel economy standards, or that are the de facto equivalent of mileage regulation, or that do not meet the requirements established by the Clean Air Act for waiver of preemption under section 209.

Both parties agree that the proposed California AB 1493 Regulations, if granted preemption of waiver by EPA, will require substantial improvements in average fuel efficiency performance in passenger cars and light trucks. By the same token, the parties do not dispute that such factors as air conditioning offsets, hybrid and plug-in hybrid credits, and up-stream carbon offsets for ethanol-gasoline blends and other fuel-source considerations mean that the relationship between carbon dioxide reduction requirements under AB 1493 and increases in average fleet fuel efficiency that would be required to achieve those reductions is not one-to-one.

Plaintiffs' and AIAM's argument with respect to EPCA preemption can be summarized as contending that the fact implementation of the California AB 1493 Regulations would require substantial improvement in average fleet fuel efficiency standards under the CAFE program is sufficient to bring the proposed standards within the ambit of EPCA's preemption provision. Defendants' argument, on the other hand, can be summarized as asserting that the fact that the California AB 1493 Regulations do not have a one-to-one correspondence to average fleet fuel efficiency standards under the CAFE program and that the California AB 1493 Regulations are "other Government standards" that NHTSA must consider in formulating average fleet mileage standards takes the California AB 1493 Regulations out of the scope of EPCA's preemption provision. Given the narrow scope the court must accord EPCA's "related to" language, it is this court's opinion that Defendants have the better of the argument.

*   *   *

The court finds that the preemptive force of 49 U.S.C. § 32919 extends very narrowly. State laws that are granted waiver of preemption under the Clean Air Act that have the effect of requiring even substantial increases in average fuel economy performance are not preempted where the required increase in fuel economy is incidental to the state law's purpose of assuring protection of public health and welfare under the Clean Air Act. The court also finds that a law that requires substantial improvement in average fleet mileage standards incidentally to its purpose of protecting public health and welfare does not constitute a de facto regulation of fuel economy standards unless there is a narrow one-to-one correlation between the pollution reduction regulation and the fuel efficiency standard. Where, as here, various considerations including fuel type and source and other sources of emission may have the effect of mitigating fuel efficiency improvement requirements, the pollution control standard does not constitute a de facto regulation of fuel efficiency.

*   *   *

B. Conflict Preemption

In its September 25 Order, the court noted:

> "[A] state law is invalid to the extent it 'actually conflicts with a . . . federal statute.'" *Int'l Paper v. Ouellette*, 479 U.S. 481, 491–92 (1987). Such a conflict can result in preemption where it is impossible for a private party to comply with both the state and federal requirements. *English v. Gen. Elec. Co.*, 496 U.S. 72, 79 (1990). Conflict preemption can also be found where "the state law 'stands as an obstacle to the accomplishment and execution of the full purposes and objectives of Congress.'" *Int'l Paper*, 479 U.S. at 491–92 (*quoting Hines v. Davidowitz*, 312 U.S. 52, 67 (1941)).

Doc. # 363, at 8:13–19.

*   *   *

Based on the discussion in *Massachusetts*, and on the text of EPCA, it is apparent that the objective of EPCA's efforts in establishing fuel economy standards is to conserve fuel by establishing the "maximum feasible average fuel economy" level. *Id.*; 49 U.S.C. § 32902(f); *see also Center for Biological Diversity*, 508 F.3d at 551–52 (overarching goal of EPCA is energy conservation). Considerations such as pricing, consumer choice, safety for the consumer, and dealer profitability are not goals or objectives in and of themselves, they are factors against which the possibility of increased fuel efficiency is weighed in order to determine feasibility. *Massachusetts*, 127 S. Ct. at 1461. Similarly, EPA's central mandate under the Clean Air Act is protection of public health and welfare. Factors such as technological feasibility, cost, and the like are factors against which the effort to promote public health and welfare is balanced.

In the context of concerns over carbon dioxide emissions, EPA's mandate to protect public health and welfare and DOT's mandate to establish the highest feasible level of fuel efficiency are aligned. DOT's goal of increasing fuel efficiency to the maximum feasible level promotes EPA's goal of limiting greenhouse gas air pollution and vice versa. *Center for Biological Diversity*, 508 F.3d at 551–52. Both EPA-promulgated standards or EPA-approved state standards must balance reductions in pollution emissions against factors that are specified by Clean Air Act, just as DOT, through NHTSA, must balance its determination of maximum feasible fuel economy against certain factors specified by EPCA. Neither the Clean Air Act nor EPCA, however, require any particular balance as a matter of law. *See, e.g., Center for Biological Diversity*, 508 F.3d at 527–28 (noting in the context of EPCA that NHTSA has "discretion to balance the factors-as long as NHTSA's balancing does not undermine the fundamental purpose of the EPCA: energy conservation").

* * *

At the core of Plaintiffs' action is a concern that the California AB 1493 Regulations, if granted waiver of preemption under section 209, will substantially burden auto manufacturers, who will be required to invest in fuel economy improvement technology; consumers, who will be required to bear higher new car costs and decreased choice; and automobile dealers, who will suffer loss of potential sales from the combination of increased pricing and decreased selection. In this context, Plaintiffs and AIAM see the mileage standards as set through EPCA as providing a level of protection from economic uncertainty by preventing states from promulgating regulations that upset the balance struck through the EPCA process. EPCA's preemptive provision is seen as protecting manufacturers, dealers and customers from state regulations that would impose costly technological modifications or limit consumer choice by prohibiting sales of non-conforming vehicles.

At oral argument Plaintiffs noted that under EPCA, NHSTA was required to factor "economic practicability" into its determination of maximum feasible fuel efficiency. Plaintiffs contend the term "economic practicability" incorporates considerations such as job loss, consumer impacts, and revenue losses from lost sales. The implication of Plaintiffs' argument is that there is actual conflict between California's AB 1493 Regulations and EPCA's purposes because California was not required to consider "economic practicability" and its AB1493 Regulations conflict with what NHTSA determined is economically practicable. Plaintiffs' argument is not persuasive. While California may not be required to engage in precisely the same weighing as NHTSA or to consider precisely the same factors, California is required to give consideration to the factors set forth in 42 U.S.C. § 7521; namely technological availability, cost, and safety factors associated with the application of emission-reduction technology-the same factors EPA would have to consider in promulgating regulations under its own authority. While EPCA and the Clean Air Act use somewhat different words to describe the factors that must be considered in setting standards or promulgating regulations, the court finds the weighing process covers substantially the same ground in both cases insofar as an assessment of economic impacts is concerned.

* * *

Because California's AB 1493 Regulations, if granted waiver under section 209 will fulfill both EPA's objective of "greatest degree of emission reduction achievable through the application of technology . . . ," 42 U.S.C. § 7521(a)(3)(A), and EPCA's objective of implementing the "maximum feasible average fuel economy" standards, 49 U.S.C. § 32902(f), the enforcement of the California AB 1493 Regulations will not conflict with EPCA for purposes of conflict preemption. To the extent the enforcement of the AB1493 Regulations may be incompatible with existing CAFE standards, NHTSA is empowered to revise its standards taking into account the AB 1493 Regulations. To the extent the implementation of technology to meet the AB 1493 Regulations will be forced by enforcement of the standards, that technology forcing does not constitute an interference with EPCA's purpose of setting average fleet mileage standards to the maximum feasible level.

DEFENDANTS' MOTION FOR SUMMARY JUDGMENT ON PLAINTIFFS' CLAIM OF FOREIGN POLICY PREEMPTION

Intrusions of state law on the Federal Government's exercise of its authority to conduct foreign affairs are subject to preclusion. *Zschernig v. Miller*, 389 U.S. 429, 440–441, 88 S. Ct. 664, 19 L. Ed. 2d 683 (1968).

* * *

[T]he court's analysis of Plaintiffs' claim of foreign policy preemption will track to some extent the analysis the court undertook with respect to Plaintiffs' claim with regard to EPCA preemption. That is, the court will first examine whether considerations of foreign policy limit EPA's authority to regulate the emission of greenhouse gasses. If executive branch policy does not prevent EPA from promulgating regulations to limit greenhouse gas emissions, then the court will address whether Congress intended that California regulations that are granted waiver of preemption under section 209 should be regarded any differently than EPA-promulgated regulations. Finally, the court will determine whether there is actual conflict between California's AB 1493 Regulations and United States foreign policy in light of all the information submitted by the parties and now before the court.

I. Authority of EPA to Regulate

[Relying heavily on *Massachusetts v. EPA*, the Court concluded that "Congress intended that EPA should have authority to regulate greenhouse gas emissions, including specifically carbon dioxide, recognizing that whatever the foreign policy of the executive branch might be, it does not conflict with or prevent EPA from carrying out its congressionally mandated regulatory duties."]

* * *

II. Congressional Intent Regarding California Regulations

* * *

Because it is Congress's express intent that California be empowered to develop alternative regulations subject to congressionally-specified conditions, executive branch policy may not interfere with that intent. The court again declines to cast the issue as being one of "federalization" of the proposed California standards. Rather, the court refers to its discussion on EPCA preemption in which it determined that there is no indication of congressional intent that a proposed California state regulation that is granted waiver of preemption under section 209 of the Clean Air Act is different for any purpose from a regulation that is promulgated directly by EPA. The court concludes that an executive branch policy cannot interfere with Congress's manifest intent to empower EPA to address the issue of regulation of carbon dioxide emissions from motor vehicles. It follows that the same executive branch policy cannot interfere with the congressionally-established pathway in the Clean Air Act that enables California to seek and receive a waiver of preemption so that California, and any other state that chooses to follow the California's lead, may require compliance with the more protective California regulations.

III. Conflict Between California's AB 1493 Regulations and Foreign Policy

[The Court then summarized three cases it claims shape the extent of the foreign policy preemption: *Zschernig v. Miller*, 389 U.S. 429 (1968) (holding an Oregon law invalid that conflicted with a treaty with Germany); *Crosby v. Nat'l Foreign Trade Council*, 530 U.S. 363 (2000) (holding invalid a Massachusetts law that restrictively regulated contracts with the military dictatorship of Myanmar, finding that it interfered with the President's power, as authorized by congressional enactment, to apply limited sanctions to Myanmar); *American Ins. Ass'n v. Garamendi*, 539 U.S. 396 (2003) (invalidating California's Holocaust Victim Insurance Relief Act of 1999, because the President was in intensive negotiations with the German government to institute a broader program of reparations to holocaust survivors).]

*   *   *

The court concludes that *Zschernig*, together with cases that follow it, including *Garamendi*, hold that a party asserting preemption on the ground of foreign policy preemption must show "clear conflict" between a state law or program and the functioning of some agreement, treaty, or program that is the product of negotiations between the administrative branch and a foreign government. In the context of the present case, this means that Plaintiffs, in order to adequately state a claim for foreign policy preemption must show what the policy of the United States is and precisely how California's AB 1493 Regulations, if granted waiver of preemption by EPA and implemented, would interfere with the United States' foreign policy.

*   *   *

In sum, the exhibits submitted by Plaintiffs establish that United States foreign policy with respect to global climate change is: (1) integrated with the broader policy of promotion of international economic growth; (2) aimed at programs in foreign countries that result in poverty reduction, enhancement of energy security reduction of pollution and mitigation of greenhouse gas emissions; and (3) expressed through individually negotiated voluntary agreements, partnerships or economic initiatives with foreign countries (rather than through binding international treaties, such as Kyoto, that omit developing nations). *See, e.g.*, Harlan Watson, Seminar of Government Experts, *U.S. Climate Change Policy* (2005), Doc. # 649-1; *Fact Sheet: A New International Climate Change Framework*, May 31, 2007, Doc. # 648-2.

The materials submitted adequately support Plaintiff's contention that it is United States foreign policy to: (1) approach climate change through voluntary agreements or partnerships negotiated with single or multiple foreign states; (2) that aim to reduce the carbon dioxide intensity (units of carbon dioxide produced per unit of economic activity) of their economies; (3) while maintaining a robust economy. It is important to note, however, that this statement of policy is different than what Plaintiffs allege constitutes current United States foreign policy.

In attempting to show conflict between California's efforts to regulate and United States foreign policy, Plaintiffs emphasize only the first part of the foregoing policy statement. That is, Plaintiffs look to the President's avowed intent to seek voluntary bilateral or multilateral agreements with foreign countries, including developing countries, and characterize this intent to negotiate as being the "policy." From there, Plaintiffs contend that the "policy" that California's attempt to regulate greenhouse gas emissions is in conflict with is the government's "policy" of leveraging foreign agreements by "speaking with one voice."

"Speaking with one voice" does not constitute a actual policy within the meaning of any of the cases heretofore cited. The "policy" in evidence in *Garamendi* was evinced by the results of the President's negotiations and was embodied in an agreement; in *Crosby*, the "policy" was embodied in an act of Congress setting forth specific limited sanctions against a country; in *Zschernig*, the "policy" was evinced by a negotiated treaty that covered the same subject as the state law. What Plaintiffs label as a policy in this case is actually nothing more than a commitment to negotiate under certain conditions and according to certain principles.

The term "policy" as used in *Zschernig* and its progeny refers to a concrete set of goals, objectives and/or means to be undertaken to achieve a predetermined result. A commitment to negotiate falls short of this definition. The President's commitment to engage in negotiations that include developing nations does not set any particular goals or means, does not guide the actions of any actors with respect to greenhouse gas reduction, and imparts no information to guide future actions that may increase or decrease greenhouse gas production. It is merely a statement of an intent to negotiate on the terms specified.

Rather, what Plaintiffs contend is United States "policy" is more accurately described as a strategy; that is, a means to achieve an acceptable policy but not the policy itself. It is the agreements, or partnerships themselves that are the results of the Administration's negotiation that are or can be evidence of the President's exercise of foreign policy. When the court looks for conflict or interference, the question necessarily arises as to the object of the interference. In order to conflict or interfere with foreign policy within the meaning of *Zschernig*, *Garamendi* or related cases, the interference must be with a policy, not simply with the means of negotiating a policy. Thus, in order to prove conflict in the instant case, Plaintiffs must make a showing that California's efforts to implement regulations limiting the emission of greenhouse gasses from automobiles will interfere with the efforts of this government or a foreign government to reduce the intensity of their greenhouse gas emissions pursuant to a negotiated agreement, treaty, partnership or the like.

When the court looks to the undisputed facts of this case to find "clear conflict" between California's proposed AB 1493 Regulations and the foreign policy of the United State Government, it finds none.

The Supreme Court's decision in *Massachusetts* impliedly recognized that EPA's contention that it should not regulate greenhouse gas emissions even if it is empowered to do so is little more than a post-hoc rationalization for inaction. Massachusetts, 127 S. Ct. at 1462–1463. Plaintiffs' contention that unilateral efforts to regulate greenhouse gas emissions might interfere with United States foreign policy is an apparent attempt to bootstrap EPA's rationalization into a pronouncement of foreign policy. When the court looks to the additional exhibits that Plaintiffs have submitted to the court to demonstrate United States foreign policy, there are two facts that are important to Plaintiffs' argument that are conspicuous by their absence. First, there is absolutely nothing in any of the exhibits submitted to support the contention that it is United States foreign policy to limit its own current efforts or the efforts of individual states in controlling greenhouse gas emissions in order to leverage agreements with foreign countries. Second, there is nothing in any of the evidence submitted to indicate that with respect to the Administration's conduct of foreign policy, the effort to reduce carbon dioxide from motor vehicle emissions is to be considered separate for any purpose from other efforts to reduce these emissions.

While the court will accept as factual Plaintiffs' allegation that it is United States foreign policy to secure commitments of other developing nations before committing itself to international treaty obligations to reduce greenhouse gas emissions, the court finds that Plaintiffs' contention that it is also United States foreign policy to hold in abeyance internal efforts to reduce greenhouse gas emissions in order to leverage foreign cooperation is completely without factual support.

Neither can the court make any presumptions in Plaintiffs' favor as a matter of logic. There is absolutely no reason in logic for any presumption that the efforts of California or any other state to reduce greenhouse gas emissions would interfere with efforts by the Executive Branch to negotiate agreements with other nations to do the same. Plaintiffs offer no evidentiary basis for the proposition that the United State would get farther in its efforts to negotiate agreements with other nations by withholding efforts to limit greenhouse gas emissions than by leading the way by example. In essence, Plaintiffs' "bargaining chip" theory of interference only makes logical sense if it would be a rational negotiating strategy to refuse to stop pouring poison into the well from which all must drink unless your bargaining partner agrees to do likewise. The court declines to make any presumptions to that effect.

The "bargaining chip" theory of interference also embraces an impermissibly broad range of activities that fall within the traditional powers of states to regulate under their own police powers for the health and welfare of their own citizens. If states can be barred from taking action to curb their greenhouse emissions, then the efforts of the various states to encourage the use of compact florescent light bulbs, subsidize the installation of solar electric generating panels, grant tax rebates for hybrid automobiles, fund renewable energy start-ups, specify enhanced energy efficiency in building codes, or any other activity that results in lower fuel or energy use would likewise constitute an interference with the President's alleged "bargaining chip policy."

Based on all the evidence submitted by Plaintiffs and AIAM, the court finds no indication of any "policy" by the President or Secretary of State to differentiate efforts to decrease greenhouse gas emissions from automobiles from efforts to decrease greenhouse gas emissions from any other source. The court further finds absolutely no evidence of any "policy" on the part of the Administration to restrain state-based activities to curb greenhouse gas emission in order to leverage international cooperation. The court concludes Plaintiffs' foreign policy preemption claim must fail because the evidence submitted does not identify any "policy" with which California's AB 1493 Regulations might conflict.

CONCLUSION

Pursuant to the foregoing discussion, the court concludes that both EPA and California, through the waiver process of section 209, are equally empowered through the Clean Air Act to promulgate regulations that limit the emission of greenhouse gasses, principally carbon dioxide, from motor vehicles. The court further concludes that the promulgation of such regulations does not interfere or conflict with NHTSA's duty to set maximum feasible average mileage standards under EPCA. The court finds EPCA's preemption of state laws that regulate vehicle fuel efficiency does not expressly preempt California's effort to reduce greenhouse gas emissions through AB 1493. Because Congress intended there should be no conflict between EPA's duty to protect public health and welfare and NHTSA's duty to set fuel efficiency standards through EPCA, the doctrine of conflict preemption does not apply. To the extent the enforcement of California's AB 1493 Regulations may be inconsistent with existing CAFE standards, EPCA provides that NHTSA has authority to reformulate CAFE standards to harmonize with the AB 1493 Regulations if, and when, such standards are granted waiver of preemption by EPA.

The court also concludes that Plaintiffs have failed to make a prima facie showing that it is the foreign policy of the United States to hold state-based efforts to reduce greenhouse gas emissions in abeyance in order to leverage agreements with foreign countries. Plaintiffs have also failed to demonstrate that implementation of California's AB 1493 Regulations will conflict in any way with United States foreign policy.

The court expresses no disagreement with the Green Mountain court's conclusion that California regulations that are granted waiver of preemption under section 209 of the Clean Air Act become laws of the federal government not subject to preemption. The court has offered here an alternative analysis that avoids the issue of "federalization" in the hope of adding a measure of clarity to the discussion.

D.   Challenges to Coal-Fired Power Plants

By ruling that carbon dioxide is an "air pollutant" under the Clean Air Act, *Massachusetts v. EPA* arguably opens the door for environmentalists to challenge individual permitting decisions made under the Act. In fact, environmental organizations led by the Sierra Club are challenging every approval of coal-fired power plants that do not take into account their CO_2 emissions. As can be seen from the following case from Georgia, the initial legal issue is whether CO_2 is a "regulated" air pollutant. Beyond this narrow question, however, environmentalists are raising a number of other issues in the permitting of new coal-fired power plants. These issues are explored following the case.

FRIENDS OF THE CHATTAHOOCHEE, INC. v. COUCH
No. 2008 CV146398 (Ga. Superior Ct., June 30, 2008)

As to . . . carbon dioxide, it is undisputed that no BACT analysis was done. There was no effort to identify, evaluate, or apply available technologies that would control CO_2 emissions, and the permit contains no CO_2 emission limits.

The ruling of the ALJ can be upheld on this issue only if carbon dioxide is not an air "pollutant subject to regulation under the Act." Otherwise, the statute requires a BACT emission limit for CO_2. The argument had been advanced before the permit issued here that CO_2 was not an "air pollutant" under the Act, but that argument was rejected by the United States Supreme Court in *Massachusetts v. EPA*, 127 S. Ct. 1438 (2007). Faced with the ruling in *Massachusetts* that CO_2 is an "air pollutant" under the Act, Respondents are forced to argue that CO_2 is still not a "pollutant *subject to regulation* under the Act." Respondents' position is untenable. Putting aside the argument that any substance that falls within the statutory definition of "air pollutant" may be "subject to" regulation under the Act, there is no question that CO_2 is "subject to regulation under the Act."

Respondents acknowledge, for example, that the regulatory regime under the Clean Air Act mandates monitoring of CO_2 emissions. The failure to conduct required monitoring under the Act's regulations is subject to criminal sanction, and a person who knowingly submits false monitoring reports may be subject to a felony prosecution. *See, e.g.*, 42 U.S.C. § 71 13(c) (2); 18 U.S.C. § 1001. Respondents do not dispute that the failure to comply with these CO_2 regulations is enforceable by criminal sanction.

In addition to the CO_2 monitoring regulations in Part 75 of Title 40 of the Code of Federal Regulations, Petitioners have provided the Court with many other examples of Clean Air Act regulations that address CO_2. Respondents effectively ignore these regulatory structures by contending that BACT limits should apply to a pollutant only if it is also capped or controlled by some other general limit. Thus, Longleaf argues that CO_2 is not "controlled or limited" by the Clean Air Act as the basis for contending that BACT should not apply. The BACT statute is plainly broader than that, however, encompassing all pollutants that are "subject to regulation" under the Act, whether or not they are independently subject to NAAQS or other general limits. The ALJ clearly erred, in light of the regulatory schemes that in fact address CO_2, in stating that "EPA has not promulgated a [NAAQS] for CO_2, has not listed CO_2 as a regulated pollutant in any section of the CAA, *and has not established any other regulations for CO_2.*" (italics added).

If the BACT requirement were limited as Respondents urge, Congress presumably would have used narrower language in the BACT provision, as it did elsewhere in the Act. *See, e.g.*, 42 U.S.C. § 7602(k) (addressing quantitative "emission limitations"). The regulatory definition of air pollutants that require[s] BACT determinations is also inconsistent with Respondents' position. The parties agree that a BACT analysis and emission limitation is required for all "regulated NSR2 pollutants." 40 C.F.R. § 52.2 l(j)(2). The parties also agree that a "regulated NSR pollutant" is defined in EPA's regulations as follows:

> *(50)* Regulated NSR pollutant, for purposes of this section, means the following:
>
> (i) Any pollutant for which a national ambient air quality standard has been promulgated and any constituents or precursors for such pollutants identified by the Administrator (e.g., volatile organic compounds and NOX are precursors for ozone);
>
> (ii) Any pollutant that is subject to any standard promulgated under section III of the Act;
>
> (iii) Any Class I or II substance subject to a standard promulgated under or established by title VI of the Act; or
>
> (iv) Any pollutant that otherwise is subject to regulation under the Act. . . .

40 C.F.R. § 52.2 1(b)(50).

The interpretation of this regulation urged by Respondents, and accepted by the ALJ, contradicts the plain meaning of the regulation. Limiting BACT determinations to those air pollutants for which there is a separate, general numerical limitation effectively ignores part (iv) of the regulation that sweeps in all pollutants that are "otherwise subject to regulation under the Act." Since CO_2 is "otherwise subject to regulation under the Act," a PSD permit cannot issue for Longleaf without CO_2 emission limitations based on a BACT analysis.

If, as the Georgia Superior Court held, new source review under the Clean Air Act must address carbon dioxide emissions, then a wide range of conditions or requirements could be placed on future coal-fired power plants. In this regard, consider the following article arguing for just such conditions:

GREGORY B. FOOTE, CONSIDERING ALTERNATIVES: THE CASE FOR LIMITING CO2 EMISSIONS FROM NEW POWER PLANTS THROUGH NEW SOURCE REVIEW
34 ENVTL. L. REP. 10,642 (2004)[*]

For the first time in a generation, large numbers of new coal-fired power plants are being planned in the United States. These plants are the largest emitters of greenhouse gases, and under business as usual, each would release hundreds of millions of tons of CO_2 over an expected lifespan of half a century or more. These plants are not entitled to a free pass on greenhouse gases. Instead, they should be seen as a prime opportunity for both limiting CO_2 emissions using currently available production processes and stimulating future technological advancement here and in the developing world. The Clean Air Act's (CAA's) new source review (NSR) permit program can fulfill these purposes.

The NSR program embodies a basic congressional judgment that proposed major new sources of air pollution should assess their environmental impacts . . . and mitigate those impacts. Considering reasonable alternatives to proposed sources is a key component of this scheme. Due to their huge CO_2 emissions and longevity, new coal-fired power plants merit careful scrutiny because there is no regulatory structure in place to remedy the problem of climate change. In these circumstances, both sound policy and the legal obligation of permitting authorities to make reasonable decisions, call for a "pay-as-you-go" approach that minimizes CO_2 emissions using available technologies and provides offsetting CO_2 reductions elsewhere for emissions that cannot be avoided.

* * *

The CAA sets two basic substantive requirements for both PSD [prevention of significant deterioration] and NNSR [non-attainment new source review] permits. First, the permit applicant must agree to use the best available technology to minimize emissions. This is termed lowest achievable emissions rate (LAER) under NNSR and best available control technology (BACT) under PSD. Second, the applicant must demonstrate that the project will be consistent with applicable air quality planning goals. Under NNSR, the new or modified source must obtain "offsets" — emissions reductions from other sources of pollution in an amount equal to or greater than the emissions of the newly permitted source. Under PSD, the applicant must ensure that the air quality impacts of the proposed source will not violate the NAAQS and that the available "increment" of increased air pollution allowed in the area will not be exceeded. Final permit terms are established following an extensive analysis by the state permitting agency and after an opportunity for public comment and a public hearing. PSD and NNSR permitting is "pollutant-specific" in that most specific requirements of both programs apply with respect to emissions of particular pollutants. Consequently, a prospective new or modified source may be subject to both PSD and NNSR requirements for different pollutants, depending on the amount of each pollutant it will emit and the attainment status of the area for that pollutant. Despite the pollutant-specific focus of NSR on two main provisions, it is comprehensive and open-ended in considering the environmental impacts of any proposed new source.

* * *

III. Considering Alternatives: The Factors That Should Be Addressed in Reviewing Applications for New Power Plants

* * *

B. Fuels and Production Processes

. . . NSR permit proceedings must seriously address reasonable alternatives to an applicant's preferred mix of production designs and processes, fuel types, and fuel sources. Most explicitly, in the PSD context the definition of BACT expressly requires "taking into account" such alternatives as "production processes," "clean fuels," and "innovative fuel combustion techniques." Likewise, the "most stringent emission limitation which is achieved in practice" for a source category cannot be ascertained for LAER purposes without considering these factors, since they can affect the final emissions rate.

This conclusion is especially compelling with respect to coal-fired power plants for two additional reasons. First, . . . these alternatives merit consideration because of the magnitude of the air quality and other adverse environmental consequences of coal-fired plants. Second, these alternatives should be considered because adopting them can substantially reduce emissions, and hence, other adverse environmental impacts from these plants. * * *

Alternative fuels and production processes also should be treated as mandatory elements of the preconstruction review that the company must include in its permit application and the permitting authority must address in its draft permit decision. They are central, not peripheral, concerns because they can substantially affect emissions rates and have in fact been widely considered in past permit proceedings. It follows that a permit decision failing to address these factors should be considered deficient on its face. Certainly, such a deficiency would be found if commenters were to place these alternatives at issue in particular permit proceedings.

1. The Choice of Fuels

With respect to fuels in particular, . . . the CAA explicitly requires that "clean fuels" be considered in determining BACT. It follows that permit applications to construct new or expanded coal-fired facilities should address the alternative of instead constructing plants burning natural gas, since gas is an inherently lower polluting fuel. Likewise, a BACT or LAER analysis should include cleaner forms of the fuel in question, such as coals with lower sulfur content than the applicant would prefer. This aspect of considering alternative fuels in turn raises the issue of choice of fuel source, and related siting issues. In particular, an applicant may intend to construct a "mine-mouth" power plant to eliminate transportation costs, or a state may desire to use coals mined within the state, to provide jobs and promote economic growth. These certainly are legitimate reasons to prefer a particular choice of fuels in a permit application, but they cannot legitimately prevent consideration of different fuel choices.

2. The Choice of Production Processes

. . . [I]n considering emissions from new sources the choice of production process using a given material to be processed or fuel to be combusted can have a profound effect on final emissions rates and other relevant factors in the permitting decision. It is likewise clear as a legal matter that considering available production processes is a proper component of BACT and LAER determinations, and indeed, is best viewed as a mandatory element in all cases.

* * *

In cases involving power plants, once a well-considered decision has tentatively been made to construct some type of coal-fired plant, there is little doubt about the need for a full and detailed analysis of the choices of production processes. This is so because, as will be seen, the choice of currently available production processes is especially important in determining the final emissions rate for NAAQS pollutants and toxic pollutants — mercury in particular — and also because this choice is critical with respect to CO_2 emissions. Accordingly, applications for permission to construct new or expanded coal-fired facilities using conventional pulverized coal boilers should also carefully consider inherently less-polluting production processes. These choices include circulating fluidized bed (CFB) boilers. Another option with even lower inherent emissions is the IGCC. The CAA legislative history is clear that BACT was intended to encompass consideration of both CFB and IGCC technology.

In the IGCC process, coal (or petcoke or other solid or liquid fuel) is gasified and processed to remove acidic and particulate components. The resulting "syngas" then feeds a combustion turbine whose exhaust heat produces steam for a second-generation cycle (as is done in a natural gas-fired combined-cycle system). Because pollutants are removed from a highly concentrated stream prior to combustion, IGCC is the lowest emitting among all coal production processes as to NAAQS pollutants. For the same reason, IGCC used in conjunction with available control technologies also provides vastly superior performance and dramatically lower cost in removing mercury and other toxic metals as compared to pulverized coal boilers. The IGCC technology is also substantially more thermally efficient — by 10% or more, according to the U.S. Department of Energy (DOE) — than other available technologies. This thermal advantage reduces total emissions of all pollutants, including CO_2, by a corresponding amount. In addition, IGCC can be configured to produce liquid fuels and hydrogen in addition to or in place of electricity as an end product, which provides a range of environmental benefits, including those resulting from use in fuel cells for vehicles and other "hydrogen economy" applications. Finally, IGCC is unique among available technologies in its ability to economically capture the CO_2 emissions from coal combustion, making the CO_2 available for storage rather than being vented to the atmosphere as a greenhouse gas.

Gasification technology has been used extensively in the chemical industry for many years, and is now coming into use for power production as well. Worldwide electrical output of IGCC totals about 5,800 megawatts (MW), with approximately 5,000 MW of additional capacity in the planning stage. Existing IGCC commercial applications include two full-scale electric-generating plants in the United States. Given this record of technical availability and actual usage, there is no doubt that IGCC should be considered an "available" technology that must be considered in determining BACT and LAER. Indeed, several states have treated IGCC as an available technology for NSR purposes. IGCC also has been required as BACT or LAER for some full-scale commercial operations. Even these few instances are sufficient to demonstrate that IGCC can be "achievable" from a cost standpoint.
* * *

C. Production Efficiency as a Component of BACT and LAER

[I]t is clear that BACT and LAER must take production efficiency into account in order to fully address the methods for minimizing emissions from, and air quality and other environmental effects of, new sources of pollution. Doing so involves measuring the effect of the efficiency of a production process on the total amount of emissions from the source. This is accomplished by assessing the amount of pollution emitted as a function of a unit of output.

With respect to sources combusting fossil fuels, "output-based" emissions limitations address thermodynamic efficiency, i.e., the amount of useful work that can be obtained from a given fuel input. For a simple example of the concept of output-based emissions standards, consider two alternatives for a proposed new power plant intended to produce a specified amount of electricity. The first plant emits X tons of pollution per unit of fuel combusted. The second plant also emits X tons of pollution per unit of fuel combusted, but because it is more efficient uses 10% less fuel to produce the same amount of electricity. The second plant's total emissions are the same as the first plant's measured on a fuel input basis, but 10% lower when measured on a power output basis. This translates directly into improved cost-effectiveness for the more efficient process.

As this example demonstrates, total releases to the environment from a source of air pollution indisputably are affected by the efficiency of the production process used. Just as logic demands that production efficiency be incorporated into the calculus for determining how emissions from a new source can be minimized, it is likewise clear that production efficiency is a legitimate component of BACT and LAER from the statutory terms themselves. More specifically, efficiency is a subset of the larger category of "production processes" and "fuel combustion techniques" under BACT, and affects the "most stringent emission limitation" for LAER purposes. This is no mere legalistic point; some production processes are more efficient than others and thus have significantly lower emissions. Disregarding efficiency would, as a practical matter, ignore important aspects of the present state of knowledge regarding available technologies for minimizing emissions and their associated costs. * * *

IV. The Case for Construction of a Truly Clean Coal-Fired Power Plant That Uses IGCC Technology to Minimize Emissions of All Pollutants and Offsets CO_2 Emissions

This section presents the case for weighing an application to construct a coal-fired power plant in light of the CO_2 emissions from such a plant. The discussion here assumes that . . . the environmentally preferable alternatives of conservation, renewable energy, and cleaner fuels tentatively have been rejected on appropriate grounds, and that the focus of the NSR permitting exercise has shifted to the conditions under which a coal- fired plant will be built. The analysis proceeds to outline the reasons why the plant should be constructed using IGCC technology to minimize emissions of both regulated pollutants and CO_2, and requiring that CO_2 emissions from the plant be offset by reductions elsewhere. The analysis also refutes likely counterarguments. The reasons why IGCC technology must be carefully considered in an NSR proceeding for purposes of regulated pollutants have already been addressed and will only be summarized here. Rather, this section will focus on . . . why such consideration presents a strong case for use of IGCC technology, and why CO_2 offsets should be required as a permit condition.

* * *

B. How CO_2 Emissions Should Be Considered in NSR Permitting

1. Use of IGCC Technology as a Production Process

* * *

. . . IGCC should be adopted for new and modified coal-fired facilities, for two additional reasons.

First, any newly constructed coal-fired plant will be in operation for many, many years, and this longevity should be taken into account. . . . These units are now known to have a life-span of at least 50 to 60 years, and quite possibly longer. * * *

Second, there is a high likelihood that mandatory CO_2 regulation will be adopted early in the life-span of any coal-fired plant constructed during the next several years. . . . In short, the prospect of CO_2 regulation presents a question of when, and not whether, comprehensive reductions will be mandated. The best answer, in the context of the long life-span of newly constructed coal-fired units, is "soon." Indeed some utilities are beginning to acknowledge the inevitability of CO_2 regulation by factoring its cost and financial risks into their corporate planning and reporting.

Given the likelihood of future CO_2 regulation, it would be unreasonable for NSR permitting authorities to simply ignore CO_2 emissions now. Whether or not states are made directly responsible for managing CO_2 emissions under a future regulatory regime, they will certainly retain substantial regulatory authority over power plants. States and ratepayers likewise will inevitably bear the environmental and economic consequences flowing from permitting decisions today when steps are taken tomorrow to reduce CO_2 emissions. In light of these foreseeable events, it is incumbent upon permitting authorities to undertake a full analysis of the regulatory and financial risks to which the state may be exposed by virtue of a decision to approve a coal-fired plant that does not minimize CO_2 emissions.

A comprehensive assessment of the cost of CO_2 emissions is necessary under BACT to understand the true costs of control technology alternatives for *regulated* pollutants alone, even before taking account of the environmental benefits of reduced CO_2 emissions as such. That analysis favors IGCC since it is the most cost-effective technology for both limiting CO_2 emissions from coal-fired units now and for retrofitting CO_2 capture-and-storage technology in the future. Thus, quantitative assessments conclude that if CO_2 is regulated in the future, that factor alone renders IGCC the cheapest of available production processes for new coal-fired units. The prospect of those future, additional regulatory costs needs to be considered in order to determine the full cost of the options for minimizing emissions of *currently* regulated pollutants. In addition, a comprehensive assessment also is needed in order to take account of the status of CO_2 as an "unregulated pollutant" emitted by coal-fired power plants. It is in this respect that the environmental benefits of CO_2 reductions are taken into account in the permit decision.

Permitting authorities could apply standard methodologies for assessing the cost-effectiveness of control technology alternatives in considering emissions of CO_2, both as it affects the full cost of control options for regulated pollutants and in taking account of its status as an "unregulated pollutant." For example, in determining the costs and benefits of IGCC as part of their review of that technology for purposes of BACT for regulated pollutants, a state could determine the number of tons of CO_2 removed by virtue of IGCC's superior thermal efficiency compared to a baseline of CO_2 emissions from a pulverized coal boiler. Such an analysis should also take into account the likely future cost of controlling that same amount of CO_2 from the pulverized coal boiler, since that cost flows directly from the production process technology decision. In considering future CO_2 regulation and its impact on the relative merits of IGCC and other combustion process technologies, the analysis should also take into account the cost of future retrofits to accommodate carbon capture and storage using IGCC versus pulverized coal or other technologies. The combination of the likelihood of the need to make future CO_2 reductions and lower costs in doing so with IGCC militates in favor of using IGCC technology today.

Analytically distinct from consideration of CO_2 as it affects both the cost of controlling regulated pollutants and as an "unregulated pollutant" in a BACT analysis is the need to address CO_2 under the environmental impacts component of NSR. Although this form of assessment is, like the others, grounded in dollars-and-cents quantification, it should also take account of concerns that either are not amenable to quantification or entail a larger degree of uncertainty. As discussed previously, the statutory purposes of PSD, and the provisions requiring consideration of alternatives under both NNSR and PSD all call for a permitting decision that takes into account the uncertainty of the environmental risks posed by construction of a new source and the overriding legislative goal of environmental protection. These factors point toward a precautionary decision that errs on the side of protection.

Finally, in assessing CO_2 emissions, permitting authorities should insist that the permit applicant make a full disclosure of its own project and corporate financial risks with respect to future climate change regulations. Doing so is a necessary component of the state's analysis of its own potential liabilities, since the permit decision could lead to adverse consequences for the state both as an environmental regulator and as a regulator of electric utilities. Full disclosure is likewise necessary for citizens to protect their own interests as ratepayers, investors, and taxpayers. In short, climate change regulatory uncertainty might reasonably dissuade a utility company from investing in any new coal-fired power plant, and dissuade a state from approving that investment. But once a tentative decision to proceed with new coal capacity is reached, it seems apparent that the best way to minimize that risk is to use IGCC production technology, since doing so reduces CO_2 emissions now and holds the prospect of additional future reductions through carbon capture and storage.

2. CO_2 Offsets as a Permit Condition

A new coal-fired power plant that employs IGCC to minimize CO_2 emissions will still add millions of tons annually to an already harmful level of emissions at a time when there is no comprehensive plan to address the climate change problem. This combination of acknowledged environmental harm and indefinite regulatory gap may be unprecedented in the modern era of environmental protection, and obliges states to seriously consider CO_2 offsets to prevent the largest new sources from making the climate change problem even worse. These offsets could be required as a condition of a NSR permit until comprehensive CO_2 regulations account for the plant's CO_2 emissions in a manner consistent with meeting climate change goals. Although offsetting emissions reductions are only mandated for emissions of NAAQS pollutants from new sources locating in nonattainment areas, permitting agencies have in the past called for nonstatutory offsets to address other environmental impacts of new sources. The legal authority to establish such permit conditions is a necessary corollary to the state's ability to deny a permit application altogether on any reasonable ground related to the comprehensive environmental concerns of NSR. Moreover, there are many reasons to support a state conclusion that some or all of the CO_2 emissions from a new coal-fired unit actually should be offset.

First, offsets under NSR are well suited to fill a regulatory gap of this nature by requiring that new sources be constructed on a "pay-as-you-go" basis in the absence of an air quality program that effectively addresses the environmental problem at issue. Indeed, offsets were originally required under NSR for this very reason. The current issue of climate change and the absence of a program of CO_2 regulation present a remarkably similar problem and calls for a similar solution.

Second, offsets work in tandem with the NSR emissions minimization tool by providing an economic incentive for use of IGCC to reduce the amount of offsets needed. Doing so will in turn stimulate the further development of both IGCC technology and associated carbon capture and storage technology by providing a market for both. Requiring offsets also provides a stimulus to other CO_2 reduction efforts, including improved production efficiency at existing utility units, by providing a market value to CO_2 reductions resulting from those actions.

Third, CO_2 offsets are not an untried regulatory tool; there are numerous available means of obtaining such offsets outside of a comprehensive program of CO_2 regulation, including market mechanisms. Oregon provides an example of a permitting structure that integrates available CO_2 emissions reduction mechanisms into planning for new power plants. The state's approach establishes a nominal output-based CO_2 emission limit, and then allows sources to achieve that limit, in part, through use of offsets. Oregon has designated a broad, flexible range of qualifying mechanisms that are quantifiable and verifiable, including reliance on CO_2 markets through payment of a per-ton cash fee to a third party to actually obtain CO_2 reductions. The state of Washington has enacted a similar program, under which 20% of CO_2 emissions from new or modified plants must be offset over a period of 30 years through direct CO_2 reduction projects, purchase of credits, or third-party mitigation. New Zealand has also required CO_2 offsets for a new coal-fired power plant in at least one instance in the absence of a regulatory system that comprehensively limits CO_2. The examples of these jurisdictions demonstrate that new and modified utility plants are an appropriate first target for CO_2 limitations, and provide confidence that a broad array of mechanisms are available to enable companies to obtain those limitations in conjunction with new source permitting.

QUESTIONS AND DISCUSSION

1.   The Foote article above notes that IGCC technology reduces CO_2 emissions and is necessary for any future efforts to capture and sequester the carbon through CCS technologies. But IGCC technologies should also be a part of all BACT and LAER analyses anyways because they lower other pollutants regulated under the CAA. In fact, the court in *Friends of the Chatahoochee* also held that the state needed to review IGCC technology as part of the BACT analysis, rejecting the claim that gasification was a totally different type of facility:

> Petitioners' final argument concerning BACT requirements involves an alternative "fuel combustion technique." The Longleaf plant as proposed would consume coal to generate electricity. Under Longleaf's proposed design, the coal would be burned in a boiler; the heat from the boiler would generate steam; and that steam would drive a turbine, which, in turn, would drive a generator to generate electricity. The IGCC technology (integrated

gasification combined cycle) is a different way of using the coal to generate heat to drive the turbines. 40 C.F.R. § 60.4 IDa. IGCC works by first converting the coal to a gas — called "gasification" — and then burning the gas to drive turbines both directly from the hot gas and from steam, which again is created by the heat of combustion. And once again, the turbines drive the generator to create electricity.

Respondents argue that they are not required by the BACT statute and regulations to do a full analysis of IGCC combustion technology, and that the permit limitations need not incorporate lower pollution limits that would occur if IGCC were used. Longleaf advances this argument, which was accepted by the ALJ, by focusing not on the overall proposed plant, but on just one aspect of the facility. At the hearing, Longleaf argued that the legal analysis here should focus only on the proposed "boiler," not on the "facility," which is a much broader term.

Respondents' approach is too narrow and cannot be squared with the provisions of the law that control the Court's decision on this issue. The BACT statute is explicit in this regard. It requires a BACT analysis and permit emission limitations based on the "emitting facility" as a whole. 42 U.S.C. § 7479(3). In addition, the statute was amended in 1977 to require, as part of the BACT analysis, consideration of "innovative fuel combustion techniques." IGCC is an "innovative fuel combustion technique."

The proposed "major emitting facility" is still the same kind of statutorily defined "facility" under the Clean Air Act whether the coal is burned directly in a boiler or is first converted to gas and then burned to create the heat of combustion that drives the turbines. The ALJ erred in ruling that IGCC would "redefine the air pollution source" so that it need not be part of the BACT analyses. . . . Under the statutory definition, one kind of "major emitting facility" is a "fossil-fuel fired steam electric plant." 42 U.S.C. § 7479(1). With or without IGCC technology, the Longleaf plant thus falls under the same "facility" definition — a "fossil-fuel fired steam electric plant." * * *

While the statute and regulation are clear on their face, the Court would also note that the proponent of the 1977 amendment that added the BACT language at issue addressed this specific question on the Senate floor. In his explanation to the Senate concerning the amendment, Senator Huddleston explained that, while he believed BACT already included "such technologies as . . . gasification," the amendment was added nevertheless "to be more explicit, to make sure there is no chance of misinterpretation." 123 Cong. Rec. S. 9434–35 (June 10, 1977).

The Court's opinion is opposite that taken by EPA; EPA argues that, "where an applicant proposes to construct a [pulverized coal-fired] unit, . . . the IGCC process would redefine the basic design of the source being proposed. [A]ccordingly, . . . we would not require an applicant to consider IGCC in a BACT analysis for [such a] unit. . . . [and] we would not include IGCC in the list of potentially applicable control options that is compiled in the first step of a top-down BACT analysis. Instead, we believe that . . . IGCC . . . is an alternative . . . " BEST AVAILABLE CONTROL TECHNOLOGY REQUIREMENTS FOR PROPOSED COAL-FIRED POWER PLANT PROJECTS, Memorandum of Stephen D. Page, Director of EPA's Office of Air Quality Planning and Standards (Dec. 13, 2005) (the Page memo). Environmental organizations challenged the Page memo in federal court, arguing that EPA had impermissibly issued the memo without providing public notice or an opportunity for comment on EPA's interpretation. In a settlement of the case, EPA agreed that the Page memo was not final agency action and did not create any legal rights or obligations. *See* EPA, Proposed Settlement Agreement, Clean Air Act Citizen Suit, 71 Fed. Reg. 61771 (Oct. 19, 2006); *see also* Natural Resources Defense Council v. EPA, Settlement Agreement, No. 06- 1059 (consolidated with Nos. 06-1062 and 06-1063) (D.C. Cir. 2006).

Although the Page memo does not have the force of law, EPA continues to distinguish between technologies and alternatives for BACT purposes. In *Sierra Club v. EPA*, 499 F.3d 653 (7th Cir. 2007), the Seventh Circuit upheld EPA's refusal to require a new "mine-mouth" coal plant to burn low-sulfur (and thus cleaner burning) coal. A "mine-mouth" plant, as the name suggests, is located at the mouth of a coal mine. If EPA had required the facility to use low-sulfur coal, the mine operator would have needed to redesign its plant to receive coal from outside the mine. The Seventh Circuit accepted EPA's argument that BACT does not require a facility to fundamentally redesign its existing proposal. *Id.* at 654-57. Regarding the statute's reference to "clean fuels," the court found the term ambiguous, as a literal reading could require all owners of proposed new coal plants to construct nuclear or wind turbines instead, since nuclear and wind energy are indisputably cleaner than coal. *Id.* at 655. Having found the term ambiguous, the court then deferred to EPA's determination of when a technology qualifies as BACT and when it constitutes a fundamental redesign excluded from BACT review. *Id.* at 656. However, the court emphasized that the Sierra Club had not asked EPA to consider low-sulfur fuels as an alternative to the proposal and suggested that EPA's broader leeway in considering alternatives may have provide Sierra Club with a better basis for its challenge. *Id.* at 655.

How will the *Sierra Club* decision affect future challenges to new coal plant proposals that do not use IGCC technology? On the one hand, *Sierra Club* defers to EPA's expert judgment regarding the requirements of BACT. On the other hand, the court recognized "the difference between low-sulfur (clean) and high-sulfur (dirty) coal as a fuel source for a power plant, and the difference between a plant co-located with a coal mine and a plant that obtains its coal from afar. The former is a difference in control technology, the latter a difference in design." *Id.* at 657. In which category does IGCC fit?

2.   The Georgia Superior Court in *Friends of the Chatahoochee* is unlikely to be the last word. First, the Georgia Court of Appeals agreed to review the case and a decision from that court is pending. Second, a large number of permit applications for coal-fired power plants have been challenged in the past year. Four days before the Georgia court rejected the Longleaf power plant, the State of Virginia approved a 585 mega-watt coal-fired power plant without taking carbon dioxide emissions into account, and environmentalists are likely to appeal. *See* David A. Fahrenthold, *Dominion's Coal-Fired Electric Plant to Advance*, The Wash. Post, p. B1, June 26, 2008.

Perhaps the most widely watched case is the Sierra Club petition to the EPA's Environmental Appeals Board (EAB) seeking review of an EPA-issued permit for the addition of a coal-fired unit to an existing power plant on tribal lands near Bonanza, Utah. EPA had issued a construction permit for the facility, which is located in an attainment area for all criteria pollutants. Petition, *In re Deseret Power Elec. Coop. (Bonanza)*, PSD Appeal No. 07-03 (EAB, file date Oct. 1, 2007). Industry groups filed amici curiae briefs in opposition to the ruling, arguing that EPA should be allowed to take a more comprehensive approach to the regulation of carbon dioxide. *See* Brief of Amici Curiae American Petroleum Inst., et al, *In re Deseret Power Elec. Coop. (Bonanza)*, PSD Appeal No. 07-03 (EAB, filed Mar. 21, 2008). EPA had argued that carbon dioxide is not a regulated NSR pollutant under its regulations, because it is not "otherwise subject to regulation" under the CAA. Environmental groups argued that CO_2 is subject to regulation, and, indeed is actually regulated, because facilities are required to monitor and report CO_2 emissions. EPA argued the term "subject to regulation" applies only to pollutants subject to actual pollution controls. On November 13, 2008, the EAB rejected EPA's arguments and remanded the Bonanza permit to EPA to reconsider whether to impose a CO_2 BACT limit and to develop an adequate record regarding its decision. Order Denying Review in Part and Remanding in Part, *In re Deseret Power Elec. Coop. (Bonanza)*, PSD Appeal No. 07-03 (EAB, file date Nov. 13, 2008). The EAB found it ambiguous whether carbon dioxide is "otherwise subject to regulation" under the CAA and thus a pollutant regulated under PSD. It directed EPA to make this decision on remand.

In response to the EAB's decision in *Bonanza*, then-EPA Administrator Stephen Johnson issued a memorandum in which he interpreted the term "subject to regulation" to mean subject to control. Memorandum from Stephen L. Johnson, EPA Administrator, to Regional Administrators, re: EPA's Interpretation of Regulations that Determine Pollutants Covered by Federal Prevention of Significant Deterioration (PSD) Permit Program (Dec. 18, 2008) (the Johnson memo). In effect, the Johnson memo repeated the litigation position of EPA, but did it in a non-litigation context which could receive more deference under administrative law principles. As with the Page memo, environmental groups challenged the Johnson memo as a final agency action issued without notice and comment. The groups also petitioned EPA to rescind the Johnson memo. On February 17, 2009, the new EPA Administrator, Lisa Jackson, agreed to reconsider the Johnson memo. While she declined to stay the effectiveness of the Johnson memo pending reconsideration, she advised other permitting authorities to not assume the Johnson memo is the final word on the CAA's application to carbon dioxide. Letter from Lisa P. Jackson, EPA Administrator, to David Bookbinder, Chief Climate Counsel, Sierra Club (Feb. 17, 2009).

From these notes, it should be obvious that the scope of CAA regulation of greenhouse gases is a moving target at this point. How should EPA regulate greenhouse gases from stationary sources? Is the CAA the best law for the job?

3.   Opposition to coal-fired power plants may also manifest itself in more than just litigation. On March 2, 2009, thousands of climate activists, including Dr. James Hansen, NASA's chief climate scientist, James Gustave Speth, the Dean of the Yale School of Forestry, and noted author Bill McKibben, locked arms to block entrance to the Capital Power Plant, a coal-fired power plant that serves the U.S. Capitol. Although the activists failed in their efforts to get arrested, what was billed as the "largest act of civil disobedience relating to climate change yet" probably portends additional protests throughout the country. *See* www.capitolclimateaction.com. If you were representing a utility that needed to expand its energy supply, would such actions make you think twice about coal? What other purposes do such strategies serve?

4.   Coal-fired power plants are unlikely to be the only category of stationary sources that will be challenged because of their climate change impacts. Concentrated Animal Feeding Operations (CAFOs), for example, are significant contributors of methane, a potent greenhouse gas. Because emissions at CAFOs come from thousands of individual animals; whether emissions from agricultural operations qualify as a "stationary source" emissions is hotly debated. Generally speaking, the emissions must be capable of "reasonably pass[ing] through a stack, chimney, vent or other functionally equivalent opening." 40 C.F.R. § 51.165(a)(1)(ix). If emissions do not meet this test, they are considered "fugitive emissions." *Id.* Fugitive emissions are not considered in an assessment of whether a particular source is a "major source" under the NSR programs.

In 2005, EPA released its Animal Feeding Operations Consent Order and Final Order, 70 Fed. Reg. 4958 (Jan. 31, 2005). The Consent Order allows AFO operators to avoid prosecution by EPA under the Clean Air Act and other laws, if the operators sign onto the agreement, pay a small penalty, and agree to participate in a monitoring study of emissions (although only a small number of operators will be selected for the study). Several environmental organizations have challenged the Consent Order in court, but the D.C. Circuit upheld the Consent Order as a reasonable exercise of EPA's enforcement discretion. Association of Irritated Residents v. EPA, 494 F.3d 1027 (D.C. Cir. 2007). Notwithstanding this decision, citizens may retain the ability to sue CAFOs for violations of the Clean Air Act, because it is unclear whether the Consent Order precludes third-party suits and because many facilities did not sign onto the agreement in any event. If you represented an organization concerned about methane emissions from CAFOs, would you recommend it file suit under the CAA to enjoin the emissions? What hurdles would you expect to face? What other options would the organization have to abate the emissions?

E.   Future Regulation of Climate Change

The long-term implications of *Massachusetts v. EPA*, California's desire for a waiver, and other actions under the Clean Air Act are not altogether clear. The Obama Administration is not as reluctant to regulate greenhouse gas emissions, but that does not necessarily mean that use of the Clean Air Act is the best approach.

The Act does not take a comprehensive approach to global warming and it is not clear that the structure of the Act is appropriate for dealing with a global air pollutant. Although several provisions could apply to greenhouse gases, it is not clear that the sum of the parts would add up to a comprehensive approach. This is to some extent the argument EPA makes in delaying the "endangerment" finding under *Massachusetts v. EPA* until it has time to develop a comprehensive approach.

Given the *Massachusetts v. EPA* decision, a climate-friendly Administration would seem to have authority to regulate greenhouse gases if it so chooses — and it may even be required to do so. This begs the question as to what EPA would or could do if it chooses to regulate greenhouse gas emissions under the Clean Air Act. Assuming the Obama Administration issues the "endangerment" finding mandated by the Court, then EPA would be required to regulate the pollutants emitted from new mobile sources. Moreover, any endangerment finding is likely to cover stationary sources as well as mobile sources. This could trigger additional regulatory authorities.

First, the EPA could identify carbon dioxide as a criteria pollutant and issue a National Ambient Air Quality Standard for it. Normally, areas of the country are then categorized according to whether they are in attainment or non-attainment with the NAAQS. But given the global mixing of carbon dioxide and other greenhouse gases, presumably the entire country would be in non-attainment. Under the Act, states are required to issue State Implementation Plans for all non-attainment areas, which paradoxically could mean that the application of the federal Clean Air Act would shift responsibility for reducing greenhouse gases to the states.

Second, as suggested by the current challenges to newly proposed power plants (discussed above in Section D), we would expect EPA to require as part of future permits that power plants, cement manufacturers, and many other industries reduce their greenhouse gas emissions as part of their application for a PSD permit. In addition, EPA could issue new source performance standards in many industry sectors to take account of greenhouse gas emissions.

Use of the Clean Air Act in this way, although useful for addressing greenhouse gases, may not be the optimal approach. Not only is it somewhat ad hoc, but we can imagine that any innovative use of the Act will be met with resistance from industry-side lawsuits challenging EPA's interpretations of the statute — just as environmentalists challenged the Bush Administration's interpretations.

On the other hand, regulation under the Clean Air Act may have several significant benefits. First, the CAA is an existing statute that EPA has administered for nearly 40 years, and EPA has developed considerable expertise in regulating all sorts of different pollutants. When compared to the significant administrative hurdles experts expect EPA to face in establishing a cap-and-trade program (*see* Chapter 11 for a discussion of anticipated administrative costs), CAA regulation may appear streamlined, simple, and cost-effective. Second, many provisions of the CAA are either technology-based or technology-forcing, and they therefore have the potential to require immediate installation of pollution controls that could achieve quick pollution reductions. Cap-and-trade programs, in contrast, will likely only spur technological development and innovation when the costs of carbon credits exceed the costs of pollution control. Experiences with the EU ETS (*see* Chapter 6 for a discussion of that program) and preliminary results from the Regional Greenhouse Gas Initiative (*see* Chapter 17) suggest that carbon credits will cost far less than most experts consider necessary to spur significant technological innovation. Third, once the scope of the CAA is resolved, the Act itself provides for a degree of certainty that a market-based program may not provide. For example, major emitters of carbon dioxide will know that they must obtain PSD or NNSR permits and can readily access application forms and materials through EPA and state agencies. Fourth, while CAA regulation may impose significant costs on regulated entities, many observers believe that high costs are necessary to trigger a movement towards more sustainable energy sources. Finally, the CAA authorizes citizens to sue for violations of the CAA's mandates. While regulated entities understandably do not view citizen suits as a benefit, citizen suits do provide additional incentives for compliance and provide members of the public a means to effectively participate in the CAA's success.

An Administration that wants to address climate change may be more likely to support comprehensive greenhouse gas legislation in the Congress. Depending on how that legislation is crafted, it may replace all, some or none of the authorities currently existing in the Clean Air Act. In this way, the future importance of the Clean Air Act is dependent as much on what Congress does as what the Administration or courts do.

II.   THE NATIONAL ENVIRONMENTAL POLICY ACT

In the United States, the National Environmental Policy Act of 1969 (NEPA), 42 U.S.C. §§ 4321–4370e, establishes a broad national commitment to protecting and promoting environmental quality by focusing an agency's attention on the environmental consequences of a proposed project. NEPA thus ensures that important environmental impacts will not be overlooked or underestimated only to be discovered after resources have been committed. Another fundamental purpose of NEPA is to guarantee "that the relevant information will be made available to the larger audience that may also play a role in both the decisionmaking process and the implementation of that decision." *See* Robertson v. Methow Valley Citizens Council, 490 U.S. 332, 349 (1989).

To fulfill these goals, NEPA provides:

> [A]ll agencies of the Federal Government shall . . . include in every recommendation or report on proposals for . . . major federal actions significantly affecting the quality of the human environment, a detailed statement . . . on the environmental impact of the proposed action.

42 U.S.C. § 4332(2)(C).

This "detailed statement" is known as an environmental impact statement (EIS) (and more commonly called an environmental impact assessment (EIA) in other countries). NEPA's mandate to prepare an EIS has several important threshold questions: Is the action federal? Is the action major? Are the impacts of the action significant?

Assuming these threshold questions are answered in the affirmative, NEPA and its implementing regulations, 40 C.F.R. §§ 1500–1517, require an agency to assess the direct, indirect, and cumulative impacts of the proposed action and propose measures to mitigate any adverse impacts. It also requires the relevant agency to evaluate reasonable alternatives to the proposed project, as well as each alternative's potential direct, indirect, and cumulative impacts and possible mitigation measures.

NEPA's regulations allow an agency to prepare a less detailed Environmental Assessment (EA) to determine whether the proposed action is one that requires a full EIS. 40 C.F.R. § 1501.4(b). The EA must briefly describe the proposal, examine alternatives, and assess the environmental impacts. 40 C.F.R. § 1508.9. Based on the information included in the EA, an agency may issue a "finding of no significant impact" (FONSI), which relieves the agency of its obligation to prepare a full EIS. Although an EA need not "conform to all the requirements of an EIS," it must be "sufficient to establish the reasonableness of th[e] decision" not to prepare an EIS. Found. for N. Am. Wild Sheep v. U.S. Dep't of Agric., 681 F.2d 1172, 1178 n. 29 (9th Cir. 1982). If the EA establishes that the agency's action may have significant environmental impacts, the agency must prepare an EIS.

Importantly, the duty to prepare an EIS is procedural only and does not trigger a specific environmental outcome. *Robertson v. Methow Valley Citizens Council*, 490 U.S. at 350–351. Thus, even if the EIS indicates that one alternative is clearly preferable from an environmental perspective, the agency is under no obligation to choose that alternative. Nevertheless, plaintiffs have been challenging agency actions for failure to incorporate the impacts of climate change in their EAs and EISs. As you read the cases below, ask yourself what the value of the NEPA process is if the EA or EIS does not force the agency to take any particular action.

A.   Is an EIS Needed?

As noted above, several threshold issues determine whether a federal agency must prepare an EIS. Under NEPA and cases interpreting it, "action" has been defined broadly to include "new and continuing activities, including projects and programs entirely or partly financed, assisted, conducted, regulated, or approved by federal agencies." 40 C.F.R. § 1508.18. An action is "federal" if it is "potentially subject to federal control or responsibility." *Id.* To date, these threshold issues have not factored in climate change litigation. Whether impacts of a federal project are "significant," however, has.

A number of cases have challenged the adequacy of EAs, claiming that a full-blown EIS was required. In an early climate change case, a group of cities, states, and environmental groups challenged the failure of the National Highway Traffic Safety Administration (NHTSA) to prepare an EIS addressing climate change impacts when it relaxed the Corporate Average Fuel Economy (CAFE) standards for automobiles. City of Los Angeles v. NHTSA 912 F.2d 478 (D.C. Cir 1990); *overruled in part by* Florida Audubon v. Bentsen, 94 F.3d 658 (D.C. 1996). The Energy Policy and Conservation Act of 1975 (EPCA) made 27.5 miles per gallon (mpg) the presumptive CAFE standard for Model Year 1985 (MY 85) and thereafter. The Act also authorized the NHTSA to set a different standard, not lower than 26.0 mpg, for any individual model year at the level it determines to be "the maximum feasible average fuel economy level" for that year (CAFE standards are discussed in more detail in Chapter 15 on transportation). The NHTSA exercised this authority to set the standard at 26.0 mpg for MYs 87–88 and at 26.5 mpg for MY 89. After preparing an EA for each of these findings, the NHTSA issued its FONSI, stating that the lower CAFE standards would not "significantly affect[] the quality of the human environment." The petitioners claimed that the NHTSA should have prepared an EIS to consider, among things, the adverse climatic effects of the increase in fossil fuel consumption that would result from setting a CAFE standard lower than 27.5 mpg. The court held that the small percentage increase in greenhouses gas emissions from the proposed standard would not cause significant environmental impacts. Thus, the NHTSA's decision not to prepare an EIS was not "arbitrary, capricious, or otherwise contrary to law."

In *Center for Biological Diversity v. National Highway Traffic Safety Administration*, almost two decades after *City of Los Angeles*, the courts had a chance to revisit fuel economy standards and NHTSA's approach to determining those standards.

CENTER FOR BIOLOGICAL DIVERSITY v. NATIONAL HIGHWAY TRAFFIC SAFETY ADMINISTRATION
508 F.3d 508 (9th Cir. 2007)

BETTY B. FLETCHER, CIRCUIT JUDGE:

Eleven states, the District of Columbia, the City of New York, and four public interest organizations petition for review of a rule issued by the National Highway Traffic Safety Administration (NHTSA) entitled "Average Fuel Economy Standards for Light Trucks, Model Years 2008–2011," 71 Fed.Reg. 17,566 (Apr. 6,

2006) ("Final Rule") (codified at 49 C.F.R. pt. 533). Pursuant to the Energy Policy and Conservation Act of 1975 (EPCA), 49 U.S.C. §§ 32901–32919 (2007), the Final Rule sets corporate average fuel economy (CAFE) standards for light trucks, defined by NHTSA to include many Sport Utility Vehicles (SUVs), minivans, and pickup trucks, for Model Years (MYs) 2008–2011. For MYs 2008–2010, the Final Rule sets new CAFE standards using its traditional method, fleet-wide average (Unreformed CAFE). For MY 2011 and beyond, the Final Rule creates a new CAFE structure that sets varying fuel economy targets depending on vehicle size and requires manufacturers to meet different fuel economy levels depending on their vehicle fleet mix (Reformed CAFE).

*   *   *

Petitioners argue that NHTSA's Environmental Assessment is inadequate under NEPA because it fails to take a "hard look" at the greenhouse gas implications of its rulemaking and fails to analyze a reasonable range of alternatives or examine the rule's cumulative impact. Petitioners also argue that NEPA requires NHTSA to prepare an Environmental Impact Statement.

I. FACTUAL AND PROCEDURAL BACKGROUND

*   *   *

NHTSA issued the Final Rule on April 6, 2006. 71 Fed.Reg. at 17,566. NHTSA set the CAFE standards for MY 2008–2010 (Unreformed CAFE) at the same levels as proposed in the NPRM [notice of proposed rulemaking].[30] Unreformed CAFE sets a fleet-wide average fuel economy standard "with particular regard to the 'least capable manufacturer with a significant share of the market.'" NHTSA has reformed the structure of the CAFE program for light trucks, effective MY 2011 (Reformed CAFE). Under Reformed CAFE, fuel economy standards are based on a truck's footprint, with larger footprint trucks subject to a lower standard and smaller footprint trucks subject to higher standards. Instead of six footprint categories (a step function) as proposed in the NPRM, Reformed CAFE would be based on a continuous function, meaning a separate fuel economy target for each vehicle of a different footprint. "A particular manufacturer's compliance obligation for a model year will be calculated as the harmonic average of the fuel economy targets for the manufacturer's vehicles, weighted by the distribution of manufacturer's production volumes among the footprint increments." A manufacturer's CAFE compliance obligation will vary with its fleet mix. A manufacturer that produces more large footprint light trucks will have a lower required CAFE standard than one that produces more small footprint light trucks.

During MYs 2008–2010, manufacturers may choose to comply with Unreformed CAFE or Reformed CAFE.

*   *   *

II. STANDARD OF REVIEW

The Administrative Procedure Act (APA), 5 U.S.C. §§ 701–706 (2007), provides that agency action must be set aside by the reviewing court if it is " 'arbitrary, capricious, an abuse of discretion, or otherwise not in accordance with law.' "

*   *   *

---

[30] MY 2008: 22.5 mpg; MY 2009: 23.1 mpg; MY 2010: 23.5 mpg.

NHTSA's compliance with NEPA is reviewed under an arbitrary and capricious standard pursuant to the APA. *See, e.g., Nat'l Parks & Conservation Ass'n*, 241 F.3d at 730. With respect to NEPA documents, the agency must take a "hard look" at the impacts of its action by providing " 'a reasonably thorough discussion of the significant aspects of the probable environmental consequences.' " *Thomas*, 137 F.3d at 1149 (quoting *Or. Nat. Res. Council v. Lowe*, 109 F.3d 521, 526 (9th Cir.1997)). We must determine whether the EA " 'foster[s] both informed decision-making and informed public participation.' " *Native Ecosystems Council v. U.S. Forest Serv.*, 418 F.3d 953, 960 (9th Cir.2005) (quoting *California v. Block*, 690 F.2d 753, 761 (9th Cir.1982)).

III. DISCUSSION

* * *

An agency must prepare an EIS "if 'substantial questions are raised as to whether a project . . . *may* cause significant degradation of some human environmental factor.' " *Idaho Sporting Cong. v. Thomas*, 137 F.3d 1146, 1149 (9th Cir.1998). Petitioners "need not show that significant effects *will in fact occur*," but only that there are "substantial questions whether a project may have a significant effect." *Id.* at 1150 (internal quotation marks omitted); *see also Blue Mountains Biodiversity Project v. Blackwood*, 161 F.3d 1208, 1212 (9th Cir.1998); *Nat'l Parks & Conservation Ass'n v. Babbitt*, 241 F.3d 722, 730 (9th Cir.2001). "If an agency decides not to prepare an EIS, it must supply a 'convincing statement of reasons' to explain why a project's impacts are insignificant. 'The statement of reasons is crucial to determining whether the agency took a 'hard look' at the potential environmental impact of a project.' " *Blue Mountains Biodiversity Project*, 161 F.3d at 1212 (quoting *Save the Yaak Comm. v. Block*, 840 F.2d 714, 717 (9th Cir.1988)); *see also Nat'l Parks & Conservation Ass'n*, 241 F.3d at 730.

"Whether there may be a significant effect on the environment requires consideration of two broad factors: 'context and intensity.' " *Nat'l Parks & Conservation Ass'n*, 241 F.3d at 731 (quoting 40 C.F.R. § 1508.27). A number of factors should be considered in evaluating intensity, including, "[t]he degree to which the proposed action affects public health or safety," "[t]he degree to which the effects on the quality of the human environment are likely to be highly controversial," "[t]he degree to which the possible effects on the human environment are highly uncertain or involve unique or unknown risks," "[t]he degree to which the action may establish a precedent for future actions with significant effects or represents a decision in principle about a future consideration," "[w]hether the action is related to other actions with individually insignificant but cumulatively significant impacts," and "[t]he degree to which the action may adversely affect an endangered or threatened species or its habitat." 40 C.F.R. § 1508.27(b)(2), (4), (5), (6), (7), (9). An action may be "significant" if one of these factors is met. *Ocean Advocates v. U.S. Army Corps of Eng'rs*, 361 F.3d 1108, 1125 (9th Cir.2004); *see also Nat'l Parks & Conservation Ass'n*, 241 F.3d at 731 (either degree of uncertainty or controversy "may be sufficient to require preparation of an EIS in appropriate circumstances.").

NHTSA's finding of no significant impact (FONSI) stated that the agency determined that its Final Rule "will not have a significant effect on the human environment. This finding of no significant impact is based on the attached Final Environmental Assessment (EA). . . . " In the Final EA, NHTSA explained that compared to the "baseline" alternative of extending the MY 2007 light truck CAFE standard through MYs 2008–2011, its evaluated alternatives would have a minor beneficial impact on various environmental resources. NHTSA concluded that "the final rule would produce, compared to U.S. emissions of CO_2, a small decrease in emissions of CO_2, the primary component of greenhouse gas emissions, under the selected alternative. Accordingly, the agency determined that the action we are adopting today will not have a significant impact on the environment."

Petitioners argue that the evidence raises a substantial question as to whether the Final Rule *may have* a significant impact on the environment and that NHTSA failed to provide a convincing statement of reasons for why a small decrease (rather than a larger decrease) in the growth of CO_2 emissions would not have a significant impact on the environment. Petitioners note that NHTSA has never evaluated the impacts of carbon emissions from light trucks or other vehicles, much less the effect of any reduction or increase in those emissions on climate change. Petitioners presented evidence that continued increase in greenhouse gas emissions may change the climate in a sudden and non-linear way. Without some analysis, it would be "impossible for NHTSA to know . . . whether a change in GHG emissions of 0.2% or 1% or 5% or 10% . . . will be a significant step toward averting the 'tipping point' " and irreversible adverse climate change.

NHTSA argues that its "conclusion that a 0.2 percent decrease in carbon dioxide emissions will not have a significant impact upon the environment is self-evidently reasonable and consistent" with *City of Los Angeles v. NHTSA*, 912 F.2d 478 (D.C.Cir.1990), and *Public Citizen v. NHTSA*, 848 F.2d 256 (D.C.Cir.1988). NHTSA also argues that the impact of the rule on global warming is too speculative to warrant NEPA analysis.

We conclude that NHTSA's FONSI is arbitrary and capricious and the agency must prepare an EIS because the evidence raises a substantial question as to whether the Final Rule may have a significant impact on the environment. *See Idaho Sporting Congress*, 137 F.3d at 1149 (holding that an EIS must be prepared "if substantial questions are raised as to whether a project . . . *may* cause significant degradation of some human environmental factor" (alteration in original; internal quotation marks omitted)). Moreover, NHTSA has failed to provide a convincing statement of reasons for its finding of insignificance. *See, e.g., Blue Mountains Biodiversity Project*, 161 F.3d at 1212; *Nat'l Parks & Conservation Ass'n*, 241 F.3d at 730.

Petitioners have raised a "substantial question" as to whether the CAFE standards for light trucks MYs 2008–2011 "*may* cause significant degradation of some human environmental factor," particularly in light of the compelling scientific evidence concerning "positive feedback mechanisms" in the atmosphere. Among the evidence Petitioners presented to the agency was the following:

[concerns relating to increases in temperature, rising sea levels, impacts on biodiversity, breakdown in marine ecosystems, and many of the other issues discussed in Chapter 1 of this book].

Finally, Petitioners have satisfied several of the "intensity" factors listed in 40 C.F.R. § 1508.27(b) for determining "significant effect." For example, the Final Rule clearly may have an "individually insignificant but cumulatively significant" impact with respect to global warming. Evidence that Petitioners submitted in the record also shows that global warming will have an effect on public health and safety. Petitioners do not claim (nor do they have to show) that NHTSA's Final Rule would be the *sole* cause of global warming, and that is NHTSA's only response on this point.

Petitioners have also satisfied the "controversy" factor. *See* 40 C.F.R. § 1508.27(b)(4); *see Blue Mountains Biodiversity Project*, 161 F.3d at 1212 (" 'controversial' is 'a substantial dispute [about] the size, nature, or effect of the major Federal action rather than the existence of opposition to a use.' " (alteration in original)). NHTSA received over 45,000 individual submissions on its proposal. We reject NHTSA's argument that "petitioners' controversy does not concern the 'size, nature, or effect' of the new CAFE standards, but rather the desire of some commenters for different regulations that they have not described in any detail." The entire dispute between Petitioners and NHTSA centers on the *stringency* of the MY 2008–2011 light truck CAFE standards — their "size" or "effect."

In light of the evidence in the record, it is hardly "self-evident" that a 0.2 percent decrease in carbon emissions (as opposed to a greater decrease) is not significant. NHTSA's conclusion that a small reduction (0.2% compared to baseline) in the growth of carbon emissions would not have a significant impact on the environment was unaccompanied by any analysis or supporting data, either in the Final Rule or the EA.

Nowhere does the EA provide a "statement of reasons" for a finding of no significant impact, much less a "convincing statement of reasons." For example, the EA discusses the amount of CO_2 emissions expected from the Rule, but does not discuss the potential impact of such emissions on climate change. In the "Affected Environment" section of the EA, NHTSA states that "[i]ncreasing concentrations of greenhouse gases are likely to accelerate the rate of climate change." The agency notes that "[t]he transportation sector is a significant source of greenhouse gas (GHG) emissions, accounting for approximately 28 percent of all greenhouse gas emissions in the United States." From this, NHTSA jumps to the conclusion that "[c]oupled with the effects resulting from the 2003 light truck rule, the effects resulting from the agency's current action are expected to lessen the GHG impacts discussed above."

Table 3-2 of the EA, which shows the potential health effects of criteria air pollutants, is similarly devoid of meaningful analysis or a statement of reasons why the effects would be insignificant. The potential health effect for CO_2 is described: "Increase in greenhouse gases can lead to climate change. Hot temperatures can lead to cardiovascular problems, heat exhaustion, and some respiratory problems. There may be an increased risk of infectious diseases due to increased temperatures. Heat can also increase the concentration of ground-level ozone."

Nor is there any analysis or statement of reasons in the section of the EA that discusses environmental impacts. The EA states that reduction in fuel production and consumption would reduce "contamination of water resources," acid rain, risk of oil spills and contamination, and "lead to minor reductions in impacts to biological resources . . . includ[ing] habitat encroachment and destruction, air and water pollution, greenhouse gases, and oil contamination from petroleum refining and distribution." [Final EA] at 32–33; *see also id.* at 39 (Table 4-7 compares the impacts under the baseline CAFE standard of 22.2 mpg and the analyzed alternatives. It cursorily summarizes the impacts as "slower rate of growth in fuel consumption for light trucks," "reduction of GHG emissions," and "minor benefit [to water and biological resources] from reductions in energy consumption, GHG emissions and extremely small changes in criteria pollutant emissions."); *id.* at 32–33 (citing no supporting data for its conclusions regarding impacts on water and biological resources).

NHTSA's EA "shunted aside [significant questions] with merely conclusory statements," failed to "directly address[ ]" "substantial questions," and most importantly, "provide[d] no foundation" for the important inference NHTSA draws between a decrease in the rate of carbon emissions growth and its finding of no significant impact. *Found. for N. Am. Wild Sheep*, 681 F.2d at 1179. NHTSA makes "vague and conclusory statements" unaccompanied by "supporting data," and the EA "do[es] not constitute a 'hard look' at the environmental consequences of the action as required by NEPA." *Great Basin Mine Watch v. Hankins*, 456 F.3d 955,

973 (9th Cir.2006). Thus, the FONSI is arbitrary and capricious. *See Klamath-Siskiyou Wildlands Center*, 387 F.3d at 994 ("[T]he problem with the entire table is that it does not provide any objective quantification of the impacts. Instead, the reader is informed only that a particular environmental factor will be 'unchanged,' 'improved,' or 'degraded' and whether that change will be 'minor' or 'major.' The reader is not told what data the conclusion was based on, or why objective data cannot be provided.").

The only reason NHTSA provided for why the environmental impact of the Final Rule would be insignificant is that it results in a decreased rate of growth of GHG emissions compared to the light truck CAFE standard for MY 2007. But simply because the Final Rule may be an improvement over the MY 2007 CAFE standard does not necessarily mean that it will not have a "significant effect" on the environment. NHTSA has not explained *why* its rule will not have a significant effect.

Petitioners have raised a substantial question of whether the Final Rule *may* significantly affect the environment. NHTSA acknowledges that carbon emissions contribute to global warming, and it does not dispute the scientific evidence that Petitioners presented concerning the significant effect of incremental increases in greenhouses gases. NHTSA has not provided a "statement of reasons *why* potential effects are insignificant," much less a "convincing statement of reasons." *See Blue Mountains Biodiversity Project*, 161 F.3d at 1211 (emphasis added) (internal quotation marks omitted). It asserts simply that the insignificance of the effects is "self-evident[ ]." In order that the public and the agency be fully advised, we remand and order the agency to prepare a full EIS.

*   *   *

Reversed and Remanded.

QUESTIONS AND DISCUSSION

1. In *City of Los Angeles v. NHTSA*, the majority upheld NHTSA's decision not to prepare an EIS covering its CAFE standards for MYs 1987–1988 and 1989. 912 F.2d at 482. Then-Judge Ruth Bader Ginsburg joined in Judge D. Ginsburg's opinion on NRDC's NEPA challenge, and she provided two reasons for her concurrence: "(1) NRDC's apparent acceptance of NHTSA's finding that the 1.0 mpg CAFE rollback at issue would yield a 'maximum theoretical increase of less than one percent in greenhouse gases,' . . . and (2) NRDC's failure even to allege that such an increase 'would produce any *marginal* effect on the probability, the severity, or the imminence' of the global warming disaster petitioners project." *Id.* at 504 (citation omitted). The court in *Center for Biological Diversity* stated that "These reasons do not apply here." 508 F.3d at 557, n. 76. What was different in *Center for Biological Diversity*?

2. Other recent cases have concluded that an EIS was not required. In *North Slope Borough v. Minerals Management Service*, No. 07-CV-0045 (D. Alaska Jan. 8, 2008) (Unpublished, Doc No. 59), the plaintiffs challenged the failure of the Minerals Management Service to prepare a new EIS for oil and gas lease sales in the Beaufort Sea that assessed the climate change impacts of those sales on subsistence and polar bears. The court upheld the decision not to prepare an EIS, concluding that the rate and impact of climate change are largely independent of whether the new lease sales are permitted. Id. at 11. In denying injunctive relief to plaintiffs, the court concluded that "the public interest in energy development favors upholding the scheduled sales. To conclude otherwise would require the Court to engage in multiple levels of speculation regarding climate change, animal migration, and economics, and to conclude that existing federal regulations would not effectively address Plaintiffs' environmental concerns. This the Court cannot do." *Id.* at 13.

B.   The Scope of the "Effects" Analysis

An essential question for any EA or EIS is the range of effects that must be considered. Under NEPA and regulations promulgated by the Council for Environmental Quality (CEQ), agencies must describe the direct, indirect, and cumulative effects of a proposed project. These environmental effects may include impacts that are ecological, aesthetic, historical, cultural, economic, social, or health related. 40 C.F.R. § 1508.8. Because a great many actions contribute to climate change, agencies will be challenged to identify which impacts are reasonably related to the project and which impacts are reasonably foreseeable.

1.   *Direct and Indirect Effects*

MID STATES COALITION FOR PROGRESS v. SURFACE TRANSPORTATION BOARD
345 F.3d 520 (8th Cir. 2003)

ARNOLD, J. Petitioners challenge the decision of the Surface Transportation Board issued January 30, 2002, giving final approval to the Dakota, Minnesota & Eastern Railroad Corporation's (DM&E) proposal to construct approximately 280 miles of new rail line to reach the coal mines of Wyoming's Powder River Basin (PRB) and to upgrade nearly 600 miles of existing rail line in Minnesota and South Dakota. They maintain that in giving its approval the Board violated . . . the National Environmental Policy Act (NEPA). * * *

The Sierra Club argues that SEA [Surface Transportation Board's Section of Environmental Analysis (SEA)] wholly failed to consider the effects on air quality that an increase in the supply of low-sulfur coal to power plants would produce. Comments submitted to SEA explain that the projected availability of 100 million tons of low-sulfur coal per year at reduced rates will increase the consumption of low-sulfur coal vis-à-vis other fuels (for instance, natural gas). While it is unlikely that this increase in coal consumption would affect total emissions of sulfur dioxide (which are capped nationally at maximum levels by the Clean Air Act Amendments of 1990), the Sierra Club argues that it would significantly increase the emissions of other noxious air pollutants such as nitrous oxide, carbon dioxide, particulates, and mercury, none of which is currently capped as sulfur dioxide is.

Before this court, the Board admits that because of the need to comply with the restrictions in the Clean Air Act Amendments on sulfur dioxide emissions, many utilities will likely shift to the low-sulfur variety of coal that the proposed project would make available. It argues, however, that this shift will occur regardless of whether DM&E's new line is constructed, since the proposed project will simply provide a shorter and straighter route for low-sulfur coal to be transported to plants already served by other railroad carriers. But the proposition that the demand for coal will be unaffected by an increase in availability and a decrease in price, which is the stated goal of the project, is illogical at best. The increased availability of inexpensive coal will at the very least make coal a more attractive option to future entrants into the utilities market when compared with other potential fuel sources, such as nuclear power, solar power, or natural gas. Even if this project will not affect the short-term demand for coal, which is possible since most existing utilities are single-source dependent, it will most assuredly affect the nation's long-term demand for coal as the comments to the DEIS [Draft EIS] explained. Tellingly, DM&E does not adopt the Board's argument that the proposed project will leave demand for coal unaffected: Instead, it adopts the more plausible position that SEA was not required to address the effects of increased coal generation because these effects are too speculative.

NEPA requires that federal agencies consider "any adverse environmental effects" of their "major . . . actions," 42 U.S.C. § 4332(C), and the CEQ regulations, which are binding on the agencies, explain that "effects" include both "direct effects" and "indirect effects," 40 C.F.R. § 1508.8. Indirect effects are defined as those that "are caused by the action and are later in time or farther removed in distance, but are still reasonably foreseeable." *Id.* "Indirect effects may include . . . effects on air and water and other natural systems, including ecosystems." *Id.* The above language leaves little doubt that the type of effect at issue here, degradation in air quality, is indeed something that must be addressed in an EIS if it is "reasonably foreseeable," *see id.* As in other legal contexts, an environmental effect is "reasonably foreseeable" if it is "sufficiently likely to occur that a person of ordinary prudence would take it into account in reaching a decision." *Sierra Club v. Marsh,* 976 F.2d 763, 767 (1st Cir. 1992).

DM&E argues in its brief that "if the increased availability of coal will 'drive' the construction of additional power plants . . . the [Board] would need to know where those plants will be built, and how much coal these new unnamed power plants would use. Because DM&E has yet to finalize coal-hauling contracts with any utilities, the answers to these questions are pure speculation — hardly the reasonably foreseeable significant impacts that must be analyzed under NEPA." Even if this statement is accurate (the Sierra Club has asserted that it is not), it shows only that the *extent* of the effect is speculative. The *nature* of the effect, however, is far from speculative. As discussed above, it is reasonably foreseeable — indeed, it is almost certainly true — that the proposed project will increase the long-term demand for coal and any adverse effects that result from burning coal.

Contrary to DM&E's assertion, when the *nature* of the effect is reasonably foreseeable but its *extent* is not, we think that the agency may not simply ignore the effect. The CEQ has devised a specific procedure for "evaluating reasonably foreseeable significant adverse effects on the human environment" when "there is incomplete or unavailable information." 40 C.F.R. § 1502.22. First, "the agency shall always make clear that such information is lacking." *Id.* Then, "if the information relevant to reasonably foreseeable significant adverse impacts cannot be obtained because the overall costs of obtaining it are exorbitant or the means to obtain it are not known," the agency must include in the environmental impact statement:

> (1) A statement that such information is incomplete or unavailable; (2) a statement of the relevance of the incomplete or unavailable information to evaluating reasonably foreseeable significant adverse impacts on the human environment; (3) a summary of existing credible scientific evidence which is relevant to evaluating the reasonably foreseeable significant adverse impacts on the human environment; and (4) the agency's evaluation of such impacts based upon theoretical approaches or research methods generally accepted in the scientific community.

Id. at § 1502.22(b).

We find it significant that when the Board was defining the contours of the EIS, it stated that SEA would "evaluate the potential air quality impacts associated with the increased availability and utilization of Powder River Basin Coal." Yet, the DEIS failed to deliver on this promise. Interested parties then submitted comments on the DEIS explaining, for the reasons that we have summarized, why this issue should be addressed in the FEIS [Final EIS]. These parties even identified computer models that are widely used in the electric power industry to simulate the dispatch of generating resources to meet customer loads over a particular study period. According to the commenting parties, these programs could be used to forecast the effects of this project on the consumption of coal. These efforts did not convince SEA, which asserted that "because the 1990 Clean Air Act Amendments mandate reductions in pollutant emissions . . . an assumption of SEA's analysis was that emissions will definitely fall to the mandated level, producing whatever effect the emissions will have on global warming." SEA's "assumption" may be true for those pollutants that the amendments have capped (including, as we have said, sulfur dioxide) but it tells the decision-maker nothing about how this project will affect pollutants not subject to the statutory cap. For the most part, SEA has completely ignored the effects of increased coal consumption, and it has made no attempt to fulfill the requirements laid out in the CEQ regulations.

The Board has stated that this project "is the largest and most challenging rail construction proposal ever to come before [us]," and that the total cost of the project is estimated to be $1.4 billion, not counting the cost of environmental mitigation. We believe that it would be irresponsible for the Board to approve a project of this scope without first examining the effects that may occur as a result of the reasonably foreseeable increase in coal consumption.

QUESTIONS AND DISCUSSION

1. The court in *Mid States Coalition for Progress* makes a distinction between the extent of an impact and the nature of the impact. What is this distinction? With climate change, will agencies ever be able to evaluate the extent of climate change impacts? Do you think there is any difference between evaluating the nature of a climate change impact versus other types of impacts? How should the Surface Transportation Board evaluate the nature of climate change impacts of the decision to construct hundreds of miles of new rail line to the coal mines of the Powder River Basin?

2. On remand, SEA's supplemental EIS (SEIS) declared that little additional coal would be consumed as a result of the new rail line and that air emissions of various pollutants, including carbon dioxide, would increase less than 1 percent nationally and regionally as a result of the minimal increase in coal use. In finding that this increase was minimal, the SEA noted that demand for coal would increase even without the new rail line and that the new rail line was just one way of transporting the coal to market. Surface Trans. Board, Decision, Dakota, Minnesota & Eastern RR Corp. Const. into the Powder River Basin, STB Fin. Docket No. 33407, at 11, 16 (Feb. 13, 2006), *available at* http://www.stb.dot.gov/decisions/readingroom.nsf/unid/53fe263777b8a00485257116004c24d7/$file/36665.pdf.   The plaintiffs filed suit again, this time claiming that the SEIS did not address CO_2 from the coal and ignored climate impacts if national coal use expanded by up to 10 percent.

To study the impacts of the project, the Board used the Energy Information Administration's (EIA) National Energy Modeling System (NEMS), which forecasts coal supply and demand as well as quantifies environmental impacts.

The Board explained that NEMS is "essentially a national and regional modeling tool" that could not be used to obtain the same level of predictive information for the local level. The Board stated that such predictive information was relevant since "there could be an increase in certain air emissions because more PRB coal would be consumed as a result of this project." With respect to existing credible scientific evidence and its potential impacts, the Board explained further that in order "to reasonably foresee the likely impacts of this project on a local level, [it] would need to know not only what existing or new power plants would actually use DM & E's service, but also whether they would otherwise not burn PRB coal, not burn as much coal, or burn a different mix of coal." The Board concluded that this could not "be determined in advance here with any degree of confidence."

After noting that "the impacts of this project on coal consumption and resulting air emissions would be small" on a national and regional basis and that any potential local air quality impacts were "speculative" and "ultimately unforeseeable," the Board concluded that it was not necessary to impose additional mitigating conditions on the project.

Mayo Found. v. Surface Transp. Bd., 472 F.3d 545, 555–556 (8th Cir. 2006). After reviewing this information, the court concluded that the Board adequately analyzed the impacts. What, if anything, has changed between the time of the first lawsuit and this one to lead to a different outcome?

3.   In *City of Los Angeles* and more recently in *Mayo*, the courts have found one percent contributions to climate change insignificant to trigger NEPA's requirement to conduct an EIS. In light of the recent information released by the IPCC regarding the impacts of climate change — as well as the Supreme Court's decision in *Massachusetts v. EPA*, finding a small impact on motor vehicle emissions substantial enough to support Article III standing — do you think the courts have been correct to dismiss these impacts as insignificant? What threshold level of emissions should an agency's action reach before it is deemed significant? If each agency action must amount to a certain threshold, how many agency actions will go through full NEPA review?

In the next case, *Border Power Plant Working Group v. Dept. of Energy*, plaintiffs challenged an EA for approval of two Presidential Permits, which are required for the siting of a transmission line across a border of the United States. *See* Exec. Order No. 12038; 10 C.F.R. 300. The transmission lines would connect new power plants in Mexico to the southern California power grid. Must the EA consider only the impacts of the power lines or must it also evaluate emissions from the new power plants in Mexico?

BORDER POWER PLANT WORKING GROUP v. DEPT. OF ENERGY
260 F. Supp. 2d 997 (S.D. Cal. 2003)

GONZALEZ, J.

As a threshold matter, the Court must first determine the scope of the environmental review required by NEPA to determine whether the construction of the power plants is within that scope. Plaintiff assumes in its arguments that the actions whose impacts must be analyzed include not only the construction and operation of the actual transmission lines, but also the operation of the power plants in Mexico to which the lines will be connected. In fact, all, or at least the vast majority, of the complaints of impacts to air quality, water quality, and human health set forth by plaintiff are actually caused by the power plants. Because of this, amicus BCP [Baja California Power] argues that if the "action" at issue here is narrowly limited to the construction and operation of the transmission lines, without regard to the generation of the power, and the emissions of the power plants are not "effects" of that action, then plaintiff's complaints are immaterial to the permits at issue.

. . . The Council for Environmental Quality (CEQ), which is charged with implementing NEPA, has defined a "major federal action" as including "actions with effects that may be major and which are potentially subject to Federal control and responsibility." *40 C.F.R. § 1508.18*. Similarly, defendant Department of Energy has defined "action" for NEPA purposes as "a project, plan, or policy . . . that is subject to DOE's control and responsibility." *10 C.F.R. § 1021.104(b)*. BCP argues that the latter definition necessarily excludes the Mexican power plants from the scope of the action because these plants are outside the regulatory jurisdiction of the United States.

The first key question under the regulatory definitions is whether the plants will be "projects" that are "subject to [Federal] control and responsibility." *10 C.F.R § 1021.104(b)*. Clearly, they are not because they are outside the jurisdiction of the United States. Accordingly, defendants correctly did not include the power plants themselves when defining the scope of the proposed action.

Nonetheless, the environmental analysis of the actions might still require consideration of the operation of the power plants if such operation constitutes an "adverse environmental effect" of the granting of the permit to construct and operate the transmission lines. *42 U.S.C. § 4332(C)(ii)*. NEPA's implementing regulations define "effects" and categorize them as "direct" or "indirect." *40 C.F.R. § 1508.8(a)*. "Direct effects" are those "which are caused by the action and occur at the same time and place." Id. "Indirect effects" are those "which are caused by the action and are later in time or farther removed in distance, but are still reasonably foreseeable." Id. Thus, as BCP notes, the question is one of causation.

The question of whether the power plants are effects of the proposed action is central to assessing both the legality of the FONSI and to assessing the adequacy of the environmental assessment (EA). First, in deciding whether to prepare an EIS, an agency must consider "significant indirect effects." *Sylvester v. U.S. Army Corps of Engineers, 884 F.2d 394, 400, 871 F.2d 817 (9th Cir. 1989)*. Second, the question of the adequacy of the EA's analysis of the air impacts, water impacts, and alternatives of the proposed actions, depend on whether the plants' adverse environmental impacts are effects of the proposed transmission lines.

* * *

[T]he Sylvester court held that in order for an agency to be required to consider secondary (indirect) and cumulative impacts (or effects) of an action other than the proposed action under NEPA, the proposed action and the second action must be "two links of a single chain." In so holding, the Sylvester court collected and analyzed the prior cases discussing the question in the Ninth Circuit. Id. (citing *Port of Astoria. Oregon v. Hodel, 595 F.2d 467, 480 (9th Cir. 1979)* (agency's EIS had to consider the supply of federal power and the construction of a private magnesium plant that used the power); *Thomas v. Peterson, 753 F.2d 754, 761 (9th Cir. 1985)* (agency's EIS had to consider both a federal road and the federal timber sales that the road would facilitate); and *Colorado River Indian Tribes v. Marsh, 605 F. Supp. 1425, 1433 (C.D.Cal.1985)* (agency had to prepare an EIS that considered both the federal action of stabilizing a river bank and the private housing built as a result)); see also *id. at 401* (citing *Friends of the Earth v. Hintz 800 F.2d 822, 832 (9th Cir. 1986)* (agency considered only filled wetlands and not other aspects of a harbor facility in deciding not to prepare an EIS); *Enos v. Marsh 769 F.2d 1363, 1371–72 (9th Cir. 1985)* (agency's EIS did not have to consider non-federal shore facilities for a new deep draft harbor); *Friends of Earth, Inc. v. Coleman 518 F.2d 323, 328 (9th Cir.1975)* (agency did not have to prepare an EIS for state funded projects in a partially federally funded airport development)). The court concluded that these cases did not mandate a different result because "the federal and private portions of the projects considered in these cases were joined to each other (links in the same bit of chain) in a way that the golf course [the proposed action under consideration in Sylvester] and the remainder of the resort complex (a separate segment of chain) are not."

Importantly, the basis for the Sylvester court's determination of whether two related actions constituted links of a single chain involved determining whether "each [action] could exist without the other." It was not enough that the actions might be related or that each "might benefit from the other's presence." Accordingly, the question in the present case narrows to whether the transmission lines and the power plants at issue would exist in the absence of the other.

Somewhat confusingly, the Sylvester court cites two other Ninth Circuit cases in a footnote, dismissing them because they involved "the impact of federal action rather than the scope of federal action." *Id. at 401 n.3* (citing *Methow Valley Citizens Council v. Regional Forester 833 F.2d 810, 816 (9th Cir. 1987)* and *City of Davis v. Coleman 521 F.2d 661, 671 (9th. Cir. 1975)*). While it is clear, as the Sylvester court implies, that the scope of the proposed action and the impacts of that action are separate questions under NEPA, this appears confusing only because "scope" may also refer to the variety of impacts that a sufficient EA or EIS must address. It is helpful to differentiate then between the scope of the proposed action and scope of the NEPA review. Thus, in the present case, the proposed action does not include the operation of the Mexican power plants. The question remains, however, whether the operation and emissions of those plants must be included within the scope of the NEPA review because they are effects of the proposed federal action. It seems to the Court that many of the cases cited by Sylvester court involved both the impact (or effects) of a proposed federal action and the scope of the action. While those cases treated the two concepts as coextensive, this Court finds the cases relevant to the present inquiry only to the extent that they discuss the effects of the proposed action. Thus, the two additional cases cited by Sylvester dealing exclusively with the effects of federal action are central to the present analysis.

First, in *Methow Valley Citizens Council v. Regional Forester 833 F.2d 810, 816–817 (9th Cir. 1987)*, rev'd on other grounds, *Robertson v. Methow Valley Citizens Council*, 490 U.S. 332, 109 S. Ct. 1835, 104 L. Ed. 2d 351 (1989), the court first emphasized that NEPA does not recognize any distinction between primary and secondary effects when requiring environmental review of the effects. *Id. at 816*. In discussing how proximate any effects must be to the proposed action to require their inclusion in the NEPA analysis, the Court held:

> This court would not require the government to speculate on impacts in order to "foresee the unforeseeable". However, it must be remembered that the basic thrust of an agency's responsibilities under NEPA is to predict the environmental effects of proposed action before the action is taken and those effects fully known. Reasonable forecasting and speculation is thus implicit in NEPA, and we must reject any attempt by agencies to shirk their responsibilities under NEPA by labeling any and all discussion of future environmental effects as "crystal ball inquiry". Thus we

find it imperative that the [agency] evaluate the reasonably foreseeable significant effects which would be proximately caused by implementation of the proposed action.

Id at 816–17. Similarly, though perhaps more narrowly, the court in City of Davis v. Coleman, found that effects must be included in the environmental review when the action is an "indispensible prerequisite" or an "essential catalyst" to the effects. *521 F.2d 661, 674 (9th Cir. 1975).*

More recently, the Ninth Circuit reaffirmed that an agency may "limit the scope of its NEPA review to the activities specifically authorized by the federal action where the private and federal portions of the project could exist independently of each other." *Wetlands Action Network v. U.S. Army Corps of Engineers (WAN), 222 F.3d 1105, 1116 (9th Cir. 2000).* In general that Court instructed that "deciding whether federal and non-federal activity are sufficiently interrelated to constitute a single federal action for NEPA purposes will generally require a careful analysis of all facts and circumstances surrounding the relationship."

The WAN court faced a situation, like here, where the federal agency did not have independent jurisdiction over the non-federal action that was a potential effect of the proposed action. See *id., at 1117.* Furthermore, the court found that the non-federal action "certainly *could* proceed without the [federal action] and . . . is currently proceeding without the [federal action]."*Id.* The non-federal action at issue in WAN, as here, was not financed by federal funding, and federal regulations did not control the design of the non-federal action. *Id.* Finally, the WAN court derived comfort from the fact that the non-federal action had already been subjected to extensive state environmental review.

In sum, Ninth Circuit precedent makes clear that effects must be causally linked to the proposed federal action in order for NEPA to require consideration of those effects in an EA or EIS. In the present case, only BCP puts much weight on the argument that the power plant emissions are not effects of the transmission line project. BCP's principle argument is that the power transmission lines are not a but-for cause of the LRPC [La Rosita Power Complex] emissions because the LRPC would generate some of its power for the Mexican market without regard to whether the transmission lines are completed, and it could send its export power through the Mexican power grid to the United States via an alternative transmission line. Amicus T-US [Termoelectrica-US] does not make the same argument, presumably because the TDM plant will only be producing power for export to the United States, and the only planned transmission line connecting that plant is the one requiring the permit under consideration. The federal defendants appear to concede, both in the EA itself and their briefs, that they were required to analyze to some extent the impacts of the power plants, although they argue, correctly, that the power plants are not within the scope of the proposed action.

*   *   *

The LRPC plant is divided into three EAX turbines and one EBC turbine. Two of the EAX turbines are designed to produce power exclusively for sale to a Mexican utility, and it is reasonably foreseeable that very little of this power will flow through the BCP transmission line into the United States. The EA does acknowledge the possibility that under limited circumstances, the domestic generation turbines may provide power to the BCP line. The record shows that the third EAX turbine is anticipated to produce power exclusively for export to the United States. However, the power produced by the EAX export turbine could be transmitted to the United States through an alternative interconnection site. Finally, the EBC turbine is configured and licensed only to sell electricity over the BCP line.

*   *   *

Considering only the information that the federal defendants had before them at the time they made their final decisions, the Court finds that it was reasonably foreseeable that the two export turbines in the LRPC would use the BCP transmission line to export the entirety of their power. Furthermore, given that the BCP line is the only current means evidenced by the record through which the EBC turbine could transmit its power, the Court finds that the BCP line was a but-for cause of the generation of power at the EBC turbine. Because the EBC turbine and the BCP transmission line are two links in the same chain, the emissions resulting from the operation of the EBC turbine are "effects" of the BCP transmission line that must be analyzed under NEPA. For the same reasons, the Court finds that the operation of the TDM plant is an effect of the T-US transmission line.

Conversely, the Court finds that the two turbines in the LRPC dedicated almost exclusively to the generation of power for the Mexican market are not causally linked to the BCP line in a way that makes the BCP line a necessary prerequisite or essential catalyst to their operation. Because the line of causation is too attenuated between these turbines and the federal action permitting the BCP line, Ninth Circuit authority makes clear that the emissions of the non-export turbines were not effects of the BCP line and that the federal defendants were therefore under no NEPA obligation to analyze their emissions as effects of the action. Additionally, because the record makes clear that the EAX export turbine has an alternative to the BCP line to export its power, the BCP line cannot be considered the but-for cause of the EAX export turbine's operation. Indeed, the EA concludes that the EAX export turbine would be built regardless of whether the BCP line is permitted. For this reason, the EAX turbine is also not an effect of the action.

[The court then found the EA inadequate because it failed to disclose and analyze the potential environmental impacts from carbon dioxide emissions.]

QUESTIONS AND DISCUSSION

1. In *Border Power*, the court emphasized that the EIS need not consider the Mexican power plants themselves as within the scope of the proposed action. Yet, it declares that the effects of the Mexican power plants must be considered. What is the significance of this distinction?

2. *Connected Actions.* Indirect effects are sometimes confused with "connected actions." The CEQ regulations define "connected actions" as actions that are "closely related and therefore should be discussed in the same impact statement." 40 C.F.R. § 1508.25(a). Actions are "connected" if they:

(i) Automatically trigger other actions which may require environmental impact statements.

(ii) Cannot or will not proceed unless other actions are taken previously or simultaneously.

(iii) Are interdependent parts of a larger action and depend on the larger actions for their justification.

Id. For example, courts have considered logging operations and the construction of a road to be "connected actions." Save the Yaak Committee v. Block, 840 F.2d 714, 719 (9th Cir. 1988); Thomas v. Peterson, 753 F.2d 754, 758 (9th Cir. 1985). Can you explain how "indirect effects" differ from "connected actions"? Why are the power plants in *Border Power Working Group* evaluated as indirect effects of the construction of transmission lines into the United States but logging roads and logging operations are connected actions?

3. The construction of new power plants in Mexico to provide electricity in the United States can present interesting international issues as well. Consider that, under the cap-and-trade structure of the Kyoto Protocol discussed in Chapter 5, a country is responsible for those emissions that take place in their country's territory. In a post-Kyoto agreement, the United States might agree to a cap, but Mexico might not. Would it then be possible for the United States to expand its energy consumption by importing coal-generated electricity from Mexico free from any restrictions? How would you recommend the negotiators address such a situation?

---

2.   *Cumulative Impacts*

NEPA regulations define "cumulative" impacts as the "incremental impact of the action when added to other past, present, and reasonably foreseeable future action regardless of what agency (Federal or non-Federal) or person undertakes such other actions. Cumulative impacts can result from individually minor but collectively significant actions taking place over a period of time." 40 C.F.R. § 1508.7. Courts have made clear the importance of assessing cumulative impacts:

> Cumulative impacts of multiple projects can be significant in different ways. The most obvious way is that the greater total magnitude of the environmental effects . . . may demonstrate by itself that the environmental impact will be significant. Sometimes the total impact from a set of actions may be greater than the sum of the parts.

Klamath-Siskiyou Wildlands Ctr. v. Bureau of Land Mgmt., 387 F.3d 989, 994 (9th Cir. 2004).

Despite the importance of understanding cumulative impacts, knowing where to draw the line, particularly concerning climate change, is difficult. Consider the following discussion of cumulative impacts from *Center for Biological Diversity*, where plaintiffs challenged the adequacy of the NHTSA's discussion of cumulative impacts when setting fuel economy standards.

CENTER FOR BIOLOGICAL DIVERSITY v. NATIONAL HIGHWAY TRAFFIC SAFETY ADMINISTRATION
508 F.3d 508 (9th Cir. 2007)

The EA catalogues the total tonnage of CO_2 emissions for light trucks for MYs 2005–2011. Table 4-5 of the Final EA lists the amount of fuel consumption and emissions of criteria pollutants and CO_2 emissions. For example, it shows that under Unreformed CAFE, the lifetime CO_2 emissions for light trucks MY 2005–2011 would be 4,979 million metric tons (mmt). Under Reformed CAFE . . . CO_2 emissions would be 4,966 million metric tons. NHTSA estimated that:

> together with the previous action raising MY 2005–07 light truck CAFE standards, the various alternatives for the current action will reduce lifetime carbon dioxide (CO_2) emissions from MY 2005–11 light trucks by 122 to 196 million metric tons, or by 2.4 to 3.8 percent *from their level if neither action had been taken*. . . . MY 2008–11 light truck CAFE standards are projected to result in cumulative reductions from the

previous and current actions ranging from 0.2 to 0.3 percent of U.S. greenhouse gas emissions over the lifetimes of MY 2005–11 light trucks.

We conclude that the EA's cumulative impacts analysis is inadequate. While the EA quantifies the expected amount of CO_2 emitted from light trucks MYs 2005–2011, it does not evaluate the "incremental impact" that these emissions will have on climate change or on the environment more generally in light of other past, present, and reasonably foreseeable actions such as other light truck and passenger automobile CAFE standards. The EA does not discuss the *actual* environmental effects resulting from those emissions or place those emissions in context of other CAFE rulemakings. This is a similar deficiency as that found in the Bureau of Land Management's EA in *Klamath-Siskiyou Wildlands Center*, where this court held that the BLM's cumulative impacts analysis was inadequate because "[a] calculation of the total number of acres to be harvested in the watershed is a necessary component of a cumulative effects analysis, but it is not a sufficient description of the actual environmental effects that can be expected from logging those acres" and "stating the total miles of roads to be constructed is similar to merely stating the sum of the acres to be harvested — it is not a description of the *actual* environmental effects." 387 F.3d at 995.

*   *   *

We agree with Petitioners that "[b]y allowing particular fuel economy levels, which NHTSA argues translate directly into particular tailpipe emissions, NHTSA's regulations are the proximate cause of those emissions just as EPA Clean Air Act rules permitting particular smokestack emissions are the proximate cause of those air pollutants and are unquestionably subject to NEPA's cumulative impacts requirements." Thus, the fact that "climate change is largely a global phenomenon that includes actions that are outside of [the agency's] control . . . does not release the agency from the duty of assessing the effects of *its* actions on global warming within the context of other actions that also affect global warming." The cumulative impacts regulation specifically provides that the agency must assess the "impact of the action when added to other past, present, and reasonably foreseeable future actions *regardless of what agency (Federal or non-Federal) or person undertakes such other actions.*" 40 C.F.R. § 1508.7; *see also Res. Ltd., Inc. v. Robertson*, 35 F.3d 1300, 1306 (9th Cir.1994) ("The Forest Service says that cumulative impacts from non-Federal actions need not be analyzed because the Federal government cannot control them. That interpretation is inconsistent with 40 C.F.R. § 1508.7, which specifically requires such analysis.").

The impact of greenhouse gas emissions on climate change is precisely the kind of cumulative impacts analysis that NEPA requires agencies to conduct. Any given rule setting a CAFE standard might have an "individually minor" effect on the environment, but these rules are "collectively significant actions taking place over a period of time." 40 C.F.R. § 1508.7; *see also Native Ecosystems Council*, 304 F.3d at 897 (holding that the Forest Service's road density standard amendments must be subject to cumulative impacts analysis because otherwise, "the Forest Service will be free to amend road density standards throughout the forest piecemeal, without ever having to evaluate the amendments' cumulative environmental impacts."); *City of Los Angeles v. NHTSA*, 912 F.2d 478, 501 (D.C.Cir.1990) (Wald, C.J., dissenting) ("[W]e cannot afford to ignore even modest contributions to global warming. If global warming is the result of the cumulative contributions of myriad sources, any one modest in itself, is there not a danger of losing the forest by closing our eyes to the felling of the individual trees?"), *overruled on other grounds by Fla. Audubon Soc. v. Bentsen*, 94 F.3d 658 (D.C.Cir.1996). Thus, NHTSA must provide the necessary contextual information about the cumulative and incremental environmental impacts of the Final Rule in light of other CAFE rulemakings and other past, present, and reasonably foreseeable future actions, regardless of what agency or person undertakes such other actions.

QUESTIONS AND DISCUSSION

The potential scope of a cumulate impacts analysis is very broad — agencies must evaluate the incremental impact of the action when added to past, present, and reasonably foreseeable actions. In the climate change context, what are past, present, and reasonably foreseeable actions?

C. Alternatives

The CEQ regulations describe an EIS's discussion of alternatives to the proposed project as the heart of the EIS. 40 C.F.R. § 1502.14. Agencies must "rigorously explore and objectively evaluate all reasonable alternatives," including a "no action" alternative and alternatives within the jurisdiction of other agencies. *Id.* It should "present the environmental impacts of the proposal and the alternatives in comparative form, thus sharply defining the issues and providing a clear basis for choice among options by the decisionmaker and the public." *Id.* "The rule of reason guides both the choice of alternatives as well as the extent to which the [NEPA analysis] must discuss each alternative." Public Citizen v. Department of Transp., 316 F.3d 1002, 1028 (9th Cir. 2003). Agencies must consider alternatives in an EA. In climate change litigation, the question of alternatives will be central to most litigant's claims. Is 35 mpg a reasonable alternative to CAFE standards of 27.5 mpg? Is a nuclear power plant and a range of conservation measures reasonable alternatives to a coal-fired power plants? Consider the range of alternatives presented by the NHTSA when considering fuel economy standards.

CENTER FOR BIOLOGICAL DIVERSITY v. NATIONAL HIGHWAY TRAFFIC SAFETY ADMINISTRATION
508 F.3d 508 (9th Cir. 2007)

In the EA, NHTSA considered a very narrow range of alternatives. All the alternatives evaluated were derived from NHTSA's cost-benefit analysis. * * *

These alternatives are hardly different from the option that NHTSA ultimately adopted. . . . The entire range of alternatives considered in the EA ranged from "22.2 to 22.7 mpg for MY 2008, 22.2 to 23.3 mpg for MY 2009, and 22.2 to 23.6 mpg for MY 2010." The estimated lifetime fuel and energy use by MY 2008–2011 light trucks under the alternatives ranged from a 1.8 to 2.6 percent decrease from "baseline,", and the estimated lifetime emissions of CO_2 ranged from 2,767 to 2,840 mmt, which is extremely small compared to the overall volume of emissions.

NHTSA acknowledged that "the range of impacts from the considered alternatives is very narrow and minimal." However, the agency justified its choice of range and refusal to consider other alternatives on the ground that "standards more stringent than those represented by the alternatives would not satisfy the statutory requirement to establish standards . . . that are both technologically feasible and economically practicable. . . . NEPA's requirements must be applied in light of the constraints placed on the agency by EPCA." Once again, NHTSA falls back on its contention that it had no discretion to consider setting higher

CAFE standards. As before, we conclude that this argument is flawed.

NHTSA also erroneously contends that Petitioners have not identified any specific alternative the agency should have considered. To the contrary, Environmental Defense submitted a detailed appendix to its comment titled, "Revised Benefit-Cost Analysis for Calculating Optimal CAFE Targets." In this document, Environmental Defense performed a marginal cost-benefit analysis, using a variety of different assumptions and inputs. Table A-1 set forth 28 different possible CAFE standards for MY 2011 (including NHTSA's figure). On the basis of its calculations, it recommended a final rule that would increase CAFE standards at a rate of 4% per year and achieve a standard of 26 mpg by MY 2011.

QUESTIONS AND DISCUSSION

1.   The court in *Center for Biological Diversity* called the NHTSA's range of alternatives inadequate. What do you think constitutes a reasonable fuel economy standard?

2.   Recall that in *Border Power Plant Working Group*, the Department of Energy was required to assess the environmental impacts relating to the construction of transmission lines as well as the effects of the new power plants. What are reasonable alternatives to this project? The Department of Energy analyzed three alternatives to the proposed project: a "no action" alternative and two alternative locations for the transmission lines. Is that sufficient? Should reasonable alternatives relate to the construction and operation of the power plants themselves, even if they are not within the jurisdiction of any U.S. agency? Plaintiffs argued that the Department of Energy could condition permits to operate the transmission lines on the commitment of the project proponents to implement state-of-the-art emissions control systems, mitigation through offsets in existing sources, and the use of dry cooling or parallel dry-wet cooling to condense steam for producing energy. The court agreed:

> [T]he agencies were obligated to set forth in the EA "the range of alternatives . . . sufficient to permit a reasoned choice." *Methow Valley Citizens Council*, 833 F.2d at 815. Although defendants argue that "international sensitivities" preclude conditioning the permits from being a reasonable and feasible alternative, such a discussion belongs in the EA's alternative analysis rather than a litigation brief. Furthermore, the Court is unconvinced that the federal government's conditioning of a permit to construct transmission lines within the government's jurisdiction to ameliorate negative environmental effects within the United States necessarily offends international principles of law. The condition would not be a direct regulation of the Mexican power plants; those plants could still choose to sell their power to the Mexican market or transmit their power via an alternate route rather than meet the condition.

> Plaintiff bears the burden of showing that the agency was alerted to the specific alternative at issue before it prepared the EA in question. This requirement helps ensure that the alternative was not so remote and speculative as to have precluded the agencies from ascertaining the possibility. In the present case, commenters, including plaintiff, clearly proposed withholding the permits until the federal defendants could be certain that the power generation met certain environmental standards. Accordingly, the Court is hard-pressed to find that the proposed alternative could not be reasonably ascertained by the agencies during their delibera-

tions. Because the Court finds that the conditioning of the permits is a reasonable and feasible alternative within the nature of the proposed actions, the Court finds that the analysis of alternatives in the EA was inadequate in this regard.

Border Power Plant Working Group v. Dept. of Energy, 260 F. Supp. 2d at 1030–1031. Do you agree that those alternatives are reasonable?

3. ***Mitigation Measures.*** An EIS must also include a discussion of mitigation measures. 40 C.F.R. § 1502.16. Mitigation includes avoiding the impact altogether, minimizing impacts by limiting the degree and magnitude of the action, rectifying the impact through rehabilitation or restoration, reducing or eliminating the impact over time by preservation and maintenance operations during the life of the project, and compensating for the impact by replacing or providing substitute resources or environments. *Id.* at § 1508.20. When making its final decision concerning a proposed project, the agency must "[s]tate whether all practicable means to avoid or minimize environmental harm from the alternative selected have been adopted, and if not, why they were not." 40 C.F.R. § 1505.2(c). While courts have found an agency's discussion of mitigation inadequate, *Neighbors of Cuddy Mountain v. U.S. Forest Serv.*, 137 F.3d 1372, 1381 (9th Cir. 1998), the Supreme Court has also stated that NEPA does not include "a substantive requirement that a complete mitigation plan be actually formulated and adopted[.]" Robertson v. Methow Valley Citizens Council, 490 U.S. 332, 352 (1989). What kind of mitigation measures could NHTSA propose? In *Border Power Plant Working Group*, what kind of measures could the Department of Energy propose to mitigate the impacts of the transmission lines?

4. Having read this section, what do you think the benefits are of discussing the climate change impacts of a proposed action in an EIS? How do you think the legal analysis will change if climate science continues to show increasingly significant impacts?

5. On February 28, 2008, the International Center for Technology Assessment (ICTA), Natural Resources Defense Council, and Sierra Club petitioned the CEQ to clarify that climate change analyses must be included in all federal environmental review documents. The groups specifically requested that CEQ (1) amend its NEPA regulations to include language clarifying that NEPA implementing regulations require that climate change effects be addressed in NEPA compliance documents, including EAs and EISs; and (2) issue a CEQ Guidance Memorandum that includes instructions to all federal agencies on how, where, and when to best integrate climate change analyses into their respective NEPA processes. Petition Requesting that the Council on Environmental Quality Amend Its Regulations to Clarify that Climate Change Analyses Be Included in Environmental Review Documents (Feb. 28, 2008). How would such regulations and guidance be useful?

6. ***Foreign Cases.*** Courts in other countries are also addressing the climate change impacts of development projects. In Australia, when a planning panel considered an amendment to a plan to extend the operation of a major coal-fired power station by 20 years, the Victorian Civil and Administrative Tribunal declared that the Victoria Planning and Environment Act 1987 (Vic) required the panel to consider submissions about the greenhouse gas implications of using brown coal. Australian Conservation Foundation v. Minister for Planning [2004] VCAT 2029 (29 October 2004). *See also* Gray v. The Minister for Planning [2006] NSWLEC 720 (the greenhouse gas impacts of burning coal must be taken into account in the environmental impact assessment of new coal mines). *But see* Wildlife Preservation Society of Queensland Proserpine/Whitsunday Branch Inc v. Minister for the Environment & Heritage & Ors [2006] FCA 736 (15 June 2006) (finding that the limited discussion of the indirect effects of GHG emissions on Australian World Heritage properties resulting from two coal mines was adequate under the

Australian Environmental Protection and Biodiversity Conservation Act of 1999).

In New Zealand, a Court of Appeal ruled that the Resource Management Act (RMA) did not require Genesis Energy, a State-owned enterprise wanting to build a gas-fired power plant, to consider the impact of greenhouse gases on climate change when the greenhouse gases are from non-renewable energy sources. Genesis Power Limited v. Greenpeace New Zealand Incorporated, Court of Appeal [2007] NZCA 569 (*Genesis Power*), *available at*: http://jdo.justice.govt.nz/jdo/Search.jsp. The decision overruled a 2007 decision in Greenpeace New Zealand v. Northland Regional Council, [2007] NZRMA 87 (the *Mighty River* case). *Genesis Power* involved an application for consent to build a gas-fired electricity generating plant. Under Section 104E of the RMA, the consent authority, when considering an application to discharge greenhouse gases, must *not* have regard to the effects of such a discharge on climate change, except to the extent that the use and development of renewable energy enables a reduction in the discharge into air of GHGs. The Environment Court in the *Mighty River* case concluded that Section 104E allowed the consent authority to consider the effects of climate change only in the context of applications to use or develop renewable energy that would enable a lowering of GHGs. The High Court overturned that decision, declaring:

> If the application for a discharge permit . . . includes no proposal which . . . would enable a "reduction into air of greenhouse gases" by the "use and development of renewable energy" then that . . . is a factor the consent authority is entitled to take into account in deciding whether to exercise its discretion and grant the resource consent.

> *   *   *

> [Section 104E] enables the consent authority to balance [the] proposed activity alongside any proposal by the applicant which would effect "reduction in the discharge into air of greenhouse gases" by an activity which involves the "use and development of renewable energy . . . relative to the use and development of non-renewable energy" and to that extent to have regard to climate change.

The court in *Genesis Power*, however, found that the *Mighty River* approach would impose substantial burdens on consenting authorities to identify alternatives using renewable energy and the significance of the project's GHG emissions on climate change. The Court of Appeal thus concluded that Section 104E only requires a consenting authority to consider the effects of climate change in applications involving the use of renewable sources of energy production. Genesis Power, at para. 40. Moreover, it concluded that in applications involving non-renewable energy production, a consent authority is *not* required to:

a. Compare the proposal advanced by the applicant with a hypothetical proposal using renewable sources.

b. Treat the non-use of renewable sources of energy as a negative factor counting against the grant of consent.

c. Assess the extent to which GHG emissions associated with the proposal would have an effect on climate change.

Id. at para. 41.

7. For a summary of all NEPA litigation related climate change, see Joseph Mendelson III, *Surveying the National Environmental Policy Act and the Emerging Issues of Climate Change, Genetic Engineering and Nanotechnology* (Feb. 13, 2008).

III. THE ENDANGERED SPECIES ACT

Scientists have long argued that climate change will cause species to migrate as habitat and other biological needs change in response to increasing water and atmospheric temperatures, changes in salinity of estuaries, changes in precipitation and snow pack, and increases in pests, among many other factors. *See* Chapter 1. Unlike flooding, wildfires, and other natural disturbances, climate change will have more profound, long-lasting impacts on species. The challenge for wildlife managers is anticipating how climate change will affect specific species:

> [N]ew climates are expected to cause ecosystem reshuffling as individual species, constrained by different environmental factors, respond differently. One tree may be limited by summer rains that hold back seedling recruitment, for instance, whereas another species may be limited by winter freezes that control insect pests. Some species may migrate up-latitude or up-elevation, while others may stay put. An ecosystem may see many species vanish — but also new arrivals.

Douglas Fox, *Back to the No-Analog Future?*, 316 SCIENCE 823, 823 (2007).

Unable to adapt quickly enough to changing conditions, some species may become endangered or even extinct. Some species may simply run out of room. The pika, an inhabitant of cold, high-altitude mountaintops, may eventually be unable to climb any higher to avoid rising mountain temperatures. Other species may have their habitat literally vanish beneath their feet. Polar bears and some species of seals, for example, rely on floating ice to hunt. With the decline of ice in the Arctic, the future of these species is uncertain.

As populations of some species have declined due to climate change, advocates have turned to the U.S. Endangered Species Act (ESA), 16 U.S.C. §§ 1531–1544, to protect species from the adverse impacts of climate change and mitigate U.S. greenhouse gas emissions. In response to petitions from environmental organizations, the U.S. Fish & Wildlife Service (FWS) has listed elkhorn and staghorn corals as threatened species in part due to the effects of climate change. Most recently, the FWS listed the polar bear as a threatened species due to climate change. Section A introduces the main provisions of the ESA before Section B looks at how the ESA may help protect polar bears and other species from the effects of climate change.

A.   Introduction to the ESA

Through the ESA, Congress wished "to halt and reverse the trend towards species extinction, whatever the cost." TVA v. Hill, 437 U.S. 153 184 (1978). To that end, the ESA establishes a framework for conserving species listed as endangered or threatened. An endangered species is "any species which is in danger of extinction throughout all or a significant portion of its range" other than insects considered to be pests. 16 U.S.C. § 1532(6). A "threatened species" is "any species which is likely to become an endangered species within the foreseeable future." 16 U.S.C. § 1532(20). The decision to list a species is based on an assessment of five factors: (A) the present or threatened destruction, modification, or curtailment of its habitat or range; (B) overutilization for commercial, recreational, scientific, or educational purposes; (C) disease or predation; (D) the inadequacy of existing regulatory mechanisms; or (E) other natural or manmade factors affecting its continued existence. 16 U.S.C. § 1533(a). The Secretary of Interior, through the FWS, administers the ESA for terrestrial and freshwater species, as well as polar bears, dugongs, walruses, and sea otters. The Department of Commerce, through the National Marine Fisheries Service (NMFS), administers the ESA for most marine species, including whales, dolphins, seals, and anadromous fish, such as salmon. *See* 50 C.F.R. § 402.01.

The ESA offers a range of measures that may help conserve listed species: a prohibition against taking, development of a recovery plan, consultation to ensure that Federal actions do not jeopardize the continuing survival of listed species or adversely affect their critical habitat, and, in the absence of a special rule for threatened species, a prohibition against "taking." The FWS and NMFS have used these obligations to protect more than 1100 endangered or threatened animal and plant species. Although "few species brought under the ESA's protection have recovered to full health, the ESA is credited with preventing the vast majority of protected species from ultimate extinction." J.B. Ruhl, *Climate Change and the Endangered Species Act: Building Bridges to the No-Analog Future*, 88 B.U.L. REV. 1, 5 (2008).

1. *Prohibition against "Taking"*

Section 9 of the ESA prohibits the "take" of endangered species. 16 U.S.C. § 1538. The ESA defines "take" to mean "harass, harm, pursue, hunt, shoot, wound, kill, trap, capture or collect or to attempt to engage in any such activity." 16 U.S.C. § 1532(19). The ESA also prohibits "harm" to endangered species, including "significant habitat modification or degradation." 50 C.F.R. § 17.2; *see also* Babbitt v. Sweet Home Chapter of Communities for a Great Oregon 515 U.S 687 (1995). Section 9 further prohibits the import, export, possession, and sale, among other things, of endangered species. While the ESA itself only prohibits the take of endangered species, regulations apply the prohibition against taking to threatened species unless the Secretary adopts a special rule. *See* 16 U.S.C. § 1533(d), 50 C.F.R § 17.31, 50 C.F.R. §§ 17.40–17.48 (special rules).

The ESA also includes a number of exceptions to the take prohibition. Section 10 allows the take of listed species by non-Federal property owners or as a consequence of a Federally operated or permitted project, provided that the take is incidental to carrying out an otherwise lawful activity and the landowner or relevant agency develops an approved Habitat Conservation Plan. The ESA also allows takes for scientific purposes, to enhance the propagation or survival of the species, zoological exhibitions, educational purposes, or special purposes consistent with the purposes of the ESA. 16 U.S.C. § 1539.

2. *Designation of Critical Habitat*

The ESA requires the FWS (or NMFS), "to the maximum extent prudent and determinable," to designate critical habitat at the time a species is determined to be endangered or threatened. 16 U.S.C. § 1533(a)(3). "Critical habitat" includes those geographical areas, within the jurisdiction of the United States, occupied by the species which contain the essential physical and biological features necessary for the survival and recovery of the species. It also includes areas outside the current range of the species if that habitat is essential to the conservation of the species. 16 U.S.C. §§ 1532(3), 1532(5)(A).

When the FWS designates critical habitat, it must "tak[e] into consideration the economic impact" of designating any particular area as critical habitat. The FWS may refuse to designate critical habitat if the benefits of exclusion outweigh the benefits of designating the area. However, it may not refuse to designate an area if it determines, based on the "best scientific and commercial data available, that the failure to designate such area as critical habitat will result in the extinction of the species." 16 U.S.C. § 1533(b)(2).

The ESA implementing regulations provide that designation of critical habitat is not prudent when one or both of the following situations exist: (1) the species is threatened by taking or other activity and the identification of critical habitat can be expected to increase the degree of threat to the species, or (2) such designation of critical habitat would not be beneficial to the species. The regulations further provide that that critical habitat is not determinable when one or both of the following situations exist: (1) information sufficient to perform required analysis of the impacts of the designation is lacking, or (2) the biological needs of the species are not sufficiently well known to permit identification of an area as critical habitat. 50 C.F.R. § 424.12(a). Once critical habitat is designated, it is subject to the consultation provisions described below.

---

3. *Consultation and the Duty to Avoid Jeopardy*

Section 7 of the ESA directs each federal agency to insure that its actions are "not likely to jeopardize the continued existence of any endangered species or threatened species or result in the destruction or adverse modification of [critical] habitat." 16 U.S.C. § 1536 (a)(2). Whereas "jeopardy" focuses on the effect of the agency action on survival and recovery of the listed species, "adverse modification" addresses the effects of the action on critical habitat. Sierra Club v. U.S. Fish & Wildlife Service, 245 F.3d 434, 441 (2001).

To effectuate this duty, the ESA requires the "action" agency to consult with an "expert" agency (FWS or NMFS) to evaluate the effects a proposed agency action may have on listed species. 16 U.S.C. § 1536(a)(2). If the action agency determines through preparation of a biological assessment or informal consultation that the proposed action is "not likely to adversely affect" listed species or critical habitat, formal consultation is not required so long as the expert agency concurs. 50 C.F.R. § 402.14(b). If, however, the agency determines that the proposed action "may affect" a listed species or its critical habitat, formal consultation is mandatory. 50 C.F.R. § 402.14(a); *see also* Bennett v. Spear, 520 U.S. 154, 158, (1997).

The final product of a formal consultation is a biological opinion ("BiOp") which sets forth the expert agency's conclusions regarding jeopardy and adverse modification. 16 U.S.C. § 1536(a)(2). In the biological opinion, the FWS or NMFS must evaluate the effects of the proposed action on the survival of species and any potential destruction or adverse modification of critical habitat, based on "the best scientific and commercial data available." *Id.* The biological opinion must include a summary of the information upon which the opinion is based, a discussion of the effects of the action on listed species or critical habitat, and the consulting agency's opinion on whether the action is likely to cause jeopardy or adverse modification."

50 C.F.R. § 402.14(h(3). In making its jeopardy determination, the FWS or NMFS must evaluate "the current status of the listed species or critical habitat," the "effects of the action," and "cumulative effects." *Id.* § 402.14(g)(2)–(3). "Effects of the action" include both direct and indirect effects of an action "that will be added to the environmental baseline." *Id.* § 402.02. The environmental baseline includes "the past and present impacts of all Federal, State or private actions and other human activities in the action area" and "the anticipated impacts of all proposed Federal projects in the action area that have already undergone formal or early Section 7 consultation." *Id.* If the biological opinion concludes that the activity will not cause jeopardy or adverse modification, or that "reasonable and prudent alternatives" to the agency action will avoid jeopardy and adverse modification and that the incidental taking of endangered or threatened species will not violate Section 7, then FWS or NMFS may issue an "Incidental Take Statement," which, if followed, exempts the action agency from Section 9's prohibition on takings. 16 U.S.C. § 1536(b)(3)–(4).

4.   *Recovery Plans*

The ESA requires the development of a recovery plan for a listed species designed to improve the status of the species to the point at which listing under the ESA is no longer necessary. 16 U.S.C. § 1533(f), 50 C.F.R. § 402.02. A recovery plan is not required, however, where "such a plan will not promote the conservation of the species." 16 U.S.C. § 1533(f). A recovery plan establishes a framework to coordinate activities among various Federal, state, and private parties for the conservation of a listed species. The recovery plans must include, to the maximum extent practicable:

(i)   a description of such site-specific management actions as may be necessary to achieve the plan's goal for the conservation and survival of the species;

(ii)   objective, measurable criteria which, when met, would result in a determination, in accordance with the provisions of this section, that the species be removed from the list; and

(iii)   estimates of the time required and the cost to carry out those measures needed to achieve the plan's goal and to achieve intermediate steps toward that goal.

16 U.S.C. § 1533(f)(1)(B).

Because of the wide variety of measures that may be needed to conserve a species, the ESA does not mandate the use of specific conservation strategies. However, courts have said that the ESA requires "the identification of management actions necessary to achieve the Plan's goals for the conservation and survival of the species. A recovery plan that recognizes specific threats to the conservation and survival of a threatened or endangered species, but fails to recommend corrective action or explain why it is impracticable or unnecessary to recommend such action, would not meet the ESA's standard." The Fund for Animals v. Babbitt, 903 F. Supp. 96, 108 (D.D.C. 1995). In addition, "[s]ince the same five statutory factors must be considered in delisting as in listing, . . . the FWS, in designing objective, measurable criteria, must address each of the five statutory delisting factors and measure whether threats to the [listed species] have been ameliorated." *Id.* at 111. Moreover, while FWS need not specify a "time certain" for completion of certain measures in a recovery plan, it is required to provide estimates of when recovery measures will be completed. *Defenders of Wildlife v. Babbitt*, 130 F. Supp. 2d 121 (D.D.C 2001).

Because each of the three elements of a recovery plan must be undertaken "to the maximum extent practicable," the FWS and NMFS have discretion to articulate a satisfactory explanation as to why, e.g., objective criteria cannot be practicably incorporated into a recovery plan. While this discretion is not "unbridled," it "is not necessary for a recovery plan to be an exhaustively detailed document." *Fund for Animals*, 903 F. Supp. at 107.

B.   Polar Bears, Climate Change, and the ESA

The ESA's mandatory duties to conserve threatened and endangered species have made it an attractive option for advocates seeking to protect species from climate change. In fact, on February 16, 2005, the Center for Biological Diversity, later joined by Greenpeace and the Natural Resources Defense Council, petitioned the FWS to list the polar bear (*Ursus maritimus*) as a threatened species under the ESA. More than three years later, on May 15, 2008, the FWS issued its final rule designating the polar bear as threatened. FWS, Final Rule, Determination of Threatened Status for the Polar Bear (*Ursus maritimus*) Throughout Its Range, 73 Fed. Reg. 28212, 28213–28214 (May 15, 2008) [hereinafter Polar Bear Determination].

But how well adapted is the ESA to climate change? To gain insight into that question, this section reviews the plight of the polar bear and the FWS's determination to designate it as a threatened species. As you read, consider the following questions:

- Does driving a CO_2-emitting car, which contributes to climate change and melting sea ice, constitute a "take" of polar bears, a species almost completely dependent on sea ice?

- For which projects should FWS consult? Does Section 7 require that FWS consult to ensure that a new coal-fired power plant in Kentucky does not jeopardize polar bears?

- Does either the take prohibition or the no jeopardy requirement mandate reductions in U.S. greenhouse gas emissions?

- What elements would you include in a recovery plan to protect polar bears and other species from the effects of climate change?

1.   *A Dependency on Diminishing Sea Ice*

Polar bears are almost completely dependent on ice. Indeed, in some languages, they are called "ice bears." Polar bears use sea ice as a platform from which to hunt and feed upon seals. They use sea ice to seek mates and breed. They use sea ice as a platform to move to terrestrial maternity denning areas and for maternity denning. They also use sea ice to make long-distance movements. FWS, Polar Bear Determination, 73 Fed. Reg. at 28,213–28,214. Polar bears are so dependent on sea ice that "[o]ver most of their range, polar bears remain on the sea ice year-round or spend only short periods on land." *Id.* at 28,213. In some regions, polar bears migrate as much as 1,000 km (621 mi) to stay with the pack ice. *Id.*

Sea ice is melting. Since 1978, scientists have documented an overall downward trend in Arctic sea ice extent (the area of the ocean with at least 15 percent ice coverage) and area (the sum of areas actually covered by sea ice). They also report that sea ice is melting more rapidly than before. For example, the FWS's Polar Bear Determination reports a decrease in summer sea ice extent of 4.5 percent per decade based on trends for late 1978 through the end of 1996. The rate of loss increased to 6.7 percent per decade when using data from 1981 to 2000. Two more recent studies, using data up to 2005 and 2006, found declines in sea ice extent up to 9.8 percent and 9.1 percent, respectively, per decade. *Id.* at 28,221.

Similarly, the area of Arctic sea ice is also declining. In fact, it reached an historic low of 2.92 million sq km (1.13 million sq mi) on September 16, 2007, 27 percent lower than the previous record low in 2005. Moreover, this record differed from previous lows, because it covered the entire Arctic Basin, not only certain sectors (North Atlantic, Beaufort/Bering Sea, etc.). *Id.* at 28,222.

Sea ice is also melting earlier than in the past. In 2005, for example, the melt season arrived approximately 17 days before the mean melt onset date. As a result of the longer melt season, the ice pack is breaking up earlier and reforming later, shortening the overall length of the "ice season." The length of the melt season is increasing at a rate of approximately 13.1 days per decade. *Id.* at 28,223.

Sea ice declines can be attributed to three conflated factors: warming, atmospheric changes (including circulation and clouds), and changes in oceanic circulation. Average Arctic temperatures have been increasing at almost twice the rate of the rest of the world in the past 100 years. Changing wind patterns are increasing ice motion and ice divergence, which increases the energy needs for the ice to reform. Warmer Atlantic Ocean water is also entering the Arctic Ocean, causing a reduction in sea ice. *Id.* at 28,224–28,225.

The loss of sea ice then accentuates the sea-ice albedo effect: "The sea-ice albedo feedback effect is the result of a reduction in the extent of brighter, more reflective sea ice or snow, which reflects solar energy back into the atmosphere, and a corresponding increase in the extent of darker, more absorbing water or land that absorbs more of the sun's energy. This greater absorption of energy causes faster melting, which in turn causes more warming, and thus creates a self-reinforcing cycle or feedback loop that becomes amplified and accelerates with time." *Id.* at 28,225.

In the IPCC's Fourth Assessment, all scenarios predict much less ice in the future, with longer melt seasons and shorter ice seasons. Looking at this data, some U.S. scientists now say that Arctic sea ice is in a "downward spiral" that will cause ice-free September conditions as early as 2030. Others believe ice-free Arctic summers will arrive much earlier — by 2013.

2.   *Polar Bears Are Threatened with Extinction*

The global population of polar bears is estimated to be 20,000 to 25,000 and distributed in 19 relatively discrete populations throughout most ice-covered seas in Russia, Norway, Greenland (Denmark), Canada, and the United States (in the Chukchi and Beaufort Seas in Alaska). Most individual populations of polar bears number between 1,500 and 2,500 individuals. In its determination, the FWS described a large number of reasons why it expects polar bear populations to decline as a result of diminishing sea ice. The following summarizes these conclusions:

FWS, POLAR BEAR DETERMINATION
73 Fed. Reg. at 28,253, 28,292–28,293

In the context of the Act, the term "endangered species" means any species or subspecies or, for vertebrates, Distinct Population Segment (DPS), that is in danger of extinction throughout all or a significant portion of its range, and a "threatened species" is any species that is likely to become an endangered species within the foreseeable future. [Although the ESA does not define the term "foreseeable future," the FWS defined it for polar bears as 45 years (three generations). It reached its conclusion based on an assessment by polar bear specialists, the life-history and population dynamics of polar bears, and documented projected changes in sea ice. The FWS also considered this time frame as "long enough to take into account multi-generational population dynamics, natural variation inherent with populations, environmental and habitat changes, and the capacity for ecological adaptation."]

Under Factor A ("Present or Threatened Destruction, Modification, or Curtailment of its habitat or range"), we have determined that ongoing and projected loss of the polar bear's crucial sea ice habitat threatens the species throughout all of its range. Productivity, abundance, and availability of ice seals, the polar bear's primary prey base, would be diminished by the projected loss of sea ice, and energetic requirements of polar bears for movement and obtaining food would increase. Access to traditional denning areas would be affected. In turn, these factors would cause declines in the condition of polar bears from nutritional stress and reduced productivity. As already evidenced in the Western Hudson Bay and Southern Beaufort Sea populations, polar bears would experience reductions in survival and recruitment rates. The eventual effect is that polar bear populations would decline. The rate and magnitude of decline would vary among populations, based on differences in the rate, timing, and magnitude of impacts. However, within the foreseeable future, all populations would be affected, and the species is likely to become in danger of extinction throughout all of its range due to declining sea ice habitat.

Under Factor B ("Overutilization for Commercial, Recreational, Scientific, or Educational Purposes") we note that polar bears are harvested in Canada, Alaska, Greenland, and Russia, and we acknowledge that harvest is the consumptive use of greatest importance and potential effect to polar bear. . . . While overharvest occurs for some populations, laws and regulations for most management programs have been instituted to provide sustainable harvests over the long term. . . . We also acknowledge that increased levels of bear-human encounters are expected in the future and that encounters may result in increased mortality to bears at some unknown level. Adaptive management programs, such as implementing polar bear patrols, hazing programs, and efforts to minimize attraction of bears to communities, to address future bear-human interaction issues, including on-the-land ecotourism activities, are anticipated.

Harvest is likely exacerbating the effects of habitat loss in several populations. In addition, continued harvest and increased mortality from bear-human encounters or other forms of mortality may become a more significant threat factor in the future, particularly for populations experiencing nutritional stress or declining population numbers as a consequence of habitat change. Although harvest, increased bear-human interaction levels, defense-of-life take, illegal take, and take associated with scientific research live-capture programs are occurring for several populations, we have determined that overutilization does not currently threaten the species throughout all or a significant portion of its range.

Under Factor C ("Disease and Predation") we acknowledge that disease pathogens are present in polar bears; no epizootic outbreaks have been detected; and intra-specific stress through cannibalism may be increasing; however, population level effects have not been documented. Potential for disease outbreaks, an increased possibility of pathogen exposure from changed diet or the occurrence of new pathogens that have moved northward with a warming environment, and increased mortality from intraspecific predation (cannibalism) may become more significant threat factors in the future for polar bear populations experiencing nutritional stress or declining population numbers. We have determined that disease and predation (including intraspecific predation) do not threaten the species throughout all or a significant portion of its range.

Under Factor D ("Inadequacy of Existing Regulatory Mechanisms"), we have determined that existing regulatory mechanisms at the national and international level are generally adequate to address actual and potential threats to polar bears from direct take, disturbance by humans, and incidental or harassment take. We have determined that there are no known regulatory mechanisms in place at the national or international level that directly and effectively address the primary threat to polar bears — the rangewide loss of sea ice habitat within the foreseeable future.

We acknowledge that there are some existing regulatory mechanisms to address anthropogenic causes of climate change, and these mechanisms are not expected to be effective in counteracting the worldwide growth of GHG emissions in the foreseeable future.

Under Factor E ("Other Natural or Manmade Factors Affecting the Polar Bear's Continued Existence") we reviewed contaminant concentrations and find that, in most populations, contaminants have not been found to have population level effects. We further evaluated increasing levels of ecotourism and shipping that may lead to greater impacts on polar bears. The extent of potential impact is related to changing ice conditions, polar bear distribution changes, and relative risk for a higher interaction between polar bears and ecotourism or shipping. Certain factors, particularly contaminants and shipping, may become more significant threats in the future for polar bear populations experiencing declines related to nutritional stress brought on by sea ice and environmental changes. We have determined, however, that contaminants, ecotourism, and shipping do not threaten the polar bear throughout all or a significant portion of its range.

On the basis of our thorough evaluation of the best available scientific and commercial information regarding present and future threats to the polar bear posed by the five listing factors under the Act, we have determined that the polar bear is threatened throughout its range by habitat loss (i.e., sea ice recession). We have determined that there are no known regulatory mechanisms in place at the national or international level that directly and effectively address the primary threat to polar bears — the rangewide loss of sea ice habitat. We have determined that overutilization does not currently threaten the species throughout all or a significant portion of its range, but is exacerbating the effects of habitat loss for several populations and may become a more significant threat factor within the foreseeable future. We have determined that disease and predation, in particular intraspecific predation, and contaminants do not currently threaten the species throughout all or a significant portion of its range, but may become more significant threat factors for polar bear populations, especially those experiencing nutritional stress or declining population levels, within the foreseeable future.

Although the FWS's determination did not attempt to pinpoint a date by which a certain number of polar bears would remain, in an earlier report the U.S. Geological Service (USGS) estimated that two-thirds of the world's polar bears will be gone by 2050. In making its projection, the USGS emphasized that because all climate models have so far underestimated the actual observed sea-ice loss, the assessment of risk to the polar bear may be conservative. STEVEN AMSTRUP, ET AL., FORECASTING THE RANGE-WIDE STATUS OF POLAR BEARS AT SELECTED TIMES IN THE 21ST CENTURY 2 (2007).

3.   *Can the ESA Save the Polar Bear from Climate Change?*

The petitioners to list the polar bear as threatened had high hopes for using the ESA to mitigate greenhouse gas emissions in the United States. Both through Section 7's consultation provisions and Section 9's take prohibitions, petitioners believed that the ESA would compel the United States to reduce emissions from a wide range of activities, including power plants, because these activities would "jeopardize the continued existence of a species" or result in a "take" of polar bears. Consider the petitioner's arguments and FWS's responses.

a.   *Jeopardy and Adverse Modification of Critical Habitat*

BRENDAN R. CUMMINGS AND KASSIE R. SIEGEL, URSUS MARITIMUS: POLAR BEARS ON THIN ICE
22 NATURAL RESOURCES & ENVIRONMENT 6–7 (2007)[*]

Section 7 consultation is required for "any action [that] may affect listed species or critical habitat." 50 C.F.R. § 402.14. Agency "action" is defined in the ESA's implementing regulations to include:

> all activities or programs of any kind authorized, funded, or carried out, in whole or in part, by Federal agencies in the United States or upon the high seas. Examples include, but are not limited to: . . . . *actions directly or indirectly causing modifications to the land, water, or air.*

50 C.F.R. § 402.02 (emphasis added). This regulatory definition of "action" should be broad enough to encompass actions that result in GHG emissions, as it would be hard to argue that such emissions are not "causing modification to the land, water or air." *Id.* The remaining question with respect to the triggering of these requirements for an action resulting in GHG emissions is whether that action "may affect" the listed species. 50 C.F.R. § 402.14. While it is clear that global warming affects listed species, attributing an individual action's contribution to global warming is more difficult.

Because the goal of Section 7 consultation is to avoid jeopardizing any listed species, the regulatory definition of "jeopardy" offers some guidance as to how the consultation requirement for a GHG-emitting action may be interpreted. To "jeopardize" a species means "to engage in an action that reasonably would be expected, directly or indirectly, to reduce *appreciably* the likelihood of both the

---

survival and recovery of a listed species in the wild by reducing the reproduction, numbers, or distribution of that species." 50 C.F.R. § 402.02 (emphasis added). If an action "appreciably" contributed to global warming, that action could then be found to jeopardize a listed species. "Appreciably" is defined in the Oxford English Dictionary as being "to the degree that can be estimated," while something is "appreciable" if it is "large or important enough to be noticed." So if an action contributes an appreciable amount of GHG emissions to the atmosphere, that action should undergo the consultation process.

While many federal actions may not contribute appreciable amounts of GHGs to the atmosphere, many clearly do. For example, the corporate average fuel economy (CAFE) standards for sport-utility vehicles and light trucks are set via regulation by the National Highway [Traffic] Safety Administration. Because the transportation sector represents a large component of United States GHG emissions, the volume of GHGs represented by this single rulemaking are certainly "appreciable." Similarly, every five years the Minerals Management Service approves a program for all offshore oil and gas leasing for the entire United States. Again, the GHGs generated through the lifecycle of the production and use of these billions of barrels if oil are very appreciable. The GHG emissions from numerous other actions present in the approval of new coal-fired power plants, oil shale leasing programs, limestone mines for cement manufacturing, and dozens, perhaps hundreds, of other projects are individually and cumulatively having an appreciable effect on the atmosphere. These are all agency "actions" as defined by the ESA, which "may affect" listed species, and therefore trigger the consultation requirements of Section 7.

FWS, POLAR BEAR DETERMINATION
73 Fed. Reg. 28,299–28,300

The 9th Circuit Court of Appeals has determined that the Service cannot use the consultation process or the issuance of an Incidental Take Statement as a form of regulation limiting what are otherwise legal activities by action agencies, if no incidental take is reasonably likely to occur as a result of the Federal action (*Arizona Cattle Growers' Association v. U.S. Fish and Wildlife Service, 273 F.3d 1229 (9th Cir. 2001)*). In that case, the court reviewed several biological opinions that were the result of consultations on numerous grazing permits. The 9th Circuit analyzed the Service's discussion of effects and the incidental take statements for several specific grazing allotments. The court found that the Service, in some allotments, assumed there would be "take" without explaining how the agency action (in this case, cattle grazing) would cause the take of specific individuals of the listed species. Further, for other permits the court did not see evidence or argument to demonstrate how cattle grazing in one part of the permit area would take listed species in another part of that permit area. The court concluded that the Service must "connect the dots" between its evaluation of effects of the action and its assessment of take. That is, the Service cannot simply speculate that take may occur. The Service must first articulate the causal connection between the effects of the action under consultation and the anticipated take. It must then demonstrate that the take is reasonably likely to occur.

The significant cause of the decline of the polar bear, and thus the basis for this action to list it as a threatened species, is the loss of arctic sea ice that is expected to continue to occur over the next 45 years. The best scientific information available to us today, however, has not established a causal connection between specific sources and locations of emissions to specific impacts posed to polar bears or their habitat.

Some commenters to the proposed rule suggested that the Service should require other agencies (e.g., the Environmental Protection Agency) to regulate emissions from all sources, including automobile and power plants. The best scientific information available today would neither allow nor require the Service to take such action.

First, the primary substantive mandate of section 7(a)(2) — the duty to avoid likely jeopardy to an endangered or threatened species — rests with the Federal action agency and not with the Service. The Service consults with the Federal action agency on proposed Federal actions that may affect an endangered or threatened species, but its consultative role under section 7 does not allow for encroachment on the Federal action agency's jurisdiction or policy-making role under the statutes it administers.

Second, the Federal action agency decides when to initiate formal consultation on a particular proposed action, and it provides the project description to the Service. The Service may request the Federal action agency to initiate formal consultation for a particular proposed action, but it cannot compel the agency to consult, regardless of the type of action or the magnitude of its projected effects.

Recognizing the primacy of the Federal action agency's role in determining how to conform its proposed actions to the requirements of section 7, and taking into account the requirement to examine the "effects of the action" through the formal consultation process, the Service does not anticipate that the listing of the polar bear as a threatened species will result in the initiation of new section 7 consultations on proposed permits or licenses for facilities that would emit GHGs in the conterminous 48 States. Formal consultation is required for proposed Federal actions that "may affect" a listed species, which requires an examination of whether the direct and indirect effects of a particular action meet this regulatory threshold. GHGs that are projected to be emitted from a facility would not, in and of themselves, trigger formal section 7 consultation for a particular licensure action unless it is established that such emissions constitute an "indirect effect" of the proposed action. To constitute an "indirect effect," the impact to the species must be later in time, must be caused by the proposed action, and must be "reasonably certain to occur" (*50 CFR 402.02* (definition of "effects of the action")). As stated above, the best scientific data available today are not sufficient to draw a causal connection between GHG emissions from a facility in the conterminous 48 States to effects posed to polar bears or their habitat in the Arctic, nor are there sufficient data to establish that such impacts are "reasonably certain to occur" to polar bears. Without sufficient data to establish the required causal connection — to the level of "reasonable certainty" — between a new facility's GHG emissions and impacts to polar bears, section 7 consultation would not be required to address impacts to polar bears.

A question has also been raised regarding the possible application of section 7 to effects posed to polar bears that may arise from oil and gas development activities conducted on Alaska's North Slope or in the Chukchi Sea. It is clear that any direct effects from oil and gas development operations, such as drilling activities, vehicular traffic to and from drill sites, and other on-site operational support activities, that pose adverse effects to polar bears would need to be evaluated through the section 7 consultation process. It is also clear that any "indirect effects" from oil and gas development activities, such as impacts from the spread of contaminants (accidental oil spills, or the unintentional release of other contaminants) that result from the oil and gas development activities and that are "reasonably certain to occur," that flow from the "footprint" of the action and spread into habitat areas used by polar bears would also need to be evaluated through the section 7 consultation process.

However, the future effects of any emissions that may result from the consumption of petroleum products refined from crude oil pumped from a particular North Slope drilling site would not constitute "indirect effects" and, therefore, would not be considered during the section 7 consultation process. The best scientific data available to the Service today does not provide the degree of precision needed to draw a causal connection between the oil produced at a particular drilling site, the GHG emissions that may eventually result from the consumption of the refined petroleum product, and a particular impact to a polar bear or its habitat. At present there is a lack of scientific or technical knowledge to determine a relationship between an oil and gas leasing, development, or production activity and the effects of the ultimate consumption of petroleum products (GHG emissions). There are discernible limits to the establishment of a causal connection, such as uncertainties regarding the productive yield from an oil and gas field; whether any or all of such production will be refined for plastics or other products that will not be burned; what mix of vehicles or factories might use the product; and what mitigation measures would offset consumption. Furthermore, there is no traceable nexus between the ultimate consumption of the petroleum product and any particular effect to a polar bear or its habitat. In short, the emissions effects resulting from the consumption of petroleum derived from North Slope or Chukchi Sea oil fields would not constitute an "indirect effect" of any federal agency action to approve the development of that field.

QUESTIONS AND DISCUSSION

1. The FWS relies on the definition of "indirect effects" to conclude that:

    For those effects beyond the footprint of the action, our regulations at *50 CFR 402.02* require that they both be "caused by the action under consultation" and "reasonably certain to occur." That is, effects are only appropriately considered in a section 7 analysis if there is a causal connection between the proposed action and a discernible effect to the species or critical habitat that is reasonably certain to occur. One must be able to "connect the dots" between the proposed action, an effect, and an impact to the species and there must be a reasonable certainty that the effect will occur.

FWS, Interim Final Rule, Special Rule for the Polar Bear, 73 Fed. Reg 28,306, 28,312 (May 15, 2008). Consider the FWS's regulatory definitions of "action area" and "effects":

    Action area means all areas to be affected directly or indirectly by the Federal action and not merely the immediate area involved in the action.
    * * *

    Effects of the action refers to the direct and indirect effects of an action on the species or critical habitat, together with the effects of other activities that are interrelated or interdependent with that action, that will be added to the environmental baseline. The environmental baseline includes the past and present impacts of all Federal, State, or private actions and other human activities in the action area, the anticipated impacts of all proposed Federal projects in the action area that have already undergone formal or early section 7 consultation, and the impact of State or private actions which are contemporaneous with the consultation in process. Indirect effects are those that are caused by the proposed action and are later in time, but still are reasonably certain to occur.

50 C.F.R. § 402.02. Is the FWS's interpretation of "indirect effects" consistent with these definitions?

2.   FWS finds support for its interpretation in *Arizona Cattle Growers' Association*. In that case, the court found that the FWS had impermissibly issued incidental take permits that restricted grazing where the FWS had not (1) determined that a listed species occurred in the grazing area at issue or (2) determined that grazing would affect a listed species. Instead, FWS based its determination to issue incidental take permits on general evidence of the possible effects of livestock grazing on the habitats of listed species. Is that the situation that exists here? Do we only have general information to conclude that emissions from a coal-fired power plant in New Jersey will affect polar bears?

3.   The Center for Biological Diversity (CBD) claims that listing the polar bear as "threatened" "will provide concrete help to polar bears and could revolutionize American climate policy," because the polar bear's protected status will trigger the ESA's consultation provisions for perhaps hundreds of projects throughout the United States. Others agree that the net cast by Section 7 is potentially very broad, because it requires federal agencies to consult with FWS or NMFS if their actions "may affect" listed species or designated critical habitat. *See* John Kostyack & Dan Rohlf, *Conserving Endangered Species in an Era of Global Warming*, 38 ELR 10,203, 10,212 (2008) (arguing that NMFS "should construe any action that results in non-trivial net increases of GHGs as meeting this threshold"). Professor Lisa Heinzerling criticized the FWS's polar bear ruling, stating that "the requirements of causation and reasonable certainty apply only to the indirect effects of an agency action on a species. It would take a subtle argument — one the Department does not provide — to explain why greenhouse gases' effects on the polar bear are not (direct) within the meaning of the Department's rules." Lisa Heinzerling, Climate Contrast: Of Polar Bears and Power Plants (May 15, 2008), *available at* http://gulcfac.typepad.com/georgetown_university_law/2008/05/climate-hypocri.html. Revisit Section A.3, above, discussing the requirements of an adequate biological opinion, and the definitions in note 1. Do you agree that Section 7 requires, for example, consultation with FWS regarding polar bears prior to issuing permits for construction of a coal-fired power plant in New Jersey or new CAFE standards for automobiles, because such activities "jeopardize" the polar bear? Are the effects from such projects direct or indirect effects?

4.   Subsequent to the listing of the polar bear as a threatened species, FWS made several changes to the ESA's consultation provisions, including several related specifically to climate change. The new rules, for example, define "direct effects" and redefine "indirect effects" as follows:

> Direct effects are the immediate effects of the action and are not dependent on the occurrence of any additional intervening actions for the impacts to species or critical habitat to occur. Indirect effects are those for which the proposed action is an essential cause, and that are later in time, but still are reasonably certain to occur. If an effect will occur whether or not the action takes place, the action is not an essential cause of the indirect effect. Reasonably certain to occur is the standard used to determine the requisite confidence that an effect will happen.

50 C.F.R. § 402.02. In its notice of the final rule, FWS explained that "if an indirect effect would occur regardless of the action, then the action is not an essential cause of that effect, and it would not be appropriate to consider its effects as an effect of an action." 73 Fed. Reg. 76,272, 76,278 (Dec. 16, 2008). Under these definitions, do you think climate change impacts can be considered direct or indirect effects of a project?

In addition, the new rules allow the action agency to decide that formal consultation is not needed without the concurrence of the FWS or NMFS in the following circumstances:

> (b)   Federal agencies are not required to consult on an action when the direct and indirect effects of that action are not anticipated to result in take and:
>
>> (1)   Such action has no effect on a listed species or critical habitat; or
>>
>> (2)   The effects of such action are manifested through global processes and:
>>
>>> (i)   Cannot be reliably predicted or measured at the scale of a listed species' current range, or
>>>
>>> (ii)   Would result at most in an extremely small, insignificant impact on a listed species or critical habitat, or
>>>
>>> (iii)   Are such that the potential risk of harm to a listed species or critical habitat is remote; or
>>
>> (3)   The effects of such action on a listed species or critical habitat:
>>
>>> (i)   Are not capable of being measured or detected in a manner that permits meaningful evaluation; or
>>>
>>> (ii)   Are wholly beneficial.

50 C.R.R. § 402.03. Paragraph 2, in particular, was intended to preclude consultation for projects having climate change impacts:

> The phrase "manifested through global processes" covers those effects that are the result of a specific source but become well mixed and diffused at the global scale such that they lose their individual identity. The combined effect of any particular source and other sources then becomes a potential contributor to a separate phenomenon with possible global impacts. Typically, however, the contribution of any particular source to the global process that then affects the local environment is very, very small. The most topical example of effects that would be manifested only through a global process is the effects of individual sources of greenhouse gas emissions and their contribution to global climate change and warming.
> * * *
>
> Even after the threshold of the effect being manifested through global processes, there are other limiting factors [under paragraph (b)(2)]. In the context of greenhouse gases, current models, though capable of quantifying the contribution to changes in global atmospheric greenhouse gas concentrations and temperature, do not allow us to quantitatively link an individual action to localized climate impacts relevant to consultation. However, based on the best scientific information available, we are presently able to conclude that the impacts of a particular source are likely to be extremely small. For example, in a recent exchange of letters, EPA provided a model-based analysis that projected that even the emissions of a very large coal-fired power plant would likely result in a rise in the maximum global mean temperature of less than one-thousandth of a degree.
>
> Finally, to attempt to regulate effects at a global scale would have the untenable consequence of transforming the "action area" for consultation into the globe itself, which would eviscerate any meaningful limit on the concept of "action area" and defy analysis. The concept of "action area," as

established in the 1986 regulations and unchanged by this rule, is an important and necessary tool to keep consultations manageable and tied to the particular action under consultation. In a global context, the concept of "action area" would be rendered meaningless.

73 Fed. Reg. at 76,282–76,283. On March 3, 2009, President Obama directed the Secretaries of the Interior and Commerce to review the December regulation to determine whether new rules would better promote the purposes of the ESA. In the meantime, he directed all agencies "to exercise their discretion, under the new regulation, to follow the prior longstanding consultation and concurrence practices involving the FWS and NMFS." Memorandum from Barack Obama to Heads of Executive Departments and Agencies: Endangered Species Act, Mar. 3, 2009

5. Whether FWS must engage in Section 7 consultation to determine whether CO_2-emitting federal activities jeopardize polar bears is one question. A separate question is whether climate change impacts must be assessed in a biological opinion where a project will have direct, non-climate change effects on a listed species. At least two courts have already said "yes," and found biological opinions to be inadequate because FWS and NMFS failed to discuss and evaluate the impacts of climate change in concluding that a project would not jeopardize protected species. NRDC v. Kempthorne, 506 F. Supp. 2d 322 (E.D.Cal.2007); Pacific Coast Federation of Fishermen's Associations v. Gutierrez, 2008 WL 1766996 (E.D. Cal. 2008). The *Kempthorne* case concerned the impacts on a threatened species of fish, the Delta smelt, of the federally-managed Central Valley Project and the State of California's State Water Project, among the world's largest water diversion projects. The court ruled that FWS must consider not only the direct impacts of the water project on the Delta smelt, but also the cumulative effects of climate change, which could affect precipitation and thus the habitat of the Delta smelt. Is this a practical way to implement the jeopardy requirements of Section 7? That is, FWS should not be asked to assess a project's indirect climate change impacts on a species. Instead, where "modeling and field observations indicate it is 'reasonably certain' that climate change will lead to changes in ecological conditions to the detriment of a protected species, the FWS must engage in a consultation to determine whether the project, taking those changes into account as cumulative effects, is (reasonably expected) to jeopardize the species." Ruhl, *Climate Change and the Endangered Species Act*, at 47 (describing the effect of the court's ruling).

6. FWS and NMFS already conduct thousands of consultations each year. If it is true that a very large range of federal projects would require Section 7 consultation, the number of consultations could skyrocket. With two Caribbean coral species and the polar bear already listed as threatened in part due to climate change, the scope of Section 7 is called into question.

It is not difficult to imagine, for instance, FWS scientists concluding that increased GHG emissions jeopardize the continued existence of polar bears or adversely affect their sea-ice critical habitat. Since the ESA forbids such a result absent a § 7 exemption by the high-level Endangered Species Committee (the God Squad), is it conceivable that the ESA would then simply ban any and all federal agency actions resulting in increased emissions? In other words, can a wildlife agency by itself apply the brakes to U.S. GHG emissions — something that Congress and the EPA have so far been unwilling or unable to do? Alternatively, will the God Squad be called upon to issue multiple — or even blanket — § 7 exemptions for federal actions that contribute to climate change? Or will we simply see increased efforts by lawmakers (via appropriations riders or indirect political pressure on agencies) or the executive branch (through backroom dealings and increased coercion of agency scientists) to soft-peddle the threats and impacts of climate change?

Kostyack & Rohlf, *Endangered Species in an Era of Global Warming*, at 10,209. Because of the potentially overwhelming number of consultations that could result from climate change, resort to the "God Squad" may provide a politically attractive solution for protecting the ESA, even if it means rejecting the ESA as a possible tool for addressing climate change. To avoid this situation, Kostyack and Rohlf suggest tying compliance with Section 7 to consistency with a national program to regulate GHG emissions. Under this proposal, emitters would certify compliance with the applicable national program capping GHG emissions once such a program is in place. *Id.* at 10,212. The authors recognize that no national cap currently exists but believe one is likely in the near future. Assuming Congress establishes a national cap, what are the strengths and weaknesses of such a proposal?

7.   The designation of critical habitat, especially critical habitat currently outside a species' range, is likely to be a crucial tool to allow wildlife to adapt to climate change because many species will shift their ranges as they respond to climate and climate-caused ecological changes. Concerning polar bears, the FWS has already identified in general terms the essential habitat features for the polar bear: annual and perennial marine sea ice habitats that serve as a platform for hunting, feeding, traveling, resting, and to a limited extent, for denning, and terrestrial habitats used by polar bears for denning and reproduction for the recruitment of new animals into the population, as well as for seasonal use in traveling or resting. Nonetheless, the FWS declined to designate critical habitat:

> [T]he identification of specific physical and biological features and specific geographic areas for consideration as critical habitat is complicated, and the future values of these habitats may change in a rapidly changing environment. Arctic sea ice provides a platform for critical life-history functions, including hunting, feeding, travel, and nuturing *(sic)* cubs. That habitat is projected to be significantly reduced within the next 45 years, and some models project complete absence of sea ice during summer months in shorter timeframes.

> A careful assessment of the designation of marine areas as critical habitat will require additional time to fully evaluate physical and biological features essential to the conservation of the polar bear and how those features are likely to change over the foreseeable future. In addition, near-shore and terrestrial habitats that may qualify for designation as critical habitat will require a similar thorough assessment and evaluation in light of projected climate change and other threats. Additionally, we have not gathered sufficient economic and other data on the impacts of a critical habitat designation. These factors must be considered as part of the designation procedure. Thus, we find that critical habitat is not determinable at this time.

FWS, Polar Bear Determination, 73 Fed. Reg. at 28,298. Do you think the FWS is right that further time is needed to determine critical habitat? Will designating critical habitat be helpful for the polar bear? In the words of the ESA, would it be "prudent" to designate critical habitat? To what extent do you think the rationale provided by FWS will apply to any species listed due to climate change?

8.   For the polar bear, anything but ice is likely to doom its existence, and in a warming environment, finding more ice will be difficult. For another species, the loss of current habitat may be accompanied by its growth someplace never before within the species' range. Should that habitat be declared "critical"? The FWS could also establish an "experimental population" under Section 10(j) of the ESA by releasing individuals of a species into a new environment, provided that the FWS

"determines that such release will further the conservation of such species." Is this a reasonable strategy for protecting species nearing extinction due to climate change?

---

b.   *Prohibitions against "Taking" Polar Bears*

As with Section 7, petitioners had hoped that Section 9 would provide a means for reducing U.S. emissions of greenhouse gases:

> While Section 7 only applies to federal actions and agencies, the prohibitions of Section 9 apply far more broadly, reaching the actions of private entities and corporations. Section 9 prohibits the "take" of listed species, which includes "harming" and "harassing" members of the species in addition to simply killing them directly. Both the legislative history and case law support "the broadest possible" reading of "take." Whether that reading is broad enough to encompass GHG emissions remains to be seen.

Cummings and Siegel, at 7.

The effect of such an interpretation could be monumental. For example, driving an automobile in Houston or New York emits carbon dioxide that contributes to climate change. Is that a "take" within the meaning of the ESA, because your actions, while not directly killing polar bears, "harm" the species? If so, are you, when you drive your car, liable under the ESA for civil penalties?

In its Polar Bear Determination, the FWS agreed that Section 9 is much "broader than a simple prohibition against killing an individual of the species." In particular, it noted that "harm" in the definition of "take" under the ESA means an act that actually kills or injures wildlife. Such act may include significant habitat modification or degradation where it actually kills or injures wildlife "by significantly impairing essential behavioral patterns, including breeding, feeding, or sheltering." The FWS was quick to add, however, that the ESA also provides for exceptions to the take prohibitions. The FWS may also develop a special rule under Section 4(d) tailored to the conservation needs of a threatened species instead of applying the general threatened species regulations.

The FWS has proposed a 4(d) rule that allows takes otherwise consistent with the Marine Mammal Protection Act (MMPA) and the Convention on International Trade in Endangered Species of Wild Fauna and Flora (CITES). Under the rule, Alaska Natives may continue to hunt polar bears for subsistence purposes and sell authentic native articles of handicrafts or clothing deriving from polar bears taken for subsistence purposes. Subject to the requirements of the MMPA, the special rule authorizes scientific research, enhancing the survival or recovery of a species, and photography, even if those activities might otherwise violate Section 9 of the ESA. The special rule closes an MMPA exception that allowed the importation of sport-hunted polar bear trophies from Canada (the exception did not apply to trophies from other range States). Moreover, the FWS will authorize incidental takes in the course of otherwise lawful activities, provided that such taking will have no more than a negligible impact on the species and, for Alaskan polar bears, will not have an unmitigable adverse impact on the availability of the species for taking for subsistence use by Alaska Natives. Incidental takes in the course of fishing activities must also comply with the requirements of the MMPA. FWS, Special Rule for the Polar Bear, 73 Fed. Reg. 28,306 (May 15, 2008).

QUESTIONS AND DISCUSSION

1. The FWS never specifically states that activities that indirectly affect polar bears, such as GHG emissions from an automobile or coal-fired power plant, do not constitute "harm" within the meaning of Section 9. However, its conclusions concerning Section 7 suggest that it does not plan to enforce Section 9 in such circumstances. Is that the correct outcome? The polar bear petitioners don't think so, and they have initiated litigation to challenge the agency's interpretation. Consider the arguments of petitioners:

> A rule promulgated pursuant to ESA Section 4(d) must be "necessary and advisable to provide for the conservation" of the species. 16 U.S.C. § 1533(d). *See, e.g.,* Sierra Club v. Clark, 755 F.2d 608, 612–13 (8th Cir. 1985) (Secretary's discretion to issue regulations under ESA Section 4(d) "is limited by the requirement that the regulations he is to issue must provide for the conservation of threatened species" (emphasis in original)); State of Louisiana, ex rel. Guste v. Verity, 853 F.2d 322, 332–33 (5th Cir. 1988). "Conservation" is defined as "the use of all methods and procedures which are necessary to bring any endangered species or threatened species to the point at which" ESA protection is no longer required. 16 U.S.C. § 1532(3). The term "conservation" includes ensuring a species' survival and promoting its recovery. Gifford Pinchot Task Force v. U.S. Fish & Wildlife Service, 378 F.3d 1059, 1070 (9th Cir. 2004). The Secretary's authority to promulgate a 4(d) rule authorizing take of polar bears is therefore limited to those measures that are "necessary and advisable" to provide for the survival and recovery of the species.

> The Interim Final 4(d) Rule exempts all activities that take polar bears from the ESA's prohibitions so long as such activities are consistent with the existing statutory requirement of the MMPA and CITES, including activities that will lead to harm to and death of polar bears. In other words, the 4(d) Rule completely eviscerates the protections of Section 9 and 50 C.F.R. § 17.31 that would apply to the bear absent the rule. The Final Rule provides no rational justification for eliminating these protections, and doing so cannot possibly be construed as "necessary and advisable" to provide for the survival and recovery of the polar bear.

Letter from Petitioners to Dirk Kempthorne, Sixty Day Notice of Intent to Sue; Failure to List the Polar Bear as an Endangered Species and Designate Critical Habitat and Unlawful Authorization of Take of Polar Bears (May 15, 2008).

Now consider the arguments of Professor J.B. Ruhl:

J.B. RUHL, CLIMATE CHANGE AND THE ENDANGERED SPECIES ACT: BUILDING BRIDGES TO THE NO-ANALOG FUTURE
88 B.U. L. Rev. 1 39–42 (2008)[*]

The harm definition projects the take prohibition from cases in which the action causes direct death or injury (e.g., hunting, shooting, and trapping), to cases in which causality is indirect — i.e., loss of habitat leads in some way to actual death or injury. However, theories of indirect take can become quite attenuated and speculative, in which case it would be unreasonable to enforce the take prohibition's rebuttable presumption against the activity as rigorously as in more obvious cases of direct take. For example, assume that a developer's plan to build a subdivision would locate new homes in an area within several hundred yards of habitat known to be occupied by members of a protected bird species, but not actually in the habitat. Opponents of the project may argue that some of the residents of the new homes will have cats as pets, some of those cat owners will allow their cats to wander outdoors, some of those cats may venture into the bird's habitat, and some of those cats may eat birds, and some of those birds may be individuals of the protected bird species. Anyone could speculate such possibilities, and it would be unreasonable to impose the burden on the developer of proving the postulated scenario is not possible.

Rather, as the [Supreme] Court pronounced when it upheld the harm definition, in many cases it is appropriate to impose the burden of proof on the proponent of the indirect harm theory. Thus, the majority emphasized that the harm rule incorporates "but for" causation, with "every term in the regulation's definition of "harm . . . subservient to the phrase 'an act which actually kills or injures wildlife.'" Furthermore, the term should "be read to incorporate ordinary requirements of proximate causation and foreseeability." The majority thus implicitly endorsed Sweet Home's "strong arguments that activities that cause minimal or unforeseeable harm will not violate the [ESA] as construed." In her concurrence, Justice O'Connor was more direct, limiting the scope of the harm rule to "significant habitat modification that causes actual, as opposed to hypothetical or speculative, death or injury to identifiable protected animals." Since the Court established these tort-like evidentiary burdens, the lower courts have steadfastly refused to enforce the take prohibition based on attenuated indirect take theories, but have enjoined case-specific instances of take when death or injury was proven to be likely.

The stiff evidentiary and proof burdens Sweet Home imposed largely explain why the government and citizen groups (through citizen suits) so infrequently attempt to prosecute take violation claims. Prosecuting a climate change case would be no mean feat either, given the generic effects of greenhouse gas emissions and the imprecision of downscaling models. Consider, for example, a scenario in which the pika is listed as endangered due to climate change. Who is taking the pika? Are greenhouse gas emissions from, say, a coal-fired power plant in Florida taking the pika? The plaintiff in such a case would have to show that the power plant emissions are the actual as well as proximate, foreseeable cause of the primary and secondary ecological effects which are in turn the actual as well as proximate, foreseeable cause of the pika's demise. Proving that would prove too much, however, as it would necessarily follow that all sources of greenhouse gases are taking the pika. This is an inherent feature of the take prohibition that makes it inapposite when take of a species occurs through large-scale, dispersed causal agents, such as water consumption and pollution — if anyone is taking the species, everyone is taking the species. Although nothing in the ESA prevents the FWS from attempting to prosecute such a case, it would be a daunting prosecutorial undertaking as well as likely political suicide. Thus far, the FWS has exhibited no stomach for it, and in the long run may determine to use its discretion — in this case prosecutorial discretion — to leave greenhouse gas emissions out of its take enforcement agenda.

The take prohibition would prove more manageable to enforce against discrete, identifiable actions that make it less likely a climate-threatened species will survive through the climate change transition. In particular, human adaptation to climate change is likely to present collisions between many species, climate-threatened or not, and human responses such as relocated agricultural and urban land uses, technological structures designed to impede sea level rise and floods, and new and intensified water diversions to sustain parched urban centers. Enforcement of the take prohibition in such settings, where proximate cause may be less difficult to establish, could help ensure that human adaptation measures are not carried out recklessly with respect to the interests of imperiled species. In this sense, section 9 would be used no differently from the way it is already used — climate change effects would simply be a reason to use it more vigilantly.

Note carefully the causal chain that Professor Ruhl describes. Plaintiffs will first need to demonstrate that emissions cause specific effects and then that those effects cause the decline of the polar bear, or in his example, the pika. Can you imagine a scenario in which that causal chain could be established? Which activities should the FWS prohibit to "conserve" polar bears?

2. While acknowledging the substantial difficulties in applying the ESA's take prohibition to greenhouse gas emitting activities, Professor Ruhl states that certain activities, such as adaptation to climate change, may lend themselves more to Section 9. Will plaintiffs, such as the Center for Biological Diversity, be satisfied with this limited application of Section 9?

3. *Incidental Takes.* Under the Marine Mammal Protection Act (MMPA), 16 U.S.C. § 1371(a)(5)(A), the FWS has authorized the non-lethal, incidental take of small numbers of polar bears and Pacific walruses during year-round oil and gas operations in the Beaufort Sea and adjacent northern coast of Alaska. This rule will be in effect through August 2, 2011. 71 Fed. Reg. 43,926 (Aug. 2, 2006). The FWS has also proposed regulations to authorize the non-lethal, incidental, unintentional take of small numbers of Pacific walruses and polar bears during year-round oil and gas industry exploration activities in the Chukchi Sea and adjacent western coast of Alaska. 72 Fed. Reg. 30,670 (June 1, 2007). In light of the conservation status of polar bears, should the FWS allow the incidental take of any polar bears?

---

c.   *Recovery Plans*

A recovery plan is supposed to provide "the process that stops or reverses the decline of a species and neutralizes threats to its existence." Fund for Animals v. Babbitt, 903 F. Supp. 96, 103 (D.D.C. 1995). In that sense, climate change and polar bears pose special challenges for recovery plans. According to attorneys for the Center for Biological Diversity, "There is no hope for recovery, much less survival, of the polar bear absent substantial reductions in GHG emissions. Any legally adequate recovery plan must therefore include mandates to reduce such emissions." Cummings & Siegel, at 7. Do you agree? In what ways, absent GHG emissions reductions, would a recovery plan benefit the polar bear? Review the provisions of the ESA concerning recovery plans. Can the FWS avoid preparing a recovery plan because the conservation of the polar bear will not benefit from one?

QUESTIONS AND DISCUSSION

1. In the context of polar bears and climate change, what are the primary limitations of this recovery plan framework? For example, what would site-specific management plans entail? In addition, assuming that reductions in GHG emissions are required, because today's emissions will continue to have climate change effects for several decades, would any restrictions on GHG be futile, at least with respect to the polar bear? Even if the ESA's recovery provisions mandate reductions in greenhouse gas emissions for the polar bear, the FWS and its parent agency, the

Department of Interior (or NMFS for species under its jurisdiction), must have authority to implement such actions. What major GHG emitting activities does the Department of Interior have jurisdiction over?

2.   In reaching its conclusion that there are no known regulatory mechanisms effectively addressing reductions in sea ice habitat at this time, the FWS reviewed a number of domestic and international treaties relating to habitat and polar bear conservation. It did not, however, refer to the UN Framework Convention on Climate Change or the Kyoto Protocol or any statute addressing emissions of GHGs. Indeed, the proposed rule does not refer to any emissions of GHGs anywhere. What effect might this have on a recovery plan or Section 7 consultation?

3.   John Kostyack and Dan Rohlf suggest that climate change may fundamentally alter the role of recovery plans:

> [M]any species now depend on habitat or ecological processes so altered by human activity that these species will need intensive management efforts on an ongoing basis simply to ensure their continued existence. Such plants and animals, sometimes called "conservation-reliant" species, may never recover as Congress contemplated in § 4 because they require on a perpetual basis the legal protections and management obligations imposed by the ESA. Given that by virtually any conceivable scenario we are not likely to solve the problem of climate change in the foreseeable future, many species now on the protected lists are likely to fall into the conservation-reliant category. This may mean that the emergency room analogy commonly used to describe the ESA, wherein the Act saves species from a disaster and then discharges them to their natural state, must for many species give way to seeing the statute more as long-term intensive care. Under this conception of the law, recovery of listed species would not serve as the ESA's principal goal for many species imperiled by climate change; instead, maintenance plans and their implementation would focus on perpetually managing targeted species so they do not experience significant declines or become extinct.

Kostyack & Rohlf, *Endangered Species in an Era of Global Warming*, at 10,208. Is it possible to reinterpret the existing provisions for recovery plans to implement "maintenance plans" envisaged by Kostyack and Rohlf? If not, what new legislation would you propose to focus on managing targeted species to avoid significant declines?

4.   Polar Bears offer an extreme case because their habitat is literally melting. For other species, it may be possible to design management plans that may actually recover the species rather than simply maintain it. For a terrestrial species, what might appropriate management measures entail? Kostyack and Rohlf suggest that recovery plans focus on specific issues related to adaptation to global warming:

> (1) corridors for species movement that allow transitions to more hospitable areas; (2) measures particularly aimed at managing and protecting vulnerable resources such as water availability and specialized habitat needs; (3) better use of population and habitat availability projections; (4) stronger adaptive management programs for long-term operations such as dams; (5) protection and acquisition of northerly or higher elevation portions of species' ranges; and (6) targeted population supplementation and reintroductions.

Id. at 10,212.

5.   In the press release accompanying the polar bear determination, Secretary of Interior Dirk Kempthorne said: "Listing the polar bear as threatened can reduce

avoidable losses of polar bears. But it should not open the door to use of the ESA to regulate greenhouse gas emissions from automobiles, power plants, and other sources. That would be a wholly inappropriate use of the ESA law. The ESA is not the right tool to set U.S. climate policy." Do you agree? Undeterred by the FWS's decisions relating to the polar bear designation, the Center for Biological Diversity has asked the FWS to list ringed, bearded, spotted and ribbon seals and the Pacific walrus, all ice-dependent species, as threatened or endangered.

IV. THE CLEAN WATER ACT

A.   Overview

Congress enacted the Clean Water Act (CWA) to "restore and maintain the chemical, physical and biological integrity of the Nation's waters." Federal Water Pollution Control Act, 33 U.S.C. §§ 1251–1387, § 1251(a). It also sought to eliminate by 1985 discharges of pollutants into navigable waters and to achieve by 1983, wherever attainable, water quality that protects fish and wildlife and provides recreation in and on the water. *Id.*

To effectuate its goals, the CWA prohibits "the discharge of any pollutant" into navigable waters unless otherwise permitted. 33 U.S.C. § 1311(a). A "discharge of a pollutant" is defined as "any addition of any pollutant into navigable waters from any point source." 33 U.S.C. § 1362(12). Any release of pollution that qualifies as a "discharge of a pollutant" is subject to stringent requirements under the CWA's National Pollutant Discharge Elimination System (NPDES) permit program of Section 402 or the dredged or fill material permit program under Section 404. 33 U.S.C. §§ 1342, 1344. The NPDES permit program forms the heart of the CWA and, along with other sections of the CWA, requires discharges to meet technology-based effluent limitations (reflecting the application of the best practicable, best conventional, or best available technology to limit pollution) as well as "any more stringent limitation necessary to meet water quality standards." 33 U.S.C. §§ 1342, 1311 (b) &(b)(1)(C). The CWA's dual emphases on technology-based treatment and protection of receiving water quality has made the CWA one of the most effective — and onerous — pollution control laws in effect in the United States.

However, these controls apply only where the "jurisdictional triggers" of Section 301(a) are satisfied. In other words, unless a release of pollution qualifies as (1) any addition, (2) of any pollutant, (3) into navigable waters, (4) from any point source, it will not trigger the Section 301(a) discharge prohibition or the Section 402 NPDES permit program. The CWA provides statutory definitions of the terms "navigable waters," "pollutant," and "point source," and a considerable body of case law has developed to further define these terms and the meaning of the word "addition." While the nuances of these definitions are beyond the scope of this section, the definitions are summarized as follows. First, a "point source" includes "any discernable, confined and discrete conveyance" such as any pipe, ditch, or tunnel, but excludes return flows from agricultural irrigation waters. 33 U.S.C. § 1362(14). (In contrast, nonpoint sources of pollution are "non-discrete sources," such as runoff from a farmland or timber harvesting, and are the responsibility of the states with certain federal oversight.). Second, the term "pollutant" includes "heat," which could become important for waters affected by climate change, as well as "industrial, municipal, and agricultural wastes." 33 U.S.C. § 1362(6). Third, "navigable waters" are defined to include any "waters of the United States." 33 U.S.C. § 1362(7). Several Supreme Court cases have limited the term to include navigable-in-fact waterways, as well as tributaries to navigable-in-fact waters, if the tributaries have a "substantial nexus" with such waters. *See* Solid Waste Agency of N. Cook County v. U.S. Army Corps of Eng'rs., 531 U.S. 159, 174 (2001) (invalidating regulation extending definition of "waters of the United States" to isolated waters with no hydrological connection to navigable-in-fact waters); United States v. Rapanos, 547 U.S. 715 (2006) (Kennedy, J.) (stating that tributaries which have a substantial nexus to navigable-in-fact waters qualify as waters of the United States under the CWA); *see also* U.S. v. Gerke Excavating, Inc., 464 F.3d 723, 724–25 (7th Cir. 2006) (holding that Justice Kennedy's concurrence in *Rapanos* is the appropriate test for determining whether a water body is subject to Clean Water Act jurisdiction); U.S. v. Lucas, 516 F.3d 316, 325 n.8 (5th Cir. 2008) (same); Northern California River Watch v. City of Healdsburg, 496 F.3d 993, 995 (9th Cir. 2007) (same). Whenever a pollution release satisfies the CWA's statutory triggers, it becomes subject to the CWA's rigorous pollution control requirements.

B.   Climate Change and the Water Quality Standards Program

In the context of climate change, it is unlikely that the CWA could directly limit the releases of greenhouse gases, since these substances are generally emitted into the atmosphere and not discharged directly into water. However, it is possible that climate change will nonetheless affect the regulatory requirements that apply to many point sources — and perhaps nonpoint sources — under the CWA, through the Act's water quality standards program.

Section 303 requires states to set water quality standards that protect designated uses for water bodies. 33 U.S.C. § 1313(c)(1). Water quality standards establish the water quality goals for a water body. 40 C.F.R. § 131.2. Water quality standards include three elements: (1) one or more designated "uses" of a waterway; (2) numeric and narrative "criteria" specifying the water quality conditions, such as maximum amounts of toxic pollutants, maximum temperature levels, and the like, that are necessary to protect the designated uses; and (3) an antidegradation policy and implementation methods that ensure that "[e]xisting instream water uses and the level of water quality to protect the existing uses [will] be maintained and protected" and that high quality waters will be maintained and protected. 33 U.S.C. §§ 1313(c)(2), 1313(d)(4)(B); 40 C.F.R. Part 131, Subpart B. Each state must develop water quality standards that specify a water body's designated uses and water quality criteria necessary to protect such uses. States establish water quality standards by "taking into consideration their use and value for public water supplies, propagation of fish and wildlife, recreational purposes, and agricultural, industrial, and other purposes [and] their use and value for navigation." 33 U.S.C. § 1313(c)(2)(A).

Whenever a state agency develops water quality standards, it must submit the standards to the Environmental Protection Agency (EPA) for review. 33 U.S.C.

§ 1313(c)(2)(A). EPA, in turn, reviews the submitted state standards to determine whether they meet the requirements of the Clean Water Act. 33 U.S.C. § 1313(c)(3). Specifically, EPA evaluates whether the standards include proper designated uses, whether those criteria will protect those uses, and whether the state's antidegradation policy conforms to federal rules. 40 C.F.R. § 131.6. In evaluating the designated uses, EPA ensures that the uses include, at a minimum, propagation of fish, shellfish, and wildlife and human recreation. 40 C.F.R. § 131.2. EPA also ensures that the criteria are "based on sound scientific rationale and [] contain sufficient parameters or constituents to protect the designated use." 40 C.F.R. § 131.11(a)(1). EPA must also determine that the criteria will protect the most sensitive designated uses. *Id.* Thus, water quality standards must include scientifically defensible criteria necessary to protect aquatic life.

In addition, Section 303(d) requires each state to identify waters within its boundaries for which "effluent limitations . . . are not stringent enough to implement any water quality standard applicable to such waters." 33 U.S.C. § 1313(d)(1)(A). A water body failing to meet any numeric criteria or narrative criteria (e.g., "no aesthetically displeasing conditions"), designated uses, or antidegradation requirements shall be included as a water-quality limited segment on the "303(d) List." 40 C.F.R. § 130.7(b)(3).

For waters identified on the 303(d) List, the states must establish a total maximum daily load (TMDL) limit for pollutants "at a level necessary to implement the applicable water quality standards." 33 U.S.C. § 1313(d)(1)(C). "A TMDL defines the specified maximum amount of a pollutant which can be discharged or 'loaded' into the water at issue from all combined sources." Dioxin/Organochlorine Center v. Clarke, 57 F.3d 1517, 1520 (9th Cir. 1995). The 303(d) List must include a priority ranking for all listed segments still requiring TMDLs. 40 C.F.R. § 130.7(b)(4).

A TMDL is, in essence, an allocation of the total allowable pollution which all known and unknown sources may release into a water body each day. Each TMDL must allocate the allowable pollution into "load allocations" ("LAs"), which apply to nonpoint sources, and "waste load allocations" ("WLAs"), which apply to point sources. 40 C.F.R. § 130.2(g), (h). All sources are then prohibited from releasing more pollution than authorized under the LAs and WLAs. The TMDLs thus "serve as a link in an implementation chain that includes federally-regulated point source controls, state or local plans for point and nonpoint source pollution reduction, and assessment of the impact of such measures on water quality, all to the end of attaining water quality goals for the nation's waters." Pronsolino v. Nastri, 291 F.3d 1123, 1129 (9th Cir. 2002).

The EPA oversees the states' implementation of Section 303(d) and must approve the identified impaired water bodies and TMDLs. 33 U.S.C. § 1313(d)(2). If EPA disapproves either, then EPA shall identify such waters and establish TMDLs as necessary to ensure water quality standards are met. 33 U.S.C. § 1313(d)(2).

Unlike the CWA's NPDES and dredged or fill material permitting programs, the CWA's water quality standards program does not apply only to discharges of pollutants from point sources. Instead, the water quality standards apply to water bodies regardless of the sources of pollution that may affect water quality. If a water body is placed on a state's 303(d) List, moreover, that placement can have significant consequences for both point and nonpoint sources of pollution. First, the CWA regulations prohibit "new discharges" of pollutants that have a reasonable likelihood of contributing to water quality standards violations from any point sources into water quality limited streams for which the state (or EPA) has not established a TMDL. 40 C.F.R. § 122.4(i). Second, once a TMDL is established, all releases of pollutants must comply with the load allocations and waste load allocations established in the TMDL. Thus, even if a particular source of pollution is not currently restricted under the Clean Water Act, degradation of a water body may ultimately result in future regulation of that source.

Scientists predict that climate change will alter water quality in a number of ways. For example, increased flooding and precipitation in many areas will likely result in increased sedimentation and pollution from runoff, which EPA acknowledges may overload storm water and waste water treatment systems. *See* Environmental Protection Agency, Climate Change — Health and Environmental Effects, Water Quality, *available at* http://www.epa.gov/climatechange/effects/water/quality.html.   Stream temperatures in many areas will also increase, leading, in turn, to a reduction in dissolved oxygen available for aquatic life and direct impacts to temperature-sensitive species. *Id.* If these alterations result in violations of applicable water quality standards, all sources of water pollution will likely face increased restrictions on the types and amounts of pollution they can release into the waters of the United States.

1.   *The 303(d) Listing Process*

Federal regulations implementing the CWA require states to submit every two years their 303(d) Lists identifying all "water quality limited" water bodies within the state. 40 C.F.R. § 130.7(d). In developing their 303(d) Lists, states must "assemble and evaluate all existing and readily available water quality-related data and information." 40 C.F.R. § 130.7(b)(5). In evaluating the data, states must expressly consider information related to any water quality problems reported by other governmental agencies and members of the public. *Id.* at § 130.7(b)(5)(iii). If a state ultimately decides not to use any existing and readily available data and information to develop its 303(d) List, the state must submit to EPA a rationale for excluding such data. 40 C.F.R. § 130.7(b)(6)(iii). The listing process thus provides an avenue for members of the public to get involved in the 303(d) List development.

The Center for Biological Diversity has petitioned California to add waters to the 303(d) List due to carbon dioxide pollution resulting in ocean acidification. As you read the petition, consider what possible actions California could take in response.

CENTER FOR BIOLOGICAL DIVERSITY, REQUEST TO ADD CALIFORNIA OCEAN WATERS TO LIST OF IMPAIRED WATERS DUE TO CARBON DIOXIDE POLLUTION RESULTING IN OCEAN ACIDIFICATION
(Feb. 27, 2007)

III. OCEAN ACIDIFICATION BACKGROUND * * *

A. Seawater Chemistry and Carbon Dioxide

The oceans freely exchange carbon dioxide with the atmosphere. The oceans have already taken up about 50% of the carbon dioxide that humans have produced since the industrial revolution, and already this has lowered the average ocean pH by 0.11 units. . . . Over time, the ocean will absorb up to 90% of anthropogenic carbon dioxide released into the atmosphere.

When carbon dioxide is dissolved in seawater it becomes reactive and changes seawater chemistry along with many other physical and biological reactions. When carbon dioxide combines with water, it forms carbonic acid and releases hydrogen ions. These hydrogen ions determine the acidity of the ocean, accounting for the change in pH. The slightly alkaline pH of the ocean is becoming more acidic. The naturally occurring pH values for the ocean were on average 8.16 and as a result of carbon dioxide pollution, the average pH value has dropped to 8.05.

Carbon dioxide pollution results in more severe pH changes than experienced in the past 300 million years. * * *

B. The Adverse Impacts of Carbon Dioxide Pollution on the Marine Environment

Scientists agree that carbon dioxide pollution is causing ocean acidification with adverse impacts on many marine organisms. Available evidence suggests that the consequences of anthropogenic carbon dioxide accumulation have already begun in surface waters.

One of the most alarming effects of ocean acidification is the impact on the availability of carbonate for calcifying organisms such as mollusks, crustaceans, echinoderms, corals, calcareous algae, foraminifera and some phytoplankton. Nearly all marine species that build shells or skeletons from calcium carbonate that have been studied have shown deterioration when exposed to increasing carbon dioxide levels in seawater. Estimates suggest that calcification rates will decrease up to 50% by the end of the century. Snails, sea urchins, starfish, lobster, crabs, oysters, clams, mussels, and scallops all build shells that are vulnerable to ocean acidification. Other marine species may experience physiological effects from acidification including lowered immune response, metabolic decline, and reproductive and respiratory problems.

[The petition then detailed the impacts of ocean acidification on a range of species. These impacts include impaired growth and development of coccolithophorids, foraminifera, and pteropods, the dominant calcifying planktonic organisms. Phytoplankton, such as these, contribute much of the organic material entering the marine food chain and are responsible for about 50% of the earth's primary production. They are food sources for a wide variety of marine organisms, including krill, whales, salmon, and other fish. Larger calcifying animals such as corals, crustaceans, echinoderms, and mollusks are also threatened by ocean acidification, because, like calcifying plankton, they are experiencing reduced calcification and erosion of their protective shells. For example, at a pH change of 0.3 units, echinoderms are significantly impacted.

Even marine animals that do not calcify are threatened by carbon dioxide increases in their habitat. Changes in the ocean's carbon dioxide concentration result in hypercapnia, an accumulation of carbon dioxide in the tissues and fluids of fish and other marine animals, and acidosis, an increased acidity in the body fluids. These impacts can cause a variety of problems for marine animals including difficulty with acid-base regulation, calcification, growth, respiration, energy turnover, and mode of metabolism. For example, even under a moderate 0.15 pH change, squid have reduced capacity to carry oxygen and higher carbon dioxide pressures are likely to be lethal. Additionally, studies have shown various impacts on fish, oysters, sea urchins, and mollusks due to changes in ocean pH. Impacts on individual species can lead to even greater ecosystem responses that will alter ecosystem productivity, nutrient availability, and carbon cycling.]

IV. CALIFORNIA'S OCEAN WATERS ARE IMPAIRED AND MUST BE ADDED TO THE 303(D) LIST

All segments of California's ocean waters must be included on the State's 303(d) List because current measures are not stringent enough to prevent ocean acidification and achieve water quality standards. 33 U.S.C. § 1313(d). The Clean Water Act requires that California protect the water quality for designated uses of its waters. California's Ocean Plan defines the designated uses of ocean waters:

> The beneficial uses of the ocean waters of the State that shall be protected include industrial water supply; water contact and non-contact recreation, including aesthetic enjoyment; navigation; commercial and sport fishing; mariculture; preservation and enhancement of designated Areas of Special Biological Significance (ASBS); rare and endangered species; marine habitat; fish migration; fish spawning and shellfish harvesting.

California Ocean Plan at 3 (2005).

The beneficial uses of California's oceans are threatened by ocean acidification. For example, many marine species are vulnerable to ocean acidification, which can impair the ocean's marine resources and economic activities dependent on these resources such as fishing, mariculture, and shellfish harvesting. Habitat for imperiled species, and their spawning, migration, and forage may be impaired. Even under conservative estimates of future carbon dioxide emissions, scientists predict chemical changes that threaten the ability of marine life to adapt to the acidifying ocean. All these impacts would severely impair Californians' aesthetic and recreational enjoyment of the ocean waters and sea life they contain.

California's ocean waters meet one or more of the 303(d) listing factors enumerated in California's Water Quality Control Policy ("WQCP"). First, California's ocean waters are experiencing a trend of declining water quality for pH. Second, ocean acidification is causing degradation of marine communities. For these reasons, which are described in detail below and supported by the attached scientific evidence, California's ocean should be placed on the 303(d) List as impaired for pH as a result of anthropogenic carbon dioxide emissions.

A. California's Oceans Are on a Trajectory for Declining Water Quality

The Clean Water Act and California's antidegradation policy prohibits any degradation of water bodies that are currently meeting water quality standards. The increasing acidification of the ocean requires that California's ocean waters be added to the 303(d) List.

> A water segment shall be placed on the section 303(d) list if the water segment exhibits concentrations of pollutants or water body conditions for any listing factor that shows a trend of declining water quality standards attainment.

WQCP § 3.10 (2004). As this listing criterion fulfills the Clean Water Act's antidegradation requirements, a water body must be listed if it has declining water quality even if water quality objectives are not exceeded. WQCP § 3.10. . . .

At present, California's ocean segments are on a trajectory of declining attainment of water quality standards for pH. California's water quality standard for the ocean states, "the pH shall not be changed at any time more than 0.2 units from that which occurs naturally." California Ocean Plan 6 (2005).

Applying the existing Ocean Plan standard for pH, all California ocean waters must be included on the 303(d) List because they are experiencing degradation. As described above, dissolved carbon dioxide lowers the pH of seawater and acidifies the ocean. Surface ocean pH has already declined by 0.11 units on average from preindustrial values. The naturally occurring pH values for the ocean were on average 8.16 and as a result of carbon dioxide pollution, the average pH value has dropped to 8.05. This is a significant change in water quality since each step is a tenfold change in acidity. * * *

The ongoing acidification of the ocean is the most severe change in ocean pH in several million years. These changes are occurring at about 100 times the rate of changes seen naturally in geological history. * * *

Meanwhile, human activities continue to release carbon dioxide, and the ocean is continuing to absorb such pollution. With the oceans absorbing about 22 million [tons] of carbon dioxide each day, seawater pH will continue to decrease. Assuming current trends of greenhouse gas emissions, the global average pH of seawater will drop another 0.3–0.4 units. Having already absorbed half of anthropogenic carbon dioxide, scientists predict that the oceans will absorb up to 90%. Unabated, carbon dioxide pollution will degrade seawater quality beyond California's water quality standards. By the end of this century, absent significant reductions in carbon dioxide emissions, this will result in a pH change up to 0.5 units.

California is among the largest producers of carbon dioxide pollution. Contributing about 492 million metric tons of greenhouse gases each year, California is the nation's second largest emitter of greenhouse gases and the world's 12th largest contributor. Carbon dioxide accounts for 84% of those emissions, much of which is quickly absorbed into the surface layers of the ocean. California's population is expected to increase from 35 million today to 55 million by 2050. Absent significant per-capita reductions in current carbon dioxide emission rates, California's emissions are likely to increase.

Increasing carbon dioxide in the atmosphere will lead to further ocean acidification.

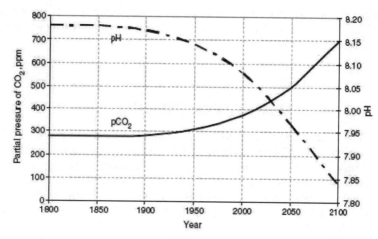

Figure 8.1 The past and projected change in atmospheric CO_2 and seawater pH assuming anthropogenic emissions are maintained at current predictions (redrawn from Zeebe and Wolf-Gladrow 2001).

Source: Turley 2006

As described above, and documented in the scientific literature submitted with this request, carbon dioxide absorption into the ocean is causing California's ocean waters to have a lower pH, increased dissolved carbon dioxide, lower concentration of carbonate ions, and increased bicarbonate ions. The result is that California's ocean waters have already been degraded by carbon dioxide pollution. California's ocean waters are on a trajectory toward nonattainment of water quality standards and therefore should be added to the 303(d) List.

B. Ocean Acidification Is Impairing Marine Communities

California's ocean waters should also be placed on the 303(d) List because they exceed the narrative water quality criteria for biological characteristics described in California's Ocean Plan. The Ocean Plan provides that "[m]arine communities, including vertebrate, invertebrate, and plant species, shall not be degraded."

California's Water Quality Control Policy ("WQCP") explicitly states that a water segment that "exhibits adverse biological response" such as "reduction in growth, reduction in reproductive capacity, abnormal development, histopathological abnormalities, and other adverse conditions" should be placed on the list. WQCP § 3.8. A segment should also be listed "if the water segment exhibits significant degradation in biological populations and/or communities" as evidenced by declining species diversity or individuals in a species. WQCP § 3.9.

As described above, the impacts of ocean acidification on marine organisms, and ultimately, marine communities are significant, diverse, and will greatly increase in severity over time. * * *

Ocean acidification is adversely affecting calcifying planktonic organisms such as coccolithophorids, foraminifera, and pteropods, larger calcifying organisms such as crustaceans, echinoderms, corals, and mollusks, non-calcifying organisms such as fish and squid, and such adverse affects will reverberate though the marine ecosystem to marine mammals, seabirds and ultimately human communities reliant upon ocean resources. In short, ocean acidification caused by anthropogenic carbon dioxide is causing degradation of California's marine communities in breach of the water quality standards. As such, California's ocean waters should be added to the 303(d) List as impaired for pH from absorption of anthropogenic atmospheric carbon dioxide.

—

QUESTIONS AND DISCUSSION

1. The Center for Biological Diversity petition seeks to place all of California's ocean waters on California's 303(d) List, because (a) the water quality in the oceans is declining, in violation of California's antidegradation policy, and (b) the acidic ocean waters do not adequately protect California's designated uses, in violation of California's narrative water quality criteria. Do you think the evidence presented in the petition justifies the action requested by the Center for Biological Diversity? Why or why not?

2. Is California required to consider the Center for Biological Diversity's petition? In *Sierra Club, Inc. v. Leavitt*, the Eleventh Circuit found that EPA had violated the Clean Water Act when it approved Florida's 303(d) List, because Florida had excluded all data that was more than 7.5 years old when it developed the list. 488 F.3d 904, 913–14 (11th Cir. 2006). Florida had chosen to exclude all older data from consideration on the basis that older data can be less reliable in assessing current conditions. *Id.* at 914. The court, however, held that Florida (and, by extension, EPA) must at least review all relevant data and then provide for specific justifications if the agencies choose to not use such data in making the 303(d) List. *Id.* What does this case suggest about how California may need to respond to the petition?

3. The Center for Biological Diversity's petition identifies airborne emissions of carbon dioxide as the primary cause of ocean acidification. While the petition also attempts to link the increased acidification to California's own carbon dioxide emissions, it is likely that global carbon dioxide emissions are responsible for increased acidification of the world's oceans. Is the 303(d) List the appropriate tool to use to address global pollution? Do you think Congress intended the Clean *Water* Act to control *air* pollution?

The answers to these questions may depend upon the particular program of the Clean Water Act. As noted above (and discussed in greater detail below), the water quality standards program is focused on the quality of water bodies generally, regardless of the source of any pollution that may impact water quality. Thus, an assessment of whether a water body is water quality limited (and thus placed on a state's 303(d) List) should focus on the designated uses in a given waterway, the criteria established to protect those uses, and the levels of pollution found in the water body. For all of these factors, the source of the pollution should be irrelevant. Indeed, many water bodies in the United States are listed on states' 303(d) Lists due to mercury pollution, even though, in many states, the primary sources of aquatic mercury pollution are air emissions of mercury from coal-fired power plants and industrial facilities located within and outside the United States.

As for controlling air emissions in order to protect water quality, various possible approaches exist. States are developing TMDLs for mercury which establish load allocations for anthropogenic sources of airborne mercury pollution. *See, e.g.*, Northeast Regional Mercury Total Maximum Daily Load 30 (Oct. 24, 2007); Oregon Department of Environmental Quality, Willamette Basin TMDL, Chapter 3: Willamette Basin Mercury TMDL 3-36 to 3-37 (Sept. 2006). These TMDLs thus treat airborne mercury emitters as nonpoint sources of mercury pollution. As discussed in the *Pronsolino* case, below, states that attempt to regulate nonpoint pollution through TMDLs will likely survive challenges to this exercise of regulatory power.

Outside of the water quality standards and TMDL context, however, it is unclear whether courts will accept regulation of airborne pollution through the Clean Water Act's point source controls. *See* Chemical Weapons Working Group, Inc. v. U.S. Dept. of Defense, 111 F.3d 1485 (10th Cir. 1997); League of Wilderness Defenders v. Forsgren, 309 F.3d 1181 (9th Cir. 2002). In *Chemical Weapons Working Group*, the Tenth Circuit rejected the plaintiffs' arguments that the Clean Water Act applied to emissions from a chemical weapons incinerator that would enter a nearby waterway, and concluded that Congress intended for the Clean Air Act to regulate such emissions. In that case, the court was particularly reluctant to allow the Clean Water Act to apply, because the Clean Water Act contains an absolute ban on discharges of chemical or biological warfare agents. 111 F.3d at 1490. Thus, regulation under the Clean Water Act would have likely resulted in closure of the facility, even though Congress had approved and funded the facility. *Id.* The court was unwilling to interpret the law in a way that would yield such a result. In *League of Wilderness Defenders*, however, the Ninth Circuit had no difficulty concluding that aerial spraying of pesticides over waters within national forests is a point source discharge requiring a NPDES permit. 309 F.3d at 1184–85 ("an airplane fitted with tanks and a mechanical spraying apparatus is a 'discrete conveyance' "). The cases, however, are distinguishable in at least one important way: in *Chemical Weapons Working Group*, the facility had received and was operating under a Clean Air Act permit, 111 F.3d at 1490–91; in *League of Wilderness Defenders*, there was never any argument that the Clean Air Act could regulate the pesticide releases. *See* 309 F.3d at 1184–90. Thus, the scope of Clean Water Act regulation may depend, at least in part, on whether a facility is already subject to Clean Air Act requirements.

4.   Several states already include water bodies on their 303(d) List for exceeding applicable water quality standards for temperature. *See* EPA, Map, *Idaho, Oregon, & Washington CWA 303(d) Listings in ESA-Listed Fish Habitat* (June 18, 2004). Many species, such as salmon and steelhead, require cold stream temperatures for spawning, rearing, and migration, and warm waters impair the species' ability to survive. In fact, multiple populations of salmon have been listed as endangered or threatened species under the Endangered Species Act due in part to elevated stream temperatures. Scientists predict that climate change will further alter water quality of streams by increasing average stream temperatures. What additional protections do you think the Clean Water Act's 303(d) listing process could provide species that are already protected under the Endangered Species Act? For a discussion of the interplay between the Clean Water Act and the ESA, *see* Craig N. Johnston, *Salmon and Water Temperature: Taking Species Seriously in Establishing Water Quality Standards*, 33 ENVTL. L. 151 (2003).

---

2.   *The Consequences of a 303(d) Listing Decision*

Once a water body is on a state's 303(d) List, important regulatory consequences result. First, federal regulations prohibit the introduction of new discharges of pollutants that may cause or contribute to violations of water quality standards into water quality limited streams for which a TMDL has not been developed. 40 C.F.R. § 122.4(i). Second, once a TMDL is developed, sources must adhere to the established load allocations and waste load allocations. As you read the following cases, consider the implications for both point and nonpoint sources if climate change alters water quality in the way most scientists predict.

a.   *Implications for Point Sources: The Prohibition against New Discharges into Water Quality Limited Streams*

FRIENDS OF PINTO CREEK v. UNITED STATES ENVIRONMENTAL PROTECTION AGENCY
504 F.3d 1007 (9th Cir. 2007)

HUG, CIRCUIT JUDGE: * * *

In this case, we determine whether the Environmental Protection Agency ("EPA") properly issued a National Pollution Discharge Elimination System ("NPDES") permit under the Clean Water Act to Carlota Copper Company ("Carlota"). The permit allows mining-related discharges of copper into Arizona's Pinto Creek, a waterbody already in excess of water quality standards for copper. . . .

I. FACTUAL BACKGROUND

. . . Due to excessive copper contamination from historical mining activities in the region, Pinto Creek is included on Arizona's list of impaired waters under § 303(d) of the Clean Water Act, 33 U.S.C. § 1313(d), as a water quality limited stream due to non-attainment of water quality standards for dissolved copper.

Carlota proposed to construct and operate an open-pit copper mine and processing facility approximately six miles west of Miami, Arizona, covering over 3000 acres while extracting about 100 million tons of ore. Part of the operation plan includes constructing diversion channels for Pinto Creek to route the stream around the mine, as well as groundwater cut-off walls to block the flow of groundwater into the mine.

. . . Because the proposed action would involve the discharge of pollutants into Pinto Creek, Carlota applied to the EPA for an NPDES permit under § 402 of the Clean Water Act, 33 U.S.C. § 1342, in 1996. The EPA ultimately issued the permit, and the Environmental Appeals Board ("Appeals Board"), the internal appellate board of the EPA, denied review.

*   *   *

V. ANALYSIS

*   *   *

Under § 303 of the Clean Water Act, 33 U.S.C. § 1313, the states are required to set water quality standards for all waters within their boundaries, regardless of the sources of the pollution entering the waters. Pursuant to § 303(d)(1), 33 U.S.C. § 1313(d)(1), each state is required to identify those waters that do not meet the water quality standard which is frequently called the "§ 303(d)(1) list." For impaired waters identified in the § 303(d)(1) list, the states must establish a TMDL for pollutants identified by the EPA. A TMDL specifies the maximum amount of pollutant that can be discharged or loaded into the waters from all combined sources, so as to comply with the water quality standards.

Each state is required to submit its § 303(d)(1) list and its TMDL to the EPA for its approval or disapproval. If the EPA disapproves either of those documents, the EPA is responsible for preparing that document. The state then incorporates its

§ 303(d)(1) list and its TMDL or the EPA's approved document into its continuing planning process as required by § 303(e), 33 U.S.C. § 1313(e).

In this case, the state had prepared the § 303(d)(1) list, but it had not prepared a TMDL. Therefore, in response to the Petitioners' objection, the EPA prepared the TMDL utilized in its awarding of the permit.

The Petitioners contend that as a "new discharger" Carlota's discharge of dissolved copper into a waterway that is already impaired by an excess of the copper pollutant violates the intent and purpose of the Clean Water Act. Under the NPDES permitting program, 40 C.F.R. § 122.4(i) addresses the situation where a new source seeks to permit a discharge of pollutants into a stream already exceeding its water quality standards for that pollutant. Section 122.4 states in relevant part:

No permit may be issued:

. . . .

(i) To a new source or a new discharger if the discharge from its construction or operation will cause or contribute to the violation of water quality standards. The owner or operator of a new source or new discharger proposing to discharge into a water segment which does not meet applicable water quality standards or is not expected to meet those standards . . . and for which the State or interstate agency has performed a pollutants load allocation for the pollutant to be discharged, must demonstrate, before the close of the public comment period, that:

(1) There are sufficient remaining pollutant load allocations to allow for the discharge; and

(2) The existing dischargers into that segment are subject to compliance schedules designed to bring the segment into compliance with applicable water quality standards.

40 C.F.R. § 122.4 (2000).

The plain language of the first sentence of the regulation is very clear that no permit may be issued to a new discharger if the discharge will contribute to the violation of water quality standards. This corresponds to the stated objectives of the Clean Water Act "to restore and maintain the chemical, physical, and biological integrity of the nation's waters." 33 U.S.C. § 1251(a) (1987). And that "it is the national policy that the discharge of toxic pollutants in toxic amounts be prohibited." 33 U.S.C. § 1251(a)(3) (1987).

The EPA contends that the partial remediation of the discharge from the Gibson Mine will offset the pollution. However, there is nothing in the Clean Water Act or the regulation that provides an exception for an offset when the waters remain impaired and the new source is discharging pollution into that impaired water.

The regulation does provide for an exception where a TMDL has been performed and the owner or operator demonstrates that *before the close of the comment period* two conditions are met, which will assure that the impaired waters will be brought into compliance with the applicable water quality standards. The plain language of this exception to the prohibited discharge by a new source provides that the exception does not apply unless the new source can demonstrate that, under the TMDL, the plan is designed to bring the waters into compliance with applicable water quality standards.

The EPA argues that under the requirements of clause (1), there are sufficient remaining load allocations to allow for the discharge because the TMDL provides a method by which the allocations could be established to allow for the discharge. There is no contention, however, that these load allocations represent the amount of pollution that is currently discharged from the point sources and nonpoint sources, and there is no indication of any plan that will effectuate these load allocations so as to bring Pinto Creek within the water quality standards. The TMDL merely provides for the manner in which Pinto Creek *could* meet the water quality standards if all of the load allocations in the TMDL were met, not that there are sufficient remaining pollutant load allocations under existing circumstances.

With regard to the requirements of clause (2), the EPA argues that the requirement of "compliance schedules" pertains only to point sources for which there is a permit. This does not correspond to the plain language of clause (2), which provides "the existing discharges into that segment [of Pinto Creek] are subject to compliance schedules designed to bring the segment into compliance with applicable water quality standards." 40 C.F.R. § 122.4(i)(2) (2000).

We examine that language utilizing the definitions provided in the regulation. The term "discharge" is defined to mean "the discharge of a pollutant." 40 C.F.R. § 122.2 (2000). The term "discharge of a pollutant," is defined as any addition of any "pollutant" or combination of pollutants to "waters of the United States" from "*any point source.*" *Id.* at § 122.2(a) (emphasis added). Thus, under the plain language of the regulation, compliance schedules are not confined only to "permitted" point source discharges, but are applicable to "any" point source.

The EPA contends that this would amount to a complete ban of the discharge of pollution to impaired waters. This is based on its misreading of the plain language of the regulation to state that the remediation has to be *completed* before Carlota's discharge. The plain language of clause (2) of the regulation, instead, provides that existing discharges into that segment (of the waters) are "subject to *compliance schedules* designed to bring the segment into compliance with applicable water quality standards." 40 C.F.R. § 122.4(i)(2) (2000) (emphasis added). This is not a complete ban but a requirement of schedules to meet the objective of the Clean Water Act.

Here the existing discharges from point sources are not subject to compliance schedules designed to bring Pinto Creek into compliance with water quality standards. Thus, Carlota has not demonstrated that clause (2) of 40 C.F.R. § 122.4(i) has been met. This is the regulation upon which Carlota and the EPA rely for issuance of the permit.

Initially, Carlota and the EPA contended that the first and second sentences of § 222.4(i) could be construed to apply independently, thus not requiring compliance with clauses (1) and (2) when an offset would result in a substantial net reduction of pollution to the impaired waters. The Petitioners, on the other hand, maintained that the two sentences must be read together, not independently. However, the EPA subsequently asked the Appeals Board to assume, for purposes of this decision, that clauses (1) and (2) do apply. *See In re Carlota Copper Co.*, 11 E.A.D. 692, 766 (EAB 2004). Thus, we are concerned in this case with whether the EPA required Carlota to fulfill all of the requirements of § 122.4(i), including clauses (1) and (2), in order to issue a permit to it as a new discharger.

The Respondents and Carlota rely on *Arkansas v. Oklahoma*, 503 U.S. 91 (1992) in support of their contentions. That case involved the issuance of a permit for a city in Arkansas to discharge effluent into a stream in Arkansas that entered a river that eventually flowed into Oklahoma. Oklahoma challenged the permit before the EPA, alleging that the discharge violated Oklahoma Water Quality Standards. In that case, the EPA found that the discharge would not lead to a "detectable change in water quality," which the Supreme Court held was supported by substantial evidence. *Arkansas*, 503 U.S. at 112. In the opinion, the Court stated that "the parties have pointed to nothing that mandates a complete ban on discharges into a waterway that is in violation of those standards. The statute does, however, contain provisions designed to remedy existing water quality violations and to allocate the burden of reducing undesirable discharges between existing sources and new sources. *See, e.g.*, § 1313(d)." *Id.* at 108. Section 1313(d) of the Clean Water Act, referred to by the Court, is the one that provides for the establishment of water quality standards and TMDLs.

The Supreme Court in *Arkansas v. Oklahoma* also referred to § 1288(b)(2), which provides for the development of area-wide programs to eliminate existing pollution in the context of area-wide waste treatment management. *Id.* That section provides details required of any plan to eliminate the pollution, including schedules, time lines, identification of agencies, and identification of measures necessary to carry out the plan.

The Appeals Board stated that prior Agency pronouncements "confirm our position that, rather than completely banning new source discharges, § 122.4(i) provides new sources with the opportunity to obtain a permit if the requirements specified in that section are met." *In re Carlota Copper Co.*, 11 E.A.D. 692, 765 (EAB 2004). The prior Agency position quoted states:

> A new source or new discharger may, however, obtain a permit for discharge into a water segment which does not meet applicable water quality standards by submitting information demonstrating that there is sufficient loading capacity remaining in waste load allocations (WLAs) for the stream segment to accommodate the new discharge and that existing dischargers to that segment are subject to *compliance schedules* designed to bring the segment into compliance with the applicable water quality standards.

Id. (emphasis added). The language quoted by the Appeals Board from the prior agency action requires compliance schedules designed to bring the water segment into compliance with the applicable water quality standards.

In Carlota's case, there are no plans or compliance schedules to bring the Pinto Creek segment "into compliance with applicable water quality standards," as required by § 122.4(i)(2), which Carlota and the EPA both acknowledge is the applicable section with which Carlota must comply. The error of both the EPA and Carlota is that the objective of that section is not simply to show a lessening of pollution, but to show how the water quality standard will be met if Carlota is allowed to discharge pollutants into the impaired waters.

The EPA has the responsibility to regulate discharges from point sources and the states have the responsibility to limit pollution coming into the waters from non-point sources. If point sources, other than the permitted point source, are necessary to be scheduled in order to achieve the water quality standard, then the EPA must locate any such point sources and establish compliance schedules to meet the water quality standard before issuing a permit. If there are not adequate point sources to do so, then a permit cannot be issued unless the state or Carlota agrees to establish a schedule to limit pollution from a nonpoint source or sources sufficient to achieve water quality standards.

*   *   *

In this case, the Petitioners do not argue for an absolute ban on discharges into a waterway that is in violation of the water quality standards. Rather, the Petitioners point to the § 122.4(i) exception by which a new discharger can comply with the Clean Water Act requirements. Those requirements simply were not met.

Thus, no conflict exists with the Supreme Court's opinion in *Arkansas v. Oklahoma*.

QUESTIONS AND DISCUSSION

1. The federal regulation at issue in *Friends of Pinto Creek* prohibits new discharges into water quality-limited streams unless a TMDL has been developed *and* 1) there are sufficient load allocations in the TMDL to accommodate the new pollution source and 2) all other existing discharges are subject to a schedule for compliance with applicable water quality standards. 40 C.F.R. § 122.44(i). How did EPA interpret this regulation before the Ninth Circuit Court of Appeals? Why did the court reject EPA's arguments? What implications could such a decision have in the climate change context? For example, if California were to grant the Center for Biological Diversity's petition and place all of its ocean waters on the 303(d) List, what additional steps would California need to take before issuing permits to new dischargers?

2. In *Friends of Pinto Creek*, the water body at issue had become polluted as a result of historic mining activities caused by other entities. If climate change has the impacts on stream quality that many predict, it is likely that many water bodies will be listed as impaired and subject to TMDLs, in which case many other companies will bear the burden of restoring water quality, even though they may not be the primary cause of water quality impairment. Consider, for example, the likely increases in stream temperatures that will result from climate change. Should industries which discharge heated water bear the burden of cooling their discharges because climate change has caused the streams to warm?

3. In *Friends of Pinto Creek*, EPA initially proposed to issue a permit to Carlota Copper Company, even though the company proposed to discharge copper into a stream listed as impaired due to excessive copper pollution and even though the state of Arizona had not yet developed a TMDL for the creek. When the environmental organizations opposed the permit, EPA then developed a TMDL. Could EPA have justified issuing the permit even absent a TMDL? Reread 40 C.F.R. § 122.4(i) and specifically consider the language regarding waters "for which the State or interstate agency has performed a pollutants load allocation." Does this language mean that EPA or the state must already have completed a TMDL before new discharges can receive permits? At least one court has determined that it does. Friends of the Wild Swan v. EPA, 130 F. Supp. 2d 1199 (D. Mont. 2000) (enjoining issuance of any NPDES permits to new sources until Montana had completed TMDLs for more than 900 streams included on Montana's 303(d) List), *aff'd in relevant part*, 74 Fed. Appx. 718 (9th Cir. 2003). Consider also the requirement that there be "sufficient remaining pollutant load allocations to allow for the [new or increased] discharge." 40 C.F.R. 122.4(i)(1). If states begin listing water bodies due to climate change-related impacts, what type of burden will the development of TMDLs place on state agencies and the EPA? How feasible will it be for agencies to develop TMDLs with remaining pollutant load allocations, when much of the carbon dioxide pollution is coming from other countries, many of which are growing at unexpected rates?

4. In *Friends of Pinto Creek*, the Ninth Circuit rejected EPA's argument that Carlota could avoid the regulatory restrictions for "new discharges" by offsetting its own pollution through pollution reductions at another mine. The Minnesota Supreme Court, however, reached a different conclusion. *See* In the Matter of the Cities of Annandale and Maple Lake NPDES/SDS Permit Issuance for the Discharge of Treated Wastewater, 731 N.W.2d 502 (Minn. 2007) ("*Annandale*"). In *Annandale*, the state issued a permit for a new facility to discharge phosphorus into a water body listed under the Minnesota 303(d) List due to insufficient oxygen. Excess phosphorus in water bodies results in oxygen depletion. The Minnesota Supreme Court upheld the permit by deferring to a state agency's conclusion that the new discharge would not result in a violation of water quality standards because an improvement to a different wastewater treatment facility would remove much more phosphorus than the new facility would add. Why did EPA's similar argument in *Pinto Creek* fail? In the climate change context, which court's approach do you think is a better one, and why?

5.   While the CWA directs states to develop TMDLs for impaired waters, the CWA does not impose rigid deadlines on the development of TMDLs; so long as the state developed its first TMDL by June 26, 1979, the state need only develop other TMDLs "from time to time" thereafter. 33 U.S.C. § 1313(d)(2). This lack of enforceable deadlines has led to a significant backlog in the development of TMDLs. *See* Oliver A. Houck, The Clean Water Act TMDL Program: Law, Policy, and Implementation 51–53 (2d ed. 2002). Do you think the *Friends of Pinto Creek* decision will spur states to develop TMDLs more quickly?

6.   What consequences would result if California grants the Center for Biological Diversity's petition to list all ocean waters in California under the 303(d) List for impairment due to increased acidity? Does this mean that no new facilities could be built on the California coast until California develops a TMDL and establishes schedules of compliance for all discharges of acidic water? Is that a fair burden for the state to bear? Could California reject the Center's petition based on such concerns?

7.   Many states have antidegradation policies that prohibit both new and *increased* discharges of pollutants into 303(d)-listed waters until the states have developed TMDLs for those streams. *See* Hells Canyon Preservation Council v. Haines, 2006 U.S. Dist LEXIS 54884 (D. Or. Aug. 4, 2006) (finding that the United States Forest Service violated Oregon's antidegradation rules by authorizing new and increased discharges into a water quality-limited stream). The court in *Friends of the Wild Swan* similarly prohibited the issuance of NPDES permits to both new and increased discharges until Montana had completed the required TMDLs. 74 Fed. Appx. 718, 723–24 (9th Cir. 2003).

---

b.   ***Implications for All Sources: Compliance with TMDLs***

PRONSOLINO v. NASTRI
291 F.3d 1123 (9th Cir. 2002)

Berzon, Circuit Judge. * * *

II. FACTUAL AND PROCEDURAL BACKGROUND

A. The Garcia River TMDL

In 1992, California submitted to the EPA a list of waters pursuant to § 303(d)(1)(A). Pursuant to § 303(d)(2), the EPA disapproved California's 1992 list because it omitted seventeen water segments that did not meet the water quality standards set by California for those segments. Sixteen of the seventeen water segments, including the Garcia River, were impaired only by nonpoint sources of pollution. After California rejected an opportunity to amend its § 303(d)(1) list to include the seventeen sub-standard segments, the EPA, again acting pursuant to § 303(d)(2), established a new § 303(d)(1) list for California, including those segments on it. California retained the seventeen segments on its 1994, 1996, and 1998 § 303(d)(1) lists.

California did not, however, establish TMDLs for the segments added by the EPA. Environmental and fishermen's groups sued the EPA in 1995 to require the EPA to establish TMDLs for the seventeen segments, and in a March 1997 consent decree the EPA agreed to do so. According to the terms of the consent decree, the EPA set March 18, 1998, as the deadline for the establishment of a TMDL for the Garcia River. When California missed the deadline despite having initiated public comment on a draft TMDL and having prepared a draft implementation plan, the EPA established a TMDL for the Garcia River. The EPA's TMDL differed only slightly from the state's draft TMDL.

The Garcia River TMDL for sediment is 552 tons per square mile per year, a sixty percent reduction from historical loadings. The TMDL allocates portions of the total yearly load among the following categories of nonpoint source pollution: a) "mass wasting" associated with roads; b) "mass wasting" associated with timber-harvesting; c) erosion related to road surfaces; and d) erosion related to road and skid trail crossings.

B. The Appellants

In 1960, appellants Betty and Guido Pronsolino purchased approximately 800 acres of heavily logged timber land in the Garcia River watershed. In 1998, after re-growth of the forest, the Pronsolinos applied for a harvesting permit from the California Department of Forestry ("Forestry").

In order to comply with the Garcia River TMDL, Forestry and/or the state's Regional Water Quality Control Board required, among other things, that the Pronsolinos' harvesting permit provide for mitigation of 90% of controllable road-related sediment run-off and contain prohibitions on removing certain trees and on harvesting from mid-October until May 1. The Pronsolinos' forester estimates that the large tree restriction will cost the Pronsolinos $750,000.

Larry Mailliard, a member of the Mendocino County Farm Bureau, submitted a draft harvesting permit on February 4, 1998, for a portion of his property in the Garcia River watershed. Forestry granted a final version of the permit after incorporation of a 60.3% reduction of sediment loading, a requirement included to comply with the Garcia River TMDL. Mr. Mailliard's forester estimates that the additional restrictions imposed to comply with the Garcia River TMDL will cost Mr. Mailliard $10,602,000.

* * *

III. ANALYSIS

B. Plain Meaning and Structural Issues

1. *The Competing Interpretations*

Section 303(d)(1)(A) requires listing and calculation of TMDLs for "those waters within [the state's] boundaries for which the effluent limitations required by section

[301(b)(1)(A)] and section [301(b)(1)(B)] of this title *are not stringent enough to implement any water quality standard* applicable to such waters." § 303(d) (emphasis added). The precise statutory question before us is whether, as the Pronsolinos maintain, the term "not stringent enough to implement . . . water quality standard[s]" as used in § 303(d)(1)(A) must be interpreted to mean *both* that application of effluent limitations will not achieve water quality standards *and* that the waters at issue are subject to effluent limitations. As only waters with point source pollution are subject to effluent limitations, such an interpretation would exclude from the § 303(d)(1) listing and TMDL requirements waters impaired only by nonpoint sources of pollution.

The EPA, as noted, interprets "not stringent enough to implement . . . water quality standard[s]" to mean "not adequate" or "not sufficient . . . to implement any water quality standard," and does not read the statute as implicitly containing a limitation to waters initially covered by effluent limitations. According to the EPA, if the use of effluent limitations will not implement applicable water quality standards, the water falls within § 303(d)(1)(A) regardless of whether it is point or nonpoint sources, or a combination of the two, that continue to pollute the water.

2. *The Language and Structure of § 303(d)*

Whether or not the appellants' suggested interpretation is entirely implausible, it is at least considerably weaker than the EPA's competing construction. The Pronsolinos' version necessarily relies upon: (1) understanding "stringent enough" to mean "strict enough" rather than "thorough going enough" or "adequate" or "sufficient"; and (2) reading the phrase "not stringent enough" in isolation, rather than with reference to the stated goal of implementing "any water quality standard applicable to such waters." Where the answer to the question "not stringent enough for what?" is "to implement any [applicable] water quality standard," the meaning of "stringent" should be determined by looking forward to the broad goal to be attained, not backwards at the inadequate effluent limitations. One might comment, for example, about a teacher that her standards requiring good spelling were not stringent enough to assure good writing, as her students still used bad grammar and poor logic. Based on the language of the contested phrase alone, then, the more sensible conclusion is that the § 303(d)(1) list must contain any waters for which the particular effluent limitations will not be adequate to attain the statute's water quality goals.

Placing the phrase in its statutory context supports this conclusion. Section 303(d) begins with the requirement that each state "identify those waters within its boundaries. . . . " § 303(d)(1)(A). So the statute's starting point for the listing project is a compilation of each and every navigable water within the state. Then, only those waters that will attain water quality standards after application of the new point source technology are excluded from the § 303(d)(1) list, leaving all those waters for which that technology will not "implement any water quality standard applicable to such waters." § 303(d)(1)(A); *see American Wildlands v. Browner*, 260 F.3d 1192, 1194 (10th Cir.2001) ("[E]ach state is required to identify all of the waters within its borders not meeting water quality standards and establish [TMDLs] for those waters."). The alternative construction, in contrast, would begin with a subset of all the state's waterways, those that have point sources subject to effluent limitations, and would result in a list containing only a subset of that subset — those waters as to which the applicable effluent limitations are not adequate to attain water quality standards.

The Pronsolinos' contention to the contrary notwithstanding, no such odd reading of the statute is necessary in order to give meaning to the phrase "for which the effluent limitations required by section [301(b)(1)(A)] and section

[301(b)(1)(B)] . . . are not stringent enough." The EPA interprets § 303(d)(1)(A) to require the identification of any waters not meeting water quality standards only if specified effluent limitations would not achieve those standards. 40 C.F.R. § 130.2(j). If the pertinent effluent limitations would, if implemented, achieve the water quality standards but are not in place yet, there need be no listing and no TMDL calculation. *Id.*

So construed, the meaning of the statute is different than it would be were the language recast to state only that "Each State shall identify those waters within its boundaries . . . [not meeting] any water quality standard applicable to such waters." Under the EPA's construction, the reference to effluent limitations reflects Congress' intent that the EPA focus initially on implementing effluent limitations and only later avert its attention to water quality standards. * * *

Nothing in § 303(d)(1)(A) distinguishes the treatment of point sources and nonpoint sources as such; the only reference is to the "effluent limitations required by" § 301(b)(1). So if the effluent limitations required by § 301(b)(1) are "as a matter of law" "not stringent enough" to achieve the applicable water quality standards for waters impaired by point sources not subject to those requirements, then they are also "not stringent enough" to achieve applicable water quality standards for other waters not subject to those requirements, in this instance because they are impacted only by nonpoint sources. * * *

3. *The Statutory Scheme as a Whole*

The Pronsolinos' objection to this view of § 303(d), . . . is, in essence, that the CWA as a whole distinguishes between the regulatory schemes applicable to point and non-point sources, so we must assume such a distinction in applying §§ 303(d)(1)(A) and (C). We would hesitate in any case to read into a discrete statutory provision something that is not there because it is contained elsewhere in the statute. But here, the premise is wrong: There is no such general division throughout the CWA.

Point sources are treated differently from nonpoint sources for many purposes under the statute, but not all. In particular, there is no such distinction with regard to the basic purpose for which the § 303(d) list and TMDLs are compiled, the eventual attainment of state-defined water quality standards. Water quality standards reflect a state's designated *uses* for a water body and do not depend in any way upon the source of pollution. *See* § 303(a)–(c).

Nor is there any other basis for inferring from the structure of the Act an implicit limitation in §§ 303(d)(1)(A) and (C). The statutory subsection requiring water quality segment identification and TMDLs, § 303(d), appears in the section entitled "Water Quality Standards and Implementation Plans," not in the immediately preceding section, CWA § 302, 33 U.S.C. § 1312, entitled "Water Quality Related Effluent Limitations."

Additionally, § 303(d) follows the subsections setting forth the requirements for water quality standards, § 303(a)–(c) — which, as noted above, apply without regard to the source of pollution — and precedes the "continuing planning process" subsection, § 303(e), which applies broadly as well. Thus, § 303(d) is structurally part of a set of provisions governing an interrelated goal-setting, information-gathering, and planning process that, unlike many other aspects of the CWA, applies without regard to the source of pollution.

True, there are, as the Pronsolinos point out, two sections of the statute as amended, § 208 and § 319, that set requirements exclusively for nonpoint sources of pollution. But the structural inference we are asked to draw from those specialized sections — that no *other* provisions of the Act set requirements for waters polluted by nonpoint sources — simply does not follow. Absent some irreconcilable contradiction between the requirements contained in §§ 208 and 319, on the one hand, and the listing and TMDL requirements of § 303(d), on the other, both apply.

There is no such contradiction. * * * As various sections of the Act encourage different, and complementary, state schemes for cleaning up nonpoint source pollution in the nation's waterways, there is no basis for reading any of those sections — including § 303(d) — out of the statute.

There is one final aspect of the Act's structure that bears consideration because it supports the EPA's interpretation of § 303(d): The list required by § 303(d)(1)(A) requires that waters be listed if they are impaired by a combination of point sources and nonpoint sources; the language admits of no other reading. Section 303(d)(1)(C), in turn, directs that TMDLs "shall be established at a level necessary *to implement* the applicable water quality standards. . . . " *Id.* (emphasis added). So, at least in blended waters, TMDLs must be calculated with regard to nonpoint sources of pollution; otherwise, it would be impossible "to implement the applicable water quality standards," which do not differentiate sources of pollution.

QUESTIONS AND DISCUSSION

1. In *Pronsolino*, the Ninth Circuit upheld the application of restrictions upon nonpoint sources necessary to comply with a TMDL established for sedimentation. What implications could this decision have on nonpoint source activities that contribute to warmer surface waters? Logging, agriculture, and grazing, for example, all result in stream alterations and a loss of stream shading, which, in turn, cause streams and rivers to become hotter. As climate change further exacerbates problems associated with warm water temperatures, could loggers, ranchers, and farmers all face the onerous prospect of Clean Water Act compliance?

2. The EPA has appeared to back away from some of the positions it took in the *Pronsolino* case. For example, in *American Wildlands v. Browner*, 260 F.3d 1192 (10th Cir. 2001), EPA argued that Montana could choose to adopt a rule exempting nonpoint sources from compliance with water quality standards. More recently, EPA has taken the position that state water quality rules related to nonpoint sources are, categorically, not water quality standards and thus not subject to EPA review and approval. Yet, EPA continues to insist that nonpoint sources remain subject to requirements developed through TMDLs. Are EPA's positions consistent with each other? Are they consistent with the Clean Water Act?

3. As discussed in other parts of this book, land management activities (including forestry, agriculture, and grazing) are both significant sources of greenhouse gas emissions and potentially significant sinks as well. Can regulation under the Clean Water Act provide a mechanism to enhance their functions as sinks? Even if it can, should these types of activities be subject to onerous regulation to offset emissions generated by all of us?

Chapter 14

UNITED STATES LAW AND POLICY: ENERGY

Question: Does . . . President [Bush] believe that, given the amount of energy Americans consume per capita, how much it exceeds any other citizen in any other country in the world, does the President believe we need to correct our lifestyles to address the energy problem?

Answer: That's a big no. The President believes that it's an American way of life, and that it should be the goal of policy makers to protect the American way of life. The American way of life is a blessed one. And we have a bounty of resources in this country. What we need to do is make certain that we're able to get those resources in an efficient way, in a way that also emphasizes protecting the environment and conservation, into the hands of consumers so they can make the choices that they want to make as they live their lives day to day.

Ari Fleischer, White House Press Briefing (May 7, 2001)

SYNOPSIS

V. Energy Efficiency and Conservation

I. INTRODUCTION

What is the energy policy of the United States? The answer to that question is so amorphous that law scholars have devoted entire law review articles to demonstrating that the United States in fact has a national energy policy. *See, e.g.,* Joseph P. Tomain, *The Dominant Model of United States Energy Policy*, 61 U. Colo. L. Rev. 355 (1990). Even then, the most that can be said is that the country has a "dominant model" of energy policy, but no one has argued — or, indeed, could argue — that the United States has a single, purposeful energy law governing generation, transmission, and distribution of energy. To the contrary, U.S. energy law, to the extent such a thing exists, consists of dozens of separate statutes and regulations administered by state, federal, and even local agencies, many of which appear to be working toward different purposes. Added to these substantive laws are subsidies, tax credits, and other financial incentives promoting coal, petroleum and natural gas, as well as wind, solar, and other renewable energy sources. Indeed, energy bills have become so laden with subsidies and tax breaks that Senator John McCain famously dubbed one the "No Lobbyist Left Behind" bill. For years now, analysts on the political left, right, and center have called for federal lawmakers to make sense of the existing disparate energy provisions sprinkled throughout the federal statutes by developing a coherent and consistent federal energy policy. Election-year politics contributed a chorus of promises for a new approach to energy policy, in response to escalating energy prices and concern about climate change. Yet, whether the United States will adopt a cohesive, sustainable energy policy remains far from certain.

Since Thomas Edison first established the Pearl Street power station in 1882, supplying electricity to lower Manhattan, the overarching goal of U.S. energy policies has been to provide cheap, abundant, and reliable energy throughout the country. The approaches to achieving these goals have varied over time, from direct federal regulation of energy production, to efforts to deregulate, to what Professor Joseph Tomain refers to as the "dominant model," which mixes regulation with market-based approaches aimed at promoting energy production and use over energy efficiency and conservation. *See* Tomain, *The Dominant Model of United States Energy Policy*, 61 U. Colo. L. Rev. at 355. This dominant model favors traditional fossil-fueled energy sources, particularly coal, oil, and natural gas, which are abundant and can provide large amounts of electricity to be distributed along the nation's electricity transmissions lines. *Id.* at 375. The dominant model also has favored energy production by large-scale, capital-intensive and centralized facilities, rather than smaller, diverse firms more likely to supply energy from alternative and renewable sources. *Id.* Finally, the dominant model of energy regulation aims to provide energy to consumers at reasonable prices established by state or, on occasion, federal regulators. *Id.* These lower costs have typically promoted energy consumption and stifled the market for higher-priced alternative energies.

The results of the dominant model can be seen in the country's energy production and consumption patterns. In 2007, more than 86 percent of the energy used in the United States came from fossil fuel sources, and overall energy consumption in the United States has increased dramatically since the 1970s. Excluding transportation-related energy use (which is covered in Chapter 15), the greatest increase in electricity consumption has occurred in the residential and building sectors, as Americans have built larger homes and offices with more appliances, electronics, and expansive heating and air conditioning systems. Perhaps lured into believing that energy would always be cheap and abundant, many new homeowners have been caught off-guard by escalating prices. The response on the national level has been to call for more energy production, rather than conservation. Even when gas prices spiked above $4 a gallon in 2008, politicians called for gas tax holidays, tax credits, and other schemes to maintain consumption levels while providing little economic relief to consumers.

However, while high energy prices lead to calls for more energy production, concerns about climate change have prompted proposals for the United States to change its model of energy production. Former Vice President Al Gore recently challenged the United States to supply all of its energy from renewable resources within the next decade (*See* Chapter 19 for an excerpt of the speech). Less ambitious proposals aim for the U.S. to obtain at least 15 percent of its energy from renewable resources within the same period. As the public waits for federal lawmakers to develop an energy plan that addresses climate change while responding to public demands for lower energy prices, states, local governments, and some private companies are taking things into their own hands. Several states now require a certain percentage of energy to come from renewable sources; other states have enacted aggressive energy conservation measures; and companies have increased their own investment in renewable energy production facilities and energy efficiency programs. The overarching question is whether these sub-federal actions will spur a broader reform of U.S. energy policy.

This chapter explores U.S. energy policy and how it may change as a result of climate change. It focuses in particular on the electricity sector, which is one of the largest sectors of greenhouse gas (GHG) emissions in the country. Section II first discusses how traditional electricity regulation has favored fossil fuel-based energy production and how concerns about climate change may lessen the dominance of coal and other fossil fuels in the future. Section III then reviews existing proposals to alter energy production, which range from increased reliance on "clean coal" and nuclear energy to a complete shift away from traditional fuels toward renewable energy sources, such as wind and power. Section IV explores proposals to restructure electricity regulation to better accommodate renewable energy sources. Section V discusses the role that energy conservation and efficiency may play in reducing GHG emissions from the electricity sector.

II.   TRADITIONAL ELECTRICITY REGULATION AND FOSSIL FUELS

The electricity sector is the single largest source of carbon dioxide emissions in the United States, contributing more than 40 percent of all CO_2 emissions. Although taxes, subsidies, and other incentives contribute to the sector's large carbon footprint, the regulatory program governing electricity likely plays an even larger role. Since the early 20th Century, electric utilities and their regulators have favored fossil fuels as the dominant energy source for electricity in the United States. While some regulators have signaled their doubts about continued reliance on fossil fuels for future electricity needs, the historical background of electricity regulation is key to understanding how the electricity sector became such a large emitter of greenhouse gases.

This section explores how the laws governing electricity production and delivery incentivized fossil fuel use. It begins with a brief introduction of the major components of electricity systems and a basic overview of traditional electricity regulation in the United States and the roles of states and the federal government in this regulatory scheme. Part B of this section takes a closer look at how traditional electricity regulation has incentivized fossil fuel-based electricity production. Part C then explores recent decisions in which electricity regulators have questioned the electricity sector's continued reliance on fossil fuels, and especially coal, as carbon regulation makes it likely that coal-based electricity costs will rise in the future.

A.   An Introduction to the U.S. Electricity System

To understand electricity regulation, it is helpful to become familiar with some key components of the electricity system. In addition, students should understand the basic framework of electricity regulation and the respective roles of states and the federal government.

1.   *The Electricity System*

Electricity production and delivery includes three main components: generation, transmission, and distribution.

- **Generation** refers to the actual production of electricity, from sources such as coal-fired power plants, nuclear plants, natural gas plants, hydropower facilities, wind farms, and solar panels. Although electricity generation facilities vary in types and sizes, they are often divided according to whether they provide baseload power or peak power. Baseload plants are those which can provide adequate and reliable electricity during normal consumption periods (i.e., non-peak). Facilities that use coal, hydropower, or nuclear materials as their energy sources typically serve as baseload plants, because they run all hours of the day to serve baseload energy needs. So long as the energy source remains available and energy needs remain consistent, baseload plants will operate continuously. When electricity needs peak during a day or season, peak power plants frequently come on line to provide supplemental electricity. Peak power plants are often smaller than baseload plants, and they may use different types of fuels as their power source. Peak power plants must start up and shut down relatively quickly and easily to respond to peaking energy needs. They often use natural gas and oil as their main fuel sources, and they may operate similarly to a diesel generator (indeed, diesel generators are sometimes used as peak power sources).

- Electricity **transmission** refers to the long-distance conveyance of electricity over high-voltage power lines. Power companies will typically take power from generation facilities, use transformers to increase the voltage over the transmission lines, and then use other transformers to decrease the voltage to distribute lower voltages power to end-users.

- **Distribution** refers to the delivery of electricity to end-users, including industries, commercial buildings, residences, and any other consumer of electricity.

2. *Regulation of Electricity in the United States*

Electricity regulation is a complex and evolving area of law. Although this book will not attempt to provide a detailed description of electricity regulation, the following overview may help students obtain a basic overview of electricity regulation.

---

a. *The Traditional Electricity Regulatory Model*

As discussed in greater detail below, electricity production and delivery has long been viewed as a natural monopoly, in which economies of scale prevent competitors from entering an established market. Under a typical monopolistic scheme, a monopoly will initially lower its prices to drive out competitors. Once all competitors have exited the market, the monopoly will have unlimited power to increase prices and lower production to maximize its profit. To prevent this type of conduct, regulators have two possible responses. Most commonly, regulators will "break up" the monopoly and restrict the monopoly's behavior to promote competition. However, in some circumstances, regulators will determine that a particular industry will never be competitive and that monopolies within that industry are inevitable. Where regulators determine such natural monopolies exist, they will increase regulation over the monopoly's behavior and its prices.

For many years, regulators viewed the electricity system as a natural monopoly. The high costs associated with construction of power plants and transmission and distribution lines made it economically infeasible for competitors to enter a market where infrastructure already existed. Moreover, additional power lines were considered unnecessary; once one system had been installed, there was simply no need for additional, redundant power lines. Therefore, regulators considered it highly unlikely that competition in the electricity sector would ever develop.

To prevent abuses from the monopolistic electricity utilities, state Public Utility Commissions (PUCs) regulate many components of an electric company's operations. In particular, utilities must receive PUC approval before making capital investments (such as building new power plants) and must receive PUC approval over all rates the utilities seek to pass onto their customers. The overarching goal for PUCs is to ensure utilities provide cheap, abundant, and reliable electricity.

PUCs set rates for utilities based on a formula that allows utilities to recover their operating expenses — which include expenditures for labor costs, fuel costs, administrative costs, and the like — and to earn a profit (called a rate of return) on their capital expenditures — which include expenses associated with building new power plants, transmission lines, and other facilities. This ratemaking formula therefore rewards utilities for constructing new power plants. Indeed, utilities earn a profit only if they make capital expenditures. Moreover, utilities must demonstrate their capital expenditures will provide cheap and reliable electricity. As noted above, reliable electricity traditionally has come from coal, nuclear energy, and hydropower. Of these, coal has typically been viewed as a cheap energy source (although hydropower is a much cheaper source in some parts of the country). Thus, for many PUCs, coal plants provided the best source of electricity in the United States. Since utilities can earn a profit only by constructing new facilities that will receive PUC approval, traditional rate regulation has incentivized coal plant construction in most of the country.

---

b.   *Electricity Restructuring and Alternatives to the Traditional Model*

Although many regulators continue to treat the entire electricity system as a natural monopoly, it is likely more accurate to distinguish between the generation, transmission, and distribution components of the electricity system when regulating utilities. Electricity generation has proven to be a competitive industry in some areas, as demonstrated by the increased number of power plants owned by independent companies that sell their power to utilities. Electricity distribution may also provide room for competition; instead of having a single power company that "sells" electricity to consumers within a geographical area, it may be possible for electricity distributors to compete with each other for customers, much like phone companies compete for customers in a deregulated system. Because it is likely true that electricity generation is already competitive and that distribution may become competitive, many scholars have called for a restructuring of the electricity system.

Under a restructured system, energy consumers would pick their own power generators and perhaps their power distributors, while regulators would continue to oversee the monopoly controlling electricity transmission. In the late 1990s and early 2000s, several states experimented with electricity restructuring that would force utilities to surrender their monopolistic control over generation and to instead buy electricity on the open market. A few states also attempted to infuse competition at the distribution end. While these initial programs met with varying degrees of success, electricity restructuring has yet to take hold. Indeed, in response to California's well publicized fiasco with electricity restructuring, in which Enron's manipulations of the California power market resulted in sky-high prices, rolling blackouts, and bankruptcies, many states withdrew plans to increase electricity competition. It remains to be seen whether utilities will reconsider electricity restructuring in the future, and whether such restructuring could increase the viability of renewable energy sources.

Many states have developed alternatives to traditional utility regulation that take into account factors beyond whether electricity will be cheap, abundant, and reliable. For example, some states have required utilities to engage in integrated resource planning, through which utilities evaluate long-term options and costs for meeting their customers' energy needs. Some PUCs require utilities to include the environmental costs of energy into their integrated resource plans. PUCs may also require utilities to include energy efficiency and efforts to reduce energy demand in their long-range planning. Utilities will receive approval for new fossil fuel plants only if they can show that such plants are the least-cost option when compared to other energy sources, energy efficiency, and demand reduction. Thus, even in a state that has not restructured its electricity system to increase competition, states have altered traditional utility regulation to consider more than just cost, abundance, and reliability.

c.   *The Role of States and the Federal Government*

As you may have noted, most of the above discussion focuses on state regulation. This is because states have authority to regulate electricity systems that involve production, transmission, and distribution of "retail" power. Retail electricity sales are sales from the electricity producer directly to the end user. In a traditional monopolistic system, one utility will generate electricity, transmit that electricity along its own transmission lines, and sell that electricity directly to customers who then use that power. These retail transactions remain subject to state control.

However, the federal government plays an important — and expanding — role in electricity regulation. The Federal Power Act (FPA) gives the Federal Energy Regulatory Commission (FERC) authority over the "sale of electric energy at wholesale in interstate commerce" and over "the transmission of electric energy in interstate commerce." FPA § 201(b)(1), 16 U.S.C. § 824(b)(1). Wholesale electricity sales involve sales of electricity to any entity that intends to then sell the electricity at resale. FPA § 201(d), 16 U.S.C. § 824(d). So, for example, if a wind power company sells electricity to a utility, and that utility then sells that electricity to you for use in your home, the wind company's sale to the utility is a wholesale electricity sale. FERC has power over the rates charged by the wind company to the utility. FERC would also have control over the transmission of the electricity, because the FPA controls transmission in interstate commerce.

FERC has adopted, and the Supreme Court has approved, a very expansive definition of "interstate commerce" under the FPA. Federal Power Comm'n v. Florida Power & Light Co., 404 U.S. 453 (1972). In effect, so long as a state is connected to an interstate transmission grid, its electricity transactions are considered to be in interstate commerce, because the "elusive nature of electrons" makes it nearly impossible for a utility to demonstrate that its electricity did not actually move out of state. *Id.* Thus, even if Florida company A sells power to Florida company B to be used by a consumer in Florida, the wholesale sale of power from A to B will be in interstate commerce because Florida is connected to an interstate grid. *See id.* Under FERC's expansive definition of interstate commerce, *all* transmissions outside of Alaska, Hawaii, and Texas (*see* note 2 below) could be subject to FERC control. Thus far, FERC has asserted authority only over transmission of wholesale electricity. *See* New York v. Federal Energy Regulatory Comm'n., 535 U.S. 1 (2002). However, the Supreme Court has recognized that FERC could preempt states' traditional regulation of electricity transmission. *Id.*

FERC and various states have engaged in numerous jurisdictional battles regarding FERC's authority to order utilities to transmit electricity from independent power producers (i.e., non-utilities) to end users, FERC's authority to regulate wholesale electricity rates, and Congress' authority to direct utilities to purchase power from certain renewable energy generators. Time and again, the Supreme Court has upheld the federal government's assertion of power over certain aspects of electricity regulation. Many observers believe the federal government must play a much larger role in electricity regulation for renewable energy sources to become viable. For example, if the United States chooses to promote wind energy development in North Dakota, FERC may need to intervene to ensure wind power producers have adequate access to transmission lines to carry power to New York or Seattle. FERC's intervention will likely spur considerable backlash from states intent upon retaining their control over regulated utilities. This issue, and many others, will require resolution for the U.S. electricity sector to move towards carbon neutrality.

QUESTIONS AND DISCUSSION

1. Do you think electricity production and delivery should be regulated as a natural monopoly, or should government regulators break up electric utility monopolies, much like they deregulated the railroads and telephone companies? What benefits might monopoly regulation provide if the U.S. attempts to lower the carbon footprint of the electricity sector? What climate change benefits could result from a more competitive electricity market? You may want to return to these questions after you read the rest of the chapter.

2. *Interstate Commerce Under the FPA.* FERC's definition of interstate commerce subjects any utility connected to the interstate grid to FERC regulation unless the utility can demonstrate that its electrons do not cross state lines. This test is impossible to meet, and, as a result, all utilities connected to an interstate grid could be subject to some type of FERC regulation over their wholesale transactions or power transmissions. There are 3 interstate transmission systems (or grids) in the United States: the Eastern Interconnect, the Western Interconnect, and the Texas Interconnect. Only three states—Alaska, Hawaii, and parts of Texas—are not connected to an interstate grid. While Alaska and Hawaii's separation results from geographic isolation, Texas has intentionally kept itself free of the interstate grid to shield itself from FERC interference. What benefits do you think Texas may derive from retaining exclusive control over its transmission lines?

3. *Wholesale Power Sales, Distributed Generation, and FERC Control.* Many renewable energy advocates believe that states should promote distributed generation from small-scale renewable energy sources. As the name suggests, distributed generation refers to power generation from numerous sources, rather than from a single baseload plant. For example, distributed generation could include solar photovoltaic cells installed on residential roofs. Renewable energy advocates hope to increase distributed generation production through enactment of net metering laws, which would require utilities to pay residential customers for any power sent back to the grid from the residential solar panels. If utilities do end up buying electricity through renewable generation, are they now buying wholesale electricity (since the power produced through the solar arrays would be sold to other utility customers)? If so, should FERC have control over these distributed generation power sales? If you worked for a state PUC, would you oppose distributed generation and net metering laws to avoid FERC regulation?

4. *FERC v. California.* When California restructured its electricity system in the late 1990s, it ordered its utilities to "functionally unbundle" all of their transmission operations from their power generation operations. Functionally unbundled power generation is considered a type of wholesale generation subject to FERC control. Thus, California's restructuring decision gave FERC control over all generation in the state.

California's restructuring experience turned into a crisis due to reduced power production, a long drought, extremely hot summer temperatures (which increased energy needs), market manipulation by Enron and other companies, and structural flaws in California's program that are too complicated to explore in this Chapter. As the crisis elevated, it became clear to California that energy companies like Enron were manipulating the system to drive electricity prices up. However, because California had restructured its system, it had no authority over wholesale electricity prices and was therefore unable to compel Enron to cease its activity or reduce the electricity costs. When California asked FERC to intervene to prevent Enron's behavior, FERC repeatedly refused. FERC intervened only after the crisis had subsided and California had lost billions of dollars. Although California's experience was unique, does this help you understand why states may work to retain jurisdiction over utilities, even if they are not true "natural monopolies"?

B.   Utility Regulation and Fossil Fuel Use

A major factor contributing to the dominance of fossil fuels is electricity regulation. As the following excerpt describes, regulation of electric utilities has created a system promoting capital investment in large power-generating facilities. Although this system is slowly changing, the "dominant model" of regulation continues to favor fossil fuel power sources.

JOSEPH P. TOMAIN, THE PAST AND FUTURE OF ELECTRICITY REGULATION
32 ENVTL. L. 435, 443–68 (2002)[*]

III. Electricity Transmission and Natural Monopoly

The electricity industry provides an excellent case study of government regulation. Like other network industries such as natural gas, telephone, and railroad, the regulation of electricity was based on the central political economic idea that the industry had natural monopoly characteristics and that electricity served the public interest. As a fundamental matter of political economy, markets and the property exchanged and valued in them exist only because of government protection. Still, it is the degree of protection that distinguishes government treatment of some industries from the treatment of others. It is also the case that the degree of government intervention changes over time.

In its beginning at the end of the nineteenth century, electricity was an unregulated competitive industry. The industry, for the most part, consisted of investor owned utilities (IOUs) that owned and operated generation, transmission, and distribution. Later, as the industry consolidated, government regulation was justified as a way to stem the abuses of market power exercised by these vertically integrated utilities. The particular market imperfection in the electric industry was natural monopoly and government responded with command-and-control regulations setting the prices that could be charged by utilities and limiting the profits that utilities could earn. Price and profit controls are a form of heavy-handed economic regulation that comes with costs of its own. Starting in the mid-1960s, traditional utility regulation appeared to have run its course as market distortions arose and as policymakers began to look at regulatory reform and deregulation. * * *

B. The Growth and Regulation of the Electricity Industry

As noted, natural monopoly has been the justification for electricity regulation. A simple definition of natural monopoly is that product costs for some time "will be lower if they consist in a single supplier." While more technical definitions exist, the central idea is that one firm can realize economies of scale throughout a range of production, thus continually lowering cost. * * * Politically, it was socially desirable to distribute electricity as a public good. Thus, the economic definition of, and the public policy arguments for, natural monopoly coalesced into a political justification for the regulation of public utilities, including electricity.

Natural monopoly theory puts policy makers in something of a bind. On the one hand, the utility's product is seen as desirable and is most cheaply delivered by one provider. On the other hand, a lone provider is a monopolist. Because state ownership was not likely, the regulatory solution, ironically, was a state controlled monopoly — the regulatory compact — as described in the following quotation from Judge Kenneth Starr:

> The utility business represents a compact of sorts; a monopoly on service in a particular geographical area (coupled with state-conferred rights of eminent domain or condemnation) is granted to the utility in exchange for a regime of intensive regulation, including price regulation, quite alien to the free market. . . . Each party to the compact gets something in the bargain. As a general rule, utility investors are provided a level of stability in earnings and value less likely to be attained in the unregulated or moderately regulated sector; in turn, ratepayers are afforded universal, non-discriminatory service and protection from monopolistic profits through political control over an economic enterprise.

Monopoly regulation was able to preserve scale economies while avoiding competitors' economically wasteful investments for a period of time. The regulatory compact imposes significant obligations on both the government and on the regulated firm. In exchange for a government-protected monopoly, the utility lets government set its prices through ratemaking. The utility is given the power of eminent domain to lower its transaction costs in constructing its network; is given an exclusive franchise or service area thus preventing competition; and is, therefore, the only firm authorized to sell its product in that area under an obligation to serve. The government, through ratemaking, sets the price of its service at rates that allow a prudently managed utility to cover its operating expenses and earn a reasonable return on its capital investment, thus yielding a profit. The regulatory control of natural monopoly, then, occurs by 1) limiting entry, 2) setting prices, 3) controlling profits, and 4) imposing a service obligation.

The traditional formula accomplished its public interest purpose by enabling the capital expansion of the industry and the construction of the country's utility infrastructure. The formula also kept rates reasonable for most of the last century. However, with the traditional formula, a utility had no economic incentive to reduce expenses and had an economic incentive to make capital investments because the more a firm invested, the more it earned for its shareholders.

1. Economic and Political Justifications

Starting roughly in 1965, the industry reached technological and financial plateaus at which industry expansion slowed considerably; economies of scale were not being realized, costs were increasing, generation was overbuilt, and alternative providers were coming into the market. Economic indicators were such that utilities could no longer rely on the annual seven percent growth rate they had enjoyed since the end of World War II. The traditional rate formula which encouraged capital expansion put utilities in the position of continuing to dump money into the rate base, thus increasing costs. Inflation and other economic indicators caused marginal costs to exceed average costs as utilities ran into trouble with cost overruns, plant cancellations, and the like. In short, competition was peeking from behind regulatory blankets.

Politically, things also changed dramatically in the mid-1960s. Production costs began to increase and rates began to rise for a number of reasons. General economic inflation, increased concern about the environment and an attendant increase in regulatory costs, Vietnam War expenditures, an unstable world economy, the 1965 Northeast blackout, and the failure of nuclear power all contributed to unsettling the electric industry and its customers. The Organization of Petroleum Exporting Countries (OPEC) added to this state of affairs by flexing its cartel muscles and closing the oil spigot, which pushed inflation to double digits, and increased energy prices generally. Also, the price elasticity of demand for electricity was more elastic than anticipated, and consumers both reduced their electricity consumption and sought energy from alternative sources, further reducing their dependence on traditional utilities. . . . All of these events made the formerly staid public utility commissions politically charged agencies, as critics attacked the basis of traditional rate regulation from both sides. Producers wanted rates to be more market sensitive and ratepayers wanted to avoid rate shock.

2. PURPA's Surprise: Increased Competition

The combined effects of the political and economic events in the late 1960s and early 1970s raised public concern about the country's energy future and raised particular concern in the Carter White House, which viewed the Energy Crisis as the "moral equivalent of war." Jimmy Carter addressed the Energy Crisis through two major legislative initiatives. The first was the massive and ambitious National Energy Act, which addressed conventional fuels. The National Energy Act had several purposes, including moving the country away from dependence on foreign oil, promoting the use of coal, increasing energy efficiency, modernizing utility ratemaking, stimulating conservation, encouraging the creation of a new market in electricity, and restructuring a distorted market in natural gas. Carter's second initiative, the Energy Security Act of 1980, addressed conservation and alternative fuels from biomass, wind and solar to tar sands and oil shale. The surprising part of the National Energy Act was the Public Utility Regulatory Policies Act (PURPA), which was aimed at securing reasonably priced energy for the nation through conservation, increasing use of alternative sources, and moving toward market-based rates.

PURPA encouraged states to move away from declining block ratemaking because it promoted consumption, and to move toward marginal cost pricing because it was more efficient; it also encouraged independent power production through cogeneration and small power generation as energy source alternatives to large public utilities. What surprised everyone was how much new nonutility generated electricity was available and how eager independent power producers (IPPs) were to enter the market. The success of PURPA revealed that traditional regulation had run its course. Generating units, with then existing technologies, could not continue to get bigger and commercial nuclear power was not "too cheap to meter." In microeconomic terms, the traditional, regulated electric industry had reached the end of its scale economies. In other words, unregulated producers existed that were willing to supply the market with electricity priced lower than the electricity being supplied by incumbent regulated utilities, and the new entrants profited by doing so with a little help from government. This situation was a free marketer's dream.

Congress passed PURPA in small part to encourage the growth of generation not owned by utility companies as a conservation measure. PURPA required local electric utilities to buy the power produced by two types of nonutility generators (NUGs), which PURPA calls "qualifying small power production facilit[ies]" (QFs) — small electric generators (eighty megawatts or less) and cogenerators. Utilities were required to purchase excess QF power at that utility's "avoided cost," that is, the price the utility would have paid for that power had it generated or bought the power itself. Because QFs could produce electricity more cheaply than the local public utility, they would produce as much as they could under the statute, use as little as they could for their business, and sell as much as they could to the local utility, which was obligated to buy at the higher price.

It is at this point in the regulatory story that transmission became noticeably important and that regulators began to rethink their regulation. While QFs could sell their power to the local utility, they did not have access to the utility's transmission lines to "wheel" their power to any other utility or end user. Consequently, the creation of QFs had two dramatic effects. First, their existence marked the formal introduction of competition into generation. Second, the purchase requirement began to force open the access door. The program was notably successful. From 1989 through 1993, both the number of QFs and installed QF capacity doubled.

PURPA . . . caused a rethinking of regulation at both ends of the fuel cycle. At the generation end, the existence of NUGs indicated that the market was competitive. At the buyers' end, consumers wanted to purchase the cheaper electricity. Unfortunately, a full-scale move to market rates was problematic not only because of the transmission problem, but also because market rates had uneven effects on consumers. All consumers are not similarly situated. Large consumers have more leverage to bargain for discounts because they buy larger quantities of electricity and they can switch fuels more easily. Further, small users are often cross-subsidized and market prices may not be favorable to them.

*   *   *

Energy Policy

The United States's energy economy can be characterized as one-half oil and one-half electricity. The oil and electricity industries share common features. Both are large, capital-intensive industries, and both provide products that consumers treat as indispensable for their daily lives. Small consumers heat their homes with natural gas and drive cars with gasoline. Larger industrial consumers use oil and natural gas fuel stocks in the production process. For small consumers, electricity has perhaps an even more significant impact because they need electricity to turn on the lights, open the refrigerator, or switch on a computer.

As a matter of the regulatory state, the oil industry is largely unregulated at the retail level while electricity is heavily regulated throughout its production, distribution, and end use. Consumers recognize the distinction because as they drive to any gas station they fill their cars up at unregulated prices, whereas their monthly electricity bill has gone through a price-setting process. Why is it that the retail price of gasoline is unregulated and society sees it as an indispensable part of life where electricity is not? There are two explanations. The first is that, while we are in the midst of electricity restructuring, we have not deregulated prices at the retail level, although plans to do so seem appropriate if not in the immediate future. The other is that electricity is a unique product because it cannot be stored — it must always be available.

It may be fair to say that electricity is even more indispensable than gasoline, particularly in today's wired economy. Certainly, electricity's importance has grown. In the past, an electric outage meant that the TV and refrigerator were off. Rarely, however, did food spoil and the second half of the game was yet to be played when the electricity was turned back on. Computers are different entities. Without proper backup, down time can mean significant data losses, not only in our homes, but in banks, work places, and in the national defense system, for example. There is no doubt that the economy will become more wired before it becomes less so, thus maintaining, if not increasing, the significance of electricity.

It is odd then that, as the demand for electricity increases, additions to generation may lag behind or remain level, yet transmission lags further behind both. This situation is understandable because investors find it risky to invest in an uncertain transmission market. Thus the problem: there is no workable competitive market in electricity, and it is the movement from large-scale, heavy-handed government regulation to such a competitive market that is the object of restructuring. The best guess is that the transition will take considerable time . . . .

A. Dominant Energy Policy

For most of the twentieth century, the United States developed and followed a dominant energy policy. That policy is not to be found in any one document nor is it a consciously coordinated whole. Yet the policy consists of large scale, capital intensive energy projects, significantly favoring fossil fuels such as oil, coal, and natural gas. Although there have been attempts throughout the twentieth century to coordinate and develop a comprehensive national energy plan, none has materialized even after the creation of the Department of Energy, which is required to report a comprehensive national energy plan to Congress annually.

QUESTIONS AND DISCUSSION

1.   Why does the dominant model favor large-scale electricity generation by fossil fuels? Although a number of reasons likely exist, at least two appear to have played a significant role in promoting this type of development. First, the historical approach to utility regulation favored investment in large, capital-intensive projects. Historically, public utilities operated vertically integrated systems, in which they controlled electricity generation, transmission over high-voltage power lines, and distribution to retail customers. Retail rates are established by multiplying a rate base by the utility's "fixed costs," which include its capital costs. The higher the capital costs, the higher the overall revenue the utility could collect. Second, in return for receiving a monopoly, utilities were required to provide a constant power source (i.e., reliable power). Fossil fuel plants can produce power under any weather conditions, day or night, so long as the fossil fuels are available, which coal always is. Renewable power sources, in contrast, have historically lacked the reliability of fossil fuels, because they depend on weather conditions and cannot be stored effectively or in large quantities.

2.   *The Transmission Bottleneck.* One issue that has plagued regulators, particularly as new sources of power became available due to deregulation, is the lack of available transmission capacity. When utilities were vertically integrated, they controlled the power entering transmission lines and could thus usually ensure that transmission lines had sufficient capacity to convey the utilities' own electricity. However, deregulation of the generation phase placed new burdens on transmission lines. Utilities initially tried to restrict access to their transmission lines, until Congress ordered the lines open to other sources of power. Since then, utilities have pointed to inadequate transmission lines as a primary cause of power outages. The lack of transmission capacity has also discouraged construction of new renewable energy sources.

C.   Addressing Carbon Dioxide Emissions through Utility Regulation

As regulation of carbon dioxide becomes more likely in the United States, public utility commissions (PUCs), which regulate intra-state electricity transmission and sales, have begun to use their regulatory power to deny utilities permission to construct new coal-fired power plants. In many cases, PUCs are not basing their decisions on the environmental consequences of coal-based electricity, but instead have determined that cost considerations require the PUCs to protect consumers from increased rates that carbon dioxide regulation may create.

1.   *An Overview of PUC Authority*

The following excerpt describes the give-and-take of utility regulation and, in particular, explains the rate-setting process that PUCs employ. While the excerpt specifically discusses the role of the Oregon PUC, the Oregon PUC's authority mirrors that of many other state commissions.

SANDRA L. HIROTSU, REMEMBERING THE BOTTOM LINE: WHY THE OREGON PUBLIC UTILITY COMMISSION'S OBLIGATION TO PROTECT UTILITY RATEPAYERS REQUIRES SAYING NO TO COAL
3–4, 6–8, 9–15 (Unpublished, Apr. 2008)*

In the United States, investor owned utilities (IOUs) generate seventy-five percent of all electricity. Their decisions to build new coal-fired power plants have significant adverse environmental impacts. Despite the environmental consequences, Americans' dependence on low-cost electricity has led to a regulatory dynamic favoring coal over less carbon-intensive fuels. As privately-owned businesses, IOUs strive to maximize profit for their investors, but as public utilities, IOUs are limited to charging customers "fair and reasonable" rates." State regulators generally allow IOUs to pass to their customers any costs reasonably necessary to build, buy, and operate coal plants. State regulators also allow IOU investors the opportunity to earn a return on their investment. Coal's low cost thus enables IOUs to fulfill their obligation to provide power at reasonable rates while still returning a profit for their investors.

As the regulatory bodies overseeing IOUs' resource planning and retail rates, state public utility commissions have historically approved plans to build coal-fired power plants. Where commissions have an obligation to protect consumers and the public from economic harm, coal's low price keeps retail electricity rates low. Moreover, where commissions have an obligation to ensure IOUs provide sufficient electricity to meet both present and future demand, commissions typically allow IOU shareholders a profit on their investments in coal plants. Allowing investors a return on their investment ensures continued investment in generation facilities such that a reliable supply of electrical power is maintained. * * *

II. Regulation of Investor Owned Utilities

In the United States, there are approximately 240 IOUs. The Federal Energy Regulatory Commission (FERC) regulates their interstate electrical transmission and wholesale electricity sales. State public utility commissions regulate IOUs' intrastate transmission and retail power rates. Since IOUs are privately owned companies providing a public service, government regulation ensures IOUs' profit motive does not interfere with their public obligation to provide adequate service while charging reasonable rates.

As public utilities, IOUs have four principal obligations and rights that distinguish them from traditional private industry. First, public utilities are obligated to serve all persons willing to pay for service. To fulfill this obligation, they must anticipate and build or acquire generation facilities ahead of demand. Second, public utilities must provide adequate and safe service. Adequate service means utilities must have sufficient generation in reserve to meet customer demand despite daily, seasonal, and yearly demand fluctuations. Third, public utilities must serve all customers on equal terms, meaning they cannot discriminate against some customers to benefit others. Fourth, public utilities may only charge just and reasonable rates for service as determined by state regulators.

Along with their obligations as public utilities, IOUs enjoy rights not held by traditional private industry. First, IOUs have the right to collect a reasonable price for services. State regulators cannot force IOUs to operate at a loss. Second, they have the right to render service subject to <u>reasonable</u> rates and regulations. Third, IOUs have the right of protection from competitors offering identical service in the same area. Thus, state regulators will grant IOUs service monopolies if the IOUs meet certain conditions such as obtaining franchise certification. * * *

A. Rate-making authority

While the [Oregon Public Utility] Commission has authority to regulate virtually every aspect of IOUs' business, one of the Commission's primary obligations is setting IOUs' retail rates. Thus, unlike other industries which price services based on a competitive marketplace, the Commission decides how much IOUs can charge customers. The goal of utility ratemaking is to set future rates that allow a utility to collect enough revenue in the period when the rates are in effect to cover the utility's costs and an adequate, but not excessive, return on investment. While there is a minimum amount, the confiscatory amount, which constitutes a rate floor, the Commission is free to set rates anywhere above that amount limited only by the mandate that rates must be "fair and reasonable." Thus the Commission has broad discretion to set customer rates and courts reviewing rate decisions have generally deferred to the Commission's expertise.

1. Ensuring fair and reasonable rates

The Commission can only approve rates that are "fair, just and reasonable." In determining what constitutes fair, just and reasonable rates, the Commission must balance the interests of an IOU's ratepayers and investors. By statute, rates are fair and reasonable if they provide adequate revenue both for operating expenses and capital costs with a return to shareholders commensurate with the return on investments in other enterprises having corresponding risks. Rates must also be sufficient to ensure confidence in the IOU's financial integrity, thus allowing the utility to maintain its credit and attract capital. The latter requirement recognizes utility customers have an interest in both low cost and reliable power. Only by attracting investment can an IOU accumulate enough money to build the infrastructure necessary to guarantee reliable electrical power.

2. Approving the revenue requirement

When an IOU seeks a rate increase, it files a request to increase its revenue requirement with the Commission. The revenue requirement represents an IOU's estimate of its expenses coupled with a rate of return for the period the rates will be in effect. The revenue requirement thus determines the total amount the IOU can collect from its customers. Only when the Commission is satisfied that the rates derived from the IOU's revenue requirement are fair and reasonable, will the Commission approve the revenue requirement. An IOU's revenue requirement can be expressed in basic terms, as follows:

Revenue requirement = (rate base x rate of return) + operating expenses.

The IOU's rate base represents the company's undepreciated assets and includes the IOU's electrical generating facilities such as coal plants. The rate of return is the return the Commission allows on capital invested to provide service. Operating expenses, which do not earn a rate of return, include infrastructure maintenance, power purchases at market-based rates, taxes, and fuel costs.

3. Approving the rate base

Because the rate base is the only part of the revenue requirement on which the Commission allows a return, IOUs prefer building or buying coal plants they can operate in contrast to purchasing electricity on the market that someone else generates to satisfy power demand. Also, since IOUs earn more profit the larger their rate base, IOUs are motivated to build or buy the most expensive resources. This reality encourages IOUs to invest in resources such as coal plants that require significant capital to build or buy.

To include a resource investment in its rate base, the Commission requires an IOU to prove that 1) the resource is "used and useful" and 2) the investment was prudent. A resource qualifies as "used" if it has actually been placed in service. A resource is "useful" as long as the IOU demonstrates the resource is reasonably necessary to provide electrical service. Once the Commission determines that a resource is "used and useful," the Commission will allow the IOU to place the resource in its rate base. However, the Commission does not allow the IOU to place the full investment cost of the resource in the rate base until the IOU demonstrates its decision to build or acquire the resource was prudent. The Commission judges prudence, not in hindsight, but based on what was "known and knowable" at the time of the initial decision to build the resource continuing through each stage of construction. Only the portion of the investment the Commission considers prudently invested does the Commission allow in the rate base. Thus if an IOU builds a resource at an unnecessarily high cost, only the costs the Commission considers prudently incurred will the Commission allow in the rate base. The prudence test makes certain the Commission does not reward risky or uneconomic investment decisions by automatically including the full investment amount in the rate base.

For example, for an IOU to include the full cost of a coal plant in its rate base, the IOU must show the plant is "used and useful" by demonstrating the plant is operating and is reasonably necessary to provide its customers with electrical service. The IOU must next demonstrate that its initial decision to build the coal plant was prudent based on what was "known and knowable" to the IOU when it decided to build the coal plant. Finally, the IOU must prove it continued to act prudently through each stage of constructing the coal plant based on what was "known and knowable." Thus the Commission's prudence test does not focus on one particular point in time. Rather, the test looks at the objective reasonableness of the IOU's actions throughout the process of building the coal plant.

B. Commission Review of Resource Plans

One of the factors the Commission considers when reviewing the prudence of resource investments is whether the initial investment decision is consistent with the IOU's resource plan. A resource plan analyzes and identifies resources the IOU needs to meet its customers' demand. The Commission requires IOUs use a planning horizon consisting of at least twenty years. The IOU's technical analysis, along with the portfolio of chosen resources constitutes the IOU's proposed resource plan.

1. Substantive requirements

The Commission requires resource plans meet four substantive criteria: 1) all plans must evaluate resources on a consistent and comparable basis; 2) all resource comparisons must consider risk and uncertainty; 3) the primary goal of resource planning must be the selection of a portfolio with the best combination of expected costs and associated risks and uncertainties for the utility and its customers; and 4) the resource plan must be consistent with the long-run public interest as expressed in Oregon and federal energy policies. Using these substantive criteria, the Commission evaluates the reasonableness of an IOUs' individual resource decisions in the context of the overall resource strategy. If the Commission finds an IOU's resource selection and overall plan reasonable, it acknowledges the resource plan. If not, the Commission can ask the IOU to modify the plan, or the Commission can refuse to acknowledge a specific part or the entire plan.

2. Commission acknowledgement

An IOU can use Commission acknowledgement of its resource plan as evidence that subsequent investments, consistent with the plan, were prudent. Thus if the Commission acknowledges a resource plan calling for building or buying new coal plants, the IOU can use the acknowledgement as evidence the IOU acted prudently in actually building or buying the new coal plants when arguing for inclusion of the full investment amount in the rate base. Acknowledgement is therefore valuable to IOUs' investors who build and acquire resources in hopes of making a profit. While an IOU can proceed with its resource plan even if the Commission refuses to acknowledge the plan, the IOU faces a higher burden of proof when arguing to rate base the full cost of a resource that was not acknowledged by the Commission. So an IOU that obtains Commission acknowledgement and acts consistently therewith, has a better chance of including the full cost of the resource in its rate base (thereby recovering the cost and a rate of return) than an IOU who does not receive Commission acknowledgement. Put another way, the Commission, in acknowledging a particular resource, makes it more likely the Commission will allow the IOU to recover the full cost of the resource from its customers along with a rate of return.

QUESTIONS AND DISCUSSION

1. ***PUC Authority to Consider Environmental Concerns in Ratemaking Decisions.*** Historically, PUCs were thought to not have the authority to consider environmental issues in their decision-making processes. However, a review of state

utility laws by Professor Michael Dworkin shows that several laws give PUCs express authority to consider energy efficiency and environmental effects. *See* Michael Dworkin et al., *The Environmental Duties for Public Utilities Commissions for 2006*, 7 Vt. J. Envtl. L. 6 (2006).

2. Where states lack the express authority to consider the environment, they may nonetheless be required to consider the economic consequences of carbon dioxide regulation. As Ms. Hirotsu argues:

> Traditional coal plants are such significant producers of carbon dioxide, any meaningful legislative effort to control carbon dioxide production will necessarily have to include coal plants. Because new coal plants represent an enormous long-term increase in carbon dioxide emissions, any plans to build or buy new coal plants carry the risk of being adversely affected by future federal carbon dioxide restrictions. Given a regulatory system that allows investment and operating costs to pass to ratepayers, the economic risks associated with future carbon regulation will likely fall on IOU ratepayers in the form of significantly higher rates.

Hirotsu, *Remembering the Bottom Line*, at 21–22.

------

2.   *PUC Decisions Regarding Coal-Fired Power Plants*

Recently, a number of PUCs have restricted utilities from building new coal-fired power plants or conditioned the construction of the plants in a number of ways. Although some PUCs have acted out of concern for the environment, others have instead based their decisions on the economic consequences new coal plants may produce. These recent decisions may signal a change in whether PUCs will continue to allow coal to be a dominant energy source for regulated utilities.

IN RE PETITION FOR DETERMINATION OF NEED FOR GLADES POWER PARK UNITS 1 AND 2 ELECTRICAL POWER PLANTS IN GLADES COUNTY, BY FLA. POWER & LIGHT CO.

Docket No. 070098-EI, Order No. PSC-07-0557-FOF-EI, Order Denying Petition for Determination of Need (July 2, 2007)

On February 1, 2007, Florida Power & Light Company (FPL) filed its petition for a determination of need for the proposed Glades Power Park Units 1 and 2 (FGPP) electrical power plants in Glades County, pursuant to Section 403.519, Florida Statutes (F.S.), and Rule 25-22.080, Florida Administrative Code (F.A.C.). FPL proposed two ultra-supercritical pulverized coal (USCPC) generating units, each having summer net capacities of approximately 980 megawatts (MW) for a combined net capacity of 1,960 MW, with proposed in-service dates of 2013 and 2014. A 4,900-acre site located west of Lake Okeechobee, approximately four miles northeast of the town of Moore Haven in an unincorporated area of Glades County is the proposed location of the units.

In its petition, FPL sought an affirmative determination of need as well as cost recovery for the FGPP. * * *

Florida's Electrical Power Plant Siting Act, Sections 403.501–403.518, F.S., recognizes that the selection of sites and the routing of associated transmission lines will have a significant impact upon the welfare of the population, the location and growth of industry, and the use of the natural resources of the state. To that end, the Act is designed so that a permit application is centrally coordinated and all permit decisions can be reviewed on the basis of standards and recommendations of the deciding agencies. Further, it is the intent of the Act to seek courses of action that will fully balance the increasing demands for electrical power plant location and operation with the broad interests of the public.

Pursuant to Section 403.519, F.S., this Commission is the sole forum for the determination of need for major new power plants. Section 403.519(3), F.S., sets out the factors we are to consider:

> In making its determination, the Commission shall take into account the need for electric system reliability and integrity, the need for adequate electricity at a reasonable cost, the need for fuel diversity and supply reliability, and whether the proposed plant is the most cost-effective alternative available. The Commission shall also expressly consider the conservation measures taken by or reasonably available to the applicant or its members which might mitigate the need for the proposed plant and other matters within its jurisdiction which it deems relevant.

The Legislature did not assign the weight that this Commission is to give each of these factors. The power plant siting process is designed so that final decisions will be rendered within certain statutory time frames based on the best information and evidence available at the time.

To support the cost-effectiveness of its FGPP proposal, FPL performed sixteen economic scenarios combining four different fuel and four different environmental compliance cost projections. Each scenario calculated the cumulative present value revenue requirement for two generation expansion plans, one with coal and one without coal. The difference between the two plans was intended to demonstrate each plans' relative cost-effectiveness compared to available alternatives. The four fuel price forecasts are ongoing, long-range estimates of the price differential between coal and natural gas. The four price estimates included a low, medium, and high price differential between coal and natural gas, as well as a "shocked" differential which was developed to show the impact of what a significant price increase in oil or natural gas may have on the value of adding FGPP to FPL's portfolio of assets. The relative price differential between coal and natural gas is the driving force behind the system revenue requirement calculations. FPL projected a net present value impact between the low and high cost differentials of approximately $72 billion.

FPL also provided four different environmental cost projections. These projections addressed environmental costs for three currently regulated emissions — sulfur dioxide, nitrogen oxides, and mercury — combined with various scenarios of future carbon allowance costs. The projected carbon costs were based upon Federal legislation under current debate before Congress. FPL projected the net present value impact between the low and high environmental costs to be approximately $22 billion. If more stringent regulations are enacted in the future, environmental costs will have an even greater impact on the overall cost-effectiveness of the FGPP.
* * *

As with any capital-intensive project, an increase in total costs will occur until lower fuel costs overcome the higher capital costs. FPL estimated that the FGPP would not show a positive net present value benefit until the year 2022. Even after this length of time, only the two most optimistic scenarios projected ratepayer savings. FPL acknowledged that the FGPP was not a clear winner from a cost standpoint; rather, the need for the FGPP was driven by the need for increased fuel diversity on FPL's system. Such a strategic benefit is difficult to quantify.

As noted above, the Commission's decision on a need determination petition must be based on a case-by-case review of facts with underlying assumptions tested for reasonableness and certainty. Taking into account each of the factors referenced in Section 403.519, F.S., we find it is in the public interest to deny FPL's petition for determination of need. Our decision is based upon our analysis of the record, . . . and our determination that FPL has failed to demonstrate that the proposed plants are the most cost-effective alternative available, taking into account the fixed costs that would be added to base rates for the construction of the plants, the uncertainty associated with future natural gas and coal prices, and the uncertainty associated with currently emerging energy policy decisions at the state and federal level. This Commission recognizes the need for fuel diversity. Section 403.519, F.S., in fact, was amended in 2005 to expressly authorize the Commission to consider fuel diversity as a factor in determining need. Nuclear and other generating technologies, as well as the use of solid fuels, may play an appropriate part in a utility's generation mix for promoting fuel diversity and affordable supply reliability. We further recognize the need for additional generation to meet current and future growth. Finally, we recognize that, in light of the inherent variability of necessary assumptions about fuel costs, capital costs, and other resource planning matters, uncertainty about cost-effectiveness alone will not necessarily control the outcome of every need determination decision. We find in this case, however, that the potential benefits regarding fuel diversity offered by FPL in support of the FGPP fail to mitigate the additional costs and risks of the project, given the uncertainty of present fuel prices, capital costs, and current market and regulatory factors.

QUESTIONS AND DISCUSSION

1. *Undertones of the Florida Decision.* Although the Florida PSC did not directly mention the effects of climate change on the utility's operations, some commentators believe that climate change was an underlying concern for the PSC:

> The FPSC's decision was the first time it rejected a new power plant since 1992. The decision did not mention climate change or GHG emissions. Instead, it was couched vaguely in terms of uncertainty over fuel prices, capital costs, and unidentified "regulatory factors." Nevertheless, environmental concerns contributed to the outcome. FPL had claimed that the plants would have included filters, scrubbers, and other systems that would have cut CO_2 emissions generated by the burning of coal by as much as 90%. Still, the plants would have emitted more mercury than any of FPL's existing plants. The fact that the plant would have been located in the middle of the Everglades also may have been a factor in the denial. Climate change also played a role. FPSC members indicated that they were concerned that the price of coal could become unstable if Congress decides to regulate GHGs. They also indicated that they regarded CO_2 as well as mercury emissions as risks if the plant were approved. An environmental consultant testified before the FPSC that FPL could incur annual penalties for emitting CO_2 between $120 to $400 million under climate change legislation being considered by Congress. Governor Charlie Crist had previously made it clear that he preferred that no new coal-fired power plants be licensed, and had issued an executive order requiring the adoption of standards to reduce greenhouse gas emissions from power plants to 2000 levels by 2017 and to 1990 levels by 2025.

According to one account, the decision in the Glades Power Park case mark[ed] the first time global warming has played a role in a PSC decision. . . . The PSC's decision was motivated by its belief that not building the plant would save customers huge costs, including the cost of cutting GHG emissions. The decision could be the harbinger of the PSC's approach to the five other proposals for new coal-fired power plants that are pending. The Executive Director of Associated Industries of Florida asserted that "[t]his idea that somehow this plant is going to help control climate change for the world is a joke when China is putting up a power plant every day." Nonetheless, FPL reacted to the decision by claiming that it was likely to decide to build more natural gas-fired plants to meet Florida's growing energy needs and to intensify its efforts to build one or two nuclear reactors.

Robert L. Glicksman, *Coal-Fired Power Plants, Greenhouse Gases, and State Statutory Substantial Endangerment Provisions: Climate Change Comes tTo Kansas*, 56 U. KAN. L. REV. 517, 540–42 (2008)

2.   PUCs have denied utilities' request to build coal plants in other states as well:

Recent proposals to build coal-fired power plants in other states also have foundered. Although the decisions in these states restricting the ability of utilities to rely on coal-fired power have been based primarily on need rather than environmental factors, regulators have also expressed concern over the GHGs emitted by coal-fired electricity generation. The Oregon Public Utility Commission ("OPUC") rejected a bid by PacifiCorp to build two new coal-fired power plants on the ground that the utility failed to justify the need for that much baseload capacity. In addition, the agency concluded that the proposal to build a combined 1109 megawatts of new coal-fired generation was inconsistent with the utility's own OPUC-approved plan to focus on conservation, renewable resources, and demand-side measures to meet electricity demand. According to one Commissioner, OPUC "really skated on the CO_2 issue in this ruling." But OPUC stated that it expected the utility to explore "bridging strategies" that would allow it to delay a commitment to coal until cleaner technologies, such as IGCC [integrated gassification combined cycle], become commercially feasible. In addition, regulators viewed skeptically PacifiCorp's plan to sell surplus power to customers in other states in light of the aversion to coal-fired generation in those states. OPUC noted, for example, that California had recently limited imports of coal-fired power from other states to plants whose emissions are comparable to natural gas-fired plants.

State regulators have also wounded proposed coal-fired projects more indirectly. In late 2007, the Minnesota Public Utilities Commission ("MPUC") refused to require Xcel Energy to buy power from a 600-megawatt coal-fired power plant proposed by Excelsior Energy. The MPUC had declared just a few months earlier that it would consider requiring a number of utilities to enter power-purchase agreements with the proposed plant, which would have been an "innovative" coal-gasification facility potentially capable of capturing its CO_2 emissions. It cited growing disillusionment with coal, assurances from Xcel that it did not need the additional power, and the high cost to Xcel's customers of the proposed plant's output as reasons for refusing to compel Xcel to purchase power from the proposed plant.

The Chairman of the MPUC described the regulatory environment for coal-fired power plants as having undergone a "paradigm shift," noting the delay or cancellation of coal-gasification projects in several other states.

Glicksman, *Coal-Fired Power Plants*, at 550–53.

3.   Most recently, the Texas PUC granted a utility a certificate of convenience and necessity, but conditioned it expressly on the utility not passing on high carbon taxes or emissions trading prices to the customers:

1. Capital Costs

The estimated cost of the Turk Plant, with September 2008 as the anticipated start of construction, is $1.522 billion. The Commission determines that it is unreasonable to expect Texas retail consumers to be responsible for the Texas jurisdictional allocation of any additional costs that exceed $1.522 billion. This cap on the capital costs of the Turk Plant limits the financial risk to Texas ratepayers arising out of uncertainties identified in the testimony including, but not limited to, the following: increased material and labor costs because of delays; costs as a result of changes in certification or approval of the Turk Plant by other jurisdictions; 14 changes in the currently proposed ownership participation; and additional costs of plant construction, including those associated with the use of ultra-supercritical technology.

2. Carbon Mitigation Costs.

The Commission carefully studied the various price tags for carbon mitigation in the record that may be attributable to the energy generated from the Turk Plant. The amounts range from as low as $13 to $15 per ton of CO_2 emissions to as high as $70 per ton. The average numbers for a coal plant range from $30 to $45 per ton. The lower numbers in this vast range are predictions of allowances to be mandated in the early phases of federal regulations on carbon dioxide emissions, growing to the larger numbers where the trade-off between a carbon "tax" and the implementation of carbon sequestration and capture technologies on coal and gas plants would occur sometime in the future. Based on these estimates and predictions, the Commission seeks to place a limit on the extent to which the Turk Plant's costs of carbon mitigation will be passed on to Texas retail ratepayers. It is unreasonable to expect the retail ratepayers to be responsible for these costs that exceed $28 per ton of CO_2 emissions through the year 2030. To the extent that carbon legislation or implementation of mitigation technology results in costs that exceed that amount per ton, those costs shall not be borne by Texas ratepayers.

Application of Southwestern Electric Power Co. for a Certificate of Convenience and Necessity Authorization for Coal Fired Power Plant in Arkansas, PUC Docket No. 33891, Order, 7–8 (Aug. 12, 2008). Will this decision encourage electricity generation from renewable sources or the continued use of older, dirtier coal-fired power plants? The Texas PUC will allow the Turk Plant to pass on costs of carbon dioxide credits valued at up to $28 per ton, even though average costs for coal plants are between $30 and $45 per ton. Due to the PUC's order, if the actual costs of carbon dioxide exceed $28 per ton, then the utility will be on the hook for those extra costs. Do you think the utility may rethink its decision to build the facility?

4.   Are PUCs acting appropriately in denying utilities permission to install new coal-fired power plants? In some cases, the proposed plants would have used integrated gasification combined cycle (IGCC) technology, which operates more efficiently and produces far fewer pollutants than older pulverized coal plants. If PUCs deny utilities the right to build these more advanced facilities, are they

simply ensuring that older, dirtier coal-fired power plants will remain on line? How could PUCs address this issue?

III.   REVISING THE ENERGY PORTFOLIO IN THE UNITED STATES

Although the United States has attempted to restructure its energy portfolio since at least the 1970s, concerns about climate change have accelerated efforts to develop alternative energy sources. Recent spikes in energy and oil prices have triggered renewed interest in the United States becoming "energy independent," through development of "cleaner" traditional energy sources, such as coal and oil. In addition, many energy experts believe that nuclear energy should be back on the table as a carbon-free power source. Finally, the renewable energy industry is growing at a remarkable pace, due largely to state mandates and federal tax incentives. This section explores the types of energy sources that the United States is developing to mitigate climate change. As you read this section, recall the article in Chapter 2 by Pakala and Sokolow. How do their wedges relate to the various energy sources described in this section?

A.   Traditional Fuels as Sustainable Energy Sources?

Can traditional fuels provide the United States with low-carbon, sustainable energy sources? Many energy experts believe that efforts to restructure the energy system are misguided, and that "clean coal," natural gas, and nuclear power provide the best hope for the United States to meet energy demands, protect the U.S. economy, and reduce overall greenhouse gas emissions. For those who believe that the United States should become energy independent, coal and nuclear power have particular promise, because the United States has ample coal and uranium supplies and would therefore not need to import any of its energy. Moreover, use of these traditional fuels would not require a restructuring of the electricity system, since it is already designed to deliver power from large, capital-intensive facilities. This section explores some of these issues.

1.   *"Clean Coal"*

The term "clean coal" technology generally refers to coal energy technologies that achieve substantial reductions in conventional air pollutants, such as sulfur dioxide, mercury, and nitrogen compounds. More recently, "clean coal" has also been equated with carbon capture and sequestration (CCS) technologies, which promise to collect carbon dioxide before it is emitted from coal-fired power plants and then store the collected carbon dioxide underground. Whether CCS can become a viable technology remains an open question. In addition, the use of CCS technology has generated considerable debate within and beyond the environmental community.

a.   *Carbon Sequestration*

For CCS to succeed, scientists must develop technologies to first capture carbon dioxide as it is released from coal-fired power plants and then to permanently store the carbon dioxide underground. New coal-fired power plants are being built to enable capture of carbon dioxide from the emissions stack. While older coal-fired power plants will require retrofitting for carbon capture, which may become feasible in the near future. However, technologies for carbon sequestration remain much more elusive. The following excerpt describes the options for sequestration of coal-fired power plant emissions.

NATIONAL ENERGY TECHNOLOGY LABORATORY, CARBON SEQUESTRATION, CO_2 STORAGE (2008)

Geologic formations considered for CO_2 storage are layers of porous rock deep underground that are "capped" by a layer or multiple layers of non-porous rock above them. Sequestration practitioners drill a well down into the porous rock and inject pressurized CO_2 into it. Under high pressure, CO_2 turns to liquid and can move through a formation as a fluid. Once injected, the liquid CO_2 tends to be buoyant and will flow upward until it encounters a barrier of non-porous rock, which can trap the CO_2 and prevent further upward migration.

There are other mechanisms for CO_2 trapping as well: CO_2 molecules can dissolve in brine, react with minerals to form solid carbonates, or adsorb in the pores of the porous rock. The degree to which a specific underground formation is amenable to CO_2 storage can be difficult to discern. Research is aimed at developing the ability to characterize a formation before CO_2 injection to be able to predict its CO_2 storage capacity. Another area of research is the development of CO_2 injection techniques that achieve broad dispersion of CO_2 throughout the formation, overcome low diffusion rates, and avoid fracturing the cap rock. These areas of site characterization and injection techniques are interrelated because improved formation characterization will help determine the best injection procedure.

There are three priority types of geologic formations in which CO_2 can be stored, and each has different opportunities and challenges:

Depleted oil and gas reservoirs. These are formations that held crude oil and natural gas over geologic time frames. In general, they are a layer of porous rock with a layer of non-porous rock above such that the non-porous layer forms a dome. It is the dome shape that trapped the hydrocarbons. This same dome offers great potential to trap CO_2 and makes these formations excellent sequestration opportunities.

As a value-added benefit, CO_2 injected into a depleting oil reservoir can enable recovery of additional oil. When injected into a depleted oil bearing formation, the CO_2 dissolves in the trapped oil and reduces its viscosity. This "frees" more of the oil by improving its ability to move through the pores in the rock and flow with a pressure differential toward a recovery well. Typically, primary oil recovery and secondary recovery via a water flood produce 30–40% of a reservoir's original oil in place (OOIP). A CO_2 flood enables recovery of an additional 10–15% of the OOIP.
* * *

Unmineable coal seams. Unmineable coal seams are too deep or too thin to be mined economically. All coals have varying amounts of methane adsorbed onto pore surfaces, and wells can be drilled into unmineable coal beds to recover this coal bed methane (CBM). Initial CBM recovery methods, dewatering and depressurization, leave a fair amount of CBM in the reservoir. Additional CBM recovery can be achieved by sweeping the coal bed with nitrogen. CO_2 offers an alternative to nitrogen. It preferentially adsorbs onto the surface of the coal, releasing the methane. Two or three molecules of CO_2 are adsorbed for each molecule of methane released, thereby providing an excellent storage sink for CO_2. Like depleting oil reservoirs, unmineable coal beds are a good early opportunity for CO_2 storage. More than 180 billion metric tons of CO_2 sequestration potential exists in unmineable coal seams . . . .

Saline formations. Saline formations are layers of porous rock that are saturated with brine. They are much more commonplace than coal seams or oil and gas bearing rock, and represent an enormous potential for CO_2 storage capacity. However, much less is known about saline formations than is known about crude oil reservoirs and coal seams and there is a greater amount of uncertainty associated with their amenability to CO_2 storage.

Saline formations tend to have a lower permeability than do hydrocarbon-bearing formations, and work is directed at hydraulic fracturing and other field practices to increase injectivity. Saline formations contain minerals that could react with injected CO_2 to form solid carbonates. The carbonate reactions have the potential to be both a positive and a negative. They can increase permanence but they also may plug up the formation in the immediate vicinity of an injection well. Researchers seek injection techniques that promote advantageous mineralization reactions. [Recent studies] estimated a range of 919 to 3,300 billion metric tons of sequestration potential in saline formations.

Shale. Shale, the most common type of sedimentary rock, is characterized by thin horizontal layers of rock with very low permeability in the vertical direction. Many types of shale contain 1–5 percent organic material, and this hydrocarbon material provides an adsorption substrate for CO_2 storage, similar to where CO_2 can be stored in coal seams. Given the generally low permeability of shale, research is focused on achieving economically viable CO_2 injection rates.

Basalt formations. Basalts are geologic formations of solidified lava. Basalt formations have a unique chemical makeup that could potentially convert all of the injected CO_2 to a solid mineral form, thus permanently isolating it from the atmosphere. Research is focused on enhancing and utilizing the mineralization reactions and increasing CO_2 flow within a basalt formation. Although oil- and gas-rich organic shales and basalts research is in its infancy, these formations may, in the future, prove to be optimal storage sites for stranded CO_2 emissions.

---

b.   *Should Governments Invest in CCS Technology?*

The viability of CCS technology to mitigate climate change has generated considerable controversy. Not surprisingly, those in the coal industry support CCS technology as a means to retain U.S. energy independence and reduce greenhouse gas emissions from the coal industry. Environmentalists, however, are divided on the issue. Some organizations view CCS as a necessary technology to address the inevitable use of coal throughout the world. Other organizations believe that focus on CCS diverts attention and funding away from renewable energy technologies.

BEN BLOCK, U.S. ENVIRONMENTAL GROUPS DIVIDED ON "CLEAN COAL"
(Worldwatch Institute, Mar. 19, 2008)[*]

At a Senate press conference held last week to urge national action on climate change policy, 16 major U.S. environmental organizations shared the stage in solidarity. But while it appears the nation's green groups are united in the fight against global warming, they remain divided on which technologies would best

---

create a carbon-free economy. This division may cause major roadblocks as Congress prepares to debate several climate change policies that could lead to sweeping changes.

Environmental organizations agree that global warming is a serious concern and that emissions from coal-fired power plants must be drastically curtailed. To do so, many support carbon capture and sequestration, commonly known as CCS. CCS technology is designed to trap and store (either in the Earth's crust or the deep oceans) the massive quantities of carbon dioxide spewed from coal power plants.

Groups like the Natural Resources Defense Council (NRDC) and Environmental Defense Fund are already lobbying on behalf of CCS. Others, such as the Sierra Club and the World Wildlife Fund, are more cautious about promoting CCS. They insist that affordable and proven technologies, such as energy efficiency and wind or solar energy, should be more fully implemented before CCS is considered. Greenpeace specifically opposes the technology.

A divided environmental community is reflective of a still unproven technology. Although CCS is almost certainly technically feasible, both the timing and the cost are highly uncertain. A Massachusetts Institute of Technology report released last year, *The Future of Coal*, concluded that the U.S. CCS program is not on track to achieve large-scale commercial operation for at least a decade.

Carbon liability concerns have led major investors and the U.S. government to rein in financing for coal-fired power plants. As a result, the coal industry has embraced CCS as essential to its survival. Some environmentalists say CCS is critical to creating a political deal that would dissuade power companies from blocking new climate legislation. "Congress should require planned new coal plants in the United States to employ CCS without further delay," NRDC said in a statement last year.

According to NRDC science fellow George Peridas, as long as China continues its surge in coal emissions and the U.S. coal industry wants to build new plants, the coal industry must be presented with an alternative. "There are cheaper ways and cleaner ways and preferable ways to meet energy demands, but I think CCS will ultimately be needed too," Peridas said. "I'd love to be actively campaigning against all use of coal, but I don't think that's the best way to reduce emissions."

U.S. Representatives Henry Waxman of California and Edward Markey of Massachusetts introduced a bill last week that would ban any coal plants that do not capture and store at least 85 percent of carbon dioxide emissions. The Sierra Club supports the legislation because it places a moratorium on coal plants until CCS is ready. The group's support, however, does not reflect an embrace of CCS. "We need to make sure that the technology to capture and store carbon is feasible and in place," said Bruce Nilles, The Sierra Club's national coal campaign director. "While we are evaluating the role coal should play in our energy future, we should continue to move forward with the clean, affordable energy solutions that are available today, like wind and solar power."

Greenpeace has taken a hard-line approach against CCS. "We are opposed to CCS technology," said Kate Smolski, Greenpeace USA global warming campaigner. "The No. 1 reason is it's a way the dirty polluting coal industry can prop itself up. It's an unproven technology. And it takes resources away from solutions that we can use right now."

The main concern with CCS is whether carbon stored inside empty aquifers would leak and pollute groundwater reserves. "If people think this is *the* solution, think again. A lot of research is needed," said Steven Chu, director of the

Lawrence Berkeley National Laboratory at last week's "Summit on America's Energy Future," sponsored by the National Academies of Sciences and Engineering. [Editors' Note: Steven Chu is now Secretary of Energy.]

Researchers are calling for "urgent" expansion of CCS research and development funding. Massachusetts Institute of Technology physicist Ernest Moniz, also director of the Energy Initiative, said experimental CCS power plants are needed to improve cost and performance. The U.S. government's plans for its first large CCS plant were halted in January when the Department of Energy canceled major pilot program FutureGen after concluding that the costs had mushroomed out of control. "What we need is several demonstrations in parallel," Moniz said at the Academies' summit. * * *

For his part, Worldwatch Institute President Christopher Flavin is skeptical of CCS. "It will be many years before we know for sure whether large-scale carbon sequestration is practical and affordable," Flavin says. "The only thing that's certain today is that we shouldn't assume CCS will be a major solution to climate change — unlike solar, wind, and energy efficiency, all of which are being deployed on a significant scale today."

QUESTIONS AND DISCUSSION

1.   How do you think environmental organizations should treat CCS? Is it realistic for organizations to oppose CCS when coal provides such a large percentage of energy in the United States and the world?

2.   One of Greenpeace's major concerns with CCS is that it will deflect research, development, and investment away from renewable energy sources. Greenpeace, False Hope: Why Carbon Capture and Storage Won't Save the Climate 7 (May 2008). Do you think Greenpeace's concerns are valid?

3.   Recent research suggests that carbon sequestration may require significant amounts of energy — perhaps as much as 20 percent of the electricity that a power plant generates would be used for carbon sequestration. Reuters News Service, *Power Needed to Bury CO_2 a Coal Issue — Experts* (June 30, 2008), *available at* http://www.planetark.org/dailynewsstory.cfm?newsid=49079. Does this suggest that CCS technology should not proceed, or does the abundance of coal make this a non-issue?

4.   *Potential Leakage from CCS Sites.* One risk of geological sequestration is that carbon dioxide may leak from sequestration sites. Under certain conditions, leakage could contaminate drinking water sources or exacerbate the effects of other environmental contaminants.

> Leaking CO_2 may affect [underground sources of drinking water] overlying the sequestration reservoir or reach the land surface where it could accumulate in soil and affect biotic respiration, or in structures where it could harm human health. The most probable routes of human exposure to CO_2 leaking from [onshore geological sequestration] sites are through inhalation or skin contact. Although CO_2 is harmless at low concentrations it can displace air and asphyxiate or cause chronic health effects at high concentrations. In areas where radon gas is prevalent, rising CO_2 could displace radon gas causing radon to accumulate in structures exacerbating human health concerns.

Jeffrey W. Moore, *The Potential Law of On-Shore Geologic Sequestration of CO_2 Captured from Coal-Fired Power Plants*, 28 ENERGY L.J. 443, 452 (2007). Do these concerns outweigh the risks from climate change? If CO_2 leaks into drinking water supplies or leaks into the atmosphere, who should be liable? What existing principles of liability would apply to a leak?

5. As noted in Chapter 11, Congress has dedicated hundreds of millions of dollars to a CCS facility known as the FutureGen facility. For a brief time, the Department of Energy suspended funding for the FutureGen plant, because DOE thought the project economically wasteful and technologically unachievable. Congress, however, reinstated the funding. The CCS facility appears to be years away from coming on line.

2.　*Nuclear Power*

Energy experts have long engaged in a heated debate regarding the role of nuclear power in the United States. On the one hand, nuclear advocates believe that nuclear energy — which emits no carbon dioxide — presents the most realistic option for providing sufficient baseload energy. On the other hand, nuclear opponents believe that the use of nuclear energy will perpetuate a flawed centralized energy program and present other environmental risks.

FRED BOSSELMAN, THE ECOLOGICAL ADVANTAGES OF NUCLEAR POWER
15 N.Y.U. ENVTL. L.J. 1 (2007)[*]

Will a new generation of nuclear plants be built in the United States? The United States is the world's largest supplier of commercial nuclear power. In 2005, there were 104 U.S. commercial nuclear generating units that were fully licensed to operate, and they provided about 20% of the Nation's electricity. But no new nuclear plants have been built in the United States for over twenty years. * * *

This article concentrates only on one issue related to that decision — an issue that often receives less attention than it deserves: How will the decision affect ecological processes and systems, both in the United States and globally? The article makes three arguments: (1) if nuclear power plants are not built, the gap will be filled by more coal-fired power plants; (2) the impact of coal-fired power plants on ecological processes and systems is likely to be increasingly disastrous; and (3) nuclear power's ecological impacts are likely to be neutral or even positive.

I. Coal and Nuclear Power Are the Realistic Choices to Meet the Need for Reliable Base-Load Electric Generation in the United States

A. Electric Utilities Need Access to an Assortment of Different Types of Power Plants

Electric utilities need to be able to have access to a "portfolio" of different types of generating plants. Because electricity cannot be stored on a large scale, power generators must continually produce power as it is consumed. Some users of electric power produce a relatively constant and predictable demand for electricity, and this amount is known as "base-load." Electric utilities need reliable generation sources with low operating costs for meeting base-load needs. Base-load power plants run virtually without interruption to supply the continuous portion of electricity needs, as compared to the needs that expand and contract seasonally or diurnally. Base-load plants are often called "must-run" plants, because they will run for as long as possible at full load, and will produce the lowest overall power-generating costs for this type of use. Today, many observers consider coal and nuclear power to be the only reliable future sources of base-load power. * * *

B. Conservation Will Not Prevent the Need for New Power Generating Capacity

Demand for electricity is influenced by many different factors, including the weather, the strength of the economy, the price of electricity, and the use of high-demand equipment and buildings. The history of the last fifty years has provided many examples of over- and under-estimation of demand growth, but no evidence of any decline in demand for any multi-year period. * * *

D. Renewables Can Play a Valuable but Limited Role

The goal of a completely renewable system of electric generation appeals to almost anyone who does not have vested interests in the continued use of non-renewable energy sources. The currently available renewable sources of electrical energy on a large scale are primarily hydroelectric power (hydro), wind, and solar. The United States and individual states have provided some incentives for the creation of renewable generating systems, and some European countries have provided even more, but renewable energy resources can meet only a small fraction of reliable base-load electricity needs within the next decade because: (1) their availability depends on external factors beyond human control, requiring backup by reliable generation; (2) their potential location is also dependent on factors beyond our control; and (3) new renewable technologies, although promising, are more than ten years away from large scale production. * * *

II. From an Ecological Standpoint, Nuclear Power Is Much Better than Coal

Examining coal and nuclear power solely from an ecological standpoint, the advantages of nuclear power are clear.

A. The Ecological Impacts of Every Stage of the Use of Coal Are Disastrous

Virtually all of the coal mined in the United States is used as boiler fuel to generate electricity, and although few users of that electricity realize it, half of the nation's electric energy is provided by coal. In his recent book, Big Coal, Jeff Goodell points out that in the United States, the mining and combustion of coal typically occur in such remote locations that most Americans have no idea "what our relationship with this black rock actually costs us." This is particularly true with regard to public understanding of ecological systems that are being destroyed in remote places or through chains of causation that only experts understand. Coal is ecologically destructive through (1) mining, (2) air pollution, (3) greenhouse gas emissions, and (4) water pollution; and (5) while so-called "clean-coal" technology is a long-range hope, it is not likely to be common in the next decade. * * *

B. Nuclear Power Has Much Less Effect on Ecological Systems than Coal

Like coal, nuclear power is made from a mineral substance that comes from a mine, is transported to the power plant and removed from the plant when its usefulness has ended. The uranium used in nuclear power plants, however, has only a small fraction of the ecological impact of coal at any stage of its cycle, both in total effect and per unit of power produced. The nuclear industry claims that:

> Nuclear energy has perhaps the lowest impact on the environment — including air, land, water, and wildlife — of any energy source, because it does not emit harmful gases, isolates its waste from the environment, and requires less area to produce the same amount of electricity as other sources.

The evidence supports these claims, as will be shown below. Moreover, the risk of a serious accident or terrorist attack on the next generation of nuclear plants will be slight.

1. The Amount of Uranium Used Is a Tiny Fraction of the Coal Used

The mining of uranium admittedly can create some of the same adverse ecological impacts as the mining of coal. The difference, however, is that while the coal-fired power plants in the United States used slightly over a billion tons of coal in 2005, nuclear power plants used only 66 million pounds of uranium oxide. Thus the scale of the impact from uranium mining is not in the same ball park as the impact of coal mining. Virtually all uranium mines currently operating in the United States are underground mines or use the *in situ* leaching method, which both have much less impact on the environment than open pit uranium mining. Moreover, coal-fired power plants produce half the electricity in the United States while nuclear power plants produce one-fifth.

In addition, unlike coal, uranium used in power plants can be recycled and used again. At the present time, the United States does not reprocess its nuclear fuel, but countries such as Great Britain, France, Japan, and Russia do so on a regular basis.
* * *

2. Nuclear Power Plants Cause No Air or Radiation Pollution

Whereas coal burning creates large amounts of sulfur dioxide and nitrogen oxides, nuclear power generation emits none. The reason that nuclear power plants produce no air pollutants when generating power is that in a nuclear power plant, nothing is burned; the heat used to spin the turbines and drive the generators comes from the natural decay of the radionuclides in the fuel. It is the burning of fossil fuels, and particularly coal, that causes air pollution from electric power plants.

Nor does a nuclear power plant pollute its surroundings with dangerous radiation, as its opponents often imply. The population exposure from the normal operation of nuclear power plants is far lower than exposure from natural sources. "The civilian nuclear power fuel cycle, involving mining, fuel fabrication, and reactor operation, contributes a negligible dose [of radiation] to the general public." Life cycle air pollutant emissions from nuclear plants are comparable to those of the wind, solar, and hydro facilities — in other words, minimal.

Concern is sometimes raised about the possibility of releases of large amounts of radiation from an accident at a nuclear power plant. In the four decades of commercial power plant operation in the United States, such a release has never occurred. The only serious accident at a commercial nuclear reactor in the United States caused no radiation damage to people outside the plant and little environmental damage.

4. Dry Cask Storage Is a Safe Way to Store Spent Fuel

In the United States, one of the most common arguments against nuclear power relates to the current proposal to bury spent fuel from power plants in a permanent storage facility at Yucca Mountain, Nevada. In my opinion, resolution of this debate is really unnecessary for the construction of new nuclear power plants because recent studies have shown that dry cask storage is a safe and secure method of handling spent fuel for the next century. Dry casks are designed to cool the spent fuel to prevent temperature elevation from radioactive decay and to shield the cask's surroundings from radiation without the use of water or mechanical systems. Heat is released by conduction through the solid walls of the cask (typically made of concrete, lead, steel, polyethylene, and boron-impregnated metals or resins) and by natural convection or thermal radiation. The cask walls also shield the surroundings from radiation. Spent fuel is usually kept in pools for five years before storage in dry casks in order to reduce decay heat and inventories of radionuclides. As the bipartisan National Commission on Energy Policy recently explained, dry cask storage "is a proven, safe, inexpensive waste-sequestering technology that would be good for 100 years or more, providing an interim, back-up solution against the possibility that Yucca Mountain is further delayed or derailed — or cannot be adequately expanded before a further geologic repository can be ready."

At present, most spent fuel is initially stored in water-filled pools on each nuclear power plant site. After five years, the fuel has cooled enough to be transferred to dry casks for storage, and many plants have built such casks onsite. The National Research Council has pointed out that the temporary storage of spent fuel in a retrievable form, such as dry cask storage, might provide opportunities for re-use of the material if new ways of using it were developed in the future. In any event, the current availability of dry cask storage means that the problem of spent fuel no longer appears to be an insurmountable barrier to building new nuclear plants.

C. "But What About Chernobyl?"

In 1986, an explosion at the Chernobyl nuclear power plant in the Ukraine caused the release of large amounts of radiation into the atmosphere. Initially, the Soviet government released little information about the explosion and tried to play down its seriousness, but this secrecy caused great nervousness throughout Europe, and fed the public's fears of nuclear power all over the world. Now a comprehensive analysis of the event and its aftermath has been made: In 2005, a consortium of United Nations agencies called the Chernobyl Forum released its analysis of the long-term effects of the Chernobyl explosion.

The U.N. agencies' study found that the explosion caused fewer deaths than had been expected. Although the Chernobyl reactor was poorly designed and badly operated and lacked the basic safety protections found outside the Soviet Union, fewer than seventy deaths so far have been attributed to the explosion, mostly plant employees and firefighters who suffered acute radiation sickness. The Chernobyl reactor, like many Soviet reactors, was in the open rather than in an American type of pressurizable containment structure, which would have prevented the release of radiation to the environment if a similar accident had occurred.

Perhaps the most surprising finding of the U.N. agencies' study was that "the ecosystems around the Chernobyl site are now flourishing. The [Chernobyl exclusion zone] has become a wildlife sanctuary, and it looks like the nature park it has become." Jeffrey McNeely, the chief scientist of the World Conservation Union, has made similar observations:

Chernobyl has now become the world's first radioactive nature re-serve. . . . 200 wolves are now living in the nature reserve, which has also begun to support populations of reindeer, lynx and European bison, species that previously were not found in the region. While the impact on humans was strongly negative, the wildlife is adapting and even thriving on the site of one of the 20th century's worst environmental disasters.

QUESTIONS AND DISCUSSION

1. What do you think of Professor Bosselman's analysis? Is nuclear power the best choice for climate-friendly energy production? Does his article sufficiently address the ecological concerns surrounding nuclear production? For example, the U.N. Report, Chernobyl's Legacy: Health, Environmental and Socio-Economic Impacts, reports that Chernobyl caused 4,000 cases of thyroid cancer, mostly in children. While most have recovered, nine died. In addition, Ukraine, Belarus, and Russia withdrew 784,320 hectares of agricultural land and 694,200 hectares of timberland from production. Moreover, the nature reserve exists because an area of roughly 30 kilometers surrounding the reactor is highly contaminated.

2. *Skepticism about Nuclear Power.* Not everyone agrees that nuclear energy has a bright future ahead of it. *See, e.g.*, Joseph P. Tomain, *Nuclear Futures*, 15 DUKE ENVTL. L. & POL'Y F. 221 (2005). Professor Tomain argues that nuclear energy "does not appear to pass a market test, has increasing safety concerns, and does not have great promise for replacing fossil fuels." *Id.* at 246. Regarding the market power of nuclear energy, Professor Tomain notes that nuclear energy has never been financially competitive. Instead, even during the heyday of nuclear production, the nuclear industry relied heavily on government subsidies and tax breaks. *Id.* at 241–43. Studies show that any revival of the nuclear energy industry will require substantial government assistance. *Id.* Tax credits for nuclear production would need to range from $6 billion to $19.5 billion, and research and development would cost another $2 billion, for nuclear energy to survive. *Id.* at 242. Concerns regarding waste disposal and weapons proliferation also lead many observers to doubt the political viability of nuclear energy. *Id.* at 244–46. How should policymakers address these concerns? Do the benefits of carbon-free power production justify the risks and financial costs that nuclear power may present?

3. Just as with CCS technologies, environmental groups are split with respect to nuclear power's role in a green energy economy.

B.   Renewable Energy Sources

Americans have become increasingly concerned about rising energy prices, climate change, and the United States' dependence upon foreign oil. As a result, American support for, and investment in, renewable energy has continued to grow. Wind energy, in particular, has boomed, and the solar energy industry has similarly experienced substantial growth. Yet, at the same time, local opposition to some renewable energy facilities has increased out of fears that large-scale renewable energy sources will destroy the scenery, threaten wildlife, or otherwise create unintended consequences. This section will highlight the potential and limitations of the dominant renewable energy resources.

1. *Wind Power*

On August 5, 2008, the American Wind Energy Association (AWEA) announced that the United States had become the world's largest wind energy producer, surpassing Germany's production rates for the first time. Press Release, AWEA, Looming Expiration of Federal Incentive Threatens Wind Power's New-Found Growth: AWEA Second Quarter Market Report Solar (Aug. 5, 2008). Wind energy has quickly become the dominant renewable energy source in the United States, and it likely has room to grow. The Department of Energy estimates that the Midwest states alone (including all states in the Great Plains) have the capacity to support energy generation for the entire country. *See* U.S. Gov't. Accountability Office, Renewable Energy: Wind Power's Contribution to Electric Power Generation and Impact on Farms and Rural Communities 17 (2004). While development of this capacity will take time, most experts agree that the U.S. capacity for wind energy is more than sufficient to meet the nation's energy needs.

Wind power technology is also readily available. Indeed, wind turbines are the modern equivalent of centuries-old technology — windmills. Stand-alone wind turbines can be used for water pumping or communications, two applications that might otherwise require electricity, as well as by property owners to generate electricity. They can also be connected to power grids, combined with other electrical systems, or connected to each other to form wind plants.

Some of the advantages of wind power are obvious. Because they are emissions free, they do not generate GHG emissions (or acid rain emissions). In addition, wind energy is among the least expensive renewable energy technologies, costing between 4 and 6 cents per kilowatt-hour, depending upon the wind resource and financing of the particular project. National Renewable Energy Laboratory, Wind Power Basics (2008).

Despite its low cost relative to other renewable energy sources, it still must compete with cheap, and often subsidized, fossil fuels. Wind power technology also requires a higher initial investment than fossil-fueled generators. Department of Energy, Wind Energy Basics (2008). In addition:

> The major challenge to using wind as a source of power is that the wind is intermittent and it does not always blow when electricity is needed. Wind energy cannot be stored (unless batteries are used); and not all winds can be harnessed to meet the timing of electricity demands.

> Good wind sites are often located in remote locations, far from cities where the electricity is needed.

> Wind resource development may compete with other uses for the land and those alternative uses may be more highly valued than electricity generation.

> Although wind power plants have relatively little impact on the environment compared to other conventional power plants, there is some concern over the noise produced by the rotor blades, aesthetic (visual) impacts, and sometimes birds have been killed by flying into the rotors. Most of these problems have been resolved or greatly reduced through technological development or by properly siting wind plants.

Id.

QUESTIONS AND DISCUSSION

1. *Wind Farm Siting Controversies.* Debates regarding siting of wind generation facilities have been particularly contentious. Wind opponents have concerns about the impacts on migrating bird and bat populations. Early wind farms, most notably a massive facility located in Altamont Pass, California, have caused the deaths of thousands of birds. While technology in the wind power sector has advanced to avoid many bird deaths, fears still exist that an increase in wind energy facilities will likewise increase migratory bird and bat mortality.

Aesthetic concerns also lead many neighbors to oppose wind development, because they think wind facilities will mar otherwise pristine views. Concerns about aesthetics have created opposition to wind projects in Maine, where a wind project was planned in a location close to the Appalachian Trail; Montana, where local residents fear that wind development will diminish the Big Sky state's scenic vistas; and, most famously, Massachusetts, where the Cape Wind project is proposed for Nantucket Sound, off the coast of Cape Cod.

As opposition to wind projects has increased, so have calls to alter the way in which wind farms are permitted. In many states, local governments have the ability to veto wind projects under local land-use laws or energy facility siting laws. One scholar has proposed to limit the power of local governments — and thus the force of "Not in My Backyard" (NIMBY) decision-making — by giving state agencies the power to permit wind facilities. *See* Ronald H. Rosenberg, *Making Renewable Energy a Reality — Finding Ways to Site Wind Power Facilities*, 32 WM. & MARY ENVTL. L. & POL'Y REV. 635, 670–84 (2008). Is this a good idea? Should local governments be denied the ability to control what happens in their jurisdiction?

2. *Economic Impacts of Wind in Rural Areas.* Wind farms have faced much less opposition from rural communities, which have welcomed the economic boost wind power can provide. In many areas, rural landowners have leased their lands for wind turbines. Rural landowners may command $3,000–$4,000 in lease fees per turbine per year. Am. Wind Energy Ass'n., *Wind Energy for Your Farm or Rural Land,* 1, *available at* http://www.awea.org/pubs/factsheets/ WindyLandownersFS.pdf. At the same time, landowners can continue to use their land for farming or ranching. Finally, wind power could provide rural communities with other economic opportunities, from construction jobs associated with installation of the wind facility, to long-term employment associated with maintaining the wind turbines:

> Assembling the pre-fabricated wind turbines and towers employs construction workers at an estimated rate of 4.8 job-years (direct and indirect employment) per 1 MW of wind power construction. Using this ratio, a 50 MW wind farm would produce 240 job-years of employment for those workers who constructed the facility. A 2005 estimate of employment impact suggested that by 2015 wind energy projects in California alone would produce 2,690 construction jobs and 450 permanent operational jobs just for facilities built on U.S. Bureau of Land Management lands.

> After the construction phase of the wind farm project, a smaller number of permanent jobs would be added to local economies usually experiencing little job growth. It has been estimated that between 9 to 10 full-time service personnel would be needed to maintain a 100 MW wind farm. Although this continuing employment benefit would not be extremely large, it would occur in rural areas with small populations and few incoming job opportunities, and it would be distributed over a large rural area.

Rosenberg, *Making Renewable Energy a Reality*, at 664. Not surprisingly, given wind power's benefits for rural areas, the top ten states in terms of wind energy production — Texas, California, Minnesota, Iowa, Washington, Colorado, Oregon, Illinois, Oklahoma, and New Mexico — all have significant amounts of rural land.

While it might seem wise for wind energy companies to focus their efforts only on rural areas to avoid costly and time-consuming siting battles, long-term development strategies will require a significant expansion of wind facilities throughout the United States.

> The optimistic goal of the federal government's Wind Powering America initiative is to have at least 24 states with at least 1,000 MW of installed wind power capacity by 2010. In 2007, there were 16 states that already meet that goal with an additional 6 states currently meeting the 1,000 MW goal when projects under construction were considered. Although achieving the 10,000 MW milestone in 2006 represented a ten-fold growth in 20 years, it must be kept in mind that American wind power still accounts for approximately 1% of existing, domestic electricity generation. This total may be small but it is still significant. Providing 48 billion kWh of electricity, which is sufficient to power 4.5 million American homes, represents a significant accomplishment for the wind power industry. However, achieving the proclaimed national goal of reaching the 5% level by 2020 will require substantial expansion of American wind power even beyond these levels and continued government encouragement. To reach this achievement, thousands of wind turbines must be sited across the country and in offshore locations.

Rosenberg, *Making Renewable Energy a Reality*, at 657–58.

3.   Renewable energy sources also face a myriad of regulatory hurdles as companies seek to locate them on public or private lands. Depending on the energy source, energy producers may need to comply with the Outer Continental Shelf Lands Act, the National Environmental Policy Act, the Surface Mining Control and Reclamation Act, among many others. Moreover, the siting, generation, and transmission of electricity will implicate another range of legislation. This book is not intended to teach all that legislation. Instead, we provide this short excerpt relating to producing and generating wind energy to stimulate discussion about how, if at all, U.S. energy policy needs alter decision-making processes to promote renewable energy development.

DEPARTMENT OF ENERGY, 20% WIND ENERGY BY 2030: INCREASING WIND ENERGY'S CONTRIBUTION TO U.S. ELECTRICITY SUPPLY
119–21 (prepublication vers., May 2008)

States can control siting decisions either through specific decision-making bodies or by virtue of rules set for projects on state-controlled land. In addition, a state agency — such as a wildlife agency — might establish guidelines for siting wind projects. State guidelines can include requirements such as maintaining certain sound levels or conducting studies.

A few states have an energy siting board, which means that they have placed the authority to review energy facilities with the state utility commission (i.e., a public service commission). The governor or legislature usually appoints representatives, and because they are more accountable to the public, they tend to be generally more familiar with this sector. The charge of these state commissions or boards often includes supplying reliable electric service at reasonable prices.

Concerned individuals or project opponents have legal recourse to raise objections by formally challenging a commission decision.

The federal government participates in regulating wind energy projects through several different agencies, depending on the circumstances. Unless there is a federal involvement, such as when developers propose a project on federally managed land, wind energy projects are not usually subject to the National Environmental Policy Act (NEPA). An agency can trigger the provisions of NEPA by undertaking a major federal action, such as allowing construction of a large energy project on federal lands (NEPA 1969).

The federal agencies that follow have mandates that may be related to wind energy:

- The **FAA [Federal Aviation Administration]** conducts aeronautical studies on all structures higher than 60 m above ground level for potential conflicts with navigable airspace and military radar, and ensures proper marking and lighting. Developers are required to submit an application for each individual turbine. From 2004 to 2006, the FAA approved almost 18,000 wind turbine proposals and issued only eight determinations of hazard. The FAA completed nearly half of these turbine proposals in 2006.

- The **Bureau of Land Management (BLM)** manages 105 million hectares of public land, mostly in the western United States. In 2005, the BLM finalized a programmatic environmental impact statement for wind energy development on BLM lands in the West. This statement includes best management practices for wind energy projects, sets standard requirements for projects, and allows for site-specific studies. As an alternative, wind developers can rely on the previous programmatic NEPA document and provide a development plan without having to do a full EIS at each site, which can save valuable resources and time (BLM).

- The **U.S. Army Corps of Engineers (USACE)** issues permits for any development that will affect wetlands. Roads, project infrastructure, and foundations at some wind project sites have the potential to affect wetlands. Projects must also comply with the Endangered Species Act if any threatened or endangered species will be adversely affected.

- **The U.S. Fish & Wildlife Service (USFWS)** can pursue prosecution for violations of the Migratory Bird Treaty Act, which prohibits the killing or harming of almost all migratory birds. Some migratory birds, however, can be taken under a permit or license. The USFWS also enforces the Bald and Golden Eagle Protection Act, which gives additional protection to eagles. The USFWS exercises prosecutorial discretion under these statutes. To date, no wind energy companies have faced action under either law, but flagrant violations without mitigation could be subject to prosecution (USFWS).

- The **Minerals Management Service (MMS)** oversees permitting for offshore ocean-based wind energy projects proposed for the outer continental shelf (OCS). MMS is developing the rules and issued a programmatic environmental impact statement for all alternative energy development on the OCS. New regulations are expected in 2008.

- The **U.S. Department of Agriculture Forest Service (USFS)** manages 78 million hectares of public land in national forests and grasslands (USDA). Projects sited on any Forest Service lands are subject to NEPA, and potentially to siting guidelines that the Forest Service is currently developing.

2. *Solar Power*

Since 2000, the United States and California have launched several programs aimed at increasing the use of solar power and improving solar technology. As a result of these efforts, the solar industry has experienced remarkable growth. California, for example, expects the solar industry in its state to grow by 35–40 percent between 2007 and 2008. Nationally, the solar industry is also expected to expand, albeit at a slower pace.

NATIONAL RENEWABLE ENERGY LABORATORY, SOLAR ENERGY BASICS (2008)

Concentrating Solar Power

Many power plants today use fossil fuels as a heat source to boil water. The steam from the boiling water rotates a large turbine, which activates a generator that produces electricity. However, a new generation of power plants, with concentrating solar power systems, uses the sun as a heat source. There are three main types of concentrating solar power systems: *parabolic-trough, dish/engine,* and *power tower.*

Parabolic-trough systems concentrate the sun's energy through long rectangular, curved (U-shaped) mirrors. The mirrors are tilted toward the sun, focusing sunlight on a pipe that runs down the center of the trough. This heats the oil flowing through the pipe. The hot oil then is used to boil water in a conventional steam generator to produce electricity.

A dish/engine system uses a mirrored dish (similar to a very large satellite dish). The dish-shaped surface collects and concentrates the sun's heat onto a receiver, which absorbs the heat and transfers it to fluid within the engine. The heat causes the fluid to expand against a piston or turbine to produce mechanical power. The mechanical power is then used to run a generator or alternator to produce electricity.

A power tower system uses a large field of mirrors to concentrate sunlight onto the top of a tower, where a receiver sits. This heats molten salt flowing through the receiver. Then, the salt's heat is used to generate electricity through a conventional steam generator. Molten salt retains heat efficiently, so it can be stored for days before being converted into electricity. That means electricity can be produced on cloudy days or even several hours after sunset.

Passive Solar

Step outside on a hot and sunny summer day, and you'll feel the power of solar heat and light. Today, many buildings are designed to take advantage of this natural resource through the use of passive solar heating and daylighting.

The south side of a building always receives the most sunlight. Therefore, buildings designed for passive solar heating usually have large, south-facing windows. Materials that absorb and store the sun's heat can be built into the sunlit floors and walls. The floors and walls will then heat up during the day and slowly release heat at night, when the heat is needed most. This passive solar design feature is called *direct gain.*

Other passive solar heating design features include *sunspaces* and *trombe walls*. A sunspace (which is much like a greenhouse) is built on the south side of a building. As sunlight passes through glass or other glazing, it warms the sunspace. Proper ventilation allows the heat to circulate into the building. On the other hand, a trombe wall is a very thick, south-facing wall, which is painted black and made of a material that absorbs a lot of heat. A pane of glass or plastic glazing, installed a few inches in front of the wall, helps hold in the heat. The wall heats up slowly during the day. Then as it cools gradually during the night, it gives off its heat inside the building.

Many of the passive solar heating design features also provide daylighting. Daylighting is simply the use of natural sunlight to brighten up a building's interior. To lighten up north-facing rooms and upper levels, a *clerestory* — a row of windows near the peak of the roof — is often used along with an open floor plan inside that allows the light to bounce throughout the building.

Of course, too much solar heating and daylighting can be a problem during the hot summer months. Fortunately, there are many design features that help keep passive solar buildings cool in the summer. For instance, overhangs can be designed to shade windows when the sun is high in the summer. Sunspaces can be closed off from the rest of the building. And a building can be designed to use fresh-air ventilation in the summer.

Photovoltaics

Solar cells, also called photovoltaics (PV) by solar cell scientists, convert sunlight directly into electricity. Solar cells are often used to power calculators and watches. They are made of semiconducting materials similar to those used in computer chips. When sunlight is absorbed by these materials, the solar energy knocks electrons loose from their atoms, allowing the electrons to flow through the material to produce electricity. This process of converting light (photons) to electricity (voltage) is called the *photovoltaic (PV) effect.*

Solar cells are typically combined into modules that hold about 40 cells; about 10 of these modules are mounted in PV *arrays* that can measure up to several meters on a side. These *flat-plate* PV arrays can be mounted at a fixed angle facing south, or they can be mounted on a tracking device that follows the sun, allowing them to capture the most sunlight over the course of a day. About 10 to 20 PV arrays can provide enough power for a household; for large electric utility or industrial applications, hundreds of arrays can be interconnected to form a single, large PV system.

Thin film solar cells use layers of semiconductor materials only a few micrometers thick. Thin film technology has made it possible for solar cells to now double as rooftop shingles, roof tiles, building facades, or the glazing for skylights or atria. The solar cell version of items such as shingles offer the same protection and durability as ordinary asphalt shingles.

Some solar cells are designed to operate with concentrated sunlight. These cells are built into *concentrating collectors* that use a lens to focus the sunlight onto the cells. This approach has both advantages and disadvantages compared with flat-plate PV arrays. The main idea is to use very little of the expensive semiconducting PV material while collecting as much sunlight as possible. But because the lenses must be pointed at the sun, the use of concentrating collectors is limited to the sunniest parts of the country. Some concentrating collectors are designed to be mounted on simple tracking devices, but most require sophisticated tracking devices, which further limit their use to electric utilities, industries, and large buildings.

The performance of a solar cell is measured in terms of its efficiency at turning sunlight into electricity. Only sunlight of certain energies will work efficiently to create electricity, and much of it is reflected or absorbed by the material that make up the cell. Because of this, a typical commercial solar cell has an efficiency of 15% — about one-sixth of the sunlight striking the cell generates electricity. Low efficiencies mean that larger arrays are needed, and that means higher cost. Improving solar cell efficiencies while holding down the cost per cell is an important goal of the PV industry, NREL researchers, and other U.S. Department of Energy (DOE) laboratories, and they have made significant progress. The first solar cells, built in the 1950s, had efficiencies of less than 4%.

QUESTIONS AND DISCUSSION

1. *Solar and Nighttime Energy.* Solar energy has long been viewed as a daytime-only power source, due to the inefficient and prohibitively expensive solar energy storage options in existence. However, in July 2008, scientists with the Massachusetts Institute of Technology (MIT) announced a breakthrough in solar technology that could allow for highly efficient, and cheap, storage of solar energy through a process that mimics photosynthesis. Press Release, Massachusetts Institute of Technology, "Major Discovery" from MIT Primed to Unleash Solar Revolution: Scientists Mimic Essence of Plants' Energy Storage System (July 31, 2008), *available at* http://web.mit.edu/newsoffice/2008/oxygen-0731.html. If the technology succeeds, the MIT scientists believe that homes could be powered solely through solar technology and will no longer depend on centralized power delivery for nighttime electricity. *Id.*

2. *Public Lands and Energy Development.* On June 26, 2008, the United States announced a freeze on the development of solar energy projects on public lands managed by the Bureau of Land Management (BLM) in six western states so that the agency could prepare a programmatic Environmental Impact Statement (EIS). *See* 73 Fed. Reg. 30,907 (May 29, 2008). According to BLM officials, a number of factors must be assessed, including the impact of construction and transmission lines on native vegetation and wildlife, the impact of operating a solar facility on water use because certain solar plants may require water to condense the steam used to power the turbine, and reclamation of land after the 20- to 30-year life span of the solar plant. Dan Frosch, *Citing Need for Assessments, U.S. Freezes Solar Energy Projects*, N.Y. TIMES, June 27, 2008. A week later, however, BLM announced that it would lift the ban on solar energy applications, citing concerns by commenters who thought the ban would stifle renewable energy development. Press Release, BLM, BLM to Continue Accepting Solar Energy Applications (July 2, 2008), *available at* http://www.blm.gov/wo/st/en/info/newsroom/2008/July/NR_07_02_2008.html.

The agency initially thought the freeze necessary to address the 125 current proposals submitted by solar companies to develop solar energy on BLM-managed lands in Arizona, California, Colorado, Nevada, New Mexico and Utah. The proposals cover almost one million acres with the potential to generate 70 billion watts of electricity, or enough to power more than 20 million average American homes. BLM, BLM Initiates Environmental Analysis of Solar Energy Development (May 29, 2008, updated June 12, 2008), *available at* http://www.blm.gov/wo/st/en/info/newsroom/2008/may_08/NR_053008.html.

Taken at face value, the need for a programmatic EIS seems essential as the projects range across a vast amount of land as many solar companies agree. Yet, others consider the solar freeze unwarranted or, worse, a "spiteful" move by the Bush Administration to slow the development of alternative energy resources while at the same time promoting fossil fuels. David Sassoon, *U.S. Freezes Solar Projects to Study Environmental Impact of Collecting Sunshine in the Desert* (SolveClimate, June 27, 2008).

The temporary ban nonetheless raises questions about the role public agencies should play in managing public lands for energy production. In fact, a week before the freeze, President Bush asked Congress to open up the Green River Basin, straddling Colorado, Utah, and Wyoming, for development of oil shale (as well as the Arctic National Wildlife Refuge and the Outer Continental Shelf to oil and gas drilling). *President Bush Discusses Energy* (June 18, 2008), *available at* http://www.whitehouse.gov/news/releases/2008/06/20080618.html. The development of oil shale is currently banned by federal law. Large-scale development has so far not occurred "due to substantial cost and technical challenges associated with processing the shale and safely disposing of the waste." ANN BORDETSKY, ET AL., DRIVING IT HOME: CHOOSING THE RIGHT PATH FOR FUELING NORTH AMERICA'S TRANSPORTATION FUTURE 12 (NRDC et al., 2007). As is clear from the following excerpt, oil shale development is likely to have significantly greater environmental impacts than solar energy:

> Oil shale contains kerogen, a precursor to petroleum. Extracting the petroleum from oil shale involves heating the rock to temperatures reaching 900° F to turn the kerogen into a liquid . . .

> Producing oil from shale takes an enormous amount of energy and causes the emission of higher amounts of global warming pollution than conventional oil development. The RAND Corporation in 2005 found that the production of just 100,000 barrels of shale oil a day using Shell's proposed *in-situ* process would require 1,200 megawatts of power. Development of this scale would call for construction of a power plant as large as any in Colorado history, large enough to serve a city of 500,000 people. Such a plant would consume 5 million tons of coal each year, requiring construction of new coal mines that would devastate wildlife habitat and create huge scars on the landscape . . . . The power plant required for producing 100,000 barrels of shale oil a day — a very small industry — would also emit 10 million tons of global warming pollution. Oil shale boosters like to talk about producing 1 million barrels of shale oil a day, which would require construction of 10 new power plants that could generate up to 121 million tons of CO_2 per year. This would represent a 90 percent increase in the CO_2 emitted by all existing electric utility generating units in 2005 in Colorado, Wyoming, and Utah combined. Added to this horrific amount of global warming pollution is the CO_2 that would result from actually burning the produced shale oil. . . .

> The scarcity of water in the American West makes it a valuable resource, and oil shale development threatens to cut into water availability even more. Each barrel of shale oil produced using the mine-and-retort process will likely use from 2.1 to 5.2 barrels of water. In 1996, the Bureau of Land Management (BLM) found that oil shale development would result in up to an 8.2 percent reduction in the annual flow of Colorado's White River where it meets the Green River in northeastern Utah.

Id. at 12. How should BLM prioritize energy development on public lands? BLM is charged under the Federal Land Policy and Management Act (FLPMA) to manage public lands for multiple uses. Its mission under FLPMA is to sustain the health and productivity of the public lands for the use and enjoyment of present and future generations. Does this mission provide BLM any meaningful guidance?

3. *Solar Power v. Trees.* Under California's 1978 Solar Shade Control Act, Cal. Pub. Res. Code §§ 25980-25966, tree owners may not allow their trees to cast a shadow over more than 10 percent of a solar collector during the hours of 10 a.m. to 2 p.m. *Id.* § 25982. Among its various exemptions, the law exempts trees planted before 1979 from the shading prohibition. *Id.* It also exempts trees which cast shadows over the solar panels within one year of installation of the solar panels. *Id.* However, existing trees that ultimately grow enough to cast the offending shade are not exempt. *Id.* Tree owners who violate the law are subject to both civil and criminal prosecution. If a tree owner receives an abatement notice from a prosecuting attorney ordering removal or alteration of the tree, a tree owner may be held liable for $1,000 per day for each day the owner retains the tree in violation of the abatement notice. *Id.* § 25983.

In May 2008, the Solar Shade Control Act received attention when a California court convicted a couple for violating the Act. The couple had planted eight redwood trees in 1993. Their neighbor had installed rooftop solar panels in 2001. In 2005, a deputy district attorney initiated a prosecution against the couple, and the judge ultimately found that 3 trees violated the Act. The other trees, the judge found, were exempt because they had cast shadows over the solar panels within a year of the panels' installation. *See* Felicity Barringer, *Trees Block Solar Panels, and a Feud Ends in Court*, N.Y. TIMES, Apr. 7, 2008, at A14. In response to the dispute, the California legislature amended the law to establish a first-in-time, first-in-right system that would allow trees that shade solar panels to remain in place if they were planted before the installation of the solar panels. S.B. 1399 (Jul. 22, 2008), codified at Cal. Pub. Res. Code §§ 25980-25966.

Do you think the California legislature's amendment is the correct response? California has enacted a "million solar roofs" program to encourage the installation of residential solar arrays. While the revision to the Solar Shade Control Act will, as the bill's sponsor suggested, avoid "a million neighborhood arguments," *see* Barringer at A14, doesn't it also have the potential to stifle solar installations? Is there a better way to promote neighborhood harmony while encouraging solar development? Do common law rules of property and nuisance inform this discussion? *See* Tenn v. 889 Associates Ldg, 500 A.2d 366 (N.H. 1985) (addressing rights of homeowners to sunlight).

---

3. *Hydropower*

Hydropower currently supplies between 70 and 80 percent of the renewable energy produced in the United States. Most of the nation's hydropower facilities were constructed during the middle part of the 20th century, often without full consideration of the impacts that dams could have on aquatic ecosystems. As the consequences of large dams became clearer, public opposition to major dam projects increased. No major hydropower dam has been built in the United States since the 1970s. Indeed, the trend in the U.S. has been to remove dams in order to provide migratory fish passage to upstream spawning grounds. However, some lawmakers have begun to explore the possibility of building additional hydropower facilities in an effort to expand the U.S. renewable energy portfolio.

U.S. DEPARTMENT OF ENERGY,
HYDROPOWER BASICS (2008)

Advantages * * *

Hydropower is generally available as needed; engineers can control the flow of water through the turbines to produce electricity on demand.

Hydropower plants provide benefits in addition to clean electricity. Impoundment hydropower creates reservoirs that offer a variety of recreational opportunities, notably fishing, swimming, and boating. Most hydropower installations are required to provide some public access to the reservoir to allow the public to take advantage of these opportunities. Other benefits may include water supply and flood control.

Disadvantages

Fish populations can be impacted if fish cannot migrate upstream past impoundment dams to spawning grounds or if they cannot migrate downstream to the ocean. Upstream fish passage can be aided using fish ladders or elevators, or by trapping and hauling the fish upstream by truck. Downstream fish passage is aided by diverting fish from turbine intakes using screens or racks or even underwater lights and sounds, and by maintaining a minimum spill flow past the turbine.

Hydropower can impact water quality and flow. Hydropower plants can cause low dissolved oxygen levels in the water, a problem that is harmful to riparian (riverbank) habitats and is addressed using various aeration techniques, which oxygenate the water. Maintaining minimum flows of water downstream of a hydropower installation is also critical for the survival of riparian habitats.

Hydropower plants can be impacted by drought. When water is not available, the hydropower plants can't produce electricity.

New hydropower facilities impact the local environment and may compete with other uses for the land. Those alternative uses may be more highly valued than electricity generation. Humans, flora, and fauna may lose their natural habitat. Local cultures and historical sites may be impinged upon. Some older hydropower facilities may have historic value, so renovations of these facilities must also be sensitive to such preservation concerns and to impacts on plant and animal life.

QUESTIONS AND DISCUSSION

1. *Greenhouse Gas Emissions from Hydropower Projects.* In 2000, a study published in *BioScience* reported that hydropower dams could contribute up to seven percent of global greenhouse gas emissions. Vincent L. St. Louis, et al., *Reservoir Surfaces as Sources of Greenhouse Gases to the Atmosphere: A Global Estimate*, 50 BioScience 766 (2000). In particular, the study noted that reservoirs behind hydroelectric dams could release significant amounts of methane and carbon dioxide, and that annual emissions from twenty-one of the studied dams would equal emissions of greenhouse gases released from three large coal-fired power plants. The exact type and nature of the emissions from dams depend, however, on factors such as climate, soil type, and vegetation in the reservoir. Nonetheless, this

study suggests that climate change may not necessarily lead to a new era of dam construction.

2. As noted above, the generation of renewable sources of energy creates adverse environmental impacts, not just climate change impacts. Which renewable energy sources should the United States promote? How should it promote renewable energy sources?

3. *Biomass and Geothermal Energy.* Biomass and geothermal energy are also potential sources of renewable energy. Geothermal energy is simply heat from the earth, usually in the form of hot water or steam. Shallow reservoirs provide a ready source of energy, while deeper sources usually require drilling to access. Geothermal sources have the potential to provide baseload powers for electricity systems, because geothermal sources release heat constantly. The Energy Information Administration estimates that geothermal sources could provide approximately 22,000 megawatts (MW) of power. While this figure is significantly higher than the current 2,200 MW of power currently produced by geothermal sources, it is a small fraction of the existing capacity of the U.S. electric power system, which is currently more than one million MW.

Biomass refers to any energy derived from plants and other organic materials, including waste. Wood is the largest biomass energy source in use in the United States, but plants and landfills also produce biomass energy. Current efforts to increase biomass production have focused on developing biofuels, which are discussed in Chapter 15, *infra*.

4. *Price.* As the above readings indicate, one of the principle hurdles for renewable energy is its cost-ineffectiveness vis-à-vis fossil fuels.

Table 14-1: Price Comparison of Electricity from Various Sources

Source	Price per kilowatt-hour
Coal	4.8 to 5.5 cents
Natural Gas	3.9 to 4.4 cents
Nuclear	11.1 to 14.5 cents
Wind	4 to 6 cents
Concentrated solar power plants	10 to 14 cents
Electricity from solar panels installed on homes and businesses	25 to 40 cents
Biofuels Power plants that burn biomass directly	Variable depending on fuel source, how it is converted to electricity, and size of plant 7 to 9 cents

To some extent, this price disparity is likely due to the amount of support the various energy sources receive. The General Accounting Office estimated that between 2002 and 2007, fossil fuels energy sources received $3.2 billion dollars in appropriations for research and development (mostly aimed at clean coal technology) and another $13.7 billion to promote electricity production from fossil fuels. Nuclear energy research and development received $6.2 billion. In comparison, Congress allocated $1.4 billion for research and development, and $2.8 billion for electricity production from renewable energy. Thus, the amount provided to fossil fuels ($16.9 billion) was more than four times that given to renewable energy sources ($4.2 billion). GAO, REPORT ABSTRACT, FEDERAL ELECTRICITY SUBSIDIES: INFORMATION ON RESEARCH FUNDING, TAX EXPENDITURES, AND OTHER ACTIVITIES THAT SUPPORT ELECTRICITY PRODUCTION, GAO-08-102 (Oct. 26, 2007). In addition, as discussed in greater detail below, renewable energy sources have been particularly vulnerable to uncertainty resulting from tax credit phase-outs, which suspend or reduce the available tax credits after only one or two years.

IV. RENEWABLE ENERGY GENERATION: REGULATION AND INCENTIVES

If renewable energy sources are ever to become the dominant source of power in the United States, the regulatory structure governing energy production and delivery must change. The current regulatory model favors large-scale, centralized power plants. Renewable energy sources, however, will likely never be able to compete with traditional sources of power under this model. Thus, energy experts believe that the electricity system must undergo restructuring if it will ever be able to support renewable energy. Other types of regulation, including federal renewable portfolio standard and federal tax credits and subsidies, will likely also need further development and reform if renewable energy is to succeed on a grand scale. This section discusses some of the regulatory reforms and incentives that may enable a transition to a renewable energy portfolio.

A. Reforming the Electricity System

Most energy experts believe that a thriving renewable energy system will require significant changes to the current electricity structure. In part, as discussed above in Professor Bosselman's excerpt regarding nuclear power, this is because the U.S. electricity system has been structured around baseload power plants which provide the vast majority of the nation's power. Baseload power plants are larger, capital-intensive structures that can deliver massive amounts of reliable energy to the power system. Due to the intermittent nature of wind and solar energy, most utilities have not viewed them as viable sources of baseload power. While this is slowly changing, experts continue to believe that a shift toward renewable energy sources will require a shift in the electricity system. The challenge for energy reform involves not only overcoming the technological hurdles associated with developing new energy sources, but also requires a new legal structure to accommodate diverse sources of electric power.

SIDNEY A. SHAPIRO & JOSEPH P. TOMAIN, RETHINKING REFORM OF ELECTRICITY MARKETS,
40 Wake Forest L. Rev. 497, 517–29 (2005)[*]

IV. The Smart Generation Model

In this Part, we discuss four prominent examples of generation of electricity under a Smart Model: distributed generation, renewable energy, renewable portfolio standards, and the Smart Grid. All of these options are potential improvements in the generation and delivery of electricity that respond to the concerns about energy, the environment, and security. While these ideas have been part of energy policy discussions for many years, they have stayed at the periphery of those discussions, mostly because they have been too costly and have not passed a market test. To date, investors have been reluctant to invest in these alternatives

---

because they have not been promised a sufficient return on their investment.

One reason, we believe, for the limited attractiveness of Smart Model generation options is the lack of accurate price signals in electricity markets. Through greater price accuracy, which we discuss in the next Part of the article, consumers can make smarter consumption choices, producers can make smarter investment decisions, and the industry can perform more efficiently. Simply, COS [cost of service] ratemaking can no longer be relied upon to continue to regulate the industry. Instead, we examine marginal cost pricing and real time pricing models that are intended to bring prices closer to the market and are intended to give consumers more accurate price signals.

One other preliminary observation is pertinent. Each of the alternatives that we discuss must connect with the transmission and distribution grid to greater or lesser degrees. Distributed generation needs backup access to backup power. Renewable resources need to connect with the market. Renewable energy portfolios have the same needs. And, the Smart Grid is an improved grid. In other words, as much as we might like to get away from the Traditional Model, the grid remains central to the electricity industry, and the grid retains its natural monopoly characteristic, thus necessitating regulation in one form or another. The grid will remain a necessary component until electricity production and distribution become localized, and that decentralization is starting through distributed generation.

A. Distributed Generation

Distributed generation ("DG") is an alternative source of electricity generation that focuses on small-scale power production. The core concept behind DG is that power will be produced locally, instead of relying on large regional grids for transmission and distribution. DG power producers will be much smaller and will rely on a variety of energy sources and technologies such as solar cells and wind turbines.

DG technologies include gas or diesel-fired engines, small turbines, fuel cells, and photovoltaic cells. While some of these fuel sources are fossil fuels, it is contemplated that DG technologies will capture both heat and power, thereby increasing energy efficiency. Other fuel sources are renewable and therefore cleaner than the fossil fuels burned in large-scale plants.

DG and micropower are dependent upon significant technological improvements throughout electricity production, transmission, distribution, storage, and consumption. Most simply, the scale of generation units is reduced significantly, and they are widely dispersed. "Smart energy" technologies are intended to reduce the size of power generation units, to be closer to the source of consumption, to utilize "Smart Grids" which will transmit power more efficiently, and to use "smart meters" which will provide consumers with more information about their consumption patterns and about their choice of providers.

Another term for DG is micropower, which also involves new technologies including microturbines, hydrogen fuels, solar cells, landfill gases, and the like. In this regard, micropower is touted as a clean energy alternative. According to the International Energy Agency, these technologies are increasing in importance. . . . [I]t is fair to assert that we are witnessing a worldwide rise in DG and micropower. * * *

C. Renewable Portfolio Standards

According to the federal government, a renewable portfolio standard ("RPS") is a "market-based strategy to ensure that renewable energy constitutes a certain percentage of total energy generation or consumption." The government creates a RPS when it requires electricity generators or sellers to supply a percentage of their electricity generation or sales with electricity from renewable resources or technologies. Although there are no federal RPS programs to date, they are operating in various states. As of 2004, eighteen states had programs in place.

Acknowledging that the renewable resources are often not cost competitive with traditional resources does not end consideration of them in our energy future. Rather, the question becomes how to encourage the development and deployment of smaller, cleaner renewable energy resources and technologies. A standard regulatory response is through subsidies, financial incentives, standards, and other regulatory devices. State governments have developed a different response through standard setting. In particular, several state governments now require that electricity producers must provide specified percentages of generation from renewable energy sources by specified dates. As examples, California has set a target portfolio requirement of twenty percent by 2017, and Maine set a thirty percent goal to be achieved by 2000. Hydroelectricity, however, is included in Maine's definition of renewable resources. Often, RPS programs include a trading provision through which regulated firms can trade renewable energy credits, thus creating a market like the emissions trading market. This market gives producers more flexibility in meeting the standards imposed upon them because a generator that cannot meet its requirement can purchase credits, while generators that can exceed the goal will sell credits.

RPS programs can be designed such as to encourage the development and use of particular technologies. Nevada, for example, encourages the use of photovoltaic cells by giving literally extra credits for electricity produced by those cells. [Editor's Note: For more on RPSs, *see* below and Chapter 17.]

D. Smart Electricity Grids

Each of the previous smart energy activities depends on a reliable distribution system, and the grid is in need of improvement as attested to by the August 2003 Blackout. New technologies, under the rubric "Smart Grid," promise to improve the grid and enable it to move electricity more efficiently and more effectively.

The Smart Grid promises "important economic, security, and environmental benefits by promoting substantial upgrades to the performance of the transmission and distribution network that connects electricity generators and consumers." Contemporary thinking, then, integrates energy, environment, and security into the distribution and transmission system by incorporating "sophisticated sensing and monitoring technology, information technology, and communications to provide better grid performance and to support a wide array of additional services to consumers."

There is a general consensus that investment in the electricity infrastructure is lagging behind our electricity needs and that additional, more reliable, transmission and distribution capacity is necessary. Given the need for a system upgrade, there is no reason not to improve upon the technology while simultaneously addressing environmental and security needs. Such improvements can occur through the so-called Smart Grid that involves:

- Infrastructure with "smarter" controls to support robust market activity; rapid recovery from cascading outages, natural disasters and potential terrorist attacks;

- High quality and highly reliable electricity for our digital economy;

- An infrastructure connected with advanced communications to form an energy web;

- An energy web which increases economic productivity;

- "Clean . . . power generation technologies" and "universal access to affordable electricity."

Smart Grid technologies are attractive not only because they are responsive to the increasing environmental sensitivity of progressive electricity policies but also because they increase grid security and contribute to greater demand sensitivities. Security is heightened as the grid operates more rapidly to recognize and isolate problem areas. The Smart Grid will also be one that can easily accommodate distributed and small-scale generation technologies, which, by their size alone, make less attractive targets. The Smart Grid is intended to be consumer friendly in other ways as well by providing communications and power to "smart" buildings to make the most intelligent use of equipment. Such portals enable residential, commercial and industrial customers to "manage electricity use in a manner that improves efficiency and reduces consumer energy costs, while at the same time enhancing customer control of electrical equipment."

QUESTIONS AND DISCUSSION

1. *Distributed Generation.* Distributed generation used to be the dominant model of electricity generation before scientists had discovered how to move electricity over high-voltage, long-distance transmission lines. The term simply refers to localized, small-scale distribution of power from a wider number of power sources. While the concept is simple, PUCs are only now beginning to adjust their regulatory policies to enable distributed generation to become a more prevalent element of electricity service.

2. *Cogeneration.* One increasingly popular type of distributed generation involves the use of cogeneration technology. Cogeneration converts the waste heat from conventional energy generation technologies into a usable source of energy. For industrial facilities that already generate their own electricity, cogeneration technologies may result in significant energy efficiencies.

> Both conventional electric generation technologies and industrial process heat applications are inefficient. Conventional electric generating technologies typically exhaust as much as two-thirds of the heat energy produced to power electric generators. Industry uses process steam most often in applications below 400 degrees Fahrenheit. However, combustion of fossil fuels to produce that heat results in temperatures of more than 3000 degrees Fahrenheit, much of which is wasted. The next major leap in efficiency must come from recovering and reusing waste heat. Machines that recover all waste heat and produce electricity have the capability to achieve efficiencies from 50 to 90%, much better than the typical thirty-plus percent of the existing central station utility fossil fuel steam system.

> Cogeneration technologies make use of the otherwise wasted heat from the combustion process. Cogeneration technologies produce electricity and a second form of useful energy, heat. The use gets two forms of useful energy for the effort and price of one. Thus, cogeneration facilities operate

at overall thermal efficiencies as great as 250 to 300% higher than conventional electric generating technologies. The very best cogeneration technologies are more than twice as efficient as new coal-fired power plants. As generating technologies become more efficient, they diminish the residual heat energy wasted. This, in turn, diminishes the by-product or cogeneration potential application of heat energy.

The heat recovered from a cogenerating energy system, a system generating heat and electricity, can be used for direct application heat, for industrial process heat, or for pre-heating the combustion air for a utility boiler. By capturing waste heat in the process of electric generation, greater efficiency is achieved. This means that more useful energy can be produced while generating a lower amount of environmental pollutants and emissions. It also means that less transmission capability would be required if there is development of dispersed electric and total energy systems, located close to load centers. Not only will additional transmission capacity not be required in certain areas, but capacity requirements of existing transmission grids will be alleviated. One way to view this phenomenon is that if natural gas cogeneration or total energy systems replace centrally dispatched electricity, energy will be moved more in its primary form by natural gas pipelines and less in its derived form as electricity.

Steven Ferrey, N*othing But Net: Renewable Energy and the Environment, Midamerican Legal Fictions, and Supremacy Doctrine*, 14 DUKE ENVTL. L. & POL'Y F. 1, 6–9 (2003).

3. *Net Metering.* Many PUCs have enacted "net metering" laws to promote the use of renewable energy sources.

Net metering enables customers to use their own generation to offset their consumption over a billing period by allowing their electric meters to turn backwards when they generate electricity in excess of their demand. This offset means that customers receive retail prices for the excess electricity they generate. Without net metering, a second meter is usually installed to measure the electricity that flows back to the provider, with the provider purchasing the power at a rate much lower than the retail rate.

Net metering is a low-cost, easily administered method of encouraging customer investment in renewable energy technologies. It increases the value of the electricity produced by renewable generation and allows customers to "bank" their energy and use it at a different time than it is produced giving customers more flexibility and allowing them to maximize the value of their production. Providers may also benefit from net metering because when customers are producing electricity during peak periods, the system load factor is improved.

U.S. Department of Energy, *Energy Efficiency and Renewable Energy, Net Metering Policies* (2008), *available at* http://www.eere.energy.gov/greenpower/markets/netmetering.shtml.

B.   Renewable Portfolio Standards

Although many states have passed their own renewable portfolio standards (RPS), Congress has repeatedly declined to do so. In 2007, Congress considered and then rejected a bill that would have required electricity utilities to purchase a certain percentage of the energy from renewable energy sources. Only after this RPS provision was stripped from the Energy Independence and Security Act of 2007 did Congress pass, and the President sign, major federal energy legislation.

Federal proposals for RPSs establish a gradual increase in the amount of renewable energy utilities must purchase over a period of time. For example, the Renewable Energy and Energy Conservation Tax Act of 2007 would have required utilities to purchase 2.75 percent of their electricity from renewable sources in 2010 and increased that amount to 15 percent by 2020. H.R. 3221, 110th Cong. (as passed by the House, Aug. 4, 2007). Federal proposals also allow utilities to trade renewable energy credits (RECs), which are meant to provide flexibility by allowing utilities that cannot produce their own renewable energy to pay for credits instead. Although this model has been adopted and implemented in at least twenty states, the federal government has to date refused to adopt a national RPS. State RPS programs are discussed in Chapter 17. As you read the following excerpt, consider whether concerns regarding the economic impacts of an RPS demonstrate why a national RPS is infeasible.

JOSHUA P. FERSHEE, CHANGING RESOURCES, CHANGING MARKET: THE IMPACT OF A NATIONAL RENEWABLE PORTFOLIO STANDARD ON THE U.S. ENERGY INDUSTRY
29 ENERGY L.J. 49, 55–62 (2008)*

2. The Goals: The Case for a National RPS

Congressional proponents of the Proposed RPS (and most versions of an RPS) cite several goals, including: reduced pollution, improved national security, job creation, and lower consumer prices. Additionally, a national program, rather than a state-by-state program, is more likely to provide a strong national market, thus leading to more renewable energy projects.

* * * One of the broader descriptions of the potential benefits of a national RPS can be found in the Union of Concerned Scientists' response, which stated that a national RPS "standard can provide many benefits for the nation, including increasing energy security, fuel diversity, price stability, jobs, farm and ranch income, tax revenues, technology development, customer choices, and reduced environmental impacts, water consumption, and resource depletion, as well as reduced compliance costs with current and future environmental regulations."

There are several ways in which these benefits would be achieved. Probably the most obvious would be the potential environmental benefits. Although electricity accounts for less than 3% of U.S. economic activity, "the burning of coal, oil, and natural gas for power currently accounts for more than 26 percent of smog-producing nitrogen oxide emissions, one-third of toxic mercury emissions, and 64 percent of acid rain-causing SO_2 emissions." One expert has asserted that if "20 percent of our electricity in 2020 were to be provided by renewables, then we would be displacing the equivalent of 71 million cars from the nation's highway." Others have noted that the increased use of renewable energy would reduce harmful emissions or reduce the cost of compliance with requirements to reduce pollution.

"And by reducing the need to extract, transport, and consume fossil fuels, a national RPS would limit the damage done to our water and land and conserve natural resources for future generations."

From a national security perspective, the primary benefit would come from a reduced dependence on foreign energy supplies, because renewable resources such as wind, sun, and biomass, tend to come from domestic sources. In the electricity sector, the most significant source would be reduced need for natural gas, which is increasingly coming (in liquefied form) from overseas. Enormous amounts of natural gas are used for electric generation, including as much as 90% or more of new electric generation.

A reduction in the use of natural gas would also, by many accounts, lead to lower prices for consumers. A recent study by Woods Mackenzie, an energy-industry consultancy, indicated that a 15% national RPS would "drive down" the demand for, and price of, natural gas and "lower the overall price of power." The company found that regardless of whether a national RPS is implemented, the "United States needs to build 420 GW of capacity over the next twenty years to replace aging facilities and meet its ever-growing need for electricity." A national RPS would create incentives ensuring, essentially requiring, that some of that new generation be fueled by renewable sources. This switch, according to the Woods MacKenzie study, to renewable generation sources would lower fuel costs and reduce fossil fuel consumption, leading to lower electricity costs, amounting to approximately $100 billion in savings.

Perhaps the most important, if not the most obvious, potential benefit of a national RPS is economic development and job creation. In projecting the impact of a 20% national RPS, the Union of Concerned Scientists determined that, by 2020, such an RPS "would generate more than 355,000 jobs in manufacturing, construction, operation, maintenance, and other industries — nearly twice as many as fossil fuels, representing a net increase of 157,480 jobs . . . " Further, it was determined that renewable energy would "provide an additional $8.2 billion in income and $10.2 billion in gross domestic product in the U.S. economy in 2020." Although premised on a national RPS percentage higher than that in the Proposed RPS, these numbers nonetheless indicate that a national RPS could provide significant economic benefits.

The most compelling job creation claims come from a report developed by the Renewable Energy Policy Project. The group determined that more than 16,000 firms in all fifty states have the technical potential to enter the growing wind turbine manufacturing sector. The twenty states that would potentially benefit the most, receiving 80% of the job creation, are the same states that account for "76% of the manufacturing jobs lost in the [U.S. over the] last 3 1/2 years."

The report considered the impact on U.S. manufacturing jobs if there were eight times more wind energy installations, which would mean a capital investment of $50 billion. Again, while this report is an estimate based on a number of major assumptions, the conclusions are still compelling, especially in states that have lost hundreds of thousands of jobs in the past six years.

3. The Criticisms: The Case Against a National RPS

* * * The primary arguments against a national RPS are that it could lead to increased consumer costs, that the RPS amounts to a wealth transfer from states with lower levels of renewable resources to states with high levels, and that it is unnecessary and better handled at the state level. * * *

Some major studies indicate a potential increase in consumer electricity costs if a national RPS were implemented. The Energy Information Administration (EIA) released a study in June 2007 of a proposed 15% RPS by 2030, which indicated that "cumulative residential expenditures on electricity from 2005 through 2030 are $7.2 billion (0.4 percent) higher, while cumulative residential expenditures on natural gas are $1.0 billion (0.1 percent) lower." For a 25% RPS by 2025, the costs would likely be much more significant: "the cost of complying with the [25% RPS] is projected to increase the price of electricity by about 3.3 percent and 6.2 percent in 2025 and 2030, respectively." On a more local level, opponents of the Proposed RPS have claimed that consumers in some states could see electricity bills rise as much as $15 per month.

Such increased costs are also part of the second major argument against a national RPS — that it essentially amounts to a wealth transfer from states with few renewable resources to those with significant renewable resources. States like North Dakota, Montana, Texas, and Kansas have significant renewable energy sources available, especially wind. Southeastern states, like Florida and Virginia, have very limited wind resources available, which could mean that such states would need to purchase RECs from renewable-rich states to stay in compliance with the national RPS requirements. The risk of this wealth transfer is apparent in certain scenarios. For example, the EIA [Energy Information Administration] determined that under a 25% RPS by 2025, the RPS would lead to higher overall electricity prices, but could,

> result in lower electricity prices in some areas of the United States. The Western Regions have considerable renewable resources that could enable suppliers to provide renewable generation in excess of their own requirements and sell surplus credits to producers in other areas with less economical renewable options. The resulting revenue could more than offset the costs of building renewable plants in the West.

A major component of the wealth-transfer complaint of a national RPS is that it unfairly promotes wind and solar energy, thus requiring states with limited solar and wind resources to pay other states for the renewable resources. However, there are indications that other renewable sources, biomass in particular, would help balance this potential inequity. "[B]iomass generation is considerably higher than the output from wind capacity . . . because of a higher biomass capacity factor." Additionally, energy efficiency provisions, like those in the Proposed RPS, could further assist in the "uneven geography of renewable resources." Nonetheless, this risk remains a significant criticism of a national RPS.

Finally, many opponents of a national RPS argue that it is unnecessary to have a national plan because state and regional initiatives are already handling the issue in regions where it is appropriate and the states, individually or regionally, are better situated to implement plans that account for regional differences. For example, in the case of the Proposed RPS, a major complaint is that a "one-size-fits-all Federal mandate does not take into account the specific energy and economic needs of individual States by requiring that 15 percent of retail electricity sales be generated from specific renewable resources which are not prevalent" in all regions. Although there are arguably benefits that a national plan can achieve that individual state plans cannot . . . many state plans are already well established and effective.

QUESTIONS AND DISCUSSION

1. ***Are States Better Equipped to Manage RPSs?*** One of the arguments against a federal RPS is that most states already have renewable requirements, and a federal RPS would merely be redundant or conflict with the goals underlying state RPSs. Many states that have adopted their RPSs have done so to boost their own renewable energy industries or to reduce local pollution. *See* Chapter 17. If the federal government were to adopt its own RPS, there could be the potential for utilities to purchase RECs from out-of-state sources and thereby stifle their own state's industry or environmental goals. Does this suggest that federal lawmakers who want an RPS may be misguided in their approach?

2. ***Costs of RECs and Trading Limitations.*** To address concerns regarding the high costs of RECs and potential increases in consumer electricity prices, some federal RPS proposals have proposed setting a cost cap on renewable energy credits. For example, the Renewable Energy and Energy Conservation Tax Act of 2007 proposed to cap REC prices at 1.9 cents per kilowatt-hour. The Energy Information Administration (EIA) calculated that this price cap would actually stifle the renewable energy market *and* likely result in REC prices that would be higher than under a trading program without a price cap. If utilities knew at the outset how much each REC would cost, the EIA found that many utilities would simply pay for RECs rather than investing in their own renewable energy technology. Renewable energy producers, moreover, would not have economic incentives to increase their production of energy, because the cost of the RECs would never be able to go above the 1.9 cent cap. In contrast, the lack of a cap would provide producers with the incentive to enter the market early (when fewer producers exist and the cost of RECs could presumably be higher) and would spur new renewable energy facilities to enter the market.

3. ***Stifling the Long-Term Market.*** Another issue with existing federal RPS proposals is the time frame for compliance and how that affects the renewable energy market. Under the Renewable Energy and Energy Conservation Tax Act of 2007, once utilities attained the goal of purchasing 20 percent of their electricity from renewable sources by 2020, the RPS would remain at 20 percent until 2039. The EIA found that the RPS would initially spur entry into the renewable energy market as the RPS climbs from 2.75 percent to 15 percent. However, as the 15 percent goal nears, renewable energy producers will have little incentive to enter the market unless Congress enacts another RPS requirement extending beyond 2020. This uncertainty, which is also present in Congress' use of subsidies and tax incentives, has been a primary concern of the renewable energy industry as it plans to move forward.

4. In contrast to the United States, the 27 member States of the European Union have agreed to a mandatory target to derive 20 percent of their energy needs from renewable energy by 2020, including a 10 percent biofuels target. While setting an overall EU goal, the EU directive establishes specific targets for each member State. Each member State's share will be determined based on the amount of energy produced from renewable resources in 2005, as well as that country's population and Gross Domestic Product. Moreover, it allows trading of renewable energy through a "guarantee of origin" regime. This facilitates domestic or international trade in renewable electricity by creating a system to ensure that the electricity was created from renewable energy sources. Should the United States develop a similar regime?

C.   Tax Credits, Deductions, and Other Incentives

The predominant method Congress has used to spur renewable energy development involves the use of tax credits and other incentives for renewable energy production and use. Since the 1970s, Congress has established a number of tax incentives for solar, biomass, and geothermal energy production. In 1992, Congress established a renewable electricity production tax credit (PTC) for qualified facilities that produce energy from qualified energy resources (QERs), including wind, biomass, and poultry waste facilities. In 2004, Congress expanded the list of QERs to include solar energy, municipal solid waste, geothermal energy, and other sources. Most studies show that tax incentives are necessary for the renewable energy industry to establish itself and compete with other fossil fuel energy sources (all of which also receive substantial subsidies and credits as well). Mona Hymel, *The United States' Experience with Energy-Based Tax Incentives: The Evidence Supporting Tax Incentives for Renewable Energy*, 38 Loy. U. Chi. L.J. 43, 74–75 (2006).

Perhaps the biggest concern with the use of tax credits and subsidies is their temporary nature. Since 1978, when Congress enacted tax incentives for wind power and solar power, those industries have expanded and contracted as tax incentives have varied. As Professor Hymel explains:

> [I]n 1992, Congress enacted the production tax credit (PTC) to further encourage the production of electricity from wind. At the time of enactment, Congress indicated that the credit was "intended to enhance the development of technology to utilize the specified renewable energy sources and to promote competition between renewable energy sources and conventional energy sources." After enactment, the wind industry took off and the United States quickly became the world leader in the development of wind technologies. In large part due to Congress's failure to make the production tax credit permanent and to adopt renewable production standards, the United States has since fallen behind while other countries have recognized the immense benefits from this renewable energy source.

Id. at 75–76. Wind advocates argue that the "on-again, off-again" nature of the PTC disrupts the industry's growth and puts it at a disadvantage to fossil fuel energy sources, all of which receive consistent tax incentives.

UNION OF CONCERNED SCIENTISTS, RENEWABLE ENERGY TAX CREDIT EXTENDED AGAIN, BUT RISK OF BOOM-BUST CYCLE IN WIND INDUSTRY CONTINUES
(Feb. 14, 2007)[*]

In one of the last measures taken by the 109th Congress, an important federal policy for promoting the development of renewable energy received a one-year extension. The production tax credit (PTC) provides a 1.9-cent per kilowatt-hour (kWh) benefit for the first ten years of a renewable energy facility's operation. The PTC was set to expire on December 31, 2007, but due to the efforts of a coalition of clean energy supporters — including UCS — it was extended for one year as part of the Tax Relief and Health Care Act of 2006 (H.R. 6408). Strong growth in U.S.

wind installations is now projected through 2008.

The legislation extending the PTC provides a one-year extension (through December 31, 2008) of the 1.5-cent/kWh credit for wind, solar, geothermal, and "closed-loop" bioenergy facilities (Adjusted for inflation, the 1.5 cent/kWh tax credit is currently valued at 1.9 cents/kWh). Other technologies, such as "open-loop" biomass, incremental hydropower, small irrigation systems, landfill gas, and municipal solid waste (MSW), receive a lesser value tax credit.

This marks just the second time that the PTC was extended by Congress before it had been allowed to expire. In August 2005, a two-year extension of the PTC was included in a large package of tax incentives in the Energy Policy Act of 2005 (H.R. 6). The PTC was set to expire at the end of 2005, and its extension was one of the few bright spots for renewable energy in this energy bill.

From 1999 until 2004, the PTC had expired on three separate occasions. Originally enacted as part of the Energy Policy Act of 1992, the PTC — then targeted to support just wind and certain bioenergy resources — was first allowed to sunset on June 30, 1999. In December of 1999, again due to the efforts of UCS and other organizations, the credit was extended until December 31, 2001. The PTC expired at the end of 2001, and it was not until March 2002 that the credit was extended for another two years. Congress allowed the PTC to expire for the third time at the end of 2003. From late 2003 through most of 2004 attempts to extend and expand the PTC were held hostage to the fossil-fuel dominated comprehensive energy bill that ultimately failed to pass during the 108th Congress. In early October 2004, a one-year extension (retroactive back to January 1, 2004) of the PTC was included in a larger package of 'high priority' tax incentives for businesses signed by President George Bush. A second bill — extending the PTC through 2005 and expanding the list of eligible renewable energy technologies — was enacted just a few weeks later.

Combined with a growing number of states that have adopted renewable electricity standards, the PTC has been a major driver of wind power development over the past six years. Unfortunately, the "on-again/off-again" status that has historically been associated with the PTC contributes to a boom-bust cycle of development that plagues the wind industry (see Figure below). The cycle begins with the wind industry experiencing strong growth in development around the country during the years leading up to the PTC's expiration. Lapses in the PTC then cause a dramatic slow down in the implementation of planned wind projects. When the PTC is restored, the wind power industry takes time to regain its footing, and then experiences strong growth until the tax credits expire. And so on.

U.S. Wind Power Capacity Additions 1999–2006

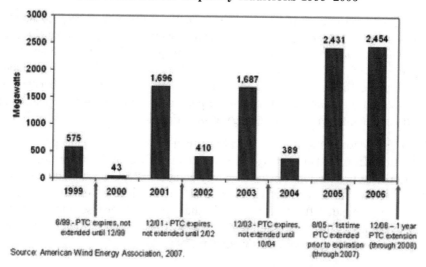

Source: American Wind Energy Association, 2007.

The last lapse in the PTC — at the end of 2003 — came on the heels of a strong year in U.S. wind energy capacity growth. In 2003, the wind power industry added 1,687 megawatts (MW) of capacity — a 36 percent annual increase. With no PTC in place for most of 2004, U.S. wind development decreased dramatically to less than 400 MW — a five-year low. With the PTC re-instated, 2005 marked the best year ever for U.S. wind energy development with 2,431 MW of capacity installed — a 43 percent increase over the previous record year established in 2001. With the PTC firmly in place, 2006 was another near record year in the U.S. wind industry. Wind power capacity grew by 2,454 MW — a 27 percent increase. The American Wind Energy Association projects similar growth in 2007.

Extending the PTC through 2008 will allow the wind industry to continue building on previous years' momentum, but it is insufficient for sustaining the long-term growth of renewable energy. The planning and permitting process for new wind facilities can take up to two years or longer to complete. As a result, many renewable energy developers that depend on the PTC to improve a facility's cost effectiveness may hesitate to start a new project due to the uncertainty that the credit will still be available to them when the project is completed.

QUESTIONS AND DISCUSSION

How should the federal government structure tax incentives for the renewable energy industry? On the one hand, renewable energy advocates argue that tax credits and other incentives are necessary to level the playing field with other industries, and that so long as other industries receive tax assistance, so should the renewable energy industry. On the other hand, some policymakers believe that tax credits for renewable sources distort the market and drive up overall energy prices. Should renewable energy sources receive tax credits for an indefinite period of time? If not, what time frame is appropriate?

V. ENERGY EFFICIENCY AND CONSERVATION

Energy experts believe the United States could reduce its energy consumption by at least 25 percent simply by improving energy efficiency throughout the United States. Energy conservation efforts work to reduce overall energy use and to shift energy use out of peak usage periods and into off-peak times. These "peak-shaving" strategies have the potential to reduce overall energy production, because U.S. energy generation is targeted at providing peak energy; to the extent peak energy demand declines, so will overall energy production.

The U.S. electricity system is not structured to encourage widespread energy conservation. In part, this is because prices established by PUCs reflect average costs of energy production. Because energy consumers are protected from paying the highest costs associated with providing electricity during peak use times, they are generally shielded from price signals that would otherwise encourage lower energy use. The following article identifies ways that regulators could restructure energy pricing to encourage energy conservation.

SIDNEY A. SHAPIRO & JOSEPH P. TOMAIN, RETHINKING REFORM OF ELECTRICITY MARKETS
40 Wake Forest L. Rev. 497, 528–41 (2005)

V. The Smart Consumption Model

A smart electricity generation policy will not displace the Traditional Model. It is, however, responsive to protecting the environment and serving other important national interests. The evaluative test for the success of the smart generation alternatives will come in the market, and, for this reason as well as others, the market must contain a pricing mechanism that is cost sensitive. We therefore turn next to new thinking about electricity pricing.

More specifically, this section investigates the potential of marginal cost pricing to promote energy conservation. Our analysis reveals that marginal cost pricing requires the installation of new meters that should result in significant energy conservation, which in turn will reduce some of the environmental harm associated with electricity generation, and that the benefits of reduced consumption should outweigh the problems of achieving it.

A. Meters and Prices

Most retail consumers purchase electricity according to how much electricity they consume over some period of time, usually a month. The price usually does not vary, except possibly for fuel costs, even if the cost of producing the electricity goes up because retail prices are based on the average cost of producing and delivering electricity. By comparison, electricity production costs vary significantly by hour in almost all systems across the country.

Average cost pricing is used in large part because marginal cost pricing requires the use of meters that measure the time of day that electricity is consumed. If electricity prices are based on marginal costs, consumers will have an incentive to reduce electricity use during periods of peak demand or to switch to less expensive sources of energy because the cost of generating and delivering electricity is normally greater during such peaks. There is little marginal cost pricing in both regulated and unregulated generation markets because neither market generally employs meters that measure time-of-day demand.

1. Regulated Markets

Consumers do not pay any more for electricity when the costs of generating and delivering it increase in regulated markets (except for fuel costs) because the normal method of setting utility prices uses average cost. Regulators, however, could adopt marginal cost pricing if they required utilities to install time-of-use meters.

a. Traditional Regulation. Under cost-of-service ratemaking, regulators first determine the revenue requirement of a utility. Regulators calculate the revenue requirement by estimating the cost of producing electricity and how much money the utility must earn to provide a sufficient rate of return for stockholders and bondholders who invest in the company. Once the revenue requirement is determined, regulators determine the price that the utility can charge for each unit of electricity. Regulators can do this by dividing the revenue requirement by the quantity of electricity that they estimate the utility will sell, but regulators may also make adjustments to reflect differences in the cost of producing and transmitting electricity. For example, a commission will set a lower price for large industrial users because it is less expensive for a utility to deliver a large volume of electricity to one location than much smaller amounts to thousands of households. None of these prices reflect actual marginal costs since they are based on regulators' estimates of the differences in cost of providing service to different classes of customers. More importantly, once a price is established for a class of customers, it does not change over the period of time in which it is in effect. In other words, price is the average cost of producing electricity for that class of customers. Thus, even after these adjustments, other than the actual fixed price paid, there is no further incentive for any class of consumers under this regulatory system to use less electricity when the cost of producing it rises.

The current method of structuring prices does not take into account that the cost of producing electricity normally increases during periods of peak demand. The cost goes up for several reasons. During periods of peak demand, electrical utilities typically include older, more inefficient generation plants in their portfolio of generators, which are not normally used because they are more expensive to operate and because they cause more air pollution than other generation units. In restructured electricity markets, local utilities can purchase additional supplies of electricity from other generators, but the cost of electricity purchased from other suppliers can be expected to rise as demand increases unless there is sufficient excess efficient generation. Furthermore, the marginal transportation costs rise according to the distance over which electricity is transported because megawatts are lost in the act of transmitting electricity. In addition, the cost of transmission increases because high demand for electricity creates transmission congestion.

The cost differences between peak and non-peak demand can be substantial
* * *

b. Regulatory Reform. If regulators decided to employ marginal cost pricing, there are a number of difficult issues that they will have to overcome. These include the choice of a pricing method, the scope of the marginal cost pricing, and methods to protect consumers who still purchase electricity from monopoly suppliers.

i. Pricing Method. Regulators have two general options to adopt marginal cost pricing: consumers receive rebates for reducing electricity usage during periods of peak demand or retail prices are actually based on the marginal cost of producing electricity.

a. Rebates. Under this approach, consumers are rewarded for reducing electricity use during periods of high demand. Thus, in this approach, consumers reduce their electricity loads in response to actual or forecasted demand. In return, they are entitled to rebates based on the amount that they reduce their electricity use during these periods of high demand. For example, a consumer might receive fifty percent of the amount of money a utility saves because the consumer reduced its electricity use during a period of high demand. The utility saves money because it does not have to generate (or buy) electricity for that customer at a time when the cost of producing the electricity (or buying it) has increased.

As compared to marginal cost pricing, this approach creates less incentive for consumers to reduce their electricity use because consumers capture only some percentage of the amount of money that the utility saves because it does not have to pay higher marginal costs to generate and deliver electricity. If, by comparison, marginal cost pricing is used, the consumer can save the full amount of the increase in cost. For example, if the marginal cost of producing electricity during a period of high demand is 50¢ per kilowatt ("kW") and the consumer is entitled to fifty percent of that amount, the consumer is entitled to a 25¢ rebate per kW. If, however, the consumer will have to pay the entire 50¢ per kW for any electricity used during a peak period, the consumer can save 50¢ for each kW that electricity usage is reduced or deferred to a period when prices are lower. Marginal cost pricing therefore provides more incentive for consumer to engage in conservation efforts. Nevertheless, this plan may be attractive to regulators because it protects consumers from a run-up in prices during periods of peak demand while still providing an incentive for consumers to reduce their electricity usage.

b. Variable prices. Regulators can also pursue marginal cost pricing through use of "time-of-use" or "real-time" pricing. In time-of-use pricing, meters record when consumption occurs (for example, hourly), and rates are assigned to time blocks much like monthly rates are presently assigned. For example, Florida Gulf Power normally charges customers three different rates (low cost, medium, and high cost) depending when the electricity is used. Real-time pricing, in contrast, uses an even smarter meter than the time-of-use meter to communicate the actual price of electricity in real time.

The biggest advantage of time-of-use pricing is that it is easier for consumers to understand and therefore for utilities and their regulators to embrace. Nevertheless, the incremental benefits of real-time pricing over time-of-use pricing may be significant relative to the small incremental cost of a real time meter over a time-of-use meter. Unlike real-time pricing, time-of-use pricing does not distinguish between hot days and cool days because the rate for blocks of time is set in advance. In addition, a key issue is how consumers will react to each type of pricing. Assuming that the time periods are designed such that the average customer consumes half of his demand during peak hours at 10¢ per kilowatt-hour ("kWh") and half during off-peak hours at 4¢ per kWh, consumers may behave as if they are charged 7¢ per kWh regardless of when power is consumed. By comparison, real time pricing seems more likely to cause consumers to engage in conservation efforts since they are immediately aware of the costs of not doing so.

Nevertheless, some critics claim real-time pricing will not work unless consumers have smart devices that shut off appliances when electricity costs rise or reduce the amount of electricity that they use. There are, however, a number of studies that indicate residential and small business consumers are able to shift their electricity demand in response to prices that vary by time.

Moreover, consumer response can be enhanced if utilities and regulators alert consumers to potential price increases. This would be similar to efforts to inform people about the quality of air during periods of potentially unhealthy smog. Most morning newspapers and television broadcasts convey this information to consumers. Similarly, the news media can warn consumers about weather conditions that will result in high demand for electricity and therefore higher electrical prices. Regulators could require utilities to maintain websites that indicate current prices, or even send email alerts, which may make it easier for consumers to keep abreast of changes in price.

The adoption of real-time pricing would also create a market demand for devices to assist consumers in reducing their energy costs. Utilizing a Smart Grid, as discussed earlier, real-time pricing meters can be designed to give consumers immediate information on the rate of consumption and the current cost per hour. It will also be possible to automate some consumer responses. For example, the meter can be connected to "smart" appliances that shut off or cut back on electricity use when they receive a signal of higher prices.

B. Prices and Conservation

Economic theory predicts that consumer demand will fall as the price of a product or service goes up. Thus, if consumers pay higher prices for electricity during periods of higher demand, the demand for electricity should fall. This "economic law," however, is subject to some important caveats. The extent to which consumers will reduce demand depends on the elasticity of demand. If consumers do not have a readily available substitute for a product or service, demand will not fall as rapidly as when less expensive substitutes are available. Consumers have three potential substitutes for purchasing electricity: They can reduce demand during peak periods when prices are higher, invest in products that reduce energy use, or switch to lower cost sources of energy. According to economic theory, consumers will choose these options only if they cost less than paying for more electricity, and the consumer will choose among these options based on their comparative costs.

While all three of these options will reduce the demand for electricity, the last may not produce an environmental improvement if consumers switch to an alternative source of energy that creates as much or more pollution. For example, some consumers may switch to a diesel unit that produces pollution emissions that greatly exceed those produced by the plant whose electricity the consumer is replacing. Most households, however, are unlikely to keep a generator in the backyard, and most industrial users will likely rely on less expensive sources of energy, such as natural gas, to fuel self-generation.

Since marginal cost pricing is not widely used, there is only limited evidence concerning the extent to which consumers will reduce demand in response to higher prices. The results of voluntary programs, however, suggest that it will be possible to obtain significant reductions of demand during periods of peak usage. A program offered to industrial users by the Georgia Power Company, for example, has produced as much as a 500 MW reduction in the utility's load, which represents about ten percent of the utility's total industrial demand. When the utility charges its highest prices, it gets an eighteen percent reduction in demand. Similarly, a voluntary program for industrial users in New York took an average of 668 MW in load off the grid during the hottest summer days, which is the equivalent of the generating capacity of a large turbine power plant.

There have also been positive results concerning residential consumers. Residential consumers who volunteered for a variable rate program offered by Gulf Power in Florida consumed only 20% of the power they purchased during high-cost periods, producing an annual average 14% savings in their electricity bills. An experimental plan in California that used marginal cost pricing including a very high price for critical peak periods resulted in a reduction of over 12% in peak demand. A marginal price plan that did not include a critical rate produced a 4% decrease in demand during peak periods. Prices during the peak period were about three times higher under the plan with the higher prices.

These results suggest that at least some industrial and residential consumers will reduce demand in response to price increases or rebates. The critical issue is how many consumers are sensitive to price and how they will act when prices go up (or when there is an opportunity to earn a rebate). Some commentators predict that many residential consumers will not react to high prices by reducing electrical use during peak periods of demand, at least in the short run. This will happen if the purchase of more energy-efficient appliances or of more insulation costs more than paying higher electricity bills, which may be the situation for persons who do not consume much electricity, even during periods of peak demand. Since, however, the benefits of lower demand are benefits for everyone using electricity, these commentators argue regulators may be justified in using additional financial incentives to encourage conservation. This argument anticipates that the cost of the incentives will be substantially less than the benefits of protecting the environment and having a more reliable and less expensive generation and delivery system. Fifteen states currently have established benefit funds for this purpose funded by a small charge of all kWh flowing through the transmission and distribution grids.

C. Capital Costs

There are good reasons to believe that marginal cost pricing (or some variation of it) will lead to conservation efforts by at least some consumers. Marginal cost pricing will cause consumers to use less electricity during periods of high demand and, to the extent that such use cannot be rescheduled to periods of lower cost, to purchase energy saving products. Nevertheless, for this reform to succeed, regulators will need to require utilities to install new meters in millions of homes and small businesses. Although this is by no means an inexpensive proposition, it does appear to be cost-effective. * * *

The actual total cost . . . would be less since it would be offset by the amount of money that consumers would save by decreasing peak purchases in favor of cheaper power during non-peak periods. While it is difficult to estimate how much money people will save, rudimentary calculations suggest consumers should quickly recoup the cost of the new meter. For a ballpark estimate, assume that the capital markets require a 10% internal rate of return on the investment in metering over a ten year period. Annual savings of about $4 billion per year would be necessary to generate such a return on investment. Since residential consumers spent over $100 billion on power in 2002, a 4% reduction in energy costs would be sufficient to amortize the investment in metering. * * *

This analysis suggests that large electricity consumers should be able to recoup the cost of the meters without much difficulty. For example, the Marriott Hotel in New York saved more than $200,000 in the first summer of experimental testing of Consolidated Edison's real time pricing by reducing its use of energy during peak periods of demand. The experience of residential consumers, however, indicates that they also will be able to recoup the cost of a new meter through decreased demand or shifts in the use of electricity. Customers of Gulf Power in Florida who purchased electricity under a voluntary variable rate plan saved, on average, 14% on their annual electricity costs.

There are additional savings. Capital costs will be saved as peak day loads grow less rapidly than total demand due to consumption switching away from peak periods. It is difficult to know how much money will be saved by additional conservation by consumers, but the United States is facing a very large bill for construction of new generation and transmission facilities in the next decade. A study commissioned by Edison Electric Institute estimates that $56 billion of transmission investments will be required during the current decade. The Energy Information Agency, an arm of the U.S. DOE, estimates that 88 gigawatts ("gW") of generation will be required by the year 2010. Using industry rules of thumb, 88 gW of capacity would require an investment of between $26 billion and $44 billion.

Moreover, the potential to save money is substantial because this household use of electricity in the residential segment is the largest consumer of power, and more importantly, it has the lowest load factor of the three major market segments. The residential segment accounts for about 37% of annual electricity consumption, while the commercial and industrial segments represent 32% and 28%, respectively, of demand. The amount of electricity consumed, however, understates the true burden that the residential segment places on the power grid. Since power cannot be stored, each utility must have the ability to generate or purchase enough power to meet peak day demand; therefore, peak usage is a better indicator of the demand that a segment makes upon the power grid. Assuming 40%, 60%, and 80% load factors for residential, commercial, and industrial consumers, respectively, residential consumers represent 51% of peak day demand, while commercial and industrial consumers represent 30% and 19%, respectively.

Experimental programs appear to confirm the previous analysis. A pilot program in Little Rock, Arkansas found that each new real-time pricing customer helped to avoid the installation of 1.5 kW of electricity, saving $1,200 in capital costs. The net savings was $350 per customer after paying $850 to install the necessary metering.

QUESTIONS AND DISCUSSION

1. **Real-time Pricing.** What are the conservation benefits of real-time pricing? Policymakers believe real-time pricing sends consumers price signals that will encourage them to restrict their energy use during the times of the day when energy rates are highest. But does this necessarily mean that overall energy use will decline, or simply that consumers will use the same amount of energy but adjust the times when they use it?

2. **Conservation and Efficiency Programs.** The federal government has employed a number of programs to promote energy conservation. For example, the Energy Star program identifies products, such as appliances, that meet certain efficiency requirements. The Environmental Protection Agency and Department of Energy oversee the program, establish the efficiency requirements, and certify those products that meet the requirements. The agencies estimate that the Energy Star program has resulted in a 40 million metric ton reduction in greenhouse gas emissions in 2007. Green building techniques, which focus on resource efficiency, are also promoted through the Energy Star program. In addition, the U.S. Green Building Council has promoted sustainable building through its Leadership in Energy and Environmental Design (LEED), which sets rigorous requirements and rewards "green builders" with LEED certifications for qualifying buildings. Public utilities and many state governments also promote energy efficiency through rebates and other financial incentives.

3. **The Jevons Paradox.** In 1865, the English economist William Stanley Jevons turned his attention to the increasing use of coal to power England's

industrial revolution. Given the possibility of diminishing coal supplies, Jevons concluded that "we cannot long continue our present rate of progress." In searching for ways to prolong the use of coal, he rejected efficiency as a policy strategy: "It is a confusion of ideas to suppose that economical use of fuel is equivalent to diminished consumption. The very contrary is the truth." THE COAL QUESTION (1865). Jevons neatly captured this paradox by noting that energy efficiency may increase energy consumption:

> The number of tons of coal used in any branch of industry is the product of the number of separate works, and the average number of tons consumed in each. Now, if the quantity of coal used in a blast-furnace, for instance, be diminished in comparison with the yield, the profits of the trade will increase, new capital will be attracted, the price of pig-iron will fall, but the demand for it increase; and eventually the greater number of furnaces will more than make up for the diminished consumption of each. And if such is not always the result within a single branch, it must be remembered that the progress of any branch of manufacture excites a new activity in most other branches, and leads indirectly, if not directly, to increased inroads upon our seams of coal. . . . [T]he more we render it efficient and economical, the more will our industry thrive, and our works of civilization grow.

Id. The extent or even existence of the Jevons Paradox, since recast as the "Khazzoom-Brookes postulate," after the economists Daniel Khazzoom and Leonard Brookes, has been acrimoniously debated. *See* Horace Herring, *Does Energy Efficiency Save Energy: The Economists Debate*, OPEN UNIVERSITY ENERGY AND ENVIRONMENT RESEARCH UNIT REPORT, 74, (July 1998). Nonetheless, there is mounting evidence that at the national level it is not uncommon for total resource consumption to grow even while efficiency improves, suggesting at least that improvements in efficiency are not necessarily sufficient for curtailing consumption (although, once again, this does not necessarily demonstrate that resource consumption grows *because of* improvements in efficiency). Moreover, what might be true at the microeconomic level may not be true at the macroeconomic level:

> . . . At this microeconomic level, for instance in the case of an individual household, savings that are made through, for instance, improved insulation, release money that will be spent on other goods. These will entail some energy consumption, creating a "rebound effect," but in practice the money that has been released, which was previously being spent essentially on either primary fuel (e.g., gas or oil) or on electricity, is unlikely to be spent on anything equally energy intensive. Absolute reductions in energy consumption are thus possible at the microeconomic level.
>
> However, this does not mean that an analogy can be made with macroeconomic effects. Apart from anything else, the substitution effects observable at the macroeconomic level cannot be replicated by households, where demand for a range of goods is relatively inelastic. If energy becomes, in effect, cheaper, there is very limited scope for the individual simply to divert money, say from food to energy. A business, on the other hand, could respond to cheaper energy by deliberately increasing consumption — using a more energy intensive process, which would allow savings to be made elsewhere, for instance in manpower.

United Kingdom, Parliament, SELECT COMMITTEE ON SCIENCE AND TECHNOLOGY, SCIENCE AND TECHNOLOGY: SECOND REPORT, paras. 3.8–3.9 (2005). Assuming, despite these uncertainties, that the Jevons Paradox is true, what policies can be employed to avoid it? To what extent should the Jevons Paradox curb our efforts to promote energy conservation?

Chapter 15

UNITES STATES LAW AND POLICY: TRANSPORTATION

Until 1999, the industrial sector was the largest end-use emitter of carbon dioxide emissions in the United States. Since then, however, transportation emissions have outpaced industrial emissions. Approximately 33 percent of U.S. carbon dioxide emissions comes from the transportation sector. Personal vehicle use contributes more than 60 percent of these transportation emissions, and more than 80 percent comes from "on-road" vehicles, which include passenger cars, sport utility vehicles, vans, motorcycles, trucks, and buses. The remainder comes from railway transportation, aircraft, and shipping.

Three major factors account for the large carbon footprint from the transportation sector: the number of vehicle miles traveled, vehicle fuel efficiency, and fuel type. Climate change policy must therefore address all three factors.

However, the U.S. legal system lacks a single, cohesive approach to regulating vehicle emissions. At least four federal agencies — the Department of Transportation, the Federal Highway Administration, the National Highway Traffic Safety Administration, and the Environmental Protection Agency — play significant roles in managing the transportation sector. In addition, state and local governments have considerable influence over many transportation decisions. By and large, the laws governing highway construction, fuel efficiency, and fuel type operate in isolation from each other. The laws rarely overlap and may, at times, conflict with each other. The agencies administering the laws, moreover, typically do not coordinate to harmonize the various goals of each law. As a result, the benefits gained through one federal program — such as the vehicle fuel efficiency requirements of the Energy Policy and Conservation Act — are often undermined through implementation of another law — such as highway construction funded through the Federal Highway Act. Not surprisingly, these inconsistencies have generated calls for a coordinated federal transportation program to reduce greenhouse gas emissions from the transportation sector.

While reform policies are debated, existing laws have important impacts on the carbon footprint of the United States. This chapter explores these laws and their effects on domestic greenhouse gas emissions. Section I discusses the federal laws governing fuel economy standards. Section II analyzes transportation system design and its impacts on greenhouse gas emissions. Finally, Section III discusses U.S. policies promoting alternative fuel development.

I. AUTOMOBILE FUEL EFFICIENCY STANDARDS

In 1975, in response to the 1973 national oil crisis triggered by the Arab oil embargo, Congress passed the Energy Policy and Conservation Act (EPCA), 49 U.S.C. §§ 32904–32919, and established the Corporate Average Fuel Economy (CAFE) program. The CAFE program establishes average fuel efficiency requirements for passenger cars and other vehicles. A manufacturer's compliance with a CAFE standard is measured by comparing the standard to the average fuel economy of the manufacturer's entire fleet of passenger vehicles produced for each model year. Thus, a manufacturer has discretion to produce some cars which exceed the allowable CAFE standard so long as it also produces enough fuel-efficient cars to bring the fleet's average fuel economy into compliance with the CAFE standard.

In the EPCA, Congress initially required new passenger automobiles to meet a standard of 18 miles per gallon (mpg) for model year (MY) 1978. By MY 1985, manufacturers were to achieve a standard of 27.5 mpg. However, Congress delegated to The National Highway Traffic Safety Administration (NHTSA) the authority to modify the presumed statutory standards. NHTSA must set any modified CAFE standards based upon "the maximum feasible average fuel economy level which such manufacturers are able to achieve in each model year." 49 U.S.C. § 32902(a). In deciding which standards represent the "maximum feasible" levels, NHTSA must consider technological feasibility, economic practicability, the effect of other Federal motor vehicle standards on fuel economy, and the need of the nation to conserve energy. *Id.* at 32902(f). NHTSA's weighing of these factors, and its establishment of standards, has been subject to litigation and controversy since the inception of the CAFE program.

The CAFE program initially yielded significant improvements in overall vehicle mileage. In 1974, before CAFE took effect, new cars achieved an average fuel economy of 12.9 mpg. By the late 1980s, average fuel economy for passenger cars exceeded 28 mpg. *See* Brent D. Yacobbucci & Robert Bamberger, CRS Report For Congress: Automobile and Light Truck Fuel Economy: The Cafe Standards (Jan. 19, 2007). By that measure, the CAFE program might appear to be an unequivocal success.

However, EPCA established separate regulatory requirements for different categories of vehicles, and these separate requirements resulted in a loophole that yielded much lower overall fuel economy standards. EPCA's minimum 18 mpg standard and presumptive 27.5 mpg standard applied only to passenger cars, which EPCA defined as vehicles weighing less than 6,000 pounds. 49 U.S.C. § 32904(a)(1)(B) (2006). For other vehicles ("non-passenger cars") weighing between 6,000 and 10,000 pounds, NHTSA had discretion to establish CAFE standards, if such regulation is feasible and would result in significant energy conservation, or if the heavier vehicles are used for substantially the same purpose as passenger cars weighing less than 6,000 pounds. 49 U.S.C. § 32902. Legislative history suggests Congress established these different requirements to distinguish between passenger vehicles and vehicles used for agriculture and construction. H.R. Rep. No. 94-340, at 89-90 (1975) *reprinted in* 1975 U.S.C.C.A.N. 1762, 1851-52. NHTSA had exercised its discretion to classify light trucks, minivans, and sport utility vehicles (SUVs) as non-passenger cars and thus subject them to much lower average fuel economy standards. These lower standards became known as the "SUV loophole."

When Congress enacted EPCA in 1974, light trucks (vehicles weighing between 6,500 and 8,000 pounds) were a fraction of the U.S. automobile market. However, when gas prices declined in the 1980s, automobile manufacturers increased their production of light trucks, particularly SUVs, and consumers responded by purchasing unprecedented amounts of these larger vehicles. From 1980 to 1990, light trucks increased from 19.9 percent of the auto market to 47.5 percent. In numerical terms, the number of SUVs on the road increased from 200,000 in 1975 to more than 3 million in 1999. As the numbers of these vehicles on the road increased, CAFE standards did not keep pace. Initially, technological limitations prevented NHTSA from establishing stringent CAFE standards for the light trucks category. The primary fuel efficiency "technology" involved reducing the size and weight of vehicles; however, various studies showed that larger, heavier vehicles provided passengers greater safety during collisions. Thus, automakers were able to paint fuel economy standards as presenting consumers with a choice of purchasing either safe vehicles or fuel-efficient vehicles, but not both. Once other fuel efficiency technologies — such as the hybrid engine — began to develop, they were considered cost-prohibitive for many consumers. Finally, consumers simply preferred trucks and SUVs over smaller vehicles. As a result, overall fuel economy (combining passenger cars and light trucks) in the United States declined from an all-time high of 26.2 in 1987 to only 23.8 mpg in 1999. In fact, the 1999 overall levels were only slightly higher than the 23.1 fuel economy standard set in 1980.

Several factors have contributed to the relative inefficiency of the United States automotive fleet. First, the increased production of and demand for light trucks, particularly SUVs, offset the fuel economy improvements in passenger cars. Second, when public pressure to increase fuel economy requirements for light trucks began to build, Congress passed a series of appropriations bills prohibiting NHTSA from revising CAFE standards. *See* Department of Transportation and Related Agencies Appropriations Act, Pub. L. 104-50, 109 Stat. 436, § 330 (Nov. 15, 1995). Third, until December 2007, Congress had not revised CAFE to amend the presumed 27.5 mpg standard for passenger cars established in 1975 with the initial passage of the EPCA. Thus, average fuel economy standards for passenger cars remained stagnant at 27.5 mpg for more than 20 years.

Recent activity in the courts, Congress, and the agencies suggests that the CAFE program may be on the cusp of reform. In December 2001, Congress lifted the moratorium against NHTSA revising the CAFE standard for light trucks. Department of Transportation and Related Agencies Appropriations Act for FY 2002, Pub. L. 107-87, 115 Stat 833 (Dec. 21, 2001). NHTSA responded with its first increased CAFE standards for light trucks since 1994. In December 2007, Congress increased the average CAFE standard for passenger and non-passenger cars to 35 mpg by 2020 and revised laws governing light trucks. In August 2008, the Ninth Circuit Court of Appeals issued a decision invalidating NHTSA's 2008–2011 standards for light trucks, ruling that the standards were too low. Center for Biological Diversity v. National Highway Traffic Safety Admin., 538 F.3d 1172 (9th Cir. 2008). This decision represents the first time in decades (if not ever) in which a federal court has ordered NHTSA to justify its failure to require more stringent fuel economy standards. Thus, as concerns about fuel economy, oil prices, and climate change increase, it appears likely that fuel economy standards will as well.

A.   Early Case Law and Deference to NHTSA

Many of the early fuel economy standards for passenger cars and light trucks were challenged in court, first by conservation organizations arguing that the CAFE standards were too weak, and later by consumer groups and conservative think tanks arguing that the CAFE standards were too stringent and threatened public safety. Many of the initial challenges by conservation organizations generated significant dispute within the D.C. Circuit regarding whether the organizations had Article III standing to challenge the standards (*see* Chapter 12). Although the court usually found the organizations had standing (but often over a vigorous dissent in opposition), NHTSA typically prevailed on the merits. The following case provides an example of how the D.C. Circuit typically resolved challenges to CAFE standards set by the NHTSA.

CENTER FOR AUTO SAFETY v. NATIONAL HIGHWAY TRAFFIC SAFETY ADMIN.
793 F.2d 1322 (D.C. Cir. 1986)

HARRY T. EDWARDS, CIRCUIT JUDGE:

The National Highway Traffic Safety Administration ("NHTSA") is required to set mandatory fuel economy standards for passenger cars and light trucks pursuant to the Energy Policy and Conservation Act of 1975 ("EPCA"). In October 1984, NHTSA issued a final rule that amended its previously published fuel economy standards for light trucks for the 1985 model year and established light truck standards for the 1986 model year. The new 1985 standard required each manufacturer to achieve a fleetwide average fuel economy of 19.5 miles per gallon ("mpg") for its light trucks, a reduction of 1.5 mpg from the original 1985 standard of 21.0 mpg. The 1986 model year standard was set at 20.0 mpg, which also represented a retreat from the original 1985 requirement.

The petitioners, four non-profit consumer organizations that work to promote energy conservation, challenge this rule. They allege that NHTSA has violated EPCA's requirement that the agency designate standards at "the maximum feasible average fuel economy level." The gravamen of their complaint is that the 1985 and 1986 model year standards are too low because in determining those standards, NHTSA gave impermissible weight to shifts in consumer demand toward larger, less fuel-efficient trucks. * * *

I. BACKGROUND

A. *Statutory Framework*

The CAFE standards set a minimum performance requirement in terms of an average number of miles a vehicle travels per gallon of gasoline or diesel fuel. Individual vehicles and models are not required to meet the mileage standard; rather, each manufacturer must achieve *an average* level of fuel economy for all specified vehicles manufactured in a given model year.

Section 502(b) of the Act directs the Secretary of DOT ("Secretary") to prescribe, by rule, standards for light trucks. The Secretary may set separate standards for different classes of light trucks, and they "shall be set at a level which the Secretary determines is the maximum feasible average fuel economy level which such manufacturers are able to achieve in each model year. . . ." Congress directed the Secretary to consider four factors in determining the "maximum feasible" fuel economy level:

(1)   technological feasibility;

(2)   economic practicability;

(3)   the effect of other Federal motor vehicle standards on fuel economy; and

(4)   the need of the Nation to conserve energy.

The Secretary may amend the standard, but amendments must also require the "maximum feasible average fuel economy level." All standards are to be set at least 18 months prior to the beginning of the model year and any amendment that makes a CAFE standard more stringent must also be promulgated at least 18 months prior to the start of the model year.

At the end of each model year, the Environmental Protection Agency ("EPA") calculates the fuel economy level each manufacturer has achieved based on the fuel economy of each model and the number of vehicles manufactured in each model line. If a manufacturer fails to meet a standard, the Secretary "shall assess" civil penalties.[17] The Secretary has limited authority to modify or cancel the penalty.

---

[17] The penalties are calculated by multiplying $5 by the number of tenths of mpg by which the fleet average fails to attain the standard and by the number of vehicles subject to the standard in the fleet manufactured that year. A 1978 amendment allows the Secretary to base the calculation on $10 per tenth of a mpg if he finds such a step is necessary to improve conservation efforts and would not have "substantial deleterious impacts" on the economy.

* * *

B. *Rulemaking Proceedings*

For the model years at issue here, NHTSA issued separate standards for four-wheel drive and two-wheel drive light trucks. . . . In addition, NHTSA issued a "combined" standard. Manufacturers have two options: they may meet the combined standard for their entire light truck fleet or they may meet the separate standards for the two-wheel drive and four-wheel drive categories. The combined standard is set at a level intermediate to the two-wheel drive and four-wheel drive standards.

1. *The Standard for Model Year 1985*

In 1980, NHTSA set the light truck combined CAFE standards for 1984 and 1985 at 20.0 mpg and 21.0 mpg, respectively. These standards were based on projections of sales of various models calculated on the assumption that manufacturers would introduce new models of fuel-efficient light trucks and that consumer demand for these vehicles would be strong due to high prices and reduced supplies of gasoline. The standards for 1984 and 1985 were set at the fuel economy levels attainable by the "least capable" manufacturer, Ford Motor Company ("Ford"). The agency acknowledged that higher standards could result in the introduction of new models or technologies by Ford, but also recognized the uncertainty of financing to undertake such ventures. It also cited the possibility that Ford might restrict the sale of its larger trucks or choose to pay penalties, thus further eroding its position in the marketplace.

In November 1983, Ford petitioned NHTSA to lower the light truck CAFE standards for model years 1984 and 1985. . . . Ford argued that a change in the standards was necessary due to changes in the "price of fuel, the attendant consumer reaction to falling fuel prices and stable fuel availability, and the increasing import penetration into the truck market." On January 30, 1984, Ford followed up its initial request with a petition for even greater reductions in standards for the 1985 model year. . . .

In response to Ford's request, NHTSA published a Notice of Proposed Rulemaking on the 1984 and 1985 light truck standards in May 1984. The agency proposed to deny Ford's requested weakening of the 1984 standards because the model year was already underway. However, for the 1985 model year, NHTSA proposed to adopt Ford's requested level of 19.5 mpg, although it estimated that this amendment could eliminate gasoline savings of up to 1.1 billion gallons. In discussing the proposed modifications, the agency noted that consumer demand for small trucks was "significantly higher" than NHTSA had projected in 1980. However, although small truck sales by domestic companies accounted for a greater proportion of sales than had been anticipated, the bulk of the demand for small models was being satisfied by foreign imports. Significantly, domestic manufacturers were selling a higher proportion of trucks with larger displacement engines than the agency had projected in 1980, while experiencing lower sales of the smaller, more fuel-efficient engines and diesels.

In October 1984, NHTSA issued a final rule adopting Ford's proposed amendments for 1985. . . . Similar revised projections suggested that General Motors Corporation ("GM") and Chrysler would achieve fuel economy levels of 20.0 mpg and 20.3 mpg, respectively. * * *

2. *The Standards for Model Years 1986–1987*

In March 1984, NHTSA published a Notice of Proposed Rulemaking for light truck fuel economy standards for the 1986 and 1987 model years. Rather than proposing a specific standard, it suggested a range of 20.0 to 21.5 mpg for model year 1986 and 20.0 to 22.5 mpg for model year 1987.

After comment, NHTSA set the light truck combined standard for 1986 at 20.0 mpg and deferred issuance of the 1987 standards. The agency projected that Ford would be able to achieve an overall fuel economy level of 20.4 mpg in 1986, a gain of 0.9 mpg over the 1985 projection, due to technological improvements and growth in demand for small vans. It projected a composite average fuel economy of 20.6 mpg for GM and 21.5 mpg for Chrysler in 1986. NHTSA considered the possibility of requiring greater gains in fuel economy than it projected Ford would achieve, which would be possible if manufacturers restricted their production of larger trucks. However, based on Ford's predictions, the agency concluded that the effects of requiring a 1.5 mpg improvement would be "beyond the realm of 'economic practicability' as contemplated in the Act."[38] * * *

Petitioners Center for Auto Safety and Environmental Policy Institute filed timely petitions for reconsideration with NHTSA. Both petitions challenged NHTSA's reliance on consumer demand as a major factor in setting CAFE standards, which they argue undercuts EPCA's goal of energy conservation. They further alleged that technology permitted greater fuel savings and that the statutorily required "maximum feasible" level of fuel economy is higher than the standard produced by accommodating Ford's capabilities, a practice they dubbed the "lowest common denominator" approach. They urged the agency to require marketing strategies to shift demand and advocated the imposition of penalties, rather than the lowering of standards, when manufacturers fail to comply with the standards. NHTSA denied the petitions for reconsideration and this appeal followed. * * *

III. MERITS

* * *

Congress delegated the determination of fuel economy standards to the Secretary, who in turn assigned this task to NHTSA. On its face, the statute gives the agency discretion to designate the classes of light trucks subject to standards. It then requires the standards to be set at the "maximum feasible" level and outlines four general categories of factors to be considered in making that determination. Consumer demand is not specifically designated as a factor, but neither is it excluded from consideration; the factors of "technological feasibility" and "economic practicability" are each broad enough to encompass the concept. Thus, the unadorned language of the statute does not indicate a congressional intent concerning the precise objections raised by the petitioners.

The legislative history of EPCA is similarly unilluminating. . . . The agency is directed to weigh the "difficulties of individual automobile manufacturers;" there is no reason to conclude that difficulties due to consumer demand for a certain mix of vehicles should be excluded. . . . [W]hile Congress rejected market forces as the *sole* means of improving energy conservation, that does not then mean that

---

[38] Ford predicted that in order to achieve a 1.5 mpg benefit in fuel economy, sales losses of 100,000 to 180,000 units with an accompanying loss of 12,000 to 23,000 jobs could occur. It also suggested that sales restrictions on its part would simply shift consumer demand for large trucks to other manufacturers, with no net gain in fuel economy.

consumer demand is *irrelevant* to the determination of the mandatory standards.
* * *

It is axiomatic that Congress intended energy conservation to be a long term effort that would continue through temporary improvements in energy availability. Thus, it would clearly be impermissible for NHTSA to rely on consumer demand to such an extent that it ignored the overarching goal of fuel conservation. At the other extreme, a standard with harsh economic consequences for the auto industry also would represent an unreasonable balancing of EPCA's policies.

The agency concluded that if manufacturers had to restrict the availability of larger trucks and engines in order to adhere to CAFE standards, the effects "would go beyond the realm of 'economic practicability' as contemplated in the Act." The original projections of technological feasibility for the 1985 model year standards were based on the assumption that gasoline prices would remain high and consumer demand for fuel-efficient vehicles would remain strong. No one disputes that actual circumstances have deviated from these assumptions. NHTSA acted within the reasonable range of interpretations of the statute in correcting the 1985 standards to account for these changed conditions. Consideration of product mix effects was also reasonable in setting the standards for 1986, as there is no evidence that the same trends in consumer demand will not continue. * * *

In short, while it may be disheartening to witness the erosion of fuel conservation measures in the face of changes in consumer priorities, this court is nonetheless compelled to uphold the agency's standards. They are the result of a balancing process specifically committed to the agency by Congress, and, in this case, the weight given to consumer demand was not outside the range permitted by EPCA.

QUESTIONS AND DISCUSSION

1. On what basis did the D.C. Circuit uphold the CAFE standards set by NHTSA? Do you believe the court decided the case correctly? Why or why not? If you represented the Center for Automotive Safety, what other arguments, if any, would you have made challenging the NHTSA standards? Does the ruling mean that the agency is held hostage to consumer demands? Is Congress?

2. The EPCA established a $5.00 penalty per vehicle for each 0.1 mpg by which a manufacturer's fleet exceeds the applicable CAFE standards. For example, if the CAFE requirement is 27.5 mpg, and if the average fuel economy for a manufacturer's fleet is 26.5 mpg, with 3.5 million passenger vehicles produced for sale in the United States, then the penalty to the manufacturer will be $5.00 x 3.5 million x 10 = $175 million.

Some European luxury car manufacturers — such as Mercedes and BMW — frequently opted to pay the penalty rather than meet the standard. U.S. and Japanese car manufacturers, in contrast, always met the standards. PAUL R. PORTNEY ET AL., THE ECONOMICS OF FUEL ECONOMY STANDARDS 1 (Resources for the Future, Nov. 2003). What does this dynamic suggest about the efficacy of the CAFE program and its penalty provision? Do you think automakers should be able to effectively opt out of CAFE by paying a per car penalty for exceeding the standard? Does the penalty provision encourage NHTSA to set low standards to protect U.S. automakers?

In an effort to prevent companies from building too many models of cars with low fuel economy, Congress also imposes a gas guzzler tax on inefficient vehicles. The gas guzzler tax of the Energy Tax Act of 1978, 26 U.S.C. §§ 4064 et seq., imposes a tax on the sale by the manufacturer (including the importer) of each automobile within a "model type" whose fuel economy fails to meet certain fuel economy requirements. The legislation exempts "non-passenger" automobiles, such as light trucks, mini-vans, recreational vehicles, and emergency vehicles (as well as the subsequently-developed sport-utility vehicle). The Energy Tax Act required the Environmental Protection Agency (EPA) to separate cars for gas guzzler tax purposes according to the fuel economy of a "model type" for a model year on the basis of characteristics likely to significantly affect fuel economy. Gas guzzler liability calculations are performed before vehicles enter into commerce so that the tax can be displayed on the fuel economy label at the beginning of the model year, thus allowing the consumer to be aware of the fuel economy value and the extra cost at the time of sale.

Cars with an average fuel economy (based on both highway and city driving) of at least 22.5 mpg are not subject to the gas guzzler tax. For cars with fuel economies below 22.5 mpg, the tax per vehicle increases as fuel economy decreases, as the following chart shows.

GAS GUZZLER TAX	
Unadjusted MPG (combined)*	Tax
at least 22.5	No tax
at least 21.5, but less than 22.5	$1000
at least 20.5, but less than 21.5	$1300
at least 19.5, but less than 20.5	$1700
at least 18.5, but less than 19.5	$2100
at least 17.5, but less than 18.5	$2600
at least 16.5, but less than 17.5	$3000
at least 15.5, but less than 16.5	$3700
at least 14.5, but less than 15.5	$4500
at least 13.5, but less than 14.5	$5400
at least 12.5, but less than 13.5	$6400
less than 12.5	$7700

See Environmental Protection Agency, Gas Guzzler Tax, Program Overview, Tax Schedule, *available at* http://www.fueleconomy.gov/FEG/info.shtml.

Each year, EPA publishes a list of car models subject to the gas guzzler tax. Most of the cars on the list are foreign and domestic sports and luxury cars. For example, the 2009 list of gas guzzlers includes cars manufactured by Aston Martin (the brand preferred by 007 James Bond), BMW, Audi, Ferrari, Mercedes Benz, and Rolls Royce, as well as the Ford Mustang, the Corvette, and the Viper. Environmental Protection Agency, Vehicles Subject to the Gas Guzzler Tax for Model Year 2009 (Oct. 2008). Thus, despite the penalties imposed by CAFE and the gas guzzler tax, luxury automakers continue to produce and sell inefficient cars. What policies would you propose that Congress adopt if you wanted to ensure that luxury vehicle manufacturers improve fuel economy?

3.   Two years after issuing its decision in *Center for Auto Safety*, the D.C. Circuit again rejected a challenge to CAFE standards that NHTSA lowered on the basis of economic practicability. Public Citizen v. Nat'l Highway Traffic Safety Admin., 848 F.2d 256 (D.C. Cir. 1988). The court found that the agency properly considered increased consumer demand for larger, but less fuel-efficient vehicles when it allowed average fuel economy standards to fall below the presumptive 27.5 mpg standard for passenger automobiles. *Id.* at 264–265. The court also rejected the argument that the agency violated its duty to consider the "need of the Nation to conserve energy," noting that the standards adopted by NHTSA, while weaker than the presumed statutory standard, would result in only a 0.09 percent yearly increase in fuel consumption. *Id.* at 265.

4.   In a series of decisions, the safety of larger vehicles became a factor underlying NHTSA's establishment of CAFE standards. *See* Competitive Enterprise Institute v. Nat'l Highway Traffic Safety Admin., 956 F.2d 321 (D.C. Cir. 1992) ("*CEI I*"); Competitive Enterprise Institute v. Nat'l Highway Traffic Safety Admin., 45 F.3d 481 (D.C. Cir. 1995) ("*CEI II*"). In *CEI I*, the court remanded a 27.5 mpg CAFE standard for model years 1989 and 1990 for passenger automobiles on the basis that NHTSA did not respond to the "contention that the standard will force carmakers to produce smaller, less safe cars, thus making it more difficult and expensive for consumers to buy larger, safer cars." 956 F.2d at 323. The court accepted CEI's contention that "the 27.5 mpg standard will increase traffic fatalities if, as a general matter, small cars are less safe than big ones," *id.* at 326, and went on to state:

> Nothing in the record or in NHTSA's analysis appears to undermine the inference that the 27.5 mpg standard kills people, although, as we observed before, we cannot rule out the possibility that NHTSA might support a contrary finding. Assuming it cannot, the number of people sacrificed is uncertain. . . . Yet the actual number is irrelevant for our purposes. Even if the 27.5 mpg standard for model year 1990 kills "only" several dozen people a year, NHTSA must exercise its discretion; that means conducting a serious analysis of the data and deciding whether the associated fuel savings are worth the lives lost.

Id. at 327. On remand, NHTSA again concluded that the 27.5 mpg standard would not price consumers out of larger, and presumably safer cars, and the D.C. Circuit upheld NHTSA's conclusion. *CEI II*, 45 F.3d 481. Nonetheless the court emphasized, and NHTSA appeared to concede, that large cars are safer than small cars. *Id.* at 485. This influenced CAFE standards for several years thereafter.

Several studies published in the late 1980s and early 1990s concluded that CAFE standards would result in increased traffic fatalities, because they would encourage companies to produce lighter, smaller, and thus less safe cars. Smaller cars have less "crash space," or room to absorb the impact of vehicle collisions. Lighter cars may also have a lower capacity to withstand collisions. Thus, studies routinely concluded that, in collisions between vehicles and stationary objects, passengers in small, light-weight cars have a greater chance of dying than those in large, heavy cars. The studies also found that passengers in larger vehicles have a higher survival rate in collisions involving other cars or trucks. These studies played an important role in keeping CAFE standards low. As discussed below, more recent studies have challenged the older conclusions regarding the safety of larger vehicles and may influence the development of future CAFE standards.

5. *The Moratorium on Revised CAFE Standards.* In the late 1980s and early 1990s, the CAFE program met with particular criticism. In addition to contending that fuel economy standards increased traffic fatalities, critics also argued that fuel economy standards undermined fuel efficiency, because consumers that bought more fuel-efficient vehicles would simply drive more. This is called the "rebound effect." In addition, because the CAFE program established more stringent requirements on passenger cars than light trucks and SUVs, observers claimed that the CAFE program would simply result in higher sales of light trucks and SUVs, which would likely cost less than cars subject to heavier regulation. *See, e.g.,* Paul E. Godek, *The Regulation of Fuel Economy and the Demand for "Light Trucks"*, 40 J.L. & Econ. 495 (1997). On the other hand, conservationists stepped up their criticism of the "light truck loophole," especially after sales of minivans and SUVs grew by 42 percent between 1988 and 1994. When NHTSA began rulemaking proceedings in 1994 to address the "light truck loophole," Congress intervened to prohibit NHTSA from spending any money on CAFE standard revisions.

Instead, Congress directed the Department of Transportation and the National Academy of Sciences to study CAFE standards. The NAS study concluded that it was technologically and economically feasible for average CAFE standards for passenger cars and light trucks to increase to 33 mpg by 2012 and to 37 mpg before 2017. *See* National Research Council, Effectiveness and Impact of Corporate Average Fuel Economy (CAFE) Standards (2002) [hereinafter NAS report]. Second, the NAS report signaled a potential shift in how costs and benefits of fuel economy would be analyzed. The study analyzed the "cost efficiency" to consumers of fuel economy standards by comparing the added costs of purchasing cars with fuel efficiency technologies to the benefits from purchasing less gas. *Id.* at 64. At the time of the report's release, in 2002, gasoline prices were around $1.50 per gallon, and the NAS concluded that consumers would save approximately $2,500 more than they would spend buying a fuel-efficient car. Third, the report concluded that the CAFE program has improved overall fuel economy and that the "rebound effect" would offset only about 10–20 percent of the efficiency achievements of the CAFE standards. *Id.* at 19. Finally, although the NAS report did not reach definitive conclusions regarding the safety of large cars, a dissenting opinion challenged the majority's conclusion that heavier vehicles are necessarily safer. *Id.* at 117.

Since the NAS released its 2002 report, several events have suggested the report may have been overly conservative regarding the advantages of fuel efficiency. Technologies, particularly those involving hybrid engines, have advanced much more quickly than the NAS committee members anticipated. Moreover, fuel prices have fluctuated above the $1.50 figure used in the NAS report, hitting $4.00 per gallon in the summer of 2008 before retreating again. Finally, several studies called into doubt the safety of larger vehicles, and in fact suggested that larger vehicles may present greater safety risks than smaller ones. These issues all came to a head once Congress lifted the moratorium against NHTSA revising the CAFE standards.

B.   Recent Developments in the CAFE Program: A New Era?

After the publication of the draft NAS report in July 2001, Congress lifted the moratorium prohibiting NHTSA from spending budget allocations on revisions to the CAFE standards. Shortly thereafter, changes to the CAFE program began to develop. First, in 2005, NHTSA proposed to adopt a "reformed" approach to establishing CAFE standards. Second, in 2007, Congress adopted the Energy

Independence and Security Act, which establishes a minimum statutory CAFE standard of 35 mpg by MY 2020 for passenger and non-passenger vehicles combined. These developments, and the litigation that has surrounded them, suggest the CAFE program has entered a new era.

1.   *Reformed CAFE and Light Trucks*

The 2002 NAS report proposed alternative ways in which NHTSA could establish CAFE standards. One proposal suggested that NHTSA establish standards based on vehicle attributes, rather than overall fleet average:

> The government could change the way that fuel economy targets for individual vehicles are assigned. The current CAFE system sets one target for all passenger cars (27.5 mpg) and one target for all light-duty trucks (20.7 mpg). Each manufacturer must meet a sales-weighted average (more precisely, a harmonic mean . . .) of these targets. However, targets could vary among passenger cars and among trucks, based on some attribute of these vehicles such as weight, size, or load-carrying capacity. In that case a particular manufacturer's average target for passenger cars or for trucks would depend upon the fractions of vehicles it sold with particular levels of these attributes. For example, if weight were the criterion, a manufacturer that sells mostly light vehicles would have to achieve higher average fuel economy than would a manufacturer that sells mostly heavy vehicles.

NAS report, *supra* at 87. NHTSA decided to pursue the NAS's recommendation by adopting a Reformed CAFE program for light trucks.

Under the Reformed CAFE program, NHTSA has established "footprint" categories of light trucks, based on the trucks' size (as measured by its wheelbase times its average track width). For each footprint category, NHTSA established a target fuel economy level. As a truck's footprint increases, the fuel economy standard declines. In addition, NHTSA refused to establish a fleet-wide average fuel economy requirement for all trucks covered under Reformed CAFE. Instead, the manufacturers' fuel economy requirements depend upon the manufacturers' vehicle production levels; if a manufacturer chooses to produce several trucks with large footprints and only a handful of trucks with smaller footprints, its fuel economy requirements will be lower. In essence, then, the automaker determines its own fleet-wide average fuel economy standard by determining its production levels of each truck model.

At the same time NHTSA proposed adopting a Reformed CAFE program, it also developed revised CAFE standards for light trucks for MY 2008–2011. Finally, in response to many requests, NHTSA established CAFE standards for certain medium-duty passenger vehicles between 8,500 and 10,000 pounds, but refused to establish CAFE standards for other vehicles over 8,500 pounds. The following litigation ensued.

CENTER FOR BIOLOGICAL DIVERSITY v. NATIONAL HIGHWAY TRAFFIC SAFETY ADMIN.
538 F.3d 1172 (9th Cir. 2008)

BETTY B. FLETCHER, CIRCUIT JUDGE:

Eleven states, the District of Columbia, the City of New York, and four public interest organizations petition for review of a rule issued by the National Highway

Traffic Safety Administration (NHTSA) entitled "Average Fuel Economy Standards for Light Trucks, Model Years 2008–2011," 71 Fed.Reg. 17,566 (Apr. 6, 2006) ("Final Rule"). The Final Rule sets corporate average fuel economy (CAFE) standards for light trucks, defined by NHTSA to include many Sport Utility Vehicles (SUVs), minivans, and pickup trucks, for Model Years (MYs) 2008–2011. For MYs 2008–2010, the Final Rule sets new CAFE standards using its traditional method, fleet-wide average (Unreformed CAFE). For MY 2011 and beyond, the Final Rule creates a new CAFE structure that sets varying fuel economy targets depending on vehicle size and requires manufacturers to meet different fuel economy levels depending on their vehicle fleet mix (Reformed CAFE).

*   *   *

I. FACTUAL AND PROCEDURAL BACKGROUND

*   *   *

D. The Final Rule: CAFE Standards for Light Trucks MYs 2008–2011

NHTSA issued the Final Rule on April 6, 2006. NHTSA set the CAFE standards for MY 2008–2010 (Unreformed CAFE) at the same levels as proposed in the [Notice of Proposed Rulemaking (NPRM)]. Unreformed CAFE sets a fleet-wide average fuel economy standard "with particular regard to the "least capable manufacturer with a significant share of the market." NHTSA has reformed the structure of the CAFE program for light trucks, effective MY 2011 (Reformed CAFE). Under Reformed CAFE, fuel economy standards are based on a truck's footprint, with larger footprint trucks subject to a lower standard and smaller footprint trucks subject to higher standards. A manufacturer's CAFE compliance obligation will vary with its fleet mix. A manufacturer that produces more large footprint light trucks will have a lower required CAFE standard than one that produces more small footprint light trucks.

During MYs 2008–2010, manufacturers may choose to comply with Unreformed CAFE or Reformed CAFE.

NHTSA used the manufacturers' preexisting product plans as the baseline for its analyses of technical and economic feasibility under both Unreformed and Reformed CAFE. NHTSA made adjustments to the product plans by applying additional technologies in a "cost-minimizing fashion," and stopping at the point where marginal costs equaled marginal benefits. . . . However, NHTSA did not monetize the benefit of reducing carbon dioxide emissions, which it recognized was "the main greenhouse gas emitted as a result of refining, distribution, and use of transportation fuels." NHTSA acknowledged the estimates suggested in the scientific literature, but concluded:

> [T]he value of reducing emissions of CO_2 and other greenhouse gases [is] too uncertain to support their explicit valuation and inclusion among the savings in environmental externalities from reducing gasoline production and use. There is extremely wide variation in published estimates of damage costs from greenhouse gas emissions, costs for controlling or avoiding their emissions, and costs of sequestering emissions that do occur, the three major sources for developing estimates of economic benefits from reducing emissions of greenhouse gases.

*   *   *

NHTSA rejected the idea of a "backstop" under Reformed CAFE. NHTSA stated that a backstop, or a required fuel economy level applicable to a manufacturer if its required level under Reformed CAFE fell below a certain minimum, "would essentially be the same as an Unreformed CAFE standard." NHTSA argued that "[the Act] permits the agency to consider consumer demand and the resulting market shifts in setting fuel economy standards," and that a backstop "would essentially limit the ability of manufacturers to respond to market shifts arising from changes in consumer demand. If consumer demand shifted towards larger vehicles, a manufacturer potentially could be faced with a situation in which it must choose between limiting its production of the demanded vehicles, and failing to comply with the CAFE light truck standard."

Finally, NHTSA declined to change the regulatory definition of cars and light trucks to close the SUV loophole and refused to regulate vehicles between 8,500 and 10,000 lbs. GWVR, other than MDPVs.

* * *

III. DISCUSSION

A. Energy Policy and Conservation Act Issues

[The court agreed with the D.C. Circuit that NHTSA properly used a cost-benefit analysis to set CAFE standards at the "maximum feasible fuel economy level."]

2. Failure to monetize benefits of greenhouse gas emissions reduction

Even if NHTSA may use a cost-benefit analysis to determine the "maximum feasible" fuel economy standard, it cannot put a thumb on the scale by undervaluing the benefits and overvaluing the costs of more stringent standards. . . .

To determine the "maximum feasible" CAFE standards, NHTSA began with the fuel economy baselines for each of the seven largest manufacturers — that is, "the fuel economy levels that manufacturers were planning to achieve in those years." NHTSA then "add[ed] fuel saving technologies to each manufacturer's fleet until the incremental cost of improving its fuel economy further just equal[ed] the incremental value of fuel savings and other benefits from doing so." The standard is further adjusted "until industry-wide net benefits are maximized. Maximization occurs when the incremental change in industry-wide compliance costs from adjusting it further would be exactly offset by the resulting incremental change in benefits." NHTSA claims that this "cost-benefit analysis carefully considers and weighs all of the benefits of improved fuel savings," and that "there is no compelling evidence that the unmonetized benefits would alter our assessment of the level of the standard for MY 2011."

Under this methodology, the values that NHTSA assigns to benefits are critical. Yet, NHTSA assigned no value to the most significant benefit of more stringent CAFE standards: reduction in carbon emissions. Petitioners strongly urged NHTSA to include this value in its analysis, and they cited peer-reviewed scientific literature in support. . . . The NAS committee, on which NHTSA relies for other aspects of its analysis, also valued the benefit of carbon emissions reduction at $50 per ton carbon.

NHTSA acknowledged that "[c]onserving energy, especially reducing the nation's dependence on petroleum, benefits the U.S. in several ways. [It] has benefits for economic growth and the environment, as well as other benefits, such as reducing pollution and improving security of energy supply." NHTSA also acknowledged the comments it received that recommended values for the benefit of carbon emissions reduction; however, the agency refused to place a value on this benefit. NHTSA stated:

> The agency continues to view the value of reducing emissions of CO_2 and other greenhouse gases as too uncertain to support their explicit valuation and inclusion among the savings in environmental externalities from reducing gasoline production and use. There is extremely wide variation in published estimates of damage costs from greenhouse gas emissions, costs for controlling or avoiding their emissions, and costs of sequestering emissions that do occur. . . . Moreover, . . . commenters did not reliably demonstrate that the unmonetized benefits, which include CO_2, and costs, taken together, would alter the agency's assessment of the level of the standard for MY 2011. Thus, the agency determined the stringency of that standard on the basis of monetized net benefits.

NHTSA's reasoning is arbitrary and capricious for several reasons. First, while the record shows that there is a range of values, the value of carbon emissions reduction is certainly not zero. NHTSA conceded as much during oral argument when, in response to questioning, counsel for NHTSA admitted that the range of values begins at $3 per ton carbon. NHTSA insisted at argument that it placed no value on carbon emissions reduction rather than zero value. We fail to see the difference. The value of carbon emissions reduction is nowhere accounted for in the agency's analysis, whether quantitatively or qualitatively. * * *

Second, NHTSA gave no reasons why it believed the range of values presented to it was "extremely wide"; in fact, several commenters and the NAS committee recommended the *same* value: $50 per ton carbon. . . . NHTSA argues that the problem was not simply "the ultimate value to be assigned, but the wide variation in published estimates of the three major underlying costs of carbon dioxide emissions — the cost of damages caused by such emissions, the costs of avoiding or controlling such emissions, and the costs of sequestering resulting emissions." But NHTSA fails to explain why those three "underlying costs" are relevant to the question of how carbon emissions should be valued. We are convinced by Petitioners' response:

> To monetize the benefits of reducing CO_2 emissions from automobiles, NHTSA did not need to calculate the "costs of sequestering emissions." Carbon capture and sequestration, though a feasible means of reducing emissions from large stationary sources such as coal-fired power plants, was not within the range of actions at issue in this automobile fuel economy rulemaking. Nor were "costs for controlling or avoiding [CO_2] emissions" a genuine methodological barrier here: NHTSA already performed an elaborate analysis of the costs of mandating increases in fuel economy. For purposes of this rule-making, that was the relevant category of control costs.

In sum, there is no evidence to support NHTSA's conclusion that the appropriate course was not to monetize or quantify the value of carbon emissions reduction at all. * * *

Third, NHTSA's reasoning is arbitrary and capricious because it has monetized other uncertain benefits, such as the reduction of criteria pollutants, crash, noise, and congestion costs, and "the value of increased energy security."

Fourth, NHTSA's conclusion that commenters did not "reliably demonstrate" that monetizing the value of carbon reduction would have affected the stringency of the CAFE standard " 'runs counter to the evidence' " before it. The Union of Concerned Scientists concluded that "including [a $50/tC value] in the determination of cost-efficient fuel economy could increase the 2011 targets by an average of 0.4–1.1 mpg." Given that the CAFE standards set by NHTSA increase only 1.5 mpg from MY 2008 to 2011, an additional 0.4 to 1.1 mpg increase by MY 2011 is significant. * * *

Finally, there is no merit to NHTSA's unfounded assertion that if it had accounted for the benefit of carbon emissions reduction, it would have had to account for the adverse safety effects of downweighting, and the two would have balanced out, resulting in no change to the final CAFE standards. No evidence supports this assertion. The assertion is also based on the controversial assumption that higher fuel economy standards for light trucks causes adverse safety effects from downweighting.

Thus, NHTSA's decision not to monetize the benefit of carbon emissions reduction was arbitrary and capricious, and we remand to NHTSA for it to include a monetized value for this benefit in its analysis of the proper CAFE standards. * * *

4. Backstop for Reformed CAFE

Under Reformed CAFE, a manufacturer's required CAFE level would depend on its fleet mix. Reformed CAFE (setting individual fuel economy targets for vehicles of every footprint size) plus a backstop (overall fleet-wide average) would prevent manufacturers from upsizing their vehicles or producing too many large footprint vehicles, if the backstop were set high enough. Under Unreformed CAFE, manufacturers had to meet only a fleet-wide average, which means that they could increase the number of small vehicles (with higher fuel economy) they produced in order to balance out the larger vehicles (with lower fuel economy) and achieve the required CAFE standard. NHTSA argues that Reformed CAFE will alleviate the problem of downweighting because there will no longer be a large gap between the CAFE targets for passenger cars and light trucks. . . .

Petitioners generally agree that Reformed CAFE, with its progressive fuel economy targets based on vehicle footprint, is an improvement over Unreformed CAFE. However, they argue that Reformed CAFE must include a "backstop" so that the "minimum level of average fuel economy applicable to a manufacturer in a model year" would not be determined solely by the manufacturer's fleet mix. *See* 49 U.S.C. § 32901(a)(6). They argue that the statutory language — "*maximum* feasible average fuel economy level," *id.* § 32902(a) (emphasis added), "*minimum* level of average fuel economy applicable to a manufacturer in a model year," *id.* § 32902(a)(6) (emphasis added) — and the statutory structure contemplate a fixed minimum CAFE standard for light trucks.

NHTSA argues that a backstop would unduly limit consumer choice and perpetuate the problems with Unreformed CAFE. It argues that the statutory requirement that there be a "minimum" level of average fuel economy applicable to a manufacturer does not necessarily mean a *fixed* minimum and is consistent with a minimum standard applicable to a manufacturer based on that manufacturer's fleet mix.

Neither the EPCA's language nor structure explicitly *requires* NHTSA to adopt a backstop. The issue is whether it was arbitrary or capricious in not adopting a backstop. Under Reformed CAFE, manufacturers would still be required to meet a minimum average fuel economy level — there would simply be no *corporate* minimum average fuel economy level. That is, each vehicle of a particular footprint would be required to meet a minimum average fuel economy level, but there would be no fleet-wide minimum. The corporate or fleet-wide minimum would depend entirely on the number of vehicles of each footprint that the manufacturer decided to produce.

Although Congress has not directly spoken on this issue, it has directed the agency to set the average fuel economy level for light trucks at the "maximum feasible" level, 49 U.S.C. § 32902(a), considering technological feasibility, economic practicability, the need of the nation to conserve energy, and the effect of other motor vehicle standards of the government, *id.* § 32902(f). NHTSA did not consider these factors in deciding whether to adopt a backstop. Instead, the agency explained:

> The intent of the CAFE program is not to preclude future mix shifts and design changes in response to consumer demand. A backstop would likely have this influence. . . . Such a system would be in opposition to congressional intent to establish a regulatory system that does not unduly limit consumer choice.

NHTSA may consider consumer demand, but "it would clearly be impermissible for NHTSA to rely on consumer demand to such an extent that it ignored the overarching goal of fuel conservation." We believe that NHTSA has committed this error here. Although EPCA is not intended to "unduly limit[ ] consumer choice," energy conservation is the fundamental purpose of the statute and an explicit statutory factor that NHTSA "shall" consider . . . NHTSA did not adequately consider the "need of the nation to conserve energy," as it was required to do under 49 U.S.C. § 32902(f), and it has not argued that a backstop would be technologically infeasible or economically impracticable. * * *

6. Changing the definition of passenger and non-passenger automobiles in order to close the SUV loophole

Petitioners challenge NHTSA's decision not to reform the SUV loophole. They argue that this decision is arbitrary and capricious because it runs counter to the evidence showing that the majority of SUVs, minivans, and pickup trucks function solely or primarily as passenger vehicles, and because NHTSA has not provided a reasoned explanation for why the transition to Reformed CAFE could not be accomplished at the same time as a revision in the definitions.

The EPCA defines "passenger automobile" as "an automobile that the Secretary decides by regulation is manufactured primarily for transporting not more than 10 individuals," excluding "an automobile capable of off-highway operation that the Secretary decides . . . has a significant feature except 4-wheel drive designed for off-highway operation" and is 4-wheel drive or more than 6,000 lbs. GVWR. 49 U.S.C. § 32901(a)(16). "Non-passenger automobiles" are thus defined by exclusion. NHTSA defines an automobile other than a passenger automobile as a "light truck," a term not used in the statute. 49 C.F.R. § 523.5 (2007). Under 49 U.S.C. § 32901(a)(16), the Secretary has discretion to decide what constitutes a "passenger automobile" within the confines of the listed criteria.

NHTSA initially sought input on ways to revise the regulatory distinction because the passenger automobile/light truck distinction had become obsolete: "The application of the regulation to the current vehicle fleet (designed with the regulatory distinctions in mind) less clearly differentiates between passenger cars and light trucks than it did in the 1970s." However, in the NPRM, NHTSA decided not to:

chang[e] those classification regulations at this time in part because [NHTSA] believe[s] an orderly transition to Reformed CAFE could not be accomplished if [NHTSA] simultaneously change[s] which vehicles are included in the light truck program and because, as applied in MY 2011, Reformed CAFE is likely to reduce the incentive to produce vehicles classified as light trucks instead of as passenger cars. * * *

We conclude that NHTSA's decision not to otherwise revise the passenger automobile/light truck definitions is arbitrary and capricious. First, NHTSA has not provided a reasoned explanation of why an orderly transition to Reformed CAFE could not be accomplished at the same time that the passenger automobile/light truck definitions are revised.

Second, NHTSA asserts that it reasonably decided to look to the purpose for which a vehicle is manufactured instead of consumers' use of a vehicle because it is a more objective way of differentiating between passenger and non-passenger automobiles. But this overlooks the fact that many light trucks today *are* manu-factured primarily for transporting passengers, as NHTSA itself has acknowl-edged: "Many vehicles produced today, while smaller than many other passenger cars, qualify as light trucks because they have been *designed* so that their seats can be easily removed and their cargo carrying capacity significantly enhanced." 68 Fed.Reg. at 74,927 (emphasis added); *see also* 71 Fed.Reg. at 17,621 n. 102 ("NAS Report . . . noted that [the passenger automobile/light truck fuel economy] gap created an incentive to design vehicles as light trucks instead of cars."). Today's design differences, which capitalize on the lower light truck CAFE standard, are the very reason that NHTSA sought input on ways to revise the regulatory distinction "in light of the current and emerging motor vehicle fleet."

In addition, NHTSA's new focus on the purpose for which automobiles are manufactured conflicts with its earlier assertion that "Congress intended that passenger automobiles be defined as those *used primarily* for the transport of individuals."

Third, NHTSA's decision runs counter to the evidence showing that SUVs, vans, and pickup trucks are manufactured primarily for the purpose of transporting passengers and are generally not used for off-highway operation. The NAS committee found that:

> The less stringent CAFE standards for trucks did provide incentives for manufacturers to invest in minivans and SUVs *and to promote them to consumers in place of large cars and station wagons.* . . . By shifting their product development and investment focus to trucks, they created more desirable trucks with more carlike features: quiet, luxurious interiors with leather upholstery, top-of-the-line audio systems, extra rows of seats, and extra doors.

Consumers use light trucks primarily for passenger-carrying purposes in large part because that is precisely the purpose for which manufacturers have manufactured and marketed them. A pickup truck usage study conducted by R.L. Polk & Co. showed that 73% of light pickup users use their trucks to carry passengers on a daily or weekly basis, 68% use them for personal trips on a daily or weekly basis, 58% use them for commuting on a daily or weekly basis, 59% *never* use them for towing, and 69% *never* use them for driving off-road. Seventy-three percent of medium pickup users use them for carrying passengers on a daily or weekly basis, 65% use them for commuting on a daily or weekly basis (61% daily), and 64% *never* use them for driving off-road. Even among heavy pickup users, 76% use them for carrying passengers on a daily or weekly basis, and 52% never use them for driving off-road. The NAS Committee further found:

> When CAFE regulations were originally formulated, different stan-
> dards were set for passenger vehicles and for work/cargo vehicles . . .
> because [work/cargo vehicles] needed extra power, different gearing, and
> less aerodynamic body configurations to carry out their utilitarian, load-
> carrying functions. . . . [But this] working definition distinction between a
> car for personal use and a truck for work use/cargo transport[ ] has broken
> down, initially with minivans, and more recently with sport utility vehicles
> and other "cross-over" vehicles that may be designed for peak use but
> which are actually used almost exclusively for personal transport. . . . The
> car/truck distinction has been stretched well beyond its original purpose.

One of the changes the NAS committee recommended to alleviate this problem was
to "tighten" the definition of a light truck, a step the EPA has already taken for
emissions standards purposes. We agree with Petitioners that NHTSA's decision
not to do the same was arbitrary and capricious, especially in light of EPCA's
overarching goal of energy conservation. Thus, we remand to NHTSA to revise its
regulatory definitions of passenger automobile and light truck or provide a valid
reason for not doing so. * * *

QUESTIONS AND DISCUSSION

**1. *Carbon Dioxide and CAFE. Center for Biological Diversity* is the first
decision to require NHTSA to consider carbon dioxide emissions in establishing
CAFE standards. As noted above, the EPCA requires NHTSA to consider four
factors — technological feasibility, economic practicability, the effect of other
Federal motor vehicle standards on fuel economy, and the need of the Nation to
conserve energy — when it sets CAFE standards. Under which of these factors do
carbon dioxide emissions fall? Do you agree with the Ninth Circuit that CAFE
requires NHTSA to consider carbon dioxide emission when it sets CAFE standards? Why or why not?

In an earlier decision issued by the D.C. Circuit, environmental organizations
had challenged NHTSA's failure to consider the effects of a weakened CAFE
standard on carbon dioxide emissions under the National Environmental Policy
Act. City of Los Angeles v. National Highway Traffic Safety Admin., 912 F.2d 478
(D.C. Cir. 1990). NHTSA had admitted that its weakened standard would result in
17.75 billion pounds of increased carbon dioxide emissions over the fleet's 20-year
lifespan. *Id.* at 500. While Judge Wald found this increase significant enough to
merit discussion in an Environmental Impact Statement (EIS), then-Judge Ruth
Bader Ginsburg noted that this increase represented only one percent of carbon
dioxide production over that time period, and found the increase legally insignificant. *Id.* at 501, 504. Judge Douglas H. Ginsburg concluded that the groups lacked
standing to address this global problem. *Id.* at 483–84.

**2. *Reformed CAFE.* As the Ninth Circuit notes, the environmental organiza-
tions challenging the NHTSA's rule agreed that Reformed Cafe represented an
improvement in how CAFE standards are set. Why would environmental organizations think this? Do you agree with their view?

---

2.   *The Energy Independence and Security Act of 2007*

In December 2007, Congress passed the Energy Independence and Security Act (EISA), which requires NHTSA "to achieve a combined fuel economy average for MY 2020 of at least 35 miles per gallon for the total fleet of passenger and non-passenger automobiles manufactured for sale in the United States for that model year." Unlike the previous EPCA's presumed 27.5 mpg requirement, the 35-mpg standard is a minimum standard and NHTSA may not establish CAFE requirements that fall short of the 35-mpg requirement. Moreover, all passenger cars must, at a minimum, achieve a 27.5 mpg average CAFE standard by 2011. For interim standards, as under EPCA, NHTSA must establish the CAFE standards at least 18 months before the MY to which the standards apply. It may establish standards for up to five years in a single rulemaking.

In enacting EISA, Congress attempted to address some of the problems under EPCA. Specifically, EISA attempts to remove the "SUV loophole" by redefining passenger automobile as most four-wheeled vehicles "manufactured primarily for use on public streets, roads, and highways and rated at less than 10,000 pounds gross vehicle weight." 49 U.S.C. § 32901(a)(3). The limited exceptions to this definition are vehicles defined as "work trucks," vehicles that work solely on rail lines, and vehicles manufactured in multiple stages by at least two different manufacturers (but this last exemption is limited to 10,000 vehicles per year, per manufacturer). *Id.* EISA also codifies NHTSA's new practice of setting standards based on vehicle attributes.

EISA adds new elements to the CAFE program as well. It directs NHTSA to establish fuel economy standards for commercial medium-duty and heavy-duty on-highway trucks weighing more than 10,000 pounds, as well as "work trucks" weighing between 8,500 and 10,000 pounds. NHTSA must establish these standards once NAS completes a study analyzing fuel economy requirements for these classes of trucks. In addition, EISA allows automakers to trade credits earned whenever their average fleet fuel economy falls below the mandatory standards.

QUESTIONS AND DISCUSSION

1.   Does EISA close the SUV loophole? Review the following excerpts from the EPCA, as amended by EISA. Do you understand how EISA changes EPCA? Do you think it addresses the "backstop" problem at issue in *Center for Biological Diversity?*

(b)   **Standards for automobiles and certain other vehicles.**

   (1)   **In general.** The Secretary of Transportation, after consultation with the Secretary of Energy and the Administrator of the Environmental Protection Agency, shall prescribe separate average fuel economy standards for—

      (A)   passenger automobiles manufactured by manufacturers in each model year beginning with model year 2011 in accordance with this subsection;

      (B)   non-passenger automobiles manufactured by manufacturers in each model year beginning with model year 2011 in accordance with this subsection; and

(C)   work trucks and commercial medium-duty or heavy-duty on-highway vehicles in accordance with subsection (k).

(2)   **Fuel economy standards for automobiles.**

(A)   **Automobile fuel economy average for model years 2011 through 2020.** The Secretary shall prescribe a separate average fuel economy standard for passenger automobiles and a separate average fuel economy standard for non-passenger automobiles for each model year beginning with model year 2011 to achieve a combined fuel economy average for model year 2020 of at least 35 miles per gallon for the total fleet of passenger and non-passenger automobiles manufactured for sale in the United States for that model year.

(B)   **Automobile fuel economy average for model years 2021 through 2030.** For model years 2021 through 2030, the average fuel economy required to be attained by each fleet of passenger and non-passenger automobiles manufactured for sale in the United States shall be the maximum feasible average fuel economy standard for each fleet for that model year.

(C)   **Progress toward standard required.** In prescribing average fuel economy standards under subparagraph (A), the Secretary shall prescribe annual fuel economy standard increases that increase the applicable average fuel economy standard ratably beginning with model year 2011 and ending with model year 2020.

(3)   **Authority of the Secretary.** The Secretary shall—

(A)   prescribe by regulation separate average fuel economy standards for passenger and non-passenger automobiles based on 1 or more vehicle attributes related to fuel economy and express each standard in the form of a mathematical function; and

(B)   issue regulations under this title prescribing average fuel economy standards for at least 1, but not more than 5, model years.

(4)   **Minimum standard.** In addition to any standard prescribed pursuant to paragraph (3), each manufacturer shall also meet the minimum standard for domestically manufactured passenger automobiles, which shall be the greater of—

(A)   27.5 miles per gallon; or

(B)   92 percent of the average fuel economy projected by the Secretary for the combined domestic and non-domestic passenger automobile fleets manufactured for sale in the United States by all manufacturers in the model year, which projection shall be published in the Federal Register when the standard for that model year is promulgated in accordance with this section.

49 U.S.C. § 32902(b).

2. Is the 35-mpg standard adequate? The standard includes both passenger and non-passenger cars, so the standard may require significant improvement in fuel economy for passenger cars if automakers continue to produce a substantial number of large, non-passenger cars. However, market fluctuations may alter the mix of passenger and non-passenger fleets. For example, in response to surging fuel prices in the summer of 2008 and lower sales of inefficient vehicles, many vehicle manufacturers announced their intention to reduce or suspend production of larger vehicles. If this were to happen, then smaller car fuel economy standards may stagnate. Indeed the 35-mpg standard will drive efficiency in smaller vehicles only if automakers continue to produce large ones. How should Congress have addressed these circumstances?

3. Although Congress established the 35-mpg standard as a minimum requirement and directed NHTSA to establish interim fuel economy standards with the 35-mpg requirement in mind, Congress did not modify the four factors the NHTSA must consider when it establishes fuel economy standards. How much discretion does NHTSA retain when it sets standards before 2020? If Congress does not amend the CAFE program after 2020, could NHTSA indefinitely retain the 35-mpg standard?

4. *The Auto Bailout and Fuel Efficiency.* When Congress first considered a multi-billion dollar bailout for the Big Three Detroit automakers, several environmental organizations asked Congress to attach environmental conditions to the bailout. For example, the Union of Concerned Scientists proposed that Congress require each company to improve its average fuel efficiency by four percent each year as a condition to receiving bailout funds. Press Release, Union of Concerned Scientists, Auto Bailout Should Link to Fuel Economy Boost (Nov. 18, 2008). At one point, Senator Barbara Boxer (D-California) had inserted language into the proposed bailout bill that would have required the Big Three to effectively withdraw their court challenge to California's proposed vehicle emissions (*see* note 6 below and Chapter 13). Ultimately, Congress backed away from linking bailout money to fuel economy or acquiescence to the California standards when it approved an initial bailout in December 2008. The automakers' continued participation in the litigation challenging California's standards, however, generated considerable controversy when reporters suggested the bailout money was funding litigation opposing the standards. *See* Elizabeth Kolbert, *Will the Big Three Take Our Money and Sue?*, News Desk, THE NEW YORKER (Jan. 29, 2009). A month later, when the Big Three filed viability plans required under the bailout bill, General Motors (GM) indicated its intent to meet the revised CAFE standards set through EISA. GM also appeared to soften its opposition to California's emissions standards. *See* David Doniger, *The Latest Bailout Plans II — So What Did We Find?*, NRDC SWITCHBOARD (Feb. 20, 2009). Do you think Congress should have included fuel economy requirements in the bailout bill?

5. *Credit Trading.* EISA allows two types of trading. First, each manufacturer may "trade" credits internally, by going beyond minimum efficiency requirements for one class of vehicles and using the excess fuel efficiency credits to offset shortfalls in efficiency for another class of vehicles. Second, EISA allows credit trading between manufacturers. Is credit trading a useful component in the CAFE program?

6. *Clean Air Act Emissions Standards and the EISA.* Shortly after Congress passed the EISA, the EPA denied California's request for a waiver under Section 209 of the Clean Air Act, which otherwise prohibits states from adopting vehicle emissions standards. *See* Chapter 13. EPA determined that EISA would achieve superior pollution reduction benefits, because it applies to all 50 states and would increase vehicle mileage by 40 percent when fully implemented. Do you think EPA justifiably relied on EISA to support its waiver denial?

   7.   *CAFE Standards and Heavy-Duty Trucks.* To date, medium and heavy-duty trucks weighing more than 10,000 pounds GVWR have not been regulated under the CAFE program. Various studies, however, show that regulation could yield significant reductions in fuel use. For example, a study commissioned by the National Center on Energy Policy concluded that, by 2015, tractor trailers could improve their fuel economies by 58 percent using conventional technologies and by 71 percent using hybrid technologies. Therese Langer, Energy Savings through Increased Fuel Economy for Heavy-Duty Trucks 16, tbl.6 (American Council for an Energy-Efficient Economy, 2004). Trucks weighing 10,000 to 19,500 pounds could see a 93 percent improvement in fuel economy using hybrid technology.

II.   REFORMING THE TRANSPORTATION INFRASTRUCTURE

   Many critics of the CAFE program believe that increased fuel efficiency will only result in greater vehicle miles traveled (VMT), as fuel economy standards make driving more affordable. Although this critique has been challenged, most transportation experts recognize that the U.S. transportation system encourages — and at times requires — most Americans to drive long distances to accomplish daily tasks.

   Land use policies promoting residential development in suburban and exurban areas have increased the overall VMT of the average American. Distances between the home and workplace have increased over the past two decades, while alternatives to driving have diminished. As a result, highways have become more crowded, congestion has increased, and overall greenhouse gas emissions from the transportation sector have climbed.

   The federal response to congestion has been to expand the highway system. Federal transportation policy has long prioritized highway construction over other types of transportation infrastructure. Yet, as the federal highway system has grown, so has suburban development. As a result, most new highways promote more driving, which leads to greater congestion, which leads to more highway construction.

   Federal policy does not provide the same support for public transportation as it does for highways. Indeed, most federal funding must, by law, be used for highway construction and not for public transportation. The lack of available funding for public transportation has prevented local governments from expanding bus, train, light rail, and subway systems. While some large metropolitan areas have robust public transportation systems, most cities of all sizes lack adequate public transportation. The lack of public transportation spurs the majority of Americans to use their own cars as their primary means of commuting.

   Reducing greenhouse gas emissions from the transportation sector will require several changes to the transportation infrastructure aimed at: reducing congestion; limiting single-passenger driving patterns and promoting high-occupancy vehicle use; expanding public transportation systems, bike lanes, sidewalks, and other low- or zero-carbon transportation options; and revising land use policies that reduce suburban and exurban sprawl. Many of these actions will require state and local governments to take the lead. However, the federal government will also play a key role through funding transportation infrastructure, supporting state policies, and possibly developing tax policies that discourage personal vehicle use.

A.   A Survey of Policies to Reduce Vehicle Miles Traveled (VMT)

The following excerpt summarizes several commonly proposed strategies that transportation agencies could employ to reduce overall VMT in the United States. Which of these are most likely to result in the greatest changes in driving patterns? Which have the greatest chance of receiving political support?

MICHAEL GRANT ET AL., TRANSPORTATION AND GLOBAL CLIMATE CHANGE: A REVIEW AND ANALYSIS OF THE LITERATURE

Ch. 5, at 31–63 (prepared for Federal Highway Admin., June 1998)

5.2 VEHICLE TRAVEL REDUCTION STRATEGIES

Vehicle travel reduction strategies attempt to reduce greenhouse gas emissions by reducing miles traveled in personal motor vehicles. Reductions in fuel consumption occur with the elimination of trips, reduction in trip lengths, or the replacement of vehicle trips with trips on alternative modes that consume less energy. * * *

Vehicle travel reduction strategies may be divided into the following categories:

- Travel pricing mechanisms;

- Provision of alternative modes;

- Parking management; [and]

- Land use planning measures . . .

5.2.1 TRAVEL PRICING MECHANISMS * * *

ROAD PRICING * * *

Roadway pricing involves the use of fees to increase the price of driving in specific facilities or on roadways, or within specific regions. Drivers who have more flexibility in their trip choices (therefore placing a lower value on a specific route or time) will switch to less expensive options, which can include other non-priced roads or alternate modes (such as transit, high-occupancy vehicles, bicycling, or walking). Congestion pricing is a specific type of road pricing where the per trip charge varies by the time of day, based on changes in the demand for travel and resulting congestion. Congestion pricing may encourage drivers to switch their time of travel to less congested times, resulting in a more even distribution of traffic throughout the day.

Road pricing is usually assessed at one or more points along a road. Currently, twenty states have toll roads, bridges, or tunnels with costs averaging between $0.02 and $0.10 per mile. . . . Cordon pricing is a related measure, which may be applied to a larger region where congestion is a severe problem. Cordon pricing establishes a series of pricing points in a ring around the congested area, whether it be a central business district or a greater metropolitan area. Motorists are charged as they enter the cordoned area. * * *

Low public acceptance can be a crucial roadblock to implementation of roadway pricing measures. Road pricing may be politically unpopular for a number of reasons. First, charging a fee on facilities that have traditionally been free often generates public dissatisfaction. Perhaps the leading objection to road pricing is that this measure is regressive and would disproportionately affect lower-income drivers. In the case of congestion pricing, drivers who could not alter their time of their trips due to inflexible work schedules would have no option but to pay the fees. A cordon zone pricing system around a central business district or downtown could conflict with land use strategies that seek to encourage employment in developed areas, though the land use impacts of cordon pricing are still being debated. * * *

VMT FEES * * *

A VMT fee refers to a charge that is levied on an annual or semi-annual assessment based on the number of vehicle miles traveled per year. This system could work in tandem with existing vehicle registration fees and inspection and maintenance programs. . . .

VMT fees target reductions in vehicle miles of travel. Unlike road pricing measures where costs can be reduced by switching travel times, use of routes, or type of vehicle used, the only way for an individual to reduce costs under this measure is to drive less, thus reducing traffic and emissions. * * *

Some economists believe that even though these fees are charged per mile of travel, drivers may not respond as strongly to VMT fees as to other travel pricing measures since the fees would only be charged on an annual basis or semi-annual basis. A 1994 study conducted for the Puget Sound Regional Council analyzed the potential impacts of VMT fees in the Puget Sound area as well as in the San Francisco Bay area. The fees ranged from $0.01 to $0.05 per mile and yielded 9.3 to 11 percent decreases in VMT and 8 to 20 percent decreases in carbon dioxide. * * *

Like other market-based measures, VMT fees raise concern regarding political feasibility and issues of equity. Taxpayers may suffer "sticker-shock" when they receive their VMT fee assessments. A fee of $0.05 per mile results in an annual VMT tax assessment of over $566 for the average vehicle (which traveled 11,329 miles in 1995). A household with two vehicles could easily receive a tax bill of over $1,000 annually in association with this VMT fee. * * *

FUEL PRICING * * *

Fuel taxes have long been used in this country to recover road construction and maintenance costs. However, in recent years, raising federal and/or state fuel taxes has increasingly been viewed as a potential tool to reduce VMT and improve fuel efficiency. Currently fuel taxes comprise 30 to 40 percent of fuel prices, but a very small percentage of total car ownership costs. Fuel tax advocates point out that American gasoline prices are a mere fraction of those in other industrialized nations, where the price of a gallon of gasoline can cost $2 to $3 more than in the U.S. * * *

Changes in fuel tax prices have two long-term effects:

- Increasing fuel prices raises the price of travel per mile, which encourages consumers to reduce vehicle miles of travel. . . .

- Since the amount paid for fuel is directly proportional to the amount of fuel consumed, fuel pricing provides incentives for the purchase of more efficient vehicles. . . .

The effectiveness of fuel pricing depends on consumers' responses to increases in the price of fuel. Advocates of higher fuel taxes point to their ability to levy the costs at the source of the activity, thus making the cost more visibly related to the act of driving. * * *

Although the federal government and all states levy gas taxes, the idea of increasing gas taxes may draw considerable political opposition. The contentious political debate surrounding the increase in the federal gas tax of $0.04 per gallon in 1996 suggests that large gas tax increases necessary to significantly reduce greenhouse gas emissions may be difficult. Some analysts have suggested that prices would have to be raised by more than $1.00 per gallon to have a large effect on national emissions. * * *

5.2.2 PROVISION FOR ALTERNATIVE MODES* * *

TRANSIT INVESTMENT * * *

Since transit is a motorized form of transportation, the effectiveness of transit investment at reducing greenhouse gases depends on the following factors:

- The level of improvement in transit frequency, coverage, or amenities;

- The extent to which increased transit investment reduces motor vehicle fuel consumption (which depends on the extent to which transit causes shifts in mode of travel, improvements in traffic flow, and any offsetting increases in travel due to improved traffic flow); and

- The extent to which any increases in transit fuel consumption offset these reductions.

There is some debate about the extent to which transit investment can reduce personal vehicle travel. When developing a new transit system, planners generally assume that ten trips on the new system will eliminate fewer than ten auto trips since some of the transit trips are new trips induced by building the new system and others have been captured from other transit systems or routes. Some warn that mass transit will have little effect at encouraging drivers to change their mode of travel since it is not compatible with most U.S. automobile users' travel needs for flexibility and convenience, nor is it compatible with existing low-density land use patterns. On the other hand, others claim that transit has a "magnifying effect" in reducing auto travel since transit affects land use in ways that reduces the need to travel. An analysis conducted by the Natural Resources Defense Council (NRDC) and the Sierra Club suggests that each new transit mile traveled replaces four to eight miles of auto travel due to changes in land use that might result from transit development. Assumptions about the degree to which transit eliminates vehicle trips affect estimated emissions benefits. * * *

The effectiveness of transit is closely related to land use patterns. High-capacity transit is often not cost-effective for suburb-to-suburb trip patterns, which are prevalent in urban travel. The increasing importance of non-work trips also implies that an increasing portion of travel is not part of the traditional transit commuter markets. Improvements in transit routing, publicity, and service to underserved areas may attract ridership without requiring the operation of additional vehicles.

The effectiveness of transit to reduce greenhouse gas emissions may be small at the national level. Transit comprises a small portion of national travel — only 0.9 percent of total passenger miles in the U.S. in 1994. An analysis by Apogee Research, Inc. suggested that transit improvements can reduce VMT by up to 2.6 percent in metropolitan areas, and most likely by only 1.0 percent. Despite these small effects, a significant portion of the literature suggests that transit is an important supporting measure for a variety of transportation control measures (TCMs), including road and fuel pricing. At the national level, emissions effects will depend upon the extent of increases in transit service feasible in urbanized areas. Vanpools, paratransit, and demand-responsive transit may be more appropriate for less urbanized areas. * * *

BICYCLE SUPPORT FACILITIES * * *

Strategies that enhance the environment for bicycles and bicycling as an alternative to single occupancy vehicles (SOVs) include:

- Development of bicycle routes, lanes, or paths;

- Provision of lockers, racks, other storage facilities, and ancillary facilities (such as showers, and clothing lockers);

- Integration with transit, either at stations or on vehicles;

- Educational, media, and promotional campaigns, including provision of bicycle maps; and

- Hiring of a local government or employer-site bicycle coordinator. * * *

Most estimates of VMT reduction from bicycle and pedestrian strategies are relatively low. Bicycle trips are generally limited to short trips. In addition, the potential number of trips that individuals may shift to bicycle is constrained by weather conditions, topography, and individual health and fitness. * * *

Estimates of VMT reductions from bicycle projects suggest that for a metropolitan area, bicycle projects may reduce regional VMT from under 0.01 percent to over 3 percent, with the latter figure assuming capital construction of facilities and an already existing favorable land-use configuration. * * *

HIGH OCCUPANCY VEHICLE (HOV) LANES * * *

High occupancy vehicle (HOV) lanes are specific lanes designated for use only by vehicles carrying two or more individuals (HOV-2) or three or more individuals (HOV-3). HOV lanes encourage carpooling and vanpooling by reducing travel time and reversing the time penalty generally incurred in picking up passengers. HOV lanes also reduce travel time for transit buses. They may be developed on freeway or arterial facilities. Lane restrictions are often limited to peak-hour driving periods. * * *

A number of analyses suggest that the net benefits of HOVs are positive. A study of HOV lanes on Interstate 5 in Seattle determined that adjusting for the growth in households and income, the increase in vehicles from 1978 to 1989 was less than had been projected originally without the HOV lanes for each year after the HOV lanes became available. It projected that the benefits increased over time, with a 6 percent reduction of VMT in 1984 to a 35 percent reduction in 1989.

HOV lanes are mainly effective at reducing peak-period travel on highly congested freeways and arterials. The regional effect of HOV lanes is generally smaller than the reduction in any one corridor. Apogee Research, Inc. estimated that HOV lanes could reduce regional VMT by up to 1.4 percent in major metropolitan areas. National effects would likely be somewhat smaller since HOV lanes would not be implemented in small towns and rural areas. * * *

5.2.3 PARKING MANAGEMENT * * *

PARKING PRICING * * *

Case studies of employer-based programs that involved raising employee parking fees to market rates have shown significant decreases in vehicle use, in the range of a 26 to 81 percent decrease in solo driving. Case studies of differential parking rates for SOVs [single occupancy vehicles] and HOVs also show significant reductions in vehicle travel. A 1996 study examined eight employer programs in California, where parking measures have received considerable attention. The study found that, on average, the employers reduced VMT by 12 percent per employee per year as a result of the program.

Some economists have found that parking charges may have a greater effect on travel behavior than other costs since parking charges are often incurred on a trip-by-trip basis (a separate money transaction must be undertaken with each trip), unlike fuel purchases and other operating costs which are made periodically. * * *

MANDATORY PARKING CASH-OUT * * *

About 95 percent of those who commute to work by automobile in the U.S. use free parking provided by their employers, and nearly all vehicle trips for non-commute purposes also include free parking. Part of the reason for this high rate is that the U.S. tax code has subsidized employer-provided parking by exempting employer parking costs from federal and most state income and payroll taxes as a fringe benefit, provided the employer does not offer cash salary in lieu of the parking space. The Tax Relief Act of 1997 removed the restriction against offering taxable cash in lieu of tax-exempt parking benefits. A "mandatory parking cash-out" policy would make mandatory what the new tax law made possible. It would require employers who provide subsidized parking to also offer their employees the option of receiving taxable income instead of parking. Since employees would be given the choice between a parking space and taxable income, they would perceive the opportunity cost of driving to work in terms of the income forgone. . . . [T]he Climate Change Action Plan estimated that reforming the federal tax subsidy would reduce light-duty VMT by approximately 25 billion miles, or 1.1 percent, in the year 2000. * * *

PARKING SUPPLY LIMITS * * *

A number of policy instruments are available for government to attempt to limit the supply of parking for SOVs, including:

- Maximum parking-supply ratios in zoning;

- Reduced or eliminated minimum-parking ratios in zoning;

- Area-wide parking caps; and

- Restriction of access to parking at certain times of the day, for certain durations, or to certain classes of users (i.e., preferential parking for HOVs). * * *

Experience with a number of parking supply management techniques shows mixed effectiveness. . . . Clearly, the relationship of parking supply to demand and the extent and level of parking supply restrictions will affect a policy's success. Area-wide parking caps that are set above levels of parking demand will have little effect on reducing travel. In addition, parking supply ratios in zoning are limited because they only affect new development. If maximum parking supply ratios are too restrictive, they may encourage development to shift to areas that are not within the bounds of the restriction. * * *

5.2.4 LAND-USE PLANNING

The goal of land use planning as a greenhouse gas reduction strategy is to shape development patterns to encourage less vehicle travel and fuel consumption. Land use measures may be examined at both the neighborhood (micro) level and the regional (macro) level.

. . . Micro-level measures that might reduce fuel consumption from transportation include:

- Increasing density and mix of uses to provide opportunities for pedestrian trips, trip-chaining, and transit access;

- Orienting higher-density development around commercial centers, transit lines, and community facilities to encourage non-motorized trips; and

- Supporting pedestrian and bicycling activity through facilities for non-motorized modes such as sidewalks and bike lanes, urban design improvements, and traffic calming.

. . . Macro-level measures that might reduce fuel consumption include:

- Increasing the compactness of metropolitan areas;

- Focusing regional development around transit networks; and

- Providing a sub-regional balance of jobs and housing, so that individuals do not need to commute long distances.

Specific tools outlined in the literature include the following:

- Site-based tools — developer incentives, zoning requirements, development standards (density standards, requirements for mixed uses, grid street requirements; area or sector plans); and

- Regional planning tools — urban growth boundaries, concurrency requirements, and location efficient mortgages (LEMs).

Quantitative relationships among land use, travel, and fuel consumption have been examined by various researchers. Although land use patterns may account for 40 to 50 percent of urban-travel variations across cities, there are many challenges to altering land use patterns, and some researchers suggest that even significant changes in urban spatial structure may bring about travel reductions of no more than 12 percent. At least one simulation of comprehensive land use measures and travel pricing in Portland, Oregon, has suggested greenhouse gas reductions of nearly 8 percent relative to what they would have been without these measures. Although these estimated reductions are significant and exceed many estimates of the potential of conventional transportation demand management (TDM) measures, various conclusions have been drawn about the effectiveness of strategies that attempt to alter land use patterns. It is difficult to isolate the effect of individual land use strategies since they often occur in combination, and they may have synergistic effects. * * *

STRATEGIES TO INCREASE DENSE, MIXED USE, TRANSIT-ORIENTED DEVELOPMENT * * *

Increasing land use mixing involves locating land uses with complementary functions close enough to one another such that travel distances are minimized. Focusing dense development on transit stations and corridors provides the density necessary for efficient mass transit service and encourages transit use. In combination, these land use patterns may reduce vehicle travel by allowing individuals to walk or take transit among housing, shopping, and employment; to reduce vehicle trip lengths; and to combine trips rather than taking separate vehicle trips. A regional land use strategy might target new development to specific transit corridors or encourage infill development in existing communities and raise transit ridership sufficiently to realize a net reduction in greenhouse gases.

. . . A number of regional analyses of alternative development patterns and transportation investments have suggested that more compact, transit-focused development patterns result in less vehicle travel than dispersed development patterns. * * *

In addition to simulation studies, empirical comparisons of various neighborhoods have been used to suggest that higher density, mixed use, and transit-oriented communities are associated with increased shares of transit and pedestrian travel and reduced VMT. For example, a 1994 study of the San Francisco Bay Area households found that households in newer suburban communities had substantially higher vehicle trip generation rates, a higher proportion of drive alone trips, and a lower percentage of public transportation trips than households in traditional communities. Similarly, a 1996 study that examined travel diaries of residents in three Seattle mixed-use neighborhoods concluded that the pedestrian share of work trips was 11.3 percent in mixed-use communities, as opposed to 3.6 percent in King County as a whole. An analysis of odometer readings from 27 California communities suggested that residential density and access to public transportation were the two urban form factors that most reliably predicted household auto travel behavior, and that doubling residential density reduced annual auto mileage per capita by 20 percent. Similarly, an analysis of trips reported in the 1990 National Personal Transportation Survey (NPTS) found that each doubling in density reduced VMT per capita by 28 percent over the entire urban range of densities.

Despite significant consensus that traditional and transit-oriented communities are associated with less vehicle travel than planned unit (suburban) development, there is disagreement on the total energy use implications of increasing density since denser areas are also often associated with reduced average travel speeds. In addition, nearly all of the empirical studies on land use and travel are cross-sectional. These studies show how variations in land use are associated with variations in VMT but do not prove a causal relationship or show how changes in one variable would result in changes in another. Resident self-selection may explain much of the observed correlation, since people who do not like to drive or cannot drive might tend to seek out high density neighborhoods with good transit access. Thus, some researchers assert that some studies do not support conclusions about how changes in structure will affect travel patterns.

Finally, there is some uncertainty about the effectiveness of planning strategies to alter land use. The amount of development that can be shaped by land use strategies depends on growth in population and employment and on preferences for various types of development styles. * * *

ENHANCEMENTS TO THE PEDESTRIAN ENVIRONMENT * * *

Efforts to enhance the safety and pleasantness of the pedestrian environment include the provision of sidewalks, clearly marked crosswalks, walk signals, and median strips. * * *

Modeling done in Portland, Oregon suggested that the pedestrian environment may be a significant factor in determining automobile ownership. In addition, it may also influence daily auto VMT and vehicle trips per person. In [one] study, a pedestrian environment factor (PEF) was developed that measures ease of street crossing, sidewalk continuity, street connectivity, and topography, with a qualitative assessment on a scale of four to twelve. Each unit increase in PEF resulted in a reduction in 0.7 vehicle miles traveled daily per household. Similarly, the Maryland National Capital Parks and Planning Commission (MNCPPC) has shown that pedestrian and bicycle friendliness is a significant factor in determining work trip mode choice.

Empirical analyses have come to similar conclusions. For example, a comparison of employment sites in Southern California found that areas perceived as safe and aesthetically pleasing had lower levels of drive-alone commute trips and higher proportions of transit, bicycle, and walk trips than sites perceived as less pedestrian-friendly. A recent study compared two Puget Sound area neighborhoods that were similar in terms of gross residential density and intensity of commercial development. It found that the neighborhood with a high level of pedestrian network connectivity had almost three times as much pedestrian activity as the one with a low level of pedestrian connectivity. * * *

5.2.5 OTHER VEHICLE TRAVEL REDUCTION MEASURES * * *

TELECOMMUTING * * *

. . . Although telecommuting can reduce vehicle travel for those that participate, its effect is limited for a number of reasons. In particular, telecommuting only targets commute travel, which is only about one quarter of total vehicle miles traveled. Telecommuting is feasible for only a portion of all workers — primarily information workers — and those that participate will often only eliminate one to three days of commute per week. In addition, some of those that participate may have taken transit or carpools in the past. Trips previously [combined] with the work trip will still need to be made. * * *

COMPRESSED WORK HOURS * * *

Compressed work hours is a program that allows individuals to work more hours per day and fewer days per week. A typical program involves working 10 hours, 4 days a week, rather than 8 hours, 5 days a week. For each employee working under this schedule, this strategy eliminates one round-trip to work each week. In addition, the change in daily work hours can often reduce peak-period travel. * * *

Compressed work hours programs have many of the same limitations of telecommuting programs — commute travel is only a small portion of total transportation emissions, it only reduces travel one day per week or every two weeks, not all employees will be able to participate, and there may be some offsetting increases in travel. It also is not clear to what extent government efforts will induce adoption by private employers.

According to EPA's Transportation Control Measures Information Documents, there is only one example in the literature where the transportation impacts of a coordinated compressed work-hours program have been systematically documented. Denver participated in a federal employee compressed work-week experiment from 1978–1981. Findings were favorable. Among employees participating, there was a 15 percent reduction in commute VMT, and a shifting of peak arrival and departure times. There was little change in modal share. Overall, participants reduced household VMT by almost 16 percent. Although there was some increase in non-work trips during the employees' day off, this was offset by a drop in weekend VMT. * * *

5.3 FUEL-ECONOMY-FOCUSED STRATEGIES * * *

5.3.1 IMPROVING TRAFFIC OPERATIONS

For a given vehicle, on-road fuel economy is a function of average speed and acceleration. At low speeds, a greater proportion of energy to the engine goes to internal engine friction and to operating accessories such as power steering and transmission, oil and water pumps, and air conditioners. Braking directly translates the vehicle's momentum into heat energy. Since characteristics of highway congestion — low travel speeds, increased braking and accelerations, idling — are associated with increased fuel use, strategies to reduce congestion and improve traffic flow can reduce greenhouse gas emissions.

At speeds above 55–60 mph, increasing aerodynamic drag causes fuel economy to decline. Oak Ridge National Laboratory is currently conducting tests of light-duty vehicles to characterize their fuel consumption over most of their operating ranges, to represent fuel economy as functions of vehicle speed and acceleration. Preliminary tests showed over 20 percent of fuel economy loss occurs between 55 and 75 mph. This fuel economy loss is similar to losses estimated from earlier studies in the 1970s and 1980s. Thus, policies to limit speeds to 55 mph may be used to reduce greenhouse gas emissions. * * *

TRAFFIC FLOW IMPROVEMENTS * * *

Traffic flow improvements encompass a wide range of programs to smooth traffic flow, reduce idling, and eliminate bottlenecks:

- *Signalization improvements* can reduce intersection delay on arterials and other routes in urbanized areas.

- *Incident management* and advanced traffic sensing technologies allow faster response time to remove breakdowns and accidents from the road.

- *Intelligent Transportation Systems (ITS)* encompass a range of technologies that develop more intelligent vehicles and transportation infrastructure, including use of real-time information on traffic conditions, directions to unfamiliar places, and identification of alternate routes. * * *

LIMIT FREEWAY SPEEDS TO 55 MPH * * *

Beyond 55 miles per hour, fuel economy is generally a decreasing function of speed for both cars and trucks. The national 55 mph speed limit, repealed in 1995, was originally passed by Congress in 1974 as an energy conservation measure. A greenhouse gas reduction strategy would be to re-apply the national 55 mph speed limit or encourage states to voluntarily limit speeds on interstates and freeways to 55 mph. * * *

EPA estimates that traveling at 65 mph as compared to 55 mph lowers fuel economy over 15 percent. Preliminary testing of vehicles at Oak Ridge National Laboratory for U.S. DOT suggest that an increase in speed from 55 to 65 mph may reduce fuel economy by over 11 percent and that increasing from 55 to 70 mph may reduce fuel economy by over 23 percent. * * *

Various estimates of energy savings from the national 55 mph limit indicate that despite imperfect compliance, it may reduce national fuel consumption on highways by about 1 to 3 percent. A 1984 study by the National Research Council (NRC) concluded that in 1983, the national speed limit reduced highway fuel consumption by about 2.2 percent.

———

QUESTIONS AND DISCUSSION

1. *Linking Urban and Suburban Areas.* One of the main challenges that planners face is connecting urban areas with suburban ones, and suburban areas with each other. The Metropolitan Policy Program at the Brookings Institution explains that while the suburb has become a key feature of the American economy, transportation planning has not kept pace.

> Suburbs are no longer just bedroom communities for workers commuting to traditional downtowns. Rather, they are now strong employment centers serving a variety of functions in the regional economies. An investigation into the location of jobs in the nation's largest metropolitan areas finds that over one half are located more than 10 miles outside of downtowns. Only about one in six metropolitan jobs is located near the metropolitan core, within 3 miles of downtown. * * *
>
> Although nearly half of work commutes still originate from, or terminate in, center cities, 40.8 percent of work trips are entirely suburban. Many older rail transit systems — which still move millions of daily commuters — capture very little of this market because they were laid out when the dominant travel pattern was still radial and before business and commercial development began to follow the edgeless pattern. . . . Plus, because commute trips make up only 15 percent of all trips, many other routes and options are being ill-served by these outmoded patterns.

METROPOLITAN POLICY PROGRAM, THE BROOKINGS INSTITUTION, A BRIDGE TO SOMEWHERE: RETHINKING AMERICAN TRANSPORTATION FOR THE 21ST CENTURY 15, 18–19 (2008). How should governments address transportation needs for suburban communities? Do any of the policies identified by the Federal Highway Administration do this?

2. *Cordon Pricing.* Some cities have toyed with using cordon pricing mechanisms that charge drivers a fee to enter into a central business district. Most notably, London, England, enacted a cordon pricing mechanism in the "congestion charge zone" covering about 8 miles in the heart of London. Each car entering the city between 7:30 a.m. and 6:00 p.m. must pay £5.00 (just under $10.00 in August 2008). The city estimates that at least 50 percent of workers who previously drove into London to work have switched to public transportation.

3. *Congestion and Greenhouse Gas Emissions.* Many transportation experts have promoted traffic congestion reduction as a key strategy in limiting domestic greenhouse gas emissions. The average commuter in the United States spends

approximately 38 hours per year in delayed traffic during rush hour. In large metropolitan areas, this figure increases to 54 hours per year. These congestion-caused delays waste nearly 2.9 billion gallons of fuel each year, and result in 27.2 million metric tons of carbon dioxide emissions annually. Beyond this, economists estimate that traffic delays exact an enormous financial price and account for approximately $78.2 billion in costs each year. *See* DAVID SCHRANK & TIM LOMAX, THE 2007 URBAN MOBILITY REPORT (Texas Transportation Institute, 2007).

The most common response to congestion problems has been development of new roads or new lanes on existing roads. Since congestion results from too many cars on the road at once, new roads should, in theory, reduce congestion-related delays. Recent studies, however, suggest that increased road-building may offer only temporary relief from congestion. Transportation planners believe that adding new road capacity leads to "induced travel":

> One of the reasons that road-building shows disappointing results in easing congestion is that adding capacity to highways doesn't just meet the current travel demand: it actually spurs additional driving. When a road is widened, more people will also choose to drive on it — either switching from another route, time of day, or mode, or taking additional trips. Transportation engineers and planners call this "induced travel." While there is debate about how much capacity is lost to induced travel, some studies of induced travel estimate that, in the short-term, up to half of the new roadway capacity on a given road is consumed by induced travel. Over time, as land uses around the new roadway change, the road becomes even more clogged. New and wider roads encourage new development, often on the fringe of urban areas. These new developments generate new traffic. Several recent studies document the effect of induced traffic.

SURFACE TRANSPORTATION POLICY PROJECT, EASING THE BURDEN: A COMPANION ANALYSIS OF THE TEXAS TRANSPORTATION INSTITUTE'S CONGESTION STUDY 4 (May 2001).

4. *Roundabouts.* Intersections with roundabouts (traffic circles) have the potential to dramatically reduce greenhouse gas emissions from vehicles. Studies at various intersections in different countries uniformly have found reductions in emissions of CO_2 and hydrocarbons. One study of three intersections in Kansas concluded that a roundabout reduced CO_2 emissions by 55 to 61 percent and emissions of hydrocarbons by 62 to 68 percent, depending on the time of day (i.e., the number of cars passing through the intersection). Because roundabouts reduce delay at intersections, they also reduce fuel consumption. Srinivas Mandavilli et al., ENVIRONMENTAL IMPACT OF KANSAS ROUNDABOUTS 16 (2003); *see also* Tony Redington, MODERN ROUNDABOUTS, GLOBAL WARMING, AND EMISSIONS REDUCTIONS: STATUS OF RESEARCH, AND OPPORTUNITIES FOR NORTH AMERICA (2001).

5. Some companies recognize that efficient travel plans can reduce gasoline consumption and costs. Most notably, UPS trucks famously plot their travel routes to take only right turns. Efficient route planning and the "right turn only" approach saves the company an estimated three million gallons of fuel a year, which translates directly into reduced greenhouse gas emissions. Brian Rooney, *UPS Figures Out "Right Way" to Save Money, Time, and Gas*, ABC NEWS ONLINE (Apr. 4, 2007).

6. *The Home Mortgage Interest Deduction and Climate Change.* Recently, Representative John Dingell (D.-Mich.) floated a proposal for phasing out the home mortgage interest deduction on large homes to pay for greenhouse gas reduction strategies. See Chapter 11 for a discussion of his proposal. Tax analysts also believe that restructuring the home mortgage interest deduction could play a role in climate change policy:

Americans prefer large, single family homes. This low density housing pattern, often referred to as "urban sprawl" or "sprawl development", virtually requires the use of the private automobile. The federal government helps Americans buy their large homes through the home mortgage interest deduction. The home mortgage interest deduction is facially neutral in that a home buyer can use the deduction whether buying a condominium above a transit hub or a six bedroom home fifty miles away from a major urban center with no accessible public transportation. Deciding whether the home mortgage interest deduction encouraged sprawl and therefore road construction or whether subsidized road construction facilitated sprawl, which was then enabled by the home mortgage interest deduction, presents the classic, and unanswerable, chicken and egg problem. However, economists generally agree that the home mortgage interest deduction has created a false market signal for home buyers, encouraging them to over-invest in housing, and artificially inflating the price of homes.

Accordingly, I recommend that the home mortgage interest deduction be changed to correct this market failure. . . . Changing the home mortgage interest deduction can have a significant impact on the choices of home buyers if the tax benefit is tied to the location of the home. First, the home mortgage interest deduction should be changed to a federal income tax credit, so that its benefits will be distributionally equitable. The new "shelter credit" would have two components: a base amount and a location efficiency premium (LEP). The base amount of the credit would be determined by multiplying the median national home price by the annualized long-term tax exempt interest rate, and then multiplying that product by the lowest marginal tax rate. For example, if the median national home price was $100,000, and the long-term tax exempt rate was 5%, the base credit would be $500. The base amount of the credit serves as a proxy for the average mortgage interest deduction. The amount of the credit would be capped at the actual housing cost paid by the taxpayer and would be phased out at higher income levels in a manner similar to the phase out of itemized deductions.

The LEP would be based on calculations similar to those done by urban planner John Holtzclaw in his analyses of location efficiency. Location efficient mortgages (LEMs) were developed using data created by Holtzclaw, who determined average transportation savings in four urban areas in California by examining four factors: residential density, transit accessibility, availability of neighborhood shopping, and pedestrian accessibility. Lenders use the transportation savings factor to calculate the borrower's eligibility for the loan, thus making the borrower eligible for a larger loan. LEMs facilitate purchase of higher cost transit accessible property by low to moderate income buyers. Because the LEP is based on the additional value represented by the accessibility of the home to public transportation, it would create an incentive for home buyers to purchase transit accessible homes, which generally are located close to the urban core. In addition, the LEP might encourage extension of public transportation into previously unserved areas, thereby increasing transportation choices.

Roberta F. Mann, *On the Road Again: How Tax Policy Drives Transportation Choice*, 24 VA. TAX REV. 587, 647–50 (2005)

What do you think of Professor Mann's proposal? Would it necessarily promote a move into urban centers? Would it promote development of increased transportation?

7. As Professor Mann indicates in her article, a location efficient mortgage (LEM) offers urban homebuyers the opportunity to take out a larger mortgage for property located in an area with good public transportation access. The theory behind a LEM is that homebuyers will spend less money on transportation and can therefore afford to dedicate a greater percentage of their annual income toward their mortgage payments. Most economists attribute the recent economic meltdown to inappropriate lending activities by banks. Should urban planners continue to advocate a LEM approach? Would Professor Mann's proposed LEP — which gives homebuyers an increased tax credit based on proximity to public transportation — avoid the potential downfalls of a LEM? How should the IRS calculate the LEP? Do you think it would really affect home purchasing decisions?

8. *Urban Growth Planning and Leakage Transportation Emissions.* Land use planning is not a perfect tool for reducing greenhouse gas emissions, because planning presents the risk of leakage. The case of Portland, Oregon, provides an example of this. Since the 1970s, the Portland metropolitan area has used an urban growth boundary (UGB) to limit suburban sprawl and promote relatively dense housing within the UGB. These strategies (combined with others) have yielded significant reductions in the city's overall greenhouse gas emissions. At the same time, however, property values and property taxes within the UGB climbed. To escape escalating property expenses, many people moved outside of the UGB to Vancouver, Washington, which is about 10 miles north of downtown Portland. In March 2007, an estimated 273,000 people commuted in cars to Portland from Vancouver each work day, offsetting many of the emissions reductions that Portland achieved through its land use planning policies. *See* Courtney Sherwood, *More Cross-River Commuters Leave Cars Home*, The Columbian, May 7, 2008, at A1. Without regional land use planning, leakage is difficult to avoid.

9. *Economic Equity and Transportation Planning.* Transportation planning strategies designed to reduce greenhouse gas emissions by raising transportation costs could place significant burdens on lower-income households. In 2003, the working poor spent approximately 6.1 percent of their income on commuting, and those who drove their own vehicles spent 8.4 percent. In comparison, the average worker spent 3.8 percent of her income on commuting. Elizabeth Roberto, Metropolitan Policy Program, The Brookings Institute, Commuting to Opportunity: The Working Poor and Commuting in the United States 7, 9 (2008). When all transportation expenses are factored in, the average American household spends approximately one-fifth of household income on transportation. Barbara J. Lipman, Center for Housing Policy, A Heavy Load: The Combined Housing and Transportation Burdens of Working Families 1 (2006). This percentage is higher for the working poor, who in 2003 spent more than 40 percent of their income on transportation. Surface Transportation Policy Project, Transportation Costs and the American Dream: Why a Lack of Transportation Choices Strains the Family Budget and Hinders Home Ownership 3 (2003).

Several factors make transportation particularly expensive for lower-income households. Since the 1980s, many companies have relocated their businesses out of city centers and into the suburbs. Poverty has also moved into the suburbs. "In 2005, for the first time in American history, more of America's poor live in large metropolitan suburbs than live in big cities." Metropolitan Policy Center, A Bridge to Somewhere, at 15. Lower-income workers frequently must travel either from a less affluent suburb or from an urban center to reach their places of employment. In many cases, public transportation systems do not reach the suburban areas. Even when public transportation is available, commuting can take a prohibitively long amount of time. Thus, lower-income employees do not have any option other than driving. These workers often drive older, less efficient vehicles, and thus spend more money per mile to commute. Moving into the same suburb in which their workplace is located is also often not an option due to high moving and housing expenses.

How should transportation planners address these issues? Do any of the above proposals present viable options for lower-income households?

B.   The Role of the Federal Government in Transportation Policies

In contrast to the dominant role the federal government plays in administering most of the laws discussed throughout this book, there is little national leadership or direction regarding transportation infrastructure. This is true even though federal funding accounts for the majority of funds committed to highway projects. Indeed, the federal highway agencies play such a limited role in transportation planning that the U.S. Government Accountability Office (GAO) has described the federal transportation program as a "cash transfer, general purpose grant program." U.S. GAO, FEDERAL-AID HIGHWAYS: TRENDS, EFFECT ON STATE SPENDING, AND OPTIONS FOR FUTURE PROGRAM DESIGN, at 5 (2004).

The limited role of the federal government dates back to the early and mid-20th Century, when expansion of the federal highway system was a national goal. In 1916, Congress passed the Federal-Aid Road Act of 1916, 39 Stat. 355, which was the "first authorized federal financial participation in the construction of the nation's roads." Stephen McDonald, Note, *Why VEETC is Not Enough: Protecting the National Highway Transportation Infrastructure*, 30 WM. & MARY ENVTL. L. & POL'Y REV. 731, 736 (2006) (quoting Craig J. Albert, *Your Add Goes Here: How the Highway Beautification Act Thwarts Highway Beautification*, 48 U. KAN. L. REV. 463, 469 (2000)). The Federal-Aid Road Act created a cooperative dynamic between the federal government and state governments, pursuant to which the federal government would fund, and state governments would build, highway construction projects. Since that time, the role of the federal government has been to promote and enable highway construction and expansion. States, meanwhile, have had primary decision-making authority in transportation planning.

In 1956, Congress reinforced these respective roles with its passage of the Federal Highway Act of 1956, which launched the construction of the interstate highway system, and the Highway Revenue Act of 1956, which established the Highway Trust Fund as the method for funding highway building and maintenance. As under the earlier law, the Federal Highway Act placed the decision-making power in the states and the funding responsibility largely in the federal government. The Highway Revenue Act established a tax system under which gasoline taxes are deposited into the Highway Trust Fund and then distributed to the states for construction of the interstate highway system. *See* McDonald, *supra*, at 735–41.

The use of gasoline taxes to pay for highway funding, and the requirement that gasoline taxes would fund highway construction, significantly affected the transportation system in the United States. Following the federal government's lead, many state governments passed their own laws establishing state gasoline taxes and dedicating the revenues to highway and road construction. As a result, under both the federal and state programs, highway building received ample funding, while mass transit and alternative forms of transportation often received very little financial support. Not surprisingly, the highway system expanded while mass transit systems atrophied in many places or were simply never developed in others.

In 1991, Congress briefly adopted a new vision for federal transportation with its passage of the Intermodal Surface Transportation Efficiency Act (ISTEA). That law declared that "it is the policy of the United States to develop a National Intermodal Transportation System that is economically efficient and environmentally sound, provides the foundation for the Nation to compete in the global economy, and will move people and goods in an energy efficient manner." Pub. L. No. 102-240, § 2, 105 Stat. 1914, 1915 (December 18, 1991). It also expanded the range of projects that are eligible for federal funding to include transit capital projects, transit improvements, and transportation planning. In addition, ISTEA dedicated funding to high-speed transportation development. ISTEA also directed greater attention to long-range planning by directing state governments and separate metropolitan planning organizations to develop long-range transportation plans. The metropolitan plans were to consider specifically land use, intermodal connectivity, and improved transit service. Finally, through the Congestion Mitigation and Air Quality (CMAQ) program, ISTEA authorized additional funding for congestion relief measures, including public transit improvements, development of bicycle and pedestrian facilities, and programs promoting carpools and high-occupancy vehicle use.

While ISTEA signaled a shift away from the federal government's almost exclusive focus on road-building to a more expansive role in transportation planning, the actual priorities of the federal government remain focused on highway construction. In part, this is due to the funding allocations under ISTEA and later statutes, the 1998 Transportation Equity Act for the 21st Century (TEA-21) and the 2005 Safe, Accountable, Flexible, Efficient Transportation Act: A Legacy for Users (SAFETEA-LU). These laws allocate federal transportation funds to states primarily based on the amount of roads, miles driven, and fuel consumed in each state, and thus disincentivize reduced consumption, since lower consumption will lead to less funding. In addition, the laws require federal approval before new transit projects are developed and funded, whereas highway projects may proceed without prior federal approval. Finally, even though ISTEA authorized federal funding to go to transit projects, later laws have capped the amount. Whereas federal funds can contribute as much as 90 percent for highway improvements and maintenance, new transit projects are limited to a 60 percent federal share. In practice, the federal government contributes closer to 40 percent of transit costs. As a result, state and local governments bear a greater burden in funding metropolitan transportation programs aimed at reducing VMT and greenhouse gas emissions.

QUESTIONS AND DISCUSSION

1. **The Role of the Federal Government.** What role do you think the federal government should play in transportation planning? Although some policy analysts have called for the federal government to create a federal transportation program, others believe the federal government would be overstepping its role if it were to dictate how local governments should design their own transportation policies. Is transportation planning an inherently local process? Should it be?

2. *Gasoline Taxes and Highway Funding.* Since 1916, gasoline taxes assessed at both the federal and state level have provided the primary revenue for highway construction and repair. As gas prices climb and gas purchases decline, revenues from gas taxes accordingly fall. If gas prices remain high, states will continue to lose money for transportation infrastructure. This funding dynamic creates a somewhat perverse incentive for governments to favor increased driving to generate higher gas tax revenue. What other funding mechanisms should governments use to pay for transportation systems?

———

III. ALTERNATIVE FUELS

The type of fuel used in automobiles and other forms of transportation heavily affects the U.S. carbon footprint. Oil and gasoline account for more than 95 percent of all fuels used in transportation sources. While alternative fuels have begun to play an increasingly important role in transportation, they account for less than 1 percent of all vehicle fuels. However, this percentage is expected to increase as Congress dedicates more subsidies to alternative fuel production. In fact, federal subsidies and mandates have generated an explosion in domestic production and use of alternative fuels, particularly biofuels. Corn-based ethanol production rose from 1.6 billion gallons in 2000 to 5 billion gallons in 2006 to a projected 7.7 billion gallons in 2008. Whether or not these production rates can or should continue to rise is debatable; but there is little doubt that alternative fuel policy will play a key role in U.S. transportation policy development in the future.

All alternative fuels, however, are not created equal. Within the transportation sector, the most common alternatives fuels are: natural gas; ethanol derived from corn; biofuels derived from soybeans, switchgrass, and other crops; second-generation biomass-to-liquid (BTL) biofuels; and hydrogen. Most of these fuel sources do not actually have lower end-of-pipe emissions than gasoline and diesel. However, depending upon how alternative fuels are produced, their lifecycle greenhouse gas emissions may be significantly lower than petroleum-based fuels. Determining which alternative fuels have the greatest impact in terms of climate change mitigation involves a number of considerations and calculations. For example, corn-based ethanol typically requires significant inputs of petroleum-based pesticides and herbicides, as well as energy-intensive processing, before it can be used as an automotive fuel. Natural gas and other alternative fuels may be imported from other countries, and the energy expended in their production and transportation may offset end-of-pipe emission reductions. As scientists develop more sophisticated models to calculate overall greenhouse gas emissions from alternative fuels, it appears that first-generation biofuels may not provide the benefits policymakers initially anticipated.

The use of alternative fuels may also have unintended consequences. Recent reports suggest that crop production for biofuels has displaced food production in many parts of the world, contributing to a global food shortage and increased food prices. Policies promoting biofuels may also spur landowners and governments to convert forest land into agricultural land. The resulting greenhouse gas emissions from land conversion may eclipse any emissions reductions gained from biofuel use.

On the other hand, biofuels and alternative fuel sources present many opportunities. Technologically, alternative fuels can already substitute for gasoline and diesel in many types of engines. It is also relatively easy and inexpensive to convert other engines for alternative fuel use. If policymakers develop innovative alternative fuel policies that can assimilate new information and promote low carbon fuels, alternative fuels may have great promise for reducing greenhouse gas emissions from transportation sources.

This section begins with a summary of the types of alternative fuels that are currently available or in development. It then discusses some of the unintended consequences of biofuel production, with a particular focus on the impacts on food production and climate change mitigation. Finally, it examines the laws that currently regulate and promote alternative fuels, and asks whether the legal system is adequately addressing the many issues involved in alternative fuel production and use.

A.   An Overview of Alternative Fuel Production and Use

Alternative sources of transportation fuel are not a new concept. The first diesel engine was likely powered by peanut oil in 1900. In 1925, Henry Ford predicted that the fuel of the future would come from vegetation. Several studies in the 1930s and 1940s explored using a range of biofuel sources, including peanut oil, fish oil, animal oil, and castor oil, to power automotive engines. *See* Gerhard Knothe, *Historical Perspective on Vegetable Oil-Based Diesel Fuels*, 12 INFORM 1103 (2001). Yet, despite early interest in alternative fuels, climate change and escalating oil prices have only recently spurred modern investment in alternative fuels as viable energy sources. This investment has quickly resulted in soaring demand for certain alternative fuels.

This section will briefly describe the common types of alternative fuels, their production methods, and current uses. As you read these descriptions, consider the following questions:

1. Which fuels, if any, have the best chance of reducing greenhouse gas emissions in the short term? Which would reduce long-term greenhouse gas emissions?

2. How should the U.S. promote development of alternative fuels for vehicles? From the excerpts below, do you think the U.S. approach is successful? Why or why not?

3. Is alternative fuel development policy consistent with U.S. efforts to increase vehicle fuel efficiency and reform the transportation infrastructure? What other types of policies could the U.S. employ to reduce overall greenhouse gas emissions from motor vehicles?

1.   *Agricultural Sources of Fuels*

The most common types of agricultural sources of fuels are often divided into two categories: ethanol and biodiesel. These two types of agricultural fuels dominate the alternative fuels market in the United States.

a.   *Ethanol*

Ethanol is an alcohol derived from starchy vegetation. Ethanol production can be very energy-intensive, particularly when ethanol is produced from corn. While other sources of ethanol may require less energy to produce, most ethanol in the

United States comes from corn. The following except describes how different sources of ethanol may affect its efficiency.

L. LEON GEYER, PHILLIP CHONG & BILL HXUE, ETHANOL, BIOMASS, BIOFUELS AND ENERGY: A PROFILE AND OVERVIEW
12 DRAKE J. AGRIC. L. 61, 69–71, 73–75 (2007)[*]

Ethanol is defined as a "clear, colorless liquid" that can be "produced from any biological feedstocks that contain appreciable amounts of sugar." Since ethanol production is contingent upon the presence of simple sugars such as starch, "it works best when [it is] derived from crops that concentrate starches in their seeds." This explains why 95 percent of all U.S. produced ethanol is made from corn.

There are two common methods of ethanol production: dry milling and wet milling. As the most common method of ethanol production in the United States, dry milling occurs when "the entire corn kernel is first ground into flour and the starch in the flour is converted to ethanol via fermentation." Conversely, wet milling is "the process of separating the corn kernel into starch, protein, germ and fiber in an aqueous medium prior to fermentation." * * *

Maywa Montenegro states that the important issue within ethanol production is the fact "it can use only a relatively small portion of each plant" to make the actual fuel which leaves a lot of biomass unused and wasted. In comparison, the production of biodiesel requires "new or used vegetable oils and animal fats chemically reacted with an alcohol (methanol is the usual choice)," thus creating little or no waste. For corn, the kernel is the active agent within the ethanol production process and the stover (leaves, stalks, and cobs) is left for waste. This creates a situation where the net energy balance of different biofuels becomes a critical issue. . . .

While corn is currently the primary source of ethanol, it is possible that more efficient sources of energy may be developed. For example, switchgrass, also called tall panic grass, is a warm-season plant that is thought by many experts as the ideal alternative to corn for cellulosic ethanol production. . . . Preliminary research by USDA scientists has found that switchgrass has an energy output/input ratio more than 3.5 times greater than corn ethanol. Similarly, sugar feedstock such as sugar cane and sugar beets offer "more efficient" alternatives to corn based ethanol. According to scientific data reported by Larry Rohter, Brazil's sugar cane ethanol yields nearly eight times as much energy as corn-based options.

Aside from corn, sugar, and switchgrass based ethanol, cellulosic ethanol is another type of ethanol derived from biomass which "refers to a wide variety of plentiful materials obtained from plants — including certain forest-related resources, many types of solid wood waste materials, and certain agricultural wastes (including corn stover) — as well as plants that are specifically grown as fuel for generating electricity." Cellulosic ethanol may be seven to eight times more efficient in respect to corn-based ethanol's net energy balance ratio. Y.H. Percival Zhang of Virginia Tech stated that "[i]f we want to produce 30 to 60 billion gallons of ethanol, which is what is needed to meet the President's goal, we have to use the entire plant, or the stover (leaves, stalks, and cobs)." The technology necessary to utilize the entire plant lies in cellulosic ethanol and requires the "technologies that can break the cellulose into the sugars that are distilled to produce ethanol."

---

b. *Biodiesel*

Biodiesel is derived from vegetable oil or animal fats that can be converted into fuel. Although some engines can run directly on vegetable oil, most engines require oils to be processed through a relatively simple chemical reaction before the oils can be used as fuel. The processing uses alcohol to remove glycerin and make the oil less dense. The processing is considered relatively efficient, and each gallon of oil will yield almost one gallon of usable biodiesel.

UNION OF CONCERNED SCIENTISTS, ALTERNATIVE FUELS: BIODIESEL BASICS
available at
http://www.ucsusa.org/clean_vehicles/big_rig_cleanup/biodiesel.html[*]

Today's Use of Biodiesel

Biodiesel makes up a tiny, but growing, fraction of diesel use in the U.S. Between 2004 and 2006, biodiesel use increased tenfold, from about 25 million gallons to 250 million gallons. Yet, as of 2007, biodiesel comprised less than one percent of total highway diesel fuel use. According to the National Biodiesel Board, production capacity is continuing to grow so that nearly two billion gallons of biodiesel could be produced by mid-2008.

Due to high biodiesel costs, engine compatibility issues, and cold weather operating concerns, biodiesel is often blended with conventional diesel fuel. Common biodiesel blends are B20 (20% biodiesel and 80% petroleum diesel) and B2 (2% biodiesel and 98% petroleum diesel). The environmental benefits associated with using biodiesel scale with the percentage of biodiesel contained in the fuel blend.

Certified low-level biodiesel blends can be used in most traditional diesel vehicles without engine modification. The use of higher-level biodiesel blends tends to require engine modification and other usage considerations.

Global Warming Impacts and Benefits

According to a model developed by the Argonne National Laboratory (ANL), neat (100%) biodiesel from soybeans can cut global warming pollution by more than half relative to conventional petroleum based diesel. The emissions benefits are higher for canola oil. In the future, non-conventional sources like algae may have the potential to provide dramatic (90%) reductions in global warming pollution. * * *

Land Use, Biofuels, and Global Warming

It is important to note that the ANL model of global warming impacts does not take into account changes in land use. When soybeans are used for fuel, they are

---

taken out of the market for food. This increases prices and stimulates demand that farmers around the world respond to by bringing more land into cultivation. With soybean production increasing in the Amazon, it is possible that the lifecycle global warming pollution of soybean biodiesel is even higher than petroleum diesel, once indirect land use changes are considered. . . .

When biodiesel is made from recycled food oil or other waste products these land use considerations do not apply. Also advanced technologies including biomass gasification may allow the use of other waste streams to be converted to synthetic diesel fuels, expanding the pool of potentially low carbon diesel.

In addition to land use, there is also some controversy over the emissions impact of fertilizer use and other land use practices (such as tillage practices). As a result, the estimated emissions from biodiesel can be expected to change as our understanding of the lifecycle improves.

Large scale production of biodiesel would require more virgin plant oils or other waste stream sources to meet larger demands. However, such large-volume biodiesel use could raise concerns about genetically modified crops, pesticide use, and land-use impacts common to ethanol and all other plant-based fuels. Crops for biodiesel must be grown in a manner that supports wildlife habitat, minimizes soil erosion, avoids competition for food crops, and does not rely on the use of harsh chemicals and fertilizers.

QUESTIONS AND DISCUSSION

1. *Emissions From Corn-Based Ethanol.* Are greenhouse gas emissions from corn-based ethanol lower than emissions from petroleum-based fuels? Scientists have reached different conclusions regarding this question, and the debate appears to be far from settled. Most scientists had assumed that corn-based ethanol production would result in a 10 to 20 percent reduction in overall greenhouse gas emissions, based on the assumption that the plants would remove more carbon than the resulting fuels would release. For example, scientists at Iowa State University concluded that, when considering emissions from the refinery phase, emissions and removals from the agricultural phase, and direct land use changes associated with increased corn production, corn ethanol would still reduce greenhouse gas emissions by at least 11 percent and up to 39 percent. Bruce A. Babcock et al., *Is Corn Ethanol a Low-Carbon Fuel?*, 13 Iowa Ag. Rev. 1–3, 10 (2007). However, in August 2007, another group of scientists concluded that emissions of nitrous oxide that occur when biomass is converted into biofuels would offset any benefits of carbon dioxide removals associated with plant growth. P.J. Crutzen et al., *N_2O Release from Agro-Biofuel Production Negates Global Warming Reduction by Replacing Fossil Fuels*, 7 Atmos. Chem. Phys. Discuss. 11,191 (2007). For corn-based ethanol, the study found that global warming effects from nitrous oxide would be 0.9–1.5 times higher than any cooling effects from reduced carbon dioxide emissions. *Id.* at 11,197. How should policymakers handle these scientific disputes?

2. *Cellulosic Ethanol and Second-Generation Biofuels.* Many ethanol advocates believe that cellulosic ethanol would achieve greater greenhouse gas reductions than corn or switchgrass ethanol. If produced using wood waste and agricultural residue, cellulosic ethanol would presumably not displace food crops and would thus present less risk of causing indirect land use changes described below. *See* note 3. The U.S. Department of Energy (DOE) estimates that cellulosic ethanol would reduce greenhouse gas emissions by 85 percent, compared to refined petroleum. However, as with corn, disputes regarding the overall benefits of

cellulosic biofuels abound. One study concluded that cellulosic ethanol production requires 170 percent more energy than corn ethanol, because cellulosic ethanol starches are difficult to extract. *See* David Pimentel & Marcia Pimentel, *Corn and Cellulosic Ethanol Cause Major Problems*, 8 ENERGIES 35, 36 (2008). Others have disputed the study's findings. In the meantime, the DOE has dedicated $385 million for six new cellulosic ethanol refineries. Press Release, DOE Selects Six Cellulosic Ethanol Plants for Up to $385 Million in Federal Funding (Feb. 28, 2007).

3.   *Biofuels and Agricultural Practices.* The indirect effects of biofuels production may actually contribute to significant global increases in greenhouse gas emissions. These impacts are particularly profound when biofuels are produced from virgin sources.

In February 2008, a controversy erupted when *Science* published two separate studies claiming that biofuel production would significantly *increase* greenhouse gas emissions due to land use changes. One study concluded that corn-based ethanol production would almost "double greenhouse gas emissions over 30 years and increase[] greenhouse gasses for 167 years." Timothy Searchlinger et al., *Use of U.S. Croplands for Biofuels Increases Greenhouse Gases Through Emissions from Land Use Change*, SCIENCEXPRESS (Feb. 7, 2008), *available at* www.sciencexpress.org. To reach these conclusions, the study authors assumed that increased demand for ethanol would spur U.S. farmers to quit growing soybeans and wheat in favor of growing more lucrative corn. *Id.* at 2. The authors also assumed that feed prices for livestock would increase. *Id.* Over time, the United States' agricultural exports of these crops and animals would decline, leading to increased food production and land conversion as other countries attempt to replace U.S. exports with locally grown food. *Id.* Since much of the existing land would otherwise provide carbon benefits in the form of carbon storage and sequestration, and since land conversion would for some time remove these carbon benefits, the authors concluded that biofuel production will lead to increased greenhouse gas emissions. *Id.* A separate study found that land conversion due to biofuels production would initially release 17 to 420 times the amount of greenhouse gas emissions that biofuels will save on an annual basis. Joseph Fargione et al., *Land Clearing and the Biofuel Carbon Debt*, SCIENCEXPRESS (Feb. 7, 2008), *available at* www.sciencexpress.org.

These studies received considerable attention and criticism after their release. For example, the U.S. Department of Energy (DOE) claimed that many of the assumptions in the studies were either incorrect or unrealistic. DOE, DOE Actively Engaged in Investigating the Role of Biofuels in Greenhouse Gas Emissions from Indirect Land Use Change, 1–2 (2008). Several other scientists challenged the assumptions in the studies. As the controversy brewed, researchers with the DOE urged the California Air Resources Board (CARB) to disregard the impacts of land use conversion in developing the state's low carbon fuel standard on the basis that the science of indirect effects of biofuels is disputed. Letter from Blake A. Simmons, et al., to Mary D. Nichols, Chairman, CARB (June 24, 2008). In response, Timothy Searchinger, lead author of one of the studies, sharply criticized the DOE researchers for urging CARB to ignore a key consideration in any complete analysis of the greenhouse gas impacts of alternative fuels. Letter from Timothy D. Searchinger to Blake A. Simmons, Re: Letter to California Air Resources Board (July 2, 2008). Finally, another set of researchers who officially advise CARB regarding the low carbon fuel standard agreed with Dr. Searchinger that CARB should not ignore indirect land use change. Their letter stated that their own analyses, while not complete, had "found very similar GHG emission results to Searchinger's for ethanol from corn." Letter from Mark A. Delucchi et al., to Mary D. Nichols, Chairman, CARB (July 3, 2008).

What do these exchanges suggest about the overall potential for biofuels to mitigate climate change and the development of an effective climate change strategy? Studies concluding that biofuels will lead to increased greenhouse gas emissions largely reach this conclusion based on market models showing that reduced agricultural exports from the U.S. will spur increased crop production in other countries. They also suggest that renewable fuel standards that allow importation of biofuels could spur other countries to increase biofuel production on unsuitable lands, and thereby emit even more greenhouse gases than gasoline. How can domestic laws address these concerns? Can international law provide a solution?

4. ***Biofuels and Soaring Food Prices.*** One of the major concerns surrounding biofuels is that farmers will shift crops away from food production and toward fuel production and thus trigger a world fuel crisis. At least some organizations, including the United Nations Food and Agricultural Organization (FAO), believe that biofuels have already contributed to this effect. In 2006, 2007, and 2008, world food prices soared to unprecedented levels: 8 percent in 2006, 24 percent above 2006 levels in 2007, and 53 percent above 2007 levels in 2008. By April 2008, the price of grains had climbed by 87 percent compared to 2006 levels. FAO, HIGH-LEVEL CONFERENCE ON WORLD FOOD SECURITY: THE CHALLENGES OF CLIMATE CHANGE & BIOENERGY, SOARING FOOD PRICES: FACTS, PERSPECTIVES, IMPACTS AND ACTIONS RE-QUIRED 3 (June 3–5, 2008). While no one contends that biofuels are the sole cause of rising food prices, many experts believe that the biofuels market, which is tapping important agricultural commodities such as sugar, maize, cassava, oilseeds and palm oil for biofuels production, is playing an important role. *Id.* at 7. In this way, expanding biofuel production could affect food security and interfere with the right to food. How would you balance the right to food with the need for expanding biofuels production?

5. ***Waste Vegetable Oil.*** Some companies and local governments have at-tempted to avoid the indirect negative consequences of using virgin feedstock by using waste vegetable oil (WVO) as a source of biodiesel. Using waste oil reduces pressure on agricultural lands that virgin oil production causes and also reduces impacts on landfills and sewer systems caused by waste oil disposal. The city of Jacksonville, Florida, has created its own biodiesel distillation facility, where it converts waste oil from local restaurants into 100 percent biodiesel (B100). *See* Karen Gardner, *City Makes Biodiesel from Used Cooking Oil*, JACKSONVILLE BUS. J., Jun. 27, 2008, at 3. The city provides the restaurants stainless steel tanks in which they can dump their waste oil and then collects the oil on a regular basis. *Id.* Jacksonville anticipates that its recycling enterprise will save the city a great deal of money and ultimately generate a profit, since it was able to process the waste oil for approximately $1.50 per gallon in the summer of 2008 and biodiesel sold in Jacksonville for more than $4.00 per gallon. SeQuential BioFuels, a commercial biodiesel production facility in Oregon, primarily processes biodiesel from waste oil collected from Kettle Foods (a potato chip company) and Burgerville (a fast food restaurant). *See* SeQuential Pacific Biodiesel, The Fuel, http://salembiodiesel.com/Fuel.htm.

6. Airlines have also explored the viability of using biodiesel as fuel. In April 2007, Virgin Atlantic and Boeing announced a partnership to develop biofuels for use as commercial jet fuel. In September 2007, Boeing and Air New Zealand announced their intention to conduct a demonstration flight using biofuels in the second half of 2008. Boeing, News Release, Boeing, Air New Zealand and Rolls-Royce Announce Biofuel Flight Demo (Sept. 27, 2007).

7. ***Algae-based Biofuels.*** In April 2008, the first algae biofuel production facility went online. Many scientists believe that algae could serve as a viable source

of biofuels, both because of algae's quick growth rate and because algae would not displace existing food crops. Consider the following:

MICHAEL BRIGGS, WIDESCALE BIODIESEL PRODUCTION FROM ALGAE
(Revised Aug. 2004), *available at*
http://www.unh.edu/p2/biodiesel/article_algae.html[*]

For any biofuel to succeed at replacing a large quantity of petroleum, the yield of fuel per acre needs to be as high as possible. At heart, biofuels are a form of solar energy, as plants use photosynthesis to convert solar energy into chemical energy stored in the form of oils, carbohydrates, proteins, etc. The more efficient a particular plant is at converting that solar energy into chemical energy, the better it is from a biofuels perspective. Among the most photosynthetically efficient plants are various types of algaes.

The Office of Fuels Development, a division of the Department of Energy, funded a program from 1978 through 1996 under the National Renewable Energy Laboratory [NREL] known as the "Aquatic Species Program". The focus of this program was to investigate high-oil algaes that could be grown specifically for the purpose of wide scale biodiesel production. The research began as a project looking into using quick-growing algae to sequester carbon in CO_2 emissions from coal power plants. Noticing that some algae have very high oil content, the project shifted its focus to growing algae for another purpose — producing biodiesel. Some species of algae are ideally suited to biodiesel production due to their high oil content (some well over 50% oil), and extremely fast growth rates. From the results of the Aquatic Species Program, algae farms would let us supply enough biodiesel to completely replace petroleum as a transportation fuel in the U.S. (as well as its other main use — home heating oil). * * *

NREL's research showed that one quad (7.5 billion gallons) of biodiesel could be produced from 200,000 hectares of desert land (200,000 hectares is equivalent to 780 square miles, roughly 500,000 acres). . . . [T]o replace all transportation fuels in the U.S., we would need 140.8 billion gallons of biodiesel. . . . To produce that amount would require a land mass of almost 15,000 square miles. To put that in perspective, consider that the Sonora desert in the southwestern U.S. comprises 120,000 square miles. Enough biodiesel to replace all petroleum transportation fuels could be grown in 15,000 square miles, or roughly 12.5 percent of the area of the Sonora desert. . . . That 15,000 square miles works out to roughly 9.5 million acres — far less than the 450 million acres currently used for crop farming in the U.S., and the over 500 million acres used as grazing land for farm animals.

The algae farms would not all need to be built in the same location, of course (and should not for a variety of reasons). . . . It would be preferable to spread the algae production around the country, to lessen the cost and energy used in transporting the feedstocks. Algae farms could also be constructed to use waste streams (either human waste or animal waste from animal farms) as a food source, which would provide a beautiful way of spreading algae production around the country. Nutrients can also be extracted from the algae for the production of a fertilizer high in nitrogen and phosphorous. By using waste streams (agricultural, farm animal waste, and human sewage) as the nutrient source, these farms essentially also provide a means of recycling nutrients from fertilizer to food to waste and back to fertilizer. Extracting the nutrients from algae provides a far safer and cleaner method of doing this than spreading manure or wastewater

---

treatment plant "bio-solids" on farmland.

These projected yields of course depend on a variety of factors, sunlight levels in particular. The yield in North Dakota, for example, wouldn't be as good as the yield in California. Spreading the algae production around the country would result in more land being required than the projected 9.5 million acres, but the benefits from distributed production would outweigh the larger land requirement. * * *

---

8. ***Caffeinating Your Car.*** Researchers have recently found a new source for biodiesel that should put some pep in your car — used coffee grounds. It turns out that coffee grounds yield 10 to 15 percent biodiesel by weight. Over 7 million tons of coffee are consumed every year, which could produce an estimated 340 million gallons of biodiesel. At the end of the process, the coffee grounds can still be composted and, best of all, unlike cars that run on French fry grease that smell like a fast food restaurant, caffeinated cars smell a little like a morning latte from your favorite coffee house. *See Fuelled by Coffee*, THE ECONOMIST'S TECH Q., Mar. 7, 2009, at 6.

---

2. *Natural Gas*

Compressed natural gas (CNG) is another source of transportation fuel currently used in a number of public transportation systems in the United States. CNG burns much cleaner than other petroleum-based fuels. For example, CNG vehicles emit approximately 80 percent fewer ozone-forming emissions than gasoline and diesel engines. Thus, the initial impetus for CNG vehicles was abating localized air pollution problems. In terms of climate change, CNG may reduce a vehicle's greenhouse gas emissions by up to 25 percent. However, these benefits may be offset depending upon how the natural gas is produced and transported.

CNG vehicles have both practical and environmental limitations. Vehicles using CNG must be specifically designed to accommodate this alternative fuel. In addition, fuel stations must have CNG-specific facilities. These practical constraints have generally limited the use of CNG to public buses (which fuel up at specified transportation facilities) and other vehicles owned by municipalities. Although some states, like California, have expanded their CNG infrastructure, the number of CNG fueling stations is still relatively small. There are approximately 1,300 CNG stations in the United States, compared to more than 190,000 gasoline stations in the country. Even in California, which has around 200 CNG stations, this number pales in comparison to that state's 14,000 gas stations.

CNG is pumped out of natural gas wells, oil wells, and coalbed-methane wells. The gas extraction process can result in localized contamination of groundwater and other environmental problems. In addition, importation and transportation of CNG has become contentious. The Energy Information Administration (EIA) estimates that most increases in natural gas in the United States will occur through imports of liquefied natural gas (LNG). However, attempts to build new on-shore LNG facilities face serious opposition, due to various environmental and public safety concerns. Thus, it is unclear whether natural gas production could satisfy a significant increase in the demand for CNG vehicles.

---

3.   *Hydrogen Fuel Cells*

Many policymakers believe that hydrogen could serve as the fuel of the future. The United States Department of Energy has devoted significant resources and time to developing viable hydrogen technology. People within the program believe that hydrogen technology could serve as a viable alternative energy resource for vehicles and other end-uses. However, other researchers assert that investment in hydrogen technology diverts funding and resources away from other viable alternative fuel sources that could come on-line much sooner, at lower costs, and with longer term benefits. The following excerpts briefly explain the technologies involved in hydrogen production and discuss the benefits and downsides of hydrogen.

U.S. DEPARTMENT OF ENERGY, HYDROGEN PRODUCTION BASICS

Hydrogen is an energy carrier, not an energy source — it stores and delivers energy in a usable form. It is abundant in nature but must be produced from compounds that contain it.

Diverse and Domestic Supply Resources

Hydrogen can be produced using diverse, domestic resources, including fossil fuels, such as coal (with carbon sequestration) and natural gas; nuclear; and biomass and other renewable energy technologies, such as wind, solar, geothermal, and hydroelectric power. Great potential for diversity of supply is an important reason why hydrogen is such a promising energy carrier.

Central, Semi-Central, and Distributed Production

Hydrogen can be produced at large central plants as far as several hundred miles from the point of end-use; semi-centrally, 25 to 100 miles from the point of end-use; or in small distributed units located at or very near the point of end-use, such as at refueling stations or stationary power sites.

How Is Hydrogen Produced?

Researchers are developing a wide range of technologies to produce hydrogen economically from a variety of resources in environmentally friendly ways.

Natural Gas Reforming

Hydrogen can be produced from methane in natural gas using high-temperature steam. This process, called steam methane reforming, accounts for about 95 percent of the hydrogen used today in the U.S. Another method, called partial oxidation, produces hydrogen by burning methane in air. Both steam reforming and partial oxidation produce a "synthesis gas," which is reacted with water to produce more hydrogen.

Renewable Electrolysis

Electrolysis uses an electric current to split water into hydrogen and oxygen. The electricity required can be generated using renewable energy technologies, such as wind, solar, geothermal, and hydroelectric power.

Gasification

Gasification is a process in which coal or biomass is converted into gaseous components by applying heat under pressure and in the presence of steam. A subsequent series of chemical reactions produces a synthesis gas, which is reacted with steam to produce more hydrogen that then can be separated and purified. Producing hydrogen directly from coal by gasification and reforming processes is much more efficient than burning coal to make electricity that is then used to make hydrogen. Researchers are developing carbon capture and sequestration technologies to separate and store the carbon dioxide (CO_2) produced in this process. With carbon capture and sequestration, hydrogen can be produced directly from coal with near-zero greenhouse gas emissions.

Like coal, biomass can be gasified using high temperatures and steam to produce hydrogen. Because biomass resources consume CO_2 in the atmosphere as part of their natural growth process, producing hydrogen through biomass gasification releases near-zero net greenhouse gases.

Renewable Liquid Reforming

Biomass can also be processed to make renewable liquid fuels, such as ethanol or bio-oil, that are relatively convenient to transport and can be reacted with high-temperature steam to produce hydrogen at or near the point of end-use.

Nuclear High-Temperature Electrolysis

Heat from a nuclear reactor can be used to improve the efficiency of water electrolysis to produce hydrogen. By increasing the temperature of the water, less electricity is required to split it into hydrogen and oxygen, which reduces the total energy required.

High-Temperature Thermochemical Water Splitting

Another water-splitting method uses high temperatures generated by solar concentrators (special lenses that focus and intensify sunlight) or nuclear reactors to drive a series of chemical reactions that split water. All of the chemicals used are recycled within the process.

Photobiological and Photoelectrochemical

When certain microbes, such as green algae and cyanobacteria, consume water in the presence of sunlight, they produce hydrogen as a byproduct of their natural metabolic processes. Similarly, photoelectrochemical systems produce hydrogen from water using special semiconductors and energy from sunlight.

What Are the Challenges?

Cost Reduction

The greatest technical challenge to hydrogen production is cost reduction. For transportation, hydrogen must be cost-competitive with conventional fuels and

technologies on a per-mile basis. This means that the cost of hydrogen —
regardless of the production technology and including the cost of delivery — must
be in the range of $2.00 to $3.00 per gallon gasoline equivalent (untaxed).

Current and Future Production Technologies

Hydrogen production technologies are in various stages of development. Some
technologies, such as steam methane reforming, are becoming well-developed and
can be used in the near term. Others, such as high-temperature thermochemical
water-splitting, photobiological, and photoelectrochemical, are in the very early
stages of laboratory development and considered potential pathways for the long-
term.

JOSEPH ROMM, CALIFORNIA'S HYDROGEN HIGHWAY RECONSIDERED
36 GOLDEN GATE U. L. REV. 393, 401–05 (2006)*

A pollution-free hydrogen car rests on two pillars: a pollution-free source for the
hydrogen itself and a fuel cell for efficiently converting it into useful energy
without generating pollution. Fuel cells are small, modular electrochemical devices,
similar to batteries, but which can be continuously fueled. For most purposes, a
fuel cell can be thought of as a "black box" that takes in hydrogen and oxygen and
puts out only water plus electricity and heat. The electricity runs an electric motor,
and from that perspective, the rest of the vehicle is much like an electric car.
Internal combustion engine cars can also be modified to run on hydrogen, although
they are considerably less efficient than fuel cell vehicles.

The transition to a transportation system based on a hydrogen economy will be
much slower and more difficult than widely realized. In particular, it is unlikely
that hydrogen vehicles will achieve significant (>5%) market penetration by 2030.

A variety of major technology breakthroughs and government incentives will be
required for hydrogen vehicles to achieve significant commercial success by the
middle of this century. "Continued research and development ("R&D") in
hydrogen and transportation fuel cell technologies remains important because of
their potential to provide a zero-carbon transportation fuel in the second half of the
century. But neither government policy nor business investment should be based
on the assumption that these technologies will have a significant impact in the
near- or medium-term." Bill Reinert, United States manager of Toyota's advanced
technologies group, said in January 2005, absent multiple technology
breakthroughs, there will not be high-volume sales of fuel cell vehicles until 2030 or
later. When Reinert was asked when fuel cell cars would replace gasoline-powered
cars, he replied "If I told you 'never,' would you be upset?"

Hydrogen cars face enormous challenges in overcoming each of the major
historical barriers to AFV success. The central challenge for any alternative fuel
vehicle seeking government support beyond R&D is that the deployment of the
AFVs and the infrastructure to support them must cost effectively address some
energy or environmental problems facing the nation. Yet two hydrogen advocates,
Dan Sperling and Joan Ogden of University of California at Davis, concede,
"[h]ydrogen is neither the easiest nor the cheapest way to gain large near- and
medium-term air pollution, greenhouse gas, or oil reduction benefits." A 2004

---

analysis by Pacific Northwest National Laboratory concluded that even "in the advanced technology case with a carbon constraint . . . hydrogen doesn't penetrate the transportation sector in a major way until after 2035." (emphasis in original) "A push to constrain carbon dioxide emissions actually delays the introduction of hydrogen cars because sources of zero-carbon hydrogen, such as renewable power, can achieve emissions reductions far more cost-effectively by simply replacing planned or existing coal plants . . . [O]ur efforts to reduce GHG emissions in the vehicle sector must not come at the expense of our efforts to reduce GHG emissions in the electric utility sector." The 2004 report noted:

> In fact, Well-to-Wheels Analysis of Future Automotive Fuels and Powertrains in the European Context, a January 2004 study by the European Commission Center for Joint Research, the European Council for Automotive R&D, and an association of European oil companies, concluded that using hydrogen as a transport fuel might well increase Europe's greenhouse gas emissions rather than reduce them. That is because many pathways for making hydrogen, such as grid electrolysis, can be quite carbon-intensive and because hydrogen fuel cells are so expensive that hydrogen internal combustion engine vehicles may be deployed instead (which is already happening in California). Using fuel cell vehicles and hydrogen from zero-carbon sources such as renewable power or nuclear energy has a cost of avoided carbon dioxide of more than $700 a metric ton, which is more than a factor of ten higher than most other strategies being considered today.

> A number of major studies and articles have recently come out on the technological challenges facing hydrogen . . . transportation fuel cells currently cost about $5,000/kw, some 100 times greater than the cost of internal combustion engines.

A 2004 article for the Society of Automotive Engineers noted, "[e]ven with the most optimistic assumptions, the fuel cell powered vehicle offers only a marginal efficiency improvement over the advanced [diesel]-hybrid and with no anticipation yet of future developments of I[nternal] C[ombustion] engines ("ICE"). At $100/kW, the fuel cell does not offer a short term advantage even in a European market."

Furthermore, another study concluded that "a new material must be discovered" to solve the storage problem. Another analysis found, "[f]uel-cell cars, in contrast [to hybrids], are expected on about the same schedule as NASA's manned trip to Mars and have about the same level of likelihood."

There is a tendency in analyses of a future hydrogen economy to assume the end state — mass production of low-cost fuel cells, pipeline delivery, and so on. Yet while transportation fuel cells would undoubtedly be far cheaper if they could be produced at quantities of one million units per year, the unanswered question is who will provide the billions of dollars in subsidies during the many years when vehicle sales would be far lower and vehicle costs far higher. Additionally, while hydrogen pipelines are the desired end result, and "the costs of a mature hydrogen pipeline system would be spread over many users," as the National Academy panel noted, "the transition is difficult to imagine in detail." The AFV problem is very much a systems problem where the transition issues are as much of the crux as the technological ones. It therefore follows that AFV analysis should be conservative in nature, stating clearly what is technologically and commercially possible today, and, when discussing the future, be equally clear that projections are speculative and will require both technology breakthroughs and major government intervention in the marketplace. Analysis should treat the likely competition fairly: If major advances in cost reduction and performance are projected for hydrogen technologies, similar advances should be projected for hybrids, batteries, biofuels, and the like. After all, AFVs must compete against the most efficient gasoline-powered vehicles for market share.

QUESTIONS AND DISCUSSION

1. In the 2003 State of the Union speech, President George W. Bush announced a White House initiative to promote hydrogen research and development. Combined with the FreedomCAR (Cooperative Automotive Research) Initiative, which supports research for hydrogen fuel cell technology, the President proposed dedicating $ 1.7 billion to the hydrogen initiative.

2. The debate regarding hydrogen is, in many ways, a debate regarding prioritization. Advocates of hydrogen believe that it should be pursued, along with other alternative energy technologies, because of its great promise. Opponents believe that the focus on hydrogen distracts from other alternative technologies that may be cheaper and easier to deploy in the near-term. Alternative energy advocates have engaged in similar debates regarding biofuels, natural gas, hybrids, and other technologies. In what ways do these debates promote better energy policy? In what ways do they stifle it?

B.   The Legal Framework Regulating Alternative Fuels

The United States and many state governments have enacted laws promoting research and development of alternative fuels. These laws generally take two forms: 1) financial incentives in the form of subsidies, grants, and tax credits, which promote production and use of alternative fuels; and 2) renewable fuel standards (RFS) specifying a minimum percentage of vehicle fuel which must come from renewable sources.

1.   *Tax Incentives and Subsidies*

The primary way that the United States has promoted alternative fuel development is through tax incentives and subsidies. The vast majority of these subsidies are aimed at corn production and corn-based ethanol. Only recently has the United States begun subsidizing other forms of alternative fuel. This section starts with a summary of subsidies and incentives that Congress has given the biofuels industry from the late 1970s to 2005. It then describes how the Energy Independence and Security Act (EISA) of 2007 and the 2008 Farm Bill further incentivize biofuels.

a.   *Subsidies and Incentives: 1978–2005*

The United States began financially supporting the biofuel industry with tax incentives in 1978 when the Energy Tax Act was signed by President Carter. That act exempted alcohol fuels such as methanol and ethanol from the $.04/gallon excise tax on petroleum fuel. Since then, a producer's credit and substantial changes in the structure of biofuel excise tax incentives have been introduced.

The ethanol tax incentive policy began with an excise tax reduction for alcohol fuels such as ethanol and methanol. This has historically been the primary tax incentive for ethanol and other alcohol-blended fuels. . . . Minor changes reflecting inflation and shifts in federal tax policy were implemented between 1978 and 2003, and a larger overhaul of the excise tax incentive system occurred in 2004, when Congress passed the American Jobs Creation Act of 2004 (Jobs Act).

Christine C. Benson, *Putting Your Money Where Your Mouth Is: The Varied Success of Biofuel Incentive Policies in the United States and the European Union*, 16 Transnat'l L. & Contemp. Probs. 633, 650–54 (2007).

JOHN A. SAUTTER et al., CONSTRUCTION OF A FOOL'S PARADISE: ETHANOL SUBSIDIES IN AMERICA
Sustainable Dev. L. & Pol'y 26, 26–27 (Spring 2007)[*]

RECENT HISTORY OF ETHANOL SUBSIDIES

On October 22, 2004 President Bush signed into law the American Jobs Creation Act. By providing a new excise tax credit system for all ethanol blends and biodiesel, this law significantly changed the way taxes are collected on gasohol (a fuel mixture containing ethanol and gasoline) and other ethanol blends. Effective January 1, 2005, the Act eliminated the reduced rate of excise tax for gasohol blends containing ten percent, 7.7 percent, and 5.7 percent ethanol. It replaces this tax with the Volumetric Ethanol Excise Tax Credit ("VEETC"), a $0.51 per gallon excise tax credit for each gallon of ethanol blended with gasoline. Additionally, the Act extends the ethanol tax incentive to 2010 and deposits all taxes paid on gasohol and other ethanol blends into the Highway Trust Fund (while the credits are paid for out of the General Fund). Furthermore, farmer cooperatives may now also claim the small ethanol producer tax credit that was created in the Omnibus Budget Reconciliation Act of 1990 under this Act.

CORN SUBSIDIES

Perhaps most importantly, U.S. taxpayers subsidize the production of corn itself, to the tune of $51.3 billion from 1995 to 2005, according to the Environmental Working Group. Without these subsidies, no corn-based ethanol would be produced in the United States. The Department of Agriculture reported that corn ethanol's variable production costs are $0.96 per gallon, with capital costs averaging $1.57 per gallon. In total, ethanol costs an average of $2.53 per gallon to produce in the United States. A recent study published by the International Institute for Sustainable Development ("IISD") estimates that U.S. subsidies for ethanol totaled approximately between $5.1 billion and $6.8 billion in 2006. These subsidies translate into $1.05 to $1.38 per gallon of ethanol, or 42 to 55 percent of its wholesale market price.

IMPORT TARIFFS

Today, importers of Brazilian ethanol pay a $0.54 per gallon import duty plus a 2.5 percent tax. This import tariff shields U.S. producers from their Brazilian counterparts, whose sugar-derived ethanol is far cheaper to produce and has higher energy content than corn-based fuel. Even with the tariffs in place, about half of the 160 million gallons of ethanol that the United States imported in 2004 came from Brazil, and Brazil is spending $9 billion on new facilities to export even more. This could pay off, as soaring U.S. wholesale prices are making Brazilian imports more competitive with domestic supplies. The import tariff will expire at the end of September 2007, but many federal legislators hope to see it extended because it has generated revenues of $53 million and $22 million in 2004 and 2005, respectively. Additionally, a most-favored nation *ad valorem* tariff is applied on imports of un-denatured ethyl alcohol (80 percent volume alcohol or higher) and denatured alcohol. Revenues under the *ad valorem* tariff have been less than $8 million per year in recent years.

VOLUMETRIC ETHANOL EXCISE TAX CREDIT

Enacted in 2004 under the Jumpstart Our Business Strength Act, the VEETC provision is the single largest subsidy to ethanol. VEETC provides a tax credit based on ethanol blended into motor fuel. According to IISD's Global Subsidies Initiative, "[i]t is awarded without limit, and regardless of the price of gasoline, to every gallon of ethanol blended in the marketplace, domestic or imported." The cost to the U.S. Treasury from the subsidy is rising rapidly. In 2005, the Joint Committee on Taxation ("JTC") estimated that tax losses from the VEETC would average $1.4 billion per year for the period 2005 to 2009. A year later, the JTC's estimate increased more than 50 percent, averaging $2.2 billion per year for the period 2006 to 2010. The U.S. Treasury estimated an even higher cost value, an average of $2.6 billion per year from 2005 to 2011.

Actual demand growth, however, is outstripping government estimates. Sales for 2006 resulted in VEETCs worth $2.5 billion, higher than either the Treasury's or the JTC's projections for the year. Demand is expected to continue to grow greatly during the coming years. Projecting the cost of the VEETC provision is difficult in such a quickly expanding market, but the Renewable Fuel Standard mandates "provide one stable benchmark against which to estimate VEETC subsidies." Presupposing that the nation will meet these targets, revenue losses will increase to $3.8 billion a year by 2012, when 7.5 billion gallons of ethanol must be expended. This equates to a $3.05 billion per year average for revenue losses for the period 2007 to 2012, which is well above both Treasury and JTC estimates. In its 2006 *Annual Energy Outlook*, the Energy Information Agency ("EIA") projects corn ethanol consumption of $9.64 billion in 2012, far surpassing the $7.5 billion mandate, which the EIA expects to be passed in 2010.

*   *   *

THE ENERGY POLICY ACT OF 2005

The Chart entitled "Government Support for Bio-Fuels" lists the amount of money earmarked for each subsidy program, as it was outlined in the Energy Policy Act of 2005 ("EPACT 2005"). [T]his monetary support does not displace the amount of money already being given to farmers for corn production. Rather, this money adds to the total amount that all individuals involved in ethanol production will consume from U.S. taxpayers. For example, Section 1342, Title XIII, Subtitle D of EPACT 2005:

Provides a tax credit equal to 30 percent of the cost of alternative refueling property, up to $30,000 for business property. Qualifying alternative fuels are natural gas, propane, hydrogen, E85 [(85 percent ethanol)], or biodiesel blends of [twenty percent] [(]B20[)] or more. Buyers of residential refueling equipment can receive a tax credit for $1,000. For non-tax-paying entities, the credit can be passed back to the equipment seller. The credit is effective on purchases put into service after December 31, 2005. It expires December 31, 2009.

Additionally, EPACT 2005 modifies the definition of "small ethanol producer" so that facilities that produce up to 60 million gallons per year (previously 30 million gallons per year) are eligible for the tax credit.

GOVERNMENT SUPPORT FOR BIOFUELS
ENERGY POLICY ACT OF 2005

Program	Fiscal Years	Total Amount
Sugarcane Ethanol Program	2005–2007	$36 million
Cellulosic Biomass Ethanol and Municipal Solid Waste Loan Guarantee Program	N/A	$1 billion
Cellulosic biomass ethanol conversion assistance	2006–2008	$750 million
Ethanol production at Mississippi State and Oklahoma State universities	2005–2007	$12 million
Renewable Fuels Research and Development Grants	2006–2010	$125 million
Advanced Biofuels Technology Program	2005–2009	$550 million
Sugarcane Ethanol Loan Guarantee Program	N/A	Up to $50 million per project

b.   *The Energy Independence and Security Act of 2007 and the 2008 Farm Bill*

In December 2007 and May 2008, Congress passed additional legislation that increases subsidies and tax credits for biofuels production. EISA authorizes the Department of Energy to issue up to $500 million in grants to promote production of advanced biofuels. It defines "advanced biofuels" as:

renewable fuel, other than ethanol derived from corn starch, that has lifecycle greenhouse gas emissions that achieve at least a 50 percent reduction over baseline lifecycle greenhouse gas emissions. The types of fuels eligible for consideration as "advanced biofuel" may include: ethanol derived from cellulose or lignin, sugar or starch (other than corn starch), or waste material, including crop residue, other vegetative waste material, animal waste, and food waste and yard waste; biomass-based diesel; biogas produced through the conversion of organic matter from renewable biomass; butanol or other alcohols produced through the conversion of organic matter from renewable biomass; and other fuel derived from cellulosic biomass.

The Energy Independence and Security Act of 2007, Pub. L. No. 110-140, Title II, § 201(1)(B)(i)–(ii), 121 Stat 1492, 1519 (2007). While "advanced biofuels" are defined as those fuels that achieve at least a 50 percent reduction in lifecycle greenhouse gas emissions, the grants may be issued only for projects that achieve at least an 80 percent reduction in lifecycle greenhouse gas emissions compared to 2005 emission levels. *Id.* at § 207(b)(2). In addition, EISA authorizes $25 million for research and development of biofuel production facilities in states with low rates of biofuel production; authorizes grants and loans for advanced biofuel refineries; and establishes a tax credit of $1.01 per gallon of cellulosic ethanol produced domestically.

On June 18, 2008, Congress overrode President Bush's veto of the Food, Conservation, and Energy Act of 2008 (the Farm Bill), and in so doing, implemented more than one billion dollars of subsidies aimed at increasing biofuels production. Pub. L. No. 110-234, 122 Stat. 923 (May 22, 2008). These subsidies and incentives include: extension of the tariffs on sugar cane-based imported ethanol; a program authorizing the Secretary of Agriculture to purchase U.S. sugar for sale to domestic biodiesel producers; loan guarantees for refiners of advanced biofuels and at least $300 million to promote expanded production of advanced biofuels; tax credits for cellulosic biofuel producers; assistance for biomass crop producers; and at least $118 million for biomass research and development and at least $35 million to support biomass refineries. The Farm Bill also continues the existing tax credit for corn-based ethanol blended with gasoline, although it lowers it from $.51 per gallon to $.45 per gallon. As discussed below, this reduction will likely be offset by increased mandates for ethanol production.

QUESTIONS AND DISCUSSION

1. *Subsidies under the Farm Bill and EISA.* The Farm Bill and EISA approach subsidies for biofuels in very different ways. The Farm Bill allocates most subsidies according to fuel type, while the EISA conditions many of the subsidies on a demonstration that advanced biofuels will reduce lifecycle greenhouse gases by 80 percent below baseline levels. Are the two laws consistent? Is one approach better than the other?

2. *Political Opposition to Subsidies.* Many commentators from both conservative and liberal quarters oppose Congress' subsidies for biofuels, and particularly corn-based ethanol. The Cato Institute, a libertarian think tank that promotes free markets, and the Environmental Working Group (EWG), a liberal environmental advocacy organization, have shown that most farm-based subsidies (including those that fund ethanol) go to large agribusiness enterprises, such as Archer Daniels Midland. These organizations also believe that subsidies distort the marketplace and prevent other more effective alternative fuel technologies from taking hold. However, while the Cato Institute is categorically opposed to subsidies (because they undermine the free market), environmental advocates believe that subsidies, when appropriately designed, can promote smart energy solutions. *See* Michael Pollan, *The Farm Bill: What Went Wrong*, GRISTMILL BLOG (Jun. 4, 2008), *available at* http://gristmill.grist.org/story/2008/6/4/43736/55179.

---

2.   *Renewable Fuel Standards*

In addition to establishing subsidies and tax credits, Congress has recently taken a more directive approach to biofuels promotion by establishing a renewable fuel standard (RFS). An RFS defines which fuels qualify as renewable and establishes a minimum amount of renewable fuel that fuel refiners, blenders, and importers must incorporate into their gasoline production. An RFS will spur investment in renewable fuel production. However, by listing specific fuels as "renewable," an RFS may promote production of fuels that cause overall environmental harm.

To address the potential unintended consequences of an RFS, some policymakers have begun to distinguish between an RFS and a Low Carbon Fuel Standard (LCFS) in establishing renewable fuel requirements. An LCFS requires that a minimum percentage of fuels qualify as "low carbon." Agencies administering an LCFS will typically rank fuels after conducting a "full fuel cycle" (also called a "well to wheel" or "field to wheel") analysis, which measures the aggregate greenhouse gas emissions and reductions from all phases of alternative fuel production, including emissions from growing or extracting the fuel, processing the fuel, and transporting the fuel. If indirect land use changes are considered in the measurement, an LCFS could avoid some of the unintended consequences of a traditional RFS by prohibiting use of fuels that may actually increase greenhouse gas emissions.

Congress first established a national RFS when it adopted the Energy Policy Act of 2005 (2005 EPAct). It revised the RFS in 2007 with its passage of EISA, which now requires fuels in the United States to contain a much higher percentage of renewable fuels. This revised standard has spurred both an increase in biofuels production and calls for revisions to the RFS standard.

a.   *The 2005 EPAct RFS*

The 2005 EPAct amends the Clean Air Act to establish a nationwide RFS directing the EPA to develop regulations establishing a minimum percentage of renewable fuel that gasoline sold in the United States must contain. 42 U.S.C. § 7545. Pursuant to the 2005 RFS, at least 4.0 billion gallons of renewable fuel were to be blended into gasoline by 2006. By 2012, the amount of renewable fuel was to climb to 7.5 billion gallons.

Table 15-1: Applicable Volumes of Renewable Fuel Under the RFS Program

Calendar Year	Billion gallons 2006
2006	4.0
2007	4.7
2008	5.4
2009	6.1
2010	6.8
2011	7.4
2012	7.5

Source: Environmental Protection Agency, Regulation of Fuels and Fuel Additives: Renewable Fuel Standard Program, 72 Fed. Reg. 23,900, 23,903 tbl.1.B-1 (May 1, 2007).

Renewable fuels are defined under the 2005 EPAct to include ethanol made from starch seeds (i.e., corn), sugar, or cellulosic materials; biodiesel; fuels produced from biomass material; and fuels produced from biogas sources, including landfills, sewage treatment plants, and feedlots. *See* 42 U.S.C. § 7545(o)(1)(C).

In May 2007, EPA issued its final rules implementing the 2005 EPAct. Environmental Protection Agency, Regulation of Fuels and Fuel Additives: Renewable Fuel Standard Program, 72 Fed. Reg. 23,900 (May 1, 2007). The rule requires refiners, importers, and blenders of gasoline for consumption in the United States to blend a specified volume of renewable fuel into gasoline. Each year, EPA will convert the statutorily mandated RFS into a percentage-based requirement based on annual fuel production; each regulated entity will then be responsible for including a specific volume of renewable fuel — based on the annual percentage requirement — in the gasoline it refines, blends, or imports.

The 2005 EPAct directed EPA to establish a trading program for renewable fuel credits. To implement the trading component, EPA established a system using Renewable Identification Numbers (RIN). Renewable fuel importers or producers assign to each batch of renewable fuel a RIN, which indicates the volume and type of fuel produced. As batches of renewable fuels are sold, the RIN is transferred along with the fuel. RINs may also be traded. At the end of each year, the regulated entities must have acquired an appropriate number of RINs, demonstrating that they in fact complied with their RFS obligations. *See* 72 Fed. Reg. at 23,929–935.

In the 2005 EPAct, Congress directed that each gallon of cellulosic biomass ethanol and waste-derived ethanol must be treated as 2.5 gallons of renewable fuel. In an effort to address this mandate and the varying energy contents from each type of qualifying renewable fuel, EPA also assigned "equivalence values" to the different fuel types. Similar in concept to a global warming potential value, the equivalence value compares the energy content of each renewable fuel to that of corn ethanol. EPA randomly assigned corn ethanol an equivalence value of 1.0; cellulosic biomass ethanol and waste-derived ethanol have equivalence values of 2.5; and other renewable fuels equivalence values range from 1.3 to 1.7. 72 Fed. Reg. at 23,919–22. The equivalence values are then used to calculate each regulated entity's compliance with the RFS. For example, if a gasoline refiner has an obligation to use 1,000 gallons of renewable fuels, it may meet that obligation by using 1,000 gallons of corn ethanol or 400 gallons of cellulosic biomass ethanol.

b.   *The 2007 EISA RFS*

In December 2007, Congress increased the RFS requirements under EISA. In the near-term, overall levels of renewable fuels must increase. By 2016, however, increased renewable fuels must come from "advanced biofuels," as the Congressional Research Service explains:

> This subtitle extends and increases the renewable fuel standard (RFS) set by P.L. 109-58 (§ 1501). The RFS requires minimum annual levels of renewable fuel in U.S. transportation fuel. The previous standard was 5.4 billion gallons for 2008, rising to 7.5 billion by 2012. The new standard starts at 9.0 billion gallons in 2008 and rises to 36 billion gallons in 2022. Starting in 2016, all of the increase in the RFS target must be met with advanced biofuels, defined as cellulosic ethanol and other biofuels derived from feedstock other than corn starch — with explicit carve-outs for cellulosic biofuels and biomass-based diesel. The EPA Administrator is given authority to temporarily waive part of the biofuels mandate, if it were determined that a significant renewable feedstock disruption or other market circumstance might occur. Renewable fuels produced from new

biorefineries will be required to reduce by at least 20% the life cycle greenhouse gas (GHG) emissions relative to life cycle emissions from gasoline and diesel. Fuels produced from biorefineries that displace more than 80% of the fossil-derived processing fuels used to operate a biofuel production facility will qualify for cash awards.

FRED SISSINE, ENERGY INDEPENDENCE AND SECURITY ACT OF 2007: A SUMMARY OF MAJOR PROVISIONS 5 (CRS, Dec. 21, 2007).

QUESTIONS AND DISCUSSION

1. *The EISA Waiver Provision.* Both the 2005 EPA Act and EISA allow the EPA to waive in whole or part the RFS if a state petitions for a waiver and can demonstrate that meeting the RFS will "severely harm the economy or environment of a State, a region, or the United States." 42 U.S.C. § 7545(o)(7)(A)(i). The waiver applies to the RFS requirement as a whole; thus, a state's petition, if granted, could reduce or eliminate the national RFS. If EPA receives a waiver request, it must, after notice and comment, issue a decision granting or denying the waiver. *Id.* § 7545(o)(7)(B)

In its final rule implementing the 2005 EP Act, EPA declined to establish regulations governing the waiver provision. 72 Fed. Reg. at 23,928. EPA explained:

> If EPA, after public notice and opportunity for comment, approves a state's petition for a waiver of the RFS program, the Act stipulates that the national quantity of renewable fuel required may be reduced in whole or in part. This reduction could reduce the percentage standard applicable to all obligated parties. However, there is no provision in the Act that would permit EPA to reduce or eliminate any obligations under the RFS program specifically for parties located within the state that petitioned for the waiver. Thus all refiners, importers, and blenders located in the state would still be obligated parties if they produce gasoline. In addition, an approval of a state's petition for a waiver may not have any impact on renewable fuel use in that state since it would not be a prohibition on the sale or consumption of renewable fuels in that state. In fact, the Act prohibits the regulations from restricting the geographic areas in which renewable fuels may be used. Renewable fuel use in the state in question would thus continue to be driven by natural market forces and, perhaps if the economics of ethanol blending were less favorable than today, the nationally-applicable renewable fuel standard.

> Given that state petitions for a waiver of the RFS program appear unlikely to affect renewable fuel use in that state, we have not finalized regulations providing more specificity regarding the criteria for a waiver or the ramifications of Agency approval of such a waiver in terms of the level or applicability of the standard. However, states can still submit petitions to the Agency for a waiver of the RFS requirements under the provision in the Energy Act and such petitions will be addressed by EPA on a case-by-case basis.

Id.

On April 25, 2008, Texas Governor Rick Perry asked EPA for a 50 percent waiver from the RFS requirement. Letter from Rick Perry, Governor of Texas, to The Honorable Stephen L. Johnson, Administrator, U.S. Environmental Protection Agency (Apr. 25, 2008). The petition stated that rising corn prices were causing particular harm to Texan cattle ranchers, most of whom raise corn-fed beef. *Id.* at 1–2. In response to the petition, several U.S. senators and environmental organizations asked EPA to grant the waiver due to the economic and environmental harms that ethanol production is causing. Other U.S. senators and representatives from the biofuel industry opposed the waiver on the grounds that reduced ethanol production would cause gasoline prices to rise.

On August 7, 2008, EPA denied the Texas petition. EPA, Notice of Decision Regarding the State of Texas Request for a Waiver of a Portion of the Renewable Fuel Standard, 72 Fed. Reg. 47,168 (Aug. 13, 2008). Consistent with its earlier statements in the Federal Register, EPA determined that relaxing the RFS requirement would have only a minimal effect on ethanol production in 2008. EPA determined that its inquiry under the waiver provision must focus solely on the effect that the RFS requirement, alone, has on corn, ethanol and gasoline prices during the year for which the waiver is sought. *Id.* at 10–13. Since corn prices are influenced by a number of factors, and since EPA concluded that the RFS would have no impact on ethanol demand, EPA concluded that Texas did not meet its burden to show that implementation of the RFS would severely harm the economy. *Id.* at 41–42. Based on EPA's framing of the question — i.e., whether the RFS by itself has a severe effect on the economy — do you think the agency would ever grant a waiver request? If not, what purpose does the waiver provision serve?

2. ***Renewable Fuel Standards and Low Carbon Fuel Standards.*** Both California and Massachusetts have endorsed using an LCFS instead of an RFS. For example, on January 18, 2007, Governor Arnold Schwarzenegger signed an Executive Order directing the California Air Resources Board (CARB) to adopt a low carbon fuel standard for the state. Exec. Order No. S-01-07 (Cal. 2007), *available at* http://gov.ca.gov/index.php?/executive-order/5172/. The order establishes a statewide goal of reducing the carbon intensity of California's transportation fuels by at least 10 percent by 2020. *Id.*, para. 1. It applies to "all refiners, blenders, producers or importers" of transportation fuels, and requires that the carbon emissions be measured "on a full fuels cycle basis." *Id.*, para. 4. Similarly, in April 2008, the Massachusetts governor and leaders of the state legislature announced their support for a state-wide, and ultimately, regional, LCFS.

While many policy advisors believe that an LCFS represents a significant improvement over a typical RFS, the development of an LCFS is extraordinarily complicated. The California process, which has been underway since early 2007, has generated numerous policy documents, public comments, and scientific reports, none of which reaches clear conclusions about how an LCFS should be implemented. By addressing the complexities of defining what "low carbon" means, the California process could provide a model for other states that may wish to adopt their own LCFS. On the other hand, the California process may deter states from engaging in the complicated rulemaking an LCFS necessitates.

3. ***Viability of the Biofuels Industry under EISA.*** A recent study published by Iowa State University concludes that crop-based biofuels such as corn ethanol and soy biodiesel will not be economically viable without subsidies. It also concludes that switchgrass ethanol could become viable only if switchgrass subsidies exceed current subsidies for corn. Mindy L. Baker, Crop-Based Biofuel Production under Acreage Constraints and Uncertainty, Working Paper 08-WP 460 (Feb. 2008). Recent reports also suggest that domestic consumer demand has not kept up with biofuel production. For example, a biodiesel plant in Washington state ships most of its biodiesel to Europe, because domestic needs are lower than anticipated. Les Blumenthal, *Fledgling U.S. Biodiesel Industry Facing Tough Times,* McCLATCHY (May 25, 2008), *available at* http://www.mcclatchydc.com/260/story/38261.html.

How should the legal system address these concerns? Does EISA's waiver provision already do this?

4. Cellulosic Biofuels. Many alternative fuel advocates believe that cellulosic biofuels derived from wood products and agricultural debris (such as corn stalks and other non-usable parts of food crops) could provide a better source of biofuels, because they would not compete with food crops for agricultural land. What incentives does EISA provide for cellulosic biofuels, and are they adequate to abate the problems that biofuel development has generated?

C.   Are Hybrids and Plug-In Vehicles the Solution?

Some advocates believe that hybrid and plug-in hybrid electric vehicles (PHEVs) could provide the best solution for reducing greenhouse gas emissions from automobiles. A hybrid vehicle contains both an internal combustion engine and an electric motor. The electric motor assists the engine with acceleration, passing, and hill climbing, and thus enables the use of smaller, more efficient engines. Energy generated during braking and coasting is stored in a battery that the electric motor can then use. With PHEVs, the battery can be powered from stationary electricity sources. Existing batteries can store enough energy for a vehicle to travel approximately 35 miles before the battery requires recharging. For most urban drivers, whose commutes average less than 30 miles, PHEVs could allow drivers to power their cars solely through the electric grid. The hybrid technology would enable drivers to have assurance that their cars will continue to run on fuel once the power in the battery drains.

1.   *An Overview of PHEV Technology*

DAVID SANDALOW, ENDING OIL DEPENDENCE: PROTECTING NATIONAL SECURITY, THE ENVIRONMENT AND THE ECONOMY
in OPPORTUNITY 08: INDEPENDENT IDEAS FOR AMERICA'S NEXT PRESIDENT, 8–9 (Michael E. O'Hanlon, ed., 2008)[*]

Plug-In Hybrid Electric Vehicles (PHEVs)

To end oil dependence, nothing would do more good more quickly than making cars that could connect to the electric grid. The United States has a vast infrastructure for generating electric power. However that infrastructure is essentially useless in reducing oil dependence, because cars can't connect to it. If we built cars that ran on electricity, the potential for displacing oil would be enormous. Fortunately, we can. Several small companies are already doing this. General Motors recently announced plans to produce light duty plug-ins.

Historically, electric cars have been limited by several factors, including short range (think golf carts), battery weight, and cost. The range problem is solved by hybrid engines that automatically switch over to a standard gas tank when the battery is drained. The weight problem is being addressed with new kinds of batteries made with nickel or lithium. Upfront costs are still high — roughly $8,000 to $11,000 more than a car with an internal combustion engine — but well within range of commercial acceptability. Purchase costs will drop once plug-in hybrids are in mass production.

The potential benefits are enormous. Electric utilities typically have substantial unused capacity each night, when electricity demand is low. Further, utilities maintain reserve generating capacity — known as "peaking power" — for days of unusually high demand. This unused and excess capacity could provide an important cushion for vehicles in case of a sudden disruption in oil supplies or steep rise in oil prices. Furthermore, driving on electricity is cheap. Even a first-generation plug-in hybrid car would travel about 3–4 miles per KwH — equivalent to about 75 cents per gallon, based on the national average for electricity prices.

Plug-in hybrids would dramatically cut local air pollutants and would be better from a global warming standpoint than cars with standard internal combustion engines. True, the energy to recharge a plug-ins vehicle needs to come from somewhere, and in much of the United States that somewhere would be a coal-fired power plant. However, the thermal efficiency of even an old-fashioned pulverized coal plant is roughly 33 to 34 percent, while that of an internal combustion engine is roughly 20 percent. In terms of heat-trapping gases emitted, plugging a car with an electric motor directly into a coal plant is better than running it on oil with an internal combustion engine.

How much oil could plug-in hybrids displace how quickly? A lot, although the data available on U.S. driving habits allow only a rough estimate. According to the Department of Transportation, 40 percent of Americans travel 20 miles or less per day and 60 percent travel 30 miles or less. One possible scenario, in which plug-ins hybrids replace one-third of the oil in U.S. light duty vehicles by 2025 is illustrated in Table 15-2. It assumes strong policies supporting early deployment of plug-ins and steady penetration in the vehicle fleet thereafter.

Table 15-2: Potential Fleetwide Oil Savings from Plug-in Hybrids (PHEVs) — An Illustrative Scenario

Year	PHEVs as a % of new car sales	% of PHEV's in U.S. auto fleet	Fleetwide Oil Savings
2008	0	0	0
2010	5%	0.3%	0.2%
2015	35%	7.2%	4.8%
2020	75%	27.6%	18.4%
2025	75%	52.0%	34.7%

Notes: New car sales are roughly 6.5 percent of the total U.S. fleet each year. Calculations assume that each PHEV uses 2/3 the gasoline of a conventional vehicle.

Finally, tens of millions of PHEVs could be added to the fleet without the need for new electric generating capacity. Even with PHEVs making up half the U.S. fleet, electricity demand would increase by only 4–7%. PHEVs could be recharged at night, when electricity demand is low. In fact, PHEVs could even sell electricity back to the grid to ease peak loads.

QUESTIONS AND DISCUSSION

1.   Several PHEVs are already in use around the country thanks to entrepreneurial creativity, but PHEVs have yet to be produced commercially. However, both Toyota and Chevrolet have announced that they are in the process of developing PHEVs for commercial release in 2010. The DOE is also funding projects that convert existing hybrids to PHEVs. *See* Fact Sheet, *Plug-in Hybrid Electric Vehicle (PHEV) Demonstration Project* (Oct. 24, 2007). The city of Seattle estimates that converted vehicles will generate half the carbon dioxide emissions of a Prius. *Id.* It also estimates that converted hybrids will achieve a mileage of at least 100 mpg. *Id.*

2.   One critique of electric vehicles is that most electrical motors cannot maintain highway speeds over long distances. PHEVs address this problem through the use of the internal combustion engine. Electricity powers the car at speeds of 35 mph or lower; however, once the car exceeds 35 mph or the electric motor loses power, the internal combustion engine would kick in.

3.   ***PHEVs and Greenhouse Gas Emissions from Electricity Sources.*** One concern about PHEVs is that they would simply shift the source of greenhouse gas emissions from vehicles to stationary sources, without actually resulting in a net reduction. However, a study published by the Electric Power Research Institute (EPRI) and Natural Resources Defense Council (NRDC) concluded that overall greenhouse gas emissions would decline as a result of PHEV use, even if inefficient coal-fired power plants continue to provide the bulk of electricity. EPRI & NRDC, EXECUTIVE SUMMARY, ENVIRONMENTAL ASSESSMENT OF PLUG-IN HYBRID ELECTRIC VEHICLES, VOLUME I: NATIONWIDE GREENHOUSE GAS EMISSIONS (July 19, 2007). According to the study, if greenhouse gas intensity from the power sector remains high, PHEV use would still result in overall emissions reductions. *Id.* at 2. Depending upon the PHEV market and the emissions reductions from the power sector, annual reductions would range from 163 to 612 million metric tons, and cumulative reductions between 3.4 to 10.3 billion metric tons by 2050. *Id.*

---

2.   *Policies Affecting PHEV Use*

Advocates of PHEVs have identified several policy and legal tools that would promote and increase their use. These include federal and state purchasing programs, subsidies for the U.S. automakers to promote production of PHEVs, and tax credits for purchasers of PHEVs. *See* Sandalow, *Ending Oil Dependence*, at 11–12, 15. Each of these policies has been employed in other contexts. As you read the following, consider which would most successfully promote PHEV use.

a.   *Federal and State Purchasing Programs*

Purchasing programs are a common tool used by governments to reduce their own vehicle emissions and to create a market for newer low-emission vehicles. For example, the Energy Policy Act of 1992 (1992 EPAct) requires federal agencies to ensure that alternative fuel vehicles account for at least 75 percent of all annual light-duty vehicle acquisitions for metropolitan areas. State governments with more than 50 vehicles in their fleets (20 of which must be used in metropolitan areas) must also ensure that 75 percent of newly acquired vehicles in metropolitan areas qualify as alternative fuel vehicles. Qualifying vehicles include vehicles powered by electricity, ethanol, and 100 percent biodiesel.

While the 1992 EPAct provides a model for how a purchasing program could be structured, it does not currently define commercial gasoline/electric hybrid vehicles as qualifying alternative fuel vehicles (AFVs). Thus, state governments that wish to increase their purchases of gasoline/electric hybrids or PHEVs must continue to ensure that 75 percent of their vehicles are qualifying AFVs. They could do this either by purchasing hybrids that use a qualifying alternative fuel (such as 100 percent biodiesel) instead of gasoline, by purchasing hybrids that run primarily on the electric motor (commercially available vehicles, such as the Prius, do not meet this requirement), or by seeking a waiver from the 75 percent AFV requirement. If a state seeks a waiver, it must establish an alternative compliance plan for reducing its petroleum use.

As a result of the 1992 EPAct, more than 70,000 federal vehicles and tens of thousands of state-owned vehicles now use alternative fuels. The vast majority of the vehicles — 94 percent of the nearly 13,000 state vehicles bought in 2006 — use E85, an ethanol/gasoline blend containing 85 percent ethanol. The 1992 EPAct appears to have effectively achieved Congress' goal of spurring production of alternative fuels. The next challenge for EPAct will likely be spurring a transition to other sources of vehicle energy.

QUESTIONS AND DISCUSSION

Purchasing Requirements and the Clean Air Act. Many states and municipalities have enacted their own purchasing laws requiring government vehicles to be low-emission or zero-emission vehicles (LEVs and ZEVs, respectively). As the popularity of these laws has increased, automakers have challenged the authority of these governments to establish these laws. Specifically, the automakers have alleged that the Clean Air Act preempts all non-federal purchasing requirements aimed at reducing vehicle emissions. Under the Clean Air Act, states are preempted from adopting their own vehicle emissions standards. 42 U.S.C. § 7543(a). However, Section 209(b) of the CAA allows California to adopt separate state emissions standards if EPA grants California a waiver from the preemption provision. If California receives a waiver, other states may adopt the California standards. *See* Chapter 13 for a more detailed overview of this provision.

In Engine Mfrs. Ass'n v. South Coast Air Quality Mgmt. Dist., 541 U.S. 246 (2004), the Supreme Court concluded that California's laws establishing purchasing requirements qualified as "standards" subject to the Clean Air Act's preemption provision. The South Coast Air Quality Management District had enacted Fleet Rules requiring public and private operators of six types of vehicle fleets — street sweepers; government-owned passenger cars, light-duty trucks, and medium-duty vehicles; public transit vehicles and urban buses; solid waste collection vehicles; airport passenger transportation vehicles, including shuttles and taxicabs picking up airline passengers; and government-owned heavy-duty on-road vehicles — to purchase LEVs, ZEVs, or alternative fuel vehicles whenever they add or replace vehicles in their fleets. *Id.* at 249–51. The Supreme Court rejected California's argument that its purchasing requirements were not "standards" under the CAA, because they did not establish emissions limitations. *Id.* at 254–55. However, the Court did not decide whether all the standards were in fact preempted, and it specifically declined to resolve the question of whether the CAA preempts internal state purchase decisions. *Id.* at 258–59.

On remand, the Ninth Circuit concluded that California's Fleet Rules established for state and local government entities were not preempted under the

CAA. *Engine Mfrs. Ass'n v. South Coast Air Quality Mgmt. Dist.*, 498 F.3d 1031 (9th Cir. 2007). The court based its holding on the "market participant doctrine" — which states that actions taken by a state (or its subdivisions) as a market participant, as opposed to actions a state takes as a regulator, are generally protected from federal preemption. *Id.* at 1041–1049. Specifically, the court found that the state's "proprietary action" in establishing rules governing the purchase and procurement of government vehicles did not amount to regulatory action preempted by the CAA. *Id.* at 1045–46. The Ninth Circuit remanded to the district court the question of whether the rules setting purchasing requirements for private entities were preempted. *Id.* at 1049–50.

b.   *Tax Credits for Purchasers of PHEVs*

A common way of promoting energy-efficient technology is through the establishment of tax credits for specific purchases. Tax credits are meant to offset the increased purchase price of most advanced technology vehicles. One of the most well known tax credits applied to hybrid vehicles. The available credit that a consumer could take depended upon the type of vehicle purchased, the year in which the vehicle was purchased, and the total number of vehicles that consumers had purchased.

IRS, HYBRID CARS AND ALTERNATIVE FUEL VEHICLES
(Dec. 11, 2007)

The Energy Policy Act of 2005 replaced the clean-fuel burning deduction with a tax credit. A tax credit is subtracted directly from the total amount of federal tax owed, thus reducing or even eliminating the taxpayer's tax obligation. The tax credit for hybrid vehicles applies to vehicles purchased or placed in service on or after January 1, 2006.

The credit is only available to the original purchaser of a new, qualifying vehicle. If a qualifying vehicle is leased to a consumer, the leasing company may claim the credit. * * *

Quarterly Sales

Consumers seeking the credit may want to buy early since the full credit is only available for a limited time. Taxpayers may claim the full amount of the allowable credit up to the end of the first calendar quarter after the quarter in which the manufacturer records its sale of the 60,000th hybrid or advance lean burn technology. For the second and third calendar quarters after the quarter in which the 60,000th vehicle is sold, taxpayers may claim 50 percent of the credit. For the fourth and fifth calendar quarters, taxpayers may claim 25 percent of the credit. No credit is allowed after the fifth quarter.

For example, F Company is a manufacturer of hybrid motor vehicles, but not advanced lean burn technology motor vehicles. F Company sells its 60,000th hybrid car on March 31, 2006.

- Ms. Smith buys an F Company hybrid car on June 30, 2006, and claims the full credit.

- Ms. Maple buys an F Company hybrid car on Dec. 31, 2006, and claims 50 percent of the credit.

- Mr. Grey buys an F Company hybrid car on June 30, 2007, and claims 25 percent of the credit.

- Mr. Green buys an F Company hybrid car on July 1, 2007, and is unable to claim the credit, because the credit has phased out for F Company vehicles.

QUESTIONS AND DISCUSSION

1. How effective are tax credits in promoting hybrids? It depends, in large part, on the perceived quality of the hybrids at issue. For example, the tax credit spurred a buying frenzy of the Toyota Prius, the most popular of all the hybrid cars available in the United States. Toyoto sold its 60,000th vehicle by the summer of 2006, and, under the phaseout schedule, the tax credit phased out in September 2007. Even after the tax credit phased out for Toyota, its overall sales of the Prius continued to increase. Sales of other hybrid vehicles sold at varying rates. Sales of hybrids produced by Toyota, Lexus, and Honda all reached the 60,000 mark and the credit has since been phased out. In contrast, as of March 2008, none of the U.S. automakers had sold 60,000 vehicles, and the full tax credit remained available for cars purchased from these companies. *See* Peter Valdes-Dapena, *Hybrid Tax Credit Shock*, CNNMONEY.COM (Mar. 7, 2008), *available at* http://money.cnn.com/ 2008/03/07/pf/taxes/2007_hybrid_tax_credit_confusion/ index.htm?section=money_pf. Does this suggest that tax credits merely provide refunds to people who would have bought a Prius anyway?

2. In the 2005 EPAct, the value of the tax credit depended in part upon the fuel efficiency and reduced emissions from each vehicle. However, the most efficient vehicle, the Honda Insight (60 mpg) qualified for only a $1,450 credit, compared to credits of $3,150 for the Prius (46 mpg) and $2600 for the Toyota Highlander (29 mpg). Does this make sense? Perhaps. Because the Insight could seat only two passengers whereas the other cars all seat four, it may be that the Insight will not yield the same overall pollution reductions.

3. How would you design a tax policy to promote PHEV use? Would you offer tax credits to a limited number of purchasers? If so, what would the value of the credits be? Who would be eligible for the credits? Would the credits phase out?

4. Tax credits for new vehicles tend to provide subsidies for wealthier car drivers. Most drivers who can afford to purchase hybrid cars are already driving relatively fuel-efficient vehicles. Yet recent studies show that replacing very inefficient cars for even moderately efficient cars would actually result in much greater fuel savings. *See* Duke University, *Gallons Per Mile Would Help Car Shoppers Make Better Decisions*, SCIENCEDAILY (June 20, 2008) *available at* http://www.sciencedaily.com/releases/2008/06/080619142118.htm. For example, replacing a car with a fuel efficiency of 34 mpg for a car with 40 mpg would, over 10,000 miles, save 98 gallons of gas, whereas replacing an 18-mpg car for a 24-mpg car would save 140 gallons of gas. *Id.* How would you design a tax policy to promote greater efficiency?

5. Is it possible that doing nothing is the best way to promote hybrids and other fuel efficiency technology? From February 2008 to June 2008, gasoline prices rose approximately $1.12 per gallon nationwide. In May 2008, gas prices were up nearly 40 percent from the prior year, and the Energy Information Administration expected gas prices to continue to climb. In response, driving and car ownership patterns changed at least temporarily. For example, in the first quarter of 2008, sales of SUVs and pickups fell by 28 percent and 14 percent, respectively. Moreover, overall driving in the United States fell by approximately 7.5 percent.

See Christopher Palmeri, *Gas May Finally Cost Too Much*, BusinessWeek, Apr. 23, 2008, *available at* http://www.businessweek.com/magazine/content/08_18/b4082000518114.htm. Use of mass transit increased by 10 to 15 percent in cities throughout the southern and western U.S. *See* Clifford Kraus, *Gas Prices Send Surge of Riders to Mass Transit*, NY Times, May 10, 2008, at A1. On the other hand, gas prices plummeted by the end of the year. Would you expect a return to past driving and car-buying habits? CNN reported increased sales of SUVs and large trucks in December 2008, when gasoline prices averaged about $1.67 a gallon. Peter Valdes-Dapena, *With Gas Falling, Trucks Come Back*, CNNMoney.com (Dec. 29, 2008). Do these changes suggest that the best policy is maintaining high gas prices while letting consumers make their own decisions in response? What other policy choices would you promote?

Chapter 16

CLIMATE CHANGE AND TORTS

SYNOPSIS

I. INTRODUCTION

It may at first be difficult to think of climate change in terms of the common law. What could the crusty old doctrine of torts have to do with a global environmental problem such as climate change? When we discuss mitigation measures through negotiation or legislation, we naturally tend to think of climate change as an environmental management or policy issue. But if a client walked in the door whose life-time investment in sugar maple trees was being threatened by changing climate, we as lawyers will be forced to think of climate change more as an infringement on someone's rights.

Climate-related tort cases are no longer theoretical. Several torts cases relating to climate change have already been brought in the United States, and for several reasons we can expect more torts cases in the future. First, climate change impacts will only become more pervasive, and more people are going to be injured by climate change. If one reviews the climate impacts identified in Chapter 1, the potential categories of people who will be damaged are astounding: farmers affected by drought, coastal property owners who lose their homes to rising seas, and flood victims who lose their homes to hurricanes, to name just a few. Not only will the impacts of climate change increase, but the ability to attribute those damages to climate change — to show causation — will also increase. As science clarifies the impacts of climate change and demonstrates the causal link between specific harms and climate change, then the call for liability will grow louder.

At the same time, the objectives of tort law would seem to be met by attention to climate change. The purposes of tort liability is (1) to compensate those injured by the acts of others, (2) to deter socially dangerous or undesirable activities, and (3) to set norms for socially desirable behavior. Take the case of the Inupiat village of Kivalina (the focus of the complaint is excerpted *infra*) as an example. One identifiable set of people (Inupiat villagers) are being forced to relocate their homes and businesses because their village is literally slipping into the ocean as warming temperatures melt the ice that formerly protected their coast from winter storms. The villagers have contributed negligibly, if anything at all, to global warming, but yet they are clearly injured. Assuming that they can prove their case — including causation — why should they not be compensated? Why should those responsible not pay? Isn't this exactly what torts is meant to do?

But is the old common law of torts appropriate for such a quintessentially modern problem? At first glance the obstacles to bringing a tort claim seem insurmountable. Where almost everyone in the world is affected and thus is a potential plaintiff, why should anyone be compensated? Moreover, everyone (or at least everyone who drives a car or uses electricity from fossil fuels) is partly responsible for climate change. The challenge for the tort system is how to assign liability when everyone is simultaneously a plaintiff and a defendant.

To some extent the debate over torts and climate change is a battle over how to characterize climate change. Is it just another form of nuisance where the behavior of one set of actors infringes on the rights of other property owners, or is it a broad, complex issue better left to legislatures and agencies to manage? Legally, this question raises the application of the political question doctrine, which is discussed in Chapter 12. This chapter looks at the issues that arise if climate change is viewed as a nuisance.

The early climate-related tort cases suggest that those who would characterize climate change as a political question are prevailing. But torts cases are unlikely to go away soon. As mentioned above, the increasing ability to link anthropogenic climate change with real impacts on real people will likely result in more cases. Whereas early tort cases were brought by state Attorneys General and were clearly motivated at least in part by broad climate policy concerns, future cases are likely to be brought by private plaintiffs who are primarily seeking compensation for damage they have incurred. With this background, consider the analysis in the following article:

DAVID A. GROSSMAN, WARMING UP TO A NOT-SO-RADICAL IDEA: TORT-BASED CLIMATE CHANGE LITIGATION
28 Colum. J. Envtl. L. 1, 3–7 (2003)[*]

In evaluating whether a tort suit is an appropriate vehicle for addressing climate change, one must consider the central concerns and goals of tort law. Many of climate change's costs are harms to property produced at least partially as a result of human actions. Harm caused by human activity is a central concern of tort law. Further, because of the uneven nature and distribution of the effects of climate change, some localized groups (e.g., those living in coastal areas or at high

---

latitudes) are bearing, and will continue to bear, the brunt of global warming's harms and costs. This existing allocation raises the question of whether we should leave these costs on the victims of climate change or should transfer them to those who arguably have contributed to creating the harm. Allocation of the costs of harms is another central tort concern.

In deciding who should bear the costs of global warming, it is helpful to look at two of tort law's basic goals: (1) reducing the costs of accidents, and (2) providing corrective justice. Consider first which allocation of costs will best reduce the costs of climate change "accidents." Leaving the costs of climate change on its victims ensures that climate-changing activities occur at higher than optimal levels, resulting in higher "accident" costs. This is true because victims and potential victims, for three principal reasons, cannot effectively organize to bargain with or to force producers of fossil fuels to reduce fossil fuel use. First, climate change has global effects, so in that regard, the transaction costs involved in organizing the vast numbers of potential victims are immense. Second, . . . the effects of climate change are unevenly distributed. While the transaction costs of organizing victims are lower in more localized areas, it is likely that any such local organization would have insufficient economic clout to bargain meaningfully with fossil fuel companies. Third, the lack of public knowledge about climate change, caused by the evolving and complicated science of climate change and compounded by some fossil fuel companies' efforts to encourage public uncertainty and inaction on global warming, further hinders fruitful organization and collective action. Lack of organization and imperfect knowledge therefore enable producers to continue producing their climate-changing products at higher than optimal levels and to keep externalizing the costs of climate change. Fossil fuel prices thus do not accurately reflect climate change's costs when these costs are left on victims.

Unlike the consumer public, fossil fuel companies and some of the principal industries reliant on them have large amounts of resources with which they can acquire the expertise needed to assess information about climate change and its costs. With such information and resources, these entities are in a better position to carry out a cost-benefit analysis comparing increased consumption with the increased "accident costs" produced by that consumption, and then to act on that analysis by internalizing the costs of climate change into the price of fossil fuels. Internalizing the costs of climate change would raise the price of fossil fuels, making alternative energy sources and more efficient consumption of fossil fuels more desirable, thereby reducing the level of greenhouse gas emissions. Placing climate change "accident" costs on the fossil fuel companies would thus minimize these costs.

Consider now which allocation of the costs of climate change would best serve the principles of corrective justice. Some harms of climate change are more easily attributable and identifiable, such as damage caused by rising sea levels, while others may be harder to distinguish from background processes, such as damage due to more frequent and more severe storms. Either way, people are harmed by climate change who otherwise would not have been. Conceptions of equity and corrective justice suggest that those who have been harmed by others' negligent or morally dubious actions should be compensated in some way. Notions of corrective justice thus also seem to support shifting the costs of climate change onto these fossil fuel companies. * * *

B. Obstacles to Climate Change Litigation

While a tort framework might be appropriate, tort-based climate change litigation could face significant institutional, practical, and legal obstacles. The main institutional question is one of judicial authority and competence to deal with this kind of problem. Courts generally focus on the particular plaintiffs and defendants in front of them; however, in this instance, the major issues of causation, multiple defendants and plaintiffs, the variety of remedies, and present and future harms all suggest a more comprehensive approach to climate change that might be better taken by a legislature or agency. Although a tort approach to climate change might be possible, therefore, some would dispute its desirability, seeing global warming as something requiring a political rather than a legal solution. As noted, however, there is a widely perceived lack of meaningful political action in the United States to address global warming, potentially leaving litigation as the best tool for addressing climate change in the foreseeable future.

Two practical obstacles to climate change litigation could also arise. First, as in tobacco litigation, the extensive financial resources of potential defendants would likely facilitate their ability to challenge everything, including issues like general causation that appear to be well-established. This reality could make a climate change suit quite expensive and time-consuming, potentially deterring many plaintiffs and attorneys from pursuing such litigation. Second, at least in public nuisance actions, the typical plaintiffs are state executives (e.g., attorneys general). The reliance of some key coastal states' economies on fossil fuel extraction, however, could make it more difficult to find states willing to take on these industries in a climate change lawsuit.

Finally, one must acknowledge the potential legal hurdles facing tort-based climate change litigation. For instance, the state of current scientific knowledge might not be sufficient to adequately prove specific causation in a court of law for some of climate change's current and future harms. Identifying potential defendants, tracing harms to their actions, and apportioning damages among them could also be a complicated and onerous task.

QUESTIONS AND DISCUSSION

1. Do you agree with Grossman's assessment of the applicability of torts law to a field like climate change? What other arguments would you make that climate change should not be the subject of a common law action? Are any of these arguments relevant for the person injured by climate change?

2. Before reading further, consider some of the basic causes of action in torts: intentional torts, negligence, nuisance, public nuisance, and products liability. Which of these could apply to the climate change situation? How would you shape a case under each of these theories? What are the basic elements of each cause of action, and what evidence would you need to meet them? Is that evidence available with respect to climate change?

3. Tobacco tort cases suffered continual losses in the courts for more than a decade before finally prevailing through a combination of innovative lawyering, clearer scientific and health information, and the disclosure of important information from defendants. Many observers believe climate change tort cases may follow a similar trajectory. What major differences do you see in the case of climate change as compared to tobacco litigation? Or to litigation over hand guns? Or to other environmental torts such as litigation over asbestos or lead. *See, e.g.*, Timothy D. Lytton, *Using Tort Litigation to Enhance Regulatory Policymaking: Evaluating Climate Change Litigation in Light of Lessons from Gun Industry and Clergy Sexual Abuse Lawsuits*, 86 TEX. L. REV. (forthcoming); Hamilton v. Accu-Tek, 62 F. Supp.2d 802, 818 (E.E. N.Y.1999) (finding a duty to victims for negligent marketing and distribution of guns) *with* Hamilton v. Beretta U.S.A. Corp., 96 N.Y.2d 222, 727

N.Y.S. 2d 7 (2001) (finding no duty was owed).

4.   In international environmental law, the twin goals of torts — compensation and deterrence or accident prevention — are reflected in the "polluter pays principle" and "state responsibility" (compensation) and the "pollution prevention principle" (deterrence). In this way, tort liability can be seen as simply one approach for implementing these broader principles. *See* Chapter 2, discussing the polluter pays principle and cost internalization, and Chapter 8, discussing the pollution prevention principle. Do these broad international environmental law principles have any applicability to the tort context?

5.   Although this chapter only addresses the common law of torts, climate change may also eventually raise interesting issues of the law of contracts. If a client believes his agreement to purchase carbon emissions credits was not adequately fulfilled, climate change raises significant issues of what exactly was being contracted for and what the remedies should be for a failure to provide the credits. The carbon trading market is burgeoning around the world and soon will be in the United States as well. The first climate-related contract suit has already been filed; the International Finance Corporation (an arm of the World Bank) sued a company for failing to provide the carbon reduction credits promised under the IFC's financing agreement. For further discussion of the way in which contract law is being used to further the carbon market, review the discussion of the Chicago Climate Exchange in Chapter 18.

II.   A REVIEW OF CURRENT CLIMATE-RELATED TORT CASES

As of January 2009, six climate-related tort cases had been filed in the United States. Two had been brought by state Attorneys General, and the remainder had been brought by private claimants. The Attorneys General claims were limited primarily to public nuisance actions and not surprisingly raised questions of broad public policy. The claims brought by private parties raised a wider range of causes of actions and sought compensation for specifically identified damage. Each of these is discussed below.

A.   The State Attorneys General Cases

In the first case, *Connecticut v. American Electric Power (AEP)*, 406 F. Supp. 2d 265 (S.D.N.Y. 2005), eight states and the city of New York sued five fossil-fuel burning utilities (allegedly the five largest emitters of greenhouse gases in the United States) and the Tennessee Valley Authority. The Complaint alleges that the utilities together emit 650 million tons of CO_2, which is approximately 10 percent of all anthropogenic CO_2 emissions in the United States. The action was filed under federal common law and state law, charging that the utilities have knowingly contributed to a public nuisance:

> Defendants, by their emissions of carbon dioxide from the combustion of fossil fuels at electric generating facilities, are knowingly, intentionally or negligently creating, maintaining, or contributing to a public nuisance — global warming — injurious to the plaintiffs and their citizens and residents. . . .

Defendants' emissions of carbon dioxide, by contributing to global warming, constitute a substantial and unreasonable interference with public rights in the plaintiffs' jurisdictions, including, *inter alia*, the right to public comfort and safety, the right to protection of vital natural resources and public property, and the right to use, enjoy, and preserve the aesthetic and ecological values of the natural world. . . .

Defendants know or should know that their emissions of carbon dioxide contribute to global warming and to the resulting injuries and threatened injuries to the plaintiffs, their citizens and residents, and the environment.

Complaint, *Connecticut v. American Electric Power*, ¶ 98, at 45–49 (S.D.N.Y.) (July 24, 2004). The plaintiffs did not seek monetary damages but rather sought injunctive relief against the defendants. The plaintiffs essentially wanted the court to impose some cap on the emissions of the mostly mid-western utilities that were defendants.

The District Court ultimately dismissed the case as presenting a non-justiciable political question. The case has been appealed and is pending in the Second Circuit. Connecticut v. American Electric, 2005 WL 2347900 (2006). This decision and the political question doctrine are discussed further in Chapter 12.

After dismissal of the *Connecticut* complaint, the State of California filed a separate action against automobile companies in September 2006. *See* Complaint, *California v. General Motors*, (N.D. Cal. Sept. 20, 2006). Brought by the California Attorney General, the suit charges that General Motors and five other major motor vehicle manufacturers committed a common law public nuisance under both federal and state law. According to the Complaint, defendants' vehicle emissions in the United States contribute to 9 percent of the world's global carbon dioxide emissions, 20 percent of U.S. emissions and 30 percent of emissions from California. California's allegations against the automobile industry were similar to those of the New England states against the utilities, claiming that "Defendants have for many years produced millions of automobiles that collectively emit massive quantities of carbon dioxide in the United States and have thus contributed to an elevated level of carbon dioxide in the atmosphere. . . ." They also claimed that the defendants "know or should know, that their emissions of carbon dioxide and other greenhouse gases contribute to global warming and to the resulting injuries and threatened injuries to California. . . ." *California v. General Motors Complaint*, at 2, 3, 12, 13. In an effort to avoid the appearance that this was "legislating" climate change as the courts had ruled in *Connecticut*, California primarily sought monetary damages for expenses and damages it is currently incurring due to global warming. The strategy did not work (yet) and the case was also dismissed on political question grounds and an appeal is pending.

B.   Private Causes of Action

The state attorney general cases clearly reflect a variety of motivations, including some which were overtly political. The same can not be said, however, of the torts cases brought by private parties claiming injuries from climate change. The first such case, *Comer v. Murphy Oil*, was filed in February 2006 in the aftermath of Hurricane Katrina. *See* Third Amended Complaint, *Comer v. Murphy Oil Co.*, 2006 WL 1474089 (S.D. Miss. Apr. 19, 2006). Ned Comer and thirteen other individuals displaced by Hurricane Katrina brought an action against nine oil companies, thirty-one coal companies, and four chemical companies. They proposed a range of causes of action, including nuisance, negligence, unjust enrichment, civil conspiracy, fraudulent misrepresentation and concealment, and trespass. This case, too, was also ultimately dismissed on political question grounds and is pending appeal.

The most recent tort-based climate case to be filed and in some ways the most interesting was filed by inhabitants of an Inupiat village in Alaska whose village (Kivalina) is slowly subsiding into the sea. No decisions have yet been made in this case, but the complaint excerpted below illustrates the evolving nature of climate-related tort cases.

KIVALINA v. EXXONMOBIL, COMPLAINT FOR DAMAGES
Civ. Action No. 08-cv-01138 (N.D. Cal., filed Feb. 26, 2008)

I. Nature of Action

1. This is a suit to recover damages from global warming caused by defendants' actions. Plaintiffs, the Native Village of Kivalina and the City of Kivalina (collectively "Kivalina"), are the governing bodies of an Inupiat village of approximately 400 people. Kivalina is located on the tip of a six-mile barrier reef located between the Chukchi Sea and the Kivalina and Wulik Rivers on the Northwest coast of Alaska, some seventy miles north of the Arctic Circle. . . . Kivalina residents are Inupiat Eskimo whose ancestors occupied the area since time immemorial. Global warming is destroying Kivalina and the village thus must be relocated soon or be abandoned and cease to exist. Relocating will cost hundreds of millions of dollars and is an urgent matter. . . .

2. Kivalina brings this action against defendants under federal common law and, in the alternative, state law, to seek damages for defendants' contributions to global warming, a nuisance that is causing severe harms to Kivalina. Kivalina further asserts claims for civil conspiracy and concert of action for certain defendants' participation in conspiratorial and other actions intended to further the defendants' abilities to contribute to global warming.

3. Defendants contribute to global warming through their emissions of large quantities of greenhouse gases. Defendants in this action include many of the largest emitters of greenhouse gases in the United States. All Defendants directly emit large quantities of greenhouse gases and have done so for many years. Defendants are responsible for a substantial portion of the greenhouse gases in the atmosphere that have caused global warming and Kivalina's special injuries.

4. Greenhouse gases trap atmospheric heat and thus cause global warming. Global warming is destroying Kivalina through the melting of Arctic sea ice that formerly protected the village from winter storms. . . . The result of the increased storm damage is a massive erosion problem. Houses and buildings are in imminent danger of falling into the sea as the village is battered by storms and its ground crumbles from underneath it. . . . Critical infrastructure is imminently threatened with permanent destruction. If the entire village is not relocated soon, the village will be destroyed.

5. Each of the defendants knew or should have known of the impacts of their emissions on global warming and on particularly vulnerable communities such as coastal Alaskan villages. Despite this knowledge, defendants continued their substantial contributions to global warming. Additionally, some of the defendants,

as described below, conspired to create a false scientific debate about global warming in order to deceive the public. Further, each defendant has failed promptly and adequately to mitigate the impact of these emissions, placing immediate profit above the need to protect against the harms from global warming.

6. Kivalina seeks monetary damages for defendants' past and ongoing contributions to global warming, a public nuisance, and damages caused by certain defendants' acts in furthering a conspiracy to suppress the awareness of the link between these emissions and global warming. * * *

[The Complaint summarizes the emissions from the various defendants and the general impacts from climate change in the Arctic region.]

C. Special Injuries to Kivalina's Property Interests

185. While the global warming to which defendants contribute injures the public at large, Kivalina suffers special injuries, different in degree and kind from injuries to the general public. Rising temperatures caused by global warming have affected the thickness, extent, and duration of sea ice that forms along Kivalina's coast. Loss of sea ice, particularly land-fast sea ice, leaves Kivalina's coast more vulnerable to waves, storm surges and erosion. Storms now routinely batter Kivalina and are destroying its property to the point that Kivalina must relocate or face extermination. The U.S. Army Corps of Engineers . . . concluded that global warming has affected the extent of sea ice adjacent to Kivalina: "[W]ith global climate change the period of open water is increasing and the Chukchi Sea is less likely to be frozen when damaging winter storms occur. Winter storms occurring in October and November of 2004 and 2005 have resulted in significant erosion that is now threatening both the school and the Alaska Village Electric Cooperative (AVEC) tank farm." The United States Government Accountability Office, in a December, 2003 report . . . reached similar conclusions regarding Kivalina: "[I]t is believed that the right combination of storm events could flood the entire village at any time." The GAO concluded that "[r]emaining on the island . . . is no longer a viable option for the community."

186. The Army Corps of Engineers' report projects that it would cost between $95 and $125 million to relocate Kivalina. The GAO report projects that it would cost between $100 and $400 million to relocate Kivalina.

187. In testimony dated June 29, 2004, by the General Accounting Office, before the U.S. Senate Committee on Appropriation, the GAO asserted that flooding and erosion in the coastal area of Alaska were due in part to rising temperatures that cause the protective shore ice to form later in the year, leaving villages, including Kivalina, vulnerable to storms.

188. Plaintiffs are discrete and identifiable entities that have contributed little or nothing to global warming. The impact of global warming on Plaintiffs is more certain and severe than on others in the general population.

D. Civil Conspiracy Allegations

1. The Use of Front Groups

189. There has been a long campaign by power, coal, and oil companies to mislead the public about the science of global warming. Defendants ExxonMobil, AEP, BP America Inc., Chevron Corporation, ConocoPhillips Company, Duke Energy, Peabody, and Southern ("Conspiracy Defendants") participated in this

campaign. Initially, the campaign attempted to show that global warming was not occurring. Later, and continuing to the present, it attempts to demonstrate that global warming is good for the planet and its inhabitants or that even if there may be ill effects, there is not enough scientific certainty to warrant action. The purpose of this campaign has been to enable the electric power, coal, oil and other industries to continue their conduct contributing to the public nuisance of global warming by convincing the public at-large and the victims of global warming that the process is not man-made when in fact it is.

190. The campaign has been conducted directly by the Conspiracy Defendants, and through trade associations such as the Edison Electric Institute ("EEI") (which represents the electric power industry), the National Mining Association (which represents the coal industry), and the Western Fuels Association (which represents coal-burning utilities that own Wyoming coal fields). The industries have also formed and used front groups, fake citizens' organizations, and bogus scientific bodies, such as the Global Climate Coalition ("GCC"), the Greening Earth Society, the George C. Marshall Institute, and the Cooler Heads Coalition. The most active company in such efforts is and has been defendant ExxonMobil.

*   *   *

FIRST CLAIM FOR RELIEF

Federal Common Law: Public Nuisance

250. Defendants' emissions of carbon dioxide and other greenhouse gases, by contributing to global warming, constitute a substantial and unreasonable interference with public rights, including, *inter alia*, the rights to use and enjoy public and private property in Kivalina. In the exercise of those rights, Plaintiffs suffer special injuries from defendants' contributions to global warming, in that global warming will diminish or destroy Plaintiffs' public and private real property (and the real property of their residents and Tribal members). The Plaintiffs' entire village must be relocated because of the nuisance at a cost of millions of dollars.

251. Defendants' greenhouse gas emissions are a direct and proximate contributing cause of global warming and of the injuries and threatened injuries Plaintiffs suffer.

252. Defendants know or should know that their emissions of greenhouse gases contribute to global warming, to the general public injuries such heating will cause, and to Plaintiffs' special injuries. Intentionally or negligently, defendants have created, contributed to, and/or maintained the public nuisance.

253. Defendants, both individually and collectively, are substantial contributors to global warming and to the injuries and threatened injuries Plaintiffs suffer.

254. Carbon dioxide and other greenhouse gas emissions resulting in global warming are inherently interstate in nature. Emissions of carbon dioxide and other greenhouse gases from defendants' operations, no matter where such operations are located, rapidly mix in the atmosphere and cause an increase in the atmospheric concentration of carbon dioxide and other greenhouse gases worldwide. The heating that results from the increased carbon dioxide and other greenhouse gas concentrations to which defendants contribute cause specific, identifiable impacts in Kivalina.

255. Defendants knew that their individual greenhouse gas emissions were, in combination with emissions and conduct of others, contributing to global warming

and causing injuries to entities such as the Plaintiffs.

256. Plaintiffs' injuries and threatened injuries from each defendant's contributions to global warming are indivisible injuries.

257. Plaintiffs have been and will continue to be injured by global warming.

258. Plaintiffs do not have the economic ability to avoid or prevent the harm.

259. Plaintiffs, due in part to their way of life, contribute very little to global warming.

260. Defendants, individually and collectively, are substantial contributors to global warming and to the injuries and threatened injuries Kivalina claims in this action. The injuries have caused Kivalina to suffer millions of dollars in damages in lost property value and revenue, including millions of dollars of funds necessary to relocate the entire community due to the harms caused by global warming.

261. Defendants are jointly and severally liable to Kivalina under the federal common law of public nuisance. * * *

[The Second Claim for Relief repeated most of the allegations above but alleged a public nuisance under state common law.]

THIRD CLAIM FOR RELIEF

Civil Conspiracy

* * *

269. Defendants ExxonMobil, AEP, BP America Inc., Chevron Corporation, ConocoPhillips Company, Duke Energy, Peabody, and Southern ("Conspiracy Defendants") have engaged in agreements to participate in an unlawful act or a lawful act in an unlawful means. The Conspiracy Defendants have engaged in agreements to participate in the intentional creation, contribution to and/or maintenance of a public nuisance, global warming. The Conspiracy Defendants participated and/or continue to participate in an agreement with each other to mislead the public with respect to the science of global warming and to delay public awareness of the issue — so that they could continue contributing to, maintaining and/or creating the nuisance without demands from the public that they change their behavior as a condition of further buying their products. At all times the Conspiracy Defendants were concerned that the public would become concerned by global warming and that the growing concern would force a change in the Conspiracy Defendants' behavior which would be costly. Delaying these costs was the major objective of the conspiracies described herein.

270. The Conspiracy Defendants have committed overt acts in furtherance of their agreements. The Conspiracy Defendants have participated in an agreement with each other to mislead the public with respect to the science of global warming, either individually or through their various industry fronts or trade associations, and have included overt acts that furthered their intentional creation, contribution to and/or maintenance of a public nuisance, global warming.

271. The Conspiracy Defendants intentionally created, contributed to and/or maintained a public nuisance, global warming, pursuant to their agreements.

272. The Conspiracy Defendants' conspiracies had as their objective creating unwarranted doubts about the existence of global warming and/or its specific causes among the general public and was intended to and did further the Conspiracy

Defendants' interests in maintaining a public nuisance.

273. The Conspiracy Defendants' overt acts contributed to and caused Plaintiffs' injuries. The Conspiracy Defendants' campaign to deceive the public about the science of global warming has caused Plaintiffs' injuries and/or is a substantial contributing factor.

274. The Conspiracy Defendants' overt acts were a direct and proximate cause of Plaintiffs' injuries.

275. The Conspiracy Defendants understood the general objectives of the scheme, accepted them, and agreed, explicitly and/or implicitly, to do their part to further the objectives of the scheme.

276. The Conspiracy Defendants are jointly and severally liable under federal common law to Plaintiffs for their injuries caused by global warming.

277. In the alternative, if federal common law were not to apply, The Conspiracy Defendants are jointly and severally liable under the common law of conspiracy under applicable state law to Plaintiffs for their injuries caused by global warming.

FOURTH CLAIM FOR RELIEF

Concert of Action

*   *   *

279. Defendants have engaged in and/or are engaging in tortious acts in concert with each other or pursuant to a common design. Defendants have engaged in and/or are engaging in concert with each other over the creation, contribution to and/or maintenance of a public nuisance, global warming.

280. Defendants know that each other's conduct constitutes a breach of duty and each defendant gives substantial assistance or encouragement to each other to so conduct itself. Defendants know that each other participated in the creation, contribution to and/or maintenance of a public nuisance, global warming.

281. Defendants give substantial assistance to each other in accomplishing a tortious result and each defendant's own conduct, separately considered, constitutes a breach of duty to Plaintiffs. Defendants give substantial assistance to each other's participation in the creation, contribution to and/or maintenance of a public nuisance, global warming.

282. Defendants are jointly and severally liable under the applicable federal and/or state law to Plaintiffs for their injuries caused by global warming pursuant to a concert of action.

RELIEF REQUESTED

Plaintiffs request that this Court:

1. Hold each defendant jointly and severally liable for creating, contributing to, and maintaining a public nuisance;

2. Hold the Conspiracy Defendants jointly and severally liable for civil conspiracy;

3. Hold each defendant jointly and severally liable for concert of action;

4. Award monetary damages on the basis of joint and several liability according to proof;

5. Enter a declaratory judgment for such future monetary expenses and damages as may be incurred by Plaintiffs in connection with the nuisance of global warming; . . .

QUESTIONS AND DISCUSSION

1. *Problem Exercise.* Assume that you were representing one of the named defendants in the Kivalina complaint. Outline the major defenses you would expect to raise in filing a motion to dismiss this complaint. Consider both threshold issues such as standing or the political question doctrine and tort-based issues such as whether plaintiffs can prove a breach of duty. Which of your defenses do you think are the strongest? Which of your arguments are the weakest?

2. If, as suggested by the GAO report, that "remaining on the island is no longer a viable option for the [Kivalina] community," what options does the community have? Putting aside the validity of the legal actions raised in the complaint, who should pay the $95 to $400 million cost of moving the village? The defendants? The villagers? Federal taxpayers? Can you see how tort cases like this one relate to the more general policy debate over who should pay for adaptation? What does the concept of cost internalization, discussed in Chapter 2, tell us about who should pay for the costs incurred by Kivalina?

3. What significance would you place on the fact that defendants in *Kivalina* likely knew that they were contributing to a nuisance? Under many formulations, a public nuisance can be demonstrated where the defendant "knowingly contributes to" a public nuisance. This requires that the defendant have knowledge that their actions may lead to the nuisance — for example, climate change — but it does not require that the underlying conduct be measured against any objective standard of reasonableness. In *Connecticut v. AEP*, for example, the complaint alleged that each defendant *knowingly* contributed to climate change and cited as support particular steps or pronouncements each defendant had taken to address climate change. In this way, the defendant utilities' initial steps to study climate change or to reduce emissions were actually used *against* them to show that they acknowledged climate change.

4. What additional evidence do you think would need to be alleged in the complaint to support the civil conspiracy cause of action? Is this action rooted in the common law of torts? What advantages do you think the plaintiffs hope to gain by including this count in the complaint?

5. A second, consolidated case was filed along with the states' complaint in *Connecticut v. AEP*. That complaint was brought by three private land trusts against the same defendants. Open Space Institute, Inc. v. American Electric Power Co., No. 04-CV-05670 (S.D.N.Y.) (July 24, 2004). Why do you think the states in that case wanted to have a private action filed along with them?

6. In *Korsinsky v. U.S. Environmental Protection Agency*, 2005 WL 2414744 (S.D.N.Y. 2005), the pro se plaintiff sued the U.S. Environmental Protection Agency (EPA), the New York State Department of Environmental Protection, and the New York City Department of Environmental Protection based on a public nuisance theory. The plaintiff alleged that the defendants contributed to climate change both by emitting carbon dioxide and by failing to implement measures that would reduce CO_2. According to the court, much of the plaintiff's complaint was taken verbatim from the *Connecticut v. AEP* complaint, described above. The plaintiff sought an injunction preventing the defendants from continuing to pollute and requiring them to use plaintiff's own invention to reduce greenhouse gas emissions. The case was dismissed for lack of standing because of a failure to allege a specific injury. The plaintiff had alleged that he was more sensitive to pollution than the general public and that he had developed a fear of pollution. The court argued that the injuries were either conjectural in the case of the sensitivity to pollution or not related to the remedies the plaintiff sought in the case of the fear of pollution.

7.   Three broad categories of potential defendants could be the target of climate tort actions. The first are *producers of fossil fuels*, such as oil and coal companies, the combustion of which directly increases greenhouse gas emissions. One study estimates that one oil company, ExxonMobil (and its corporate predecessors), has contributed approximately "five per cent of global, man-made, climate changing carbon dioxide emissions over the last 120 years." Press Release, Friends of the Earth, Exxonmobil's contribution to global warming revealed (Jan. 29, 2004). The second category includes direct *users of fossil fuels*. Although this might theoretically include virtually every person in the United States, the primary target in this category are the relatively small number of large utilities that contribute a substantial portion of total U.S. emissions. (According to the complaint in *Connecticut v. American Electric Power*, the five largest fossil fuel burning utilities account for approximately 10% of *all* anthropogenic carbon dioxide emissions in the country). The last category includes those companies that manufacture or market *products whose use contributes to climate change*. The automobile companies in *California v. General Motors* are a prime example. Which of these categories of defendants do you think are the most vulnerable to a lawsuit? What different defenses might be available to each category of defendant?

III.   EVALUATING THE ELEMENTS OF A TORT ACTION IN THE CLIMATE CONTEXT

The basic elements of a tort cause of action in negligence are the following: (1) the defendant must have breached a duty — i.e., behaved unreasonably towards the plaintiff; (2) that breach must have caused, both factually and legally (proximately), injury to the plaintiffs; and (3) the plaintiff must in fact have suffered harm. All of the climate-related tort actions brought thus far have included public nuisance claims under both federal and state common law as their primary claims, although the private party plaintiffs in *Comer* and *Kivalina* included other theories as well. The basic elements of a public nuisance as noted above are that the defendant is contributing to a condition that unreasonably interferes with a public right. Although the elements of a public nuisance claim are different in important ways, such actions in most states require an inquiry into the reasonableness of the defendants' actions (the duty), proof of causation, and a demonstration of damages. These elements are discussed generally below, but this section is meant to stimulate your thinking about the applicability of torts generally to climate change. Given the status of the relatively few cases brought thus far, this section presents more questions than answers.

A.   Breach of Duty: The Reasonableness of Defendants' Actions

In negligence cases, the general standard of care is "to conform to the legal standard of reasonable conduct in light of the apparent risk. What the defendant must do, or must not do, is a question of the standard of conduct required to satisfy the duty." W. PAGE KEETON, ET AL., PROSSER AND KEETON ON THE LAW OF TORTS, § 53 (W. PAGE KEETON ED., 5TH ED. 1984). This simple formulation, of course, masks the complex and nuanced discussion of what standard of care in a particular circumstance — for example, with respect to the emissions of greenhouse gases — a particular defendant owes to a particular plaintiff. The following excerpt begins to explore the negligence standard of care in the context of climate change:

DAVID HUNTER & JAMES SALZMAN, NEGLIGENCE IN THE AIR: THE DUTY OF CARE IN CLIMATE CHANGE LITIGATION
155 U. PA. L. REV. 1741, 1746–49 (2007)*

For negligence actions, the general level of the duty of care is well known — to act reasonably or not to act in such a way that creates an unreasonable risk of harm. * * * But how would we define the unreasonable behavior of energy utilities whose emissions contribute to an increase in temperature that reduces snow pack? Or a car company whose products do the same thing? How do we analyze whether the utility or the car company's behavior was reasonable or unreasonable?

The duty of care analysis will be similar, although not identical, for tort actions based on theories other than negligence. For cases based on product liability, for example, the duty is to avoid selling a defective product or one that is unaccompanied by an adequate warning. For nuisance, the obligation is not to interfere unreasonably or knowingly with the use and enjoyment of another's property, and with public nuisance it is not to contribute unreasonably or knowingly to an interference with the public's resources. In each case, the determination of a breach of duty can be analyzed in terms of the "reasonableness" of defendant's conduct (or of its product design), which in turn can be analyzed through a risk-utility (i.e., cost-benefit) analysis of the underlying conduct (or product) and the foreseeable resulting harms. Also relevant to each of the tort actions is the availability of alternative approaches, technologies or products that could reduce the foreseeable risk. * * *

One frequently used method for analyzing whether a defendant has acted negligently is to compare the costs of avoiding the negligent behavior with the likely damages caused by the activity. Learned Hand's famous B<PL formula, sometimes known as the "Calculus of Negligence," provides the classic example of this approach in determining whether or not to impose a duty. In *Carroll Towing*, 159 F.2d 169 (2d Cir. 1947), Hand proposed that tort liability for negligence should be imposed when the burden of preventing injury is less than the product of the magnitude of the injury and its likelihood ($B < P \times L$). The main insight of this heuristic is that the duty to prevent harm is dependent on comparing the costs of avoiding damage or preventing harm with the expected damages from the activity. * * *

In determining the reasonableness of a certain action, a defendant cannot emphasize only the costs he faces, but must also consider the external social costs

---

of his activity. Where the costs of avoiding large amounts of potential damages would be reasonable, defendants have a duty to incur those costs. Where such costs would be unreasonable in light of potential risk, the defendant is under no such duty. Under this view, a principle purpose of tort law is to maximize social utility, because where the costs of accidents exceed the costs of preventing them, the law will impose liability.

In the climate change context, scientific developments over the past decade have shifted, and continue to shift, each element of the BPL formula in the direction of liability. The identifiable risks of climate changes are becoming better understood and most of them have become more likely with greater consequences than was thought even a decade ago. In addition, new technologies are lowering the costs of pollution control equipment, carbon storage, fuel switching and renewable and other energy alternatives. * * *

1. The Likelihood (P) and Severity of the Damage (L)

[A]n emerging scientific consensus now broadly accepts that climate change is happening, is caused by human activities, and is resulting in specific injuries or will do so in the foreseeable future. For example, the [IPCC] concluded in 2001 . . . that "most of the observed warming over the last 50 years is likely to have been due to the increase in greenhouse gas concentrations." "Likely" is defined by the IPCC to mean there is a confidence level of between 66%–90%. The scientific evidence and consensus linking anthropogenic GHG emissions and increased temperature has only increased since 2001.

That the planet is now warming is also well accepted. Long-term climate data suggest that the planet's average surface air temperature has increased significantly since the late 19th century. Moreover, average global temperatures are now expected to be much higher, much sooner, than was predicted even a decade ago. . . . . According to the IPCC . . . , global average temperatures are estimated to rise between 2 to 4.5° C by the year 2100, with an additional 1.5° C possible due to potential positive feedback loops. Such a rate of warming is without precedent for at least the last 10,000 years.

So what if the planet's temperature increases? The key issue is whether that temperature increase has an impact on human health and the environment. The 2001 IPCC Assessment found that climate change was *already* having a discernible impact on many different environmental systems. [The article then summarizes many of the impacts and associated long-term trends identified in Chapter 1.] * * *

What then are the global costs of climate — the L in the BPL formula? Various estimates exist and provide vastly different numbers. Most analysts put the costs at somewhere between 0 and 3% GDP. Nordhaus, for example in a widely cited analysis, has estimated the global costs at approximately 2.4% of GDP or approximately $30 per ton of carbon. More recently, a study commissioned by the UK government, known as the Stern report, and released in October, 2006, based its estimates on more recent higher estimates of global temperature increases. The Stern Report places the costs of climate change under business as usual scenarios at 5 to 10% of global GDP, with more pessimistic assumptions putting the loss at 20% of GDP by the end of the century. Assuming a global GDP of roughly 20 trillion dollars, the estimated annual impacts range from $500 billion to $4 trillion dollars.

Those who follow the climate change debate have become accustomed to long lists of potential impacts (and in fact have become rather inured to them), but tort litigation forces the courts, defendants and others to focus on these impacts more closely, particularly as they impact particular plaintiffs or categories of plaintiffs. The IPCC's willingness to state that increases in temperature are likely to be caused by human activities and that such increases are already having discernible impacts not only supports causation in a torts case, but also responds generally to the BPL formula. The likelihood is high and the potential impacts are severe. . . . The IPCC's practice of bounding its statements in probabilities is also helpful to litigants in climate change cases. * * *

Although the IPCC's periodic reviews of the climate change science and the economic estimates of total costs are important, just as important for specific tort cases is the growing research on particularized impacts in specific geographic regions. * * *

[U]nlike even a decade ago, today strong evidence links climate change to specific anticipated impacts at the local or state level. This understanding supports moving the debate over climate policy from general policy debates to case-specific adjudications over identifiable harms. As these types of regional impacts become better known and studied, and buttressed by the stronger consensus findings. In the Fourth IPCC Assessment, the causal link between human activities, increased temperatures, changing climate, and specific impacts to identifiable litigants will be more clearly demonstrated. Put another way, the probability (and thus foreseeability) of specific damage caused by climate change is increasingly being documented. This will not only allow for stronger arguments on causation but would also satisfy two prongs of the BPL formula (the probability of harm (P) and the severity of the harm (L)) and thus strengthen plaintiff's case for a breach of the duty of reasonable care.

2. Burden or Cost of Avoiding Harm

At the same time the probability of serious injury from climate change is increasing, the costs of reducing carbon emissions are decreasing. Over time the efficiency of the economy is increasing as measured by the carbon intensity or amounts of carbon emitted per dollar of GDP produced. From 1990 to 2002, carbon intensity was reduced 17% in the United States and 15% on average among the 25 countries with the highest emissions. Carbon intensity is dependent on fuel mix and energy use efficiency. Particularly in the absence of regulatory mandates, declines in carbon intensity suggest that either through fuel switching, new methodologies, new technologies or similar changes, the economy is finding it less costly over time to reduce emissions.

The same cost trends can be seen in the energy sector. The cost of alternative energy sources such as wind and solar are dropping steadily and are becoming increasingly competitive. Costs of wind power have declined from 40 cents/kw-h in 1979 to 3–5 cents/kw-h today. Installed costs of solar power have dropped 5% per year over the past decade. Similarly, in the automobile industry, new technologies such as the hybrid technology have increased efficiency at affordable costs. Fuel-switching is also available to the transport system as a growing percentage of road transport is being run by natural gas (3%) or biofuels (5%).

Clearly many efficient technologies now exist and are increasingly cost-effective. One survey of 74 companies from 18 sectors in 11 countries, for example, found GHG emission reductions of up to 60% with total gross cost *savings* of $11.6 billion (mostly because of reduced energy costs). In fact, considerable progress on addressing climate change can be simply through the dissemination and "scaling up" of technologies and practices already well known. * * *

What then are the costs of addressing climate change? Estimates have varied, although most estimates put the costs of stabilizing GHG emissions at safe levels at up to 1% of the global economy. This is a staggering amount, except when it is compared to the estimated costs of climate change. As noted above, most estimates put the costs of climate change at roughly 3% of the global economy (three times as much), with more recent estimates ranging from 5–20%.

Just as with impacts, for purposes of analyzing a specific climate change claim, the BPL formula may be less about global costs and benefits and more about the costs and benefits present in the specific case. The complaints that have been filed thus far recognize this, focusing on the steps that are available to the specific defendants to reduce their climate impact. Thus, for example, in the *Connecticut v. AEP* complaint, the Attorneys General allege that:

> Defendants have available to them practical, feasible and economically viable options for reducing carbon dioxide emissions without significantly increasing the cost of electricity to their customers. These options include changing fuels, improving efficiency, increasing generation from zero- or low-carbon energy sources such as wind, solar, and gasified coal with emissions capture, co-firing wood or other biomass in coal plants, employing demand-side management techniques, altering the dispatch order of their plants, and other measures.

Later, the Attorneys General assert that "defendants could generate the same amount of electricity while emitting significantly less carbon dioxide by employing readily available processes and technologies." Complaint, Connecticut v. AEP, at para. 156.

An incomplete, though instructive, back-of-the-envelope method to assess costs is to price the emission reductions sought in the climate complaints [discussed further below]. The *Connecticut* complaint, for example, seeks an injunction to require the companies to cap their emissions (allegedly 650 million tons per year) and then to reduce by some set amount each year. If we assume reductions of 7%, arbitrarily set at the level of reduction to which the U.S. would have committed under the Kyoto Protocol), then companies would be asked to reduce 45 million tons each year. If one uses current carbon market prices in Europe and the United States, this would cost the utilities in total from $180 to $450 million per year (based on the over-simple assumption that the current range of carbon costs of $4.00 ton in the Chicago Climate Exchange to $10.00 ton in the European Climate Exchange would remain unchanged). If divided equally among the five defendants, the cost per defendant would have been $36 to $90 million. * * *

We should make clear that these estimates are based on several over-simple assumptions (i.e., market price won't change in the face of increased demand), but they do provide a first-order estimate for the costs of avoiding the negligent behavior (i.e., emissions beyond Kyoto-level reductions). The point is not to develop a precise estimate of the compliance costs but to show that a BPL inquiry both could be conducted and could show that the likely costs of avoidance may in some cases be less than the likely damages from climate change. Under the Hand formula, the defendant's conduct not to take those steps could be considered a breach of their duty to act reasonably under the circumstances.

Moreover, trends in carbon intensity and in the declining costs of renewables and other green technologies mean that the cost of addressing climate change is declining over time. This suggests that in future cases, the burden of avoiding harm will be lower than today, making findings of liability more likely.

QUESTIONS AND DISCUSSION

1. Do you agree with the analysis of the Hand formula above? Are all the trends moving toward liability?

2. Courts have come up with additional factors beyond the BPL formula for determining the reasonableness of an activity. For example, in *Vu v. Singer Co.*, 538 F. Supp. 26, 29 (N.D.Cal. 1981), the court held that the extent of the duty depended on what was reasonable under the circumstances, judged by the following standards:

(1)   foreseeability of harm to plaintiff;

(2)   degree of certainty that plaintiff suffered injury;

(3)   closeness of connection between defendant's conduct and injury suffered;

(4)   moral blame attached to defendant's conduct;

(5)   policy of preventing future harm;

(6)   extent of burden to the defendant and the consequences to the community of imposing a duty to exercise care with resulting liability for breach; and

(7)   availability, cost, and prevalence of insurance for the risk involved.

Id. at 29. How would you analyze these factors in the context of climate change?

3. We often think that imposing liability on a defendant presupposes that they have been blameworthy in some respect. Indeed, this is one of the factors identified above in Note 2. What factors would be relevant to you in arguing that a defendant should be morally (and legally) blamed for its contribution to climate change? To some extent, this requires placing the defendant's specific conduct in the context of what was known or suspected about climate change at the time. Thus, a plan to expand oil development or coal-fired utilities or to market inefficient SUVs may not have been blameworthy or "unreasonable" in 1990. What about 2000? Or 2010? Consider this question in light of the timeline of the climate negotiations in Table 4-2. Given the emerging understanding of climate change, determining what an appropriate response should have been at any specific time is difficult, imprecise and un-scientific. It is in fact a subjective judgment about reasonableness — one that is often left in the tort context to juries. What about decisions today to build coal-fired power plants in the United States? Are those plans reasonable?

4. Contributing to an analysis of the moral blameworthiness in many tort cases is the degree of defendant's recklessness or intention in undertaking the risky activity. But in the case of climate change, almost all of the potential corporate defendants are acting deliberately or intentionally in ways they now know contribute to climate change. Most utilities, energy companies, or automobile manufacturers have either made public pronouncements or taken policy steps that show they are aware of climate change threats and of their contribution to the problem. How does this affect their potential liability, if at all? If you were representing a fossil fuel-based company, what advice would you give them to lower their potential exposure to future climate change actions?

5. According to the Restatement's treatment of public nuisance, the following are "circumstances that may sustain a holding that an interference with a public right is unreasonable":

(a)   whether the conduct involves a significant interference with the public health, the public safety, the public peace, the public comfort or the public convenience, or

(b)   whether the conduct is proscribed by a statue, ordinance or administrative regulation, or

(c)   whether the conduct is of a continuing nature or has produced a permanent or long-lasting effect, and as the actor knows or has reason to know, has a significant effect upon the public right.

Restatement (Second) of Torts, § 821B(2). Given the widespread, serious, and long-lasting impacts that are increasingly attributed to climate change, does it seem far-fetched to argue that climate change constitutes a "significant interference" with the public's welfare? See Matthew F. Pawa & Benjamin A. Krass, *Global Warming as a Public Nuisance: Connecticut v. American Electric Power*, 16 FORDHAM ENVTL. L. REV. 407 (2005); *see also* Bruce Ledewitz & Robert D. Taylor, *Law and the Coming Environmental Catastrophe*, 21 WM & MARY ENVTL. L. & POL'Y REV. 599, 614 (1997).

B.   Causation

Just as difficult as demonstrating a breach of a legal duty for plaintiffs will be the challenges they face on causation. Causation is divided into two different elements: (1) cause in fact, where plaintiffs must prove that but for the breach of duty, injury would have occurred; and (2) proximate causation or legal causation where the court determines whether the injury was sufficiently foreseeable to allow for the imposition of liability. The following excerpt explores the difficult issues of causation that arise in the climate change context:

DAVID A. GROSSMAN, WARMING UP TO A NOT-SO-RADICAL IDEA
28 COLUM. J. ENVTL. L. 22–25 (2003)

In many toxic tort cases, as in a climate change case, the clear causal chains examined in first-year torts classes usually do not exist. Instead, plaintiffs must rely on more statistical or probabilistic means. In mass exposure cases such as Agent Orange, for instance, plaintiffs often had to rely on epidemiological studies to try to demonstrate the association between exposure to a substance and deleterious health effects. These studies attempt to establish generic causation — whether it can be said that the substance, as a general proposition, causes the sort of injuries afflicting the plaintiffs. In the climate change context, climate scientists use computer models to project the past and future course of Earth's climate and to demonstrate the probabilistic association between increased greenhouse gas emissions and climatic effects. Despite the uncertainties that remain in climate science, the studies and models such as those the IPCC relied upon provide a solid basis for arguing that a general causal link exists between greenhouse gas emissions, climate change, and effects such as sea-level rise, thawing permafrost, and melting sea ice — all probably beyond the "more likely than not" standard used in the legal arena.

Generally speaking, courts have not considered statistical associations like those produced by epidemiological studies to be adequate proof of specific causation — whether it can be said that the substance caused plaintiffs' particular injuries. This individual causation is often the most problematic for toxic tort plaintiffs. Determination of specific causation is complicated by the existence of background levels of the injuries and of other risk factors that may contribute to the victims' chances of developing the disease ("confounding factors"). These complications mean that even where it can be shown that the defendant is responsible for a significant proportion of the cases of harm, no single plaintiff can prove that he or she is one of those cases. . . . Many courts and scholars have concluded that plaintiffs who rely on epidemiological evidence must show that, more probably than not, their individual injuries were caused by the risk factor in question, as opposed to any other cause. This has sometimes been translated to a requirement of a relative risk of at least two.

Showing specific causation in the climate change context could be particularly difficult. First, climate change's effects involve shifts in climatic activity, such as more intense and more frequent storms, not the creation of distinctive new phenomena, like the "signature diseases" of asbestosis in asbestos cases and clear cell adenocarcinoma in DES cases [Diethylstilbestrol, or DES, is a drug once prescribed during pregnancy to prevent miscarriages or premature deliveries, but which later was found to cause a rare form of cancer]. Unlike those cases, the complexity of the climate system means that several factors are involved in producing climatic phenomena, making it difficult to show the probability that defendants' contributions to anthropogenic climate change caused any particular phenomenon. Second, unlike cancer or other typical toxic tort effects, the natural phenomena affected by climate change are subject to natural fluctuations in frequency and severity. The chaotic system underlying climatic effects makes it quite difficult to differentiate a particular pattern change in temperature or sea level caused by anthropogenic climate change from one caused by natural variability.

The obstacle posed by specific causation is mitigated, however, when governments as opposed to individuals are the plaintiffs. When states bring tort claims, the plaintiffs have almost infinite lifespans and cover large amounts of territory, allowing for an aggregation of effects over both space and time. The harms mentioned above — sea-level rise, temperature increases, thawing permafrost, and melting and thinning sea ice — are among the harms most clearly tied to climate change, asserted by the IPCC with high levels of confidence. The aggregation of these harms makes it easier to rule out confounding factors; one sinkhole in a road or one particular storm surge is more easily attributed to factors other than climate change than is a state full of damaged roads or with a lengthy and retreating shoreline. Natural fluxes and confounding factors still exist, since some portion of the harms within the aggregation would not actually be caused by global warming, but aggregation allows plaintiffs to better establish that some present harms from climate change exist in the broader geographic and temporal range. Once these harms are established, the question is no longer whether defendants have caused harms. Rather, the pertinent question becomes whether the amount of their contributions is sufficient to find liability for damages.

QUESTIONS AND DISCUSSION

1. The above discussion of the aggregation of impacts in actions brought by states presaged the first climate change cases. As discussed above, the states in *Connecticut* and in *California* did not premise their public nuisance cases on any one specific weather event, so they arguably would not have to show that climate change has resulted in a specific hurricane or drought — but just that generally over time climate change may have certain impacts (e.g., declines in snow pack, more intense storms, warmer temperatures, etc.). Contrast this to the *Comer* complaint, which would require plaintiffs to show that Hurricane Katrina was at least exacerbated by the defendants' contribution to climate change. Can you see why the state cases would appear to be stronger?

2. Moreover, under the plaintiffs' theory of public nuisance, they would not have to prove that the injury was "more likely than not" *caused* by the defendants' conduct, but rather simply that the defendants' conduct more likely than not *contributed* to the nuisance and thus the injury. In this way, the fact that the defendant utilities in *Connecticut* or the defendant automobile manufacturers in *California* contribute only a fraction of global greenhouse gas emissions would not necessarily bar the suit.

3. *Joint and Several Liability.* Under plaintiffs' public nuisance theory, defendants could arguably be held jointly and severally liable for the entire injury (even if their contribution alone is insufficient to cause the damage). Under basic tort law theories, defendants that contribute to an indivisible harm or injury may be held jointly and severally liable. This is particularly true in nuisance and public nuisance cases. In this regard consider the following quote from an 1881 nuisance action brought by a downstream landowner against an upstream slaughterhouse:

> It is no answer to a complaint of nuisance that a great many others are committing similar acts of nuisance upon the stream. Each and every one is liable to a separate action, and to be restrained.

> The extent to which the appellee has contributed to the nuisance, may be slight and scarcely appreciable. Standing alone, it might well be that it would only, very slightly, if at all, prove a source of annoyance. And so it might be, as to each of the other numerous persons contributing to the nuisance. Each standing alone, might amount to little or nothing. But it is when all are united together, and contribute to a common result, that they become important as factors, in producing the mischief complained of. And it may only be after from year to year, the number of contributors to the injury has greatly increased, that sufficient disturbance of the appellant's rights has been caused to justify a complaint.

> One drop of poison in a person's cup, may have no injurious effect. But when a dozen, or twenty, or fifty, each put in a drop, fatal results may follow. It would not do to say that neither was to be held responsible.

Woodyear v. Schaefer, 57 Md. 1, 9–10 (Md. 1881). Is there any reason that this approach should not apply 125 years later to global warming? For a further discussion of these and other issues raised by public nuisance climate cases, see Matthew F. Pawa & Benjamin A. Krass, *Global Warming as a Public Nuisance: Connecticut v. American Electric Power*, 16 Fordham Envtl. L. Rev. 407 (citing *California v. Gold Run Ditch & Mining Co.*, 4 Pac. 1152, 1157 (Cal. 1884) ("in an action to abate a public or private nuisance, all persons engaged in the commission of the wrongful acts which constitute the nuisance may be enjoined, jointly or severally."); *Lockwood Co. v. Lawrence*, 77 Me. 297 (Me. 1885) (holding that each of sixteen sawmill operators that were polluting a stream could be held jointly and severally liable, notwithstanding that each defendant's contribution alone might have been harmless); *United States v. Luce*, 141 F. 385 (C.C.D. Del. 1905) (holding under federal common law that one of two sources of air pollution were jointly and severally liable for a public nuisance). *See also* Michie v. Great Lakes Steel Division, 495 F.2d 213 (6th Cir. 1974), *cert. denied* 419 U.S. 997 (1974) (finding that under Michigan law the three U.S. defendants could be held liable jointly and severally for maintaining a nuisance for harm caused to plaintiffs in Canada).

4. The use of public nuisance theories is one possible way to circumvent the general rule that plaintiffs must prove that the defendants' actions were "more likely than not" the cause of their injuries. What other possible theories are available to plaintiffs, where, as in the case of climate change, not all of the parties who contributed to the injury will be before the court? Consider the famous case of *Sindell v. Abbott Laboratories*, 607 P.2d 924 (Cal. Sup. Ct. 1980), where the California Supreme Court imposed liability on five manufacturers of diethylstilbestrol (DES) based on their market share of the drug. Plaintiff recovered, although she could not know which of the manufacturers produced the DES that injured her and was thus unable to prove which of the five companies was more likely than not the one that caused her specific injuries. In what ways are plaintiffs in a climate change case in a similar position? Would market share liability be an appropriate means of imposing and allocating liability? Could liability be imposed based on a company's historical greenhouse gas emissions? What advantages or disadvantages would you anticipate with such an approach?

5.   The evidence for demonstrating causation seems to be increasing. The IPCC's Fourth Assessment clearly provides substantial weight for the general issues of causation — i.e., whether humans are causing climate change. But just as important have been developments in climate science that have led experts to attribute certain events at least partly to anthropogenic climate change. A 2007 study, for example, found that the human contribution to the 2003 European heat wave, which contributed to the deaths of more than 30,000 people, increased the potential of risk of such weather from 4 to 10 times. *See, e.g.*, Myles Allen, et al., *Scientific Challenges in the Attribution of Harm to Human Influence on Climate*, 155 U. Pa. L. Rev. 1353 (2007); Myles Allen, *Liability for Climate Change*, 421 Nature 891–92 (Feb. 27, 2003); Peter Stott, et al., *Human Contribution to Europe Heat Wave of 2003*, 432 Nature, 610 (Dec. 2, 2004); Simone Bastianoni, Federico M. Pulselli & Enzo Tiezzi, *The Problem of Assigning Responsibility for Greenhouse Gas Emissions*, 49 Ecological Econ. 253 (2004) (discussing difficulties in assigning responsibility for greenhouse gas emissions). How will such studies shape future climate litigation strategies? Do you see any obstacles to using such studies in court?

6.   ***Admissibility of Evidence.*** Many corporate defense lawyers believed that testimony regarding climate change and its impacts would not be allowed into evidence under the Federal Rules of Evidence's criteria for expert testimony. In *Daubert v. Merrell Dow Pharmaceuticals, Inc.*, 113 S. Ct. 2786, 125 L. Ed. 2d 469 (1993), the Supreme Court announced a two-part test for the admissibility of expert testimony: (1) is the expert's testimony the product of "good science," reflecting scientific knowledge derived from the scientific method and (2) the science relevant to the legal question at hand. In the only case thus far to rule on a motion to dismiss expert testimony regarding climate change, the District Court in Vermont admitted affidavits from two climate change experts. Green Mountain Chrysler Plymouth Dodge Jeep v. Crombie, 508 F. Supp. 2d 295, 316 (D.Vt. 2007). As climate science gets better able to attribute specific events or impacts to anthropogenic climate change, such rulings may be easier for plaintiffs in the future.

C.   Damages

To some extent, proving damages may be the most straight-forward element in a climate-change tort case. In both the *Connecticut* and *California* cases, the plaintiff states identified specific damage to their natural resources and economies that they alleged were caused by anthropogenic climate change. In *Connecticut*, for example, the states alleged impacts that included declining snow pack and ice; increased loss of life and public health threats from heat-related illnesses and smog; impacts on coastal resources from storm surges and permanent sea-level rise; declining water levels and increasing temperatures in the Great Lakes; and rapid declines in forest resources, including New York's Adirondack State Park. In addition to identifying current and future impacts, in *California* the state detailed costs that it was already incurring to adapt to climate change, including, for example, the costs of re-building levees to prevent sea water infiltration and beach preservation efforts to reverse increased beach erosion from sea level rise. Similarly, the damages in the *Kivalina* complaint are straight-forward — the costs of relocating the village — and supported by an official U.S. government report.

Putting aside the question of causation (discussed above), whether damage has occurred or is likely to occur in the future can be readily demonstrated. There can be no doubt, for example, that the plaintiffs in *Comer* had suffered harm from Hurricane Katrina or that the Village of Kivalina is indeed subsiding into the ocean. In this regard, review the climate change impacts summarized in Chapter 1 and consider how many of those impacts could form the basis of damages to real plaintiffs in a lawsuit.

Not all damages from climate change may be eligible for a tort case, however. In public nuisance actions, for example, plaintiffs must demonstrate that their specific injuries are different in nature or degree than that suffered by the general public. Generally speaking, plaintiffs who have suffered only economic losses without any physical damage to a proprietary interest cannot recover in tort. In *State of Louisiana ex rel Guste v. M/V Testbank*, 752 F.2d 1019, *cert. denied*, 477 U.S. 903 (1986), for example, the court addressed liability for a massive pentachlorophenol (PCP) spill in the Mississippi River Gulf outlet. The U.S. Coast Guard closed the outlet to navigation for nearly a month and temporarily suspended fishing, crabbing, shrimping, and other activities. The impacts of the spill rippled through the Louisiana economy, and a wide variety of affected parties filed suit. The court held that only those plaintiffs who suffered a direct, physical loss to their interests could maintain their suit, while plaintiffs with more indirect damages — for example, restaurants that could not purchase fish — could not.

Just as in *Louisiana*, the reverberations of climate change through local and regional economies is, and will be, substantial. A severe drought that destroys the Great Plains wheat crop may impact breadmakers, restaurants, and truckers. Tort law would typically limit liability only to those whose economic losses resulted from a physical loss — in this example the wheat farmer — and not those breadmakers, restaurants, and truckers whose economic loss arises only through contract or other financial relationships.

QUESTIONS AND DISCUSSION

Although limiting recovery only to those who suffered a physical deprivation of their interests may hinder some climate claims, do you think it may also help courts to view climate-related cases more positively? Given that so many people and interests are affected either directly or indirectly from climate change, this doctrine might provide a convenient and reasonable approach to setting limits on climate claims.

IV. DEFENSES TO TORT ACTIONS

A. Political Question Doctrine and other Threshold Issues

As noted above, thus far all three of the climate-related tort cases have been dismissed on the grounds that climate change raises a political question that is inappropriate for the judiciary. The political question doctrine, along with several other threshold issues such as standing that apply in climate-law related cases are discussed further in Chapter 12. Below we address the additional threshold defense — relevant to common law claims — that both federal and state common law tort actions may be pre-empted by the Clean Air Act.

B. Are Common Law Claims Pre-Empted by the Clean Air Act?

When Congress exercises its constitutional authority, it may preempt states from enacting legislation concerning the same subject. As discussed in more detail in Chapter 13 in the context of California's and other states' attempts to issue vehicle emissions standards, the Supremacy Clause "invalidates state laws that 'interfere with, or are contrary to,' federal law." Gibbons v. Ogden, 9 Wheat. 1, 211 (1824) (Marshall, C. J.). Federal statutes may also preempt federal common law claims. Preemption of state law and common law claims may be express or implied. Implied preemption has two forms: field preemption and conflict preemption. Field preemption occurs when "the depth and breadth of a congressional scheme" that occupies the legislative field is "so pervasive as to make reasonable the inference that Congress left no room for the States to supplement it." *Lorillard Tobacco Co. v. Reilly*, 533 U.S. 525, 541, (2001); *Rice v. Santa Fe Elevator Corp.*, 331 U.S. 218, 230 (1947). Field preemption also occurs when the federal interest in a subject area that it regulates is "so dominant" that federal law "will be assumed to preclude enforcement of state laws on the same subject." *Rice*, 331 U.S. at 230. Conflict preemption exists either when "compliance with both federal and state regulations is a physical impossibility," *Florida Lime & Avocado Growers, Inc. v. Paul*, 373 U.S. 132, 142–43 (1963), or where state law "stands as an obstacle to the accomplishment and execution of the full purposes and objectives of Congress." *Hines v. Davidowitz*, 312 U.S. 52, 67 (1941).

Plaintiffs have raised public nuisance claims under both federal and state common law in all of the climate change-related claims filed thus far. None of the courts have yet to reach the preemption issue.

Given the history of using the common law, particularly nuisance law, to redress injuries resulting from air and water pollution, *see. e.g., Georgia v. Tennessee Copper Co.*, 206 U.S. 230, 236 (1907), one could have expected Congress to speak clearly as to preemption of common law claims in modern environmental statutes. However, in the context of climate change and other air pollution, it is not clear whether Congress intended the Clean Air Act to preempt state law and federal common law. Although the court in *Green Mountain Chrysler* as well as in *Central Valley Chrysler Jeep v. Goldstene*, 529 F. Supp. 2d 1151 (E.D. Ca. 2007), held that regulation of greenhouse gas emissions from automobiles was not preempted by the Clean Air Act or the Energy Policy and Conservation Act, the court relied heavily on the express waiver provisions of Section 208 of the Clean Air Act. See Chapter 13. The Clean Air Act does not otherwise expressly preempt or save state law or federal common law claims. Thus, the operative question is whether the Clean Air Act impliedly preempts such claims.

1. *Is Federal Common Law Preempted?*

No court has ever answered whether the Clean Air Act preempts common law claims. But cases involving the Clean Water Act, formally known as the Federal Water Pollution Control Act, provide an analogous situation. Like the Clean Air Act, the Clean Water Act is a comprehensive statute. That alone, however, is not enough for a federal statute to preempt federal common law. The following two cases, decided nine years apart, both involve the State of Illinios suing Milwaukee and other municipalities in Wisconsin for polluting Lake Michigan. In the first case, decided prior to passage of the 1972 Clean Water Act Amendments, Illinois' federal common law claim is upheld. Nine years later, the Court rules that the 1972 Amendments preempt Illinois' claims.

ILLINOIS v. MILWAUKEE
406 U.S. 91 (1972) (Milwaukee I)

Mr. Justice Douglas delivered the opinion of the Court.

This is a motion by Illinois to file a bill of complaint under our original jurisdiction against four cities of Wisconsin, the Sewerage Commission of the City of Milwaukee, and the Metropolitan Sewerage Commission of the County of Milwaukee. The cause of action alleged is pollution by the defendants of Lake Michigan, a body of interstate water. According to plaintiff, some 200 million gallons of raw or inadequately treated sewage and other waste materials are discharged daily into the lake in the Milwaukee area alone. Plaintiff alleges that it and its subdivisions prohibit and prevent such discharges, but that the defendants do not take such actions. Plaintiff asks that we abate this public nuisance.

*   *   *

III

Congress has enacted numerous laws touching interstate waters. In 1899 it established some surveillance by the Army Corps of Engineers over industrial pollution, not including sewage, Rivers and Harbors Act of March 3, 1899, 30 Stat. 1121, a grant of power which we construed in *United States v. Republic Steel Corp.*, 362 U.S. 482, and in *United States v. Standard Oil Co.*, 384 U.S. 224.

The 1899 Act has been reinforced and broadened by a complex of laws recently enacted. The Federal Water Pollution Control Act, 62 Stat. 1155, as amended, 33 U.S.C. § 1151, tightens control over discharges into navigable waters so as not to lower applicable water quality standards. . . . Congress has evinced increasing concern with the quality of the aquatic environment as it affects the conservation and safeguarding of fish and wildlife resources.

Buttressed by these new and expanding policies, the Corps of Engineers has issued new Rules and Regulations governing permits for discharges or deposits into navigable waters. 36 Fed.Reg. 6564 *et seq.*

The Federal Water Pollution Control Act in § 1(b) declares that it is federal policy "to recognize, preserve, and protect the primary responsibilities and rights of the States in preventing and controlling water pollution." But the Act makes clear that it is federal, not state, law that in the end controls the pollution of interstate or navigable waters. While the States are given time to establish water quality standards, § 10(c)(1), if a State fails to do so the federal administrator promulgates one. § 10(c)(2). Section 10(a) makes pollution of interstate or navigable waters subject "to abatement" when it "endangers the health or welfare of any persons." The abatement that is authorized follows a long-drawn out procedure unnecessary to relate here. It uses the conference procedure, hoping for amicable settlements. But if none is reached, the federal administrator may request the Attorney General to bring suit on behalf of the United States for abatement of the pollution. § 10(g).

The remedy sought by Illinois is not within the precise scope of remedies prescribed by Congress. Yet the remedies which Congress provides are not necessarily the only federal remedies available. "It is not uncommon for federal courts to fashion federal law where federal rights are concerned." *Textile Workers v. Lincoln Mills*, 353 U.S. 448, 457. When we deal with air and water in their ambient or interstate aspects, there is a federal common law,[5] as *Texas v. Pankey*, 441 F.2d 236, recently held.

The application of federal common law to abate a public nuisance in interstate or navigable waters is not inconsistent with the Water Pollution Control Act. Congress provided in § 10(b) of that Act that . . . "(s)tate and interstate action to abate pollution of interstate or navigable waters shall be encouraged and shall not . . . be displaced by Federal enforcement action."

The leading air case is *Georgia v. Tennessee Copper Co.*, 206 U.S. 230, where Georgia filed an original suit in this Court against a Tennessee company whose noxious gases were causing a wholesale destruction of forests, orchards, and crops in Georgia. * * *

The nature of the nuisance was described as follows:

> It is a fair and reasonable demand on the part of a sovereign that the air over its territory should not be polluted on a great scale by sulphurous acid gas, that the forests on its mountains, be they better or worse, and whatever domestic destruction they have suffered, should not be further destroyed or threatened by the act of persons beyond its control, that the crops and orchards on its hills should not be endangered from the same source. If any such demand is to be enforced this must be, notwithstanding the hesitation that we might feel if the suit were between private parties, and the doubt whether for the injuries which they might be suffering to their property they should not be left to an action at law. Id., at 238, 27 S. Ct., at 619.

Our decisions concerning interstate waters contain the same theme. Rights in interstate streams, like questions of boundaries, "have been recognized as presenting federal questions."[6] *Hinderlider v. La Plata Co.*, 304 U.S. 92, 110. The question of apportionment of interstate waters is a question of "federal common law" upon which state statutes or decisions are not conclusive. *Ibid.*

---

[5] While the various federal environmental protection statutes will not necessarily mark the outer bounds of the federal common law, they may provide useful guidelines in fashioning such rules of decision. . . .

[6] Thus, it is not only the character of the parties that requires us to apply federal law. *See Georgia v. Tennessee Copper Co.*, 206 U.S. 230, 237; *cf. Wisconsin v. Pelican Ins. Co.*, 127 U.S. 265, 289; The Federalist No. 80 (A. Hamilton). As Mr. Justice Harlan indicated for the Court in *Banco Nacional de Cuba v. Sabbatino*, 376 U.S. 398, 421–427, where there is an overriding federal interest in the need for a uniform rule of decision or where the controversy touches basic interests of federalism, we have fashioned federal common law. Certainly these same demands for applying federal law are present in the pollution of a body of water such as Lake Michigan bounded, as it is, by four States.

In speaking of the problem of apportioning the waters of an interstate stream, the Court said in *Kansas v. Colorado*, 206 U.S. 46, 98, that "through these successive disputes and decisions this court is practically building up what may not improperly be called interstate common law." * * *

When it comes to water pollution this Court has spoken in terms of "a public nuisance," *New York v. New Jersey*, 256 U.S., at 313; *New Jersey v. New York City*, 283 U.S. 473, 481, 482. In *Missouri v. Illinois*, 200 U.S. 496, 520–521, the Court said, "It may be imagined that a nuisance might be created by a State upon a navigable river like the Danube, which would amount to a casus belli for a State lower down, unless removed. If such a nuisance were created by a State upon the Mississippi the controversy would be resolved by the more peaceful means of a suit in this court."

It may happen that new federal laws and new federal regulations may in time pre-empt the field of federal common law of nuisance. But until that comes to pass, federal courts will be empowered to appraise the equities of the suits alleging creation of a public nuisance by water pollution. While federal law governs,[9] consideration of state standards may be relevant. *Cf. Connecticut v. Massachusetts*, 282 U.S. 660, 670; *Kansas v. Colorado*, 185 U.S. 125, 146–147. Thus, a State with high water-quality standards may well ask that its strict standards be honored and that it not be compelled to lower itself to the more degrading standards of a neighbor. There are no fixed rules that govern; these will be equity suits in which the informed judgment of the chancellor will largely govern.

So ordered.

MILWAUKEE v. ILLINOIS
451 U.S. 304 (1981) (Milwaukee II)

JUSTICE REHNQUIST delivered the opinion of the Court.

When this litigation was first before us we recognized the existence of a federal "common law" which could give rise to a claim for abatement of a nuisance caused by interstate water pollution. *Illinois v. Milwaukee*, 406 U.S. 91 (1972). Subsequent to our decision, Congress enacted the Federal Water Pollution Control Act Amendments of 1972. We granted certiorari to consider the effect of this legislation on the previously recognized cause of action

I

Petitioners, the city of Milwaukee, the Sewerage Commission of the city of Milwaukee, and the Metropolitan Sewerage Commission of the County of Milwaukee, are municipal corporations organized under the laws of Wisconsin. Together they construct, operate, and maintain sewer facilities serving Milwaukee

---

[9] Federal common law and not the varying common law of the individual States is, we think, entitled and necessary to be recognized as a basis for dealing in uniform standard with the environmental rights of a State against improper impairment by sources outside its domain. The more would this seem to be imperative in the present era of growing concern on the part of a State about its ecological conditions and impairments of them. In the outside sources of such impairment, more conflicting disputes, increasing assertions and proliferating contentions would seem to be inevitable. Until the field has been made the subject of comprehensive legislation or authorized administrative standards, only a federal common law basis can provide an adequate means for dealing with such claims as alleged federal rights. And the logic and practicality of regarding such claims as being entitled to be asserted within the federal-question jurisdiction of § 1331(a) would seem to be self-evident." Texas v. Pankey, 441 F.2d 236, 241–242.

County, an area of some 420 square miles with a population of over one million people. The facilities consist of a series of sewer systems and two sewage treatment plants located on the shores of Lake Michigan 25 and 39 miles from the Illinois border, respectively. On occasion, particularly after a spell of wet weather, overflows occur in the system which result in the discharge of sewage directly into Lake Michigan or tributaries leading into Lake Michigan. The overflows occur at discrete discharge points throughout the system.

Respondent Illinois complains that these discharges, as well as the inadequate treatment of sewage at the two treatment plants, constitute a threat to the health of its citizens. Pathogens, disease-causing viruses and bacteria, are allegedly discharged into the lake with the overflows and inadequately treated sewage and then transported by lake currents to Illinois waters. Illinois also alleges that nutrients in the sewage accelerate the eutrophication, or aging, of the lake.

Illinois' claim was first brought to this Court when Illinois sought leave to file a complaint under our original jurisdiction. *Illinois v. Milwaukee, supra.* We declined to exercise original jurisdiction because the dispute was not between two States, and Illinois had available an action in federal district court. The Court reasoned that federal law applied to the dispute, one between a sovereign State and political subdivisions of another State concerning pollution of interstate waters, but that the various laws which Congress had enacted "touching interstate waters" were "not necessarily the only federal remedies available." *Id.*, at 101, 103. Illinois could appeal to federal common law to abate a public nuisance in interstate or navigable waters. The Court recognized, however, that:

> "It may happen that new federal laws and new federal regulations may in time pre-empt the field of federal common law of nuisance. But until that time comes to pass, federal courts will be empowered to appraise the equities of the suits alleging creation of a public nuisance by water pollution." *Id.*, at 107.

*   *   *

Five months later Congress, recognizing that "the Federal water pollution control program . . . has been inadequate in every vital aspect," passed the Federal Water Pollution Control Act Amendments of 1972. The Amendments established a new system of regulation under which it is illegal for anyone to discharge pollutants into the Nation's waters except pursuant to a permit. To the extent that the Environmental Protection Agency, charged with administering the Act, has promulgated regulations establishing specific effluent limitations, those limitations are incorporated as conditions of the permit. Permits are issued either by the EPA or a qualifying state agency. Petitioners operated their sewer systems and discharged effluent under permits issued by the Wisconsin Department of Natural Resources (DNR), which had duly qualified under § 402(b) of the Act, 33 U.S.C. § 1342(b), as a permit-granting agency under the superintendence of the EPA. See *EPA v. State Water Resources Control Board, supra,* at 208,. Petitioners did not fully comply with the requirements of the permits and, as contemplated by the Act, § 402(b)(7), 33 U.S.C. § 1342(b)(7), the state agency brought an enforcement action in state court. On May 25, 1977, the state court entered a judgment requiring discharges from the treatment plants to meet the effluent limitations set forth in the permits and establishing a detailed timetable for the completion of planning and additional construction to control sewage overflows.

Trial on Illinois' claim commenced on January 11, 1977. On July 29 the District Court rendered a decision finding that respondents had proved the existence of a nuisance under federal common law, both in the discharge of inadequately treated sewage from petitioners' plants and in the discharge of untreated sewage from sewer overflows. The court ordered petitioners to eliminate all overflows and to achieve specified effluent limitations on treated sewage. A judgment order entered on November 15 specified a construction timetable for the completion of detention facilities to eliminate overflows. Both the aspects of the decision concerning overflows and concerning effluent limitations, with the exception of the effluent limitation for phosphorus, went considerably beyond the terms of petitioners' previously issued permits and the enforcement order of the state court.

On appeal, the Court of Appeals for the Seventh Circuit affirmed in part and reversed in part. 599 F.2d 151. The court ruled that the 1972 Amendments had not pre-empted the federal common law of nuisance, but that "[i]n applying the federal common law of nuisance in a water pollution case, a court should not ignore the Act but should look to its policies and principles for guidance." *Id.*, at 164. The court reversed the District Court insofar as the effluent limitations it imposed on treated sewage were more stringent than those in the permits and applicable EPA regulations. The order to eliminate all overflows, however, and the construction schedule designed to achieve this goal, were upheld.

II

Federal courts, unlike state courts, are not general common-law courts and do not possess a general power to develop and apply their own rules of decision. *Erie R. Co. v. Tompkins*, 304 U.S. 64, 78 (1938). The enactment of a federal rule in an area of national concern, and the decision whether to displace state law in doing so, is generally made not by the federal judiciary, purposefully insulated from democratic pressures, but by the people through their elected representatives in Congress. *Erie* recognized as much in ruling that a federal court could not generally apply a federal rule of decision, despite the existence of jurisdiction, in the absence of an applicable Act of Congress.

When Congress has not spoken to a particular issue, however, and when there exists a "significant conflict between some federal policy or interest and the use of state law,"7 the Court has found it necessary, in a "few and restricted" instances, to develop federal common law. Nothing in this process suggests that courts are better suited to develop national policy in areas governed by federal common law than they are in other areas, or that the usual and important concerns of an appropriate division of functions between the Congress and the federal judiciary are inapplicable. We have always recognized that federal common law is "subject to the paramount authority of Congress." It is resorted to "[i]n absence of an applicable Act of Congress," and because the Court is compelled to consider federal questions "which cannot be answered from federal statutes alone." Federal common law is a "necessary expedient," and when Congress addresses a question previously governed by a decision rested on federal common law the need for such an unusual exercise of lawmaking by federal courts disappears. This was pointedly recognized in *Illinois v. Milwaukee* itself, 406 U.S., at 107 ("new federal laws and new federal regulations may in time pre-empt the field of federal common law of nuisance"), and in the lower court decision extensively relied upon in that case, *Texas v. Pankey*, 441 F.2d 236, 241 (10th Cir. 1971) (federal common law applies "[u]ntil the field has been made the subject of comprehensive legislation or authorized administrative standards").

*   *   *

Contrary to the suggestions of respondents, the appropriate analysis in determining if federal statutory law governs a question previously the subject of federal common law is not the same as that employed in deciding if federal law pre-empts state law. In considering the latter question " 'we start with the assumption that the historic police powers of the States were not to be superseded by the Federal Act unless that was the clear and manifest purpose of Congress.' " *Jones v. Rath Packing Co.*, 430 U.S. 519, 525 (1977) (quoting *Rice v. Santa Fe Elevator Corp.*, 331 U.S. 218, 230 (1947)). While we have not hesitated to find pre-emption of state law, whether express or implied, when Congress has so indicated, see *Ray v. Atlantic Richfield Co.*, 435 U.S. 151 (1978), or when enforcement of state regulations would impair "federal superintendence of the field," *Florida Lime & Avocado Growers, Inc. v. Paul*, 373 U.S. 132, 142 (1963), our analysis has included "due regard for the presuppositions of our embracing federal system, including the principle of diffusion of power not as a matter of doctrinaire localism but as a promoter of democracy." *San Diego Building Trades Council v. Garmon*, 359 U.S. 236, 243 (1959). Such concerns are not implicated in the same fashion when the question is whether federal statutory or federal common law governs, and accordingly the same sort of evidence of a clear and manifest purpose is not required. Indeed, as noted, in cases such as the present "we start with the assumption" that it is for Congress, not federal courts, to articulate the appropriate standards to be applied as a matter of federal law.

III

We conclude that, at least so far as concerns the claims of respondents, Congress has not left the formulation of appropriate federal standards to the courts through application of often vague and indeterminate nuisance concepts and maxims of equity jurisprudence, but rather has occupied the field through the establishment of a comprehensive regulatory program supervised by an expert administrative agency. The 1972 Amendments to the Federal Water Pollution Control Act were not merely another law "touching interstate waters" of the sort surveyed in *Illinois v. Milwaukee*, 406 U.S., at 101–103, and found inadequate to supplant federal common law. Rather, the Amendments were viewed by Congress as a "total restructuring" and "complete rewriting" of the existing water pollution legislation considered in that case. Congress' intent in enacting the Amendments was clearly to establish an all-encompassing program of water pollution regulation. *Every* point source discharge is prohibited unless covered by a permit, which directly subjects the discharger to the administrative apparatus established by Congress to achieve its goals. The "major purpose" of the Amendments was "to establish a *comprehensive* long-range policy for the elimination of water pollution." S.Rep.No.92-414, at 95, 2 Leg.Hist. 1511 (emphasis supplied). No Congressman's remarks on the legislation were complete without reference to the "comprehensive" nature of the Amendments. . . . The establishment of such a self-consciously comprehensive program by Congress, which certainly did not exist when *Illinois v. Milwaukee* was decided, strongly suggests that there is no room for courts to attempt to improve on that program with federal common law.

Turning to the particular claims involved in this case, the action of Congress in supplanting the federal common law is perhaps clearest when the question of effluent limitations for discharges from the two treatment plants is considered. The duly issued permits under which the city Commission discharges treated sewage from the Jones Island and South Shore treatment plants incorporate, as required by the Act, the specific effluent limitations established by EPA regulations pursuant to § 301 of the Act. There is thus no question that the problem of effluent limitations has been thoroughly addressed through the administrative scheme established by Congress, as contemplated by Congress. This being so there is no basis for a federal court to impose more stringent limitations than those imposed under the regulatory regime by reference to federal common law. . . . Federal courts lack authority to impose more stringent effluent limitations under federal common law than those imposed by the agency charged by Congress with administering this comprehensive scheme.

The overflows do not present a different case. They are point source discharges and, under the Act, are prohibited unless subject to a duly issued permit. As with the discharge of treated sewage, the overflows, through the permit procedure of the Act, are referred to expert administrative agencies for control. All three of the permits issued to petitioners explicitly address the problem of overflows. . . .

It is quite clear from the foregoing that the state agency duly authorized by the EPA to issue discharge permits under the Act has addressed the problem of overflows from petitioners' sewer system. The agency imposed the conditions it considered best suited to further the goals of the Act, and provided for detailed progress reports so that it could continually monitor the situation. Enforcement action considered appropriate by the state agency was brought, as contemplated by the Act, again specifically addressed to the overflow problem. There is no "interstice" here to be filled by federal common law: overflows are covered by the Act and have been addressed by the regulatory regime established by the Act. Although a federal court may disagree with the regulatory approach taken by the agency with responsibility for issuing permits under the Act, such disagreement alone is no basis for the creation of federal common law.

*   *   *

The invocation of federal common law by the District Court and the Court of Appeals in the face of congressional legislation supplanting it is peculiarly inappropriate in areas as complex as water pollution control.

*   *   *

Not only are the technical problems difficult — doubtless the reason Congress vested authority to administer the Act in administrative agencies possessing the necessary expertise — but the general area is particularly unsuited to the approach inevitable under a regime of federal common law. Congress criticized past approaches to water pollution control as being "sporadic" and "ad hoc," S. Rep. No. 92-414, p. 95 (1971), 2 Leg. Hist. 1511, apt characterizations of any judicial approach applying federal common law. . . .

It is also significant that Congress addressed in the 1972 Amendments one of the major concerns underlying the recognition of federal common law in *Illinois* v. *Milwaukee*. We were concerned in that case that Illinois did not have any forum in which to protect its interests unless federal common law were created. See 406 U.S., at 104, 107. In the 1972 Amendments Congress provided ample opportunity for a State affected by decisions of a neighboring State's permit-granting agency to seek redress. Under § 402 (b)(3), . . . a state permit-granting agency must ensure that any State whose waters may be affected by the issuance of a permit receives notice of the permit application and the opportunity to participate in a public hearing. Wisconsin law accordingly guarantees such notice and hearing. Respondents received notice of each of the permits involved here, and public hearings were held, but they did not participate in them in any way. Section 402 (b)(5) . . . provides that state permit-granting agencies must ensure that affected States have an opportunity to submit written recommendations concerning the permit applications to the issuing State and the EPA, and both the affected State and the EPA must receive notice and a statement of reasons if any part of the recommendations of the affected State are not accepted. Again respondents did not avail themselves of this statutory opportunity. Under § 402 (d)(2)(A), . . . the EPA may veto any permit issued by a State when waters of another State may be affected. Respondents did not request such action. Under § 402 (d)(4) of the Act, . . . added in 1977, the EPA itself may issue permits if a stalemate between an issuing and objecting State develops. The basic grievance of respondents is that the permits issued to petitioners pursuant to the Act do not impose stringent enough controls on petitioners' discharges. The statutory scheme established by Congress provides a forum for the pursuit of such claims before expert agencies by means of the permit-granting process. It would be quite inconsistent with this scheme if federal courts were in effect to "write their own ticket" under the guise of federal common law after permits have already been issued and permittees have been planning and operating in reliance on them.

QUESTIONS AND DISCUSSION

1. In early public nuisance litigation, the Supreme Court recognized the existence of federal common law to address interstate pollution. Georgia v. Tennessee Copper, 206 U.S. 230 (1907). *Milwaukee I* also acknowledges federal common law specifically with respect to interstate water pollution. It did so even in light of the Federal Water Pollution Control Act (FWPCA), which had existed as federal law since 1948. In its earlier incarnations, the FWPCA provided states financial incentives to reduce their water pollution and protect water quality. What elements of the 1972 amendments to the Clean Water Act were critical for convincing the Supreme Court that, with respect to interstate water pollution, federal common law was preempted?

2. Shortly after it decided *Milwaukee II*, the Supreme Court issued yet another decision regarding the preemptive scope of the Clean Water Act as it applies to common law actions, in which it broadly stated, "the federal common law of nuisance in the area of water pollution is entirely preempted by the more comprehensive scope of the [Clean Water Act]." Middlesex County Sewerage Auth. v. Nat'l Sea Clammers Ass'n, 453 U.S. 1, 22 (1981). Does this language suggest that the Clean Air Act, which is also a comprehensive federal statute, fully occupies the field of air pollution control and thus preempts public nuisance claims regarding climate change? Does it matter that EPA has not regulated carbon dioxide under the Clean Air Act? *See* Chapter 13 (describing the application of the Clean Air Act to climate change).

2.   *Is State Common Law Preempted?*

Whether state common law claims to abate climate change are preempted by a federal statute such as the Clean Air Act will be subject to the same type of analysis that applies to preemption of federal common law (e.g., express, field, or conflict preemption). However, the Supreme Court's analysis of preemption of state common law claims has evolved over time. The Court's decision in *Milwaukee I, supra*, at 107, n.9 appeared to suggest that federal common law would, as a matter of course, apply to all interstate pollution disputes: "Federal common law and not the varying common law of the individual States is, we think, entitled and necessary to be recognized as a basis for dealing in uniform standard with the environmental rights of a State against improper impairment by sources outside its domain." Illinois v. Milwaukee, 406 U.S. 91, 107, n.9 (1972) (quoting Texas v. Pankey, 441 F.2d 236, 241–242).

Later, however, in *Milwaukee II*, the Supreme Court declared that the analysis "start[s] with the assumption that the historic police powers of the States were not superceded" by federal law. It thus may be more willing to find that a federal law preempts federal common law. *See* Milwaukee v. Illinois, 451 U.S. 304, 317 (1981) (excerpted above). Four years later, the Court appeared to recognize the ongoing viability of state common law to address pollution.

INTERNATIONAL PAPER CO. v. OUELLETTE
479 U.S. 481; 107 S. Ct. 805; 93 L. Ed. 2d 883 (1987)

JUSTICE POWELL delivered the opinion of the Court.

This case involves the pre-emptive scope of the Clean Water Act, 86 Stat. 816, as amended, 33 U.S.C. § 1251 *et seq.* (CWA or Act). The question presented is whether the Act pre-empts a common-law nuisance suit filed in a Vermont court under Vermont law, when the source of the alleged injury is located in New York.

I

Lake Champlain forms part of the border between the States of New York and Vermont. Petitioner International Paper Company (IPC) operates a pulp and paper mill on the New York side of the lake. In the course of its business, IPC discharges a variety of effluents into the lake through a diffusion pipe. The pipe runs from the mill through the water toward Vermont, ending a short distance before the state boundary line that divides the lake.

Respondents are a group of property owners who reside or lease land on the Vermont shore. In 1978 the owners filed a class action suit against IPC, claiming, *inter alia*, that the discharge of effluents constituted a "continuing nuisance" under Vermont common law. Respondents alleged that the pollutants made the water "foul, unhealthy, smelly, and . . . unfit for recreational use," thereby diminishing the value of their property. The owners asked for $20 million in compensatory damages, $100 million in punitive damages, and injunctive relief that would require IPC to restructure part of its water treatment system. The action was filed in State Superior Court, and then later removed to Federal District Court for the District of Vermont.

*   *   *

II

[W]e turn to the question presented: whether the Act pre-empts Vermont common law to the extent that law may impose liability on a New York point source. We begin the analysis by noting that it is not necessary for a federal statute to provide explicitly that particular state laws are pre-empted. Although courts should not lightly infer pre-emption, it may be presumed when the federal legislation is "sufficiently comprehensive to make reasonable the inference that Congress 'left no room' for supplementary state regulation." In addition to express or implied pre-emption, a state law also is invalid to the extent that it "actually conflicts with a . . . federal statute." Such a conflict will be found when the state law " 'stands as an obstacle to the accomplishment and execution of the full purposes and objectives of Congress.' "

A

As we noted in *Milwaukee II*, Congress intended the 1972 Act amendments to "establish an all-encompassing program of water pollution regulation." 451 U.S., at 318. We observed that congressional "views on the comprehensive nature of the legislation were practically universal." *Id.*, at 318, n. 12. An examination of the amendments amply supports these views. The Act applies to all point sources and virtually all bodies of water, and it sets forth the procedures for obtaining a permit in great detail. The CWA also provides its own remedies, including civil and criminal fines for permit violations, and "citizen suits" that allow individuals (including those from affected States) to sue for injunction to enforce the statute. In light of this pervasive regulation and the fact that the control of interstate pollution is primarily a matter of federal law, *Milwaukee I*, 406 U.S., at 107, it is clear that the only state suits that remain available are those specifically preserved by the Act.

Although Congress intended to dominate the field of pollution regulation, the saving clause negates the inference that Congress "left no room" for state causes of action. Respondents read the language of the saving clause broadly to preserve both a State's right to regulate its waters, 33 U.S.C. § 1370, and an injured party's right to seek relief under "any statute *or common law*," § 1365(e) (emphasis added). They claim that this language and selected portions of the legislative history compel the inference that ongress intended to preserve the right to bring suit under the law of any affected State. We cannot accept this reading of the Act.

*   *   *

Given that the Act itself does not speak directly to the issue, the Court must be guided by the goals and policies of the Act in determining whether it in fact pre-empts an action based on the law of an affected State. Cf. *City of Rome v. United States*, 446 U.S. 156, 199 (1980) (POWELL, J., dissenting) ("We resort to legislative materials only when the congressional mandate is unclear on its face"). After examining the CWA as a whole, its purposes and its history, we are convinced that if affected States were allowed to impose separate discharge standards on a single point source, the inevitable result would be a serious interference with the achievement of the "full purposes and objectives of Congress." See *Hillsborough County v. Automated Medical Laboratories, Inc., supra*, 471 U.S. at 713. Because we do not believe Congress intended to undermine this carefully drawn statute through a general saving clause, we conclude that the CWA precludes a court from applying the law of an affected State against an out-of-state source.

B

In determining whether Vermont nuisance law "stands as an obstacle" to the full implementation of the CWA, it is not enough to say that the ultimate goal of both federal and state law is to eliminate water pollution. A state law also is pre-empted if it interferes with the methods by which the federal statute was designed to reach this goal. . . . In this case the application of Vermont law against IPC would allow respondents to circumvent the NPDES permit system, thereby upsetting the balance of public and private interests so carefully addressed by the Act.

By establishing a permit system for effluent discharges, Congress implicitly has recognized that the goal of the CWA — elimination of water pollution — cannot be achieved immediately, and that it cannot be realized without incurring costs. The EPA Administrator issues permits according to established effluent standards and water quality standards, that in turn are based upon available technology, 33 U.S.C. § 1314, and competing public and industrial uses, § 1312(a). The Administrator must consider the impact of the discharges on the waterway, the types of effluents, and the schedule for compliance, each of which may vary widely among sources. If a State elects to impose its own standards, it also must consider the technological feasibility of more stringent controls. Given the nature of these complex decisions, it is not surprising that the Act limits the right to administer the permit system to the EPA and the source States. See § 1342(b).

An interpretation of the saving clause that preserved actions brought under an affected State's law would disrupt this balance of interests. * * *

Application of an affected State's law to an out-of-state source also would undermine the important goals of efficiency and predictability in the permit system.

C

Our conclusion that Vermont nuisance law is inapplicable to a New York point source does not leave respondents without a remedy. The CWA precludes only those suits that may require standards of effluent control that are incompatible with those established by the procedures set forth in the Act. The saving clause specifically preserves other state actions, and therefore nothing in the Act bars aggrieved individuals from bringing a nuisance claim pursuant to the law of the *source* State. By its terms the CWA allows States such as New York to impose higher standards on their own point sources, and in Milwaukee II we recognized that this authority may include the right to impose higher common-law as well as higher statutory restrictions. 451 U.S., at 328 (suggesting that "States may adopt more stringent limitations . . . through state nuisance law, and apply them to in-state dischargers".

QUESTIONS AND DISCUSSION

1. The Supreme Court's underlying rationale in *Ouellette* for preempting Vermont common law claims is concern for imposing a variety of out-of-state standards on a single point source. Would the success by private plaintiffs on their nuisance claim result in standards being imposed? Wouldn't it be possible for the court to impose, in the words of the District Court, "compensatory damage awards and other equitable relief for injuries caused . . . [that] merely supplements the standards and limitations imposed by the Act." Ouellette v. International Paper Co., 602 F. Supp. 264, 271 (D.Vt. 1985). In fact, Vermont and other plaintiffs sought damages and an injunction ordering relocation of the plant's water intake system closer to the source of its waste discharge system. Does that change your opinion of whether Vermont state law should be preempted? Despite losing their chance to use Vermont common law, the plaintiffs used New York common law to reach a settlement for $5 million.

2. After *Ouellette* and *Milwaukee II*, what do you think is the status of federal and state common law claims for air pollution? In 1972, in a suit brought by several states against the big 4 auto manufacturers for conspiring to restrain the development of vehicle pollution controls, the Supreme Court issued a decision that discussed, in dicta, the preemptive nature of the Clean Air Act:

> Air pollution is, of course, one of the most notorious types of public nuisance in modern experience. Congress has not, however, found a uniform, nationwide solution to all aspects of this problem and, indeed, has declared "that the prevention and control of air pollution at its source is the primary responsibility of States and local government." 81 Stat. 485, 42 U.S.C. § 1857(a)(3). To be sure, Congress has largely pre-empted the field

with regard to "emissions from new motor vehicles," 42 U.S.C. § 1857f-6a(a); 31 Fed.Reg. 5170 (1966); and motor vehicle fuels and fuel additives, 84 Stat. 1699, 42 U.S.C. § 1857f-6c(c)(4). It has also pre-empted the field so far as emissions from airplanes are concerned, 42 U.S.C. §§ 1857f-9 to 1857f-12. So far as factories, incinerators, and other stationary devices are implicated, the States have broad control to an extent not necessary to relate here. But in certain instances, as, for example, where federal primary and secondary ambient air quality standards have been established, 42 U.S.C. §§ 1857c-4 and 1857c-5, or where "hazardous air pollutant(s)" have been defined, 42 U.S.C. § 1857c-7, there may be federal pre-emption. See 42 U.S.C. § 1857c-8 et seq. Moreover, geophysical characteristics which define local and regional airsheds are often significant considerations in determining the steps necessary to abate air pollution. Thus, measures which might be adequate to deal with pollution in a city such as San Francisco, might be grossly inadequate in a city such as Phoenix, where geographical and meteorological conditions trap aerosols and particulates.

Washington v. General Motors Corporation, 406 U.S. 109 (1972).

In 1981, the Second Circuit refused to determine whether the Clean Air Act preempted common law claims. It noted, however, that while the Clean Water Act regulates every point source of water pollution, the Clean Air Act requires states and the EPA to regulate only those sources that threaten national ambient air quality standards (NAAQS). *New England Legal Foundation v. Costle*, 666 F.2d 30, 32 n.2 (2d Cir. 1981). At that time, the Clean Air Act required the states to develop NAAQS for certain pollutants and charged EPA with setting new source performance standards for new polluting entities, hazardous air pollutants, and national emissions for automobiles, but it did not comprehensively address national air pollution through a permitting program similar to the Clean Water Act's National Pollutant Discharge Elimination System program. Since that ruling, however, Congress amended the Clean Air Act to require operating permits for certain major sources of air pollution. 42 U.S.C. § 7661. Does this progression appear similar to the Clean Water Act and the decisions in *Milwaukee I* and *Milwaukee II*? *See, e.g.*, Robert V. Percival, *The Clean Water Act and the Demise of the Federal Common Law of Interstate Nuisance*, 55 ALA. L. REV. 717, 768 (2004) (arguing that the Clean Air Act is widely assumed to preempt federal common law in disputes over transboundary air pollution, while state common law nuisance actions remain viable so long as the law of the source state is applied). Consider the following analysis:

ANDREW JACKSON HEIMERT, KEEPING PIGS OUT OF PARLORS: USING NUISANCE LAW TO AFFECT THE LOCATION OF POLLUTION
27 ENVTL. L. 403, 473–475 (1997)[*]

The Supreme Court has yet to address whether the CAA [Clean Air Act] preempts federal or state common law. It would, however, likely apply much of the reasoning from Milwaukee II and Ouellette. The greatest similarity between the two Acts is the technology requirements. Both Acts stipulate that sources use some prescribed level of pollution-reduction equipment as the primary means of achieving the Acts' goal. If the justification for preemption relies on the expert setting of technology by EPA, then the Court should reach the same result for the

CAA as it did for the CWA. The differences between the Acts are unlikely to alter the result. For example, the CWA more comprehensively covers sources than does the CAA. For covered sources, however, preemption justifications are just as strong under each Act — only noncovered sources present a problem. The Acts also set ambient levels differently. The CWA directs states to determine uses for bodies of water, which allows states to determine how much pollution should be allowed in any particular water. In contrast, the CAA establishes national ambient levels for air pollution, although these may be made more strict by states. States, therefore, must take additional action to lower ambient level requirements under the CAA. This probably makes preemption a more troubling proposition for the CAA, as legislative inertia may lead states not to reconsider ambient standards, whereas the CWA requires states to think about each body of water. Overall, however, the Acts' minor differences are not likely to lead the court to come to a different conclusion about the preemptive effect of the CAA than it did for the effect of the CWA.

One circuit has partially addressed the preemption issue, and another considered it but found it unnecessary to decide. In New England Legal Foundation v. Costle [666 F.2d 30 (2d Cir. 1981)], a New York utility sought a variance from New York's state implementation plan (SIP) in order to use high sulfur coal in its plant. EPA granted the variance. A Connecticut environmental group, fearing greater amounts of pollution coming across Long Island Sound, sought an injunction through federal nuisance law. The Second Circuit, relying on Milwaukee II, found that EPA's administrative approval of the coal countenanced preemption of the federal common law claim; otherwise the actions spawned would be counterproductive. The court did not decide whether the CAA preempted all nuisance law, or just if the administrative approval had created a defense.

The Ninth Circuit also considered the issue of federal common-law nuisance for air pollution in National Audubon Society v. Department of Water [869 F.2d 1196 (9th Cir. 1989)]. The Society brought a nuisance action to restrain California's Water Department from undertaking actions that would create substantial particulate matter pollution. Because the air pollution would potentially travel interstate, the Society argued federal common law should apply. The Court of Appeals rejected this theory because the controversy did not involve one state seeking to challenge pollution in another state. Having found federal common law inapplicable, the court declined to consider the preemptive effect of the CAA on federal common law.

In a vigorous dissent, Judge Reinhardt argued that because clean air is an inherently federal interest, federal common law should apply. He would apply federal common law regardless of the plaintiff's residence — the nature of the pollution determines the applicable common law. Reinhardt then considered whether the CAA preempted the federal common law he would apply. He argued that because the CAA "does not control emissions from every source, but only from those sources that are found to threaten the air quality standards promulgated by the EPA," there should be no preemption. Reinhardt likened the CAA regime to that under the pre-1972 FWPCA, which concentrated primarily on ambient standards and less on point-source emissions regulation. Because federal common law survived that regime, he reasoned that it should under the CAA as well.

The regime that the Supreme Court likely would implement would prohibit states from applying their common law to air pollution sources emitting from out of state. A downwind plaintiff, therefore, has only two options. One is to show that the additional emissions will contribute significantly to nonattainment or that it will use up the PSD increment. Alternatively, a downwind plaintiff may turn to the nuisance law of the source state, which may require entry into a hostile forum. This option, too, may not carry great efficacy if that state has low nuisance standards. Furthermore, it may not provide the optimal deterrent.

---

3. In *Ouellette*, the plaintiffs were told that they could bring public nuisance claims under the laws of the source's state. In *Connecticut v. AEP*, all of the defendant power plants were located in the Midwest; only one power plant was located in one of the plaintiff states. Although that case was dismissed on political question grounds, what might be the implications of this dynamic for preemption claims in the climate change context?

4. The Supreme Court's ruling in *Massachusetts v. EPA* may have actually clouded the issue of preemption. Had the Court ruled that the Clean Air Act does not mandate or allow the EPA to regulate carbon dioxide, then there should be no conflict preemption of the plaintiffs' nuisance claims. By ruling that carbon dioxide is a pollutant and that EPA has the authority to regulate it, if it so chooses, the Court strengthens the claims for preemption. Even if EPA has not regulated carbon dioxide, could the court find that the Clean Air Act's regulatory scheme is "so pervasive" or "so dominant" that it occupies the entire field of air pollution and thus preempts nuisance claims aimed at carbon dioxide emissions?

5. Probably the most important question of preemption in the climate change context is one that still cannot be analyzed — the preemptive effect of new comprehensive climate change legislation. Once such legislation is passed, state common law tort claims could be preempted. If you were an industry lobbyist working on new climate legislation, what would you want included in the legislation to ensure all state tort cases would be preempted? What if you represented states interested in preserving common law claims?

V. FUTURE IMPLICATIONS OF TORT LITIGATION

The filing of tort-based climate change cases has prompted considerable debate over whether an issue as complex and difficult as climate change is really appropriate for the courts. Were the state attorneys general, in particular, just grandstanding or using the courts to promote a political agenda? Indeed, this is partly the issue raised successfully by the defendants in invoking the political question doctrine.

Regardless of the motives of the state attorneys general, several things are certainly clear. Climate-based litigation does play a political role — it is motivated at least in part to build pressure for more sweeping changes. Yet, the courts are not going to solve climate change, even if the plaintiffs prevail. And it is likely going to be years before any tort-based case prevails, if one ever does. If these cases are intended partly to move the climate debate, is their "success" necessarily dependent on winning? What value, if any, do cases like this have in the climate change policy debate? In thinking about this question, consider the following essay on the value of climate change litigation strategies generally:

DAVID HUNTER, THE IMPLICATIONS OF CLIMATE CHANGE LITIGATION FOR INTERNATIONAL ENVIRONMENTAL LAW-MAKING

in ADJUDICATING CLIMATE CONTROL: SUB-NATIONAL, NATIONAL AND SUPRA-NATIONAL APPROACHES (Hari Osofsky & W. Burns eds, forthcoming Cambridge Press 2009)*

The primary focus here is on the implications of the climate litigation strategies simply by virtue of their having been filed. In fact, the debate over whether specific theories will prevail or what remedies can be fashioned in a specific case misses much of the significance of these litigation strategies. Just the acts of preparing, announcing, filing, advocating and forcing a response have significant impacts — and of course some will prevail. * * *

1. The Focus on Victims

Indeed, climate advocates' focus on specific injuries in specific situations has far-reaching implications for climate policy more generally. In the Kyoto negotiations or in previous national climate policy debates, the focus has primarily been on climate change's global impacts: average temperature increases, average sea level rise, average changes in precipitation. With the rise of climate litigation strategies, however, the focus necessarily shifts to the specific injuries being asserted by the plaintiffs or claimants: the impacts on New England's ski industry, California's coastline, the life and culture of the Inuit, the survival of polar bears or penguins, or the grandeur of Mount Everest or Glacier National Park. * * *

This focus on specific injuries is critical for building political support; such cases link climate change with the lives of ordinary people. Reports of a global increase in temperature of 1° or even 5° have little meaning to most people. The impact is much more understandable when an Inuit expresses implications of climate change for their lives, when the glaciers of Nepal are melting, or when descriptions of drowning or cannibalistic polar bears are reported on the news. The Inuit human rights petition, for example, provides thirty-five pages on impacts of climate change on their life and culture. The petition details changes in Arctic ice conditions and the resulting dangers for Inuit travel, the reduction in materials (thick ice) for building traditional igloos, and the deterioration of wildlife harvests because of declining populations of caribou, seals, polar bears and other animals. In short, the petition tells a story about the impacts of climate change in human terms far removed from the antiseptic discussion of GHG concentrations or global mean temperatures that have traditionally predominated international climate negotiations.

The story-telling quality of "cases" thus makes climate change more tangible and more immediate, which significantly changes the tone of the climate debate. If real victims — such as islanders or the Inuit — are in a room pressing their stories, it is harder for others to bluster about how climate change is a hoax or is unimportant because some regions may benefit from warming or will be able to adapt relatively easily. At the very least, addressing climate change takes on a renewed urgency when one moves from the abstraction of sea level rise, for example, to questions of how to treat climate refugees from South Pacific islands or how to shore up the eroding California coastline. A focus on victims increases the saliency of questions about compensation and adaptation to climate change, and the urgency of mitigating climate change to avoid even worse impacts in the future.

This builds momentum at both the national and international levels for stronger climate policy making.

2. Implications for Climate Policy

Climate litigation's focus on victims and on specific impacts has implications for how we use climate science and on what climate science is conducted. Every litigation strategy requires the collection, synthesis, and presentation of climate science in support of its claims. This process highlights and makes more accessible to a wider audience the expanding research and analysis on specific local and regional climate impacts.

This is proven particularly true of the reports issued by the Intergovernmental Panel on Climate Change (IPCC), which have been cited as the scientific basis by most of the climate plaintiffs or petitioners. The IPCC reports attract particular attention because they compile and summarize the international consensus on climate science at a specific point in time. Moreover, the IPCC's practice of explicitly bounding its views of the likelihood of certain scientific conclusions in terms of numeric probabilities not only assists international policymakers at the UNFCCC, but also offers lawyers scientific conclusions that are useful in explaining and meeting the standards for causation. This reliance on the IPCC's reports presents a two-way validation: the IPCC's prestige and international status provides a convenient and effective affirmation of the claimant's factual allegations (at least with respect to global climate trends) and, at the same time, use of the IPCC . . . adds legitimacy and prestige to the IPCC and its reports. [The IPCC won the the Nobel Peace Prize after publication of the Fourth Assessment, in part because of the way in which the report swept through the world as the authoritative statement on climate science.] * * *

More generally, climate litigation efforts may provide an incentive to some scientists to prioritize certain questions that they might otherwise ignore. Questions of attribution, for example, become particularly relevant for litigation strategies aimed at securing compensation for those affected or for driving corrective action by identifying those responsible. The science of attribution is gaining ground; one recent study, for example, found that the human contribution to the 2003 European heat wave increased the potential of risk of such weather from 4 to 10 times. Approximately 22,000 to 35,000 people died from heat-related deaths, 75% of whom would have been likely to survive for more than a year without such heat. Such studies will be critical in shaping future climate litigation strategies.

Finally, climate litigation is shaping the tone of the debate over climate science. In journalistic or political approaches to climate, the views of climate skeptics were previously given equal weight to the broad consensus views regarding science. In climate litigation forums, however, such skeptics may be asked to submit affidavits or even face cross-examination of their views. This ground-truthing of climate science may screen out and discredit those fringe scientists whose positions can not withstand the scrutiny that comes from adversarial proceedings, particularly in domestic courts. To be sure, some opinions questioning the adequacy of climate science for judicial review have and will occur, but recent cases, including the U.S. Supreme Court decision in *Massachusetts v. EPA*, are tending to support and recognize the general scientific consensus regarding climate change. When courts and other highly credible institutions validate the basic science of climate change, the general public's perception of the climate debate shifts from *whether* climate change is occurring to what the appropriate remedies should be. For the public, Judicial decisions can move the debate from an esoteric one among scientists to an issue *decided* by impartial judges whose job it is to resolve such matters.

Implications for the Climate Negotiations

Climate change litigation strategies have been at least partly a response to the perceived weakness of the international climate regime. Initially, many of the litigation strategies were designed as an indirect response to the decisions by Australia and the United States to withdraw from the Kyoto Protocol. More recently, a Canadian environmental group filed a lawsuit asking the courts to declare Canada in noncompliance (or imminent noncompliance) with the UNFCCC and Kyoto Protocol. [Application, Friends of the Earth v. Her Majesty the Queen, Minister of the Environment & Minister of Health, No. T-914-07 (Federal Court Ottawa, May 28, 2007) (application for judicial review of the Canadian government's actions, emitting greenhouse gases, in violation of sect. 166 of the Canadian Environmental Protection Act, the UNFCCC and the Kyoto Protocol).] . . . According to the application, the Government of Canada's own reports estimate that its actual emissions will be nearly 40% higher than that which is allowed under the Kyoto Protocol. Although this is the first lawsuit in the world aimed specifically at enhancing compliance with the international climate regime, many of the other climate litigation strategies have also been designed at least in part to increase the political will for stronger international climate change policy.

The litigation efforts thus should not be seen in isolation from the negotiations. . . . Many of the principle players in climate litigation are also active in international negotiating and policy-making processes. In the "epistemic community" that has emerged around climate negotiations, climate advocates find both a ready audience for spreading the news of litigation and for seeking the same goals that they are seeking through the litigation. The CoP/MoP community is thus a critical venue for developing strategies, identifying partners, reaching out to the press, building legitimacy and credibility for the litigation, and developing factual experts that can help in the litigation. * * *

High profile climate litigation strategies in the United States have also helped to undermine the U.S. opposition to the Kyoto Protocol, including particularly its efforts to derail the launch of negotiations for the second reporting period under Kyoto. At the 2005 CoP/MoP in Montreal, the U.S. sought to enlist Australia, China and India in a united front against the European push for negotiations of future commitments under the Kyoto Protocol. The U.S. strategy failed in part because of the multiplicity of U.S. voices at the negotiations (including local government officials, former President Bill Clinton, and several Senators) that argued action was occurring in the United States, that the Administration was isolated, and that the United States would likely engage in future international negotiations after the next President took office. The presence of high profile alternative U.S. voices and actions thus emboldened negotiators to set out a future negotiation schedule, more confident that the United States would eventually come back to the table. * * *

The focus on remedies that is inherent to climate litigation may influence future debates at the UNFCCC over adaptation. Certainly, the portrayal of specific harm to victims *today*, as opposed to general impacts tomorrow, is likely to force climate negotiators and the UNFCCC secretariat to focus on adaptation and compensation sooner than it otherwise would. This could increase funding available under the regime to respond to the needs of victims. In the most extreme scenarios, the threat of civil liability could conceivably lead industry and others to promote a liability regime under the UNFCCC that would both clarify the rules of liability and essentially cap private sector liability — much as has been done with environmental damage from nuclear facilities and oil spills.

The relationship between remedies in climate litigation and in the climate regime goes both ways. Steps identified and supported by the UNFCCC may help shape remedies in climate litigation, which could remove a major obstacle for successful climate advocacy. Some analysts, for example, have already proposed that remedies in climate litigation should include the requirement to buy carbon offsets endorsed in the climate regime. [*See Mandatory CO₂ Credit Purchases Eyed as Remedy in Climate Change Suits*, INSIDE EPA.COM (Nov. 24, 2006), *available at* http://www.law.arizona.edu/news/Press/Engel112706-2.pdf (quoting proposal from Professor Kirsten Engels).] The climate regime may also be the appropriate forum for a broader remedial response for those who are victims of climate change. If the number of climate refugees increases, for example from sea level rise, a more comprehensive UN remedial response may be necessary and would likely come under the auspices of the UNFCCC. Viewed in this light, the climate change litigation strategies are clearly supportive of and a potential catalyst for a stronger and more comprehensive UNFCCC regime.

QUESTIONS AND DISCUSSION

1.   The motivation of the private plaintiffs in *Kivalina* and *Comer* are arguably less political than the cases brought by state attorneys general. The village of Kivalina primarily seeks compensation to pay for their relocation. Can you see the linkage between their claims and the policy issues inherent in adaptation, discussed in Chapter 3? Why should the villagers in *Kivalina* or the property owners in *Comer* shoulder such a disproportionate amount of the climate change burden?

2.   It is hard to determine the success of the state cases. Obviously, the cases have been dismissed and are pending trial, but that may not be the end of the story. Matt Pawa, a lawyer for plaintiffs in a companion case to *Connecticut* notes that shortly after the lawsuit was filed, one of the defendants, Cinergy Corp., subsequently announced its support for regulation of carbon dioxide emissions, and another, American Electric Power Co., announced it would build a clean coal plant that can capture and sequester carbon dioxide emissions. Another defendant, Xcel Energy, recently joined the Plains CO₂ Reduction Partnership to "further investigate various strategies to reduce carbon dioxide emissions into the atmosphere." *See* Matthew F. Pawa & Benjamin A. Krass, *Global Warming as a Public Nuisance: Connecticut v. American Electric Power*, 16 FORDHAM ENVTL. L. REV. 407 (2005). Do you think the tort litigation influenced their decisions?

3.   Climate litigation strategies not only rely on emerging science, but also will influence the development of climate science both directly and indirectly. Some domestic climate cases in several countries have been filed with the goal of improving the assessment of climate impacts and the use of climate science. In *Massachusetts v. EPA*, the U.S. Supreme Court required the government to make a reasoned judgment on whether emissions of carbon dioxide are endangering public health and welfare as an initial step in determining whether to regulate carbon dioxide as an air pollutant under the Clean Air Act. *Massachusetts v. EPA*, 127 S. Ct. at 1462–63. At the project level, cases in the United States, Germany, and Australia have sought (sometimes successfully) to require under national law the consideration of climate impacts in project finance or permitting. *See, e.g., Friends of the Earth v. Mosbacher*, No. C02-4106 JSW, 2007 WL 962955 (N.D. Cal. Mar. 30, 2007) (order denying plaintiffs' motion for summary judgment and granting in part and denying in part defendants' motion for summary judgment); *Friends of the Earth v. Watson*, No. C02-4106 JSW, 2005 WL 2035596 (N.D. Cal. Aug. 23, 2005) (order denying defendants' motion for summary judgement); *Bund & German-watch v. German Federal Ministry of Economics and Labour [BMWA]*, Beschluss, Verwaltungsgericht [VG Berlin] [Local Administrative Court] Jan. 10, 2006, VG 10

A 215.04 (2006), *translated at* http://www.climatelaw.org/media/Germany/ de.export.decision.eng.doc. (order entering settlement with legal opinion); *Wildlife Preservation Soc. of Queensland Proserpine/Whitsunday Branch v. Ministry for Environment & Heritage*, (2006) FCA 736 (upholding decisions by the Australian environment ministry to license two coal mines, despite their failure to consider climate impacts on natural heritage sites). In Australia, for example, greenhouse gas emissions and resulting climate impacts must be assessed in coal mining and power plant operations, which presumably increase the scientific basis for decision-making in those sectors. Australian Conservation Foundation v. Minister for Planning, Administrative Decision, (2004) VCAT 2029 (holding that the Australian Planning and Environment Act requires consideration of greenhouse gas emissions and resulting climate impact in licensing coal mining and power plant operations); For information on climate-related cases brought in Australia, see the website of the Australian Climate Justice Program, *available at* http://www.cana.net.au/ ACJP/ (last visited at May 28, 2007). A recent lawsuit in the United States compelled the United States to complete a National Assessment of climate impacts, which was required by Congress to be completed by 2004. Center for Biological Diversity v. Brennan, 2007 WL 2408901, No. C06-7061 (N.D. Cal., Aug. 21, 2007). The assessment was finally released in the Spring of 2008, forcing a reluctant Bush Administration to release a scientific document that basically confirms the substantial current and future impacts of climate change.

Chapter 17

STATE AND LOCAL RESPONSES TO CLIMATE CHANGE

I.   INTRODUCTION

Many state and local governments in the United States have responded to the lack of a comprehensive national climate change law by adopting regional, statewide, and local measures to reduce greenhouse gas emissions. These measures vary in their approaches to regulation, which include incentive-based programs promoting voluntary energy conservation efforts, market-based emissions trading programs, and direct regulatory controls mandating reductions in greenhouse gas emissions. On a regional level, emissions trading programs dominate the legal landscape. State and local actions, in contrast, typically employ more specific directives, such as renewable portfolio standards, which require utilities to obtain electricity from renewable sources; emissions limitations; and broad "climate action plans," which establish statewide goals for climate change mitigation and adaptation. As of June 2008, all states had developed at least some sort of climate change measures, nearly half of the states had entered into regional agreements to reduce greenhouse gases, and several states had adopted emissions reduction targets similar to the "targets and timetables" under the Kyoto Protocol.

State and local action to address climate change began in fits and starts in the 1980s. A few states, such as New Jersey, developed policies in the late 1980s aimed at improving energy and fuel efficiency and passed laws signaling the states' concern regarding climate change. These initial measures were followed in the mid-1990s by several states working to inventory their greenhouse gas emissions and to develop action plans to reduce their emissions levels. By the late 1990s, some states had begun in earnest to develop climate change policies. During the same period, several other states enacted legislation criticizing the Kyoto Protocol and prohibiting state agencies from taking any action to reduce greenhouse gas emissions. This backlash, however, was short-lived, and the years between January 2000 and June 2008 have witnessed a remarkable proliferation of state and local measures aimed at mitigating climate change. *See* BARRY C. RABE, GREENHOUSE AND STATEHOUSE: THE EVOLVING STATE GOVERNMENT ROLE IN CLIMATE CHANGE (Pew Center on Global Climate Change, Nov. 2002).

These local actions raise several legal and practical questions. On a practical level, perhaps the dominant question is what benefits these varying actions can yield, in light of the global nature of climate change. On the one hand, due to the significant amount of greenhouse gases emitted by each state, their efforts to reduce emissions would appear to have a significant global effect. Texas, the United States' largest emitting state, releases more carbon dioxide annually than Germany, which ranks 7th in terms of the world's largest national carbon dioxide emitters. *See* World Resources Institute, Climate Analysis Indicators Tool (2003), *available at* http://cait.wri.org. From this lens, it would appear that state action to mitigate climate change could yield important global benefits.

On the other hand, actions taken by state and local governments seem likely to fall to the "Tragedy of the Commons," because any climate change benefits of local actions will only be subsumed by global emissions:

> As some commentators note . . . there is an apparent illogic in the flurry of sub-federal activity directed at climate change. When viewed through the lens of traditional commons analysis, it would seem that rational sub-federal actors should eschew unilateral (or even regional) actions to reduce their GHG emissions, given that the atmosphere is a true global commons wherein GHG emissions from one part of the world are entirely fungible with emissions from any other part of the world. Viewed in this light, to the extent that sub-federal GHG reductions actually result in climatic benefits, any such benefits would be lost through such market inefficiencies as free-riding, hold-outs, leakage, and even insouciance. Moreover, regardless of these inefficiencies, the impact of GHG reductions by sub-federal actors on global temperature will necessarily be statistically inconsequential — for all their efforts, the benefits such actors will accrue in terms of avoided global warming will, in practical terms, be nonexistent.

Kevin L. Doran, *U.S. Sub-Federal Climate Change Initiatives: An Irrational Means to a Rational End?*, 26 VA. ENVTL. L.J. 189, 191–93 (2008). To be sure, such concerns exist on the international level as well, since any emissions reductions obtained by a developed country party to the Kyoto Protocol may be readily offset by increased emissions from developing countries. Indeed, Germany and Texas (with roughly equivalent emissions) would seem to be in similar situations. However, whereas national governments may negotiate on an international level to resolve the problems created through this dynamic, state and local governments lack the power to directly participate in management of the global commons. It would seem, then, that sub-federal governments would avoid unilateral emissions reductions. Yet, this has not been the case. What practical reasons exist for this seemingly irrational state behavior?

One answer is that state and local-level actions may, in the aggregate, yield meaningful greenhouse gas reductions. Collectively, the 17 states that have enacted state-wide greenhouse gas-reduction targets include nearly half of the U.S. population, account for about half of the U.S. gross domestic product, and emit approximately 30 percent of the U.S. greenhouse gas emissions and 6.5 percent of global greenhouse gas emissions. *Id.* at 213–14. Thus, it might seem rational for state and local governments to act to limit their emissions, at least if the governments believe that the international community will succeed in reducing global greenhouse gas emissions as well.

In addition, many state and local governments believe that their efforts will result in significant, long-term economic benefits. Renewable energy sources, for example, typically require a larger workforce to operate than fossil-fueled electricity plants. Venture capitalists stand to make a great deal of money by funding successful mitigation technologies. Moreover, "green collar" jobs may promise to pay higher wages and offer greater job security than other traditional industries. Finally, state and local policies that reduce greenhouse gas emissions typically also reduce other localized pollutants.

Regardless of the incentives driving state and local actions, these actions may run into several Constitutional restraints. For example, state emissions requirements could violate the Commerce Clause if they discriminate against or unduly burden interstate commerce. Regional initiatives may conflict with the Compacts Clause of the Constitution. Unilateral state actions may also intrude upon the federal government's powers over foreign affairs.

This chapter will review the legal questions surrounding the proliferation of state and local climate change laws. It begins with a summary of some of the major state and local regulatory programs aimed at reducing greenhouse gas emissions and otherwise mitigating climate change. Section II.A discusses the three major regional initiatives that states have negotiated with each other: the northeastern states' Regional Greenhouse Gas Initiative (RGGI), the Western Climate Initiative, and the Midwestern Regional Greenhouse Gas Reduction Accord. Section II.B discusses several state and local approaches to climate change mitigation, including the proliferation of renewable portfolio standards, emissions targets, environmental assessment requirements, and climate action plans. Section III then explores whether state and local measures violate the Commerce Clause and questions how subnational governments may act to reduce greenhouse gas emissions effectively without unduly interfering with interstate commerce. Finally, Section IV assesses the role that states and municipalities should play in the future, if the federal government adopts national climate change legislation.

II.   STATE AND LOCAL ACTIONS TO MITIGATE CLIMATE CHANGE

In the 1990s, only a handful of states and cities had adopted climate change mitigation strategies. By 2008, however, more than 850 mayors had signed onto the U.S. Conference of Mayors Climate Protection Agreement committing them to take action to mitigate climate change, and every single state had adopted at least one policy to limit or offset greenhouse gas emissions. As it became increasingly clear that the federal government would neither ratify the Kyoto Protocol nor establish a binding national climate regime (*see* Chapters 4 and 11 for a discussion of the U.S. domestic and international approaches to climate change mitigation), state governments also began to form their own regional alliances to enhance the overall impact of their mitigation strategies and create more favorable economic conditions for regulated entities. This section first describes the regional agreements and identifies some of the legal challenges that states may face as they work to implement the regional programs. The section then discusses the most prevalent forms of climate change mitigation measures adopted by state and local governments.

A.   Regional Measures

The development of regional climate change initiatives began in 2003, when George Pataki, then governor of New York, invited other governors from the northeastern United States to discuss the creation of a regional emissions trading program for CO_2 emissions from power plants. At that time, most of the northeastern states already had statewide emissions goals or limitations, and most of the states figured that entry into an emissions trading program would enhance the states' ability to meet their existing limitations. The states thus agreed to develop the Regional Greenhouse Gas Initiative (RGGI) and to establish a region-wide cap-and-trade program for carbon dioxide emissions. The states ultimately completed development of RGGI in 2005.

RGGI establishes a regional cap-and-trade program for CO_2 emissions from power plants. The initial cap requires facilities to meet 2005 emissions levels by 2009 and then reduces emissions by 10 percent below 2009 levels by the end of 2018. Ten states (Connecticut, Delaware, Maine, New Hampshire, New Jersey, New York, Vermont, Massachusetts, Rhode Island, and Maryland) have signed the Memorandum of Understanding (MOU) establishing RGGI's trading program.

More recently, the governments of the western and midwestern states have created their own regional initiatives. The Western Climate Initiative was signed in February 2007, and the midwestern states established the Midwestern Regional Greenhouse Gas Reduction Accord in November 2007. While the western and midwestern initiatives are still in their early stages, the programs anticipate using a cap-and-trade program similar to that in RGGI.

REGIONAL GREENHOUSE GAS INITIATIVE
Memorandum of Understanding (Dec. 20, 2005), as amended
(Aug. 8, 2006)

NOW THEREFORE, the Signatory States express their mutual understandings and commitments as follows:

1. OVERALL ENVIRONMENTAL GOAL

The Signatory States commit to propose for legislative and/or regulatory approval a CO_2 Budget Trading Program (the "Program") aimed at stabilizing and then reducing CO_2 emissions within the Signatory States, and implementing a regional CO_2 emissions budget and allowance trading program that will regulate CO_2 emissions from fossil fuel-fired electricity generating units having a rated capacity equal to or greater than 25 megawatts.

2. CO_2 BUDGET TRADING PROGRAM

A. *Program Adoption.* Each of the Signatory States commits to propose, for legislative and/or regulatory approval, the Program substantially as reflected in a Model Rule that will reflect the understandings and commitments of the states contained herein. The Program launch date will be January 1, 2009 as provided in 3.C. below.

B. *Regional Emissions Cap.* The regional base annual CO_2 emissions budget will be equal to 121,253,550 short tons.[1]

C. *State Emissions Caps.* The regional base annual CO_2 emissions budget will be apportioned to the States so that each state's initial base annual CO_2 emissions budget is as follows:

Connecticut: 10,695,036 short tons

Delaware: 7,559,787 short tons

Maine: 5,948,902 short tons

New Hampshire: 8,620,460 short tons

New Jersey: 22,892,730 short tons

New York: 64,310,805 short tons

Vermont: 1,225,830 short tons

For the years 2009 through 2014, each state's base annual CO_2 emissions budget shall remain unchanged.

D. *Scheduled Reductions.* Beginning with the annual allocations for the year 2015, each state's base annual CO_2 emissions budget will decline by 2.5% per year so that each state's base annual emissions budget for 2018 will be 10% below its initial base annual CO_2 emissions budget.

E. *Compliance Period and Safety Valve.*

(1) Compliance Period. The compliance period shall be a minimum of three (3) years, unless extended after a Safety Valve Trigger Event (described below). A subject facility must have a sufficient number of allowances at the end of each compliance period to cover its emissions during that period.

(2) Safety Valve Trigger.

(a) Safety Valve Trigger. If, after the Market Settling Period (as defined below), the average regional spot price for CO_2 allowances equals or exceeds the Safety Valve Threshold (defined below) for a period of twelve months on a rolling average (a "Safety Valve Trigger Event"), then the

---

[1] Editors' Note: One short ton equals approximately 0.91 metric tons.

compliance period may be extended by one year, for a maximum compliance period of 4 years.

(b) Safety Valve Threshold. The Safety Valve Threshold shall be equal to $10.00 (in 2005$), as adjusted by the Consumer Price Index (CPI) plus 2% per year beginning January 1, 2006.

(c) Market Settling Period. The Market Settling Period is the first 14 months of each compliance period.

F. *Offsets.* The Program will provide for the award of offset allowances to sponsors of approved CO_2 (or CO_2 equivalent) emissions offset projects for reductions that are realized on or after the date of this MOU. Offset allowances may be used for compliance by units subject to the Program. Among the key features of the offset component of the Program are:

(1) General Requirements.

(a) Minimum Eligibility Requirements. At a minimum, eligible offsets shall consist of actions that are real, surplus, verifiable, permanent and enforceable.

(b) Initial Offset Types. The initial offset project types that may be approved by a Signatory State are: landfill gas (methane) capture and combustion; sulfur hexafluoride (SF_6) capture and recycling; afforestation (transition of land from non-forested to forested state); end-use efficiency for natural gas, propane and heating oil; and methane capture from farming operations. . . . The measurement and verification protocols and certification processes will be consistent across the Signatory States and incorporated into each State's program.

(c) Additional Offset Types. The Signatory States agree to continue to cooperate on the development of additional offset categories and types, including other types of forestry projects, and grassland revegetation projects. Additional offset types will be added to the Program upon approval of the Signatory States.

(2) Initial Offsets Geography and Limits.

(a) Geographic Location of Offset Projects. Offset allowances may be awarded to projects located anywhere inside the United States, provided offset allowances for projects located outside the Signatory States shall be awarded only if the state or jurisdiction where the project is located has:

(1) established a cap-and-trade program in which a specific tonnage limit has been placed on the greenhouse gas emissions from one or more significant economic sectors in such state; and/or

(2) entered into a memorandum of understanding with the implementing environmental agencies in the Signatory States, pursuant to which the state or other jurisdiction agrees to carry out certain administrative responsibilities to ensure the credibility of offset allowances from that state or other jurisdiction.

(b) Limit on Offsets Use. In each compliance period, a source may cover up to 3.3% of its reported emissions with offset allowances.

(3) Offsets Trigger and Reset.

(a) Offsets Trigger. If, after the Market Settling Period (defined above), the average regional spot price for CO_2 allowances equals or exceeds $7.00

(2005\$) per ton for a period of twelve months on a rolling average (an "Offsets Trigger Event"), then the percentage of offsets that a source may use to cover its emissions shall increase to 5.0% of its reported emissions for the compliance period in which the Offsets Trigger Event occurs.

(b) Offset Trigger Reset. After an Offset Trigger Event, the limits on use of offsets set forth in Section F.2. shall once again apply commencing at the start of the subsequent compliance period.

(4) Safety Valve Offsets Trigger and Reset.

(a) Safety Valve Trigger. Upon occurrence of a Safety Valve Trigger Event:

(1) offset allowances may be awarded for the retirement of allowances or credits from international trading programs; and

(2) the percentage of offsets that a source may use to cover its emissions shall increase to 10.0% of its reported emissions for the entire compliance period during which the Safety Valve Trigger Event occurs.

(b) Safety Valve Trigger Reset. After a Safety Valve Trigger Event, the limits on use of offsets set forth in Section F.2. shall once again apply commencing at the start of the subsequent compliance period.

G. *Allocations of Allowances.* Each Signatory State may allocate allowances from its CO_2 emissions budget as determined appropriate by each Signatory State, provided:

(1) each Signatory State agrees that 25% of the allowances will be allocated for a consumer benefit or strategic energy purpose. Consumer benefit or strategic energy purposes include the use of the allowances to promote energy efficiency, to directly mitigate electricity ratepayer impacts, to promote renewable or non-carbon-emitting energy technologies, to stimulate or reward investment in the development of innovative carbon emissions abatement technologies with significant carbon reduction potential, and/or to fund administration of this Program; and

(2) the Signatory States recognize that, in order to provide regulatory certainty to covered sources, state-specific rules for allocations should be completed as far in advance of the launch of the Program as practicable.

H. *Early Reduction Credits.* Each Signatory State may grant early reduction credits for projects undertaken after the date this Memorandum is signed and prior to the launch of the Program as defined in 3.C. at facilities subject to the Program, which projects have the effect of reducing emissions from the facility by (a) an absolute reduction of emissions through emission rate improvements; or (b) permanently reducing utilization of one or more units at the facility.

I. *Banking.* The banking of allowances, offset allowances and early reduction credits will be allowed without limitation.

3. MODEL RULE FOR ESTABLISHMENT OF THE CO_2 BUDGET TRADING PROGRAM

A. *Model Rule.* The Signatory States are collectively developing a draft Model Rule to serve as the framework for the creation of necessary statutory and/or regulatory authority to establish the Program. The Signatory States will use their best efforts to collectively release this draft Model Rule within 90 days after the execution of this MOU for a 60-day public review and comment period. Comments received during this comment period shall be reviewed by the Signatory States, and revisions to the draft Model Rule will be considered. A revised Model Rule will be developed and released within 45 days of the close of the public comment period after consultation among the Signatory States.

B. *Legislation and/or Rulemaking.* Each Signatory State commits to seek to establish in statute and/or regulation the Program and have that State's component of the regional Program effective as soon as practicable but no later than December 31, 2008.

C. *Launch of Program.* The Signatory States intend that the first compliance period of the Program will commence January 1, 2009.

4. REGIONAL ORGANIZATION

In order to facilitate the ongoing administration of the Program, the Signatory States agree to create and maintain a regional organization ("RO") with a primary office in New York City. The RO will be a non-profit entity incorporated in New York and will operate pursuant to by-laws agreed upon by the Signatory States. The RO shall have an Executive Board comprised of two representatives from each Signatory State. The RO may employ staff and acquire and dispose of assets in order to perform its functions.

A. *RO Functions.* The RO will have the following functions:

(1) Deliberative Forum. Act as the forum for collective deliberation and action among the Signatory States in implementing the Program . . . .

(2) Emissions and Allowance Tracking . . . .

(3) Offsets Development. Provide technical support to the States for the development of new offset standards to be added to state rules.

(4) Offsets Implementation. Provide technical assistance to the States in reviewing and assessing applications for offsets projects . . . .

(5) Limitation on Powers. The RO is a technical assistance organization only. The RO shall have no regulatory or enforcement authority with respect to the Program . . . .

B. *Funding for the RO.* The Signatory States agree that the RO shall be funded at least in part through payments from each Signatory State in proportion to the State's annual base CO_2 Emissions Budget . . . .

5. ADDITION OR REMOVAL OF SIGNATORY STATES

A. *New Signatory States.*

(1) New Signatories. A Non-Signatory State may become a Signatory State by agreement of the Signatory States as reflected in an amendment to this MOU.

*   *   *

(3) Massachusetts and Rhode Island. The Signatory States recognize the contributions of Massachusetts and Rhode Island to the design and development of the Program and the negotiation of this MOU. The Signatory States agree that Massachusetts and Rhode Island may become signatories to this MOU at any time prior to January 1, 2008, without any amendment to the terms of this MOU. In the event that authorized representatives of Massachusetts and/or Rhode Island execute this MOU before such date, they shall receive the following CO_2 emissions budgets:

Massachusetts: 26,660,204 short tons

Rhode Island: 2,659,239 short tons

In the event that Massachusetts and/or Rhode Island become Signatory States under this paragraph, then the regional emissions budget set forth in Section 2.B. of this MOU shall be increased to include the allowance budgets of Massachusetts and/or Rhode Island. * * *

QUESTIONS AND DISCUSSION

1. *Basic Elements of the MOU.* Review RGGI and answer the following questions:

- What are the main elements of RGGI?

- What is the first emissions cap?

- What are the later caps?

- What are the relevant compliance periods?

- Which facilities are covered under RGGI?

- What is the safety valve and how is it triggered?

2. *Offsets.* The cap in RGGI applies only to emissions of carbon dioxide from power plants. However, RGGI allows offsets to come from activities including "landfill gas (methane) capture and combustion; sulfur hexafluoride (SF_6) capture and recycling; afforestation (transition of land from non-forested to forested state); end-use efficiency for natural gas, propane and heating oil; methane capture from farming operations." RGGI, MOU, ¶ (2)(F)(1)(b). Both the Western Climate Initiative and the Midwestern Regional Greenhouse Gas Reduction Accord intend to establish emissions trading programs for all six greenhouse gases covered under the Kyoto Protocol. What advantages or disadvantages result from limiting emissions caps or offsets to certain types of activities and gases?

RGGI also limits the amount of offsets sources may use to meet their emissions allowances. If average prices for carbon dioxide allowances remain below $7.00 per ton (adjusted for inflation) over a twelve-month rolling average period, sources may cover up to 3.3% of their emissions with offsets. A rolling average period means that the average price is calculated every month for the previous twelve months, rather than calculated based on average prices during the calendar year. However, if allowance prices increase, one of two "triggers" may result and allow sources to increase their use of allowances. First, if average prices equal or exceed $7.00 per ton, an "Offsets Trigger Event" occurs, and facilities may increase the use of offsets to cover up to 5 percent of their reported emissions during that compliance period. Second, if average prices exceed $10.00 per ton (adjusted for inflation), a "Safety Valve Trigger Event" occurs. During the compliance period in which a Safety Valve Trigger Event occurs, sources may use offsets to cover up to 10 percent of their emissions. They may also include emissions credits obtained through any international trading programs.

RGGI initially placed significant limitations on the use of offsets obtained from activities in states that are not signatories to the MOU. Specifically, sources would receive one allowance for each ton of emissions reductions created within the Signatory States, but they would receive only one-half allowance for each ton of emissions reductions in other states. In other words, offsets would have twice the value if they came from within the Signatory States. The 2006 Amendments to the MOU changed this formula and weighed all offsets from within the United States equally. However, sources may use offsets from another states only if that state has either 1) established a cap-and-trade program limiting greenhouse gas emissions, or 2) entered into a memorandum of understanding with the Signatory States which ensures credibility of the offset allowances. What legal challenges would the Signatory States have faced if they had maintained the initial offset allocation based on geographical origin? Do you think RGGI's current requirements for use of offsets from non-Signatory States raises any legal concerns?

3. As with the European Union's Emissions Trading Scheme (ETS), RGGI must address issues of additionality, leakage, supplementarity, and linkages to other systems. *See* Chapter 6. Compare how RGGI has addressed these issues to the ETS. What advantages and disadvantages are there to the RGGI approach as compared to that of the European Union? What steps are included to increase the linkages of the systems? Can, for example, entities subject to RGGI buy credits from the ETS or Kyoto's Clean Development Mechanism?

4. *Allocations.* Unlike most emissions trading programs, the Model Rule implementing RGGI anticipates that states will use an auction to distribute initial allowances.

Auctions under RGGI began in September 2008, and as this book went to publication, RGGI had conducted two auctions before the RGGI compliance period began on January 1, 2009. During the first auction, held on September 25, 2008, Signatory States released approximately 12.5 million CO_2 allowances, which sold for an average price of $3.07 each. The second auction on December 17, 2008, involved an additional 31.5 million CO_2 allowances, and these sold for an average price of $3.38 each. Interestingly, the maximum amount bid for the allowances declined from more than $12.00 per allowance during Auction 1 to $7.20 per allowance during Auction 2. *See* POTOMAC ECONOMICS, POST-SETTLEMENT AUCTION REPORT, REGIONAL GREENHOUSE GAS INITIATIVE, CO_2 AUCTION 1 (OCT. 17, 2008); POTOMAC ECONOMICS, POST-SETTLEMENT AUCTION REPORT, REGIONAL GREENHOUSE GAS INITIATIVE, CO_2 ALLOWANCE AUCTION 2 (Jan. 5, 2008). Demand for carbon allowances was about three times greater than the number of allowances available during the second auction. Based on that, are you surprised by the prices of the allowances?

States participating in other regional initiatives have not reached agreement regarding the processes they will employ to distribute allowances. For example, Washington and California, both participants in the Western Climate Initiative, appear to have very different philosophies regarding allowance distribution; while Washington's governor has expressed an intent to distribute allowances for free, California's governor appears likely to use an auction to distribute the allowances. *See* Warren Callwell, *Governor Favors Mostly Free Permits for Polluters*, SEATTLE TIMES, Dec. 13, 2008. Should states have the option of how they will distribute credits to sources that will ultimately trade the credits in a regional trading program? Won't that create inequity between sources in different states and disrupt the trading market? How should states resolve these issues if they wish to move forward with the regional agreement?

5. *Participation.* Nearly half of the states in the country now participate in one of the regional programs. RGGI currently has the largest membership, with ten participating states, identified above, and Pennsylvania and the District of Columbia acting as observers. Observers participate in policy discussions but have not committed to emissions caps. The Western Climate Initiative has seven participating states: Arizona, California, Montana, New Mexico, Oregon, Utah, and Washington. Alaska, Colorado, Idaho, Nevada, and Wyoming are observers. Finally, the Midwestern Regional Greenhouse Gas Reduction Accord has six states — Illinois,

Iowa, Kansas, Michigan, Minnesota, and Wisconsin — participating, and three states — Indiana, Ohio, and South Dakota — observing. Not to be left out, in August 2008 Governor Tim Kaine of Virginia called for Southern states to launch a unified regional approach to climate change and energy, although it is not yet clear what that will entail. What does this level of participation suggest about future prospects of national climate legislation?

6. ***Foreign Affairs.*** Canadian provinces have also signed on either as observers or participants to the three initiatives. For example, British Columbia, Manitoba, and Quebec are all participating in the Western Climate Initiative. Manitoba is also a participant in the Midwestern Regional Greenhouse Gas Reduction Accord. The Western Climate Initiative participants hope that other Canadian provinces, as well as Mexican states, will join the initiative.

The inclusion of foreign governments in the regional programs raises questions under the Compacts Clause of the Constitution, Art. I, § 10, cl. 3, and the broader prohibition against states interfering in foreign affairs. The Constitution vests the power to conduct foreign affairs exclusively in the federal government by giving the President the power to make treaties and Congress the power to raise an army and declare war. Courts rarely invalidate state laws for interfering with foreign affairs, except for "state or local laws purporting to set up their own authorities as mini-state-departments, with power to oversee and either approve or disapprove foreign regimes or the negotiation efforts of the U.S. Executive Branch[.]" Robert K. Huffman & Jonathan M. Weisgall, *Climate Change and the States: Constitutional Issues Arising from State Climate Protection Leadership*, Sust. Dev. L. & Pol'y, 6, 12 (Winter 2008) (quoting personal correspondence with Prof. Laurence Tribe, Feb. 2, 2008). However, as sub-federal governments increase their efforts to limit greenhouse gas emissions, challenges to these efforts have similarly increased. Do regional initiatives that include Canadian provinces impermissibly interfere with foreign affairs? Would a decision by the states participating in RGGI to allow regulated entities to purchase offsets from the Kyoto Protocol's Clean Development Mechanism or the EU ETS violate the Constitution?

ROBERT K. HUFFMAN & JONATHAN M. WEISGALL, CLIMATE CHANGE AND THE STATES: CONSTITUTIONAL ISSUES ARISING FROM STATE CLIMATE PROTECTION LEADERSHIP
Sust. Dev. L. & Pol'y, 12–13 (Winter 2008)[*]

In *Zschernig v. Miller*[, 389 U.S. 429 (1968)], the Supreme Court invalidated an Oregon law that prevented a nonresident alien from inheriting property unless certain conditions were met — primarily, a reciprocal right for Americans in the alien's country and the assurance that any property received in Oregon would not be confiscated at home. Noting that states are the typical forum for probate matters, the Court still found the law problematic. "The several States, of course, have traditionally regulated the descent and distribution of estates. But those regulations must give way if they impair the effective exercise of the Nation's foreign policy." *Zschernig* involved a citizen of East Germany, a country with which the United States had no treaties regarding inheritance. Regardless, "even in absence of a treaty, a State's policy may disturb foreign relations."

Crosby v. National Foreign Trade Council [530 U.S. 363 (2000)] is the first in a line of recent foreign affairs cases that focus on state attempts to limit contact with foreign countries. The *Crosby* court heard a challenge to a Massachusetts law that prohibited state entities from buying goods or services from companies doing business with Burma. At the time the law was passed, there was no similar federal prohibition, although a federal law providing for sanctions on Burma was enacted a few months later. Although the Court spoke specifically of the Supremacy Clause, the decision's rationale focused heavily on how the Massachusetts law tied the President's hands and thus reduced his leverage against Burma.

We need not get into any general consideration of limits of state action affecting foreign affairs to realize that the President's maximum power to persuade rests on his capacity to bargain for the benefits of access to the entire national economy without exception for enclaves fenced off willy-nilly by inconsistent political tactics.

*   *   *

Finally, in *American Insurance Ass'n v. Garamendi*[, 539 U.S. 396 (2003)], the Supreme Court extended the ruling in *Crosby* to areas where there was no explicit federal statute, but merely executive agreements between the President and heads of foreign states. *Garamendi* involved a California law requiring any insurer in the state to disclose information about all policies sold in Europe between 1920 and 1945. This was seen as a way of ensuring that claims belonging to Holocaust victims were paid to any survivors and their heirs living in California.

President Clinton, however, had made executive agreements with Germany, Austria, and France so that all claims against German insurance companies relating to the Holocaust would be heard by an international commission established for that purpose. The Court noted that the President has considerable authority in the area of foreign relations and can act independently of Congress. "While Congress holds express authority to regulate public and private dealings with other nations in its war and foreign commerce powers, in foreign affairs the President has a degree of independent authority to act." Thus, congressional silence does not undermine the executive agreements, which can, even without an explicit conflict, preempt state laws.

Garamendi was a 5-4 decision, with Justices Rehnquist and O'Connor in the majority. Justice Ginsburg's dissent, which was joined by Justices Stevens, Scalia, and Thomas, focused on whether there was an explicit conflict between the executive agreement and the state law. Without such a conflict the dissenting Justices would not allow an executive agreement to preempt a state law. Justice Ginsburg also noted that "the notion of 'dormant foreign affairs preemption' with which *Zschernig* is associated resonates most audibly when a state action 'reflects a state policy critical of foreign governments and involves 'sitting in judgment' on them.' "

Applying the case law above to a scenario in which states attempted to link to a foreign trading system, the lack of a coherent federal policy on GHG regulation at this point strongly points to the constitutionality of such a linkage. The biggest potential problem would occur if there is federal legislation that makes mention of international linkages, or if the President makes clear statements concerning national priorities for GHG regulation that conflict with linking domestic trading systems with their international counterparts.

Perhaps just as important, any attempt to link to foreign emissions trading systems will be viewed very differently from the *Crosby* and *Giannoulias* cases. States attempting linkages will not be disparaging or otherwise passing negative judgment on foreign parties, as occurred in those cases involving state laws prohibiting or restricting commerce with rogue nations. Without that factor, it is difficult to imagine how courts could find any sort of interference with America's foreign policy prerogatives. Thus, cap-and-trade system linkages are likely permissible overtures to international partners, particularly if the federal government still has not undertaken a comprehensive scheme of carbon regulation.

Do you agree with the authors' conclusions that state initiative linkages with foreign governments would not intrude upon the federal power to conduct foreign affairs? Why, for example, wouldn't the U.S. repudiation of the Kyoto Protocol and ongoing actions of the Bush Administration to negotiate alternative strategies be considered "clear statements concerning national priorities for GHG regulation that conflict with linking domestic trading systems with their international counterparts"? For an alternative perspective regarding foreign policy preemption, *see* Norman E. Fichthorn & Allison D. Wood, *Constitutional Principles Prohibit States from Regulating CO$_2$ Emissions*, 20 Legal Backgrounder 47 (2005).

7. *The Compacts Clause.* The Compacts Clause of the Constitution states that "No state shall, without the consent of Congress, . . . enter into any Agreement or Compact with another state, or with a foreign power[.]" U.S. Const. art. I, § 10, cl. 3. None of the regional initiatives have received Congressional approval. Do they run afoul of the Compacts Clause? Consider the following.

ROBERT K. HUFFMAN & JONATHAN M. WEISGALL, CLIMATE CHANGE AND THE STATES: CONSTITUTIONAL ISSUES ARISING FROM STATE CLIMATE PROTECTION LEADERSHIP
Sust. Dev. L. & Pol'y, 10–11 (Winter 2008)

In reviewing claims under the Compacts Clause, courts look generally to whether states are attempting to enhance their power at the expense of the federal government.

> Where an agreement is not "directed to the formation of any combination tending to the increase of political power in the States, which may encroach upon or interfere with the just supremacy of the United States," it does not fall within the scope of the Clause and will not be invalidated for lack of congressional consent.

[Cuyler v. Adams, 449 U.S. 433, 440 (1981).] The first question that courts look at is whether a contractual arrangement, such as a cap-and-trade system, reaches the point of being a "compact" under the Compacts Clause. If it is a compact, then it generally must be approved by Congress or it will be invalid. Once approved by Congress, it reaches the level of federal law. Thus, for an unapproved state-to-state or state-to-foreign-party relationship to be valid, it must not reach the formality of being a "compact" for these purposes.

To answer the first question, whether an arrangement is an agreement or compact, the courts look to the general indicia of a compact. The Supreme Court summarized the relevant factors in *Northeast Bancorp v. Federal Reserve*[, 472 U.S. 159 (1985)], a decision involving an agreement by holding companies to purchase banks:

> The . . . statutes . . . both require reciprocity and impose a regional limitation . . . . But several of the classic indicia of a compact are missing. No joint organization or body has been established to regulate regional banking or for any other purpose. Neither statute is conditioned on action by the other State, and each State is free to modify or repeal its law

unilaterally. Most importantly, neither statute requires a reciprocation of the regional limitation.

From the passage above, one can draw some general criteria for determining whether a contractual relationship is an agreement or compact. There should be some sort of joint organization or body to govern the agreement, if necessary. It should be binding; that is, no state can freely remove itself from the agreement. And it must require a reciprocity of the regional limitation, meaning that one party cannot agree to a nationwide program while another believes the agreement only covers a handful of states.

Regarding a regional cap-and-trade program, courts are unlikely to find that RGGI or a similar program is a compact, unless the agreement contains language that conditions actions (in one state) on actions by other states and is not freely revocable by participant states. It appears, based on *Northeast Bancorp*, that a voluntary union, which allows for a state to back out should it not want to participate, would not be considered a compact for the purposes of the Clause.

However, it is difficult to see how a linked international cap-and-trade framework could be crafted so as not to constitute a compact or even a treaty, which would be impermissible under Article I, § 10, cl. 1, regardless of the presence or absence of congressional approval. In order to have a properly functioning linkage between markets, there would need to be guarantees regarding enforceability and permanence. Without legally enforceable guarantees about the quality of the credits being traded, the markets are unlikely to succeed. There would be a serious problem, for example, if an offset project in California created credits that were purchased by a steel manufacturer in France, and California de-linked itself from the markets. The problem of how the French manufacturer would account for the credits in the absence of a monitoring or verification mechanism to account for what is happening in California is a significant one. The only way to ensure the integrity of the credits being traded in the marketplace is to create a framework that is robust enough to protect all of the parties involved. This would presumably include the inability to voluntarily leave the program and would be most easily accomplished with some sort of central emissions registry that aggregates and processes data from all participants. These components are almost certain to create a compact under the Compacts Clause, which would then require congressional approval in order to be valid.

The states participating in RGGI seem to have taken particular care to lay out their agreement in an MOU, rather than a contract. The MOU also calls for the states to develop a "Model Rule" to serve as recommended regulations for each state to adopt when implementing the MOU. Do these softer approaches save RGGI from being considered a "compact" under the Compacts Clause? Why or why not?

8. An independent power producer, Indeck Corinth, in New York has filed suit against the New York governor, Department of Protection (DEP) and others challenging the state's participation in RGGI. *See* Indeck Corinth, L.P. v. Patterson, Complaint (N.Y. Sup. Ct., Jan. 29, 2009). Indeck alleges, among other things, that RGGI violates the Compacts Clause. Perhaps more significantly, it alleges that the governor entered into RGGI without statutory authority, because the New York legislature has not expressly granted the executive authority to enter into climate change agreements or emissions trading programs. Finally, Indeck alleges that RGGI will impose unfair and illegal costs on Indeck, because Indeck is bound by a long-term, fixed contract to deliver power to a New York utility and will be unable to pass the costs of its carbon allowances onto the utility or its consumers. Other

independent power producers who are locked into long-term contracts have raised similar concerns regarding RGGI. Danny Hakim, *Paterson Draws Fire on Shift in Emissions*, N.Y. Times, Mar. 6, 2009, at A1 (stating that Governor Paterson had agreed to reconsider the rules for allowance auctions by making more credits available for free to energy generators).

B.   State and Local Measures

Municipalities and states have also initiated independent actions to mitigate climate change. Several states and a few cities have adopted renewable portfolio standards specifying a minimum level of electricity which must come from renewable energy sources. States have also adopted emissions caps for particular industries, or, in California, for the economy as a whole. In addition, some states have enacted laws aimed at reducing or mitigating carbon dioxide emissions from coal-fired power plants. Beyond these more directed approaches, most states and many cities have enacted climate action plans, applied environmental assessments to activities emitting greenhouse gases, and taken other actions aimed at reducing greenhouse gas emissions. This section describes some of the most common types of mitigation measures subnational governments have adopted. Readers interested in learning about more measures should explore the website of the Pew Center on Global Climate Change, which contains an expansive database describing local, state, regional, and federal actions.

1.   *Renewable Portfolio Standards*

As explained in greater detail in Chapter 14, the federal government has contemplated establishing a federal renewable portfolio standard (RPS), which would require that a certain percentage of all electricity produced in the United States come from renewable energy sources. However, Congress has yet to pass federal legislation establishing a national RPS. States, however, have been quite active in developing their own RPS laws.

Iowa enacted the first RPS in 1991, but few states immediately followed. In the late 1990s, however, a few more states adopted RPSs, and by June 2008, 26 states and the District of Columbia had adopted mandatory RPSs. *See* Pew Center on Global Climate Change, States with Renewable Portfolio Standards (Aug. 2007).

While RPSs vary from state-to-state, they typically consist of a requirement that utilities obtain a specific quantity or percentage of power from renewable sources and a definition or list of qualifying renewable energy sources. Under many programs, the percentage requirement will increase over time. Most state programs also allow utilities to either generate the renewable energy directly or to purchase renewable energy credits from other suppliers. Renewable energy credits (RECs) function much like offset credits in a cap-and-trade program, in that utilities may buy and sell the credits at market rates and use the credits generated by other companies to offset the utilities' direct emissions.

Broadly speaking, RPSs have received broad support in state legislatures, particularly when the programs allow for renewable energy credits. Most lawmakers believe that RPSs provide economic growth and employment opportunities, by spurring investment in and development of renewable energy technologies. Since renewable energy production typically requires more human labor than conventional, fossil-fuel electricity production, renewable energies are often promoted as good sources of "green jobs." In addition, the availability of RECs creates a type of market-based system, in which renewable energy producers will be able to sell their emissions credits to utilities at whatever price the market demands. As market demand rises due to the increasing RPS requirement, new renewable energy sources should go on-line. Over time, RPSs are expected to help create vigorous renewable energy industries.

Despite the general support for RPSs, state RPS programs have been difficult to implement for a few reasons. *See* BARRY G. RABE, RACE TO THE TOP: THE EXPANDING ROLE OF U.S. STATE RENEWABLE PORTFOLIO STANDARDS 22–27 (Pew Center on Global Climate Change 2006). First, the market-based system has not always succeeded in diversifying renewable energy sources, in large part because the monetary value of RECs has remained too low to spur development of new sources or technologies. As a result, most RECs come from wind power, which is relatively inexpensive to generate. To diversify sources of renewable energy, some states have begun to specify that a certain percentage of power must come from more expensive technologies, such as solar. While these types of requirements have the laudable goal of expanding renewable energy production, they alter the market-based system around which many RPS programs are designed.

Second, RPSs can struggle under their own success if energy transmission systems lack the capacity to handle excess input from renewable energy sources. In Texas, for example, an RPS led to growth of wind farms in West Texas. The wind farms generated far more wind power than the transmission lines were designed to conduct. Unless states account for transmission in establishing an RPS, they may end up with a bottleneck in the transmission line, which, in turn, may harm the economic viability of the renewable energy source (because it will not be able to deliver its product) or may detract investors from building new sources (because they will not have certainty regarding the return on their investments).

Third, RPSs do not guarantee local approval of specific renewable energy projects, and local opposition may prevent construction of these sources. In Massachusetts, for example, local opposition to the Cape Wind facility, which would be located in the ocean about 5 miles from Cape Cod, has thus far prevented the facility from being constructed. If siting concerns remain barriers to renewable energy projects, utilities in states with an RPS will likely end up buying energy from nearby states. To the extent a state developed its RPS to promote its own renewable energy industry, local opposition could defeat that goal.

Finally, the market-based approach may undermine some of the very goals of a state-enacted RPS. If the law allows regulated entities to purchase out-of-state credits as part of an RPS, local renewable energy development may suffer. This, in turn, will undermine state goals of reducing local air pollution, expanding renewable energy production, and creating local employment. On the other hand, if a state restricts utilities from purchasing out-of-state credits, but allows the utilities to purchase locally generated credits, the state may run afoul of the Commerce Clause. An easy solution to these problems would be elimination of the market-based approach; however, few states have been willing to mandate renewable energy standards without providing utilities the flexibility a market-based approach provides.

Despite these potential downfalls, RPSs remain a popular and overall successful state mechanism, and it seems likely that more states will develop RPSs in the future. However, many questions remain about the design and legality of state RPSs.

QUESTIONS AND DISCUSSION

1. Professor Barry Rabe has described in great detail the states' roles in developing RPSs and the limitations state programs may face. *See* BARRY G. RABE, RACE TO THE TOP: THE EXPANDING ROLE OF U.S. STATE RENEWABLE PORTFOLIO STANDARDS 22-27 (Pew Center on Global Climate Change 2006). Students interested in this topic should review his report.

2. Just what constitutes "renewable energy"? In Pennsylvania, the state definition includes waste coal and coal produced using integrated gasification combined cycle (IGCC) technology. Although IGCC plants are typically 10–20 percent more efficient than older coal-fired power plants, they nonetheless emit significant quantities of greenhouse gases. Considering the stated goals underlying RPSs, does it make sense to include fossil-fuel energy sources as "renewable" energy? Maine defines renewable energy sources to include small hydropower facilities but not hydroelectric facilities with a production capacity of more than 100 megawatts. Under Maryland's RPS, eligible hydroelectric facilities must generate 30 megawatts of power or less. Code of Maryland, § 7-701 *et seq.* Why aren't larger hydroelectric facilities "renewable"? In Maine, at least, do you think it matters that small hydroelectric facilities are abundant and that facilities generating more than 100 megawatts are prevalent in Canada? Do you think a uniform definition (i.e., federal definition) of renewable energy would be useful?

3. As noted above, many states have enacted RPSs to spur their own renewable energy industries. However, these efforts can be undermined if the RPS allows utilities to purchase renewable emissions credits from out-of-state sources. The RPS may run afoul of the Commerce Clause if the state seeks to restrict use of out-of-state emissions credits while allowing utilities to obtain renewable emissions credits from in-state sources. (*See infra.*) On the other hand, industries may resist RPSs that do not allow renewable emissions credits at all. If you were advising a state, how would you structure an RPS that promotes in-state alternative energy development, provides utilities with flexibility in meeting the RPS, and complies with the Constitution?

4. Some observers argue that RPSs are suboptimal policies for encouraging the development and adoption of renewable energy. Instead, they point to European experience, particularly that of Germany, which has employed policies known either as renewable energy payments (REPs) or feed-in tariffs (FITs) to become a renewable powerhouse. FITs require utilities to enter into long-term purchase contracts with any renewable energy provider, no matter how small, and guarantee a rate of return above the cost of energy production. Proponents of FITs argue that they encourage small-scale renewables that are ignored by utilities in meeting their requirements under an RPS. The experience in Germany would seem to support this view:

> German utilities enter into 20-year contracts to purchase power from nonutility power producers. . . . [C]ompensation depends on the actual cost of each renewable source. And in Germany, ordinary citizens can become producers and compete with utilities.

> Proponents of the RPSs praise the U.S. approach for being more efficient; after all, FITs make relatively costly small projects just as

profitable as big ones. In the process, however, RPSs stymie investments by homeowners and small businesses, leaving renewable power generation up to wholesalers. The largest U.S. wind farm in 2006, Horse Hollow in Texas, has as much generating capacity as a large coal-fired plant and is owned by a single company, FPL Energy. In contrast, although Germany had twice the renewable generating capacity of the United States in 2006, the largest German wind farm is less than one-seventh the size of Horse Hollow, and ownership is spread across numerous local companies and individual investors.

. . . Germany benefits from FITs in several key ways. First, 14 percent of Germany's total electricity supply (or 8.4 percent of total energy supply) is already accounted for by renewables. Second, Germany is progressing rapidly toward even larger shares (Germany was striving for 12 percent renewable electricity by 2010, and got only 3 percent of total energy supply from renewables as recently as 2002). Third, the policy has helped avoid the emission of millions of tons of CO_2 — more than 100 million tons in 2006. . . .

But the ultimate benefit of Germany's FITs is the technology, industry, and infrastructure that are being created for the global turn to renewable energy, which Germans are betting is inevitable.

*   *   *

German FITs [also require little bureaucracy]; no approval is required. If people . . . wish to put solar panels on their roof, they need not request forms for governmental subsidies and hope for approval and quick processing. German homeowners simply call a local solar contractor and set a date. In this way, German FITs leave everything but the price up to the market. The result is that all worthwhile projects can go online, not just a select few deemed by utilities to be most efficient.

Craig Morris & Nathan Hopkins, *Home-Gown Juice*, WORLD WATCH, May–June 2008, at 20, 23–24. As explained in greater detail in Chapter 14, the United States has also used mandatory purchase requirements to spur renewable energy development. In 1978, Congress passed the Public Utilities Regulatory Policy Act (PURPA), which required facilities to purchase power from any qualifying facility (QF) at just and reasonable rates. Qualifying facilities included small renewable energy producers and cogenerators (facilities which produce both power and steam). Regulations implementing PURPA required utilities to pay rates equal to the "avoided costs" — the costs the utilities would otherwise have spent if they had produced the energy themselves. Many utilities entered into long-term contracts with QFs, and, ultimately, PURPA resulted in approximately 1200 QFs coming on line. However, most of the QFs are natural gas-fired plants, which are cheaper to build and operate than many renewable sources.

At the time of PURPA's passage, most utilities' avoided costs were quite high. In the 1980s, however, costs of oil and coal began to decline, and utilities found it much cheaper to produce their own electricity. However, PURPA demanded that utilities continue to purchase power from QFs and long-term contracts meant that utilities were paying QFs much more money than they would spend generating their own electricity. As a result of this dynamic, many utilities oppose PURPA's mandatory purchase requirements and have called for PURPA's repeal.

Many of the early long-term contracts with the small renewable energy producers have begun to expire. Unlike in the 1970s, current avoided costs are quite low. As a result, renewable energy producers may find avoided costs uneconomical and go out of business.

Is a FIT, like that in Germany, the solution? Do you think utilities would support a mandatory purchase requirement after their experience with PURPA? Based on the current economic situation, do you think states would impose a FIT on the utilities they regulate? Are RPSs, with tradable RECs, a more viable way to spur future renewable energy development?

Do you think there are any obstacles to states adopting feed-in policies in the future? For more information on feed-in policies, see the Alliance for Renewable Energy's website at www.allianceforrenewableenergy.org.

5.   State RPSs may raise international trade issues where they discriminate against foreign producers, as the Maine standards may do *vis-à-vis* Canadian producers of hydropower. This issue is addressed in Chapter 10.

---

2.   *Greenhouse Gas Emission Reduction Goals*

In the wake of the United Nations Framework on Climate Change and the Kyoto Protocol, several states adopted statewide greenhouse gas emissions targets. As of June 2008, 19 states had adopted such targets, which range from Utah's goal of reaching 2005 emissions levels by 2020 to Minnesota's goal of reducing emissions by 80 percent below 2005 levels by 2050. Many other states have set goals similar to Minnesota's. However, most state targets are aspirational. California, in contrast, has established mandatory emissions reductions.

a.   *Statewide Emissions Reductions: California*

In passing the Global Warming Solutions Act, AB 32, California became the first state law to establish a mandatory economy-wide emissions cap, violations of which are subject to penalties.

GLOBAL WARMING SOLUTIONS ACT
Assembly Bill No. 32
Cal. Health & Safety Code § 38500-00

Under existing law, the State Air Resources Board (state board), the State Energy Resources Conservation and Development Commission (Energy Commission), and the California Climate Action Registry all have responsibilities with respect to the control of emissions of greenhouse gases, as defined, and the Secretary for Environmental Protection is required to coordinate emission reductions of greenhouse gases and climate change activity in state government.

This bill would require the state board to adopt regulations to require the reporting and verification of statewide greenhouse gas emissions and to monitor and enforce compliance with this program, as specified. The bill would require the state board to adopt a statewide greenhouse gas emissions limit equivalent to the statewide greenhouse gas emissions levels in 1990 to be achieved by 2020, as specified. The bill would require the state board to adopt rules and regulations in an open public process to achieve the maximum technologically feasible and cost-effective greenhouse gas emission reductions, as specified. The bill would authorize the state board to adopt market-based compliance mechanisms, as defined, meeting specified requirements. The bill would require the state board to monitor compliance with and enforce any rule, regulation, order, emission limitation, emissions reduction measure, or market-based compliance mechanism adopted by the state board, pursuant to specified provisions of existing law. The bill would authorize the state board to adopt a schedule of fees to be paid by regulated sources of greenhouse gas emissions, as specified.

Because the bill would require the state board to establish emissions limits and other requirements, the violation of which would be a crime, this bill would create a state-mandated local program.

*   *   *

PART 3. STATEWIDE GREENHOUSE GAS EMISSIONS LIMIT

38550. By January 1, 2008, the state board shall, after one or more public workshops, with public notice, and an opportunity for all interested parties to comment, determine what the statewide greenhouse gas emissions level was in 1990, and approve in a public hearing, a statewide greenhouse gas emissions limit that is equivalent to that level, to be achieved by 2020. In order to ensure the most accurate determination feasible, the state board shall evaluate the best available scientific, technological, and economic information on greenhouse gas emissions to determine the 1990 level of greenhouse gas emissions.

38551. (a) The statewide greenhouse gas emissions limit shall remain in effect unless otherwise amended or repealed.

(b) It is the intent of the Legislature that the statewide greenhouse gas emissions limit continue in existence and be used to maintain and continue reductions in emissions of greenhouse gases beyond 2020.

(c) The state board shall make recommendations to the Governor and the Legislature on how to continue reductions of greenhouse gas emissions beyond 2020.

PART 4. GREENHOUSE GAS EMISSIONS REDUCTIONS

38560.5. (a) On or before June 30, 2007, the state board shall publish and make available to the public a list of discrete early action greenhouse gas emission reduction measures that can be implemented prior to the measures and limits adopted pursuant to Section 38562.

(b) On or before January 1, 2010, the state board shall adopt regulations to implement the measures identified on the list published pursuant to subdivision (a).

(c) The regulations adopted by the state board pursuant to this section shall achieve the maximum technologically feasible and cost-effective reductions in greenhouse gas emissions from those sources or categories of sources, in further-ance of achieving the statewide greenhouse gas emissions limit.

38562. (a) On or before January 1, 2011, the state board shall adopt greenhouse gas emission limits and emission reduction measures by regulation to achieve the maximum technologically feasible and cost-effective reductions in greenhouse gas emissions in furtherance of achieving the statewide greenhouse gas emissions limit, to become operative beginning on January 1, 2012.

PART 5. MARKET-BASED COMPLIANCE MECHANISMS

38570. (a) The state board may include in the regulations adopted pursuant to Section 38562 the use of market-based compliance mechanisms to comply with the regulations.

(b) Prior to the inclusion of any market-based compliance mechanism in the regulations, to the extent feasible and in furtherance of achieving the statewide greenhouse gas emissions limit, the state board shall do all of the following:

(1)   Consider the potential for direct, indirect, and cumulative emission impacts from these mechanisms, including localized impacts in communities that are already adversely impacted by air pollution.

(2)   Design any market-based compliance mechanism to prevent any increase in the emissions of toxic air contaminants or criteria air pollutants.

(3)   Maximize additional environmental and economic benefits for California, as appropriate.

(c) The state board shall adopt regulations governing how market-based compliance mechanisms may be used by regulated entities subject to greenhouse gas emission limits and mandatory emission reporting requirements to achieve compliance with their greenhouse gas emissions limits.

PART 6. ENFORCEMENT

38580. (a) The state board shall monitor compliance with and enforce any rule, regulation, order, emission limitation, emissions reduction measure, or market-based compliance mechanism adopted by the state board pursuant to this division.

(b) (1) Any violation of any rule, regulation, order, emission limitation, emissions reduction measure, or other measure adopted by the state board pursuant to this division may be enjoined pursuant to Section 41513, and the violation is subject to those penalties set forth in Article 3 (commencing with Section 42400) of Chapter 4 of Part 4 of, and Chapter 1.5 (commencing with Section 43025) of Part 5 of, Division 26.

———

QUESTIONS AND DISCUSSION

1.   The California legislature adopted AB 32 to implement one of the interim goals established by Governor Schwarzenegger through an Executive Order. The Executive Order established an initial goal of lowering California's greenhouse gas emissions to 2000 levels by 2010, and then established more progressive reductions of reaching 1990 levels by 2020 and achieving an 80 percent reduction below 1990 levels by 2050. Exec. Order No. S-3-05 (Cal. 2005). AB 32 codifies the goal of reaching 1990 levels by 2020.

2.   On June 26, 2008, the California Air Resources Board (CARB) released its draft Scoping Plan, describing how CARB would meet the goal of reaching 1990 emissions levels by 2020. *See* CARB, Climate Change Draft Scoping Plan, Executive Summary (June 26, 2008). The draft plan proposes to adopt a state-wide cap-and-trade program that would ultimately link to the cap-and-trade program to be developed under the Western Climate Initiative. *Id.* at ES-3. Unlike many states, it was not a foregone conclusion that California would implement AB 32

through emissions trading or any other type of market-based system. As Professor Alice Kaswan explains:

> During negotiations over AB 32, the legislature rejected the Governor's effort to mandate a cap and trade program, instead leaving the decision about whether to adopt a market-based system to the primary implementing agency, the CARB. *See* [Mark Martin, *Núñez Slams Governor on Emission Law*, S.F. Chron., Oct. 17, 2006, at B1]. When the Governor then mandated the development of a cap and trade system through a subsequent Executive Order, some California leaders believed he had betrayed the legislative agreement. *Id.* Assembly Speaker Fabian Núñez, one of AB 32's co-authors, stated that the "governor was reinterpreting the law based on proposals he had suggested to lawmakers during negotiations over the legislation . . . but that had been rejected by the Legislature." *Id.* The tension continues. When Governor Schwarzenegger slated 24 out of 123 new positions at the CARB for development of a market-based system, the legislature cut the number to two, displaying its preference for requiring mandatory reductions rather than cap and trade.

Alice Kaswan, *The Domestic Response to Global Climate Change: What Role for Federal, State, and Litigation Initiatives?*, 42 U.S.F. L. REV. 39, 57 n.95 (2007). Many environmental organizations were opposed to emissions trading due to environmental justice concerns. Although most greenhouse gases themselves do not cause localized harm, other pollutants typically emitted with greenhouse gases do. A market-based program could allow levels of locally harmful pollutants to remain high. *Id.* at 57–58. To address these concerns, the California legislature added paragraph (b)(1) to Section 38570 (*supra*). Does this adequately address environmental justice concerns?

3. AB 32 is the first climate change law that establishes civil and criminal penalties for violations of any emissions limitations established for greenhouse gases. As with other violations of California's air pollution laws, violators of AB 32 will be subject to penalties ranging from $25,000 to $75,000 per violation per day.

4. AB 32 gives the CARB responsibility for developing a greenhouse gas regulatory program. It also vests considerable discretion in the state board to develop the regulatory mechanism to limit statewide greenhouse gas emissions. What type of regulatory model would you advise the state board to employ to meet AB 32's goals, and why? Should the state use a cap-and-trade program, as it appears likely to do? For a discussion of the European Union's experience with emissions trading, *see* Chapter 6. Should California impose one-size, fits-all emissions controls without allowing for emissions trading? Would such a program be politically viable? Would it be practically feasible, in light of the scope of AB 32? Are there other types of regulatory programs California could employ?

5. In addition to AB 32, California enacted Senate Bill 1368, which directs the California Public Utilities Commission (CPUC) to establish emissions standards for power plants supplying electricity to California. Cal. S.B. 1368, 2006 Cal. Stat., ch. 598 (codified at Cal. Pub. Util. Code §§ 8340–8341). Pursuant to this bill, the CPUC established emissions requirements for "all new utility-owned generation and all procurement contracts that exceed three years in length." *See* Order Instituting Rulemaking to Implement the Commission's Procurement Incentive Framework and to Examine the Integration of Greenhouse Gas Emissions Standards into Procurement Policies, Rulemaking 06-04-009, 9 (Cal. Pub. Util. Comm'n., Apr. 13, 2007). Under the CPUC regulations, the greenhouse gas emissions levels for newly generated or procured electricity must not exceed the emissions rates of combined-cycle natural gas turbine. *Id.* Coal-derived electricity can emit almost three times more carbon dioxide than combined-cycle natural gas plants, and some observers believe that the CPUC regulations will effectively prohibit California utilities from building new coal-fired power plants or entering into long-term contracts with out-of-state coal-fired electricity generators. *See* Brian H. Potts, *Regulating Greenhouse Gas Leakage: How California Can Evade the Impending Constitutional Attacks*, 19 ELECTRICITY J. 43 (2006). As a result, utilities have challenged the regulations as violating the Commerce Clause. *See* Section III, *infra*.

---

b.   *Local Emissions Reductions: Portland, Oregon*

Portland, Oregon was probably the first local government to adopt greenhouse gas emissions limitations in 1993, when it established a goal of reducing its emissions to 10 percent below 1990 levels by 2010. Despite considerable effort to reduce its emissions, and to promote sustainability generally, it seems unlikely that Portland will meet its goal.

HARI M. OSOFSKY & JANET KOVEN LEVIT, THE SCALE OF NETWORKS?: LOCAL CLIMATE CHANGE COALITIONS
8 CHI. J. INT'L L. 409, 415–26 (2008)[*]

A. Leading The Charge From Portland

As the U.S. city with the longest effort at implementing sustainable carbon choices, Portland is an excellent laboratory for the complexities of urban emissions reduction. Portland's national leadership on issues of energy and climate began in 1979, when it became the first U.S. city to adopt an energy policy. This municipal policy was developed in the context of Oregon's state land use laws of the 1970s, which established a comprehensive scheme that included urban growth boundaries and long-range planning and encouraged citizen involvement at multiple scales. By the time Portland again led the charge in adopting a carbon dioxide emissions reduction plan in 1993, more than 150 cities had used its energy policy as a model.

Portland's goals and the substance of its plans have been ambitious and have provided an important template for cities that have begun more recently to pursue aggressive energy reduction strategies. As Timothy Grewe, Susan Anderson, and Lauren Butman — all involved in leading the administration of Portland's efforts — have noted, "[w]hat makes Portland unique is its institutionalization of sustainability as a core business driver." At least as significantly, its struggles provide an important lesson about localities and climate change. Despite impressive per capita reductions, Portland's growth has made its total emissions goals more elusive. It thus serves as an example of the difficulties of balancing growth with emissions reduction. This Section explores the mix of public leadership, private commitments, and nonprofit advocacy that shapes Portland's efforts.

1. Public Leadership

Portland first began grappling with how to frame its climate change efforts in the early 1990s under the leadership of then-Commissioners Earl Blumenauer and Mike Lindberg. Together with their counterparts in eleven other cities around the

---

world, Portland officials explored questions of how real climate change was and what cities could do to address it. Through that dialogue, they created an informal network of cities committed to reducing greenhouse gas emissions to 10 percent below 1990 levels. According to Susan Anderson, then-intern at and now-director of Portland's Office of Sustainable Development, "Back then, we didn't talk about global warming because people would've thought we were wacky. . . . We talked about making changes for the cost-saving benefits."

In 1993, as a result of these dialogues, the Portland City Council unanimously adopted a carbon dioxide reduction plan that specifically focused on the gas's contribution to climate change. The plan covered a wide range of urban policy areas, including land use planning, transportation, energy efficiency, solid waste and recycling, urban forestry, and renewable energy. Portland's carbon reduction strategy set the ambitious goal of reduction to 20 percent below 1990 levels by 2010. It also became the first city in the United States to join the international coalition of Cities for Climate Protection, which has grown to include 691 cities around the world.

Since making that commitment to aggressive greenhouse gas reduction, Portland has accumulated an impressive list of successes that include: 2 new major light rail lines and a 75 percent increase in public transit use since 1990; purchase of more than 10 percent renewable energy for its energy use; a recycling rate of 54 percent; construction of close to 40 high-performance green buildings; planting of over 750,000 trees and shrubs since 1996; weatherization of 10,000 multi-family units and over 800 family homes over a 2-year period; and establishing the Energy Trust of Oregon. It reduced per capita emissions by 12.5 percent over that period, which puts it at the leading edge of urban achievement on climate change in the United States.

And yet, despite all of these efforts and progress, its greenhouse gas emissions were still at slightly above 1990 levels in 2004, making a reduction to even its scaled back April 2000 goal of 10 percent below 1990 levels by 2010 quite difficult. The biggest problem facing Portland in reaching its total emissions target is that more and more people inhabit it each year. Each new person adds emissions. * * *

The critical question from a public policy perspective is how much further Portland can go under its current model of green economic development. From 2001 to 2004, Portland made significant additional progress. It continued monitoring emissions and supporting community education on climate change. Its per capita building energy use declined 7 percent due in large part to the work of the Energy Trust of Oregon and the programs it has created for customers of major energy utilities. It debuted its central city street car and two light rail lines during that period. By adding to its renewable energy resources, particularly wind power, Portland achieved the above-mentioned goal of purchasing 10 percent renewable energy and, in fact, reached just over 11 percent of its electricity from renewables in 2005. Its continued efforts on recycling and tree planting also had an impact. The city has ambitious goals for the future as well and will continue to be an important public policy laboratory as it leads the way.

* * * However, as of 2006, Oregon still obtains over 40 percent of its electricity from coal. Moreover, the state's ambitious work takes place against a backdrop of a deregulated utility industry that in the mid-to-late 1990s, prior to the creation of the Energy Trust, cut its energy conservation efforts by 60 to 70 percent. Fully actualizing a green business model will still take significant forward movement.

* * *

In sum, Portland represents the closest that the United States has to a success story on climate change. It demonstrates that urban areas have the capacity to change their emissions profiles dramatically through comprehensive planning efforts that rely upon partnerships between public, private, and nonprofit entities. However, the Portland example also reveals the core tensions presented by a green growth model. The cities participating in the Cities for Climate Protection now represent approximately 15 percent of global anthropogenic greenhouse gas emissions. Whether or not they can bring emissions down significantly while they grow represents a crucial question facing climate change efforts based on prevailing economic models and goals.

QUESTIONS AND DISCUSSION

1. Portland's efforts to lower its greenhouse gas emissions have received national and international attention. For example, Portland's efforts to increase bicycle ridership earned Portland a platinum rating by the League of American Bicyclists for being a "Bicycle Friendly Community." Only Portland and Davis, California, have received a platinum rating to date. As a result of the city's efforts, nearly 16 percent of Portlanders use bicycles as their primary or secondary means of transportation to work. *See* Press Release, *Portland Named a Platinum Bicycle Friendly Community* (Apr. 29, 2008). In addition, Portland was ranked as the top sustainable city in 2006. *See* The SustainLane 2006 U.S. City Rankings, *available at* http://www.sustainlane.com/us-city-rankings/overview.jsp. As noted above, Portland's efforts yielded a per capita emissions reduction of 12.5 percent. However, despite these efforts and accolades, Portland's overall greenhouse gas emissions increased by 0.7 percent between 1993 and 2005. Professors Osofsky and Levit link the increased emissions to an increase in Portland's population. What are other possible reasons that a city like Portland's overall emissions may increase over time? *See* Chapter 15 for a discussion of how Portland's restrictive land use measures have likely resulted in increased traffic congestion from workers commuting into Portland from cities located beyond Portland's urban growth boundary.

2. Local climate change mitigation measures seem particularly prone to problems associated with leakage. As Portland's experience suggests, one city's growth control measures may drive up property values within city and result in increased population growth beyond the city limits. Moreover, cities do not always have control over decisions that will affect greenhouse gas emissions within their geographic boundaries. For example, states and the Environmental Protection Agency (EPA) have the final say regarding whether facilities should receive air pollution permits under the Clean Air Act. Similarly, state governments decide how transportation funding is spent and may override local sustainability goals to implement state transportation plans. Should local governments that have invested in greenhouse gas reductions have a stronger voice in decisions that may erode these investments? What type of law could you design to protect local interests?

3. *Measures to Limit Emissions from Coal Plants*

Since 2001, approximately 178 new coal-fired power plants have been proposed throughout the United States. Environmental organizations across the country have been using existing federal laws such as the Clean Air Act, as well as state siting and zoning laws, to oppose permitting for those plants. Actions brought under the Clean Air Act are discussed further in Chapter 13. In response to public pressure, some states have also taken specific actions to mitigate carbon dioxide releases from coal-fired power plants. These include offset requirements, emissions limitations, and technology-based requirements. Most of these states have few existing coal-fired power plants and derive most of their electricity from other in-state sources, such as hydropower in the Pacific Northwest, or from power plants located in other states.

a.   *Carbon Cap or Offset Requirements for New Coal Plants*

A handful of states have enacted legislation requiring either new coal plants to offset their greenhouse gas emissions or existing coal plants to meet emissions requirements. Oregon, Washington, and Massachusetts all require new coal plants to offset a portion of their emissions from any new facility. Oregon and Washington require offsets of 17 percent and 20 percent, respectively, while Massachusetts requires a modest 1 percent offset. Massachusetts and New Hampshire also cap emissions from existing plants. New Hampshire required its three coal-fired power plants to meet 1990 emissions levels by 2006, and Massachusetts required its six plants to reduce their emissions to approximately 10 percent below 1996–1999 levels by 2006–2008 (specific dates vary with each plant). Most recently, Florida passed HB 7135, which will reduce electricity sector emissions by 80 percent below 1990 levels by 2050. Fla. Stat. § 366.92 (2008).

b.   *Carbon Capture and Sequestration Technology-based Mandates*

In an effort to develop new "clean coal" technologies, a handful of utilities have proposed constructing new coal plants with the capacity to use carbon capture and sequestration (CCS). As the name suggests, CCS facilities collect carbon dioxide emitted from a power plant and transfer the carbon dioxide to a permanent storage location. In an effort to ensure that CCS technologies would be used in Washington, the state enacted a law in 2007 requiring all new coal plants to sequester a certain level of carbon dioxide as a condition of receiving a siting permit. As you read the following excerpt, consider whether other states should adopt Washington's strategy.

IN THE MATTER OF APPLICATION NO. 2006-01, ENERGY NORTHWEST PACIFIC MOUNTAIN ENERGY CENTER POWER PROJECT

Adjudicative Order No. 2, Order Staying Adjudicative Proceeding
(Wa. Energy Facility Site Evaluation Council, Nov. 27, 2007)

Nature of the Proceeding

This matter involves Application No. 2006-1 submitted by Energy Northwest ("ENW") for certification of a site at Kalama, Washington in Cowlitz County under RCW 80.50. ENW proposes to construct the Pacific Mountain Energy Center ("PMEC") a combined cycle gasification facility for the production of electrical energy. Chapter 80.50 RCW gives the Energy Facility Site Evaluation Council ("EFSEC" or "the Council") the authority to make a recommendation to the governor as to whether the State, by action of the Governor, should enter into a site certification agreement with the applicant that would authorize the construction and operation of PMEC subject to the terms of the agreement.

At this moment, ENW proposes to construct PMEC as a 793 megawatt electrical generating facility. PMEC is proposed to operate on synthetic gas produced from petroleum coke, a byproduct of refining, or coal. ENW filed this application initially on September 12, 2006, before the enactment of Engrossed Substitute Senate Bill 6001 (ESSB 6001), codified as RCW 80.80. ENW was the first in Washington State to propose an Integrated Gasification Combined Cycle (IGCC) project with carbon sequestration. The project involves environmental technology that seeks to minimize carbon emissions, to recapture byproducts such as sulfur, and to utilize as its fuel, products such as petroleum coke, a refinery waste product that might otherwise not be recycled, and coal.

ESSB 6001, RCW 80.80

*   *   *

The new law imposes conditions on pending applications. RCW 80.80.040(11) requires new facilities generating more than 1100 pounds of greenhouse gases per megawatt hour of electricity to sequester greenhouse gases to this level or below. The project must satisfy the criteria of RCW 80.80(11)(a)–(f) . . . .

The statute, RCW 80.80.040(13), requires that an application pending on the date the law became effective must include a carbon sequestration plan, referred to herein as a greenhouse gas reduction plan (GGRP), that demonstrates how the project will meet all of the requirements of RCW 80.80(11). RCW 80.80(13) also requires the applicant to make a good faith effort to implement the plan. Only after preparing a detailed sequestration plan, receiving a site certification agreement, and making a good faith effort to implement the plan, may an applicant who finds implementation "not feasible" be excused from its terms and allowed to purchase greenhouse gas offsets.

Energy Northwest's Greenhouse Gas Reduction Plan

ENW filed the GGRP on July 30, 2007. The GGRP explained ENW's view that a plan such as contemplated by the statute is impossible to prepare at present based on the technological and economical infeasibility of geological sequestration. Instead, ENW presented a proposal to prepare a specific plan at some future time, perhaps as late as 2020, when geological sequestration becomes a proven technology for use by power plants and a number of asserted technological, engineering, and legal questions have been answered. In the interim, ENW proposed to consider offsets based on assumptions that it enumerated in its GGRP.

*   *   *

Sufficiency of the GGRP

The most significant question — and the only question posed to the parties that the Council will address in this order — is whether the GGRP as proposed legally complies on its face with the requirements of the statute.

We determine as a Council, and without dissent, that the ENW GGRP fails to meet the minimum requirements of the law, that it is therefore insufficient as a matter of law, that its provisions cannot be supplemented to the level of minimal sufficiency by mere revisions, and that its flaws are pervasive and affect the processing of the entire application. Therefore, we stay the adjudicative process and direct the Council staff to suspend application processing pending action by the applicant to cure the present flaws.

1. The Basic Flaw.

The basic flaw in ENW's GGRP is that it is not a plan at all in terms of the statute — it does not identify specific steps it will take to implement sequestration. Instead, it is a plan to make a plan, and it vows to begin making specific steps toward implementing geological sequestration at some future time, after geological sequestration becomes commercially accepted for use in reducing emissions of fossil-fueled power plants. It proposes that eventually, at some indefinite future time, it will seek to develop a specific plan for accomplishing the purposes of the statute. In the meantime, it argues, after the fifth year of operation, it may purchase offsetting greenhouse gas emission rights from unspecified sources because a specific plan is futile and it need not make a good faith effort to comply with the letter of the statute.

The reason this is a fundamental flaw is that it asks the Council to invalidate the statute — an action that is clearly beyond the power of an administrative agency. This is not an ambiguous statute, which might be cured by interpretation of its terms. Instead, the statute is detailed and specific in its requirements. The applicant must make specific plans for specific actions to accomplish a specific goal — geologic or other approved sequestration of greenhouse gases — and receive from the Governor a Site Certification Agreement, before it can ask for relief by the purchase of offsets. Then, only after ENW has made a good faith effort to implement the plan, and only after the Council has agreed that implementation is "not feasible," may it be excused from compliance with plan implementation and allowed to purchase offsetting emission rights.

ENW argues that sufficiency of the GGRP is a factual issue that must be determined only after an evidentiary hearing. We strongly disagree. We need only look to the statute and the plan that ENW presented to determine whether the plan contains the elements that the statute requires.

We determine that the GGRP simply does not contain the elements required by statute, not that a plan containing the required elements is inadequate in its measures.

2. Futility or Impossibility of Compliance.

ENW argues that compliance with the statute is futile. While futility may be true from its perspective, which would require a fully developed carbon sequestration industry before literal compliance with the statute is mandated, it is not true from the standpoint of the other parties. They point out that some projects must be within the first wave of technological development — if all waited until a technology became mainstream, technology would never reach mainstream. They also note that sequestration technology is mature in other high-volume applications, such as extraction of oil from wells.

Futility is also not true from the plain language and the clear meaning of the statute. The other parties point out that the statute was enacted specifically to deal with applications in ENW's present situation and that the legislature is presumed to know the meaning and the application of its enactments. This is not an ambiguous statute, which might be susceptible of interpretation. The law is clear and specific in its application to this project. We will not interpret the statute to disregard the plain meaning of the legislature.

ENW argues that it made a good faith effort to comply with the statute. We do not impugn its motives. The test we must apply, however, is not whether it has made a good faith effort, but whether its GGRP complies with the clear terms of the law. We determine that it does not.

ENW proposes application of the "doctrine of impossibility," citing a case in which physical incapacity excused a teacher from the duty to teach, and it argues that under terms of the "vested rights doctrine," the law is invalid in application to PMEC because the application was filed before the law became effective and because of "constitutional principles of fairness and due process." ENW does not contend that we have jurisdiction to invalidate the law on those bases and it does not address whether the vested rights principle also applies to matters such as this, which affect the public health, safety and welfare.

*   *   *

4. Conclusion.

In sum, the plain reading of the statute demands a carbon sequestration plan, with specifics, and ENW has provided only a general statement of intention that it will begin creating such a plan in the future at some indefinite time. In its brief, ENW calls this proposal "adaptive management," under a practice that allows details of compliance to be developed through different measures, over time, allowing learning from and improving upon compliance measures. RCW 80.80 does not allow adaptive management in lieu of clear statutory requirements, and ENW's proposal is a proposal to develop goals and measures later. It is not adaptive management, which pursues specific goals through clearly identified means.

We conclude that ENW's proposed greenhouse gas reduction plan fails to meet the requirements of the statute, and must be rejected.

QUESTIONS AND DISCUSSION

1. *Technology-Forcing and Technological Infeasibility.* RCW 80.80.040(11) clearly qualifies as a technology-forcing law, in that it directs new coal plants to establish particular plans for carbon capture and sequestration. Most technology-based standards are in fact "performance standards," which establish emissions limitations based on technological capacity, but do not direct regulated entities to employ specified types of technology. Do you think Washington State's approach to forcing technological innovation is effective? Is it fair? What other ways can legislatures force or promote technological innovation?

2. *Carbon Capture and Sequestration.* Many scientists believe that CCS technology is key to climate change mitigation. A CCS facility collects carbon dioxide emissions from a stationary source, transfers the carbon dioxide to a sequestration site, and then permanently stores the carbon dioxide in a sequestration facility. While the concept is rather simple, the mechanics have not yet proven to be. For example, many proposed sequestration sites are located underground, in natural formations. Depending upon the geological conditions of the site, carbon dioxide may leak into areas and ultimately be released into the atmosphere. In addition, geological sequestration may alter the natural conditions of the underground environment, resulting in unintended consequences. As a result, finding a secure, long-term sequestration area is often difficult.

Scientists involved in CCS development emphasize the importance of developing CCS testing facilities to show that CCS is a viable climate change mitigation technology. However, many conservationists oppose the construction of entirely new coal-fired power plants for the purpose of establishing CCS demonstration projects. Several groups have advocated for development of such facilities only to replace older, dirtier coal plants. Utilities object to these demands, because of the costs of replacing older facilities.

3. Another proposed new coal plant recently failed to obtain necessary approvals due, at least in part, to Washington's CCS statute. In that case, the Wallula Energy Resource Center (WERC) had proposed to build an integrated gasification combined coal plant with CCS in Walla Walla, Washington. Prior to building the facility, WERC proposed conducting sequestration tests on Washington state lands. Citing public opposition to the facility and the likelihood of future litigation, the Washington Department of Natural Resources denied WERC permission to build the sequestration site. WERC has since withdrawn its application for a siting permit from EFSEC.

4. Technology-forcing laws could present significant risks of "leakage" if adjacent states do not have similar requirements. In the case of the Washington facilities, it seems as though other laws would prevent the facilities from siting in Oregon and Idaho. Oregon law, for example, requires all new coal-fired power plants to offset 17 percent of their emissions with carbon credits, and most observers view this offset requirement as an effective barrier to new coal construction. In Idaho, the legislature imposed a two-year moratorium on new coal plants in 2006, and Idaho residents have expressed a clear disdain for new coal facilities. Montana could serve as a possible location for the facility, but several new coal-fired power plants have recently been proposed in the state, and there is likely little demand for another one. Thus, "leakage" in this case could be unlikely.

5. Some observers believe that "clean coal" technologies are too expensive to have much viability in the United States. One of the largest proposed facilities, called FutureGen, has struggled to secure private and public funding. The facility will likely cost approximately $1.8 billion to construct and operate. In June 2008, the Department of Energy withdrew its support for the facility, due to cost concerns. A month later, the Senate Appropriations Committee included $134 million dollars for the facility in an appropriations bill. More recently, Congress passed an appropriations bill that could provide the FutureGen plant with up to $1 billion. *See* Dan Eggen and Ellen Nakashima, *Despite Pledges, Package Has Some Pork*, THE WASH. POST, Feb. 13, 2009, at A06. Also in July 2008, a New York company announced it will abandon its plans to build a "clean coal" plant, citing cost concerns. *See New York Cancels Plans for Clean Coal Plant*, REUTERS UK, *available at* July 16, 2008, http://uk.reuters.com/article/governmentFilingsNews/ idUKN1648713620080716. Public utility commissions (PUC) have signaled their own doubts about the viability of CCS facilities. In Minnesota, for example, the PUC rejected a utility's request to invest in a new CCS facility due to cost concerns and fears about the unproven technology. *In the Matter of a Petition by Excelsior Energy Inc. for Approval of a Power Purchase Agreement Under Minn. Stat. § 216B.1694, Determination of Least Cost Technology, and Establishment of a Clean Energy Technology Minimum Under Minn. Stat. § 216B.1693*, Minn. Pub. Util. Comm'n, Docket No. E-6472/M-05-1993, Order Resolving Procedural Issues, Disapproving Power Purchase Agreement, Requiring Further Negotiations, and Resolving To Explore The Potential for a Statewide Market for Project Power Under Minn. Stat. § 216B.1694, Subd. 5 (Aug. 30, 2007).

4. *Other Common State and Local Measures*

State and local governments have employed a wide range of additional strategies to address and mitigate climate change. A few of these are discussed below. Other strategies, such as development of energy efficiency standards, land use plans, and transportation improvements are addressed in other chapters.

a. *Climate Action Plans*

Climate action plans are state-specific plans for mitigating and adapting to climate change. A typical climate action plan will include an estimate of baseline greenhouse gas emissions from the state, a summary of localized impacts that climate change will likely cause in the state, and a list of recommended measures for the state to take to mitigate climate change. Climate action plans are valuable in that they can identify the most appropriate mitigation actions for each state, and typically reflect state-specific concerns related to a state's political structure, economy, and natural resources. However, climate action plans typically lack regulatory requirements that mandate specific actions to reduce greenhouse gases. Thus, while climate action plans serve as a useful start for establishing initial policy, states must also enact other laws to implement the recommendations in the plans.

b. *Environmental Reviews*

Many states have laws resembling the National Environmental Policy Act (NEPA), which require government actors to conduct an environmental assessment prior to taking any action that will significantly affect the environment. The application of NEPA to climate change is discussed in Chapter 13. In addition, state and local governments have begun to apply their "little NEPA" laws to address climate change. See Michael H. Gerrard, *Climate Change and the Environmental Impact Review Process*, 22 WTR. NAT. RESOURCES & ENV'T 20 (2008). The New York Department of Transportation, for example, requires analyses of greenhouse gas emissions associated with transportation projects. King County in Washington State requires all county agencies to identify and evaluate climate change impacts for every public or private activity in which the county agency is a lead agency under the Washington State Environmental Protection Act. Massachusetts has adopted a formal policy requiring a quantification of project-related greenhouse gas emissions, as well as development of a proposed alternative to the proposed project, for many types of projects subject to review under the Massachusetts Environmental Policy Act. The proposed alternative must incorporate measures to "avoid, minimize, or mitigate" greenhouse gas emissions. Massachusetts Executive Office of Energy and Environmental Affairs, Greenhouse Gas Emissions Policy (Apr. 23, 2007). Finally, California has recently issued new guidelines explaining how state agencies should assess the effects of greenhouse gas emissions under the California Environmental Quality Act (CEQA).

The use of CEQA to address climate change has a particularly interesting history. Environmental organizations first began challenging project-specific environmental impact reports (EIRs) that had not considered the project impacts on climate change. *See* Natural Resources Def. Council v. Reclamation Board of the Resources Agency, Case No. 06 CS 01228 (Super Ct., Sacramento County, Apr. 27, 2007); American Canyon Community United for Responsible Growth v. City of American Canyon, Case No. 26-27462 (Super Ct., Napa Co., May 22, 2007). In both cases, the judges rejected the challenges because the plaintiffs did not demonstrate that significant new information had become available regarding the impacts of the project on climate change. Environmental groups, later joined by California Attorney General Jerry Brown, then submitted comments to local governments requesting that they analyze climate change in CEQA documents developed in relation to land use planning. After the Center for Biological Diversity sued the county of San Bernardino for failing to analyze climate change in its CEQA review, Attorney General Brown also sued the county. The lawsuits resulted in a settlement requiring San Bernardino — which is the largest county in the lower 48 states with one of the fastest growing populations — to inventory its greenhouse gas emissions and develop an emissions reduction plan. Following this case, in 2007, the California legislature passed Senate Bill 97, which expressly states that CEQA applies to greenhouse gas emissions.

Unlike the federal NEPA, as well as most "little NEPAs," application of CEQA to climate change could force substantive changes in agency practices. This is because CEQA prohibits an agency from approving a project that will have significant environmental impacts if feasible alternatives or feasible mitigation measures could avoid or substantially lessen those impacts. Pub. Res. Code § 21002. For a proposed building project, for example, mitigation measures may include using "green" building practices, such as constructing high-efficiency buildings, using recycled materials, and installing solar arrays or other alternative energy sources, to power the building. *See* Center for Biological Diversity, THE CALIFORNIA ENVIRONMENTAL QUALITY ACT: ON THE FRONT LINES OF CALIFORNIA'S FIGHT AGAINST GLOBAL WARMING, 10 (Sept. 2007). Land use planning decisions could also be subject to extensive mitigation requirements, such as development of public transportation systems, revised building codes and zoning requirements, and installation of methane capture and conversion facilities on county-owned landfills. *Id.* at 11. Thus CEQA review could spur significant changes in land use planning and development decisions.

III. DOES THE COMMERCE CLAUSE PROHIBIT SUB-FEDERAL REGULATION OF GREENHOUSE GAS EMISSIONS?

The Commerce Clause prohibits any state from enacting laws that either (1) facially discriminate against interstate commerce, *Philadelphia v. New Jersey*, 437 U.S. 617, 624 (1978), or (2) are facially neutral, but place an undue burden on interstate commerce. Pike v. Bruce Church, 397 U.S. 137, 145 (1970). The states' decisions to act unilaterally, or regionally, raise Commerce Clause concerns. For example, the RGGI MOU places limitations on offsets obtained from non-signatory states. At least one state RPS similarly attempts to limit the ability of utilities to obtain renewable emissions credits from out-of-state sources. Do these restrictions violate the Commerce Clause?

CITY OF PHILADELPHIA v. NEW JERSEY
437 U.S. 617 (1978)

A New Jersey law [ch. 363] prohibits the importation of most "solid or liquid waste which originated or was collected outside the territorial limits of the State. . . . " In this case we are required to decide whether this statutory prohibition violates the Commerce Clause of the United States Constitution

I

The statutory provision in question . . . provides:

> No person shall bring into this State any solid or liquid waste which originated or was collected outside the territorial limits of the State, except garbage to be fed to swine in the State of New Jersey, until the commissioner [of the State Department of Environmental Protection] shall determine that such action can be permitted without endangering the public health, safety and welfare and has promulgated regulations permitting and regulating the treatment and disposal of such waste in this State.

As authorized by ch. 363, the Commissioner promulgated regulations permitting four categories of waste to enter the State. [The regulations authorize imports of garbage to be fed to swine, materials intended for recycling, municipal solid waste intended to be uses as a heat source, and hazardous waste imported for treatment or recovery but not disposal.] Apart from these narrow exceptions, however, New Jersey closed its borders to all waste from other States.

Immediately affected by these developments were the operators of private landfills in New Jersey, and several cities in other States that had agreements with these operators for waste disposal. They brought suit against New Jersey and its Department of Environmental Protection in state court, attacking the statute and regulations on a number of state and federal grounds. In an oral opinion granting the plaintiffs' motion for summary judgment, the trial court declared the law unconstitutional because it discriminated against interstate commerce. The New Jersey Supreme Court . . . found that ch. 363 advanced vital health and environmental objectives with no economic discrimination against, and with little burden upon, interstate commerce, and that the law was therefore permissible under the Commerce Clause of the Constitution. * * *

III

A

Although the Constitution gives Congress the power to regulate commerce among the States, many subjects of potential federal regulation under that power inevitably escape congressional attention "because of their local character and their number and diversity." In the absence of federal legislation, these subjects are open to control by the States so long as they act within the restraints imposed by the Commerce Clause itself. The bounds of these restraints appear nowhere in the words of the Commerce Clause, but have emerged gradually in the decisions of this Court giving effect to its basic purpose. * * *

The opinions of the Court through the years have reflected an alertness to the evils of "economic isolation" and protectionism, while at the same time recognizing that incidental burdens on interstate commerce may be unavoidable when a State legislates to safeguard the health and safety of its people. Thus, where simple economic protectionism is effected by state legislation, a virtually *per se* rule of invalidity has been erected. The clearest example of such legislation is a law that overtly blocks the flow of interstate commerce at a State's borders. But where other legislative objectives are credibly advanced and there is no patent discrimination against interstate trade, the Court has adopted a much more flexible approach, the general contours of which were outlined in *Pike v. Bruce Church, Inc.*, 397 U.S. 137, 142:

Where the statute regulates evenhandedly to effectuate a legitimate local public interest, and its effects on interstate commerce are only incidental, it will be upheld unless the burden imposed on such commerce is clearly excessive in relation to the putative local benefits. . . . If a legitimate local purpose is found, then the question becomes one of degree. And the extent of the burden that will be tolerated will of course depend on the nature of the local interest involved, and on whether it could be promoted as well with a lesser impact on interstate activities.

The crucial inquiry, therefore, must be directed to determining whether ch. 363 is basically a protectionist measure, or whether it can fairly be viewed as a law directed to legitimate local concerns, with effects upon interstate commerce that are only incidental.

B

The purpose of ch. 363 is set out in the statute itself as follows:

The Legislature finds and determines that . . . the volume of solid and liquid waste continues to rapidly increase, that the treatment and disposal of these wastes continues to pose an even greater threat to the quality of the environment of New Jersey, that the available and appropriate land fill sites within the State are being diminished, that the environment continues to be threatened by the treatment and disposal of waste which originated or was collected outside the State, and that the public health, safety and welfare require that the treatment and disposal within this State of all wastes generated outside of the State be prohibited.

The New Jersey Supreme Court accepted this statement of the state legislature's purpose. The state court additionally found that New Jersey's existing landfill sites will be exhausted within a few years; that to go on using these sites or to develop new ones will take a heavy environmental toll, both from pollution and from loss of scarce open lands; that new techniques to divert waste from landfills to other methods of disposal and resource recovery processes are under development, but that these changes will require time; and finally, that "the extension of the lifespan of existing landfills, resulting from the exclusion of out-of-state waste, may be of crucial importance in preventing further virgin wetlands or other undeveloped lands from being devoted to landfill purposes." Based on these findings, the court concluded that ch. 363 was designed to protect, not the State's economy, but its environment, and that its substantial benefits outweigh its "slight" burden on interstate commerce.

The appellants strenuously contend that ch. 363, "while outwardly cloaked 'in the currently fashionable garb of environmental protection,' . . . is actually no more than a legislative effort to suppress competition and stabilize the cost of solid waste disposal for New Jersey residents. . . . " They cite passages of legislative history suggesting that the problem addressed by ch. 363 is primarily financial: Stemming the flow of out-of-state waste into certain landfill sites will extend their lives, thus delaying the day when New Jersey cities must transport their waste to more distant and expensive sites.

The appellees, on the other hand, deny that ch. 363 was motivated by financial concerns or economic protectionism. In the words of their brief, "[n]o New Jersey commercial interests stand to gain advantage over competitors from outside the state as a result of the ban on dumping out-of-state waste." Noting that New Jersey landfill operators are among the plaintiffs, the appellee's brief argues that "[t]he complaint is not that New Jersey has forged an economic preference for its own commercial interests, but rather that it has denied a small group of its entrepreneurs an economic opportunity to traffic in waste in order to protect the health, safety and welfare of the citizenry at large."

This dispute about ultimate legislative purpose need not be resolved, because its resolution would not be relevant to the constitutional issue to be decided in this case. Contrary to the evident assumption of the state court and the parties, the evil of protectionism can reside in legislative means as well as legislative ends. Thus, it does not matter whether the ultimate aim of ch. 363 is to reduce the waste disposal costs of New Jersey residents or to save remaining open lands from pollution, for we assume New Jersey has every right to protect its residents' pocketbooks as well as their environment. And it may be assumed as well that New Jersey may pursue those ends by slowing the flow of *all* waste into the State's remaining landfills, even though interstate commerce may incidentally be affected. But whatever New Jersey's ultimate purpose, it may not be accomplished by discriminating against articles of commerce coming from outside the State unless there is some reason, apart from their origin, to treat them differently. Both on its face and in its plain effect, ch. 363 violates this principle of nondiscrimination.

The Court has consistently found parochial legislation of this kind to be constitutionally invalid, whether the ultimate aim of the legislation was to assure a steady supply of milk by erecting barriers to allegedly ruinous outside competition, or to create jobs by keeping industry within the State, or to preserve the State's financial resources from depletion by fencing out indigent immigrants. In each of these cases, a presumably legitimate goal was sought to be achieved by the illegitimate means of isolating the State from the national economy.

Also relevant here are the Court's decisions holding that a State may not accord its own inhabitants a preferred right of access over consumers in other States to natural resources located within its borders. These cases stand for the basic principle that a "State is without power to prevent privately owned articles of trade from being shipped and sold in interstate commerce on the ground that they are required to satisfy local demands or because they are needed by the people of the State."

The New Jersey law at issue in this case falls squarely within the area that the Commerce Clause puts off limits to state regulation. On its face, it imposes on out-of-state commercial interests the full burden of conserving the State's remaining landfill space. It is true that in our previous cases the scarce natural resource was itself the article of commerce, whereas here the scarce resource and the article of commerce are distinct. But that difference is without consequence. In both instances, the State has overtly moved to slow or freeze the flow of commerce for protectionist reasons. It does not matter that the State has shut the article of commerce inside the State in one case and outside the State in the other. What is crucial is the attempt by one State to isolate itself from a problem common to many by erecting a barrier against the movement of interstate trade.

A.   Commerce Clause Challenges to Emissions Standards

When California proposed its emissions standards for electricity procurement, it received many comments that the rules would violate the Commerce Clause. It addressed these comments in its final rulemaking adopting the procurement standards.

RE: INTEGRATION OF GREENHOUSE GAS EMISSIONS STANDARDS INTO PROCUREMENT POLICIES, RULEMAKING PROCEEDING 06-04-009
Decision 07-01-039, 2007 WL 403573
(Cal. Pub. Util. Comm'n, Jan. 25, 2007)

INTERIM OPINION ON PHASE 1 ISSUES: GREENHOUSE GAS EMISSIONS PERFORMANCE STANDARD

BY THE COMMISSION:

1. Introduction and Summary

Today, we adopt an interim greenhouse gas (GHG) emissions performance standard for new long-term financial commitments to baseload generation undertaken by all load-serving entities (LSEs), consistent with the requirements and definitions of Senate Bill (SB) 1368 (Stats. 2006, ch. 598). Our adopted emissions performance standard or 'EPS' is intended to serve as a near-term bridge until an enforceable GHG emissions limit applicable to LSEs is established and in operation. At that time, as directed by SB 1368, we will reevaluate and continue, modify or replace this standard through a rulemaking proceeding. . . .

As discussed in this decision, an EPS is similar to an energy efficiency appliance standard. If a consumer wants to purchase a new refrigerator in California, for example, he or she has a variety of models to choose from — each with a different upfront purchase price, operating cost and other design attributes. However, at a minimum, each refrigerator must meet the threshold for appliance efficiency established by the standard. Similarly, SB 1368 establishes a minimum performance requirement for any long-term financial commitment for baseload generation that will be supplying power to California ratepayers. The new law establishes that the GHG emissions rates for these facilities must be no higher than the GHG emissions rate of a combined-cycle gas turbine (CCGT) powerplant.

An EPS is needed to reduce California's financial risk exposure to the compliance costs associated with future GHG emissions (state and federal) and associated future reliability problems in electricity supplies. Put another way, it is needed to ensure that there is no 'backsliding' as California transitions to a statewide GHG emissions cap: If LSEs enter into long-term commitments with high-GHG emitting baseload plants during this transition, California ratepayers will be exposed to the high cost of retrofits (or potentially the need to purchase expensive offsets) under future emission control regulations. They will also be exposed to potential supply disruptions when these high-emitting facilities are taken off line for retrofits, or retired early, in order to comply with future regulations. A facility-based GHG emissions performance standard protects California ratepayers from these backsliding risks and costs during the transition to a load-based GHG emissions cap. As directed by SB 1368, we have considered the effects on system reliability and overall costs to electricity customers in developing an EPS that will achieve these objectives.

*   *   *

8. Commerce Clause Issues

The Commerce Clause states that: 'Congress shall have [the] [p]ower . . . to regulate Commerce with foreign [n]ations, and among the several [s]tates. 'The negative implication, or dormant aspect, of the Commerce Clause limits the ability of individual states to impede the flow of interstate commerce. Dormant Commerce Clause doctrine consists of three analytical frameworks. First, a state rule that facially discriminates against other states in order to protect local economic interests will generally be found invalid. Second, when a state rule does not facially discriminate against out-of-state economic interests, the *Pike* balancing test will be applied. Under *Pike*, a state enactment 'will be upheld unless the burden imposed on such commerce is clearly excessive in relation to the putative local benefits.' Third, a state rule must not regulate extraterritorially. The EPS does not run awry of any of these tests and is thus valid under the Commerce Clause.

8.1. The EPS does not Discriminate Against Interstate Commerce

Any party challenging the constitutional validity of a regulation under the dormant Commerce Clause bears the burden of demonstrating discrimination. CEED [the Center for Energy and Economic Development] argues that the EPS has a discriminatory effect on interstate commerce that violates the dormant Commerce Clause. Citing *City of Philadelphia* for the principle that: '[a] state cannot block imports from other states, nor exports from within its boundaries, without offending the Constitution,' CEED argues that the proposed EPS is unconstitutional because it would limit the ability of out-of-state coal-fueled generation plants to export their electricity into California.

The EPS is distinguishable from the statute in *City of Philadelphia* for two reasons. First, the statute in *City of Philadelphia* prevented certain products from entering New Jersey. Under the EPS, electricity generated from high-GHG emitters can still be sold to California LSEs under existing contracts, or under new or renewal contracts of less than five years. In addition, coal-fired and other plants that use technology that reduces GHG emissions could meet the EPS.

More importantly, the EPS does not discriminate based on geographic origin. . . . In *City of Philadelphia*, the New Jersey statute prohibited the importation of 'solid or liquid waste which originated outside the territorial limits of the State.' . . . In sharp contrast, the geographic locality of a high-GHG emitter is irrelevant under the EPS. An LSE is free to enter into long-term contracts with both in-state and out-of-state generators because the EPS makes no distinctions between in-state and out-of-state sources of electricity. Indeed, the Attorney General notes that: 'under the [EPS], a substantial amount of electricity generated out-of-state would [meet the EPS and therefore] continue to be available for procurement' For these reasons, we find CEED's argument to be without merit.

* * *

CEED further argues that the EPS (and the GHG cap to be implemented in Phase 2) 'places heightened financial burdens on the construction of new coal-fueled power plants in neighboring states.' This is based on the practice of using pre-construction contracts to secure financing for powerplant construction. CEED further argues that the EPS therefore provides California firms with a 'significant competitive advantage' in securing financing.

The dormant Commerce Clause does not require California to protect the pecuniary interests of out-of-state coal burners. Moreover, CEED's argument does not show that California firms will have a significant competitive advantage. As stated above, both California firms and out-of-state firms are covered under the EPS. The Supreme Court has observed that the Commerce Clause 'protects the interstate market, not particular interstate firms, from prohibitive or burdensome regulations.' We find CEED's argument to be without merit.

*   *   *

No party has met the burden of demonstrating discrimination. Therefore, we conclude that the EPS is an evenhanded regulation that does not discriminate against interstate commerce.

8.2. *Pike* Balancing Test

When a state enactment is not facially discriminatory, the *Pike* balancing test is generally applied. In *Pike v. Bruce Church* (1970) 397 U.S. 137, the Supreme Court established this test that weighs the local benefits against the burdens on interstate commerce, in order to determine if a particular state regulation violates the dormant Commerce Clause. A regulation's burdens on interstate commerce must be 'clearly excessive' in relation to the local benefits in order for a regulation to be struck down under *Pike*. As Environmental Defense points out, the burden of proving 'excessiveness' would fall on a party challenging a regulation.

8.2.1. The EPS has Substantial Local Benefits

Despite the restrictions of the dormant Commerce Clause, a state retains general police powers to regulate legitimate local concerns. In SB 1368, the Legislature has made specific legislative findings regarding the local benefits of the EPS. SB 1368 reads: '[g]lobal warming will have serious adverse consequences on the economy, health and environment of California.'

Regarding economic benefits, the Legislature found that 'federal regulation of emissions of greenhouse gases is likely' 'over the next decade' and that SB 1368 serves to 'reduce potential exposure of California customers for future pollution-control costs.' SB 1368 also reduces 'potential exposure of California consumers to future reliability problems in electricity supplies.' Thus, the EPS serves to protect ratepayers from the costs and risks of complying with future laws and regulations that will further limit the emission of GHG gases in the process of generating electricity. If Californians are reliant on high-GHG emitting sources, whether in-state or out-of-state, future regulations could have a devastating impact on the California economy. Non-compliant energy sources could be forced to refurbish their facilities to meet these new standards, and the costs could be shifted to consumers. Whether or not costs are shifted, plants would likely be unable to continue supplying as much power to California while they are refurbishing. Further, the EPS encourages a wide range of clean energy sources, which protects the reliability of the grid. It is a legitimate local purpose to protect California consumers from financial risks in an evolving regulatory scheme, while ensuring a continuous supply of electricity for California customers.

Regarding the health and environment of California, we look to the legislative findings of AB 32 and the Final Climate Action Team Report to the Governor and the Legislature (Presented to the Legislature in March, 2006) (CATR).

In AB 32, the Legislature found that:

'(a) Global warming poses a serious threat to the economic wellbeing, public health, natural resources, and the environment of California. The potential adverse impacts of global warming include the exacerbation of air quality problems, a reduction in the quality and supply of water to the state from the Sierra snowpack, a rise in sea levels resulting in displacement of thousands of coastal businesses and residences, damage to marine ecosystems and the natural environment, and an increase in the incidences of infectious diseases, asthma, and other human health-related problems.'

GHG emissions contribute to climate change. By increasing the number of extremely hot days, and the 'frequency, duration, and intensity of conditions conducive to air pollution formation, oppressive heat, and wildfires,' the public health of Californians could be dramatically affected. Climate change is also likely to increase infectious disease vectors such as mosquitoes, ticks, fleas and rodents, which would effectuate the negative health consequences discussed in AB 32. Similarly, climate change can increase asthma triggers such as pollen, dust mites, and molds. The decreases to the Sierra Nevada snowpack mentioned in AB 32 would have far-reaching effects on California's water supply. The snowpack provides a natural water supply to Californians, including agricultural growers. Loss of the snowpack would result in decreased runoff, which would reduce the availability of the already overstretched water supply. Electric supply from hydroelectric power-plants is also likely to diminish, while demand continues to rise. The rise in sea level described in AB 32 could submerge many of California's beaches and estuaries. The occurrences of extreme oceanic events are also expected to rise with sea levels.

* * * We thus conclude that the EPS has substantial local benefits.

8.2.2. The EPS does not Excessively Burden Interstate Commerce

As noted above, CEED argues that the EPS will burden interstate commerce because it would somehow limit the construction of new coal-fueled plants and because clean coal technology is not commercially feasible. We have already shown how these alleged 'burdens' are nondiscriminatory. CEED also makes the speculative claim that the EPS would decrease the price of electricity sold by some out-of-state generators. . . . CEED is selectively characterizing the interstate market in order to inflate the purported burden. The EPS would affect electric generators that are high-GHG emitters and seek to enter into new long-term baseload contracts with California LSEs. However, this would only affect those generation companies to the extent they also refuse to refurbish their power plants, or build new power plants, with technology that limits GHG emissions such that they comply with the EPS. Beyond this very specific class, out-of-state generators would generally be able to meet the EPS. The overall interstate market is not being overly burdened.

More generally, CEED argues that: 'the reality of California's energy market dictates that the [EPS] will primarily preclude out-of-state suppliers from competing in California markets' and that the EPS burdens the economies of other states more than California. CEED further argues that through coal displacement, various interstate geographic regions of the United States would be negatively impacted in the future.

CEED presents a report by 'Energy Ventures Analysis, Inc.' (EVA) which states that: '[b]aseload power imported from the Southwest would be far harder hit than generation from the Pacific Northwest. Both major importing areas would be hit much harder than in-state California plants.' The report speculates that 8–52% of the existing Pacific Northwest imports would not meet the EPS, and that 54–86% of the existing Southwest imports would not meet the EPS. However, assuming arguendo these numbers were accurate, as much as 92% of the existing Pacific Northwest imports would meet the EPS, and as much as 46% of the existing

Southwest imports would meet the EPS. Moreover, generators may make changes to existing generation plants or construct new out-of-state generation plants, in order to meet the EPS.

We find the EVA report unpersuasive. Indeed, reducing reliance on high-GHG emitting resources is a major goal of the EPS. Whether one out-of-state geographic region may be impacted more than another is not relevant here because the concern underlying the dormant Commerce Clause is economic protectionism of in-state interests.

CEED also attaches a study purporting to show various costs that will be incurred as coal is displaced by other fuels. However, the authors of the study cautioned that their analysis 'is not intended to measure the impacts of any specific policy that could result in decreased coal production or utilization.' Environmental externalities such as pollution and GHG emissions were not considered in the study. In any event, the fact that national displacement of coal may have some economic effects does not establish an impermissible burden on interstate commerce.

Overall, the argument CEED raises is analogous to a failed argument in *Minnesota v. Clover Leaf Creamery* (1981) 449 U.S. 456. In *Clover Leaf Creamery*, the Court upheld a Minnesota statute that banned the retail sale of milk in plastic nonreturnable, nonrefillable containers, but allowed such sale in other types of nonreturnable, nonrefillable containers. The opponents of the statute argued that the 'plastic resin . . . used for making plastic nonreturnable milk jugs, is produced entirely by non-Minnesota firms, while pulpwood, used for making paperboard, is a major Minnesota product.' The Supreme Court responded: '[e]ven granting that the out-of-state plastics industry is burdened relatively more heavily than the Minnesota pulpwood industry, we find that this burden is not 'clearly excessive' in light of the substantial state interest in promoting conservation of energy and other natural resources.'

As in *Clover Leaf Creamery*, the burdens cited by CEED cannot be deemed 'clearly excessive' in light of the substantial local benefits of the EPS. * * *

For all the reasons stated above, we conclude that the alleged burdens are incidental and not clearly excessive in relation to the substantial local benefits of the EPS.

QUESTIONS AND DISCUSSION

1. *Is California's EPS Discriminatory?* A law may be invalid under the Dormant Commerce Clause if it has either a discriminatory effect or a discriminatory purpose. Minnesota v. Clover Leaf Creamery, 449 U.S. 456, 471 n. 15 (1981). In most cases where the Court has found a law discriminatory, the law imposed a burden on out-of-state commerce without placing the same burden on in-state interests. *Id.* at 472 (summarizing cases). If, however, a law applies to both in-state and out-of-state entities, the Court will generally not find that law discriminatory even if the out-of-state entities may face greater hardships in complying with the law.

2. *Undue Burden.* Do you agree with the California Public Utility Commission's (CPUC's) conclusions that the EPS does not place an undue burden on interstate commerce? As a result of energy deregulation and increased transmission capacity (*see* Chapter 14), as well as stringent California air pollution controls, more than 90 percent of California's coal-derived electricity comes from out of state. In contrast, more than 85 percent of California's natural-gas derived electricity

originates in California. *See* CALIFORNIA ENERGY COMMISSION, CALIFORNIA ENERGY ALMANAC, TOTAL ELECTRICITY SYSTEM POWER (2007). The EPS requires all electricity generation to achieve emissions rates achieved by combined-cycle natural gas plants. Combined-cycle natural gas plant emission rates are nearly one-third of the typical emissions rates of pulverized coal plants and one-half the emissions rates of integrated gasification combined-coal (IGCC) plants. Thus, the law seems to strongly favor natural gas generators (more than 85 percent of which are located in California) and strongly disfavor coal (more than 90 percent of which comes from out-of-state). Why, then, did the CPUC conclude that the law does not unduly burden interstate commerce?

In part, the CPUC's opinion seems to turn on the potential development of carbon capture and storage technologies to reduce greenhouse gas emissions from coal plants. Yet, as noted above, *supra* note 5 in Section II.B.3.b, efforts to develop "clean coal" facilities appear to have stalled. Does this mean that the CPUC erred in finding that the EPS did not unduly burden interstate commerce? Why or why not?

3. *Alternatives to the Emmissions Performance Standards.* Could the CPUC have enacted a regulation that would have less impact on interstate commerce? One of the reasons the CPUC applied the EPS to procurement contracts was to prevent "leakage" that would result if the CPUC established emissions requirements only on generators. The CPUC feared that regulation of in-state generation only would allow utilities to increase their imports of cheaper coal-derived electricity from other states, and thus negate any greenhouse gas reductions achieved through in-state regulation only. Indeed, at the time CPUC was developing the EPS regulations, six southern California cities were negotiating long-term contracts with coal-fired power generators in Utah. *See* Patricia Weisselberg, *Shaping the Energy Future in the American West: Can California Curb Greenhouse Gas Emissions from Out-of-State, Coal-Fired Power Plants Without Violating the Dormant Commerce Clause?*, 42 U.S.F. L. REV. 185, 200–202 (2007). The cities ultimately abandoned the contract negotiations due to concerns about climate change and the pending regulations. Does this suggest that the application of the EPS to procurement contracts is a necessary means to limit greenhouse gas emissions?

4. *Local Interests.* Under the *Pike* test, courts will balance the state's interest in regulating with the burden imposed on interstate commerce. The stronger the state interest, the less likely it is that a court will strike down a law, even if the law does burden interstate commerce. In the context of climate change, of course, the issue is whether a state's interest in reducing greenhouse gas emissions can ever truly be considered a "local" interest. How did the CPUC resolve this aspect of the challenge?

In *Central Valley Chrysler-Jeep v. Witherspoon*, the plaintiffs challenged California's proposed vehicle emissions standards because they burden " 'the production and sale of new motor vehicles' while providing 'no local environmental benefit, or insubstantial benefits at best.' " 456 F. Supp. 2d 1160, 1183 (E.D. Cal. 2006). However, the district court rejected the challenge on the basis that the Clean Air Act provision authorizing California to adopt its own vehicle emissions standards under Section 209 demonstrates a Congressional intent to waive application of the dormant Commerce Clause to such standards. *Id.* at 1185–86. The question therefore still remains: how "local" must the state interest be to justify burdening interstate commerce?

B.   Commerce Clause Challenges to Renewable Portfolio Standards

As noted above, many states have developed RPSs mandating a certain percentage of power that must come from renewable energy sources. For many states, an underlying motivation to adopt an RPS is to spur investment in local renewable energy industries. In fact, many states have mandated that a certain percentage of the renewable energy must be locally produced. Dr. Benjamin K. Sovacool summarizes the types of RPSs that implicate the Commerce Clause:

BENJAMIN K. SOVACOOL, THE BEST OF BOTH WORLDS: ENVIRONMENTAL FEDERALISM AND THE NEED FOR FEDERAL ACTION ON RENEWABLE ENERGY AND CLIMATE CHANGE
27 STAN. ENVTL. L.J. 397, 457–58 (2008)*

Even though these decisions would seem to serve as a stark warning to states seeking to restrict the flow of commodities in the energy sector, many state RPS statutes set geographic restrictions on renewable generation or otherwise limit the interstate trade of RECs [Renewable Energy Credits] and could be accused of violating a central tenet of the United States Constitution. Nevada and New Jersey have adopted restrictions that only count in-state renewable resources toward their RPS mandates. Pennsylvania's relatively new "Alternative Energy Portfolio Standard" (Act 213) does exactly the same thing, allowing only in-state resources or those coming from nearby service areas to meet state regulations. Similarly, Maryland and the District of Columbia require that RPS-eligible renewable resources must come from within the PJM service territory [PJM is a regional transmission operator coordinating the movement of electricity between parts of several mid-Atlantic, Midwestern, and Eastern states, including Maryland, D.C., Delaware, New Jersey, and Ohio], and in the Pacific Northwest, RECs can only be sold among the fourteen members of the Western Renewable Energy Generation Information System. California's RPS requires RECs to be bundled with the electricity generated from renewable resources, which has the practical effect of restricting unbundled RECs from other states. The California Public Utilities Commission has warned state policymakers that their position on out-of-state RECs may be constitutionally questionable.

In Texas, which recently surpassed California to become the nation's leading producer of wind energy, state lawmakers passed legislation that could spark a constitutional challenge from the state's wind generators, many of whom are profiting from selling excess wind generation to neighboring RPS states. The law requires that RECs generated in state apply toward Texas's RPS goals: "[T]he Commission shall ensure that all renewable capacity installed in this state and all renewable energy credits awarded, produced, procured, or sold from renewable capacity in this state are counted toward the goal." The problem is that

> Texas's proposed legislation effectively would ban the out-of-state sale of RECs generated from in-state renewable capacity since any certified REC tracking system would mark the RECs as having been already counted. Texas wind generators, who can sell wind credits for much higher prices in other markets, could argue that the law is a clear violation of the constitutional right to interstate commerce.

The growing tension between state and federal electricity regulators may mean that a Commerce Clause challenge is impending. While the legality of geographical RPS restrictions has yet to be challenged on Commerce Clause grounds, regulators are beginning a kind of "Commerce Clause brinksmanship."

While the states' goals may be laudable, it is not clear whether they would survive a challenge under the Commerce Clause. In fact, it is likely that at least some RPSs would be invalidated as impermissible protectionist measures.

KIRSTEN H. ENGEL, THE DORMANT COMMERCE CLAUSE THREAT TO MARKET-BASED ENVIRONMENTAL REGULATION: THE CASE OF ELECTRICITY DEREGULATION
26 ECOLOGY L.Q. 243, 271 81 (1999)[*]

3. Restricting Interstate Commerce in Marketable Goods

[A] state's willingness to implement a renewable portfolio standard through a system of tradable energy credits is likely to hinge upon the state's ability to capture the available environmental and economic benefits associated with renewable power production. To retain the tradable energy credit mechanism and yet capture a benefit other than that of reducing global warming, a state might specify that only the following will satisfy an energy retailer's renewable power purchase obligation under the state standard: (1) the energy credits generated by in-state renewable power producers (in-state credit generation restriction); or (2) energy credits representing renewable power that is sold to end-use consumers in the enacting state (in-state power sale restriction). . . . . Each of these restrictions provides advantages for the enacting state but raises distinct Commerce Clause issues.

a. In-State Energy Credit Generation Restriction

Of the options listed above, a state gains the greatest economic benefits by restricting the source of credits allowed under its renewable portfolio standard to credits generated by in-state renewable power producers. Under such a restriction, energy retailers must purchase credits from in-state renewables companies, either directly from such companies or from other suppliers. The restriction thus subsidizes in-state renewables companies, thereby fostering jobs and other economic benefits for the state. The degree to which an in-state credit generation restriction will benefit the state's environment depends, however, upon whether the restriction reduces the generating capacity of local fossil fuel fired plants. To date, only Nevada has enacted a renewable portfolio standard with an in-state credit generation restriction.

Two aspects of an in-state credit generation requirement merit scrutiny: (1) the restriction imposes a burden upon multi-state firms that wish to do business within the state; and (2) the restriction facially discriminates against credits generated by out-of-state renewable power producers solely on the basis of their geographic origin. Because states frequently impose threshold requirements upon companies

---

conducting business in-state, and courts generally allow states considerable latitude in doing so, the first aspect of the restriction does not pose serious problems. * * *

b. In-State Power Sale Restriction

An in-state power sale restriction requires that all of the renewable-based energy that a retailer uses to satisfy a state's renewable portfolio standard be sold to or made available to state customers. When enacted as part of a tradable credit scheme that implements a state's renewable portfolio standard, such a restriction limits energy credits satisfying a state's renewable power mandate to those representing renewable energy sold to in-state consumers. Such a restriction ensures that the state's renewable portfolio standard will foster the renewable power industry within the geographic region serving its energy customers and hence prevents the leakage of the environmental and economic benefits of the standard to distant regions. For the enacting state, such a restriction may be just as effective in capturing the potential environmental and economic benefits of renewable power generation as an in-state credit generation restriction. First, the state is assured of the price stability benefits of a more diverse energy portfolio. Second, to the extent that the portfolio standard displaces fossil-fuel capacity within the same geographic region, the state will reap the same clean air benefits from the in-state sale restriction as from the in-state credit generation restriction. The in-state sales requirement assures that the renewable power represented by the credits originates from renewable power plants located within distances from which power can reasonably be transmitted. While the jobs fostered by the portfolio standard may not be created in-state, they will occur within the region that transmits power to the state, which may benefit the residents of the enacting state. . . . Any renewable power generator, regardless of its location, can generate qualifying credits if it is able to send power through the electricity transmission grid to end-use consumers within the state.

QUESTIONS AND DISCUSSION

1. Professor Engel's article suggests that states face the greatest risk of having their laws invalidated under the Commerce Clause if the states establish market-based mechanisms that allow utilities to meet their RPS through purchasing renewable energy credits, but only "count" those credits that come from in-state renewable energy sources. Does this mean that states would be better off limiting market-based systems entirely? How could a state restructure its RPS to promote in-state renewable energy development without running afoul of the Commerce Clause?

2. What types of state laws do you think stand the best chance of surviving Commerce Clause challenges? Which state laws do you think are the most effective at mitigating climate change? Are your answers the same for these two questions? What does this suggest to you about the efficacy of state approaches to mitigating climate change?

IV.   THE FUTURE ROLE OF STATE AND LOCAL GOVERNMENTS

State and local governments have clearly played a leading role in developing innovative climate change policies. As these sub-federal governments have increased their regulation of greenhouse gas emissions, many regulated entities and commentators have called for federal preemption of most state and local policies. On the other hand, representatives of sub-federal governments and many conservationists have called for a type of "cooperative federalism" approach to regulation, so that all levels of government can work together to address climate change.

Those who argue for a continued role for state and local governments raise several points. First, states have traditionally acted as laboratories for new policies and thereby allowed the federal government to adopt its own policies based on the failures and successes of state innovations. Second, state and local governments are closer to those they represent, and therefore can theoretically respond quicker and more directly to their constituents' needs. Moreover, their responses can serve to drive federal action as well. Third, because states have acted before the federal government, they have gained expertise as regulators in areas that the federal government has yet to regulate. If sub-federal governments are preempted from regulating greenhouse gas emissions, the federal government will no longer benefit from the states' experiences. In addition, preemption could be perceived as undemocratic, because it could eliminate policies which have broad citizen support.

On the other hand, those who favor federal action, and especially preemption, argue that the nature of climate change calls for a uniform approach involving all fifty states. The varying state policies create an uneven regulatory environment, which is difficult and costly to navigate. In addition, for a greenhouse gas emissions trading program to succeed, it must be administered at the federal level pursuant to federal rules. Finally, because international negotiations are the domain of the federal government, many believe that climate change policies must also be established only on a federal level.

Between these poles are many who believe that all levels of government can and must work together to address climate change. The question is how government responsibilities should be allocated. Consider the following paper.

FRANZ T. LITZ, TOWARD A CONSTRUCTIVE DIALOGUE ON FEDERAL AND STATE ROLES IN U.S. CLIMATE CHANGE POLICY
24–32 (Pew Center on Climate Change 2008)[*]

V. Future U.S. Climate Policies: Settling on Federal and State Roles

Given the broad range of policies that will be necessary to tackle the climate change challenge, any future national climate action framework will require some action from both the federal government and states. This is in part due to the recognition that an economy-wide cap-and-trade program, although necessary, will not be sufficient to change behavior in certain areas of the economy where market barriers or inelasticity of demand prevent such transformation. In such areas, complementary policies will be required. Many of these complementary measures will take place in areas of traditional state authority, while others will take place in subject areas where federal and state governments have shared responsibility for accomplishing policy goals. * * *

The remainder of this paper is dedicated to outlining three possible approaches to comprehensive nationwide climate change action. All three approaches require the federal government to establish mandatory nationwide GHG reduction targets. Otherwise, the three approaches are described as follows:

- The first hypothetical approach, the "Heavy State Role" scenario, would reserve most decisions about how to achieve the reduction targets to the states through federally mandated comprehensive climate change action plans.

- (In the second scenario, the "Heavy Federal Role," the federal government would bear responsibility for achieving nationwide reductions through federal programs. The exception to this might be those programs that relate to areas over which states largely have exclusive control, such as land use decisions.

- The third, the "Federal-State Partnership" approach, calls for the federal government to enact certain key "anchor" policies that would be implemented nationwide. States would be given roles in the implementation of the federal anchor programs to the extent those roles effectively capitalize on state jurisdictional strengths. States would be also required to develop comprehensive climate change action plans to achieve reductions beyond the federal anchor programs.

*   *   *

1. Heavy State Role Approach

Under the "Heavy State Role" approach, the federal government would enact mandatory nationwide reduction targets and require every state to develop, implement and periodically revise a comprehensive state climate action plan. The contents of the plan would be largely up to the individual states, but each state would be responsible for achieving its share of the national reduction target. The federal government would offer states technical and financial assistance to develop and implement state plans.

The Heavy State Role option presents some advantages. The federal action would deliver two key benefits: there would be clear national reduction targets and all states would have to contribute their share to the effort. Beyond these benefits, all 50 states would be allowed to experiment with individual state approaches to reduce emissions, much as many states have done to date. This would tend to be positive for those policy mechanisms that are best tailored to specific state circumstances. The approach would also engender a potentially productive competition among states to develop policies that best achieve the results while meeting other state goals.

For those policy mechanisms that benefit from wide-scale deployment, however, such as cap-and-trade programs, the Heavy State Role approach would be much less helpful. Regional efforts like the Regional Greenhouse Gas Initiative would proliferate in an attempt to offset this disadvantage, as they have in the absence of federal action. Linking regional and state programs may go further to offset the disadvantage, but differences across emissions markets would on balance be counterproductive and more costly.

The Heavy State Role approach would present additional challenges beyond the differences across states and regions. Although every state would be required to make reductions, experience to date suggests that many high-emitting states are very reluctant to impose emissions limitations. Delays would accompany federal attempts to bring unwilling states along. While different policies from state to state would yield innovative results in some states, other state attempts may fail to get reductions, while differences would bring inefficiencies as compared to uniform national programs. There is also the potential for uneven regulation across state lines.

2. The Heavy Federal Role Approach

In contrast with the Heavy State Role scenario, the Heavy Federal Role approach places responsibility for reaching nationwide goals on the federal government. The only exceptions would be the areas that are simply not practical to regulate at the federal level, such as local land use policies. Key policies under this approach might be a broad nationwide cap-and-trade program, along with other policies such as a renewable portfolio standard and a low-carbon fuel standard.

The greater reliance on federal control in all areas would maximize the uniformity of policies across all states, and create a predictable business environment. For those programs that are most effectively implemented on a national level — like a cap-and-trade program — the overall cost of the programs will be minimized, allowing for more significant reductions overall. A few potential policies are outlined below before a discussion of the benefits and challenges of the Heavy Federal Role Approach.

National Cap-and-Trade Program. In general, a cap-and-trade program presents the classic example of a policy measure that is more effectively deployed at a national level than at the state or regional level. This is true because the more sources covered by a cap, the greater the possibility for inexpensive reductions across the system as a whole, and in turn, the greater the overall reduction practically achievable. Larger cap-and-trade programs also send more robust market signals to investors who seek larger markets for new technologies to address GHG emissions. A federal program also tends to level the playing field for sources as compared to state or regional emissions trading regimes.

If implemented like the Acid Rain Program described above, a federal cap-and-trade program generally leaves little room for states to achieve deeper reductions from covered sources. A federal cap-and-trade program sets the maximum amount of emissions that may come from a set of sources — typically sources such as electric generators and industrial facilities. The federal cap establishes the total reductions regardless of more stringent state programs that affect sources in a particular state, because a reduction in one state by definition frees up allowances in the system to be used in another state. A Heavy Federal Approach would presumably not seek to change this dynamic.

National Vehicle Efficiency Standards. * * * Under current federal law, only the federal government may regulate vehicle fuel efficiency. This ensures that automobile manufacturers need only comply with one set of efficiency regulations rather than a patchwork of state regulations.

National Renewable or Low-Carbon Portfolio Standard. A national renewable or low-carbon portfolio standard could be enacted to increase the share of electricity generated from renewable and other low-carbon energy sources. A national renewable portfolio standard would have the advantage of driving renewable energy across the country, and not just in states that have adopted their own renewable energy portfolio standards. A national standard could also provide more flexibility concerning the location of renewable energy generating facilities: solar and wind installations could be sited in areas best able to capitalize on these natural resources.

As discussed above, however, electric generation resource planning has long been the province of state governments, with the exception of matters that affect interstate commerce or interstate resources. A federal renewable portfolio standard would either require a new federal authority and associated bureaucracy, or it would have to rely on state regulatory bodies for its implementation.

A Heavy Federal Role, therefore, presents the advantages that have been recited for federal action: uniform national application of requirements; involvement of all states, not just those willing to act on their own; and a level playing field for businesses operating nationwide. While it maximizes the benefits of federal action, however, the heavy federal approach does not enable states to do what they do best.

In leaving states largely out, the heavy federal scenario creates significant challenges. Because states would not be devising climate action plans, the opportunities to identify creative local solutions to problems would be substantially diminished. The federal government would be less able to address local stakeholders and other interests. Areas that were previously the state's charge, like electricity and natural gas delivery, would necessarily come under increasingly federalized control. As in the Corporate Average Fuel Economy context, states would not be in a position to drive improvements when the federal government is slow to act.

3. Federal and State Partnership Approach

While the heavy state and federal approaches take advantage of the strengths of the state or federal governments, respectively, a Federal and State Partnership Approach aims to draw on the strengths of both levels of government. Under this approach, the federal government would set nationwide greenhouse gas reduction targets and implement key national "anchor" programs that are aimed at obtaining significant uniform reductions across all 50 states. At the same time, the states would be tapped to achieve additional reductions through those policies and programs that benefit from state and local design and implementation. In developing the federal anchor programs, furthermore, states would serve as on-the-ground implementers where appropriate, and opportunities to allow states to continue to serve as "first movers" would be preserved to the extent that the benefits of national implementation are not unduly compromised.

It is important here to consider the potential need for both federal anchor programs as well as complementary policies that are designed to adjust for market failures or local circumstances. For example, much attention has been paid to the need for a national cap-and-trade program to reduce emissions across multiple sectors of the economy. Some of the federal proposals to date seek to cover transportation fuels to reduce emissions from the transportation sector. Yet while broad coverage has advantages, consumer behavior is generally not very responsive in the short term to incremental increases in the price of transportation fuels. As a result, tackling transportation emissions is likely to require more than cap-and-trade. States may be in a better position to design complementary measures designed to encourage consumers to both buy more energy efficient vehicles and travel fewer miles. Indeed, the traditionally state and local areas of transportation and land-use planning could play a significant role in this complementary effort.

Because of the potential need to achieve emissions reductions beyond those that can be accomplished through federal anchor programs, the shared approach aims to divide roles to reach the best policy outcome. Below, the federal anchor programs are revisited together with a brief discussion of how states might play constructive roles in these programs.

Potential State Roles in a Federal Cap-and-Trade Program. Recall that federal cap-and-trade programs tend to discourage action at the state level because any reductions achieved from sources covered by the federal cap simply free up federal allowances to be used outside the state. It may nonetheless be possible to provide states with the flexibility to achieve deeper reductions. If under a federal cap-and-trade program some allowances are allocated first to states for distribution to sources, and if states were permitted to unilaterally retire a portion of the allowances allocated to the state, the state could effectively impose a more stringent requirement on its own sources without enabling additional emissions at a location outside the state.

In addition, any federal cap-and-trade program could allow states to determine the appropriate method of distributing some allowances to sources in the states. Some would argue that allowance allocation is appropriately accomplished at the state level given the state's familiarity with its industries and stakeholders. Should a state decide to auction the allowances, it may invest the allowance revenue in a way that accomplishes complementary aims that are more easily achieved at the state level, such as increased investment in energy efficiency. Others would argue that treating the same industries differently in different states raises interstate competitiveness issues, and that the federal government may be in the best position to stimulate technological innovation through allocation policy.

Federal climate policy must also address how to best interact with the three regional cap-and-trade systems already under development. The federal government will need to assess whether and how to provide a transitional existence to such programs. Depending on the timing of enactment of federal policy, some state programs will have already begun trading and/or auctioning of allowances.

National and State Greenhouse Gas Vehicle Tailpipe Standards. The Clean Air Act struck a compromise between the two extremes on vehicle tailpipe standards. Vesting exclusive authority in the federal government to regulate tailpipe emissions could lead to unresponsive policies. On the other hand, allowing all 50 states to regulate tailpipe emissions would result in tremendous inefficiencies for automobile manufacturers and consumers. By limiting to two the number of different regulatory standards the automakers must meet, Congress struck a balance between state and federal authority. The outcome is a policy that preserved the ability for states to innovate and spur federal action.

By enacting certain key national anchor programs that preserve the states' ability to enact policies more stringent than the federal programs, the federal government will be achieving significant reductions through policies that make sense at a federal level. The remaining policies in other areas are then left for states to develop as appropriate. Through the state climate change mitigation planning process, states could assemble a portfolio of policies and measures across all areas, including energy efficiency, low-carbon and renewable fuels, transportation and land use policies, agriculture, forestry, and waste reduction measures.

———————

QUESTIONS AND DISCUSSION

1.   What do you think about the proposal for federal and state governments to share responsibility to implement national climate change policy? On the one hand, it appears to be a workable solution, since it would mirror many of the "cooperative federalism" statutes already in existence. It would allow states to go beyond minimum federal standards and thus preserve their sovereignty to enact measures to protect public health and welfare. On the other hand, the proposal might not result in the uniform federal standards sought by many industries.

2.   As noted in Chapter 12, many industries have called for federal preemption of state and local greenhouse gas emissions requirements. Do you believe federal preemption is appropriate? Why or why not? If you do, what type of federal law, if any, do you think Congress should adopt in preempting state and local laws? How far should preemption go? Should it extend only to the regional cap-and-trade programs? Should it cover state emissions trading programs? Renewable portfolio standards? Land use laws?

3.   What is it about climate change that makes industries' calls for broad preemption seem politically palatable? As Mr. Litz explains, the federal government and states have a long history of jointly implementing environmental laws, and the federal government has preempted states in only a few circumstances (such as with motor vehicle standards). Does the international nature of climate change present a good case for broad preemption of state laws? If yes, why? If not, what other reasons would justify preemption?

4.   For further discussion of federal-state issues, including preemption, in the climate context, *see, e.g.,* J.R. DeShazo & Jody Freeman, *Timing and Form of Federal Regulation: The Case of Climate Change,* 155 U. PA. L. REV. 1499 (2007); William Andreen, et al., *Cooperative Federalism and Climate Change: Why Federal, State and Local Governments Must Continue to Partner* (Center for Progressive Reform 2008); Nicholas Lutsey & Daniel Sperling, *America's Bottom-Up Climate Change Mitigation Policy,* 36 ENERGY POL'Y 671 (2008); Alice Kaswan, *A Cooperative Federalism Proposal for Climate Change Legislation: The Value of State Autonomy in a Federal System,* 85 DENVER U. L. REV. 791 (2008).

Chapter 18

THE PRIVATE SECTOR

"It is our judgment that climate change represents the largest single environmental challenge this century. It will have an impact on all aspects of modern life. It is therefore a major issue for our customers and our staff, as well for every organization on the planet."
— Sir John Bond, Chairman of HSBC Corporation, in announcing the financial institution's commitment to climate neutrality

SYNOPSIS

I. Introduction
II. Why Do Corporations Voluntarily Curb Emissions?
III. Voluntary Commitments And Actions
    A. Reporting and Reducing GHG Emissions
    B. Creating a Carbon Market: the Chicago Climate Exchange
IV. Greening Investment And Green Collar Jobs
V. The Private Sector And Public Climate Policy

I. INTRODUCTION

What should be clear at this point in the book is that successfully addressing climate change will take tremendous technological innovation and massive new investments, leading to a complete restructuring of the world's energy systems. None of that is possible without the proactive engagement of virtually every segment of the private sector. The good news in this regard is that in recent years significant elements of the private sector have shown substantial leadership in responding to climate change. Some companies have reversed longstanding opposition to climate policies, others have committed voluntarily to reduce their carbon footprint, and still others have invested in climate-friendly technologies as a major strategic business opportunity. Indeed, pick up any business or investment magazine and you are likely to find articles or even whole issues devoted to green business, green investment, green energy, or the newest moniker — green collar jobs. *See, e.g., Fortune* (May, 2008); *The Economist* (June 2–8, 2007); *Newsweek* (April 17, 2007).

The private sector is large and diverse, and the range of private sector responses to climate change reflects this diversity. Consider the range of private sector roles illustrated by the following statistics taken from The Climate Group, *The Growth of the Low Carbon Economy, Summary Report* (2007):

- By the end of 2006, the market capitalisation of the global solar sector had increased from US$6 billion a year earlier to reach US$22 billion. By 2010, global solar industry revenues are likely to hit US$20 billion.

- From 2002 to 2005, total installed wind capacity nearly doubled, to 59.3GW. It is set to quadruple by 2012, providing enough power for half the homes in the EU: 200GW. The total value of new wind power equipment installed just in 2006 reached US$23 billion.

- In Germany, between 1991 and 2006, the energy-efficiency index for homes improved by 9%. Germany has the highest uptake of CFLs in the EU, with 6.5 per home.

- Fuji, Toshiba and Kyocera are among the brands planning to market fuel cells for domestic use. By 2030, Japan expects the proportion of households powered by fuel cells to reach 6%.

- More than 1,400 U.S. manufacturers now use the high-efficiency *Energy Star* logo across 32,000 product models. In 2005 alone, the use of *Energy Star* products in the U.S. prevented the release of GHG emissions equivalent to 23 million cars and saved US$12 billion in energy costs.

- Global production of biofuels grew by 95% from 2000 to 2005 and as a proportion of transport fuels is expected to account for 5% by 2015. Worldwide, it is forecast that annual sales of hybrid cars will reach one million by 2010, 3.9 million by 2015 and over 7.5 million by 2020.

- In its first year on the market in Sweden, the Saab BioPower — the only commercially available car in Europe to run on E85 bioethanol (i.e., 85% ethanol) — took 30% of all new car sales.

- The "Big Three" U.S. carmakers — GM, DaimlerChrysler and Ford — have announced plans to double their annual production of flex-fuel vehicles. By 2010, global annual production of these vehicles is forecast to reach two million.

- In 2005, the amount of global energy sector investment channelled into renewables and clean-tech reached 10%. In 2006, the proportion of project finance going into renewables and clean-tech reached 15%.

- Clean technology has become the fastest-growing sector in venture capital and private equity investment. A 2005 survey revealed that 19 venture capitalists investing in 57 European clean-tech firms had made an average annual return since 1999 of almost 87%.

- By 2005, clean energy companies had a total market valuation of US$50 billion, double the 2004 level. By 2006, the value of global clean-tech IPOs (initial public offerings) had grown to US$10 billion, a twenty-fold increase from 2003.

- By March 2007, there were 57 carbon investment funds spread across multiple carbon managers with a total under management of US$8.5 billion.

In sum, many private sector actors have made remarkable progress in the past few years, mostly without significant technological breakthroughs. More promising for the future is the large amount of research and development now aimed at creating climate-friendly projects, increasing energy efficiency or facilitating the switch to clean energy. Governments support much of this research and development, but the majority is led by private sector investment. This chapter will investigate further the role of the private sector, particularly in the United States, in responding to the climate change threat. The topic is a big one and the chapter is organized around several separate questions, including what motivates corporations to respond voluntarily to climate change, what is the nature and scope of current private sector commitments, and what is the future of a green economy. As you read the chapter, consider what role the law can play to catalyze the transition to a green economy.

———————

II. WHY DO CORPORATIONS VOLUNTARILY CURB EMISSIONS?

The reasons motivating the private sector to reduce their GHG emissions are as diverse as the private sector itself. To some extent, companies are motivated by the same reasons that people are — namely out of a growing concern that humanity will suffer significantly from future climate change. But companies are also under a fiduciary obligation to maximize shareholder economic returns and must ultimately tie any proactive response to climate change to the long-term success of their company. Many arguments are used to connect a proactive approach to the bottom line.

First, responding to climate change can save companies substantial sums of money, particularly in times of high energy costs. Reducing GHG emissions typically means more efficient operations, lower energy use, and reduced operating expenses. Dow Chemical, for example, reportedly saved an estimated $4 billion between 1994 and 2005 from reduced energy use, and DuPont saved $3 billon between 1990 and 2005. And they are not alone; *Carbon Down, Profits Up* lists twenty-five other corporations that reported both emissions reductions and cost savings. Most cost-savings come from energy efficiency gains and depend significantly on the current energy intensity and fuel mix of each company. *See* The Climate Group, *Carbon Down, Profits Up*, at 5–6 (3rd ed. 2007).

Second, U.S. companies hope to benefit from a head start in responding to the anticipated nation-wide regulation of carbon. As discussed in Chapter 11, significant U.S. regulation of carbon dioxide and other greenhouse gases is a virtual certainty in the next few years. This is not lost on the private sector. According to the Pew Center on Global Climate Change, 90 percent of companies interviewed "believe that government regulation is imminent, and 67 percent believe it will come between 2010 and 2015." Andrew J. Hoffman, *Getting Ahead of the Curve: Corporate Strategies That Address Climate Change*, Pew Center on Global Climate Change (Oct. 2006), *available at* http://www.pewclimate.org/. As Cinergy CEO Jim Rogers puts it: "The greatest risk we face is 'stroke-of-the-pen' risk, the risk that a regulator or congressman signing a law can change the value of our assets overnight." *Id.* at 64. Planning for that carbon-constrained future for many companies means taking initial steps now.

Third, some corporations see climate change as a major opportunity to develop and market green technologies and products for what is seen as a huge future market. Among the best known initiatives is General Electric's "ecomagination," which reflected a major investment and commitment to meeting anticipated future green demand. See www.ecomagination.com. Toyota's Prius is another well-known and economically successful climate-friendly product. Toyota dominates the U.S. market for hybrid cars and expects hybrid vehicles to rise from six percent of its U.S. car sales in 2005 to 20% by 2012. General Motors is essentially betting the company on the success of its new electric car, the Chevy Volt, which is scheduled for production by 2010. *See Jonathan Rauch, Electro-Shock Therapy*, THE ATLANTIC MONTHLY (July/Aug. 2008), *available at* http://www.theatlantic.com/doc/200807/

general-motors. Even oil companies have shifted more resources into climate friendly energy, including for example British Petroleum's subsidiary, BP Solar, which is now one of the world's largest solar companies.

Fourth, some companies recognize that they will be substantially affected by climate change; as a matter of self-interest they are taking a leadership role with the hope of inspiring others to respond to climate change. The most well known example of this is the insurance industry, which anticipates sky-rocketing pay-outs from increased storm damage. Insurance companies have not only lowered their climate exposure by reducing the number of policies they write for coastal properties, but they have been consistent corporate voices for the need to reduce GHG emissions.

Many climate-dependent industries, particularly in the agriculture and tourism sectors, have also been leaders in raising climate awareness. Ski slopes, for example, are likely to be among the first victims of climate change. The world's highest ski resort, located in the Bolivian Andes, for example, is expected to lose all natural snow in the next decade as the glaciers continue to melt. Only 50 percent of ski resorts in the Austrian Alps will be "snow-reliable,' meaning they have enough snow for 100 days a season, if temperatures rise two degrees. In response, the National Ski Areas Association, with hundreds of members, has revised its environmental charter. Members must strive to "green" every aspect of their operations, from generating or purchasing renewable energy to building LEED-certified structures. *See* Mark Lander, *Global Warming Poses Threat to Ski Resorts in the Alps*, THE N.Y. TIMES, Dec. 16, 2006; National Ski Areas Association, Sustainable Slopes: The Environmental Charter for Ski Areas (Dec. 2005).

Finally, corporations face increasing consumer risk as consumers become more active in demanding green products and approaches. This leads many corporations to green their image to maintain consumer loyalty. BP and General Electric, two corporations that contribute heavily to GHG emissions, rarely advertise any aspect of their company without mentioning some eco-friendly feature or product. BP — formerly British Petroleum — has rebranded itself to "Beyond Petroleum" to position itself with current and future consumers.

In addition to increasing appeal among consumers, greening the corporate image also serves to establish a better relationship with the government. This appears to be a motivating factor in companies' participation in EPA-sponsored voluntary programs, such as the Climate Leaders or Climate Vision programs described further in Section III. Companies see the benefit of positive general publicity for being a part of these programs and also the benefit of working closely with EPA officials who are likely soon to be regulating GHG emissions.

QUESTIONS AND DISCUSSION

1. Reconsider the significant trends recounted above from the *Low Carbon Economy Report*. Do those trends make you more confident that we may successfully address the climate change challenge? To what extent can those trends be attributed solely to voluntary actions by the private sector? What role do you think government regulation or legislation has made in those trends.

2. *Corporate Counseling.* If you were the outside counsel for an energy-intensive manufacturing company, what arguments would you make to convince the company to take a proactive strategy to address climate change? Is that the role of an outside counsel? What advice would you give the company? What elements would you recommend that the company consider in its climate change response plan?

3. Not all companies have taken a leadership role with respect to climate change. Some companies have actively funded conservative think tanks, individuals and others to promote the idea that climate change is either a hoax, or at least is not worth significant policy response. What would be your response if you were counsel to a company that wanted to promote scientists and advocates who claim climate change is a myth? What ethical obligations, if any, would prevent you from promoting minority scientific views in answering a complaint in federal court? What if you believed the scientific views had limited support in the scientific community? For information about corporations promoting the opinions of climate change deniers, see Greenpeace's Exxonsecrets.org.

4. *Regulatory Risk.* As noted above, one of the major drivers persuading private companies to address climate change is the perception that governments, particularly the United States, will set increasingly strong regulations for GHG emissions within the next decade. How do you think this would affect a company's strategic planning? How can a company reduce its future exposure to changes in regulations? Consider in this respect the following table evaluating relative risk exposures of leading companies, assuming a future price of $50 per ton of carbon, a 20 percent emissions constraint and a 7-year compliance period. How do the differences within a sector relate to a company's potential competitiveness in a future where GHG emissions are regulated? What do they inform us of the relative regulatory risk that some companies face in each sector?

Table 18-1: Summary of Sector Risks	
Automobiles	Among top auto manufacturers, average fuel efficiency differed 25% for passenger cars sold in 2004.
Banks	Certain banks have upwards of 50% of their commercial loan portfolio directed towards "high risk" sectors with exposure to both the regulatory and weather risks of climate change.
Chemicals	The company exposed to the highest regulatory risk in the Chemicals sector could face annual compliance costs of nearly 4% of net income. Conversely, the least exposed firm faces less than 1.5%.
Electric Utilities-International	The company exposed to the highest regulatory risk in the Electric Utilities — International sector could face annual compliance costs of nearly 8% of net income. Conversely, the least exposed firm faces less than 1%. Some large emitters could see financial windfalls from carbon pricing scenarios.
Electric Utilities-North America	The company exposed to the highest regulatory risk in the Electric Utilities — North America sector could face annual compliance costs of over 20% of net income. Conversely, the least exposed firm faces less than 1%.
Metals & Mining	The Metals & Mining company exposed to the highest regulatory risk could face annual compliance costs of nearly 22% of net income. Conversely, the least exposed firm faces approximately 2%.

Table 18-1: Summary of Sector Risks	
Oil and Gas	The Oil & Gas company exposed to the highest regulatory risk could face annual compliance costs in excess of 2% of net income. Conversely, the least exposed firm faces less than 0.5%.

Carbon Disclosure Project 2005, at 7 (Innovest, 2005). Does the chart start to explain why some companies are more likely to respond proactively to climate change? Would you expect some companies in the same sector to have different approaches to public policy debates regarding climate change?

5.   In addition to the risk of new regulations, companies also face growing litigation risk as exemplified by recent tort cases brought regarding climate change. *See* Chapter 16 (discussing current climate tort litigation). How significant do you think litigation risk is compared to other climate-related risks faced by various corporations? How would you counsel a company to reduce its litigation risk? If you were representing an Inupiat village affected by climate change, would the intentional efforts of some oil, coal, and gas companies to fund climate deniers be relevant to your allegations? See Complaint, Native Village of Kivalina v. Exxon Mobil, filed N.D. Cal. (Feb. 26, 2008), discussed in Chapter 16.

6.   In addition to ski operators, what other climate-vulnerable industries have taken significant steps to abate climate change. To what extent does this approach turn the polluter pays principle on its head? Does it seem fair that those sectors most vulnerable to climate change should be asked to lead on climate mitigation efforts?

III.   VOLUNTARY COMMITMENTS AND ACTIONS

A.   Reporting and Reducing GHG Emissions

Companies in all sectors have begun to take significant, frequently voluntary, steps to reduce their greenhouse gas emissions. Some companies have adopted benchmarks based loosely on the Kyoto Protocol's caps and others have gone far beyond. The Climate Group's *Carbon Down, Profits Up* report annually compiles specific steps to address climate change reported by private companies and local governments. In 2007, the non-profit Climate Group reported that:

> 137 organisations [companies and local governments] from 20 countries have reported GHG emissions reductions. 27 corporations reported both emissions reductions and cost savings. Cumulatively, these emission reductions totaled 89.5 million tonnes CO_2eq — an average reduction of approximately 18%. Catalyst Paper, Dupont, Astrazeneca, and the Governments of Seattle (U.S.) and Woking (UK) have cut operational emissions over 60%. Energy efficiency, renewable energy and waste management are the most frequently implemented mitigation measures across all sectors, public and private. * * *

> Without pretending that mitigating climate change will be achieved without cost, the 84 corporations, 36 city and 17 regional governments profiled here demonstrate that there is considerable scope to cut emissions and reap significant financial benefits. These organisations are collectively responsible for over 3.5 billion tonnes of CO_2e (equivalent) emissions — nearly 8% of the global total. While there may be some overlap between

sectors, the corporations listed account for 1.8 billion tonnes CO_2e, the cities for 336 million tonnes CO_2e and the regions for 1.3 billion tonnes CO_2e. Together, the 137 organisations have reduced their emissions by over 497 million tonnes CO_2e, an average cut of over 14%; nearly half of these have been achieved by corporations.

Among the most impressive achievements are the 71%, 63% and 60% reductions by Catalyst Paper, AstraZeneca and DuPont respectively. * * *

The ways these cuts have been achieved also supports the conventional wisdom that: a) there is significant potential for energy efficiency improvements — 126 organisations (92%) used energy efficiency as part of their emissions reductions strategy — and b) that no single approach will be sufficient to reduce global emissions to the levels that science suggests are necessary. Almost all the organisations in this report employed more than one measure, with over 100 (73%) using some form of renewable energy, 77 (56%) improving waste management and 102 (74%) organisations using five or more different measures.

The Climate Group, *Carbon Down, Profits Up* 5–6 (3d ed. 2007). As Table 18-2 shows, many of the companies reporting to the Climate Group set a clear target, expressed either in net emission reductions, in carbon intensity, or in targets for renewables. How they define those goals, and how they intend to obtain them, varies.

Table 18–2: Examples of Corporate Reduction Targets
(adapted from The Climate Group, Carbon Down, Profits Up (Feb. 2007),
and the Pew Center on Climate Change, *Getting Ahead of the Curve:*
***Corporate Strategies that Address Climate Change* (2006))**

ABB: Achieved its goal to reduce GHG emissions by 1 percent each year from 1998 to 2005. Its next goal is to reduce CO_2 emissions from operations in Switzerland by 50 percent by 2010.

Alcoa: Reduce GHG emissions by 25 percent from 1990 levels by 2010, and by 50 per cent from 1990 levels when their inert anode technology is fully commercialized. Has actually seen a 37 percent reduction in emissions from 1990–2004, which now saves the company $20 million *annually.*

Baxter International: Reduce energy use and associated GHG emissions by 30 percent per unit of product value from 1996 levels by 2005. Baxter does not appear to have met its goal.

BP: Reduce GHG emissions by 10 percent from 1990 levels by 2010 (already achieved) and hold net GHGs stable at 1990 levels to 2012. BP has saved $1 billion from 2003–2005, and will be investing $8 billion in alternative energy from 2005–2015.

Cinergy: Reduce greenhouse gas emissions to an average of five percent below their 2000 level during the period 2010 through 2012.

> ## Table 18–2: Examples of Corporate Reduction Targets
> ### (adapted from The Climate Group, Carbon Down, Profits Up (Feb. 2007), and the Pew Center on Climate Change, *Getting Ahead of the Curve: Corporate Strategies that Address Climate Change* (2006))
>
> **DuPont:** Reduce GHG emissions by 65 percent from 1990 levels by 2010 (already achieved 67 percent reduction by 2002); hold total energy use to 1990 levels until 2010 (as of 2002 their actual use was 9 percent below 1990 levels despite a 305 increase in production) and source 10 percent of global energy use from renewable resources by 2010. DuPont has saved $3 billion through energy efficiency alone from 1990–2005.
>
> **Intel:** Its goals are to achieve an absolute 10 percent reduction in PFC emissions from 1995 levels by 2010, and reduce greenhouse gas emissions per production unit 50 percent below a 2002 baseline by 2010.
>
> **Polaroid:** Reduce CO_2 emissions 20 percent below 1994 levels by the end of 2005 and 25 percent by 2010.

As Table 18-2 shows, DuPont has been among the leading companies in reducing its greenhouse gas emissions. Since 1990, DuPont has voluntarily reduced its greenhouse gas emissions (CO_2e) by 67 percent. In so doing, it has saved *$2 billion* through energy efficiency. It saves another $10–15 million annually through use of renewables. As you read the following case study on DuPont's efforts consider the wide range of motivations, strategies and justifications that are used even within one company to maintain the focus over time on greenhouse gas reductions. How did DuPont achieve these reductions? In other words, can DuPont's success be replicated?

ANDREW J. HOFFMAN, GETTING AHEAD OF THE CURVE: CORPORATE STRATEGIES THAT ADDRESS CLIMATE CHANGE
90–92 (Pew Center on Climate Change 2007)[*]

[Dupont] began measuring and tracking their largest GHG emissions — CO_2, nitrous oxide (N_2O) and HFC-23 — in 1991 and also made an internal commitment to reduce net emissions. This action coincided with a larger expansion of environmental efforts at DuPont. In 1992, the company published its first external environmental report and an Environmental Policy Committee was created on the Board of Directors.

DuPont made its internal commitments to reduce GHGs and energy use (per pound of product) public in 1994 by becoming the first company to join the Environmental Protection Agency (EPA)/ Department of Energy (DOE) Climate Wise program. The initial goal was to reduce GHG emissions 40 percent below 1990 levels by the year 2000. Establishing the goals was a two step process. First, each business unit identified possible reductions. Then, the Safety, Health and Environment Excellence Center (a Corporate function comprised of policy and technical experts under the VP for Safety, Health and Environment, the role of which is to develop and facilitate implementation of corporate environmental policy) pushed those reductions further, creating a stretch goal.

The first actions taken toward achieving the GHG reduction goals were aimed at the "low hanging fruit" in the company's operations. At the time, there was little sense of opportunity for competitive advantage other than getting ahead of the curve on regulation. DuPont's "low hanging fruit" consisted of reducing emissions of two potent GHGs: N_2O, with a Global Warming Potential (GWP) of 310 times that of CO_2, and HFC-23, with a GWP value of 11,700. In fact, given these high GWPs, CO_2 emissions were not a major issue for the company when GHG reduction goals were first initiated.

In 1991, a scientific paper implicated Nylon production as a source of atmospheric N_2O, a GHG regulated under the Kyoto Protocol. In response, N_2O producers reached an industry-wide agreement in 1993 to reduce emissions by 1999. To reach this goal, DuPont developed an end-of-pipe capture and destroy technique which eliminated 90 percent of emissions at a cost of $50 million with no payback to the business unit's profit and loss (P&L) statement. This additional burden was acknowledged by headquarters and earnings expectations for the unit were adjusted accordingly. For DuPont, accepting the $50 million hit was not only an issue of avoiding government regulation, but also of sticking to the company's principles by "doing the right thing." DuPont shared the technology with the other N_2O producers in the agreement as it was an end-of-the-pipe addition, separate from the core process, and substantial benefits required adoption by the entire industry.

The second target GHG, HFC-23, is an unintended byproduct from the production of HCFC-22, a common refrigerant, and part of DuPont's product line. Reductions of HFC-23 were primarily achieved through a process improvement, resulting in greater yield of HCFC-22 and therefore reduced HFC-23 byproduct. Additional reductions were accomplished through thermal destruction of all or a portion of the remaining HFC-23. Unlike the N_2O reduction technology, the HFC-23 reduction was not driven by an industry-wide agreement and involved an alteration in the core process that resulted in competitive cost savings. Therefore, the technology remained proprietary.

When it was realized that the initial GHG reduction goals would be readily achieved through these two initiatives, DuPont management moved swiftly to establish new goals. The new targets, set in 1999, were expanded to incorporate energy efficiency goals and to fit with DuPont's sustainable growth initiative. They consist of three elements: hold energy flat at the 1990 baseline; source 10 percent of energy from renewable sources at cost competitive rates; and reduce net GHG emissions to 65 percent below 1990 levels, all by the year 2010. Maintaining the 1990 baseline for the GHG reduction goal was a deliberate move, consistent with the baseline for countries under the United Nations Framework Convention on Climate Change and also reflective of the company's desired baseline for early action credits.

To achieve these new goals, "We have to attack energy," says Linda Fisher, VP and Chief Sustainability Officer. "We have a heavy dependence on fuel, and so rising energy prices are a major concern." DuPont is vulnerable to energy prices on two fronts because much of the feedstock it uses is derived from hydrocarbons, especially natural gas. This vulnerability was reflected in DuPont's fourth quarter 2005 earnings, which were half the amount predicted due to higher energy and ingredient costs, as well as hurricane disruptions, plant outages and lower sales in some segments. Uma Chowdhry, VP of Central Research and Development, states it simply: "What energy prices have done to us focuses the mind very quickly."

DuPont's attention to energy efficiency is currently at a point of transition. According to John Carberry, Director of Environmental Technology, energy efficiency efforts between 1990 and 2000 were dominated by yield, capacity and utilization gains; cogeneration and power partnering; and replacing low value/high energy products with those that are high value/low energy. For example, coatings for the auto industry are being replaced with very low Volatile Organic Compound (VOC) coatings, and commodity fibers are being replaced by Pioneer HiBred's corn and soy seeds. Since 2000, he says the focus has been more fine tuned and aimed at instrumentation changes to affect yield, capacity and utilization; process changes; continuing use of combined heat and power; and modern heat management including insulation, steam traps, waste heat recovery and modern motors. The difference between the past and the future is that the latter is highly investment intensive.

Through the company's efforts, energy use has decreased seven percent compared to 1990 levels, despite a 30 percent production increase, saving the company over $2 billion since 1990 and yielding a decrease in GHG emissions of 420 million metric tons. This financial savings figure is calculated as the costs avoided through energy reductions achieved by improving yields and creating less energy-intensive product portfolios versus the business as usual scenario.

Sourcing renewable energy, the second energy goal, has the potential to reduce upstream emissions, fuel costs and exposure to volatile price fluctuations. While progress in this area has led to an annual cost savings of approximately $8 million, meeting the goal of 10 percent has proven challenging. According to Porter, this will be the "toughest goal, yet if we didn't set a goal, we wouldn't have done anything." Cost-competitive projects are relatively scarce and difficult to identify. The company has only been able to source about five percent of its energy from renewable sources, with most efforts coming from the use of landfill gas. In one example, the company partnered with a municipal landfill near its De Lisle, Mississippi plant. A third party laid seven miles of pipeline and installed compression equipment to bring low-cost gas for the plant's boilers. Although it is a less reliable source than the local gas provider, the effort has displaced 30 to 50 percent of natural gas used to run the boilers.

With regard to the third goal of GHG emission reductions, DuPont has been quite successful. As of 2003, DuPont achieved a 72 percent reduction from 1990 GHG emissions. After the 2004 divestment of the nylon business, Invista-related GHG emissions were removed both from the baseline and the realized reductions and overall reductions were recalculated as 60 percent . . . .

As the company's programs have developed, its strategies have become more sophisticated. Going forward, the challenge for DuPont is to treat climate change and energy efficiency as business opportunities by connecting them to the overall objectives of the firm. Company leadership believes that the right product mix will offer an advantage in a carbon-constrained world. Fisher, who is tasked with embedding sustainable growth into strategic planning, gives her view on what climate change means at DuPont, "It's more than just science. It is also a matter of understanding our role in both the problem itself and our opportunities to address it; and to get internal agreement on that."

For DuPont, the business aspect of the issue has two components: risk management — will DuPont be put at a competitive disadvantage from carbon constraints? — and business opportunity — can DuPont capitalize on carbon constraints to expose new market opportunities? According to Fisher, "In developing future business plans and strategies, we need to understand the implications of GHG restraints and whether they pose a risk or opportunity for our family of products." As regulation becomes more likely, such analyses will be further developed.

QUESTIONS AND DISCUSSION

1. The DuPont case study should remind us of how complicated it can be to reduce greenhouse gas emissions in large, complex companies. What were the major strategies that led to DuPont's success? What different corporate objectives motivated the reductions? What internal and external factors either encouraged or impeded the company's pro-active efforts to reduce emissions? How do you think the decline in oil prices in 2008 will affect DuPont's corporate commitment to improving energy efficiency?

2. The first step for any company to set and then meet emission reduction targets is to measure current emissions. If a company wants to trade emission reduction credits, the baseline must be one that is supported by a credible and consistent methodology. One ton of emissions reduction in one sector and in one country needs to be relatively uniform with one ton of emissions reduction in another sector or country, and this requires uniformly accepted ways of measuring and accounting for emissions. Several such methodologies for measuring a company's GHG emissions have been developed. The World Business Council on Sustainable Development and the World Resources Institute, for example, cooperated to develop the Greenhouse Gas Protocol Initiative. *See* WRI & WBCSD, *The Greenhouse Gas Protocol — A Corporate Accounting and Reporting Standard* (2005). The GHG Protocol aims at harmonizing GHG accounting and reporting standards internationally to ensure that different trading schemes and other climate related initiatives adopt consistent approaches to GHG accounting. The importance of a uniform methodology can be seen by the wide uses of the GHG Protocol, as reflected in the following excerpt from the GHG Protocol website:

The GHG Protocol Corporate Standard has been designed to be program or policy neutral. However, many existing GHG programs use it for their own accounting and reporting requirements and it is compatible with most of them, including:

- Voluntary GHG reduction programs, e.g., the World Wildlife Fund (WWF) Climate Savers, the EPA's Climate Leaders, the Climate Neutral Network, and the Business Leaders Initiative on Climate Change (BLICC);

- GHG registries, e.g., California Climate Action Registry (CCAR), World Economic Forum Global GHG Registry

- National and regional industry initiatives, e.g., New Zealand Business Council for Sustainable Development, Taiwan Business Council for Sustainable Development, Association des entreprises pour la réduction des gaz à effet de serre (AERES)

- GHG trading programs, e.g., UK Emissions Trading Scheme (UK ETS), Chicago Climate Exchange (CCX), and the European Union Greenhouse Gas Emissions Allowance Trading Scheme (EU ETS)

- Sector-specific protocols developed by a number of industry associations, e.g., International Aluminum Institute, International Council of Forest and Paper Associations, International Iron and Steel Institute, the WBCSD Cement Sustainability Initiative, and the International Petroleum Industry Environmental Conservation Association (IPIECA).

See www.ghgprotocol.org. Despite the Greenhouse Gas Protocol and other efforts, no international standard for evaluating and reporting GHG emissions and emissions reductions has emerged. According to *Carbon Down, Profits Up 2007*, less than half of the companies that reported their emissions have had their emissions independently verified. The diversity of reporting methodologies also means it is difficult to harmonize reported reductions or compare them across companies or industry sectors.

3. *Carbon Disclosure Project.* Through the Carbon Disclosure Project (CDP), a coalition of institutional investors (i.e., banks, pension funds, etc.) asks the world's largest companies to report annual GHG emissions information. The CDP harnesses the influence of investor institutions to increase transparency and disclosure about corporate actions relating to climate change. For 2008, the CDP has requested over 3,000 of the world's largest corporations to measure and disclose their greenhouse gas emissions and report their strategy for addressing climate change. The 2008 information request was signed by 3,000 institutional investors with assets of $57 trillion. It asks detailed questions regarding a company's perceived regulatory risk, its processes for measuring direct and indirect GHG emissions, strategies it has implemented for reducing GHGs, and anticipated future emissions.

More than 70 per cent of Fortune 500 companies completed the annual questionnaire in 2005 and the number of targeted companies is expanding every year. Total emissions reported now equal 13 percent of the world's total emissions. The emissions levels from hundreds of companies can be accessed through the CDP website and the CDP's annual reports summarize the responses to the questionnaire. The CDP also identifies the 60 "best in class" companies as part of a Climate Leaders Index. See www.cdproject.net.

Why do you think institutional investors would want such information about climate change? Do you think a survey sent by an NGO would gain the same attention inside the recipient companies as a letter sent by potential investors? Ultimately, the responses to the CDP are voluntary and the quality of the responses varies considerably. As a result, the database does not yet provide a reliable overall inventory of emissions. Even given the non-scientific approach to the survey, how can such information be used?

4. Despite the activities of some industry leaders in addressing climate change, most companies still have not. According to the Carbon Disclosure Project, only 13 percent of Fortune 500 companies reported any decrease in emissions, while 17 percent reported an increase in 2005. Moreover, decreasing emissions from corporate operations often misses the more important climate impacts of a company — i.e., the climate impact of the products and services it sells. Ford Motor may in fact be able to reduce its GHG emissions, but any reduction would be offset if it does not work to increase the energy efficiency of the cars it sells. Similarly, HSBC may have achieved carbon neutrality in running its banking operations, but to what extent does it take climate concerns into account when making loans or providing other financial services? Some companies have begun to set such goals. For example, Bentley Prince Street, California's largest commercial carpet manufacturer, has committed to make all its products "climate neutral," with net zero GHG emissions, by 2010. Similarly, NET, a Japanese electronics company, has committed to making its own operations *and its products* carbon neutral by 2010.

5. *Securities Regulations and Disclosures of Climate Liabilities.* As risks associated with climate change become clearer, companies may need to consider disclosure to investors under securities regulation. Under the Securities Act of 1933 and the Securities Exchange Act of 1934, public companies must disclose all "material" costs and liabilities to its shareholders. A matter is "material" if a reasonable person is likely to consider it important. Environmental groups have increasingly been invoking the federal securities laws and related state laws in an attempt to pressure large, public corporations to address climate change. The groups have urged greater investigation and disclosure of potential and actual "material" impacts deriving from climate change, submitted "shareholder proposals" for vote at annual shareholders' meetings, and asserted that corporate directors and officers have a state corporate law "fiduciary duty" to act with regard to climate change. What types of risks from climate change do you think may be material for different sectors of the economy? *See, e.g.*, Perry E. Wallace, *Climate Change, Fiduciary Duty, and Corporate Disclosure: Are Things Heating Up in the Boardroom?*, 26 Va. Envtl. L. J. 293 (2008); Perry E. Wallace, *Global Climate Change and the Challenge to Modern American Corporate Governance*, 55 So. Meth. U. L. Rev. 493, 496 (2002).

6. In September 2007, twenty-two environmental groups and institutional investors filed a formal petition with the Securities Exchange Commission, requesting that the SEC clarify corporate obligations to disclose climate-related risks. The petitioners included U.S. and European institutional investors that manage more than $1.5 trillion in assets. The following outlines the petitioners' requests:

PETITION TO THE SEC, APPENDIX G: KEY ELEMENTS OF PROPOSED SEC GUIDANCE ON CLIMATE DISCLOSURE

The Commission should issue an interpretive release clarifying registrants' obligation under existing law and regulations to assess the risks they face in connection with climate change and to disclose those risks that are material. This guidance should set forth the process by which a registrant should make this assessment and the types of information most likely to be relevant to the assessment, and should direct registrants to disclose the following risks if they are material:

1. Physical risks associated with climate change;

2. Financial risks associated with present or probable regulation of greenhouse gas emissions; and

3. Legal proceedings relating to climate change.

Basis for Interpretive Release

As explained in our petition, climate change has become increasingly important to the operations and financial condition of many registrants. Developments associated with global warming, including physical changes associated with a warming climate and regulatory measures adopted to mitigate greenhouse gas emissions, can affect companies in a variety of ways, such as by posing risks to physical assets of the registrant or its customers or suppliers, introducing new regulatory compliance costs and obligations, increasing the costs of important inputs, and opening up opportunities for new products and services. Many investors are now seeking information concerning companies' response to the physical changes, regulatory developments, and new opportunities associated with climate change.

While some registrants have been providing information on the impacts of climate change in their periodic filings, disclosures remain inconsistent and in many cases incomplete. In particular, corporate disclosure of the risks posed by climate change is lacking, even for companies that do address the impact of climate change and their own emissions. The uneven state of disclosure of climate information, the pervasive emergence of global warming as a significant influence upon the economy, the numerous and complex ways in which it may bear materially on registrants' financial condition, and the widespread adoption of greenhouse gas regulations in recent years, all indicate a need for guidance concerning registrants' disclosure obligations with respect to climate issues.

Climate-related risks that constitute material contingent liabilities must be expressed on a company's balance sheet or in footnotes to financial statements. Our petition sets forth examples of climate risk that may require such treatment.

Whether or not climate risk can be estimated with a degree of certainty warranting its classification as a material contingent liability, registrants have obligations under various provisions of Regulation S-K to disclose in narrative form material information regarding the physical risks associated with climate change and with governmental regulations intended to limit emissions of greenhouse gases. Registrants should carefully examine the potential implications of climate change and present or probable regulation of greenhouse gas emissions for their own operations and financial condition. Whether disclosure is required will depend, as in other areas, upon an informed judgment about whether the information is material. In addressing that question, companies should not limit their consideration merely to particular projects and sites, but should also consider whether the overall degree of risk posed by climate change is material to the corporation's long-term ability to create and maintain value for shareholders. * * *

Information bearing on the consequences of climate change and greenhouse gas regulation for a registrant's operations and financial condition is an important part of that expanding body of information, and registrants should review it carefully and make disclosures where appropriate.

As the . . . [Commission has] observed, "in identifying, discussing and analyzing known material trends and uncertainties, companies are expected to consider all relevant information, even if that information is not required to be disclosed." In assessing the impact of climate change and greenhouse gas regulation on their financial condition and operations, registrants should examine any corporate policies or governance structures that have been established to address climate issues, and review the company's institutional mechanisms for assembling and analyzing information about the various ways in which climate change can affect the company.

Where the company has not established internal mechanisms for assembling and assessing climate information, it may need to do so in order to exercise informed judgments concerning the nature and materiality of climate-related risk.

Process for Assessment of Material Climate Risks

To assess potential financial risks associated with present and probable regulatory requirements concerning greenhouse gases, registrants should determine their current and projected emissions levels. Companies should tabulate their current greenhouse gas emissions, including direct emissions from their own operations and emissions from purchased electricity and purchased products and services. They should estimate their past greenhouse gas emissions to the extent necessary to assess significant trends in their emissions levels, and should also project their future greenhouse gas emissions, as necessary to evaluate the costs they are likely to face from greenhouse gas regulation. Well established tools such as the Greenhouse Gas Protocol exist to aid in the calculation of greenhouse gas emissions.

Factors to Evaluate in Assessing the Materiality of Climate Risks

While disclosure obligations will depend upon individual registrants' particular circumstances, and assessment of the materiality of climate risks, the following kinds of information should be considered and may be subject to disclosure obligations under existing Commission regulations.

Physical Risks Associated with Climate Change

A registrant should review and evaluate the consequences that physical risks and effects associated with climate change may have for the registrant's business and operations, including its personnel, physical assets, supply chain, and distribution chain, and must disclose information on those consequences when they are material to corporate performance.

Examples of such physical effects may include the impact of changes in weather patterns, such as increases in the storm intensity, sea-level rise, melting of permafrost, and temperature extremes, on facilities or operations; effects of climate change upon land, water availability or quality, or other natural resources on which the registrant's business depends; damage to facilities or decreased efficiency of equipment; or effects of changes in temperature on the health of the workforce.

For some registrants, financial risks associated with climate change may arise from physical risks to entities other than the registrant itself. For example, climate change-related physical changes and hazards to coastal property may pose a material credit risks (*sic*) for banks whose borrowers are located in at-risk areas. Climate change may also affect a registrant's supply chain in a variety of ways: climatic changes may diminish supplies of important inputs, physical damage to suppliers' infrastructure may cause costly interruptions in deliveries, and physical changes associated with climate change may decrease consumer demand for products or services. Registrants should evaluate whether they are subject to such risks and disclose any material information related to them. Physical impacts associated with climate change will vary widely depending upon companies' location and the nature of their facilities and operations, but all registrants should review their exposure to such risks and, where the risks are material, must disclose them.

Financial Risks Associated with Greenhouse Gas Regulation

For many registrants, present or probable greenhouse gas regulation has material effects warranting disclosure. When compliance with any international, federal, state, or local laws and regulations concerning climate, including laws regulating greenhouse gas emissions, may have a material effect on the capital expenditures, earnings, and competitive position of the registrant and its subsidiaries, such laws should be identified and their effect discussed.

In conformity with Item 303 of Regulation S-K, registrants must describe any known trends or uncertainties in connection with the impact of climate change or greenhouse gas regulation that they reasonably expect will have a material favorable or unfavorable impact on net sales or revenues or income from continuing operations. When costs associated with compliance with such laws, or penalties for noncompliance, are material to a registrant's financial condition or operations, the registrant's disclosures must include an analysis of any such material effects, including a discussion of the financial risks and opportunities afforded by such regulations.

When a registrant concludes that legislative and regulatory proposals, although not yet enacted into law, are reasonably likely to be enacted and that such proposals, if adopted, would have a material effect on the company's financial condition or operations, the registrant should identify and discuss the proposals.

The registrant should describe and evaluate realistic alternative regulatory scenarios.

Greenhouse gas regulation may have a material effect upon a registrant that is not itself directly subject to the regulation, for example by increasing the costs or decreasing the supply of some product or service on which the registrant's business depends, or increasing or decreasing demand for the registrant's products or services. Where material, such indirect effects should be identified and analyzed.

Legal Proceedings Relating to Climate Change

Under Item 103, registrants must describe any pending judicial or administrative proceeding other than routine business litigation, arising under any Federal, State or local laws, if the proceeding is considered material to the business or financial condition of the registrant; or involves a claim for damages exceeding 10 percent of the assets of the registrant and its subsidiaries on a consolidated basis; or a government authority is a party to such proceeding(s) and the proceeding(s) involves potential monetary sanctions above $100,000. Registrants must disclose any proceedings arising under laws relating to climate change, including those regulating emissions of greenhouse gases, when the proceedings meet the Item 103 criteria.

What is the value of disclosing risks associated with climate change? Petitioners claim that "Investors of all types are aware that climate change, and greenhouse gas regulation, will have enormous implications for long-term capital investments that are being made right now by corporations. They want to know how fully (if at all) companies are taking climate change into account in making those decisions. They want to identify, and invest in, companies that are "out front" in responding to climate risks and opportunities, and to avoid firms that are "behind the curve." Do you agree? Even if investors, or at least the majority of investors, do not want this information, may disclosure still shine a light on a company's efforts, or lack thereof, to address climate change, thus encouraging companies to reduce their climate change impacts?

7. *EPA-led Voluntary Initiatives.* The EPA has launched several initiatives aimed at sparking and rewarding voluntary steps to address climate change. These include the Climate VISION program, the Climate Leadership Program, and the Energy Star Program.

Climate VISION Program. The Climate VISION (Voluntary Innovative Sector Initiatives: Opportunities Now) program is a public-private partnership launched in 2003. Thus far, trade associations representing fourteen energy-intensive industrial sectors and the Business Council on Climate have joined Climate VISION and vowed to reduce their GHG intensity. According to the Climate VISION mission statement, the program helps its members:

- Identify and implement cost-effective solutions for reducing GHG emissions;

- develop and utilize the tools to calculate, inventory, and report GHG emissions reduction, avoidance, and sequestration;

- develop strategies to speed the development and commercial adoption of advanced technologies;

- develop strategies across the commercial and residential sectors to help energy consumers reduce GHG emissions; and

- recognize voluntary mitigation actions.

For more information, see http://www.climatevision.gov/.

Climate Leaders Program. Under the Climate Leaders program, private companies are encouraged to set ambitious GHG emission reduction targets, develop a plan for achieving the targets, and report annually on their progress. Nearly 150 firms have announced their participation in Climate Leaders, but as of the end of 2007 fewer than half had set reduction targets. More information on Climate Leaders, including a current list of participants, can be found online at http://www.epa.gov/climateleaders.

Energy Star Program. The Energy Star program, launched in 1992, is a multi-faceted effort to improve energy efficiency and thus reduce GHG emissions. The program provides the most widely recognized energy efficiency label for appliances, light bulbs, and other products. EPA claims that with Energy Star's help U.S. consumers reduced their emissions by the equivalent of 25 million cars and saved $14 billion in energy costs in 2006. *See* U.S. Environmental Protection Agency, *Energy Star and Other Climate Protection Partnerships, 2006 Annual Report* 1 (Sept. 2007), *available at* http://www.energystar.gov.

How effective do you think these voluntary initiatives are? A recent Government Accounting Office (GAO) report found that the Climate VISION and Climate Leaders programs were not meeting their goals. For example, the GAO reported that the government did not track implementation of the promised commitments by industry and thus had no way of either encouraging implementation or measuring the program's actual effectiveness. The GAO report found that only eleven of the fifteen participating trade groups in Climate VISION had set targets under the program and only five had reported on their emissions, and only 38 of 74 firms in Climate Leaders had even set reduction goals, let alone met them. *See* U.S. Government Accountability Office, *Climate Change: EPA and DOE Should Do More to Encourage Progress Under Two Voluntary Programs*, GAO-06-97 (April 2006). For a more complete description of voluntary climate programs, see Tom Kerr, *Voluntary Climate Change Efforts, in* GLOBAL CLIMATE CHANGE AND U.S. LAW 591 (Michael B. Gerrard ed., 2007).

8. ***Greenwashing.*** Some environmentalists believe that many company claims to be climate-friendly are simply the latest form of greenwashing. The term "greenwashing" refers to "the act of misleading consumers regarding the environmental practices of a company or the environmental benefits of a product or service." *See* www.terrachoice.com. Greenwashing only rarely involves outright lying (such as improperly claiming a particular third-party certification). More common are environmental claims that are vague, misleading, or meaningless. A 2007 study by an environmental marketing firm TerraChoice found that of "1,018 products examined, all but one made claims that are demonstrably false or that risk misleading intended audiences." *See* TerraChoice, *Six Sins of Greenwashing: A Study of Environmental Claims in North American Consumer Markets* (2007), online at www.terrachoice.com. Do the findings from the TerraChoice survey surprise you? Is green marketing any different than other forms of marketing, for example political campaign advertising? What role, if any, should the law play in ensuring that green marketing claims are accurate? Have you seen climate-related claims that you suspect may be false, vague, or deliberately misleading?

9. ***Third-Party Evaluation and Certification.*** One of the key ways to counter greenwashing and indeed to improve the effectiveness of any voluntary environmental commitment is through the use of third-party evaluation, verification, and

certification. The best voluntary GHG emission reduction programs will rely on independent, third-party monitoring and reporting. Many non-profit and for-profit certifiers have emerged to evaluate general environmental product claims. *See, e.g.,* Scientific Certification Systems, Inc, www.scscertified.com; Green Seal www.greenseal.org. Moreover, the certification of reductions may also be required in most carbon trading markets. *See* discussion in Chapter 6.

B.   Creating a Carbon Market: the Chicago Climate Exchange

One of the more innovative voluntary responses to climate change has been the Chicago Climate Exchange (CCX). Since 2003, the CCX has operated a voluntary *and* binding cap-and-trade system for greenhouse gas emissions in North America. Unlike in Europe, no regulatory framework yet exists in the United States to create a carbon market. Members of the CCX filled this regulatory void through the use of private contracts. Companies (or universities, municipalities, etc.) that emit any of the six greenhouse gases included in the Kyoto Protocol voluntarily agree to reduce their emissions. The member institutions further agree to purchase emissions reduction allowances from one another. Through this innovative use of contracts, CCX is both voluntary and binding.

Because the CCX is not linked to the Kyoto Protocol, the European Emissions Trading Scheme, or any other carbon trading system, members of the exchange cannot use allowances to meet their Kyoto or ETS targets. Nevertheless, the CCX has built a solid membership list with more than 100 participants, including manufacturers such as Ford Motor Company, Cargill, IBM, Monsanto, Honeywell, and Rolls-Royce, as well as a number of electric power generators and forest product producers. It also includes a number of municipal governments, such as the cities of Portland, Chicago, Boulder, Berkeley and Melbourne, Australia, and educational institutions, including the University of Minnesota and Michigan State University. For a complete list, see http://www.chicagoclimatex.com.

1.   *How CCX Works*

"Members" of the CCX are allocated annual emissions allowances in accordance with their emissions baseline and the CCX Emission Reduction Schedule. In Phase I, which ran from 2003 to 2006, each "member" of the CCX committed to reduce its emissions by at least 1% per year or a total of 4% below its baseline emissions. In Phase II, which runs from 2007 to 2010, each member must reduce its emissions an additional 2%, or at least 6% below its baseline. Members that reduce emissions below their targets may sell or bank their surplus allowances for future reporting periods. Members that fail to achieve their targets agree in advance to buy emission reduction credits, which the CCX calls "Carbon Financial Instrument" (CFI) contracts. The CFI contract represents 100 metric tons of CO_2 equivalent and may be comprised of either Exchange Allowances or Exchange Offsets. Exchange Allowances are issued to members in accordance with their allowed emission levels under the CCX Emission Reduction Schedule. Exchange Offsets are generated by qualifying offset projects. The Financial Industry Regulatory Authority (FINRA) provides independent, third-party verification of emissions reductions. Trades occur through the CCX Trading Platform, an anonymous, fully electronic system for offering and accepting bids to buy and sell CFI contracts. An annual "true-up" period requires members to ascertain whether their emissions in the previous year match the number of carbon allowances each member holds. If a member's emissions exceed its individual emissions limit, it may buy additional allowances.

Another category of "associate members," comprising office-based businesses or institutions with "negligible direct GHG emissions," have different commitments. Instead of reducing their negligible direct emissions, an associate member must report and offset 100% of its indirect emissions from energy purchases and business travel from its year of entry through 2010. As with the direct emissions of members, these offsets are verified by FINRA.

---

2.   *Enforcement and Compliance*

To date, the CCX reports that all members have met their reduction targets. In addition, from 12 to 17 members each year have exceeded their emissions reduction targets and the aggregate emissions of all members have exceeded their targets by as much as 42,000,000 CO_2eq (12.1 percent below reduction objectives) in 2004. Chicago Climate Exchange, *2006 Program-Wide True-up Summary Report* (Oct. 31, 2007). As a consequence of this perfect compliance record, strict enforcement of CCX emissions targets has not been necessary. This is not surprising given the relatively modest reduction goals in Phase I. The question remains to what extent the CCX will be enforceable as the emission reduction targets get more significant in Phase II and beyond. In this regard, consider the following:

TSEMING YANG, THE PROBLEM OF MAINTAINING EMISSION "CAPS" IN CARBON TRADING PROGRAMS WITHOUT FEDERAL GOVERNMENT INVOLVEMENT: A BRIEF EXAMINATION OF THE CHICAGO CLIMATE EXCHANGE AND THE NORTHEAST REGIONAL GREENHOUSE GAS INITIATIVE
17 FORDHAM ENVTL. L. REV. 271, 277–81 (2006)[*]

Emissions control commitments are voluntarily undertaken by joining the CCX. However, subsequent compliance is arguably not voluntary at all. Because the CCX is a self-regulated, private entity, unsupervised by the CFTC [Commodity Futures Trading Commission] or other regulatory body, it is, in essence, a private contractual arrangement. When entities become CCX members, they agree "to abide by the rules of the Exchange as provided in the CCX Rulebook." Violations of CCX commitments would thus be enforceable as breaches of contractual obligations and lead to corresponding forms of liability. In other words, the CCX is as "voluntary" as any contract commitment is. CCX commitments may be made voluntarily, but they become legally binding once assumed.

What happens when a CCX member fails to limit its carbon emissions as required and then refuses to purchase the requisite carbon allowances? The rules of the CCX do not explicitly address the consequences of non-compliance with emissions limits. Presumably, the procedures governing Exchange rule violations

---

more generally would be triggered. These provisions provide for punitive sanctions, including fines and suspension of trading privileges, when any CCX rules are violated. The ultimate sanction is termination of CCX membership. Since compliance with emissions limits and true-up are a Rulebook requirement, these provisions provide a mechanism for deterring or responding to non-compliance.

Because the CCX is a privately held company, much information about its operations is not publicly available. Thus, it is not clear whether the sanctions mechanism has ever been triggered. But given the small size and voluntary membership, consisting of companies that have a commitment to reducing their own greenhouse gas emissions, it is probably safe to assume that the mechanism has not been used. Even if an emissions limit is missed, the true-up period would provide ample opportunity to purchase the necessary carbon credits. At prices fluctuating between $1 to $4 per ton of carbon equivalent, that would seem to be a minor inconvenience for any company committed to enhancing or maintaining its green reputation. For 2003 and 2004, the CCX has reported the successful reduction of program-wide carbon emissions by over 8% and over 13%, respectively, below the relevant emissions reduction objectives.

Nevertheless, it would be premature to hail the CCX's success — so far — as a harbinger of the future viability and effectiveness of private carbon trading programs more generally. Several issues critical to the implementation of an environmentally effective emission trading program remain unresolved. For example, questions have been raised about how the CCX measures credits and ensures the additionality of emissions reductions. The Economic Growth Provisions of the CCX Rule Book also limit the total extent to which a CCX member's non-compliance is recognized by the Exchange. Thus, the maximum CO2 equivalent emissions that will be recognized for the purpose of True-up by each CCX Member or Associate Member will be 102% of that Member's or Associate Member's Baseline Emission level during each of the years 2003 and 2004, and 103% of its Baseline during each of the years 2005 and 2006.

When combined with the CCX Emission Reduction Schedule, the Economic Growth Provision implies that the maximum amount of net purchases of Exchange Allowances and/or Exchange Offsets . . . required for Compliance is limited to 3% of each CCX Member's and Associate Member's emission baseline during 2003, 4% of its baseline during 2004, 6% of its baseline during 2005 and 7% of its baseline during 2006.

Depending on the particular year, no CCX member can be considered to be out of compliance by more than 3 to 7%. Any non-compliance above those values would be ignored by the CCX, limiting the compliance pressure once non-compliance has crossed a certain threshold.

There are additional, less-readily addressable problems. If private trading arrangements become more widespread, membership will inevitably grow to include companies whose voluntary commitment to addressing global climate change may be much less serious than that of current CCX members. There is also no assurance that carbon prices will always stay low. To prevent opportunism, bad faith, or other forms of deliberate non-compliance, the necessity for a credible and effective set of non-compliance sanctions would become much more important. In such circumstances, would the CCX compliance provisions provide adequate deterrence? The CCX's present structure suggests that they might not for two reasons: 1) lack of sufficient coerciveness, and 2) lack of sufficient certainty.

With respect to sanctions sufficiency, no information is available about the range of fines that have been imposed, if any, nor of any other consequences. Thus, it is unclear whether the compliance mechanisms will be sufficient to induce compliance by businesses that care little about the environment or their environmental image.

The operational success of the CCX also provides little guidance to future behavior of current members if conditions were to change significantly. For example, with carbon credit prices relatively low, the price of "true-up" through allowance purchase has been low. If carbon prices and compliance costs rise significantly, will the commitment of CCX members to their green image still provide sufficient pressure to comply with the limits? * * *

If non-compliance is to be expected under certain circumstances, can the CCX itself be expected to properly police its members in all relevant situations? The question goes to the issue of sanctions certainty. The CCX Rulebook allows for non-compliance sanctions ranging from fines and suspension of trading privileges to expulsion. Arguably, the CCX has an institutional interest in preventing compliance failures and maintaining the integrity of the market. Failure to respond to significant instances of non-compliance could attract attention by regulators and deplete its goodwill and environmental reputation. The practical consequence would also be to lessen the utility of Exchange participation to members interested in promoting their green image.

But it is questionable how readily such sanctions, especially severe ones, can be deployed. For example, it is not clear how the most severe sanction, expulsion from the CCX, is always a credible deterrent. If carbon credit prices rise to such high levels that non-compliance with true-up becomes attractive, would CCX membership still be desirable? Arguably, under such circumstance, expulsion might not be viewed as punitive in nature. More importantly, even if other punitive sanctions remain available, for example significant monetary fines, would the CCX actually exercise that authority?

QUESTIONS AND DISCUSSION

1.   In light of the issues raised in Professor Tseming Yang's excerpt, how much do you think the CCX will reduce GHG emissions? The reduction goals of the CCX are modest and most of the participants would probably achieve those reductions with or without the exchange. What, then, do you think the value of the CCX is? To the companies? To the environment?

2.   In 2006, allowances worth 10.3 $MtCO_2$ — seven times the amount in 2005 — and $38.1 million were traded through the CCX. Karan Capoor & Philippe Ambrosi, *State and Trends of the Carbon Market 2007*, at 18 (2007). The prices for allowances in the CCX have been low relative to the European Emissions Trading Scheme (ETS) described in Chapter 6. Prices have ranged from below $1 per ton of CO_2 to nearly $5 per ton. As of July 2008, the trading price was just over $4.00 per ton.

3.   Prices for emissions reduction credits in the ETS have fluctuated even more than in the CCX, but the selling price for a ton of carbon has typically been much higher (and in early 2008 were selling for approximately $20 per ton). What do you think explains the difference in price between a ton of carbon reductions in Europe and one in the United States? What do you think would happen if the markets became more integrated? How could they become more integrated?

4.   As with other membership-based organizations, establishing deterrent mechanisms is challenging. Members are generally reluctant to support severe penalties, because it is not in their self-interest. Severe penalties may deter new members from joining and cause existing members to resign. Assuming the CCX remains a voluntary enterprise and that stricter compliance provisions are needed,

what would you recommend? Why do you think current CCX rules ignore noncompliance by more than 7 percent of a member's emissions reductions?

5. *Carbon Offset Markets.* The CCX is not the only voluntary carbon trading market operating in the United States. A decentralized market also exists for purchasing carbon offsets from a variety of different suppliers. Individuals, small companies, municipalities, and others have made pledges to offset their personal or institutional emissions. Although not binding contracts as in the CCX, the net result is that these voluntary pledges have created a demand for carbon offsets. A variety of companies and non-profit organizations have emerged to meet this demand, offering to plant a tree, install solar cookers, or take other actions to offset the purchaser's individual or corporate emissions. *See, e.g.,* www.carbonfund.org and www.terrapass.com The sites feature carbon offset calculators to factor in carbon from all activities, including transportation, business and home energy use, and even weddings. Then users pay on a price per ton basis to offset their personal emissions. This money then is invested in renewable energy projects (wind, solar, etc.) or forest projects that would otherwise not be possible without the collective payments of offset customers.

Many questions have emerged as to how effective this offset market is in actually reducing GHG concentrations. First, the offset market is not regulated and some credits may be more "real" than others. The problem of additionality, discussed in Chapter 6, is a significant challenge for all broad-based offset markets. Even where no deliberate fraud has occurred, questions can arise as to whether real, lasting climate benefits are being provided. *See, e.g.,* David Fahrenholt, *Value of U.S. House's Carbon Offsets is Murky,* THE WASH. POST, Jan. 28, 2008, at A1 (questioning whether carbon credits bought through the Chicago Climate Exchange to offset the Capitol's energy use resulted in any additional benefits for climate change).

6. *Green Power Market Development Group.* Another form of market was created by the Green Power Market Development Group, a collaboration of 12 leading corporations and the World Resources Institute. This Group has not created a carbon market but rather the groups are cooperating to build corporate demand for green power. Their goal is to develop corporate markets for 1000 MW of new, cost competitive green power by 2010 by:

1. Developing strategies to reduce green power costs by using innovative purchasing options, reducing transaction costs for companies, and gaining economies of scale through working as a group.

2. Reducing market barriers faced by green power suppliers and buyers by providing independent information to potential customers.

3. Defining the business case for buying green energy products by recognizing the value of renewable energy to diversify energy portfolios.

See http://www.thegreenpowergroup.org/. What do you think of this strategy? Why do you think a non-profit like World Resources Institute is involved?

IV. GREENING INVESTMENT AND GREEN COLLAR JOBS

Among the most positive and hopeful trends in recent years is the rise in "green," particularly climate-friendly, investment. Indeed, many observers believe we are entering an era where investments in renewables, energy conservation, and related green technologies present the greatest opportunity for innovation and growth since the internet boom of the 1990s. Just as that period revolutionized how we do business, shop, or socialize, some observers believe this new period will revolutionize our energy systems. In their view, this energy revolution will see solar and wind technologies, fuel cells, alternative fuels, and innovations in energy conservation spark an entirely new economy.

To some extent, this energy revolution has already begun. The American Solar Energy Society estimates that in 2006 alone, renewable energy and energy efficiency were responsible for $970 billion in revenues. Green venture capital essentially doubled in 2006, and investments in clean technology now rank third behind biotech and software in venture capital investments. *See Clean-Tech Investing Rises Sharply, Say New Studies*, GreenBiz.com (Aug. 11, 2006).

The growth in green investment has been tied to the new phenomenon of "green collar jobs." Renewable energy and conservation accounted for 8.5 million jobs in 2006. Expanding renewable electricity from 6 percent to 20 percent would create an additional 355,000 jobs by 2020. Energy efficiency is far more labor intensive than generating energy, creating 21.5 jobs for every $1 million invested, compared to 11.5 jobs for new natural gas generation. And renewable energy creates four times as many jobs per megawatt of installed capacity as natural gas and 40 percent more jobs per dollar of investment than coal. Some analysts predict that three to five million more green jobs can be created over the next 10 years as part of an energy transformation.

The potential marriage of large profits, good jobs and a clean environment has clear political implications; many observers believe the only way to gain the political commitment necessary to respond effectively to climate change is to clarify how the necessary investments will also create new U.S. jobs. This belief motivated environmental groups and labor unions to joining together in creating the Apollo Initiative (named after the program that put the United States into space). The new Apollo Initiative is aimed at reducing national energy consumption 16 percent, growing the renewable portion of electricity to 15 percent by 2015 and reducing carbon emissions by 23 percent — but what is perhaps most innovative about the Apollo Initiative is its focus on job creation:

THE APOLLO ALLIANCE, NEW ENERGY FOR AMERICA: THE APOLLO JOBS REPORT
1–13, (Jan. 2004), *available at*, www.apolloalliance.org

Energy is the lifeblood of a modern economy. And America's future prospects will depend upon the secure supply of affordable and sustainable energy that can fuel our continued growth and prosperity. But growing dependence on foreign oil, unprecedented energy failures, and mounting evidence of environmental crises are clear warning signs that America's current policies cannot be sustained. It is time for a bold initiative — with the vision and the scope of the original Apollo program — to end America's dependence on foreign oil and create millions of good jobs building the sustainable energy system of the next century.

A new Apollo initiative will address challenges that America can no longer afford to ignore: the *economic imperative* — we have lost 16% of all manufacturing jobs since Bush took office; the *national security imperative* — we import well over half of all our oil, most from unstable and undemocratic nations; the *environmental imperative* — we face mounting evidence of a global environmental crises; and the *social imperative* — we face $1.6 trillion in unmet infrastructure needs in cities and rural communities while we suffer the worst state fiscal crisis of our time.

While the Apollo project is about changing our future, it is built on an honest assessment of our past and the recognition that public leadership and meaningful public investment have historically been essential for economic development and promoting new technology. In the past, government investment in the railroads, in the national highway system, in the space program, in the research and development of the micro chip and other technologies elevated our economy and quality of life to new levels. * * *

The new Apollo Initiative calls for a large scale federal commitment, on the scale of $30 billion/year for 10 years, to achieve a new energy infrastructure that is diversified, environmentally safe, and more efficient. This initiative will turn challenge into opportunity. It will generate good jobs and help U.S. companies capture the green markets of the future. It will reduce dependence on foreign oil. It will rebuild communities, and it will make America an environmental leader again, helping put the world on a path to a sustainable future.

*   *   *

Detailed analysis of the potential economic benefits reveals the promise of Apollo. A $30 billion investment per year for 10 years would provide the following benefits:

- Add more than 3.3 million jobs to the economy

- Stimulate $1.4 trillion in new Gross Domestic Product

- Stimulate the economy through adding $953 billion in Personal Income and $323.9 billion in Retail Sales

- Produce $284 billion in net energy cost savings

*   *   *

[To achieve these benefits, the Apollo Alliance developed the following Ten-Point Plan for Good Jobs and Energy Independence]

1. Promote Advanced Technology & Hybrid Cars: Begin today to provide incentives for converting domestic assembly lines to manufacture highly efficient cars, transitioning the fleet to American made advanced technology vehicles, increasing consumer choice and strengthening the U.S. auto industry.

2. Invest In More Efficient Factories: Make innovative use of the tax code and economic development systems to promote more efficient and profitable manufacturing while saving energy through environmental retrofits, improved boiler operations, and industrial cogeneration of electricity, retaining jobs by investing in plants and workers.

3. Encourage High Performance Buildings: Increase investment in construction of "green buildings" and energy efficient homes and offices through innovative financing and incentives, improved building operations, and updated codes and standards, helping working families, businesses, and government realize substantial cost savings.

4. Increase Use of Energy Efficient Appliances: Drive a new generation of highly efficient manufactured goods into widespread use, without driving jobs overseas, by linking higher energy standards to consumer and manufacturing incentives that increase demand for new durable goods and increase investment in U.S. factories.

5. Modernize Electrical Infrastructure: Deploy the best available technology to existing plants, protecting jobs and the environment; research new technology to capture and sequester carbon and improve transmission for distributed renewable generation.

6. Expand Renewable Energy Development: Diversify energy sources by promoting existing technologies in solar, biomass and wind while setting ambitious but achievable goals for increasing renewable generation, and promoting state and local policy innovations that link clean energy and jobs.

7. Improve Transportation Options: Increase mobility, job access, and transportation choice by investing in effective multimodal networks including bicycle, local bus and rail transit, regional high-speed rail and magnetic levitation rail projects.

8. Reinvest in Smart Urban Growth: Revitalize urban centers to promote strong cities and good jobs, by rebuilding and upgrading local infrastructure including road maintenance, bridge repair, and water and waste water systems, and by expanding redevelopment of idled urban "brownfield" lands, and by improving metropolitan planning and governance.

9. Plan for a Hydrogen Future: Invest in long term research & development of hydrogen fuel cell technology, and deploy the infrastructure to support hydrogen powered cars and distributed electricity generation using stationary fuel cells, to create jobs in the industries of the future.

10. Preserve Regulatory Protections: Encourage balanced growth and investment through regulation that ensures energy diversity and system reliability, that protects workers and the environment, that rewards consumers, and that establishes a fair framework for emerging technologies.

QUESTIONS AND DISCUSSION

1.   What do you think of the Apollo Alliance's underlying strategies? Is the focus on the economic benefits — i.e., the job-creating aspects of energy transformation effective? What do you think of their ten-point plan? If you were going to write your own ten-point plan to transform our energy systems, what additional initiatives would you include?

2.   *Green Collar Jobs.* Quantifying the number of green collar jobs is difficult, because people disagree on the definition of what makes a job "green." The term typically refers to jobs ordinarily performed by blue collar workers, but in a green energy sector. For example, a coal power plant technician trained to service a series of windmills would have transitioned to a green collar job. But what about a steel worker whose product formerly went into automobiles but now goes into windmills? Is his or her job now 'green'? The Apollo Alliance describes green collar jobs in the following way:

> Green-collar jobs . . . are well paid, career track jobs that contribute directly to preserving or enhancing environmental quality. Like traditional blue-collar jobs, green-collar jobs range from low-skill, entry-level positions to high-skill, higher-paid jobs, and include opportunities for advancement in both skills and wages. * * *

> Green-collar jobs are in construction, manufacturing, installation, maintenance, agriculture, and many other sectors of the economy. . . . While some green-collar jobs (e.g., wind turbine technician) are in new occupa-

tions, most are existing jobs that demand new green economy skills. For example, construction companies building and retrofitting America's cities need workers with traditional construction skills who also have up-to-date training in energy efficiency. And employers doing solar installation need workers with conventional electrical training, in addition to specialized solar skills. * * *

In sum, spurring the creation of green-collar jobs . . . means more than creating short-term work on individual green projects. It means building a sustainable economy, where environmental goals go hand in hand with social and economic goals. It means embracing visionary policies for your community, mobilizing all of the resources at your disposal to meet those goals, and explicitly working to expand the number of long-term, high-quality green-collar jobs for local residents.

APOLLO ALLIANCE & GREEN FOR ALL, GREEN-COLLAR JOBS IN AMERICA'S CITIES: BUILDING PATHWAYS OUT OF POVERTY AND CAREERS IN THE CLEAN ENERGY ECONOMY 3 (2008), *available at* www.apolloalliance.org. Does the Apollo Alliance's definition clarify the definition of green collar jobs? Critics of the concept of green collar jobs argue that jobs are not being "created" but simply shifted from one sector to another, with little net gain. *See generally* Steven Greenhouse, *Millions of Jobs of a Different Collar*, N.Y. TIMES, Mar. 26, 2008.

3. The growth in green collar jobs is not limited to the United States. Estimates put the increase of environmental jobs in the United Kingdom at an additional 100,000 jobs by 2015. In Germany, renewables are considered the number one job creator, with an estimated 100,000 new jobs expected to be added by 2020 to the 170,000 jobs currently available in the renewables (mostly solar) sector.

4. The potential for a new generation of good, green jobs is not lost on the labor movement. Labor leaders are beginning to support greater investments in a new energy future. Consider in this regard recent remarks of the head of the AFL-CIO:

REMARKS BY JOHN J. SWEENEY, PRESIDENT, AFL-CIO
UN Summit on Climate Risk, New York, New York
Feb. 14, 2008

I want to talk with you today about how the labor movement views the challenge of global warming and the opportunity presented by investments in clean and efficient energy.

Let me begin with this: We hear again and again that we must choose between having a stable climate and having a strong global economy. This is a false choice.

The global economy cannot prosper unless we secure a stable climate and sustainable sources of energy. Global warming means global Depression, food and water shortages and drowned cities. * * *

On the other hand, we can only take on climate change because of the wealth — the human and political capital — that comes from a broad based and prosperous global economy. Mobilizing that investment capital to meet the challenge of climate change is what brings us together today. * * *

Now some will say this is really a problem for governments. And it is true that government must act. But the global investment community must not wait for governments.

Investors need to step forward in two ways. First, investors need to look at investments in new clean energy ventures and projects. Second, investors need to demand the information necessary to hold corporations accountable. Investors should ask the companies you invest in — first, are you taking responsibility for addressing the crisis? And second and most importantly, are companies taking steps to seize the opportunities created by this crisis? * * *

Investors should be looking at new technologies for generating usable energy. New technologies like solar, wind, and geothermal. And if we are serious about dealing with carbon emissions, we must expand our use of older carbon free energy sources. Older sources like hydro and nuclear power. But we can't stop there. We must pursue reengineering old energy sources such as carbon capture and sequestration for coal fired electrical generation plants.

Consider investments in renewable energy. A 10-year program to bring 18,500 megawatts of renewable energy on line annually could generate 2 million full-time equivalent jobs. And there are over 70,000 firms active in industries that could supply the components. The result? Twenty percent of our power capacity would come free of carbon emissions.

The same dynamics exist for nuclear and capturing coal emissions. These technologies require capital and developing them will create jobs — lots of jobs. * * *

But to really begin to address this crisis, we must think big. A new strategy for the global economy has to mean speed and scale. * * *

In the United States today, approximately $3 billion is invested in alternative energy venture capital. That sounds like a big number until you realize that Americans put $9 billion a year into computer games and somewhere north of $100 billion annually on the war in Iraq.

The labor movement cannot accept the status quo — a status quo of no rules and no strategy.

We know where doing nothing leads. It leads to a planet of radical inequalities of wealth and power. It leads to global economic instability. To governments each looking to their armies to pursue the hopeless mission of seizing the world's dwindling supplies of energy. And all the while all of us will face the unstoppable, unknowable consequences of radical, accelerating global climate change.

What are the political implications of a labor-environment alliance on green collar jobs? What difference does this make to the coal miner of West Virginia? Other than simply opposing polices to curb carbon emissions, what policies should the unions that represent West Virginia coal miners' support?

V. THE PRIVATE SECTOR AND PUBLIC CLIMATE POLICY

In addition to the obvious role business plays in the marketplace, business also plays a critical political role in the debate over climate policy, both internationally and nationally. For many years, this corporate involvement was overwhelmingly aimed at slowing or avoiding any significant steps to curb fossil fuel use or otherwise reduce GHG emissions. A broad array of fossil-fuel dependent companies, including oil, automobile, and coal companies, joined to form the Global Climate Coalition (GCC) in 1989 "to coordinate business participation in the international policy debate on the issue of global climate change and global warming." This benign-sounding mission belied a massive, well-funded effort to block or slow progress at the Earth Summit and then subsequently at the Kyoto Protocol negotiations. The GCC spent a reported $13 million just in television advertising in 1997 to build opposition to the Kyoto negotiations, and its lobbyist was a visible and influential figure, working closely with OPEC negotiators, to try to block or weaken the Protocol. The GCC was very influential in undermining the U.S. position during the negotiations, but soon after companies began to defect. Continued scientific evidence of climate change, coupled with environmentalist pressure, led many companies to step publicly away from the GCC's uncompromising stance. The GCC folded formally in 2002, proclaiming mission accomplished. *See, e.g.,* Lester R. Brown, *The Rise and Fall of the Global Climate Coalition* (Earth Pol'y Inst., July 25, 2000). For a lively account of the role of the GCC in the Kyoto negotiations, see JEREMY LEGETT, THE CARBON WARS (2001).

As companies have begun to address their own carbon footprint, however, some have also joined more political initiatives to support generally a broad response to climate change. The Pew Center on Climate Change, for example, created a "Business Environmental Leadership Council" (BELC) in the 1990s, motivated by the belief that business's engagement would be critical for solving the climate problem. The BELC is now the largest U.S.-based association of corporations focused on addressing the challenges of climate change, with 42 members representing $2.8 trillion in market capitalization and 3.8 million employees. Many different sectors are represented, from high technology to diversified manufacturing, from oil and gas to transportation, from utilities to chemicals. The companies must subscribe to a set of "Core Beliefs," which include:

1. We accept the views of most scientists that enough is known about the science and environmental impacts of climate change for us to take actions to address its consequences.

2. Businesses can and should take concrete steps now in the U.S. and abroad to assess opportunities for emission reductions, establish and meet emission reduction objectives, and invest in new, more efficient products, practices and technologies.

3. The Kyoto agreement represents a first step in the international process, but more must be done both to implement the market-based mechanisms that were adopted in principle in Kyoto and to more fully involve the rest of the world in the solution.

4. We can make significant progress in addressing climate change and sustaining economic growth in the United States by adopting reasonable policies, programs and transition strategies.

See www.pewclimate.org/companies_leading _the_way_belc. Can you see how convening such a group of like-minded corporations could be valuable for building and demonstrating political will for regulating GHGs?

Some industry members have taken even more overt pro-regulation positions. Most notably, many leading businesses and environmental organizations formed a U.S. Climate Action Partnership (USCAP) "to call on the federal government to enact legislation requiring significant reductions of greenhouse gas emissions." Members of USCAP include such corporate giants as Duke Energy, Dow Chemical, General Motors, and General Electric and environmental organizations such as the Natural Resources Defense Council, Environmental Defense Fund and the World Resources Institute. Their jointly released recommendations include the following:

U.S. CLIMATE ACTION PARTNERSHIP, A CALL FOR ACTION: CONSENSUS PRINCIPLES AND RECOMMENDATIONS

(2007), *available at* www.us-cap.org/USCAPCallForAction.pdf

Congress Needs to Enact Legislation as Quickly as Possible

We offer the following interconnected set of recommendations for the general structure and key elements of climate protection legislation that we urge Congress to enact as quickly as possible. The legislation should require actions to be implemented on a fast track while a cap and trade program is put in place, including the establishment of a GHG inventory and registry, credit for early action, aggressive technology research and development, and policies to discourage new investments in high-emitting facilities and accelerate deployment of zero and low-emitting technologies and energy efficiency. We recommend these fast track actions begin within one year of enactment.

The Environmental Goal

U.S. legislation should be designed to achieve the goal of limiting global atmospheric GHG concentrations to a level that minimizes large-scale adverse climate change impacts to human populations and the natural environment, which will require global GHG concentrations to be stabilized over the long-term at a carbon dioxide equivalent level between 450–550 parts per million.

Take a Stepwise, Cost-Effective Approach

While achieving our environmental goal will require a fundamental transformation of the energy system over the long-term, we cannot predict with accuracy all technological developments between now and 2100. For these reasons, legislation should focus on what we know can be cost-effectively achieved over the next twenty to thirty years while putting us on a trajectory for deeper reductions by mid-century.

Cap and Trade is Essential

Our environmental goal and economic objectives can best be accomplished through an economy-wide, market-driven approach that includes a cap and trade program that places specified limits on GHG emissions. This approach will ensure emission reduction targets will be met while simultaneously generating a price signal resulting in market incentives that stimulate investment and innovation in the technologies that will be necessary to achieve our environmental goal. The U.S. climate protection program should create a domestic market that will establish a uniform price for GHG emissions for all sectors and should promote the creation of a global market.

Establish Short and Mid-Term GHG Emission Targets

To begin the process of reducing U.S. emissions, we recommend Congress establish a mandatory emission reduction pathway with specific targets that are:

- between 100–105% of today's levels within five years of rapid enactment;
- between 90–100% of today's levels within ten years of rapid enactment;

- between 70–90% of today's levels within fifteen years of rapid enactment

The short- and mid-term targets selected by Congress should be aimed at making it clear to the millions of actors in our economy and to other nations that we are committed to a pathway that will slow, stop and reverse the growth of U.S. emissions. Furthermore, Congress should specify an emission target zone aimed at reducing emissions by 60% to 80% from current levels by 2050.

Complementary Policies and Measures will be Necessary

Climate protection policies must be complemented with U.S. energy policies that result in diverse and adequate supplies of low-GHG energy. In addition, as described below, an aggressive technology research, development, and demonstration program, along with policies aimed at deploying low- and zero-emission technologies will be necessary to achieve our policy goals. In sectors that are insensitive to price signals and that face market barriers to the introduction or utilization of low or zero-emission technology, we recommend appropriate sector-specific policies.

Scope of Coverage and Point of Regulation of the Cap and Trade Program

We recommend the cap and trade program should cover as much of the economy's GHG emissions as is politically and administratively possible. We believe there are potentially effective approaches to achieving these objectives including the following. An upstream" program that requires fossil fuel producers (or shippers in the case of natural gas) to be covered by allowances that equal the emissions released when the fuel is combusted, thereby adding the cost of the emission reduction allowance to the price of the fuel; or a "hybrid" program that includes a downstream cap applied to GHG emissions from large stationary sources (e.g., covering 80% of the emissions from the fewest possible number of sources) combined with an upstream cap or another policy tool applied to the carbon content of fossil fuels used by remaining sources.

Emission Offsets

Legislation should permit entities subject to the cap to meet part of their obligations through the purchase of verified emission offsets from a range of domestic sinks, domestic sources of emissions that are not subject to the cap, and projects outside the U.S. The offset must be environmentally additional, verifiable, permanent, and enforceable.

Emission Allowance Allocations

An emission allowance allocation system should seek to mitigate economic transition costs to entities and regions of the country that will be relatively more adversely affected by GHG emission limits or have already made investments in higher cost, low-GHG technologies, while simultaneously encouraging the transition from older, higher-emitting technologies to newer, lower-emitting technologies. A significant portion of allowances should be initially distributed free to capped entities and to economic sectors particularly disadvantaged by the secondary price effects of a cap including the possibility of funding transition assistance to adversely affected workers and communities. Free allocations to the private sector should be phased out over a reasonable period of time.

Cost Control Measures

Cost control measures are policies designed to provide capped entities with greater confidence that their cost will be limited and flexibility to manage emission reduction compliance costs. We believe the most powerful cost control measure is a robust cap and trade program since markets do the best job of controlling costs over time. If used, cost control measures must be designed to enable a long-term price signal that is stable and high enough to drive investment in low- and zero-emitting technologies, including carbon capture and storage. Any additional cost-control option considered by Congress must ensure the integrity of the emissions cap over a multi-year period and preserve the market's effectiveness in driving reductions, investment, and innovation. As policy makers weigh additional cost control options, it is important for them to consider who and what portions of the economy are impacted, the time duration of the impact and remedy, international competitiveness, the implications for international emissions trading, and how the measure impacts the price signal necessary to stimulate investment and technological innovation. Some possible additional cost control options include but are not limited to a safety valve, borrowing, strategic allowance reserve, preferential allocations, dedicated funding, technology incentives and transition assistance.

Inventory and Registry

A national emissions baseline must be established. Legislation should establish a registry by no later than the end of 2008. The final regulations establishing a national registry and inventory of GHG emissions should ensure consistency in the definition, counting, and reporting of GHG emissions from all regulated entities (i.e., those that are subjected to the cap) and from all other emission sources on a voluntary basis. The U.S. inventory should include an estimate of all GHG emissions, not just those in the registry.

Credit for Early Action

It will take time to get a cap and trade program up and running. We need to reward those firms that have acted to reduce GHG emissions and encourage others to do so while the program is being established. Legislation should require regulations to be promulgated by no later than the end of 2008 establishing an early action program that grants a credit for reductions made starting from a specified date, such as 1995, until such time as the mandatory program becomes effective. Claimants would be required to demonstrate their eligibility for the credit based on accurate data.

Technology Policies and Measures

A federal technology research, development and demonstration (RD&D) and deployment program is a necessary complement to the GHG reduction policies that will drive demand for low-carbon technology. The program should be designed with the following key characteristics.

- Joint public/private sector cost-sharing and oversight;

- Establishment of performance criteria and a technology roadmap to guide RD&D and deployment program investment decisions;

- Stable, long-term financing (e.g., a dedicated federal revenue stream or other means not reliant upon annual congressional appropriations);

- Establishment of a public/private institution to govern the administration of the RD&D and deployment program fund; and

- A mix of deployment policies to create incentives to use low-GHG technologies and address regulatory or financial barriers. Such policies could include loan guarantees, investment tax credits, and procurement standards.

Sector-Specific Policies and Measures

Policies and measures are needed to complement an economically sound cap and trade system to create additional incentives to invest in low-GHG approaches in key sectors. The need and scope of sector specific policies and measures will depend on the stringency of targets, scope of coverage, and point of regulation in the cap and trade program. Some of the sector-specific policies and measures are intended to be transitional in nature and should be phased out over time. * * *

International Engagement and Linkage

While taking the necessary first step of placing limits on our own emissions, Congress should strongly urge the Administration to safeguard U.S. interests by engaging in international negotiations with the aim of establishing commitments by all major emitting countries. The post-2012 global framework should establish international GHG markets, assist vulnerable populations in adapting to climate impacts, and boost support for climate-friendly technology in developing countries.

QUESTIONS AND DISCUSSION

1.   Can you see the areas of compromise between the environmental groups and the corporations who signed on the U.S. Climate Action Partnership? What value do you think the stakeholders received from issuing this joint statement? If you represent British Petroleum, would you have recommended they sign on to it? What about a manufacturing company like IBM? The Environmental Defense Fund?

2.   *Problem Exercise: Drafting and Negotiating U.S. Legislation.* The U.S. Climate Action Partnership *Call for Action* was meant to signal to Congress acceptable parameters for a comprehensive greenhouse gas emission reduction bill. Use the statement as a template to negotiate and draft a potential U.S. Climate Protection Act. To facilitate the negotiation and drafting, the class may be divided into different teams, representing different stakeholders including an oil or coal company, a manufacturing company like Ford Motor that is closely tied to fossil fuels, a private bank such as Citibank with limited direct carbon emissions, and the Natural Resources Defense Council, an environmental advocacy group. First, within your group draft specific statutory language for one or more of the issues highlighted above and reflecting the agreed principles. Then, share your draft language with the other groups. Finally, break into issue-based groups to try to negotiate agreed upon statutory text.

Chapter 19

TOWARD A CARBON-FREE FUTURE

"I still don't know what Bali was about, but I do know that it was incremental, not transformational — and incrementalism, when it comes to clean energy, is just a hobby."

—Thomas Friedman, *What Was That All About?*, N.Y. Times, Dec. 19, 2007.

SYNOPSIS

I. Envisioning a Carbon-Free Economy
II. How to Achieve a Carbon-Free Future
III. Building Support for a Carbon-Free Future
    A. Building Political Will for Preventing Climate Change
    B. Reframing How We Talk About Climate Change

I. ENVISIONING A CARBON-FREE ECONOMY

The scope and scale of any post-Kyoto agreement or any federal U.S. environmental legislation is conjecture at this time, but one thing will continue to be true throughout the next century — whether through multilateral or unilateral action or mitigation or adaptation, policymakers throughout the world will need to address the causes and the impacts of global climate change. Individuals, too, must reconsider the choices they make. One vehicle for governmental action will undoubtedly be the international climate change regime, but it surely will not be the only one. In Chapter 9, we reviewed the possible approaches for a post-Kyoto Protocol agreement. Those approaches, however, focused on what might be politically achievable in that forum. The growing scientific evidence, however, tells us that what may be politically achievable in the short-term is unlikely to meet the demands of climate change.

As discussed in Chapter 1, the relationship between human emissions of greenhouse gases and on-the-ground impacts necessitates taking action to transform our economy. In 2007, atmospheric concentrations of carbon dioxide (CO_2) reached 382 parts per million. When other greenhouse gases are added to the mix, concentrations now stand at 430 parts per million CO_2 equivalent. Christopher Flavin, *Building a Low-Carbon Economy, in*, State of the World 2008: Innovations for a Sustainable Economy 75 (Worldwatch Institute 2008). Many scientists argue that CO_2 concentrations above 450 parts per million and CO_2 equivalent concentrations above 500 parts per million must be avoided. Even at that level, the average global temperature would increase by 2.4° to 2.8° Celsius above pre-industrial levels, and leave us living on a "different planet." James Hansen, Address at St. James Palace, London: The Threat to the Planet: How Can We Avoid Dangerous Human-Made Climate Change? 2 (Nov. 21, 2006). More recently, James Hansen has gone further, saying that we must return to 350 ppm. The Intergovernmental Panel on Climate Change (IPCC) estimates that carbon dioxide emissions must be reduced by 50 to 85 percent relative to the year 2000 just to limit average global temperature *increases* to 2° to 2.4° Celsius above pre-industrial temperatures.

But if the world's economies continue with business as usual, emissions will go in exactly the opposite direction. The U.S. Department of Energy expects global CO_2 emissions to grow by nearly 57 percent by 2030 from 2004 levels solely from increases in energy consumption. U.S. DEPARTMENT OF ENERGY, INTERNATIONAL ENERGY OUTLOOK 2007 4 (2007). In the United States, 47 new coal-fired power plants are under construction or permitted with another 67 under development. ERIK SHUSTER, TRACKING NEW COAL-FIRED POWER PLANTS (National Energy Technology Laboratory, Feb. 18, 2008). In 2008, China was building as many as one coal-fired power plant per week. This business-as-usual scenario would take us much closer to atmospheric concentrations of CO_2 of 550 parts per million and well above a 2 Celsius temperature increase. Flavin, *Building a Low-Carbon Economy*, at 77.

The stark implications of a business-as-usual future have led to the phenomenal change in public attitudes toward climate change witnessed over the past five years, as well as to calls by many leading political leaders for dramatic cuts in greenhouse gas emissions. In short, many people recognize the need for a collective effort to retool the energy base of our modern economies. The International Climate Change Task Force, for example, has called for a "transformative technological revolution":

> Preventing dangerous climate change . . . must be seen as a precon-
> dition for prosperity and a public good, like national security and public
> health. By contrast, the cost of taking smart, effective action to meet the
> challenge of climate change should be entirely manageable. Such action
> need not undermine standards of living. Furthermore, by taking action now
> and developing a long-term climate policy regime we can ensure that the
> benefits of climate protection are achieved at least cost. Climate change,
> energy security, and the urgent need to increase access to modern energy
> services for the world's poor create an enormous need for more efficient
> low-carbon and no-carbon energy-supply options. We need a transforma-
> tive technological revolution in the twenty-first century involving the
> development and rapid deployment of cleaner energy and transportation
> technologies. By reducing greenhouse emissions and deploying new
> climate-friendly technologies, companies can create jobs and launch a new
> era of economic prosperity.

INTERNATIONAL CLIMATE CHANGE TASK FORCE, MEETING THE CLIMATE CHALLENGE: RECOMMENDATIONS OF THE INTERNATIONAL CLIMATE CHANGE TASK FORCE 1–2 (2005). Achieving such a "transformative technological revolution" will require us to contemplate what was once unthinkable: a low-carbon or carbon-free future. In 2007, Norway boldly pledged to become "carbon neutral" by 2050, vowing to offset any net emissions with vast investments in developing countries. Elisabeth Rosenthal, *Lofty Pledge to Cut Emissions Comes with Caveat in Norway*, N.Y. TIMES, Mar. 22, 2008, at A1. And in the following speech, former Vice-President Al Gore challenged the United States to produce 100 percent of its electricity from renewable energy and clean carbon sources within 10 years.

AL GORE, ADDRESS AT D.A.R. CONSTITUTION HALL: A GENERATIONAL CHALLENGE TO REPOWER AMERICA
(July 17, 2008)*

Today I challenge our nation to commit to producing 100 percent of our electricity from renewable energy and truly clean carbon-free sources within 10 years.

This goal is achievable, affordable and transformative. It represents a challenge to all Americans — in every walk of life: to our political leaders, entrepreneurs, innovators, engineers, and to every citizen.

A few years ago, it would not have been possible to issue such a challenge. But here's what's changed: the sharp cost reductions now beginning to take place in solar, wind, and geothermal power — coupled with the recent dramatic price increases for oil and coal — have radically changed the economics of energy.

When I first went to Congress 32 years ago, I listened to experts testify that if oil ever got to $35 a barrel, then renewable sources of energy would become competitive. Well, today, the price of oil is over $135 per barrel. And sure enough, billions of dollars of new investment are flowing into the development of concentrated solar thermal, photovoltaics, windmills, geothermal plants, and a variety of ingenious new ways to improve our efficiency and conserve presently wasted energy.

And as the demand for renewable energy grows, the costs will continue to fall. Let me give you one revealing example: the price of the specialized silicon used to make solar cells was recently as high as $300 per kilogram. But the newest contracts have prices as low as $50 a kilogram.

You know, the same thing happened with computer chips — also made out of silicon. The price paid for the same performance came down by 50 percent every 18 months — year after year, and that's what's happened for 40 years in a row.

*   *   *

What could we do . . . for the next 10 years? What should we do during the next 10 years? Some of our greatest accomplishments as a nation have resulted from commitments to reach a goal that fell well beyond the next election: the Marshall Plan, Social Security, the interstate highway system. But a political promise to do something 40 years from now is universally ignored because everyone knows that it's meaningless. Ten years is about the maximum time that we as a nation can hold a steady aim and hit our target.

When President John F. Kennedy challenged our nation to land a man on the moon and bring him back safely in 10 years, many people doubted we could accomplish that goal. But 8 years and 2 months later, Neil Armstrong and Buzz Aldrin walked on the surface of the moon.

To be sure, reaching the goal of 100 percent renewable and truly clean electricity within 10 years will require us to overcome many obstacles. At present, for example, we do not have a unified national grid that is sufficiently advanced to link the areas where the sun shines and the wind blows to the cities in the East and the West that need the electricity. Our national electric grid is critical infrastructure, as vital to the health and security of our economy as our highways and telecommunication networks. Today, our grids are antiquated, fragile, and vulnerable to cascading failure. Power outages and defects in the current grid system cost U.S. businesses

---

more than $120 billion dollars a year. It has to be upgraded anyway.

We could further increase the value and efficiency of a Unified National Grid by helping our struggling auto giants switch to the manufacture of plug-in electric cars. An electric vehicle fleet would sharply reduce the cost of driving a car, reduce pollution, and increase the flexibility of our electricity grid.

At the same time, of course, we need to greatly improve our commitment to efficiency and conservation. That's the best investment we can make.

America's transition to renewable energy sources must also include adequate provisions to assist those Americans who would unfairly face hardship. For example, we must recognize those who have toiled in dangerous conditions to bring us our present energy supply. We should guarantee good jobs in the fresh air and sunshine for any coal miner displaced by impacts on the coal industry. Every single one of them.

Of course, we could and should speed up this transition by insisting that the price of carbon-based energy include the costs of the environmental damage it causes. I have long supported a sharp reduction in payroll taxes with the difference made up in CO_2 taxes. We should tax what we burn, not what we earn. This is the single most important policy change we can make.

In order to foster international cooperation, it is also essential that the United States rejoin the global community and lead efforts to secure an international treaty at Copenhagen in December of next year that includes a cap on CO_2 emissions and a global partnership that recognizes the necessity of addressing the threats of extreme poverty and disease as part of the world's agenda for solving the climate crisis.

Of course the greatest obstacle to meeting the challenge of 100 percent renewable electricity in 10 years may be the deep dysfunction of our politics and our self-governing system as it exists today. In recent years, our politics has tended toward incremental proposals made up of small policies designed to avoid offending special interests, alternating with occasional baby steps in the right direction. Our democracy has become sclerotic at a time when these crises require boldness.

It is only a truly dysfunctional system that would buy into the perverse logic that the short-term answer to high gasoline prices is drilling for more oil ten years from now.

*   *   *

If you want to know the truth about gasoline prices, here it is: the exploding demand for oil, especially in places like China, is overwhelming the rate of new discoveries by so much that oil prices are almost certain to continue upward over time no matter what the oil companies promise. And politicians cannot bring gasoline prices down in the short term.

However, there actually is one extremely effective way to bring the costs of driving a car way down within a few short years. The way to bring gas prices down is to end our dependence on oil and use the renewable sources that can give us the equivalent of $1 per gallon gasoline.

*   *   *

On July 16, 1969, the United States of America was finally ready to meet President Kennedy's challenge of landing Americans on the moon.

*   *   *

We must now lift our nation to reach another goal that will change history. Our entire civilization depends upon us now embarking on a new journey of exploration and discovery. Our success depends on our willingness as a people to undertake this journey and to complete it within 10 years. Once again, we have an opportunity to take a giant leap for humankind.

QUESTIONS AND DISCUSSION

1. The IPCC has left little doubt that the climate is changing and that human activity is playing a major role in those changes. Yet, political leaders appear reluctant to act with the urgency that scientists say is necessary. Is talk of a carbon-free energy sector in 10 years or carbon-free economy within the next 40 years realistic? What approaches that you've learned about in this book do you think hold promise for facilitating a "transformative technological revolution"? What role can law play in such a revolution?

2. Some energy experts have called Al Gore's proposal for carbon-free electricity in 10 years unrealistic. Even if true, does such a proposal open up policy space for less ambitious proposals, such as carbon-free electricity in 20 years? In fact, isn't part of the value of Gore's proposal to set an inspirational goal? What is the value of laying down such a benchmark?

3. Six months after Al Gore gave this speech, oil prices had dropped 50 percent to less than $60 per barrel due to the global economic crisis. To what extent, if any, does this change Al Gore's argument? In what ways is it more difficult to transform our energy use when oil prices are lower? In what ways is it easier?

II. HOW TO ACHIEVE A CARBON-FREE FUTURE

In analyzing calls for a transformative energy revolution and a carbon-free future, it is important to revisit the practical possibilities of meeting such a goal. Do we know how to do it? Are there policies and technologies that can help us reach a carbon-free future? The following excerpt by Chris Flavin builds on the Pacala and Sokolow article excerpted in Chapter 2. The Flavin article and the one that follows by Arjun Makhijani set forth some clear recommendations for achieving a carbon-free, or at least a low-carbon, energy future. How realistic are these steps? What obstacles do you see that will hold us back?

CHRISTOPHER FLAVIN, BUILDING A LOW-CARBON ECONOMY
in STATE OF THE WORLD 2008: INNOVATIONS FOR A SUSTAINABLE ECONOMY 75, 78–86 (Worldwatch Institute 2008)[*]

For the world as a whole to cut emissions in half by 2050, today's industrial countries will need to cut theirs by more than 80 percent. Getting there depends on three elements in a climate strategy: capturing and storing the carbon contained in fossil fuels, reducing energy consumption through new technologies and lifestyles, and shifting to carbon-free energy technologies.

A variety of combinations of these three strategies can in theory do the job. Princeton scientists Robert Socolow and Stephen Pacala have broken the task down into 15 1-billion-ton "wedges" of reductions — including such options as improved fuel economy or massive construction of wind farms — that policymakers can choose from. The key question is which combination of strategies will minimize the substantial investment cost but also provide a healthy and secure energy system that will last.

Phasing out oil, the most important fossil fuel today, may turn out to be the easiest part of the problem. Production of conventional crude oil is expected to peak and begin declining within the next decade or two. By 2050, output could be a third or more below the current level. Reliance on natural gas, which has not been as heavily exploited as oil and which releases half as much carbon per unit of energy as coal, is meanwhile likely to grow. * * *

The central role of coal in the world's climate dilemma has led policymakers and industrialists to focus on so-called carbon capture and storage (CCS). Although it is only likely to be feasible for large, centralized uses of fossil fuels, many energy planners are counting on it. They hope to build a new generation of power plants equipped with devices that capture carbon either before or after the combustion of fossil fuels and then pipe the CO_2 into underground geological reservoirs or into the deep ocean, where it could in principle remain for millions of years.

* * *

In light of the lead times required for technology development and demonstration, it will be 2020 at the earliest before significant numbers of carbon-neutral coal plants come online. Nor is it guaranteed that CCS plants will be competitive with other carbon-free generators that are likely to be in the market by that date. But the bigger question is whether that would not be too late, considering the hundreds of new coal-fired power plants that are currently being considered in China, the United States, and other nations. To have any hope of halving carbon emissions by 2050, it is hard to avoid the conclusion that the uncontrolled burning of coal will need to be eliminated — and soon. In the meantime, a growing number of climate experts are calling for a moratorium on building new coal-fired power plants unless or until CCS becomes available.

The Convenient Truth

* * *

Improved energy productivity and renewable energy are both available in abundance — and new policies and technologies are rapidly making them more economically competitive with fossil fuels. In combination, these energy options represent the most robust alternative to the current energy system, capable of providing the diverse array of energy services that a modern economy requires. Given the urgency of the climate problem, that is indeed convenient.

The first step in establishing the viability of a climate-safe energy strategy is assessing the available resources and the potential role they might play. Surveys show that the resource base is indeed ample; the main factors limiting the pace of change are the economic challenge of accelerating investment in new energy options and the political challenge of overcoming the institutional barriers to change.

* * *

The greatest potential turns out to lie in the most basic element of the energy economy — buildings — which could be improved with better insulation, more-efficient lighting, and better appliances, at costs that would be more than paid for by lower energy bills. With technologies available today, such as ground-source heat pumps that reduce the energy needed for heating and cooling by 70 percent, zero-net-energy buildings are possible that do not require fossil fuels at all. All countries have untapped potential like this to increase energy productivity, but the largest opportunities are found in the developing nations, where current energy productivity tends to be lower. Future increases in energy productivity will not only reduce consumption of fossil fuels, they will make it easier and more affordable to rapidly increase the use of carbon-free energy sources. * * *

Several studies have assessed the scale of the major renewable resources and what their practical contribution to the energy economy might one day be. One study by the National Renewable Energy Laboratory in the United States, for example, concluded that solar thermal power plants built in seven states in the U.S. Southwest could provide nearly seven times the nation's existing electric capacity from all sources. And mounting solar electric generators on just half of the suitable rooftop area could provide 25 percent of U.S. electricity. In the case of wind power, the Pacific Northwest Laboratory found that the land-based wind resources of Kansas, North Dakota, and Texas could meet all the nation's electricity needs, even with large areas excluded for environmental reasons.

These reports demonstrate that resource availability will not be a limiting factor as the world seeks to replace fossil fuels. With improved technologies, greater efficiency, and lower costs, renewable energy could one day replace virtually all the carbon-based fuels that are so vital to today's economy.

*   *   *

The Economics of Change

*   *   *

According to conventional wisdom, the energy sector is far from such a transformation. New renewable energy sources represent less than 2 percent of the total energy supply, and in 2007 total U.S. government support of renewable energy R&D came to little more than $600 million — about what the government spent in Iraq in a single day. What these figures fail to capture is the recent infusion of private-sector capital and technology and the fact that today's renewable energy pioneers are not limited to "energy technology" but rather draw on fields as diverse as semiconductor physics, biotechnology, aerodynamics, and computer engineering.

Over the past five years, the manufacture of wind turbines has grown at 17 percent annually, and solar cells at a 46-percent annual rate. This rapid growth has turned these industries into lucrative businesses, with demand outrunning supply and profits soaring. Some $52 billion was invested in renewable energy in 2006, up 33 percent from 2005. At that level, investment in renewable energy is already one quarter that of the oil industry — and gaining ground rapidly. * * *

Corporate R&D on clean energy technologies reached $9.1 billion in 2006. A single company, Vestas Wind Systems, spent $120 million on R&D in 2006, while the U.S. government spent less than $50 million on wind R&D. Even these numbers understate private R&D, which is often embedded in commercial projects, and exclude R&D investments by privately held companies, many of them funded with venture capital and other forms of equity investment. Venture capital and private equity investment in clean energy totaled $8.6 billion in 2006, 69 percent above the

2005 level and 10 times the 2001 level. * * *

In Silicon Valley, clean energy is helping drive a post-dotcom revival. Although it is regrettable that serious investment in renewable energy did not begin earlier, the science and technology available today will allow the industry to achieve performance and cost goals that would not have been possible in the past.

One example is photovoltaics, where producers are pursuing a host of strategies for reducing materials requirements, raising efficiency, and lowering manufacturing costs of the crystalline cells that dominate the market. Other companies are developing new thinfilm photovoltaic materials that hold the promise of dramatic cost reductions. With demand outrunning supplies of PV materials in the past two years, price trends have temporarily reversed their usual downward course. But the industry is planning to increase its manufacturing capacity as much as eightfold over the next three years, and dramatic price declines are likely, spurring the industry to develop new applications and markets that would not be feasible today.

Beyond the advance in technology, the economics of renewable energy will further improve as the scale of production rises — the same phenomenon that has successively turned televisions, personal computers, and mobile phones from specialty products for high-income technology pioneers into massmarket consumer devices. An analysis of production costs in several manufacturing industries by the Boston Consulting Group found that each time cumulative production of a manufactured device doubles, production costs fall by 20–30 percent.

The annual production of wind turbines is now doubling every three years — and wind is already competitive with natural gas-fired power in the United States. It would be competitive with coal-fired power plants if they had to pay the current European CO_2 price of $32 per ton. Solar electricity is still twice as expensive as retail grid electricity in most markets, but annual production is doubling every two years — which should cut costs in half in the next four to six years.

ARJUN MAKHIJANI, CARBON-FREE AND NUCLEAR-FREE, A ROADMAP FOR U.S. ENERGY POLICY
165–66, 175 (2007)

The overarching finding of this study is that a zero-CO_2 U.S. economy can be achieved within the next thirty to fifty years without the use of nuclear power and without acquiring carbon credits from other countries. In other words, actual physical emissions of CO_2 from the energy sector can be eliminated with technologies that are now available or foreseeable. This can be done at reasonable cost while creating a much more secure energy supply than at present. Net U.S. oil imports can be eliminated in about 25 years. All three insecurities — severe climate disruption, oil supply and price insecurity, and nuclear proliferation via commercial nuclear energy — will thereby be addressed.

* * *

B. Recommendations: The Clean Dozen

The 12 most critical policies that need to be enacted as urgently as possible for achieving a zero-CO_2 economy without nuclear power are as follows.

1. Enact a physical limit of CO_2 emissions for all large users of fossil fuels (a "hard cap") that steadily declines to zero prior to 2060, with the time schedule being assessed periodically for tightening according to climate, technological, and eco-

nomic developments. The cap should be set at the level of some year prior to 2007, so that early implementers of CO_2 reductions benefit from the setting of the cap. Emission allowances would be sold by the U.S. government for use in the United States only. There would be no free allowances, no offsets and no international sale or purchase of CO_2 allowances. The estimated revenues — approximately $30 to $50 billion per year — would be used for demonstration plants, research and development, and worker and community transition.

2. Eliminate all subsidies and tax breaks for fossil fuels and nuclear power (including guarantees for nuclear waste disposal from new power plants, loan guarantees, and subsidized insurance).

3. Eliminate subsidies for biofuels from food crops.

4. Build demonstration plants for key supply technologies, including central station solar thermal with heat storage, large- and intermediate-scale solar photovoltaics, and CO_2 capture in microalgae for liquid fuel production (and production of . . . high solar energy capture aquatic plants, for instance in wetlands constructed at municipal wastewater systems).

5. Leverage federal, state and local purchasing power to create markets for critical advanced technologies, including plug-in hybrids.

6. Ban new coal-fired power plants that do not have carbon storage.

7. Enact at the federal level high efficiency standards for appliances.

8. Enact stringent building efficiency standards at the state and local levels, with federal incentives to adopt them.

9. Enact stringent efficiency standards for vehicles and make plug-in hybrids the standard U.S. government vehicle by 2015.

10. Put in place federal contracting procedures to reward early adopters of CO_2 reductions.

11. Adopt vigorous research, development, and pilot plant construction programs for technologies that could accelerate the elimination of CO_2, such as direct electrolytic hydrogen production, solar hydrogen production (photolytic, photoelectrochemical, and other approaches), hot rock geothermal power, and integrated gasification combined cycle plants using biomass with a capacity to sequester the CO_2.

12. Establish a standing committee on Energy and Climate under the U.S. Environmental Protection Agency's Science Advisory Board.

QUESTIONS AND DISCUSSION

1. President Obama has announced a number of new initiatives to address climate change and the 2009 Stimulus Bill also included provisions for addressing climate change. In addition, Congress is debating comprehensive climate change legislation. Review the legislative proposals discussed in Chapter 11 and research more recent proposals and initiatives. To what extent do they reflect actions identified by Flavin or Makhijani?

2. Throughout the course of this book, we have described international proposals to mitigate climate change. We have also discussed litigation under current federal law as well as legislative proposals to regulate greenhouse gas emissions. Many of these adopt an incremental approach to climate change. For example, California's attempt to regulate carbon dioxide emissions from vehicles, as well as the new federal standard, would merely slow the growth in carbon dioxide emissions. These efforts may begin to shift the economy away from business as usual, but they are inadequate to solve climate change completely. How should environmentalists address this? Should they continue to use existing statutes to slow the growth in greenhouse gas emissions and expend valuable financial and staff resources doing so, or should they put their energy and resources into advocacy for the longer term goal of a carbon-free economy?

3.   Even if we transform our society into a carbon-free economy within the next 40 years, average global temperatures will still increase by at least 2 degrees Celsius above pre-industrial levels. Species will likely go extinct, diseases will increase, precipitation will increase or decrease, depending on where you live. What are the implications for the policies of adaptation outlined in Chapter 3?

4.   Many others are also talking about and planning a carbon-free future. For example, the Club of Rome's Desertec project is a plan for supplying energy needs to a rather significant portion of the world with just solar power. For details of the program, see http://www.trecers.net.

5.   At first blush, some of the proposals by Flavin and Makhijani may seem far-fetched but technological change can happen fast. Consider, for example, the state of plug-in hybrid vehicles. Although hybrid vehicles may still be a relative novelty throughout much of the nation, General Motors and Toyota have already pledged to have plug-in hybrids on the road by 2010, if not earlier. Indeed, GM has pledged to have its plug-in Volt with a capacity to travel 40 miles on a single charge in mass production by 2010. Anticipating the change to plug-ins, Portland General Electric Co. has begun installing a dozen plug-in vehicle-charging stations in the Portland metropolitan area. Moreover, U.S. automotive companies could not give away their sport-utility vehicles because consumers could not afford to fill their tanks. Obviously, this was in response mostly to record-breaking gasoline prices, but it also shows how quickly technology and associated consumer habits can change if given appropriate market or policy signals.

6.   Gore and Makhijani note elsewhere that enough solar energy reaches Earth every 40 minutes to meet 100 percent of the *entire* world's energy needs for a full year; enough wind blows through the Midwest every day to meet 100 percent of current U.S. electricity demand. Tapping those energy resources could make the United States not only energy independent but a net exporter of energy. How can the law be used to catalyze major investments in wind and solar power?

7.   *Class Exercise.* Assume that you are the President of the United States and that you have the choice to transform one particular segment of the economy. Which would you choose? What are the opportunities and challenges of transforming that economic sector?

III.   BUILDING SUPPORT FOR A CARBON-FREE FUTURE

What should become clear from the above excerpts as well as a review of mitigation strategies in Chapter 2 is that in general terms a consensus exists for what needs to be done to reduce the risk of the worst climate change impacts — an ambitious expansion of energy conservation, fuel switching to non-fossil fuels, and efforts to capture carbon from fossil-fuel burning. Most of the technologies necessary to make this energy transformation already exist, although the costs of some must decline to compete with business-as-usual energy sources or technologies. From a legal perspective, many of the necessary policies are also familiar, involving some combination of taxing carbon, reducing subsidies to fossil fuels, capping and trading emissions, or mandating restrictions or technologies on specific industries. The problem is thus not a lack of smart technologies or policies but rather a lack of political will. How should this political will be built? Some observers, such as Gus Speth, Dean of the Yale School of Forestry, former head of United Nations Development Programme, and founder of the World Resources Institute, believe we need to build a stronger environmental movement. Others believe the use of language and the way we frame the debate — is climate change an environmental issue or a human health imperative? — could help build momentum for a carbon free future.

A.   Building Political Will for Preventing Climate Change

JAMES GUSTAVE SPETH, THE BRIDGE AT THE EDGE OF THE WORLD: CAPITALISM, THE ENVIRONMENT AND CROSSING FROM CRISIS TO SUSTAINABILITY
225–31 (2008)*

First, the new environmental politics must be broadened now so that environmental concern and advocacy extend to the full range of relevant issues. Efforts within the framework of today's environmentalism must continue; indeed, they must be strengthened. But the environmental agenda should expand to embrace a profound challenge to consumerism and commercialism and the lifestyles they offer, a healthy skepticism of growth mania and a sharp focus on what society should actually be striving to grow, a challenge to corporate dominance and a redefinition of the corporation and its goals, a commitment to deep change in both functioning and the reach of the market, and a commitment to building what Alperovitz calls "the democratization of wealth" and Barnes calls "capitalism 3.0."

The new agenda should also incorporate advocacy of human rights as a central concern. Though environmental justice has gained a foothold in American environmentalism, it is not yet the priority it should be. Across much of the world social justice concerns and environmental concerns are fused as one cause, and many environmental leaders have been persecuted, jailed, and murdered. They are brothers and sisters, and their rights to life, speech, and democracy should be vigorously defended. Many established environmental issues must be seen as human rights issues — the right to water and sanitation, the right to sustainable development, the right to cultural survival, freedom from climatic disruption and ruin, freedom to live in a nontoxic environment, the rights of future generations.

The new environmental politics should also embrace a program to address America's social problems directly and generously. . . . In particular, it is crucial for environmentalists to join with others in addressing the crisis of inequality now unraveling America's social fabric and undermining its democracy — a crisis of unprecedented profits, soaring executive pay, huge incomes, and increasingly concentrated wealth for a small minority occurring simultaneously with poverty rates near a thirty-year high, stagnant wages despite rising productivity, declining social mobility and opportunity, record levels of people without health insurance, failing schools, increased job insecurity, shrinking safety nets, and the longest work hours among the rich countries.

---

* * *

If the first watchword of the new environmental politics is "broaden the agenda," the second is "get political." Lawyering and lobbying are important, but what the new environmentalism must build now is a mighty force in electoral politics. Building the necessary muscle will require major efforts at grassroots organizing; strengthening groups working at the state and community level; and developing messages, appeals, and stories that inspire and motivate because they speak in a language people can understand, resonating with what is best in both an American tradition and the public's values and presenting compelling visions of a future worth having for families and children. Perhaps above all, the new environment politics must be broadly inclusive, reaching out to embrace union members and working families, minorities and people of color, religious organizations, the women's movement, and other communities of complementary interest and shared fate. And it is unfortunate but true that stronger alliances are still needed to overcome the "silo effect" that separates the environmental community from those working on domestic political reforms, the liberal social agenda, human rights, international peace, consumer issues, world health and population concerns, and world poverty and underdevelopment.

Environmental politics cannot succeed with only a narrowly defined environmental constituency. The new environmentalism needs to reach out to many communities and support their causes not just to build the case for reciprocal support, and not just because the objectives are worthy, but also because environmental goals will not be realized unless these other causes succeed. In the end, they are all one cause and will rise and fall together. If, for example, someone says, "We can't help others abroad because we have got to take care of Americans first," know this: they will not take care of Americans either.

The final watchword of the new environmental politics is "build the movement." Efforts to build environmental strength in America's electoral process and to join forces with a wider array of constituencies embracing a broader agenda should both contribute to the emergence of a powerful citizens' movement for change.

What we need now is an international movement of citizens and scientists, one capable of dramatically advancing the political and personal actions needed for the transition to sustainability. We have had movements against slavery, and many have participated in movements for civil rights and against apartheid and the Vietnam War. Environmentalists are often said to be part of "the environmental movement." We need a real one. It is time for we the people, as citizens and as consumers, to take charge.

The best hope we have for this new force is a coalescing of a wide array of civic, scientific, environmental religious, student, and other organizations with enlightened business leaders, concerned families, and engaged communities, networked together, protesting, demanding action and accountability from governments and corporations, and taking steps as consumers and communities to realize sustainability in everyday life.

Young people will almost certainly be centrally involved in any movement for real change. They always have been. New dreams are born most easily when the world is seen with fresh eyes and confronted with impertinent questions. The Internet is empowering young people in an unprecedented way — not just by access to information but by access to each other, and to a wider world.

One goal should be to find the spark that can set off a period of rapid change, like the flowering of the domestic environmental agenda in the early 1970s. In the end, we need to trigger a response that in historical terms will come to be seen as revolutionary — the Environmental Revolution of the twenty-first century. Only such a response is likely to avert huge and even catastrophic environmental losses.

*   *   *

Can one see the beginnings of a true citizens' movement in America? Perhaps . . . I am letting my hopes get the better of me, but I think we can. Its green side is visible, I think, in the remarkable surge of campus organizing and student mobilization occurring today, much of it coordinated by the student-led Energy Action Coalition. It's visible also in the increasing activism of religious organizations, including many evangelical groups under the banner of Creation Care, and in the rapid proliferation of community-based environmental initiatives. It's there in the joining together of organized labor, environmental groups and progressive businesses in the Apollo Alliance and in the Sierra Club's collaboration with the United Steelworkers, the largest industrial union in the United States. It's visible too in the outpouring of effort to build on Al Gore's *An Inconvenient Truth*, in the green consumer movement and in the consumer support for the efforts of the Rainforest Action Network to green the policies of the major U.S. banks. It's there in the increasing number of teach-ins, demonstrations, marches, and protests, including the fourteen hundred events across the United States in 2007 inspired by Bill McKibben's "Step it Up!" stop global warming campaign. It is there in the constituency-building work of minority environmental leaders. . . . It can be seen too in the strong presence of U.S. nonprofits in the various World Social Forums and in the convening of the first U.S. Social Forum in 2007. It's just beginning, but it's there, and it will grow.

QUESTIONS AND DISCUSSION

1.   Discussions of building alliances, broadening the environmental movement, and reframing the debate seem distant from what is typically considered the role of a lawyer. But lawyers are often the intellectual and organizing leaders of social movements. Beyond that, social movements or the organizations that compose them are often a public interest lawyer's clients. An understanding of movement objectives, strategies, and politics is thus a critical part of being a complete lawyer in the public interest, just as understanding a corporation's product line, competitors, and market dynamics is in the corporate world.

2.   One role that lawyers play in the public interest environmental community is to draft policies and legislation that can focus the environmental movement and rally it behind specific and practical policy reforms. In recent years, however, an increasing amount of attention is being paid to the importance of framing policies and goals in language that resonates with broader aspects of the public. To some extent, both Al Gore and Gus Speth's excerpts discuss the need to broaden the appeal of the environmental message generally and climate change more specifically. Gore's excerpt is an attempt to frame climate change as a great American challenge, not unlike our effort to go to the moon. Speth sees the widespread interest in climate change as an opportunity for strengthening the environmental movement, if connections can be made to labor, human rights, and other constituencies. Key to successfully building this movement will be whether lawyers and others can express their policy goals in ways that engage a broader social movement in supporting an energy transformation. The next section thus discusses the importance of how we as lawyers frame the climate change debate.

B.   Reframing How We Talk About Climate Change

Reframing the debate about climate change reflects the growing recognition that *how* we talk about issues has a significant impact on *whether* there will be political support for action. How we talk or frame an issue reflects certain values and ideas, which may or may not be values and ideas shared by the majority of the public. If responding to climate change is viewed as merely one more environmental issue, it may arguably never garner sufficient popular support for the transformative steps that are necessary. Would it be better, for example, to think of climate change as a public health issue? As a national security issue? Or as an economics and jobs issue? The following excerpt by Joe Brewer and Evan Frisch highlights the importance of thinking about the values and ideas behind our approach to climate change and seeks to reorient the language of climate change policy debates to ensure broader public support.

JOE BREWER AND EVAN FRISCH, COGNITIVE POLICY, THE ENVIRONMENTAL FORUM
Sept./Oct. 2008, at 36, 37–38*

The climate crisis is among the most serious threats we face. Getting the right framework is critical, requiring expertise in many areas — including public policy, science, economics, planning and development, and more. One area of expertise that has gone largely unnoticed so far is the application of cognitive science — an interdisciplinary study drawing from psychology, philosophy, neuroscience, linguistics, anthropology, computer science, and biology — to the political process.

*   *   *

We propose a new conceptual framework that distinguishes two kinds of policy, material and cognitive. Material policies are familiar: they outline what is to be done in the world. . . . Material policies always have a cognitive dimension, often unconscious and implicit rather than conscious and explicit, which shapes how citizens and policymakers understand them. For example, do all citizens own the air together? Or is the atmosphere a resource that each person or company has a natural right to use for its own gain? The way in which these questions are answered defines a cognitive dimension — whether the policy is perceived to be valuable and useful or interfering and injurious.

When environmentalists talk about policy, they tend to focus on material concerns such as the species or ecosystems that would be preserved by a new program or the number of tons of pollutants that won't be dumped in our nation's waterways. In addition to this material dimension, every policy has a cognitive dimension — implicit values, concepts, and modes of thought that allow the policy to make mental sense. Policy proposals without a coherent, attractive cognitive dimension risk being misunderstood by the public and are susceptible to successful attack. An example from another field can be found in the gradual chipping away of support for the inheritance tax by repositioning it as a "death tax," which sounds unfair on the face of it.

Opponents of environmental action have been successful in cognitive policy — that is, in shaping public discourse to lead the public to accept basic values and principles that undermine environmental programs. Their long-term investment in cognitive policy has paid off in making their material policies seem natural — for

---

example, investments in biofuels that require more petroleum to grow than they replace under the guise of energy independence, drilling in the Arctic National Wildlife Refuge as a means of escaping from rising gas prices, or delaying action on climate change because of scientific uncertainty.

The success of a policy depends on how it meets both material *and* cognitive criteria. Concentrating on material criteria alone can be counterproductive if a policy is either unpopular, or if it instills in the public's mind long-term values that contradict the aims of the policy.

*   *   *

We will now present a case study to demonstrate the importance of cognitive policy that compares two climate proposals — the "Climate Security" bill proposed by Senators Joe Lieberman and John Warner and policy analyst Peter Barnes's "Cap and Dividend" proposal. . . . Our purpose is to show the role of human cognition in the policymaking process, not promote a specific policy solution. We selected these particular proposals because they are illustrative of significantly different cognitive foundations that lead to distinct policy consequences.

We will begin with Cap and Dividend, since it is both the less known of the two proposals and the one with an overt cognitive policy. The central principle of the Cap and Dividend cognitive policy is a simple idea: We all own the air. The material policy linked to that idea is composed of the following: Carbon pollution is capped where it enters the economy. Any company that wants to sell fossil fuels must purchase dumping permits. Each year the number of permits made available goes down. Companies that reduce emissions below the level allowed by their permits can then trade them to other companies, creating a market for permits — a cap-and-trade system.

The money goes into a trust, and is distributed every month via bank transfer to all Americans equally. Their shares are non-transferable. As the number of permits goes down, the value of permits rises and each American gets more money. The value of the air is directly reflected in their bank accounts.

The Lieberman-Warner bill has no overt cognitive policy. It is presented as a typical material policy. Its central component is also a cap-and-trade system that places a limit on the amount of CO_2 generated each year that decreases with time.

Lieberman-Warner starts by giving a large proportion of the valuable permits away free to those companies that pollute the most. The biggest polluters can use the permits to go on polluting at slightly decreasing levels each year or they can earn profits by selling the permits. That is, the money goes to the polluters — the bigger the polluter, the more they get. The idea is that polluters have an implicit right to go on doing business just as they were — with pollution as a by-product external to the business — and that they require, and deserve, financial compensation to stop.

Over time more permits are auctioned, until 100 percent are sold at auction. As the money goes into the general treasury, it is distributed through a wide array of public projects across various industries and municipalities. Citizens have no direct role in the process.

Lieberman-Warner has no explicit cognitive dimension. But it does have an implicit cognitive policy. That is, it is based on and supports a set of ideas without conscious discussion. Since most thought is unconscious, the cognitive policy behind Lieberman-Warner functions below our mental radar screens, where it operates in dissonance with the bill's stated goals.

As a result, Lieberman-Warner fails to hold up to the Cognitive Criterion for Public Support. It is bureaucratic and complex, making it difficult to decipher. Its overarching themes focus on industry and overlook the role of citizens. This focus promotes an understanding that the policy has to do with industry, not with me.

Furthermore, as energy prices rise, it leads to the "hidden tax" scenario: The price increase is a hidden tax on consumers. People understand that higher prices come from charging companies more for carbon emissions, reinforcing the idea that climate legislation harms the economy. They infer that the cost is naturally passed on to them, with no blame to the corporations. The policy will be seen as faulty. Government can easily be blamed as prices go up and nothing compensates citizens for the price rise.

In contrast, Cap and Dividend was created with certain cognitive goals in mind. It holds up much better. First off, it is easily understood. Companies have not been paying the full cost of doing business. Now they must pay a dumping cost for damage to our air. We, the citizens, are compensated for damages through recurring payments. This leads to the "dumping cost" scenario: The price increase is a cost for businesses that pollute.

People receive recurring payments from carbon dumping permits sold to polluters and see a correlation as their returns grow with rising energy prices. This allows them to understand that companies are paying to dump carbon into our air and each person receives compensation for this damage. The polluting companies are to blame. The policy helps people by providing dividends.

If one looks only at the material policies, the two proposals seem similar. Both introduce a carbon cap that goes down each year. Both use an auction to distribute permits — all the permits for Cap and Dividend and a gradually increasing percentage for Lieberman-Warner. Both create permit trading markets. On the surface, they may seem more alike than different. This impression is false. The profound differences arise through the power of ideas. The cognitive dimensions of the policies have strategic consequences.

QUESTIONS AND DISCUSSION

1.   Joe Brewer and Evan Frisch believe that the words we use to talk about climate change and the manner in which we structure laws deeply affects how we perceive issues. Thus, even though the Lieberman-Warner bill and Peter Barnes' Cap and Dividend proposal share many of the same attributes, they believe that the Cap and Dividend proposal is far superior and thus far more likely to succeed. Do you agree? See Chapter 11 for additional discussion of possible U.S. legislative approaches.

2.   The importance of framing issues with values that resonate with larger, majoritarian values is now a central idea of both political campaigning and economic marketing. *See, e.g.*, GEORGE LAKOFF, DON'T THINK OF AN ELEPHANT: KNOW YOUR VALUES AND FRAME THE DEBATE (2004). It is also well understood in consumer marketing. *See, e.g.*, MALCOLM GLADWELL, THE TIPPING POINT: HOW LITTLE THINGS CAN MAKE A BIG DIFFERENCE (2002).

3.   Climate change of course touches all sorts of issues and can be framed in many different ways. Environmental groups are sensitive to this, which is why almost every environmental group working on climate change uses the polar bear as an iconic symbol for the environmental threats of climate change. Why do you think environmentalists place so much attention on the polar bear? Is this a good

strategy for environmental groups? What constituency is attracted to such an approach? On the one hand, such an approach may speak to the core environmental constituency, but does it help create a broader social movement like that envisioned by Gus Speth?

4. Most observers believe if climate change is viewed simply as a threat to the environment — even a massive threat — it is unlikely to garner the support necessary for transformative change. For this reason, Professor Lisa Heinzerling argues below that framing climate change as a human health issue will have significant positive policy implications:

LISA HEINZERLING, CLIMATE CHANGE, HUMAN HEALTH, AND THE POST-CAUTIONARY PRINCIPLE
96 Geo. L.J. 445, 450–451 (2008)*

"We have to give climate change a human face — it is not all about 'sinks,' 'emission trading schemes' and technology. Climate change is about people, children, families and . . . our relationship with the world around us."

What are the consequences, for public debate and public policy, of framing the problem of climate change in terms of human health? I believe framing the problem this way has at least three implications: motivating political action, enlarging the number and kinds of governmental institutions involved in the problem, and creating a strong moral case for action.

First, and most pragmatically, "environmental" threats rarely capture the attention of the public and policymakers unless and until they are linked to human health. People are worried about the polar bear, to be sure, but it is doubtful that the polar bear's plight alone — or even the added plight of the many other species threatened by climate change — will prompt the kinds of large changes necessary to address climate change. To take an example from early in the environmental era, many studies connected the pesticide DDT with harm to wildlife, even to harm to the beloved bald eagle, but it was not until DDT was tied to cancer risk in humans that the federal government decided to ban the substance. The same basic story holds for the regulation of many other pollutants. Speaking in purely practical terms, therefore, it makes a great deal of sense to highlight the consequences of climate change for human health.

Second, emphasizing the consequences of climate change for human health will affect the way we think about responses to this problem. If we think of climate change as purely an "environmental" problem, we will likely turn, in the United States, to the EPA for an answer. But as important as the EPA is domestically, with respect to this problem, I believe it is equally vital that we turn to other non-environmental institutions for assistance. Framing climate change as a human health threat naturally encourages resort to agencies charged with a traditional public health mission, such as the Centers for Disease Control and the National Institutes of Health. It also prompts attention to even less obvious institutions, like the United Nations Security Council. We will think differently about solutions to climate change as an institutional matter if we frame the problem of climate change as a human health problem.

Finally, recognizing the current and future consequences of climate change for human health makes the moral case for aggressive action on climate change unimpeachable. If we were simply talking about a more uncomfortable climate, or even the destruction of other species, it might be easier to dismiss the moral imperative of action on climate change. But humans are dying and falling ill due to our collective actions, and will continue to do so in even larger numbers if we do nothing. Emphasizing the human dimension of climate change brings a moral clarity to the problem that is not matched by worries about the polar bear.

---

5. Review the many impacts of climate change outlined in Chapter 1. How would you frame climate change to deepen the political will for transformative change? Public health like Professor Heinzerling? An economic opportunity like Al Gore? A human rights issue like the Inuit in their claim described in Chapter 10? Or a national security issue as the Pentagon views it? Of course, climate change implicates all of these issues, which is what makes it so urgent and such an exciting area of law.

6. There are many exciting opportunities emerging for law students and others interested in working towards the transformative changes necessary to address the challenge of climate change. All major national environmental organizations now have climate change programs. State and local organizations also are promoting climate change policies throughout the country. *See* Chapter 17. In addition, many state and municipal governments are creating commissions, counsels, and new departments to cut their carbon footprints. *See* Chapter 17. The carbon markets are also creating exciting new opportunities for business-minded lawyers. Virtually every large law firm now has special climate counsel. And as described in Chapter 18, many private sector corporations are trying to cut their emissions and participate in the emerging carbon market. Green venture capital firms are now the most dynamic high-tech investment funds. And even small businesses and individual households are building demand for energy audits and carbon offsets. At each of these levels, there is a need for climate lawyers.

7. Climate change is a dynamic area of the law, with laws and policies in flux at all levels. Internationally, the post-Kyoto regime may have been completed within a year of this book's publication. The U.S. Congress may have also passed comprehensive climate legislation within that same year. For certain, President Obama will substantially change federal policy towards climate change. State and local governments, unless preempted by federal law, show no sign of slowing their efforts to mitigate climate change. To what extent do changes since the publication of this book give you hope that the world and the United States may effectively meet the climate change challenge? In light of these recent developments, what would you now say is the highest priority for lawyers and policymakers?

ANNEX 1

UNITED NATIONS FRAMEWORK CONVENTION ON CLIMATE CHANGE

1771 U.N.T.S. 107
signed June 1992,
Entered into Force: March 21, 1994

The Parties to this Convention,

Acknowledging that change in the Earth's climate and its adverse effects are a common concern of humankind,

Concerned that human activities have been substantially increasing the atmospheric concentrations of greenhouse gases, that these increases enhance the natural greenhouse effect, and that this will result on average in an additional warming of the Earth's surface and atmosphere and may adversely affect natural ecosystems and humankind,

Noting that the largest share of historical and current global emissions of greenhouse gases has originated in developed countries, that per capita emissions in developing countries are still relatively low and that the share of global emissions originating in developing countries will grow to meet their social and development needs,

Aware of the role and importance in terrestrial and marine ecosystems of sinks and reservoirs of greenhouse gases,

Noting that there are many uncertainties in predictions of climate change, particularly with regard to the timing, magnitude and regional patterns thereof,

Acknowledging that the global nature of climate change calls for the widest possible cooperation by all countries and their participation in an effective and appropriate international response, in accordance with their common but differentiated responsibilities and respective capabilities and their social and economic conditions,

Recalling the pertinent provisions of the Declaration of the United Nations Conference on the Human Environment, adopted at Stockholm on 16 June 1972,

Recalling also that States have, in accordance with the Charter of the United Nations and the principles of international law, the sovereign right to exploit their own resources pursuant to their own environmental and developmental policies, and the responsibility to ensure that activities within their jurisdiction or control do not cause damage to the environment of other States or of areas beyond the limits of national jurisdiction,

Reaffirming the principle of sovereignty of States in international cooperation to address climate change,

Recognizing that States should enact effective environmental legislation, that environmental standards, management objectives and priorities should reflect the environmental and developmental context to which they apply, and that standards applied by some countries may be inappropriate and of unwarranted economic and social cost to other countries, in particular developing countries,

Recalling the provisions of General Assembly resolution 44/228 of 22 December 1989 on the United Nations Conference on Environment and Development, and resolutions 43/53 of 6 December 1988, 44/207 of 22 December 1989, 45/212 of 21

December 1990 and 46/169 of 19 December 1991 on protection of global climate for present and future generations of mankind,

Recalling also the provisions of General Assembly resolution 44/206 of 22 December 1989 on the possible adverse effects of sealevel rise on islands and coastal areas, particularly low-lying coastal areas and the pertinent provisions of General Assembly resolution 44/172 of 19 December 1989 on the implementation of the Plan of Action to Combat Desertification,

Recalling further the Vienna Convention for the Protection of the Ozone Layer, 1985, and the Montreal Protocol on Substances that Deplete the Ozone Layer, 1987, as adjusted and amended on 29 June 1990,

Noting the Ministerial Declaration of the Second World Climate Conference adopted on 7 November 1990,

Conscious of the valuable analytical work being conducted by many States on climate change and of the important contributions of the World Meteorological Organization, the United Nations Environment Programme and other organs, organizations and bodies of the United Nations system, as well as other international and intergovernmental bodies, to the exchange of results of scientific research and the coordination of research,

Recognizing that steps required to understand and address climate change will be environmentally, socially and economically most effective if they are based on relevant scientific, technical and economic considerations and continually re-evaluated in the light of new findings in these areas,

Recognizing that various actions to address climate change can be justified economically in their own right and can also help in solving other environmental problems,

Recognizing also the need for developed countries to take immediate action in a flexible manner on the basis of clear priorities, as a first step towards comprehensive response strategies at the global, national and, where agreed, regional levels that take into account all greenhouse gases, with due consideration of their relative contributions to the enhancement of the greenhouse effect,

Recognizing further that low-lying and other small island countries, countries with low-lying coastal, arid and semi-arid areas or areas liable to floods, drought and desertification, and developing countries with fragile mountainous ecosystems are particularly vulnerable to the adverse effects of climate change,

Recognizing the special difficulties of those countries, especially developing countries, whose economies are particularly dependent on fossil fuel production, use and exportation, as a consequence of action taken on limiting greenhouse gas emissions,

Affirming that responses to climate change should be coordinated with social and economic development in an integrated manner with a view to avoiding adverse impacts on the latter, taking into full account the legitimate priority needs of developing countries for the achievement of sustained economic growth and the eradication of poverty,

Recognizing that all countries, especially developing countries, need access to resources required to achieve sustainable social and economic development and that, in order for developing countries to progress towards that goal, their energy consumption will need to grow taking into account the possibilities for achieving greater energy efficiency and for controlling greenhouse gas emissions in general, including through the application of new technologies on terms which make such an application economically and socially beneficial,

Determined to protect the climate system for present and future generations,

Have agreed as follows:

ARTICLE 1 — DEFINITIONS*

For the purposes of this Convention:

1. "Adverse effects of climate change" means changes in the physical environment or biota resulting from climate change which have significant deleterious effects on the composition, resilience or productivity of natural and managed ecosystems or on the operation of socio-economic systems or on human health and welfare.

2. "Climate change" means a change of climate which is attributed directly or indirectly to human activity that alters the composition of the global atmosphere and which is in addition to natural climate variability observed over comparable time periods.

3. "Climate system" means the totality of the atmosphere, hydrosphere, biosphere and geosphere and their interactions.

4. "Emissions" means the release of greenhouse gases and/or their precursors into the atmosphere over a specified area and period of time.

5. "Greenhouse gases" means those gaseous constituents of the atmosphere, both natural and anthropogenic, that absorb and re-emit infrared radiation.

6. "Regional economic integration organization" means an organization constituted by sovereign States of a given region which has competence in respect of matters governed by this Convention or its protocols and has been duly authorized, in accordance with its internal procedures, to sign, ratify, accept, approve or accede to the instruments concerned.

7. "Reservoir" means a component or components of the climate system where a greenhouse gas or a precursor of a greenhouse gas is stored.

8. "Sink" means any process, activity or mechanism which removes a greenhouse gas, an aerosol or a precursor of a greenhouse gas from the atmosphere.

9. "Source" means any process or activity which releases a greenhouse gas, an aerosol or a precursor of a greenhouse gas into the atmosphere.

ARTICLE 2 — OBJECTIVE

The ultimate objective of this Convention and any related legal instruments that the Conference of the Parties may adopt is to achieve, in accordance with the relevant provisions of the Convention, stabilization of greenhouse gas concentrations in the atmosphere at a level that would prevent dangerous anthropogenic interference with the climate system. Such a level should be achieved within a time-frame sufficient to allow ecosystems to adapt naturally to climate change, to ensure that food production is not threatened and to enable economic development to proceed in a sustainable manner.

---

* Titles of articles are included solely to assist the reader.

ARTICLE 3 — PRINCIPLES

In their actions to achieve the objective of the Convention and to implement its provisions, the Parties shall be guided, inter alia, by the following:

1. The Parties should protect the climate system for the benefit of present and future generations of humankind, on the basis of equity and in accordance with their common but differentiated responsibilities and respective capabilities. Accordingly, the developed country Parties should take the lead in combating climate change and the adverse effects thereof.

2. The specific needs and special circumstances of developing country Parties, especially those that are particularly vulnerable to the adverse effects of climate change, and of those Parties, especially developing country Parties, that would have to bear a disproportionate or abnormal burden under the Convention, should be given full consideration.

3. The Parties should take precautionary measures to anticipate, prevent or minimize the causes of climate change and mitigate its adverse effects. Where there are threats of serious or irreversible damage, lack of full scientific certainty should not be used as a reason for postponing such measures, taking into account that policies and measures to deal with climate change should be cost-effective so as to ensure global benefits at the lowest possible cost. To achieve this, such policies and measures should take into account different socio-economic contexts, be comprehensive, cover all relevant sources, sinks and reservoirs of greenhouse gases and adaptation, and comprise all economic sectors. Efforts to address climate change may be carried out cooperatively by interested Parties.

4. The Parties have a right to, and should, promote sustainable development. Policies and measures to protect the climate system against human-induced change should be appropriate for the specific conditions of each Party and should be integrated with national development programmes, taking into account that economic development is essential for adopting measures to address climate change.

5. The Parties should cooperate to promote a supportive and open international economic system that would lead to sustainable economic growth and development in all Parties, particularly developing country Parties, thus enabling them better to address the problems of climate change. Measures taken to combat climate change, including unilateral ones, should not constitute a means of arbitrary or unjustifiable discrimination or a disguised restriction on international trade.

ARTICLE 4 — COMMITMENTS

1. All Parties, taking into account their common but differentiated responsibilities and their specific national and regional development priorities, objectives and circumstances, shall:

(a) Develop, periodically update, publish and make available to the Conference of the Parties, in accordance with Article 12, national inventories of anthropogenic emissions by sources and removals by sinks of all greenhouse gases not controlled by the Montreal Protocol, using comparable methodologies to be agreed upon by the Conference of the Parties;

(b)   Formulate, implement, publish and regularly update national and, where appropriate, regional programmes containing measures to mitigate climate change by addressing anthropogenic emissions by sources and removals by sinks of all greenhouse gases not controlled by the Montreal Protocol, and measures to facilitate adequate adaptation to climate change;

(c)   Promote and cooperate in the development, application and diffusion, including transfer, of technologies, practices and processes that control, reduce or prevent anthropogenic emissions of greenhouse gases not controlled by the Montreal Protocol in all relevant sectors, including the energy, transport, industry, agriculture, forestry and waste management sectors;

(d)   Promote sustainable management, and promote and cooperate in the conservation and enhancement, as appropriate, of sinks and reservoirs of all greenhouse gases not controlled by the Montreal Protocol, including biomass, forests and oceans as well as other terrestrial, coastal and marine ecosystems;

(e)   Cooperate in preparing for adaptation to the impacts of climate change; develop and elaborate appropriate and integrated plans for coastal zone management, water resources and agriculture, and for the protection and rehabilitation of areas, particularly in Africa, affected by drought and desertification, as well as floods;

(f)   Take climate change considerations into account, to the extent feasible,in their relevant social, economic and environmental policies and actions, and employ appropriate methods, for example impact assessments, formulated and determined nationally, with a view to minimizing adverse effects on the economy, on public health and on the quality of the environment, of projects or measures undertaken by them to mitigate or adapt to climate change;

(g)   Promote and cooperate in scientific, technological, technical, socio-economic and other research, systematic observation and development of data archives related to the climate system and intended to further the understanding and to reduce or eliminate the remaining uncertainties regarding the causes, effects, magnitude and timing of climate change and the economic and social consequences of various response strategies;

(h)   Promote and cooperate in the full, open and prompt exchange of relevant scientific, technological, technical, socio-economic and legal information related to the climate system and climate change, and to the economic and social consequences of various response strategies;

(i)   Promote and cooperate in education, training and public awareness related to climate change and encourage the widest participation in this process, including that of non-governmental organizations; and

(j)   Communicate to the Conference of the Parties information related to implementation, in accordance with Article 12.

2. The developed country Parties and other Parties included in annex I commit themselves specifically as provided for in the following:

(a)   Each of these Parties shall adopt national[1] policies and take corresponding measures on the mitigation of climate change, by limiting its anthropogenic emissions of greenhouse gases and protecting and enhancing its green-

---

[1] This includes policies and measures adopted by regional economic integration organizations.

house gas sinks and reservoirs. These policies and measures will demonstrate that developed countries are taking the lead in modifying longer-term trends in anthropogenic emissions consistent with the objective of the Convention, recognizing that the return by the end of the present decade to earlier levels of anthropogenic emissions of carbon dioxide and other greenhouse gases not controlled by the Montreal Protocol would contribute to such modification, and taking into account the differences in these Parties' starting points and approaches, economic structures and resource bases, the need to maintain strong and sustainable economic growth, available technologies and other individual circumstances, as well as the need for equitable and appropriate contributions by each of these Parties to the global effort regarding that objective. These Parties may implement such policies and measures jointly with other Parties and may assist other Parties in contributing to the achievement of the objective of the Convention and, in particular, that of this subparagraph;

(b)   In order to promote progress to this end, each of these Parties shall communicate, within six months of the entry into force of the Convention for it and periodically thereafter, and in accordance with Article 12, detailed information on its policies and measures referred to in subparagraph (a) above, as well as on its resulting projected anthropogenic emissions by sources and removals by sinks of greenhouse gases not controlled by the Montreal Protocol for the period referred to in subparagraph (a), with the aim of returning individually or jointly to their 1990 levels these anthropogenic emissions of carbon dioxide and other greenhouse gases not controlled by the Montreal Protocol. This information will be reviewed by the Conference of the Parties, at its first session and periodically thereafter, in accordance with Article 7;

(c)   Calculations of emissions by sources and removals by sinks of greenhouse gases for the purposes of subparagraph (b) above should take into account the best available scientific knowledge, including of the effective capacity of sinks and the respective contributions of such gases to climate change. The Conference of the Parties shall consider and agree on methodologies for these calculations at its first session and review them regularly thereafter;

(d)   The Conference of the Parties shall, at its first session, review the adequacy of subparagraphs (a) and (b) above. Such review shall be carried out in the light of the best available scientific information and assessment on climate change and its impacts, as well as relevant technical, social and economic information. Based on this review, the Conference of the Parties shall take appropriate action, which may include the adoption of amendments to the commitments in subparagraphs (a) and (b) above. The Conference of the Parties, at its first session, shall also take decisions regarding criteria for joint implementation as indicated in subparagraph (a) above. A second review of subparagraphs (a) and (b) shall take place not later than 31 December 1998, and thereafter at regular intervals determined by the Conference of the Parties, until the objective of the Convention is met;

(e)   Each of these Parties shall:

(i)   coordinate as appropriate with other such Parties, relevant economic and administrative instruments developed to achieve the objective of the Convention; and

(ii)   identify and periodically review its own policies and practices which encourage activities that lead to greater levels of anthropogenic emissions of greenhouse gases not controlled by the Montreal

Protocol than would otherwise occur;

(f) The Conference of the Parties shall review, not later than 31 December 1998, available information with a view to taking decisions regarding such amendments to the lists in annexes I and II as may be appropriate, with the approval of the Party concerned;

(g) Any Party not included in annex I may, in its instrument of ratification, acceptance, approval or accession, or at any time thereafter, notify the Depositary that it intends to be bound by subparagraphs (a) and (b) above. The Depositary shall inform the other signatories and Parties of any such notification.

3. The developed country Parties and other developed Parties included in annex II shall provide new and additional financial resources to meet the agreed full costs incurred by developing country Parties in complying with their obligations under Article 12, paragraph 1. They shall also provide such financial resources, including for the transfer of technology, needed by the developing country Parties to meet the agreed full incremental costs of implementing measures that are covered by paragraph 1 of this Article and that are agreed between a developing country Party and the international entity or entities referred to in Article 11, in accordance with that Article. The implementation of these commitments shall take into account the need for adequacy and predictability in the flow of funds and the importance of appropriate burden sharing among the developed country Parties.

4. The developed country Parties and other developed Parties included in annex II shall also assist the developing country Parties that are particularly vulnerable to the adverse effects of climate change in meeting costs of adaptation to those adverse effects.

5. The developed country Parties and other developed Parties included in annex II shall take all practicable steps to promote, facilitate and finance, as appropriate, the transfer of, or access to, environmentally sound technologies and know-how to other Parties, particularly developing country Parties, to enable them to implement the provisions of the Convention. In this process, the developed country Parties shall support the development and enhancement of endogenous capacities and technologies of developing country Parties. Other Parties and organizations in a position to do so may also assist in facilitating the transfer of such technologies.

6. In the implementation of their commitments under paragraph 2 above, a certain degree of flexibility shall be allowed by the Conference of the Parties to the Parties included in annex I undergoing the process of transition to a market economy, in order to enhance the ability of these Parties to address climate change, including with regard to the historical level of anthropogenic emissions of greenhouse gases not controlled by the Montreal Protocol chosen as a reference.

7. The extent to which developing country Parties will effectively implement their commitments under the Convention will depend on the effective implementation by developed country Parties of their commitments under the Convention related to financial resources and transfer of technology and will take fully into account that economic and social development and poverty eradication are the first and overriding priorities of the developing country Parties.

8. In the implementation of the commitments in this Article, the Parties shall give full consideration to what actions are necessary under the Convention, including actions related to funding, insurance and the transfer of technology, to meet the

specific needs and concerns of developing country Parties arising from the adverse effects of climate change and/or the impact of the implementation of response measures, especially on:

(a)   Small island countries;

(b)   Countries with low-lying coastal areas;

(c)   Countries with arid and semi-arid areas, forested areas and areas liableto forest decay;

(d)   Countries with areas prone to natural disasters;

(e)   Countries with areas liable to drought and desertification;

(f)   Countries with areas of high urban atmospheric pollution;

(g)   Countries with areas with fragile ecosystems, including mountainous ecosystems;

(h)   Countries whose economies are highly dependent on income generated from the production, processing and export, and/or on consumption of fossil fuels and associated energy-intensive products; and

(i)   Land-locked and transit countries.

Further, the Conference of the Parties may take actions, as appropriate, with respect to this paragraph.

9. The Parties shall take full account of the specific needs and special situations of the least developed countries in their actions with regard to funding and transfer of technology.

10. The Parties shall, in accordance with Article 10, take into consideration in the implementation of the commitments of the Convention the situation of Parties, particularly developing country Parties, with economies that are vulnerable to the adverse effects of the implementation of measures to respond to climate change. This applies notably to Parties with economies that are highly dependent on income generated from the production, processing and export, and/or consumption of fossil fuels and associated energy-intensive products and/or the use of fossil fuels for which such Parties have serious difficulties in switching to alternatives.

ARTICLE 5 — RESEARCH AND SYSTEMATIC OBSERVATION

In carrying out their commitments under Article 4, paragraph 1 (g), the Parties shall:

(a)   Support and further develop, as appropriate, international and intergovernmental programmes and networks or organizations aimed at defining, conducting, assessing and financing research, data collection and systematic observation, taking into account the need to minimize duplication of effort;

(b)   Support international and intergovernmental efforts to strengthen systematic observation and national scientific and technical research capacities and capabilities, particularly in developing countries, and to promote access to, and the exchange of, data and analyses thereof obtained from areas beyond national jurisdiction; and

(c)   Take into account the particular concerns and needs of developingcountries and cooperate in improving their endogenous capacities and capabilities to participate in the efforts referred to in subparagraphs (a) and (b) above.

ARTICLE 6 — EDUCATION, TRAINING AND PUBLIC AWARENESS

In carrying out their commitments under Article 4, paragraph 1 (i), the Parties shall:

(a)   Promote and facilitate at the national and, as appropriate, subregional and regional levels, and in accordance with national laws and regulations, and within their respective capacities:

   (i)   the development and implementation of educational and public awareness programmes on climate change and its effects;

   (ii)   public access to information on climate change and its effects;

   (iii) public participation in addressing climate change and its effects and developing adequate responses; and

   (iv)   training of scientific, technical and managerial personnel.

(b)   Cooperate in and promote, at the international level, and, where appropriate, using existing bodies:

   (i)   the development and exchange of educational and public awareness material on climate change and its effects; and

   (ii)   the development and implementation of education and training programmes, including the strengthening of national institutions and the exchange or secondment of personnel to train experts in this field, in particular for developing countries.

ARTICLE 7 — CONFERENCE OF THE PARTIES

1. A Conference of the Parties is hereby established.

2. The Conference of the Parties, as the supreme body of this Convention, shall keep under regular review the implementation of the Convention and any related legal instruments that the Conference of the Parties may adopt, and shall make, within its mandate, the decisions necessary to promote the effective implementation of the Convention. To this end, it shall:

(a)   Periodically examine the obligations of the Parties and the institutional arrangements under the Convention, in the light of the objective of the Convention, the experience gained in its implementation and the evolution of scientific and technological knowledge;

(b)   Promote and facilitate the exchange of information on measures adopted by the Parties to address climate change and its effects, taking into account the differing circumstances, responsibilities and capabilities of the Parties and their respective commitments under the Convention;

(c)   Facilitate, at the request of two or more Parties, the coordination of measures adopted by them to address climate change and its effects, taking into account the differing circumstances, responsibilities and capabilities of the Parties and their respective commitments under the Convention;

(d)   Promote and guide, in accordance with the objective and provisions of the Convention, the development and periodic refinement of comparable methodologies, to be agreed on by the Conference of the Parties, inter alia, for preparing inventories of greenhouse gas emissions by sources and removals by sinks, and for evaluating the effectiveness of measures to limit the emissions and enhance the removals of these gases;

(e)   Assess, on the basis of all information made available to it in accordance with the provisions of the Convention, the implementation of the Convention by the Parties, the overall effects of the measures taken pursuant to the Convention, in particular environmental, economic and social effects as well as their cumulative impacts and the extent to which progress towards the objective of the Convention is being achieved;

(f)   Consider and adopt regular reports on the implementation of the Convention and ensure their publication;

(g)   Make recommendations on any matters necessary for the implementation of the Convention;

(h)   Seek to mobilize financial resources in accordance with Article 4, paragraphs 3, 4 and 5, and Article 11;

(i)   Establish such subsidiary bodies as are deemed necessary for the implementation of the Convention;

(j)   Review reports submitted by its subsidiary bodies and provide guidance to them;

(k)   Agree upon and adopt, by consensus, rules of procedure and financial rules for itself and for any subsidiary bodies;

(l)   Seek and utilize, where appropriate, the services and cooperation of, and information provided by, competent international organizations and intergovernmental and non-governmental bodies; and

(m)   Exercise such other functions as are required for the achievement of the objective of the Convention as well as all other functions assigned to it under the Convention.

3. The Conference of the Parties shall, at its first session, adopt its own rules of procedure as well as those of the subsidiary bodies established by the Convention, which shall include decision-making procedures for matters not already covered by decision-making procedures stipulated in the Convention. Such procedures may include specified majorities required for the adoption of particular decisions.

4. The first session of the Conference of the Parties shall be convened by the interim secretariat referred to in Article 21 and shall take place not later than one year after the date of entry into force of the Convention. Thereafter, ordinary sessions of the Conference of the Parties shall be held every year unless otherwise decided by the Conference of the Parties.

5. Extraordinary sessions of the Conference of the Parties shall be held at such other times as may be deemed necessary by the Conference, or at the written request of any Party, provided that, within six months of the request being communicated to the Parties by the secretariat, it is supported by at least one-third of the Parties.

6. The United Nations, its specialized agencies and the International Atomic Energy Agency, as well as any State member thereof or observers thereto not Party

to the Convention, may be represented at sessions of the Conference of the Parties as observers. Any body or agency, whether national or international, governmental or non-governmental, which is qualified in matters covered by the Convention, and which has informed the secretariat of its wish to be represented at a session of the Conference of the Parties as an observer, may be so admitted unless at least one-third of the Parties present object. The admission and participation of observers shall be subject to the rules of procedure adopted by the Conference of the Parties.

ARTICLE 8 SECRETARIAT

1. A secretariat is hereby established.

2. The functions of the secretariat shall be:

(a)   To make arrangements for sessions of the Conference of the Parties and its subsidiary bodies established under the Convention and to provide them with services as required;

(b)   To compile and transmit reports submitted to it;

(c)   To facilitate assistance to the Parties, particularly developing country Parties, on request, in the compilation and communications of information required in accordance with the provisions of the Convention;

(d)   To prepare reports on its activities and present them to the Conference of the Parties;

(e)   To ensure the necessary coordination with the secretariats of other relevant international bodies;

(f)   To enter, under the overall guidance of the Conference of the Parties, into such administrative and contractual arrangements as may be required for the effective discharge of its functions; and

(g)   To perform the other secretariat functions specified in the Conventionand in any of its protocols and such other functions as may be determined by the Conference of the Parties.

3. The Conference of the Parties, at its first session, shall designate a permanent secretariat and make arrangements for its functioning.

ARTICLE 9 — SUBSIDIARY BODY FOR SCIENTIFIC AND TECHNO-LOGICAL ADVICE

1. A subsidiary body for scientific and technological advice is hereby established to provide the Conference of the Parties and, as appropriate, its other subsidiary bodies with timely information and advice on scientific and technological matters relating to the Convention. This body shall be open to participation by all Parties and shall be multidisciplinary. It shall comprise government representatives competent in the relevant field of expertise. It shall report regularly to the Conference of the Parties on all aspects of its work.

2. Under the guidance of the Conference of the Parties, and drawing upon existing competent international bodies, this body shall:

(a)   Provide assessments of the state of scientific knowledge relating to climate change and its effects;

(b)   Prepare scientific assessments on the effects of measures taken in the implementation of the Convention;

(c)   Identify innovative, efficient and state-of-the-art technologies and know-how and advise on the ways and means of promoting development and/or transferring such technologies;

(d)   Provide advice on scientific programmes, international cooperation in research and development related to climate change, as well as on ways and means of supporting endogenous capacity-building in developing countries; and

(e)   Respond to scientific, technological and methodological questions that the Conference of the Parties and its subsidiary bodies may put to the body.

3. The functions and terms of reference of this body may be further elaborated by the Conference of the Parties.

ARTICLE 10 — SUBSIDIARY BODY FOR IMPLEMENTATION

1. A subsidiary body for implementation is hereby established to assist the Conference of the Parties in the assessment and review of the effective implementation of the Convention. This body shall be open to participation by all Parties and comprise government representatives who are experts on matters related to climate change. It shall report regularly to the Conference of the Parties on all aspects of its work.

2. Under the guidance of the Conference of the Parties, this body shall:

(a)   Consider the information communicated in accordance with Article 12, paragraph 1, to assess the overall aggregated effect of the steps taken by the Parties in the light of the latest scientific assessments concerning climate change;

(b)   Consider the information communicated in accordance with Article 12, paragraph 2, in order to assist the Conference of the Parties in carrying out the reviews required by Article 4, paragraph 2 (d); and

(c)   Assist the Conference of the Parties, as appropriate, in the preparation and implementation of its decisions.

ARTICLE 11 — FINANCIAL MECHANISM

1. A mechanism for the provision of financial resources on a grant or concessional basis, including for the transfer of technology, is hereby defined. It shall function under the guidance of and be accountable to the Conference of the Parties, which shall decide on its policies, programme priorities and eligibility criteria related to this Convention. Its operation shall be entrusted to one or more existing international entities.

2. The financial mechanism shall have an equitable and balanced representation of all Parties within a transparent system of governance.

3. The Conference of the Parties and the entity or entities entrusted with the operation of the financial mechanism shall agree upon arrangements to give effect to the above paragraphs, which shall include the following:

(a) Modalities to ensure that the funded projects to address climate change are in conformity with the policies, programme priorities and eligibility criteria established by the Conference of the Parties;

(b) Modalities by which a particular funding decision may be reconsidered in light of these policies, programme priorities and eligibility criteria;

(c) Provision by the entity or entities of regular reports to the Conference of the Parties on its funding operations, which is consistent with the requirement for accountability set out in paragraph 1 above; and

(d) Determination in a predictable and identifiable manner of the amount of funding necessary and available for the implementation of this Convention and the conditions under which that amount shall be periodically reviewed.

4. The Conference of the Parties shall make arrangements to implement the above-mentioned provisions at its first session, reviewing and taking into account the interim arrangements referred to in Article 21, paragraph 3, and shall decide whether these interim arrangements shall be maintained. Within four years thereafter, the Conference of the Parties shall review the financial mechanism and take appropriate measures.

5. The developed country Parties may also provide and developing country Parties avail themselves of, financial resources related to the implementation of the Convention through bilateral, regional and other multilateral channels.

ARTICLE 12 — COMMUNICATION OF INFORMATION RELATED TO IMPLEMENTATION

1. In accordance with Article 4, paragraph 1, each Party shall communicate to the Conference of the Parties, through the secretariat, the following elements of information:

(a) A national inventory of anthropogenic emissions by sources and removals by sinks of all greenhouse gases not controlled by the Montreal Protocol, to the extent its capacities permit, using comparable methodologies to be promoted and agreed upon by the Conference of the Parties;

(b) A general description of steps taken or envisaged by the Party to implement the Convention; and

(c) Any other information that the Party considers relevant to the achievement of the objective of the Convention and suitable for inclusion in its communication, including, if feasible, material relevant for calculations of global emission trends.

2. Each developed country Party and each other Party included in annex I shall incorporate in its communication the following elements of information:

(a) A detailed description of the policies and measures that it has adopted to implement its commitment under Article 4, paragraphs 2 (a) and 2 (b); and

(b) A specific estimate of the effects that the policies and measures referred to in subparagraph (a) immediately above will have on anthropogenic emissions by its sources and removals by its sinks of greenhouse gases during the period referred to in Article 4, paragraph 2 (a).

3. In addition, each developed country Party and each other developed Party included in annex II shall incorporate details of measures taken in accordance with

Article 4, paragraphs 3, 4 and 5.

4. Developing country Parties may, on a voluntary basis, propose projects for financing, including specific technologies, materials, equipment, techniques or practices that would be needed to implement such projects, along with, if possible, an estimate of all incremental costs, of the reductions of emissions and increments of removals of greenhouse gases, as well as an estimate of the consequent benefits.

5. Each developed country Party and each other Party included in annex I shall make its initial communication within six months of the entry into force of the Convention for that Party. Each Party not so listed shall make its initial communication within three years of the entry into force of the Convention for that Party, or of the availability of financial resources in accordance with Article 4, paragraph 3. Parties that are least developed countries may make their initial communication at their discretion. The frequency of subsequent communications by all Parties shall be determined by the Conference of the Parties, taking into account the differentiated timetable set by this paragraph.

6. Information communicated by Parties under this Article shall be transmitted by the secretariat as soon as possible to the Conference of the Parties and to any subsidiary bodies concerned. If necessary, the procedures for the communication of information may be further considered by the Conference of the Parties.

7. From its first session, the Conference of the Parties shall arrange for the provision to developing country Parties of technical and financial support, on request, in compiling and communicating information under this Article, as well as in identifying the technical and financial needs associated with proposed projects and response measures under Article 4. Such support may be provided by other Parties, by competent international organizations and by the secretariat, as appropriate.

8. Any group of Parties may, subject to guidelines adopted by the Conference of the Parties, and to prior notification to the Conference of the Parties, make a joint communication in fulfilment of their obligations under this Article, provided that such a communication includes information on the fulfilment by each of these Parties of its individual obligations under the Convention.

9. Information received by the secretariat that is designated by a Party as confidential, in accordance with criteria to be established by the Conference of the Parties, shall be aggregated by the secretariat to protect its confidentiality before being made available to any of the bodies involved in the communication and review of information.

10. Subject to paragraph 9 above, and without prejudice to the ability of any Party to make public its communication at any time, the secretariat shall make communications by Parties under this Article publicly available at the time they are submitted to the Conference of the Parties.

ARTICLE 13 — RESOLUTION OF QUESTIONS REGARDING IMPLE-MENTATION

The Conference of the Parties shall, at its first session, consider the establishment of a multilateral consultative process, available to Parties on their request, for the resolution of questions regarding the implementation of the Convention.

ARTICLE 14 — SETTLEMENT OF DISPUTES

1. In the event of a dispute between any two or more Parties concerning the interpretation or application of the Convention, the Parties concerned shall seek a settlement of the dispute through negotiation or any other peaceful means of their own choice.

2. When ratifying, accepting, approving or acceding to the Convention, or at any time thereafter, a Party which is not a regional economic integration organization may declare in a written instrument submitted to the Depositary that, in respect of any dispute concerning the interpretation or application of the Convention, it recognizes as compulsory ipso facto and without special agreement, in relation to any Party accepting the same obligation:

    (a)   Submission of the dispute to the International Court of Justice, and/or

    (b)   Arbitration in accordance with procedures to be adopted by the Conference of the Parties as soon as practicable, in an annex on arbitration.

A Party which is a regional economic integration organization may make a declaration with like effect in relation to arbitration in accordance with the procedures referred to in subparagraph (b) above.

3. A declaration made under paragraph 2 above shall remain in force until it expires in accordance with its terms or until three months after written notice of its revocation has been deposited with the Depositary.

4. A new declaration, a notice of revocation or the expiry of a declaration shall not in any way affect proceedings pending before the International Court of Justice or the arbitral tribunal, unless the parties to the dispute otherwise agree.

5. Subject to the operation of paragraph 2 above, if after twelve months following notification by one Party to another that a dispute exists between them, the Parties concerned have not been able to settle their dispute through the means mentioned in paragraph 1 above, the dispute shall be submitted, at the request of any of the parties to the dispute, to conciliation.

6. A conciliation commission shall be created upon the request of one of the parties to the dispute. The commission shall be composed of an equal number of members appointed by each party concerned and a chairman chosen jointly by the members appointed by each party. The commission shall render a recommendatory award, which the parties shall consider in good faith.

7. Additional procedures relating to conciliation shall be adopted by the Conference of the Parties, as soon as practicable, in an annex on conciliation.

8. The provisions of this Article shall apply to any related legal instrument which the Conference of the Parties may adopt, unless the instrument provides otherwise.

ARTICLE 15 — AMENDMENTS TO THE CONVENTION

1. Any Party may propose amendments to the Convention.

2. Amendments to the Convention shall be adopted at an ordinary session of the Conference of the Parties. The text of any proposed amendment to the Convention shall be communicated to the Parties by the secretariat at least six months before the meeting at which it is proposed for adoption. The secretariat shall also

communicate proposed amendments to the signatories to the Convention and, for information, to the Depositary.

3. The Parties shall make every effort to reach agreement on any proposed amendment to the Convention by consensus. If all efforts at consensus have been exhausted, and no agreement reached, the amendment shall as a last resort be adopted by a three-fourths majority vote of the Parties present and voting at the meeting. The adopted amendment shall be communicated by the secretariat to the Depositary, who shall circulate it to all Parties for their acceptance.

4. Instruments of acceptance in respect of an amendment shall be deposited with the Depositary. An amendment adopted in accordance with paragraph 3 above shall enter into force for those Parties having accepted it on the ninetieth day after the date of receipt by the Depositary of an instrument of acceptance by at least three-fourths of the Parties to the Convention.

5. The amendment shall enter into force for any other Party on the ninetieth day after the date on which that Party deposits with the Depositary its instrument of acceptance of the said amendment.

6. For the purposes of this Article, "Parties present and voting" means Parties present and casting an affirmative or negative vote.

ARTICLE 16 — ADOPTION AND AMENDMENT OF ANNEXES TO THE CONVENTION

1. Annexes to the Convention shall form an integral part thereof and, unless otherwise expressly provided, a reference to the Convention constitutes at the same time a reference to any annexes thereto. Without prejudice to the provisions of Article 14, paragraphs 2 (b) and 7, such annexes shall be restricted to lists, forms and any other material of a descriptive nature that is of a scientific, technical, procedural or administrative character.

2. Annexes to the Convention shall be proposed and adopted in accordance with the procedure set forth in Article 15, paragraphs 2, 3, and 4.

3. An annex that has been adopted in accordance with paragraph 2 above shall enter into force for all Parties to the Convention six months after the date of the communication by the Depositary to such Parties of the adoption of the annex, except for those Parties that have notified the Depositary, in writing, within that period of their non-acceptance of the annex. The annex shall enter into force for Parties which withdraw their notification of non-acceptance on the ninetieth day after the date on which withdrawal of such notification has been received by the Depositary.

4. The proposal, adoption and entry into force of amendments to annexes to the Convention shall be subject to the same procedure as that for the proposal, adoption and entry into force of annexes to the Convention in accordance with paragraphs 2 and 3 above.

5. If the adoption of an annex or an amendment to an annex involves an amendment to the Convention, that annex or amendment to an annex shall not enter into force until such time as the amendment to the Convention enters into force.

ARTICLE 17 — PROTOCOLS

1. The Conference of the Parties may, at any ordinary session, adopt protocols to the Convention.

2. The text of any proposed protocol shall be communicated to the Parties by the secretariat at least six months before such a session.

3. The requirements for the entry into force of any protocol shall be established by that instrument.

4. Only Parties to the Convention may be Parties to a protocol.

5. Decisions under any protocol shall be taken only by the Parties to the protocol concerned.

ARTICLE 18 — RIGHT TO VOTE

1. Each Party to the Convention shall have one vote, except as provided for in paragraph 2 below.

2. Regional economic integration organizations, in matters within their competence, shall exercise their right to vote with a number of votes equal to the number of their member States that are Parties to the Convention. Such an organization shall not exercise its right to vote if any of its member States exercises its right, and vice versa.

ARTICLE 19 — DEPOSITARY

The Secretary-General of the United Nations shall be the Depositary of the Convention and of protocols adopted in accordance with Article 17.

ARTICLE 20 — SIGNATURE

This Convention shall be open for signature by States Members of the United Nations or of any of its specialized agencies or that are Parties to the Statute of the International Court of Justice and by regional economic integration organizations at Rio de Janeiro, during the United Nations Conference on Environment and Development, and thereafter at United Nations Headquarters in New York from 20 June 1992 to 19 June 1993.

ARTICLE 21 — INTERIM ARRANGEMENTS

1. The secretariat functions referred to in Article 8 will be carried out on an interim basis by the secretariat established by the General Assembly of the United Nations in its resolution 45/212 of 21 December 1990, until the completion of the first session of the Conference of the Parties.

2. The head of the interim secretariat referred to in paragraph 1 above will cooperate closely with the Intergovernmental Panel on Climate Change to ensure that the Panel can respond to the need for objective scientific and technical advice. Other relevant scientific bodies could also be consulted.

3. The Global Environment Facility of the United Nations Development Programme, the United Nations Environment Programme and the International Bank

for Reconstruction and Development shall be the international entity entrusted with the operation of the financial mechanism referred to in Article 11 on an interim basis. In this connection, the Global Environment Facility should be appropriately restructured and its membership made universal to enable it to fulfil the requirements of Article 11.

ARTICLE 22 — RATIFICATION, ACCEPTANCE, APPROVAL OR ACCESSION

1. The Convention shall be subject to ratification, acceptance, approval or accession by States and by regional economic integration organizations. It shall be open for accession from the day after the date on which the Convention is closed for signature. Instruments of ratification, acceptance, approval or accession shall be deposited with the Depositary.

2. Any regional economic integration organization which becomes a Party to the Convention without any of its member States being a Party shall be bound by all the obligations under the Convention. In the case of such organizations, one or more of whose member States is a Party to the Convention, the organization and its member States shall decide on their respective responsibilities for the performance of their obligations under the Convention. In such cases, the organization and the member States shall not be entitled to exercise rights under the Convention concurrently.

3. In their instruments of ratification, acceptance, approval or accession, regional economic integration organizations shall declare the extent of their competence with respect to the matters governed by the Convention. These organizations shall also inform the Depositary, who shall in turn inform the Parties, of any substantial modification in the extent of their competence.

ARTICLE 23 — ENTRY INTO FORCE

1. The Convention shall enter into force on the ninetieth day after the date of deposit of the fiftieth instrument of ratification, acceptance, approval or accession.

2. For each State or regional economic integration organization that ratifies, accepts or approves the Convention or accedes thereto after the deposit of the fiftieth instrument of ratification, acceptance, approval or accession, the Convention shall enter into force on the ninetieth day after the date of deposit by such State or regional economic integration organization of its instrument of ratification, acceptance, approval or accession.

3. For the purposes of paragraphs 1 and 2 above, any instrument deposited by a regional economic integration organization shall not be counted as additional to those deposited by States members of the organization.

ARTICLE 24 — RESERVATIONS

No reservations may be made to the Convention.

ARTICLE 25 — WITHDRAWAL

1. At any time after three years from the date on which the Convention has entered into force for a Party, that Party may withdraw from the Convention by giving

written notification to the Depositary.

2. Any such withdrawal shall take effect upon expiry of one year from the date of receipt by the Depositary of the notification of withdrawal, or on such later date as may be specified in the notification of withdrawal.

3. Any Party that withdraws from the Convention shall be considered as also having withdrawn from any protocol to which it is a Party.

ARTICLE 26 — AUTHENTIC TEXTS

The original of this Convention, of which the Arabic, Chinese, English, French, Russian and Spanish texts are equally authentic, shall be deposited with the Secretary-General of the United Nations.

IN WITNESS WHEREOF the undersigned, being duly authorized to that effect, have signed this Convention.

DONE at New York this ninth day of May one thousand nine hundred and ninety-two.

ANNEX I

Australia
Austria
Belarus*
Belgium
Bulgaria*
Canada
Croatia* ^
Czech Republic* ^
Denmark
European Community
Estonia*
Finland
France
Germany
Greece
Hungary*
Iceland
Ireland
Italy
Japan
Latvia*
Liechtenstein ^
Lithuania*
Luxembourg
Monaco ^
Netherlands
New Zealand
Norway
Poland*
Portugal
Romania*
Russian Federation*
Slovakia* ^
Slovenia* ^
Spain
Sweden
Switzerland
Turkey
Ukraine*
United Kingdom of Great Britain
and Northern Ireland
United States of America

ANNEX II

Australia
Austria
Belgium
Canada
Denmark
European Community
Finland
France
Germany
Greece
Iceland
Ireland
Italy
Japan
Luxembourg
Netherlands
New Zealand
Norway
Portugal
Spain
Sweden
Switzerland
United Kingdom of Great Britain
and Northern Ireland
United States of America

* Countries that are undergoing the process of transition to a market economy.
^ Countries added to Annex I by an amendment that entered into force on August 13, 1998, pursuant to Decision 4/CP.3 adopted at CoP3.
Turkey was deleted from Annex II by an amendment that entered into force June 28, 2002, pursuant to Decision 26/CP.7 adopted at CoP7.

ANNEX 2

KYOTO PROTOCOL TO THE UNITED NATIONS FRAMEWORK CONVENTION ON CLIMATE CHANGE

Signed Dec. 11, 1997
Entered into Force: February 16, 2005

The Parties to this Protocol,

Being Parties to the United Nations Framework Convention on Climate Change, hereinafter referred to as "the Convention",

In pursuit of the ultimate objective of the Convention as stated in its Article 2,

Recalling the provisions of the Convention,

Being guided by Article 3 of the Convention,

Pursuant to the Berlin Mandate adopted by decision 1/CP.1 of the Conference of the Parties to the Convention at its first session,

Have agreed as follows:

Article 1

For the purposes of this Protocol, the definitions contained in Article 1 of the Convention shall apply. In addition:

1. "Conference of the Parties" means the Conference of the Parties to the Convention.

2. "Convention" means the United Nations Framework Convention on Climate Change, adopted in New York on 9 May 1992.

3. "Intergovernmental Panel on Climate Change" means the Intergovernmental Panel on Climate Change established in 1988 jointly by the World Meteorological Organization and the United Nations Environment Programme.

4. "Montreal Protocol" means the Montreal Protocol on Substances that Deplete the Ozone Layer, adopted in Montreal on 16 September 1987 and as subsequently adjusted and amended.

5. "Parties present and voting" means Parties present and casting an affirmative or negative vote.

6. "Party" means, unless the context otherwise indicates, a Party to this Protocol.

7. "Party included in Annex I" means a Party included in Annex I to the Convention, as may be amended, or a Party which has made a notification under Article 4, paragraph 2 (g), of the Convention.

Article 2

1. Each Party included in Annex I, in achieving its quantified emission limitation and reduction commitments under Article 3, in order to promote sustainable development, shall:

(a) Implement and/or further elaborate policies and measures in accordance with its national circumstances, such as:

    (i) Enhancement of energy efficiency in relevant sectors of the national economy;

    (ii) Protection and enhancement of sinks and reservoirs of greenhouse gases not controlled by the Montreal Protocol, taking into account its commitments under relevant international environmental agreements; promotion of sustainable forest management practices, afforestation and reforestation;

    (iii) Promotion of sustainable forms of agriculture in light of climate change considerations;

    (iv) Research on, and promotion, development and increased use of, new and renewable forms of energy, of carbon dioxide sequestration technologies and of advanced and innovative environmentally sound technologies;

    (v) Progressive reduction or phasing out of market imperfections, fiscal incentives, tax and duty exemptions and subsidies in all greenhouse gas emitting sectors that run counter to the objective of the Convention and application of market instruments;

    (vi) Encouragement of appropriate reforms in relevant sectors aimed at promoting policies and measures which limit or reduce emissions of greenhouse gases not controlled by the Montreal Protocol;

    (vii) Measures to limit and/or reduce emissions of greenhouse gases not controlled by the Montreal Protocol in the transport sector;

    (viii) Limitation and/or reduction of methane emissions through recovery and use in waste management, as well as in the production, transport and distribution of energy;

(b) Cooperate with other such Parties to enhance the individual and combined effectiveness of their policies and measures adopted under this Article, pursuant to Article 4, paragraph 2 (e) (i), of the Convention. To this end, these Parties shall take steps to share their experience and exchange information on such policies and measures, including developing ways of improving their comparability, transparency and effectiveness. The Conference of the Parties serving as the meeting of the Parties to this Protocol shall, at its first session or as soon as practicable thereafter, consider ways to facilitate such cooperation, taking into account all relevant information.

2. The Parties included in Annex I shall pursue limitation or reduction of emissions of greenhouse gases not controlled by the Montreal Protocol from aviation and marine bunker fuels, working through the International Civil Aviation Organization and the International Maritime Organization, respectively.

3. The Parties included in Annex I shall strive to implement policies and measures under this Article in such a way as to minimize adverse effects, including the adverse effects of climate change, effects on international trade, and social, environmental and economic impacts on other Parties, especially developing country Parties and in particular those identified in Article 4, paragraphs 8 and 9, of the Convention, taking into account Article 3 of the Convention. The Conference of the Parties serving as the meeting of the Parties to this Protocol may take

further action, as appropriate, to promote the implementation of the provisions of this paragraph.

4. The Conference of the Parties serving as the meeting of the Parties to this Protocol, if it decides that it would be beneficial to coordinate any of the policies and measures in paragraph 1 (a) above, taking into account different national circumstances and potential effects, shall consider ways and means to elaborate the coordination of such policies and measures.

Article 3

1. The Parties included in Annex I shall, individually or jointly, ensure that their aggregate anthropogenic carbon dioxide equivalent emissions of the greenhouse gases listed in Annex A do not exceed their assigned amounts, calculated pursuant to their quantified emission limitation and reduction commitments inscribed in Annex B and in accordance with the provisions of this Article, with a view to reducing their overall emissions of such gases by at least 5 per cent below 1990 levels in the commitment period 2008 to 2012.

2. Each Party included in Annex I shall, by 2005, have made demonstrable progress in achieving its commitments under this Protocol.

3. The net changes in greenhouse gas emissions by sources and removals by sinks resulting from direct human-induced land-use change and forestry activities, limited to afforestation, reforestation and deforestation since 1990, measured as verifiable changes in carbon stocks in each commitment period, shall be used to meet the commitments under this Article of each Party included in Annex I. The greenhouse gas emissions by sources and removals by sinks associated with those activities shall be reported in a transparent and verifiable manner and reviewed in accordance with Articles 7 and 8.

4. Prior to the first session of the Conference of the Parties serving as the meeting of the Parties to this Protocol, each Party included in Annex I shall provide, for consideration by the Subsidiary Body for Scientific and Technological Advice, data to establish its level of carbon stocks in 1990 and to enable an estimate to be made of its changes in carbon stocks in subsequent years. The Conference of the Parties serving as the meeting of the Parties to this Protocol shall, at its first session or as soon as practicable thereafter, decide upon modalities, rules and guidelines as to how, and which, additional human-induced activities related to changes in greenhouse gas emissions by sources and removals by sinks in the agricultural soils and the land-use change and forestry categories shall be added to, or subtracted from, the assigned amounts for Parties included in Annex I, taking into account uncertainties, transparency in reporting, verifiability, the methodological work of the Intergovernmental Panel on Climate Change, the advice provided by the Subsidiary Body for Scientific and Technological Advice in accordance with Article 5 and the decisions of the Conference of the Parties. Such a decision shall apply in the second and subsequent commitment periods. A Party may choose to apply such a decision on these additional human-induced activities for its first commitment period, provided that these activities have taken place since 1990.

5. The Parties included in Annex I undergoing the process of transition to a market economy whose base year or period was established pursuant to decision 9/CP.2 of the Conference of the Parties at its second session shall use that base year or period

for the implementation of their commitments under this Article. Any other Party included in Annex I undergoing the process of transition to a market economy which has not yet submitted its first national communication under Article 12 of the Convention may also notify the Conference of the Parties serving as the meeting of the Parties to this Protocol that it intends to use an historical base year or period other than 1990 for the implementation of its commitments under this Article. The Conference of the Parties serving as the meeting of the Parties to this Protocol shall decide on the acceptance of such notification.

6. Taking into account Article 4, paragraph 6, of the Convention, in the implementation of their commitments under this Protocol other than those under this Article, a certain degree of flexibility shall be allowed by the Conference of the Parties serving as the meeting of the Parties to this Protocol to the Parties included in Annex I undergoing the process of transition to a market economy.

7. In the first quantified emission limitation and reduction commitment period, from 2008 to 2012, the assigned amount for each Party included in Annex I shall be equal to the percentage inscribed for it in Annex B of its aggregate anthropogenic carbon dioxide equivalent emissions of the greenhouse gases listed in Annex A in 1990, or the base year or period determined in accordance with paragraph 5 above, multiplied by five. Those Parties included in Annex I for whom land-use change and forestry constituted a net source of greenhouse gas emissions in 1990 shall include in their 1990 emissions base year or period the aggregate anthropogenic carbon dioxide equivalent emissions by sources minus removals by sinks in 1990 from land-use change for the purposes of calculating their assigned amount.

8. Any Party included in Annex I may use 1995 as its base year for hydrofluorocarbons, perfluorocarbons and sulphur hexafluoride, for the purposes of the calculation referred to in paragraph 7 above.

9. Commitments for subsequent periods for Parties included in Annex I shall be established in amendments to Annex B to this Protocol, which shall be adopted in accordance with the provisions of Article 21, paragraph 7. The Conference of the Parties serving as the meeting of the Parties to this Protocol shall initiate the consideration of such commitments at least seven years before the end of the first commitment period referred to in paragraph 1 above.

10. Any emission reduction units, or any part of an assigned amount, which a Party acquires from another Party in accordance with the provisions of Article 6 or of Article 17 shall be added to the assigned amount for the acquiring Party.

11. Any emission reduction units, or any part of an assigned amount, which a Party transfers to another Party in accordance with the provisions of Article 6 or of Article 17 shall be subtracted from the assigned amount for the transferring Party.

12. Any certified emission reductions which a Party acquires from another Party in accordance with the provisions of Article 12 shall be added to the assigned amount for the acquiring Party.

13. If the emissions of a Party included in Annex I in a commitment period are less than its assigned amount under this Article, this difference shall, on request of that Party, be added to the assigned amount for that Party for subsequent commitment periods.

14. Each Party included in Annex I shall strive to implement the commitments mentioned in paragraph 1 above in such a way as to minimize adverse social, environmental and economic impacts on developing country Parties, particularly those identified in Article 4, paragraphs 8 and 9, of the Convention. In line with relevant decisions of the Conference of the Parties on the implementation of those paragraphs, the Conference of the Parties serving as the meeting of the Parties to this Protocol shall, at its first session, consider what actions are necessary to minimize the adverse effects of climate change and/or the impacts of response measures on Parties referred to in those paragraphs. Among the issues to be considered shall be the establishment of funding, insurance and transfer of technology.

Article 4

1. Any Parties included in Annex I that have reached an agreement to fulfil their commitments under Article 3 jointly, shall be deemed to have met those commitments provided that their total combined aggregate anthropogenic carbon dioxide equivalent emissions of the greenhouse gases listed in Annex A do not exceed their assigned amounts calculated pursuant to their quantified emission limitation and reduction commitments inscribed in Annex B and in accordance with the provisions of Article 3. The respective emission level allocated to each of the Parties to the agreement shall be set out in that agreement.

2. The Parties to any such agreement shall notify the secretariat of the terms of the agreement on the date of deposit of their instruments of ratification, acceptance or approval of this Protocol, or accession thereto. The secretariat shall in turn inform the Parties and signatories to the Convention of the terms of the agreement.

3. Any such agreement shall remain in operation for the duration of the commitment period specified in Article 3, paragraph 7.

4. If Parties acting jointly do so in the framework of, and together with, a regional economic integration organization, any alteration in the composition of the organization after adoption of this Protocol shall not affect existing commitments under this Protocol. Any alteration in the composition of the organization shall only apply for the purposes of those commitments under Article 3 that are adopted subsequent to that alteration.

5. In the event of failure by the Parties to such an agreement to achieve their total combined level of emission reductions, each Party to that agreement shall be responsible for its own level of emissions set out in the agreement.

6. If Parties acting jointly do so in the framework of, and together with, a regional economic integration organization which is itself a Party to this Protocol, each member State of that regional economic integration organization individually, and together with the regional economic integration organization acting in accordance with Article 24, shall, in the event of failure to achieve the total combined level of emission reductions, be responsible for its level of emissions as notified in accordance with this Article.

Article 5

1. Each Party included in Annex I shall have in place, no later than one year prior to the start of the first commitment period, a national system for the estimation of anthropogenic emissions by sources and removals by sinks of all greenhouse gases not controlled by the Montreal Protocol. Guidelines for such national systems, which shall incorporate the methodologies specified in paragraph 2 below, shall be decided upon by the Conference of the Parties serving as the meeting of the Parties to this Protocol at its first session.

2. Methodologies for estimating anthropogenic emissions by sources and removals by sinks of all greenhouse gases not controlled by the Montreal Protocol shall be those accepted by the Intergovernmental Panel on Climate Change and agreed upon by the Conference of the Parties at its third session. Where such methodologies are not used, appropriate adjustments shall be applied according to methodologies agreed upon by the Conference of the Parties serving as the meeting of the Parties to this Protocol at its first session. Based on the work of, inter alia, the Intergovernmental Panel on Climate Change and advice provided by the Subsidiary Body for Scientific and Technological Advice, the Conference of the Parties serving as the meeting of the Parties to this Protocol shall regularly review and, as appropriate, revise such methodologies and adjustments, taking fully into account any relevant decisions by the Conference of the Parties. Any revision to methodologies or adjustments shall be used only for the purposes of ascertaining compliance with commitments under Article 3 in respect of any commitment period adopted subsequent to that revision.

3. The global warming potentials used to calculate the carbon dioxide equivalence of anthropogenic emissions by sources and removals by sinks of greenhouse gases listed in Annex A shall be those accepted by the Intergovernmental Panel on Climate Change and agreed upon by the Conference of the Parties at its third session. Based on the work of, inter alia, the Intergovernmental Panel on Climate Change and advice provided by the Subsidiary Body for Scientific and Technological Advice, the Conference of the Parties serving as the meeting of the Parties to this Protocol shall regularly review and, as appropriate, revise the global warming potential of each such greenhouse gas, taking fully into account any relevant decisions by the Conference of the Parties. Any revision to a global warming potential shall apply only to commitments under Article 3 in respect of any commitment period adopted subsequent to that revision.

Article 6

1. For the purpose of meeting its commitments under Article 3, any Party included in Annex I may transfer to, or acquire from, any other such Party emission reduction units resulting from projects aimed at reducing anthropogenic emissions by sources or enhancing anthropogenic removals by sinks of greenhouse gases in any sector of the economy, provided that:

     (a)   Any such project has the approval of the Parties involved;

     (b)   Any such project provides a reduction in emissions by sources, or an enhancement of removals by sinks, that is additional to any that would otherwise occur;

(c)   It does not acquire any emission reduction units if it is not in compliance with its obligations under Articles 5 and 7; and

(d)   The acquisition of emission reduction units shall be supplemental to domestic actions for the purposes of meeting commitments under Article 3.

2. The Conference of the Parties serving as the meeting of the Parties to this Protocol may, at its first session or as soon as practicable thereafter, further elaborate guidelines for the implementation of this Article, including for verification and reporting.

3. A Party included in Annex I may authorize legal entities to participate, under its responsibility, in actions leading to the generation, transfer or acquisition under this Article of emission reduction units.

4. If a question of implementation by a Party included in Annex I of the requirements referred to in this Article is identified in accordance with the relevant provisions of Article 8, transfers and acquisitions of emission reduction units may continue to be made after the question has been identified, provided that any such units may not be used by a Party to meet its commitments under Article 3 until any issue of compliance is resolved.

Article 7

1. Each Party included in Annex I shall incorporate in its annual inventory of anthropogenic emissions by sources and removals by sinks of greenhouse gases not controlled by the Montreal Protocol, submitted in accordance with the relevant decisions of the Conference of the Parties, the necessary supplementary information for the purposes of ensuring compliance with Article 3, to be determined in accordance with paragraph 4 below.

2. Each Party included in Annex I shall incorporate in its national communication, submitted under Article 12 of the Convention, the supplementary information necessary to demonstrate compliance with its commitments under this Protocol, to be determined in accordance with paragraph 4 below.

3. Each Party included in Annex I shall submit the information required under paragraph 1 above annually, beginning with the first inventory due under the Convention for the first year of the commitment period after this Protocol has entered into force for that Party. Each such Party shall submit the information required under paragraph 2 above as part of the first national communication due under the Convention after this Protocol has entered into force for it and after the adoption of guidelines as provided for in paragraph 4 below. The frequency of subsequent submission of information required under this Article shall be determined by the Conference of the Parties serving as the meeting of the Parties to this Protocol, taking into account any timetable for the submission of national communications decided upon by the Conference of the Parties.

4. The Conference of the Parties serving as the meeting of the Parties to this Protocol shall adopt at its first session, and review periodically thereafter, guidelines for the preparation of the information required under this Article, taking into account guidelines for the preparation of national communications by Parties included in Annex I adopted by the Conference of the Parties. The Conference of the Parties serving as the meeting of the Parties to this Protocol shall also, prior to

the first commitment period, decide upon modalities for the accounting of assigned amounts.

Article 8

1. The information submitted under Article 7 by each Party included in Annex I shall be reviewed by expert review teams pursuant to the relevant decisions of the Conference of the Parties and in accordance with guidelines adopted for this purpose by the Conference of the Parties serving as the meeting of the Parties to this Protocol under paragraph 4 below. The information submitted under Article 7, paragraph 1, by each Party included in Annex I shall be reviewed as part of the annual compilation and accounting of emissions inventories and assigned amounts. Additionally, the information submitted under Article 7, paragraph 2, by each Party included in Annex I shall be reviewed as part of the review of communications.

2. Expert review teams shall be coordinated by the secretariat and shall be composed of experts selected from those nominated by Parties to the Convention and, as appropriate, by intergovernmental organizations, in accordance with guidance provided for this purpose by the Conference of the Parties.

3. The review process shall provide a thorough and comprehensive technical assessment of all aspects of the implementation by a Party of this Protocol. The expert review teams shall prepare a report to the Conference of the Parties serving as the meeting of the Parties to this Protocol, assessing the implementation of the commitments of the Party and identifying any potential problems in, and factors influencing, the fulfilment of commitments. Such reports shall be circulated by the secretariat to all Parties to the Convention. The secretariat shall list those questions of implementation indicated in such reports for further consideration by the Conference of the Parties serving as the meeting of the Parties to this Protocol.

4. The Conference of the Parties serving as the meeting of the Parties to this Protocol shall adopt at its first session, and review periodically thereafter, guidelines for the review of implementation of this Protocol by expert review teams taking into account the relevant decisions of the Conference of the Parties.

5. The Conference of the Parties serving as the meeting of the Parties to this Protocol shall, with the assistance of the Subsidiary Body for Implementation and, as appropriate, the Subsidiary Body for Scientific and Technological Advice, consider:

    (a)   The information submitted by Parties under Article 7 and the reports of the expert reviews thereon conducted under this Article; and

    (b)   Those questions of implementation listed by the secretariat under paragraph 3 above, as well as any questions raised by Parties.

6. Pursuant to its consideration of the information referred to in paragraph 5 above, the Conference of the Parties serving as the meeting of the Parties to this Protocol shall take decisions on any matter required for the implementation of this Protocol.

Article 9

1. The Conference of the Parties serving as the meeting of the Parties to this Protocol shall periodically review this Protocol in the light of the best available scientific information and assessments on climate change and its impacts, as well as

relevant technical, social and economic information. Such reviews shall be coordinated with pertinent reviews under the Convention, in particular those required by Article 4, paragraph 2 (d), and Article 7, paragraph 2 (a), of the Convention. Based on these reviews, the Conference of the Parties serving as the meeting of the Parties to this Protocol shall take appropriate action.

2. The first review shall take place at the second session of the Conference of the Parties serving as the meeting of the Parties to this Protocol. Further reviews shall take place at regular intervals and in a timely manner.

Article 10

All Parties, taking into account their common but differentiated responsibilities and their specific national and regional development priorities, objectives and circumstances, without introducing any new commitments for Parties not included in Annex I, but reaffirming existing commitments under Article 4, paragraph 1, of the Convention, and continuing to advance the implementation of these commitments in order to achieve sustainable development, taking into account Article 4, paragraphs 3, 5 and 7, of the Convention, shall:

(a)   Formulate, where relevant and to the extent possible, cost-effective national and, where appropriate, regional programmes to improve the quality of local emission factors, activity data and/or models which reflect the socio-economic conditions of each Party for the preparation and periodic updating of national inventories of anthropogenic emissions by sources and removals by sinks of all greenhouse gases not controlled by the Montreal Protocol, using comparable methodologies to be agreed upon by the Conference of the Parties, and consistent with the guidelines for the preparation of national communications adopted by the Conference of the Parties;

(b)   Formulate, implement, publish and regularly update national and, where appropriate, regional programmes containing measures to mitigate climate change and measures to facilitate adequate adaptation to climate change:

   (i)   Such programmes would, *inter alia*, concern the energy, transport and industry sectors as well as agriculture, forestry and waste management. Furthermore, adaptation technologies and methods for improving spatial planning would improve adaptation to climate change; and

   (ii) Parties included in Annex I shall submit information on action under this Protocol, including national programmes, in accordance with Article 7; and other Parties shall seek to include in their national communications, as appropriate, information on programmes which contain measures that the Party believes contribute to addressing climate change and its adverse impacts, including the abatement of increases in greenhouse gas emissions, and enhancement of and removals by sinks, capacity building and adaptation measures;

(c)   Cooperate in the promotion of effective modalities for the development, application and diffusion of, and take all practicable steps to promote, facilitate and finance, as appropriate, the transfer of, or access to, environmentally sound technologies, know-how, practices and processes pertinent to climate change, in particular to developing countries, including the formulation of policies and programmes for the effective transfer of environmentally sound technologies that are publicly owned or in the public domain and the creation of an enabling environment for the private sector, to promote and enhance the transfer of, and access to, environmentally sound technologies;

(d) Cooperate in scientific and technical research and promote the maintenance and the development of systematic observation systems and development of data archives to reduce uncertainties related to the climate system, the adverse impacts of climate change and the economic and social consequences of various response strategies, and promote the development and strengthening of endogenous capacities and capabilities to participate in international and intergovernmental efforts, programmes and networks on research and systematic observation, taking into account Article 5 of the Convention;

(e) Cooperate in and promote at the international level, and, where appropriate, using existing bodies, the development and implementation of education and training programmes, including the strengthening of national capacity building, in particular human and institutional capacities and the exchange or secondment of personnel to train experts in this field, in particular for developing countries, and facilitate at the national level public awareness of, and public access to information on, climate change. Suitable modalities should be developed to implement these activities through the relevant bodies of the Convention, taking into account Article 6 of the Convention;

(f) Include in their national communications information on programmes and activities undertaken pursuant to this Article in accordance with relevant decisions of the Conference of the Parties; and

(g) Give full consideration, in implementing the commitments under this Article, to Article 4, paragraph 8, of the Convention.

Article 11

1. In the implementation of Article 10, Parties shall take into account the provisions of Article 4, paragraphs 4, 5, 7, 8 and 9, of the Convention.

2. In the context of the implementation of Article 4, paragraph 1, of the Convention, in accordance with the provisions of Article 4, paragraph 3, and Article 11 of the Convention, and through the entity or entities entrusted with the operation of the financial mechanism of the Convention, the developed country Parties and other developed Parties included in Annex II to the Convention shall:

(a) Provide new and additional financial resources to meet the agreed full costs incurred by developing country Parties in advancing the implementation of existing commitments under Article 4, paragraph 1 (a), of the Convention that are covered in Article 10, subparagraph (a); and

(b) Also provide such financial resources, including for the transfer of technology, needed by the developing country Parties to meet the agreed full incremental costs of advancing the implementation of existing commitments under Article 4, paragraph 1, of the Convention that are covered by Article 10 and that are agreed between a developing country Party and the international entity or entities referred to in Article 11 of the Convention, in accordance with that Article.

The implementation of these existing commitments shall take into account the need for adequacy and predictability in the flow of funds and the importance of appropriate burden sharing among developed country Parties. The guidance to the entity or entities entrusted with the operation of the financial mechanism of the Convention in relevant decisions of the Conference of the Parties, including those agreed before the adoption of this Protocol, shall apply *mutatis mutandis* to the provisions of this paragraph.

3. The developed country Parties and other developed Parties in Annex II to the Convention may also provide, and developing country Parties avail themselves of, financial resources for the implementation of Article 10, through bilateral, regional and other multilateral channels.

Article 12

1. A clean development mechanism is hereby defined.

2. The purpose of the clean development mechanism shall be to assist Parties not included in Annex I in achieving sustainable development and in contributing to the ultimate objective of the Convention, and to assist Parties included in Annex I in achieving compliance with their quantified emission limitation and reduction commitments under Article 3.

3. Under the clean development mechanism:

(a) Parties not included in Annex I will benefit from project activities resulting in certified emission reductions; and

(b) Parties included in Annex I may use the certified emission reductions accruing from such project activities to contribute to compliance with part of their quantified emission limitation and reduction commitments under Article 3, as determined by the Conference of the Parties serving as the meeting of the Parties to this Protocol.

4. The clean development mechanism shall be subject to the authority and guidance of the Conference of the Parties serving as the meeting of the Parties to this Protocol and be supervised by an executive board of the clean development mechanism.

5. Emission reductions resulting from each project activity shall be certified by operational entities to be designated by the Conference of the Parties serving as the meeting of the Parties to this Protocol, on the basis of:

(a) Voluntary participation approved by each Party involved;

(b) Real, measurable, and long-term benefits related to the mitigation of climate change; and

(c) Reductions in emissions that are additional to any that would occur in the absence of the certified project activity.

6. The clean development mechanism shall assist in arranging funding of certified project activities as necessary.

7. The Conference of the Parties serving as the meeting of the Parties to this Protocol shall, at its first session, elaborate modalities and procedures with the objective of ensuring transparency, efficiency and accountability through independent auditing and verification of project activities.

8. The Conference of the Parties serving as the meeting of the Parties to this Protocol shall ensure that a share of the proceeds from certified project activities is used to cover administrative expenses as well as to assist developing country Parties that are particularly vulnerable to the adverse effects of climate change to meet the costs of adaptation.

9. Participation under the clean development mechanism, including in activities mentioned in paragraph 3 (a) above and in the acquisition of certified emission reductions, may involve private and/or public entities, and is to be subject to whatever guidance may be provided by the executive board of the clean development mechanism.

10. Certified emission reductions obtained during the period from the year 2000 up to the beginning of the first commitment period can be used to assist in achieving compliance in the first commitment period.

Article 13

1. The Conference of the Parties, the supreme body of the Convention, shall serve as the meeting of the Parties to this Protocol.

2. Parties to the Convention that are not Parties to this Protocol may participate as observers in the proceedings of any session of the Conference of the Parties serving as the meeting of the Parties to this Protocol. When the Conference of the Parties serves as the meeting of the Parties to this Protocol, decisions under this Protocol shall be taken only by those that are Parties to this Protocol.

3. When the Conference of the Parties serves as the meeting of the Parties to this Protocol, any member of the Bureau of the Conference of the Parties representing a Party to the Convention but, at that time, not a Party to this Protocol, shall be replaced by an additional member to be elected by and from amongst the Parties to this Protocol.

4. The Conference of the Parties serving as the meeting of the Parties to this Protocol shall keep under regular review the implementation of this Protocol and shall make, within its mandate, the decisions necessary to promote its effective implementation. It shall perform the functions assigned to it by this Protocol and shall:

(a)   Assess, on the basis of all information made available to it in accordance with the provisions of this Protocol, the implementation of this Protocol by the Parties, the overall effects of the measures taken pursuant to this Protocol, in particular environmental, economic and social effects as well as their cumulative impacts and the extent to which progress towards the objective of the Convention is being achieved;

(b)   Periodically examine the obligations of the Parties under this Protocol, giving due consideration to any reviews required by Article 4, paragraph 2 (d), and Article 7, paragraph 2, of the Convention, in the light of the objective of the Convention, the experience gained in its implementation and the evolution of scientific and technological knowledge, and in this respect consider and adopt regular reports on the implementation of this Protocol;

(c)   Promote and facilitate the exchange of information on measures adopted by the Parties to address climate change and its effects, taking into account the differing circumstances, responsibilities and capabilities of the Parties and their respective commitments under this Protocol;

(d) Facilitate, at the request of two or more Parties, the coordination of measures adopted by them to address climate change and its effects, taking into account the differing circumstances, responsibilities and capabilities of the Parties and their respective commitments under this Protocol;

(e) Promote and guide, in accordance with the objective of the Convention and the provisions of this Protocol, and taking fully into account the relevant decisions by the Conference of the Parties, the development and periodic refinement of comparable methodologies for the effective implementation of this Protocol, to be agreed on by the Conference of the Parties serving as the meeting of the Parties to this Protocol;

(f) Make recommendations on any matters necessary for the implementation of this Protocol;

(g) Seek to mobilize additional financial resources in accordance with Article 11, paragraph 2;

(h) Establish such subsidiary bodies as are deemed necessary for the implementation of this Protocol;

(i) Seek and utilize, where appropriate, the services and cooperation of, and information provided by, competent international organizations and inter-governmental and non-governmental bodies; and

(j) Exercise such other functions as may be required for the implementation of this Protocol, and consider any assignment resulting from a decision by the Conference of the Parties.

5. The rules of procedure of the Conference of the Parties and financial procedures applied under the Convention shall be applied *mutatis mutandis* under this Protocol, except as may be otherwise decided by consensus by the Conference of the Parties serving as the meeting of the Parties to this Protocol.

6. The first session of the Conference of the Parties serving as the meeting of the Parties to this Protocol shall be convened by the secretariat in conjunction with the first session of the Conference of the Parties that is scheduled after the date of the entry into force of this Protocol. Subsequent ordinary sessions of the Conference of the Parties serving as the meeting of the Parties to this Protocol shall be held every year and in conjunction with ordinary sessions of the Conference of the Parties, unless otherwise decided by the Conference of the Parties serving as the meeting of the Parties to this Protocol.

7. Extraordinary sessions of the Conference of the Parties serving as the meeting of the Parties to this Protocol shall be held at such other times as may be deemed necessary by the Conference of the Parties serving as the meeting of the Parties to this Protocol, or at the written request of any Party, provided that, within six months of the request being communicated to the Parties by the secretariat, it is supported by at least one third of the Parties.

8. The United Nations, its specialized agencies and the International Atomic Energy Agency, as well as any State member thereof or observers thereto not party to the Convention, may be represented at sessions of the Conference of the Parties serving as the meeting of the Parties to this Protocol as observers. Any body or agency, whether national or international, governmental or non-governmental,

which is qualified in matters covered by this Protocol and which has informed the secretariat of its wish to be represented at a session of the Conference of the Parties serving as the meeting of the Parties to this Protocol as an observer, may be so admitted unless at least one third of the Parties present object. The admission and participation of observers shall be subject to the rules of procedure, as referred to in paragraph 5 above.

Article 14

1. The secretariat established by Article 8 of the Convention shall serve as the secretariat of this Protocol.

2. Article 8, paragraph 2, of the Convention on the functions of the secretariat, and Article 8, paragraph 3, of the Convention on arrangements made for the functioning of the secretariat, shall apply *mutatis mutandis* to this Protocol. The secretariat shall, in addition, exercise the functions assigned to it under this Protocol.

Article 15

1. The Subsidiary Body for Scientific and Technological Advice and the Subsidiary Body for Implementation established by Articles 9 and 10 of the Convention shall serve as, respectively, the Subsidiary Body for Scientific and Technological Advice and the Subsidiary Body for Implementation of this Protocol. The provisions relating to the functioning of these two bodies under the Convention shall apply *mutatis mutandis* to this Protocol. Sessions of the meetings of the Subsidiary Body for Scientific and Technological Advice and the Subsidiary Body for Implementation of this Protocol shall be held in conjunction with the meetings of, respectively, the Subsidiary Body for Scientific and Technological Advice and the Subsidiary Body for Implementation of the Convention.

2. Parties to the Convention that are not Parties to this Protocol may participate as observers in the proceedings of any session of the subsidiary bodies. When the subsidiary bodies serve as the subsidiary bodies of this Protocol, decisions under this Protocol shall be taken only by those that are Parties to this Protocol.

3. When the subsidiary bodies established by Articles 9 and 10 of the Convention exercise their functions with regard to matters concerning this Protocol, any member of the Bureaux of those subsidiary bodies representing a Party to the Convention but, at that time, not a party to this Protocol, shall be replaced by an additional member to be elected by and from amongst the Parties to this Protocol.

Article 16

The Conference of the Parties serving as the meeting of the Parties to this Protocol shall, as soon as practicable, consider the application to this Protocol of, and modify as appropriate, the multilateral consultative process referred to in Article 13 of the Convention, in the light of any relevant decisions that may be taken by the Conference of the Parties. Any multilateral consultative process that may be applied to this Protocol shall operate without prejudice to the procedures and mechanisms established in accordance with Article 18.

Article 17

The Conference of the Parties shall define the relevant principles, modalities, rules and guidelines, in particular for verification, reporting and accountability for emissions trading. The Parties included in Annex B may participate in emissions trading for the purposes of fulfilling their commitments under Article 3. Any such trading shall be supplemental to domestic actions for the purpose of meeting quantified emission limitation and reduction commitments under that Article.

Article 18

The Conference of the Parties serving as the meeting of the Parties to this Protocol shall, at its first session, approve appropriate and effective procedures and mechanisms to determine and to address cases of non-compliance with the provisions of this Protocol, including through the development of an indicative list of consequences, taking into account the cause, type, degree and frequency of non-compliance. Any procedures and mechanisms under this Article entailing binding consequences shall be adopted by means of an amendment to this Protocol.

Article 19

The provisions of Article 14 of the Convention on settlement of disputes shall apply mutatis mutandis to this Protocol.

Article 20

1. Any Party may propose amendments to this Protocol.

2. Amendments to this Protocol shall be adopted at an ordinary session of the Conference of the Parties serving as the meeting of the Parties to this Protocol. The text of any proposed amendment to this Protocol shall be communicated to the Parties by the secretariat at least six months before the meeting at which it is proposed for adoption. The secretariat shall also communicate the text of any proposed amendments to the Parties and signatories to the Convention and, for information, to the Depositary.

3. The Parties shall make every effort to reach agreement on any proposed amendment to this Protocol by consensus. If all efforts at consensus have been exhausted, and no agreement reached, the amendment shall as a last resort be adopted by a three-fourths majority vote of the Parties present and voting at the meeting. The adopted amendment shall be communicated by the secretariat to the Depositary, who shall circulate it to all Parties for their acceptance.

4. Instruments of acceptance in respect of an amendment shall be deposited with the Depositary. An amendment adopted in accordance with paragraph 3 above shall enter into force for those Parties having accepted it on the ninetieth day after the date of receipt by the Depositary of an instrument of acceptance by at least three fourths of the Parties to this Protocol.

5. The amendment shall enter into force for any other Party on the ninetieth day after the date on which that Party deposits with the Depositary its instrument of acceptance of the said amendment.

Article 21

1. Annexes to this Protocol shall form an integral part thereof and, unless otherwise expressly provided, a reference to this Protocol constitutes at the same time a reference to any annexes thereto. Any annexes adopted after the entry into force of this Protocol shall be restricted to lists, forms and any other material of a descriptive nature that is of a scientific, technical, procedural or administrative character.

2. Any Party may make proposals for an annex to this Protocol and may propose amendments to annexes to this Protocol.

3. Annexes to this Protocol and amendments to annexes to this Protocol shall be adopted at an ordinary session of the Conference of the Parties serving as the meeting of the Parties to this Protocol. The text of any proposed annex or amendment to an annex shall be communicated to the Parties by the secretariat at least six months before the meeting at which it is proposed for adoption. The secretariat shall also communicate the text of any proposed annex or amendment to an annex to the Parties and signatories to the Convention and, for information, to the Depositary.

4. The Parties shall make every effort to reach agreement on any proposed annex or amendment to an annex by consensus. If all efforts at consensus have been exhausted, and no agreement reached, the annex or amendment to an annex shall as a last resort be adopted by a three-fourths majority vote of the Parties present and voting at the meeting. The adopted annex or amendment to an annex shall be communicated by the secretariat to the Depositary, who shall circulate it to all Parties for their acceptance.

5. An annex, or amendment to an annex other than Annex A or B, that has been adopted in accordance with paragraphs 3 and 4 above shall enter into force for all Parties to this Protocol six months after the date of the communication by the Depositary to such Parties of the adoption of the annex or adoption of the amendment to the annex, except for those Parties that have notified the Depositary, in writing, within that period of their non-acceptance of the annex or amendment to the annex. The annex or amendment to an annex shall enter into force for Parties which withdraw their notification of non-acceptance on the ninetieth day after the date on which withdrawal of such notification has been received by the Depositary.

6. If the adoption of an annex or an amendment to an annex involves an amendment to this Protocol, that annex or amendment to an annex shall not enter into force until such time as the amendment to this Protocol enters into force.

7. Amendments to Annexes A and B to this Protocol shall be adopted and enter into force in accordance with the procedure set out in Article 20, provided that any amendment to Annex B shall be adopted only with the written consent of the Party concerned.

Article 22

1. Each Party shall have one vote, except as provided for in paragraph 2 below.

2. Regional economic integration organizations, in matters within their competence, shall exercise their right to vote with a number of votes equal to the number of their member States that are Parties to this Protocol. Such an organization shall not

exercise its right to vote if any of its member States exercises its right, and vice versa.

Article 23

The Secretary-General of the United Nations shall be the Depositary of this Protocol.

Article 24

1. This Protocol shall be open for signature and subject to ratification, acceptance or approval by States and regional economic integration organizations which are Parties to the Convention. It shall be open for signature at United Nations Headquarters in New York from 16 March 1998 to 15 March 1999. This Protocol shall be open for accession from the day after the date on which it is closed for signature. Instruments of ratification, acceptance, approval or accession shall be deposited with the Depositary.

2. Any regional economic integration organization which becomes a Party to this Protocol without any of its member States being a Party shall be bound by all the obligations under this Protocol. In the case of such organizations, one or more of whose member States is a Party to this Protocol, the organization and its member States shall decide on their respective responsibilities for the performance of their obligations under this Protocol. In such cases, the organization and the member States shall not be entitled to exercise rights under this Protocol concurrently.

3. In their instruments of ratification, acceptance, approval or accession, regional economic integration organizations shall declare the extent of their competence with respect to the matters governed by this Protocol. These organizations shall also inform the Depositary, who shall in turn inform the Parties, of any substantial modification in the extent of their competence.

Article 25

1. This Protocol shall enter into force on the ninetieth day after the date on which not less than 55 Parties to the Convention, incorporating Parties included in Annex I which accounted in total for at least 55 per cent of the total carbon dioxide emissions for 1990 of the Parties included in Annex I, have deposited their instruments of ratification, acceptance, approval or accession.

2. For the purposes of this Article, Athe total carbon dioxide emissions for 1990 of the Parties included in Annex I means the amount communicated on or before the date of adoption of this Protocol by the Parties included in Annex I in their first national communications submitted in accordance with Article 12 of the Convention.

3. For each State or regional economic integration organization that ratifies, accepts or approves this Protocol or accedes thereto after the conditions set out in paragraph 1 above for entry into force have been fulfilled, this Protocol shall enter into force on the ninetieth day following the date of deposit of its instrument of ratification, acceptance, approval or accession.

4. For the purposes of this Article, any instrument deposited by a regional economic integration organization shall not be counted as additional to those deposited by

States members of the organization.

Article 26

No reservations may be made to this Protocol.

Article 27

1. At any time after three years from the date on which this Protocol has entered into force for a Party, that Party may withdraw from this Protocol by giving written notification to the Depositary.

2. Any such withdrawal shall take effect upon expiry of one year from the date of receipt by the Depositary of the notification of withdrawal, or on such later date as may be specified in the notification of withdrawal.

3. Any Party that withdraws from the Convention shall be considered as also having withdrawn from this Protocol.

Article 28

The original of this Protocol, of which the Arabic, Chinese, English, French, Russian and Spanish texts are equally authentic, shall be deposited with the Secretary-General of the United Nations.

DONE at Kyoto this eleventh day of December one thousand nine hundred and ninety-seven.

IN WITNESS WHEREOF the undersigned, being duly authorized to that effect, have affixed their signatures to this Protocol on the dates indicated.

Annex A

Greenhouse gases
Carbon dioxide (CO2)
Methane (CH4)
Nitrous oxide (N20)
Hydrofluorocarbons (HFCs)
Perfluorocarbons (PFCs)
Sulphur hexafluoride (SF6)

Sectors/source categories
Energy
    Fuel combustion
        Energy industries
        Manufacturing industries and construction
        Transport
        Other sectors
        Other
    Fugitive emissions from fuels
        Solid fuels
        Oil and natural gas
        Other
    Industrial processes
        Mineral products
        Chemical industry
        Metal production
        Other production
        Production of halocarbons and sulphur hexafluoride
        Consumption of halocarbons and sulphur hexafluoride
        Other
    Solvent and other product use
    Agriculture
        Enteric fermentation
        Manure management
        Rice cultivation
        Agricultural soils
        Prescribed burning of savannas
        Field burning of agricultural residues
    Waste
        Solid waste disposal on land
        Wastewater handling
        Waste incineration
        Other

Annex B

Party	Quantified emission limitation or reduction commitment (percentage of base year or period)
Australia	108
Austria	92
Belgium	92
Bulgaria*	92
Canada	94
Croatia*	95
Czech Republic*	92
Denmark	92
Estonia*	92
European Community	92
Finland	92
France	92
Germany	92
Greece	92
Hungary*	94
Iceland	110
Ireland	92
Italy	92
Japan	94
Latvia*	92
Liechtenstein	92
Lithuania*	92
Luxembourg	92
Monaco	92
Netherlands	92
New Zealand	100
Norway	101
Poland*	94
Portugal	92
Romania*	92
Russian Federation*	100
Slovakia*	92
Slovenia*	92
Spain	92
Sweden	92
Switzerland	92
Ukraine*	100
United Kingdom of Great Britain and Northern Ireland	92
United States of America	93

* Countries that are undergoing the process of transition to a market economy.

TABLE OF CASES

[References are to pages]

[References are to pages]

[References are to pages]

V

W

Z

INDEX

[References are to pages.]

[References are to pages.]

[References are to pages.]

[References are to pages.]

[References are to pages.]

[References are to pages.]

[References are to pages.]

[References are to pages.]

[References are to pages.]

STATE AND LOCAL RESPONSES TO CLI-MATE CHANGE
Commerce clause challenges
　Emissions standards . . . 861
　Renewable portfolio standards . . . 868
Future role of state and local governments . . . 871
Mitigation of climate change
　Coal-plant emissions
　　Carbon cap or offset requirements
　　　. . . 852
　　Carbon capture and sequestration
　　　technology-based mandates . . . 852
　　Greenhouse gas emission reduction goals
　　　California . . . 845
　　　Portland, Oregon . . . 849
　　Regional measures . . . 830
　　Renewable portfolio standards . . . 841
　　State and local measures
　　　Climate action plans . . . 857
　　　Environmental reviews . . . 857
Renewable portfolio standards
　Commerce clause challenges to . . . 868
　Mitigation of climate change . . . 841

STATE ATTORNEYS GENERAL
Climate-related tort cases . . . 787

STATE SOVEREIGNTY
United Nations Framework Convention on Climate
　Change . . . 151

STATE VEHICLE EMISSIONS STANDARDS
Preemption . . . 563
Waiver under Clean Air Act . . . 553

STATIONARY SOURCE EMISSIONS STAN-DARDS
Clean Air Act . . . 541

STERN REVIEW OF CLIMATE ECONOMICS
Generally . . . 82

SUBSIDIES(See also TAX SUBSIDIES)
International trade . . . 460

SUPPLEMENTARITY
Kyoto Protocol issues . . . 239

SUSTAINABLE DEVELOPMENT RIGHT
United Nations Framework Convention on Climate
　Change . . . 158

T

TAX CREDITS
Plug-in hybrid electric vehicles . . . 779
Renewable energy generation . . . 703

TAX DEDUCTIONS
Renewable energy generation . . . 703

TAXES, INTERNATIONAL TRADE
Automobiles . . . 450
Border tax adjustments . . . 452
Carbon . . . 451
Products made with fossil fuels . . . 452

TAX INCENTIVES
Alternative fuels
　Energy Independence and Security Act of 2007
　　. . . 769
　Farm Bill of 2008 . . . 769
　Regulation
　　1978-2005 . . . 766
　　Energy Independence and Security Act of
　　　2007 . . . 769
Renewable energy generation . . . 703

TAX SUBSIDIES, ALTERNATIVE-FUEL
1978-2005 . . . 766
Energy Independence and Security Act of 2007
　. . . 769
Farm Bill of 2008 . . . 769

TECHNOLOGY TRANSFER
United Nations Framework Convention on Climate
　Change . . . 178

TMDLS (See TOTAL MAXIMUM DAILY LOADS
(TMDLS))

TORTS, CLIMATE-RELATED (See CLIMATE-RELATED TORTS)

TOTAL MAXIMUM DAILY LOADS (TMDLS)
Compliance . . . 645

TRADITIONAL REGULATION
Internalization of external costs . . . 55

TRANSPORTATION
Alternative fuels
　Agricultural sources of fuels
　　Biodiesel . . . 756
　　Ethanol . . . 754
　Hydrogen fuel cells . . . 762
　Natural gas . . . 761
　Plug-in hybrid electric vehicles
　　Policies Federal and state purchasing pro-
　　　grams 777 Tax credits for purchasers
　　　779
　　Technology . . . 775
　Regulation
　　Renewable fuel standards Energy Inde-
　　　pendence and Security Act of 2007
　　　772 Energy Policy Act of 2005 771
　　Tax incentives and subsidies 1978-2005
　　　766 Energy Independence and Security
　　　Act of 2007 769 Farm Bill of 2008
　　　769
Automobile fuel efficiency standards
　Early case law . . . 718
　Energy Independence and Security Act of 2007
　　. . . 734
　Light trucks . . . 726
　NHTSA, deference to . . . 718
　Reformed CAFE . . . 726
Infrastructure reform
　Federal government, role of . . . 751
　Vehicle miles traveled, survey of policies to
　　reduce . . . 738

[References are to pages.]